UNIVERSITY CASEBOOK SERIES

MATERIALS ON LEGISLATION:

Political Language and the Political Process

SECOND EDITION

by

WILLIAM D. POPKIN
Walter W. Foskett Professor of Law
Indiana University School of Law, Bloomington

WESTBURY, NEW YORK

THE FOUNDATION PRESS, INC.

1997

Library of Congress Cataloging-in-Publication Data
Popkin, William D.
    Materials on legislation, political language and the political
process / by William D. Popkin. — 2nd ed.
      p.   cm. — (University casebook series)
    Includes index.
    ISBN 1–56662–519–X
    1. Legislation—United States—Cases. 2. Statutes—United States—
Cases. 3. Law—United States—Interpretation and construction—
Cases. I. Title. II. Series.
    KF4945.A7P66 1997
    348.73'2—dc21   97–1097

 *TEXT IS PRINTED ON 10% POST CONSUMER RECYCLED PAPER*

To my wife, Prema

*

PREFACE

Colleagues are essential to a book on Legislation. They feed you interesting cases and keep you aware of the subtleties in a particular field of law. At the risk of omitting someone, I give special thanks to Doug Boshkoff, Roger Dworkin, Don Gjerdingen, Bill Hicks, Joe Hoffman, Julia Lamber, Bruce Markell, Harry Pratter, Lauren Robel, John Scanlan, Jeff Stake, and a double dose to Pat Baude. Judge Benjamin Kaplan was also generous with his time and advice, for which I am grateful. The library staff was as helpful as they were tolerant of my many requests, especially Keith Buckley, Mitch Counts, Ralph Gaebler, and Marianne Mason.

I also thank F. Reed Dickerson, whose differences with me about how to approach statutory interpretation shaped my own thinking more than I care to admit.

My secretaries were Margaret Carroll and Susan Neher. I thank them for their skill, hard work, and patience.

*

PREFACE TO THE SECOND EDITION

This second edition reflects my emphasis on statutory interpretation and its history. Part I is about the history. The material on state and federal constitutional law has been moved from the early part of the book to the end, in Part III. Part II focuses on the same topics of statutory interpretation that were emphasized in the first edition.

My secretary was Jennifer Walker. I thank her for her skill, hard work, and patience.

An editorial note. I have eliminated most footnotes and citations from cases and articles, but left quotation marks from the original. I have also provided clarifying comments in brackets within the excerpted material.

*

ACKNOWLEDGEMENTS

I gratefully acknowledge permission to publish excerpts from the following material.

Ackerman & Hassler, <u>Beyond the New Deal: Coal and the Clean Air Act</u>, 89 Yale L.J. 1466, 1508–11, 1560 (1980)

> Reprinted by permission of the Yale Law Journal Company and Fred B. Rothman & Company from <u>The Yale Law Journal</u>, Vol. <u>89</u>, pp. <u>1539–1571</u>; and Reprinted by permission of Bruce A. Ackerman and William T. Hassler.

B. Asbell, <u>The Senate Nobody Knows</u> 35–36, 224, 267–68 (paperback ed. 1981), reprinted by permission of Johns Hopkins University Press, and Bernard Asbell.

G. Calabresi, <u>A Common Law for the Age of Statutes</u> 121–22, 125–27, 129–30, 133–34 (1982)

> Reprinted by permission of the publishers from A COMMON LAW FOR THE AGE OF STATUTES by Guide Calabresi, Cambridge, Mass.: Harvard University Press, Copyright © 1982 by the President and Fellows of Harvard College; and Reprinted by permission of Guido Calabresi.

Chafee, <u>The Disorderly Conduct of Words</u>, 41 Colum. L. Re. 381 (1941), pp. 398–402, 404

> Copyright © 1941 by the Directors of the Columbia Law Review Association, Inc. All Rights Reserved. This article originally appeared at 7 Colum. L. Rev. 379 (1907). Reprinted by permission.

R. Dickerson, <u>The Interpretation and Application of Statutes</u> 87–88, 90–92 (1975)

> Reproduced by permission of Little, Brown & Company © 1975, assigned to Aspen Law & Business, a division of Aspen Publishers, Inc.

Easterbrook, <u>Statutes' Domains</u>, 50 U.Chi.L.Rev. 533, 544–51 (1983), reprinted by permission of the University of Chicago Law Review, and Frank Easterbrook.

Easterbrook, <u>Foreword: The Court and the Economic System</u>, 98 Harv. L. Rev. 4, 14–18, 44, 45–46 (1984), reprinted by permission of Harvard Law Review Association, and Frank Easterbrook.

Eule, <u>Judicial Review of Direct Democracy</u>, 99 Yale L.J. 1503, 1510–13, 1555–56, 1568, 1575–77 (1990)

> Reprinted by permission of the Yale Law Journal Company and Fred B. Rothman & Company from <u>The Yale Law Journal</u>, Vol. <u>99</u>, pp. <u>1503–1590</u>; and Reprinted by permission of Julian N. Eule.

Farber & Frickey, <u>In the Shadow of the Legislature: The Common Law in the Age of the New Public Law</u>, 89 Mich. L. Rev. 875, 903–04 (1991), reprinted by permission of Michigan Law Review Association, Dan Farber, and Philip Frickey.

Friendly, <u>Reactions of a Lawyer-Newly Become Judge</u>, 71 Yale L.J. 218, 225–28 (1961)

> Reprinted by permission of the Yale Law Journal Company and Fred B. Rothman & Company from <u>The Yale Law Journal</u>, Vol. <u>71</u>, pp. <u>218 - 238</u>.

Friendly, <u>The Gap in Lawmaking-Judges Who Can't and Legislators Who Won't</u>, 63 Colum. L. Rev. 787 (1963), pp. 799–802, 805

> Copyright © 1963 by the Directors of the Columbia Law Review Association, Inc. All Rights Reserved. This article originally appeared at 63 Colum. L. Rev. 787 (1963). Reprinted by permission.

Freund, <u>Prolegomena To A Science of Legislation</u>, 13 Ill. L. Rev. 264, 269–70 (1918)

> Reprinted by special permission of Northwestern University School of Law, Volume 13, <u>Illinois Law Review</u>, (264, 269–70)—<u>Illinois Law Review</u>.

K. Kofmehl, <u>Professional Staffs of Congress</u> 121–23 (3d ed. 1977), reprinted by permission of Purdue Research Foundation.

Langevoort, <u>Statutory Obsolescence and the Judicial Process: The Revisionist Role of the Courts in Federal Banking Regulation</u>, 85 Mich. L. Rev. 672, 693–94, 696, 698 (1987), reprinted by permission of Michigan Law Review Association, and Donald Langevoort.

A. Maass, <u>Congress and the Common Good</u> 115–16 (1982)

> Excerpt from CONGRESS AND THE COMMON GOOD by Arthur Maass. Copyright © 1983 by Arthur Maass. Reprinted by permission of Basic Books, a division of HarperCollins Publishers.

MacCallum, <u>Legislative Intent</u>, 75 Yale L.J. 754, 778–81, 783 (1966)

> Reprinted by permission of the Yale Law Journal Company and Fred B. Rothman & Company from <u>The Yale Law Journal</u>, Vol. <u>75</u>, pp. <u>754–787</u>.

Morehead, <u>Private Bills and Private Laws: A Guide to the Legislative Process</u>, Vol. 9, No. 3, The Serials Librarian 115, 116, 118–19 (1985)

> Reproduced by permission of Haworth Press, Inc., 10 Alice Street, Binghampton, N.Y., Copyright © 1985.

Patterson, <u>Historical and Evolutionary Theories of Law</u>, 51 Colum. L. Rev. 681 (1951), pp. 695–98

> Copyright © 1951 by the Directors of the Columbia Law Review Association, Inc. All Rights Reserved. This article originally appeared at 51 Colum. L. Rev. 681 (1951). Reprinted by permission.

T. Plucknett, <u>Statutes and Their Interpretation</u> (William S. Hein & Co., Inc. 1980), pp. 1–2, 22, 25, 49–50

> Copyright © 1980 by William S. Hein & Co., Inc. All Rights Reserved.

Pound, <u>Spurious Interpretation</u>, 7 Colum. L. Rev. 379 (1907), pp. 380–84

> Copyright © 1907 by the Directors of the Columbia Law Review Association, Inc. All Rights Reserved. This article originally appeared at 41 Colum. L. Rev. 381 (1941). Reprinted by permission.

Pound, <u>Common Law and Legislation</u>, 21 Harv. L. Rev. 383, 383–87 (1908), reprinted by permission of Harvard Law Review Association.

Rosenthal, <u>The State of State Legislatures</u>, 11 Hofstra L. Rev. 1185, 1187–91 (1983), reprinted by permission of Hofstra Law Review Association, and Alan Rosenthal.

Ruud, <u>No Law Shall Embrace More Than One Subject</u>, 42 Minn.L.Rev. 389, 389, 391–92, 398–400, 447 (1958), reprinted by permission of Minnesota Law Review Foundation.

Scott, <u>The Politics of Article 9</u>, 80 Va. L. Rev. 1783, 1806–1817 (1994), reprinted by permission of Robert Scott, Virginia Law Review Association, and Fred B. Rothman & Co.

Stewart and Sunstein, <u>Public Programs and Private Rights</u>, 95 Harv. L.Rev. 1193, 1231 1292–93, 1294–95, 1296, 1300–01, 1306–07 (1982), (1936), reprinted by permission of Harvard Law Review Association, Richard B. Stewart, and Cass R. Sunstein.

Stone, <u>The Common Law in the United States</u>, 50 Harv. L. Rev. 4, 12–13 (1936), reprinted by permission of Harvard Law Review Association (in first edition only).

Sunstein, <u>Beyond the Republican Revival</u>, 97 Yale L.J. 1539, 1542, 1544–45, 1548–49, 1555–56, 1576–77, 1579, 1581–82 (1988)

> Reprinted by permission of the Yale Law Journal Company and Fred B. Rothman & Company from <u>The Yale Law Journal</u>, Vol. <u>97</u>, pp. <u>1539 - 1590</u>; and Reprinted by permission of Cass Sunstein.

S. Thorne, <u>A Discourse Upon the Statutes</u> 43–47 (1942)

> Reprinted with the permission of the Henry E. Huntington Library; and Reprinted by permission of Sam Thorne.

Thorne, <u>The Equity of a Statute amd Heydon's Case</u>, 31 Ill. L. Rev. 202, 203–05, 207–09, 215–17 (1936)

>Reprinted by special permission of Northwestern University School of Law, 1936, <u>Illinois Law Review</u>, (Volume 31)—202, 203–05, 207–09, 215–17; and Reprinted by permission of Sam Thorne.

Wald, <u>Some Observations on the Use of Legislative History in the 1981 Supreme Court Term</u>, 68 Iowa L.Rev. 195, 214–16 (1983), reprinted by permission of the Iowa Law Review, and Patricia Wald.

SUMMARY OF CONTENTS

*

DETAILED TABLE OF CONTENTS

TABLE OF CASES

Principal cases are in bold type. Non-principal cases are in roman type. References are to Pages.

MATERIALS ON LEGISLATION:

Political Language and the Political Process

*

CHAPTER 1

THE BOOK'S APPROACH

Legislation is all around us. When we purchase an appliance, get injured on the job, complain to a landlord about dangerous electrical wiring, clean up the environment, purchase stock, enforce civil rights, obtain social security benefits, file a tax return, or vote, we confront law created by statute. Statutes have infiltrated into traditional common law areas and created whole bodies of law to deal with the modern welfare state and to regulate activities of modern business. And yet most of what a law student studies in the first year of law school is the common law, which consists of general rules fashioned over time by judges in individual cases. Even when statutes are discussed, little attention is paid to the problems that are common to statutory law, which cut across different areas of substantive law. The purpose of this course is to take statutes as seriously as we take the common law. We want to know what it means to adopt law by statute, how it contrasts with the common law, and how courts should deal with statute law.

1.01   JUDICIAL CONCEPTIONS OF LEGISLATION AND JUDGING

The conventional answers to questions of statutory interpretation rely on either the text or legislative intent, but these answers are unsatisfactory. They provide neither a sufficient explanation nor an adequate justification for how judges interpret legislation. The critical interpretive question is always one of institutional lawmaking responsibility, based on conceptions of legislation and adjudication. When a judge interprets a statute, he or she always asks whether reaching a particular substantive result lies within the judge's or some other institution's sphere of lawmaking responsibility, such as the legislature or an agency.

The influence of text/intent is often overstated in judicial opinions about statutory interpretation because judges are reluctant to admit that they are allocating lawmaking responsibility. The easiest course for the judge is to cite evidence of meaning derived from the text and/or legislative intent as *conclusive* authority for a result, rather than as *constraints* on statutory meaning. But text and intent are never the sole considerations. The judge always takes account of both the substantive concerns which argue for a particular result and of the procedural considerations which help to justify the results reached by a particular institution. Statutory interpretation depends on working out the interaction of substance and procedure, as well as text and intent.

The interplay of substance and procedure is at the heart of all judging and is a familiar feature of administrative and constitutional law. In administrative law, the more confident the judge is about the process by which the agency reaches a decision, the more tolerant the judge will be of the agency's substantive conclusions. And, in constitutional law, the more careful the legislature has been in making substantive law, the less likely it is that the court will reject legislative conclusions as unconstitutional. Conversely, the more important the substantive values, the greater the standard of procedural care the agency or legislature must demonstrate before a court will allow those institutions to reject such values. This interaction between substance and procedure underlies the search for various levels of judicial scrutiny in constitutional law (strict scrutiny, intermediate review, and minimum rationality), and explains how courts decide whether or not to defer to an administrative decision. It is therefore not surprising that it also contributes to understanding statutory interpretation.

The judge's reluctance to admit to making lawmaking choices in statutory interpretation is counterbalanced by an inclination among academic lawyers to emphasize the radical indeterminacy of texts and legislative intent as a source of meaning. The argument is that texts and intent are not just unclear in some cases, but that they are always potentially uncertain. And, indeed, they are. The idea is as old as Aristotle, and rests on the notion that the lawmaker cannot anticipate everything that is likely to arise and to which the statute might apply. In Book V, sec. 10, of the Nicomachean Ethics, Aristotle discussed "equity" as a corrective of legal justice. The problem, he said, was "that all law is universal but about some things it is not possible to make a universal statement which shall be correct. * * * [T]he error is not in the law nor in the legislator but in the nature of the thing, since the matter of practical affairs is of this kind from the start." Aristotle's solution is as follows:

> When the law speaks universally [   ] and a case arises on it which is not covered by the universal statement, then it is right, where the legislator fails us and has erred by over-simplicity, to correct the omission—to say what the legislator himself would have said had he been present, and would have put into his law if he had known. * * * And this is the nature of the equitable, a correction of law where it is defective owing to its universality.

When we map this insight about the legislator's inability to anticipate all the particulars to which the law might apply onto the contemporary political world in which complexity and change are endemic, we soon realize that every case presents something new which the legislature has not anticipated—either the particulars of the case or the evolution of background values from which the statute originally emerged. But the indeterminacy of text and intent can be as overstated as the view that the text and intent are dispositive. The reality is that text and intent often exert a gravitational pull on statutory meaning—that is, they are constraints—even if that pull is never completely dispositive. Consequently, judges who ask where lawmaking responsibility lies do not thereby disregard evidence of what the text means or what the legislature might intend. They instead implement a conception of statutory interpretation as *the interaction of constraints on statutory meaning (evidence of text and intent) with substantive values and procedural considerations when applying particular statutes to particular cases.*

One implication of this conception of statutory interpretation is that judges must take responsibility for substantive results when interpreting legislation. And this, in turn, requires a theory of judging that survives in an age when the dominant source of law is statutory. More specifically, the theory must deal with the claim that the legislature is supreme where statute law is concerned, in contrast to constitutional or common law. The "legislative supremacy" view posits that the judge's only responsibility in statutory interpretation is to defer to the statutory text or legislative intent. In this view, statutes and the common law are sharply distinct sources of law, requiring courts to play dramatically different roles. Courts would continue to have a creative role in the common law, but their role in dealing with statutes would be very different.

The debate about the judge's role in statutory interpretation has often been framed in terms of legislative supremacy. One response is to note that, in contrast to the English and Continental European tradition, our legislature is not sovereign—the Constitution is. But that is not much help. It simply invites the argument that the Constitution allocates paramount law-making authority to the legislature. In the familiar language of Separation of Powers doctrine, the idea is that the Constitution allocates lawmaking power solely to the legislature.

The better response is to focus on what legislative supremacy and Separation of Powers means. It can mean that legislatures have the first, last, and only word in determining law in those areas in which it chooses to legislate. This puts legislation in a watertight compartment, allowing judges no lawmaking authority when they interact with statutes. But there is a rival view, which posits that legislative supremacy means only that legislatures have the first and last word but that, in between, there is a wide range of judicial lawmaking potential, left to the prudential judgment of the court. This is consistent with another view of Separation of Powers, that the branches of government often share government power, subject to mutual checks and balances (such as the executive veto of legislation, and judicial review of unconstitutional legislation). In this view, statutes and common law are both sources of law with a common objective—to move towards the best possible legal resolution of disputes. A pervasive question in this book is whether we are in a period where there is no sharp division between statutes and common law, where the judge's role is to participate in a political dialogue with other institutions to determine what the law means. More specifically, we want to know whether and how courts can participate in this dialogue *through statutory interpretation.*

Put somewhat differently, the debate about legislative authority and statutory interpretation can be framed in terms of "legislative will." The "will" of the legislature prevails (subject to constitutional constraints), but its "will" can prevail in different ways. It can be a source of authority, a final veto on someone else's action, or a part of a colloquy. The perspective adopted in these materials is that legislation is a much richer phenomenon than a command of a willful legislative sovereign to which courts defer. It is part of a dynamic, ongoing relationship among political institutions. Opponents of this approach are wary of judicial power and frequently quote Humpty Dumpty's comment to Alice as a warning: Humpty Dumpty says that a word "means just what I [the interpreter] choose it to mean * * *. The question is * * * which is to be master—that's all." Lewis Carroll, Through the Looking Glass 274 (Penguin ed. 1970). But Lewis Carroll reminded us not only that the interpreter has power, but also that meaning itself—presumably what the interpreter seeks—is a complex phenomenon. When the March Hare admonishes Alice to "say what you mean" and Alice responds, "I do, at least—at least I mean what I say—that's the same thing you know," the Hatter cautions Alice: "Not the same thing a bit!" As we will see, legislatures may say more or less than they mean and statutes may mean more or less than they say.

A judge may be concerned with the interaction of statutory meaning and text without coming close to engaging in Humpty–Dumptyism. Prudence often suggests great care in reaching certain decisions, which should not be confused with an absence of constitutional authority in courts to decide how prudent to be. This is as true in statutory interpretation as it is in constitutional and common law. The following excerpt from P.H. Investment v. Oliver, 778 P.2d 11 (Utah App.1989), is a rare example of a judicial statement distinguishing carefully between the constitutional and prudential rationales for a judicial decision. Although it deals with the common law, it has relevance for statutory interpretation as well. The question in the case was whether to create an implied warranty of habitability to enable a tenant to reduce her rent obligation based on defects in the condition of the premises. The court refrained from judicially creating an implied warranty, stating:

> Our holding is based on considerations of public policy, rather than on an inherent lack of judicial power. Separation of powers principles delimit the outer reaches of judicial lawmaking power, but changing the judge-made rules at issue in this case would not approach those outer reaches. The courts of many states have found alteration of these rules to be within the scope of judicial power, and Utah courts have not hesitated to overrule outmoded or ill-founded case law doctrines. Courts are thus engaged in an ongoing dialogue with the Legislature in lawmaking, from a somewhat contrasting institutional frame of reference. With their constant immersion in the law, courts are in a better position than the Legislature to note defects in the law, and their partial independence from the shifting and perhaps, in rare instances, harsh or extreme tides of popular opinion gives them a perspective and an ability to assure a minimum of liberty to persons who may not be able to meaningfully assert their interests in the legislative process. Therefore, we abstain at this time from undertaking an extensive revision of the law in this area, not because judges today are unable to

revise what judges of yesteryear have written, but because we believe that the Legislature is better able to undertake such a revision.

1.02   OUTLINE OF BOOK

Our conception of legislation and adjudication is an artifact of our legal history and so we begin our study with an historical review of how the legal culture reacted to statutes. Part I is about the history and theory of statutory interpretation. It traces that history from a time when legislation and adjudication were not distinct to the contemporary legal world in which separation of powers concerns must be addressed, recounting the changes in judicial attitude that accompanied the displacement of the common law by legislation. Chapter 2 reviews the reception of statutes from the middle ages to the end of the 19th Century, during which period courts were confident of their dominant legal role and skeptical of legislation, but during which legislatures also evolved towards lawmaking dominance, both in theory and practice, and courts were eventually put on the defensive. Chapter 3 discusses the emergence of purposive statutory interpretation in the 20th Century, when legislators became confident of their ability to make law and judges conceded that legislatures were the dominant lawmakers. Chapter 4 discusses contemporary theories of statutory interpretation, which respond to a loss in confidence in *both* judging and legislating.

Part II deals with the technique and theory of statutory interpretation, focusing on how courts and legislatures interact. Contemporary analyses of statutory interpretation emphasize the perspective of the statutory text, the legislative writer's intent, and the role of the judicial reader, and the focus of Part II is about which of these perspectives to prefer. It is difficult, however, to know which point of view a judicial reader can legitimately adopt without also being as clear as we possibly can about what counts as evidence of the text's meaning and the writer's intent, and what it means for judges to to take account of background considerations to interpret a statute.

Part II–A is therefore as concerned with what we mean by the criteria of statutory meaning—the text, intent or purpose, and background considerations—as about which normative interpretive theory to adopt. Chapter 5 discusses the text. Chapter 6 deals with purpose, which we refer to as a type of external context. Chapter 7 looks at *substantive* background considerations, which is another type of external context. Chapter 8 examines the impact on statutory interpretation of statutory detail, the legislative process, and the interaction between the two. Chapter 9 deals with the impact of change on statutory meaning, paying close attention to *institutional* background considerations.

Part II–B focuses on a special problem of determining statutory meaning: the role played by legislative history. Topics include the effect of committee reports, legislative debates reported in the congressional record, and post-legislative developments (such as reenactment of statutes and legislative inaction) on statutory meaning.

Part II–C considers some less familiar ways in which statutes might become a source of law. Statutes might influence common law development or become a source of rights and obligations in areas not traditionally covered by the common law. Patterns of statutes might develop over time so that the overall pattern takes on a meaning not obvious from examining a single statute. For example, we are concerned with efforts by earlier legislatures to control future lawmaking, with deciding when later law repeals earlier legislation, and with whether multiple statutes should be interpreted as though they are part of an integrated text. In these situations, we confront the most basic questions of how legislation can enter into the broad fabric of the law in a rich and meaningful way, like the common law itself.

Part III deals with how courts monitor the lawmaking process, through state and federal constitutional law, rather than statutory interpretation. Topics include: electoral groundrules; controlling the influence of money on politics; state constitutional rules about legislative procedure and special interest legislation; requirements of legislative rationality; and legislative-executive relationships (such as line item vetoes and impoundment). Some of these issues are also discussed in constitutional law classes. This course looks for a "legislation" spin on material studied elsewhere.

1.03 PEDAGOGY

It is no secret that Legislation courses have never penetrated very deeply into the law school curriculum.[1] When legislation became a dominant source of law in the first four decades of the 20th century, the major argument for a Legislation course was that the legislative process deserved study in its own right. The argument was made most forcefully by Ernst Freund,[2] who contrasted adjudication with legislation in the following ways: the judicial decision is concerned with logic, not empirical data; cases reason out propositions, rather than consider the fitness of means to ends; teaching about cases leads the student to think critically, but teaching about statutes requires constructive thinking; judicial thought is incapable of producing certain types of legal reforms. This led Freund to conclude that a course in statutes cannot be conducted profitably by reading only cases.

Edward Rubin presents a modern version of Freund's point of view.[3] He notes that most legal scholarship is restricted to "an increasingly secondary legal institution, namely the judiciary," even though legislators and adminis-

---

1. Williams, Statutory Law in Legal Education: Still Second Class After All These Years, 35 Mercer L. Rev. 803 (1984); Eskridge & Frickey, Legislation Scholarship and Pedagogy in the Post–Legal Process Era, 48 U.Pitt.L.Rev. 691 (1987).

2. Freund, A Course in Statutes, 4 Am. L. Sch. Rev. 503 (1919)

3. Rubin, The Concept of Law and the New Public Law Scholarship, 89 Mich. L. Rev. 792 (1991).

trators have become the principal law-creating officials. Because legal scholarship, alone among the social sciences, is prescriptive, legal scholars must expand their object of study if they want to address decisionmakers.

Rubin observes the following major differences between common law judges and legislative and administrative decisionmakers. Common law judges appeal to principles, act incrementally, rely on analogy, and justify decisions by reference to process. By contrast, legislators and administrators act instrumentally to achieve a purpose; do not act incrementally, except by choice; do not rely on analogies to prior law; and justify their actions by how well they achieve a purpose, not by their process of decisionmaking. Because of these differences, someone addressing legislators and administrators must focus on legislative and administrative lawmaking techniques, such as enforcement. For example, what should a statute say about allocating burden of proof, the award of attorney's fees, the use of mediation, the imposition of civil and criminal penalties, and private vs. administrative remedies? Drafting is also important. For example, what is the optimum level of specificity vs. generality in a law? Rubin notes lack of interest in the immensely important Financial Institutions Reform, Recovery, and Enforcement Act, Pub. L. No. 101–73, 103 Stat. 183 (1989), dealing with the savings-and-loan crisis, as a failure of legal scholarship.

Robin West also criticizes a focus on judicial lawmaking. She advocates reorienting progressive legal discourse towards a legislative rather than a judicial audience. She argues that the "idea of 'adjudicative law' may be antithetical to the progressive understanding of the Constitution * * *."[4] Adjudication, she argues, is authoritarian in practice, requiring positive authority, rather than being probabilistic and open-ended, which is characteristic of at least some legislation. Instrumentally, adjudication is corrective and compensatory and is therefore unlikely to abolish subordinating relationships or adopt radically redistributionist goals, both of which are sometimes achieved by legislation. Finally, the morality of adjudicative law is conservative and traditional, not aspirational and utopian, and the forms and processes of adjudication are elitist, hierarchical, and nonparticipatory. Legislation is at least potentially more aspirational and participatory.

Despite these criticisms of a pedagogical emphasis on adjudication, this book focuses on statutes-in-court. Judging will continue to be what most occupies lawyers, and law school is the only place where judging is the central concern. At least political science departments consider legislation and public administration schools study agency decisionmaking. As for Robin West's comparison of adjudication and legislation, there is plenty of material in this course to help the student compare what courts and legislatures can do.

We do not neglect the legislative process. It is important to understand how legislation is made, not least so that we may understand how courts

4. West, Progressive and Conservative Constitutionalism, 88 Mich. L. Rev. 641 (1990).

should determine the meaning of statutes. Too much of what courts say about the legislative process is descriptively wrong or at least naive. This course therefore deals with such matters as the role of private interest groups in shaping legislation, logrolling and legislative compromise, the problem of legislative inertia and careless drafting, how committees and their staffs operate, what happens on the floor of Congress, and what the executive line item veto can accomplish. We pay attention to the legislative process, however, primarily to understand statutes-in-court.

You should be careful how you read cases dealing with statutes. They are harder to read than common law cases. They do not usually tell stories about litigants the way common law cases do. Nor do they invite the speculation about principle associated with the common law. Statutes seem to freeze the law in some middle ground between evolving principle and particular facts, adopting rules that seem arbitrary and less susceptible to the speculations associated with common law principles. (Common law rules may also be arbitrary, but it is less obvious.) Once you get the hang of reading cases dealing with statutes, you should not be bored. The intellectual challenge is considerable, because it requires mastering not only judicial reasoning but also understanding what the legislative process was trying to accomplish and working out the relationship between legislatures and courts.

PART I

THE HISTORY AND THEORY OF STATUTORY INTERPRETATION

Part I consists of three chapters, tracing the history and theory of statutory interpretation. It provides a necessary framework for the in-depth study of statutory interpretation in subsequent chapters.

Chapter 2 examines statutory interpretation from the 13th Century through (approximately) 1900, discussing the rise of legislation and the reaction of common law courts. There are two primary themes—(1) the evolution of separation of powers between legislatures and courts, on which the conception of interpretation depends; and (2) the shift from the common law courts' historical sense of lawmaking dominance towards the primacy of legislation. Common law courts originally operated on the assumption that they had a superior ability to identify law, which consisted of objectively determinable custom and which evolved gradually in response to contemporary needs. Legislation, by contrast, was viewed as a secondary source of law, declaring the common law and correcting its defects. On a more technical note, statutes were criticized as carelessly drafted and rigid, creating rather than eliminating uncertainty.

This negative view of statutes came under intense scrutiny in both England and the United States in the 18th Century and thereafter. During the period between the Revolution and the Founding (1776–1789) and throughout the 19th Century, there was a tug-of-war between courts and legislatures in the United States, marked by debates over the relative legitimacy and competence of legislative and judicial lawmaking. The first half of the Century witnessed a shift towards judicial deference to statutes, at least compared to earlier periods, although differences of opinion about the judicial role persisted among judges and commentators. Then, towards the middle and end of the Century, judges developed a marked hostility towards statutes, as courts tried to preserve common law principles in the face of reform legislation.

Chapter 3 looks at the changes in attitude towards statutes and statutory interpretation that began in the early 20th Century and evolved through the 1960s. This period witnessed a reaction against judicial hostility towards legislation and the completion of the trend towards statutes as the dominant form of lawmaking. It was accompanied by a greater faith in the ability of legislatures to make law (there was now a "science" of legislation); and a

9

correlative suspicion of judge-made law, which was revealed to be riddled with political choices rather than objective principle. The dynamic source of law was now located at least as much if not more in legislation, rather than common law. An active judicial role was preserved in statutory interpretation through the imaginative reconstruction of legislative purpose applied to specific cases.

Chapter 4 examines contemporary history since the 1960s, which has witnessed the disintegration of those foundations on which judges might confidently engage in statutory interpretation. The Law and Economics movement argued against the view that legislation had a purpose on which judges could or should rely. Critical Legal Studies further developed the theme that judge-made law embodied political choices—systematically tilted towards the dominant social/political point of view—but without confidence that legislation would develop into a science in the service of the public good. Feminist and Critical Race Theory, and Gay legal studies, emphasized the shortcomings of both courts and legislatures in omitting the voices of significant elements of the population. Loss of faith in law in general and judging in particular contributed to the rise of modern textualism in statutory interpretation. It also contributed to interest in a "pragmatic" approach to statutory interpretation, which rejects reliance on any single foundation to justify judging, but eclectically embraces multiple approaches, suitable to the occasion. It remains to be seen whether such eclecticism can sustain a robust conception of judging.

CHAPTER 2

THE RISE OF LEGISLATION AND THE REACTION OF COMMON LAW COURTS

This Chapter presents an historical review of how courts interpreted statutes from common law beginnings to the end of the 19th Century. We encounter a variety of ways to characterize the relationship between courts and legislatures. Consider these possibilities: (1) the words of the statute merely suggest the content of legislation to the court; (2) the "equity of the statute" (a) limits the strict application of the language, (b) expands the statutory language so that it applies to events not within the words but within the intention of the statute, or (c) enters the law as a generating legal principle; (3) legislative intent determines statutory meaning; (4) the text determines statutory meaning; (5) the statute is narrowly or expansively interpreted to implement certain substantive values.

The general point is that interpretation depended and still depends on the judges' conception of the relationship between courts and the legislature and that this relationship has changed over time. The history reveals a gradual separation of legislation from judging, without which the very conception of interpretation could not exist. This distancing of legislatures from courts eventually matured into modern concerns about separation of powers and the legitimate role courts could play in determining statutory meaning.

2.01   13TH–15TH CENTURY

T. Plucknett, Statutes and Their Interpretation
(William S. Hein & Co., Inc. 1980).

§ 1.   The Forms of Legislation

 * * * [The judges of the 19th century] had the inestimable advantage [over judges of the 13th and 14th centuries] of knowing the exact meaning of several highly important words—"Parliament," "Statute," "Proclamation," "Court," "Sovereignty," and the like. Contrast this with the state of legal knowledge in the reigns of

Edward I and Edward II [Editor—1272–1307 and 1307–1327 respectively]. Who could then say what a statute was, or be certain that any particular document was a statute? Who could say, even, what the actual words of any acknowledged statute really were? * * *

§ 2.   The Nature of the Legislature

Then again, what of those new devices, parliaments? Recurring periods of discontent, followed by threats of serious trouble, had several times produced crises which the Crown had successfully met by summoning meetings of notables—who grumbled, and dispersed. The result was generally a tax, sometimes a promise or even a measure of reform. Indeed, there were two especially remarkable years, 1275 and 1285, when the larger part of the law of England was drastically overhauled at the parliaments then held, but it would have been difficult to regard a tactical device employed by the king when in military or financial extremity as an acknowledged source of English law. Still less could one have said that parliament or anyone else was sovereign, for sovereignty at this time was more a theological than a constitutional conception, and was confronted with insuperable theoretical difficulties when applied to earthly monarchies. * * *

§ 4.   Judicial Legislation and Administration

Judicial interpretation, moreover, was frankly acknowledged to be virtually legislation. * * *

* * * [T]he lawyers of Edward I's time took no especial pains to distinguish adjudication from legislation. If the two functions could be conveniently performed together and by the same routine, then they were, and no theory of the separation of powers was in existence to force a distinction. * * *

§ 6.   The Legal Results of the Fusion of Powers

Our period is remarkable for this fusion of powers, which frustrates all attempts to make the mediaeval constitution look like a system. These facts must be borne in mind when we come to the examination in detail of the relations between the courts and the legislature * * *, for they will explain the absence of that feeling that a statute is something imposed upon a court from without, which is so typical of modern conditions. At the same time the great familiarity with which the statutes were treated will also be seen to have its justification in the fusion of powers and institutions which we have attempted to describe. * * *

It was only gradually that the courts made a practice of examining the intention of a statute in order to find a clue to its interpretation. * * *

[When judges first looked for legislative intent, they] had no difficulty whatever in discussing the intention of the legislature since the judges themselves bore the principal share in lawmaking. Examples already quoted may be supplemented with further details here: thus, in many quarters there was doubt as to whether Westminster II, c.3 would allow the receipt of a wife to defend her right when her husband was about to surrender it, unless the writ against the husband mentioned her also. HENGHAM, J. settled the matter at once by declaring the intention of the legislature—of which he was a member—"We agreed in Parliament that the wife if not named in the writ, should not be received"; and again, "Do not gloss the statute for we know better than you; we made it". It is noteworthy that when HENGHAM'S inside knowledge of the legislature's intention is no longer available, the court is put to an examination of the wording of Westminster II, c.3 and only after some difficulty reached the same conclusion—that the wife was only receivable if named in the writ.

The critical point made by Plucknett is that we cannot begin to understand how courts deal with statutes until we have some idea of what a statute is, which in turn requires understanding what is meant by a legislature. The early Parliaments of the 13th and 14th Century were nothing like a modern legislature. They were a shifting group of powerful people summoned and discharged by the King. Their job was to hear cases (like a court), agree to pay taxes (they did not legislate taxes so much as agree to requests for money), deal with matters of state (often foreign affairs), and transmit petitions for particular benefits or relief to the King and his Council (initiating what we might call private legislation). Parliament was not so much a body as an occasion at which people met to cooperate with the King (to parley or speak with the King) as they saw fit.

The lack of organizational structure (compared to a modern legislature) corresponded to a lack of developed sense of lawmaking. Law was not something that was created; it was custom (that is, common law). Judges and Parliament thought of themselves (1) as declaring customary law, a sense of role which long outlasted reality; and (2) as responding to particularized grievances, not making general law.

There was, moreover, no inkling of separating the legislative and judicial functions, as illustrated by Judge Hengham's confident assertion that he had first hand knowledge of what the law provided. This judicial sense of knowing about legislative intent persisted long after judges were not legislators. Indeed, the decline of judicial confidence in identifying such intent is one of the major features of modern statutory interpretation.

In the following excerpts we begin to see the separation of legislators and judges, and the beginnings of "interpretation." This should not be confused with a well-defined sense of separation of legislative and judicial powers as we know it today. Pay particular attention to the conception of "equitable interpretation," and the distinction between extending and limiting the reach of statutes.

Thorne, The Equity of a Statute and Heydon's Case
31 Ill. L. Rev. 202 (1936).

The interpretation of statutes in its modern sense is a latecomer to English law: it must be obvious that so long as the law maker is his own interpreter the problem of a technique of interpretation does not arise. Only when he is forced to delegate the function of interpretation to a different person does the matter become urgent. The extension or contraction of a statute's words in the light of the legislator's actual intention, known to the judge in fact, or in the light of the judges' own intention when they themselves drew it, is a very different thing from the extension or contraction of its words under a doctrine of equitable interpretation. In the first case there is no interpretation at all: the words of the provision are little more than a faint and distant echo of a very real and well understood intention, and it is in its light that the judge gives or withholds a remedy; the words may seem to expand, contract, or disappear completely, but in fact they have played no part in the result. It is only after the middle of the fourteenth century, when judges find themselves no longer able to draw either upon the actual intention of the legislator or upon the royal dispensing power, that they are forced to construct a body of rules of statutory interpretation: a document, and no longer the verbal explanations of one man to another, becomes the sole basis for the judge's action, and if the facts do not fall within the statute's precise words, then perhaps it may be possible to resort to some doctrine of equitable interpretation which, on its face, can mean nothing unless by its side there exists the contrary view of strict interpretation from which it is distinguished. Just how far equitable interpretation will permit the judge to expand the express words of a statute we shall see later, but it seems clear that a doctrine of equitable interpretation does not appear until early in the fifteenth century, after, as we should expect, the doctrine of strict interpretation from which it relieves, and which itself first takes form late in the preceding century, has made its rigors felt. * * *

* * * Prior to the reign of Edward III [Editor—1327–1377] the court frequently restricted the scope of a statute by excepting particular cases from its operation * * *.

But the reverse of the medal yields a very different picture. * * * It soon must have become evident in practice that a refusal to extend the words of a statute led frequently to injustice when applied to legislative acts drawn with the lack of attention to exact meaning and careful phraseology exhibited by the statutes of the time, and in the light of what we have said above of the judge's willingness to except cases out of the statute, it perhaps is difficult to understand their corresponding unwillingness to extend legislation beyond its exact words. That they are unwilling cannot be denied for, as we shall see below, the appearance of the doctrine of equitable interpretation is itself strong evidence of the existence of a vigorous policy of strict interpretation. Statutes are to be taken as they stand; though they may be restricted in scope without comment, any extension, however slight, must be justified by reference to a definite doctrine of interpretation. But these methods of dealing with statutes are not inconsistent: the general attitude during the later Year Book period is one of jealousy for the common law which was not to be modified by statute more than could be avoided. Statutes will be held to do no more than they literally say in changing or adding to common law rules, and on the other hand, common law policy will be read into statutes to restrict general words that change common law principles too violently. The two seemingly opposite views of the nature of a statute—one requiring strict adherence to its words, the other permitting the words to be disregarded—are both based upon the feeling that common law ought not to be changed, a policy that develops during the reign of Edward III, and that may be observed dominating the action of the court during the entire later Year Book period along three parallel lines of force: increasing strictness in interpreting statutes beyond their literal meaning; no change in the free policy of an earlier day permitting cases to be excepted out of the statute's general words; [Editor—third "line of force" omitted] * * *.

S. Thorne, A Discourse Upon the Statutes
(1942).

In the early fourteenth century, if the words of an act supplied a remedy for one complex of facts but did not provide for a comparable situation that deserved equal treatment, no difficulty was experienced in achieving justice by permitting the same result in the analogous case. [Editor—In statutory interpretation lingo, extending a statute beyond its text deals with a "casus omissus," an omitted case.] To a modern mind such an extension, though it would today be regarded as judicial legislation on an excessively broad scale, is less drastic than others that were contemporaneously made, since it is interstitial in character and therefore more limited in scope. But a distinction of this kind, dependent as it is upon a more sophisticated concept of legislation, is not visible in the undifferentiated practice of the early fourteenth century, for at that time all extensions, whether circumscribed by the words of the statute or not, were equally proper or, with the advent of a stricter approach toward legislation, correspondingly improper. After the third quarter of the century, however, judicial action with respect to statutes is distinguished into that which is equivalent to legislation and that which falls short of it—a separation reflected in the emergence of the doctrine of "lequity de lestatut." * * * The appearance of that doctrine reflects the fact that a definition of legislation had been formulated, during the middle years of the fourteenth century, which now made it possible [to distinguish] between judicial action that was completely legislative in character and that which did not overstep the proper function of courts. * * * Put more precisely, the terms in which an act was phrased had gained greater importance than they had possessed earlier and could not be easily augmented without parliamentary action, but, on the other hand, a statute was not yet thought to provide solely for the one set of circumstances it mentioned, and thus its words had not acquired the sanction that was later to force courts to take the position that a case similar to that dealt with in a statute, but entirely unprovided for by it, must remain so.

The bold supplementation of statutes, recognized after the middle fourteenth century to be legislative action, was no longer within the province of judges, but, just as analogous cases were within a common-law rule, so situations unmentioned in an act but in the same mischief as that toward which it was directed were aided by "lequity de lestatut." Though the doctrine is framed in terms that do not suggest a judicial authority to extend a statute beyond its words, but rather a vague penumbra of essentially similar cases surrounding the precise words of an act to which it must in justice apply, later usage has come to regard it as an example of a power exercised by judges which enabled them to bring within reach of a statute situations that admittedly lay outside its express provisions. But to describe the process in terms of conflicting legislative and judicial authority or, in other words, to visualize it as an illustration of the power of the judiciary to supplement legislative fiat, is to conceive it in modern and therefore anachronistic form. It was simply a facet of the administration of justice * * *. Whatever liberties judges may seem to be taking with statutes, and whatever powers would be needed to justify their actions today, they were themselves conscious of performing nothing more than an ordinary, routine step in the administration of justice between party and party * * *.

2.02   16th–17th Century

a) Introduction

During the 16th and 17th Centuries, Parliament completed an evolutionary process of becoming an organized lawmaking body. It asserted the right to determine its members' qualifications, to impeach officials, and to avoid arrest. It developed an affirmative sense of lawmaking authority, evidenced by growing use of general legislation, publishing sessions laws, writing preambles for statutes, initiating legislation (not just agreeing to legislation proposed by the Crown), conducting business by formal internal procedures, and keeping journals (the House of Lords beginning in 1509;

the House of Commons in 1547). Parliament finally established its right to convene and remain in session without depending on the Crown's pleasure.

Parliament also completed a more revolutionary process of acquiring sovereignty by the end of the 17th Century. In response to the Crown's claims to sovereignty, Parliament asserted its rights—initiating a civil war in 1642, disposing of Charles I in 1649 (by beheading), and setting up a non-monarchical commonwealth from 1649–1660. Thereafter, England restored the monarchy, but further conflict with the Crown resulted in the Glorious Revolution of 1688, which established Parliamentary sovereignty.

These changes in Parliament's organization and legal authority had some effect on the relationship of legislation to judging, including statutory interpretation—or at least on the judicial rhetoric. Some of that story is recounted in the following pages. It would be premature, however, to view the evolution of 16th–17th Century approaches to statutory interpretation against a background of modern separation of powers doctrine. During the period we are discussing, the serious rival to Parliament was the Crown, not the courts. Parliament and the courts both appealed to the common law in their battles with the Crown and the common law was viewed as Parliament's source of privilege and authority. Both Parliament and courts were under the law and the common law lawyers were the oracles of the law. Law students who study how judges disposed of the 16th Century Statute of Uses and the 17th Century Statute of Frauds are aware of how cavalierly judges dealt with some legislation.

Thorne summarizes the evolution of statutory interpretation in the 16th–17th Centuries, focusing on extensive equitable interpretation, as follows.

S. Thorne, A Discourse Upon the Statutes
(1942).

> In the sixteenth century, then, the extension of an enactment to a situation not within its precise words could be justified by means of the doctrine of a controlling "equity" which was "no part of the law, but a moral virtue which corrects the law." This was a more generalized form of the Year Book concept of "lequity de lestatut," which in turn reflects the new attitude toward statutes which were now being recognized as a body of material to be treated as a whole * * *.

> As acts of Parliament take on the attributes of modern legislation, the intention of the legislator must grow in importance and take the place of the equity, conjectured purpose, or reason that had controlled earlier. It is therefore significant that only during the middle years of the sixteenth century did the intention of the makers begin to form the justification for extending a statute beyond its words. * * *

* * * The appearance of the term "interpretation" provides another indication of the growing sanction back of acts of Parliament, for as enactments acquire formal rigidity their words must be saved by regarding departures from them as "interpretations" made by judges. These were founded, as has been indicated, upon reason or equity—words substantially synonymous with justice—and in the later sixteenth century they were being made as well in the light of the intention of the legislature. * * *

* * * [Although the seventeenth Century] fall[s] outside the scope of the present essay, there was evidently no acceptance, prior to Blackstone's day, of the rule that, Parliament having spoken only of specific things and specific situations, all others were *casus omissi* * * *. As Parliament became the sovereign and the duty of the judge was recognized to be merely to determine what Parliament has said and to "apply" it, omitted particulars could no longer be supplied, since that would amount to a usurpation of or encroachment upon the power of the legislature. This is a view of the judicial function that differed fundamentally from that which had prevailed earlier * * *. Its acceptance marks both the final abandonment of the powers of equitable construction assumed by judges in the sixteenth century (and thus of the older undifferentiated practice best described in terms of "lequity de lestatut") and the beginning of a long series of apologetic explanations for their past use.

b) PLOWDEN'S COMMENTARIES

The leading statement of the "equitable interpretation" approach to statutory interpretation in the 16th Century comes from Plowden's Commentaries, appended to his report of the decision in the case of Eyston v. Studd, 75 Eng.Rep. 692, 2 Plowden 463 (1587). Here is some of what Plowden said:

> * * * [O]ur law (like all others) consists of two parts, viz. of body and soul, the letter of the law is the body of the law, and the sense and reason of the law is the soul of the law * * *.

Plowden analogizes law to a nut with a shell (the letter) and kernel (the sense) and makes his preference for the kernel very clear: "the fruit and profit of the nut lies in the kernel, and not in the shell [and] the fruit and profit of the law consists in the sense more than in the letter." Consequently, Plowden says, you may know the letter, but not the sense, "for sometimes the sense is more confined and contracted than the letter, and sometimes it is more large and extensive." Plowden goes on to state that it is "equity" which

> enlarges or diminishes the letter according to its discretion. * * * And this correction of the general words is much used in the law of England.

And:

[I]f there is any defect in the law, it should be reformed by equity, which is no part of the law, but a moral virtue which corrects the law.

Plowden then paints the image of the judge as someone who carries on a conversation with the hypothetical law-maker.

In order to form a right judgment when the letter of a statute is restrained, and when enlarged by equity, it is a good way, when you peruse a statute, to suppose that the law-maker is present, and that you have asked him the question you want to know touching the equity, then you must give yourself such an answer as you imagine he would have done, if he had been present.

A modern reader might infer from Plowden's description of the judicial role that the judge had great power. Enlarging or diminishing the law in the judge's discretion, to implement the fruit and profit of the law (the kernel), suggests a bold assertion of judicial authority.[1] We need to look more closely, however, at just what that claim of judicial power meant. Like so many famous quotes about statutory interpretation, we can only understand their meaning by looking at illustrative examples. At least some of Plowden's examples reveal a more innocent objective than a modern reader might infer—simply helping the legislature to achieve its more or less obvious goal. Plowden's first two examples limit the reach of the criminal law: a statute defines a crime in general language, but the court exempts infants and people of unsound mind from the letter; and a statute defines as an accessory to a crime anyone who gives food to the criminal, but the court interprets the law to excuse the wife who feeds her husband. These are commonsensical exceptions, providing relief from the overbreadth of general language, and implementing traditional common law rules about criminal responsibility and spousal relationships.

Moreover, Plowden is probably not adopting any special rule of lenity to limit the reach of criminal statutes. In his comments on Eyston v. Studd, he rejects any special rule for penal laws, stating: "* * * [E]quity knows no difference between penal laws and others, for the intent, (which is the only thing regarded by equity * * *) ought to be followed and taken for law, as well in penal laws as in others." The actual judicial practice of the time regarding penal statutes is unclear. Thorne suggests that penal statutes could not be extended by equity, but could be limited (e.g., "park" cannot be extended to include "forest").[2] But Baade quotes Hatton, a 17th Century

---

1. See also 75 Eng.Rep. 130, 1 Plowden, p. 82: "For words, which are no other than the verberation of the air, do not constitute the statute, but are only the image of it, and the life of the statute rests in the minds of the expositors of the words, that is, the makers of the statutes. And if they appear dispersed, so that their minds cannot be known, then those who may approach nearest to their minds shall construe the words, and these are the sages of the law, whose talents are exercised in the study of such matters."

2. Thorne, The Equity of a Statute and Heydon's Case, 31 Ill. L. Rev. 202, 213 (1936)(hereafter "Thorne").

commentator, for the view that penal laws might be either extended or limited.[3]

Other Plowden examples limiting, and in some cases extending, the reach of a statute are similarly commonsensical: a statute aimed at preventing jailers from extorting money from inmates was interpreted not to apply to a traditional award of money to pay for certain services performed by the jailer; a requirement that the sheriff retain and not sell goods from a shipwreck, so that ownership could be determined later, did not apply to perishables; "executors" includes administrators; and the phrase "life or for years" also applied to a transaction of only one year.

There is, however, substantial evidence that judges went well beyond simply helping legislatures to achieve their more or less obvious goals. Some commentators characterized judging in this early period as a "process [which] has occasionally been carried to such an unwarrantable extent as to justify the expression of driving a coach and four through Act[s] of Parliament."[4] Certainly, judges approached statutes with a degree of lawmaking confidence that seems unfamiliar to us. One judge in 1616 referred to "that liberty and authority which judges have over laws, *especially over statute laws*, according to reason and best convenience, to mould them to the truest and best use (emphasis added)."[5] Judicial self-confidence is obvious in the following quote from Matthew Hale, one of the most distinguished lawyers and judges writing in the mid–17th Century: "As to exposition of Acts of Parliament and written laws certainly he that hath been educated in the study of the law hath a great advantage over those that have been otherwise exercised * * *."[6] We also encounter the beginnings of an explicit canon (not just a practice) of narrowly interpreting statutes in derogation of common law in a 1678 case dealing with the Statute of Frauds—"all acts which restrain the common law ought themselves to be restrained by exposition."[7]

One way judges dominated legislation was to find that a statute was declaratory of the common law, from which it followed "that a statute made in the affirmative, without any negative expressed or implied, doth not take away the common law."[8] Judicial discretion in deciding whether the statute was simply declaratory gave judges considerable power to work out the interaction of statutes and the common law. Another way courts could (if they wanted) preserve the common law was to find that remedies supplemented rather than displaced the common law. A famous example concerns the 18th Century dispute over whether a statutory remedy for copyright violation eliminated common law remedies. In Millar v. Taylor, 4 Burr. 2303 (1769), the court held that the statutory remedy did *not* preclude common

---

3. Baade, The *Casus Omissus*: A Pre-History of Statutory Analogy, 20 Syr. J. Int'l. Law & Comm. 45, 79 (1994)(hereafter "Baade").

4. Quoted in McIlwain, High Court of Parliament and Its Supremacy, p. 260 (1910)(hereafter "McIlwain").

5. Quoted in Baade, p. 76, from the decision in Sheffield v. Radcliffe.

6. Quoted in Baade, p. 84.

7. Quoted in Baade, pp. 84–85.

8. Quoted in McIlwain, p. 269.

law remedies, but the Law Lords reversed in Donaldson v. Beckett, 4 Burr. 2408 (1774).

c) HEYDON'S CASE

Another landmark of statutory interpretation, which occurred near the end of the 16th Century, is Heydon's Case (1584). It set forth an approach to statutory interpretation which explained how courts and legislature would interact. The case is especially interesting as an example of equitable interpretation, because it *extends* rather than limits the statute's reach. The court adopted the following set of interpretive rules:

> It was resolved by the Barons of the Exchequer that for the sure and true interpretation of all statutes in general (be they penal or beneficial, restrictive or enlarging of the Common Law) four things are to be discussed and considered: 1st, What was the Common Law before the making of the Act; 2nd, What was the mischief and defect for which the Common Law did not provide; 3rd, What remedy the Parliament hath resolved and appointed to cure the disease of the commonwealth; and 4th, The true reason of the remedy; and then the office of all the judges is always to make such construction as shall suppress the mischief and advance the remedy, and to suppress subtle inventions and evasions for continuance of the mischief, and *pro privato commodo*, and to add force and life to the cure and remedy according to the true intent of the makers of the Act *pro bono publico*.

In the following excerpt, Thorne discusses what these rules might have meant to a 16th Century lawyer. Of special interest is his discussion of the 4th consideration—"true reason of the remedy"—which has survived and been transformed into the modern approach to statutory interpretation which favors interpreting a statute in light of its purpose. Thorne suggests that we cannot equate 16th Century practice with modern purposive judging, a conclusion which we cannot evaluate until we have looked more closely at 20th Century purposivism in later chapters. Thorne argues that extensive equitable interpretation at this time allowed only for "the strict, literal meaning of a statute [to] be extended, but only slightly extended." (He gives as an example the application of a statute dealing with the "death of a husband" to a case of a dissolved marriage.[9] Is that a "slight" extension?)

Thorne, The Equity of a Statute and Heydon's Case
31 Ill. L. Rev. 202 (1936).

> * * * [The rules] are phrased in very wide terms, and on their face may seem to envisage the idyllic picture they are said to describe. But that picture is brought by the words only to a modern mind. Their kernel lies in the fourth rule—"the true reason of the

---

9. Thorne, pp. 210–11.

remedy"—the purpose of the remedy—the *Sinn* of the remedy. The rules cannot be taken anachronistically as an early effort to inculcate in judges a view that the statute revealed an attitude that the appropriate exercise of judicial power permitted courts to advance. * * * The resolutions in *Heydon's Case* are [close] to what courts were groping toward by means of the equity of the statute; an understanding of the *ratio legis* rather than the *ratio verborum*, an effort to make the interpretation of statutes, whether they be phrased in the singular or plural, something more than merely a grammatical exercise. The words, and not their sense, had heretofore absorbed complete attention: *Heydon's Case* points toward another side, and gives a rule of thumb for illuminating the words by reference to that which they are to do. The choice is not the modern one between what a statute said and what a statute intended to do, but rather between what it said in abstract, *in vacuo*, so to speak, and what it intended to do. It is needless * * * to pretend that it is easy to think in these unfamiliar dimensions, and it may be urged that the distinction put forward here is a distinction without a difference. Nevertheless we think it one of much importance and one too frequently overlooked.

[Editor—It *is* hard to think in these terms. What do you think Thorne means? Consider this modern example. Suppose the text of a statute dealing with worker safety referred to "cars." The question in the case is application of this statute to those working with "trucks" and "trains." Would considering an extension to either trucks or trains be an example of the "modern" contrast between what the statute said and what it intended, or between what the statute said in the abstract and what it intended? Is extension in one case but not the other a "slight" extension?]

Let us turn to the case itself. The statute of 31 Hen. VIII, c. 13, as quoted by Coke, provided that "if any abbot, etc., or other religious and ecclesiastical house or place * * * make any lease or grant for life, or for term of years, of any manors, messuages, lands, etc., and in the which any estate or interest for life, year or years * * * then had his being or continuance * * * every such lease shall be utterly void." It would be difficult to find an act whose purpose is as evident as that of this Suppression Act of 1539. [Editor—The statute was an attempt to prevent avoidance of Henry VIII's seizure of Church property.] This *ratio legis*, if no other, was known to all, even to the common lawyers, and likewise it was common knowledge that the monasteries were evading the provisions of the act wherever possible. The Abbot of Dieulacres caused blank forms to be prepared, sealed with the convent seal, on which [   ] leases were subsequently made out, much to the benefit of his own family. The manor of Rialton was leased by the prior of Bodmin Priory to his brother for ninety-nine years. The monks of Newenham by means of a disused seal (the real one having been removed by the Commissioners) could grant leases long after the dissolution.

Yet there was great doubt, in Coke's words, "whether a copyhold estate * * * at the will of the lord, according to the custom of the said manor, should in judgment of law be called an estate and interest for lives, within the said general words and meaning of the said act." Though Coke does not give the debates, we may assume that they centered around the fact that the statute clearly abridged the common law, and as such was to be strictly construed, for before the statute religious and ecclesiastical persons might have made leases for as many years as they pleased, and also about the nice problem of whether a copyhold estate fell within the statute's provisions. For although a copyholder had in judgment of law but an estate at will, yet custom had so established and fixed his estate that he possessed many advantages, and for most practical purposes he was owner of an estate, subject only to services analogous to the services due from a great deal of other land. It was not a violent extension to provide, as did the Barons, that "when an act of Parliament is generally made for the good of the weal public, and no prejudice can accrue by reason of alteration of any interest, service, tenure or custom of the manor, there many times copyhold and customary estates are within the general purview of such acts." If in the course of the case they took occasion to lay down rules of statutory interpretation, we may be sure that these rules are not completely unconnected with the case in hand: that of a restrictive statute viewed in the light of a very clear and apparent *ratio legis*. That they thought it necessary to recite these very wide rules is itself an interesting commentary upon the strict rule of interpretation we have spoken of above at length.

d) BONHAM'S CASE

This period of legal history is also famous for another statement relevant to the relationship between statutes and courts. In Dr. Bonham's Case (1610), Lord Coke stated:

> [I]t appears in our books that in many cases the common law will control Acts of Parliament and adjudge them to be utterly void. For when an Act of Parliament is against common right or reason, or repugnant, or impossible to be performed, the common law will control it and adjudge such Act to be void.[10]

This statement has often been taken to assert a power of judicial review to strike down statutes, an obviously bold claim which might also imply broad interpretive powers. Thorne argues in the cited article that something much less dramatic was going on in Bonham's Case. The specific issue was whether a doctor could be fined for unlicensed practice of medicine. The occasion for the statement about the statute violating "common right or reason" was that doctors acted as judges to determine whether the fine should be imposed

---

10. See generally Thorne, Dr. Bonham's Case, 54 Law Quart. Rev. 543 (1938).

and this violated the principle that no person should decide a case in which he could benefit (because the doctors would derive some benefit from the fine).[11] According to Thorne, application of this principle fell comfortably within the judge's traditional interpretive power to interpret a statute to avoid "absurd" results, and that the case did not stand for any broader claim of judicial power.

This more limited reading of Bonham's Case fits well with what we know about Coke's views of judging and Parliament.[12] Coke's professional life was concerned with opposing both the common law and Parliament to the Crown, not with opposing Parliament. While Speaker of the House of Commons, he worked to preserve Parliamentary privilege against the Crown. Later, as a member of Parliament, he urged adoption of the Petition of Right, which protected common law rights from the exercise of the Crown's prerogative. And his famous statement about the law being *artificial* reason, known to judges, was directed against King James' claim to know *natural* reason, which could prove a rival to judicial authority.[13] (Coke also told the King that the King was protected by the law. Other judges—perhaps influenced by the fact that judges at this time did not have tenure, but served at the pleasure of the Crown[14]—affirmed the contrary. They stated that rex is lex, not that lex is rex.) It is certainly true that the judge's privileged access to artificial reason reflected judicial confidence in the ability to identify law (judges at this time would never have spoken of "making" law). But there was little sense that this power was invoked in conflict with Parliament. If Coke was claiming the extraordinary power to declare statutes void, we might have expected some Parliamentary objection, but there was none. Interpreting a text to prevent overriding a strong common law principle simply prevented the unthinkable (the "absurd"), rather than confronting Parliament with a rival claim of judicial power.

2.03   18TH-19TH CENTURY—ENGLISH MATERIAL

By the 18th Century, there is some evidence of a developing separation of powers not only between the legislature and the Crown but also between

---

11. Coke was generally concerned with the widespread potential for judicial corruption at this time and advocated replacing the system of judicial fees with salaries. Veall, The Popular Movement for Law Reform, 1640–1660, p. 68 (1970).

12. The material in this paragraph is taken primarily from Catherine Drinker Bowen, The Lion and the Throne, pp. 20, 304–05, 316, 483–504 (1956).

13. "Then, the king said, that he thought the law was founded upon reason, and that he and others had reason as well as the judges: to which it was answered by me, that true it was, that God had endowed his Majesty with excellent science, and great endowments of nature; but his Majesty was not learned in the laws of his realm of England, and causes which concern the life, or inheritance, or goods, or fortunes of his subjects are not to be decided by natural reason, but by the artificial reason and judgment of law, which law is an act which requires long study and experience before a man can attain to the knowledge of it." Coke, 12 Coke's Reports 63, 65.

14. See Hallam, Constitutional History of England, Vol. I, pp. 335, 441 (1850).

the legislature and courts. Thorne's observation that Parliamentary sovereignty affected statutory interpretation, or at least its rhetoric, seems accurate. A 1742 opinion stated: [15]

> When the words of an Act are doubtful and uncertain, it is
> proper to inquire what was the intent of the Legislature: but it is very
> dangerous for Judges to launch out too far in searching into the
> intent of the Legislature, when they have expressed themselves in
> plain and clear words.

(Note the court's reference to legislative "intent," not "equity," and the
apparent importance of the words of the statute.) A 1785 opinion denies
judges the power to extend a statute to cover a *casus omissus*.[16] Moreover, the
ascendance of Parliament meant a severe reduction in powers associated with
the Royal Prerogative, as a result of the 1689 Bill of Rights. One such power
was to dispense with the rigors of the law (in effect, a power to suspend the
operation of the law), and some judges had relied on this power to justify
equitable interpretation.[17]

The leading 18th Century writer on statutory interpretation and the
common law generally was Blackstone. In the following excerpt from his
Commentaries on the Laws of England, what role do words play in statutory
interpretation? What does Blackstone mean by the "reason and spirit" of the
law? Is it the same thing as the "true reason of the remedy" in Heydon's
Case? In a conflict between the text and the "reason and spirit" of the law,
which prevails?

> Blackstone, Vol. 1, Commentaries on the Law of England, pp.
> 58–62 (1765)
>
> * * * [I]t may not be amiss to add a few observations concern-
> ing the *interpretation* of laws.
>
> When any doubt arose upon the construction of the Roman
> laws, the usage was to state the case to the emperor in writing, and
> take his opinion upon it. This was certainly a bad method of
> interpretation. To interrogate the legislature to decide particular
> disputes, is not only endless, but affords great room for partiality
> and oppression. * * *
>
> The fairest and most rational method to interpret the will of the
> legislator, is by exploring his intentions at the time when the law was
> made, by *signs* the most natural and probable. And these signs are
> either the words, the context, the subject matter, the effects and
> consequence, or the spirit and reason of the law. Let us take a short
> view of them all.
>
> 1. Words are generally to be understood in their usual and
> most known signification; not so much regarding the propriety of

---

15. Colehan v. Cooke, 125 Eng.Rep.
1231, 1233 (1742).

16. Baade, p. 89.

17. Baade, p. 88. See generally, May,
Presidential Defiance of "Unconstitutional"
Laws: Reviving the Royal Prerogative, 21
Hastings Const. L.Q. 865 (1994).

grammar, as their general and popular use. Thus the law mentioned by Puffendorf, which forbad a layman to *lay hands* on a priest, was adjudged to extend to him, who had hurt a priest with a weapon. Again; terms of art, or technical terms, must be taken according to the acceptation of the learned in each art, trade, and science. So in the act of settlement, where the crown of England is limited to the princess Sophia, and the heirs of her body, "being protestants," it becomes necessary to call in the assistance of lawyers, to ascertain the precise idea of the words "*heirs of her body*;" which in a legal sense comprise only certain of her lineal descendants. * * *

2.   If words happen to be still dubious, we may establish their meaning from the *context*; with which it may be of singular use to compare a word, or a sentence, whenever they are ambiguous, equivocal, or intricate. Thus the proeme, or preamble, is often called in to help the construction of an act of parliament. * * *

3.   As to the subject-matter, words are always to be understood as having a regard thereto; for that is always supposed to be in the eye of the legislator, and all his expressions directed to that end. Thus, when a law of our Edward III forbids all ecclesiastical persons to purchase *provisions* at Rome, it might seem to prohibit the buying of grain and other victual; but when we consider that the statute was made to repress the usurpations of the papal fee, and that the nominations to benefices by the pope were called *provisions*, we shall see that the restraint is intended to be laid upon such provisions only.

4.   As to the *effects* and *consequence*, the rule is, that where words bear either none, or a very absurd signification, if literally understood, we must a little deviate from the received sense of them. Therefore the Bolognian law, mentioned by Puffendorf, which enacted "that whoever drew blood in the streets should be punished with the utmost severity," was held after long debate not to extend to the surgeon, who opened the vein of a person that fell down in the street with a fit.

5.   But, lastly, the most universal and effectual way of discovering the true meaning of a law, when the words are dubious, is by considering the reason and spirit of it; or the cause which moved the legislator to enact it. For when this reason ceases, the law itself ought likewise to cease with it. [Editor—Notice how the language in Heydon's Case about the "true reason of the remedy" has been transformed to "the reason and spirit" of the law.] * * * There was a law, that those who in a storm forsook the ship should forfeit all property therein; and the ship and lading should belong entirely to those who stayed in it. In a dangerous tempest all the mariners forsook the ship, except only one sick passenger, who by reason of his disease was unable to get out and escape. By chance the ship came safe to port. The sick man kept possession, and claimed the benefit of the law. Now here all the learned agree, that the sick man

is not within the reason of the law; for the reason of making it was, to give encouragement to such as should venture their lives to save the vessel: but this is a merit, which he could never pretend to, who neither stayed in the ship upon that account, nor contributed anything to its preservation.

From this method of interpreting laws, by the reason of them, arises what we call *equity*; which is thus defined by Grotius, "the correction of that, wherein the law (by reason of its universality) is deficient." For since in laws all cases cannot be foreseen or expressed, it is necessary, that when the general decrees of the law come to be applied to particular cases, there should be somewhere a power vested of defining those circumstances, which (had they been foreseen) the legislator himself would have expressed. * * *

Equity thus depending, essentially, upon the particular circumstances of each individual case, there can be no established rules and fixed precepts of equity laid down, without destroying it's very essence, and reducing it to a positive law. And, on the other hand, the liberty of considering all cases in an equitable light must not be indulged too far; lest thereby we destroy all law, and leave the decision of every question entirely in the breast of the judge. And law, without equity, though hard and disagreeable, is much more desirable for the public good, than equity without law: which would make every judge a legislator, and introduce infinite confusion; as there would then be almost as many different rules of action laid down in our courts, as there are differences of capacity and sentiment in the human mind.

As for Lord Coke's possible assertion in Dr. Bonham's Case—that a court could void an Act of Parliament against common right or reason—Blackstone affirms legislative sovereignty, stating:[18]

* * * [I]f the parliament will positively enact a thing to be done which is unreasonable, I know of no power that can control it; * * *. But where some collateral matter arises out of the general words, and happens to be unreasonable; there the judges are in decency to conclude that this consequence was not foreseen by the parliament, and therefore they are at liberty to expound the statute by equity, and only [to that extent] disregard it.

Blackstone then gives an example of interpreting a statute to disregard an unreasonable result—a statute authorizing a judge to hear *all* types of cases should be interpreted to exclude judging a case in which the judge is a party. Thus, the specific holding in Dr. Bonham's Case (that no judge should decide a case in which he could benefit) is reduced simply to interpreting a *generally-worded* statute to exclude unreasonable *specific* applications.

---

18. Blackstone, Vol. 1, Commentaries on the Law of England, p. 91 (1765) (hereafter "Blackstone").

The language of Blackstone's Commentaries suggests a commitment to law over equity—to the text over equitable interpretation—that may or may not accurately describe judicial practice. Blackstone certainly did not believe that legislation was a superior form of lawmaking. To Blackstone,[19] the common law was the "perfection of reason." He complained of the "mischiefs * * * from the inconsiderate alterations of our laws," most of which were traced to "innovations that have been made by acts of parliament." (The sheer size of the statute book had come in for considerable comment in the 18th Century; Coke had complained about the number of statutes in the 17th Century but their number had grown ten-fold during the 18th Century).[20] One reason Blackstone wrote his Commentaries was to remedy the "defective education of our senators," and make "the penners of our modern statutes [   ] better informed [   ] in the knowledge of the common law." (Another leading 18th Century jurist, Lord Mansfield—who was largely responsible for updating the common law to include what was then modern commercial law—also believed in the superiority of the common law: "the common law that works itself pure by rules drawn from the fountain of justice is for this reason superior to an act of parliament."[21])

Reconciling these negative views of legislation with an apparent deference to the statutory text and an affirmation of legislative sovereignty is not easy for the modern mind. The answer probably lies in the 18th Century understanding of legislative sovereignty. There are several ways legislative sovereignty can work its way into a legal system. First, all law is (formally) legislative. This was the view associated with Jeremy Bentham,[22] writing at the end of the 18th and the beginning of the 19th Century. He argued that law was a command, an act of will. The common law, riddled with the uncertainties of unclear and multiple judicial decisions, did not fit that definition. But the 18th Century legal culture certainly did not adopt the view that legislation is the only form of law.

Second, legislative sovereignty might permit the judge to be resourceful in developing the common law but subservient regarding statute law. The judge's formal lawmaking role would be restricted to the common law. Undoubtedly, the seeds of that view were planted during the 18th Century, but it is unlikely that this describes either the theory or practice of judicial interaction with legislation at that time. Common law judges simply had too much confidence in their ability to determine the law.

Third, the legislature might be sovereign in the sense of having the first and last word but the judge has significant discretion to work things out in between. This seems to be the reality of 18th Century judicial practice. As David Lieberman notes, the courts' attitude towards parliamentary lawmak-

19. The quotes from Blackstone in the remainder of this paragraph appear at Blackstone, p. 10.

20. David Lieberman, Blackstone's Science of Legislation, 27 J Brit. Stud. 117, 141 (1988)(hereafter "Lieberman, Science").

21. David Lieberman, The Province of Legislation Determined, p. 91 (1989) (hereafter "Lieberman, Province").

22. Lieberman, Province, pp. 222–36.

ing was not "fully disclosed in [ ] formal doctrines of constitutional sovereignty."[23] Courts paid greater heed to what Parliament did (especially the text) in light of the growing importance of legislation, but judges still played an important role in working out how the statute fit into the legal system. Haines suggests a middle ground, as follows:[24]

> [There were instances] in which the courts interpreting the common law changed the meaning of statutes, refused to give them the effect intended, or to apply a rule [ ] until [the legislature issued] an unmistakable mandate, which the courts reluctantly at times conceded it was their duty to obey. Short of such mandates clearly and unequivocally expressed there was a wide realm in which the courts applied the basic principles of reason of the common law and were seldom interfered with by either the king or Parliament.

This middle ground is developed more fully by Postema, in his discussion of the views of the influential mid–17th Century English judge and lawyer, Matthew Hale.[25] Hale argues that changes in the law occur both from changes in the common law and by Acts of Parliament, but that statutes have no impact on the law until they gain community acceptance—that is, they are incorporated into the common law. Postema argues that this perspective accommodates legislative sovereignty on the theory that "[w]ithout finding a place in [the common law], legislation can be only a matter of isolated rules having no *general* impact on the law beyond the narrow application of the statutory language * * *." In this respect, legislation is like a judicial opinion, which (Blackstone affirmed) is only "evidence" of the law, and that, if later found to be "absurd or unjust," was not "bad law," but was "not law" in the first place.[26] The judge's exceedingly cautious reaction to statutes fit with this view that the "law" existed independent of its statement by either judge or legislator.

This may sound sophistic to our modern ears. Sovereignty is sovereignty and that's it. But the 18th Century understanding of sovereignty meant legislative ascendance over the Crown, not judicial passivity. In 17th Century England, the Crown had claimed sovereignty and, in the ensuing dispute, Charles I had even been beheaded in 1649. Faced with this monarchical claim, it was only natural that Parliament would make a claim rival to the Crown's—that is, a claim to sovereignty. And, after the Revolution of 1688, legislative sovereignty was in fact primarily asserted in dealings with the Crown—in what we would consider constitutional legislation about the

---

23. Lieberman, Province, p. 55. See also Plucknett, Bonham's Case and Judicial Review, 40 Harv. L. Rev. 30, 57–58 (1926)(18th Century judges "treat[ed] statutes with scant respect, but without giving any constitutional justification * * *;" Statutes of Frauds is an example).

24. Haines, The American Doctrine of Judicial Supremacy, p. 36 (1959) (hereafter "Haines").

25. Postema, Bentham and the Common Law Tradition, pp. 25–26 (1986) (hereafter "Postema").

26. Blackstone, pp. 69–70.

powers of government institutions. Typical examples were statutes dealing with succession to the Crown (1689), limits on the power of the Crown set forth in the Bill of Rights (1689), the Toleration Act protecting Protestant dissenters (1689), and the Act of Settlement establishing judicial tenure independent of the Crown (1701).[27] The age of statutory dominance, for which parliamentary sovereignty was a necessary but not sufficient condition, lay in the future. Until that reality developed, abstract notions of sovereignty could not relegate the "equity of the statute" approach to the historical dust bin. As Richard Posner puts it:[28]

> Blackstone emphasized the role of courts in making law because, when he wrote, most law was judge-made. But he did not neglect the role of legislation. * * * [H]e assigned a limited role to statutory law; its proper office was to resolve conflicts between common law precedents and otherwise to supplement and patch common law doctrine.

And, as Baade states: Parliamentary sovereignty "was [ ] more apparent than real."[29]

Commentators on Blackstone certainly failed to see in him a deferential view of the judge's role in statutory interpretation. The leading critic of the common law was Jeremy Bentham, who criticizes Blackstone's invocation of "reason and spirit" in statutory interpretation because it would not defer to the legislature. Bentham viewed Blackstone's reference to "unreasonable" law in his discussion of Bonham's Case as authorizing too much judicial discretion because the standard is not "fixed and certain." Apparently, whatever Blackstone said, Bentham anticipated that Blackstone-trained lawyers would exercise equitable interpretation (through applying "reason and spirit"). In Bentham's view, "[t]he question [ ] is whose opinion shall be the standard? that of the Legislature, or that of the Judge? of him whose office is to *make* his Will be the law, or of him whose office is no other than to find out that Will and carry it into effect?" Bentham feared that the judicial "license of interpretation" is just "another branch of customary" (that is, common) law, which should be rejected.

Bentham probably correctly perceived judicial practice, even if there was a change in judicial rhetoric. With the rise of Parliamentary sovereignty, it almost certainly become harder to refer to equitable interpretation. This actually suited those common law judges who were hostile to the expanding role of legislation, insofar as *extensive* equitable interpretation was concerned. The court could say that Parliament was sovereign as far as it had spoken, that courts had limited powers, and that therefore the statute could not be

27. G.M. Trevelyan, The English Revolution 1688–1689, pp. 76, 79–80, 88 (1965 paperback edition). See also Lieberman, Science, p. 132; Michael Lobban, Blackstone and the Science of Law, 30 Historical Jl. 311, 326–27 (1987).

28. Richard Posner, Blackstone and Bentham, 19 J. Law and Econ. 569, 585 (1976).

29. Baade, p. 90.

extended—there was nothing courts could do about a *casus omissus*. But when the statute impinged on the common law, the courts could apply a canon of statutory interpretation which required narrow interpretation of statutes in derogation of the common law, without relying explicitly on equitable interpretation. Indeed, judicial reliance on explicit canons of construction to limit the reach of statutes (strict interpretation of penal law; the "deroga-tion" canon; liberal interpretation of remedial laws) may have developed in the 18th Century, as a rhetorical substitute for equitable interpretation.[30]

The "Golden Rule".[31] There is one final way to explain Blackstone's views, which expands on his reference to avoiding "absurd" results. In the 19th Century, interpreting statutory texts to avoid "absurdity" came to be known explicitly as the Golden Rule, but interpretive practice before that time could often be explained in these terms. Here are two formulations of the Golden Rule. Notice that one formulation is not limited to preventing "absurdity," but includes preventing "inconvenience." If the Golden Rule applies to "inconvenience," is it any different from equitable interpretation, applied to narrow the statute's reach?

> It is a very useful rule in the construction of a statute to adhere to the ordinary meaning of the words used, and to the grammatical construction, unless that is at variance with the intention of the Legislature to be collected from the statute itself, or leads to any manifest absurdity or repugnance, in which case the language may be varied or modified so as to avoid such inconvenience, but no further. Becke v. Smith, 2 M. & W. 191, 195 (1836):

And:

> [I]nconsistence, absurdity or inconvenience will permit judges to attribute a "less proper" meaning to statutory language. River Wear Comm'rs. v. Adamson, (1877) 2 App. Cas. 742, 764.

Does drawing the line between absurdity and inconvenience leave the judge too free to make law? The statutory "absurdity" in the River Wear Comm'rs. case was the imposition of statutory liability without fault.

The dominant version of the Golden Rule is that interpretation will avoid "absurd," not just "inconvenient" results. "Absurdity" focuses the judge's attention on some conception of fundamental values that the judge should protect (see, e.g., Coke's opinion in Bonham's Case). A concern with "inconvenience" focuses more on helping the legislature reach results which make sense, either in terms of the legislature's goals or in working out the interaction of legislation and the common law. Watch carefully for the absurdity-inconvenience distinction as you go through the material in this course.

---

30. Corry, Administrative Law and the Interpretation of Statutes, 1 U. Toronto L. Rev. 286, 296 (1936).

31. See generally Dougherty, Absurdity and the Limits of Literalism: Defining the Absurd Result Principle in Statutory Interpretation, 44 Amer. Univ. L. Rev. 127 (1994).

Note also that the Golden Rule is concerned with limiting, not extending a statute. That, too, is an important distinction that runs throughout the history of statutory interpretation.

2.04   18TH-19TH CENTURY—UNITED STATES MATERIAL

a) 1776–1789

We are so accustomed today to considering the original intent of the constitutional structure that we run the risk of oversimplifying the evidence. This is certainly true of the constitutional background regarding the extent of judicial power to interpret statutes. The following material about the period from 1776–1789 (from the Revolution to the Founding of the Constitution) suggests a picture of almost purposeful uncertainty regarding the judicial role. You might, of course, disagree with this evaluation of the evidence, and you might also conclude that original intent is not, in any event, the dispositive criterion.

i) INTRODUCTION[32]

In the Colonial America of 1776, the potential conflict between judges and the legislature was *not* an abstract matter of legal theory, as it might have been in 18th Century England. It was very much a part of political reality because judges were associated with the power of the English Crown. The politics of 1776 differentiated sharply between judge-made common law and law made by the people through legislatures and juries.

On the one hand, Americans came to view legislation as something creative, not simply the declaration or patching up of the common law. On the other hand, judge-made common law was, to put it mildly, suspect. The Declaration of Independence lists among its complaints that the King "made judges dependent on his will, for the tenure of their offices, and the amount and payment of their salaries." Equity judges could exercise discretion without juries. And the common law, especially in its more technical manifestations, was a foreign import ill-suited to the needs of the new republic, which was free of the trappings of a feudal and aristocratic society.

The constitutions in the newly independent states overcame judicial power in a variety of ways. Most legislatures either shared in or completely controlled the appointment of judges, and further confined judges through a power of removal from office and controlling salaries. The equity power of courts was often eliminated or limited[33] and juries were empowered to

---

32. The paragraphs in this introduction rely on Gordon Wood, The Creation of the American Republic, pp. 160–61, 264–66, 275–76, 300–03, 403–08, 453–63 (1969)(hereafter "Wood"); Edward Corwin, The Progress of Constitutional Theory Between the Declaration of Independence and the Meeting of the Philadelphia Convention, 30 Amer. Hist. Rev. 511, 514–15, 518–19 (1925)(hereafter "Corwin"); Shannon Stimson, The American Revolution in the Law, pp. 48–56 (1990)(hereafter "Stimson").

33. Corwin, p. 515.

decide the *law*, not just the facts.[34] Only English common law that was suited to the conditions in the new States was adopted by the new constitutions,[35] and, in any event, it was expected that the subtleties of English common law would be replaced by legislation (many state constitutions explicitly stated that the adopted common law could be altered by statute). Instead of the sense of legislative incompetence, which characterized the 18th Century English image of Parliament, there was a sense of legislative lawmaking potential.

Legislatures not only attempted to control judges but also passed laws that we would describe as adjudication. Some of this was familiar legislative practice in the 18th Century—most legislation at that time was in the nature of private laws, such as granting corporate charters and divorces to specific people and providing individual legal relief (often from debts). But, in many instances, legislation directly impinged on judging, by retroactively overriding judicial decisions and granting new trials.[36]

Regarding interpretation, Gordon Wood quotes one 1977 author as saying that "no axiom is more dangerous than that the spirit of the law ought to be considered, and not the letter." Horwitz argues that, for the colonists, judicial discretion in statutory interpretation was considered more dangerous than common law adjudication.[37] And, somewhat later, Associate Justice John Dudley in New Hampshire (who served from 1785–97), charged a jury "to do justice between the parties not by any quirks of law out of Coke or Blackstone—books that I never read and never will—but by common sense as between man and man."[38] The *jury*'s common sense would replace the artificial reason of *judges*.

This focus on perspectives current around the time of the 1776 Revolution does not capture the ambiguity towards judging that evolved during the 1776–1789 period. The experience with legislation during the Revolutionary period produced a reaction against legislatures, at least in the formation of the federal constitution. The proliferation of statutes turned out to increase rather than decrease judicial discretion. And even Jefferson, an early proponent of expansive legislative power and always a critic of judicial lawmaking,[39] came to fear legislative encroachment on individual rights; and he characterized the mixture of legislative, executive, and judicial functions in

---

34. Note, The Changing Role of the Jury in the Nineteenth Century, 74 Yale L.J. 170, 173 (1964).

35. Seminole Tribe of Florida v. Florida, 116 S.Ct. 1114, 1174 n. 55 (1996)(Souter, J. dissenting).

36. See Plaut v. Spendthrift Farm, Inc., 115 S.Ct. 1447, 1453–55 (1995) (discussing the history of legislative reversal of court judgments).

37. Horwitz, The Transformation of American Law, 1780–1860, pp. 4–5 (1977).

38. Maxwell Bloomfield, American Lawyers in a Changing Society, 1776–1876, p. 57 (1976).

39. Jefferson objected to the "honeyed Mansfieldism" of Blackstone, which he associated with excessive judicial discretion, and to teaching new lawyers primarily through Blackstone's Commentaries. Julius Waterman, Thomas Jefferson and Blackstone's Commentaries *in* Essays in the History of Early American Law, pp. 459, 468–72; Wood, p. 304, n.75 (objecting to "construing texts equitably").

legislative hands as "despotic government."[40] Substantively, legislation alarmed many people by threatening creditors rights. Legislation providing equitable relief to specific individuals seemed to usurp the judicial function. And, of course, there were always those who had not favored shifting power from judges to legislatures in the first place. For many, the common law retained a mystic attraction as a source of rights, enforceable by courts. The Continental Congress in 1774 had stressed that the common law was the source of rights which the colonies claimed,[41] and this resulted in the early state constitutions adopting a Declaration of Rights and the federal constitution incorporating a Bill of Rights (whose first eight articles embodied the traditional common law rights enjoyed by Englishmen). By the 1780s, many people viewed legislatures as at least as great a threat as judicial power had been a decade earlier. Some courts, relying on Coke's statement that statutes might be void, developed doctrines of judicial review to strike down legislation.[42]

A basic problem with drawing inferences about the judge's role in statutory interpretation from examining the 1776–1789 period is that statutory interpretation was not a major focus of attention when the federal and state constitutions were being constructed. *First*, judging itself was not the major concern. Much more important were issues of the legislature's composition (one or two houses), representation in the legislature, the selection of the executive, and the executive veto. *Second*, when judging was an issue, the primary focus was not on interpretation but on *control* of judges—through (1) selection (appointment by the legislature or executive or some combination thereof); (2) conditions of removal (tenure during good behavior vs. a term of years; impeachment for wrongdoing; removal at the request of a majority or ⅔rds of the legislature, with or without the governor's consent); and (3) control of salary (should judicial salary be immune from increase or decrease while in office). *Third*, when interpretation was discussed, it focused primarily on the United States Constitution.

If we are to learn much about statutory interpretation from what happened between 1776–1789, we must therefore construct a sense of judicial role from constitutional provisions concerned with the relationship of legislatures to judges, and not from any specific provisions dealing with statutory interpretation. Unfortunately, this effort is fraught with uncertainty.

First, what does the degree of legislative control over judges suggest? One view is that greater legislative control—characteristic of the early state constitutions—is an expression of hostility towards judicial creativity, meant to eliminate judicial lawmaking. There is no doubt that the drafters of state

---

40. Jefferson, Notes on the State of Virginia, p. 120 (W. Peden, ed. 1955).

41. First Continental Congress Declaration and Resolves (1774), *in* Documents Illustrative of the Formation of the Union of American States, H.R. Doc. No. 398, 69th Cong., 1st sess., pp. 1,3 (C. Tansill, ed. 1927).

42. Haines, pp. 88–121; Goldstein, Popular Sovereignty, the Origins of Judicial Review, and the Revival of Unwritten Law, 48 J.Pol. 51, 62 (1986).

constitutional provisions controlling the appointment, removal, and salary of judges shared the view that judicial discretion was a serious danger to the republican principles that underlay the Revolution. But, having established popular control over judges, it is not clear that judicial discretion was meant to be completely eliminated. As we will see, the ideal of judging during this period was complex—neither completely passive nor actively willful. Legislative control may have been a method of accommodating the inevitability of some judicial creativity, rather than eliminating it altogether.

Assertions of judicial independence of legislative control—characteristic of the United States Constitution—carry the same ambiguity. Judicial independence might be taken to mean enthusiasm for judicial lawmaking, but not necessarily. It might instead be intended to reduce legislative interference with specific judicial decisions, without implying anything about an affirmative creative role for independent judges.

Second, it is not only difficult to draw inferences about the judicial role from constitutional provisions about legislative control and judicial independence, but there is also evidence of *both* legislative control and judicial independence in the constitutional materials—such as legislative appointment of judges combined with post-appointment tenure.

The ambiguity of the evidence is consistent with the historical reality that the constitution-builders were intensely pragmatic, not concerned with whether the governments they created fit some theoretically consistent mold. Indeed, the need to attract widespread support led them to compromises which avoided a rigid constitutional model. They rejected the extremes of monarchical and legislative sovereignty, but were never entirely clear what they created in between these extremes. The central message of these constitutions may be that there is no clear message about judicial lawmaking power, especially regarding statutory interpretation, and that each generation of judges must determine the approach suitable for the legal environment in which they work.

There are two additional reasons why the historical material may be of questionable use for us today. *First*, much of the concern in the 1776–1789 period was about *limiting* legislation. The focus was on liberty *from* government, and rested on a negative "original sin" image of human nature as concerned primarily with individual self-aggrandizement. It is unclear what we should do with these 18th Century perspectives in the contemporary era, where we place much greater reliance on government and a more optimistic view of human nature.

Second, the perspective on judging differed somewhat at the state and federal levels. State constitutions favored more legislative control over judges and the United States constitution titled more towards judicial independence. To the extent that evidence of legislative-judicial relationships shed any light on the judicial role in statutory interpretation, the material on state constitutions may not be dispositive regarding the role of federal courts, especially in the modern period when federal legislation is so significant.

ii) THE CONSTITUTIONAL PATTERNS

We therefore turn to the state and federal constitutional material, with some skepticism about its usefulness in shedding light on the judicial role, especially statutory interpretation. The state constitutional material is likely to be unfamiliar, given law school's focus on the federal constitution, but it is important. Most legislation in this early period was at the state level.

State constitutions. State constitutional provisions about appointment and removal of judges and control over salary are presented below in chart form. The charts sometimes refer to a Council, which needs some explanation. The states were familiar with "councils" from their colonial experience. The colonial councils were usually appointed by the King on the advice of the colonial governor and often sat as the upper house of the legislature, as the highest court of appeal, and as advisors to the governor, mixing legislative, executive, and judicial functions. Many early state constitutions provided for councils, which performed a more modest role than their colonial predecessors. They were usually elected by the legislature or people, participated with the Governor (who was referred to as "President" in some states) in making certain decisions, and acted as checks on gubernatorial power.

Appointment of judges. The first chart—Appointment Power—can be summarized this way. The dominant pattern is either appointment by the legislature, or by a governor and council, both of whom were chosen by the legislature. In only three states were judicial appointments made by a governor who was popularly elected and then only with participation by a council elected by the legislature. Pennsylvania was alone in providing for popular election of a council which, along with the President (who was chosen by the legislature and council) appointed judges.

As noted earlier, the pattern is clearly one of legislative control over judging. You should observe that, for all the discussion of Separation of Powers as an important theme during the period we are discussing, the reality (as least for judging) was a strong legislative check on the judiciary, rather than separation between judging and legislating.

APPOINTMENT POWER

State	Year Const. adopted	Appointment provision
New Jersey[a]	1776	Legislature
North Carolina	1776	Legislature
Virginia	1776	Legislature
Delaware[b]	1776	Legislature and President, chosen by legislature
South Carolina[c]	1776	Legislature
	1778	Legislature
Maryland	1776	Governor, chosen by legislature; and council, chosen by legislature
Massachusetts	1780	Governor, chosen by people; and council, chosen by legislature
New Hampshire	1784	President, chosen by people; and council, chosen by legislature

State	Year Const. adopted	Appointment provision
New York[a]	1777	Governor, chosen by people; and council, chosen by legislature
Pennsylvania	1776	President, chosen by leg. and council; and council, chosen by people
Georgia[d]	1777/1789	Legislature
Connecticut[d]	1784 statute	Legislature
Rhode Island[d]	pre–1776 charter	Legislature

[a] Legislators sat on the highest court in New Jersey (court of appeal consisted of Governor and Legislative Council (Senate)); and New York (Court of Errors consisted of senators and judges).

[b] Delaware's highest court consisted of the President and six judges, three elected by each legislative branch.

[c] In both the 1776 and 1778 Constitutions, the chancery court consisted of an executive official and a privy council; the council included legislators elected by the legislature, until the legislature provided otherwise.

[d] The information for Georgia, Connecticut, and Rhode Island is derived from Haynes, The Selection and Tenure of Judges, pp. 105, 108, 127–28 (1944)(hereafter "Haynes"). The Georgia 1777 and 1789 Constitutions are unclear. Connecticut's 1776 Constitution adopted its 1662 Charter. Rhode Island operated under its 1663 Charter.

Post-appointment control. The appointment pattern is clearly one of legislative dominance. Post-appointment control seems different. In most states, judges had tenure during good behavior, tempered by a power of (1) legislative impeachment for misconduct and, less often, (2) removal upon the address of a majority or ⅔rds of the legislature (not limited to impeachment grounds), sometimes with the consent of the Governor and/or council. As for judicial salaries, the constitutions often stated that they should be fixed, adequate, and/or permanent. However, we lack evidence about how the power of removal and control over salary was actually exercised,[43] which is important in determining whether the legislature retained effective control over judges.

POST–APPOINTMENT CONTROL[a]

State (year of const.)	Term	Removal	Salary
New Jersey (1776)	7 or 5 years	Impeach only	no provision
North Carolina (1776)	Good behavior	Impeach only	adequate
Virginia (1776)	Good behavior	Impeach only	fixed, adequate
Delaware (1776)	Good behavior	Impeach; and by address of legislature	adequate, fixed
South Carolina (1776)	Good behavior	no impeachment provision; by address of leg.	established by act
(1778)	Good behavior	Impeach; and by address of leg.	adequate, fixed
Maryland (1776)	Good behavior	no imp. provision;[b] remove by Gov. on address by ⅔ of leg.	liberal, not profuse; secured

43. See Federalist Papers, # 79, p. 403 (Max Beloff, ed.)(hereafter "Federalist")("Some [states] have declared that *permanent* salaries should be established for judges; but the experience has, in some instances, shown that such expressions are not sufficiently definite to preclude legislative evasions.")

State (year of const.)	Term	Removal	Salary
Massachusetts (1780)	Good behavior	Impeach; and by Gov. and council, on address of leg.	established by law; permanent
New Hampshire (1784)	Good behavior	Impeach; and by Gov. and council, on address of leg.	established by law; permanent
New York (1777)	Good behavior	Impeach only	no provision
Pennsylvania (1776)	7 years	Impeach; and by address of leg. for "misbehavior"	fixed
Georgia (1789)c	3 years	Impeach	no incr/decr

a The chart provides no information on Connecticut and Rhode Island, which continued to be governed by their pre-Revolutionary Charters. However, one contemporary writer states that these judges were appointed annually, and, in Connecticut, were routinely reappointed unless guilty of serious misconduct. Smith, A Comparative View of the Constitutions of Several States With Each Other, and With That of the United States, p. 33 (1796).

b Judges could be removed if convicted in a court of law.

c The 1777 Georgia Constitution is uncertain regarding tenure, but judges probably served at the pleasure of the legislature. Haynes, p. 108. The Constitution provided that every "officer [   ] shall be liable to be called to account by the [legislature]." There was no provision about salaries.

Federal constitution. The federal constitutional structure was tilted as much in favor of judicial independence as state constitutions favored legislative control of judging. The post-Revolutionary reaction against legislative dominance over judging was clear. Federal judges were *appointed* by the President with the advice and consent of the Senate. Judges had *tenure during good behavior*; removal was only possible through *impeachment* by the House and conviction by the Senate. *Salaries* could not be reduced.

Separation of Powers. Perhaps the right place to look for inferences about judicial power is not in the specifics of the legislative-judicial relationship, but in provisions about separation of powers.[44] But that, too, might prove disappointing. Only six states explicitly adopted such provisions, the most famous of which is in the 1780 Massachusetts Constitution.

> The legislative department shall never exercise the executive and judicial powers, or either of them; the executive shall never exercise the legislative and judicial powers, or either of them; the judicial shall never exercise the legislative and executive powers, or either of them; to the end it may be a government of laws, and not of men.

The original proposal at the 1780 Massachusetts convention focused only on judicial independence—"The judicial department of the state ought to be separate from, and independent of, the legislative and executive powers."[45]

44. Observers often state that most states had such provisions; see Corwin, p. 514, citing Federalist #47. But Federalist, #47 discusses how state constitutions provide for checks and balances, not separation of powers.

45. 4 Works of John Adams 230 (Charles Adams 1851).

Another proposed section stated: "In the government of the Commonwealth of Massachusetts, the legislative, executive, and judicial power, shall be placed in separate departments, to the end that it might be a government of laws and not of men." However, without any explanation of which we are aware, the text of the two proposals was combined and modified to read as above.

The New Hampshire 1784 constitution was more modest:

> In the government of this state, the three essential powers thereof, to wit, the legislative, executive and judicial, ought to be kept as separate from and independent of each other, as the nature of a free government will admit, or as is consistent with that chain of connection that binds the whole fabric of the constitution in one indissoluble bond of union and amity.

There were four other explicit separation of powers provisions in the 1776–1789 constitutions:

North Carolina (1776)

> —That the legislative, executive, and supreme judicial powers of government, ought to be forever separate and distinct from each other.

Virginia (1776)

> —The legislative, executive, and judiciary department, shall be separate and distinct, so that neither exercise the powers properly belonging to the other.

Maryland (1776)

> —That the legislative, executive, and judicial powers of government, ought to be forever separate and distinct from each other * * *.

Georgia (1777)

> —The legislative, executive, and judiciary departments, shall be separate and distinct, so that neither exercise the powers properly belonging to the other.

There was no explicit Separation of Powers clause in the federal constitution. Madison proposed amending the constitution to provide as follows:

> The powers delegated by the constitution, are appropriated to the departments to which they are respectively distributed: so that the legislative department shall never exercise the powers vested in the executive or judicial; nor the executive exercise the powers vested in the legislative or judicial; nor the judicial exercise the powers vested in the legislative or executive departments.

The House passed the amendment but the Senate did not.[46]

The problem with drawing inferences about the judicial role (especially statutory interpretation) from separation of powers provisions is that their meaning is unclear. There were at least three relevant views of Separation of Powers,[47] and neither has clear implications for statutory interpretation.

"Airtight compartment." Under one view of Separation of Powers—the *airtight compartment* view—legislatures legislate and courts do not. Even if we accept the "airtight compartment" view of Separation of Powers, however, it leaves us with an unanswered question—what is meant by judging and does it include *some* element of what we would call lawmaking.

We might take our cue about the meaning of judging from Hamilton's observations in Federalist # 78, contrasting legislatures and judges—legislatures had "will," but judges had "merely judgment."[48] The implication we might draw from this statement is that judgment is a passive activity, bearing no resemblance to what we would call lawmaking. But that is not how people in the late 18th Century would have understood judicial "judgment."

It is not easy for us to grasp what judicial judgment meant at that time, in part because late 18th Century lawyers and judges would never have used the term "lawmaking" to describe what they did. The dominant image was one of "discovering" the law. But there are three aspects to the process of discovery which suggest that judgment included elements of discretion that we would comfortably label as lawmaking, even though we would not equate it with an exercise of legislative will.

First, there were two different traditions about discovering the law. One tradition required what Coke had called "artificial reason," possessed by those with the expertise that came with legal training.[49] Coke himself preached the view that there actually *was* an earlier common law in the English past which was out there to be discovered. Although it is very obvious from studies of Coke's decisions that his discoveries of ancient law involved a lot of creative judgment, the "discovery" myth did not acknowledge anything that we would call lawmaking choice.

But a second and more dominant view of the common law and judging in the United States at this time was that inherited from Hale, an author who was well known to U.S. lawyers in the late 18th Century,[50] and whose view of the common law was quite different from Coke's. His image of the common law is captured by the following vivid metaphor, comparing the evolution of

---

46. Casper, An Essay in Separation of Powers: Some Early Versions and Practices, 30 Wm. & Mary L. Rev. 211, 221–22 (1989).

47. See generally Gwyn, The Meanings of the Separation of Powers (1965).

48. Federalist, # 78, p. 396.

49. The explanation in this and the following paragraph relies on Postema, Ch. 1, pp. 3–38 (1986).

50. Hamburger, The Constitution's Accommodation of Social Change, 88 Mich. L. Rev. 239, 255 (1989).

the common law to "the Argonauts Ship [which] was the same when it returned home, as it was when it went out, tho' in the long Voyage it had successive Amendments, and scarce came back with any of its former Materials."[51] In this view, the common law, though connected to the past, still changed. Obviously, whatever expertise the judges had involved some element of choice, as the judge helped the law adapt to current needs.

Second, both Blackstone and Hale had an image of the judicial role which fit comfortably with the idea that judicial judgment had some creative role to play in effecting legal change. Blackstone explicitly affirmed that the judicial opinion was only evidence of law (although, admittedly, he had a strong commitment to judicial precedent, absent a showing that the decisions were "manifestly absurd or unjust").[52] And Hale envisioned judgments becoming part of the law only when they were incorporated into custom by popular acceptance. This 18th Century image of judicial decision making as tentative and experimental (which contributed to Bentham's view that it was not law) requires an element of lawmaking discretion, although the judges and lawyers of that time would not have put it that way. One can even hear echoes of this view that judging is associated with legal change in some of Hamilton's statements in the Federalist Papers—in Federalist # 22, he acknowledges the "diversities in the opinions" of judges,[53] and, in Federalist # 78, he refers to "judicial discretion."[54]

Third, the term "judgment," outside the judicial context, would also have been understood to involve the kind of "creative discovery" that was part of the legal tradition. This is apparent from the writings of Kames, a Scottish judge and philosopher, who (like Hale) was well known to late 18th Century United States lawyers.[55] Kames wrote extensively about the judicial role in law reform arguing that "[m]atters of law are ripened [   ] by warmth of debate at the bar and coolness of judgment on the bench," and that law had to "keep pace with historical development."[56] Of special interest, however, was the way Kames captured the late 18th Century view of accounting for "taste," often taken as a synonym for "judgment." Although the modern view is that "there is no accounting for taste," the late 18th Century view was different. Judgment and taste *had* to be accounted for. This was best expressed in Kames's book, Elements of Criticism,[57] the final chapter of which was "devoted to disproving the 'dangerous' maxim: 'There is no disputing about taste.'" Kames argued that people had standards of taste, based on a "sense or conviction of a common nature." This parallels the

51.   Quoted in Postema, p. 6.

52.   Blackstone, pp. 69–70.

53.   Federalist, p. 108.

54.   Federalist, p. 399. He was not alone in his willingness to use the word "discretion" to describe judging. See United States v. The William, 28 Fed. Cases 614, 620 (1808)("Legal discretion is limited. * * * Political discretion has a far wider scope.").

55.   Hamowy, Jefferson and the Scottish Enlightenment: A Critique of Garry Wills' Inventing America: Jefferson's Declaration of Independence, 36 Wm. & Mary Quart. 503, 521 (1979).

56.   Lieberman, Province, p. 165. Regarding Kames, see generally Lieberman, Province, Chs. 7–8, pp. 144–75.

57.   Jay Fliegelman, Declaring Independence, p. 74 (1993).

image of law as a set of principles beyond whatever individual judges asserted and required the same kind of creative discovery that Hale and Blackstone affirmed as an element of judicial judgment.

There was, in addition to these inherited conceptions of judgment, a distinctly United States point of view associated with the Scottish "common sense" philosophy that was current during the period we are examining and that influenced such diverse thinkers as the Anti–Federalist Jefferson and the Federalist Wilson.[58] The general idea was that people had a common sense that enabled them to make right judgments, although it was possible that self-interest and poor education might cloud this mental faculty. (Recall Kames argument that people had standards of taste, based on a "sense or conviction of a common nature.") The implications of the "common sense" philosophy for judging were varied. Jefferson stressed the role of the jury as the most obvious link to popular common sense[59] (recall the New Hampshire judge's charge to the jury that they rely on "common sense"). Other writers found a more affirmative role for judges. Hamilton referred to the "common sense" of the judicial rules of legal interpretation.[60] Wilson relied on the common sense of *both* judges and juries, arguing (as Stimson notes) that the "reasoned and discursive 'common sense' judgment of the people was vested in [the Supreme Court] * * *."[61] The distinctly American variation on common sense philosophy was to transform the English idea of discretionary judgment, which was admittedly cramped, into a more robust conception of "common sense" judgment that could claim a link to the people, from whom all power in the new Republic arose. In other words, common sense would replace artificial reason.

In sum, there was (1) an English tradition of judging that envisioned judicial discretion in the process of discovering and applying the law; (2) a United States commitment to the notion that "common sense" contributed to making judgments; and (3) these perspectives combined to constitute the "separate" powers held by judges.

There were, to be sure, many advocates of Separation of Powers who thought of separation doctrine as denying judicial discretion. But the evolution of attitudes towards legislating and judging from 1776 to 1789 marks these advocates as one of two polar views of law—the view that law is predominately legislative and the view that judging remains an important source of law. The United States Revolutionary experience made legislative dominance a real possibility, rather than just a technical matter of sovereignty (as was true in 18th Century England). But it did not end the uncertainty about how legislating and judging should interact. Separation of Powers

---

58. May, The Enlightenment in America, pp. 344, 346 (1976)(Jefferson referred to Dugold Stewart, called "the most popular spokesman of Common Sense in America," as "one of the greatest thinkers."); Stimson, pp. 92, 128 (Reid's influence on Jefferson and Wilson)(hereafter "Stimson").

59. Stimson, pp. 87–89.

60. Federalist, # 83, p. 424.

61. Stimson, pp. 131–36.

doctrine contained within it that uncertainty, rather than resolving it in favor of one extreme or the other.

At the very least, Madison honestly described the uncertain borderline between judgment and will in Federalist # 37 when he said:

> The faculties of the mind itself have never yet been distinguished and defined, with satisfactory precision, by all the efforts of the most acute and metaphysical philosophers. Sense, perception, *judgment*, desire, volition, memory, imagination, are found to be separated, by such delicate shades and minute gradations, that their boundaries have eluded the most subtle investigations, and remain a pregnant source of ingenious disquisition and controversy (emphasis added).[62]

Checks and balances. Even if we understood what the "airtight compartment" approach to Separation of Powers meant for judging in 1789, there was still another conception of Separation of Powers that we must consider. *Checks and balances*—in which governmental power is shared and each department checks the other—was at least as important as the compartmentalizing of the legislative and judicial functions. Madison in Federalist # 47 makes this point. He argues that Separation of Powers precludes one branch from having the *whole* power of another branch. (A likely example would be when the legislative branch possesses the whole power of the judiciary by appointment and post-appointment control.) It is quite another matter, Madison argued, if one branch has a "partial agency in" or some control over the activities of another branch—what we would call checks and balances—as when the executive can veto a statute.

In the context of judging, the legislature has *some* judicial power through impeachment of judges. Conversely, judges can control the legislature through judicial review of statutes to assure that they are constitutional.[63] Hamilton even argued in Federalist # 78 that *statutory interpretation* provided a check on the legislature, stating: "[T]he independence of the judges may be an essential safeguard against the effects of occasional ill-humours in the society," not just when there is an "infraction of the constitution," but also when there is "injury of the private rights of particular classes of citizens, by unjust and partial laws;" the "firmness of the judicial magistracy is of vast importance in mitigating the severity, and confining the operation of such laws."[64]

Hamilton's view sounds a lot like a version of the Golden Rule, whereby judges *limited* the reach of statutes. Assuming courts could do this in 1789, how can that power be generalized to justify judicial lawmaking discretion in the 20th Century?

Multiple office-holding. A further complication in deciding what "separation of powers" meant for judging is that, for some, it meant primarily a

---

62. Federalist, # 37, p. 178. Cf. Federalist, # 51, p. 264 ("each department [executive, legislative, and judiciary] should have a will of its own").

63. Hamilton, Federalist, # 78, p. 398.

64. Hamilton, Federalist, # 78, pp. 400–01.

prohibition of multiple office-holding.[65] For example, when Essex County, Massachusetts, rejected the proposed 1778 Massachusetts constitution, a major point was that the "three powers [of government] ought to be in different hands;" and "[i]f the legislative and judicial powers are united, the maker of the law will also interpret it * * *."[66] Notice that objection to judicial interpretation is in the setting of a merged legislative and judiciary. Similarly, Essex County objections to "artful [judicial] constructions" was *not* a free-floating concern about judicial interpretation, but was explicitly tied to the problem of united executive and judicial powers. If it turns out that multiple office-holding was the major separation of powers concern at the state level, that would be especially important, because most legislation in this period came from the states. Most of our attention to separation of powers has focused on debates about the federal constitution, where the relationship of the federal government to states rights complicates the effort to understand the more general question of the interaction between courts and legislatures.

The majority of state constitutions from 1776–1789 explicitly prohibited judges from holding political office. Three states restricted judges from holding legislative office—North Carolina and Virginia prohibited judges from being legislators; New Jersey allowed judges to be senators but not members of the Assembly. Four states prohibited judges from holding any other office—Delaware, Maryland, Massachusetts, and New Hampshire. Two states made further distinctions—New York prohibited judges from holding other office, except that they could be delegates to the general congress of the United States, and the first county judges could also be senators; Pennsylvania prohibited supreme court judges from holding other office, but prohibited admiralty judges from holding only legislative office.

The federal constitution prohibits any office holder (including judges) from being a member of congress. U.S. Const, Art I, sec. 6.

iii) JUDICIAL POLITICAL INVOLVEMENT

Another feature of early constitution-building that might shed some light on the judicial lawmaking role is the extent to which judges could and did engage in political activity. One might, for example, infer that, if judges can act politically, they might also have a political role to play when judging. Prohibition or refusal to act politically, might suggest the contrary. But not necessarily. Judges might be able to compartmentalize their multiple roles, being political where appropriate and judicial when judging. Conversely, if judges could not or did not act politically, that is also ambiguous regarding the judicial role. It might signify minimal lawmaking authority, or it might protect judges from public disaffection, preserving whatever lawmaking role they have.

---

65. Corwin, p. 516.

66. Massachusetts, Colony to Commonwealth: Documents on the Formation of Its Constitution, 1775–1780, pp. 79–80 (Robert Taylor ed. 1961).

Political role for judges; Council of Revision. Even if judges could not hold political office, they might act politically in their judicial capacity. The most famous example was the New York Council of Revision.[67] The Council had the power to veto legislation when laws were "inconsistent with the spirit of the constitution, or with the public good." It originated as a compromise between too much legislative and too much executive power—a veto on legislation was considered necessary, but a governor-veto seemed too monarchical. The solution was to involve judges in the veto process. Council membership included the Governor, the chancellor (chief judge for the equity branch of the judiciary), and state Supreme Court justices. Although some people favored a Council of Revision to protect judges from legislative encroachment, the Council's power clearly extended further, to include political policy judgments.

A Council of Revision including judges was also actively considered in the federal constitutional convention. Some delegates, including Madison, favored a New York style Council of Revision with power to veto legislation, consisting of the "Executive and a convenient number of the National Judiciary" (this was Resolution 8 of the Virginia Plan proposed to the constitutional convention). Madison gave two reasons. First, he favored the Council to give greater weight and respectability to the Executive check on legislative dominance. Second, he argued that legal wisdom would help provide "consistency, conciseness, perspicuity, and technical propriety in the laws."

The proposal for a Council of Revision in the federal constitution was defeated. Some of the objections were prudential—judges who passed on proposed legislation might be biased when the law came up later for judicial review; and political involvement by judges might damage their judicial reputation and make their other work more difficult. But the more fundamental point was the "airtight compartment" version of Separation of Powers—the Council of Revision would give judges a legislative power. Elbridge Gerry was the foremost opponent of the Council on Separation of Powers grounds, stating: "It was quite foreign from the nature of [the judicial] office to make them judges of the policy of public measures."[68]

What can we infer from the defeat of a federal Council of Revision about more selective judicial exercises of lawmaking power, such as judicial review and statutory interpretation? The question is especially important because it is not uncommon for those objecting to too much judicial lawmaking to rely on the fact that judges do *not* sit as a Council of Revision. It appears that the major protagonists did not see a link between a judicial role on such a Council and more selective opportunities for judicial discretion. Gerry, who opposed the Council, did not oppose judicial review of statutes for unconsti-

---

67. Barry, The Council of Revision and the Limits of Judicial Power, 56 U. Chi. L. Rev. 235 (1989); Street, The Council of Revision of the State of New York (1859).

68. The discussion of the Constitutional Convention's consideration of the Council of Revision is based on Farrand, The Records of the Federal Convention, Vol. I, pp. 97–98; Vol II, pp. 74–78.

tutionality. And Madison favored the Council of Revision, in part because it would discourage judicial review regarding unconstitutionality.[69]

Judicial role for legislators. Two states preserved a political role for judges, not by giving judges a role in politics, but by giving legislators a role in judging. The highest court in New Jersey and New York consisted in part of legislators.

Other political activity. In the early years of the Republic judges often engaged in political activity.[70] For example, two federal Supreme Court Justices served as treaty negotiators and two ran for state governor while they were Justices. But they were usually careful to refrain from taking on political tasks in an *official* judicial capacity. Thus, federal judges refused to recommend eligibility for veterans benefits to the Secretary of War—because the recommendation could be rejected by the Secretary and was therefore only advisory, not judicial—but they were willing to make these recommendations *out of court*.[71]

Another example of drawing judges into what might appear to be political activity is giving advisory opinions to political officials who ask about the legality of specific legislation or other government action. The Supreme Court refused to give an advisory opinion to President Washington in 1793 in its official capacity, but some individual federal judges advised Presidents and responded to legislator's requests for advice about improving legislation. A few state constitutions were more accommodating to judges giving officially-authorized advisory opinions. For example, the 1780 Massachusetts constitution provided as follows: "Each branch of the legislature, as well as the governor and council, shall have authority to require the opinions of the justices of the supreme judicial court upon important questions of law, and upon solemn occasions."[72]

iv) JUDICIAL PRACTICE; STATUTORY INTERPRETATION

If it is difficult to construct the appropriate judicial role from the legislative-judicial relationships based on state and federal constitutions (especially about statutory interpretation), we might still learn something from examining judicial practice. Unfortunately, the evidence is both uncertain and sparse.

During the Revolutionary–Founding period, there were *three* ways courts might interact with statutes. The first two allowed for judicial review: (1) strike down statutes as unconstitutional; (2) strike down statutes as violating natural law. The third way judges might interact with statutes concerned statutory interpretation: (3) interpret statutes to protect certain

69. The Writings of James Madison, Vol. 8, p. 406 (Hunt, ed. 1908).

70. Westin, Out-of-Court Commentary by United States Supreme Court Justices, 1790–1962: Of Free Speech and Judicial Lockjaw, *in* Westin, An Autobiography of the Supreme Court, pp. 6–7 (1963).

71. Marcus, Separation of Powers in the Early National Period, 30 Wm. & Mary L. Rev. 269, 272–74 (1989).

72. Mass. Const. 1780, Chapter III, Art. II. Of the original 13 states, New Hampshire was the only other state to provide for advisory opinions.

values in the absence of a clear statutory statement to the contrary. None of these roles was uncontroversial and the courts did not always distinguish carefully among them.

First, judicial review based on the Constitution was vigorously debated in connection with ratification of the Constitution. Hamilton argued for judicial review in Federalist # 78 on the theory that the Constitution was "law," and that courts always had the power to determine which of two laws prevailed, whether it was two statutes, or a statute and the constitution. Although later history settled this question in favor of judicial review, the issue was not completely settled at the time of the Founding.[73]

Second, whatever Coke's decision in Bonham's case meant in England, it was often appealed to on this continent for the proposition that a statute in violation of common right or natural law was void. This was a common practice before adoption of written constitutions,[74] but also persisted in both federal and state courts even after adoption of written constitutions, most famously by Justice Chase in Calder v. Bull ("vital principles [ ] will overrule an apparent and flagrant abuse of legislative power;" an "act [ ] contrary to the great first principles of the social compact [ ] cannot be considered a rightful exercise of legislative authority").[75] Even though this judicial role was controversial at the time (e.g. Justice Iredell in Calder v. Bull denied courts a power to void statutes on natural justice grounds),[76] and even though judicial review based explicitly on natural justice has since been discredited, it was one of several ways a judge could interact with statutes in the late 18th Century.

Third, judges injected substantive values into the process of statutory interpretation. As noted earlier, somewhere between Coke's voiding of statutes for violation of common right and absolute Parliamentary sovereignty lay a middle way in 18th England:

> * * * [There were instances] in which the courts interpreting the common law changed the meaning of statutes, refused to give them the effect intended, or to apply a rule [ ] until the [legislature issued] an unmistakable mandate, which the courts reluctantly at times conceded it was their duty to obey. Short of such mandates clearly and unequivocally expressed there was a wide realm in which the courts applied the basic principles of reason of the

73. See generally Nelson, Changing Conceptions of Judicial Review: The Evolution of Constitutional Theory in the States, 1790–1860, 120 U. Pa. L. Rev. 1166 (1972)(hereafter "Nelson").

74. See the argument for plaintiff in Robin v. Hardaway (1772), citing Bonham's Case, reported by Jefferson, Report of Cases Determined by the General Court of Virginia, pp. 112–13 (1981).

75. 3 U.S. (3 Dall.) 386, 388 (1798). See also Haines, The Law of Nature in State and Federal Decisions, 25 Yale L. J. 617, 625–31 (1916)

76. 3 U.S. at 399. Cover argues that a "constitutional positivism" prevailed at the time of the Founding, which did not confuse constitutional law with natural justice. Cover, Justice Accused: Antislavery and the Judicial Process, p. 27 (1975).

common law and were seldom interfered with by either the king or Parliament.[77]

This was the traditional English judicial method of dealing with statutes—applying clear statement rules to interpret statutory meaning. We are so accustomed to observing that United States constitutional theory justifying judicial review was a sharp departure from English 18th Century constitutional *theory*—which affirmed Parliamentary sovereignty—that we overlook the similarity in *practice* between clear statement rules in statutory interpretation and judicial review. The effect of the two practices is certainly different—because judicial review can be overturned only by constitutional amendment and statutory interpretation remands an issue for legislative reexamination—but the historical practices were more closely linked than we realize.

The link between judicial review and clear statement rules was most obvious when courts used such rules to preserve fundamental values. Indeed, courts did not always distinguish carefully between judicial review and statutory interpretation for this purpose. For example, in Ham v. M'Claws, 1 Bay 93, 97 (S.Car. 1789), the South Carolina court stated that

> statutes passed against the plain and obvious principles of common right, and common reason, are absolutely null and void * * *. [W]e would not do the legislature who passed this act [ ] so much injustice, as to sit here and say that it was their intention [to do such an act.] We are, therefore, bound to give such a construction [to this act] as will be consistent with justice, and the dictates of natural reason, though contrary to the strict letter of the law * * *.

And, in Gardner v. Newburgh, 2 Johns. Ch. 162, 168 (N.Y.1816), Chancellor Kent held that a statute was unconstitutional and then interpreted it to avoid that result, stating that

> [I]t would be unjust, and contrary to the first principles of government, and equally contrary to the intention of this statute to [take property without compensation].

Other courts *did* make a distinction between striking down legislation and statutory interpretation, but affirmed that equitable interpretation was alive and well, despite acknowledging legislative supremacy. Rutgers v. Washington, a well-known 1784 New York case, involved a suit against a British subject who entered and used the property of a New York resident who had fled the invading British troops. The question was whether the defendant could rely on the law of nations, which was part of the substantive common law, or whether a statute abrogated this defense. In adopting an "equitable interpretation" approach to preserve the common law defense (urged upon the court by Alexander Hamilton for the defendant), the court stressed the substantively-laden judicial role envisioned by Plowden in fitting statutes into the broader fabric of the law:[78]

---

77. Haines, p. 36.

78. The Law Practice of Alexander Hamilton, Vol I, p. 396 (Julius Goebel, Jr.

In order, [Plowden] says, to form a right judgment whether a case be within the equity of a statute, it is a good way to suppose the law maker present, and that you asked him the question—did you intend to comprehend the case? Then you must give yourself the answer as you may imagine, he *being an upright and reasonable man*, would have been given (emphasis in original).

The court did not question the "supremacy of the Legislature," but held that "unreasonable" results arising from "general words" regarding some "collateral matter" are presumed "not foreseen by the Legislature" and are not included in the statute, by "expound[ing] the statute by equity. * * * [T]his is the language of Blackstone in his celebrated commentaries, and this is the practice of the courts of justice, from which we have copied our jurisprudence * * *."[79]

The decision created a great stir in New York, leading to calls in the New York Assembly for replacement of the judicial official (which did not pass) because the court had in effect engaged in legislation, altering rather than declaring law.[80] It is unclear, however, whether the judge's interpretive approach would have been replicated on appeal. Defendants were probably unsure what interpretive standard the appeals court would adopt and the case was settled by compromise before an appeal was perfected.[81]

b) THE DEBATE OVER CONSTITUTIONAL INTERPRETATION

The primary focus of discussion about interpretation at the time of the Founding was the Constitution, as part of the ratification debates. These disputes shed some light on how interpretive issues were analyzed at that time, although their relevance for *statutory* interpretation is unclear.

Opponents of ratifying the Constitution (known as Anti–Federalists) expressed fear that federal judges would apply Blackstone's interpretive approach to constitutional interpretation to enhance the Federalist's political agenda of expanding the power of the national government. Whatever anyone else thought Blackstone meant, these opponents (writing under the pseudonym of Brutus) thought that Blackstone favored "equitable interpretation." Explicitly citing Blackstone as the source of interpretive method, Brutus states: "By [equity the judges] are empowered, to explain the constitution according to the reasoning spirit of it, without being confined to the words or letter."[82] And: "[T]his [Supreme] court will be authorized to decide upon the meaning of the constitution, [ ] not only according to the natural and obvious meaning of the constitution, but also according to the spirit and intention of it."[83] And, in the spirit of the constitutional preamble

ed.)(1964)(hereafter "Hamilton, Law Practice").

79. Hamilton, Law Practice, p. 415. See also Cover, p. 35 (post-Revolutionary canons of construction express a preference for "liberty").

80. Stimson, pp. 115–16 (1990).

81. Hamilton, Law Practice, pp. 311–15.

82. The Debate on the Constitution, Part Two, Brutus XI, 1/31/1788, p. 131 (Bernard Bailyn selection 1993)(hereafter "Brutus").

83. Brutus, XV, 3/20/1788, p. 375.

(referring to a "more perfect union"), reliance on the "reason and spirit of the constitution" will tend towards enhancing the power of the general government in accordance with Federalist views.[84] In sum, the supreme court was vested with a "power of giving an *equitable* construction to the constitution (emphasis in original)."[85]

Brutus had nothing to worry about if the anti-federalist *substantive* view of the constitutional *spirit* prevailed, resulting in strict construction of federal power. If the Constitution was a compact among states—if that was its spirit—the general government's powers would be narrowly construed. Justice Chase, in an early Supreme Court case, adopted this substantive view of the constitution's spirit, to decide that the *ex post facto* clause applied only to criminal and not civil state laws. "It appears to me a self-evident proposition, that the several State Legislatures retain all the powers of legislation, delegated to them by the State Constitutions; which are not expressly taken away by the Constitution of the United States."[86] And, in 1803, Tucker's comments on Blackstone's Commentaries explicitly referred to the spirit of the constitution,[87] but argued for a *narrow* reading of the central government's powers to preserve the rights of the people and to avoid destroying the states by implication.[88] But Brutus did have a lot to worry about. He accurately feared equitable construction by Federalist judges, which would embrace a substantive view of the constitution that would aggrandize federal power.

Brutus wrote his comments on constitutional interpretation between January 31 and March 30, 1788. Hamilton responded to Brutus in Federalist ## 78–84, the first of which appeared on May 28, 1788. Essentially, Hamilton said not to worry. Judicial interpretation was no threat. He denied that judges had the interpretive freedom that Brutus feared. But he was at best disingenuous. Hamilton knew full well that judges had interpretive potential which could pose a threat to Anti–Federalist values.

Most of Hamilton's remarks dealt with the issue of judicial review of potentially unconstitutional legislation. But he also commented on "equitable" interpretation, presenting what we would recognize as a nondenial denial. "[T]here is not a syllable in the plan under consideration, which *directly* empowers the national courts to construe the laws according to the spirit of the constitution * * * (emphasis in original)."[89]

Hamilton's confidential opinion to President Washington on the constitutionality of the national bank is much more forthright about judicial interpretation than the Federalist papers. He makes all the arguments Brutus anticipated. Liberality is a formal judicial principle of interpretation; and, in addition, the substantive spirit of the constitution calls for liberal (that is, expansive) interpretation of federal power. "[T]he powers contained

84. Brutus, XII, 2/7/1788 & 2/14/1788, p. 173.

85. Brutus, XV, 3/20/1788, p. 372.

86. Calder v. Bull, 3 U.S. (3 Dall.) 386, 387 (1798).

87. St. George Tucker, Blackstone's Commentaries, Vol. I, pp. 354–55, 364 (1803)(hereafter "Tucker").

88. Tucker, pp. 154, 423.

89. Federalist, # 81, p. 412.

in a constitution of government, especially those which concern the general administration of the affairs of the country * * * ought to be construed liberally * * *;" and, in response to the Attorney General Randolph's argument to "construe[ ] with greater strictness" a federal rather than a state constitution, Hamilton states that the "reason of the rule" is otherwise.[90] The same point of view appears in his notes for a response to the Attorney General's opinion on the bank: "There is a real difference between the rule of interpretation, applied to a law and a constitution. The one comprises a summary of matter, for the detail of which numberless Laws will be necessary; the other is the very detail. The one is therefore to be construed with a discreet liberality; the other with a closer adherence to the literal meaning."[91] (This distinction between constitutional and statutory interpretation recurs in Marshall's opinions, discussed below.)[92]

Judicial decisions interpreting the Constitution also reflect the tension apparent in the debate between Brutus and Hamilton. The best known statement with which Brutus would have agreed is by Justice Chase in Priestman v. United States.[93] Chase stated that no rule of construction "can be more dangerous, than that, which distinguishing between the intent, and the words, of the legislature, declares, that a case not within the meaning of a statute, according to the opinion of the Judges, shall not be embraced in the operation of the statute, although it is clearly within the words: or, vice versa, that a case within the meaning, though not within the words, shall be embraced;" and he implies a contrast between British and American courts—"For my part, however, sitting in an American Court, I shall always deem it a duty to conform to the expressions of the legislature, to the letter of the statute, when free from ambiguity and doubt; without indulging a speculation, either upon the impolicy, or the hardship, of the law."

A good example of the Hamiltonian approach is from Justice Wilson's decision in Chisholm v. Georgia.[94] Wilson, more than any of the Founders, stressed that the people were sovereign *and* that the courts, as well as the legislature, spoke for the people. Not only was the Constitution a product of "We the People," but (for Wilson) the common law itself was the embodiment of custom, which derived support from popular consent.

Wilson's opinion in Chisholm embodied this sense of judicial lawmaking power. The decision affirmed that states were not immune from lawsuits in federal courts. (Hamilton had assured readers of the Federalist Papers to the contrary, that immunity from suit without consent was "the general sense,

---

90. The Papers of Alexander Hamilton, Vol. VIII, p. 105 (hereafter "Hamilton, Papers").

91. Hamilton Papers, p. 48.

92. An argument has been made that constitutional and statutory interpretation were governed by the same principles, but the primary point of the argument is that 18th Century interpreters rejected reliance on evidence of subjective intent, especially through legislative history. See Powell, The Original

Understanding of Original Intent, 98 Harv. L. Rev. 885 (1985). It is true that subjective intent was rejected as a evidence of meaning for both documents, but the similarity in interpretive approaches disappears if we focus on the text and equitable interpretation as interpretive criteria.

93. Priestman v. United States, 4 U.S. (4 Dall.) 28, 31 (1800).

94. 2 U.S. (2 Dall.) 419, 465 (1793).

and the general practice of mankind.")[95] Wilson relies heavily on what he calls "the general texture of the Constitution of the United States." That texture is "to form an union more perfect" and to "form themselves into a nation for national purposes." He asks rhetorically: "Is it congruous, that, with regard to such purposes, any man or body of men, any person natural or artificial, should be permitted to claim successfully an entire exemption from the jurisdiction of the national Government? Would not such claims, crowned with success, be repugnant to our very existence as a nation?"

Someone reading Wilson's opinion cannot help but notice how different it is in tone from the English approach to equitable interpretation. The text is not so much corrected (to use Plowden's phrase) by his vision of the constitution's texture as it is *imbued* with it. This was Wilson the Justice elaborating the common sense of the people for whom he spoke.[96] By contrast, Justice Jay's opinion in the same case relied on a more traditional interpretive approach, invoking the common law maxim that remedial statutes should be liberally interpreted—in this case, to permit suits against states.[97]

c) FEDERAL STATUTORY INTERPRETATION—CHIEF JUSTICE MARSHALL

It is unclear what relevance the material on interpreting the constitution has for statutory interpretation. Indeed, there is evidence (noted earlier from Hamilton's Papers and explained below for Chief Justice Marshall) that interpreting statutes should be less free-wheeling than interpreting the constitution—at least at the federal level.[98] Unlike some of Marshall's constitutional interpretation opinions, which adopt an equitable interpretation approach (without using the term),[99] Marshall writes about statutes (both as a Supreme Court and Circuit Court judge) as though they were very different from the Constitution. The opinions emphasize the statutory text, not substantive background principles.[100] Thus: the "law is the best expositor of

95. Federalist, # 81, p. 417.

96. It did not take long (1798) for the people to correct Wilson by passing the Eleventh Amendment, preserving state sovereign immunity in federal court.

97. 2 U.S. at 476.

98. See generally Yoo, Marshall's Plan: The Early Supreme Court and Statutory Interpretation, 101 Yale L.J. 1607 (1992).

99. An example of Chief Justice Marshall's liberal "equitable interpretation" approach to the Constitution is his dissent in Ogden v. Saunders, 25 U.S. (12 Wheat.) 213, 344 (1827). In this, his only dissent in a constitutional case, Marshall argued that the "no impairment of contract" clause of the U.S. Constitution applied to contracts formed *after* as well as before passage of a state statute. He

rejected the view that a "contract is a mere creature of society, and derives all its obligation from human legislation." Instead, contracts impose "pre-existing intrinsic obligation[s] which human law enforces," which exist "anterior to, and independent of society." Marshall invokes the "state of nature" to support his interpretation of the constitution.

100. Marshall was, however, willing to correct a text which contained an obvious drafting error—for example, where the text refers to two time periods, only one of which is possible; Huidekoper's Lessee v. Douglass, 7 U.S. (3 Cranch) 1, 64–72 (1805). See also Ross v. Doe, 26 U.S. (1 Pet.) 655, 667 (1828) (Trimble, J.)(correcting statute which specified date on which nothing relevant to the law happened).

itself;"[101] "Men use a language calculated to express the idea they mean to convey;[102] 'intention of the legislature * * * searched for in the words;'[103] 'By the spirit of the law, I understand, the intention of the legislature, to be collected from the general language of the act, the scope of its provisions, and the objects to be attained.' "[104]

He is very clear that his approach to statutory interpretation has evolved away from the historical practice of equitable interpretation, noting that the older practice of going "far beyond the words" has "in modern times [   ] been a good deal restrained."[105] Nonetheless, a more modest judicial discretion to tilt the text *might* survive: "Courts still construe words liberally, to reach that intention which the words themselves import, [but they] seldom insert a description of persons omitted by the statute, because, in the opinion of the court, there is the same reason for comprehending those persons within its provisions, as for comprehending those who are actually enumerated."[106]

Marshall's most famous statutory interpretation decision is United States v. Fisher.[107] It contains a quote about statutory interpretation which can drastically mislead when taken out of context: "Where the mind labours to discover the design of the legislature, it seizes every thing from which aid can be derived * * *." But the immediate setting for this statement is Marshall's use of the act's title, which (he says) "claims a degree of notice, and will have its due share of consideration," but cannot "control plain words in the body of the statute;" and: "Where the intent is plain, nothing is left to construction."

The core of Marshall's view of statutory interpretation appears later in the same opinion.[108] His approach was to distinguish between, on the one hand, fundamental principles and, on the other, political regulation and inconvenience, leaving the latter to the legislature. "Where rights are infringed, where fundamental principles are overthrown, where the general system of the laws is departed from, the legislative intention must be expressed with irresistible clearness to induce a court of justice to suppose a design to effect such objects." Marshall here sounds a lot like Hamilton, whose only comment on statutory interpretation in the Federalist Papers asserts an interpretive power to *limit* statutes to prevent injustice.[109]

However, Marshall advocates a different more textual approach when less than fundamental values are at stake. "But where only a political regulation is made, which is inconvenient, if the intention of the legislature be expressed in terms which are sufficiently intelligible to leave no doubt in

101. Pennington v. Coxe, 6 U.S. (2 Cranch) 33, 52 (1804).

102. Oneale v. Thornton, 10 U.S. (6 Cranch) 53, 68 (1810).

103. Schooner Paulina's Cargo, 11 U.S. (7 Cranch) 52, 60 (1812).

104. Thomson v. United States, 23 F.Cas. 1108, 1109 (1820).

105. Kirkpatrick v. Gibson, 14 F.Cas. 683, 684 (1828).

106. 14 F.Cas. at 684.

107. 2 Cranch 358, 6 U.S. 358, 386 (1805).

108. 6 U.S. at 390.

109. Federalist, # 78, pp. 400–01.

the mind when the words are taken in their ordinary sense, it would be going a great way to say that a constrained interpretation must be put upon them, to avoid an inconvenience which ought to have been contemplated in the legislature when the act was passed, and which, in their opinion, was probably overbalanced by the particular advantages it was calculated to produce." In matters of political regulation, "[i]t is for the legislature to appreciate them. They are not of such magnitude as to induce an opinion that the legislature could not intend to expose the citizens of the United States to them, when words are used which manifest that intent." Marshall's views sound a lot like the dominant conception of the Golden Rule—stick to the text except to avoid absurdity or injustice, but not inconvenience.

Marshall's focus on the "fundamental" might have reflected an important aspect of United States legal culture at the time of the Founding. English statutory interpretation had always been concerned with fundamental values, as Coke's decision in Bonham's Case illustrated. But this was not a separate element in English equitable interpretation. Equitable interpretation was broadly conceived as the way for courts to make sense of how statutes fit into the law. In Marshall's terms, this traditional view of equitable interpretation was concerned with *both* the fundamental and the inconvenient.

United States experience put significant pressure on this traditional approach. As Wood argues, *the* significant break with English legal theory was to highlight the existence of fundamental as opposed to ordinary law and the court's role in enforcing fundamental law.[110] This justified adopting the Constitution to embody fundamental values and judicial review to enforce them. But emphasis on constitutionalized fundamental values created a serious problem for statutory interpretation for a society equally intent on giving legislatures (at least state legislatures) a dynamic lawmaking role, not just technical sovereignty. One way to reconcile these two objectives was to bifurcate law into the fundamental, for which courts continued to show special concern, and the inconvenient, which was left to the legislature. Marshall's approach to statutory interpretation achieved that goal.

Of course, everything turns on what is a mere "inconvenience" and what is fundamental. Marshall would have been the first to admit that it is hard to sort out what a judge is actually doing based on generalities. He notes that there is "no difference of opinion" about "abstract principles" of statutory interpretation but "in the application of those principles [ ] the difference discovers itself."[111] In this respect, he is like other common law lawyers, such as Hale, Blackstone, and Hamilton, who believed that there were general legal principles, but that specific judicial opinions did not always agree on their proper application.

d) STATE STATUTORY INTERPRETATION IN THE 19TH CENTURY

Any picture of statutory interpretation which dwells on federal courts in the 19th Century is woefully incomplete. The federal government had only

---

110. Wood, pp. 261–66, 291–92.   **111.** 6 U.S. at 386.

limited governmental powers and it was not until the 20th Century that federal legislation began to dominate much of our law. Indeed, Chief Justice Marshall's reluctance to assert too much power to interpret statutes might have reflected his position as a federal judge, anxious to preserve his authority for constitutional cases, and content to leave the much less important field of statutory interpretation well enough alone.

Most statutes were passed by state legislatures. National independence brought with it a sense of control over lawmaking that created new political opportunities for state legislation.[112] There had always been more statutes than common law lawyers liked to admit, as evidenced by their frequent complaints about the quantity and well as quality of legislation. Although these complaints persisted in the 19th Century United States, early 19th Century legislatures had a sense of lawmaking potency and confidence that the earlier British Parliament had not enjoyed. State legislatures responded, for example, with statutes creating mechanics liens and rights for married women in property. Numerous private bills authorized specific corporations to construct public works, such as canals and bridges. Control of banking and bankruptcy was a constant legislative concern. And most states "revised" their statutes, in the sense of updating, correcting, and (in some cases) making substantial changes, putting them all together in a statutory code. Even as conservative a common law lawyer and judge as Chancellor Kent of New York spoke favorably, if cautiously, of some statutory modifications of the common law in his 1826 Commentaries on American Law.[113] It is true that, by comparison to modern legislation, early 19th century statutes were not broadly programmatic. There were no comprehensive statutes, such as tax and welfare laws, or broad regulatory statutes controlling large areas of political and social life, such as the National Labor Relations Acts and various Securities laws. Still, legislation was experienced as an affirmative force for legal change in the first half of the 19th Century.

This period was, in fact, one of dynamic legislation *and* judicial revision of the common law. The traditional common law perspective on law as a set of discoverable principles (though susceptible of change through application), gradually gave way somewhere around the 1820s to an instrumental vision of judge-made common law. Judges were much more self-conscious in creatively reshaping the common law to serve the needs of economic development.[114]

It is not clear what instrumentalism in common law judging and the increasing sense of legislative potency actually meant for the development of statutory interpretation. Much more research needs to be done on statutory

---

112. See generally William Novak, Salus Populi: The Roots of Regulation in America, 1787–1873 (1992).

113. See Raack, "To Preserve the Best Fruits": The Legal Thought of Chancellor James Kent, 33 Amer. J. Leg. Hist. 320, 339, 357 (1989) (hereafter "Raack"). Kent was not usually so generous; he referred to the com-mon law as a "nursing father," but a "statute is like a tyrant." Quoted in Raack, p. 354.

114. Horwitz, The Transformation of American Law, 1780–1860, pp. 1–2 (1977)("judges began to conceive of common law adjudication as a process of making and not merely discovering legal rules").

interpretation during this period. There is little doubt that equitable interpretation lost ground, both rhetorically and in its more extreme forms of disregarding the statutory text. But it is my perception that there was also less of a sense of antagonism between statutes and the common law in the first half of the 19th Century, compared to the attitudes that characterized earlier centuries in England or that would come to characterize later 19th Century judging in the United States (see Chapter 2.04div). A more harmonious relationship between statutes and common law would certainly be a sensible approach in a legal climate in which *both* legislating and judging were creative forces for legal change.

i) FIRST HALF OF THE 19TH CENTURY—CASES

The growing sense of legislative competence and legitimacy altered the rhetoric of many judicial decisions. For example, in a 1798 Delaware case,[115] the judge was reluctant to expand a statute: "Inconveniences may arise, but they will not warrant the court to apply the law to a case not within it. Our powers are judicial, not legislative." In fact, the statute in the case was in derogation of the common law and the judge could just as easily have said that he would not on that account expansively interpret the law. Instead, he appealed to a separation of powers notion to deny judicial discretion to expand the statute's coverage.[116]

Similarly, in an 1855 Georgia case,[117] the tension between equitable interpretation and sticking to the statutory text is apparent. The issue was whether a judgment creditor had to take certain steps to preserve his rights as a creditor. The court first observed that the statute was "one [ ] to which this Court has applied the principle of *equitable* interpretation." But the opinion went on to reject that approach for contemporary statutes:

> [I]n my opinion, the rule of rules in the interpretation of Statutes, is to follow the words, if their meaning is plain. This rule, it is true, I should feel myself at liberty to depart from, in the case of some old English Statutes, and some Statutes of our own which pursue old English Statutes, such as the Statute of Frauds * * *.
>
> But as a general thing, with respect to the Acts of our own Legislature, I should feel myself rigorously bound down to the words. The words of those Acts are, what the great majority of the people of the State shape their actions by. It is the words only, that are published to them—and when, after they have followed the words of the law, they are told by the Courts that they have not followed the law, they feel, that for them, the law has been turned into a snare. And it is difficult to say that they have not the right so to feel.

115. Brown v. Brown, 1 Del. Cases, 188, 190–91 (Ct. Common Pleas 1798).

116. Note also that the reference to "inconvenience" implicitly echoes the Golden Rule and affirms that "absurd" results might still be avoided, an approach affirmed in Laws v. Davis, 1 Del. Cases. 256, 259 (Ct. Common Pleas 1800).

117. Strawbridge v. Mann, 17 Ga. 454, 456 (1855).

New York; Mayor of New York v. Lord. Disputes about the judicial role in statutory interpretation—and about the surviving role of equitable interpretation—are also apparent in two New York cases in 1837 and 1840, both dealing with a statute which provided compensation when the government destroyed a burning building to prevent the spread of fire.[118] The earlier case involved a claim for compensation by a tenant who owned goods lost in the destroyed building (a department store); the later case involved a claim by the tenant for loss of goods owned by someone who was *neither* owner nor tenant of the destroyed building, but whose goods were in the building when the fire occurred. The statutory text (sec. 81) permitted the city to "pull down[ ] or destroy" a building to prevent the spread of fire, but imposed an obligation on the city to "assess the damages which the owners of such building, and all persons having any estate or interest therein, have respectively sustained by the pulling down or destroying thereof." The statute also provided a procedure to assess the amount of the loss which would be paid "in full satisfaction of all demands by reason of the pulling down or destroying such building." Sec. 83 specified that the "sum assessed [ ] for any building so pulled down or destroyed" shall be defrayed by the city.

In the 1837 case, which awarded compensation to the tenant by a vote of 16–6, the court's interpretive credo was as follows: "Among [the] fixed principles or rules for the interpretation or construction of statutes, which has been adopted in this country and England, is that of construing the statute by equity, so as to produce neither injustice nor absurdity, where the language of the statute is such as to admit of different interpretation." This neatly combines the language of "equity" and the Golden Rule (injustice or absurdity), with a bow to the text ("where the language [ ] admit[s] of different interpretation"). The court argued that "natural equity"—meaning the constitutional principle that private property shall not be taken for public use without just compensation—could be considered to resolve doubts about meaning.

The dissenting judges argued that the majority had been too cavalier with the text. They favored applying equitable construction only when the statute contained "doubtful" words; and argued that "we are not at liberty to act upon the supposed intention of the legislature," and that it was "dangerous" to "go beyond the letter, for the purpose of carrying into effect the intent of the law-maker."

In the later 1840 case, the tenant of a destroyed building sought compensation for goods in his possession but which were owned by others who had no "estate or interest" in the building. By a vote of 15–3, the court held *against* compensation. One judge made general statements that were as hostile to equitable interpretation as the prior opinion was generous—the "experience of later years had taught courts the danger of excess in bold interpretation, according to the presumed intent and against the plain language of acts." Interestingly, the 1840 court still acknowledged an inter-

---

118. The material about Mayor of New York v. Lord appears in 17 Wend. 285, 286, 291–94, 304 (1837); 18 Wend. 126, 131–32, 139 (1837); Stone v. The City of New York, 25 Wend. 157, 177, 179–80 (1840).

pretive principle which sounded a lot like the Golden Rule by distinguishing between an "acknowledged rule of justice or right" and matters of "legislative discretion alone":

> If courts were ever authorized to go beyond [some reasonable meaning of the language of the statute], it would only be done where there was some acknowledged rule of justice or right wholly independent of the statute, to which its provisions failed to give effect * * *. But when a statute rests upon legislative discretion alone, or judgment upon public policy, then, any assumption by courts, varying, abridging, or extending the clear provisions of a statute, upon the ground of carrying out the policy or intention of the enacting body, appears [ ] to be usurpation of power, transgressing the fixed boundaries between the judicial and legislative authority.

The distinction between a "rule of justice" and "legislative discretion" is also reminiscent of Marshall's distinction between the "fundamental" and matters of "inconvenience."

There are several points worth noting about these cases. First, the rhetoric favoring and opposing equitable interpretation is more extreme than the decisions warrant, at least in my reading of the statutory text. The text seemed doubtful enough, as the majority in the earlier 1837 case stated, to justify considering additional factors when the destroyed property belonged to the tenant. The dissent stressed sec. 83's reference to the "sum assessed [ ] for any building so pulled down or destroyed," but (as the majority noted) sec. 81 contained broader language regarding damages "sustained by the pulling down or destroying" of the building. This was not a case in which the court paid little attention to the statutory language, which was arguably true of many older applications of equitable interpretation. Indeed, when confronted in the 1840 case with a request to extend the statute to provide compensation for property owned by people with no estate in the destroyed building—on the ground that the statute was "designed to assist the common law as a remedial statute"—the court refused the request.

Second, the rhetoric about statutory interpretation may have reflected the judges' views of their judicial role. The deciding court was the Court of Errors in New York, which included both the Chancellor *and* Senators. The report of the 1837 case contains two opinions, one by the Chancellor favoring equitable interpretation, and one by Senator Edwards speaking against equitable interpretation. The 1840 case reports three decisions by Senators, some of which contain language opposing equitable interpretation. The New York Chancellor was a more traditional judge, expected to favor judicial discretion, and the Senators most likely reflected the "popular" point of view, favoring public control over judges and less judicial discretion.

Third, the real dispute was probably about the judges' views of fundamental values. This was a period of intense conflict over the respective rights of private property and public claims on private property for the public good. The older view had required people to commit their property to the community for the common good without compensation[119] (one judge in the 1840 case stated that there is "no reason of justice why that large portion of the city wholly out of hazard should" pay for the loss). But there was a rival and increasingly weighty view, that private property owners had a strong claim to compensation whenever their property was committed to the public good. This latter view may have led the majority in the 1837 case to tilt the statutory text in favor of a statutory purpose with which the judges were in strong sympathy (one judge who favored compensation in the 1837 case saw the "equity and justice" in providing compensation). As we will see in Chapter 3, this approach bears a strong resemblance to many examples of 20th Century purposive interpretation, in which fundamental principles favor *extending* a statute, rather than (as in the Golden Rule) limiting the statute's reach.

Massachusetts; Chief Judge Shaw. We can get a more complete picture of state statutory interpretation in the 19th Century by looking at a whole series of decisions, not just a few selected cases. For that purpose, I selected the opinions of Massachusetts Chief Judge Lemuel Shaw (serving from 1830–1860). Shaw shared with many 19th Century judges a skepticism about legislation. Although "[i]n the multitude of legislators, [ ] there is much learning, prudence, and experience," there is also "a great deal of ignorance, vanity, and pretension," and "it is not always easy to distinguish between the restless impatience of things as they are, a wanton love of innovation, and a sincere and ardent zeal for improvement."[120] This wariness of legislation sometimes led him to be cautious about interpreting "positive" law (that is, statutes) to make dramatic changes:[121]

> [A] wide departure from established rules of law, founded in considerations of public policy, and depending solely upon provisions of positive law [ ] is, therefore, to be construed strictly, and not extended beyond the limits to which it is plainly carried by such provisions of statute.

And, like Marshall, he would limit a statute which "disturb[ed] the fundamental principles of right."[122] One issue which Shaw obviously viewed as "fundamental" was that juries should not decide questions of law. He interpreted a statute which sought to make juries the judge of the law as simply "a declaratory act, making no substantial change in the law regulating the relative rights and functions of the court and of the jury."[123] The statute had, however, stated the contrary:—"In all trials for criminal offenses, it shall be the duty of the jury * * * to decide at their discretion [ ] both the fact

---

119. See generally William Novak, Salus Populi: The Roots of Regulation in America, 1787–1873 (1992); Note, The Origins and Original Significance of the Just Compensation Clause of the Fifth Amendment, 94 Yale L.J. 694 (1985).

120. Lemuel Shaw, Profession of the Law in the United States, 7 American Jurist 67 (1831)(hereafter "Shaw, Profession").

121. Gray v. Coffin, 63 Mass. 192, 199 (1852).

122. Jacquins v. Commonwealth, 63 Mass. 279, 282 (1852).

123. Commonwealth v. Anthes, 71 Mass. 185 (1855).

and the law * * *."[124] As the dissent noted: "Legislation is usually resorted to not to reaffirm existing laws or decisions of the court, but to correct some supposed defect or omission in former statutes, or to introduce some change in the law and administered and declared by the court."[125]

But Shaw was certainly no blind devotee of the old common law—he spent much of his judicial life revising and updating common law. Whatever suspicions he had about legislation were balanced by a realistic view of the common law. He considered placing exclusive reliance on "a system of artificial and technical rules having very little regard to principle" to be a "partial and erroneous" view of the law.[126] And he would not narrowly construe a statute just because it was in derogation of the common law. In response to an argument "that this statute disturbs the symmetry of the common law," he observed that "[a]ll statutes are intended to modify the common law to affect remedies * * *."[127] He approved of some statutory changes in the common law, such as changing the "established and inflexible rule of the common law, that [ ] lands [acquired after making a will] will not pass by devise."[128]

The most interesting aspect of Shaw's approach to statutory interpretation was not his occasional willingness to limit statutes which made dramatic changes or impinged on fundamental values, but his nondoctrinaire approach to legislation. He avoided extreme statements about whether interpretation depended on text, statutory purpose, or equity, and did his best to fit statutes into the legal system, relying on whatever helped him figure out their meaning. Perhaps, as a state rather than a federal judge, he had less of Marshall's doubts about the judge's power of statutory interpretation. He also wrote in an environment of frequently changing statutes written against a common law background, which was a much more complex statutory world than Marshall encountered in early 19th Century federal legislation. In that setting, Shaw *really* did "seize every thing from which aid c[ould] be derived" to interpret statutes. Or, as G. Edward White put it, "Shaw grounded [his decisions] on rough common sense."[129]

Shaw's statutory interpretation opinions often appeal to *both* the text and the spirit or reason underlying the statute (or, analogously, to statutory purpose, policy, or intent), without distinguishing between the weights attributable to these criteria. Here are some sample quotes: "within the letter of the present statute, and [ ] equally within its spirit and purpose";[130] "certainly not within the words of the statute, and [ ] not within its reason";[131] "nothing in the terms, and nothing in the object or purpose of

---

124. 71 Mass. at 186–87.

125. 71 Mass. at 239.

126. Shaw, Profession, p.68.

127. Jacquins v. Commonwealth, 63 Mass. 279, 282 (1852).

128. Winchester v. Forster, 69 Mass. 366, 369 (1849).

129. White, The American Judicial Tradition, p. 43 (1988).

130. Commonwealth v. Dimond, 57 Mass. 235, 237 (1849).

131. Drake v. Curtis, 55 Mass. 395, 410 (1848).

the statute";[132] "nothing in the terms or spirit."[133] Given Shaw's concern about the "reason and 'spirit' " of legislation, it is not surprising to find him supporting equitable interpretation, with none of the anxiety that afflicted many 19th Century commentators (discussed later). Sometimes he even sounds like Plowden:[134]

> * * * [I]t is well established, that in the construction of remedial statutes, cases not within the letter of the statute, are taken to be within its spirit and equity, upon a reasonable certainty arising from a consideration of the statute and of every part and clause of it, and from the obvious end and purpose to be accomplished by it, that it was so intended by the legislature: and also that a case may come within the letter, which shall not be judicially construed to be within the act, because it is alike manifest, to a reasonable certainty, that it was not so intended by the makers of the act.

Moreover, Shaw would also rely on fundamental principles to advance a statute's remedial purposes, reminiscent of the 1837 N.Y. court's decision in New York v. Lord—"This construction appears to us to be entirely reasonable and necessary. It is a remedial act, intended to carry into execution that most equitable provision of the constitution"[135] (providing compensation when private property is taken for public use).

The effort to figure out what the legislature was trying to do also led Shaw, as it had Marshall and other 19th Century judges, to the " 'whole act' over 'literal' meaning."[136] Moreover, the "whole text" extended beyond the specific statute to include other related legislation: "[w]ere this a new act of legislation," one meaning might be inferred, but it is a revision and "some light may be thrown on the subject by considering the course of legislation";[137] it is "necessary to examine the other parts of the revised statutes and earlier laws, indicating the course of policy [ ] upon the subject of taxation."[138]

Shaw's determination to understand what the legislature was trying to do even led him to rely on legislative history in the form of materials generated by the legislative process. This history consisted of reports of commissioners who drafted the revised laws for codification into a state statutory code. Most of the references to this legislative history were to drafting history; [139] these are changes made in the text of drafts as they work

---

132. Brigham v. Bigelow, 53 Mass. 268, 271 (1844).

133. Hartwell v. Inhabitants of Littleton, 30 Mass. 229, 232 (1832).

134. Brown v. Thorndike, 32 Mass. 388, 402 (1834).

135. Parks v. Boston, 32 Mass. 198, 203 (1834).

136. Sawyer v. Inhabitants of Northfield, 61 Mass. 490, 494 (1851).

137. Harwood v. City of Lowell, 58 Mass. 310, 312–313 (1849).

138. Inhabitants of Newburyport v. Essex County Commissioners, 53 Mass. 211, 216–217 (1846).

139. Kidder v. Browne, 63 Mass. 400, 401 (1852); Howard v. Merriam, 59 Mass. 564, 565 (1850); Britton v. Commonwealth, 55 Mass. 302, 305 (1848); Commonwealth v. Mash, 48 Mass. 472, 474 (1844); Williams v. Hadley, 36 Mass. 379, 380 (1837); Tower v. Tower, 35 Mass. 262, 263 (1836).

their way to final legislative passage. But some of the references are to statements in commissioner's reports about legislative goals, analogous to modern legislative history found in committee reports.[140]

I do not mean to suggest that Shaw was disrespectful of the statutory text. His opinions contain statements which are quite deferential to statutory language and which lean away from relying on equity, spirit, and reason. He argues that the "inconvenience" of an interpretation is relevant only when language is "doubtful"; there is "no construction" in cases "where terms are plain and explicit."[141] And, like Marshall, he says that "[a] statute is no doubt to be construed according to the intent of the legislature; but it is the intent gathered from the words of the enactment."[142] But the dominant pattern in his statutory interpretation opinions is an eclectic approach to the text, purpose, and equity of the law.

ii) MID–CENTURY—THE SHIFT TOWARDS AN ELECTED JUDICIARY

Constitutional changes. The prior discussion of state statutory interpretation is pre-Civil War. It suggests a shift away from equitable interpretation in some of its more extreme forms and a sensitivity towards the growing competence and legitimacy of legislation. This temporal focus is too narrow, however. We need to take account of the constitutional developments towards democratic selection of state judges in the middle of the 19th Century and consider whether they had any impact on statutory interpretation.

State constitutions, unlike the federal constitution, were often amended in the 19th Century. This reality may, in fact, undermine the relevance of the 1776–1789 material regarding state constitutions that we read earlier in this chapter. We might instead be more justified in looking at later constitutional moments for evidence about the interaction between legislating and judging.[143]

The most significant result of the 19th Century process of amending state constitutions was the democratizing of elections, eliminating most property qualifications (as long as the voter was male and white). Thus, in 1800, there were three states with universal manhood suffrage; by 1828, liberal though not quite universal suffrage existed in all states except two of the original thirteen. And, whereas the original constitutions were not

---

140. Wright v. Oakley, 46 Mass. 400, 402 (1843)("reasons [   ] stated by the commissioners [   ] in their note to [   ] their report"); Morrison v. Underwood, 59 Mass. 52, 54 (1849)("report of the revising commissioners, in their comments"); Marshall v. Crehore, 54 Mass. 462, 466 (1847)("the commissioners, by their note, (*in loco*,) indicate what was their purpose"); Newcomb v. Williams, 50 Mass. 525, 536 (1845) ("fully explained by the re-

port of commissioners for making that revision").

141. Abbott v. Bullard, 62 Mass. 141, 144 (1851).

142. Barnicoat v. Folling, 69 Mass. 134, 136 (1854).

143. See generally Tarr, Understanding State Constitutions, 65 Temple Law Rev. 1169 (1992).

generally ratified by the people (Massachusetts being the exception), between 1830–1850 all but two had to be approved at the polls.[144]

Despite some earlier calls for popular election of judges, however, the movement towards democracy did not directly affect judging until much later than the 1820s.[145] Mississippi was the first state (in 1832) to elect all judges,[146] but it was not until New York did so in its 1846 constitution that the movement spread rapidly. Within ten years thereafter, 15 of 29 states existing in 1846 provided for popular election of judges; and all states entering the Union after 1846 so provided.[147]

The move to democratize judicial selection was not universal. The Massachusetts 1820 constitutional convention headed off such attempts. Justice Story chaired the committee on the judiciary at the convention, which proposed *less* popular accountability by increasing the legislative vote needed to remove judges to ⅔rds.[148] The move failed but, perhaps, took some of the steam out of any moves towards electing judges. The 1853 Massachusetts convention also diverted attempts to provide for election of judges, but did propose ten year terms, which was defeated at the polls.[149] Still, the dominant mood in the 19th Century favored popular election of judges.

We should not assume, however, that the election of judges necessarily rejected judicial discretion. First, there was the same ambiguity about the impact of judicial selection by popular election as there was when legislatures chose judges. Does popular election signify less judicial discretion or does the connection to popular representation mean that there is room for creative judging, subject to electoral influence? It is one of the curious features of our legal history (at least to this observer) that there has been no apparent effort to justify judicial discretion *because* of the judicial link to popular election.

Second, popular election of judges did not necessarily signify faith in legislatures. The contrast between popular elections and faith in the legislature would not be clearly demarcated until the late 19th and early 20th Centuries, when the Populist and Progressive movements led to initiatives and referendums to bypass and impose checks on legislative lawmaking. But the observation that popular election of judges in the mid–19th Century did

---

144. Haynes, pp. 88–89.

145. In New York, dissatisfaction with judging did lead to ending their political role in 1821 by eliminating the Council of Revision, in which appointed judges had a veto over proposed legislation. The Council had frequently objected to legislation on grounds that the law would violate the constitution and/or the "public good." One study states that 55.6% of the vetoes were on policy grounds, 21.8% on constitutional grounds, and 12.4% both. Barry, The Council of Revision and the Limits of Judicial Power, 56 U. Chi. L. Rev. 235, 245–46 (1989). See generally, Dougherty, Constitutional History of the State of New York (2d ed. 1915); Peterson, Democracy, Liberty, and Property: The State Constitutional Conventions of the 1820's, pp. 125–270 (1966).

146. Haynes, p. 117.

147. Haynes, p. 100.

148. Osgood, Isaac Parker: Republican Judge, Federalist Values *in* The History of the Law in Massachusetts: The Supreme Judicial Court: 1692–1992, p. 168 (1992); Journal of Debates and Proceedings in the Massachusetts Constitutional Convention, 1820–21, p. 136 (1853 De Capo Press 1970).

149. Grinnell, The Judicial System and the Bar (1820–1861) *in* Commonwealth History of Massachusetts, pp. 59–60 (1930 ed. Hart).

not signify confidence in the legislature is not entirely anachronistic. 19th Century legislatures tended to pass special interest legislation that favored only a few economically powerful interests and to undermine state credit by excessive borrowing. This led to state constitutional prohibitions of "special legislation"—that is, statutes which favored narrow groups of people—and of practices which threatened to bankrupt state government, some of which we discuss later in Chapter 17. Undoubtedly, judges drew on this suspicion of legislatures to justify a more aggressive lawmaking role during the latter half of the 19th Century, which is described in subsequent pages. Do you think that such suspicion, backed up by constitutional provisions embodying doubts about legislative competence, can help to justify judicial discretion in statutory interpretation?

Legal culture; law vs. democracy. As it turned out, something more fundamental than the state constitutional structure dominated the development of the judicial role regarding statutes. The constitutional shift towards democracy had less to do with judging than a change in the legal culture, which led to judges resisting the dominance of legislation over the common law. The legal culture, at the same time that it stressed democracy in the selection of public officials, moved towards a sharp split between the law and the people.

To understand that change, we must look back again to the 1776–1789 period that we discussed earlier. In this early period, there had been faith in an ideal that the people and the law shared a common objective, resulting in part from what Nelson describes as "the early nineteenth century view [of] 'the people' as a politically homogenous and cohesive body possessing common political goals and aspirations, not as [factions]."[150] It is also implicit in the observation in Federalist, # 51 that all appointments, including judicial, should be "drawn from [ ] the people," if it were not for the fact that judicial independence from the legislature was necessary.[151]

There were certainly intense disputes about *who* would best implement this ideal. Some placed more confidence in the legislature as the people's voice. Others suspected that the legislature would destroy liberties protected by law. (The skeptics drew sustenance from Shay's 1786 Rebellion in Western Massachusetts, an uprising of debtors directed largely towards disrupting the government and the legal system, and from the success of this movement at the state ballot box.). Others, such as Jefferson, relied heavily on the jury as the popular voice of the law. And Wilson linked the law to popular consent by conceiving of judicial opinions as jury-like expressions of custom embodied in the common law. Indeed, even the Bill of Rights (which we consider the quintessential assertion of legal rights from popular dominance) was meant to assure majoritarian participation in preserving justice, most notably illustrated by the important role it provided for juries.[152] As we

---

150. Nelson, p. 1177. See also White, The Marshall Court and Constitutional Change 1815–35, pp. 195–200 (1988)(drawing a distinction between partisan politics and the consensual political theory).

151. Federalist, # 51, p. 264–65.

152. Amar, The Bill of Rights as a Constitution, 100 Yale L. J. 1131, 1133 (1991).

discussed earlier in this Chapter, the influence of "common sense" philosophy provided the glue that held the law and people together.

This idealized image of a conjunction between the law and the people disintegrated in the middle and later decades of the 19th Century, no doubt because more and more of "the people" were entitled to vote. The "people" became less and less an abstraction and more and more a numerical reality. We can symbolically date the beginning of this view to the inauguration of President Jackson in 1829, where masses of people were invited to attend the White House reception, resulting in danger to life and limb and destruction of property; Justice Story was prompted to observe that "the reign of king 'Mob' seemed triumphant."[153] With the extension of the franchise and real democracy, the dissolution of politics into factions and the threat *to* law *from* the people seemed assured, at least from certain political perspectives.

Consequently, law once again came to be viewed as the embodiment of timeless and immutable principles, capable of protecting the individual's legal rights from popular encroachment. This was encouraged by the revitalization of the notion that judges and lawyers were experts, with access to technical knowledge ("artificial reason") that enabled them to determine the law. In the first half of the 19th Century, Kent and Story wrote law treatises which made claims of legal expertise plausible in a country where there had previously been a dearth of law reports and organized legal doctrine.[154] Over time, this view was eventually reinforced by the creation and influence of professional bar associations in the last third of the 19th Century,[155] which further nurtured the view that there was an expert body of knowledge to which lawyers and judges had access.

In an age of increasing pressure for legislative change, however, attempts to revive the older common law lawyers' image of discoverable common law principles and of the expertise that lawyers had in working out those principles was bound to produce serious political conflict. Constitutional law courses recount how common law property and contract rights were read into the Due Process clause of the United States Constitution to strike down state and federal statutes. We will soon see that statutory interpretation was infused with a similar animus—through the doctrine that statutes in derogation of the common law should be narrowly construed.

Evolution of New York Constitution. The evolution of New York's constitutional provisions dealing with the selection of judges supports these observations about the separation of democracy from law.[156] What began in 1846 as

---

153. Ellis, The Union at Risk, p. 15 (1987).

154. Kent's Commentaries on American Law were published in 1826. Story's treatises appeared between 1832 and 1845; Newmyer, Supreme Court Justice Joseph Story, p. 281 (1985).

155. The first modern organized bar association was the New York City Bar Association, formed in 1870. The New York State

Bar Association was organized in 1876; the American Bar Association in 1878. Pound, The Lawyer From Antiquity to Modern Times, pp. 253–78 (1953).

156. This material on New York developments is based on Bergan, The History of the New York Court of Appeals, 1847–1932, pp. 96, 100, 102, 107, 124, 129–30, 245–47 (1985). See also Bishop and Attree, Report of the Debates and Proceedings of the Convena serious effort to force popular accountability of judges gradually changed into a system where judges were removed from politics, as much as the system allowed and the organized bar could achieve.

The 1846 Constitution embodied democratic principles, providing that the Justices of the Court of Appeals (the highest court in the state) and the Supreme Court (the highest court of original jurisdiction) would be elected for eight year terms.[157] Four of the eight member Court of Appeals were elected to eight year terms, except that the first four judges would take office for two, four, six and eight years respectively so that eventually one judge would be elected every two years. The other four Court of Appeals judges would be chosen from Supreme Court judges with the shortest time to serve. This made it almost impossible for the Court of Appeals to develop a sense of collegial cohesion independent of popular control.

In 1867–68 there was a new Constitutional Convention which resulted in amending the constitution so that the Court of Appeals consisted of seven members elected for concurrently-running 14 year terms. (The public was asked to vote in 1873 on whether judges should still be elected and they continued this practice.) The 1867–68 change "was a sharp turning away from the 1846 Convention's policy, based on a conviction that the court and public would benefit by short, staggered terms for judges calling for frequent public review of individual judicial performance." The court could now develop as a coherent body, with independent legal expertise. Moreover, although the election process was technically partisan, the political parties made efforts to take the elections out of politics, relying in large part on the organized bar. Bergan states: "[I]n the vast majority of cases, the nomination of the incumbents of the office of judge * * * has been nomination by the profession." Although intense debates over appointment vs. election persisted in the 1867–68 convention, the ideological fervor did not match the reality. The growing influence of the New York City and State Bar Associations, which helped select the party's candidates, contributed to removing selection of judges from substantive partisan politics (although party loyalty still played an important role in nominations).

This did not mean that political issues were always unimportant in electing judges. When the New York Court of Appeals in 1911 held that the Workers Compensation law was unconstitutional because it provided for no-fault liability, rather than negligence, the Chief Justice's support of this decision contributed to his defeat for reelection. The response of the political parties and the bar, however, was to circle the wagons and take the election of the Chief Justice out of politics (the senior associate justice would be backed by both parties for promotion to chief judge).

It is, of course, possible that New York's experience was atypical. But there is no firm evidence that electoral accountability has affected judicial behavior in the state generally. There is some anecdotal evidence that "hot button" decisions in criminal law and sentencing have been influenced by the

tion for the Revision of the Constitution of the State of New York (1846).

157. N.Y. Const, 1846, Art. VI, secs. 2,4,12.

electoral process. And there may also be some effect when the decision is close to the end of an election cycle and the judge is running for reelection. My own guess is that electoral accountability has influenced at least some state judges to adopt interpretive rhetoric stressing that statutory interpretation is a passive activity (deferring to text and/or legislative intent), but that the link between the rhetoric and reality is tenuous.[158]

iii) MID–TO–LATE 19TH CENTURY—NARROW INTERPRETATION OF STATUTES IN DEROGATION OF COMMON LAW

In the area of statutory interpretation, the split between democracy and law is illustrated by the application of the doctrine that statutes in derogation of the common law should be narrowly construed. State courts invoked this canon in the middle to late 19th Century to preserve prior common law in the face of legislative change. Here are a few examples dealing with interpretation of the Married Women's Property Acts.[159] The cases are from New York and Pennsylvania, both of which elected judges when the cases were decided.[160]

Married Women's Property Acts. Statutes protecting the separate property rights of married women were passed in significant numbers beginning in the 1840s and continuing after the Civil War. At the very least, they protected a wife's property from her husband's creditors. Some of them provided (more broadly) that a wife had a certain amount of control over her own property, although these provisions sometimes had to be made very explicit to overcome hostile judicial interpretation.

In Vallance v. Bausch,[161] the issue was whether the statute eliminated a husband's common law property right called tenancy by the curtesy, which gave the husband a life interest in certain property obtained by a wife during marriage after the wife died, if they had a child during the marriage.[162] The statutory text provided that the wife's property[163]

> "shall not be subject to the disposal of her (future) husband, nor be liable for his debts, and shall continue her sole and separate property, as if she were a single female;" and "that any married female may take by inheritance, or by gift, grant, devise or bequest, * * * and hold to her sole and separate use, and convey and devise * * *, in the same manner, and with like effect, as if she was unmarried, and the same shall not be subject to the disposal of her husband, nor liable for his debts."

158. See generally Eule, Judicial Review of Direct Democracy, 99 Yale L.J. 1503, 1580–83 (1990).

159. See generally Richard Chused, Married Women's Property Law: 1800–1850, 71 Geo. L. J. 1359 (1983); Chused, Late Nineteenth Century Married Women's Property Law: Reception of the Early Married Women's Property Acts by Courts and Legislatures, 29 Amer. J. Leg. Hist. 3 (1985).

160. Haynes, pp. 123, 127.

161. 28 Barb. 633 (N.Y.1859).

162. See generally Haskins, Curtesy in the United States, 100 U.Pa.L.Rev. 196 (1951).

163. The quote is from Billings v. Baker, 28 Barb. 343, 347–48 (N.Y.1859).

The judge held that the statute gave the wife a lifetime power to dispose of and use property during the marriage and to protect her property from her husband's disposition and his creditors, but did not allow her to eliminate the husband's tenancy by the curtesy by will, if she had not conveyed the property during her lifetime. The judge characterized as "simply absurd" the statute's statement that a married woman shall own property as if she were single—"What principle of public policy or political economy would have induced the legislature to take away" the husband's curtesy rights?[164] (Notice the reference to "absurdity" and, by implication, to the Golden Rule.)

In Walker v. Reamy,[165] the statute stated that property acquired by a married woman "shall be owned, used, and enjoyed by her as her own separate property, and the said property shall not be subject to levy and execution for the debts of her husband * * *." The court rewrote the text so that the "and" at the beginning of the second clause said "and therefore" or "so that," limiting the statutory protection to seizure for the husband's debts. The husband's curtesy interest therefore survived and, in addition, the wife was not free to invest funds without her husband's consent. Otherwise, the statute "is hardly consistent with the plain common sense of the law." The court "presume[s] that no innovation on the old law was intended further than was absolutely required." The rest of the opinion praises the traditional husband-centered family—"It is impossible that a woman can use and enjoy her property as fully and separately after marriage as before;" "[t]he husband is still the head of the family."

Not all judges were hostile to Married Women's Property Acts. Some characterized the Acts as remedial, with no particular preference for survival of the prior common law. One example is Judge Potter in New York, who later authored the American edition of Dwarris' English treatise on statutory interpretation. Billings v. Baker[166] raised the same question as Vallance v. Bausch—whether the New York statute eliminated the husband's tenancy by the curtesy. Judge Potter called the statute "remedial" and refused to narrow what he thought was the plain import of the text: "The language of this act is entirely inconsistent with the idea that there is a tenancy for life existing in another person." "[T]he courts should adhere strictly to the sensibly expressed intention of the legislature, [rather] than [ ] permit old maxims [ ] to control the construction of our own abrogating statutes." Judge Potter directly linked his interpretive approach to a rejection of Kent's idealized view of the common law: "Is the glory of the ancient common law so dazzling, that the learning of the present day, and all the attempted reforms upon the system to meet the wants of the age, are to be regarded as dangerous experiments?"

---

164. 28 Barb. at 642–43. A New Jersey decision, Johnson v. Cummins, 16 N.J.Eq. 97, 107 (1863), agreed with Vallence, citing a large number of supporting New York cases. The New Jersey judges were appointed by the Governor with consent of the Senate.

165. 36 Pa. 410, 414–16 (1860).

166. 28 Barb. 343, 346, 350–51, 361 (N.Y.1859).

From a late 20th Century perspective, we are likely to view the narrow interpretation of Married Women's Property Acts as reflecting judicial hostility to statutes. But it is worth asking whether that results from our own perception of appropriate legal relationships between husbands and wives, rather than an objective view of what statutory interpretation should have been at the time. Was it "hostile" to ask the legislature if it really meant to get rid of a traditional property right designed to protect the economic welfare of the children of the marriage after the wife's death. After all, it *is* true that the major purpose of the early Married Women's Property Acts was to protect their property from the husband's creditors. Even if we give credence to another purpose, which was to allow women to engage in their own commercial activity with their own property,[167] would that purpose be defeated by reducing the woman's right to dispose of her property by will, after her death?   Perhaps the rhetoric of these judicial opinions is much more hostile to legislative reform than the decisions.

Nonhostile applications of derogation canon. From this discussion, you might assume that every invocation of the "derogation" doctrine reflected hostility to statutes. That is not true. There are many ways to limit the reach of statutes in derogation of common law, some of which are not at all antagonistic to legislation. Sometimes narrow interpretation of statutes meant simply a refusal to extend a statute to *negate* the concurrent operation of both statutory and common law remedies. In such cases, the common law survived to provide a parallel remedy. The narrow interpretation of statutes in derogation of common law meant only that statutes *supplemented* the common law; and the interpreter should not extend the statutory remedy by negative implication to reject common law remedies. This application of the derogation canon is not likely to be hostile to statutes, unless there is strong evidence that the statute meant to completely replace the common law remedial scheme.

A 1797 Supreme Court case, sometimes cited as an early example of federal adoption of a hostile "derogation" canon, is actually another example of using prior common law to reach a sensible interpretation of a later statute, rather than to denigrate statutes to favor the common law.[168] The case interpreted new legislation which provided that repeal of a statute which had itself repealed an earlier statute did *not* revive the original statute. This new legislation overrode a common law rule that the earliest statute revived when a repealing statute was repealed. For example, under the common law rejected by the new legislation, if statute 3 repealed statute 2 which had repealed statute 1, statute 1 revived. The new legislation changed

---

167. Not all courts took a generous view of a married woman's business acumen, however. In Frarey v. Wheeler, 4 Or. 190, 195 (1871), the court rejected an interpretation of a state statute which would have overridden a married woman's common law disability to enter into covenants to convey real estate, stating: "[I]t is the generally received opinion that the sphere of married women's duties [ ] precludes the means of acquiring by them that knowledge of law and commercial transactions necessary to enable them [ ] to safely and understandingly enter into covenants concerning their real estate."

168. Brown v. Barry, 3 U.S. (3 Dall.) 365 (1797).

this common law rule—statute 3's repeal of statute 2 would not revive statute 1. In the Supreme Court case, a 1792 statute *suspended* another 1792 statute which had repealed a 1748 law, but the suspension only lasted until October 1793. The Court held that the 1748 law revived until October 1793, narrowly construing the new legislation about repeals not reviving the earliest statute, so that it did not apply to *suspending*, as opposed to *repealing* a prior law. Although the Court noted that the new legislation was in derogation of common law, it is hard to view this case as a precursor of "hostile" application of the derogation doctrine. The fact that the suspension-until-October–1793 statute and the prior (but suspended) repealing law were both passed in the same 1792 legislative session strongly suggested a legislative intent that the 1748 statute survived until October 1793.

e) THE 19TH CENTURY COMMENTATORS

The increasing importance of statutes in the 19th Century was paralleled by an increase in published commentaries about statutory interpretation. Initially, statutory interpretation did not attract nearly as much attention as the Constitution in the late 18th and early 19th Century. Tucker's notes to his 1803 edition of Blackstone's Commentaries contained a few comments on constitutional interpretation (favoring strict construction to preserve the spirit of the constitution), but nothing about statutory interpretation.[169] Commentaries on law written in 1826 by Kent (formerly the New York Chancellor) devote one lecture to statutes and their interpretation.[170] Story (a Supreme Court Justice) wrote a major work about the constitution— Commentaries on the Constitution—and contributed a piece on statutes and statutory interpretation to the Encyclopaedia Americana in 1831.[171] Lieber (a professor) wrote a book on hermeneutics in 1839 discussing statutory interpretation as part of an essay on the interpretation of written documents generally.[172]

As the century progresses, the literature on statutory interpretation increases. A New York lawyer, E. Fitch Smith, wrote commentaries on both statutes and constitutional law in 1848, placing statutory construction first. He observed that there was no American work on the construction of statutes and rejected advice that the issue was unworthy of a moment's consideration because it was so familiar.[173] And Sedgwick, also a New York lawyer, wrote a treatise in 1857 that gives far more consideration to statutes than the

---

169. Tucker, pp. 354–55, 364.

170. James Kent, Commentaries on American Law, Vol. I, Lecture XX (1826).

171. Joseph Story, Law, Legislation and Codes, in Encyclopaedia Americana, App. VII, p. 576–92 (F. Lieber ed. 1831)(hereafter "Story, Encyclopaedia"). Citation is to the 1836 New Edition of Encyclopaedia Americana.

172. Francis Lieber, Legal and Political Hermeneutics (2d ed., Boston, Charles C. Little & James Brown 1839)(hereafter "Lieber"). The 1839 book was an expanded version of an 1837 essay entitled "Political Hermeneutics." See Editor's Note, A Symposium on Legal and Political Hermeneutics, 16 Cardozo L. Rev. 1879, 1879 (1995).

173. E. Fitch Smith, Commentaries on Statute and Constitutional Law and Statutory and Constitutional Construction, pp. x-xi (1848)(hereafter "Smith").

constitution.[174]

Separate treatises on statutes appeared after the Civil War, two of which were English treatises with notes and comments by U.S. authors: Potter, a New York Judge, published an American 1871 edition of Dwarris' English treatise on statutes, with comments appropriate to the United States system;[175] Pomeroy (a law professor) published an 1874 edition of Sedgwick's 1857 Treatise, with numerous updated notes about statutory interpretation; and Endlich, a Pennsylvania judge, published an 1888 American Edition of Maxwell's English treatise on interpretation.[176]

U.S. authored treatises on statutory interpretation also appeared: Bishop, wrote his commentaries on statutory interpretation in 1882.[177] In 1891, Sutherland's Statutes and Statutory Construction appeared.[178] And, in 1896, West Publishing Company brought out Black's Construction and Interpretation of the Laws.[179] In addition, Cooley's 1872 Commentaries on Blackstone, unlike Turner's 1803 edition, discussed statutory interpretation.[180]

These treatises, especially after the Civil War, seemed to fill a widespread need among the practicing bar for material on statutory interpretation. Consistent with the spirit of the late 19th Century, Bishop argued that interpretation law could be reduced to organized rules and that "statutory interpretation [was] governed as absolutely by rules as anything else in the law."[181] Sutherland's 1891 treatise states that, unlike contracts and other private documents, "law for the construction of Written Laws" is not "well defined;" and "When it is considered how many legislative bodies there are," it is important that "principles [be] generalized, with a view to maintaining the domain of the law as a science."[182] Black stated that his work followed "the general plan of the Hornbook Series * * * after the manner of a code, expressed in brief black-letter paragraphs."[183]

More significantly, no one had to apologize (as Smith had done) for writing about statutory interpretation. Bishop states that "in practical importance, there is no legal subject which approaches this."[184] Still, even at this date Sutherland admitted that "statutes are but a small part of our jurisprudence."[185]

---

174. Theodore Sedgwick, A Treatise on the Rules Which Govern the Interpretation and Application of Statutory and Constitutional Law (1857) (all cites are to the Pomeroy edition, 1874)(hereafter "Sedgwick").

175. Platt Potter, A General Treatise on Statutes by Dwarris (1871)(all citations are to the 1885 edition)(hereafter "Potter").

176. G.A. Endlich, A Commentary on the Interpretation of Statutes Founded on Maxwell's Treatise (1888)(hereafter "Endlich").

177. Joel Bishop, Commentaries on the Written Law and Their Interpretation (1882)(hereafter "Bishop").

178. J.G. Sutherland, Statutes and Statutory Construction (1891) (hereafter "Sutherland, 1st").

179. Henry Black, Construction and Interpretation of the Laws (1896) (hereafter "Black").

180. Thomas Cooley, Commentaries on Blackstone's Laws of England, pp. 85–91 (1873)(hereafter "Cooley").

181. Bishop, p. 3, sec. 2.

182. Sutherland, 1st, pp. iii-iv.

183. Black, p. iii.

184. Bishop, p. 3, sec. 2.

185. Sutherland, 1st, p. 373, sec. 289.

The general theme among the commentators progresses from the traditional equitable interpretation approach (see Kent) to strong questioning of this practice. Most commentators after Kent urged paying greater respect to the legislature, relying less on courts and more on legislatures to correct textual shortcomings. As always, the shifting vision of the judicial role rested on changing views about legislative and judicial lawmaking competence and legitimacy. It is my perception, however, that commentators were often critical rather than descriptive of judicial practice. The pendulum may have been swinging away from traditional judge-dominated interpretation but not as fast as the commentators urged.

Kent.[186] The earliest of the commentators is Kent, whose Commentaries on American Law, Vol. I (1826), discusses statutory interpretation in Lecture XX (Of Statute Law). He affirms that the "true meaning of the statute is generally and properly to be sought from the body of the act itself" (the reference to "body" shows how far from Plowden we have come). Nonetheless, Kent did not express the kind of confidence in legislation that leads some later commentators to question too much judicial discretion in statutory interpretation. He refers not only to the "imperfection of language," but also to the "want of technical skill in the makers of the law." He cites Plowden, as well as Heydon's Case, for the view that the common law is the "perfection of reason." No wonder he believed that "[s]tatutes are to be construed in reference to the principles of the common law, for it is not to be presumed the legislature intended to make any innovation upon the common law, further than the case absolutely required." And, in a letter to Livingston, the codifier of Louisiana law, he states: "I think [ ] Lord Mansfield, or Burke [ ] possessed ten times as much practical good sense and sound wisdom as [ ] Jeremy Bentham."[187]

Story.[188] Story's 1831 essay on statutory interpretation lacks originality—it is mainly a rehashing of Blackstone. But it is worth noting that his view of legislation is more positive and his view of the common law less favorable than Kent's. The problem with statutes is not anything inherent about language or lack of technical skill, but the (Aristotelian) problem of lack of foresight regarding the particulars to which a statute might apply. Speaking of statutes, he asks rhetorically: "But is it possible to foresee, or to provide beforehand, for all [ ] cases?"

As for the common law, he is not quite as reverential as Kent. Not that he did not place immense faith in the common law. He clearly viewed it as the dominant source of law ("a man may live a century and feel [ ] but in few instances the operation of statutes [ ]; but the common law [is] like the

---

186. James Kent, Commentaries on American Law, Vol. I., pp. 431–34 (Da Capo Press 1971)(1826)(hereafter "Kent").

187. Letter from Chancellor Kent, to Edward Livingston.—Penal Code, 16 American Jurist 361, 370 (1837).

188. The material in these paragraphs about Story is from Story, Encyclopaedia, pp. 585–88, 591.

atmosphere in which he breathes"); and legislation, though coextensive with sovereignty, "is in fact employed, if not universally, at least generally in mere acts of amendment and supplement to existing laws and institutions. Its office is ordinarily not so much to create systems of laws, as to supply defects, and cure mischiefs in the systems already existing." But Story also admitted that the common law could become atrophied, "quite as unyielding as any code can be," which could require legislative change.

Lieber.[189] Lieber's 1839 book on Legal and Political Hermeneutics deals with the entire range of legal and political texts and does not focus explicitly on statutes. He is a complex thinker who embodies the ambivalence towards statutory interpretation that we observed earlier in debates over constitutional interpretation and among state court judges.[190] He is best known for his distinction between interpretation and construction, and for the related view that interpretation must precede construction. In making this distinction, he appears to commit to the text, suspicious of judicial "construction" that takes judges beyond the interpretation of textual meaning ("construction is dangerous if it goes beyond the sense of the text").

But Lieber's attitude towards "construction" is ambivalent. He defines it in familiar "equity of the statute" language, though with a textualist tinge— as "the drawing of conclusions respecting subjects, that lie beyond the direct expression of the text, from elements known from and given in the text— conclusions which are in the spirit, though not within the letter of the text." Although construction is "dangerous," it is "unavoidable." And he acknowledges the difficulty of confining the occasions for statutory construction. Although he states that "nothing is so favorable to that great essential of all civil liberty—the protection of individual rights, as close interpretation and construction," he elsewhere advocates a liberal construction to prevent flogging a Christian Native Indian in the British Army. "[T]here are considerations, which ought to induce us to abandon interpretation, or with other words to sacrifice the direct meaning of a text to considerations still weightier; especially not to slaughter justice, the sovereign object of laws, to the law itself, the means of obtaining it." There is a sense that construction responds to selected substantive concerns, incapable of precise description in advance, but which necessarily play a role in determining statutory meaning. Perhaps we should understand Lieber's reference to justice as echoing Marshall's concern that statutory interpretation be sensitive to fundamental values.

E.   *Fitch Smith.*[191] Smith's views (1848) are less complex than Lieber's. He is resolutely opposed to equitable interpretation (Chapter X—Of Legislative and Judicial Interpretation). He asks: "Are the courts to proceed upon established principles—to be governed by fixed rules; or, exercising a liberal discretion, to have recourse, in doubtful cases to natural principles,—to aid

---

189. The material in these paragraphs about Lieber is from Lieber, pp. 56, 64, 113, 115–17, 121, 127, 134, 136, 139–40.

190. See generally A Symposium on Legal and Political Hermeneutics, 16 Cardozo L. Rev. 1879–2351 (1995).

191. The material in these paragraphs is from Smith, pp. 580, 584, 588, 591, 827–35.

and to moderate the law according to equitable considerations,—to include in their deliberations those cases and circumstances, which the legislator himself would have expressed, had he foreseen them?" His answer is that it is "the duty of the judge in a land jealous of its liberties, to give effect to the expressed sense, of words, of the law." If this means omission of something within the mischief but not within the meaning, so be it (it is just a casus omissus). "The duty of the judge is to adhere to the legal text, as his sole guide."

It is clear from Smith's text, however, that he is criticizing not describing judicial practice. He acknowledges that "able judges" have had to "correct[ ] abuses and introduc[e] improvements" and blames this judicial practice on the "supineness" of the legislature, and on "the want of a proper understanding at what point interpretation ought to end, and legislation should begin." In his comments on City of New York v. Lord, he agrees with the dissenters in the 1837 case, who would have denied compensation for goods lost by a tenant as a result of destroying a building to prevent the spread of fire. He states:

> Where the legislature have used words of plain and definite import, it would be dangerous to put upon them a construction which would amount to holding that the legislature did not mean what they had clearly expressed.

And he quotes Dwarris' warning that "judges are not to be encouraged to direct their conduct 'by the crooked cord of discretion, but by the golden metwand of the law.' " Otherwise, "equitable construction [will] usurp legislative authority."

Sedgwick.[192] Sedgwick (1857) is the most modern-sounding of the commentators—"Common sense and good faith are the leading stars of all genuine interpretation." He sounds almost pragmatic, without any of the passion for black letter rules that we see in some of the post-Civil War treatises.

> What is required * * * is not formal rules, or nice terminology, or ingenious classification; but that thorough intellectual training, that complete education of mind, which lead it to a correct result, wholly independent of rules, and, indeed, almost unconscious of the process by which the end is attained;

and he argues that

> [o]urs is eminently a practical science. It is only by an intimate acquaintance with its application to the affairs of life, as they actually occur, that we can acquire that sagacity requisite to decide new and doubtful cases.

Or, as he puts it in the motto to his treatise: "Great is the mystery of judicial interpretation."

---

192. The material in these paragraphs about Sedgwick is from Sedgwick, pp. 179, 184, 192–93, 205, 253, 261, 263, 265–75, 314.

Despite this "practical" strain, Sedgwick leaves no doubt that he opposes equitable interpretation. He describes both "liberal and strict construction" as an example of the "judicial function [ ] blended with and lost in the legislative attributes." Consequently, "if [the] intention is expressed in a manner devoid of contradiction and ambiguity, there is no room for interpretation or construction, and the judiciary are not at liberty, on consideration of policy or hardship, to depart from the words of the statute * * *." He cites favorably both Justice Chase in the Priestman case and the dissent in the 1837 decision in City of New York v. Lord.

Sedgwick's opposition to equitable interpretation is based on a view of legislative competence, just as Blackstone and others had been concerned with legislative *in*competence. Equitable interpretation is obsolete because "the legislator has now time to frame his statute in simple and intelligible language." He sounds especially modern in worrying about the practical impact of equitable interpretation in encouraging "unbounded [legislative] carelessness."

Equally as important as legislative competence was judicial incompetence. In Sedgwick's view, the judge's ability to know what the legislature wanted is much reduced, compared to an earlier time.

> It may very well be that, in the condition of English jurisprudence in former times, when laws were few and rarely passed, when the business of legislation was confined to a small and select class, to which practically all the judiciary belonged, when the legislative and judicial bodies sat in the same place, and, indeed, in the same building,—in such a state of things, it may well be that they might indeed really possess, a considerable personal knowledge of the legislative intent, and that they might come almost to consider themselves as a co-ordinate body with the Legislature.

But times had changed. Striking a note that will sound familiar to modern students of legislation, Sedgwick argues that "where the business of legislation has become multifarious and enormous, and especially in this country where the judiciary is so completely separated from the Legislature, it must be untrue in fact that they can have any personal knowledge sufficient really to instruct them as to the legislative intention; and if untrue in fact, any general theory or loose idea of this kind must be dangerous in practice."

Sedgwick took special aim at the narrow interpretation of statutes in derogation of common law. He traces this approach to Coke's now-obsolete view that the common law was perfect ("It is difficult, if not impossible, now to understand this enthusiastic loyalty to a body of law, the most peculiar features of which the activity of the present generation has been largely occupied in uprooting and destroying.") Sedgwick also claims that his views reflect judicial practice. He says that equitable discretion has been discredited in courts:

> [T]he judges themselves set limits to the powers they had arrogated; and abandoning all pretensions of a right to exercise any control over legislation, to correct its errors or supply its deficien-

cies, they confined their power of construction to admitted cases of doubt. Such is now the settled doctrine both in England and in this country.

But the wish was probably father to the thought. Sedgwick admits that "[t]he notion of a restricted or an enlarged construction has been introduced and practiced upon rather with reference to the kind or class of laws to which the statute in question belonged than to the clearness or ambiguity of the letter of the enactment." And a book review of Sedgwick's work further suggests that his opposition to equitable interpretation was neither unanimous nor uniformly reflected in judicial practice.[193]

Commentary about statutory interpretation increased after the Civil War but without any evident increase in sophistication or change in theme. There was very little in the way of sustained innovative thinking.

Opposition to equitable interpretation rested on the idea that it was obsolete, as Sedgwick had argued. Bishop argued that extension of statutes was more appropriate for briefer older statutes than modern "plethoric" legislation.[194] Sutherland locates equitable interpretation in a time when acts of parliament were brief and general and the line between legislating and judging was unclear; it is now obsolete, a relic of ancient hermeneutics.[195] Potter's Dwarris makes a more political statement: "The judiciary, are removed too far from the people to share much in their prepossessions."[196] Black links the obsolescence of equitable interpretation to decline in the sanctity of the common law.[197]

Endlich's Maxwell[198] argues that the "court [can] exercise the power of controlling the language in order to give effect to what they suppose to have been the real intention of the law makers," only when the text is ambiguous or doubtful. The judge cannot mold meaning to "meet an alleged convenience or an alleged equity." It is "inaccurate to speak of the meaning or intent of a statute as something separate or distinct from the meaning of its language;" and that to do so would be an "assumption of legislative powers by the court." (Still, Endlich was not a naive textualist—"it is not always safe" to assume that the draftsman "understood the rules of grammar.")

Most commentators were also opposed to any special rule narrowly interpreting statutes in derogation of the common law. Cooley's 1872 Commentaries on Blackstone was an exception—speaking favorably of this canon

193. On Construing Statutes by Equity, 3 Quart. L. J. 150, 152–53 (1858) (favoring equitable construction).

194. Bishop, pp. 180–81, sec. 190.

195. Sutherland, 1st, pp. 524–31, secs. 413–14.

196. Potter, p. 89.

197. Black, p. iii.

198. The material in this paragraph on Endlich appears in Endlich, pp. 6–7, 11–12. 48–52, 111.

and arguing (reminiscent of Kent) that preservation of the common law was important.[199]

> But where the new statute does not in terms repeal the old law, the two will stand together so far as effect can be given to both. * * * A statute which makes an innovation on the established principles of the common law must be strictly construed.

But most other commentators were critical of the preference for the common law, while generally acknowledging its prevalence.

Pomeroy's 1874 edition of Sedgwick contained a long note criticizing the narrow interpretation of statutes in derogation of the common law, but leaving little doubt that this was a common practice in many jurisdictions.[200] Endlich's Maxwell states that it is easier to alter statute than common law, though his own view is critical of a narrowing interpretation to preserve common law; he argues that prior law of any kind, whether statute or common law, should not be impliedly repealed, but the common law has no special place.[201] Bishop[202] and Black[203] also argue that the relationship of both prior common and statute law to a later statute is the same; there is a general rule against implied repeals in both situations but there is nothing special about prior common law.

Potter's Dwarris also seems to be an exception to criticism of the derogation canon. He affirmed that "our courts, federal and state" hold that there should be no "innovation upon the common law, further than the case absolutely required,"[204] citing Kent's eulogy of the common law as the perfection of reason. But we know from Judge Potter's opinion in Billings v. Baker,[205] identifying the Married Women's Property Acts as remedial, that he objected to the Kentian approach. Recall that, in Billings, Potter stated: "Is the glory of the ancient common law so dazzling, that the learning of the present day, and all the attempted reforms upon the system to meet the wants of the age, are to be regarded as dangerous experiments?" Perhaps Potter's treatise was meant to be descriptive rather than critical of judicial practice.[206]

There are a few hints that the narrow interpretation of statutes in derogation of common law might make some sense if they protected important rights. Sutherland states that "statutes in derogation of [common law], and especially of common right, are strictly construed, and will not be extended by construction beyond their natural import."[207] And Endlich suggests a somewhat greater concern to preserve the prior common law from statutory innovation when the prior common law protects personal and

---

199. Cooley, Vol. I, p. 89 n. 21.
200. Sedgwick, pp. 267–69, note(a).
201. Endlich, pp. 172–75.
202. Bishop, pp. 113, 140–41, 178, secs. 119, 155, 189a.
203. Black, pp. 243–45.
204. Potter, p. 185.
205. 28 Barb. 343, 361 (N.Y.1859).

206. Sutherland, also apparently in a descriptive mode, that "in all doubtful matters, and when the statute is in general terms, it is subject to the principles of the common law * * *." Sutherland, 1st, pp. 374–75, sec. 291.

207. Sutherland, 1st, p. 374, sec. 290.

property rights, with the qualification that this is true only "so far as that rule has any legitimate force or application."[208]

Nonetheless, the general tone of late 19th Century commentary opposed the judicial hostility toward legislation which was embodied in the "derogation" canon.

2.05   INTERPRETATION AS COMMON LAW POWER

It is obvious that United States judges have been unsure what approach to statutory interpretation they should adopt. But one thing is certain. There was never any doubt that statutory interpretation was a common law power. That is what Hamilton meant in Federalist, # 83 when he said that "[t]he rules of legal interpretation are rules of *common sense*, adopted by the courts in the construction of the laws (emphasis in original);"[209] and, in Federalist, # 78, that the rule favoring the statute which is past last in time is "not derived from any positive law, but from the nature and reason of the thing. It is a rule not enjoined upon the courts by legislative provision, but adopted by themselves, as consonant to truth and propriety, for the direction of their conduct as interpreters of the law."[210] And Alexander Hamilton's notes for argument in the New York case of Rutgers v. Washington explicitly allude to the fact that "Statutes are to be construed by the rules of the common law."[211] Similarly, Justice Washington in 1805 stated, echoing Hamilton, that the "rules [of interpretation] * * * are as clearly founded in plain sense, as they are certainly warranted by the principles of common law."[212]

19th Century commentaries also agreed that interpretation was a common law power. Justice Story affirmed that "the rules of interpretation belong[ ] to and [are] fixed in the common law [and] we shall enumerate a few, some of which, indeed, may be truly said to belong to the universal elements of rational jurisprudence."[213] Sedgwick's treatise stated:[214] "The rules of construction and interpretation of acts of Congress, and of statutes of State Legislatures, except where, in regard to the latter, the State Constitutions otherwise determine, are to be derived from the common law." Bishop affirmed that "statutory interpretation is governed as absolutely by rules as anything else in the law. And the rules are of common-law origin."[215] And Sutherland agreed: "Rules of interpretation and construction are derived from the common law."[216]

---

208. Endlich, pp. 473–74.

209. The Federalist, # 83, p. 424.

210. Federalist, # 78, p. 399.

211. Hamilton, Law Practice, p. 357.

212. United States v. Fisher, 6 U.S. (2 Cranch) 358, 400 (1805).

213. Story, Encyclopaedia, p. 583.

214. Sedgwick, at p. 223 note(a).

215. Bishop, at p. 3, sec. 2.

216. Sutherland, 1st, p. 373, sec. 289. 20th Century federal and state judges also describe interpretation as a common law power. Lang v. United States, 133 Fed. 201, 205 (7th Cir.1904)(common-law canon of construction); Howell v. Deady, 48 F.Supp. 104, 108 (D.Or.1939)(canons of construction applied at common law); Western Metal Supply Co. v.

There are two inferences to be drawn from interpretation being a common law power. *First*, there is no need for the courts to be given an interpretive power explicitly in the constitution. It is inherent in the grant of judicial power to the courts. *Second*, as a common law power, interpretation is as susceptible to evolution as any other rule of common law. The fact that the nature of federal legislation has changed and that theories of legislative-judicial relations have altered should influence contemporary theories of statutory interpretation. Even a textualist approach to statutory interpretation, whether or not that was the original conception of the judicial role in statutory interpretation, might be acceptable under an evolutionary view of the common law interpretive power.

2.06   CODIFICATION

We have alluded several times in this Chapter to codification. Pressure to codify statute law predated the 19th Century and has always been a battleground in the ongoing dispute about the role of courts and legislatures. Indeed, it received far more attention in 19th Century legal periodicals than statutory interpretation.[217] It therefore deserves special attention. You should notice, however, that the debates about codification reflect the same attitudes towards legislative and judicial competence and legitimacy that play such an important role in determining how judges should interpret statutes.

Definition; political implications. The political implications of codification differ greatly depending on which of several meanings you consider. First, existing statutes can simply be compiled into a code, arranged by subject matter for easy access and comprehension. Second, existing statutes can be compiled and revised, with varying effects on changing the law. More modest revisions weed out obsolete and redundant statutes and correct errors. More ambitious codification changes the law (even the common law) to meet contemporary needs and lays the groundwork for future evolution. Third, the common law, as well as statute law, can be codified, again either to compile or change the law.

Codification of all law into statutory form tends to be favored when there is a vacuum in the law or there is a political revolution. An example of a vacuum is the early codification of Massachusetts law in 1648,[218] when there was a dearth of lawyers and law books. This reliance on statutory

---

Pillsbury, 156 P. 491, 499 (Cal.1916)(Henshaw, J., dissenting)(principles of construction embraced and declared in the common law, repeated in our code rules of construction [ ], and reinforced by the added provision of the code to the effect that the common law of England is the rule of decision in all courts of this state); Missouri v. Griffin, 848 S.W.2d 464, 471 (Mo.1993)(the common law canons of construction).

217. See generally Charles Cook, The American Codification Movement: A Study of Antebellum Legal Reform (1981); Gordon, Book Review of Cook, supra, 36 Vand. L. Rev. 431 (1983).

218. The Book of the General Lawes and Libertyes Concerning the Inhabitants of the Massachusetts (Huntington Library 1975)(Thomas Barnes, ed.)

codification did not survive the eventual importation of both lawyers and lawbooks into the Colonies.

The most successful example of political revolution giving rise to statutory codification is the French Napoleonic Code, which swept away prior customary law after the French Revolution.[219] Short of revolution, codification of all law tends to be favored by those who want to replace the old legal order, frequently salted with a heavy dose of antagonism to lawyers and a belief that the law can be simplified by adoption of plain statutory language. More modest efforts at compiling and revising the statute books, stopping short of codification of all law, is often favored by the more conservative bar, both to head off more radical change and to provide them with easier access to legal materials.

Pre–Civil War. Codification has been an important issue in United States law since the time of Independence. Some of the arguments for codification were very political, such as objections to relying on British law (which meant primarily common law), antagonism towards an elite legal profession, and the democratic impulse to develop indigenous law. These arguments favored comprehensive codification of both statute and common law. They often drew on Jeremy Bentham's writings, advocating elimination of archaic common law.

The more conservative argument for codification favored minimizing legal uncertainty and the difficulty of access to law, and eliminating errors and obsolete provisions. These "moderate" advocates of codification were opposed to sweeping away the common law because it was associated with protection of private rights and they feared the political changes that codification might bring. They also made more technical arguments: statutory language would not provide for all new situations; would not be adaptable to change; and would contain errors. They preferred to place their faith in the comprehensive nature of the common law and its adaptability to change without disrupting settled expectations. The codification "moderates" therefore sought codification of only statute law, with modest revisions. Lawyers frequently supported this limited type of codification.

Before the Civil War, many states "revised" their statute law, usually to update and correct the law, but sometimes with substantive effect. For example, the New York revision in the 1820s made substantial changes in the common law property rules.[220] Even Story participated in the revision process, serving on the Massachusetts Commission,[221] yielding to the "present state of popular opinion [making] it necessary to do something on the

---

219. For a discussion of failed attempts at codification during the English Commonwealth period (1649–1660) and how it fit into the broader legal history of 17th Century England, see Shapiro, Codification of the Laws in Seventeenth Century England, 1974 Wisc. L. Rev. 428.

220. Raack, p. 356–57.

221. Joseph Story, Codification of the Common Law in Massachusetts: Report of the Commissioners etc., 17 American Jurist 17, 30 (1837). See also Codification of the Common Law in Massachusetts: Report of a Special Committee of the House of Representatives of the Massachusetts Legislature [ ] as Relates to the Subject of Codifying the Common Law, 15 American Jurist 111 (1836).

subject."[222] But there was no general codification of the common law. The most serious effort at 19th Century codification of the entire common law was associated with David Dudley Field in New York. As one of three members of a commission established by the New York legislature, he succeeded in obtaining passage of a New York Procedure Code in 1848. However, his efforts to win legislative approval of more substantive civil and criminal "Field Codes" in the following decades met with little success.

Post-Civil War. After the Civil War the codification debate continued, with the Field Codes being the focus of debate. The terms of the debate are summarized in the following excerpt.

Patterson, Historical and Evolutionary Theories of Law

51 Colum. L. Rev. 681 (1951).

* * * Some of the arguments to be used or avoided in the debate over [codification] may be derived from a study of those made by David Dudley Field (1805–1894) in support of the adoption in New York of his civil code, and by James Coolidge Carter (1827–1903), a prominent New York lawyer who, as chairman of a bar association committee, led the attack against it. Field was a follower of the great English law reformer, Jeremy Bentham, and his arguments for codification were substantially those of his master. Summarized briefly, they were: 1. Judges should not be lawmakers, as they are under case law. 2. Codification will make the law "cognoscible" to laymen, who cannot understand case law. 3. Codification will make the law systematic and clear, so that prediction will be more reliable. 4. The code will permit flexibility of interpretation and will not be a strait-jacket. 5. Even an imperfect code is better than none; no nation that has once adopted a code has ever gone back to uncodified law. 6. The code can be amended as imperfections develop.

Carter's arguments against the adoption of Field's civil code may be outlined thus: 1. Judges will continue to make law after the code is adopted, because they will be unable to apply the code to novel situations without resorting to the case law that preceded it. Furthermore judges will torture the language of the code to mean what they think it should mean. 2. The code will be no more accessible to laymen than is case law. 3. The code will not make prediction more reliable if its terms are general and vague, thus making possible different judicial constructions. 4. If the code is phrased in very specific terms, it will be arbitrary and unjust for new cases, and the judges will have to distort the language to cover them. 5. There is no short cut to the mastery of the law. The bulk of case law is greatly exaggerated. While public law and procedure have often been codified, there is no successful code of private law.

---

222.   Quoted in Raack, p. 356.

6. A code will impede the growth of law since amendments can come only after the mischief has been done; a code overgrown by amendments will be an incoherent mass. 7. Codifiers assume the superhuman task of anticipating all future conditions.

The arguments match each other roughly * * *. Field might have retorted that to find a small group of wise and far-seeing lawmakers is easier than to find a host of judges capable of reading, understanding and applying the amorphous body of case law. As for Carter's other arguments, No. 1 parallels Gray's position that statutes are not law but only sources of law. Carter exaggerated the possibilities of judicial interpretation just as did Gray and the judges of the eighteen nineties. The present realization that judges inevitably "make law" by adding to the sum total of legal meanings but are limited in what they can add at any one time, makes it possible to argue that codification will reduce the scope of judicial law making even though it can never eliminate it. Carter's assertion that the judges would resort to the case law which preceded the code was confirmed by the New York decisions interpreting Field's code of procedure, which for a half century after its enactment in 1848 was rendered partly ineffective by historical interpretations. And in California and the states which borrowed most of its civil code, based in turn upon the Field Code, English and American precedents are still blithely cited as if a code had never been adopted. But civil procedure in New York today is vastly better, as a result of legislation and judicial interpretation, than that which preceded adoption of the Field Code. The improvements made by codification may not be immediately apparent, yet, given reasonably adequate treatment, over a few decades a code counts enormously. Carter's second argument, that the laymen will not resort to the code for guidance, seems correct, but neither will he resort to case law. His arguments Nos. 3 and 4 state the dilemma of codification: either vague and futile or precise and harsh. Yet careful terminology and system can reduce both risks. As for Carter's argument that no successful code of private law had ever been drafted, Field pointed to codes in Europe and South America. The French, approaching the sesquicentennial of the Code Napoleon, are engaged in thoroughly revising it, but would never dream of going back to their eighteenth century chaos of local custom and Roman law. Field's statement that no nation has abandoned codification is, I believe, still correct.

Carter's work in opposition to the Field Code led to his preparing a series of lectures which, though never delivered, were published posthumously. Rejecting natural law as too vague and idealistic and Austin's positivism as a theory which based law on fiat, he turned to history for the true meaning of law, and found it in custom: "Human nature is not likely to undergo a radical change, and, therefore, that to which we give the name of Law always has been, still is, and will forever continue to be Custom." Justice derives its supremacy among the moral sentiments from the profound convictions of custom. No written law can ever inspire men's loyalty as does customary law. A statute which runs contrary to custom cannot be enforced, and an unenforced law is a "law" in name only. * * *

The arguments for and against codification will continue. The best argument of its opponents is the probability of serious defects in drafting. * * * Aside from a few state codes, American substitutes for the European type of codification have thus far been threefold: 1. The Uniform Laws written and sponsored by the National Conference of Commissioners on Uniform Laws. 2. The Restatement of Law, a valuable systematic summary of fundamental portions of private case law, not enacted but having the unofficial authority of its able and learned redactors. 3. The amendments drafted by the New York Law Revision Commission and similar bodies in a few other states, which are admittedly merely piecemeal improvements on case law.

Codification in the broad sense of replacing common law was not generally successful after the Civil War. Although the Field Civil Code passed the New York legislature in both 1878 and 1887, the Governor vetoed it.[223] Some Western states,[224] including California in 1872, did adopt a civil code based on Field's work,[225] but the motivation in California had nothing to do with resolving conflict over lawmaking authority between the legislature and the judiciary. It was more a reflection of California's effort to strike out confidently on its own in contrast to the East. And even that effort faltered. California judges often interpreted the code as though it had adopted the common law,[226] a position ratified by the state legislature in 1901.[227] See also State v. Britton, 178 P.2d 341 (Wash.1947)(1881 statute defining when harmless error shall be disregarded on appeal is not cited by state Supreme Court until 1947).

Eventually, the pressure to codify law weakened after the Civil War because the need for greater certainty and uniformity was satisfied in other ways: by commentaries, treatises, and the developing national digest system; through national law schools fostering an image of the law as having unifying principles; and because federal commercial law developed under Swift v. Tyson.[228]

Modern uniform laws and restatements. By the end of the 19th century, there was another flurry of interest in codification. A major factor was the concern with nonuniformity of law in a society where legal activity increasingly crossed state borders. At the urging of the American Bar Association,

---

223. Lewis Grossman, Codification and the California Mentality, 45 Hastings L. J. 617, 621 n.16 (1994)(hereafter "Grossman").

224. The states were California, the Dakotas, Idaho, and Montana. Cook, The American Codification Movement: A Study of Antebellum Legal Reform, p. 198 (1981).

225. Harrison, The First Half–Century of the California Civil Code, 10 Calif. L. Rev. 185 (1922).

226. See Sharon v. Sharon, 16 P. 345 (Cal.1888)

227. Grossman, pp. 618–21, 636.

228. 41 U.S. 1 (1842).

the National Conference of Commissioners on Uniform State Laws (NCCUSL) was established in 1892, consisting of commissioners appointed from each state by the Governor.[229] The Commissioners are usually lawyers, judges, and academics. The Conference (acting through its committees) drafts uniform laws which are presented to the Conference's annual meeting for approval. Approved drafts are then presented to the state legislatures for adoption.

The Conference has had mixed success. Over 200 uniform acts have been proposed. One commentator reports that 107 of these have been enacted by fewer than 10 states; 77 by fewer than 5. More than 40 states have enacted only 22 of the uniform acts.[230] White finds that the more widely-adopted proposals cluster in three areas: commercial law (e.g., the UCC); acts of special interest to lawyers and courts (e.g., Uniform Reciprocal Enforcement of Support Act); and descent and estate law (e.g., Uniform Anatomical Gift Act). Mere professional interest in improving the technical aspects of law has not been a dynamic force for passage. The Conference also drafts model acts when it wants to influence law reform but believes that an area is too unsettled for a uniform law.

The original conception underlying adoption of uniform laws was to distill established principles from case law, not to reform the law. Such distillation was consistent with the common law lawyers optimism about the common law (there *were* such principles to extract) and suspicion of statutes (legislative reform was suspect). The Commissioners were unable to avoid entirely the taint of "reform," however, once they yielded to the temptation to propose statutes in areas unknown to the common law (for example, the 1923 Uniform Workmen's Compensation Law). The same reform orientation supported the decision in 1958 to propose Model (not Uniform) Acts in areas of "emergent need."

Another institutional strand in the codification movement is the American Law Institute (ALI), founded in 1923. The ALI is a private body consisting of lawyers, judges, and academics, which appoints its own members. Like the NCCUSL, it operates through committees of experts in the field. Each project has a reporter—sometimes more than one—who is usually an academic. The resulting draft proposals are presented for approval of the entire membership at the annual meeting.

The ALI was concerned with the lack of uniformity in the law, but opposed codification of the common law. Its best known products are the Restatements of the Law, which were intended in part to take the wind out of the movement for statutory codification. There was limited support for statutory enactment of the Restatements, having the binding effect of a decision of the highest court of the state (that is, subject to judicial modification). The ALI has dealt not only with traditional common law subjects, but has also been influential in selected statutory areas of law, such as tax. The

---

229. See generally Dunham, A History of the National Conference of Commissioners on Uniform State Laws, 30 Law & Cont. Prob. 233 (1965).

230. White, Ex Proprio Vigore, 89 Mich. L. Rev. 209 (1991).

ALI's income tax project was the foundation for much of the Internal Revenue Code of 1954. The most famous Code to emerge from the codification movement in this country is the Uniform Commercial Code, developed jointly by the NCCUSL and the American Law Institute.

The self-image of both the National Conference and the ALI is of a group of technical experts committed to public service working in areas of law with a minimum of policy conflict. In practice, however, the law on which these experts work is often riddled with important policy implications (banks, for example, are intensely concerned with the secured transactions portion of the Uniform Commercial Code).[231]

Codification of United States statutes. United States statutes were codified just after the Civil War, in the narrower sense of compiling the annually-published statutes into a single code, with minor revisions to correct and update the law. They were published as the Revised Statutes of 1874. The United States experience illustrates one of the problems with this type of codification—the chance of error. The Revised Statutes of 1874 were enacted into law, but many mistakes were later found in the revision. A Revised Statutes of 1878 was then published, with the aim of making necessary corrections, but it was only *evidence* of the law, not itself "the law." Later efforts at codification produced the United States Code, the first edition of which appeared in 1926. Because of fears that the codification would contain errors, only some of the United States Code is enacted into law. Those Titles of the Code not enacted into law are only *prima facie* evidence of the law and the researcher must examine the Statutes at Large or Revised Statutes of 1874 for the official version.[232]

Occasionally, there is a question about the legal effect of a change made by the Reviser, even when the change is enacted into codified law. In Third National Bank of Nashville v. Impac Limited, Inc., 432 U.S. 312 (1977), the Court held that the close juxtaposition of two statutory provisions by the Reviser, enacted in 1874, was relevant in determining what the statute meant. The minority opinion, however, thought the Reviser had simply made an error with no substantive significance. In United States v. Falcone, 934 F.2d 1528 (11th Cir.1991), the court cited the statute authorizing the Reviser to "revise, simplify, arrange and consolidate" the law as evidence that the Reviser's omission of a phrase did *not* differ from the meaning that the statute would have had *with* the omitted text.

---

231. See generally Schwartz and Scott, The Political Economy of Private Legislatures, 143 U. Pa. L. Rev. 595 (1995); Schwarcz, A Fundamental Inquiry Into the Statutory Rule-making Process of Private Legislatures, 29 Georgia L. Rev. 909 (1995).

232. Independent Insurance Agents of America, Inc. v. Clarke, 955 F.2d 731

(D.C.Cir.1992)(Statutes at Large consulted to see whether words omitted from U.S. Code were in fact omitted from the legislation).

CHAPTER 3

FROM 1900 TO THE 1960S—
PURPOSIVE INTERPRETATION

20th Century legislation, at both the state and federal levels, had a vitality and scope that earlier legislation lacked. It often replaced the common law and created whole new bodies of statute law. Federal regulatory statutes established the Food and Drug Commission (1906),[1] the Federal Reserve Board (1913),[2] and the Federal Trade Commission (1914).[3] Workers Compensation replaced much of tort law regarding employer and employee relationships, both at the state level (beginning in the first decade of the 20th Century)[4] and at the federal level for federal employees (in 1916)[5] and longshoremen (in 1927).[6] Some purely redistributionist state statutes appeared—such as state Mothers' Pensions Acts in the second decade of the 20th Century.[7] The federal income tax (in 1913)[8] also had a redistributionist populist tinge, despite rates which would strike us as ridiculously low. And all of this was before the New Deal explosion of regulatory and redistributionist legislation.

State and federal legislative reforms continued to meet with judicial hostility. Statutes interfering with common law rights were still struck down as unconstitutional and state courts narrowly interpreted statutes in derogation of the common law. New York even held its Workers Compensation law unconstitutional because it eliminated the common law requirement of fault as a basis of liability.[9] But there were signs of a change.

19th Century commentators had criticized judicial hostility to statutes but, except for occasional references to increased legislative competence, their critique lacked an affirmative defense of legislation. By contrast, those favoring the narrow interpretation of statutes in derogation of common law had a well developed theory and affirmative image of the common law as custom, sanctified by long usage and popular consent, and as a science, both

---

1. Federal Food and Drug Act of 1906, ch. 3915, 34 Stat. 768 (1906).

2. Federal Reserve Act, ch. 6, 38 Stat. 251 (1913).

3. Federal Trade Commission Act, ch. 311, 38 Stat. 717 (1914).

4. Roy Lubove, The Struggle for Social Security, pp. 52–54 (1968) (hereafter "Lubove").

5. Federal Employees Compensation Act, ch. 458, 39 Stat. 742 (1916).

6. Longshoreman's and Harbor Workers' Compensation Act, ch. 509, 44 Stat. 1424 (1927).

7. Lubove, p. 99.

8. 38 Stat. 114 (1913).

9. Ives v. South Buffalo Ry. Co., 94 N.E. 431 (N.Y.1911).

of which gave courts the confidence to limit the reach of legislation. In the early years of the 20th Century, commentators corrected that imbalance. They explained why legislation was good—it was a *science* and it was capable of dealing with the kinds of change to which the slow-moving common law could not adjust. And, as the century progressed, a commitment to implementing democratic will replaced science as the justification for placing judicial faith in legislation.

There had been enthusiasm for democratic principles before, but it was always controversial.[10] Throughout the 19th Century, it was always respectable to object to "too much democracy," playing on fears of the mob and anarchy. The 20th Century was different. As Morton Horwitz explains, the 20th Century witnessed the widespread acceptance of democracy as a political principle, rejecting the prior negative "mob tyranny" image. Democratic principles were widely embraced, for example, in the amendments to the U.S. Constitution providing that the U.S. Senate should be popularly elected (1913) and that women could vote (1920).[11]

Not all images of legislation were positive, but the remedy was in the direction of "more," rather than less, democracy. The Populist and Progressive movements at the end of the 19th and beginning of the 20th Centuries had considerable success in reviving the old idea of *direct* democracy.[12] The dominant idea behind direct democracy was to bypass special interest obstacles to popular reform legislation and to check the legislature's proclivity to favor narrow interest groups. Politically, these movements were a farmer-labor coalition opposed to big business, and had their major successes in the West and South. Between 1898 and 1918, 18 states adopted both initiatives (which allow voters to adopt legislation) and referendums (which allow the voters to approve of legislation passed by the legislature), 3 states adopted referendums only, and one adopted only the initiative; all but four of these states were in the West or South.

Between 1908 and 1933, 12 states also provided for recall of elected state officials; all but one of the recall states were in the West or South. Seven of these recall provisions included judges. The issue of judicial recall was so contentious that Arizona's request for admission to the Union was denied because its constitution contained such a provision. Admission was granted only when judicial recall was removed, after which Arizona adopted judicial recall on its own.[13] The Progressive Party, led by Theodore Roosevelt, even favored recall of specific judicial decisions by popular vote, as

---

10. Horwitz, The Constitution of Change: Legal Fundamentality Without Fundamentalism, 107 Harv. L. Rev. 1, 57–65 (1993).

11. Senatorial election: U.S. Const., 17th Amendment (passed Congress in 1912; state ratification in 1913); women suffrage: U.S. Const, 19th Amendment (passed Congress in 1919; ratification in 1920).

12. The material in these paragraphs about the Populist and Progressive movements is based on Cronin, Direct Democracy: The Politics of Initiatives, Referendums and Recall, pp. 38–39, 125–56 (1989).

13. Bates, The United States, 1898–1928: Progressivism and a Society in Transition, pp. 117–18 (1976).

follows:[14]—

> That when an Act [ ] is held unconstitutional under the State
> Constitution, by the courts, the people, after an ample interval for
> deliberation, shall have an opportunity to vote on the question
> whether they desire the Act to become law, notwithstanding such
> decision.

The changing image of democracy and legislation had significant implications for statutory interpretation. The vitality and scope of modern reform
legislation invited the view that statutes embodied a purpose which was the
guide to their interpretation. Although some observers analogized purposive
interpretation to traditional "equitable interpretation," that was an oversimplification. The old "equity" often allowed the judge to help out a careless
legislature which overlooked problems or failed to update laws, either by
extending the statute a bit or limiting coverage, or by making sense of the
whole text and related statutes. Purposivism, in at least some of its manifestations, was different. It reconceived the text as embodying vital legislative
purposes. The closest analogy in past practice was to the way Wilson and
Marshall approached the constitution. The spirit of the document did not so
much "correct" its language (in Plowden's terms) as imbue it with meaning.
Moreover, where late 19th Century equitable interpretation narrowed the
reach of statutes through application of the "derogation" canon (whether or
not they employed the phrase "equitable interpretation"), purposivism extended statutes. Though no one said it quite this way—it was statutes that
20th Century judges were expounding.

3.01   Giving Statutes Their Due—Pound

Roscoe Pound wrote two influential articles (excerpted below) at the
beginning of the 20th Century, which reconceptualized statutes as a source
of principle and objected to "spurious" interpretation which favored common law over statutes. These views had implications both for statutory
interpretation (rejecting reliance on the "derogation" canon) and for the
influence of statutes on the evolution of the common law.[15] They also

---

14. The Progressive Party Platform of
1912, reprinted in The Progressive Movement, p. 130 (Hofstadter ed. 1963).

15. There was an occasional breadth of
vision in late 19th Century commentary that
anticipated Pound. For example, Joel Bishop,
Commentaries on the Written Law and Their
Interpretation, p. 4, secs. 5–6 (1882), describes
statutes this way:

> * * * A new statutory provision, cast
> into a body of written and unwritten laws,
> is not altogether unlike a drop of coloring
> matter to a pail of water. Not so fully, yet

to a considerable extent, it changes the
hue of the whole body; and how far and
where it works the change can be seen by
him who comprehend the relations of the
parts, and discerns how each particle acts
upon and governs and is governed by the
others. * * *. [I]t is a thread of woof
woven into a warp which before existed.
It is never to be contemplated as a thing
alone, but always as a part of a harmonious whole.

foreshadowed the arrival of purposive interpretation, without explicitly saying so.

a) POUND, COMMON LAW AND LEGISLATION, 21 HARV. L. REV. 383 (1908)

Not the least notable characteristics of American law today are the excessive output of legislation in all our jurisdictions and the indifference, if not contempt, with which that output is regarded by courts and lawyers. Text-writers who scrupulously gather up from every remote corner the most obsolete decisions and cite all of them, seldom cite any statutes except those landmarks which have become a part of our American common law, or, if they do refer to legislation, do so through the judicial decisions which apply it. The courts, likewise, incline to ignore important legislation; not merely deciding it to be declaratory [of the common law], but sometimes assuming silently that it is declaratory without adducing any reasons, citing prior judicial decisions and making no mention of the statute. In the same way, lawyers in the legislature often conceive it more expedient to make of a statute the barest outline, leaving details of the most vital importance to be filled in by judicial law-making. It is fashionable to point out the deficiencies of legislation and to declare that there are things that legislators cannot do try how they will. It is fashionable to preach the superiority of judge-made law. It may be well, however, for judges and lawyers to remember that there is coming to be a science of legislation and that modern statutes are not to be disposed of lightly as off-hand products of a crude desire to do something, but represent long and patient study by experts, careful consideration by conferences or congresses or associations, press discussions in which public opinion is focused upon all important details, and hearings before legislative committees. It may be well to remember also that while bench and bar are never weary of pointing out the deficiencies of legislation, to others the deficiencies of judge-made law are no less apparent. To economists and sociologists, judicial attempts to force Benthamite conceptions of freedom of contract and common law conceptions of individualism upon the public of today are no less amusing—or even irritating—than legislative attempts to do away with or get away from these conceptions are to bench and bar. The nullifying of these legislative attempts is not regarded by lay scholars with the complacent satisfaction with which lawyers are wont to speak of it. They do not hesitate to say that "the judicial mind has not kept pace with the strides of industrial development." They express the opinion that "belated and anti-social" decisions have been a fruitful cause of strikes, industrial discord, and consequent lawlessness. They charge that "the attitude of the courts has been responsible for much of our political immorality."

There are two ways in which the courts impede or thwart social legislation demanded by the industrial conditions of today. The first is narrow and illiberal construction of constitutional provisions, state and federal. "Petty judicial interpretations," says Professor Thayer, "have always been, are now, and will always be, a very serious danger to the country." The second is a narrow and illiberal attitude toward legislation conceded to be constitutional, regarding it as out of place in the legal system, as an alien element to be held down to the strictest limits and not to be applied beyond the requirements of its express language. The second is by no means so conspicuous as the first, but is not on that account the less unfortunate or the less dangerous. Let us see what this attitude is, how it arose, and why it exists in an industrial community and an age of legislation.

Four ways may be conceived of in which courts in such a legal system as ours might deal with a legislative innovation. (1) They might receive it fully into the body of the law as affording not only a rule to be applied but a principle from which to reason, and hold it, as a later and more direct expression of the general will, of superior authority to judge-made rules on the same general subject; and so reason from it by analogy in preference to them. (2) They might receive it fully into the body of the law to be reasoned from by analogy the same as any other rule of law, regarding it, however, as of equal or co-ordinate authority in this respect with judge-made rules upon the same general subject. (3) They might refuse to receive it fully into the body of the law and give effect to it directly only; refusing to reason from it by analogy but giving it, neverthe-less, a liberal interpretation to cover the whole field it was intended to cover. (4) They might not only refuse to reason from it by analogy and apply it directly only, but also give to it a strict and narrow interpretation, holding it down rigidly to those cases which it covers expressly. The fourth hypothesis represents the orthodox common law attitude toward legislative innovations. Probably the third hy-pothesis, however, represents more nearly the attitude toward which we are tending. The second and first hypotheses doubtless appeal to the common law lawyer as absurd. He can hardly conceive that a rule of statutory origin may be treated as a permanent part of the general body of the law. But it is submitted that the course of legal development upon which we have entered already must lead us to adopt the method of the second and eventually the method of the first hypothesis. * * *

We are told commonly that three classes of statutes are to be construed strictly: penal statutes; statutes in derogation of common right; and statutes in derogation of the common law. An eminent authority has objected to all of these categories and has pointed out that all classes of statutes ought to be construed with a sole view of ascertaining and giving effect to the will of the law-maker. But there is more justification for some of these categories than for others. For the rule that penal statutes are to be construed strictly something may be said. When acts are to be made penal and are to be visited with loss or impairment of life, liberty, or property, it may well be argued that political liberty requires clear and exact definition of the offense. So also the rule that statutes in derogation of common right are to be construed strictly has some excuse in England where there are no constitutional restrictions. * * * Whenever it is applied beyond these limits, it is without excuse and is merely an incident of the general attitude of courts toward legislation. The proposition that statutes in derogation of the common law are to be construed strictly has no such justification. It assumes that legislation is something to be deprecated. As no statute of any consequence dealing with any relation of private law can be anything but in derogation of the common law, the social reformer and the legal reformer, under this doctrine, must always face the situation that the legislative act which represents the fruit of their labors will find no sympathy in those who apply it, will be construed strictly, and will be made to interfere with the *status quo* as little as possible. * * *

It is reasonable to see Pound's views in this article as a precursor of modern purposive interpretation. His third way of dealing with legislation—"a liberal interpretation to cover the whole field it was intended to cover"—can be understood as a nod towards purposivism. But it would be a mistake to understand him as a full-fledged purposivist. His description of legislation as the embodiment of principle had two primary objectives—(1) to allow statutes to influence the evolution of common law (that is the point of the first two ways of dealing with statutes, by treating them as superior or co-ordinate sources of principle from which to reason; and (2) to counterbalance the judicial tendency to limit legislation based on substantive values extraneous to the statute, such as the common law (that was the point of Pound's fourth way to deal with statutes, by "strict and narrow interpretation," which he severely criticized). After all, he was writing in the first decade of the 20th Century and the explosion of modern regulatory and redistributionist legislation still lay in the future. That may explain why he relies primarily on a developing "science" of legislation, rather than on democratic principles, to assert the primacy of statutes over judge-made law.

b) POUND, SPURIOUS INTERPRETATION, 7 COLUM. L. REV. 379 (1907)

I have said that one of the points of contact between law and morals is to be found in interpretation. This is true to some extent of all interpretation. But it is more especially true of that form of interpretation—or rather that form of judicial law-making under the guise of interpretation—which Austin has styled "spurious interpretation." The name given by Austin has been objected to as "depreciatory." But the distinction is entirely valid, and deserves more attention than it has received. Nor is the depreciation of the process, involved in the name Austin applies to it, a sound objection. For if the process is not in fact what it pretends to be, but operates "by side winds and in underhand ways" to bring about results not attainable directly, it is not merely destructive of clear legal thinking to use one term to cover both the genuine and the pretended, but in a time when we ought to have outgrown fictions, the pretended interpretation by virtue of which the law grows judicially, deserves to be so branded that no one shall be deceived. Austin's analysis will be found in the fragment of his Essay on Interpretation. In substance, it is this: The difficulty calling for interpretation may be, (a) which of two or more co-ordinate rules to apply, or (b) to determine what the law-maker intended to prescribe by a given rule, or (c) to meet deficiencies or excesses in rules imperfectly conceived or enacted. The first two are cases for genuine interpretation. The third case, when treated as a matter of interpretation, calls for spurious interpretation.

The object of genuine interpretation is to discover the rule which the law-maker intended to establish; to discover the intention with which the law-maker made the rule, or the sense which he attached to the words wherein the rule is expressed. Its object is to enable others to derive from the language used "the same idea which the author intended to convey." Employed for these purposes, interpretation is purely judicial in character; and so long as the ordinary means of interpretation, namely the literal meaning of the language used and the context, are resorted to, there can be no question. But when, as often happens, these primary indices to the meaning and intention of the law-maker fail to lead to a satisfactory result, and recourse must be had to the reason and spirit of the rule, or to the intrinsic merit of the several possible interpretations, the line between a genuine ascertaining of the meaning of the law, and the making over of the law under guise of interpretation, becomes more difficult. Strictly, both are means of genuine interpretation. They are not covers for the making of new law. They are modes of arriving at the real intent of the maker of existing law. The former means of interpretation tries to find out directly what the law-maker meant by assuming his position, in the surroundings in which he acted, and endeavoring to gather from the mischiefs he had to meet and the remedy by which he sought to meet them, his intention with respect to the particular point in controversy. The latter, if the former fails to yield sufficient light, seeks to reach the intent of the law-maker indirectly. It assumes that the law-maker thought as we do on general questions of morals and policy and fair dealing. Hence it assumes that of several possible interpretations the one which appeals most to our sense of right and justice for the time being is most likely to give the meaning of those who framed the rule. If resorted to in the first instance, or without regard to the other means of interpretation, this could not be regarded as a means of genuine interpretation. But inherent difficulties of expression and want of care in drafting require continual resort to this means of interpretation for the legitimate purpose of ascertaining what the law-maker in fact meant.

[Editor—(1) Does Pound sound a lot like Blackstone in rank ordering interpretive criteria, from text/context, to reason and spirit, to intrinsic merit? (2) Is Pound correct in claiming that intrinsic merit, if not relied on prematurely, is a way of determining what the law-maker in fact meant? If not, why might he incorrectly insist that the judge is doing nothing more than identify legislative intent?]

On the other hand, the object of spurious interpretation is to make, unmake, or remake, and not merely to discover. It puts a meaning into the text as a juggler puts coins, or what not, into a dummy's hair, to be pulled forth presently with an air of discovery. It is essentially a legislative, not a judicial process, made necessary in formative periods by the paucity of principles, feebleness of legislation, and rigidity of rules characteristic of archaic law. So long as law is regarded as sacred, or for any reason as incapable of alteration, such a process is necessary to growth, but surviving into periods of legislation, it becomes a source of confusion. Such survival, however, like the survival of fictions, of implications in law, and of such phrases as "constructive" trust and constructive fraud, is inevitable in any system. While it is the chief means of growth in the formative period, in the period of growth by juristic speculation, which is the classical period in every legal system, it becomes a settled doctrine, and passes into succeeding periods of legislation as an undoubted judicial attribute. As legislation becomes stronger and more frequent, examples of this type of so-called interpretation will finally become less common. Outside of constitutional law, where special reasons operate to keep it alive, the most conspicuous example in recent American case-law is the attempt in some jurisdictions to read into the statutes governing descent an exception excluding the heir who murders his ancestor, a holding now generally repudiated. None the less the genuine character of this so-called interpretation remains for the most part unquestioned. Jurists continue to discuss it as a form of interpretation *ex ratione legis*, and courts confuse the two in one and the same sentence.

Spurious interpretation is an anachronism in an age of legislation. It is a fiction. * * * Spurious interpretation, moreover, is a fiction which has done its legitimate work. Men have long seen that special fictions are unnecessary and unsuited to a developed system of law. But general fictions tend to become so deep-rooted, that eradication is well nigh impossible. Spurious interpretation and genuine interpretation are so generally confused by institutional writers, that few who study the law realize that there is any difference. * * * So long as the bulk of a legal system is in the form of case-law, this is no great matter. When the growing-point shifts to legislation, and judicial law-making, being at variance with constitutional theory, is confined within constantly narrowing limits, it becomes a matter of the first importance, since it leads of necessity to exercise of legislative powers by the courts.

Pound's sharp distinction between genuine and spurious interpretation may need rethinking. He may have exaggerated that distinction because he associated spurious interpretation with hostility towards legislation and he wanted to end that hostility. In the modern context, where courts are no longer hostile to legislation, drawing such a sharp distinction may obscure the element of judicial creativity in "genuine" interpretation, and suppress judicial lawmaking potential, just because it would be considered "spurious" by some observer. For example, is Pound right to object to reading an exception into a statute specifying the effect of a will so as to prohibit inheritance by a named beneficiary who murdered the testator (the case of Riggs v. Palmer, 22 N.E. 188 (N.Y.1889))?

Moreover, as we will see, the source of modern judicial lawmaking potential has shifted away from limiting statutes in light of substantive values extraneous to the statute (such as the common law), towards the selectively sympathetic embrace of statutory purpose, whose reach and vitality might not be evident without judicial elaboration. In Pound's terminology, there is an element of judicial judgment about "intrinsic merit" in identifying and advancing the reason and spirit (that is, the purpose) of the law. It is unclear whether Pound would have viewed as "spurious" the judge's lawmaking role in elaborating purpose.

3.02   THE FUNCTION OF STATUTES

The hostility to statutes to which Pound reacted could not last. This was the era of progressive legislation, of legislative law reform. There was optimism that a scientific spirit of fact-gathering and public debate would bring about desirable political results. This heady optimism about legislation was best expressed in the legal literature by Professor Freund, a political scientist on the Chicago Law faculty.

a) FREUND, PROLEGOMENA TO A SCIENCE OF LEGISLATION, 13 ILL. L. REV. 264 (1918)

> Leaving then aside the formulation of principles in statutory form, a science of legislation as a distinctive branch of jurisprudence is concerned mainly with tasks for which the upbuilding of the common law furnishes no precedents or standards; with those aspects of statutes, in other words, that find no analogy in principles developed by judicial reasoning. *The special province of the science of legislation must be to carry the development of the law beyond what the processes of the unwritten law can possibly do for it.*
>
> Judicial reasoning is by its very nature incapable of producing many rules which may be the only or the most adequate rules for

dealing with a legal situation. The instrument of reasoning is logic, and its product a principle. If a principle were always sufficient for the practical adjustment of affairs, we might rest content with the processes of judge-made law, but a mere principle often fails to furnish the needed direction. Principle can determine that a female employee shall not be overworked, it cannot say, ten hours, not eleven. *Reasoning from principle does not produce measured quantities*; the period of the rule against perpetuities and the period of prescription, which seem anomalous exceptions, followed the analogy of previously established periods. The former was taken from the age of minority which was fixed by custom and not by reason, just as it was a custom-the custom of merchants-which introduced the definite number of days of grace in the law of commercial paper. *Nor can principle produce form*; where the common law requires form for acts, they are due to custom, as the feoffment and livery of seisin, or the seal as a requisite of deed; neither writing nor attestation is anywhere in private law a judge-created requirement. And equity never solved the problem of priorities between successive purchasers or mortgagees, because the only effective means of publicity, the public record of instruments, was entirely incapable of being established or required by the exercise of judicial power.

Measured quantity, conventional form, administrative arrangements, and (it should be added), compromise and concession, constitute the exclusive province of statute law, and if these matters are amenable to principle, it must be principle quite different in kind from that represented by common law rules. The legislator has always the choice between a number of valid rules, and if this choice is controllable by considerations that may aspire to the dignity of principles, the principle is that of constant relations, the relation between methods and results, the law to which human action is subject irrespective of human authority, and largely dependent upon empirical, psychological, and sociological factors. Such a law the lawyer regards as being on the whole beyond his science, and as characteristic of the social and political sciences, and he will look with skepticism upon a proposed extension of jurisprudence in that direction.

Workers Compensation statutes are typical examples of what Freund is talking about. Workers Compensation laws were a response to common law tort rules, which were perceived as unduly restrictive of an employee's right to recover for industrial accidents. Industrial accidents were taking a heavy toll and the common law was considered inadequate both as a method of encouraging safety and as a compensation scheme for injured workers and their families. At common law, an employee suing an employer had to prove fault and the employer could interpose the defenses of contributory negligence, assumption of risk and the fellow servant rule. Courts could have abolished these defenses and they sometimes did, but elimination of the fault requirement would have seemed too radical. The problem was ripe for legislation that broke with the past, made concessions to employers by way of compromise, fixed recovery amounts applicable to all cases, and established administrative agencies to handle the litigation.

Workers Compensation did all that. Common law defenses were eliminated and employers were liable without fault for injuries occurring by accident if they arose out of and in the course of employment. In exchange, employers were usually liable only to the extent of fixed amounts set forth in schedules, based on prior wages and the severity of the physical impairment. Industrial accident commissions (or similarly named agencies) were established to administer the program. Funding came from insurance premiums or self-insurance financed by employers, which varied with accident experience. It took a statute to achieve these reforms. Courts could not have done the job, at least not courts as we know them.

These points are generalized in the following observations by Judge Friendly about the advantages of legislation.

b) FRIENDLY, REACTIONS OF A LAWYER–NEWLY BECOME JUDGE, 71 YALE L.J. 218 (1961)

[In McWeeney v. New York, New Haven & Hartford R. Co.,] the issue that had to be decided was not one adapted to the techniques of judicial law making [ ]. The issue was whether, in a personal injury action under the Federal Employers' Liability Act, the jury should be instructed to make a deduction, from the portion of the award representing loss of earning power, for the income taxes the plaintiff would have had to pay on the lost earnings. The precedents in our own Court were conflicting * * *. The decisions in other jurisdictions were divided. The legal principles invoked by the two sides—for the defendant that damages are intended to make a plaintiff whole but no more, for the plaintiff that a recovery is not to be reduced for benefits from "collateral sources"—were so far away that resort to them would have been rationalization rather than reasoning—the lines of force were too remote to exert any real pull.

Here was a case where, of Cardozo's various methods of decision, only "the method of sociology" was available; the problem was of the broad sort normally dealt with by elected legislators and the Court had in effect to act as such. Since logic and philosophy afforded no aid, it is not surprising that the result was lacking in them. Looking at the great mass of personal injury cases, of which this one was typical, we held that the administrative problems of income tax determination by juries or even by judges, plus the tendency to under-compensation arising from inflation and from the inability of plaintiffs to recover their attorneys' fees, rendered the proposed instruction improper. If we had stopped there, we would have been on ground that could not be attacked as illogical, whether or not one thought it wise. However, the case of the very large earner was pressed upon us. How absurd to present a plaintiff with an award based on annual earnings of $100,000 when his effective income would have been less than half! We said therefore that at some point in the income scale the balance of interests between plaintiff and defendant would shift; later decisions will have to determine that point's location more precisely and also how the deduction in the case of the large earner shall be determined. I would hope, although I confess without much real expectation, that before the courts have to do this, the legislature will step in.

The reason why I think McWeeney's case was inappropriate for judicial solution is not so much that the precedents afforded no guidance—judges in a tradition that * * * introduced the action for money had and received into the common law would hardly cavil at that. The more important reasons are that we lacked the factual data needed for a right answer and, still worse, there was no right answer we could give even if the data had been available. Let me explain.

A judge desiring to make a truly intelligent answer to the question posed in McWeeney's case would need to know much more of what takes place in the jury room than courts have yet learned—although some light from the Middle West, in the shape of the University of Chicago jury study, may not be far away. Also, I should think, he would have to know much else. He would wish to know how much of the verdicts go for attorney's fees and other expenses of litigation, what plaintiffs do with the sums awarded, and whether the lump sum recovery, determined in advance of the fact on the basis of averages, is still suitable, especially in an age of new cures that may make it too high, and of increased longevity and inflation which may make it too low. But when all this information was at hand, judges still would not be able to give a good answer to the question presented. A court has only three choices—to deduct the tax in all cases, to deduct it in none, or to deduct it in the big income cases but not in the medium or small. The last course, which we adopted, was satisfactory only in the limited sense of seeming better than either of the others, but it leaves future problems of drawing the line, and of determining the tax in cases beyond the line, which courts are ill equipped to handle.

Contrast the resources available to the legislature. The legislature might establish a small—or no—percentage deduction on awards up to a certain annual figure, and a higher percentage on those above. In fixing these percentages, it could determine whether they should reflect the under-compensation from probable future inflation or from the lack of recovery of attorney's fees and, if so, to what degree. Percentage deductions thus determined could apply regardless of idiosyncracies of the particular plaintiff in the way of exceptions, deductions or outside income, and hence would free the courts from the burden of inquiry about these in every case. Alternatively, the legislature might decide to require the portion of the award representing loss of earnings, or so much of it as was left after deducting expenses of litigation, to be paid into court and disbursed over a period of years, then being subject to income tax, and thereby end the whole problem. Almost any of these solutions would be better than the best a court can achieve.

The moral is pointed out by the English experience with the related question of the effect, in personal injury cases, of benefits receivable under the national insurance scheme. After much investigation, Parliament enacted the Law Reform (Personal Injuries) Act, 1948, section 2(1) of which provides that in an action for damages for personal injuries there shall be taken into account against any loss of earnings or profits half the value of any rights in respect of national security benefits for five years from the time when the cause of action accrued. No judge could have arrived at a solution so Solomonic. Yet who is to say that it is not wiser than a court's universal yea or nay? * * *

3.03   PURPOSIVISM AND LEGAL REALISM

a)   INTRODUCTION

Before purposive interpretation could come into its own, something more was needed than Pound's commitment to scientific legislation and that something was an affirmative sense of legislative vitality. The early years of the 20th Century were not quite up to that reconceptualization of statutes. The New Deal had not yet arrived and state legislatures were still suspect both from the Left and the Right. From the Left, Populist and Progressive movements in the states sought to bypass state legislatures through referendums and initiatives, because the legislature was captive to private interests. (Not all democratic impulses favored legislation!) And, from the Right, there were still those who associated legislation with "mob" rule—indeed, some explain the progressive movement to bypass state legislatures as a middle class attempt to block the efficacy of machine politics in aiding the lower classes.[16]

By the time of President Franklin D. Roosevelt's New Deal in 1933, however, legislation acquired a more positive image. Landis, in 1934, still dwelled on "science" as the source of legislative vitality, but this was becoming more obviously a rhetorical device.[17] Scientific expertise was now

---

16. Julian Eule, Judicial Review of Direct Democracy, 99 Yale L. J. 1503, 1513–14 (1990).

17. James Landis, Statutes and the Source of Law, in Harvard Legal Essays, p.

213 (1934)(referring to the influence of "the rise of social sciences" on legislation and a "science of statutory interpretation") (hereafter "Landis").

associated as much with administrative decision making as with legislation, as agencies were delegated the task of applying their knowledge to flesh out general legislative principles. Legislatures came to be viewed as the place where popular democratic will was expressed, where the common good was enacted into law.[18] Statutes now replaced the common law as the source of social consensus. Eventually, this emphasis on democracy would evolve into a countermajoritarian anxiety about judging, including judicial choices associated with purposive interpretation. But in this time of heady optimism about science, democracy, and legislatures, courts could enthusiastically adopt a role as the creative expositors of legislative purpose. Thus, when Landis said that "legislation [ ] is assuming a creative aspect of purpose" *and* that the judge is a "creative artist," he made the connection between creative legislating and judging that has characterized purposive interpretation ever since.[19] And he was quite explicit about that link: "The consciousness that the judicial and legislative processes are closely allied both in technique and in aims will inevitably make for greater interdependence in both."[20] Landis also claimed an ancient lineage for purposivism in the 16–17th Century practice of equitable interpretation—arguing that, even in that early period, "behind the formal fiat of the statute lay an aim that challenged [the judge's] sympathetic attention, [and] the appropriate exercise of judicial power permitted courts to advance ends so emphatically asserted."[21]

The judicial-legislative link which was at the heart of purposivism was most famously stated by the Supreme Court in United States v. American Trucking Associations, Inc.[22] The Court affirmed the importance of the text as evidence of purpose ("There is, of course, no more persuasive evidence of the purpose of a statute than the words by which the legislature undertook to give expression to its wishes."); and the Golden Rule ("When that meaning has led to absurd or futile results, however, this Court has looked beyond the words to the purpose of the act."). But there was more. "Frequently, however, even when the plain meaning did not produce absurd results but merely an unreasonable one 'plainly at variance with the policy of the legislation as a whole' this Court has followed that purpose, rather than the literal words." And the Court was explicit in addressing the question of judicial role, shunting aside Separation of Powers concerns. Indeed, it was the court's "duty" to interpret the statute in light of legislative policy. Any danger that the judges' own views would intrude into the decision was worth taking. "The interpretation of the meaning of statutes, as applied to justiciable controversies, is exclusively a judicial function;" it was a "duty [which] requires one body of public servants, the judges, to construe the meaning of what another body, the legislators, has said." As for the "danger that the courts' conclusion as to legislative purpose will be unconsciously influenced

---

18. Note, Legislative Materials to Aid Statutory Interpretation, 50 Harv. L. Rev. 821, 822 (1937).

19. Landis, pp. 213, 219.

20. Landis, p. 233.

21. Landis, p. 216. Thorne argued in the Illinois Law Review article, excerpted in Chapter 2, that 16th Century equitable interpretation was less bold than modern purposive interpretation.

22. 310 U.S. 534, 543–44 (1940).

by the judges' own views or by factors not considered by the enacting body," the best way to address that concern was through a "lively appreciation of the danger."

b) JUDGE LEARNED HAND

The leading and most articulate judicial exponent of purposivism, as well as of the need for a "lively appreciation of the danger" of purposivism, was Judge Learned Hand. One of his more famous statements is the following:[23]

> Of course it is true that the words used, even in their literal sense, are the primary, and ordinarily the most reliable, source of interpreting the meaning of any writing: be it a statute, a contract, or anything else. But it is one of the surest indexes of a mature and developed jurisprudence not to make a fortress out of the dictionary; but to remember that statutes always have some purpose or object to accomplish, whose sympathetic and imaginative discovery is the surest guide to their meaning.

Lehigh Valley Coal Co. v. Yensavage,[24] is a typical example of a purposive Hand opinion. The decision interpreted "employee," not in accordance with its common law meaning, as though the term had been borrowed from some storehouse of meaning outside the statute, but more broadly, to achieve the statute's purpose. The statute was meant to protect miners who were "employees" and worked in potentially unsafe conditions. The defendant had established a relationship with his workers which avoided the traditional "employment" relationship but Hand said that did not matter because it would "miss[ ] the whole purpose of such statutes, which are meant to protect those who are at an economic disadvantage."[25] He continued:[26]

> It is true that the statute uses the word 'employed,' but it must be understood with reference to the purpose of the act, and where all the conditions of the relation require protection, protection ought to be given. It is absurd to class such a miner as an independent contractor * * *. He has no capital, no financial responsibility. * * *
>
> Such statutes [ ] upset the freedom of contract, and for ulterior purposes put the two contesting sides at unequal advantage; they should be construed, not as theorems of Euclid, but with some imagination of the purposes which lie behind them.

See also Borella v. Borden Co.:[27]

23. Cabell v. Markham, 148 F.2d 737, 739 (2d Cir.1945).

24. 218 Fed. 547 (2d Cir.1914). A later Supreme Court case also read "employee" in light of the history, context, and purpose of the statute, rather than adopt its common law or local law meaning. N.L.R.B. v. Hearst Publications, 322 U.S. 111 (1944).

25. 218 Fed. at 552.

26. 218 Fed. at 552–53.

27. 145 F.2d 63, 64–65 (2d Cir.1944).

We can best reach the meaning here, as always, by recourse to the underlying purpose, and, with that as a guide, by trying to project upon the specific occasion how we think persons, actuated by such a purpose, would have dealt with it, if it had been presented to them at the time. To say that that is a hazardous process is indeed a truism, but we cannot escape it, once we abandon literal interpretation—a method far more unreliable.

Hand's purposivism was pervasive, not limited to social welfare labor legislation. For example, it also extended to interpretation of the income tax law. In Commissioner v. Ickelheimer,[28] the statute disallowed loss deductions on "direct" and "indirect" sales between related parties, including husband and wife. The wife sold bonds on the stock market and the husband bought the same bonds a day or two later on the stock market. There was no use of a friend as a go-between and the taxpayers were subject to the risks of the market during the gap in time between sale and repurchase. The majority (Hand was in dissent) applied the term "indirect" sale to the use of a friend as a go-between, but not to sales where the parties were at the risk of market fluctuations. Hand disagreed:[29]

> * * * [O]ne would have to be a very convinced literalist to say that the section did not cover a device by which the plain purpose of the statute could be frustrated * * *. Unless we must confine "indirectly" to cases where the seller passes title to an intermediary who has agreed to pass it to the ultimate buyer at the same price, we should call [what the taxpayer did] an "indirect sale." I can see no reason so to confine it.

And:

> * * * [T]he colloquial words of a statute have not the fixed and artificial content of scientific symbols; they have a penumbra, a dim fringe, a connotation, for they express an attitude of will, into which it is our duty to penetrate and which we must enforce ungrudgingly when we can ascertain it, regardless of imprecision in its expression. Here we can have no doubt of the purpose, of what Congress was aiming at; and that, I submit, we truncate, if we do not include transactions by which, in accordance with a preexisting design, property passes by whatever combination of moves at a substantially unchanged price from one member to the other of any of the specified pairs.

c) LEGAL REALISTS; RADIN

Purposive interpretation was accompanied not only by a developing sense that legislation was a desirable source of law but also by a rejection of

---

28. 132 F.2d 660 (2d Cir.1943). The Supreme Court reached the same result in McWilliams v. Commissioner, 331 U.S. 694 (1947).

29. 132 F.2d at 662.

the traditional view that common law courts simply discovered objective legal principles. As Holmes said: "The life of the law has not been logic, it has been experience."[30] This perspective on law eventually matured into the Legal Realist movement, which revealed judging (especially the common law) to be riddled with lawmaking policy choices.[31] The Legal Realist critique made it virtually impossible for anyone to appeal to the judge's "artificial reason" in expounding the law, and also called into question reliance on "fundamental principles," which were also political in nature. This perception that law and politics intersected had significant implications for statutory interpretation.

First, if the common law was based on judicial policy choices, then legislation seemed to have a comparative advantage over courts in making law; and judges could claim no special insight into the "law" to limit the reach of legislation, especially if the appeal was to the "derogation" canon privileging the common law. Second, the traditional substantive canons of interpretation did not provide objective judicial guidelines, but were easily manipulated by judges to reach desired results. One of the more famous articles in the Legal Realist genre argued that the interpretive canons came in pairs—each with an equal and opposite principle.[32] The classic example of such pairing was the derogation canon and the contrary principle that remedial statutes should be liberally construed.

At this point, one might expect Legal Realists to wholeheartedly embrace a purposivist approach to statutory interpretation, but it was not that simple. When some Legal Realists looked at the legislative process, they were unable to identify "legislative intent" with any degree of certainty. For example, Max Radin doubted that the vast bulk of legislators had given any thought at all to the specifics of most litigated cases; or that, even if the thought had occurred to them, they would have agreed about how to apply the statute; and, in any event, such thoughts were not law. He made a similar point about the indeterminacy of legislative purpose, adding that legislators as a group usually had a concatenation of purposes, often ranging from the more specific to the more general.[33]

Nonetheless, there was a strong tendency among many Legal Realists to embrace purposivism. Many of them retained an optimistic belief in a value-free humanistic social science and in the ability of legislatures and agencies to make law based on that science. Many of the Legal Realists worked on legislation during the New Deal and readily embraced the notion that there was a science of legislation at the same time that they were skeptical of a

---

30. Oliver Wendell Holmes, The Common Law 1 (1881).

31. See Morton Horwitz, The Transformation of American Law, 1870–1960: The Crisis of Legal Orthodoxy, Chapter 6 (1992); Laura Kalman, Legal Realism at Yale, 1927–1960 (1986).

32. Karl Llewellyn, Remarks on the Theory of Appellate Decision and the Rules or Canons About How Statutes Are to be Construed, 3 Vand. L. Rev. 395 (1950). See also Stephen Ross, Where Have You Gone, Karl Llewellyn? Should Congress Turn Its Lonely Eyes To You?, 45 Vand. L. Rev. 561 (1992).

33. Max Radin, Statutory Interpretation, 43 Harv. L. Rev. 863, 870–72, 876–78 (1930).

science of judicial lawmaking. And the best way to implement what the legislature had done was through a sympathetic purposive approach to statutory interpretation.

Even Radin spoke favorably of the purposivist approach, except that he was quite realistic about the extent to which it required creative judicial judgment. He was unable to pretend that purposivism eliminated judicial creativity. Nor did this bother him much. He authored an updated version of Heydon's Case in which he frankly admitted that the judge exercises judgment about the value attributed to whatever legislative purpose the judge identifies.[34] He based his view on a theory of judging and legislating that was much more hospitable to creative judging than many purposivists allowed—a statute was a "ground design," and judges were "statesmen," who could "exercise a judgment on the value of the [statutory] purpose."[35] The following statements are typical of Radin's views:[36]

> "[O]ur legislature is no more or less sovereign than administrators or judges"; "[t]he legislature has no constitutional warrant to demand reverence for the words in which it frames its directives."

Radin was therefore led to "rewrite" Heydon's Case as follows (emphasis added):[37]

> The first question the interpreter asks is: What is the purpose of the statute as a whole? * * * Second, *Is the statutory purpose one that the court feels is good?* We need not trouble ourselves about the statement that the court must not legislate. Both the judicial and the executive branches participate in the legislative process. * * * They may not rephrase the statute. They may not reject the purpose, even if they do not find it to be good. *But they may [   ] exercise a judgment on the value of the purpose,* and make that judgment the basis of enforcement of the law. * * * Third, Is the implemental portion of the statute declared to be exclusive? If so, it is clear that those who framed the statute were uncertain about the value of its program and the court may not disregard that fact even if the court is quite certain.

d) JUDICIAL ROLE

Although Radin may have been comfortable (and honest) about the mix of purposivism and judicial creativity, not all purposivists were quite so sanguine about this judicial role. Learned Hand, for example, wrote at length about judging in several essays brought together in a book entitled "The Spirit of Liberty."[38] Some of his comments seem quite cautionary about

---

34. Max Radin, A Short Way With Statutes, 56 Harv. L. Rev. 388, 407–11 (1942)(hereafter "Radin, Short Way").

35. Radin, Short Way, pp. 407, 411.

36. Radin, Short Way, p. 406, 422.

37. Radin, Short Way, p. 422.

38. Learned Hand, The Spirit of Liberty (ed. Irving Dilliard 1952) (hereafter "Dilliard").

purposivist statutory interpretation. For example, he appears to describe purposive interpretation in almost grudging tones:[39]

> When a judge tries to find out what the government would have intended which it did not say, he puts into its mouth things which he thinks it ought to have said, and that is very close to substituting what he himself thinks right. Let him beware, however, or he will usurp the office of government, even though in a small way he must do so in order to execute its real commands at all.

Hand argues that the judge "must not enforce whatever he thinks best; he must leave that to the common will expressed by the government."[40] But, having left matters to the "common will," he then says some things about legislatures and "common will" that are quite strange coming from a purposivist—suggesting that there is not much coming from the legislature on which the judge can elaborate except what the "powerful" can legislate:[41]

> We think of the legislature as the place for resolving [major conflicts], and so indeed it is. But if we go further and insist that there we have an expression of a common will, it seems to me that for the most part we should be wrong again. * * * The truth appears to be that what we mean by a common will is no more than that there shall be an available peaceful means by which law may be changed when it becomes irksome enough to powerful people who can make their will effective.

A judge who makes these statements might seem an unlikely candidate for spearheading the purposive approach to statutory interpretation, which rests on a shared sense of legislative vitality and creative judging, sympathetic to legislative purpose. And yet that is exactly what Hand does in his judicial opinions. Indeed, as Gerald Gunther notes, Hand usually enforced New Deal laws "more sympathetically than even the post–1937 Supreme Court."[42]

Why would a judge with Hand's concern about judicial lawmaking have been so enthusiastic about purposivism as a technique of statutory interpretation, despite his awareness of its potential for judicial lawmaking?[43] Hand was certainly distrustful of the "masses"—he favored judicial restraint in large part because he feared that the voters would react against "political" judging by interfering with judicial independence and he vigorously opposed judicial recall. But he was also distrustful of wealth—Frankfurter called him a "democratic aristocrat." Politically, he was active as a young man in the pro-labor and pro-regulatory causes advanced by Theodore

---

39. Learned Hand, How Far Is a Judge Free in Rendering a Decision (1935), Dilliard, p. 108 (hereafter "Rendering").

40. Rendering, p. 109.

41. Learned Hand, Is There a Common Will (1929), Dilliard, p. 53. Hand also did not believe that the common will resided in the common law, an idea which he labeled a "fiction." Id., pp. 52–53.

42. Gerald Gunther, Learned Hand, p. 451 (1994)(hereafter "Gunther").

43. The material in this paragraph is based on Gunther, pp. xii, xvi, 62, 64, 110, 113, 205, 209, 215, 223, 246, 250, 348, 380, 394, 407, 433 (1994).

Roosevelt's Progressive Party, and even ran for the New York Court of Appeals as a Progressive while he was a sitting federal District Court judge. Purposivism, in the historical context of progressive legislation, may have allowed Hand (as well as other judges) to advance political principles with which they were in sympathy, while at the same time fairly claiming that they were advancing the legislature's will. Moreover, unlike judicial review striking down a statute, interpretation did not prohibit legislatures from responding by enacting clarifying legislation.

In the broader context of his other writings, Hand's caution about purposive interpretation may therefore be nothing more than admonishing himself to do what the Supreme Court urged in *American Trucking*—to have a "lively appreciation" of the "danger that the courts' conclusion as to legislative purpose will be unconsciously influenced by the judges' own views or by factors not considered by the enacting body." Having alerted himself to this concern, he then advocates a robust purposivism:[44]

> [The judge] must try as best he can to put into concrete form what that [legislative] will is, not by slavishly following the words, but by trying honestly to say what was the underlying purpose expressed. * * * Thus, on the one hand, he cannot go beyond what is said [   ]; on the other, he cannot suppose that what has been said should clearly frustrate or leave unexecuted its own purpose.[45]

> Courts must reconstruct the past solution imaginatively in its setting and project the purposes which inspired it upon the concrete occasions which arise for their decision.[46]

And, sounding a lot like Plowden, Hand asserts that[47]

> what [the judge] really does is to take the language before him, [   ] and try to find out what the government [   ] would have done, if the case before him had been before them. * * * To apply [the words] literally may either pervert what was plainly their general meaning, or leave undisposed of what there is every reason to suppose they meant to provide for.

The better reading of Hand's entire body of work is that he was simply incapable of resolving the potential conflict between creative and deferential judging that he was both perceptive and honest enough to see implicit in

44. Rendering, p. 109. See also Guiseppi v. Walling, 144 F.2d 608, 624 (2d Cir. 1944)(Hand, J., concurring)("There is no surer way to misread any document than to read it literally"); Peter Pan Fabrics, Inc. v. Martin Weiner Corp., 274 F.2d 487, 489 (2d Cir.1960)(rejecting "relentless literalism").

45. Rendering, pp. 106–07.

46. Learned Hand, The Contribution of an Independent Judiciary to Civilization (1942), Dilliard, p. 157.

47. Rendering, p. 106. Learned Hand made a similar statement in his judicial opinions: "As nearly as we can, we must put ourselves in the place of those who uttered the words, and try to divine how they would have dealt with the unforeseen situation; and, although their words are by far the most decisive evidence of what they would have done, they are by no means final." Guiseppi v. Walling, 144 F.2d 608, 624 (2d Cir.1944) (Hand, J., concurring).

purposive interpretation. This may not have bothered Radin, but it bothered Hand.

3.04 LEGAL PROCESS

The most influential attempt to resolve the tension between creative and deferential statutory interpretation is the Hart & Sacks Legal Process materials, which appeared in unpublished form in 1958 and has recently been published by Foundation Press.[48]

The Legal Process judge has an "ought" role in determining statutory meaning, as many Legal Realists had urged:—"The function of a court in interpreting a statute is to decide what meaning ought to be given to the directions of the statute in the respects relevant to the case before it * * *."[49] And:[50]

> In interpreting a statute a court should:
>
> 1. Decide what purpose ought to be attributed to the statute * * *;
>
> 2. Interpret the words * * * to carry out the purpose as best it can. * * *

Moreover, "[i]n determining the more immediate purpose which ought to be attributed to a statute * * * a court should try to put itself in imagination in the position of the legislature which enacted the measure," and "should not do this in a mood of cynical political observer, taking account of all the short-run currents of political expedience that swirl around any legislative session."[51]

The "oughtness" of the judge's role in the Legal Process formulation suggests a judge with considerable lawmaking discretion. But there are strong contrary indications, reminiscent of Hand's more cautionary comments.[52]

> In trying to discharge this function the court should:
>
> 1. Respect the position of the legislature as the chief policy-determining agency of the society * * *;
>
> 4. Be mindful of the nature of language and, in particular, of its special nature when used as a medium for giving authoritative general directions; * * *

---

48. Henry M. Hart, Jr. & Albert M. Sacks, The Legal Process (eds. William N. Eskridge, Jr. & Philip Frickey 1994)(hereafter "Hart & Sacks"). All citations are to the published version.

49. Hart & Sacks, p. 1374.

50. Hart & Sacks, p. 1374.

51. Hart & Sacks, p. 1378.

52. Hart & Sacks, p. 1374.

And, in deciding what meaning ought to be attributed, the judge must "mak[e] sure [ ] that it does not give the words [ ] a meaning they will not bear * * *."[53]

The fundamental question about the Legal Process approach was what to make of the most famous Legal Process injunction of all: "[The court] should assume, unless the contrary unmistakably appears, that the legislature was made up of reasonable persons pursuing reasonable purposes reasonably."[54] Was the judge supposed to hold the legislature to an external standard of reasonableness, by interpreting the statute in light of that presumption? Or was the judge supposed to be confident that the legislature acted reasonably and not do too much judging?

The broader Legal Process message favors the more restrained version of the judicial role. Judicial restraint derives from the Legal Process view of the respective competence of legislature and judge. In a section entitled "The Process of Reasoned Elaboration of Purportedly Determinate Decisions,"[55] Hart & Sacks first urge the judge to "make as sure as he can that the claimed uncertainty is a real one which he actually has the power to resolve. Respect for the principle of institutional settlement demands this. What a legislature has determined ought not to be set at naught by any other agency or person."[56] Judicial caution is justified by what Eskridge and Frickey refer to as the "centrality of process" in the Legal Process approach,[57] based on the following statement by Hart & Sacks—"[D]ecisions which are the duly arrived at result of duly established procedures [ ] ought to be accepted as binding upon the whole society * * *."[58]

The innate caution of the Hart & Sacks approach is apparent in their flight from the word "discretion":[59]

> * * * [T]here may be thought to be a justification for describing the act of interpretation as one of discretion. * * * But this would be to obscure what seems to be the vital point—namely, the effort, and the importance of the effort, of each individual deciding officer to reach what *he* thinks is *the* right answer (emphasis in original).

Underlying this tilt towards judicial restraint is an optimistic image of the legislative process, in which well-represented groups work out their differences in the public interest. That is, legislatures functioned like the progressive New Deal legislature was supposed to function. Along with faith in the legislature went a reluctance to give the judge too much to do, deferring instead to other more competent decisionmakers. Interpretation requires "an appreciation [ ] of the official's own function. There may be a

---

53. Hart & Sacks, p. 1374.

54. Hart & Sacks, p. 1378.

55. Hart & Sacks, pp. 145–50.

56. Hart & Sacks, pp. 146–47.

57. Introduction to Hart & Sacks, pp. xciv.

58. Hart & Sacks, p. 4.

59. Hart & Sacks, pp. 149–50. Recall that even Hamilton had spoken of "judicial discretion" in Federalist # 78.

difference in this respect, for example, between a court and an administrative agency."[60]

It may be something of an exaggeration to call the Legal Process approach a "procedure-based positivism," as Eskridge and Frickey do.[61] "Reasoned elaboration" of purpose *did* give the judge a lot to do and there is no denying the tensions in the Legal Process formulation regarding just how much discretion the judge had (whether or not Hart & Sacks liked the word). But as long as there was optimism about legislation, the broader goals of a democratic legal system and reasoned elaboration by judges of legislative purpose converged to a common end. The contemporary wilting scrutiny of the legislative process (explored in the next chapter) has, however, exposed what Eskridge describes as the "failure of legal process to develop a robust normative theory of democratic legitimacy," which he views as "a striking deficiency in its usefulness in thinking about law, a thinking that becomes glaring in light of the willingness of legal process theory to turn over so many policy decisions to unelected judges."[62]

————

By now it should be apparent that statutory interpretation depends on an image of both judging and legislating. When the common law was dominant, courts developed various approaches which allowed them to shape statutory meaning based on the assumption that legislatures did not always get things right and needed help making law. The rise of legislation and the exposure of judicial lawmaking choices forced courts to be less arrogant regarding statutes and their own lawmaking potential, and this eventually evolved into purposive interpretation. But what if courts lose faith in *both* judging and legislating? That is most likely where we are today and we are now struggling with the implications of that decline in confidence for statutory interpretation? It is difficult to revive a robust pre–20th Century sense of judicial lawmaking (and we probably would not want to), but what is a court to do when the optimism about legislation which supported purposivism and which persisted during the first six decades of the 20th Century has evaporated? An exploration of these issues would bring us to the contemporary debates about statutory interpretation, to which we turn in Chapter 4.

3.05   INTERACTION OF PURPOSE AND SUBSTANTIVE CANONS

Before looking at contemporary history, however, we should consider how contemporary courts work out the relationship between statutory pur-

---

60. Hart & Sacks, p. 147.

61. Introduction to Hart & Sacks, p. xcvi.

62. William Eskridge Jr., Dynamic Statutory Interpretation 161 (1994) (hereafter "Eskridge, Dynamic").

pose and substantive background considerations, some of which courts have relied on in the past to limit statutes, often in a spirit of hostility towards legislation. We look at two substantive canons of interpretation mentioned by Pound—the rule of lenity and the narrow interpretation of statutes in derogation of common law. This will provide us with an understanding of how courts *actually* interpret statutes and with an insight into how the interaction of purposivism and substantive canons requires judicial lawmaking discretion. It will turn out that this interaction calls for a more subtle appreciation of the complexities of statutory interpretation than are captured by either the hostility towards legislation embodied in some 19th Century applications of the derogation canon or the equal and opposite reaction by Pound's early 20th Century critique of that canon.

Pound's antagonism towards the "derogation" canon might have meant rejection of judicial reliance on all substantive values external to the interpreted statute. But that would be too extreme a position for courts to sustain. After all, purposivism also requires the judge to be more than the passive oracle of legislative will; as Radin observed, the judge has a creative role to play in working out values implicit in the legislative purpose. And, if that is true, perhaps the judge can also take account of other substantive values, even those inherent in substantive canons, such as the "derogation" canon; recall that Pound, without explanation, had spoken favorably of the rule of lenity

We look in this section at the interaction of legislative purpose with the values underlying two substantive canons of interpretation—(1) the rule of lenity, which tilts interpretation of criminal statutes in favor of the accused; and (2) the narrow interpretation of statutes in derogation of the common law. The material carries these two lessons—(1) the weight of the canons varies with the statutory context; and (2) their weight is not fixed but evolves over time.

Interpretive presumptions. To help you evaluate how substantive values interact with statutes, here is a three-part typology—the values can operate as strong, weak, or in-between presumptions.

A *weak* presumption operates as a tie-breaker when the evidence of statutory meaning is otherwise in equipoise (a "burden of proof" standard favoring specific values).

A *strong* presumption insists on powerful evidence that the statute overrides certain substantive values, such as a plain or clear statement in the statutory text. General nonspecific statutory texts and legislative history are not enough to override a strong presumption (a "beyond reasonable doubt" standard).

Finally, an *in-between* presumption inserts values as a significant factor in the interpretive mix of text, purpose, and substantive background considerations which determine a statute's meaning (analogous to an intermediate "clear and convincing" burden of proof). I do not pretend that it is easy in individual cases to fit the decision into such neat categories. It may be hard to distinguish between using substantive values as a tie-breaker and, more aggressively, as a stronger presumption in the interpretive mix. It may also be difficult to know when the text "plainly" overrides the values embodied in a substantive canon. But something like this approach seems essential to understand what courts are doing.

a) RULE OF LENITY

There is a long tradition of construing penal statutes to favor the criminal accused, often referred to as the "rule of lenity." Even Pound, who objected strongly to narrow interpretation of statutes in derogation of the common law, favored this canon because it protected against deprivation of political liberty. The following case selection emphasizes statutes involving possession or use of guns. Does the court use the rule of lenity as a strong, weak, or in-between presumption? Is there anything about the behavior regulated by the statute that helps to explain the strength of the presumption in the particular case?

(1) *Scarborough v. United States*, 431 U.S. 563 (1977). In Scarborough, the petitioner was convicted of possessing a firearm in violation of Title VII of the Omnibus Crime Control and Safe Streets Act of 1968 (Omnibus Crime Control Act), 18 U.S.C.A. App. §§ 1201–1203. The statute provided:

> Any person who—"(1) has been convicted * * * of a felony
> * * *
>
> "and who receives, possesses, or transports in commerce or affecting commerce * * * any firearm shall be fined not more than $10,000 or imprisoned for not more than two years, or both." 18 U.S.C. App. § 1202(a).

The issue was whether the statutorily required nexus between the possession of a firearm by a convicted felon and interstate commerce could be satisfied by proof that the possession of the firearm which traveled in interstate commerce occurred *prior* to the felony conviction. The Government's position was that a nexus was established if the firearm possessed by the convicted felon traveled at some time in interstate commerce, whether prior to or after the felony conviction. The defendant first contended that the nexus with interstate commerce must be "contemporaneous" with the possession of the firearm. "Contemporaneous" meant that at the time of the felony the possessor must be engaging in commerce or must be carrying the gun at an interstate facility. The defendant then conceded, however, that conviction for possession would be allowed without any proof of a contemporary connection with commerce so long as the firearm which had traveled in interstate commerce was acquired *after* the felony conviction.

The Court admitted that the statute was not "a model of clarity," but nonetheless held that the statute applied to the defendant. The defendant argued that Congress knew how to "specify an offense based on firearms that had previously traveled in commerce" when it wanted to, citing another statute which "prohibited a convicted felon from receiving a firearm 'which has been shipped or transported in interstate or foreign commerce.'" The Court rejected this argument on the ground that the other statute was carefully drafted, but this statute "was a last-minute amendment to the Omnibus Crime Control Act enacted hastily" without reference to a legislative committee and with little discussion. The Court stated that "Congress' choice of language was ambiguous at best." In other words, the statute's ambiguity was the product of carelessness in the legislative process.

The Court explained at length how legislative intent was at least clear, even if the language was not. It relied on legislative history in comments made on the floor of the Senate by Senator Long when he introduced the statutory provision.

> The legislative history in its entirety, while brief, further supports the view that Congress sought to rule broadly—to keep guns out of the hands of those who have demonstrated that "they may not be trusted to possess a firearm without becoming a threat to society." [114 Cong. Rec. 14773 (1968)]. There is simply no indication of any concern with either the movement of the gun or the possessor or with the time of acquisition.

The Court adds that the defendant's theory would "create serious loopholes in the congressional plan to 'make it unlawful for a firearm * * * to be in the possession of a convicted felon,'" because a person who obtained a firearm prior to his conviction could retain it forever so long as he was not caught with it in an interstate facility.

Concerning the rule of lenity, the Court made the following statement about how much doubt the judge must have before indulging a substantive presumption about the statute's meaning.

> Finally, petitioner seeks to invoke the [principle of lenity]. * * * Petitioner, however, overlooks the fact that we did not turn to these guides [in an earlier case] until we had concluded that "[a]fter 'seizing every thing from which aid can be derived,' * * * we are left with an ambiguous statute." The [rule is] applicable only when we are uncertain about the statute's meaning. * * * Here, the intent of Congress is clear. We do not face the conflicting pull between the text and the history that confronted us in [another case]. In this case, the history is unambiguous and the text consistent with it. Congress sought to reach possessions broadly, with little concern for when the nexus with commerce occurred.

The dissent, however, concluded that the Court's result was "inconsistent with the time-honored rule of lenity in construing federal criminal statutes."

> [W]e are under no mandate to construe this statute so that a person in lawful possession of a firearm, and presumed to be innocent of a felony until proved guilty, must upon his conviction of a felony also be automatically and instantly guilty of a wholly different serious criminal offense. The statute could equally be read to apply only when a person first comes into possession of a firearm after his felony conviction. [Therefore,] "it is appropriate, before we choose the harsher alternative, to require that Congress should have spo-

ken in language that is clear and definite. We should not derive criminal outlawry from some ambiguous implication."

Relying on legislative history. In Scarborough the Court looks behind the text to legislative history to resolve ambiguity. In United States v. R. L. C., 503 U.S. 291 (1992), Justice Scalia wrote that "it is not consistent with the rule of lenity to construe a textually ambiguous penal statute against a criminal defendant on the basis of legislative history." He acknowledged that courts had looked at legislative history in the past but could identify only one case in which the legislative history was used to reject the more lenient reading of the text.

(2) *Smith v. United States*, 508 U.S. 223 (1993). In Smith, a federal statute mandated sentence enhancement for someone who "during and in relation to any crime of violence or drug trafficking crime * * * uses * * * a firearm." The issue was whether the statute applied when the defendant bartered a firearm for cocaine. The Court cited both Webster's and Black's Dictionaries to support its view that "use" had an ordinary meaning which includes bartering. The dissent (Justices Scalia, Stevens and Souter) argued that the statutory phrase was "use a firearm" and that this ordinarily implied use as a weapon. The Court also stated (as it had in Scarborough) that the rule of lenity only applied "[a]fter 'seiz[ing] every thing from which aid can be derived.' "[63] The dissent responded:

> Even if the reader does not consider the [meaning] as clear as I do, he must at least acknowledge, I think, that it is eminently debatable—and that is enough, under the rule of lenity, to require finding for the petitioner here.

The dissent also objected to the majority's use of statutory purpose to shed light on statutory meaning. The majority had described the congressional purpose this way:

> * * * When Congress enacted the current version of § 924(c)(1), it was no doubt aware that drugs and guns are a dangerous combination. In 1989, 56 percent of all murders in New York City were drug related; during the same period, the figure for the Nation's Capital was as high as 80 percent. The fact that a gun is treated momentarily as an item of commerce does not render it inert or deprive it of destructive capacity. Rather, as experience demonstrates, it can be converted instantaneously from currency to cannon. We therefore see no reason why Congress would have intended courts and juries applying § 924(c)(1) to draw a fine metaphysical distinction between a gun's role in a drug offense as a

---

63. In Bailey v. United States, 116 S.Ct. 501 (1995) a unanimous Court refused to extend Smith to a case where the gun was locked in the trunk of a car in a bag. It adopted an "active employment" test, rejecting application of the statute to a case in which the gun was merely possessed, even though the gun was concealed nearby "at the ready." For a linguistic perspective on the statutory text ("use a firearm"), see Clark Cunningham & Charles Fillmore, Using Common Sense: A Linguistic Perspective on Judicial Interpretations of "Use a Firearm," 73 Wash.U.L.Quart. 1159 (1995)(discussing Smith and Bailey cases).

weapon and its role as an item of barter; it creates a grave possibility of violence and death in either capacity.

The dissent responded:

> The Court contends that giving the language its ordinary meaning would frustrate the purpose of the statute, since a gun "can be converted instantaneously from currency to cannon." Stretching language in order to write a more effective statute than Congress devised is not an exercise we should indulge in.

(3) *United States v. Thompson/Center Arms Co.*, 504 U.S. 505 (1992). The rule of lenity was unavailing in *Scarborough* and *Smith*, but was favorably invoked in the Thompson case. The statute taxed anyone "making" a "firearm." The question was whether a gun manufacturer "makes" a firearm when it packages a mail-order kit which can be used to make both a firearm and another weapon, which did not fit the technical statutory definition of "firearm." A majority of the Court applied the rule of lenity, with a plurality explicitly noting that violation of the statute attracted not only a tax but also a criminal sanction (without proof of willfulness). Does the fact that the defendant here was the gun manufacturer—not the gun user—help explain why the values embodied in the rule of lenity carried more weight in this case?

Dual civil/criminal penalties. The *Thompson* case poses a special problem that must be confronted with many modern criminal statutes—the fact that the same behavior may be subject to both criminal and civil sanctions. If the rule of lenity applies because of the potential for criminal sanctions, the application of the civil penalty may also be narrowed. There are a number of ways a court might deal with this problem, besides treating the entire statute as a criminal statute and applying the rule of lenity. First, Justice Stevens' dissent in *Thompson* emphasized that imposition of a criminal sanction was in fact a remote possibility (the government made this a test case to interpret the statute and agreed to impose only a tax), and that the statute had important regulatory goals, but the Court was not impressed with this argument.

Second, it might be possible to interpret the statute differently depending on whether civil or criminal penalties are imposed. In United States v. United States Gypsum Co., 438 U.S. 422 (1978), the Court interpreted the Sherman Act to require proof of intent as an element of a criminal antitrust violation, applying the rule of lenity. No intent requirement, however, was read into the civil liability portion of the statute.

Third, Justice Jackson came up with yet another suggestion in S.E.C. v. C.M. Joiner Leasing Corp., 320 U.S. 344 (1943), to deal with dual criminal/civil penalty statutes. The issue in the case was whether the Securities and Exchange Commission could enjoin certain trading activities under the Securities Act of 1933 based on fraud. The defendant sold assignments of oil leases and the question was whether these items were "securities" covered by the Act. Although the case involved an injunction, behavior which could be enjoined was also criminal.

Jackson noted that "[i]t would be necessary in any case for any kind of relief to prove that documents being sold were securities under the Act. In some cases it might be done by proving the document itself, which on its face would be a note, a bond, or a share of stock. In others proof must go outside the instrument itself as we do here. Where this proof is offered in a civil action, as here, a preponderance of the evidence will establish the case; if it were offered in a criminal case, it would have to meet the stricter require-ment of satisfying the jury beyond reasonable doubt." Is Jackson correct that the statutory definition of the regulated behavior could be left to the jury, with different burdens of proof in civil and criminal cases? Isn't the definition of a "security" an issue of law for the judge, not the jury?

(4) *Staples v. United States; Mens rea*. In the following case, the Court interpreted the statute to require *mens rea*—knowledge that the gun he possessed was in fact a "machinegun" and therefore illegally possessed. But the Court argues that this favorable pro-defendant interpretation was *not* an application of the rule of lenity. Is it accurate to say that reading the *mens rea* requirement into the statute is not an application of the rule of lenity?

Why might the Court deny that it is applying the rule of lenity in reading a *mens rea* requirement into the statute? Does that avoid confront-ing the fact that the rule of lenity has lost some of its historic force, which would tilt *away* from requiring mens rea? Does it avoid confronting the element of discretion involved in working out the interaction of statutory purpose and the lenity canon?

Staples v. United States

511 U.S. 600 (1994).

■ JUSTICE THOMAS delivered the opinion of the Court. * * *

The National Firearms Act makes it unlawful for any person to possess a machinegun that is not properly registered with the Federal Government. Petitioner contends that, to convict him under the Act, the Government should have been required to prove beyond a reasonable doubt that he knew the weapon he possessed had the characteristics that brought it within the statutory definition of a machinegun. We agree * * *.

[Editor—A machinegun is a gun which can fire automatically more than one shot without manual reloading. The defendant owned a gun which had been modified to be capable of automatic fire but the defendant denied knowledge of this capability.]

Whether or not [the statute] requires proof that a defendant knew of the characteristics of his weapon that made it a "firearm" under the Act is a question of statutory construction. * * * Thus, we have long recognized that determining the mental state required for commission of a federal crime requires "construction of the statute and * * * inference of the intent of Congress." * * *

The language of the statute, the starting place in our inquiry, provides little explicit guidance in this case. [It] is silent concerning the mens rea required for a violation. It states simply that "it shall be unlawful for any person * * * to receive or possess a firearm which is not registered to him in the National Firearms Registration and Transfer Record." Nevertheless, silence on this point by itself does not necessarily suggest that Congress intended to dispense with a conventional mens rea element, which would require that the defendant know the facts that make his conduct illegal. On the contrary, we must construe the statute in light of the background rules of the common law, in which the requirement of some mens rea for a crime is firmly embedded. As we have observed, "the existence of a mens rea is the rule of, rather than the exception to, the principles of Anglo–American criminal jurisprudence." * * *

According to the Government, however, the nature and purpose of the National Firearms Act suggest that the presumption favoring mens rea does not apply to this case. The Government argues that Congress intended the Act to regulate and restrict the circulation of dangerous weapons. Consequently, in the Government's view, this case fits in a line of precedent concerning what we have termed "public welfare" or "regulatory" offenses, in which we have understood Congress to impose a form of strict criminal liability through statutes that do not require the defendant to know the facts that make his conduct illegal. In construing such statutes, we have inferred from silence that Congress did not intend to require proof of mens rea to establish an offense. * * *

Such public welfare offenses have been created by Congress, and recognized by this Court, in "limited circumstances." Typically, our cases recognizing such offenses involve statutes that regulate potentially harmful or injurious items. In such situations, we have reasoned that as long as a defendant knows that he is dealing with a dangerous device of a character that places him "in responsible relation to a public danger," he should be alerted to the probability of strict regulation, and we have assumed that in such cases Congress intended to place the burden on the defendant to "ascertain at his peril whether [his conduct] comes within the inhibition of the statute." Thus, we essentially have relied on the nature of the statute and the particular character of the items regulated to determine whether congressional silence concerning the mental element of the offense should be interpreted as dispensing with conventional mens rea requirements. * * *

The Government argues that * * * all guns, whether or not they are statutory "firearms," are dangerous devices that put gun owners on notice that they must determine at their hazard whether their weapons come within the scope of the Act. * * *

The Government seeks support for its position from our decision in United States v. Freed, 401 U.S. 601 (1971), which involved a prosecution for possession of unregistered grenades * * *. The defendant knew that the items in his possession were grenades, and we concluded that [the statute] did not require the Government to prove the defendant also knew that the grenades were unregistered. To be sure, in deciding that mens rea was not required with respect to that element of the offense, we suggested that the Act "is a regulatory measure in the interest of the public safety, which may well be premised on the theory that one would hardly be surprised to learn that possession of hand grenades is not an innocent act." Grenades, we explained, "are highly dangerous offensive weapons * * *." But that reasoning provides little support for dispensing with mens rea in this case. * * *

[Editor—The Court goes on to distinguish grenades from guns, as follows.]

Neither [ ] can all guns be compared to hand grenades. * * * [T]he fact remains that there is a long tradition of widespread lawful gun ownership by private individuals in this country. Such a tradition did not apply to the possession of hand grenades in Freed * * *. Here, the Government essentially suggests that we should interpret the section under the [ ] assumption that "one would hardly be surprised to learn that owning a gun is not an innocent act." That proposition is simply not supported by common experience. Guns in general are not "deleterious devices or products or obnoxious waste materials," that put their owners on notice that they stand "in responsible relation to a public danger."

The Government protests that guns, * * * like grenades [ ], are potentially harmful devices. * * * But that an item is "dangerous," in some general sense, does not necessarily suggest, * * * that it is not also entirely innocent. Even dangerous items can, in some cases, be so commonplace and generally available that we would not consider them to alert individuals to the likelihood of strict regulation. As suggested above, despite their potential for harm, guns generally can be owned in perfect innocence. Of course, we might surely classify certain categories of guns—no doubt including the machineguns, sawed-off shotguns, and artillery pieces that Congress has subjected to regulation—as items the ownership of which would have the same quasi-suspect character we attributed to owning hand grenades in Freed. But precisely because guns falling outside those categories traditionally have been widely accepted as lawful possessions, their destructive potential, while perhaps even greater than that of some items we would classify along with narcotics and hand grenades, cannot be said to put gun owners sufficiently on notice of the likelihood of regulation to justify interpreting [the statute] as not requiring proof of knowledge of a weapon's characteristics.

In note 17 to its opinion, the Court stated:

In reaching our conclusion, we find it unnecessary to rely on the rule of lenity, under which an ambiguous criminal statute is to be construed in favor of the accused. That maxim of construction "is reserved for cases where, 'after' 'seizing every thing from which aid can be derived,' the Court is 'left with an ambiguous statute.' " Here, the background rule of the common law favoring mens rea and the substantial body of precedent we have developed construing statutes that do not specify a mental element provide considerable interpretive tools from which we can "seize aid," and they do not leave us with the ultimate impression that [the statute] is "grievously" ambiguous. Certainly, we have not concluded in the past that statutes silent with respect to mens rea are ambiguous.

Has the rule of lenity lost some of its bite? If it has, why might that be so? Has the nature of crimes changed; has the judicial attitude towards protecting the accused and protecting society changed?

Might the courts be taking clues from legislative action? For example, the RICO statute (the Racketeer Influenced and Corrupt Organizations Act) contains a statement that "the provisions of this title shall be liberally construed to effectuate its remedial purposes." Pub. L. 91–452, § 904(a). And, sometimes, Congress amends a statute to explicitly reject the Court's "lenient" reading of a statutory text. See Pub. L. 100–690, § 7603, 102 Stat. 4181, 4508 (1988), overriding McNally v. United States, 483 U.S. 350 (1987)(mail fraud statute not given "harsher" reading; so the statute did not apply to kickbacks to government officials); P.L. 103–325 103rd Cong., 2d sess. (1994), amending 31 U.S.C.A. § 5324, overriding Ratzlaf v. United States, 510 U.S. 135 (1994)(breaking up transaction to avoid reporting requirements applicable to transactions over $10,000 is not criminal unless the individual knows that his conduct is illegal; it is insufficient that the individual knows his action evades the bank's obligations).[64]

Does United States v. X–Citement Video[65] suggest a general reinvigoration of the rule of lenity? The statute prohibited "knowingly" transporting, shipping, receiving, distributing, or reproducing a visual depiction, 18 U.S.C.A. §§ 2252(a)(1) and (2), if such depiction "involves the use of a minor engaging in sexually explicit conduct," §§ 2252(a)(1)(A) and (2)(A). The Court held that "knowingly" applied to both transporting, etc. *and* the fact that the conduct involved a minor, invoking the rule of lenity (citing Staples!). The Court conceded that this result violated the "most natural grammatical reading."

---

64. The Congressional Record for August 2, 1994 (140 Cong Rec H 6642) contains Representative Gonzalez' explanation that the amendment overriding Ratzlaf "restores [ ] clear Congressional intent."

65. 513 U.S. 64 (1994).

b) STATUTES IN DEROGATION OF THE COMMON LAW

Many statutes alter the substantive results that would be reached under the common law. The statutes are, in other words, "in derogation of the common law." In many of the older cases, a narrow interpretation of a statute to preserve specific common law rules protected those private interests which benefited from the 19th Century evolution of the common law, often property owners, sellers, and employers.[66] The willingness to adopt a narrow interpretation was reinforced by the view of statutes as unwelcome public intrusions into private activity, which was the subject of the common law. This attitude produced a reaction among commentators like Pound that denigrated any reference to the doctrine as a throwback to an earlier time when statutes were suspect and courts were biased against statutes which altered the political framework implicit in the common law.

In this section, we want to understand and critique the narrow interpretation of statutes in derogation of common law. You should be alert to the fact that not all invocations of the canon reflect hostility towards legislation. Here are some examples:

(1) We earlier noted instances in which the statute created remedies which did not preclude continued reliance on common law remedies. That will often (though not always) make a lot of sense, and invoking the derogation canon only prevents extending the statutory specifics to negative survival of the common law.

(2) As noted below, some statutes appear to incorporate common law concepts, in which case the survival of the common law and reliance on the derogation canon for this purpose is innocent enough.

(3) Sometimes it really does make sense to be cautious about interpreting a statute to override the prior common law. Is there a legitimate way to state the criteria for being cautious without suggesting that changes in the common law are necessarily suspect? After all, you may recall from the discussion in Chapter 2.04e of the 19th Commentators that implied repeal of any law—whether statutory or common law—was doubtful. See whether the following framework is useful for explaining the cases:

> Consider the common law that would be displaced;
>
> Determine how much of a departure from prior law the statute would achieve, how clear the statute is, and how strong the statutory and common law policies are;
>
> The greater the departure, the less clear the statute, the weaker the statutory policy, and the stronger the common law policy, the less likely it is that the statute alters the common law.

66. Page, Statutes in Derogation of Common Law: The Canon as an Analytical Tool, 1956 Wis. L. Rev. 78, 107.

i) WORKERS COMPENSATION

Workers Compensation statutes displaced the common law by creating tort liability without fault. A famous early case noted that the "statute, judged by our common-law standards, is plainly revolutionary." Ives v. South Buffalo Ry. Co., 94 N.E. 431, 436 (N.Y.1911). It then struck down the statute for violating constitutional due process requirements. The court would have permitted abolition of the contributory negligence, assumption of risk, and fellow servant defenses, which existed at common law, but liability without fault was too much for the court to swallow.

Finding a statute in derogation of the common law unconstitutional is a more dramatic step than interpreting it to avoid displacing the common law. The more usual reaction by judges hostile to Workers Compensation was to interpret the legislation to preserve the common law. There were plenty of opportunities. Workers Compensation statutes made the employer liable for "injury by accident" if the accident "arose out of and in the course of employment." Both phrases gave the court an opportunity to limit coverage.

For example, in Carter v. International Detrola Corp., 43 N.W.2d 890, 891 (Mich.1950), the court stated that an "injury by accident" within the meaning of the statute, required "causes and conditions which are characteristic of and peculiar to the business of the employer"—the "peculiar risk" doctrine. Catching pneumonia from a fellow worker with a cold, for example, would not normally be covered. However, if the disease was transmitted because one phone operator coughed into the mouthpiece later used by the next phone operator, it was covered because that was "peculiar" to the job.

Similarly, some courts held that an accident did not "arise out of and in the course of employment" unless its cause was an "added peril" created by the job, not a cause common to everyday life. An accident to a pedestrian-worker who was doing nothing unusual while delivering a parcel might thereby be excluded from coverage. See, e.g., New Amsterdam Casualty Co. v. Hoage, 62 F.2d 468 (D.C.Cir.1932)(greater weight of modern opinion rejects earlier view that hazards common to the community at large are not covered).

The impetus for these decisions confining employer liability was the court's reluctance to hold the employer liable when the employer was unable to do much to prevent the disability. After all, diseases are contracted in many ways and the employer can not do much to prevent normal accidents. Some but not all of the cases taking a restrictive view of coverage specifically invoked the "derogation of common law" doctrine,[67] but they were all probably influenced by attitudes favoring preservation of the common law.

Was preserving the common law proper in these cases? The common law required fault as a condition of liability and there is no doubt that the Workers Compensation statutes abolished the fault requirement. Fault is a species of responsibility, however, and it was by no means clear that the new

---

67. See, e.g., Sutter v. Kalamazoo Stove & Furnace Co., 297 N.W. 475, 477 (Mich. 1941); Wagner v. La Salle Foundry Co., 75 N.W.2d 866, 871–72 (Mich.1956).

statutes entirely abolished all standards based on employer responsibility. Narrowly interpreting the definition of an injury by accident and the work connection requirement was a way of preserving some standard of employer responsibility for the worker's safety, even if fault was no longer required. If the employer could do very little to prevent the disability, perhaps the Workers Compensation statute should not apply because the employer could not be held responsible.

Invocation of the employer responsibility principle was not simply judicial devotion to the past embodied in the common law. Surely the text— "injury by accident" and "arise out of and in the course of employment"—is not so clear. Moreover, the adoption of Workers Compensation statutes had been preceded by widespread publicity about Germany's experience with similar legislation in encouraging employers to adopt safety measures. In addition to expanding employee compensation, Workers Compensation was intended to give employers the incentive to provide safety. Invoking the common law to limit statutory change was a way of testing how to balance the statutory policies of accident prevention and employee compensation.

As time passed, courts expanded statutory coverage. The "peculiar risk" and "added peril" requirements have pretty much faded from the scene. And some modern cases can be only explained on the theory that these requirements are a dead letter. See, e.g. City of New Castle v. Workmen's Compensation Appeals Board, 546 A.2d 132 (Pa.Cmwlth.1988)(employee was covered by Workers Compensation when he contracted rare disease by kissing fellow female employee on the cheek prior to her taking maternity leave). Nonetheless, even though employer responsibility is of diminished importance, the interpretive question remains whether courts were acting improperly in the early days of Workers Compensation statutes by narrowly interpreting statutory coverage.

ii) UNIFORM COMMERCIAL CODE

The question of interpreting statutes in derogation of the common law has also arisen in cases involving the Uniform Commercial Code. The court in the following case adopted an approach which has been severely criticized and rarely followed,[68] but it gives you a sense of what a court determined to preserve the common law in the face of a statute might do.

What evidence is there that the court is engaged in spurious interpretation—disregarding the statutory text to preserve the common law?

Roto–Lith Ltd. v. F.P. Bartlett Co.

297 F.2d 497 (1st Cir.1962).

■ KNOCH, CIRCUIT JUDGE: * * *

[Editor—Plaintiff bought emulsion for use as a cellophane adhesive from the defendant, but it failed to adhere. The plaintiff had

---

68. See C. Itoh Co. (America) Inc. v. Jordan International Co., 552 F.2d 1228 (7th Cir.1977).

sent its order to the defendant and the defendant had responded with its forms, consisting of an acknowledgement and invoice, identical in all important respects to the plaintiff's offer, except that it stated that there would be no warranties and that, if the seller's terms were "not acceptable, a buyer must so notify the seller at once." The plaintiff did not notify the seller. The first question was whether there was a contract based on the writings exchanged between the parties. The second question was whether, if the writings did not create a contract, there was nonetheless a contract based on the parties' conduct and, if so, whether the warranties were excluded from the conduct-created contract. The court dealt as follows with section 2–207 of the Uniform Commercial Code.]

* * * Section 2–207 provides:

"(1) A definite and seasonable expression of acceptance or a written confirmation which is sent within a reasonable time operates as an acceptance even though it states terms additional to or different from those offered or agreed upon, unless acceptance is expressly made conditional on assent to the additional or different terms."

"(2) The additional terms are to be construed as proposals for addition to the contract. Between merchants such terms become part of the contract unless:

"(a) the offer expressly limits acceptance to the terms of the offer;

"(b) they materially alter it; or

"(c) notification of objection to them has already been given or is given within a reasonable time after notice of them is received."

Plaintiff exaggerates the freedom which this section affords an offeror to ignore a reply from an offeree that does not in terms coincide with the original offer. According to plaintiff defendant's condition that there should be no warranties constituted a proposal which "materially altered" the agreement. As to this we concur. Plaintiff goes on to say that by virtue of the statute the acknowledgment [by defendant-offeree] effected a completed agreement without this condition, and that as a further proposal the condition never became part of the agreement because plaintiff did not express assent. We agree that section 2–207 changed the existing law, but not to this extent. Its purpose was to modify the strict principle that a response not precisely in accordance with the offer was a rejection and a counteroffer. Now, within stated limits, a response that does not in all respects correspond with the offer constitutes an acceptance of the offer, and a counteroffer only as to the differences. If plaintiff's contention is correct that a reply to an offer stating additional conditions unilaterally burdensome upon the offeror is a binding acceptance of the original offer plus simply a proposal for the additional conditions, the statute would lead to an absurdity. Obviously no offeror will subsequently assent to such conditions.

The statute is not too happily drafted. Perhaps it would be wiser in all cases for an offeree to say in so many words, "I will not accept your offer until you assent to the following: * * *" But businessmen cannot be expected to act by rubric. It would be unrealistic to suppose that when an offeree replies setting out conditions that would be burdensome only to the offeror he intended to make an unconditional acceptance of the original offer, leaving it simply to the offeror's good nature whether he would assume the additional restrictions. To give the statute a practical construction we must hold that a response which states a condition materially altering the obligation solely to the disadvantage of the offeror is an "acceptance * * * expressly * * * conditional on assent to the additional * * * terms." [Editor—Why *must* the court hold that way? Is there any language in the UCC dealing with "material alteration" of an offer, which suggests that such alteration does *not* prevent creation of a contract based on the exchange of writings between the parties?]

Plaintiff accepted the goods with knowledge of the conditions specified in the acknowledgment. It became bound [by the counter-offer].

[Editor—This last sentence is a statement that, although the writings did not create a contract, performance did; and that performance by accepting the goods constituted acceptance of the counter-offer. This is the common law rule and that is all the court said about this issue. In fact, the UCC had a specific provision on contract formation when Section 2–207(1) did not produce a contract. Section 2–207(3) of the Code provides that "[c]onduct by both parties which recognizes the existence of a contract is sufficient to establish a contract for sale although the writings of the parties do not otherwise establish a contract." The second sentence of Section 2–207(3) provides that where a contract has been consummated by the conduct of the parties, "the terms of the particular contract consist of those terms on which the writings of the parties agree, together with any supplementary terms incorporated under any other provisions of this Act." The UCC overturned the common law, which had created a contract in accordance with the counter-offeror's terms when the original offeror performed under the contract.]

iii) STATUTES BASED ON THE COMMON LAW

The prior cases dealt with statutes which appeared to reject the common law. There is one situation in which survival of the common law after passage of a statute is unproblematic, indicating no hostility to statutes. When the statute itself is based on the common law, its incorporation into the statute makes sense. For example, in Norfolk R. & H. Authority v. Chesapeake & Potomac Tel., 464 U.S. 30 (1983), a utility sought compensation for being forced to relocate its telephone transmission lines. A statute based on the common law of eminent domain provided that any person "displaced" from his home or business was entitled to compensation. At common law, however, utilities were not entitled to compensation for relocating telephone lines from a public right-of-way. The Court held that the statute incorporated the common law coverage limitations.

The Court also interpreted an anti-trust statute in the light of its common law underpinnings in Associated General Contractors v. California State Council of Carpenters, 459 U.S. 519, 529 (1983). Broad language allowing recovery by "any person who shall be injured * * * by anything forbidden in the antitrust laws" was interpreted to exclude union plaintiffs who would have been excluded under traditional common law doctrine. And in NLRB v. Amax Coal Co., 453 U.S. 322, 329 (1981), the Court stated that the use of statutory "terms that have accumulated settled meaning under either equity or the common law * * * [implies] that Congress means to incorporate the established meaning of these terms."[69]

iv) LEGISLATING RULES OF INTERPRETATION

States often adopt generally-worded laws which reject a narrow interpretation of statutes in derogation of the common law.[70] Some of these laws are applicable to the entire statute book and require that statutes be "liberally construed with a view to effect their objects and to promote justice." Fordham & Leach quote Sutherland's treatise on Statutory Interpretation to the effect that these interpretation statutes have generally effectuated their purpose, but the authors doubt they have had decisive weight. It is extremely difficult to know what effect these statutes have because we do not know what courts would have done in their absence. They are often adopted when courts are moving in a similar interpretive direction, without regard to a legislative nudge.

The general point raised by statutes dealing with statutory interpretation is the efficacy of this type of legislation. Statutes are intended to solve specific problems, but a statutory rule of interpretation lacks specificity. It is a general principle of law, like "wrongdoers should not profit from their wrongs," which floats about as part of our general legal tradition. Legislating such general principles is difficult because principles tend to have meaning only in the context of a specific problem. When a statute dealing with a specific problem is passed, the court is drawn to the reality surrounding the adoption and interpretation of that specific legislation. An abstract interpre-

---

69. The point made in these paragraphs should be distinguished from two issues to which we return in Chapters 8 and 9—whether an evolving common law power is delegated by statute to a court, or survives adoption of a statute.

70. See Fordham & Leach, Interpretation of Statutes in Derogation of the Common Law, 3 Vand. L.Rev. 438 (1950).

tive principle might have little weight when the court confronts the reality of applying a specific law, even if that principle is embodied in a statute.

Suppose, as sometimes happens, a "liberal construction" rule appears in a *specific* statute, such as a Workers Compensation law. Are such rules more effective than general statutes applicable to all laws? Do they overcome whatever inferences might be reached based on the compromise origins of the legislation? As noted earlier, it is hard to prove what would happen without the liberal interpretation rule. The fact that courts cite the rule does not tell us whether they would have done the same thing without the statutory language.

Perhaps the explicit *repeal* of a liberal interpretation rule applicable to a specific statute will have an effect on statutory interpretation. For example, on June 30, 1985, the Maine legislature repealed a section of the Workers Compensation law, stating: "In interpreting this Act, the [Workers' Compensation] commission shall construe it liberally," and replaced it with the following:

> All workers' compensation cases shall be decided on their merits and the rule of liberal construction shall not apply to those cases. Accordingly, this Act is not to be given a construction in favor of the employee, nor are the rights and interests of the employer to be favored over those of the employee.

But perhaps this Maine law simply reflects a general trend away from increasing employer insurance costs by holding employers liable, so that the courts would, in any event, have retreated from a liberal interpretation of Workers Compensation laws which would favor employees over employers, whatever the new law stated.[71]

---

71. See generally Marsella v. Bath Iron Works Corp., 585 A.2d 802 (Maine 1991)(citing the new law establishing a level employer-employee playing field when interpreting the Workers Compensation law).

CHAPTER 4

CONTEMPORARY HISTORY—THE DECLINE OF FOUNDATIONALISM

4.01 INTRODUCTION

It is always dangerous, if not impossible, to write contemporary legal history. We are too close to separate the important from the trivial. But we must try or else we cannot understand how current theories of statutory interpretation have evolved from earlier approaches and how the past sheds light on the limitations and potential of modern approaches to statutory interpretation.

The significant feature of contemporary history is that the optimism about legislation, which had held the Legal Process approach together, has evaporated. The optimism was based on faith in a policy science of legislation and the democratic process from which statutes were supposed to originate. This permitted an uneasy combination of purposive interpretation and skepticism about judging, overlooking or accepting elements of judicial creativity associated with the imaginative reconstruction of legislative intent.

But faith in "policy science" did not survive World War II. "Science" had failed to head off fascism and an international conflagration and now seemed more associated with the destructive power of the physical sciences (symbolized by the atom bomb) than the creative potential of political science.

That left democracy. The emphasis on democracy highlighted the contrast between legislatures and courts to the apparent disadvantage of judicial lawmaking discretion. Still, as long as there was faith in democracy, purposivism could reconcile democratic values with creative judging. Judges had some leeway to elaborate democratically declared purposes. But once faith in the democratic process declined, courts seemed without a rudder to guide their role in statutory interpretation.

Soon after the 1958 Hart & Sacks Legal Process materials, the comfortable notion that "the legislature was made up of reasonable persons pursuing reasonable purposes reasonably" evaporated under assault from both the Left and Right. From the Left, the optimism that legislation was the product of a political system representing all groups was shattered by the civil rights revolution, as excluded groups (defined by race, gender, etc.) called attention to defects in the electoral and legislative processes. From the Right, optimism was shattered by the observation that many interests had a hard time organizing to be politically efficacious against well-organized private interest groups, and that political bargaining and agenda manipulation drained the legislative results of anything deserving the label "purposive."

This left statutory interpretation without a foundation on which to justify judicial discretion in working out the meaning of legislation. Some tried to overcome anxiety about how free the judge was in rendering a decision by finding new justifications for judicial lawmaking discretion—often going under the label of "Republicanism." They focused on both procedure and substance. Procedurally, judges made up for shortcomings in the legislative process. Substantively, they brought public values to the determination of statutory meaning. Essentially, substance-based Republicanism (as it related to statutory interpretation) was an attempt to do what Chief Justice Marshall had suggested—to define those values which were sufficiently fundamental that they influenced statutory meaning. Even if the legislature lacked purpose, the law did not and courts were charged with implementing that purpose.

The other major response was textualist—giving the courts as little to do as possible by sticking closely to the statutory language (or, at least, that was what the textualists hoped). Modern textualism differs radically in its objectives from reliance on the text in 19th Century. In the earlier period, the text was contrasted with judicial reliance on substantive background considerations (often the common law), which many judges thought superior to statutes. Textualism was one way to urge the *priority* of legislation over judging. However, the evolution of legislation through the middle of the 20th Century and the rise of purposivism ended judicial hostility to statutes. Modern textualism is therefore less an effort to defer to legislatures than to prevent what it perceives to be too much judging inherent in purposivism.

Finally, as the 20th Century comes to a close and the Republicans and textualists have had their say, "pragmatists" have attempted to take account of all the major approaches—purposivism, Republicanism, and textualism—by giving each their due, as well as adding a few more criteria to the interpretive mix. Their rigorous anti-foundationalism imparts a sense of realism to the interpretive process. It calls for interpretive flexibility, adopting different approaches for different statutes, and for multiple reinforcing approaches which (they hope) will produce a stronger result than any single approach could support. Whether pragmatism has a sufficiently robust conception of judging to sustain an affirmative judicial role in statutory interpretation remains to be seen.

4.02   THE IMPORTANT QUESTIONS

All approaches to statutory interpretation must address empirical and normative questions about legislation and the judicial role. A casual and often biased empiricism about legislative incompetence was always near the surface in the pre–20th Century attitudes towards statutes. Moreover, the link between the empirical image of the legislature and the normative conception of the judicial role was clear, though controversial—if legislatures were not good at what they were doing, judges might be justified in paying less deference to statutes. 20th Century purposivism tended to sweep these issues under the rug. A shift towards optimism about the legislative process was not matched by careful empirical studies of what legislatures were actually doing; and, despite the caution raised by Judge Hand and Hart & Sacks, normative concerns about judges elaborating legislative purpose were muted.

Modern empirical critiques of the legislative process have revived a strong negative view of the legislative process but it is difficult to respond with an affirmative view of the judicial role. The 20th Century commitment to democracy, along with the Legal Realist critique of political judging, has made judicial lawmaking discretion suspect. Even if the democratic legislative process lacks the creative vitality that supported purposivism, the judge's competence and legitimacy in making up for legislative deficiencies remain in question.

Or at least that is the challenge posed by modern empirical and normative critiques of legislation and judging. It remains to be seen (and you should critically examine) whether those critiques are accurate and what their implications are for statutory interpretation. What should judges do now that an innocent confidence in *both* legislating and judging has evaporated?

In the remainder of this Chapter, we look closely at contemporary empirical models and descriptions of the legislative process, and at various normative theories of how judges should react to this reality. These questions will continue to occupy us throughout Part II, when we deal with statutory interpretation. You should begin to develop your own theory of statutory interpretation, which can then be tested against the specific examples in Part II.

Before looking closely at modern empirical and normative approaches, however, it is useful to keep in mind the following basic questions which these approaches address.

a) EMPIRICAL QUESTIONS

(1) What Interests Influence the Legislative Process?

A. *Voters or interest groups?* Whose interests have the greatest impact on the legislature? Are they (a) voter interests; or (b) interest groups (i) within the electoral district, or (ii) outside the electoral district? Why aren't voter preferences always the major influence on legislation?

B. *How do politically influential groups form?* Which interests are best able to organize politically? Is it useful to distinguish in this regard between economic interests and public values; between benefits for a small group vs. benefits for a large diffuse group of people?

C. *Defining interests—"public values" and "economic interests."* We often refer in this chapter to "public values" and "economic interests." What is a public value and how does it differ from an economic interest?

Consider these efforts at a definition. A claim based on public values asserts that someone deserves to get a benefit or avoid a burden, or that it advances some conception of the public good. A claim based on economic interests asserts simply that someone wants something that will impose costs on others.

The definition of public values is not quantitative. The number of people wanting a program does not mean that it serves a public purpose. "Public" refers to a vision of social and political life that transcends counting up interests, whatever their number. Imagine, for example, the different ways you might justify a statute favoring the following groups: the poor; the bottom 90% of the population, paid for by the top 10%; minority groups who have been discriminated against; all groups except white protestant anglo-saxons.

The concept of public values is often associated with left of center politics, advocating inclusion of groups which have been omitted from the political process. Public values can, however, just as readily include economically conservative points of view. The claims of private property can be based on the link between private property and various public values—for example: private centers of power limit government control and support democracy; private property rewards effort; limiting the vote to property owners preserves political stability. Public values may also be socially conservative, illustrated by pro-life positions.[1] The pursuit of public values is not only substantively ambiguous, but may also present special problems for the political process. A lot of public values attract single issue commitment from their advocates. You may or may not think this is a good thing, depending on your own political persuasion. Single issue politics is, however, different from traditional politics in this country, which tends to avoid polarization of the electorate.

Is the pursuit of economic interests generally bad and the pursuit of public values good?

(2) How Does the Legislative Process Produce Legislation?

A. FROM INTERESTS TO LEGISLATION

(i) *Bargaining.* Is legislation the result of a bargaining process? If so, what do legislators bargain about—economic interests or public values?

(ii) *Indeterminate majority will.* Is majority will indeterminate, until legislative leaders manipulate voting through agenda control to produce statutes?

---

1. The conception of "public" values at the time of the Founding was often militaristic, hierarchical, male, and white. See Sun- stein, Beyond the Republican Revival, 97 Yale L.J. 1539 (1988)(hereafter "Sunstein, Revival").

(iii) *Deliberation*. The assumption underlying both the bargaining and indeterminacy views of the legislative process is that legislators *reflect* interests, which are bargained about or manipulated to a statutory conclusion. Is the legislative process instead deliberative, transforming interests into public values through discussion and debate?

B. INSTITUTIONAL REALITIES—LEGISLATIVE INCENTIVES AND LEADERSHIP

(i) *Legislators' incentives*. What incentives operate on legislators (future wealth; reelection; higher office, such as legislative leadership, the Senate, or the Presidency; their own values)? Do these incentives operate differently on different legislators, such as the rank and file or legislative leaders?

(ii) *Legislative leaders*. Who are legislative leaders? Do certain members of the legislature control the legislative process? If so, who are they (members of committees, committee chairs, legislative leaders, anyone else)? Is the arena of control the legislative committee, the floor debates, the conference committee between House and Senate, anything else? What role does the President play as a legislative leader?

(iii) *Impact of legislative leadership*. How does the exercise of legislative leadership affect the way interests are translated into legislation?

(3) Types of Legislation

There are many ways to categorize statutes, such as authorization vs. appropriations bills, and public vs. private laws. Some empirical generalizations about statutes may fit some types of legislation better than others. For example, appropriations bills may be used for economic interest logrolling—providing dams, roads and other public works to different regions of the country. Bargaining here consists of little more than "you scratch my back and I'll scratch yours." By contrast, broad programmatic legislation, such as civil rights or environmental statutes, may be shaped by bargaining among affected economic interests, or by deliberation and/or bargaining about public values, or both. Data about one type of statute may not be useful for understanding other types of legislation.

b) NORMATIVE QUESTIONS

What are the normative implications of the empirical reality? Describing the legislative process does not tell us what is right or wrong with the process. Nor does it tell us who should fix it. Those are normative questions.

(1) Normative Models of Legislatures

What is the preferred normative model of the legislative process? Should we simply accept the dominant role of economic interests and try to assure that political bargaining occurs on a level playing field? Or should we instead encourage a deliberative process, either as an end in itself, or as a means to produce more "public value" oriented statutes?

What does deliberation consist of: procedures to prevent legislative surprise and hidden legislation; or, more ambitiously, to encourage careful debate about ends and the means/end fit?

Is concern with process too limited? Should we instead focus directly on the public values that should result from legislation?

(2) Normative Models of Judging

A. *Legislation vs. judging.* Should improvement in legislation be left primarily to legislative reform, with courts playing only a minimal role? Are legislators even more ineffective at reforming the political process of which they are a product, at least regarding certain issues? Will judges turn out to be ineffective protectors of under-represented interests, yielding to traditional biases rather than implementing progressive public values?

B. *What can judges do?* If judges should play a role, what can they do effectively?

(i) Can judges define groups in need of political protection? Are such groups discrete and insular minorities, such as racial minorities; are they diffuse and therefore political powerless interests, such as the poor?

(ii) Is political power simply a matter of effective organization of people with common interests, or does the political culture shape the rhetoric and reality of political debate to the disadvantage of some groups? (For example, will attitudes towards women shape political judgment about females in the armed services, regardless of political organization?)

(iii) Should courts directly identify substantive values which should be advanced politically and, if so, how can they identify those values?

C. *Constitutional law or statutory interpretation.* Even if courts should play an active role, what are the respective roles of constitutional law and statutory interpretation in judicial implementation of political norms?

D. *Interaction of legislation with broader law?* Is legislation a radically separate source of law from judging? Or are both statutes and judge-made law part of a broader fabric of the law, with judges playing a discretionary role in working out the interactions?

4.03   THE LAW AND ECONOMICS CRITIQUE

The Law and Economics (or Public Choice) perspective on the legislative process undermined optimism that the legislature had any purpose from which judges could reason. (If this is your first encounter with the phrase "public choice," do not be misled by the use of the word "public" in this context. It does not connote a broad concept of "public interest," or refer to "public values." It simply describes the "public" arena in which the choice is made.)[2]

First, the Public Choice perspective took aim at the optimistic assumption that legislators adequately represented the many political views extant in the society and explained why this optimism might be misguided. Legislators responded to strong interest groups (those who could contribute to campaigns and lobby for their preferences), while electoral politics tended to be about atmospherics or single issues which focused on a limited number of concerns. Interest groups which were effective in the legislature usually consisted of those with strong economic interests (or, perhaps, those with a single-issue commitment to certain values), which enabled them to overcome obstacles to organization and to become politically effective.

Second, the legislative process did not produce a purpose from which the judge could reason for two reasons. Legislation was, first of all, a product of bargaining, often about private interests but also about public values. Legislation was therefore the result of offsetting pressures, not expansive public purposes. Moreover, whatever groups achieved legislative clout, their ability to prevail was subject to agenda manipulation by those who controlled the legislative process. The majoritarian winner was an accident of agenda control, not legislative purpose.

This critique drained the judge's confidence that legislation had a purpose which judges could elaborate. If statutory interpretation was strongly tied to the democratic ideal of implementing legislative will, judges apparently had little to do in determining statutory meaning, once legislative will was exposed as little more than compromise and/or agenda manipulation. All they could do was defer to the text.

Notice also how the Law and Economics critique transformed the "science" of legislation. "Science" was no longer associated with solving political problems (pragmatic science), but with building empirical models and describing the political process (positive science). Moreover, as so often happens with social science, the findings mirrored public perception. The public had come to view advocates of public values as special interest pleaders. Protectors of Social Security now came across less as bearers of public values—helping the less fortunate who contributed to the economy in their youth—and more as economic interest advocates, unwilling to modify claims to soften burdens on a younger working generation. The dominant public mood was to object to "special interest" politics, which appeared to consist of disparate claims made on the government without a sense of common public interest.

––––––––––

The Law and Economics critique specifically addressed two of the empirical questions noted earlier—what interests influence the legislative

2. See generally D. Mueller, Public Choice (1979); J. Buchanan and G. Tullock, The Calculus of Consent (1962); A. Downs, An Economic Theory of Democracy (1957).

process and how does the legislative process produce legislation?[3] We explain and evaluate this critique in the following pages. Always keep in mind that the empirical data and models do not answer the normative question of judicial role, although they provide material which any normative approach must consider.

a) WHAT INTERESTS INFLUENCE THE LEGISLATIVE PROCESS?

i) VOTERS

Do voter preferences have a critical impact on legislators? If so, are these preferences economic interests or a concern with public values? Are voters in fact public spirited? One bit of evidence in this direction is that voters vote, despite the fact that their chances of influencing the election's outcome are slight. Perhaps voters express different views depending on the office—focusing on character when voting for the President; public values for the Senate; and self-interest for the House.

Remember that the voters with impact are the marginal voters who give the legislator victory. If 70% of the voters generally split along party lines, the remaining 30% have an impact. What preferences are these voters likely to have?

ii) INTEREST GROUPS

Why aren't voters alone the source of political pressure for legislation, assuming at this point that legislators care only about getting elected? Why interest groups and not voters? One reason is that voters lack the time, money, and inclination to get information needed to form an opinion about many issues. Votes are often based on general atmospheric impressions, which pigeonhole a candidate as an economic or social liberal or conservative, or which emphasize character. Moreover, when voters do react to specifics, they do so only periodically, and their concerns tend to be narrow, focused on a limited range of issues.

Single issue voters may hold the balance of power based on a legislator's position on one issue, but not care much about votes on other issues, leaving the legislator unconstrained on those issues by voter preferences. What are some prominent single issues in today's politics—pro-life, pro-choice, gun control, concerns of the aged, anything else?

If economic interest is the voter's major concern, what does that imply for the content of legislation? For example, the voters in a farm district will care a lot about farm legislation but not necessarily about other issues. This may leave the farm legislator with discretion to vote on non-farm issues without worrying about the voter's self-interest. However, there is a counter-vailing possibility—the farm legislator may have bargained to obtain pro-

---

3. For a review of the empirical literature, see Daniel Farber & Philip Frickey, Law and Public Choice (1991); Jerry Mashaw, The Economics of Politics and the Understanding of Public Law, 65 Chi–Kent L.Rev. 123 (1989). See also Farber & Frickey, Foreword: Positive Political Theory in the Nineties, 80 Geo. L.J. 457 (1992).

farm votes from urban legislators in exchange for supporting an "urban" position in a later vote, thereby constraining the legislator's freedom of action.

Interest groups, in contrast to voters, often have the commitment, money and work force to support a candidate and to contribute directly to the candidate's campaign, giving them significant leverage to obtain legislation which specifically interests them, without too much attention to what the voters in the electoral district might want. Indeed, interest groups are often far more national than the representative's constituency. Their leverage increases as the cost of campaigning increases because money becomes more critical. The expense of TV and long campaigns increases the importance of interest groups who provide campaign funding.

Collective goods and group formation. How do politically powerful interest groups form? This issue is important for a number of reasons, discussed later in the course: what legal controls should be imposed on money in politics (Chapter 16); how vigorously should courts enforce state constitutional rules about legislative procedures and federal constitutional rationality standards (Chapter 17); should statutes be interpreted to protect people unable to form effective groups (discussed throughout Subparts IIA and IIC on statutory interpretation); should legislative history be suspect because of control by organized groups (Chapters 10 and 12)?

In the literature, the problem of organizing political groups is analyzed as a problem of "collective action" to obtain "collective goods."[4] A "collective good" is one characterized by non-exclusion of people from benefits, once the benefits have been provided. (The term "benefit," as used here, includes the avoidance of burdens or costs.)

Law often provides collective goods.[5] Once a law is passed, all those eligible can enjoy its benefits. This is true of both legislation implementing public values and, in many cases, economic goods. All of society, for example, enjoys the benefit of implementing a fair distribution of income (a "public value"). Economic goods distributed politically may also be a collective good, because all those eligible share in the benefits once the law is adopted. All farmers enjoy price supports; all workers get minimum wages; and many manufacturers benefit from trade protection. An example of burden avoidance as a collective good is lower taxes on all those eligible for tax relief.

The collective enjoyment of legislation suggests this question. Why would anyone contribute money or time to a political interest group when they can sit back and let others organize the group and still enjoy its benefits (the "free-rider" problem)? Assume that joint efforts by a significant number of people would produce a collective good, providing enjoyment worth $10

---

4. See M. Olsen, The Logic of Collective Action (1965).

5. The discussion of collective goods relies heavily on R. Hardin, Collective Action (1982).

per person, at a cost of $4 per person. This produces a clear $60 gain for the group of 10 people ($100 − $40). Would you help form a group to obtain these benefits? Consider this explanation for why you might not join. If I do not pay my dues (or provide equivalent value in labor), the benefit will be provided anyway by the efforts of the other nine people cooperating to form a politically effective group, so I will enjoy $10 in any event. Why spend $4 for nothing? If this strategy of free riding occurs to everybody, however, everyone will hold back and no political group will form. Instead of a $6 gain for everyone ($10 per person for a $4 cost), everyone will get $0.

This decision making process can be represented schematically in the following chart, based on the earlier example. Each cell presents a combination of payoffs to you and to each other person in the potential political group, depending on whether you join or do not join, and whether the rest of the potential group joins or does not join together to produce the benefit. Your payoff is always the first of the two figures.

Be sure you understand where each number comes from in each cell of the chart and why I have labeled each cell—cooperate; sucker; free rider; uncooperative.

	REST OF THE GROUP	
YOU	Join	Do not join
Join	6,6 (cooperate)	–4,0 (sucker)
Do not join	10,6 (free rider)	0,0 (uncooperative)

One reason why the % result might not occur is that it will be obvious to all potential free riders that nothing will happen if they do not join together. In politics, sufficient political clout is often an all or nothing proposition. Unless enough people join together, nothing gets done. This fact will appear obvious to all potential free riders and they might therefore have an incentive to band together.

But the obvious inability to free ride successfully does not necessarily produce a decision to join. If joining means pouring $4 down the drain, because others may not join, it might seem better to leave the status quo where it is (no one joins = %), rather than be a sucker and lose $4. The decision to join will therefore depend on what each person thinks others are likely to do and that in turn depends on the gains that appear likely from joining together. If there is a 50/50 chance that $10 gain per person will be produced, the $10 is the equivalent of a $5 benefit (50% of $10). This suggests that the size of the gain per person is a critical factor in whether the group will form. If the potential gains, discounted for uncertainty that the gain will not be realized, exceed the $4 cost, the potential joiners will conclude that the $4 cost will not go down the drain and the group will form.

What might increase the size of the collective good to potential group members and therefore favor group formation? Consider the following: (1) a large money value per group member; (2) continuity of benefits over time, compared to a one-shot benefit; and (3) caring more about avoiding burdens than obtaining opportunities not previously enjoyed.

This discussion lends some support to the commonly held view that political group formation is more likely when the benefits of political action are concentrated on a small group of people than when benefits are distributed widely over a large group of people. First, when benefits are concentrated on a small group, it will be obvious to each potential member that nothing will happen unless they all join together; or at least that the political impact will depend on each person contributing. Moreover, it will be easier to work out the interrelationships between potential group members (that is, minimize transaction costs) when the group is small. Second, benefits concentrated on a small group are more likely to provide group members with large political pay-offs, especially when the benefit is economic. Examples of concentrated benefits include a tariff favoring an industry, or a tax break for one industry. Widely distributed benefits are illustrated by a tax decrease for all taxpayers. "Benefits" in the sense of avoiding burdens can also be concentrated or diffuse. Concentrated burdens include a potential tax on one industry (a tax on cigarettes or alcohol) and regulation of a profession. Widely distributed burdens are illustrated by an increase in taxes for the general public and higher prices from inflation.

Are some ideological commitments so intense that they provide the economic equivalent of a large dollar payoff? Can you think of some examples?

Notice, however, that concentrated benefits do not necessarily result in greater benefits per person than diffuse benefits. That depends on whether the political pie is fixed. Sometimes there are resource limits, to be spread out over the beneficiaries of a government program (e.g. appropriations of money may be capped, or drilling rights may be available for limited amounts of offshore land). In that case, the more beneficiaries the less benefit per person. However, in some programs, additional beneficiaries obtain the same benefits as others (more Social Security is paid out to additional beneficiaries; everyone can buy guns without gun control). Benefits do not necessarily decline just because they are not concentrated on a small number of people. However, given budget constraints, benefits which do not decline with increased numbers of beneficiaries may be small.

The emphasis in this discussion on benefits and free riders should not obscure what may be a more serious problem for group formation—the costs of joining. Even if there are no free rider problems and even if everyone perceives the benefit from group formation to exceed the cost, there may be alternative uses of time and money that produce a greater return than political group formation. In the prior example, we assumed that $4 produced a $10 political benefit. If spending $4 on something else produces an $11 benefit, joining the group would not make sense. Does this problem affect the poor more than others, because their most basic needs must be met before political organization seems attractive?

Incentives to group formation other than political benefits. The analysis of the free rider problem focused solely on specific political advantages. Groups may form, however, in part for nonpolitical reasons and then develop political clout once the significant problems of group formation are overcome. Consider the following reasons for group formation: do they reinforce the formation of political groups by those who already anticipate large political gains; do they explain why political groups which are otherwise very vulnerable to free rider problems might nonetheless form? Will groups formed for these reasons be politically strong?

1. Do economic goods, such as low cost insurance, provide incentives for group formation? Are they generally provided after a group has formed for other reasons, thereby helping to maintain but not create the group?

2. Is a sense of professionalism a sufficient incentive to form a group? For example, will lawyers and doctors organize for that reason alone? Will businesses form trade associations, regardless of collective political benefits?

3. Are there other sources of solidarity that might produce political groups, independent of collective political benefits? Do social interaction benefits explain group formation by minorities, women, unions, or trade associations? Do they suggest that it is easier to form small rather than large groups; that it is easier to form than expand the group?

4. Are there noninstrumental reasons for wanting to cooperate, not already captured by the notion of social or ideological solidarity? (Some people refer to such reasons as "nonrational".) Perhaps we are cooperative animals, unless those with whom we cooperate betray us. The idea is that we are disposed to cooperate and will do so, tit-for-tat, until others defect from the group. Does the propagation of information about the free rider problem have an adverse impact on people's willingness to cooperate by making them suspicious of others? If so, should we suppress the theory?

Group Leadership. One of the factors discouraging group formation is the absence of group leadership which can bring potential free riders together or can substitute for difficulties in group formation. There are many ways such leadership can be provided.

1. Does the government play a role in forming some groups? For example, do some government programs require that a recipient group receive technical or financial aid, such as farm or poverty programs? Government organizations might even substitute for private group formation through executive agencies (for example, the Veterans Administration).

2. Are there private policy entrepreneurs, whose ideological careers are tied up with working for and financing group formation? Sometimes a few dynamic individuals might be important. Is Ralph Nader an example? Sometimes large private foundations

and/or wealthy people give money to create and sustain interest groups. These foundations may be financed by aggregations of individual and corporate wealth and reflect the political ideology of the founder or current board of directors. In this way, the need for broad-based group membership support is lessened.

b) How Does the Legislative Process Produce Legislation?

Legislation is the product not only of outside influence but also of how legislators respond. The Public Choice model of legislative behavior posits (1) that legislation results primarily from bargaining about economic interests; and (2) that majority will is indeterminate until manipulated by those controlling the agenda. In this section, we first explain and critique both elements of this model and then pay special attention to institutional realities.

i) PUBLIC CHOICE MODEL

First, the "Public Choice" model tends to view legislation as the result of bargaining about economic interests. The general idea is that the political process is like the economic marketplace; statutes are agreements written in a public forum. Economic interests either legislate benefits for themselves (occupational licensing, for example, is an effort to keep out competitors); or compromise conflicting preferences to produce legislation (Workers Compensation is a bargain between employers and employees, both seeking to advance economic interests by limiting liability and obtaining benefits respectively).

(A) Bargaining

Easterbrook, Foreword: The Court and the Economic System
98 Harv. L. Rev. 4 (1984).

Why are there laws?—There are two basic styles of statutory construction. In one the judge starts with the statute, attributes to it certain purposes (evils to be redressed), and then brings within the statute the class of activities that produce the same or similar objectionable results. The statute's reach goes on expanding so long as there are unredressed objectionable results. The judge interprets omissions and vague terms in the statute as evidence of want of time or foresight and fills in these gaps with more in the same vein. The maxim "Remedial statutes are to be liberally construed" sums up this approach.

In the other approach the judge treats the statute as a contract. He first identifies the contracting parties and then seeks to discover what they resolved and what they left unresolved. For example, he may conclude that a statute regulating the price of fluid milk is a pact between milk producers and milk handlers designed to cut back output and raise price, to the benefit of both at the expense of consumers. A judge then implements the bargain as a faithful agent but without enthusiasm; asked to extend the scope of a back-room deal, he refuses unless the proof of the deal's scope is compelling. Omissions are evidence that no bargain was struck: some issues were left for the future, or perhaps one party was unwilling to pay the price of a resolution in its favor. Sometimes the compromise may be to toss an issue to the courts for resolution, but this too is a term of the bargain, to be demonstrated rather than presumed. What the parties did not resolve, the court should not resolve either. The maxim "Statutes in derogation of the common law are to be strictly construed" sums up this approach.

* * * A judge cannot set about rearranging economic relations on the basis of an ambiguous statute without first resolving a question about the nature of legislation. If statutes generally are designed to overcome 'failures' in markets and to replace the calamities produced by unguided private conduct with the ordered rationality of the public sector, then it makes sense to use the remedial approach to the construction of statutes—or at least most of them. If, on the other hand, statutes often are designed to replace the outcomes of private transactions with monopolistic ones, to transfer the profits ("rents") of productive activity to a privileged few, then judges should take the beady-eyed contractual approach. * * *

One of the implications of modern economic thought is that many laws are designed to serve private rather than public interests. People demand laws just as they demand automobiles, and some people demand more effectively than others. Laws that benefit the people in common are hard to enact because no one can obtain very much of the benefit of lobbying for or preserving such laws. Smaller, more cohesive groups are more effective lobbyists. These groups can obtain a greater share of the benefits of laws targeted to assist people who have common characteristics, and so they will raise more money and campaign for legislation more effectively. The tobacco lobby is not large, but it is effective in obtaining subsidies. It also turns out that small, cohesive groups can get more for them-selves by restricting competition and appropriating rents than by seeking rules that enhance the welfare of all. Thus we should expect regulatory programs and other statutes to benefit the regulated group—they need not "capture" the programs, because they owned them all along. The burgeoning evidence showing that regulatory programs increase prices for consumers and profits for producers supports this understanding.

How is a court to decide whether a particular statute is general-interest legislation or private-interest legislation? Some laws (the prohibition of murder, for example) are general-interest laws, and others (such as tobacco subsidies) are private-interest laws, but most reflect a mixture of objectives. * * *

One way to approach the problem is to ask whether the statute is specific or general. The more detailed the law, the more evidence of interest-group compromise and therefore the less liberty judges possess. * * *

Another approach is to look for the indicia of rent-seeking legislation: limitations on new entry into the business, subsidies of one group by another, prohibitions of private contracting in response to the new statutory entitlements.

Still a third way is to look at process. Who lobbied for the legislation? What deals were struck in the cloakrooms? Who demanded what and who gave up what? Knowing the contending parties conveys information. So does knowing the grounds of contention. A statute in which two rent-seeking groups fought to a deadlock, each unsatisfied but unable to get more, is different from a statute over which there was no serious contest among self-interested groups. The closer the contest, and the more the parties were looking to their own interests (rather than the public interest more broadly defined), the more appropriate it is to treat the statute as a contract and to decline to give either party an advantage it failed to get explicitly. * * *

No statute has a single genesis. Members of Congress are not automata manipulated by today's group; they have their own goals. Most statutes are interest-group compromises only in part, and the question is, "Which part?" Some statutes are designed to implement principles of morality rather than to influence economic conduct, and these statutes cannot easily be analyzed on a continuum between public interest and private interest. * * *

* * * [T]he question is not whether the Court sometimes finds statutes to be interest-group legislation, but whether it looks for this possibility pervasively. Are the Justices alert to the private-interest nature of legislation? Do they use principles of construction appropriate to that recognition?

QUESTIONS AND COMMENTS

1. Easterbrook is not arguing that the Public Choice model explains all legislation. He only wants judges to be more alert to the possibility that legislation has such origins. Still, his argument has implications for specific cases. First, he suggests some indicia of the contractual approach—detailed text, evidence of rent-seeking legislation; behind-the-scenes legislative lobbying. Second, and perhaps more importantly, suppose the evidence about whether a statute implements the "general interest" or "private interest" is uncertain, as will often be true when busy judges and lawyers try to understand legislation. Would Easterbrook take the "beady-eyed contractual approach" or the more expansive purposive approach? Isn't this the main objective of the Public Choice models—to change the judge's assumptions about legislation in the absence of specific evidence about what prompted the legislation?

2.   The bargaining to which Easterbrook refers is private interest bargaining. He does not discuss how bargaining about public values should influence statutory interpretation. Suppose bargaining is critical in the legislative process, but that it is about public values, not private economic interests. Should that alter the judge's decision about whether a statute has expansive purposes? Does a bargain limit the judge whatever the subject of the bargain?

Models and facts. One of the problems with any model of legislation is that its devotees may assume corroborating evidence which does not exist. The point is important because a great deal of modern law and economics critique is concerned with empirical *models*, not empirical data. These models have an important function. When judges interpret statutes, they have an image of legislation which influences statutory meaning. The purposive approach thrived on an affirmative image of the legislature. The major impact of the law and economics approach may be to alter the judge's presumptive image of legislation. More specifically, it may shift the burden of proof to those who argue that there is a vital legislative purpose relevant to statutory interpretation, absent which the judge will assume the contrary.

A study of a banking law statute by Langevoort suggests that the law and economics model may mislead observers about the origin of legislation. The Glass–Steagall Act, adopted in 1933, imposes barriers to investment banking by commercial banks. In the older view of banking, investment bankers offer securities for sale to the public; commercial banks lend to businesses. The Public Choice analysis of this legislation concludes that the statute originated in efforts by investment bankers to protect themselves from commercial banks. The facts, Langevoort finds, are otherwise. He acknowledges that commercial banks moved into investment banking in the 1920s but notes that no major study cites special interest pleading as a significant factor in the passage of legislation separating commercial and investment banking. He concedes the possibility of a "cover-up" but then provides an alternative explanation.

Langevoort, Statutory Obsolescence and the Judicial Process: The Revisionist Role of the Courts in Federal Banking Regulation

85 Mich. L. Rev. 672 (1987).

* * * By all accounts, the legislative history begins with Senator Carter Glass of Virginia, principal drafter of the Federal Reserve

Act in 1914, and the preeminent congressional authority on the business of banking. Glass * * * was an old-fashioned banking theorist; he believed that the proper role of a commercial bank was lending evidenced by short-term commercial paper. * * * Glass believed that [this] would make future long-term economic depressions unlikely.

Glass was extremely troubled during the later 1920s by extensive bank lending to finance securities purchases, not because he was opposed to the stock market itself, but because he believed that such lending was taking money away from local businesses in need of credit. * * *

* * * [A]s the Depression lengthened, public demand for Congress to "do something" and a growing opinion that bankers were somehow to blame for economic conditions kept the issue alive. Though apparently willing to compromise, Glass insisted that the proper response was divorce * * *. [Editor—The author notes two factors contributing to passage of the law separating commercial and investment banking—congressional hearings implicating bank wrongdoing in the stock market's troubles, and the banking industry's desire to head off the more drastic step of federal deposit insurance. In the end, both separation and deposit insurance passed.]

Thus, there is an explanation for the separation of investment and commercial banking that does not involve special-interest pressure from the private investment bankers. For Carter Glass and those closest to this portion of the legislation the principal motivation was pursuit, perhaps more emotional than rational, of the channeling objective—an attempt to force banks to redirect their resources, efforts, and energies to the traditional business of commercial and agricultural lending by foreclosing the securities temptation. If any special interest group was instrumental in this regard, it was probably the smaller businesses and farmers (not surprisingly, Glass' Virginia constituents) who considered the unavailability of credit at least partially responsible for their current woes. Many in Congress (and probably Glass as well), also viewed separation as a politically attractive way of appearing to respond punitively to the bankers' recently exposed excesses. Others saw it as simply part of a legislative package that contained something far more important, federal deposit insurance. * * *

Even more interesting is the conduct of the investment banking firms after enactment. One bit of history that on first glance might seem to support the special interest theory is Carter Glass' fairly close relationship with the most influential of the private investment firms, J.P.Morgan. Two Morgan partners, Russell Leffingwell and S. Parker Gilbert, were Glass' good friends and had been his close advisors as Secretary of the Treasury. Glass reportedly tried to protect the Morgan interests during the stock market hearings.

There, if anywhere, is the link between Glass and Wall Street and the opportunity for pursuit of monopoly rents. Yet upon passage of the legislation, J.P. Morgan & Co. chose to quit the *investment banking* business in order to comply with the law and retain its ability to accept deposits at what is today Morgan Guaranty Trust Co. Approximately one-third of the other private investment bankers (including Brown Brothers Harriman and Drexel & Co.) did the same. That seems strange behavior for a group that had just been successful in obtaining special-interest legislation on its behalf.

COMMENTS

1. *Who is more naive?* Those committed to the Public Choice model would respond to claims that it makes unproven and oversimplified assumptions about politics with the argument that it is at least as naive to assume that legislation embodies public purposes. For example, affirmative action, tax breaks for homeowners, price supports for farmers, workers compensation, restrictive licensing, and social security will never be defended explicitly on the ground that its advocates simply *want* it, but on the grounds that these programs implement public values. Legislative preambles and purpose clauses are often drafted in this rhetorical vein but cannot always be trusted to explain the statute. Someone predisposed to assume that legislation embodies public values may too quickly trust the rhetoric without looking to see what the statute really does or what deals lay behind the law.

2. *Proving the specifics.* As you read about the empirical models concerning collective action and legislative bargaining, you must be struck by the difficulty of determining what is really going regarding specific legislation. Will judges (or lawyers) have the resources to make judgments about which model of the legislative process best fits the facts? What does your answer suggest about judging in the absence of reliable information—should judges expansively interpret statutes or take the beady-eyed approach?

(B) Indeterminacy of Majority Rule; Control of Legislative Process

Another branch of public choice analysis is concerned with the impact of agenda control on legislation. We like to think that there is a majority will independent of the political process through which it is expressed. Pound's view that statutes embody purposes from which courts can reason was based on this assumption. The work of Kenneth Arrow suggests otherwise.[6]

If there are three (or more) voters with different rank ordering of preferences, they will often be unable to agree on a majority position unless outside intervention structures the vote. This leads to the pessimistic conclusion that political results are arbitrary and subject to manipulation by nondemocratic forces. Notice that the following analysis is independent of whether preferences are economic interests or public values. Notice also that bargaining about legislative results is consistent with this manipulative view

---

6. See K. Arrow, Social Choice and Individual Values (2d ed. 1963).

of politics because different bargains may win or lose depending on agenda control. Bargaining can, however, be an alternative to agenda control, if legislators forge a majority position to avoid manipulation of the legislative result.

An example will illustrate how agenda control might manipulate political results. Assume voters A (industry), B (charities), and C (unions) with the following preferences for positions N,M, and $ on adopting Workers Compensation. Preference N is for (N)o Workers Compensation program at all; preference M is for a (M)oderate program with modest dollar benefits; and preference $ is for a program with generous $ benefits.

Vote	Rank Order of Preferences
A (industry)	N, M, $
B (charities)	M, $, N
C (unions)	$, N, M

This array of preferences might occur for the following reasons. Voter A represents an industry group which believes that tort reform is not coming, so there is no need to compromise, and that Workers Compensation will be expensive for the industry. Hence, voter A opposes any program, but his second choice is one with modest benefits—that is, N,M,$ in that order. Voter B represents charities, who would be covered by the bill, and whose sense of public values results in favoring Workers Compensation coverage (even for themselves), despite their immunity from tort liability. However, they prefer more modest payment schedules to the more generous program. Hence, M,$,N in that order. Voter C represents the unions, which believe that tort reform is coming. Voter C prefers a generous Workers Compensation program, because of the certainty it provides, but would otherwise like to gamble on tort reform, rejecting a modest Workers Compensation program that might dampen political enthusiasm for more thorough reform. Hence, $,N,M in that order.

As a result of this set of preferences, the order and pairing of votes is critical. If the vote is taken first on N vs. M, N wins, eliminating M. In the next vote between N and $, $ wins. If the first vote had been between N and $, however, $ would have won, but a runoff between $ and M produces a victory for M. Work out the results of M vs. $, followed by the winner's runoff against N.

This example illustrates that results can be manipulated so that one point of view wins. Party leadership might force an all or nothing showdown between N (no program) and $ (generous program), by prohibiting consideration of an amendment for modest benefits (M). Or, if such an amendment were allowed, the first vote might be between N and M (none vs. modest), which would reject the modest proposal. The run-off between N and $ would result in a victory for $. Agenda control is therefore very important.[7]

---

7. Legislators might try to counteract agenda control by engaging in strategic voting—that is, voting against interest so that the final vote will be more palatable. Here is an example. Assume that the first vote in the earlier Workers Compensation example is

There are several responses to the view of politics as indeterminate and manipulative, based on the role of political ideology, intensity of preferences, and the impact of deliberation.

First, ideology may array preferences along a liberal/conservative spectrum (rather than in the form of unstructured rank orderings, as in the prior Workers Compensation example). In such cases, votes will be resolved in accordance with the views of the median voter. For example, the union might be hard pressed to view "no Workers Compensation program" as preferable to some modest program, because of its liberal ideology. The union would then adopt $, M, N ordering (rather than $, N, M). When that happens, M (the modest program) will always beat N and $ (no program and generous program) in any series of run-offs.

The tendency to structure issues along a liberal/conservative spectrum may be minimal in the United States, however, where political parties are less ideologically oriented and much weaker than in Europe. Politicians have decentralized state and local power bases that discourage central party control, which might otherwise impose a more ideological perspective. Various "reforms" have also weakened the party structure. Campaign spending rules have encouraged formation of Political Action Committees (PACs), which give a legislator some independence of traditional party control.

Second, another way to avoid voting indeterminacy is to account for preference intensity. Even though each legislator has one vote, intensity can still be recognized through logrolling. Assume that the union is so intent on $ (generous program) winning, that it strikes a deal with the charities, that it will oppose a bill opening a charity's finances to attorney general inspection in exchange for the charities placing $ at the top of their preference list. Now, with charities wanting $, M, N, in that order, $ will win regardless of which votes are taken first.

Third, legislators may not enter political deliberation with completely fixed and pre-formed points of view. Discussion (often outside of public view) may shape and reshape the legislator's position.[8] While this is not a complete bar to indeterminacy and manipulation of political results, it makes it more difficult to identify each legislator's preferences and engage in agenda control.

ii) INSTITUTIONAL REALITIES—LEGISLATIVE INCENTIVES AND LEADERSHIP

The discussion of the Public Choice model has paid too little attention to the institutional realities through which the legislative process is filtered—specifically, the incentives which motivate legislators and the legislative

(N)o benefits vs. (M)oderate benefits. We saw that the most generous program, $, would eventually win in that case. As an industry representative with an N,M,$ preference structure, you might be well advised to vote for (M)oderate, instead of (N)o benefits on the first vote, so that the next choice will be between (M)oderate and $, in which case (M)oderate wins.

8. See generally Sunstein, Naked Preferences and the Constitution, 84 Colum. L. Rev. 1689 (1984).

leadership, and how the legislative leadership interacts with legislators. Is there anything about such incentives and interaction which undercuts some of the inferences from the Public Choice model?

(A) Legislative Incentives

Models of legislation must take account not only of voters and interest groups but also the incentives to which legislators respond. A legislator's propensity to serve strong interest groups, to bargain, or to deliberate may vary depending on whether the legislator pursues private financial gain, reelection objectives, higher office, or his or her own political agenda.

Legislators who pursue private gain are obviously vulnerable to those who can provide rewards. The resulting legislative process violates all norms of correct legislative behavior because it corrupts legislative judgment regarding issues favored by those providing the legislator with the opportunity for private gain. The private gain may take many forms: a bribe; financial benefits creating conflicts of interest, such as profits attributable to doing business with the government; or job opportunities after leaving the legislature. Although these practices are for the most part illegal, some enforcement slippage undoubtedly occurs, especially regarding subsequent employment. Nonetheless, there is probably little outright corruption in most legislatures today.

The most powerful legislative incentive is probably reelection. Whether legislators want private gain, public service, power, or a Washington social life, reelection is necessary. Reelection incentives often affect the legislative process through the influence of campaign financing, which enhances reelection prospects. Those who finance campaigns have special influence and access to the legislator. There is undoubtedly a connection between the ability to form politically powerful interest groups, discussed earlier in this chapter, and the wherewithal to finance campaigns. The reelection-campaign finance link does not, however, produce the worst kind of corruption because political influence and access do not equate with a specific political quid pro quo exchanged for private gain.[9] Moreover, multiple sources of campaign financing may offset each other, leaving the legislator at best free to vote independently, or at worst paralyzed by conflicting pressures.

One way to question the impact of the reelection incentive is to suggest that the legislator might be more like an independent "political entrepreneur," with ambitions beyond reelection, and to see what consequences that might have for the legislative process. Some legislators want to achieve committee or party leadership within the body to which they belong; or advance to a position of greater prominence (perhaps the Senate or the Presidency); or simply to have an impact on public policy in *some* field of law for personal reasons. To achieve these goals legislators may have to stake out

---

9. Until 1992, a retiring legislator could use campaign contributions left over from prior campaigns for personal purposes after paying income taxes. The law has been prospectively changed to prohibit this practice. Pub. L. 101–194, § 504(b), 103 Stat. 1716, 1755 (1989).

broader public positions, rather than yield to the influence of interest groups who finance reelections. And once in a position of leadership, the legislator has opportunities to help constituents, which diminishes the need for campaign financing. Some particular legislators come to mind in this connection. Senator Magnuson staked out a position as a specialist in consumer concerns to offset his image as the Senator from Boeing (he was from Washington). Senator Muskie specialized in environmental legislation. Both used committee chairmanships to this end. Senator Bradley was somewhat unusual in making tax reform a specialty without a legislative leadership base, but he may have had Presidential ambitions.

There are some countervailing considerations, however, which diminish the independence of the political entrepreneur. First, legislative leadership still depends on being reelected. Second, leadership positions on important legislative committees provide opportunities to help not only constituents but also those throughout the country who finance campaigns. Campaign money is therefore attracted to legislators controlling important committees with national impact, at the same time that such control reduces the need for the funds. Moreover, some legislative leaders consolidate their position by forming political action committees (PACs) which dole out contributions to other members of Congress for their campaigns. These members obviously develop loyalty to the leader, linking PAC funding to leadership positions.

If political entrepreneurs are important, a critical question is where they find their ideas. There is a ready supply produced by academics, think tanks, and interest groups, with the help of media publicity. These sources work up ambitious projects for political change which may never see the light of day, but which, at the right moment, may have unexpected influence. Studies of worker accidents and the German social insurance program at the end of the 19th Century helped pave the way for Workers Compensation. More recently, the filtering into public consciousness of a tax expenditure budget, which analogized tax breaks to public spending, laid the groundwork for lowering tax rates and eliminating many special tax preferences in the Tax Reform Act of 1986. The tax expenditure budget had been developed in academic circles and publicized by the media many years earlier.

———————

How would term limits affect a legislator's incentives?[10] Although states cannot constitutionally impose term limits on federal legislators,[11] they can (and many states do) impose term limits on state officials. There is also some wide but probably shallow support for a constitutional amendment to limit the terms of Members of Congress.

    1. Would term limits cause legislators to be less interested in long term projects which benefit voters or the public outside their districts?

10. See generally Cohen & Spitzer, Term Limits, 80 Geo. L.J. 477 (1992).

11. U.S. Term Limits, Inc. v. Thornton, 115 S.Ct. 1842 (1995).

2.   What post-term prospects would most attract legislators and what effect would those prospects have on the legislative process? Would legislators seek jobs as lobbyists or as employees in the private sector; political appointments controlled by the President or political parties; higher office?

3.   What is the impact of term limits on losing senior legislative leaders: will we get new blood or lose experience or both?

4.   What impact will term limits have on cooperation among legislators to achieve legislation; is such cooperation good or bad; does that depend on the type of legislation (e.g., pork barrel logrolling or civil rights legislation)?

5.   Will term limits attract a new type of legislator, one who is less concerned with narrow economic interests or with voters? What will these legislators be concerned about?

Even if term limits for legislative membership are not adopted, each chamber can limit terms for *committee chairs*. The House Rules now provide that no member can serve as chair of the same committee or subcommittee for more than three consecutive terms. House of Representatives, House Rules, Rule X(6)(c)(1995).

So far we have emphasized Members of Congress. Do not forget that the President has a legislative role, exercised through threat of veto, party leadership, control of patronage, force of personality, and media access. The President may take the broadest view of public policy and have considerable influence on those issues to which he gives attention and commits his leadership. Deregulation of the airline industry, which undermined the oligopolistic control enjoyed by private economic interests, benefited from Presidential leadership favoring deregulation. And protectionist tariff legislation that would be bad for the nation overall has been discouraged by Presidential leadership, even though particular legislators would be inclined to vote otherwise.

Blame avoidance. One legislative incentive deserves special attention—the legislator's desire to avoid blame. It is often said that legislators try harder to avoid blame than garner credit, because the electorate is more ungrateful than thankful. There is a lot of anecdotal evidence to support this view. When the Senate voted a salary increase, the influential Chair of the Appropriations Committee, who had been assiduously harvesting votes, excused Senators running in the next election from following the party's lead. Members of Congress will often watch the vote tally board to see how others are voting so that they are not alone in taking a potentially unpopular position which can be used against them in a later election. And interest group pressure may be more effective closer to an election than during the early part of a congressional term, because there is time to atone for "early" legislative sins.

The most dramatic examples of blame avoidance occur when legislators try to avoid voting on controversial legislation because someone will be very unhappy. This is especially true when there are well organized groups on both sides of an issue. The legislative leadership will sometimes hold back legislation from floor consideration if the vote will make too many enemies for too many legislators.

Some important legislation may be explained on the ground that it permits legislators to avoid blame. An example is the indexing of Social Security benefits for inflation. Congress had traditionally voted specific benefit increases around election time and claimed credit each time. The benefit increases were getting out of hand, but voting against the benefits by fiscal conservatives was a difficult blame-attracting vote. Indexing eliminated the pressure for periodic increases and therefore the need to vote against them. It was also attractive to beneficiaries, who (after all) were guaranteed inflation adjustments, so the inflation adjustment was not obviously perceived as anti-beneficiary legislation.[12]

One commentator argues that reelection incentives and blame avoidance combine to explain which activities are important to legislators. Fiorina identifies three types of legislative activity—pork barreling (providing economic benefits such as dams and military bases), casework for constituents, and legislation (a separate category).[13] For reelection purposes, pork and casework have advantages. Unlike controversial legislative programs, which will always make some voters unhappy, helping constituents is always safe and profitable. This perspective helps to explain the following events: the growth of federal government and legislative staff, both of which create opportunities for legislators to help constituents; the decline of party influence, because candidates rely less on the party for reelection support; the decline in close races in the House of Representatives, because constituent casework makes it easier for a legislator to retain his seat, and incumbency in turn enhances the legislator's ability to help constituents.

Multiple incentives. Multiple incentives probably influence legislative behavior. Two examples of legislative behavior illustrate how multiple incentives might operate—(1) the search for legislative "cover," (2) and voting "both ways."

"Cover" in the legislative process is an umbrella which allows legislators to deflect blame for abandoning a strong interest group for a broader principle. An example is the enforcement mechanism for spending ceilings on federal expenditures in the now-abandoned Gramm–Rudman–Hollings

---

12. See R. Weaver, Automatic Government: The Politics of Indexing (1988) (hereafter "Weaver").

13. M. Fiorina, Congress: Keystone of the Washington Establishment (1989).

legislation. Expenditures which exceeded the budget ceilings caused a more-or-less pro-rata reduction of all expenditures. A legislator could deflect blame for not supporting specific expenditures benefiting constituents or interest groups on the ground that it would exceed the spending ceilings, which could be rhetorically billed as budget busting. Congress could always have voted explicitly to exceed the ceilings, but this carried a high political price, there were House and Senate procedural rules making this difficult, and there was strong collegial pressure not to abandon the ceilings.

For exceedingly controversial blame-generating statutes, legislators may seek the umbrella of a prior agreement by selected legislators to spread the burdens widely, as with military base closings, or to certify the public need for the legislation, such as correcting errors in the Social Security benefit formula which counted inflation twice to provide excessive benefits.[14] Blame can also be avoided by passing the buck to the courts by adopting a generally-worded statutory text or remaining silent about an important issue (such as retroactivity—we return to this issue in Chapter 7, using the Civil Rights Act of 1991 as an example). A voice vote (which conceals voter identity), rather than a recorded vote, may also avoid publicity for unpopular positions. The opposition can usually force a recorded vote but does not always take advantage of the opportunity.

Legislators may also try to have it "both ways." Sometimes, there are actually two votes: for example, a vote to authorize a program and against significant funding; or a vote to table a bill followed by a vote to pass it, if the tabling motion is defeated.

Frequently, a statute combines provisions which satisfy more than one political position. This is illustrated by the Tax Reform Act of 1986. The statute implemented tax equity by eliminating many tax benefits previously thought invulnerable because of special interest lobbying. For some, this was a public policy worth pursuing in its own right. For others, including the President, it was the price paid for lowering tax rates without increasing the federal budget deficit. Passage was finally assured only by adopting $5 billion of transition rules which preserved benefits enjoyed by a limited group of voters and interest groups in constituencies represented by legislators with critical votes.

There is a more troublesome illustration of voting "both ways" on a statute. A statute may contain symbolic but not very effective reassurances to one group while protecting the interests of another more powerful interest group. Symbolic assurances are often provided to those least capable of effective political organization, because it is harder to fool the lawyers and lobbyists for well-organized interest groups who specialize in watching legislation. Preambles, purpose clauses, and titles of laws may therefore promise much more than the law delivers, allowing the legislator to posture as a supporter of the public interest, while still protecting well-organized interest groups. Delegation to an agency is sometimes motivated by these considerations. The agency is created to serve some perceived public need, but the

14. Weaver, pp. 81–82.

expectation is that interest groups will effectively restrain the statute's rhetorical promise through intra-agency lobbying.

(B) Legislative Leadership

The legislative product depends in large part on legislative leadership. There is some truth to the public choice image of "manipulative" leaders, in the sense that they have considerable control over what gets voted on and when. Whether this deserves the pejorative "manipulative" label is another matter. Perhaps legislative leaders improve legislation. Just as representative government may be preferable to town meeting democracy, so leadership in a representative legislature may have advantages. Consider what features of the leadership-membership relationship might increase or decrease deliberation or the influence of strong interest groups or public values in the political system.

The following material discusses leadership in the United States Congress. Patterns in state legislatures may be quite different.

There are many sources of leadership control in Congress. The most important are the party leaders in each house and the chairs of committees and subcommittees. In addition, the House Rules Committee, for which there is no Senate counterpart, controls House procedure by specifying what bills will come up for a vote, structuring floor consideration, and resolving turf battles among committees. Below the legislative leaders are committee members and, ultimately, the Members of Congress who may try with varying degrees of success to have their way. Patterns of control vary between House and Senate.[15]

Committees. Most bills are referred to legislative committees for consideration. Committee membership generally reflects party alignment in each chamber. The committee chair has considerable power, based in part on control over when and for how long hearings will be held and whether a bill will be reported to the legislature for action. The chair will also usually manage the bill on the floor of Congress. For these reasons the committee and especially the committee chair are often gatekeepers controlling the destiny of legislation.

The committees may be broadly representative of the parent body, or they may be unrepresentative, consisting of "outliers" who are either more to the political left or right of the parent body or more representative of special interests.[16] As outliers, committee members might advance legislation not favored by the legislative majority, or frustrate the majority by stalemating proposals whenever the committee consists of outliers located at both political extremes. In practice, committee composition probably varies, with some committees consisting of political or special interest outliers and others more broadly representative.

---

15. For extensive discussion of congressional procedures, see C. Tiefer, Congressional Practice and Procedure: A Reference, Research, and Legislative Guide (1989).

16. See generally Krehbiel, Are Congressional Committees Composed of Preference Outliers?, 84 Amer. Pol. Sci. Rev. 149 (1990).

Several recent developments have complicated power relationships within committees and reduced the chair's power. The basic trend has been towards greater dispersion of power. First, seniority is no longer the only criterion for being a committee chair. Second, committee membership has been expanded to permit new members to serve, with less regard to seniority. Third, subcommittees with genuine power have been created; they no longer lapse after holding hearings on a bill, and subcommittee chairs often manage bills on the floor. Fourth, a bill can be referred to more than one committee with somewhat greater frequency than in the past. Although these trends occurred in both the House and Senate, they were more dramatic in the House.

House leadership. The role of the party leadership varies greatly in the House and Senate, in part because of the relative sizes of the two bodies. The House is a large unwieldy body which can only operate effectively under close control. One source of control is the Speaker of the House, who has much greater power than the Senate Majority Leader. The Speaker strongly influences committee assignments, including the Rules Committee, based to a considerable extent on loyalty. He also influences which committee has jurisdiction over a bill when there is a dispute, sometimes assigning a bill jointly, sequentially, or in parts to different committees.

Another source of leadership control in the House is the power wielded by the House Rules Committee. Its importance is reflected in a greater than proportionate membership for the majority party.

The Rules Committee's best known function is to establish the groundrules for considering bills.[17] To govern this process, the Rules Committee issues Special Rules defining what amendments and motions are in order. It can specify that no amendments are in order (a "closed" rule) or that only certain amendments are in order ("restrictive" or "complex" rules). Restrictive rules range from those allowing many amendments to those allowing only one amendment or, very broadly, one substitute for the bill under consideration. Sometimes only amendments proposed by the committee with bill jurisdiction are allowed. An "open" rule, permitting unlimited amendment, was once common but is now rare. The Rules Committee can also waive points of order raising procedural objections against violations of House rules, such as the requirement that amendments be germane.

The Special Rules are recommended by the Rules Committee for House acceptance. The normal pattern is for the House to adopt the rule for considering legislation, although the House occasionally rejects the Rules Committee's proposal on very controversial bills. After adopting a rule governing consideration of a bill, the House then resolves itself into a Committee of the Whole to take tentative votes, and eventually reports the bill back to the House for a final vote. This gives one final chance for the House to reject amendments made in the Committee of the Whole or to

17. Sometimes the Rules Committee will block House consideration of legislation which is so controversial that legislators would prefer not to risk making enemies by taking either side.

recommit the entire bill to a committee. Recommittal with instructions is the minority's last opportunity to get a vote on amendments which a restrictive rule may have precluded.

A bill can also come up for consideration under "suspension of the rules." This procedure is usually used only for minor bills, but occasionally for more important legislation, especially in the rush to adjournment. It provides the equivalent of a special rule—the bill manager moves to suspend the rules and pass a bill, with such amendments as the mover specifies. No other amendments are allowed and no points of order lie against the bill. Passage of a bill pursuant to the suspension procedure requires a two-thirds vote of the House.

In recent decades, there has been some shift away from centralized leadership control in the House. First, there has been a greater opportunity for members to obtain floor consideration of bill amendments, especially during the 1970s. Second, committee size increased and there was greater use of subcommittees, both of which reduced leadership power. Third, the ethos of apprenticeship and deference to committee chairs also diminished. More powerful interest groups and the declining importance of parties created more complex pressures on legislators, which made them more resistant to leadership control.

In the 1980s floor debate and amendments were still more important than before the 1970s, but leadership control was reasserted. First, the rules governing consideration of omnibus budget bills (massive legislation with provisions covering many different appropriations provisions) discouraged floor amendment. Second, "restrictive" rules governing floor consideration of a bill became more common, especially on more controversial legislation. Committee chairs and House leadership played a significant role in shaping these restrictive rules.[18]

Senate leadership. The Senate is another story altogether. There is nothing comparable to the House practice of centralized control. The Majority Leader lacks the power of the House Speaker and there is nothing like the House Rules Committee. Senate tradition and rules permit floor amendment, including nongermane amendments. (Germaneness is, however, required for appropriations and budget reconciliation legislation and after cloture has shut off a filibuster.) The Senate will also vote as a body to overrule the chair on points of order for political reasons, in contrast to the House, where the Speaker's decision is usually final. These politically oriented votes can undermine whatever germaneness requirements exist. The Senate also has a tradition of open discussion. For example, Senate debate on the Tax Reform Act of 1986 lasted twelve days and considered many amendments, but House debate was limited to a few hours and one amendment in the nature of a Republican substitute. The best known example of open discussion in the Senate is the filibuster, which can only be ended by a cloture vote of 60% of the membership. These opportunities for Senators to act independent of the leadership may be one reason why there is less

18.   See S. Smith, Call to Order (1989).

objection to seniority and centralized committee power in the Senate than in the House.

The Senate leadership still has various techniques of control. First, there is a procedure to control debate, called the "unanimous consent agreement" (UCA), which can do all that a restrictive special rule in the House can do. Since the early 1970s, the leadership has taken primary responsibility for working out UCAs, but unanimous consent is far from guaranteed and has been increasingly difficult to arrange in the 1990s. Second, majority leader prerogatives usually include power over adjournment and a motion to "proceed to consideration" to move Senate business along and determine what bills will be considered, although this prerogative is not dictatorially exploited. Less formally, majority leadership uses the motion to table to prevent minority member amendments, relying largely on party loyalty for support. The motion to table is nondebatable and has a high priority in competition with other claims on Senate business (it is "privileged"). Third, the majority leader and bill managers have priority of recognition from the presiding officer. Fourth, the bill's floor manager retains some control through the "call for the regular order," which brings the Senate back to committee amendments temporarily deferred.

Fifth, a tradition of comity among Senators may offset some of the body's anarchic tendencies. Comity plays an important role because Senators are elected for long periods and are more likely to interact frequently with each other (assuming no term limits). There is, however, a contrary tradition of respecting a Senator's claims to individual power. One example is the majority leader's tradition of allowing Senators to request "holds" on legislation, which can slow down or block consideration of a bill. Another example is the filibuster, permitted by rule and tradition.

In recent years, the centrifugal forces have been ascendant, as the filibuster has been more widely used (not just against civil rights legislation, as was generally true until the 1970s), and techniques for post-cloture filibustering have developed, such as extensive quorum calls and requests for recorded votes. Indeed, the tendency towards expanding the filibuster and preventing UCAs has contributed (along with fund-raising) to the growing dissatisfaction among incumbent Senators and has accelerated the pace of voluntary retirements.

Conference. Disagreements between the House and Senate are often resolved through conference committees, usually consisting of selected members of the relevant House and Senate committees. In recent years, however, the ability of House and Senate committee members to control conferences has been reduced by expanding conferees to include members of more than one committee and, occasionally, legislators not serving on a relevant committee. In addition, the House and Senate are now somewhat more willing to reject conference agreements, which further limits the ability of a conference committee to disregard the wishes of the parent body. One reason a parent chamber might vote down a conference compromise is that the conference might have rejected amendments which had previously been passed by floor amendment (usually in the Senate), often over the opposition of committees in the parent chamber.

Shifting patterns of leadership control. Patterns of leadership control are neither permanent nor airtight. First, the patterns described above are only current practice. At the turn of the 19th century, for example, the Speaker of the House had almost dictatorial control of committee assignments and floor procedure (as Chair of the Rules Committee). In the 1980s, the Democratic House leadership was vulnerable to coalitions of Republicans and conservative Democrats. In the Senate, the importance of UCAs and the majority leader's reliance on the motion to table to prevent amendments is a recent phenomenon.

Second, the foregoing discussion may overstate control by legislative leadership. With enough commitment, the leadership loses. For example, in 1982, a comprehensive tax bill had extended income tax withholding to interest payments. Next year, opponents struck back. Millions of letters arrived in Washington from the elderly and others who objected to their interest being taxed (of course, interest had always been taxable, but debtors did not withhold tax). Banks were in fact behind the letter campaign. House and Senate leaders blocked a vote on repeal, which would have increased the budget deficit. Repeal advocates bypassed the Senate committee process and attached their proposal as a non-germane amendment to another bill. A filibuster by repeal opponents was cut off by a 60% cloture vote. The Senate leadership's effort to prevent defeat by adjourning was rejected, even though Senators usually support the leadership on adjournment motions. In the House, the rarely used petition to discharge a bill from committee, where it was languishing, brought repeal of withholding to a House vote. The bill passed under suspension of the rules, for which a two-thirds vote is required. The overwhelming vote demonstrated that the bill was veto proof.

Third, the legislative leadership is itself fragmented among different committee chairs and the House Speaker and Senate majority leader. In fact, a dominant complaint about Congress today is the absence of effective leadership—too many committees considering important legislation; increased partisanship; and committee chairs unresponsive to party leaders.

Would you favor any of the following proposals, which were floated in Congress in 1992,[19] to deal with these problems:

House Speaker can appoint (not just influence the appointment) of committee chairs;

create more ad hoc panels across current committee lines to consider multi-issue legislation;

reduce the number of committees?

---

19. See 50 Cong. Quart. Weekly Rep. 1579 (1992). See generally Solomon and Wolfensberger, The Decline of Deliberative Democracy in the House and Proposals for Reform, 31 Harv. J. Leg. 321 (1994).

Are any of the "problems" you perceive with the legislative process amenable to "reforms," or are they the result of deeper causes, such as a party split between the White House and Congress; PAC campaign funding independent of the party; anything else?

Discharge petition dispute. A recent challenge to the House legislative leadership changed the rules about discharge petitions. A discharge petition permits a majority of House Members to force floor consideration of a bill which is bottled up in committee. Before a change in the House rules in September, 1993 (H. Res. 134, sponsored by Congressman Inhofe), signatures on a discharge petition remained secret until the necessary majority signed. This permitted Members to say publicly that they wanted the House to consider the bill without signing the discharge petition to back their claims. The new rules require public availability of signatures prior to reaching the necessary majority for discharge. House of Representatives, House Rules, Rule XXVII, clause 3 (1995).

Is greater publicity for discharge petition signatures and the expected increase in their successful use a plus or a minus for the legislative process? In the following excerpt (printed in 139 Cong Rec E 2389, 103rd Cong. 1st Sess. (Oct. 7, 1993)), Representative Mike Synar praises the prior practice for its contribution to the democratic process. How can greater secrecy and preventing an issue from coming to the entire legislative body *improve* the democratic process?

Mr. Speaker, much has been made of proposal to change the rules governing discharge petitions. * * *

* * * While I ultimately supported the Inhofe resolution, my decision was not an easy one. I have some serious concerns about the impact of this resolution on the legislative process and about the tone of the debate surrounding the House's consideration of the resolution.

Proponents of the Inhofe proposal alleged its consideration was being hindered by the heavy-handed tactics of house leaders who sought to retain a policy of secrecy and dishonest representation. * * *

Proponents also claimed that passing this legislation would bring sunshine to government. All that congressman Inhofe's resolution does is change the timing of when signatures on discharge petitions are released. Not whether they are, but when.

In addition, Mr. Inhofe and others argued that not releasing the names of signers before the petition receives a majority allows members to deceive their constituents about their support for a bill. Members may say they support legislation, may even cosponsor it, but stop short of taking the final step that will bring it to the floor for a vote. This lack of action, Mr. Inhofe contends, is indicative of deception on the part of members.

I disagree. Refusal to sign a discharge petition does not mean a member is not supportive of legislation. Even if a member supports legislation, he or she may be reluctant to bring it to the floor outside the proper process. A discharge petition precludes process.

The discharge petition was originally brought into being as a means to circumvent the committee process by a determined majority of the house. It was intended as a procedure of last resort. A procedure to be used only when normal channels failed. As such, it is a necessary safeguard to our democratic process. A life preserver, if you will, to be used to keep the process afloat when it has been tossed overboard. You do not use a life preserver unless you're in danger of drowning: a discharge petition is much the same.

By discharging a committee of legislation, an opportunity for public input and involvement is lost. Hearings, wherein information is made available to members by proponents of different sides of the issue are foregone.

Congressman Inhofe suggests that by changing the timing of when the names on the petitions are released, members will be forced to be more candid in their statements of support for legislation. If this is the case, then releasing the names earlier may indeed be beneficial. However, this benefit is of limited application as only 31 discharge petitions have been entered in the last 57 years.

Furthermore, releasing the names of signers before a majority is garnered may have serious drawbacks that could outweigh that single benefit. Rather than benefiting the public, the Inhofe proposal may instead bolster groups with narrow interests who would use the disclosed names of discharge petition signers as a lobbying tool.

Special interests are even now plotting ways to use the discharge procedure to promote their agendas. They see it as a way to circumvent committees where they do not have "friends." I cannot emphasize enough how unwise the increased use of this procedure would be as it undermines the committee process the House relies on to consider complex policy issues. That said, in the end, I still found myself supporting this measure during the house's vote.

What the whole debate boils down to is this: substantively, does the Inhofe proposal make a difference in the discharge procedure? The answer is no. After studying the issue for some time, I realized that while there is potential for good and bad to result from this change, it is not innately one or the other. By its existence, this bill will not make individual members do other than what is within them to do. In the past, the discharge petition has been used by members only as a last resort. I have faith that each of my colleagues will continue to act within the bounds of his or her own conscience.

Some may wonder, then why vote for it? The primary reason is this: this whole debate has enhanced the perception of secrecy that surrounds the congress. I believe that the previous rule entailed no real secrecy. In terms of the damage this issue has wrought, however, it may as well have been the most secret rule in existence.

Despite the fact that this is probably the most open congress in the history of the body, the institution is plagued by a perception of secrecy. In this case, that perception is more important than the realities surrounding this issue. It distracts the congress from tackling the many substantive issues that face us today. It enforces the perception shared by many of the American people that they are not participants in the process. That no matter what they do, or how they vote, or what they say, the power structure of Washington will do as it will.

Democracy is not a spectator sport. It is important that people participate in the process. If in passing this bill, we in some measure reassured the American people that this is a responsive body, then we did right in passing it.

4.04 THE CRITIQUE FROM THE LEFT

The empirical critique of the legislative process by those associated with Law and Economics (Public Choice) came from the political Right. As Easterbrook's article indicated, it has been used by its proponents to justify the beady-eyed judicial approach—limiting judicial discretion as much as possible. We will see in a later section that these empirical insights into the legislative process have also been used to justify a more aggressive normative conception of judging—one associated with the political Left—but the historical link has been with the political Right.

There was also an empirical critique of the legislative process from the Left, which emerged from the country's experience during the 1960s and 1970s. The civil rights movement made it clear that various groups were shut out of both (1) the electoral process (African–Americans often could not vote and women often could not get elected), and (2) the legislative process (for example, seniority rules in the Senate usually kept civil rights legislation in committee). Opposition to the Vietnam War proved effective precisely because it bypassed the legislature and moved to the streets. By the late 1960s, the assassination of Martin Luther King when he was forging multi-racial links among the economically less privileged suggested that political reform coalitions were doomed to failure. And, by the 1970s, Watergate confirmed lack of confidence in the political system.

The critique from the Left characterized the political process as exclusionary, resulting from traditional social and cultural blindness to the needs and experiences of others. The Public Choice insights about the problems of collective action were not neglected; but they were seen as misleadingly incomplete. The problem lay with social and cultural attitudes, not just with political mechanics. Overcoming the free rider problem to political organization, for example, would still leave many groups out in the political cold. The problem was that excluded groups were seen as the "other," not as full participants in the political process. It would be difficult, in Legal Process terms, for the dominant political groups to include the "others" among the "reasonable persons" who could "pursu[e] reasonable purposes reasonably." Moreover, those excluded were also more and more unwilling to view the dominant groups as "reasonable."

These views appeared under several banners—critical legal studies, feminist jurisprudence, critical race theory and gay legal studies. Though far from homogeneous in their view of the political system, they agreed that the legislative process often produced a systematic (if not always self conscious) pattern of exclusion. From their perspective, the most striking feature of the Legal Process view of the legal system was not its optimism about the reasonableness of legislating but its inattention to minority rights. One of the more surprising aspects of the legal literature in the late 1950s was the difficulty legal academics encountered in justifying desegregation decisions protecting African–Americans from discrimination. Learned Hand, for example, in his later years, criticized the Supreme Court's 1954 decision in Brown v. Board of Education as an example of judicial second-guessing of legislative choices.[20]

There was an irony in the fact that the 1960s and 1970s, when these views took shape, were periods of considerable legal reform, often to include omitted groups. The Voting Rights Acts ended many of the old exclusionary practices. The legislature relaxed some of its procedures which entrenched seniority. And post-Watergate legislation tried to do something about the impact of money in politics. Government also did more than simply adjust the political process. The War on Poverty and civil rights legislation tried to end disadvantage and discrimination in the workplace, which would (it was hoped) eventually result in meaningful participation in both the economic and political life of the country. "Maximum feasible participation,"[21] a phrase which has disappeared from our political language, was supposed to bring previously excluded groups into grass roots political participation.

Ultimately, these reforms did little to head off loss of faith in the government generally and the legislature in particular. Indeed, by creating expectations that were not realized, they contributed to the view that there was not much the government could do about these problems. Those left out saw themselves fall further behind and those included often expressed the frustrations associated with rising expectations. Moreover, legislation aimed at limiting the influence of money in politics proved ineffective (PAC contributions exploded), suggesting that the legislative process could not fix itself.

20. Gerald Gunther, Learned Hand, pp. 656–67 (1994).

21. Daniel P. Moynihan, Maximum Feasible Misunderstanding (1970).

None of this surprised many on the Left. If politics was primarily a reflection of broader cultural forces, no wonder that the economically disadvantaged were not helped by legislative reforms and no wonder that old biases did not yield to legislative correction.

4.05 RECONSTRUCTING THE JUDICIAL ROLE

There have been two responses to the decline of faith in a democratically purposeful legislature—find something for judges to do besides simply elaborating legislative purpose (Republicanism), or not let judges do much of anything at all (textualism). Underlying both approaches is a normative theory of judging.

Republicanism adopts the view that law strives for an ideal to which all government (legislatures and judges) contribute. Judges must do more than passively implement the (arguably purposeless) legislative results but must collaborate with the legislature in making law, although prudential considerations allow for a wide range of judicial discretion in how to collaborate. This conception of judging rejects the airtight compartment view of legislating and judging. It instead views both statutes and judge-made law as part of a broader legal framework, with the judge bearing some responsibility for working out the interactions among the various components of the law. This is reminiscent of the Hale and Blackstone conception of statutes and judicial opinions as only evidence of the law.

Textualism, by contrast, gives the judge little to do on the theory that judging (at least statutory interpretation) is concerned only with implementing what the legislature says. This follows from a very different view of the law from that adopted by Republicanism. It adopts the airtight compartment view of Separation of Powers—legislatures legislate, judges "merely" judge, and the two tasks are radically distinct.

The law and economics empirical critique of legislation arrives at textualism by the following chain of reasoning—part empirical, part normative. It initially adopts an intentionalist view of legislation but fails to find any intent worth elaborating—that is the empirical part. This leads to the text by default, *because* the judge has no role in fitting statutes into the broader fabric of the law; the text becomes the only way to defer to what the legislature has done, once there is no purpose to elaborate—that is the normative part.

a) FINDING SOMETHING FOR JUDGES TO DO—"REPUBLICANISM"

Modern "Republicanism" adopts an ideal of an inclusive political process in which all groups (without exclusion) deliberate respectfully for the common good or public interest. The historical roots of Republicanism are traceable to the time of the Founding—to the Anti–Federalists' conception of civic virtue. This is illustrated by Jefferson's view that "[t]he moral sense is as much a part of our constitution as that of feeling, seeing, or hearing; * * * [and] every human mind feels pleasure in doing good to another."[22] That moral sense would operate in the political arena to produce deliberation leading to a common commitment to the public interest. The historical details of this ideal in 1789 are obviously too narrow for us today (excluding women, minorities, and the unpropertied), but the ideal was capable of shaking off its limits and growing into an attractive model of politics. Indeed, contemporary feminist writings are a dominant strain in the modern updating of Republican ideals.[23]

Contemporary discussion of "Republicanism" has also revived interest in the original conception of politics that produced the federal Constitution. James Madison's view of factions, expressed in the Federalist papers, was that one faction might prevail over others, oppressing the political loser. He contrasted politics in a large republic, like the United States, with smaller governmental units, like the states. Only in a large republic, with properly constructed checks and balances, could oppression by a dominant faction be minimized. The Anti–Federalists objected to this negative image of state and local politics, as susceptible to majority oppression. They envisaged politics as expressing the ideals of Republican civic virtue, usually understood today as a synonym for deliberation about public values. They were also concerned that a stronger federal government would in fact adopt political positions associated with industry and commerce, which would encourage personal aggrandizement and discourage civic virtue.

Modern Public Choice models of legislation usually claim to be descendants of Madison's view of factions. There is, however, a strong case to be made that checks and balances in the federal government were intended not only to deal with the reality of factions but also to transform legislative and representative politics into a deliberative process about public values. A significant strain in Madison's thinking, in other words, was to advance the Anti–Federalists goals but by different means. He sought ways to adapt the republican traditions of civic virtue, which were historically associated with small city-states, to the needs and circumstances of a large nation-state.[24]

———————

The Republican ideal has both procedural and substantive features. Procedural republicanism stresses procedural due process, in which the dominant concern is with adequate representation of political interests. "As if" republicanism is substantively more ambitious, though it remains tied to a procedural foundation—stressing the judge's role in simulating the substan-

---

22. Henry May, The Enlightenment in America, p. 296 (1976).

23. See Martha Minow, Making All the Difference: Inclusion, Exclusion, and American Law (1990); Martha Minow, Justice Engendered, 101 Harv. L. Rev. 10 (1987); Mar-

garet Radin, The Pragmatist and the Feminist, 63 So. Cal. L. Rev. 1699 (1990).

24. See Sunstein, Interest Groups in American Public Law, 38 Stan. L. Rev. 29 (1985); Ackerman, Discovering the Constitution, 93 Yale L. J. 1013 (1983).

tive results of an inclusive and deliberative process seeking the common good.

(1) Procedural Republicanism

Procedural Republicanism relies on judges to make up for procedural defects in the give-and-take process of making legislation.[25] It tries to be substantively unaggressive, accepting the Public Choice view that interests are brought to the political bargaining table to secure the best possible deal, not to rework positions to secure the common good (that is, the interests are exogenous to the political process). Procedural Republicanism's goal is to compensate for shortcomings in this political process.

Reliance on procedure has always seemed an attractive escape hatch for judges intent on avoiding the appearance of substantive lawmaking.[26] Most procedural protections deal with the application, not the formation of rules. There is a well-developed body of constitutional, statutory, and common law about notice and hearing requirements when courts and administrative agencies apply law.[27] Procedural requirements for rulemaking are less well developed. Judges, as a matter of practice, usually write and publish opinions explaining how judicial rules evolve. Administrative agencies are usually required by statute to provide notice and an opportunity for written comment before they make rules. But the legislative rulemaking process is relatively untouched by explicit procedural standards.

There are *some* process requirements for legislative rulemaking (see Chapter 17). State constitutions often require reading a bill three times and waiting several days before a vote, limit a bill to one subject, prohibit changing a bill's subject matter as it passes through the legislature, forbid substantive law in appropriations bills, and require bills to contain titles describing their subject matter. The rationale for these rules is to improve the legislator's and public's awareness of what the legislature is doing and to reduce the impact of powerful private interests groups who might otherwise capture the legislative process.[28] (One prominent state judge has suggested forcing legislatures to stick to their own internally-adopted procedural rules—as a requirement of due process of law—to improve the deliberative process.[29] Is that a good idea?)

At the federal level, there are very few explicit constitutional requirements about how statutes are made, certainly nothing like the detailed rules

---

25. Frank Michelman, Law's Republic, 97 Yale L. J. 1493, 1526 (1988).

26. Laurence Tribe, The Puzzling Persistence of Process–Based Constitutional Theories, 89 Yale L. J. 1063 (1980).

27. Henry Friendly, Some Kind of Hearing, 123 U. Pa. L. Rev. 1267 (1975).

28. The efficacy of these constitutional rules is uncertain. A minority of states (by judicial fiat) adopt an "enrolled bill" approach, which precludes judicial review for violations of state constitutional rules about legislative procedures. And some states which review for procedural error excuse lapses which seem "harmless" (such as failure to read the bill three times; or violation of the one-subject rule if the title is accurate). See Chapter 17 *infra*.

29. See Linde, Due Process of Lawmaking, 55 Neb. L. Rev. 197, 246 (1976).

found in state constitutions to encourage a meaningful deliberative process.[30] Each house of Congress has its own procedural rules, but these are not legally enforceable in court.[31] Although participation in the legislative process is routinely permitted on important legislation (assuming someone knows about the bill and has the means to participate), there is no explicit constitutional requirement that the legislature permit such participation.[32] This gap in procedural protections at the legislative level seemed ripe for judicial attention, providing a substantively neutral way to improve the substantive results of the political process, and Procedural Republicanism sought to fill the void.

Concerns about procedural defects in the legislative process had its greatest impact on thinking about constitutional law, in the work of John Hart Ely.[33] Groups which were excluded from politics deserved special constitutional protection—implementing what Ely called the "representation-reinforcing" principle.[34] This insight built on the famous Carolene Products footnote,[35] which expressed concern for those discrete and insular minorities which had been excluded from the "pluralist bazaar"[36] ("pluralist" is a synonym for the Public Choice image of multiple interest groups bargaining about pre-determined interests). Ely's conception of exclusion was expansive, taking account of the fact that some people could not (really) get a hearing because no one would listen. Prejudice could as effectively foreclose access as more obvious barriers—such as overcoming obstacles to the vote, to effective political organization, and legislative inertia.

Application to statutory interpretation. Procedural concerns also had an impact on statutory interpretation. *First,* one way courts could make up for inadequate access to the political process was to tilt interpretation in favor of those groups who are least able to organize effectively. This suggested extending protection beyond those discrete and insular minorities who are better able to organize than many groups, to include the poor, who lack the time or money to be politically active.[37] The Supreme Court in fact took a generous pro-poor approach to interpreting welfare legislation in the late 1960s and 1970s.[38] Another way to help the politically less well organized was

---

30. For example, revenue bills must originate in the House of Representatives (U.S. Const., Art. I., sec. 7); and 20% of those present can force recording of the yeas and nays (U.S.Const., Art. I., sec. 5).

31. Metzenbaum v. Federal Energy Regulatory Commission, 675 F.2d 1282 (D.C.Cir. 1982).

32. Minnesota State Board for Community Colleges v. Knight, 465 U.S. 271, 283 (1984). But cf. Vander Jagt v. O'Neill, 699 F.2d 1166, 1170 (D.C.Cir.1982)(Member of Congress sues unsuccessfully to require party representation on congressional committees to reflect percentage of party membership in the parent chamber).

33. John Hart Ely, Democracy and Distrust: A Theory of Judicial Review, pp. 79–83, 102–03, 151–53 (1980)(hereafter "Ely").

34. Ely, p. 87.

35. United States v. Carolene Products Co., 304 U.S. 144, 152 n. 4 (1938) (stricter scrutiny to protect "discrete and insular minorities").

36. Ely, p. 152.

37. Bruce Ackerman, Beyond Carolene Products, 98 Harv. L. Rev. 713 (1985).

38. See, e.g., King v. Smith, 392 U.S. 309 (1968)(state's definition of "father" to include a man living with the mother but who has no duty to support children violates the federal AFDC grant-in-aid statute).

to rely on the public values rhetoric which so often works its way into statutory language.[39] Legislators like to have it "both ways," voting for texts which seem to implement public values while hoping that legislative history or agency restraint will lead courts to confine the statute to protect well organized political interests. Courts could counter this ploy by implementing the public values language.

Second, statutory interpretation could help to level the political playing field by interpreting a statute in favor of the group which is least likely to be listened to in the legislature, even if they are politically active. For example: what chance does an unpopular gay couple have to persuade a legislature that it is a "family"? Chapter 5.02b discusses what the term "family" means in a older statute.

These procedural concerns, which are most closely associated with Republicanism, raise issues of fundamental fairness—assuring a level political playing field. There are other procedural concerns which deserve mention here, however, even though they do not necessarily raise such fundamental issues. Legislatures may exhibit other procedural shortcomings and courts might have a role to play in helping the law overcome them. As you work through the materials later in the course, you should consider exactly which procedural problems within the legislature the court might be addressing.

First, interpretation can compensate for legislative inertia—the tendency for the legislature not to act. Various factors contribute to inertia. Legislators are very busy and do not have time to address many problems. A few legislators in key positions can control the agenda, blocking legislation that would otherwise have a good chance of passage. And legislators are often more concerned with negative rather than positive reactions from constituents, favoring inaction to avoid making enemies. These factors contribute to the ability of well organized groups to control the legislative process, but the concern about legislative inertia extends beyond the problem of inadequate representation. A legislature cannot be expected to react to every change that occurs. Consequently, courts might extend statutes to events not within the historical legislature's contemplation, to obviate the need for the legislature to revisit the law. Or a court might either deny or extend application of the law to contemporary facts when that is best way to force the legislature to overcome inertia and revisit a political issue. These questions are discussed in Chapter 9, dealing with change.

Second, a procedure-based approach can also correct for situations in which legislators are unaware of what they are doing, rather than being indifferent or even hostile to certain underrepresented interests. In constitutional law, this can be accomplished by carefully scrutinizing claims that a law has a public purpose and that there is a good fit between statutory means and the alleged purpose, whenever there is evidence that the legislature acted with little awareness of what it was doing.[40] (See Chapter 17.03, dealing

---

39. Jonathan Macey, Promoting Public–Regarding Legislation Through Statutory Interpretation: An Interest Group Model, 86 Colum. L. Rev. 223 (1986).

40. United States Railroad Retirement Board v. Fritz, 449 U.S. 166, 182 (1980)(Bren-

with legislative rationality.) In statutory interpretation, careless legislating can justify inferring a meaning that does not implement the careless result. Thus, when a statute requires filing "*before* December 31," the court could infer that this was a drafting error and substitute the more sensible "on or before December 31" language.[41] This case is discussed in Chapter 6.04biv.

(2) "As if" Republicanism[42]

A.   NO PROCEDURE WITHOUT SUBSTANCE

The central criticism of a focus on procedure is that making up for procedural defects cannot fully explain the judicial role. First, procedural values are often as contested as substantive concerns, and the debate over procedure quickly becomes a debate over substantive implications. Not everyone agrees, for example, that legislative inertia is a defect requiring a judicial remedy. Inertia might be built into the constitutional structure to minimize legislative activity.[43] But minimal legislation is itself a contested substantive value. The case for legislative inertia is that, like checks and balances, it limits government power, but that may not make much sense in contemporary society where so much power rests with unregulated private aggregations of authority.

Second, decisions about which groups to protect is substantively based. Proceduralism purports to identify those excluded from politics, not those whose exclusion was "unjustified."[44] But justification is necessarily part of the judge's concern in deciding whom to protect. It is usually too hard for courts to distinguish the political loser from the politically excluded, once we get over the problem of extreme examples of blocking access to the ballot. Difficulty of political organization may simply reflect lack of political intensity, which cannot be characterized as a defect in the democratic process.

Moreover, the concept of prejudice (the refusal to listen) is hard to distinguish from political disagreement.[45] For example, regarding gender issues, it is often said that men just don't get it; hence, arguments made by women, though they are an electoral majority and are well organized

---

nan, J., dissenting)(Congress inattentively omits group from retirement benefits, deferring to private interest bargain in which bargaining parties inadequately represented in group); Schweiker v. Wilson, 450 U.S. 221, 243 (1981)(Powell, J., dissenting)(deference to legislature rests in part on principle of responsive and aware political process); Fullilove v. Klutznick, 448 U.S. 448, 548–53 (1980)(Stevens, J., concurring)(busy congress acted precipitately and failed to address important questions regarding racial preferences).

41. United States v. Locke, 471 U.S. 84, 122 (1985)(Stevens, J. dissenting).

42. The phrase is borrowed from Jerry Mashaw, As if Republicanism, 97 Yale L. J. 1685 (1988)(hereafter "Mashaw").

43. Frank Easterbrook, Statutes' Domains, 50 U. Chi. L. Rev. 533, 548–49 (1983).

44. Ely, p. 153.

45. Cf. Postema, Bentham and the Common Law Tradition, p. 67 (1986), discussing Burke's view that prejudice is "unlearned intuition," not "blind, unthinking bias,"and that the "wise and prudent person" seeks the "latent wisdom" in prejudices which "initially appear [ ] ungrounded."

politically, are not "heard." Homophobia creates similar problems for gays. Although it is certainly possible to characterize unheard voices as a procedural defect, if we really listen carefully to those who (allegedly) do not hear certain arguments, we quickly uncover a substantive world view that might express itself this way—"Sure, I hear you. You're just wrong. My embrace of traditional gender values is self-conscious and purposeful. It is the backbone of our society." People with old prejudices have often given them quite a bit of thought, although people with newer prejudices do not like to admit it. None of us is immune from that charge (the "liberal" attitude towards religious fundamentalism strikes me as an example). We are, quite simply, a diverse society, where the "problem" is as much diversity as prejudice. There is no avoiding the fact that the appropriate vision of society, the individual, and their mutual relationship is a substantive issue which affects judicial decisions.

Third, our legal tradition does not unlink procedure from substance. Procedures are fine-tuned to account for substantive impact. The "beyond a reasonable doubt" rule in criminal law is the best known example, but judicial review of agency rules has always been sensitive to the substantive values at stake—for example, prior hearings are constitutionally required before cutting off needs-based welfare but not when the benefits are not needs-based.[46]

Although the constitution does not explicitly impose procedural requirements on the federal legislature, it does so indirectly through the equal protection and due process clauses, with adjustments to account for substantive considerations. Thus, when a statute imposes burdens on fundamental interests or certain traditionally disadvantaged groups, the courts require information about the legislature's actual purpose (the legislative end) and a close fit between legislative means and ends. As substantive concerns diminish, the court requires less assurance that the deliberative process worked well. The court will accept a weaker fit between statutory means and ends and may even accept the government's claim about legislative purpose (with little solid evidence). Short of accepting the most tenuous fit between means and ends, a court may rely on evidence from the legislative history about how carefully the legislature considered the ends and the means-end fit and the extent to which affected parties were able to present their concerns to the legislature.[47] The fundamental point is that the legislative process deserves deference to the extent that legislatures were aware of the public purposes which the legislation implements and gave due consideration to how best to implement those purposes, and that the degree of procedural care is a function of the substantive values at stake.

---

46. Compare Goldberg v. Kelly, 397 U.S. 254 (1970) with Mathews v. Eldridge, 424 U.S. 319 (1976)(social security disability benefits).

47. Schweiker v. Wilson, 450 U.S. at 243–44 (Powell, J., dissenting). See also United States v. Lopez, 115 S.Ct. 1624, 1631–32 (1995)(no showing that Congress made any findings about connection of regulated activity to interstate commerce).

B.   SUBSTANTIVE ASSUMPTIONS OF A REPUBLICAN PROCESS

"As if" Republicanism attempts to make up for the substantive weaknesses of Procedural Republicanism,[48] by deciding cases "as if" the Republican ideal worked well, not stopping with procedural concerns. It urges judges to implement public values more directly—to simulate the results of an inclusive and deliberative process producing legislation for the common good. There are two ways to accomplish this objective in the context of *statutory interpretation*—first, by enthusiastic elaboration of statutory purposes which further such values (as Radin suggested in Chapter 3.03c); and, second, by imposing clear statement rules which protect such values from anything but the most precise legislative interference.

There are five normative assumptions at the core of "as if" Republicanism.[49] First, people bring their concerns to the legislative process, but they do so only tentatively and provisionally; second, the alteration of initial positions is not bargaining to an accommodation but a re-vision in accordance with a commitment of mutual respect and concerns for others; third, mutual respect and concern imply a normative conception about which views are entitled to special attention in the deliberate process (the proceduralist approach was concerned only with correcting for exclusion, not with whether exclusion was justified or unjustified);[50] fourth, the re-vision is concerned with public values, either transforming private interests which were initially advanced or rethinking public value positions originally held; fifth, the final product embodies public values for the common good.

These assumptions hold procedural and substantive concerns in a very delicate balance. "As if" Republicanism is committed to substantive concerns which are implicit in the commitment to a deliberative and inclusive political process—respect and concern for those with whom deliberation occurs. Procedure is not only an instrumental value, enabling participants to get what they want, but also a substantive value, encouraging respect and concern for others with whom they are thrown together in political interaction.

Frank Michelman's version of Republicanism rests clearly on such assumptions. First, the respect/concern requirement insists that points of view are entitled to political inclusion when they involve "self-identification" whose recognition is a precondition for mutual respect. He develops this theme in discussing homosexuality,[51] which is "not just a certain sort of inclination that 'anyone' might feel, but a more personally constitutive and distinctive way, or ways, of being." It has "come to be experienced, claimed, socially reflected and—if ambiguously—confirmed as an aspect of identity demanding respect."

---

48. See generally Frank Michelman, Law's Republic, 97 Yale L.J. 1493 (1988)(hereafter "Michelman, Republic"); Frank Michelman, Traces of Self-Government, 100 Harv. L. Rev. 4 (1986)(hereafter "Michelman, Traces"); Cass Sunstein, Beyond the Republican Revival, 97 Yale L.J. 1539 (1988).

49. See generally Sunstein, Revival, pp. 1542, 1544–45, 1548–49, 1555–56, 1576–77, 1579, 1581–82.

50. Ely, p. 153.

51. Michelman, Republic, pp. 1532–37.

Second, the requirement of respect/concern affirms that "difference is what we have in common," "that 'openness to "otherness" [is] a way toward recognition not only of the other, but also of oneself.' "[52] The emphasis is on a particular way of deliberating—hearing voices that are conventionally unheard, or in Michelman's image, "confront[ing] the parties in the flesh" (a theme he discusses in the context of an army rule forbidding a Jew from wearing a Yarmulke). This is not substantively innocent. It insists that the judge replicate a result that listens empathetically to the multiple points of view included in the deliberative process.[53]

The substantive focus of "as if" Republicanism is, however, modest. Thus, Michelman refers to a "process-based, republican-not-pluralist" approach.[54] There is no doubt that a judicial world which listens to conventionally unheard voices is different from one which does not make this effort, but this description of the judicial process lends some credence to observations that "as if" Republicanism has a "relative[ly] empt[y]"[55] normative vision and is "a flight from substance."[56] Michelman's substantivism is, by his own admission, relatively weak—it seeks "a process of normative justification without ultimate objectivist foundations."[57]

Further evidence of the weak substantive content of "as if" Republicanism is the emphasis on "practical reason." "Practical reason" is, in Michelman's definition, a "process, in which the meaning of the rule emerges, develops, and changes in the course of applying it."[58] Although advocates of Republicanism probably expect traditionally excluded minorities to gain a voice they would otherwise lack, there is no guarantee that careful listening will privilege their point of view. In practice, it may turn out that Ely's representation-reinforcing approach does more to justify helping excluded points of view, by protecting their interests directly, than a Republicanism that tries to replicate a process which pays attention to multiple perspectives.

C. *JUDICIAL PROCESS*

There is, however, enough substance in "as if" Republicanism for Michelman to be concerned with finding a justification for judges to play an active lawmaking role. His route to the Republican ideals of "civic virtue and the general good" lies through the courts, which "represent to us of the possibility of practical reason."[59] The most refreshing element of his argument is abandoning the fiction of democratic rhetoric, frankly admitting that the "Court is, vis-a-vis the people, irredeemably an undemocratic institution"[60] and that the justification for the judge's lawmaking role "must sound

---

52. Michelman, Traces, pp. 32–33.

53. See generally Lynne Henderson, Legality and Empathy, 85 Mich. L. Rev. 1574 (1987); Jane Schacter, Metademocracy: The Changing Structure of Legitimacy in Statutory Interpretation, 108 Harv L. Rev. 593, 623–24 (1995)(hereafter "Schacter").

54. Michelman, Republic, p. 1526.

55. Mashaw, p. 1686.

56. Richard Epstein, Modern Republicanism—Or the Flight from Substance, 97 Yale L.J. 1633 (1988).

57. Michelman, Traces, p. 23.

58. Michelman, Traces, pp. 28–29.

59. Michelman, Traces, pp. 24, 72–76.

60. Michelman, Traces, p. 16.

in virtual representation."[61] But in justifying the judicial role, Michelman refocuses our attention from legislative process to judicial process. He stresses the procedural advantages judges have in playing an affirmative role in constructing Republican values. In his view, judges are uniquely situated to decide about public values. The judicial process is insulated from interest-group politics and is capable of "listening for voices at the margins."[62] More important is the courts' deliberative tradition consisting of reflective thought (fostered by a collegial bench) and the need to write publicly-available opinions justifying results and taking responsibility.[63]

This procedural defense of what judges do invites a closer look at judging, not always with Michelman's optimism. The Left's critique of an exclusionary political process also applies to judging. Where the Legal Realists saw more or less random political choices by judges, the Left perceived a more systematic political bias to disadvantage those who had traditionally been left out of society. The optimism underlying "as if" Republican judging therefore provides false comfort. Judges exercise power, with a tendency toward what Cover called the "jurispathic" rather than the "jurisgenerative."[64] "Interpretation always takes place in the shadow of coercion,"[65] excluding meaning in the act of creating it. The facade of Republicanism or any other "ism" that conceals the exercise of power through the determination of meaning can even deflect rather than bring about real reform and change.

Courts may indeed be dominated by particular ideologies or class biases, perhaps the very traditions that ought to be questioned. Judicial decisions unfavorable to homosexuals and the poor are often cited in this connection. For example, the Court's negative attitude toward gays is not limited to the decision in Bowers v. Hardwick, 478 U.S. 186 (1986), upholding a sodomy conviction of gay partners. In Boutilier v. INS, 387 U.S. 118 (1967), the Court interpreted "psychopathic personality" in the immigration law to include homosexuality. It was Congress which overrode Boutilier in the Immigration Act of 1990, Pub. L. No. 649, § 601, 104 Stat. 4978, 5067. (But see Romer v. Evans, 116 S.Ct. 1620 (1996), which held that a state constitutional amendment prohibiting laws and policies protecting gays from discrimination violates minimum rationality test.) In this vein, Robin West

---

61. Not everyone finds abandoning democratic rhetoric refreshing. See Schacter, pp. 607, 646–50. Schacter insists (p. 647) that Republican approaches are best understood as serving substantive democratic values and that "democracy represents perhaps our most potent vocabulary for expressing basic ideals about collective self-government, the conditions that make meaningful self-government possible, and, most importantly, the numerous and diverse values with which self-government is associated." See also Guido Calabresi, A Common Law for an Age of Statutes, pp. 96–97 (1982)("legal fabric [is] a good approximation of one aspect of the popular will, of what

a majority in some sense desires."). But see Morton Horwitz, The Constitution of Change: Legal Fundamentality Without Fundamentalism, 107 Harv. L. Rev. 30, 57–65 (1993)(tracing recent rise of democracy as central legitimating concept).

62. Michelman, Republic, p. 1537.

63. Michelman, Traces, pp. 33, 76–77.

64. Robert Cover, Nomos and Narrative, 97 Harv. L. Rev. 4, 16 (jurisgenerative), 39 (jurispathic)(1983)(hereafter "Cover").

65. Cover, p. 40.

objects to the collapsing of the distinction between interpretation and politics on the ground that judging is traditional and incremental; legislatures, for all their faults, are where we should look for political change.[66]

In sum, Republicanism's efforts to recreate an ideal of inclusive and deliberative politics has just enough substance to attract the concerns that plague all substantively aggressive approaches to judging—the difficulty in privileging certain substantive values. We lack a consensus regarding substantive goals (otherwise natural law approaches would be more enthusiastically received),[67] and that in turn undermines the efforts of judges to explain who deserves how much empathy in the process of practical reasoning and how to replicate the results of such a reasoning process.

Acknowledging the substance in Republican interpretation also puts into bold relief a problem with relying too heavily on Republicanism as a theory of statutory interpretation. Its historical role has been to correct Legal Process's oversight of the exclusionary aspects in our political system. But statutory interpretation is about much more than the concerns of excluded groups. Viewed from the perspective of the long history of statutory interpretation, Republicanism is an effort to define those "fundamental" values that influence statutory meaning, something which Chief Justice Marshall and others advocated many years ago. Interpretation is, however, as much about courts helping to work out statutory meaning in more mundane settings—what Marshall called "political regulation" and "inconvenience"—and Republicanism does not seem very concerned with those issues. Republicanism will not provide us with a theory of ordinary judging, addressed to the day-to-day problems of statutory interpretation.

b) GIVING JUDGES AS LITTLE TO DO AS POSSIBLE—TEXTUALISM

Another response to the decline of purposivism was to suggest that judges should do as little as possible by falling back on the text—resting on the normative view that judges have no role in fitting legislation into the broader fabric of the law. If there is no democratic purpose to implement, all that is left is the statutory language—assuming, of course, that the judge has no affirmative role to play in fitting legislation into the broader fabric of the law. Professor Easterbrook explains the textualist's point of view from the Law and Economics perspective. (Later chapters will consider how easy it is to stick to the text.)

66. Robin West, Progressive and Conservative Constitutionalism, 88 Mich. L. Rev. 641, 650–51, 713–20 (1990).

67. Eskridge, Dynamic Statutory Interpretation, p. 182 (1994)(not a homogenous enough culture)(hereafter "Eskridge, Dynamic").

Ronald Dworkin claims that the judge can identify the right answer by working out "the best constructive interpretation of the community's legal practice." Ronald Dworkin, Law's Empire, p. 225 (1986). Some consider this claim vulnerable to the same objections as natural law approaches (Eskridge, Dynamic, p. 148). Others characterize the approach as "internal" to the judge's decision making process, which avoids the objections applicable to natural law, but deprives the claim of any "value [ ] for the *community* (emphasis in original)." Michelman, Traces, p. 71.

Easterbrook, Statutes' Domains

50 U.Chi.L.Rev. 533 (1983).

My suggestion is that unless the statute plainly hands courts the power to create and revise a form of common law, the domain of the statute should be restricted to cases anticipated by its framers and expressly resolved in the legislative process. Unless the party relying on the statute could establish either express resolution or creation of the common law power of revision, the court would hold the matter in question outside the statute's domain. The statute would become irrelevant, the parties (and court) remitted to whatever other sources of law might be applicable. * * *

* * * If [the legislature] enacts some sort of code of rules, the code will be taken as complete (until amended); gaps will go unfilled. If instead it charges the court with a common law function, the court will solve new problems as they arise, but using today's wisdom rather than conjuring up the solutions of a legislature long prorogued.

This is just a slightly different way of making the point that judicial pursuit of the "values" or aims of legislation is a sure way of defeating the original legislative plan. A legislature that seeks to achieve Goal X can do so in one of two ways. First, it can identify the goal and instruct courts or agencies to design rules to achieve the goal. In that event, the subsequent selection of rules implements the actual legislative decision, even if the rules are not what the legislature would have selected itself. The second approach is for the legislature to pick the rules. It pursues Goal X by Rule Y. The selection of Y is a measure of what Goal X was worth to the legislature, of how best to achieve X, and of where to stop in pursuit of X. Like any other rule, Y is bound to be imprecise, to be over— and under—inclusive. This is not a good reason for a court, observing the inevitable imprecision, to add to or subtract from Rule Y on the argument that, by doing so, it can get more of Goal X. The judicial selection of means to pursue X displaces and directly overrides the legislative selection of ways to obtain X. It denies to legislatures the choice of creating or withholding gapfilling authority. The way to preserve the initial choice is for judges to put the statute down once it becomes clear that the legislature has selected rules as well as identified goals.

This approach is faithful to the nature of compromise in private interest legislation. It also gives the legislature a low-cost method to signal its favored judicial approach to public interest legislation. A legislature that tries to approach the line where costs begin to exceed benefits is bound to leave a trail of detailed provisions, which on this approach would preclude judges from attempting to fill gaps. The approach also is supported by a number of other considerations. First, it recognizes that courts cannot reconstruct an original meaning because there is none to find. Second, it prevents legislatures from extending their lives beyond the terms of their members. Third, it takes a liberal view of the relation between the public and private spheres. Fourth, it takes a realistic view of judges' powers. I elaborate on these below.

1. **Original meaning**. Because legislatures comprise many members, they do not have "intents" or "designs," hidden yet discoverable. Each member may or may not have a design. The body as a whole, however, has only outcomes. It is not only impossible to reason from one statute to another but also impossible to reason from one or more sections of a statute to a problem not resolved.

This follows from the discoveries of public choice theory. Although legislators have individual lists of desires, priorities, and preferences, it turns out to be difficult, sometimes impossible, to aggregate these lists into a coherent collective choice. Every system of voting has flaws. The one used by legislatures is particularly dependent on the order in which decisions are made. Legislatures customarily consider proposals one at a time and then vote them up or down. This method disregards third or fourth options and the intensity with which legislators prefer one option over another. Additional options can be considered only in sequence, and this makes the order of decision vital. It is fairly easy to show that someone with control of the agenda can manipulate the choice so that the legislature adopts proposals that only a minority support. [Editor—Easterbrook is referring to the problem of determining majority choice when three or more voters rank order their preferences in certain ways, which we discussed earlier in this chapter.] The existence of agenda control makes it impossible for a court— even one that knows each legislator's complete table of preferences—to say what the whole body would have done with a proposal it did not consider in fact.

One countervailing force is logrolling, in which legislators express the intensity of their preferences by voting against their views on some proposals in order to obtain votes for other proposals about which their views are stronger. Yet when logrolling is at work the legislative process is submerged and courts lose the information they need to divine the body's design. A successful logrolling process yields unanimity on every recorded vote and indeterminacy on all issues for which there is no recorded vote.

In practice, the order of decisions and logrolling are not total bars to judicial understanding. But they are so integral to the legislative process that judicial predictions of how the legislature would have decided issues it did not in fact decide are bound to be little more than wild guesses, and thus to lack the legitimacy that might be accorded to astute guesses. Moreover, because control of the agenda and logrolling are accepted parts of the legislative process, a court has no justification for deciding cases as it thinks the legislature would in their absence. It might as well try to decide how the legislature would have acted were there no threat of veto or no need to cater to constituents.

[Editor—Points 2 and 3 are omitted.]

4. **Judicial Abilities**. Statutory construction is an art. Good statutory construction requires the rarest of skills. The judge must find clues in the structure of the statute, hints in the legislative history, and combine these with mastery of history, command of psychology, and sensitivity to nuance to divine how deceased legislators would have answered unasked questions.

It is all very well to say that a judge able to understand the temper of 1871 (and 1921), and able to learn the extent of a compromise in 1936, may do well when construing statutes. How many judges meet this description? How many know what clauses and provisos, capable of being enacted in 1923, would have been unthinkable in 1927 because of subtle changes in the composition of the dominant coalitions in Congress? It is hard enough to know this for the immediate past, yet who could deny that legislation that could have been passed in 1982 not only would fail but also could be repealed in 1983? The number of judges living at any time who can, with plausible claim to accuracy, "think [themselves] * * * into the minds of the enacting legislators and imagine how they would have wanted the statute applied to the case at bar," may be counted on one hand.

To deny that judges have the skills necessary to construe statutes well—at least when construction involves filling gaps in the statutes rather than settling the rare case that arises from conflicts in the rules actually laid down—is *not* to say that stupid and irresponsible judges can twist any rule. Doubtless the "judge's role should be limited, to protect against willful judges who lack humility and self-restraint." Yet there is a more general reason for limiting the scope of judicial discretion. Few of the best-intentioned, most humble, and most restrained among us have the skills necessary to learn the temper of times before our births, to assume the identity of people we have never met, and to know how 535 disparate characters from regions of great political and economic diversity would have answered questions that never occurred to them. Anyone of reasonable skill could tell that some answers would have been beyond belief in 1866. After putting the impossible to one side, though, a judge must choose from among the possible solutions, and here human ingenuity is bound to fail, often. When it fails, even the best intentioned will find that the imagined dialogues of departed legislators have much in common with their own conceptions of the good.

———————

COMMENTS AND QUESTIONS

1. Compromise and statutory interpretation

a. *Private interest and public values.* The relevance of Easterbrook's approach to statutory interpretation may not depend on the private interest origins of legislative bargaining and compromise. A major target of his article is judicial reliance on substantive presumptions favoring one side of a legislative compromise, which by definition has no favorites. Objections to favoring one side of a legislative bargain do not depend on the compromise originating in private interest negotiations. The bargaining could just as well result from negotiation over public values. Justice Harlan once characterized the results of bargaining over welfare reform as producing a "child born of the silent union of legislative compromise." Rosado v. Wyman, 397 U.S. 397, 412 (1970). Easterbrook might say that judges should not give voice to these silences, whether or not the legislative bargain is about private interests or public values.

Are compromises about public values the same as private interest bargains? Does one side of a public value compromise have more growing power than another, in accordance with the public values that side represents?

b. *How far can a court go in furthering one side of a compromise?* For example, in Potomac Electric Power Co. v. Director, Office of Workers' Compensation Programs, 449 U.S. 268 (1980), an injured worker covered by the fixed schedule of monetary damages in a Workers Compensation statute argued that he should receive a larger award, measured by actual loss of wage-earning capacity. The majority disagreed. It supported reliance on the plain meaning of the statute with the comment that the remedial nature of the statute, imposing more certain recovery for employees without proof of fault, was balanced by assuring employers of definite and lower limits on potential liability than would prevail at common law. As a compromise, the statute did not guarantee a completely adequate remedy. These comments were a response to Justice Blackmun's dissent, which argued that it was possible to construe the statute to allow the claimant to choose between the scheduled award and actual loss of wage earning capacity and that therefore the choice should be permitted, because a liberal construction was more in keeping with the overall remedial purposes of the act.

c. *Compromise for administrative reasons.* It is possible to dwell too much on broad theories which might confine judicial discretion—such as those advanced by the law and economics perspective. There are also more mundane reasons why judges might not have too much to do when interpreting statutes, suggested by Easterbrook's observation that Goal X might be implemented by Rule Y. One reason why that might happen, dampening the inclination to rely on statutory purpose, is that direct implementation of Goal X might be administratively difficult. Rule Y is a compromise between substantive goals and administrative reality.

2. Normative foundations of textualism

a. *Judicial role and legislative intent.* Easterbrook purports to link the Law and Economics image of legislation without purpose to textualism on the ground that the judge's job is simply to implement legislative will; and, when that will is as undynamic as the Law and Economics perspective suggests, there is little for the judge to do except do what the text says (unless the text "plainly hands" the courts a "common law" power). But judicial deference to legislative will does not come close to explaining what drives the modern textualist. The textualist's real objective is to stop judges from being too creative, except to the extent necessary to establish the principle of minimal judging in the first place. Easterbrook's last point—about judicial power—suggests that the major defect in creative statutory interpretation is the amount of judicial power it permits, not that it would violate legislative will.

The distinction between limiting judging and violating legislative will calls attention to an ambiguity in the countermajoritarian anxiety, which plagues contemporary efforts to justify judging. In the constitutional setting, where it originated, striking down statutes obviously threatens to reject (run "counter" to) legislative choice. When a court freely interprets a statute, however, it often does not reject a legislative decision. The gaps in legislation are not, as Easterbrook might seem to suggest, purposefully left out of the statutory bargain. They are often the result of the legislature overlooking issues, either because of haste or carelessness, or because they have not kept up with changes over time. The exercise of judicial discretion in statutory interpretation usually makes guesses about how to deal with issues the legislature did not consider at all or did not consider carefully.

Textualists are not impressed, however, by the difference between rejecting legislative decisions and making guesses when the legislature was silent. The core of Easterbrook's argument for textualism is that judges must avoid the risk of implementing their own views when interpreting statutes because that violates Separation of Powers principles, intruding judging into lawmaking domains where it should not reach. That is why textualists object so strongly to purposivism, because it enables the judge to camouflage judicial lawmaking in the guise of elaborating historical legislative purpose. The modern textualist sees purposivism as an excuse for a free rendering of statutory meaning beyond what the legislature has determined or delegated to the court. It is a different matter, Easterbrook argues, if the legislature delegates authority to judges by plainly handing them a common-law-like power.[68] In that case, judges can openly and honestly rely on their own best guess about *contemporary* policy, because the legislature grants them this authority.

b. *Rule of law.* I do not want to leave the impression that the only normative foundation for textualism is Separation of Powers. Judges charged with the responsibility of fitting statutes into the broader fabric of the law might opt for "rule of law" values as the dominant feature of that broader

68. Easterbrook, Domains, p. 544.

fabric. Textualism (it is hoped) would implement the rule of law goals of certainty and reliability, giving the statutory reader a firm ground on which to plan activities, without fear that plans will be undermined by free judicial interpretation or disrupted by an administrator relying on a statute's potential uncertainty. This implements the substantive value of individual autonomy, allowing private parties to plan transactions (economic or otherwise). It also protects people from arbitrary government, a value in its own right.[69]

c. *Determining the meaning of a "text."* We have proceeded with this discussion of textualism as though it were easy to determine textual meaning. Textualists prefer that assumption. They prefer an image of the text as an independently observable fact on which judges can rely. This view is obviously essential if the text is to implement the "rule of law" values of certainty and reliability. But it also helpful to those who adopt the Separation of Powers approach to statutory interpretation, because it makes it appear that there is something out there on which the judge can rely without doing too much judging. In fact, the conception of a text is quite murky. Its meaning is subject to more uncertainties than modern textualists admit. And what counts as a text *follows* from a normative view of judging, rather than being an independent fact to which the judge can defer. As we will see in Chapter 5 and later chapters, textualists tend to define the text in ways that minimize judicial discretion (once the definition of the text is out of the way), but nothing inherent in the conception of a text demands that view of how a text acquires meaning.

4.06 PRAGMATISM

When the Legal Process synthesis collapsed, Republicanism and textualism suggested responses. Republicanism appeared to place too much faith in judging; textualism too little. Pragmatism (often discussed under the rubric of "practical reasoning") attempts a synthesis of approaches to statutory interpretation that gives both Republicanism and textualism their due.[70]

"Pragmatism" requires the judge to be a problem solver without privileging any single interpretive approach. Sometimes the text is more important; sometimes purpose. In addition, the judge must also be ready to update the statute either to imaginatively reconstruct legislative purpose or to make the statute fit with contemporary values (often called the "legal landscape"). Account must also be taken of what other institutions, such as agencies and later legislatures, have done or are likely to do. Moreover, the judge is not just a pragmatist—she is "critical," willing to "criticize existing

---

69. See Antonin Scalia, The Rule of Law as a Law of Rules, 56 U. Chi. L. Rev. 1175 (1989).

70. See William Eskridge, Jr. & Philip Frickey, Statutory Interpretation as Practical Reasoning, 42 Stan. L. Rev. 321 (1990)(hereafter "Eskridge, Practical Reasoning"); William Eskridge, Jr. & Philip Frickey, Law as Equilibrium, 108 Harv. L. Rev. 26, 56–76 (1994).

conventions and traditions."[71] This is an aggressively anti-foundationalist view of interpretation, unbeholden to any one approach.[72]

This anti-foundationalism goes beyond denying a privileged place to any single interpretive approach. One might, for example, be anti-foundationalist in the limited sense of rejecting a single factor in favor of a multi-factor analysis—including text, purpose, and background considerations. The results of a multi-factor analysis are hard to predict but are not indeterminate. An astute observer could theoretically assign weights to the relevant interpretive criteria. But pragmatists reject even this amount of determinism. The interpretive process is one in which the judge learns about the meaning of the text as she engages in the act of interpretation. The point is not just that it is almost impossible to do a study that reliably assigns weights to interpretive factors (it would be very hard, for example, to assign a weight to the "text" because people disagree on what counts as the text and whether it is unclear). The point is that whatever weight the judge assigns is provisional and exploratory, subject to adjustment as the text is applied to the facts in an interpretive setting.[73]

At first blush, this might seem like a full blooded tilt in favor of unanchored judicial discretion—a modern version of Legal Realism—rather than a synthesis of interpretive approaches. But pragmatism contains features which hold the judge back. First, its anti-foundationalism rejects not just single-minded textualism but also other -isms which might justify too much judicial power. The judge is not, for example, a confident Republican. In this respect, pragmatism shares a common bond with the skeptical legal culture from which modern textualism has emerged. Second, it recognizes that, despite the potential for uncertainty, the text and purpose are coherent ideas capable of influencing the judge, of anchoring a decision. The judge is not a radical deconstructionist or a renegade hermeneutical updater of texts.[74]

The central descriptive thrust of pragmatism is indisputably correct. After the dust has settled on what is left from the decline of purposivism and the rivalry between Republicanism and textualism, we cannot improve on the description of statutory interpretation beyond that of multiple interpretive perspectives. Justice Stevens is a good example of the quintessential pragmatist judge (what I have referred to elsewhere as a "common law" judge)[75] and you should watch for evidence of this in later chapters.

---

71. Eskridge, Dynamic, p. 201.

72. Eskridge, Practical Reasoning, p. 348 ("[W]hen statutory interpreters make [   ] choices, they are normally not driven by any single value—adhering to majoritarian commands *or* encouraging private reliance on statutory texts *or* finding the best answer according to modern policy—but are instead driven by multiple values.").

73. Michelman, Traces, p. 33.

74. Eskridge, Practical Reasoning, p. 347 ("[T]he interpreter's choice is somewhat constrained by the text, the statute's history, and the circumstances of its application * * *.").

75. William Popkin, A Common Law Lawyer on the Supreme Court: The Opinions of Justice Stevens, 1989 Duke L. J. 1087 (1989).

The challenge for pragmatism is to provide not only a description of judging but also a normative theory. After all, Legal Process purposivism, Republicanism, and textualism do not purport to be complete accounts of judging. (As Hart and Sacks counseled: "Do not expect anybody's theory of statutory interpretation [   ] to be an accurate statement of what courts actually do with statutes.")[76] They are theories of judging meant to tilt interpretation in a particular direction by exerting a normative pull which cannot in practice eliminate the pragmatic approach that has always dominated judging. Legal Process posited a link between democratic purpose and a judge who elaborated that purpose. Republicanism relies either on the judge's perception of weaknesses in the democratic process or on the judge's procedural advantages as a substantive decision maker. The textualist has a negative theory of judging, based on Separation of Powers and Rule of Law considerations, which argue against giving the judge too much to do. What theory of judging can sustain the pragmatist who works with multiple interpretive criteria, creating meaning as she goes?

The problem pragmatism encounters is suggested by an uncertainty in how the judge marshals multiple perspectives to interpret statutes. Eskridge hopes that the result will be a "cable, weav[ing] together several mutually supporting threads"[77] to provide the strongest interpretation. But that may not be how it works. The strands may combine opportunistically, in judicial opinion writing, as the judge puts together several arguments to avoid concurrences and dissents on a collegial bench, to prevent reversal by a higher court, or to adopt rhetoric that gives a facade of legitimacy to an opinion that might otherwise be criticized (as when the beginning of an opinion parades thinly supported claims to rely on the text and/or legislative intent). This kind of "weaving" together of disparate approaches may be good judicial statecraft. It may even be less opportunistic than I have suggested. It may indicate respect for different positions taken by other judges, refusing to choose among competing theories of how to determine the meaning of statutes. But it does not provide a satisfactory model of practical judicial reasoning on which to justify a theory of statutory interpretation.

The "cable" image has another possible meaning, however, that can support a more robust theory of judging. Sensitivity to the various threads of interpretive theory might produce stronger judging because different statutes have different value implications and institutional settings, which call for different interpretive approaches. The major challenge for modern statutory interpretation is to work out the best approach for interpreting statutes in different areas of the law, based on a clear understanding of the raw material of statutory meaning and the methodological issues raised by different interpretive approaches.

---

76.   Hart & Sacks, p. 1169.

77.   Eskridge, Dynamic, p. 200.

The reality of statutory interpretation will always be more complex than the interpretive theories which predominate at any point in time. It is certainly important to keep in mind the empirical and normative assumptions about judging and legislating, based on the Public Choice and Republican critiques, but it is also important to remember that these critiques do not exhaust questions about statutory interpretation.

There is, first, the daunting task of understanding what we mean by text, legislative intent and purpose, and substantive and institutional background considerations, about which these critiques have so much to say. Without such an understanding, we cannot appreciate the points of controversy between different interpretive approaches or decide which one to prefer. Chapters 5 through 9 directly address these questions.

Second, the dominant critiques may have too little to say about a wide range of interpretive issues—those which deal with matters of inconvenience, political regulation, or legislative discretion, rather than fundamental values. There may be something about the dynamics of judging which draws the judge into the process of working out answers to legal questions that is not captured by any theory yet developed—something, as Hand says, that the judge "cannot escape" once literalism is rejected. We are, of course, accustomed to judges doing this in the common law and, to some extent, in constitutional law. Why not statute law as well?

As you read the materials in Part II dealing with technique and theory, look for evidence which implicitly or explicitly supports any of the theories developed in Part I and for evidence that these theories do not fully capture what judging and statutory interpretation is all about. Can you work out a theory of "ordinary judging" that helps to explain statutory interpretation?

PART II

THE TECHNIQUE AND THEORY OF STATUTORY INTERPRETATION

What techniques should a court use to determine the meaning of a statute? By asking about techniques of interpretation, we do not leave behind the historical material in Part I. The historical relationship between common law courts and legislatures both calls attention to the limits beyond which courts cannot go in the use of various interpretive techniques and also raises possibilities for a judicial role based on a common law power of statutory interpretation. Whether we define the judicial role by reference to constitutional patterns at the time of the Founding or the evolution of judicial-legislative relationships in the subsequent centuries, we are necessarily operating in the shadow of these historical practices. We are, moreover, asking the same questions courts have always asked—what are legislatures and judges good at, what are their limitations—even though the answers may differ.

The language of statutory interpretation—of the techniques judges use—has also been handed down to us from prior practice, but we must be careful in using language developed in earlier periods. Some language has hardly survived. We do not hear much about equitable interpretation any more. But the decline in usage can be misleading. Modern purposive interpretation and judicial use of substantive background considerations are related to extensive and limiting equitable interpretation respectively, though in modified form.

Other terms have survived and are used with as much if not more frequency today—such as "text" and "legislative intent." The "text" has always had a variety of meanings and it is hard to be sure whether it was used the same way in earlier times as it is today. And "legislative intent" is often used today in connection with legislative history, whereas it was once a judicial synonym for judicial second-guessing of the legislature, based on all evidence the judge could muster (text, purpose, substantive background considerations).

We need, in other words, to develop our own vocabulary and to incorporate it into a theory of statutory interpretation, based on an awareness of what has gone before and of the potential for future evolution.

QUESTIONS AND OUTLINE

Subpart II–A discusses the criteria for determining statutory meaning. It deals with the concept of text and context and with how a court uses such criteria to interpret statutes. Here are some of the questions we address:

1. What is the role of author and audience in determining the text's meaning? What authors and audiences have a claim on the text?

2. What is the role of the linguistic canons in determining the meaning of the statutory text?

3. Is there a difference between textualism and literalism?

4. What is the role of context in determining textual meaning or qualifying a meaning otherwise indicated by the text? What are the different meanings of "context"—what counts as "internal context" and "external context"?

5. What do we mean by "legislative intent" and "legislative purpose"?

6. How does the judge take account of institutional considerations—of the institutional competence of the legislature and the judge—in determining statutory meaning.

7. What is the impact of statutory detail on statutory meaning and the judicial role?

8. How do the compromise origins of a statute affect its interpretation?

9. To what extent can a court consider change to give a statute a contemporary meaning that might not be faithful to the historical meaning of the text or the intent of the enacting legislature?

Subpart II–B considers legislative history. This term is defined broadly to include not only the committee reports and other legislative material that accompany passage of a statute, but also events occurring after passage of a statute, such as administrative rules, subsequent legislative history, and reenactment of a law.

Subpart II–C deals with some specific problems that explore the outer boundaries of interpretive theory. We consider whether statutes can be a source of judge-made law, even when the court has no common law authority over the subject matter of the legislation. We also encounter clusters of statutes dealing with a particular subject, where the court may create patterns of law that are greater than the sum of the legislative parts.

The Writer, the Text, and the Reader

When asked to determine what the legislature intended, Justice Frankfurter once said that he didn't "care what the [　] intention was. I only want to know what the words mean." Frankfurter, Some Reflections on the Meaning of Statutes, 47 Colum.L.Rev. 527, 538 (1947). This statement captures the tension in statutory interpretation between two approaches. One approach focuses on the intent of the writer of the document (the legislature) and the other approach stresses the text.

If you are focusing on the statute's text, how do you know the meaning of words? You must look at the context in which they are used. But what counts as the context of legislative language for someone interested in what the words mean? Consider the following: the common understanding of language shared by author and audience when the statute was written; the surrounding text of the statute; the historical mischief the statute dealt with; the statute's general purpose; the social, political, moral, and legal background out of which the statute emerged (including the common law)?

If you look for legislative intent, what counts as evidence of statutory meaning? Is legislative intent determined by the same elements of text and context noted above, or is there a difference of emphasis, drawing the interpreter away from the text and its common understanding to broader elements of context?[1] Is there a coherent notion of legislative intent? After all, a federal statute is the product of over 500 people voting in two legislative houses and an executive branch. And, as Chapter 4 explained, legislative leaders may manipulate the agenda to control the statutory result. Whose intent counts? What weight does legislative history, such as committee reports and legislative hearings, have in the search for legislative intent? Is the search for "intent" really a search for how legislative purpose applies to the facts of the case; and, if so, what is the relevance of legislative compromise in making that judgment? Recall Plowden's and Hand's reference to the judge carrying on a hypothetical conversation with the "legislator" to determine how the legislator would reach a decision.

The emphasis on the writer and the text overlooks the judicial interpreter of the statute. If we look at what the interpreter does, we may want to shift our attention away from both the historical author and audience and the statutory text. The judicial reader interpreting the text brings various perspectives to interpretation, which may not be what the author/audience

---

1. See generally, MacCallum, Legislative Intent, 75 Yale L.J. 754 (1966); Radin, Statutory Interpretation, 43 Harv. L. Rev. 863 (1930). In Knapp & Michaels, Against Theory, 8 Critical Inquiry 723, 724 (1982), the authors state that the "meaning of a text is simply identical to the author's intended meaning." Is that correct?

had in mind. The spirit with which the judge brings her own perspective to statutory interpretation can vary considerably. The judge may do this grudgingly, acknowledging but not embracing its inevitability, as Judge Learned Hand did. Or the judge may consider this to be an essential feature of the court's role in deciding cases and controversies, as many judges did in the 19th and earlier centuries, and as Radin suggested the judge should do in deciding how vigorously to elaborate purpose.

One way to look at these issues is to ask what a statute is. Only then can we know how the interpreter should determine its meaning. Some years before Justice Frankfurter made his statement about wanting to know what the statutory words meant, Justice Holmes said that he did not want to know what the legislature meant, only what the statute means. Holmes, The Theory of Legal Interpretation, 12 Harv. L. Rev. 417, 419–20 (1899). But what is a statute? Is it what the writer intends, what the text means, or what the reader creatively derives from the evidence of statutory meaning? A statute may not say all that it means or mean all that it says.

Some commentators approach the debate about defining a statute by examining the relationship between law and literature.[2] They point out that both texts seek to persuade and instruct, relying on the reader's understanding of how the text applies to specific cases to give the document meaning. A text always contains potential meaning, which unfolds over time, and the judicial reader plays a role in developing that potential. Opponents of this view argue that it confuses literature and politics. They argue that a statute is a political command, with the power to impose burdens, not an invitation to judicial readers to collaborate in the process of determining meaning. They view the emphasis on the text's potential to persuade and instruct as slipping dangerously into textual indeterminacy, which accords the judge far too much power to make law.

Advocates of a significant judicial role often acknowledge that law should not be confused with literature. They concede that works of literature, unlike statutes, are read for pleasure, which necessarily draws the reader into a more collaborative role. They also accept the view that legal texts are more political than literature.[3] They nonetheless assert that political texts are not inert commands, but embodiments of purpose whose significance is deter-

2. Writings on this subject include the following: Legal Hermeneutics (G. Leyh, ed.)(1992); Eskridge, Gadamer/Statutory Interpretation, 90 Colum. L. Rev. 609 (1990); Weisberg, The Law-Literature Enterprise, 1 Yale J. Law & Human. 1 (1988); West, Communities, Texts, and Law: Reflections on the Law and Literature Movement, 1 Yale J. Law & Human. 129 (1988); Popkin, The Collaborative Model of Statutory Interpretation, 61 S. Cal. L. Rev. 541 (1988); R. Posner, Law and Literature: A Misunderstood Relation (1988); Hoy, Interpreting the Law: Hermeneutical and Poststructuralist Perspectives, 58 S. Cal. L. Rev. 135 (1985); Fish, Fish v. Fiss, 36 Stan. L. Rev. 1325 (1984); Fiss, Objectivity and Interpretation, 34 Stan. L. Rev. 739 (1982); Cover, Foreword: Nomos and Narrative, 97 Harv. L. Rev. 4 (1983); Dworkin, Law as Interpretation, 60 Texas L. Rev. 527 (1982).

3. Literature's nonpolitical status is not apparent in all cultures. Totalitarian regimes fear literary works for their political potential. Some Islamic fundamentalists view Salmon Rushdie's novels as having important political consequences. And Shelley argued that "poets were the unacknowledged legislators of the world." P. Shelley, A Defense of Poetry 80 (Jordan ed. 1965).

mined through application to cases in light of historical antecedents and subsequent evolution. This necessarily requires the judge to consider the text's potential meaning. Moreover, the fear of textual indeterminacy is overdone. The judge is subject to many constraints, and judicial choice within those constraints is not the equivalent of choosing willfully from among indeterminate options.

The relevance of the empirical and normative perspectives on statutes which we discussed in Chapter 4 should be apparent at this point. The empirical models and data about the legislative process are concerned with legislative intent, about what the legislature is likely to have meant. The normative perspectives are concerned with how the judicial reader should approach the statute. All judges have some normative perspective, which identifies the appropriate interpretive criteria. Even the most committed textualist has a normative conception of judging that mandates sticking as closely to the text as possible. Other normative perspectives require a more aggressive judicial role in determining what the statute means.

Judicial rhetoric. The point of these introductory comments about interpretation is that the critical issue is what counts as evidence of statutory meaning. Unfortunately, judicial rhetoric is often misleading. Judges often say that they are only looking for the legislative intent or the plain meaning of the statutory text, but then do whatever they think is right in interpreting the statute without paying too much attention to their broad statements of interpretive philosophy.

The reasons for judicial invocation of either legislative intent or statutory text are not hard to discover. Both legislative intent and the plain meaning of the text lay strong claims to being *the* critical criterion of statutory meaning. In a country where statutes emerge from the legislative process and democratic principles are strong, no one has to apologize for relying on legislative intent. And commitment to the text has an equal claim. After all, the statute is a text passed by a legislature, signed by the chief executive, and read by the public, or at least by their legal advisors.

The difficulty of making sense of judicial rhetoric is compounded by the fact that important opinions are often written by courts consisting of more than one judge. The opinion may be a "committee" effort, accommodating the views of several judges, as well as the rhetorical requirements of the legal culture. Consider the following judicial statements, all more or less contemporary:

Rubin v. United States, 449 U.S. 424, 430 (1981):

> * * * When we find the terms of a statute unambiguous, judicial inquiry is complete, except "in rare and exceptional circumstances." TVA v. Hill, 437 U.S. 153, 187 n. 33 (1978)(quoting Crooks v. Harrelson, 282 U.S. 55, 60 (1930)).

A somewhat less rigid approach appears in the following statement in another recent case, North Dakota v. United States, 460 U.S. 300, 312 (1983):

> As with any case involving statutory interpretation, "we state once again the obvious when we note that, in determining the scope of a statute, one is to look first at its language." Dickerson v. New Banner Institute, Inc., 460 U.S. 103, 110 (1983). * * * "Absent a clearly expressed legislative intention to the contrary, the language must ordinarily be regarded as conclusive." Consumer Product Safety Comm'n. v. GTE Sylvania, Inc., 447 U.S. 102, 108 (1980).

Even less confining are the following statements:

Train v. Colorado Public Interest Research Group, Inc., 426 U.S. 1, 9–10 (1976):

> To the extent that the Court of Appeals excluded reference to legislative history * * *, the court was in error. As we have noted before: "When aid to construction of the meaning of words, as used in the statute, is available, there certainly can be no 'rule of law' which forbids its use, however clear the words may appear on 'superficial examination.'" United States v. American Trucking Ass'ns, 310 U.S. 534, 543–44 (1940).

F.B.I. v. Abramson, 456 U.S. 615, 625 n. 7 (1982)(quoting Justice Frankfurter in United States v. Monia, 317 U.S. 424, 431 (1943)):

> The notion that because the words of a statute are plain, its meaning is also plain, is merely pernicious oversimplification.

Boston Sand & Gravel Co. v. United States, 278 U.S. 41, 48 (1928):

> It is said that when the meaning of language is plain we are not to resort to evidence in order to raise doubts. That is rather an axiom of experience than a rule of law, and does not preclude consideration of persuasive evidence [of statutory meaning] if it exists.

In sum, judicial rhetoric is often an unreliable guide to what the courts are doing. That makes it hard to read cases interpreting statutes. But there may still be coherent approaches to statutory interpretation. Specific judges almost certainly have some more or less general approach, whatever the opinions may say. Our primary task is to decide what *should* count as evidence of meaning, and to develop our own clear understanding of how to use the language of statutory interpretation. How would *you* write an opinion interpreting the statute being considered?

CHAPTER 5

THE TEXT

5.01 INTRODUCTION

There is nothing plain about the concept of a text or how an interpreter determines whether it has a plain meaning.

a) ROUTINE SOURCES OF UNCERTAINTY

Some sources of textual uncertainty are quite routine. Everyone, textualist and nontextualist alike, agrees that the judge must resolve the uncertainty—often from material outside the text (although they might disagree about where to look).

1. *Vagueness.* Vagueness is the phenomenon of one meaning shading off into another, black or white into grey. An example is determining whether a person is a "guest" in a car, as defined in a statute prohibiting "guests" from suing the driver. Someone sitting in the front seat is a guest; someone waiting to be picked up by a car is not. But what of someone alighting from a vehicle during a temporary stop in the drive? Concerns about fraudulent lawsuits, financed by deep pocket insurance companies, undeniably influence the answer to this question. Whether judicial reliance on such concerns implements legislative purpose or contemporary values is unclear.[4]

2. *Ambiguity.* An ambiguous text is one which can refer to two clearly divergent meanings, as understood in two clearly divergent settings. Examples of semantic ambiguity include the phrase "foul play," referring to a criminal or baseball event; and "heat," referring to temperature or a track and field event. Legislative purpose, evidenced by the surrounding text (that is, internal context), often resolves this type of uncertainty. It will be immediately obvious, for example, from other statutory language whether the subject matter of a statute using the term "foul play" is crime or baseball. Indeed, semantic ambiguity is often resolved so effortlessly that the text hardly seems unclear in the first place. (Not all ambiguity is so routinely resolved, however, as we will see in a moment.)

Syntactic ambiguity is also possible, as when the placement of a comma might affect meaning. (A typical problem is whether a modifying phrase applies to every item on a prior list. A comma before the modifying phrase and after the last-listed item, *suggests* application to the entire list, as in "A,B,

---

4. See, e.g., Tallios v. Tallios, 112 N.E.2d 723 (Ill.App.1953).

and C, on condition that * * *," compared to "A, B, and C on condition that * * *.") There is considerable disagreement about how to resolve syntactic uncertainty. Some judges would remain on the surface of the text, applying an ideal drafter's conception of grammar and style to resolve the ambiguity. Other judges would emphasize legislative purpose and substantive background considerations.

(Notice that I am not following the common practice of calling all uncertainties "ambiguities." I prefer to distinguish between ambiguities and other sources of linguistic uncertainty.)

3. *Open-ended.* Some texts are described as "open-ended," in the sense that uncertainty can only be resolved by weighing multiple factors whose meaning evolves over time. Terms like "reasonable," "unconscionable," and "good faith" are examples. In such cases, the court might rely primarily on legislative purpose or selected substantive background considerations, or might treat the law as a delegation of judicial "common law" authority, which the court is relatively free to develop.

4. *Generality.* The use of general language might not belong on a list of routine examples of uncertainty. Generality refers to language which appears to cover a range of facts, even though some applications may seem very strange. The text is not obviously fragile and seems to have a plain meaning. On occasion, questioning the apparent meaning of general language is no more disquieting than observing and resolving other doubts about statutory meaning. We probably react that way to Wittgenstein's famous example involving the meaning of "game." When you tell someone supervising a young child to play a "game" with the child, you will be surprised and understandably annoyed if they play poker for money. In a case like that, the plain application of general language produces a strange result (is it "absurd"?), and avoiding that application "goes without saying." Most cases of limiting general language are not so unproblematic.

Many sources of textual uncertainty are not routine or are not routinely resolved. Indeed, a major point of this chapter is that the concept of a "text" contains many more uncertainties than we might at first recognize. First, there are uncertainties in identifying the author and audience whose understanding creates plain meaning in the first place. After all, a synonym for "plain meaning" is "common understanding," and what is "common" is the understanding of an author and audience about how language is used. Chapter 5.02 discusses the choice of the author and audience.

Second, author/audience problems do not exhaust the problems of determining textual meaning. An old canon of statutory interpretation requires the judge to take account of the whole text (referred to as "internal context") to interpret its parts and this can also give rise to textual uncertainty. (Judge Shaw, as noted in Chapter 2, made frequent reference to the "whole text.") But how should the various elements of the whole text interact to determine meaning? More specifically, how probative of textual meaning are the linguistic canons of statutory interpretation, which deal with such interactions?   Chapter 5.03 discusses "internal context."

Chapter 5.04 explains the difference between literalism and textualism.

b) STATUTORY VS. COMMON LAW TEXTS

As you consider how judges determine the meaning of a statutory text, keep in mind a distinction between common law and statutory language. The words of a statute serve a different function from the words in a common law decision. In the common law, the words with legal relevance are found in earlier decisions. The legal impact of those words depends on what is essential to the decision (we distinguish holding from dictum) and whether the facts of a later case are similar to those of the prior case. The criteria for determining what is essential and similar are not determined by the text of the prior decision, however; the judge's craft consists in making that determination. Moreover, the words themselves are usually viewed as embodying principles which can be qualified or abandoned if our attachment to the principles weakens. (If the reason for the rule ceases, the rule ceases. Cessante ratione legis, cessat ipsa lex.)

Statutes are not the same as common law decisions. The text cannot be so easily subverted when the facts of a case are different from those which led to the statute's adoption or the principle underlying adoption of a statute weakens. This difference is illustrated by the way courts deal with pre-independence British statutes which became the law of the various United States after independence. These statutes "have almost universally been regarded as having the effect of judicial precedent, rather than legislative enactment."[5] Consequently, they are applied to the facts of a case in the manner of the common law. In the above-cited case, the statute said that a devise to a witness to a will who attests to its validity "shall * * * be utterly null and void." Because the statute was treated like the common law, however, the statutory rule was qualified to allow the witnesses to take their inheritance up to the amount they would have received as an intestate share. The court applied to the statute the principle that "the peculiar circumstances of a particular case may justify departure from a rule of the common law to reach a sensible result."

If a statutory text is more authoritative than a judicial opinion, why is that so?

1.   Does the statutory author intend the text to have more authoritative application than does the author of a judicial opinion, thereby making the text more important?

2.   Is it much harder to determine the factual and policy context of a statute than a judicial opinion?   Is the context of an opinion more fully contained in the four corners of the document, making it easier to distinguish "holding" from "dictum" in an opinion than a statute?

---

5. Manoukian v. Tomasian, 237 F.2d 211 (D.C.Cir.1956).

3. Is statute law more "textual" because the text is passed by the legislature and signed by the chief executive?

Are there nonetheless ways in which a statutory and common law text are similar, drawing on understandings from historical background and application to facts in both instances? Are the common law and statute law all *that* different?

――――――――――

Given the potential indeterminacy of a text's meaning discussed in this Chapter, some might argue that the effort to salvage the concept of "plain meaning" is not worth the effort. But that would be a mistake. Judges (and the rest of us) frequently experience plain meaning and will not look kindly on an argument that starts from the premise that there is no such thing. The proper way to question plain meaning is to identify what there is about meaning in a particular case that prevents it from being plain.

It is, however, important to remember that, when we experience language as having a plain meaning, it is usually because the facts in a case satisfy all plausible references that the text might have. *Plain meaning is really the plain application of a text to the facts at hand. It is not the text which is plain, but its application to the facts.*

5.02   AUTHORS AND AUDIENCES

We discuss two author/audience problems in this section. First, not all ambiguities are readily resolved by internal context. Multiple authors and audiences, with textual understandings derived from different language communities, have legitimate claims on the text which are not eliminated by looking at the entire document. The example we address is the distinction between lay and technical meanings.

Second, many words derive meaning from a conjunction of specific characteristics, only some of which may be present in specific situations. There is no ambiguity, in the sense of clearly divergent meanings—for example, a gay and traditional family share characteristics in ways that a foul play in the criminal law and baseball do not. That is why these types of uncertainties are often said to arise when there is a "family resemblance" between two different uses of a term. But there *is* linguistic uncertainty, even if it does not deserve to be called an ambiguity.[6] Frequently, the problem of deciding which characteristics determine the meaning of a text is problematic when the statute is old, and new situations arise which may not fit the historical understanding. We therefore discuss this question under the heading of "future audience."

―――――――

6. See generally Winter, The Metaphor of Standing and the Problem of Self–Governance, 40 Stan. L. Rev. 1371, 1385–86 (1988); Winter, Transcendental Nonsense, Metaphoric Reasoning and the Cognitive Stakes for Law, 137 U. Pa. L. Rev. 1105, 1153 (1989).

a) LAY VS. TECHNICAL MEANING

Plain meaning requires a shared understanding between author and audience. The following case is typical in presuming a lay meaning, absent evidence that a technical meaning is more appropriate. Does the opinion tell us anything about what criteria determine whether a technical meaning *is* more appropriate?

Nix v. Hedden

149 U.S. 304 (1893).

■ Mr. Justice Gray, after stating the case, delivered the opinion of the court.

The single question in this case is whether tomatoes, considered as provisions, are to be classed as "vegetables" or as "fruit," within the meaning of the Tariff Act of 1883.

The only witnesses called at the trial testified that neither "vegetables" nor "fruit" had any special meaning in trade or commerce, different from that given in the dictionaries; and that they had the same meaning in trade today that they had in March, 1883.

The passages cited from the dictionaries define the word "fruit" as the seed of plants, or that part of plants which contains the seed, and especially the juicy, pulpy products of certain plants, covering and containing the seed. These definitions have no tendency to show that tomatoes are "fruit," as distinguished from "vegetables," in common speech, or within the meaning of the Tariff Act.

There being no evidence that the words "fruit" and "vegetables" have acquired any special meaning in trade or commerce, they must receive their ordinary meaning. Of that meaning the court is bound to take judicial notice, as it does in regard to all words in our tongue; and upon such a question dictionaries are admitted, not as evidence, but only as aids to the memory and understanding of the court.

Botanically speaking, tomatoes are the fruit of a vine, just as are cucumbers, squashes, beans and peas. But in the common language of the people, whether sellers or consumers of provisions, all these are vegetables, which are grown in kitchen gardens, and which, whether eaten cooked or raw, are, like potatoes, carrots, parsnips, turnips, beets, cauliflower, cabbage, celery and lettuce, usually served at dinner in, with or after the soup, fish or meats which constitute the principal part of the repast, and not, like fruits generally, as dessert.

Botanical usage and colloquial usage differed, but the case was easy once the author and audience for the statute were identified as non-scientific. The plain meaning of the text for the relevant legislative author and audience was that tomatoes were vegetables. Presumably, it would have been easy to determine whether a technical botanical meaning was appropriate from internal context—other language indicating that the subject matter of the statute dealt with botanical issues.

What did the Court assume about the author and audience in the following case—is it a group with a specialized understanding of the statutory language?[7]   In United States v. Wells Fargo Bank, 485 U.S. 351 (1988), the Court unanimously held that the following statutory language did *not* grant an exemption from the estate tax: "[Certain property] * * * shall be exempt from all taxation now or hereafter imposed." How could this language *not* apply to an estate tax?   The Court stated: "Well before [this Act] was passed, an exemption of property from all taxation had an understood meaning: the property was exempt from *direct* taxation, but certain privileges of ownership, such as the right to transfer property, could be taxed." The property was therefore subject to estate tax, which was a tax on a transfer of property, not a "direct" tax on property. If you were a general practitioner (not a tax specialist) in a small county seat, what would you think of this decision?   Would you object that you *were* an audience for this statute and the more technical understanding of the text—as excluding indirect taxes—was inappropriate.

Evaluate this response to the general practitioner. The text had two possible meanings—a more technical and more colloquial meaning. The legislative author, familiar with this technical area of the law, intended the more technical meaning.

Does this response turn the textualist into an intentionalist—someone concerned with legislative intent rather than the meaning of the text?   Why can the legislative author determine the relevant audience by virtue of its intent regarding the audience to whom the statute is directed?   Don't other audiences have a claim on the text as well?   Is your answer affected by whether the statute deals with taxes or creates a crime?

Occasionally, a court self-consciously addresses the question of rival authors and audiences.

1.   Who are the potential authors and audiences in the following case—is the author or audience a group of lay people or people with more specialized knowledge?

2.   What was the evidence for the court's conclusion in choosing an author and/or audience?

----

7.   Cf. United States v. Calamaro, 354 U.S. 351 (1957)(a statute dealing with gambling was interpreted so that the phrase "receiving wagers" had the technical meaning familiar to professional gamblers).

3. What justifies the Court of Appeals relying on the congressional committee as the author? Would a textualist rely on a committee's understanding rather than the likely understanding of the entire legislature?

4. Is the statute's audience the one aimed at by the author; and, if so, what allows the author to choose the audience?

St. Luke's Hospital Ass'n. v. United States

333 F.2d 157 (6th Cir.1964).

■ Edwards, J.: * * *

Plaintiff–Appellee—a Cleveland hospital—filed suit in the United States District Court for the Northern District of Ohio to recover $19,301.39 from Defendant–Appellant, United States of America. This amount represents Federal Insurance Contributions Act (Social Security) taxes and interest thereon assessed against the hospital and paid by it under protest. The assessment was based upon the employment by the hospital of "residents." The hospital claimed these residents were "doctors-in-training" and as such were exempt under an amendment to the Federal Insurance Contributions Act which, in its terms, exempted "interns" from the statutory definition of "employment." * * *

The District Judge gave a judgment for the hospital. His careful and well-reasoned opinion argued that the word "intern" in the applicable statute should be construed as encompassing "residents-in-training." He based this conclusion first on the fact that although the terms "intern" and "resident" had totally different meanings in medical and hospital circles in 1939 when the amendment excluding interns was passed, this was not true in relation to the usage of the terms in the public vocabulary. And he held that it was the congressional intent to apply the public rather than the specialized meaning.

[Editor—The District Judge supported reliance on the more colloquial meaning, as follows:

> In the case before the Court the statute is not restricted to any one segment of society or to any one special field. There is no prior Congressional usage of the language which the Court can look to. The statute in question bears no title from which it can be ascertained as to whom it was directed.

> The fact of the matter is that [the statute] contains eleven major divisions. [The relevant exclusion section for "interns" appears in] one of the eleven divisions, [which] contains exclusions from coverage for fifteen major categories with twenty subgroupings, relating to many individuals in various unrelated fields of endeavor.

The Court does not believe that the technical meaning ascribed in medical circles to the words "intern" and "resident" must be said to be the understanding and intent of Congress in its use of the word "intern" in a statute of such breadth and scope which did not deal solely with hospitals and the medical profession.

What is the relevance for the District Judge of the "breadth and scope" of the statute in determining the author and audience?]

* * *

As to the interpretation of the 1939 amendment, we are unable to agree—albeit we recognize that reasonable minds could easily differ on issues of interpretation as finely spun as these. * * *

In our view the term "intern" as used and understood by doctors and hospitals in 1939 generally referred to a medical student who was seeking a year of hospital training in order to complete his requirements for a medical degree and admission to practice. * * *

We recognize, of course, that [   ] we have concerned ourselves with the definitions of the word "intern" as it was and is used by doctors and hospitals, and that it was this usage which the Federal District Judge rejected in favor of a more general definition.

There is no doubt that "intern" does have an older and more general meaning found in dictionaries, which would include any person residing in an institutional setting for educational or training purposes. Thus, in its older and less specific meaning, the word "intern" was the opposite of "extern."

Contrary, however, to the view of the matter taken by the Federal District Judge, we believe that in 1939 Congress was thoroughly familiar with and had every intention of using the newer, the more specific, and by then the more common definition of the word "intern."

* * * [T]he language involved was embodied in an exception to the definition of employment. Thus it was specifically addressed to prospective "interns" and to the employers of "interns," i.e. the hospitals of the United States, who were, as indicated above, thoroughly familiar with the newer and more technical definition.

Congressional committees which draft amendments to federal legislation acquire a definite expertise which certainly extends in our opinion to knowing the difference between an intern and a resident, or between an intern and a resident-in-training. [Editor—The court then cites evidence of Congressional Committee usage of the term "intern" in contrast to the term "resident."]

* * *

In all of the above we do not ignore the fact that distinctions between interns and residents-in-training have been substantially reduced in the years since 1939. The resident training program has been greatly expanded and its educational aspects have been greatly enhanced. No doubt these developments lend some weight to the argument for expansion of the intern exemption to cover residents-in-training. It seems clear to us, however, that meeting these changed conditions, if indeed there is warrant for doing so at all, is the function of legislation and not that of judicial interpretation.

b) Future Audience

There is an old discredited theory of language which posited that words were linked to a fixed objective reality as a container would be to its contents or a pointer to the object pointed at. The word contained or pointed to reality and the only task was to make sure that it properly conveyed that reality to the listener (or reader). The task of determining meaning was to define the necessary and sufficient conditions for the meaning of a word. If reality did not satisfy those conditions, the word did not have that meaning. A dictionary is a privileged tool of interpretation in this approach.

Language is no longer viewed this way. It is a cultural phenomenon, produced by the experiences of the community in which words are used. These experiences determine meaning in a complex way, not captured by the container or pointer view of language. There are no necessary or sufficient conditions defining a term. Instead, a text has potential characteristics and the meaning in specific circumstances depends on identifying both the author and the audience and how they would understand the text.

Interpreters sometimes fall into the habit of unconsciously privileging one or more of the potential characteristics of a text, which often has deep political implications. For example, the word "mother" has these potential references: someone who provides the ovum (genetic mother), bears the child to term (birth mother), cares for the child, and is married to the biological father. But is caring for a child or bearing the child in the womb a necessary condition of motherhood; what of the person who provides the ovum?

The problem becomes extremely controversial if there are different language communities with different conceptions of what lies at the "core" meaning of a text. And some of these differences can be politically charged, as with the different definition of "family" in the gay and straight communities? These differences *may* exist when the text was first adopted (what does "discriminate" mean to minority groups; to other groups?). But they often arise when meaning changes over time, as might occur with the meaning of "family."

Some of the uncertainties about textual references are easily resolved by the context in which language is used. For example, whether "mother" refers to the woman who supplies the ovum (genetic mother) may depend on whether the statute deals with testing for inherited genetic defects. And some potential uses of a word, to which students of language might refer, will never trouble a legal interpreter—the context will eliminate some meanings by a process of which the interpreter is not even aware. For example, "mother" might refer to a "Reverend Mother," by analogy to one of the conditions mentioned above—the care of (metaphorical) children—but this possibility is unlikely to cause problems for an interpreter. Still, many uncertainties about textual references are not so easily resolved.

The following case involves the meaning of "family." It raises the question of how closely future facts must fit the characteristics which contribute to the historical meaning of a text before the future facts will come within the statutory language. In more theoretical terms, what claims does the future audience have on the historical text?

Is it proper for a court disposed to incorporate new facts into old texts to make the following observation—if the legislature wanted to limit the court's power to read the future into the historical text, it could have explicitly stated that the text only included certain historically-bound specifics? Why might a legislature *not* want to write such a law? (The relationship of change to statutory interpretation is discussed further in Chapter 9.)

In Braschi v. Stahl Associates Co., 543 N.E.2d 49 (N.Y.1989), the issue was whether a gay couple was a family. Right after World War II, New York City adopted a statute providing rent control. Pursuant to that statute, a regulation prohibited eviction from a rent controlled apartment of "either the surviving spouse of the deceased tenant or some other member of the deceased tenant's family who has been living with the tenant." The landlord argued that "family" meant "blood, consanguinity, and adoption," as defined in intestacy laws. The court held that "family" should not be

rigidly restricted to those people who have formalized their relationship by obtaining, for instance, a marriage certificate or an adoption order. The intended protection against sudden eviction should not rest on fictitious legal distinctions or genetic history, but instead should find its foundation in the reality of family life. In the context of eviction, a more realistic, and certainly equally valid, view of a family includes two adult lifetime partners whose relationship is long-term and characterized by an emotional and financial commitment and interdependence. This view comports both with our society's traditional concept of "family" and with the expectations of individuals who live in such nuclear units. * * *

The determination as to whether an individual is entitled to non-eviction protection should be based upon an objective examination of the relationship of the parties. In making this assessment, the lower courts of this State have looked to a number of factors, including the exclusivity and longevity of the relationship, the level of emotional and financial commitment, the manner in which the parties have conducted their everyday lives and held themselves out to society, and the reliance placed upon one another for daily family services. These factors are most helpful, although it should be emphasized that the presence or absence of one or more of them is not dispositive since it is the totality of the relationship as evidenced by the dedication, caring and self-sacrifice of the parties which should, in the final analysis, control.

In the following New Jersey case the court refused to interpret "wife" to include someone living with a man in a spouse-like relationship under a Workers Compensation law. How is this case different from several others with which it can be compared:

(1) the case you have just read involving eviction;

(2) the other Workers Compensation cases the New Jersey court distinguished, in which someone who was not technically married was treated as married; and

(3) the definition of "family" for the common law tort of negligent infliction of emotional distress in the case cited at the end of the New Jersey opinion? Is the court's power to apply language very different when the language comes from a prior common law opinion?

Toms v. Dee Rose Furniture

621 A.2d 91 (N.J.Super.1993).

■ Skillman, J.A.D. * * *

Petitioner appeals from the dismissal of her claim for workers compensation dependency benefits based on the death of John Brinker.

Petitioner and the decedent began living together in 1975, when they were both in their early twenties, and maintained an exclusive romantic relationship for the next twelve years until decedent was shot and killed during the course of his employment by a mentally disturbed boyfriend of a coemployee. Petitioner and decedent maintained joint bank and utility accounts and purchased a home as joint tenants with a right of survivorship. Although petitioner and decedent lived together as though they were husband and wife and planned to get married eventually, they were not married as of the date of decedent's tragic death. * * *

To be entitled to dependency benefits under N.J.S.A. 34:15–13, a claimant must fit within one of the classes of beneficiaries enumerated in N.J.S.A. 34:15–13(f), which include a "wife." Petitioner acknowledges that she never married the decedent and thus was not legally recognized as his wife. However, petitioner contends, relying upon Dawson v. Hatfield Wire & Cable Co., 280 A.2d 173 (1971) and Parkinson v. J & S Tool Co., 313 A.2d 609 (1974), that she is entitled to benefits as a "de facto" wife.

In Dawson, the claimant and decedent were married ceremonially and lived together for sixteen years until the husband's death in a work-related accident. However, unbeknownst to the wife, her husband had never divorced his first wife. Consequently, their marriage was void. Nonetheless, the court found that the ceremonial marriage and petitioner's good faith reasonable belief that she was married qualified her as a "wife."

In Parkinson, the claimant and decedent were married ceremonially before a Catholic priest, but subsequently divorced. The parties reunited ten years later and asked a priest to remarry them. However, the priest said a marriage ceremony was unnecessary because the couple was "already married in the eyes of God." The couple accepted the priest's explanation, assumed they were married and resumed cohabitation. The husband was subsequently killed in a work- related accident. In holding that petitioner was entitled to compensation benefits, the Court emphasized that the parties had been ceremonially married, that their marriage had been reaffirmed before a priest, and that the only reason they did not have a second marriage ceremony was the mistaken advice given them by the priest. The Court contrasted these circumstances with an unlawful common law marriage.

Solemnity, publicity, and deliberation distinguish a legitimate marriage ceremony from an illegitimate common law union. Inherent in the common law marriage are a non-recognition of the legal process, and a lack of commitment which often gives rise to an impermanent and ephemeral arrangement, such that economic support, let alone dependency, may be withheld randomly. The union, which in the eyes of the public remains an uncertainty, may dissolve at any time. Such a couple may not both use an identical surname, file joint tax returns, or be deemed an entity for census-taking, welfare or social security eligibility. Oftentimes while they both may reside at one address, only one name may appear, and the other party may have legal residence elsewhere * * * . The Legislature and this Court have both declared that common law marriages are prohibited.

Notwithstanding the closeness and longevity of the relationship between petitioner and decedent, they were not married and therefore petitioner was not the decedent's wife. * * *

This case is fundamentally different from Dunphy v. Gregor, 617 A.2d 1248 (App.Div.1992), which involved the scope of the common law tort action for negligent infliction of emotional distress * * * , if a person suffers severe emotional distress from observing the death or serious injury of a family member caused by another party's negligence. In that context, we held that parties who were engaged and living together had an "intimate, familial relationship" which could form the basis for a [ ] cause of action. In contrast, petitioner's claim is based upon a statute which limits benefits to a person who qualifies as a "wife." Petitioner did not occupy that status in relation to the decedent.

The following case also involves change and its impact on the application of an older statute to new facts. Is it an easier or harder case than those we have discussed so far, and why?

In Anna J. v. Mark C., 286 Cal.Rptr. 369 (Ct.App.1991), a dispute arose about who was the "mother" of an unborn child. Mark and Crispina wanted a child but Crispina was medically unable to bear children. She did, however, provide an egg which was fertilized by sperm from her husband outside her womb. The embryo was then implanted in Anna's womb for a fee. The contract with Anna provided that Anna waived parental rights. Later, Anna wanted to keep the child.

The relevant statute for determining parental rights was the Parentage Act. The Act was adopted to eliminate the legal distinction between legitimate and illegitimate children, following a United States Supreme Court decision that distinctions based on illegitimacy violated the Constitution's guarantee of equal protection. The statute stated:

> As used in this part, "parent and child relationship" means the legal relationship existing between a child and his natural or adoptive parents * * * . (Civ.Code, § 7001.)

The court held that Crispina (who supplied the ovum) was the "natural mother" under this statute. In reaching this conclusion, it examined three other statutory rules. First, the statute provides that a blood test can exclude a man as the "father." In this case, a blood test had excluded Anna as the genetic mother. The court thought this was a strong analogy disfavoring Anna's claim.

Second, the statute states: "A parent and child relationship may be established as follows: (1) Between a child and the natural mother it may be established by proof of her having given birth to the child * * *." § 7003(1). Anna argued that this section established her status as the mother. The court rejected Anna's argument, stating that this section applied *only after* determining who the natural mother was. Because Crispina was the natural mother, using blood tests, Crispina's role as birth mother was irrelevant.

Third, sperm donors are denied status as a "parent." Anna argued by analogy to this provision that the ovum donor was not the mother. Although the court had previously relied on the blood test analogy against Anna, it now refused to apply the sperm donor provision to help her. The court reasoned that denying parental status to a sperm donor was meant to "protect both sperm donors and married couples who employ artificial insemination" and had no bearing on who the mother was.

The court concluded, heroically, that "the law of California, as worded by our Legislature, requires us to conclude Mark and Crispina are the natural and legal parents of the child." Is that true? Didn't the word "mother" simply fall apart when the genetic and child bearing functions were split?

The California Supreme Court affirmed the appellate court decision, finding that Crispina was the "natural mother." Johnson v. Calvert, 851 P.2d 776 (Cal.1993). But it rejected the lower court's reasoning. It held that the statute showed no preference for either mother, both of whom "presented acceptable proof of maternity." The court decided to rely on the intentions of the parties in entering the surrogacy relationship, rejecting the argument that the contract was against public policy. It also rejected using a "best interests of the child" test, although it suggested that the "intent" test will usually produce a result in the child's best interests. The court argued that a "best interests" approach would confuse parentage with custody.

5.03   INTERNAL CONTEXT

The text consists of many words, not just the specific language that seems to be the focus of attention. The surrounding text (internal context) often sheds light on the text's meaning. Many linguistic canons of statutory construction deal with how features of the surrounding text interact to produce meaning. We are concerned in this section with two questions. First, how does surrounding text shed light on meaning? Second, which rules about relying on internal context are genuinely concerned with how authors communicate with an audience and which rules serve some other purpose?

If the rules are not concerned with how authors and audiences communicate, what function do they serve? Could it be any of the following: (1) make up for lack of legislative history at the state level; (2) avoid the kind of judicial discretion that accompanies purposivist interpretation; (3) force legislatures to draft carefully by telling them what standards of good drafting the court will follow in statutory interpretation?

We defer to Chapter 15 the question of identifying the whole text. For example, is it just the four corners of the relevant public law; the code into which the law was codified; other related acts passed at the same or different times?

a) WORDS IN CLOSE PROXIMITY

Here are two cases in which the surrounding text was used to resolve uncertainty—applying the *noscitur a sociis* canon, that words are known by their neighbors. The first case, Morton, is a simple example. In the second case, IMPAC, the court looks not only to surrounding text but also to other arguments to support its conclusion. Is this just an example of conservative opinion writing—to buttress a result with every possible argument? Is it a consequence of trying to get as much concurrence as possible from judges on a multi-judge court? Or is the argument from internal context weaker than in Morton, in need of support?

i) UNITED STATES v. MORTON

467 U.S. 822 (1984).

■ Justice Stevens delivered the opinion of the Court.

The question presented is whether the United States is liable for sums withheld from the pay of one of its employees because it complied with a direction to withhold those sums contained in a writ of garnishment issued by a court without personal jurisdiction over the employee.

On December 27, 1976, respondent, a Colonel in the United States Air Force, was stationed at Elmendorf Air Force Base in Alaska. On that date Elmendorf's Finance Office received by certified mail a writ of garnishment, accompanied by a copy of a judgment against respondent that had been issued by the Circuit Court for the Tenth Judicial Circuit of Alabama in a divorce proceeding. The writ, which was in the regular form used in Alabama, directed the Air Force to withhold $4,100 of respondent's pay to satisfy sums due under the judgment "for alimony and child support." The Finance Office promptly notified respondent that it had received the writ. On advice from an Air Force attorney, respondent told the Finance Office that the state court's order was void because the Alabama court had no jurisdiction over him. Nevertheless, the Finance Officer honored the writ and paid $4,100 to the Clerk of the Alabama court, deducting that amount from respondent's pay. Subsequently additional writs of garnishment were served on the Air Force with similar results.

Respondent * * * collaterally attacked the garnishment by bringing this action against the United States to recover the amounts that had been withheld from his pay and remitted to the Alabama court. The Government took the position that it had a complete defense since Congress has by statute provided:

"Neither the United States, any disbursing office, nor governmental entity shall be liable with respect to any payment made from moneys due or payable from the United States to any individual pursuant to legal process regular on its face, if such payment is made in accordance with this section and the regulations issued to carry out this section." 42 U.S.C. § 659(f).

The trial judge first noted that the Alabama writ was on the regular form used by the Alabama courts. Thus, he did not disagree with the Government's position that the writ was "regular on its face" within the meaning of the statute. He held, however, that the writ was not "legal process" within the meaning of § 659(f) because the statutory definition of that term requires that it be issued by a "court of competent jurisdiction." [Editor–The statute provides: "The term 'legal process' means any writ, order, summons, or other similar process in the nature of garnishment, which—(1) is issued by (A) a court of competent jurisdiction * * *."] He reasoned that the portion of the divorce decree ordering respondent to make alimony and child support payments had not been issued by a court of competent jurisdiction because the Alabama court did not have personal jurisdiction over respondent. Since respondent was not domiciled in Alabama at the time of the divorce proceedings, and since Alabama did not then have a statute authorizing personal service on nonresidents for child support or alimony and could not assert jurisdiction under either its own law or the Due Process Clause because it lacked sufficient contacts with respondent, the trial judge concluded that the Alabama judgment on which the garnishment orders were based was void for lack of jurisdiction. Accordingly, the trial judge held that respondent was entitled to recover the amounts withheld from his pay from the United States. * * *

We assume, as does the Government, that the Alabama court lacked jurisdiction over respondent when it issued its writs of garnishment. Based on that assumption, respondent defends the judgment below by arguing that the Alabama court was not a "court of competent jurisdiction," and hence its orders could not satisfy the statutory definition of "legal process."

If we were to look at the words "competent jurisdiction" in isolation, we would concede that the statute is ambiguous. The concept of a court of "competent jurisdiction," though usually used to refer to subject-matter jurisdiction, has also been used on occasion to refer to a court's jurisdiction over the defendant's person. We do not, however, construe statutory phrases in isolation; we read statutes as a whole. Thus, the words "legal process" must be read in light of the immediately following phrase—"regular on its face." That phrase makes it clear that the term "legal process" does not require the issuing court to have personal jurisdiction.

Subject-matter jurisdiction defines the court's authority to hear a given type of case, whereas personal jurisdiction protects the individual interest that is implicated when a nonresident defendant is haled into a distant and possibly inconvenient forum. The strength of this interest cannot be ascertained from the "face" of the process; it can be determined only by evaluating a specific aggregation of facts, as well as the possible vagaries of the law of the forum, and then determining if the relationship between the defendant—in this case the obligor—and the forum, or possibly the particular controversy, makes it reasonable to expect the defendant to defend the action that has been filed in the forum State. The statutory requirement that the garnishee refer only to the "face" of the process is patently inconsistent with the kind of inquiry that may be required to ascertain whether the issuing court has jurisdiction over the obligor's person.

ii) THIRD NATIONAL BANK v. IMPAC LIMITED, INC.

432 U.S. 312 (1977).

■ Mr. Justice Stevens delivered the opinion of the Court.

A federal statute enacted in 1873 provides that certain prejudgment writs shall not be issued against national banks by state courts. The question presented by this case is whether that prohibition applies to a preliminary injunction restraining a national bank from holding a private foreclosure sale, pending adjudication of the mortgagor's claim that the loan is not in default. We conclude that the prohibition does not apply. * * *

The critical statutory language reads as follows:

"[N]o attachment, injunction, or execution, shall be issued against such association or its property before final judgment in any suit, action, or proceeding, in any State, county, or municipal court." 12 U.S.C. § 91.

At least three different interpretations might be placed on that language. Most narrowly, because the rest of § 91 relates to insolvency, this language might be limited to cases in which a national bank is insolvent, or at least on the verge of insolvency. Secondly, regardless of the bank's financial circumstances, it might be construed to prohibit any prejudgment seizure of bank assets. Most broadly, it might be given a completely literal reading and applied not merely as a shield for the bank's assets but also as a prohibition against prejudgment orders protecting the assets of third parties, including debtors of the bank. * * *

The National Currency Act of 1864 authorized the formation of national banks. Section 52 of that act contained the first part of what is now 12 U.S.C. § 91. It prohibited any transfer of bank assets in contemplation of insolvency or with a view to preferring one creditor of the bank over another. The 1864 statute did not, however, include the prohibition against the issuance of prejudgment writs now found in 12 U.S.C. § 91.

That prohibition was enacted in 1873 as § 2 of "An Act to require national Banks to restore their Capital when impaired, and to amend the National–Currency Act." 17 Stat. 603. If the prohibition had been added to § 52 of the 1864 Act, the amended section would have been virtually identical with the present 12 U.S.C. § 91. It was, however, added to § 57 of the 1864 Act, which authorized suits against national banks in the state courts. Petitioner therefore infers that the amendment was intended to qualify the jurisdiction of state courts over national banks and that the amendment should be given its full, literal meaning. * * *

When the first edition of the Revised Statutes of the United States were prepared in 1873, the prohibition against prejudgment writs was combined with the provision concerning preferential transfers and acts in contemplation of insolvency to form § 5242, which is now 12 U.S.C. § 91. [Mortgagors] argue that this revision placed the provision in the context which was originally intended.

For the past century the prohibition against prejudgment writs has remained in the preferential-transfer section. * * *

* * * [I]n Earle, the first Justice Harlan stated that the ban on prejudgment writs must "be construed in connection with the previous parts of the same section" concerning preferential transfers. 178 U.S., at 453. * * *

Petitioner argues, however, that the Court erred in Earle by reading the anti-attachment and preferential-transfer provisions together. It contends that the two were simply combined by mistake in the Revised Statutes. The burden is on petitioner, we think, to show that the present form of the statute—which, after all, constitutes the legal command of Congress—does not reflect congressional intent. If any mistake occurred, it seems at least as likely that the 1873 amendment was incorrectly added to § 57 as that the revisors, that very year, made an error which has gone undetected for over a century. But there are three stronger reasons for rejecting the argument.

First, the historical evidence supports the revisors. It appears likely that when originally passed the provision barring prejudgment writs actually was aimed at preventing preference by creditors. As noted earlier, the threat of insolvency was a serious national problem in 1873, and there had been a number of cases just before in which state courts had allowed creditors to obtain preferences in this manner. There does not seem to have been any similar problem with actions by noncreditors. It seems improbable, for instance, that there were many actions by mortgagors to enjoin foreclosures by national banks, because at that time national banks were allowed to accept mortgages only in very limited circumstances

Second, the anti-injunction provision itself bears strong signs that it was meant to have a limited scope. It is a familiar principle of statutory construction that words grouped in a list should be given related meaning. The word "injunction" is sandwiched between the words "attachment" and "execution." Both are writs used by creditors to seize bank property. On the other hand, the word "garnishment" is conspicuously absent from the list. That writ is directed at the bank, but is used to seize property belonging to others which happens to be in the hands of the bank. The inference is strong that Congress intended only to prevent state judicial action, prior to final judgment, which would have the effect of seizing the bank's property.

Third, petitioner completely fails to identify any national or local interests which its reading of the statute would serve. That reading would give national banks engaged in the business of making loans secured by mortgages on real estate a privilege unavailable to competing lenders. No reason has been advanced for assuming that Congress intended such disparate treatment. We cannot believe that Congress intended to give national banks a license to inflict irreparable injury on others, freed from the normal constraints of equitable relief. * * *

Even though petitioner's reading of the act can be supported by its text and by fragments of history, accepted principles of construction require that the provision in question be construed in its present context and given a rational reading. Fairly read, the statute merely prevents prejudgment seizure of bank property by creditors of the bank. It does not apply to an action by a debtor seeking a preliminary injunction to protect its own property from wrongful foreclosure.

■ Mr. Justice Blackmun, with whom the Chief Justice and Mr. Justice White join, dissenting. * * *

* * * [T]he Court's confidence in the reliability of the compilation is misplaced. It is hard to believe that the revisers, faced with the task of compiling for the first time the mass of congressional legislation from 1789 to 1873, could have performed the delicate task of determining what Congress "really" intended in adopting the 1873 amendment and of "correcting" its error. It is far more likely that the revisers' "placement" of the provision governing prejudgment writs was just one of the many errors that marred the first compilation. See M. Price and H. Bitner, Effective Legal Research 29 (3d ed. 1969); Dwan and Feidler, The Federal Statutes—Their History and Use, 22 Minn.L. Rev. 1008, 1014 (1938). * * *

QUESTIONS

1. Why was Justice Stevens nervous about relying on the Reviser's placement of the "no injunction" provision with the "no preferential transfer" provision? Remember (from the discussion in Chapter 2) that the Reviser made so many mistakes that later codifications were treated only as *prima facie* evidence of the statute, but that what the Reviser did in 1873 was enacted into law. Does enactment into law eliminate any argument that the internal juxtaposition of the two provisions should be disregarded?

2. Do you agree with the following statement from Justice Thomas' dissent in Gustafson v. Alloyd Co., Inc., 513 U.S. 561 (1995), about the limited use of the *noscitur a sociis* canon.

The majority uses the [noscitur] canon in an effort to create doubt, not to reduce it. The canon applies only in cases of ambiguity, which I do not find in [the statute]. "Noscitur a sociis is a well-established and useful rule of construction where words are of obscure or doubtful meaning; and then, but only then, its aid may be sought to remove the obscurity or doubt by reference to the associated words."

Why would a textualist like Justice Thomas be so anxious to deny that the whole text should be considered as part of the process of deciding whether the text is clear or uncertain in the first place? Consider the following explanation for Justice Thomas' position. The "whole text" approach raises the possibility that a statute *creates* its own textual meaning and that is something the textualist is reluctant to admit. After all, in the IMPAC case, the meaning of the word "injunction" seemed to be created by its statutory environment.

b) Ejusdem Generis

Another way in which the surrounding text sheds light on the meaning of particular words is captured by the phrase "ejusdem generis"—the same generic category. A statute will often set forth a specific detailed list followed by a general catch-all phrase. The general phrase must be interpreted. The "ejusdem generis" canon of construction states that the general phrase is limited to the same types of things that are listed more specifically.

This canon is probably based on a genuine attempt to understand how authors use and audiences understand language. Its application can still be troublesome, however. In Cleveland v. United States, 329 U.S. 14 (1946), petitioners were members of a Mormon sect who practiced polygamy. They transported at least one plural wife across state lines, either for the purpose of cohabiting with her, or for the purpose of aiding another member of the group to do so. They were convicted of violating the Mann Act, which makes it an offence to transport in interstate commerce "any woman or girl for the purpose of prostitution or debauchery, or for any other immoral purpose." The decision turned on the meaning of the latter phrase, "for any other immoral purpose." The defendants argued that "other immoral purpose" did not include polygamy, being of a different genus from prostitution and debauchery. The Court agreed that prostitution implied sexual relations for hire, but noted that debauchery did not. Polygamy was therefore in the same genus as the other immoral practices listed in the Act. Does the verb "debauch" (if not the noun "debauchery") imply any relation between sex and money? Does debauching lead to prostitution?

c) Avoid Surplusage

Courts often state that a statute will be interpreted to avoid surplusage, so that every word adds something to what you are saying. Exxon Corp. v. Hunt, 475 U.S. 355, 369 n. 14 (1986); Hassan v. Fraccola, 851 F.2d 602, 604 (2d Cir.1988). Is this canon of construction about internal context concerned with how language is commonly used? It is far from clear that avoiding surplusage describes ordinary speech. In State v. Stovall, 648 P.2d 543, 547 n. 1 (Wyo.1982), the court noted that Americans tend to be redundant in everyday conversation, rather than concise. Moreover, statutes are political language and may not follow the conventions of ordinary speech. See also White v. Roughton, 689 F.2d 118, 120 (7th Cir.1982)(Posner, J.)(statutes, like contracts, often have surplusage). The legislature may want to be sure to cover all possibilities and therefore speak redundantly. The canon against surplusage is therefore applied with caution. At most, it is a presumption, probably a weak one, which is rejected when its application defeats statutory objectives.

d) PRESUMPTION THAT WORDS HAVE A CONSISTENT MEANING THROUGHOUT THE STATUTE

Another often-cited canon of construction about the internal context of a statute is that the same words are used with the same meaning throughout the statutory text. This is as questionable an assumption about common usage as "no surplusage." Not surprisingly, courts often disregard this maxim when a more sensible result is indicated.

For example, in Lawson v. Suwanee Fruit & Steamship Co., 336 U.S. 198 (1949), a Workers Compensation statute provided benefits for work-related disability. To achieve that purpose, the statute defined "disability" to mean an incapacity resulting from a work-related injury. Another portion of the statute provided a "second injury" fund, which provided that if an employee who was partially disabled prior to acquiring a job then suffers a job-related injury which results in permanent and total disability, the employer will be liable only for the disability resulting from the second injury. This rule is intended to encourage employers to hire the partially disabled, who are more likely to become totally disabled on the job, by removing the employer's concern about Workers Compensation liability for total disability. The statutory language dealing with the second injury fund presented some interpretation problems, however, as explained below.

■ Mr. Justice Murphy delivered the opinion of the Court. * * *

Section 8(f)(1) of the Act provides that "if an employee receive an injury which of itself would only cause permanent partial disability but which, combined with a previous disability, does in fact cause permanent total disability, the employer shall provide compensation only for the disability caused by the subsequent injury: Provided, however, That in addition to compensation for such permanent partial disability, and after the cessation of the payments for the prescribed period of weeks, the employee shall be paid the remainder of the compensation that would be due for permanent total disability. Such additional compensation shall be paid out of the special fund established in section 44." The court below held that this section is "clear and unambiguous, and therefore needs no construction. When read in its ordinary sense it can have but one meaning: liability for the second injury fund."

But the word "disability" is defined in the statute. Section 2 provides that "when used in this Act * * * (10) 'Disability' means incapacity because of *injury* * * *." (Emphasis supplied.) The word "injury" is, in turn, defined as "accidental injury or death arising out of and in the course of employment * * *." 2(2). If these definitions are read into the second injury provision, then, it reads as follows: "If an employee receive an injury which of itself would only cause permanent partial disability but which, combined with a previous incapacity because of accidental injury or death arising out of and in the course of employment, does in fact cause permanent total disability, the employer shall provide compensation only for the disability caused by the subsequent injury." Because Davis' previous injury was nonindustrial, this reading points to liability for the employer.

If Congress intended to use the term "disability" as a term of art, a shorthand way of referring to the statutory definition, the employer must pay total compensation. If Congress intended a broader and more usual concept of the word, the judgment below must be affirmed. Statutory definitions control the meaning of statutory words, of course, in the usual case. But this is an unusual case. If we read the definition into § 8(f)(1) in a mechanical fashion, we create obvious incongruities in the language, and we destroy one of the major purposes of the second injury provision: the prevention of employer discrimination against handicapped workers. We have concluded that Congress would not have intended such a result. * * *

On the basis of the incongruity involved in applying the definition mechanically, the unmistakable purpose of the second injury fund, * * * we conclude that the term "disability" was not used as a term of art in § 8(f)(1), and that the judgment must be affirmed.

The Court's interpretation, although it meant that the term "disability" was interpreted colloquially in one place in the statute and in accordance with the statutory definition in another, implemented the statute's obvious purpose. Would the decision be easier if the second injury fund provision had been adopted some years after initial adoption of the Workers Compensation statute?

However, in Sullivan v. Stroop, 496 U.S. 478, 484 (1990), the Court applied the maxim that "identical words used in different parts of the same act are intended to have the same meaning." The statute dealt with Title IV of the Social Security Act, Part A of which provided that the state "shall disregard the first $50 of any child support payments * * * "in determining the AFDC welfare claimant's income. Inclusion in income would reduce welfare benefits. The statute unquestionably applied to payments made by a parent to support the child. The case involved *government* payments made under the "child's insurance benefits" program established by Title II of the Social Security Act.

The Court observed that the $50 disregard provision was found in Title IV–A and that Part D of Title IV included a provision to enforce an absent parent's obligation of child support. It concluded that "child support" was a "term of art" used throughout Title IV to refer to payments from absent parents. The Court also quoted Black's Law Dictionary to the effect that child support meant legally compulsory payments from parents.

The dissent by Justice Blackmun noted the history of the various statutory provisions. The $50 disregard in Part IV–A postdated adoption of Part IV–D dealing with parental support. Part IV–A was adopted in 1984 when, for the first time, the statute mandated inclusion of the child's income in the income of the family unit. The disregard was added in the House–Senate conference and had not previously been in either the House or Senate bill. According to the dissent, the "only plausible explanation for its sudden appearance is that it was meant to assuage the concerns of some members of Congress about the harsh impact of the [ ] amendments * * *." That hardship would be experienced by the welfare family who included either parental *or* government child support in family income. Although Part IV–D unquestionably dealt with child support from absent parents, Justice Blackmun noted that the maxim favoring identical construction of identical words in the same or related statutes was only a general assumption, not to be applied if the sections had different purposes.

QUESTIONS

If parts of a statutory text are drafted at different times, as was true of Parts IV–A and IV–D in Stroop, what justifies interpreting the document so that the same words have the same meaning throughout? Is the text really a single text, written and read as an integrated document? In this connection, consider the following questions.

1. Can we really expect the legislative author to worry about how the same words are used throughout a statute whose parts are drafted at different times? Was there evidence in Stroop that the legislative authors did not treat Part IV as an integrated document?

2. Should we care about what the author thought? Maybe all we care about is how an audience reads the text. Would the statutory audience in Stroop treat Part IV as an integrated document?

3. Or, perhaps, we do not care about real authors and audiences at all. Is there some other justification for assuming that words have the same meaning throughout a statute? Will it force better drafting or is Congressional drafting so chaotic that the drafters will not respond to judicially-crafted incentives? Will sticking to canons of interpretation, such as "consistent textual meaning" and "no surplusage," limit judicial discretion in statutory interpretation?

e) EXPRESSIO UNIUS EST EXCLUSIO ALTERIUS

Another canon of construction based on language is *expressio unius est exclusio alterius*, which asserts that the express inclusion of one (or more) thing(s) implies the exclusion of other things from similar treatment. For example, if a tax break is explicitly made available for one person (X), the implication is that the statute does not otherwise provide that benefit under other general provisions of the tax law to other people (Y and Z). The idea is that, if the tax break had been generally available in the first place, there would have been no need for an express provision helping X. The possibility that courts would apply the *expressio unius* canon led to the 9th Amendment to the U.S. Constitution, stating: "The Enumeration in the Constitution, of certain rights, shall not be construed to deny or disparage others retained by the people."

As a statement about ordinary language usage, this canon is doubtful. Sometimes, statutory context indicates that an express statement determines who in the entire universe should be covered by a statute, but we need to know a lot about context to know whether inferring the exclusion of others is reasonable.

As a statement about political language, the canon is even more doubtful. Busy legislatures are concerned with matters brought to their attention. Moreover, political groups seeking a benefit do not care much about how a statute might be interpreted without an express provision. They want an express statement on which they can rely, regardless of whether the best interpretation of the statute would have provided the benefit in any event. In other words, expressly helping person X may say nothing about whether persons X, Y and Z are already helped under the statute. Person X may just have the legislature's ear.

In Dobson v. Commissioner, 320 U.S. 489 (1943), for example, the taxpayer had deducted a loss on the sale of stock but derived no tax advantage from the deduction because she had no income. She later sued and recovered some of the loss. She argued that the recovery was not taxable income because the earlier deduction was useless; it provided no "tax benefit." Congress had adopted a rule specifying that *certain* recoveries—such as the recovery of a bad debt after a prior deduction of what earlier appeared to be a worthless debt—would not be taxable if the original deduction was of no tax benefit. The statute dealing with recoveries did not, however, include the situation affecting the Dobson taxpayer. The issue was whether an express tax break for some payments excluded the same tax break for others under a general "tax benefit" rule. The Court stated:

> [T]he history of the bad debt recovery question illustrates the mischief of overruling the Tax Court in matters of tax accounting. Courts were persuaded to rule as matter of law that bad debt recoveries constitute taxable income, regardless of tax benefit from the charge-off. The Tax Court had first made a similar holding, but had come to hold to the contrary. [Taxing bad debt recoveries] led to such hardships and inequities that the Treasury appealed to

Congress to extend relief. It did so. The Government now argues that by extending legislative relief in bad debt cases Congress recognized that in the absence of specific exemption recoveries are taxable as income. We do not find that significance in the amendment. A specific statutory exception was necessary in bad debt cases only because the courts reversed the Tax Court and established as matter of law a "theoretically proper" rule which distorted the taxpayer's income. Congress would hardly expect the courts to repeat the same error in another class of cases, as we would do were we to affirm in this case.

Sometimes the statute explicitly answers the question whether specific rules comprehensively deal with an area of the law, negating application of a general principle. For example, the tax law had developed a general principle taxing income to a person who retained dominion and control over property. This was very important for trusts, where grantors created trusts but retained control. Specific provisions of the Internal Revenue Code, sections 671–77, deal with the problem, stating when a trust grantor will be taxed, and the last sentence of sec. 671 specifies that these detailed rules are exclusive:

> No items of a trust shall be included in (the grantor's income) solely on the grounds of his dominion and control over the trust * * *, except as specified in this part.

By contrast, Comment to sec. 2–318 of the Uniform Commercial Code, which abolishes privity for suing on a seller's warranty for certain injured parties, states:

> This section expressly includes as beneficiaries within its provisions the family, household, and guests of the purchaser. Beyond that, the section is neutral and is not intended to enlarge or restrict the developing case law on whether the seller's warranties, given to his buyer who resells, extend to other persons in the distributive chain.

Evaluate the court's decision in Wilson v. Harris Trust & Sav. Bank, 777 F.2d 1246 (7th Cir.1985). In this case a *private* employer laid off an employee who filed for bankruptcy. The statute explicitly prohibited a *government* employer from discriminating against such employees. Before this explicit provision was passed, litigants argued that the "fresh start" principle underlying the Bankruptcy law prevented discrimination against employees who filed for bankruptcy. The issue was whether the explicit rule prohibiting discrimination by government employers had an impact on the court's ability to apply the "fresh start" principle to private employers. The court held that "the terms of the statute are unambiguous" (!) in providing a negative inference that *private* employers were not covered. The decision was especially strange because there was explicit legislative history stating that, even though the legislature was *not* adopting a proposal to extend the explicit prohibition to private employers, "[n]evertheless, [the statute] is not limited either * * *. The courts will continue to mark the contours of the anti-discrimination provision in pursuit of sound bankruptcy policy."

———

This review of various canons of construction suggests that they sometimes have little to do with how people ordinarily use and understand language. Is it possible that a judge who invokes at least some of the canons is unconcerned with how people communicate but with something else? The rhetorical appeal of textualism might make citation of text-based canons of construction irresistible but conceal some basis for decision other than a genuine concern with meaning shared by author and audience.

f) OUTLANDISH STATUTORY DEFINITION

The most obvious case of internal context is a statutory definition of words used in the text. To what extent can the statute legislate its own definition that departs from any sensible linguistic meaning? On the one hand, courts say that "[t]he legislature may create its own dictionary, and its definitions may be different from ordinary usage." Commonwealth v. Massini, 188 A.2d 816 (Pa.Super.1963)("domestic animal" defined to exclude cats in a statute making it a crime to kill a domestic animal). On the other hand, courts say that a statutory definition cannot totally distort linguistic usage. Careful examination of the cases rejecting distorted usage, however, reveals that the defect in the statutes was probably the substantive effect of the unusual definition, not the mere fact that the definition was unusual. See, e.g., Central Television Service, Inc. v. Isaacs, 189 N.E.2d 333 (Ill.1963)(statute defining a seller for the sales tax to include certain TV service providers violated the state constitutional requirement that taxes be uniform).

What should a court do if the only thing questionable about the statute is the weird definition? Suppose the statute defines "four" to mean "five." See G. Orwell, Nineteen Eighty–Four 252–61 (1949)(protagonist states that "Freedom is the freedom to say that two plus two make four;" he is then made to believe that five fingers are being held up by his interrogator, rather than the four that he thinks he sees).

g) CONFLICTING EVIDENCE FROM INTERNAL CONTEXT

Internal context consists of a number of indicators about statutory meaning, some of which may conflict. In United States National Bank of Oregon v. Independent Insurance Agents, 508 U.S. 439 (1993), the Court resolves such a conflict between punctuation and other features of internal context. It concluded, *unanimously*, that the statute's punctuation was an error, relying instead on the statute's structure, text, and subject matter. The substantive issue was whether banks in towns with populations not exceeding 5,000 could act as insurance company agents. This "small-bank" rule was adopted in 1916, and might have been repealed in 1918. The rule's possible 1918 repeal was the issue in the case.

The case is an example of how a textualist judge can build up a sense of the statute's objective or purpose, without necessarily going outside the text's boundaries.

The Revised Statutes of 1874 adopted a rule in § 5202 that national banks cannot incur excessive debt, but listed four types of debt exempt from the calculation. Later, the Federal Reserve Act of 1913 created the federal reserve banking system. § 13 of that Act, in addition to listing five powers held by the new reserve banks, also amended § 5202 to add a fifth type of exempt debt.

In 1916, Congress amended many sections of the Federal Reserve Act of 1913, including § 13. One of the amendments added the small-bank rule, giving banks the power to act as insurance agents. The punctuation used by the amendment suggested that this 1916 small-bank rule was accomplished by an amendment to § 5202 of the Revised Acts of 1874, not § 13 of the Federal Reserve Act. This was important because, in 1918, Congress explicitly amended and restated § 5202 to add a sixth type of debt exempt from the excessive debt rules, but the restatement of § 5202 left out the small-bank rule. If, beginning in 1916, the small-bank rule had in fact been part of § 5202 (rather than the Federal Reserve Act of 1913), it was repealed by the 1918 statute.

The first codification of the U.S.Code in 1926 included the small-bank rule in Title 12, § 92. (Although some titles of the U.S.Code have been enacted into law, Title 12 has *not* been so enacted.) Then, in 1952 and thereafter, the codifiers concluded that the 1918 law had repealed the small-bank rule. A House subcommittee report agreed that repeal had occurred, but the Report was not attached to any legislation dealing with the issue. The relevant regulatory agencies (Comptroller General and Federal Reserve Board) disagreed; they thought the small-bank rule was still the law.

Why the confusion? It arose from the punctuation in the 1916 law amending § 13 of the Federal Reserve Act of 1913. The punctuation made it look as though the small-bank rule was placed in § 5202, which was later repealed. The 1916 law, which amended various sections of the Federal Reserve Act of 1913, looked as follows (the brackets are provided by the Court in its opinion and in my explanation of the statute, but are not in the legislation itself; the italicized provisions dealing with § 13 of the Federal Reserve Act of 1913 and Revised Statutes § 5202 are the provisions causing the problem):

[1]   At the end of section eleven insert a new clause as follows:

"* * *"

[2]   *That section thirteen be, and is hereby, amended to read as follows:*

" * * [Editor—Listing and modifying bank powers]"*

[3]   Section fifty-two hundred and two of the Revised Statutes of the United States is hereby amended so as to read as follows: "No national bank association shall at any time be indebted [in excess of capital stock], except on account of demands of the nature following:

"First, Notes of circulation.

"Second, Moneys deposited with or collected by the association.

"Third * * *.

"Fourth * * *.

"Fifth * * *.

[Editor—Then followed three paragraphs with beginning quotes, dealing with bank powers, the second of which contained the small bank insurance agent exception.]

"The discount and rediscount * * * of any bills receivable and of domestic and foreign bills of exchange, and of acceptances authorized by this Act, shall be subject to such restrictions * * * as may be imposed by the Federal Reserve Board.

"That * * * *(a small bank)* may * * act as the agent for any fire, life, or other insurance company * * *.

"Any member bank may accept drafts * * * etc."

[4]   That subsection (e) of section fourteen, be, and is hereby, amended to read as follows:

"* * *"

[5–7] [Editor—That section sixteen, section twenty-four, and section twenty-five be amended to read as follows:

"* * *"]

Here is the difficulty. Each bracketed paragraph appears to contain its own specific amendments, *placed within quotation marks.* The Court concludes, however, that the bracketed paragraph [3], dealing with § 5202, was part of an amendment to § 13 of the Federal Reserve Act, accomplished by the bracketed paragraph [2]. A simple change in punctuation—deleting and adding quotation marks (as indicated in capital letters below)—achieves that result:

[2]   That section thirteen be, and is hereby, amended to read as follows:

"[Editor—Listing and modifying bank powers (DELETE CLOSE QUOTATION MARKS)

"(ADD OPEN QUOTATION MARKS) *Section fifty-two hundred and two of the Revised Statutes of the United States is hereby amended so as to read as follows:* [DELETE OPEN QUOTATION

MARKS] *No national bank association shall at any time be indebted [in excess of capital stock], except [listing five categories of exempt debt, and setting forth the three bank powers, including the small bank rule].*"

This redoing of the quotation marks means that the small-bank rule is an amendment to the Federal Reserve Act of 1913, not § 5202, and was not repealed in 1918.

In reaching this result, the Court first stated its interpretive approach as follows:

> A statute's plain meaning must be enforced, of course, and the meaning of a statute will typically heed the commands of its punctuation. But a purported plain-meaning analysis based only on punctuation is necessarily incomplete and runs the risk of distorting a statute's true meaning. Along with punctuation, text consists of words living "a communal existence," in Judge Learned Hand's phrase, the meaning of each word informing the others and "all in their aggregate tak[ing] their purport from the setting in which they are used." Over and over we have stressed that "[i]n expounding a statute, we must not be guided by a single sentence or member of a sentence, but look to the provisions of the whole law, and to its object and policy." No more than isolated words or sentences is punctuation alone a reliable guide for discovery of a statute's meaning. Statutory construction "is a holistic endeavor," and, at a minimum, must account for a statute's full text, language as well as punctuation, structure, and subject matter.

The Court then concluded that "though the deployment of quotation marks in the 1916 Act points in one direction, all of the other evidence from the statute points" to the conclusion that "the punctuation marks were misplaced and that the 1916 Act put section 92 not in Rev. Stat. § 5202 but in § 13 of the Federal Reserve Act."

To reach this conclusion the Court marshaled several arguments. First, it noted the structure of the 1916 Act, observing that:

> only the third [amendment dealing with § 5202] does not in terms refer to a section of the Federal Reserve Act. Congress, to be sure, was free to take a detour from its work on the Federal Reserve Act to revise the Revised Statutes. But if Congress had taken that turn, one would expect some textual indication of the point where once its work on Rev. Stat. § 5202 was done it returned to revision of the Federal Reserve Act. None of the directory phrases that follow the phrase mentioning Rev. Stat. § 5202, however, refers back to the Federal Reserve Act.

Second, the Court relied on the Act's title, which was: "An Act to amend certain sections of the Act entitled 'Federal Reserve Act.'" It observed that "[d]uring this era the titles of statutes that revised pre-existing laws appear to have typically mentioned each of the laws they revised."

Third, the Court relied on the "language and subject matter of section 92 and the paragraphs surrounding it, paragraphs within the same opening and closing quotation marks." (Section 92 is the section of 26 U.S.C. in which the small-bank provision was codified.) It noted that in the paragraph preceding section 92, the 1916 Act granted the Federal Reserve Board authority to regulate the "discount and rediscount and the purchase and sale by any Federal reserve bank of any bills receivable and of domestic and foreign bills of exchange, and of acceptances authorized by this Act * * *." Because "this Act" must mean the Federal Reserve Act, and because "section 92 travels together with the paragraphs that surround it," the Court concluded that both paragraphs were placed in the Federal Reserve Act. The Court also noted that the subject matter of the paragraphs before and after the small-bank rule dealt with Federal Reserve Bank powers, whose placement in the Federal Reserve Act, but not § 5202, made sense. It concluded that "the 1916 Act placed section 92 in the same statutory location as it must have placed its neighbors, in § 13 of the Federal Reserve Act." The Act's punctuation was too weak to trump what the Court called "the overwhelming evidence from the structure, language, and subject matter of the 1916 Act." The placement of the quotation marks was deemed a scrivener's error, "a mistake made by someone unfamiliar with the law's object and design." In conclusion, the Court held that the "true meaning of the 1916 Act is clear beyond question," and that the "statute's meaning is unambiguous."

5.04   TEXTUALISM VS. LITERALISM

Literalism should be distinguished from the genuine search for textual meaning based on the way people commonly understand language. Literalism is a kind of "spurious" textualism, unconcerned with how people actually communicate—with how the author wanted to use language or the audience might understand it. It holds up the text in isolation from actual usage.

Judge Learned Hand was probably being critical of literalism when he observed that "the meaning of a sentence may be more than that of the separate words, as a melody is more than the notes." Helvering v. Gregory, 69 F.2d 809, 810–11 (2d Cir.1934), affirmed, 293 U.S. 465 (1935). And that "it is one of the surest indexes of a mature and developed jurisprudence not to make a fortress out of the dictionary; but to remember that statutes always have some purpose or object to accomplish, whose sympathetic and imaginative discovery is the surest guide to their meaning." Cabell v. Markham, 148 F.2d 737, 739 (2d Cir.1945), affirmed, 326 U.S. 404 (1945).

An example of literalism is Kissinger v. Reporters Committee for Freedom of the Press, 445 U.S. 136, 151 (1980). The Court interpreted "withhold" to mean a government agency's retention of *physical* possession or control, emphasizing that any other reading would "read the 'hold' out of 'withhold.'" It rejected an interpretation of "withhold" to mean refusing to turn over documents which the agency could legally obtain. If your professor refused to exercise authority he possessed to order the registrar to give you a grade which was in the registrar's possession, would the professor be "withholding" the grade?

Does reference to the Latin root meanings of words amount to literalism? See Coy v. Iowa, 487 U.S. 1012, 1016 (1988)("confrontation" of witness by defendant requires that the witness see the defendant and vice-versa; "Simply as a matter of Latin [ ], the word 'confront' [ ] derives from the prefix 'con-' (from 'contra' meaning 'against' or 'opposed') and the noun 'frons' (forehead)").

Do at least some of the uses of some of the linguistic canons amount to literalism? For example, how would you characterize a decision in which a court insists on applying the *expressio unius est exclusio alterius* canon without any reliable evidence that the legislature was considering the entire universe of possibilities when it made an explicit statement in the statutory text?

You must be careful, however, not to confuse textualism and literalism. Sometimes the charge of literalism is made against a linguistic argument made by a textualist—such as the textualist's view favoring historical over current usage, and the textualist's rejection of purpose to trump or tilt statutory meaning away from a more probable meaning derived from ordinary usage. But that is unfair. Whether or not the textualist's linguistic argument is the best way to interpret statutes, the textualist's attempt to determine how language is understood cannot always be equated with literalism.

Literalism might also occur by emphasizing grammar and style. Is that what happens in the following Scalia opinion, written while he was on the D.C. Court of Appeals? Is he concerned with shared understanding of meaning between author and audience, with how the author is likely to have used language, with how the audience is likely to have understood language, or with something else? To what extent is it "literalism" to disregard the realities of the political drafting process, which may differ from how other written instruments may be drafted?

In Church of Scientology of California v. I.R.S., 792 F.2d 153 (D.C.Cir. 1986), affirmed, 484 U.S. 9 (1987), Judge Scalia dealt with an exception to a provision of the tax law, which otherwise limited access to income tax return information. "Return information" was defined in the statute as follows (26 U.S.C. § 6103(b)(2)):

> (A) a taxpayer's identity, the nature, source, or amount of his income, * * * receipts, deductions, exemptions, * * * tax liability, tax withheld, * * * or tax payments, whether the taxpayer's return was, is being, or will be examined or subject to other investigation or processing, or any other data, received by, recorded by, prepared by * * * or collected by the Secretary with respect to a return or with respect to the determination of the existence, or possible

existence, of liability [ ] of any person under this title for any tax, penalty, interest, fine, forfeiture, or other imposition, or offense, and

(B) any part of any written determination or any background file document relating to such written determination (as such terms are defined in section 6110(b)) which is not open to public inspection under section 6110, *but such term does not include data in a form which cannot be associated with, or otherwise identify, directly or indirectly, a particular taxpayer.*

The italicized clause was the Haskell Amendment, so named because it was inserted into the committee-proposed bill by a floor amendment introduced by Senator Haskell at the end of legislative deliberations. The case considered whether the Haskell amendment allowed access to data that did not identify a particular taxpayer because names, identifying numbers and other similar information had been deleted (for example, tax returns with the material deleted or schedules of information attached to returns that did not identify particular taxpayers). Long v. United States I.R.S., 596 F.2d 362 (9th Cir.1979), held that such access was allowed. However, the Seventh Circuit in King v. I.R.S., 688 F.2d 488, 493 (7th Cir.1982), reached a conclusion different from Long. It held that the statute "protects from disclosure all non-amalgamated items listed in subsection (b)(2)(A), and that the Haskell Amendment provides only for the disclosure of statistical tabulations which are not associated with or do not identify particular taxpayers."

Judge Scalia agreed with the King case. One part of his argument relies heavily on internal context, particularly on what he calls "natural" usage, and on avoiding surplusage. How "natural" is the usage on which he relies?

The starting point of analysis, of course, is the text of the provision at issue, which, we agree with the Seventh Circuit, is ill suited to achieve the result pronounced in Long. It would be most peculiar to catalogue in such detail, in subparagraph (A) of the body of the definition, the specific items that constitute "return information" (e.g., "income, payments, receipts, deductions, exemptions, credits, assets, liabilities, net worth, tax liability, tax withheld, deficiencies, over-assessments, or tax payments, * * * or any other data, received by, recorded by, prepared by, furnished to, or collected by the Secretary with respect to a return") while leaving to an afterthought the major qualification that none of those items counts unless it identifies the taxpayer. Such an intent would more naturally have been expressed not in an exclusion ("but such term does not include * * *")but in the body of the definition—by stating, for example, that "the term 'return information' means the following information that can be associated with or identify a particular taxpayer: * * *." If the intended scope of the exclusion is as broad as Long holds, the structure of the provision is akin to defining mankind as "all mammals in the world, but excluding those that are not relatively hairless bipeds with the power of abstract reasoning." While such a form of definition is conceivable, it would constitute "everyday language" (as the dissent characterizes it) only

for one of Lewis Carroll's characters, and it hardly takes "talmudic dissection" or "microscopic scrutiny," to reject it as implausible.
* * *

We also agree with the Seventh Circuit that the formulation of the Haskell provision itself suggests something other than merely the absence of identifying information.   It would be strange to express the latter thought by excluding "data *in a form* which cannot be associated with, or otherwise identify * * * a particular taxpayer" (emphasis added).   The emphasized phrase would be superfluous for that purpose, as reading the provision without it will demonstrate. A more natural formulation for the purposes which Long assigns would be similar to that contained in the provision of FOIA that "any agency may *delete identifying details*," 5 U.S.C. § 552(a)(2)(emphasis added); or similar to the formulation used elsewhere in this same Subchapter of the Internal Revenue Code, that no publication shall "permit * * * information * * * to be associated with, or otherwise identify, directly or indirectly, a particular taxpayer," 26 U.S.C. § 6108(c). * * *

This Scalia opinion is typical in claiming to identify how English writers would "naturally" write. But it may not pay much attention to the environment in which the authors were writing. The Haskell amendment was adopted in a rush to adjournment. The dissent relied on this fact to reject what it called Judge Scalia's "talmudic" approach. Hurried drafting was bound to produce some carelessness.

Perhaps at least some textualists are not really concerned with how people communicate but with how they *should* communicate. Justice Scalia writes from a good grammar and style perspective, as though he knows good drafting standards. Interpretation in accordance with those standards might be intended to force the drafter to achieve a higher standard of drafting. The court is telling Congress that failure to adhere to that standard runs the risk that the court will not implement legislative intent.

Will judicial interpretation influence statutory drafting? Is drafting such a chaotic process in a busy legislature that judicial incentives for good drafting will be ineffectual? Are there differences between federal and state legislatures? Perhaps state legislative staff, who actually draft statutes, pay more attention to judicially mandated linguistic canons of interpretation than federal drafters.

What is the alternative to remaining on the surface of the text and looking for good grammar and style? Does your answer to this question suggest any other reason for Justice Scalia's surface textualism?

CHAPTER 6

EXTERNAL CONTEXT—PURPOSE

6.01 INTRODUCTION

This Chapter discusses how external context in the sense of statutory purpose influences the meaning of a statute. "Purpose" has a narrower and broader meaning. First, there is the historical mischief that prompts legislative action. Second, there is the broader purpose of the statute. In some statutes the purpose may be coextensive with the specific mischief prompting legislation. The case of Third National Bank v. Impac Limited, Inc., 432 U.S. 312 (1977), discussed in Chapter 5, may be an example. A concern with preventing debtor banks transferring property to prefer certain creditors was both the mischief prompting the legislation and the statute's purpose. In other statutes the purpose may expand beyond the historical mischief which initially prompts legislative action (or at least the Court concludes that it does). For example, in Cleveland v. United States, 329 U.S. 14 (1946), a statute prompted by a concern with commercial sex was interpreted to have the broader purpose of dealing with other kinds of immoral sex, including polygamy. And, in United States v. Turkette, 452 U.S. 576 (1981), the statute was passed in response to the historical mischief of organized crime infiltrating legitimate businesses. It was, however, interpreted to have the broader purpose of criminalizing activity related to illegitimate as well as legitimate business. The language of the statute ("enterprise") covered more than the historical mischief (infiltrating legitimate business), which had attracted most of the legislature's attention.

Another type of external context includes the political, social, moral, legal and other substantive background considerations in the shadow of which all political action occurs. Unlike purpose, these traditions may not explain why a statute is passed and may not even be consciously considered as part of the legislative process. Sometimes the most basic traditions operate at the subconscious level. They "go without saying." The narrow interpretation of statutes in derogation of the common law (discussed in Chapter 2) was a controversial example. "Background considerations" are the focus of attention in the next chapter. You should, however, be alert to the influence of substantive background considerations on the use of purpose to interpret statutes—recall Radin's view (discussed in Chapter 3) that judges "exercise a judgment on the value of the purpose."

It is important at the outset to keep in mind what this chapter is *not* about. First, it is not about how purpose, inferred from the internal textual context, determines meaning. That was discussed in Chapter 5. Most textualists will consider internal context (the "language, structure, and subject matter" of the law) to help interpret the text.

Second, the emphasis in this Chapter is on how purpose, inferred from external context, can produce meaning different from what the text suggests or can tilt meaning in a particular direction. It is important to remember, however, some external context is always needed to identify the plain meaning of a text. Plain meaning depends on what an author and audience share about understanding language, which in turn depends on their common experiences, as any one trying to explain what words mean to a non-native speaker will tell you.[1]

Chapter 6.02 first notes a distinction between intent and purpose that is too often overlooked. We then consider some relatively easy cases in Chapter 6.03, where the text does not make sense. We then turn in Chapter 6.04 to cases where the plain meaning of the text makes sense but conflicts with very persuasive evidence of statutory purpose. Can purpose *trump* the text? Chapter 6.05 deals with the more usual case of disagreement about how clear the text is and with how to resolve conflicts between purpose and the probable meaning of the text. Can purpose *tilt* the text toward a particular statutory meaning? Chapter 6.06 presents decisions in the Lenroot case, which permits you to review your understanding of the materials in Chapters 5 and 6, and of the different ways the text acquires meaning and how purpose might influence statutory meaning.

6.02   LEGISLATIVE PURPOSE AND INTENT

Before we look too closely at how purpose can influence statutory meaning, there is an uncertainty about what purpose means that must be clarified. "Legislative purpose" is a variation on the much-used and abused phrase "legislative intent." Judges often use "legislative intent" without distinguishing between "intent" and "purpose," which Dickerson explains in the following excerpt.

Dickerson seems most concerned with the fact that "legislative purpose" is elusive because it can be defined with ever increasing levels of generality. Workers Compensation, for example, was adopted to help workers injured on the job, to help the disabled, to provide replacement for lost income, to

---

1.   Purpose can also call attention to textual uncertainties that are not at first apparent. My favorite example is the income tax provision which permits deduction of "a reasonable allowance for salaries." Internal Revenue Code of 1986, § 162(a)(1). The provision has always been understood as a *limit* on deductible salary, but its statutory purpose was to help businesses, permitting them to lower their excess profits taxes by reducing net income, whether or not they paid salaries.

Armed with knowledge of this statutory purpose, the reader now finds the reference to a deduction of a reasonable "allowance" (rather than a reasonable "amount") for salaries a little strange as a limit on the deduction of actual compensation payments. Deduction of an "allowance" makes sense, however, as a rule helping rather than hurting taxpayers. See Griswold, New Light on "A Reasonable Allowance for Salaries," 59 Harv. L. Rev. 286 (1945).

redistribute income, and to provide for the general welfare. The "level of generality" problem is the older critique of judicial reliance on legislative purpose. The modern critique—derived from the Law and Economics perspective—emphasizes conflicting compromised purposes, such as helping workers and limiting employer liability for work-related injuries. Which purpose is dominant, if any?

R. Dickerson, The Interpretation and Application of Statutes
(1975).

Whereas the concept of "legislative intent" is in disfavor with many legal writers, that of "legislative purpose" enjoys not only favor but preeminence. For most, it is the touchstone of statutory interpretation. It is important, therefore, to distinguish it from legislative intent and examine it in some detail.

In their widest senses the two concepts overlap. Thus, if it may be said that when a legislature took particular action it had a range of ever-widening purposes, beginning at the inner extreme with the specific purpose of taking that action and ending at the outer extreme with the very general purpose of helping to advance the total public good, the former is coextensive with the legislative intent to effectuate the specific purpose. The important fact is that lawyers tend to identify the immediate legislative purpose with "legislative intent" and to reserve the term "legislative purpose" for any broader or remote ("ulterior") legislative purpose.

Thus, in general legal usage the word "intent" coincides with the particular immediate purpose that the statute is intended to directly express and immediately accomplish, whereas the word "purpose" refers primarily to an ulterior purpose that the legislature intends the statute to accomplish or help to accomplish. Although some ulterior purposes, like the immediate purpose, tend to be fully served by the statute in the sense that compliance with its working provisions will fully carry them out, most ulterior purposes are broad enough that they can be only partly served by such compliance.
* * *

The reasons for supposing an actual consensus on legislative purpose are sometime stronger, but usually weaker, than they are on legislative intent. True, it is sometimes easier for a group of persons subjectively to share the same general purpose than it is for them subjectively to share the same intent. But, although this might make the supposition of an actual legislative purpose more palatable to some of the skeptics of subjective legislative intent, there are countervailing considerations.

The disciplines of the legislative process are directed more to attaining agreement on the specific action to be taken in a bill than to attaining agreement on its legislative purposes, even when these purposes have been memorialized in the bill itself. Even those who are closest to the bill are likely to focus more sharply on the specific action taken in the bill than on any general statements of purpose. Other legislators, whose knowledge of the bill tends to be general only, are likely to have their own notions of the broader or more remote purposes that it will serve and not so likely, therefore, to adopt the states of mind of others. Indeed, even those who are closely familiar with the specific terms of the bill may agree on the same specific action for a variety of reasons. As a result, there is likely to be less actual agreement on specific ultimate objectives than there is on the action taken in the bill itself. This may explain why most formal statements of purpose in bills or committee reports tend to be innocuous generalities designed to offend the least number of people, a fact that destroys most of their usefulness for resolving specific uncertainties of meaning. As a general result, there are likely to be fewer reliable evidences of legislative purpose than there are to be of legislative intent. * * *

This is not to say that actual legislative purpose cannot and does not exist, or that there is no reliable basis for inferring it. Rather, it says that the elements that have made the concept of subjective legislative intent unacceptable to many exist in many cases to an even greater degree for subjective legislative purpose. In the face of these considerations, it is ironic that the amorphous and elusive "legislative intent" has been spurned by many in favor of the even more amorphous and elusive "legislative purpose."

This raises the general question of how subjective legislative purpose is to be determined. * * *

Whether we search for actual legislative purpose or for actual legislative intent, we can infer it only from external materials. Unfortunately, in the ascertainment of legislative purpose, it cannot always be assumed that there is in fact such a purpose or, if there is, that there is reliable evidence of it. For most state legislatures, there is only the statute and the backdrop of proper context. The statute normally includes no preamble or purpose clause, and there is little recorded legislative history. Even where they exist, there is no assurance that either will be relevant.

As with legislative intent, the danger in presuming an actual legislative purpose beyond what is expressly or impliedly revealed is that the interpreter will either attribute to the statute a purpose of his own contriving or search for actual purpose so relentlessly that he goes beyond the limits of the appropriate available evidence. Because the reliable indicia of any purpose are more likely to be found beyond the mere words of the statute, the temptation to scavenge among the materials of legislative history is at least as great as it is for legislative intent.

In the following excerpt, is Chafee critical of judicial reliance on "intent" or "purpose," as those terms have been defined by Dickerson?

Chafee, The Disorderly Conduct of Words

41 Colum. L. Rev. 381 (1941).

* * * My first suggestion is, that we should firmly resolve never to speak of the intention of a testator or other writer on a given point except after we have carefully convinced ourselves that that point was actually in his mind when he wrote the words in question. For example, we will never say "He intended this result" when we merely think that if he had foreseen the present contingency (which he didn't) then he would have intended this result. That consideration may be helpful, but it is not his intention. Again, what the judge would have intended in the circumstances of the writer or what a reasonable man would have intended or what the normal speaker of English would have intended may also be helpful, but they have even less to do with the mind of the man who used the words. My guess is, that if we stick by this resolve, we shall soon find that his intention is a much less important factor in the decision than the frequent uncritical use of the word in judicial opinions and law books would lead us to suppose. * * *

* * * To clarify the problem, go back to my earlier statement that legal interpretation is a passing from the word to the object through somebody's mind. Whose mind? Not that of the author of the document. Indeed, if it be a will he is dead. It must be the mind of the judge. Although his mind may be influenced by what he believes the testator or other user to have thought, the mental operations of the two men cannot fully correspond. Other important factors beside the supposed intention of the testator, etc., contribute to the thought which the judge ultimately frames before applying the words to the outside world.

Therefore, my next suggestion is that the "meaning" of language in operative documents is a combination of several of the different senses in which judges use "meaning", only one or two of which involve the intention of the writer; and that the relative importance of his intention varies considerably with the type of document under consideration. It is most important in a will, which Lord Blackburn called "the language of a testator, soliloquizing." It is less important in a contract, where the fair expectation of the other party has to be given effect. * * * Intention is even less important, I venture to say, in the interpretation of a statute, in writing which hundreds of persons participated with widely varying degrees of attention and with very little chance of envisaging the contingencies that have arisen later. * * *

In short, what is commonly called "the intention of the parties" is in large measure the intention of the judge, subject to all sorts of traditional restraints on his range of choice. When all is said and done, the court of last resort in an interpretation case can echo quite a bit of the famous boast of Humpty Dumpty:

> "When I use a word," Humpty Dumpty said, in rather a scornful tone, "it means just what I choose it to mean-neither more nor less."

> "The question is," said Alice, "whether you can make words mean so many different things."

> "The question is," said Humpty Dumpty, "which is to be master-that's all."

* * *

Nor is it always sufficient to determine what objects the words were applied to at the time they were written. A grant of the dramatic rights in a popular novel, given before the invention of motion pictures, may conceivably include screen rights; and few will follow the lawyer who wrote a book to prove that Congress could not regulate railroad rates under its powers over "commerce" because the only transportation in 1787 was by boats and wagons. When those who used words contemplated their long continued application, these words must eventually acquire a new content, especially when, as Marshall said, "It is a Constitution that we are interpreting."

Let me end with a story about Robert Browning. Toward the close of his life he received a letter from Professor Hiram Corson of Cornell, asking whether one of his early obscure poems meant what Corson supposed it did. Browning replied, "I didn't mean that when I wrote it, but I mean it now."

Would it reduce confusion about the meaning of "intent" to refer to the intent of the statute, rather than legislative intent?

6.03 MAKING SENSE OF THE STATUTE

a) SCRIVENER'S ERRORS

If the text itself makes no sense, going outside the statutory text to determine legislative intent is not so controversial, because there is no text-based conclusion worth following. Moreover, the judge is rarely exercising much lawmaking discretion, except to fix up a defective text.

United States v. R. & J. Enterprises

178 F.Supp. 1 (D.Alaska 1959).

■ McCarrey, Judge. * * *

Chapter 80, S.L.A. 1959, provides as follows:

"Be it enacted by the Legislature of the State of Alaska:

"Section 1. No female person shall be employed by [Editor—here comes the strange part. The text of the law omitted *'or associated with the holder or operator of'*] any liquor or beverage dispensary, club, road house, restaurant, or common carrier dispensary license issued under the laws of the State of Alaska, to solicit, entice or encourage the purchase by patrons of any such licensed premises of alcoholic beverages upon a rebate, percentage, or share the profit basis, or any other basis; nor shall any such female person receive any salary or other compensation from any person for the solicitation, enticement, or encouragement of the purchase of alcoholic beverages as hereinabove set forth. [Editor—Without the omitted text, the statute prohibited 'employment by any * * * license,' which makes no sense.] Bona fide entertainers, hat check girls and female employees not directly or principally employed to solicit sales of intoxicants shall be exempt herefrom.

"Sec. 2. Any female person or the holder or operator of any liquor dispensary, club, restaurant, or common carrier dispensary license violating the provisions of this Act shall be guilty of a misdemeanor and shall be punished by a fine of not less than $300,000 or more than $1,000,000, or by imprisonment for not more than sixty days, or by both such fine and imprisonment."

The court concluded that the omitted language should be read back into the statute. It relied on the title of the Act ("To prohibit employment of certain or the taking of compensation by females for certain purposes in connection with the sale of intoxicating liquors and providing penalties"); the text of the original "correct" draft of the bill; and the Governor's statement reiterating the statute's purpose. Although the statute was "an example of careless legislation," the court found that "the intent of the legislators is clear * * *."

Why shouldn't the court refuse to bail out the legislature when the text is gibberish by holding that there is no statute? Should courts discourage careless drafting by nullifying the statute?

———————

Do not assume that all scrivener's errors produce gibberish. Sometimes "not" is included or excluded. For example, in 1984, Congress delayed the effective date of a new statutory provision, which would have eliminated a tax loophole. The delay was *not* supposed to apply to sales for large amounts of money, specifically those over $100 million. Only smaller sales were to be entitled to the delay. Due to a drafting error, the delay was provided for sales *over* $100 million. Specifically, the statute delaying the new law said that the new law would not apply to "the sale or exchange of property * * * the sale price of which is greater than $100 million."[2]

The mistake was in omitting the word "no" before "greater than $100 million." The error was spotted after passage and before adjournment, but Congress failed to correct the error. A bill making the correction passed the House and Senate, but the Senate version contained some additional controversial amendments which required House approval. The House failed to give its approval on the day of adjournment because of a point of order raised by one member of the House.

The House enrolling clerk, assuming the word "no" would be inserted, included it in the bill sent to the Federal Register for publication on October 23. On October 24, however, a corrected version of the bill was sent to the Federal Register, omitting the word "no."

What should the Treasury do in implementing this law? (1) Should it exempt sales for no more than $100 million, as Congress intended? If it did, who could complain? (2) Must it exempt sales greater than $100 million, as the statute says?

b) Preventing Statutory Nullification

Cabell v. Markham
148 F.2d 737 (2d Cir.1945), affirmed, 326 U.S. 404 (1945).

■ L. Hand, Circuit Judge.

[Editor—The statute dealt with the rights of a creditor of an enemy alien during wartime after the U.S. government, through the Alien Property Custodian, had seized the alien's property.]

This appeal depends upon the meaning of a part of the proviso to § 9(e) of the Trading with the Enemy Act, as amended on March 10, 1928, 50 U.S.C.A. Appendix, § 9(e), which we quote * * *. [Editor—Quote is as follows: "nor in any event shall a debt be allowed under this section unless it was owing to and owned by the claimant prior to October 6, 1917, and as to claimants other than citizens of the United States unless it arose with reference to the money or other property held by the Alien Property Custodian or Treasurer of the United States hereunder; nor shall a debt be allowed under this section unless notice of the claim has been filed, or application therefor has been made, prior to the date of the enactment of the Settlement of War Claims Act of 1928."] The plaintiff filed a complaint under § 9 (a) of that act, alleging that he was a creditor of an Italian insurance company, whose assets in this country the predecessor in office of the defendant, Markham, had seized, as Alien Property Custodian; and that he had presented his

2. See Timberlake, Drafting Error Alters Effect of Imputed Interest Rule Changes; Ramifications Unclear, 25 Tax Notes 389 (1984).

claim in due form to the Custodian, who refused to recognize it. The defendants moved to dismiss the complaint because of its insufficiency in law, on the ground that the claim had not been in existence before October 6, 1917, and had not been filed before the date of the enactment of the Settlement of War Claims Act of 1928. The judge held that, since both these facts appeared in the complaint, the proviso of § 9(e) just quoted covered the situation; and for this reason he dismissed the complaint.

When the Trading with the Enemy Act was first passed on October 6, 1917, it contained the substance of what is now subdivision (a), but nothing more. It was amended again and again, but subdivision (e) was not added until 1920 (41 St. L. 980), though from the first it provided that no debt should be paid which had not been "owing" before October 6, 1917. The addition that the claim should be presented before March 10, 1928, dates from the amendment of that year. The statute was not re-enacted when the present war broke out; nor was that necessary, for it automatically went into effect again. * * *

It is at least arguable that the whole of subdivision (e) is limited to seizures made during the first war. It begins with a provision that "a citizen or subject of any nation which was associated with the United States in the prosecution of the war" may recover his property or collect his debt only in case that nation gave reciprocal rights to citizens of the United States. The use of the preterit is significant, particularly when coupled with the word, "associate," which it will be remembered was chosen during the last war in sedulous avoidance of any implication that we had "allies." If this be true, it would be indeed unreasonable not to confine the proviso similarly: that is, to read it otherwise than as limited to seizures made during that war. If we do not so read it, the result is really nonsense, for the remedy given in subdivision (a), which is prospective, is completely defeated by subdivision (e). Nobody can seriously believe that a general plan designed to be successively suspended and revived, as peace and war should alternate, was meant to be permanently mutilated by a statute of limitation expressly made applicable to only the first of its phases. The defendants have no answer except to say that we are not free to depart from the literal meaning of the words, however transparent may be the resulting stultification of the scheme or plan as a whole.

Courts have not stood helpless in such situations; the decisions are legion in which they have refused to be bound by the letter, when it frustrates the patent purpose of the whole statute. * * * As Holmes, J., said in a much-quoted passage from Johnson v. United States, 163 F. 30, 32: "it is not an adequate discharge of duty for courts to say: We see what you are driving at, but you have not said it, and therefore we shall go on as before." Of course it is true that the words used, even in their literal sense, are the primary, and ordinarily the most reliable, source of interpreting the meaning of any writing: be it a statute, a contract, or anything else. But it is one of the surest indexes of a mature and developed jurisprudence not to make a fortress out of the dictionary; but to remember that statutes always have some purpose or object to accomplish, whose sympathetic and imaginative discovery is the surest guide to their meaning. Since it is utterly apparent that the words of this proviso were intended to be limited to seizures made during the last war, and could not conceivably have been intended to apply to seizures made when another war revived the Act as a whole from its suspension, it does no undue violence to the language to assume that it was implicitly subject to that condition which alone made the Act as a whole practicable of administration.

Judgement reversed.

COMMENTS

1. This case contains one of the most famous quotes about statutory interpretation:

it is one of the surest indexes of a mature and developed jurisprudence not to make a fortress out of the dictionary; but to remember that statutes always have some purpose or object to accomplish, whose sympathetic and imaginative discovery is the surest guide to their meaning.

This quote appears on every anti-literalist's banner and also appears in numerous cases which reject textualism. Regardless of where you come out on the literalist/textualist/purposivist debate, notice that this case does not involve a conflict between the text and a speculative legislative purpose. The only purpose you need to attribute to the statute is one of survival into the next war. Moreover, Judge Hand does not "scavenge" legislative history for evidence of legislative purpose, but relies on internal statutory context.

2. Suppose a statute states that an employer is exempt from liability to a multi-employer pension plan if it withdraws from the plan "before January 12." The intended and *only* beneficiary of the law was an employer who acted *on* January 12. The legislative drafter made a mistake. Does this statute apply to the employer who withdraws *on* January 12? See Central States v. Lady Baltimore Foods, Inc., 960 F.2d 1339 (7th Cir.1992)(Posner, J.).

c) SUBSTANTIVE ABSURDITY

The Golden Rule, mentioned in Chapter 2, precludes substantively absurd interpretations.[3] The primary impact of this rule is to prevent

---

3. Becke v. Smith, 2 M. & W. 191, 195 (1836)("It is a very useful rule in the construction of a statute to adhere to the ordinary meaning of the words used, and to the gram- matical construction, unless that is at variance with the intention of the Legislature to be collected from the statute itself, or leads to any manifest absurdity or repugnance, in which

substantive results which are dramatically out of step with the society's substantive background values, which we will discuss in the next chapter. One branch of the interpretive principle that allows judges to prevent absurdity, however, is concerned with the disjunction between purpose and text. If the statutory text seems to create a result that is absurd with respect to the statute's underlying purpose, the judge can read an exception into the text.

You should, however, observe an important difference between preventing absurdity based on substantive values rather than the disjunction between legislative purpose and the apparent meaning of the text. Think back to the 19th Century emphasis on fundamental values vs. inconvenient results, which we encountered in Justice Marshall's statutory interpretation opinions and elsewhere. A judge is most likely to avoid an absurd substantive result when the values to be protected are "fundamental," whether the judge says so explicitly or not. When the absurd result occurs because of a disjunction between legislative purpose and the text, there is no reason why the disjunction must violate fundamental values (although, of course, it could).

Textualists are apparently willing to invoke the "absurdity" principle, when there is a very tenuous link between statutory purpose and text. (Why is that true? Is there minimal opportunity for too much second-guessing about purpose and making judgments about its value?) A good example of the textualist's approach is suggested in the sparring between Justice Brennan's purposivist opinion and Justice Scalia's absurdity approach in K Mart Corp. v. Cartier, Inc., 486 U.S. 281, 316, 328 n. 2 (1988). Justices Brennan and Scalia argued about the impact of "postenactment developments" on the meaning of language. Justice Brennan claimed that a statute can become "ambiguous" if the developments "implicate the statute's purpose." Brennan gave a hypothetical of a 19th Century legislature requiring a utility commission to "inspect all ovens installed in a home for propensity to spew flames." He stated that

> the statute would not unambiguously apply to microwave or electric ovens. Although it would not be absurd to read the statute to cover such developments, a court might decline to do so, depending on the extent to which the statute's purpose would be furthered by inspection of ovens that spew fewer flames than do conventional ovens.

Justice Scalia gives the textualist's response. He says that

> with respect to microwave ovens there may indeed be an ambiguity—not because the purpose would not be served but because the term "oven" connotes "a heated enclosure," Webster's Third International Dictionary 1605 (1981), and may or may not embrace

case the language may be varied or modified   further.")
so as to avoid such inconvenience, but no

microwave ovens. With respect to electric ovens, there seems to me
no ambiguity at all.

Scalia then suggests that, despite the absence of ambiguity, the statute might
not apply to electric ovens because it would be *absurd* to inspect ovens which
do not spew flames.

Notice that the evidence of purpose in the K–Mart hypothetical came
from internal context (the textual reference to "spew flames"). Would Scalia
have been equally willing to limit statutory coverage on absurdity grounds if
the evidence of purpose was not derived from the statutory text? For
example, how might he decide the following case?

In Sanders v. Hisaw, 94 So.2d 486 (La.App.1957), a statute made it a
crime to pass a car without honking the horn. When the statute was passed,
all highways were two lane and honking was meant to warn oncoming
drivers. Would the statute apply to passing cars going in the same direction
on today's four lane highways?

6.04 CONFLICT OF TEXT AND CONTEXT

a) LEGISLATIVE OR JUDICIAL RESPONSIBILITY

Now come the hard cases. The text is not absurd, but it seems to be out
of step with the statutory purpose. What should a court do? In this section,
we read cases in which the judge goes behind the text and uses purpose to
decide the case. Remember to consider why the legislature might have failed
to be more precise in meshing purpose and text and whether the judicial
role varies depending on the reason for legislative failure. Here are some
possible reasons for such failure:

(1) legislative haste or carelessness;

(2) failure to discharge a political or lawmaking responsibility;

(3) political powerlessness of an affected group;

(4) changes over time.

Are some lapses of legislative responsibility to write the text carefully more
serious than others, arguing against the court bailing out the legislature? Are
some lapses so easy for the legislature to prevent that the court should not
come to the legislature's rescue?

You should also watch for cases in which judicial appeals to legislative
purpose seem to involve the judge in exercising some lawmaking discretion.
Not every case of judicial reliance on purpose involves the exercise of such
discretion, but some do. In this connection, recall Judge Hand's view that
the judge is always trying to determine what the historical legislature would
have done if confronted by the facts of the case, not what they specifically
intended to do, because there is often no specific intent regarding the facts of
the particular case. See, e.g., Hand, Thomas Walter Swan, 57 Yale L.J. 167,
171 (1947):

[The task] is no less than to decide how those who have passed the "enactment" would have dealt with the "particulars" before [the judge], about which they have said nothing whatever.

See also Burnet v. Guggenheim, 288 U.S. 280, 285 (1933)("[W]hich choice is it the more likely that Congress would have made?")(Justice Cardozo). Is it ever possible for a court to apply historical purpose to a contemporary fact situation and still be completely faithful to the historical legislature? How do judges living today recreate historical purpose from another era? What do they assume the legislature knows about the contemporary world?

b) Cases

i) RECTOR OF HOLY TRINITY CHURCH v. UNITED STATES

143 U.S. 457 (1892).

■ Mr. Justice Brewer delivered the opinion of the court.

Plaintiff in error is a corporation, duly organized and incorporated as a religious society under the laws of the State of New York. E. Walpole Warren was, prior to September, 1887, an alien residing in England. In that month the plaintiff in error made a contract with him, by which he was to remove to the city of New York and enter into its service as rector and pastor; and in pursuance of such contract, Warren did so remove and enter upon such service. It is claimed by the United States that this contract on the part of the plaintiff in error was forbidden by the act of February 26, 1885, 23 Stat. 332, c. 164, and an action was commenced to recover the penalty prescribed by that act. [Editor—If you are wondering how this case could ever have been brought, the statute authorized "any person" to bring the suit and required the District Attorney to prosecute these suits out of United States funds. According to an interview with the Pastor Warren reported in the New York Daily Tribune, March 1, 1892, the suit was "an entirely friendly one," brought by Mr. Kennedy, a member of another church, with the object of "mak[ing] odious the attempt to apply the law to clergymen." Warren stated that Mr. Kennedy "begged us to try the case squarely on the merits to the end, and not try to have it dismissed on any side issue."] The Circuit Court held that the contract was within the prohibition of the statute, and rendered judgment accordingly, (36 Fed. Rep. 303;) and the single question presented for our determination is whether it erred in that conclusion.

The first section describes the act forbidden, and is in these words:

"Be it enacted by the Senate and House of Representatives of the United States of America in Congress assembled, That from and after the passage of this act it shall be unlawful for any person, company, partnership, or corporation, in any manner whatsoever, to prepay the transportation, or in any way assist or encourage the importation or migration of any alien or aliens, any foreigner or foreigners, into the United States, its Territories, or the District of Columbia, under contract or agreement, parol or special, express or implied, made previous to the importation or migration of such alien or aliens, foreigner of foreigners, to perform labor or service of any kind in the United States, its Territories, or the District of Columbia."

It must be conceded that the act of the corporation is within the letter of this section, for the relation of rector to his church is one of service, and implies labor on the one side with compensation on the other. Not only are the general words labor and service both used, but also, as it were to guard against any narrow interpretation and emphasize a breadth of meaning, to them is added "of any kind;" and, further, as noticed by the Circuit Judge in his opinion, the fifth section, which makes specific exceptions, among them professional actors, artists, lecturers, singers and domestic servants, strengthens the idea that every other kind of labor and service was intended to be reached by the first section. While there is great force to this reasoning, we cannot think Congress intended to denounce with penalties a transaction like that in the present case. It is a familiar rule, that a thing may be within the letter of the statute and yet not within the statute, because not within its spirit, nor within the intention of its makers. This has been often asserted, and the reports are full of cases illustrating its application. This is not the substitution of the will of the judge for that of the legislator, for frequently words of general meaning are used in a statute, words broad enough to include an act in question, and yet a consideration of the whole legislation, or of the circumstances surrounding its enactment, or of the absurd results which follow from giving such broad meaning to the words, makes it unreasonable to believe that the legislator intended to include the particular act. * * *

* * * [T]he title of this act is, "An act to prohibit the importation and migration of foreigners and aliens under contract or agreement to perform labor in the United States, its Territories and the District of Columbia." Obviously the thought expressed in this reaches only to the work of the manual laborer, as distinguished from that of the professional man. No one reading such a title would suppose that Congress had in its mind any purpose of staying the coming into this country of ministers of the gospel, or, indeed, of any class whose toil is that of the brain. The common understanding of the terms labor and laborers does not include preaching and preachers; and it is to be assumed that words and phrases are used in their ordinary meaning. So whatever of light is thrown upon the statute by the language of the title indicates an exclusion from its penal provisions of all contracts for the employment of ministers, rectors and pastors.

Again, another guide to the meaning of a statute is found in the evil which it is designed to remedy; and for this the court properly looks at contemporaneous events, the situation as it existed, and as it was pressed upon the attention of the legislative body. The situation which called for this statute was briefly but fully stated by Mr. Justice Brown when, as District Judge, he decided the case of United States v. Craig, 28 Fed. Rep. 795, 798: "The motives and history of the act are matters of common knowledge. It had become the practice for large capitalists in this country to contract with their agents abroad for the shipment of great numbers of an ignorant and servile class of foreign laborers, under contracts, by which the employer agreed, upon the one hand, to prepay their passage, while, upon the other hand, the laborers agreed to work after their arrival for a certain time at a low rate of wages. The effect of this was to break down the labor market, and to reduce other laborers engaged in like occupations to the level of the assisted immigrant. The evil finally became so flagrant that an appeal was made to Congress for relief by the passage of the act in question, the design of which was to raise the standard of foreign immigrants, and to discountenance the migration of those who had not sufficient means in their own hands, or those of their friends, to pay their passage."

It appears, also, from the petitions, and in the testimony presented before the committees of Congress, that it was this cheap unskilled labor which was making the trouble, and the influx of which Congress sought to prevent. It was never suggested that we had in this country a surplus of brain toilers, and, least of all, that the market for the services of Christian ministers to which the attention of Congress, or of the people, was not directed. So far, then, as the evil which was sought to be remedied interprets the statute, it also guides to an exclusion of this contract from the penalties of the act.

A singular circumstance, throwing light upon the intent of congress, is found in this extract from the report of the senate committee on education and labor, recommending the passage of the bill: "* * * The committee report the bill back without amendment, although there are certain features thereof which might well be changed or modified, in the hope that the bill may not fail of passage during the present session. Especially would the committee have otherwise recommended amendments, substituting for the expression, 'labor and service,' whenever it occurs in the body of the bill, the words 'manual labor' or 'manual service,' as sufficiently broad to accomplish the purposes of the bill, and that such amendments would remove objections which a sharp and perhaps unfriendly criticism may urge to the proposed legislation. The committee, however, believing that the bill in its present form will be construed as including only those whose labor or service is manual in character, and being very desirous that the bill become a law before the adjournment, have reported the bill without change." Page 6059, Congressional Record, 48th Cong., [1st Sess.] * * *

[Editor—You might infer from the Senate Committee Report that the Senate made a drafting error because it was rushed. That inference is unwarranted. The Senate had already amended the text so the statute had to go back to the House for concurrence. Faced with this delay, the Senate adjourned (Congressional Record, 48th Cong., 1st Sess. 6065 (1884)), and resumed discussions in February of the next year. There was much discussion in the Senate of how badly the statute had been drafted, perhaps based on a text prepared by interest groups favoring the law (one Senator referred to the "folly of a class of men who suppose that bills can be better prepared for the consideration of Congress * * * by those who are not familiar with legal phraseology and with the legal profession"— Congressional Record, 48th Cong., 2d Sess. 1781 (1885)). Many amendments were eventually adopted by the Senate, and accepted by the House, including permission to contract to bring in domestic servants and "personal friends." Id., page 2032.]

We find, therefore, that the title of the act, the evil which was intended to be remedied, the circumstances surrounding the appeal to Congress, the reports of the committee of each house, all concur in affirming that the intent of Congress was simply to stay the influx of this cheap unskilled labor.

[Editor—The rest of the opinion does not deal with purpose, but with an important substantive background consideration—the country's religious roots. This argument is not edited out of the readings because you should consider whether purpose or this background consideration is the more critical factor in the Court's decision. Real-world opinions are often like that—they include multiple criteria and you are left to determine their respective weights.]

But beyond all these matters no purpose of action against religion can be imputed to any legislation, state or national, because this is a religious people. This is historically true. From the discovery of this continent to the present hour, there is a single voice making this affirmation. * * *

Even the Constitution of the United States, which is supposed to have little touch upon the private life of the individual, contains in the First Amendment a declaration common to the constitutions of all the States, as follows: "Congress shall make no law respecting an establishment of religion, or prohibiting the free exercise thereof," etc. And also provides in Article 1, section 7, (a provision common to many constitutions,) that the Executive shall have ten days (Sundays excepted) within which to determine whether he will approve or veto a bill.

There is no dissonance in these declarations. There is a universal language pervading them all, having one meaning; they affirm and reaffirm that this is a religious nation. These are not individual sayings, declarations of private persons: they are organic utterances; they speak the voice of the entire people. * * *

Suppose in the Congress that passed this act some member had offered a bill which in terms declared that, if any Roman Catholic church in this country should contract with Cardinal Manning to come to this country and enter into its service as pastor and priest; or any Episcopal church should enter into a like contract with Canon Farrar; or any Baptist church should make similar arrangements with Rev. Mr. Spurgeon; or any Jewish synagogue with some eminent Rabbi, such contract should be adjudged unlawful and void, and the church making it be subject to prosecution and punishment, can it be believed that it would have received a minute of approving thought or a single vote? Yet it is contended that such was in effect the meaning of this statute. The construction invoked cannot be accepted as correct. It is a case where there was presented a definite evil, in view of which the legislature used general terms with the purpose of reaching all phases of that evil, and thereafter, unexpectedly, it is developed that the general language thus employed is broad enough to reach cases and acts which the whole history and life of the country affirm could not have been intentionally legislated against. It is the duty of the courts, under those circumstances, to say that, however broad the language of the statute may be, the act, although within the letter, is not within the intention of the legislature, and therefore cannot be within the statute.

QUESTIONS

1. Is there any satisfactory way to deny the plain application of the text to Pastor Warren? I do not think so. The word "labor" might include only manual labor, but "service" seems much broader. The addition of the phrase "of any kind" implies the broadest coverage. The exclusion of some brain toilers from the statute implies that brain toilers would otherwise be covered. For what it is worth, Pastor Warren (in the interview cited earlier) expressed surprise that he was not a "contract worker."

2. Would the statute cover a professor or a business manager? If it would cover such brain toilers, does that indicate that the Court was primarily concerned with the impact on religion? In other words, is the case really about absurd substantive results—the impact on religion—rather than about the relationship of legislative purpose to the statutory text?

3. What if the defendant had been a Muslim preacher? If you think the Court would have allowed the prosecution, does that give you pause about relying on substantive background considerations to interpret a statute?

ii) HOLY TRINITY TODAY

How much vitality does Holy Trinity have today? How does the following case answer this question?

Public Citizen v. United States Department of Justice

491 U.S. 440 (1989).

■ Justice Brennan delivered the opinion of the Court.

The Department of Justice regularly seeks advice from the American Bar Association's Standing Committee on Federal Judiciary regarding potential nominees for federal judgeships. The question before us is whether the Federal Advisory Committee Act (FACA), 5 U.S.C. App. § 1 et seq. (1982 and Supp. V), applies to these consultations and, if it does, whether its application interferes unconstitutionally with the President's prerogative under Article II to nominate and appoint officers of the United States; violates the doctrine of separation of powers; or unduly infringes the First Amendment right of members of the American Bar Association to freedom of association and expression. We hold that FACA does not apply to this special advisory relationship. We therefore do not reach the constitutional questions presented. * * *

* * * FACA directs the Director of the Office of Management and Budget and agency heads to establish various administrative guidelines and management controls for advisory committees. It also imposes a number of requirements on advisory groups. For example, FACA requires that each advisory committee file a charter, § 9(c), and keep detailed minutes of its meetings. § 10(c). Those meetings must be chaired or attended by an officer or employee of the Federal Government who is authorized to adjourn any meeting when he or she deems its adjournment in the public interest. § 10(e). FACA also requires advisory committees to provide advance notice of their meetings and to open them to the public, § 10(a), unless the President or the agency head to which an advisory committee reports determines that it may be closed to the public in accordance with the Government in the Sunshine Act. § 10(d). In addition, FACA stipulates that advisory committee minutes, records, and reports be made available to the public, provided they do not fall within one of the Freedom of Information Act's exemptions, and the Government does not choose to withhold them. § 10(b). Advisory committees established by legislation or created by the President or other federal officials must also be "fairly balanced in terms of the points of view represented and the functions" they perform. §§ 5(b), (c). Their existence is limited to two years, unless specifically exempted by the entity establishing them. § 14(a)(1). * * *

Section 3(2) of FACA defines "advisory committee" as follows:

"For the purpose of this Act—

"(2) The term 'advisory committee' means any committee, board, commission, council, conference, panel, task force, or other similar group, or any subcommittee or other subgroup thereof (hereafter in this paragraph referred to as 'committee'), which is—

"(A) established by statute or reorganization plan, or

"(B) established or utilized by the President, or

"(C) established or utilized by one or more agencies, in the interest of obtaining advice or recommendations for the President or one or more agencies or officers of the Federal Government, except that such term excludes (i) the Advisory Commission on Intergovernmental Relations, (ii) the Commission on Government Procurement, and (iii) any committee which is composed wholly of full-time officers or employees of the Federal Government."

Appellants agree that the ABA Committee was not "established" by the President or the Justice Department. Equally plainly, the ABA Committee is a committee that furnishes "advice or recommendations" to the President via the Justice Department. Whether the ABA Committee constitutes an "advisory committee" for purposes of FACA therefore depends on whether it is "utilized" by the President or the Justice Department as Congress intended that term to be understood. * * *

Where the literal reading of a statutory term would "compel an odd result," Green v. Bock Laundry Machine Co., we must search for other evidence of congressional intent to lend the term its proper scope. "The circumstances of the enactment of particular legislation," for example, "may persuade a court that Congress did not intend words of common meaning to have their literal effect." Watt v. Alaska, 451 U.S. 259, 266 (1981). Even though, as Judge Learned Hand said, "the words used, even in their literal sense, are the primary, and ordinarily the most reliable, source of interpreting the meaning of any writing," nevertheless "it is one of the surest indexes of a mature and developed jurisprudence not to make a fortress out of the dictionary; but to remember that statutes always have some purpose or object to accomplish, whose sympathetic and imaginative discovery is the surest guide to their meaning." Cabell v. Markham, 148 F.2d 737 (2d Cir.1945). Looking beyond the naked text for guidance is perfectly proper when the result it apparently decrees is difficult to fathom or where it seems inconsistent with Congress' intention, since the plain-meaning rule is "rather an axiom of experience than a rule of law, and does not preclude consideration of persuasive evidence if it exists." Boston Sand & Gravel Co. v. United States, 278 U.S. 41, 48 (1928)(Holmes,J.).

Consideration of FACA's purposes and origins in determining whether the term "utilized" was meant to apply to the Justice Department's use of the ABA Committee is particularly appropriate here, given the importance we have consistently attached to interpreting statutes to avoid deciding difficult constitutional questions where the text fairly admits of a less problematic construction. It is therefore imperative that we consider indicators of congressional intent in addition to the statutory language before concluding that FACA was meant to cover the ABA Committee's provision of advice to the Justice Department in connection with judicial nominations. * * *

[Editor—The Court then considers the history of FACA, noting the following. First, a House Report does not mention the ABA or similar advisory committee as raising problems in need of a statutory solution. Second, the words "or utilized" were added in the Conference Committee and the Conference Committee Report offered no indication that the addition was significant. It was apparently added "to clarify that FACA applied to advisory committees established by the Federal Government in a generous sense of the term, encompassing groups formed indirectly by quasi-public organizations such as the National Academy of Sciences 'for' public agencies as well as 'by' such agencies themselves." The Academy "utilized" advisory groups whose expenses were met by the government and it was such advisory groups whose coverage the statute intended.]

* * * Weighing the deliberately inclusive statutory language against other evidence of congressional intent, it seems to us a close question whether FACA should be construed to apply to the ABA Committee, although on the whole we are fairly confident it should not. There is, however, one additional consideration which, in our view, tips the balance decisively against FACA's application. [Editor—The Court then appeals to the principle that excluding consultations with the ABA Committee from statutory coverage avoided constitutional doubts about the statute.]

Justice Kennedy, with whom the Chief Justice and Justice O'Connor join, concurring in the judgment. [Editor—Justice Scalia did not participate in the decision.] * * *

The Framers of our Government knew that the most precious of liberties could remain secure only if they created a structure of government based on a permanent separation of power. See, e.g., The Federalist Nos. 47–51 (J. Madison). Indeed, the Framers devoted almost the whole of their attention at the Constitutional Convention to the creation of a secure and enduring structure for the new Government. It remains one of the most vital functions of this Court to police with care the separation of the governing powers. That is so even when, as is the case here, no immediate threat to liberty is apparent. * * *

* * * The only [statutory] question we face * * * is whether the ABA Committee is "utilized" by the Department of Justice or the President.

There is a ready starting point, which ought to serve also as a sufficient stopping point, for this kind of analysis: the plain language of the statute. * * * Reluctance to working with the basic meaning of words in a normal manner undermines the legal process. * * *

Although I believe the Court's result is quite sensible, I cannot go along with the unhealthy process of amending the statute by judicial interpretation. Where the language of a statute is clear in its application, the normal rule is that we are bound by it. There is, of course, a legitimate exception to this rule, which the Court invokes, citing Church of the Holy Trinity v. United States, and with which I have no quarrel. Where the plain language of the statute would lead to "patently absurd consequences," that "Congress could not *possibly* have intended," we need not apply the language in such a fashion. When used in a proper manner, this narrow exception to our normal rule of statutory construction does not intrude upon the lawmaking powers of Congress, but rather demonstrates a respect for the coequal Legislative Branch, which we assume would not act in an absurd way.

This exception remains a legitimate tool of the judiciary, however, only as long as the Court acts with self-discipline by limiting the exception to situations where the result of applying the plain language would be, in a genuine sense, absurd, i.e., where it is quite impossible that Congress could have intended the result, and where the alleged absurdity is so clear as to be obvious to most anyone. * * * In today's opinion, however, the Court disregards the plain language of the statute not because its application would be patently absurd, but rather because, on the basis of its view of the legislative history, the Court is "fairly confident" that "FACA should [not] be construed to apply to the ABA Committee." I believe the Court's loose invocation of the "absurd result" canon of statutory construction creates too great a risk that the Court is exercising its own "WILL instead of JUDGMENT," with the consequence of "substituti[ng] [its own] pleasure to that of the legislative body." The Federalist No. 78, p. 469 (C. Rossiter ed. 1961)(A. Hamilton). * * *

Unable to show that an application of FACA according to the plain meaning of its terms would be absurd, the Court turns instead to the task of demonstrating that a straightforward reading of the statute would be inconsistent with the congressional purposes that lay behind its passage. To the student of statutory construction, this move is a familiar one. It is, as the Court identifies it, the classic Holy Trinity argument. "[A] thing may be within the letter of the statute and yet not within the statute, because not within its spirit, nor within the intention of its makers." I cannot embrace this principle. Where it is clear that the unambiguous language of a statute embraces certain conduct, and it would not be patently absurd to apply the statute to such conduct, it does not foster a democratic exegesis for this Court to rummage through unauthoritative materials to consult the spirit of the legislation in order to discover an alternative interpretation of the statute with which the Court is more comfortable. It comes as a surprise to no one that the result of the Court's lengthy journey through the legislative history is the discovery of a congressional intent not to include activities of the ABA Committee within the coverage of FACA. The problem with spirits is that they tend to reflect less the views of the world whence they come than the views of those who seek their advice.

Lest anyone think that my objection to use of the Holy Trinity doctrine is a mere point of interpretive purity divorced from more practical considerations, I should pause for a moment to recall the unhappy genesis of that doctrine and its unwelcome potential. * * *

The central support for the Court's ultimate conclusion that Congress did not intend the law to cover Christian ministers is its lengthy review of the "mass of organic utterances" establishing that "this is a Christian nation," and which were taken to prove that it could not "be believed that a Congress of the United States intended to make it a misdemeanor for a church of this country to contract for the services of a Christian minister residing in another nation." I should think the potential of this doctrine to allow judges to substitute their personal predilections for the will of the Congress is so self-evident from the case which spawned it as to require no further discussion of its susceptibility to abuse. * * *

The Court's final step is to summon up the traditional principle that statutes should be construed to avoid constitutional questions. Although I agree that we should "first ascertain whether a construction of the statute is fairly possible by which the [constitutional] question may be avoided," Crowell v. Benson, 285 U.S. 22, 62 (1932), this principle cannot be stretched beyond the point at which such a construction remains "*fairly* possible." And it should not be given too broad a scope lest a whole new range of government action be proscribed by interpretive shadows cast by constitutional provisions that might or might not invalidate it. The fact that a particular application of the clear terms of a statute might be unconstitutional does not provide us with a justification for ignoring the plain meaning of the statute. If that were permissible, then the power of judicial review of legislation could be made unnecessary, for when ever the application of a statute would have potential inconsistency with the Constitution, we could merely opine that the statute did not cover the conduct in question because it would be discomforting or even absurd to think that Congress intended to act in an unconstitutional manner. The utter circularity of this approach explains why it has never been our rule.

The Court's ultimate interpretation of FACA is never clearly stated, except for the conclusion that the ABA Committee is not covered. It seems to read the "utilized by" portion of the statute as encompassing only a committee "established by a quasi-public organization in receipt of public funds," or encompassing "groups formed indirectly by quasi-public organizations such as the National Academy of Sciences." This is not a "fairly possible" construction of the statutory language even to a generous reader. I would find the ABA Committee to be covered by FACA. It is, therefore, necessary for me to reach and decide the constitutional issue presented.

[Editor—The concurrence then holds the application of FACA to the ABA Committee unconstitutional, because it interferes with the President's power to appoint officials (specifically, federal judges) under Article II, § 2, cl. 2 of the Constitution.]

COMMENTS

1. *Historical background.* Does the following history shed any light on the decision in Public Citizen, suggesting why the legislature might not have paid much attention to whether the statutory text covered the ABA?[4] An ABA Committee had commented on nominations since 1946, but the Committee had traditionally been viewed as pro-establishment and conservative. It was so viewed in 1972 when FACA was adopted and was still viewed that way by many when the Public Citizen case was decided ("Public Citizen" is a Ralph Nader organization). During the Reagan period, however, conservative opinion swung against the Committee, most notably as a result of the 1987 hearings on Judge Bork's nomination to the Supreme Court. Five Committee members did not find Judge Bork, a prominent conservative jurist, qualified for the Supreme Court, in part on ideological grounds. Under considerable pressure, the Committee amended its criteria in 1988. Instead of professional competence, integrity, and judicial temperament being the "primary" considerations, the amended 1988 guidelines stated that ideology would *not* be considered, except when relevant to professional criteria. The ABA's role remained politically controversial, however, and was the subject of Senate Judiciary Committee hearings in Spring 1989, when Public Citizen was decided. In 1989 the guidelines were further amended to state explicitly that political and ideological philosophy would not be considered at all.

2. *Fundamental values vs. inconvenient results.* Is the Court in Public Citizen helping the legislature avoid an "inconvenient" result, one which would not violate fundamental substantive values? That may be Justice Kennedy's point when he suggests applying the absurdity test only when the results would be "patently absurd" and not when legislative history shows that the text might be overbroad.

3. *Doubts about constitutionality.* In Public Citizen, the Court resolves uncertainty about statutory meaning by appealing to the canon that statutes should be interpreted to avoid constitutional doubts. This canon of statutory

4. See Ross, Participation by the Public   Vand. L. Rev. 1 (1990).
in the Federal Judicial Selection Process, 43

interpretation has a long tradition. A recent example is N.L.R.B. v. Catholic Bishop of Chicago, 440 U.S. 490 (1979), where the Court decided that interpreting a statute to provide NLRB jurisdiction over teachers in church-operated schools might infringe the Religion Clauses of the First Amendment.

The canon is supported by a number of policies. It allows the court, in effect, to ask the legislature whether it really meant to do something of questionable constitutionality. It allows the court to postpone judgment about difficult constitutional issues. It preserves legislation. In some cases, an interpretation which avoids constitutional doubts may also accurately identify a substantive background consideration which the legislature would have adopted.

Courts can, however, employ the "avoid constitutional doubts" canon in questionable ways. First, the invocation of the presumption might allow judges to adopt statutory interpretations they prefer without adequate support. Claims of constitutional doubt conceal advancement of principles lacking genuine constitutional justification. Second, the presumption might so distort the statute that it is completely unfaithful to the statute, which was Kennedy's objection in Public Citizen.

iii) LAWMAKING RESPONSIBILITY

The legislature in Holy Trinity obviously forgot about religious employees. But why should the court bail out the legislature? Isn't it the legislature's responsibility to be more careful? As noted earlier, your answer may depend on why the legislature was not more careful. Congress was apparently focused on the special labor union interests backing the statute, with a heavy dose of class and race bias. Labor wanted the bill (Congressional Record, 48th Cong., 2d Sess. 1785 (1885)(vote for bill because labor wants it)). In addition, the class and ethnic bias was palpable. Members of Congress spoke of laborers ignorant of our social conditions, who were from the lowest social stratum, who did not become citizens, and were not a desirable acquisition to the body politic. The Chinese exclusion laws had recently been passed and there were many references to the workers' Hungarian origins, although one Senator objected to equating Europeans with Asian coolies (id., page 1631).

One way to approach a statute like this is to force the legislature to swallow the implications of a text energized by such concerns. If the legislature gets caught up in a pro-special interest and race-bias mood, why should the court rescue the statute from its textual implications?

In this connection, consider the following case, primarily Judge Winter's dissent. In United States v. University Hospital, 729 F.2d 144 (2d Cir.1984), the United States Department of Health and Human Services (HHS) sought access to hospital records concerning a seriously deformed newborn infant. The infant suffered from spina bifida and hydrocephalus, both of which could be surgically corrected to prolong life, but also suffered from microcephaly, which produced an extremely high risk of severe retardation for which surgery was unavailing. The parents refused to consent to surgical procedures to prolong the infant's life and the hospital did not seek a court order permitting treatment. § 504 of the Rehabilitation Act of 1973 provides that

> (n)o otherwise qualified handicapped individual * * * shall, solely by reason of his handicap, * * * be subjected to discrimination under any program or activity receiving Federal financial assistance * * *.

The government identified microcephaly as a handicapping condition, and argued that the statute was violated if an infant with spina bifida and hydrocephalus, but not microcephaly, would have received corrective surgery. The government sought the hospital records to determine whether the statute had been violated, which depended on whether the treatment decision was based (properly) on a medical judgment or (improperly) on the handicap.

The court held that the statute did not apply. As the following excerpts indicate, the court makes both a language argument (about plain meaning) and an argument about statutory purpose.

> * * * As the mainstream of cases under section 504 exemplifies, the phrase "otherwise qualified" is geared toward relatively static programs or activities such as education, and transportation systems. As a result, the phrase cannot be applied in the comparatively fluid context of medical treatment decisions without distorting its plain meaning. In common parlance, one would not ordinarily think of a newborn infant suffering from multiple birth defects as being "otherwise qualified" to have corrective surgery performed or to have a hospital initiate litigation seeking to override a decision against surgery by the infant's parents. If congress intended section 504 to apply in this manner, it chose strange language indeed. * * *
>
> * * * [I]n arguing that Baby Jane may have been "subjected to discrimination" the government has taken an oversimplified view of the medical decisionmaking process. Where the handicapping condition is related to the condition(s) to be treated, it will rarely, if ever, be possible to say with certainty that a particular decision was "discriminatory". It is at this point that the analogy to race, relied on so heavily by the dissent, breaks down. Beyond the fact that no two cases are likely to be the same, it would invariably require lengthy litigation primarily involving conflicting expert testimony to determine whether a decision to treat, or not to treat, or to litigate or not to litigate, was based on a "bona fide medical judgment", however that phrase might be defined. Before ruling that congress intended to spawn this type of litigation under section 504 we would want more proof than is apparent from the face of the statute.
>
> [Editor—The court then reviews the legislative history and finds congressional attention directed to education, transportation, em-

ployment, and housing. It finds no mention of defective newborn infants.]

We are aware, of course, that "[w]here the words and purpose of a statute plainly apply to a particular situation, * * * the fact that the specific application of the statute never occurred to Congress does not bar us from holding that the situation falls within the statute's coverage." Here, however, the government's theory not only strains the statutory language but also goes well beyond Congress's overriding concern with guaranteeing handicapped individuals access to programs or activities receiving federal financial assistance. * * * Under these circumstances, the failure of Congress to focus on treatment decisions involving defective newborn infants strikes a telling blow to the government's position.

Judge Winter's dissent took a different view of the judicial role in statutory interpretation.

* * * It hardly needs stating that the underlying issues brim with political and moral controversy and portend to extend the hand of the federal government into matters traditionally governed by an interaction of parental judgment and state authority. Were I able to conclude that Congress had no reason to address these issues in its consideration of Section 504, I would concur with the majority on the grounds that specific consideration by the Congress of this political and moral mine-field would be appropriate before applying the statute as written.

However, such a conclusion is untenable since Section 504 is no first step into a hitherto uncharted legal wilderness. As the Senate Report stated:

> Section 504 was patterned after, and is almost identical to, the antidiscrimination language of section 601 of the Civil Rights Act of 1964, 42 U.S.C. § 2000d–1 (relating to race, color, or national origin), and section 901 of the Education Amendments of 1972, 42 U.S.C. § 1683 (relating to sex). The section therefore constitutes the establishment of a broad government policy that programs receiving Federal financial assistance shall be operated without discrimination on the basis of handicap.

S.Rep. No. 1297, 93d Cong., 2d Sess. Section 504 was thus enacted against a background of well understood law which was explicitly designated as a guide to interpretation. Congress was persuaded that a handicapped condition is analogous to race and that, so far as the administration of federal financial assistance is concerned, discrimination on the basis of a handicap should be on statutory par with discrimination on the basis of race.

Once Section 504's legislative heritage is acknowledged, the "void" in the legislative history is eliminated and the many issues raised by defendants with regard to medical decisions, parental judgments and state authority simply evaporate. The government has never taken the position that it is entitled to override a medical judgment. Its position rather is that it is entitled under Section 504 to inquire whether a judgment in question is a bona fide medical judgment. While the majority professes uncertainty as to what that means, application of the analogy to race eliminates all doubt. A judgment not to perform certain surgery because a person is black is not a *bona fide* medical judgment. So too, a decision not to correct a life threatening digestive problem because an infant has Down's Syndrome is not a *bona fide* medical judgment. The issue of parental authority is also quickly disposed of. A denial of medical treatment to an infant because the infant is black is not legitimated by parental consent. Finally, once the legislative analogy to race is acknowledged, the intrusion on state authority becomes insignificant.

The logic of the government's position on these aspects of the case is thus about as flawless as a legal argument can be. Any doubt must stem * * * from a disagreement as to whether a handicapped condition is fully analogous to race. Whether that doubt is justified or not, however, courts are not the proper fora in which the reasonableness of the analogy to race is to be judged. * * *

* * * I would respectfully suggest that we act outside our legitimate area of authority in declining to follow the path staked out by Title VI of the Civil Rights Act. Congress did not adopt the analogy to race merely as a legislative means to a policy goal but was persuaded and politically energized by the view that the analogy was correct. A judicial failure to follow the analogy where it leads is an outright disagreement with Congress' judgment and an unconstitutional act in itself.

Finally, we facilitate the democratic legislative process by applying the analogy to race as adopted by the Congress. A political temptation to avoid confrontations with issues of moral or prudential controversy is an inevitable aspect of legislative deliberations. If courts are perceived as ready to "correct" overbroad legislation, Congress will find it ever more tempting to avoid its responsibility to address and resolve the highly delicate issues which may lurk in seemingly unobjectionable legislative proposals. Rhetorical flourishes will be substituted for statutory precision and "voids" in legislative histories will be ever more frequent. This is particularly so in cases involving legislative analogies to race. The moral and legal successes of the civil rights movement have prompted many groups to seek legislation which puts a particular characteristic or condition on a legal par with race. So long as the courts are perceived to stand ready to consider tempering such legislation where it leads to controversial results, the path of least political resistance will always be for the Congress to avoid serious consideration of the actual consequences of legislating particular analogies to race. Only an apprehension that such legislative analogies will be enforced by courts as written can provide a counter incentive to induce Congress to address its legislative responsibilities.

Judge Winter's dissent objects to Congress shunning its responsibility to address politically sensitive issues. He refuses an interpretation which bails out the legislature when it casually drafts statutes on the basis of politically potent analogies, such as race discrimination. Should a court take a similar approach to a case like Holy Trinity, where a legislature is energized by special interests and race bias, giving the statute its full textual reach?

In the following case, the taxpayer won a large amount of money in the Irish Sweepstakes. She borrowed money to invest in very secure Treasury notes, prepaying the interest on the loan. The interest on the loan exceeded the interest earned on the notes. Under the statute, "interest paid or accrued" on "indebtedness" was deductible. The court held that the loan was not a "sham," because the loan was for a significant period of time from an independent financial institution with real control over the loan arrangement. Nonetheless, the statutory text was limited and the interest deduction was disallowed.

Who should have had the lawmaking responsibility to deal with this potential tax loophole? The legislature almost certainly overlooked this problem in 1913 when the interest deduction was originally adopted, because these tax avoidance techniques were uncommon. Still, would it have been better for the court to leave it to the legislature to deal with the problem? Does the case make it more or less likely that Congress will address the use of deductible interest to obtain tax breaks?

Notice that, in this case, relying on legislative purpose to limit the text *hurts* taxpayers. This is quite different from other cases you have read, where the statute's coverage was restricted to prevent government burdens. Does that make the case more "modern," more 20th Century in spirit?

Goldstein v. Commissioner

364 F.2d 734 (2d Cir.1966).

■ Waterman, Circuit Judge. * * *

We hold, for reasons set forth hereinafter, that Section 163(a) of the 1954 Internal Revenue Code does not permit a deduction for interest paid or accrued in loan arrangements, like those now before us, that can not with reason be said to have purpose, substance, or utility apart from their anticipated tax consequences. * * * There is at least this much truth in this oft-repeated maxim: a close question whether a particular Code provision authorized the deduction of a certain item is best resolved by reference to the underlying congressional purpose of the deduction provision in question.

Admittedly, the underlying purpose of Section 163(a) permitting the deduction of "all interest paid or accrued within the taxable year on indebtedness" is difficult to articulate because this provision is extremely broad: there is no requirement that deductible interest serve a business purpose, that it be ordinary and necessary, or even that it be reasonable. Nevertheless, it is fair to say that Section 163(a) is not entirely unlimited in its application and that such limits as there are stem from the Section's underlying notion that if an individual or corporation desires to engage in purposive activity, there is no reason why a taxpayer who borrows for that purpose should fare worse from an income tax standpoint than one who finances the venture with capital that otherwise would have been yielding income.

In order fully to implement this Congressional policy of encouraging purposive activity to be financed through borrowing, Section 163(a) should be construed to permit the deductibility of interest when a taxpayer has borrowed funds and incurred an obligation to pay interest in order to engage in what with reason can be termed purposive activity, even though he decided to borrow in order to gain an interest deduction rather than to finance the activity in some other way. In other words, the interest deduction should be permitted whenever it can be said that the taxpayer's desire to secure an interest deduction is only one of mixed motives that prompts the taxpayer to borrow funds; or, put a third way, the deduction is proper if there is some substance to the loan arrangement beyond the taxpayer's desire to secure the deduction. After all, we are frequently told that a taxpayer has the right to decrease the amount of what otherwise would be his taxes, or altogether avoid them, by any means the law permits. E.g., Gregory v. Helvering, 293 U.S. 465 (1935). On the other hand, and notwithstanding Section 163(a)'s broad scope this provision should not be construed to permit an interest deduction when it objectively appears that a taxpayer has borrowed funds in order to engage in a transaction that has no substance or purpose aside from the taxpayer's desire to obtain the tax benefit of an interest deduction: and a good example of such purposeless activity is the borrowing of funds of 4% in order to purchase property that returns less than 2% and holds out no prospect of appreciation sufficient to counter the unfavorable interest rate differential. Certainly the statutory provision's underlying purpose, as we understand it, does not require that a deduction be allowed in such a case. Indeed, to allow a deduction for interest paid on funds borrowed for no purposive reason, other than the securing of a deduction from income, would frustrate Section 163(a)'s purpose; allowing it would encourage transactions that have no economic utility and that would not be engaged in but for the system of taxes imposed by Congress. When it enacted Section 163(a) Congress could not have intended to permit a taxpayer to reduce his taxes by means of an interest deduction that arose from a transaction that had no substance, utility, or purpose beyond the tax deduction.

iv) DRAFTING ERRORS

Sometimes the legislature is careless, not by failing to address a substantive political issue, but by drafting carelessly. Is this a worse failure of legislative responsibility than failing to address an important political issue? Consider the following case.

In United States v. Locke, 471 U.S. 84 (1985), a federal statute required recording of ownership with the Bureau of Land Management to rid federal lands of stale mining claims and provide the federal government with current information. A claimant must file "prior to December 31." Failure to file is an abandonment of a claim to ownership. Appellees filed *on* December 31 and the government ruled that they forfeited ownership. The Court (per Justice Marshall) agreed, stating as follows:

> [W]e are not insensitive to the problems posed by congressional reliance on the words "prior to December 31." But the fact that Congress might have acted with greater clarity or foresight does not give courts a carte blanche to redraft statutes in an effort to achieve that which Congress is perceived to have failed to do. "There is a basic difference between filling a gap left by Congress' silence and rewriting rules that Congress has affirmatively and specifically enacted." Nor is the judiciary licensed to attempt to soften the clear import of Congress' chosen words whenever a court believes those words lead to a harsh result. On the contrary, deference to the supremacy of the legislature, as well as recognition that congressmen typically vote on the language of a bill, generally require us to assume that "the legislative purpose is expressed by the ordinary meaning of the words used." "Going behind the plain language of a statute in search of a possibly contrary congressional intent is 'a step to be taken cautiously' even under the best of circumstances." When even after taking this step nothing in the legislative history remotely suggests a congressional intent contrary to Congress' chosen words, and neither appellees nor the dissenters have pointed to anything that so suggests, any further steps take the courts out of the realm of interpretation and place them in the domain of legislation. The phrase "prior to" may be clumsy, but its meaning is clear. Under these circumstances, we are obligated to apply the "prior to December 31" language by its terms.

Justice Stevens (with Justice Brennan) dissented, stating:

> The Court's opinion is contrary to the intent of Congress, * * * and unjustly creates a trap for unwary property owners. [T]he choice of the language "prior to December 31" [is] at best, "the consequence of a legislative accident, perhaps caused by nothing more than the unfortunate fact that Congress is too busy to do all of its work as carefully as it should." In my view, Congress actually

intended to authorize an annual filing at any time prior to the close of business on December 31st, that is, prior to the end of the calendar year to which the filing pertains. * * *

A careful reading of [the statutory text] discloses [several] respects in which its text cannot possibly reflect the actual intent of Congress. * * * [Editor—Justice Stevens then refers to a textual error stating "on" instead of "or"; and to the relaxation by the agency of the statutory requirement of "filing in the office of the Bureau" to include mailing to the Bureau by December 30, even if the mailing arrives after December 30.]

In light of the foregoing, I cannot believe that Congress intended the words "prior to December 31 of each year" to be given the literal reading the Court adopts today. The statutory scheme requires periodic filings on a calendar-year basis. The end of the calendar year is, of course, correctly described either as "prior to the close of business on December 31," or "on or before December 31," but it is surely understandable that the author of [the statute] might inadvertently use the words "prior to December 31" when he meant to refer to the end of the calendar year. As the facts of this case demonstrate, the scrivener's error is one that can be made in good faith. The risk of such an error is, of course, the greatest when the reference is to the end of the calendar year. That it was in fact an error seems rather clear to me because no one has suggested any rational basis for omitting just one day from the period in which an annual filing may be made, and I would not presume that Congress deliberately created a trap for the unwary by such an omission. * * *

* * * The Bureau in this case was well aware of the existence and production of appellees' mining claims; only by blinking reality could the Bureau reach the decision that it did. It is undisputed that the appellees made the first 1980 filing on August 29, 1980, and made the second required filing on December 31, 1980; the Bureau did not declare the mining claims "abandoned and void" until April 4, 1981. Thus, appellees lost their entire livelihood for no practical reason, contrary to the intent of Congress, and because of the hypertechnical construction of a poorly drafted statute, which an agency interprets to allow "filings" far beyond December 30 in some circumstances, but then interprets inflexibly in others. * * *

In my view, this unique factual matrix unequivocally contradicts the statutory presumption of an intent to abandon by reason of a late filing. In sum, this case presents an ambiguous statute, which, if strictly construed, will destroy valuable rights of appellees, property owners who have compiled with all local and federal statutory filing requirements apart from a one-day "late" filing caused by the Bureau's own failure to mail a reminder notice necessary because of the statute's ambiguity and caused by the Bureau's information to appellees that the date on which the filing occurred would be acceptable. [Editor—The Bureau had followed a practice of mailing reminder notices about the filing date, but had not sent one to appellees. Moreover, appellees had inquired about the filing date from the Bureau, and Bureau personnel told them that the filing was due "on or before December 31, 1980."] Further, long before the Bureau declared a technical "abandonment," it was in complete possession of all information necessary to assess the activity, locations, and ownership of appellees' mining claims and it possessed all information needed to carry out its statutory functions. Finally, the Bureau has not claimed that the filing is contrary to the congressional purposes behind the statute, that the filing affected the Bureau's land-use planning functions in any manner, or that it interfered "in any measurable way" with the Bureau's need to obtain information. A showing of substantial compliance necessitates a significant burden of proof; appellees, whose active mining claims will be destroyed contrary to Congress' intent, have convinced me that they have substantially complied with the statute.

I respectfully dissent.

COMMENTS AND QUESTIONS

1. Judge Posner comments favorably on Justice Stevens approach: "I can see no harm and much good in the Court's [rewriting the clear statutory language], given the unusual circumstance."[5] The circumstance to which Judge Posner alludes was a drafting error which became a trap, destroying valuable property rights. He distinguishes the issue in Locke from the question whether the constitutional provision requiring the President to be age 35 is flexible: "To interpret 35 years to mean as mature as the average 35–year-old would [ ] undo a choice deliberately made by the framers."

2. Even if careless drafting is not the worst failure of legislative responsibility, is it nonetheless a comparatively easy lapse for the legislature to avoid? If so, perhaps the court should place the responsibility for accurate drafting on the legislature? Do not be too harsh, however, on a legislature which makes drafting errors. Time is often short, especially at the end of a session, and drafters make mistakes. The drafters of United States statutes are usually the staff of a legislative committee, or work in the House or Senate Legislative Counsel's office. Someone should be checking on their work but mistakes happen.

3. What are the substantive values protected by Stevens' opinion in Locke? Is he simply preventing an irrational legislative error or are there other substantive values worth protecting? Is he enforcing a "common law" of administrative behavior through statutory interpretation?

5. R. Posner, Law and Literature: A Misunderstood Relation, p.256 (1988).

4. Notice that the Court specifically observed that there was "nothing in the legislative history [to] remotely suggest [   ] a congressional intent contrary to Congress' chosen words." Apparently, the Court is more willing to rely on statutory purpose than on statutory purposelessness to rewrite a statutory text.

6.05   CONTEXT AND PERMISSIBLE READINGS OF THE TEXT

Clear conflict between text and external context is unusual. More often a text seems to have a more plausible meaning, which might yield to another meaning upon consideration of statutory purpose. The more text-oriented interpreter will resist the pull of context in such cases.

The following case presents as clear an example of a tension between a context- and text-oriented judge as you can find. The majority opinion by Justice Stevens begins and ends with a statement about legislative purpose to eliminate race discrimination in voting. The dissent, by Justice Scalia, just as plainly begins and ends with the textualist's credo—the importance of deference to ordinary meaning.

Is this a case where the Court adopts the general principle that purpose prevails over text, or does it enthusiastically *embrace this statute's purpose,* and, if so, why? Is this an example of the judge "exercis[ing] a judgment on the value of the purpose."

The case involved the interpretation of the following statute, § 2 of the Voting Rights Act of 1965, as amended in 1982. The critical language is italicized.

"Sec. 2. (a) No voting qualification or prerequisite to voting or standard, practice, or procedure shall be imposed or applied by any State or political subdivision in a manner which results in a denial or abridgement of the right of any citizen of the United States to vote on account of race or color, or in contravention of the guarantees set forth in section 4(f)(2), as provided in subsection (b).

"(b) A violation of subsection (a) is established if, based on the totality of circumstances, it is shown that the political processes leading to nomination or election in the State or political subdivision are not equally open to participation by members of a class of citizens protected by subsection (a) in that *its members have less opportunity than other members of the electorate to participate in the political process and to elect representatives of their choice.* * * *"
[96 Stat. 134.]

Chisom v. Roemer

501 U.S. 380 (1991).

■ Justice Stevens delivered the opinion of the Court.

The preamble to the Voting Rights Act of 1965 establishes that the central purpose of the Act is "to enforce the fifteenth amendment to the Constitution of the United States." The Fifteenth Amendment provides:

> "The right of citizens of the United States to vote shall not be denied or abridged by the United States or by any State on account of race, color, or previous condition of servitude." U.S. Const., Amdt. 15, § 1.

In 1982, Congress amended § 2 of the Voting Rights Act to make clear that certain practices and procedures that result in the denial or abridgement of the right to vote are forbidden even though the absence of proof of discriminatory intent protects them from constitutional challenge. The question presented by this case is whether this "results test" protects the right to vote in state judicial elections. We hold that the coverage provided by the 1982 amendment is coextensive with the coverage provided by the Act prior to 1982 and that judicial elections are embraced within that coverage. * * *

It is [   ] undisputed that § 2 applied to judicial elections prior to the 1982 amendment * * *. Moreover, there is no question that the terms "standard, practice, or procedure" are broad enough to encompass the use of multimember districts to minimize a racial minority's ability to influence the outcome of an election covered by § 2. The only matter in dispute is whether the test for determining the legality of such a practice, which was added to the statute in 1982, applies in judicial elections as well as in other elections. * * *

Justice Stewart's opinion for the plurality in Mobile v. Bolden, 446 U.S. 55 (1980), which held that there was no violation of either the Fifteenth Amendment or § 2 of the Voting Rights Act absent proof of intentional discrimination, served as the impetus for the 1982 amendment. * * *

Under the amended statute, proof of intent is no longer required to prove a § 2 violation. Now plaintiffs can prevail under § 2 by demonstrating that a challenged election practice has resulted in the denial or abridgement of the right to vote based on color or race. * * *

The two purposes of the amendment are apparent from its text. Subsection 2(a) adopts a results test, thus providing that proof of discriminatory intent is no longer necessary to establish any violation of the section. Subsection 2(b) provides guidance about how the results test is to be applied.

Respondents contend, and the [Court of Appeals] majority agreed, that Congress' choice of the word "representatives" in the phrase "have less opportunity than other members of the electorate to participate in the political process and to elect representatives of their choice" in subsection 2(b) is evidence of congressional intent to exclude vote dilution claims involving judicial elections from the coverage of § 2. We reject that construction because we are convinced that if Congress had such an intent, Congress would have made it explicit in the statute, or at least some of the Members would have identified or mentioned it at some point in the unusually extensive legislative history of the 1982 amendment. [Editor—The Court observes in a footnote that "Congress' silence in this regard can be likened to the dog that did not bark. See A. Doyle, Silver Blaze, in The Complete Sherlock Holmes 335 (1927)."] * * *

The [Court of Appeals] majority assumed that § 2 provides two distinct types of protection for minority voters—it protects their opportunity "to participate in the political process" and their opportunity "to elect representatives of their choice." Although the majority interpreted "representatives" as a word of limitation, it assumed that the word eliminated judicial elections only from the latter protection, without affecting the former. In other words, a standard, practice, or procedure in a judicial election, such as a limit on the times that polls are open, which has a disparate impact on black voters' opportunity to cast their ballots under § 2, may be challenged even if a different practice that merely affects their opportunity to elect representatives of their choice to a judicial office may not. This reading of § 2, however, is foreclosed by the statutory text and by our prior cases.

Any abridgement of the opportunity of members of a protected class to participate in the political process inevitably impairs their ability to influence the outcome of an election. As the statute is written, however, the inability to elect representatives of their choice is not sufficient to establish a violation unless, under the totality of the circumstances, it can also be said that the members of the protected class have less opportunity to participate in the political process. The statute does not create two separate and distinct rights. * * * It would distort the plain meaning of the sentence to substitute the word "or" for the word "and" [in subsection (b) which refers to an injury to members of the protected class who have less "opportunity" than others "to participate in the political process and to elect representatives of their choice"]. Such radical surgery would be required to separate the opportunity to participate from the opportunity to elect. [Editor—In a footnote, the Court responds to the dissent's argument "that our literal reading of the word 'and' leads to the conclusion that a small minority has no protection against infringements of its right 'to participate in the political process' because it will always lack the numbers necessary 'to elect its candidate.' In the Court's view, the dissent's 'argument [ ] rests on the erroneous assumption that a small group of voters can never influence the outcome of an election.' "]

The statutory language is patterned after the language used by Justice White in his opinions for the Court in White v. Regester, 412 U.S. 755 (1973). In both opinions, the Court identified the opportunity to participate and the opportunity to elect as inextricably linked. In White v. Regester, the Court described the connection as follows: "The plaintiffs' burden is to produce evidence * * * that its members had less opportunity than did other residents in the district to participate in the political processes and to elect legislators of their choice." And earlier, in Whitcomb v. Chavis, 403 U.S. 124 (1971), the Court described the plaintiffs' burden as entailing a showing that they "had less opportunity than did other * * * residents to participate in the political processes and to elect legislators of their choice." * * *

Both respondents and the [Court of Appeals] majority place their principal reliance on Congress' use of the word "representatives" instead of "legislators" in the phrase "to participate in the political process and to elect representatives of their choice." When Congress borrowed the phrase from White v. Regester, it replaced "legislators" with "representatives." This substitution indicates, at the very least, that Congress intended the amendment to cover more than legislative elections. Respondents argue, and the majority agreed, that the term "representatives" was used to extend § 2 coverage to executive officials, but not to judges. We think, however, that the better reading of the word "representatives" describes the winners of representative, popular elections. If executive officers, such as prosecutors, sheriffs, state attorneys general, and state treasurers, can be considered "representatives" simply because they are chosen by popular election, then the same reasoning should apply to elected judges.

Respondents suggest that if Congress had intended to have the statute's prohibition against vote dilution apply to the election of judges, it would have used the word "candidates" instead of "representatives." But that confuses the ordinary meaning of the words. The word "representative" refers to someone who has prevailed in a popular election, whereas the word "candidate" refers to someone who is seeking an office. Thus, a candidate is nominated, not elected. When Congress used "candidate" in other parts of the statute, it did so precisely because it was referring to people who were aspirants for an office.

The [Court of Appeals] majority was, of course, entirely correct in observing that "judges need not be elected at all," and that ideally public opinion should be irrelevant to the judge's role because the judge is often called upon to disregard, or even to defy, popular sentiment. The Framers of the Constitution had a similar understanding of the judicial role, and as a consequence, they established that Article III judges would be appointed, rather than elected, and would be sheltered from public opinion by receiving life tenure and salary protection. Indeed, these views were generally shared by the States during the early years of the Republic. Louisiana, however, has chosen a different course. It has decided to elect its judges and to compel judicial candidates to vie for popular support just as other political candidates do.

The fundamental tension between the ideal character of the judicial office and the real world of electoral politics cannot be resolved by crediting judges with total indifference to the popular will while simultaneously requiring them to run for elected office. When each of several members of a court must be a resident of a separate district, and must be elected by the voters of that district, it seems both reasonable and realistic to characterize the winners as representatives of that district. Indeed, at one time the Louisiana Bar Association characterized the members of the Louisiana Supreme Court as representatives for that reason: "Each justice and judge now in office shall be considered as a representative of the judicial district within which is situated the parish of his residence at the time of his election." * * *

Finally, both respondents and the [Court of Appeals] majority suggest that no judicially manageable standards for deciding vote dilution claims can be fashioned unless the standard is based on the one-person, one-vote principle. They reason that because we have held the one-person, one-vote rule inapplicable to judicial elections, see Wells v. Edwards, 409 U.S. 1095 (1973), it follows that judicial elections are entirely immune from vote dilution claims. The conclusion, however, does not follow from the premise.

The holding in Wells rejected a constitutional challenge based on the Equal Protection Clause of the Fourteenth Amendment. It has no more relevance to a correct interpretation of this statute than does our decision in Mobile v. Bolden, supra, which also rejected a constitutional claim. The statute was enacted to protect voting rights that are not adequately protected by the Constitution itself. The standard that should be applied in litigation under § 2 is not at issue here. Even if serious problems lie ahead in applying the "totality of circumstances" described in § 2(b), that task, difficult as it may prove to be, cannot justify a judicially created limitation on the coverage of the broadly worded statute, as enacted and amended by Congress.

Congress enacted the Voting Rights Act of 1965 for the broad remedial purpose of "ridding the country of racial discrimination in voting." In Allen v. State Board of Elections, 393 U.S. 544, 567 (1969), we said that the Act should be interpreted in a manner that provides "the broadest possible scope" in combating racial discrimination. Congress amended the Act in 1982 in order to relieve plaintiffs of the burden of proving discriminatory intent, after a plurality of this Court had concluded that the original Act, like the Fifteenth Amendment, contained such a requirement. Thus, Congress made clear that a violation of § 2 could be established by proof of discriminatory results alone. It is difficult to believe that Congress, in an express effort to broaden the protection afforded by the Voting Rights Act, withdrew, without comment, an important category of elections from that protection. Today we reject such an anomalous view and hold that state judicial elections are included within the ambit of § 2 as amended.

The judgment of the Court of Appeals is reversed and the case is remanded for further proceedings consistent with this opinion.

■ Justice Scalia, with whom the Chief Justice and Justice Kennedy join, dissenting.

Section 2 of the Voting Rights Act is not some all-purpose weapon for well-intentioned judges to wield as they please in the battle against discrimination. It is a statute. I thought we had adopted a regular method for interpreting the meaning of language in a statute: first, find the ordinary meaning of the language in its textual context; and second, using established canons of construction, ask whether there is any clear indication that some permissible meaning other than the ordinary one applies. If not—and especially if a good reason for the ordinary meaning appears plain—we apply that ordinary meaning.

Today, however, the Court adopts a method quite out of accord with that usual practice. It begins not with what the statute says, but with an expectation about what the statute must mean absent particular phenomena ("we are convinced that if Congress had * * * an intent [to exclude judges] Congress would have made it explicit in the statute, or at least some of the Members would have identified or mentioned it at some point in the unusually extensive legislative history," and the Court then interprets the words of the statute to fulfill its expectation. Finding nothing in the legislative history affirming that judges were excluded from the coverage of § 2, the Court gives the phrase "to elect representatives" the quite extraordinary meaning that covers the election of judges.)

As method, this is just backwards, and however much we may be attracted by the result it produces in a particular case, we should in every case resist it. Our job begins with a text that Congress has passed and the President has signed. We are to read the words of that text as any ordinary Member of Congress would have read them, see Holmes, The Theory of Legal Interpretation, 12 Harv. L. Rev. 417 (1899), and apply the meaning so determined. In my view, that reading reveals that § 2 extends to vote dilution claims for the elections of representatives only, and judges are not representatives. As the Court suggests, the 1982 amendments to the Voting Rights Act were adopted in response to our decision in City of Mobile v. Bolden, 446 U.S. 55 (1980), which had held that the scope of the original Voting Rights Act was coextensive with the Fifteenth Amendment, and thus proscribed intentional discrimination only. I agree with the Court that that original legislation, directed towards intentional discrimination, applied to all elections, for it clearly said so. * * *

The 1982 amendments, however, radically transformed the Act. As currently written, the statute proscribes intentional discrimination only if it has a discriminatory effect, but proscribes practices with discriminatory effect whether or not intentional. This new "results" criterion provides a powerful, albeit sometimes blunt, weapon with which to attack even the most subtle forms of discrimination. The question we confront here is how broadly the new remedy applies. The foundation of the Court's analysis, the itinerary for its journey in the wrong direction, is the following statement: "It is difficult to believe that Congress, in an express effort to broaden the protection afforded by the Voting Rights Act, withdrew, without comment, an important category of elections from that protection." There are two things wrong with this. First is the notion that Congress cannot be credited with having achieved anything of major importance by simply saying it, in ordinary language, in the text of a statute, "without comment" in the legislative history. As the Court colorfully puts it, if the dog of legislative history has not barked nothing of great significance can have transpired. Apart from the questionable wisdom of assuming that dogs will bark when something important is happening, we have forcefully and explicitly rejected the Conan Doyle approach to statutory construction in the past. We are here to apply the statute, not legislative history, and certainly not the absence of legislative history. Statutes are the law though sleeping dogs lie.

The more important error in the Court's starting-point, however, is the assumption that the effect of excluding judges from the revised § 2 would be to "withdraw * * * an important category of elections from [the] protection [of the Voting Rights Act]." There is absolutely no question here of withdrawing protection. Since the pre–1982 content of § 2 was coextensive with the Fifteenth Amendment, the entirety of that protection subsisted in the Constitution, and could be enforced through the other provisions of the Voting Rights Act. Nothing was lost from the prior coverage; all of the new "results" protection was an add-on. The issue is not, therefore, as the Court would have it, whether Congress has cut back on the coverage of the Voting Rights Act; the issue is how far it has extended it. Thus, even if a court's expectations were a proper basis for interpreting the text of a statute, while there would be reason to expect that Congress was not "withdrawing" protection, there is no particular reason to expect that the supplemental protection it provided was any more extensive than the text of the statute said. * * *

[Editor—Justice Scalia next deals with the majority's argument that "to participate in the political process *and* to elect representatives of their choice" imposes two conjunctive requirements, rather than disjunctive requirements. Scalia favors the disjunctive reading, with the first phrase applying to judges and the latter phrase to "representatives." He observes that "and" often means "or" in

English usage, as in the First Amendment—"the right of the people peaceably to assemble, and to petition the Government for redress of grievances." He also rejects the majority's attempt to avoid an unfortunate implication of its "conjunctive" reading, which is that the opportunity to participate would be denied if the voters formed such a small part of the electorate that they could not "elect" a representative of their choice. To avoid that implication, the majority had interpreted "to elect" to mean "to influence the outcome of an election," which Justice Scalia thought was an impermissible construction.] * * *

The Court, petitioners, and petitioners' amici have labored mightily to establish that there is a meaning of "representatives" that would include judges, and no doubt there is. But our job is not to scavenge the world of English usage to discover whether there is any possible meaning of "representatives" which suits our preconception that the statute includes judges; our job is to determine whether the ordinary meaning includes them, and if it does not, to ask whether there is any solid indication in the text or structure of the statute that something other than ordinary meaning was intended.

There is little doubt that the ordinary meaning of "representatives" does not include judges, see Webster's Second New International Dictionary 2114 (1950). The Court's feeble argument to the contrary is that "representatives" means those who "are chosen by popular election." On that hypothesis, the fan-elected members of the baseball All-Star teams are "representatives"—hardly a common, if even a permissible, usage. Surely the word "representative" connotes one who is not only elected by the people, but who also, at a minimum, acts on behalf of the people. Judges do that in a sense—but not in the ordinary sense. As the captions of the pleadings in some States still display, it is the prosecutor who represents "the People"; the judge represents the Law—which often requires him to rule against the People. It is precisely because we do not ordinarily conceive of judges as representatives that we held judges not within the Fourteenth Amendment's requirement of "one person, one vote." The point is not that a State could not make judges in some senses representative, or that all judges must be conceived of in the Article III mold, but rather, that giving "representatives" its ordinary meaning, the ordinary speaker in 1982 would not have applied the word to judges, see Holmes, The Theory of Legal Interpretation, 12 Harv. L. Rev. 417 (1899). It remains only to ask whether there is good indication that ordinary meaning does not apply.

There is one canon of construction that might be applicable to the present case which, in some circumstances, would counter ordinary meaning—but here it would only have the effect of reinforcing it. * * * [Editor—Justice Scalia here mentions the canon that a statute should not be interpreted to intrude on state government unless there is a plain statement to the contrary. He concludes that he is "content to dispense with the 'plain statement' rule in the present case—but it says something about the Court's approach to today's decision that the possibility of applying that rule never crossed its mind."]

While the "plain statement" rule may not be applicable, there is assuredly nothing whatever that points in the opposite direction, indicating that the ordinary meaning here should not be applied. Far from that, in my view the ordinary meaning of "representatives" gives clear purpose to congressional action that otherwise would seem pointless. * * * As the Court suggests, that language for the most part tracked this Court's opinions in White v. Regester, *supra*, and Whitcomb v. Chavis, *supra*, but the word "legislators" was not copied. Significantly, it was replaced not with the more general term "candidates" used repeatedly elsewhere in the Act, but with the term "representatives," which appears nowhere else in the Act (except as a proper noun referring to Members of the federal lower House, or designees of the Attorney General). The normal meaning of this term is broader than "legislators" (it includes, for example, school boards and city councils as well as senators and representatives) but narrower than "candidates."

The Court says that the seemingly significant refusal to use the term "candidate" and selection of the distinctive term "representative" are really inconsequential, because "candidate" could not have been used. According to the Court, since "candidate" refers to one who has been nominated but not yet elected, the phrase "to elect candidates" would be a contradiction in terms. The only flaw in this argument is that it is not true, as repeated usage of the formulation "to elect candidates" by this Court itself amply demonstrates. In other words, far from being an impermissible choice, "candidates" would have been the natural choice, even if it had not been used repeatedly elsewhere in the statute. It is quite absurd to think that Congress went out of its way to replace that term with "representatives," in order to convey what "candidates" naturally suggests (viz., coverage of all elections) and what "representatives" naturally does not.

A second consideration confirms that "representatives" in § 2 was meant in its ordinary sense. When given its ordinary meaning, it causes the statute to reproduce an established, eminently logical and perhaps practically indispensable limitation upon the availability of vote dilution claims. * * *

Well before Congress amended § 2, we had held that the principle of "one person, one vote" does not apply to the election of judges. If Congress was (through use of the extremely inapt word "representatives") making vote dilution claims available with respect to the election of judges, it was, for the first time, extending that remedy to a context in which "one person, one vote" did not apply. That would have been a significant change in the law, and given the need to identify some other baseline for computing "dilution," that is a matter which those who believe in barking dogs should be astounded to find unmentioned in the legislative history. If "representatives" is given its normal meaning, on the other hand, there is no change in the law (except elimination of the intent requirement) and the silence is entirely understandable.

I frankly find it very difficult to conceive how it is to be determined whether "dilution" has occurred, once one has eliminated both the requirement of actual intent to disfavor minorities, and the principle that 10,000 minority votes throughout the State should have as much practical "electability" effect as 10,000 nonminority votes. How does one begin to decide, in such a system, how much elective strength a minority bloc ought to have? * * * The Court is stoic about the difficulty of defining "dilution" without a [one-person one-vote] standard of purity * * *. In reality, however, [ ] the Court [ ] leads us—quite unnecessarily and indeed with stubborn persistence—into this morass of unguided and perhaps unguidable judicial interference in democratic elections. * * *

All this is enough to convince me that there is sense to the ordinary meaning of "representative" in § 2(b)—that there is reason to Congress's choice—and since there is, then, under our normal presumption, that ordinary meaning prevails. I would read § 2 as extending vote dilution claims to elections for "representatives," but not to elections for judges. For other claims under § 2, however—those resting on the "to participate in the political process" provision rather than the "to elect" provision—no similar restriction would apply. Since the claims here are exclusively claims of dilution, I would affirm the judgment of the Fifth Circuit. * * *

As I said at the outset, this case is about method. The Court transforms the meaning of § 2, not because the ordinary meaning is irrational, or inconsistent with other parts of the statute, but because it does not fit the Court's conception of what Congress must have had in mind. When we adopt a method that psychoanalyzes Congress rather than reads its laws, when we employ a tinkerer's toolbox, we do great harm. Not only do we reach the wrong result with respect to the statute at hand, but we poison the well of future legislation, depriving legislators of the assurance that ordinary terms, used in an ordinary context, will be given a predictable meaning. Our highest responsibility in the field of statutory construction is to read the laws in a consistent way, giving Congress a sure means by which it may work the people's will. We have ignored that responsibility today. I respectfully dissent.

COMMENTS AND QUESTIONS

1. For this case to present a tension between text and external context, you must decide whether Justice Scalia has the better textual argument. Is Justice Scalia correct when he argues: (1) "representatives" act on behalf of the people, which excludes judges; (2) defining "representatives" to include "chosen by popular election" would include All-Star balloting; (3) "and" often means "or"; (4) "elect" does not mean "influence the outcome of an election"; (5) "candidate" is the more natural way to describe elected officials rather than "representatives"?

2. The word "representatives" seems a lot like the word "mother," discussed in Chapter 5. It has numerous possible references: elected in a political election; periodically standing for reelection; charged with acting in behalf of the short term interests of voters; charged with acting in their long term interests. Legislators fit all these qualifications and therefore obviously come within the statutory language. Do elected judges fit some criteria, enough to create a "family resemblance" sufficient to make them "representatives"?

3. Is it possible to consider how an author and audience would understand the word "representatives" without taking account of the fact that *this* statute was concerned with voting rights for minorities? Is that fact simply evidence of purpose or a background consideration that has nothing to do with understanding how authors and audiences would understand the statutory text?

Scalia seems to say that it is not only possible to exclude such considerations, but that the judge's job is to do so—to avoid "scaveng[ing] the world of English usage [for a] possible meaning." He adopts a "storehouse of meaning" approach to statutory language, in which statutes borrow meaning from "out there" somewhere, and play no role in shaping the meaning of the texts they use. Do people understand language, at least statutory language, by adopting a "storehouse of meaning" approach?

4. In Smith v. United States, 508 U.S. 223 (1993), involving the "use a firearm" (discussed in Chapter 3), Justice Scalia again argued that the Court did not understand the distinction between ordinary and possible usage. He stated:

> In the search for statutory meaning, we give nontechnical words and phrases their ordinary meaning. To use an instrumentality ordinarily means to use it for its intended purpose. When someone asks "Do you use a cane?" he is not inquiring whether you have your grandfather's silver-handled walking-stick on display in the hall; he wants to know whether you walk with a cane. Similarly, to speak of "using a firearm" is to speak of using it for its distinctive purpose, i.e., as a weapon. To be sure, "one can use a firearm in a number of ways," including as an article of exchange, just as one can "use" a cane as a hall decoration—but that is not the ordinary meaning of "using" the one or the other. The Court does not appear to grasp the distinction between how a word can be used and how it

ordinarily is used. It would, indeed, be "both reasonable and normal to say that petitioner 'used' his MAC–10 in his drug trafficking offense by trading it for cocaine." It would also be reasonable and normal to say that he "used" it to scratch his head. When one wishes to describe the action of employing the instrument of a firearm for such unusual purposes, "use" is assuredly a verb one could select. But that says nothing about whether the ordinary meaning of the phrase "uses a firearm" embraces such extraordinary employments. It is unquestionably not reasonable and normal, I think, to say simply "do not use firearms" when one means to prohibit selling or scratching with them.

Is Scalia asking the right question? Is the interpreter concerned with ordinary usage outside of the statutory text or with how the legislative author and audience might understand a phrase used in the statute?

5. You may suspect that substantive background considerations—concern about minority voting rights—influenced Justice Stevens. But is Justice Scalia's opinion innocent of such substantive concerns. First, he alludes to but does not ultimately rely on the canon that a statute should not be interpreted to intrude on state government, absent a plain statement requiring that result.

Second, he worries about applying the statute's voting dilution standard to judges. That standard includes not only meeting the one-person one-vote test but also examines whether a political group has been improperly excluded from the political process, such as by submerging their political impact in a multimember electoral district. This will lead, he says, to a "morass of unguided and perhaps unguidable judicial interference in democratic elections."

Third, and most importantly, Scalia notes that the constitutional one-person one-vote doctrine is not applied to judges *because* they represent the Law, not the People. Few values are more important to Scalia than this distinction between the Law and the People, a distinction we should recognize as the airtight compartment approach to Separation of Powers and as the rationale behind the aggressive anti-statute approach which thrived in the post-Civil War legal culture (see Chapter 2).

6. Can you avoid considering purpose and the values associated with that purpose in defining the phrase "grocery store" in the following three statutes—(1) one statute exempts a grocery store from the minimum wage for employees; (2) one prohibits sale of liquor by a grocery store; (3) one imposes health inspection requirements on a grocery store. Now assume three stores which sell groceries in the following percentages: 100% (the typical grocery store), 51% (a discount store that also sells appliances, etc.), and 5% (a pharmacy which also sells candy, chips, and the like). Is there an ordinary usage that can determine which of these three stores that sell groceries is a "grocery store" for all three statutes?

Suppose the no-liquor-sale statute was adopted in 1925 when groceries were only sold in stores which sold only groceries. Would you limit the definition of "grocery store" as narrowly as possible—using the beady-eyed contractual approach advocated by Easterbrook (see Chapter 4)—on the theory that the statute imposes barriers to entry lobbied for by liquor stores. Or do you think the statute was sponsored by anti-liquor consumption advocates, suggesting a more expansive definition? See Delaware Alcoholic Beverage Control Commission and Wal–Mart Stores, Inc. v. Newsome, ___ A.2d ___, 1996 WL 335978 (Del.1996).

6.06 Western Union Telegraph Co. v. Lenroot

By now, you have seen a number of different approaches to statutory interpretation. You might take a moment here to read the opinions in the following case, both to characterize the various interpretive approaches and to make your own choice about how you might have interpreted the statute. How do the judges use the text; how do they use purpose; are any substantive background considerations relevant?

Recall that Learned Hand (who writes the Court of Appeals opinion in this case) was a purposivist (see Chapter 3). How does his purposivism differ from the purposivism of Justice Murphy (dissenting in Lenroot) and Judge Rifkind (who writes the District Court opinion)?

If you conclude that Murphy and Rifkind are "sympathetically" elaborating the anti-child labor purpose, from where do they get the confidence that these values are part of the broader fabric of the law? Read Rifkind's opinion carefully for a clue.

Western Union Telegraph Co. v. Lenroot

323 U.S. 490 (1945).

■ Mr. Justice Jackson delivered the opinion of the Court.

A decree of the District Court in substance restrains the Western Union Telegraph Company from transmitting messages in interstate commerce until for thirty days it has ceased employment of messengers under the age of sixteen and eighteen. This was thought to be required by the Fair Labor Standards Act of 1938. * * *

The Western Union Telegraph Company collects messages in communities of origin and dispatches them by electrical impulses to places of destination where they are distributed. Messengers are employed in both collection and distribution. A little under 12 per cent of the messenger force is under sixteen years of age, and about 0.0033 per cent are from sixteen to eighteen years of age, engaged in the operation of motor vehicles, scooters, and telemotors. These messengers are employed only in localities where the law of the state permits it. It is not denied that both groups are engaged in oppressive child labor as defined by the Federal Act, if it applies. Whether it does so apply is the only issue here.

It is conceded that the Act does not directly prohibit the employment of these messengers, because it contains no prohibition against employment of child labor in conducting interstate commerce. It is conceded, too, that language appropriate directly to forbid this employment was proposed to Congress and twice rejected. * * *

Both parties contend on the basis of legislative history that the omission of a direct prohibition [of employment of child labor in conducting interstate commerce] was deliberate; the Company arguing that it was unwanted, the Government that it was believed superfluous. We think that dispassionate reading will not disclose what either advocate sees in this history.

It is nowhere stated that Congress did, and no reason is stated or is obvious why Congress should, purposely leave untouched child labor employed directly in interstate commerce. It is true that no opponent of child labor appeared to want to strike at all of it. Agriculture, which accounts for from one-half to two-thirds of it, was expressly exempted. Child actors, almost negligible in number, were exempted. Telegraph messengers, so far as the evidence reveals, although a familiar form of child labor, were in no one's mind in connection with this prohibition, although the peculiarities of that service were recognized in allowing them under certain conditions to be employed at lower than minimum wages under the Act. But whether a majority of Congress, had this question come to its attention, would have regarded messenger service as more like agriculture in being a relatively inoffensive type of child labor or as more like mining and manufacturing, considered more harmful, is a question on which we have no information whatever.

On the other hand, we find nothing to sustain the Government's position that "the omission resulted from the realization that the indirect sanction of forbidding interstate shipment, coupled with broad statutory definitions" would be construed to eliminate child labor from interstate commerce. No such realization appears in any committee report, in the speech of any sponsor of the bills, nor in debate either on the part of those supporting or of those opposing the bills. * * *

Our search of legislative history yields nothing to support the Company's contention that Congress did not want to reach such child labor as we have here. And it yields no more to support the Government's contention that Congress wanted to forego direct prohibition in favor of indirect sanctions. Indeed, we are unable to say that elimination of the direct prohibitions from the final form of the bill was purposeful at all or that it did not happen from sheer inadvertence, due to concentration on more vital and controversial aspects of the legislation. The most that we can make of it is that no definite policy either way appears in reference to such an employment as we have in this case, no legislative intent is manifest as to the facts of this case which we should strain to effectuate by interpretation. Of course, if by fair construction the indirect sanctions of the Act apply to this employment, courts may not refuse to enforce them merely because we cannot understand why a simpler and more direct method was not used. But we take the Act as Congress gave it to us, without attempting to conform it to any notions of what Congress would have done if the circumstances of this case had been put before it. [Editor—Justice Jackson was usually suspicious of claims about what Congress specifically intended.]

The Government brought this action to reach indirectly child labor in interstate commerce by bringing it under the prohibition of § 12 (a) of the Act, which so far as material reads "no producer, manufacturer or dealer shall ship or deliver for shipment in commerce any goods produced in an establishment situated in the United States in or about which within thirty days prior to the removal of such goods therefrom any oppressive child labor has been employed." Violation of this command is a crime (§§ 15 and 16) punishable by a fine and imprisonment, and threatened violations may be restrained by injunction. The Government in this case sought injunction. Its complaint charges the Western Union with a violation in that "defendant has been engaged in shipping telegraph messages in interstate commerce and in delivering telegraph messages for shipment in interstate commerce, the said goods having been produced in its said establishments in or about which the aforesaid minors were employed, suffered, and permitted to work within thirty (30) days prior to the removal of said goods therefrom."

Contention that this section is applicable to the Western Union is predicated on three steps, viz.: telegrams are "goods" within its meaning; the Company "produces" these goods within the Act because it "handles" them; and transmission is "shipment" within its terms. If it can maintain all three of these positions, the Government is entitled to an injunction; if it fails in any one, admittedly the effort to bring the employment under the Act must fail.

The Government says messages are "goods" because the Act defines "goods" as therein used to include among other things "articles or subjects of commerce of any character." § 3(i). Of course, statutory definitions of terms used therein prevail over colloquial meanings. It was long ago settled that telegraph lines when extending through different states are instruments of commerce itself. That "ideas, wishes, orders, and intelligence" are "subjects" of the interstate commerce in which telegraph companies engage has also been held. * * *. We think telegraphic messages are clearly "subjects of commerce" and hence that they are "goods" under this Act, as alleged in the complaint.

The next inquiry is whether the Western Union Telegraph Company is a producer of these goods within the Act. Congress has laid down a definition that as used in the Act "'produced' means produced, manufactured, mined, handled, or in any other manner worked on * * *." § 3(j). The company, says the Government, not only "handles" the message but "works on" it.

The Government contends that in defining "produced" the statute intends "handled" or "worked on" to mean not only handling or working on in relation to producing or making an article ready to enter interstate transit, but also includes the handling or working on which accomplishes the interstate transit or movement in commerce itself. If this construction is adopted, every transporter, transmitter, or mover in interstate commerce is a "producer" of any goods he carries. But the statute, while defining "produced" to mean "handled" or "worked on" has not defined "handled" or "worked on." These are terms of ordinary speech and mean what they mean in ordinary intercourse in this context. They serve a useful purpose when read to relate to all steps, whether manufacture or not, which lead to readiness for putting goods into the stream of commerce. One who packages a product, or bottles a liquid, or labels, or performs any number of tasks incidental to preparing for shipment might otherwise escape the Act, for in a sense he neither manufactures, produces, or mines the goods. We are clear that "handled" or "worked on" includes every kind of incidental operation preparatory to putting goods into the stream of commerce.

If we go beyond this and assume that handling for transit purposes is handling in production, we encounter results which we think Congress could not have intended. The definitions of this Act apply to the wage and hour provisions, as well as to the child labor provisions. Section 15 (a) makes it unlawful to transport or ship goods in the production of which any employee was employed in violation of the wage and hour provision. But it makes this exception: "except that no provision of this Act shall impose any liability upon any common carrier for the transportation in commerce in the regular course of its business of any goods *not produced by such common carrier*." (Emphasis added.) This recognizes a distinction between handling in transportation and producing, which is entirely put to naught by the Government's contention that by definition everyone who handles goods in carriage is thereby made a producer. The exception then is as if it read "the Act shall impose no liability on a common carrier for carrying goods that it does not carry." One would not readily impute such an absurdity to Congress; nor can we assume, contrary to the statute, that "produced" means one thing in one section and something else in another. To construe those words to mean that handling in carriage or transmission in commerce makes one a producer makes one of these results inevitable. Congress, we think, did not intend to obliterate all distinction between production and transportation. * * * We think the Government has not established its contention that the Western Union is a "producer" of the telegraph messages.

A third inquiry remains. Has the Company engaged in "shipping telegraph messages in interstate commerce and in delivering telegraph messages for shipment" as alleged? * * *

The statute applies the indirect sanctions of the Act only to those who "ship" subjects of commerce. It does not, however, define "ship". The Government says, "The verb 'ship' is an imprecise word meaning little more than to send or to transport." The term, not being artificially defined by statute, is from the ordinary speech of people. Its imprecision to linguists and scholars may be conceded. But if it is common in the courts, the market places or the schools of the country to speak of shipping a telegram or receiving a shipment of telegrams, we do not know of it, nor are examples of such usage called to our attention. * * * The fact is that to sustain the complaint we must supply an artificial definition of "ship," one which Congress had power to enact, but did not. We do not think "ship" in this Act applies to intangible messages, which we do not ordinarily speak of as being "shipped."

Another consideration convinces us that this Act did not contemplate its application by indirection to such a situation as we have in hand. Its indirect sanctions are well adapted to the producer, miner, manufacturer, or handler in preparation for commerce. They become clumsy and self-defeating when applied to telegraph companies, railroads, interstate news agencies, and the like, as this decree demonstrates. The Western Union is not forbidden by the decree to employ child labor, nor could it be, for it is not so forbidden by the Act. As construed by the courts below, what is prohibited is the sending of telegrams—so long as it employs child labor and for a period of thirty days after it quits. This, as the Company observes, is a sanction that the court could not permit to become effective. A suspension of telegraphic service for any period of time would be intolerable. * * *

* * * We think if Congress contemplated application of this Act to the Western Union it would have provided sanctions more suitable than to forbid telegrams to be sent by the only Company equipped on a nation-wide scale to serve the public in sending them. Nor will we believe without more express terms than we find here that Congress intended the courts to issue an injunction which as a practical matter they would have to let become a dead letter, or enforce at such cost to the public, if a defendant proved stubborn and recalcitrant. If the indirect sanctions of this Act were literally to be applied to great agencies of transportation and communication, the recoil on the public interest would be out of all proportion to the evil sought to be remedied.

However, the indirect sanction of cutting one's goods off from the interstate market is one which can be applied to producers, as we have defined them herein, effectively and without injury to the public interest. If such a producer using child labor is refused facilities to transport his goods, competitors usually come in, needs are still supplied, and only the offender suffers. These indirect sanctions can practically and literally be applied to the miner and the manufacturer with no substantial recoil on the public interest, and with no gestures by the courts that they cannot follow through to punish disobedience.

[Editor—Why does Justice Jackson now talk about what Congress might have contemplated? Previously he stated that Congress probably did not have anything in mind concerning the facts of the litigation.]

Reversed.

■ Mr. Justice Murphy, dissenting.

By reading into the Fair Labor Standards Act an exception that Congress never intended or specified, this Court has today granted the Western Union Telegraph Company a special dispensation to utilize the channels of interstate commerce while employing admittedly oppressive child labor. * * *

In approaching the problem of whether Western Union is a producer of goods shipped in interstate commerce we should not be unmindful of the humanitarian purposes which led Congress to adopt § 12(a). Oppressive child labor in any industry is a reversion to an outmoded and degenerate code of economic and social behavior. In the words of the Chief Executive, "A self-supporting and self-respecting democracy can plead no justification for the existence of child labor * * *." Message of the President to Congress, May 24, 1937, House Doc. No. 255 (75th Cong., 1st Sess.), p.20. * * * Courts should not disregard the legislative motive in interpreting and applying the statutory provisions that were adopted. If the existence of oppressive child labor in a particular instance falls within the obvious intent and spirit of § 12(a), we should not be too meticulous and exacting in dealing with the statutory language. To sacrifice social gains for the sake of grammatical perfection is not in keeping with the high traditions of the interpretative process. [Editor—How do you react to Justice Murphy's statement that we "should not be too meticulous and exacting in dealing with the statutory language." What does he emphasize?]

The language of § 12(a), when viewed realistically and with due regard for its purpose, compels the conclusion that Western Union has been guilty of a violation of the child labor provisions. Oppressive child labor conditions are admitted and the only issue concerns the application of the words "goods" and "producer" and "ships" to the activities of Western Union. * * *

[Editor—Justice Murphy then works his way through the critical language, consisting of "goods," "producer," and "ship." He does not dwell on "goods," because the majority held that telegraphic messages were "goods." He argues that Western Union did "handle" and "work on" the messages to put them in a condition for interstate transport. It was therefore a "producer," which did more than transport goods. He then turns to a discussion of the word "ship."]

3.   Finally, the majority does not think that the verb "ship" is applicable to the transmission either of electrical impulses or intangible messages and hence Western Union does not "ship" goods in commerce within the meaning of § 12(a). As a matter of linguistic purism, this conclusion is not without reasonableness. But proper respect for the legislative intent and the interpretative process does not demand fastidious adherence to linguistic purism. This Court does not require that Congress spell out all types of "goods" or "subject of commerce" that move in interstate commerce; no more should it require that Congress spell out every verb that may be in usage as to various goods or subjects of commerce. If the verb actually used by Congress may fairly be interpreted to cover the particular situation in a manner not at variance with the intent and spirit of the statute, no sound rule of law forbids such an interpretation. * * *

[Editor—Again, Justice Murphy refers to "intent and spirit" of the statute. Where does that come from? Why doesn't the majority opinion refer to "intent and spirit?"]

A word need be said about the Court's fear of enforcing § 12(a) against Western Union. * * *

However much we may dislike the imposition of Congressional sanctions against a particular industry or field of endeavor, the judicial function does not allow us to disregard that which Congress has plainly and constitutionally decreed and to formulate exceptions which we think for practical reasons, Congress might have made had it thought more about the problem. To read in exceptions based upon the nature or importance of the particular industry or corporation is dangerous precedent. If the suspension of telegraphic service for 30 days is so intolerable as to justify lifting the burden of § 12(a) from the shoulders of Western Union, can it not be argued with equal fervor that a 30-day injunction against interstate shipments by an airplane manufacturer, a munitions plant or some other industry vital to a war or peace time economy would be likewise intolerable? What valid distinction in this respect is there between interstate carriers and manufacturers or producers? Moreover, are we to examine the competitive situation or degree of importance of a particular company to determine the amount of intolerableness which a suspension of interstate transportation might be engender? These and countless other legislative problems present themselves when we embark upon a course of fashioned exceptions to a statute according to our own conceptions of appropriateness of the sanctions of an Act. Such a course is an open invitation to wholesale veto of valid and reasonable legislative provisions by means of judicial refusal to apply statutory enforcement measures. Adherence to the sound rule that inequities and hardships arising from the statutory sanctions are for Congress rather than the courts to remedy by way of amendment to the statute is desirable and necessary in such a situation.

We are charged with the duty of interpreting and applying acts of Congress in accordance with the legislative intent. Courts are not so impotent that they cannot perform that duty and, at the same time, grant stays or other appropriate relief in the public interest should the occasion demand it. Thus if the injunction is granted here against Western Union, we will have vindicated to that extent the public policy against oppressive child labor. If a 30 day suspension of telegraph messages would unduly harm the public interest, a stay of the mandate or of the injunction can be granted until at least 30 days have elapsed during which no oppressive child labor has been employed by Western Union. Thus by fashioning remedies through injunctions and stays we can aid in the elimination of oppressive child labor without undue hardship on the public. This can and should be done without abdicating our judicial function and assuming the role of the legislature.

The Court of Appeals and District Court, unlike the Supreme Court, both found against Western Union. Here is some of what each of them said.

Lenroot v. Western Union Telegraph Co.

141 F.2d 400 (2d Cir.1944).

■ L. Hand, Circuit Judge.

* * * Congress could unquestionably have forbidden the employment of the messengers and drivers here in question, if it had wished. That does not, however, answer the question whether [the statute] covers the business; and it does not do so, unless the defendant is a "producer" of "goods" which it "ships" in interstate commerce. While it is of course true that, taken in their colloquial sense, these words do not apply to its activities, they should not be so taken, for the statute has made its own definitions in § 203. Subdivision (i) of that section reads as follows: " 'Goods' means goods * * * wares, products, commodities, merchandise, or articles or subjects of commerce of any character." (Originally the words, "or subjects," were absent; they were added in the Senate Committee on Education and Labor.) Subdivision (j) reads: "'Produced' means produced, manufactured, mined, handled, or in any other manner worked on."

In order to learn whether the defendant's business falls within the [statute], we must consider exactly what steps sending a telegram comprises. Ordinarily, it is true, the sender thinks of the telegram as the actual transmission of his words to the addressee; and so he speaks of "sending" it and of its being "delivered," as though the same thing had left him, passed to the addressee's home or office and was there handed to him. Indeed, the defendant itself uses that very argument in order to bring itself within the exception in § 215(a)(1) which exempts common carriers from the act as to any goods not produced by them. It does no more, it says, than transport to the addressee intangible objects—the sender's words transformed into electric impulses; it "produces" no "goods," even though we read those words with their definitions. We might indeed agree, if the defendant did no more than carry written messages between the parties; conceivably the same might even be true, if it only provided means—like a telephone—by which the parties could communicate, though these consisted of pulsations of an electric current. But neither of these is what the defendant does. The sender either writes out his message on paper and delivers it to one of the defendant's messengers, or delivers it himself at one of the defendant's offices; or he dictates or telephones it to an employee at an office, who takes it down on paper in shorthand, or types it. The message so received never leaves that office; the addressee never sees it. Another employee—or perhaps the same one—either uses it as a text for pressing a key in suitable dots and dashes, having a conventional significance to him and to another employee at the opposite end of a wire; or as a text for manipulating some other suitable device—like a "teletype"—by which equivalent movements will appear upon a similar device at the end of a wire. In either case nothing can be said to be "sent" between the office except pulsations of electrical current, which are not only not the sender's message, but would be totally incomprehensible to him or to the addressee, if either could perceive them. When these have been transmitted, they are either translated, if they are in code, or transcribed, if they are not; and the message so resulting is delivered either by messenger or by telephone to the addressee. From the foregoing it is at once apparent that there is not the least similarity between what the defendant does and the transportation of goods by a common carrier. It is also apparent that the defendant's activities are within the definition of "produced" in subdivision (j) of § 203; for, not only does it "handle" the sender's message, but it "works on" it, first, by changing it into something wholly different, and then by changing it back to a form like the original.

The only remaining question is whether the defendant "ships" any "goods." First, are there any "goods" concerned? To prove that there are the plaintiff relies upon the phrase, "subjects of commerce of any character" in subdivision (i); to which the defendant answers that we must judge that phrase by its context, which necessarily limits its meaning to "tangible" objects. It is here that the Senate amendment becomes important. Until that was made the subdivision had read: "wares, products, commodities, merchandise or articles of commerce of any character." So far as we can see, no more complete enumeration could have been made of every kind of "tangible"; so that, when the Senate expanded the phrase to include, not only "articles" of commerce, but "subjects" of commerce, the opposition would have meant nothing, if it had not included "intangibles." Moreover, not only had all kinds of "tangibles" been already included, but "subjects of commerce" was not a good description of "tangibles." Its introduction into a phrase which had been sufficient to include all kinds of "tangibles," cannot be set down to tautology, or slovenly draughting; it demands that some additional significance be added. We need not with the plaintiff resort to opinions such as those of Johnson, J., in Gibbons v. Ogden, 9 Wheat. 1, 229, 230, in which the transmission of "intelligence" is spoken of as a "subject" of commerce. It is enough that we have unmistakable evidence of a purpose to extend the definition of subdivision (i) to everything which had been considered a "subject of commerce": that is, to whatever Congress could regulate as such a subject. Last, we have to say whether, assuming that a message received for transmission is "goods," and that the defendant "produces" it, it also "ships" the message, when it sends the pulsations over the telegraph wires. Although that is indeed an inappropriate word to apply to "intangibles," its unfitness for the most part disappears, once we treat messages as "goods." Certainly we should stultify ourselves, having gone so far, if we were to refuse to understand it as covering what is here involved.

Lenroot v. Western Union Telegraph Co.

52 F.Supp. 142 (D.N.Y.1943).

■ Rifkind, District Judge. * * *

Defendant is engaged in the transmission and delivery of telegraph messages throughout the United States and in foreign countries. * * *

* * * Are the activities of the defendant subject to the child labor provisions of the Act? * * * It is the contention of defendant that it is not a "producer, manufacturer or dealer," that it does not "ship or deliver for shipment in commerce any goods." It is engaged, the defendant argues, in the transmission of ideas, whereas the statute governs only the shipment of tangible goods. Plaintiff argues that there is no such limiting language expressed in the statute and that no such limiting intention can be discovered in the policy and history of the statute.

A brief description of what actually occurs at the establishments of the defendant has been stipulated. [Editor—Description omitted.]

* * *

Congressional attempts to deal with child labor nationally began with the introduction of bills in 1906. It was 10 years, however, before Congress enacted the first Federal Child Labor Law, 39 Stat. 675, c. 432, which extended only to factories, manufacturing establishments, canneries, workshops, mines and quarries. This law was declared unconstitutional. Hammer v. Dagenhart, 1918, 247 U.S. 251. Congress immediately thereafter made an attempt to regulate child labor by the use of the taxation power. 40 Stat. 1138, c. 18. This, too, was declared unconstitutional by the Supreme Court. Bailey v. Drexel Furniture Co., 1922, 259 U.S. 20. In 1924, Congress submitted to the States, for ratification, a proposed amendment to the Constitution, authorizing Congress "to limit, regulate and prohibit the labor of persons under 18 years of age." It has been ratified by 28 States.

Under the National Industrial Recovery Act, 48 Stat. 195, 576 Codes were adopted, each of them containing minimum age provisions. After Schechter Poultry Corp. v. United States, 1935, 295 U.S. 495, which declared that Act unconstitutional, the number of children leaving school for work sharply increased.

The legislative history of the child labor provisions of the Fair Labor Standards Act began with a message from the President to the Congress on May 24, 1937, Senate Report 884, 75th Congress, First Session. [Editor—The court discusses the various proposals. It notes that differences were not resolved until a conference committee reported the bill in the form in which it was enacted. And that the Act was held constitutional in United States v. Darby, 1941, 312 U.S. 100.]

The history of the statute is consistent only with the conclusion that Congress intended to keep the arteries of commerce free from pollution by the sweat of child labor. To accomplish this result with the least difficulty, the law prohibited the introduction into the stream of commerce, not only of the products of child labor but of all of the products of an establishment where any child labor had been employed within 30 days. In view of the breadth of the congressional policy, the opening hypothesis should be that the defendant is subject to the Act unless reason for lack of application is clearly shown. (I am not speaking of the burden of proof, since the case presents no issues of fact.) * * *

Defendant's chief reliance is upon the "obvious and natural import of the language." The words "producer" and "goods" especially when used in a context with "ship," it is contended, require a construction of the statute which limits its application to producers of goods that can be shipped, or tangible goods.

Reliance upon the common meaning of the terms employed is misplaced when Congress has enacted definitions which necessarily displace both the dictionary and common usage as authority for the meanings of the words employed. Thus, under the statute, "produced" includes "handled, or in any other manner worked on." Section 3(j). "Goods" includes "articles or subjects of commerce of any character." Section 3(i). * * * [T]he insertion of "subjects of commerce" seems insistently to demand that tangibility shall not be the required attribute of the goods. The phrase "subjects of commerce" has a history which the manifest professional draftsmanship of the statute must be deemed to have recognized. [Editor—Discussion of the definition of "goods" omitted.]

Once we reach the conclusion that the messages telegraphed by defendant are goods within the meaning of the statute, there is not much difficulty in finding that these goods are produced in the defendant's establishments. Clearly they are "handled" and "worked on." In the light of the statutory definition the argument that the defendant simply transmits the ideas of its customers and that it is not a producer, must fall as a matter of law. It falls also as a matter of fact, for it is the work of the defendant which transmutes the ideas of the customers into telegraphic messages by means of a series of changes and processes already described.

More troublesome is the question whether the defendant "shipped" goods in commerce. The word "ship" is not defined by the statute. Since the verb, "shipped," is derived from the noun, "ship," linguistic purists might limit its connotation to transportation by water. Common usage, however, has long sanctioned the use of the phrases, to ship by rail, or to ship by air, or to ship by truck. It is used synonymously with transport and convey. The defendant conveys its messages by wire. The Supreme Court has spoken of the telegraph companies as engaged in "transportation." It has called the defendant a "carrier of messages" and compared it to a railroad, as a "carrier of goods." Western Union Teleg. Co. v. Texas, 1881, 105 U.S. 460, 464.

I do not think that Congress intended to limit the application of the Act to the conventional modes of shipment. Its broad policy was to keep the streams of interstate commerce undefiled by the products of child labor. It is a remedial statute entitled to liberal interpretation. * * *

CHAPTER 7

EXTERNAL CONTEXT—
BACKGROUND CONSIDERATIONS

By now it should be clear why judicial use of external context can be controversial. That context includes substantive background considerations (that is, substantive values) and it is often difficult for the interpreter to avoid judging the weight to which those values are entitled when determining statutory meaning. We have already seen this in two settings—(1) in the use of substantive canons (Chapter 3—the derogation and rule of lenity canons); and (2) to influence the interaction purpose and text (Chapter 6—Chisom v. Roemer). In this Chapter we look more closely at how substantive background considerations enter into the interpretive process.

We first consider an analytical framework for thinking about how substantive background considerations influence statutory meaning—do they take the form of canons or are they less structured and more *ad hoc*; what is the source of the values embodied in the background considerations; and does the judge who relies on these values implement likely legislative intent or impose values external to the statute on the interpretive process?

We next look at how two substantive canons interact with the statute—the federalism canon protecting states from undue federal interference, and the canon presuming that statutes are prospective. We are especially interested in whether substantive background considerations in canonical form minimize judicial discretion.

Finally, we look at the most basic background consideration of all—the type of document being interpreted. Although the same interpretive criteria may be relevant for all documents, their weights vary depending on the document's function in our political/legal system.

7.01 ANALYTICAL FRAMEWORK

There are three questions a judge must address in deciding how substantive context values affect statutory interpretation. They are summarized here and then discussed below:

1. Are the values embodied in more or less clear background rules (a substantive canon of construction) or are they identified on a more *ad hoc* basis?

2. What is the source of those values—the constitution; tradition; contemporary views; something else?

3. Are the values identified by the judge likely to be those the legislature would implement, or are they brought to the statute by the judicial reader, or both?

a) SUBSTANTIVE CANONS OR AD HOC APPROACHES

Substantive background considerations have been with us for a long time in the form of substantive canons of interpretation. We saw how the derogation and lenity canons worked in Chapter 3 and this Chapter will look at the federalism and presumption-of-prospective-statutes canons.

Substantive background considerations also come in more *ad hoc* form. The Golden Rule (avoid "absurd" results), and Chief Justice Marshall's variation on that rule—requiring a clear statement to override fundamental principles (see Chapter 2)—are concerned with values that are not embodied in canonical form. And, as Chapter 6 illustrated, specific noncanonical values can influence the weight attributed to statutory purpose.

You might think that a textualist would balk at bringing substantive values to the statute but that is not an accurate description of at least some modern textualists. Recall Justice Scalia's commitment to the canons in his dissent in Chisom v. Roemer—"I thought we had adopted a regular method for interpreting the meaning of language in a statute: first, find the ordinary meaning of the language in its textual context; and second, *using established canons of construction*, ask whether there is any clear indication that some permissible meaning other than the ordinary one applies (emphasis added)."

And Scalia would also apply the Golden Rule, as he explains in the following excerpt from Green v. Bock Laundry Machine Co., 490 U.S. 504 (1989). This case involved a *civil* defendant who wanted to impeach the plaintiff's credibility with evidence of the plaintiff's prior felony conviction. Federal Rule of Evidence 609(a) provides:

> General Rule. For the purpose of attacking the credibility of a witness, evidence that the witness has been convicted of a crime shall be admitted if elicited from the witness or established by public record during cross-examination but only if the crime (1) was punishable by death or imprisonment in excess of one year under the law under which the witness was convicted, and the court determines that the probative value of admitting this evidence outweighs its prejudicial effect to the defendant, or (2) involved dishonesty or false statement, regardless of the punishment.

The Rule was, however, silent regarding impeachment of a plaintiff, apparently permitting impeachment of a plaintiff without weighing prejudicial effect. The Court held, after an exhaustive review of legislative history, that the Rule applied only to *criminal* defendants. This meant that the rule did not require balancing probative value and the prejudicial effects of impeachment evidence based on a prior conviction when either a civil plaintiff or civil defendant wanted to impeach the adversary.

Justice Scalia concurred in the judgment, based primarily on the potentially absurd result of a literal reading of the Rule. He stated:

> We are confronted here with a statute which, if interpreted literally, produces an absurd, and perhaps unconstitutional, result. Our task is to give some alternative meaning to the word "defendant" in Federal Rule of Evidence 609(a)(1) that avoids this consequence * * *.
>
> * * * The meaning of terms on the statute books ought to be determined, not on the basis of which meaning can be shown to have been understood by a larger handful of the Members of Congress; but rather on the basis of which meaning is (1) most in accord with context and ordinary usage, and thus most likely to have been understood by the whole Congress which voted on the words of the statute (not to mention the citizens subject to it), and (2) most compatible with the surrounding body of law into which the provision must be integrated—a compatibility which, by a benign fiction, we assume Congress always has in mind. [Editor—Notice Justice Scalia's reference to a "benign fiction" about what Congress had in mind, apparently conceding that judicial reliance on substantive background considerations is not an effort to identify likely legislative intent.] I would not permit any of the historical and legislative material discussed by the Court, or all of it combined, to lead me to a result different from the one that these factors suggest.
>
> I would analyze this case, in brief, as follows:
>
> (1) The word "defendant" in Rule 609(a)(1) cannot rationally (or perhaps even constitutionally) mean to provide the benefit of prejudice-weighing to civil defendants and not civil plaintiffs. Since petitioner has not produced, and we have not ourselves discovered, even a snippet of support for this absurd result, we may confidently assume that the word was not used (as it normally would be) to refer to all defendants and only all defendants.
>
> (2) The available alternatives are to interpret "defendant" to mean (a) "civil plaintiff, civil defendant, prosecutor, and criminal defendant," (b) "civil plaintiff and defendant and criminal defendant," or (c) "criminal defendant." Quite obviously, the last does least violence to the text. It adds a qualification that the word "defendant" does not contain but, unlike the others, does not give the word a meaning ("plaintiff" or "prosecutor") it simply will not bear. The qualification it adds, moreover, is one that could understandably have been omitted by inadvertence—and sometimes is omitted in normal conversation ("I believe strongly in defendants' rights"). Finally, this last interpretation is consistent with the policy of the law in general and the Rules of Evidence in particular of providing special protection to defendants in criminal cases. * * *
>
> For the reasons stated, I concur in the judgment of the Court.

Why might Justice Scalia embrace substantive canons and the Golden Rule but not otherwise countenance judges bringing substantive background considerations to the statute? Are the canons or "absurdity" so clear that they minimize judicial discretion.

b) SOURCE OF VALUES

What is the source of substantive values on which the judicial reader relies in statutory interpretation? Is it the Constitution; tradition; contemporary views; something else? Does the source of values help determine whether they are "fundamental?"

Some values fit every category, but some have a less secure pedigree. The substantive canons of construction discussed in Chapter 2 are illustrative. The narrow interpretation of statutes in derogation of common law embodied a strong tradition and had the contemporary support of some judges, but lacked a secure constitutional foundation and was a very controversial obstacle to contemporary reform legislation. By contrast, the rule of lenity echoes the Constitution's concern with protecting the criminal accused, has a long tradition, and some contemporary support. Perhaps that is why Pound did not characterize the rule of lenity canon as "spurious" (see Chapter 3).

COMMENTS AND QUESTIONS

1. Is judicial reliance on tradition self-justifying? Justice Scalia implies as much in the following case.[1] In Holmes v. Securities Investor Protection Corp., 503 U.S. 258 (1992), the Court dealt with the requirements for plaintiffs to recover civil damages under the Racketeer Influenced Organizations Act (RICO). Justice Scalia's concurring opinion read common law proximate cause requirements into the statute, which said nothing about causation, stating:

> [Proximate cause] is required in RICO not so much because RICO has language similar to that of the Clayton Act, which in turn has language similar to that of the Sherman Act, which by the time the Clayton Act had been passed, had been interpreted to include a proximate cause requirement; but rather, I think, because it has always been the practice of common-law courts (and probably of all courts, under all legal systems) to require as a condition of recovery, unless the legislature specifically prescribes otherwise, that the injury have been proximately caused by the offending conduct.

---

1. Cf. Board of County Comm'rs. v. Umbehr, 116 S.Ct. 2342 (1996)(Scalia, J., dissenting)("As I have explained, I would separate the permissible from the impermissible on the basis of our Nation's traditions, which is what I believe sound constitutional adjudication requires.")

2. The role of the Constitution as a source of context values should not be confused with judicial reliance on constitutional values to avoid an interpretation which raises constitutional doubts. In many cases there is no doubt about the legislature's constitutional power, but the legislature threatens to impinge on interests with constitutional significance. For example, although legislation creating crimes and burdening states may sometimes violate the Constitution, there is a clear range of legislative activity achieving these results which is constitutional but which nonetheless potentially harms constitutionally-inspired values (protecting the criminal accused and preserving federalism). These values support the rule of lenity (Chapter 3) and the "federalism" canon (discussed later in this chapter). Rather than let the Constitution do all the substantive work, the court might adopt constitutionally-inspired values as rebuttable presumptions about statutory meaning.

3. What is the source of the values used by judges in the following situations?

a. The canon interpreting statutes to liberally achieve a statute's remedial purposes?

b. Justice Stevens' opinion in Chisom v. Roemer?

c. Justice Jackson's concern in Lenroot about the impact of an injunction on the nation's commerce?

c) LEGISLATIVE INTENT OR JUDICIAL READER?

Are the values on which the judge relies likely to be those the legislature would implement, or are they brought to the statute by the judicial reader, or both?

Do not assume that substantive background considerations are more likely to be good guesses about legislative intent just because they influence the weight attributed to the statute's purpose. Indeed, a major objection to purposivism is that it disguises judicial preferences as legislative intent. Some background considerations that have nothing to do with purpose may provide excellent guesses about likely legislative intent. Holy Trinity's concern about religion is a prominent example—it is unlikely the legislature would have criminalized importing a pastor.

Sometimes it is very clear that the judicial reader is bringing values to bear on statutory interpretation that are not likely to be good guesses about legislative intent. This occurs frequently with the substantive canons of interpretation and the next section provides you with material to evaluate this claim.

7.02   "PLAIN STATEMENT" CANONS

In this section we look closely at two substantive canons—avoid burdening the states and the presumption that statutes are prospective. These canons are often said to impose plain statement (or clear statement) requirements if the legislature wants to reject the values they embody,[2] which should remind you of the typology of presumptions discussed in Chapter 3—*weak* presumption as a tie-breaker; *strong* presumption insists on powerful evidence that the statute overrides certain substantive values (a plain statement rule); and an *in-between* presumption inserting values as a significant factor in the interpretive mix of text, purpose, and substantive background considerations. As you read the following materials, consider whether the canons operate to impose a plain statement rule—a "strong" presumption—or something less than a strong presumption. Do the canons provide the judge with a certain enough guide to minimize judicial discretion?

a) AVOID BURDENING STATES

The canon against burdening states has been invoked in numerous settings, including the following:

1. To prevent inferring that a federal statute overrides State sovereign immunity in federal courts; Atascadero State Hosp. v. Scanlon, 473 U.S. 234, 242 (1985)("Congress may abrogate the States' constitutionally secured immunity from suit in federal court only by making its intention unmistakably clear in the language of the statute."). The state's immunity in federal court is affirmed by the Eleventh Amendment to the Constitution—"The Judicial power of the United States shall not be construed to extend to any suit in law or equity, commenced or prosecuted against one of the United States by Citizens of another State, or by Citizens or Subjects of any Foreign State."[3]

2. To prevent inferring a cause of action against States; Pennhurst State School and Hospital v. Halderman, 451 U.S. 1, 17, 23 (1981)(federal grant-in-aid legislation is like a contract; if Congress wants to impose as a grant condition that there is a cause of action against the state, "it must do so unambiguously"; the statute in this case lacks the necessary "conditional language").

3. To prevent inferring that a federal statute interferes with areas traditionally regulated by States; Gregory v. Ashcroft, 501 U.S. 452, 460, 464 (1991)(federal prohibition of mandatory retirement age did not apply to appointed state judges; the States' power to determine judicial qualifications was a "fundamental" state function, traditionally regulated by the States, and the Court "must be absolutely certain that Congress intended" such intrusion; the

---

2. See generally Eskridge & Frickey, Quasi–Constitutional Law: Clear Statement Rules as Constitutional Lawmaking, 45 Vand. L. Rev. 593 (1992); Eskridge, Public Values in Statutory Interpretation, 137 U. Pa. L. Rev. 1007 (1989); Nagle, Waiving Sovereign Immunity in an Age of Clear Statement Rules, 1995 Wis. L. Rev. 771.

3. State immunity in federal court also extends to suits against a state by its own citizens. Hans v. Louisiana, 134 U.S. 1 (1890).

Court quoted from Atascadero, supra—the intrusion must be "unmistakably clear in the language of the statute").

These cases seem to answer many of the questions posed in the prior discussion of judicial reliance on substantive context values.

First, judicial invocation of the canon against burdening States is probably not a guess about legislative intent, but a substantive norm which can only be overridden by explicit legislation. This explains why the Court's commitment to the canon perseveres in the face of several congressional overrides of its decisions.[4] It also explains why only the statutory text, not legislative history, can provide the plain statement rejecting the substantive canon. See, e.g., Atascadero, supra ("Congress may abrogate [sovereign immunity] only by making its intention unmistakably clear in the language of the statute"). This contrasts with reliance on legislative history to determine whether an absurd result was really intended by the legislature. See Green v. Bock Laundry Machine Co., 490 U.S., at 527 (Scalia, J.)("it [is] entirely appropriate to consult * * * the legislative history [ ], to verify that what seems to us an unthinkable disposition (civil defendants but not civil plaintiffs receive the benefit of weighing prejudice) was indeed unthought of * * *.").

Second, the Court bases the plain statement canon against burdening States on constitutionally-inspired values. Atascadero (473 U.S. at 242) recognized that State immunity in federal courts rested on the Eleventh Amendment; Pennhurst (451 U.S. at 17) relied on Eleventh Amendment immunity cases as an analogy for refusing to infer a cause of action against the States; (Gregory (501 U.S. at 462) relied on the Tenth Amendment, preserving to the States and the people those powers not delegated to the United States).

This claim—that the plain statement requirement rests only on constitutionally-inspired values, and not on a constitutional mandate—may need to be qualified. There is a growing number of Justices who would expand constitutional barriers against burdening the states, at least where the issue is jurisdiction over states in federal court. The Court in a 1996 case—Seminole Tribe of Florida v. Florida[5]—held (5–4) that Congress could not abrogate state immunity in federal court when acting under the Article I Commerce Clause, overruling Pennsylvania v. Union Gas Co., 491 U.S. 1 (1989). It is unclear how far this decision will carry. It rests on the view that state sovereign immunity is hard-wired into the Constitution, as a part of the "fundamental jurisprudence in all civilized nations." 116 S.Ct. at 1130. This probably means that Congress cannot abrogate state sovereign immunity in federal court when acting under other Article I powers, such as bankruptcy and copyright. To the extent there are real constitutional questions about the

---

4. After the decision in Atascadero, Congress overrode the result in Rehabilitation Act Amendments of 1988, Pub. L., 99–506, § 1003, 100 Stat. 1807, 1845. Then, in Dellmuth v. Muth, 491 U.S. 223 (1989), the Court applied the canon in another State sovereign immunity case, which Congress overrode in the Education of the Handicapped Act Amendments of 1990, Pub. L. 101–476, § 103, 104 Stat. 1103, 1106.

5. 116 S.Ct. 1114 (1996).

reach of federal legislative power, the statute might be interpreted to avoid those doubts.

However, there are some areas where Congress clearly can legislate to override state sovereign immunity in federal court and the interpretive issue, based on constitutionally-inspired values, persists. For example, the Seminole case explicitly affirmed that Congress had the power to abrogate state immunity when acting under the 14th Amendment.[6] And Congress probably can continue to condition a grant-in-aid on a waiver of state immunity in federal court.[7]

As the prior discussion suggests, the plain statement canon against burdening the States and the constitutional status of federalism concerns have been controversial. First, the canon's ascendancy to a strong plain statement requirement is (some argue) relatively new. Until recently, the canon was part of the interpretive mix, permitting persuasive evidence of legislative intent to establish that the statute burdened the States.[8]

Second, the strength of the constitutional values underlying the canon is strongly contested. The Constitution's Supremacy Clause (Article VI), stating that federal law "shall be the supreme law of the Land," is a rival to federalism principles. The current Supreme Court, however, believes strongly in federalism principles. Justice Brennan's rejection of the view that the Eleventh Amendment is grounded in "principles essential to the structure of our federal system" appeared in a *dissent* in Atascadero (473 U.S. at 247–48). And, as noted above, the Supreme Court in the Seminole case (116 S.Ct. 1114 (1996)) has denied Congress the power to legislate away the state's sovereign immunity when acting under the Article I Commerce Clause (over a long and thoroughly researched dissent by Justice Souter (116 S.Ct. at 1145–85)). The dissent argued that, although sovereign immunity existed when the Constitution was adopted as an element of the common law, it could be superseded by legislation, like other common law principles. (Souter's dissent stresses the "pervasive understanding" at the time of the Founding that the common law "was always subject to legislative amendment.") The Court claimed instead that sovereign immunity was even more basic than the common law, "[finding] its roots, not solely in the common law [ ], but in the much more fundamental 'jurisprudence in all civilized nations.' "

---

6. See Fitzpatrick v. Bitzer, 427 U.S. 445 (1976)(Congress can burden States when acting under the 14th Amendment).

7. See South Dakota v. Dole, 483 U.S. 203 (1987)(Congress can impose conditions acting under the Constitution's Spending Clause if they are based on the General Welfare). A constitutional issue remains whether the condition is sufficiently related to the grant-in-aid program to justify the federal grant imposing a waiver of state sovereign immunity.

8. Dellmuth, 491 U.S. at 239–42 (Brennan, J., dissenting). See generally Eskridge & Frickey, Quasi–Constitutional Law: Clear Statement Rules as Constitutional Lawmaking, 45 Vand. L. Rev. 593 (1992).

Third, it is unclear just what is needed to satisfy a plain statement requirement. For example, in Dellmuth v. Muth, 491 U.S. 223 (1989), Justice Scalia accepted the plain statement canon to protect States from loss of state sovereign immunity in federal court, but argued that the text did not have to refer explicitly to state sovereignty or the Eleventh Amendment (which provides immunity) to subject States to suit.

Fourth, the canon's application to cases not involving State immunity in federal courts (that is, where the Eleventh Amendment is not implicated) has been uneven.[9] For example, in Evans v. United States, 504 U.S. 255 (1992), the Court held that the federal Hobbs Act definition of "extortion" included bribery. A major impact of this decision was to apply federal criminal law to state officials. The dissent objected that

> [t]he Court's construction of the Hobbs Act is repugnant not only to the basic tenets of criminal justice reflected in the rule of lenity, but also to basic tenets of federalism. Over the past 20 years, the Hobbs Act has served as the engine for a stunning expansion of federal criminal jurisdiction into a field traditionally policed by state and local laws—acts of public corruption by state and local officials. * * *
>
> * * * [C]oncerns of federalism require us to give a narrow construction to federal legislation in such sensitive areas unless Congress' contrary intent is "unmistakably clear in the language of the statute." Gregory v. Ashcroft, 111 S.Ct. 2395, 2401 (1991).

And in City of Edmonds v. Oxford House, Inc., 115 S.Ct. 1776 (1995), the Court (in an opinion by Justice Ginsburg) held that federal anti-discrimination law *was* applicable to a city zoning rule. The federal Fair Housing Act (FHA) prohibited discrimination in housing against persons with handicaps, but exempted "any reasonable local, State, or Federal restrictions regarding the maximum number of occupants permitted to occupy a dwelling." The City's zoning code, governing areas zoned for single-family dwelling units, defined "family" as "persons [without regard to number] related by genetics, adoption, or marriage, or a group of five or fewer [unrelated] persons." The City argued that a group home for 10 to 12 adults recovering from alcoholism and drug addiction violated the zoning law because it operated in a neighborhood zoned for single-family residences.

The Court held in favor of the group home. The City's zoning code provision was not exempt from the anti-discrimination provision of the FHA because it was a *land use* restriction, not a *maximum occupancy* restriction. A dissent, written by Justice Thomas, argued that the decision violated the interpretive approach taken in Gregory v. Ashcroft because "land use—the subject of petitioner's zoning code—is an area traditionally regulated by the States rather than by Congress, and that land use regulation is one of the historic powers of the States."

9. Justice White's dissent in Pennhurst (451 U.S. at 48 n.14) argued that it did not apply outside the Eleventh Amendment context.

The Court responded to the dissent's argument by distinguishing Gregory, on the ground that Gregory involved a "state constitutional provision, not a local ordinance * * *,—a provision going beyond an area traditionally regulated by the States" to implicate "a decision of the most fundamental sort for a sovereign entity." (Gregory refused to interpret a federal prohibition of mandatory age requirements to apply to state judges.)

———

In the following case, the Court revisited the plain statement canon against burdening the States. The case involved whether a federal statute (Federal Employers' Liability Act—FELA) created a cause of action against the States enforceable in *state* court. The Eleventh Amendment was not implicated, because it only applies to suits in federal court. The Court upholds the cause of action but sends uncertain signals about whether the canon survives in its strong plain statement form when the issue is whether there is a cause of action against a state in state court. The decision rests on *stare decisis* grounds, denying that recent cases favoring the canon require overruling the earlier Parden case, which had inferred a cause of action against the States.

The Court draws a very questionable distinction between interpreting statutes to permit a lawsuit in federal court and to infer a cause of action enforceable in state court, claiming that the former involves *constitutional* law, but the latter involves only *statutory interpretation*. Isn't statutory interpretation relevant in both situations, the only question being how strong the constitutionally-inspired values are in each instance. Arguably, constitutional values are more significant when the issue is whether the statute implies a waiver of sovereign immunity in federal court (for example, by accepting federal money in a grant-in-aid program), rather than inferring a cause of action against the state in state court, because the state would be hauled into a potentially unfriendly federal court. But the issue is statutory interpretation in both instances.[10]

The Court's distinction between constitutional law and statutory interpretation is presented in response to Justice O'Connor's dissent, which appears to argue that the Constitution is as potent in preventing states from being sued for damages in state as in federal court. Her dissent comes five years before the decision in Seminole, but may have been a precursor of a broad constitutional holding that Congress cannot abrogate state sovereignty

10. You should note that the sovereign immunity issue regarding suits in federal court is no longer one of statutory interpretation based on constitutionally-inspired values in the FELA setting, because that federal legislation is based on the Commerce Clause, and the 1996 Seminole case, *supra*, held that the Constitution prohibited forcing a state to waive sovereign immunity in federal court when Congress acted under the Article I Commerce Clause. In other instances, however, such as legislation enforcing the 14th Amendment and grant-in-aid programs, the

immunity in state as well as in federal court.[11] If that is correct, it would moot any discussion of whether Congress intended to create a cause of action against the states in state court. But, under Supreme Court precedent when Hilton was decided (in 1991), Congress could constitutionally abrogate state sovereign immunity when acting under the Commerce Clause, even in *federal court*. The meaning of federal legislation regarding suits against states in federal *and* state court were issues of statutory interpretation, albeit influenced by constitutionally-inspired values. And that continues to be true when Congress clearly retains the right to abrogate state sovereign immunity (under the 14th Amendment, for example).

Hilton v. South Carolina Public Railways Comm'n.

502 U.S. 197 (1991).

■ Justice Kennedy delivered the opinion of the Court.

In this case we must decide whether the Federal Employers' Liability Act (FELA), creates a cause of action against a state-owned railroad, enforceable in state court. We hold that it does, reaffirming in part our decision in Parden v. Terminal Railway of Alabama State Docks Dept., 377 U.S. 184 (1964).

Petitioner Kenneth Hilton was an employee of the South Carolina Public Railways Commission. The Commission, which has some 300 employees, is a common carrier engaged in interstate commerce by railroad and is an agency of the State of South Carolina, having been created by statute in 1969. Hilton alleges he was injured in the scope and course of his employment and that the negligence of the Commission was the cause of the accident. In the case now before us the Commission is the respondent.

To recover for his injuries, petitioner first filed a FELA action in United States District Court. That case was pending when we announced our decision in Welch v. Texas Dept. of Highways and Public Transportation, 483 U.S. 468 (1987), which held that the Jones Act, does not abrogate the States' Eleventh Amendment immunity. The Jones Act incorporates the remedial scheme of FELA; and, based on his understanding that Eleventh Amendment immunity from Jones Act suits would apply as well to FELA, petitioner dismissed his federal court action. He refiled his FELA suit in a South Carolina state court, and this is the case now before us. * * *

issue of waiver of sovereign immunity is still an issue of statutory interpretation.

11. Creating a cause of action against the state in *state* court may violate the Tenth Amendment ("The powers not delegated to the United States by the Constitution, nor prohibited by it to the States, are reserved to the States respectively, or to the people"). In New York v. United States, 505 U.S. 144 (1992), the Court held that the federal government could not directly compel passage of a law by the state legislature. Although the New York case went out of its way to distinguish and reaffirm Testa v. Katt, 330 U.S. 386 (1947), which forces state courts to enforce federal statutes, the issue of state sovereign immunity in state court may still raise Tenth Amendment concerns.

In Parden we held that FELA authorizes suits for damages against state-owned railroads, and that by entering the business of operating a railroad a State waives its Eleventh Amendment immunity from suit in federal court. The latter holding was overruled in Welch, to accord with our more recent Eleventh Amendment jurisprudence, but the Welch Court was explicit in declining to decide whether in the Jones Act (or in FELA), Congress intended to create a cause of action against the States. In other words, the Welch decision did not disturb the statutory-construction holding of Parden.

[Editor—After the Seminole case, *supra*, the FELA could not *constitutionally* force the state to waive sovereign immunity in federal court, because it relied on the federal commerce power. The interpretive question regarding waiver of state sovereign immunity in federal court would, however, persist if Congress were legislating pursuant to the 14th Amendment.]

In addressing the latter issue [regarding inference of a cause of action against states], the South Carolina court found "dispositive" our decision in Will v. Michigan Dept. of State Police, 491 U.S. 58 (1989). Will was a suit brought in state court under 42 U.S.C. § 1983 against the State of Michigan. We held that the State is not a "person" as that term is used in § 1983, and is not suable under the statute, regardless of the forum where the suit is maintained. In so holding, we relied in part on the lack of any "clear statement" in the statute of a congressional intent to impose liability on the State. * * * [T]he South Carolina court read Will to hold that a statute will not be interpreted to create a cause of action for money damages against a State unless it contains "unmistakably clear language" showing the Congress intended to do so. * * *

Our analysis and ultimate determination in this case are controlled and informed by the central importance of stare decisis in this Court's jurisprudence. Respondents ask us to overrule a 28–year-old interpretation, first enunciated in Parden, that when Congress enacted FELA and used the phrase "[e]very common carrier by railroad," to describe the class of employers subject to its terms, it intended to include state-owned railroads. * * * The issue here is whether we should reexamine this longstanding statutory construction. * * * [Editor—The Court then observes that stare decisis is especially applicable in cases of statutory interpretation, because Congress is free to override the decision. We discuss the application of *stare decisis* to statutory interpretation cases in Chapter 15. The Court also observes that "many States specifically exclude railroad workers from [Workers' Compensation] coverage, because of the assumption that FELA provides adequate protection for those workers. * * * Our overruling Parden would require these States to reexamine their statutes, meanwhile putting at risk all employees and employers who have been acting on the assumption that they are protected in the event of injuries caused by an employer's negligence."]

* * * [W]e cannot treat the holding of Welch as determinative of the issue now presented for our decision. As we explained in Welch, our Eleventh Amendment cases do indeed hold that "Congress may abrogate the States' constitutionally secured immunity from suit in federal court only by making its intention unmistakably clear in the language of the statute." Atascadero State Hospital v. Scanlon, 473 U.S. 234, 242 (1985). Congressional intent to abrogate Eleventh Amendment immunity must be expressed in the text of the statute; the Court will not look to legislative history in making its inquiry. Dellmuth v. Muth, 491 U.S. 223, 230 (1989). These cases establish a rule of constitutional law, based on the Eleventh Amendment. That rule was developed after the Parden decision, and was found in Welch to have undercut the reasoning of Parden and to require Parden's Eleventh Amendment holding to be overruled. But as we have stated on many occasions, "the Eleventh Amendment does not apply in state courts."

The issue becomes, then, a pure question of statutory construction, where the doctrine of stare decisis is most compelling. Respondent argues, and the state courts in this case said, that the statutory-construction holding of Parden is no longer good law because of our later opinion in Will v. Michigan Dept. of State Police, supra. Respondent would make the result in Will solely a function of our Eleventh Amendment jurisprudence, reading the case to adopt a per se rule prohibiting the interpretation of general liability language to include the States, absent a clear statement by Congress to the effect that Congress intends to subject the States to the cause of action. Respondent argues that in light of Will, the same considerations which led us to a partial overruling of Parden in Welch should govern here.

We think the argument misconstrues the Will decision. Will did not import the entirety of our Eleventh Amendment jurisprudence into the area of statutory construction. It treated the Eleventh Amendment as a relevant consideration. The primary focus of Will was, as it should have been, on the language and history of § 1983. * * * The issue in Will and in this case is different from the issue in our Eleventh Amendment cases in a fundamental respect: The latter cases involve the application of a rule of constitutional law, while the former cases apply an "ordinary rule of statutory construction." This conclusion is evident from our discussion[ ] in * * * Gregory v. Ashcroft last Term. [Gregory] describe[s] the plain statement rule as "a rule of statutory construction to be applied where statutory intent is ambiguous," rather than as a rule of constitutional law; and [it did not] implicate [ ] the Eleventh Amendment. * * *

When the issue to be resolved is one of statutory construction, of congressional intent to impose monetary liability on the States, the requirement of a clear statement by Congress to impose such liability creates a rule that ought to be of assistance to the Congress and the courts in drafting and interpreting legislation. The requirement also serves to make parallel two separate inquiries into state liability: Eleventh Amendment doctrine and canons of statutory interpretation. In most cases, as in Will and Gregory v. Ashcroft, the rule can be followed. The resulting symmetry, making a State's liability or immunity, as the case may be, the same in both federal and state courts, has much to commend it. It also avoids the federalism-related concerns that arise when the National Government uses the state courts as the exclusive forum to permit recovery under a congressional statute. This is not an inconsequential argument. Symmetry in the law is more than aesthetics. It is predictability and order. But symmetry is not an imperative that must override just expectations which themselves rest upon the predictability and order of stare decisis.

In the case before us the clear statement inquiry need not be made and we need not decide whether FELA satisfies that standard, for the rule in any event does not prevail over the doctrine of stare decisis as applied to a long-standing statutory construction implicating important reliance interests. And when the rule is either overcome or inapplicable so that a federal statute does impose liability upon the States, the Supremacy Clause makes that statute the law in every State, fully enforceable in state court.

For the reasons we have stated, the judgment of the South Carolina Supreme Court is reversed, and the case is remanded for further proceedings not inconsistent with this opinion.

■ Justice O'Connor, with whom Justice Scalia joins, dissenting.
* * *

The Court invokes stare decisis while at the same time running headlong away from it. In my view, this case is cleanly resolved by applying two recent precedents, [Will and Welch]. * * *

The Court tries to drive a wedge between Will and Welch by characterizing the former as a statutory interpretation case, and the latter as a constitutional case. The clear statement rule, the Court says, was required in Welch because the Eleventh Amendment was implicated. In Will, by contrast, use of the clear statement rule was somewhat discretionary, because the issue in that case was a question of statutory interpretation in which the Constitution was not implicated. Because this case involves state sovereign immunity in state court, not federal court, and the Eleventh Amendment does not by its terms apply, the Court holds that the clear statement rule in this "nonconstitutional" context can be trumped by stare decisis.

The Court's distinction is untenable. The clear statement rule is not a mere canon of statutory interpretation. Instead, it derives from the Constitution itself. The rule protects the balance of power between the States and the Federal Government struck by the Constitution. Although the Eleventh Amendment spells out one aspect of that balance of power, the principle of federalism underlying the Amendment pervades the constitutional structure * * *. Recognizing this basic truth about our governmental structure under the Constitution, we have been wary of extending the effect of congressional enactments into areas traditionally governed by the States, unless Congress has directed us to do so by an unmistakably clear statement. Indeed, in the cases in which we have employed the clear statement rule outside the Eleventh Amendment context, we have recognized the rule's constitutional dimensions. [Editor—The dissent then quotes from several cases, including Gregory v. Ashcroft, supra ("This plain statement rule is nothing more than an acknowledgment that the States retain substantial sovereign powers under our constitutional scheme, powers with which Congress does not readily interfere").] Thus, the Court's position that we are not required to employ the clear statement rule in this context ignores the constitutional source of the rule.

The Eleventh Amendment spells out one instance, but not the only one, in which respect and forbearance is due from the national to the state governments, a respect that cements our federation in the Constitution. The clear statement rule assumes that Congress will show that respect by not lightly abridging the powers or sovereignty retained by the States. From this standpoint, it makes little sense to apply the clear statement rule to congressional enactments that make the States liable to damages suits in federal courts, but not to apply the clear statement rule to congressional enactments that make the States liable to damages suits in their own courts. Sovereign immunity, a crucial attribute of separate governments, is infringed in both cases. * * *

The Court gives no guidance to lower courts as to when it will apply the clear statement rule and when it will not. The Court's obscurity on this point does little to further the goals of stability and predictability that assertedly drive its analysis. * * *

In sum, the Court's newly created exception to the clear statement rule threatens to eliminate it altogether, except when the States' Eleventh Amendment sovereign immunity is abrogated in federal court. It will be difficult, if not impossible, for lower courts to know when they should apply the rule in interpreting statutes that upset the traditional balance between the State and Federal Government outside the context of Eleventh Amendment immunity. * * *

The concern that South Carolina Railway's employees will be without a remedy should not determine the result in this case. If we clarified our doctrine, instead of obfuscating it, States could allow other compensation schemes to fill the void left by FELA. We should not so quickly assume that South Carolina will callously ignore the fate of its own workers. Certainly, South Carolina has more of a stake in seeing that its employees are compensated than does Congress or this Court.

Instead of avoiding the implications of our previous decisions, I would adhere to them. The Court's holding, while premised on fairness, is unfair to the States, courts, and parties that must parse our doctrine applying the clear statement rule. Therefore, I respectfully dissent.

b) AVOID RETROACTIVE STATUTES

There is an old canon of interpretation which presumes that statutes are not retroactive. This canon is especially interesting because it is based on a traditional image of legislation as a product of arbitrary legislative will. Retroactive legislation is therefore potentially unfair, because arbitrariness includes an element of surprise and can destroy reliance interests. More broadly, people do not like being pushed around by arbitrary exercises of power, even if they never relied on existing rules.

As you read the following material, see whether the presumption against retroactive statutes has declined in weight. If there is a tendency for the courts to more readily accept retroactive legislation, why that might be so: (1) Is legislation less willful than we usually suppose; (2) does legislative compromise take care of concerns about retroactivity; (3) are the interests affected by retroactive legislation less important; (4) is the change wrought by statutes becoming more gradual, like the gradual evolution of common law?

i) INTRODUCTION

Some retroactive legislation, dealing with crimes, property, and contracts, is prohibited by the United States Constitution. For example, neither state nor federal law can create crimes or increase punishments *ex post facto*. Article I, sec. 9, sec. 10. The Constitution explicitly prohibits state law from impairing the obligation of contracts, Article I, sec. 9, and the Due Process Clause of the 5th Amendment imposes the same prohibition on federal law. Battaglia v. General Motors Corp., 169 F.2d 254 (2d Cir.1948). If a retroactive law amounts to a taking of property, it must serve a public purpose and provide compensation. This rule applies explicitly to the federal government through the 5th Amendment to the United States Constitution, and to the states through the Due Process Clause of the 14th Amendment. PruneYard Shopping Center v. Robins, 447 U.S. 74 (1980).

Concern about retroactive statutes runs so deep, however, that nonconstitutional presumptions are sometimes applied to interpret a statute as having only prospective effect. The presumption (1) can be strong—imposing a clear statement rule; or (2) can be applied more flexibly, to prevent retroactive application if that would result in "manifest injustice."

Courts do not always formulate the legal issue this way. They often state that a statute cannot retroactively interfere with "vested rights," unless the statute is "curative," "remedial," or "procedural." In this view, the court's job begins and ends with applying these legal categories to the facts. This is often described as "legal formalism," because the court has only the task of fitting facts within well-defined formal categories. The less formalistic appeal to a "manifest injustice" criterion is more popular today because it is more honest about exposing the judge's creative role in determining whether a statute should be retroactively applied.

Sometimes a state constitution or statute prohibits retroactive statutes or directs that the statutes shall operate only prospectively. However, these explicit provisions are usually applied the same way as judicial presumptions; they are interpreted to permit retroactivity when the statute is explicitly retroactive and when retroactivity would not have serious harmful effects. For example, the Missouri constitution (Art. I, sec. 13) explicitly prohibits retrospective legislation, but the courts still uphold statutes which are explicitly retroactive or which are procedural and do not affect substantive rights. White v. St. Louis–San Francisco Railway Co., 602 S.W.2d 748 (Mo.App. 1980). Frequently, the state statute prohibiting retroactivity will have a built-in escape clause permitting retroactivity in appropriate circumstances. See, e.g., Cooper v. Watson, 187 N.W.2d 689 (Minn.1971)("No law shall be construed to be retroactive unless clearly or manifestly so intended by the legislature.")

Modern legislation strains traditional presumptions regarding retroactive legislation. Without ever impairing a contract or taking property, government regulation and tax laws frequently disrupt prior expectations. Individuals are left with whatever they "own," in the traditional sense of the term, but the expectations they had when they made prior commitments are disturbed. An individual who spent money to educate himself for a science degree finds that there is no federal money to support scientific research. A business which purchased land for development finds that environmental legislation impairs its value. An investor in a building is hurt by new safety rules. These types of legislation generally do not impair contracts or take property, although there is a lively debate over when regulation is a taking of property which requires compensation. We tend to think of most of these government actions as similar to other changes, such as a shift in consumer preferences, which can impair the value of prior investments. In other words, these events *are* expected in the sense that there are always some risks anticipated when an investment is made and the risk of changing government policy is just one more risk to be considered.

Despite these considerations, litigants often object to retroactive statutes, appealing to both constitutional and nonconstitutional doctrines. In reading the following cases, determine whether the court's concern with retroactivity is based on the Constitution or some other source. If it is not constitutionally based, what justifies the court's concern? Would Pound consider a presumption against retroactivity an example of spurious interpretation because it originates with the court's conception of justice? By what criteria and by what authority do courts determine whether a statute should have retroactive effect?

ii) MANIFEST INJUSTICE

Gibbons v. Gibbons

432 A.2d 80, 81 (N.J.1981).

■ Pashman, J.

N.J.S.A. 2A:34–23 authorizes the trial court in divorce actions to "make such award or awards to the parties, in addition to alimony and maintenance, to effectuate an equitable distribution of the property, both real and personal, which was legally and beneficially acquired by them or either of them during the marriage." On December 31, 1980, the Legislature enacted L. 1980, c.181, which amended this statute by excluding from equitable distribution all property "acquired during the marriage by either party by way of gift, devise or bequest * * * except * * * interspousal gifts." * * *

* * * According to the committee statement accompanying the amendment, the rationale for it was that

> [I]n the majority of instances, the gift, devise or bequest in question will be from the parents or other relative of the recipient. To permit a compulsory division of the asset between the recipient and his spouse is contrary to the marital expectations of the recipient and the giving parent or relative. Since the efforts of neither spouse resulted in the gift, devise or bequest, it need not be regarded as a marital asset under the partnership concept of marriage. [Senate Judiciary Committee Statement to Assembly, No. 1229 of 1980.]

However, the amendment contained no indication as to whether it was to be applied to pending cases or only prospectively, and the legislative history offers no clear guidance on this point. This lack of direction led the Governor to state, at the time he signed the bill into law, that because of the statute's silence on the question of retroactivity and the absence of a consensus in the Legislature on the point, "I believe the courts are the more appropriate forum to resolve that issue. They will have to decide based on existing principles of law, the extent to which this new law will affect pending cases." We now undertake to resolve the retroactivity issue.

The courts of this State have long followed a general rule of statutory construction that favors prospective application of statutes. The rationale for this rule has been succinctly stated as follows:

> It is a fundamental principle of jurisprudence that retroactive application of new laws involves a high risk of being unfair. There is general consensus among all people that notice or warning of the rules that are to be applied to determine their affairs should be given in advance of the actions whose effects are to be judged by them. The hackneyed maxim that everyone is held to know the law, itself a principle of dubious wisdom,

nevertheless presupposes that the law is at least susceptible of being known. But that is not possible as to law which has not been made.

However, as we have said on at least one occasion, the rule favoring prospective application of statutes, while "a sound rule of statutory interpretation * * * is no more than a rule of statutory interpretation" and is not to be applied mechanistically to every case. Thus, there are well-settled rules concerning the circumstances in which statutes should be applied retroactively, where there is no clear expression of intent by the Legislature that the statute is to be prospectively applied only.

First, there are those statutes in which the Legislature has expressed the contrary intent; i.e., that the statute be applied retroactively. In such cases the court should, as Justice Schreiber has said, "apply the statute in effect at the time of its decision." This expression of legislative intent may be either express, that is, stated in the language of the statute or in the pertinent legislative history, or implied, that is, retroactive application may be necessary to make the statute workable or to give it the most sensible interpretation, see Hohl v. Tp. of Readington, 181 A.2d 150 (N.J.1962)(amendments to zoning ordinances given retroactive effect because proper exercise of police power to further the public health, safety, morals or welfare outweighs private rights). * * *

Another category of cases in which we have held that statutes may be given retroactive application is that in which the statute is ameliorative or curative. In re Smigelski, 154 A.2d 1 (N.J.1959). In Smigelski this rule was applied to permit retroactive application of an amendatory statute that set limits to the duration of juvenile commitments.

However, even if a statute may be subject to retroactive application, a final inquiry must be made. That is, will retroactive application result in "manifest injustice" to a party adversely affected by such an application of the statute? The essence of this inquiry is whether the affected party relied, to his or her prejudice, on the law that is now to be changed as a result of the retroactive application of the statute, and whether the consequences of this reliance are so deleterious and irrevocable that it would be unfair to apply the statute retroactively.

Applying these principles to the statute at issue in the present case, we conclude that the amendment to N.J.S.A. 2A:34–23 should be applied retroactively.

* * * [In this case,] the exceptions to the rule of prospectivity weigh in favor of retroactive application. First, the amendment in question, like that in Smigelski, supra, is curative insofar as it reflects the Legislature's attempt to improve a statutory scheme already in existence. Second, retroactive application will bring the

law into harmony with the settled expectations of many donors and donees. As was noted by the Senate Judiciary Committee * * *, "[t]o permit a compulsory division of [gift or inheritance assets] between the recipient and his spouse is contrary to the marital expectations of the recipient and the giving parent or relative." Senate Judiciary Committee Statement to Assembly, No. 1229 of 1980. * * *

Nor will retroactive application of the statute result in manifest injustice to the adversely affected party, in this case, Mary Weitzel Gibbons. She claims that it is inequitable to apply the amended statute to her because she relied upon the law as it existed at the time she brought her action. In particular, she says she chose to seek equitable distribution only and not alimony as well because of what she believed was the broad scope of assets subject to equitable distribution. But clearly no manifest injustice will result from retroactive application of the amendatory statute to her case since any orders pertaining to alimony or other support "may be revised and altered by the court from time to time as circumstances may require," N.J.S.A. 2A:34–23.

Accordingly, we reverse the judgment of the Appellate Division and remand this case to the trial court for determination of the correct equitable distribution in accordance with the statute as amended.

Note on curative statutes. Gibbons indicates that the statute in question was curative, in the sense that it improves a statutory scheme. That is not the usual way in which the term "curative" is used to support a retroactive statute. Usually a prior event, like issuing an ordinance or making a contract, was legally defective and a later statute cures the defect retroactively. The court's improper invocation of the "curative" category is a symptom of the attraction of formalistic legal reasoning, which permits the court to conceal its creative judgments by pretending that the facts fit some predetermined legal category.

A typical curative statute, in the correct sense of the term, was involved in Application of Santore, 623 P.2d 702 (Wash.App.1981). Mr. and Mrs. Santore had signed adoption papers permitting another family to adopt Mrs. Santore's child. They later tried to revoke the adoption. A statute had been passed (statute 2) which unintentionally repealed an earlier statute permitting adoption by written consent (statute 1). The repealing statute 2 was in effect when the Santores gave up their child for adoption. A later statute (statute 3) then retroactively corrected this mistake and reinstated the written consent procedure. The impact of Statute 3, reinstating the written consent procedure, was challenged by the Santores in a habeas corpus action to get back their child. The court dismissed the challenge, stating:

* * * The Santores argue [that statute 3] retroactively interferes with their "vested rights," in violation of the due process and contract clauses of the federal and state constitutions, by making effective Mrs. Santore's consent to adoption, which was ineffective under the law existing when the consent was executed. * * *

* * * [W]e note that a retroactive statute is unconstitutional under the due process or contract clauses only if the statute is unfair or unreasonable. The proper test of the constitutionality of retroactive legislation is whether a party has changed position in reliance upon the previous law or whether the retroactive law defeats the reasonable expectations of the parties, not whether the law abrogates a "vested right," which is merely a conclusory label. Curative laws [such as statute 3] which implement the original intentions of affected parties are constitutional because there is no injustice in retroactively depriving a person of a right that was created contrary to his expectations at the time he entered the transaction from which the right arose. Application of [statute 3] defeats no justifiable reliance interests of the Santores. Mrs. Santore intended to relinquish her child when she signed the consent and did not sign in reliance upon the then defective provisions of [statute 2]. Indeed, the record indicates that the Santores were unaware of [statute 2] until after they filed the habeas corpus petition.

See also State ex rel. Tomasic v. Kansas City, 636 P.2d 760 (Kan.1981), in which the Kansas Port Authority developed an industrial facility for General Motors Corp. by issuing industrial revenue bonds. Some of the necessary statutory authority related to this development had been omitted from earlier legislation, however, and a 1981 Act validated certain proceedings taken prior to April 1, 1981 by the Port Authority. The court upheld the 1981 Act because it allowed contracts entered into prior to the Act to be performed in accordance with the parties' expectations.

iii) SUPREME COURT

In Kaiser Aluminum & Chemical Corp. v. Bonjorno, 494 U.S. 827 (1990), the Supreme Court decided that a statute should not be applied retroactively, basing its conclusion on an interpretation of congressional intent. The plurality explicitly refused to takes sides in the dispute over whether and when laws should be presumed to be retroactive or prospective. It described the dispute, as follows:

The Court in Bradley v. Richmond School Bd., 416 U.S. 696 (1974), faced the issue whether an attorney's fee statute that went into effect during the pendency of the appeal was to be applied by the appellate court. Relying on Thorpe v. Durham Housing Authority, 393 U.S. 268 (1969), the Court held that "a court is to apply the law in effect at the time it renders its decision." The Court derived its holding from a broad reading of United States v. Schooner Peggy, 1 Cranch 103, 2 L.Ed. 49 (1801). * * * Under the rule set forth in Schooner Peggy, an amendment to the law while a case was pending should be applied by the appellate court only if, "by its terms," the law was to be applied to pending cases. In Thorpe, supra, the Court broadened the rule set forth in Schooner Peggy: "[E]ven where the intervening law does not explicitly recite that it is to be applied to pending cases, it is to be given recognition and effect." As a means of softening the potentially harsh impact of this broadening retrospective application of congressional enactments, the Court recognized two exceptions to the presumption that courts are to apply the law in effect at the time of decision. The presumption does not govern where retrospective application would result in manifest injustice to one of the parties or where there is clear congressional intent to the contrary. * * *

In apparent tension with the rule articulated in Bradley, supra, is our recent reaffirmation of the generally accepted axiom that "[r]etroactivity is not favored in the law . * * * [C]ongressional enactments and administrative rules will not be construed to have retroactive effect unless their language requires this result." Bowen v. Georgetown University Hospital, 488 U.S. 204, 208 (1988).

Justice Scalia would not join the plurality opinion, arguing that the Court should resolve the tension in Bradley (retroactivity if no manifest injustice) and Bowen (presumption against retroactivity). His review of the historical record revealed that cases permitting retroactivity could almost always be explained on the ground that they implemented congressional intent, that the statute was not really retroactive, or that the retroactive law was really found in a judicial decision, rather than a statute. Thorpe and Bradley, which are cited for the "manifest injustice" approach, were therefore a wrong doctrinal turn. In the remainder of his opinion, he stated his view of what the law should be:

Precedent aside, however, even as an original matter there is nothing to be said for a presumption of retroactivity—neither in the narrow context of "cases pending" or "cases on appeal" nor (a fortiori) in the logically compelled broader context of all cases. It is contrary to fundamental notions of justice, and thus contrary to realistic assessment of probable legislative intent. The principle that the legal effect of conduct should ordinarily be assessed under the law that existed when the conduct took place has timeless and universal human appeal. It was recognized by the Greeks, and by the Code Napoleon. It has long been a solid foundation of American law [Editor—citing Kent, Story, and U.S. and state constitutions]. * * * The presumption of nonretroactivity, in short, gives effect to enduring notions of what is fair, and thus accords with what legislators almost always intended. [Editor—Didn't Scalia say that relying on legislative intent was a "benign fiction"?]

The Thorpe–Bradley rule does the opposite * * *. A background rule of retroactivity is so patently contrary to probable legislative intent that it could not possibly be applied (as the presumption of nonretroactivity is applied) whenever there is no legislative indication to the contrary. So Thorpe and Bradley have invented an all-purpose exception to their counterintuitive rule: retroactivity will not be assumed where that will produce "manifest injustice." What that might mean (viz., almost anything) is well enough exemplified by Thorpe. There we did not consider it "manifestly unjust," on the basis of a federal regulation adopted 18 months after the fact, to prevent a landlord from evicting a tenant whose lease had been terminated in full compliance (as we assumed) with all applicable laws. Is there any doubt that we *would* have found it "manifestly unjust" to *evict* the tenant if the sequence were reversed—that is, if the landlord had *not* complied, at the time of the lease termination, with a regulation repealed 18 months later? "Manifest injustice," I fear, is just a surrogate for policy preferences. Indeed, it cannot be otherwise. Once one begins from the premise of Thorpe and Bradley that, contrary to the wisdom of the ages, it is not in and of itself unjust to judge action on the basis of a legal rule that was not even in effect when the action was taken, then one is not really talking about "justice" at all, but about mercy, or compassion, or social utility, or whatever other policy motivation might make one favor a particular result. A rule of law, designed to give statutes the effect Congress intended, has thus been transformed to a rule of discretion, giving judges power to expand or contract the effect of legislative action. We should turn this frog back to a prince as soon as possible.

I do not pretend that clear reaffirmation of the presumption of nonretroactivity will always make it simple to determine the application in time of new legislation. It will remain difficult, in many cases, to decide whether the presumption has been overcome by the text, and indeed to decide whether a particular application *is* retroactive. But however many obstacles may remain along the route, surely it is essential to agree upon our point of departure. * * *

I would eliminate the confusion of the past two decades and reaffirm unqualifiedly the principle of construction that reflects both our long applied jurisprudence and the reality of legislative intent: A statute is deemed to be effective only for the future unless a contrary intent appears.

The four dissenting judges permitted retroactivity, accepting "the evolution of the presumption in favor of application of new laws to pending cases reviewed [ ] in Bradley." This required some attention to the specific manifest injustice concerns raised by the case. The issue was the computation of postjudgment interest against a losing defendant. After judgment against the defendant and while the defendant's appeal was pending, the interest rate on the judgment was raised by statute. The dissent concluded that application of the new law would not disturb reliance on the state of the law prior to the amendment. The defendant in their view "was not entitled to assume much of anything about its interest rate" on judgments entered against it in view of the fact that the "parties were on notice that Congress could alter the applicable rate if it wished," and that it was not even clear how much the judgment would be until the appeal was decided. The dissent also referred to the "public interests implicated by the statutory change," and concluded that remitting the plaintiff to the old lower rate of postjudgment interest would allow the defendant, "an adjudicated violator of the antitrust laws, to escape the consequences of protracting litigation."

It is unclear what the dissenters meant when they stated that "the parties were on notice that Congress could alter the applicable rate" of interest. They might be referring to the fact that the area of law is entirely created by statute; there is no common law. But that would support a presumption favoring retroactivity.

Whatever the dissenters might have meant, what do you think of the following argument about notice of possible legislative action? Some areas of law are constantly under legislative review. A pattern might develop of frequent revisiting of statutory rules. For example, a statute might abolish contributory negligence and adopt comparative negligence if the plaintiff is no more than 49% negligent. Then, some years later, the statute might extend comparative negligence to plaintiffs who are no more than 50% negligent. Finally, legislation might adopt comparative negligence in all cases. At some point, does the legislative activity put prospective defendants on notice that the law might change adversely? How frequently must the legislation be revised to establish such notice?

The Supreme Court revisited the question of the retroactivity presumption in connection with the Civil Rights Act of 1991. Here is some historical background to this controversy.

On November 21, 1991 President Bush signed the Civil Rights Act of 1991, ending an extended controversy about civil rights legislation dealing with job bias. The law was a response to nine Supreme Court decisions issued in 1989, which were pro-defendant and which generally rejected prior pro-plaintiff decisions (some from the Court and some from lower court opinions). We will note two of them in this discussion. First, in Patterson v. McLean Credit Union, 491 U.S. 164 (1989), the Court held that the guarantee of the "right to make and enforce contracts" free of racial discrimination (42 U.S.C. § 1981) applied only to discrimination in the formation of the contract, not to discrimination during the performance of the contract. Consequently, charges of employer racial harassment on the job were not covered by § 1981, contrary to what lower courts had held. The Act reversed that decision, applying § 1981 to discrimination during performance as well as in the making of the employment contract.

Application of § 1981 was important for several reasons. There was another statute (Title VII) providing remedies for employer race discrimination during performance of the employment contract but, in some respects, it was less generous. Title VII was limited to employers with a significant number of employees; required exhaustion of administrative remedies; and, when Patterson was decided, provided only equitable relief, including some back pay. (Back pay would compensate, for example, for loss of wages between the time a worker was improperly discharged and the date of reinstatement.) By contrast, § 1981 provided full compensatory and sometimes punitive damages. (Compensatory damages would cover, for example, loss of wages if no one would hire a discharged worker in the future because her reputation was damaged by the employer's improper action, and for pain and suffering arising from what the employer did.) Finally, § 1981 also applied to contracts outside the employment setting.

Second, in Wards Cove Packing Company, Inc. v. Atonio, 490 U.S. 642 (1989), the Court dealt with the standards under Title VII for proving discrimination by employers. In some respects, Title VII was broader than § 1981. Title VII applied not only to race (to which § 1981 is limited), but also to discrimination based on sex, color, religion, and national origin. It also covered a somewhat broader range of substantive behavior than § 1981, including recruitment practices. Unlike § 1981, Title VII covers cases of disparate impact, not just discriminatory intent. The Supreme Court had earlier decided in the Griggs case that when an employer used a hiring criterion which had a disparate adverse impact on a protected group, the employer had to prove a business necessity for the criterion. Wards Cove relaxed the standard by which the employer could justify hiring practices and shifted the burden of proof regarding such need to the complaining employee. The Civil Rights Act of 1991 is unclear about exactly how much of the prior Griggs case is restored, but it clearly rejects the Wards Cove pro-defendant formulation.

In addition to rejecting the results in various Supreme Court cases, the Act also provides for compensatory and punitive damages in Title VII cases, if violation of the statute is intentional, subject to a dollar cap. As noted above, prior to the Act, the only remedy was an injunction and limited back pay relief.

The Act was the culmination of a legislative process that began soon after the Supreme Court's 1989 decisions. Hearings were held beginning in February, 1990, and a 1990 version of the Act was vetoed by the President on the ground that it would require job quotas. After the veto, a House bill was introduced in 1991 but a veto was still threatened. House passage by less than the ⅔rds needed to override a veto led to further compromise. In June, Senator Danforth introduced a Senate bill, but President Bush still objected. Yet another compromise, sponsored by Senators Danforth and Kennedy, resulted in a Senate filibuster, a cloture vote to stop the filibuster, and finally Senate and House passage by veto-proof majorities (93–5 in the Senate; 381–38 in the House). President Bush signed the bill.

The law contained the typical provision that the "Act shall become effective upon enactment." Controversy immediately erupted over whether the damage provisions were retroactive. The Equal Employment Opportunity Commission (EEOC), which is charged with enforcing certain civil rights laws, stated that it would not seek retroactive application of the damage provisions. EEOC Notice No. 915.002 (Dec. 27, 1991). It relied on the

Bowen case (cited in Kaiser Aluminum & Chemical Corp. v. Bonjorno, supra—requiring explicit statutory language to support retroactivity), on the ground that Bowen was the latest Court statement on this issue.

Legislative history regarding retroactivity in general was inconclusive. Senators inserted diverse views into the congressional record as legislative history. Danforth, joined by Senator Dole, stated that the Act was prospective. 137 Cong. Rec. S 15478 (daily ed. Oct. 30, 1991)(Dole, writing for himself and the administration); id. at S 15483 (daily ed. Oct. 30, 1991)(Danforth). Kennedy stated his view that the Act was retroactive or at least that the issue was left open for the courts to decide. Id. at S 15963 (daily ed. Nov. 5, 1991); id. at S 15485 (daily ed. Oct. 30, 1991).[12] The vetoed 1990 bill had provided some retroactive relief and deletion of a similar provision in 1991 was, in part, intended to prevent a Presidential veto. In other words, Congress self-consciously passed the buck to the courts to decide about retroactivity.

One provision of the statute might seem relevant to the retroactivity issue but is probably not important. The defendant in Wards Cove was the beneficiary of a special provision in the statute dealing with retroactivity, as follows: "Nothing in this Act shall apply to any disparate impact case for which a complaint was filed before March 1, 1975 and for which an initial decision was rendered after October 30, 1983." When the House received the Senate bill, there were numerous objections to this special legislation favoring Wards Cove, but the bill was considered in the House under a "closed" rule, which prohibited floor amendments, allegedly to prevent a veto if the protection for Wards Cove was removed by House amendment. 137 Cong. Rec. H 9506 (daily ed. Nov. 5, 1991). Sometimes a narrow provision in a statute accomplishing a result implies the absence of a similar legal rule in all other situations not mentioned by that provision—in Latin, *expressio unius est exclusio alterius*, or (in English) the express inclusion of one thing excludes the other. Here, that approach would imply that requiring prospectivity for Wards Cove meant retroactivity in other cases.[13]

The "expressio unius" approach to interpreting a statute is highly suspect, however, nowhere more so than when the specific provision responds to lobbying by a narrow interest group. All the provision does is nail down an interpretation favoring the winning group, intending nothing about how the statute should otherwise be interpreted. The courts which

---

12. This disagreement contrasts with agreement between Senators Danforth and Kennedy on legislative history regarding the most contentious portion of the statute, which was the Title VII substantive law regarding proof of disparate impact resulting from employer job qualifications. They inserted a statement in the Act that no statements other than the interpretive memorandum appearing at Vol. 137 Cong. Rec. S 15276 (daily ed. Oct. 25, 1991) shall be considered legislative history of, or relied upon in any way as legislative history in construing or applying, any provi- sion of this Act that related to Wards Cove * * *.

13. Indeed, some commentators said that liberal Senators voted *for* prospectivity regarding Wards Cove to support the view that the rest of the statute was otherwise retroactive. Senator Kennedy even supported correcting the engrossed version of the Senate bill which had inadvertently omitted the Wards Cove provision. Id. at S 15963 (daily ed. Nov. 5, 1991).

have discussed the Act's retroactivity have generally held that the special legislation favoring Wards Cove has no bearing on the general question of the Act's retroactivity.

All of the above is underbrush, indicating that the statutory text and legislative history are inconclusive about retroactivity. What then should a court do when a plaintiff seeks retroactive application of the Civil Rights Act of 1991? The following two decisions dealt with the new compensatory and punitive damages provisions of Title VII and the new law overruling Patterson.

Do these cases present yet another potential clash between statutory purpose and substantive background considerations? Are there "fundamental" values at stake? What values do the judges consider fundamental?

Notice that both Stevens and Scalia agree on the result—the statutes are prospective. What then do they disagree about?

Landgraf v. USI Film Products

511 U.S. 244 (1994).

■ Stevens, J., delivered the opinion of the Court.

The Civil Rights Act of 1991 (1991 Act or Act) [§ 102] creates a right to recover compensatory and punitive damages for certain violations of Title VII of the Civil Rights Act of 1964. The Act further provides that any party may demand a trial by jury if such damages are sought. We granted certiorari to decide whether these provisions apply to a Title VII case that was pending on appeal when the statute was enacted. We hold that they do not. * * *

Petitioner's primary submission is that the text of the 1991 Act requires that it be applied to cases pending on its enactment. Her argument, if accepted, would make the entire Act (with two narrow exceptions) applicable to conduct that occurred, and to cases that were filed, before the Act's effective date. Although only § 102 is at issue in this case, we therefore preface our analysis with a brief description of the scope of the 1991 Act.

The Civil Rights Act of 1991 is in large part a response to a series of decisions of this Court interpreting the Civil Rights Acts of 1866 and 1964. Section 3(4) expressly identifies as one of the Act's purposes "to respond to recent decisions of the Supreme Court by expanding the scope of relevant civil rights statutes in order to provide adequate protection to victims of discrimination." [Editor—References to act sections overturning prior Court cases are omitted.] * * *

A number of important provisions in the Act, however, were not responses to Supreme Court decisions. * * * Among the provisions that did not directly respond to any Supreme Court decision is the one at issue in this case, § 102. * * *

Before the enactment of the 1991 Act, Title VII afforded only "equitable" remedies. The primary form of monetary relief available was backpay. Title VII's back pay remedy * * * is a "make-whole" remedy that resembles compensatory damages in some respects. However, the new compensatory damages provision of the 1991 Act is "in addition to," and does not replace or duplicate, the backpay remedy allowed under prior law. * * *

[Editor—The 1991 Act added compensatory and punitive damages to the equitable remedy of back pay in cases of intentional discrimination. In a few situations, of which this case was an example, there could be no back pay award because the employee was not discharged, and the 1991 Act's compensatory/punitive damages scheme created a monetary remedy where none previously existed.]

In 1990, a comprehensive civil rights bill passed both Houses of Congress. Although similar to the 1991 Act in many other respects, the 1990 bill differed in that it contained language expressly calling for application of many of its provisions, including the section providing for damages in cases of intentional employment discrimination, to cases arising before its (expected) enactment. The President vetoed the 1990 legislation, however, citing the bill's "unfair retroactivity rules" as one reason for his disapproval. Congress narrowly failed to override the veto.

The absence of comparable language in the 1991 Act cannot realistically be attributed to oversight or to unawareness of the retroactivity issue. Rather, it seems likely that one of the compromises that made it possible to enact the 1991 version was an agreement not to include the kind of explicit retroactivity command found in the 1990 bill.

The omission of the elaborate retroactivity provision of the 1990 bill—which was by no means the only source of political controversy over that legislation—is not dispositive because it does not tell us precisely where the compromise was struck in the 1991 Act. The Legislature might, for example, have settled in 1991 on a less expansive form of retroactivity that, unlike the 1990 bill, did not reach cases already finally decided. A decision to reach only cases still pending might explain Congress' failure to provide in the 1991 Act, as it had in 1990, that certain sections would apply to proceedings pending on specific preenactment dates. Our first question, then, is whether the statutory text on which petitioner relies manifests an intent that the 1991 Act should be applied to cases that arose and went to trial before its enactment.

Petitioner's textual argument relies on three provisions of the 1991 Act: §§ 402(a), 402(b), and 109(c). Section 402(a), the only provision of the Act that speaks directly to the question before us, states: "Except as otherwise specifically provided, this Act and the amendments made by this Act shall take effect upon enactment."

That language does not, by itself, resolve the question before us. A statement that a statute will become effective on a certain date does not even arguably suggest that it has any application to conduct that occurred at an earlier date. Petitioner does not argue otherwise. Rather, she contends that the introductory clause of § 402(a) would be superfluous unless it refers to §§ 402(b) and 109(c), which provide for prospective application in limited contexts.

The parties agree that § 402(b) was intended to exempt a single disparate impact lawsuit against the Wards Cove Packing Company. Section 402(b) provides: "(b) CERTAIN DISPARATE IMPACT CASES.—Notwithstanding any other provision of this Act, nothing in this Act shall apply to any disparate impact case for which a complaint was filed before March 1, 1975, and for which an initial decision was rendered after October 30, 1983." Section 109(c), part of the section extending Title VII to overseas employers, states: "(c) APPLICATION OF AMENDMENTS.—The amendments made by this section shall not apply with respect to conduct occurring before the date of the enactment of this Act." According to petitioner, these two subsections are the "other provisions" contemplated in the first clause of § 402(a), and together create a strong negative inference that all sections of the Act not specifically declared prospective apply to pending cases that arose before November 21, 1991.

Before addressing the particulars of petitioner's argument, we observe that she places extraordinary weight on two comparatively minor and narrow provisions in a long and complex statute. Applying the entire Act to cases arising from preenactment conduct would have important consequences, including the possibility that trials completed before its enactment would need to be retried and the possibility that employers would be liable for punitive damages for conduct antedating the Act's enactment. Purely prospective application, on the other hand, would prolong the life of a remedial scheme, and of judicial constructions of civil rights statutes, that Congress obviously found wanting. Given the high stakes of the retroactivity question, the broad coverage of the statute, and the prominent and specific retroactivity provisions in the 1990 bill, it would be surprising for Congress to have chosen to resolve that question through negative inferences drawn from two provisions of quite limited effect.

Petitioner, however, invokes the canon that a court should give effect to every provision of a statute and thus avoid redundancy among different provisions. Unless the word "otherwise" in § 402(a) refers to either § 402(b) or § 109(c), she contends, the first five words in § 402(a) are entirely superfluous. Moreover, relying on the canon "[e]xpressio unius est exclusio alterius," petitioner argues that because Congress provided specifically for prospectivity in two places (§§ 109(c) and 402(b)), we should infer that it intended the opposite for the remainder of the statute.

Petitioner emphasizes that § 402(a) begins: "Except as otherwise specifically provided." A scan of the statute for other "specific provisions" concerning effective dates reveals that §§ 402(b) and 109(c) are the most likely candidates. Since those provisions decree prospectivity, and since § 402(a) tells us that the specific provisions are exceptions, § 402(b) should be considered as prescribing a general rule of retroactivity. Petitioner's argument has some force, but we find it most unlikely that Congress intended the introductory clause to carry the critically important meaning petitioner assigns it. Had Congress wished § 402(a) to have such a determinate meaning, it surely would have used language comparable to its reference to the predecessor Title VII damages provisions in the 1990 legislation: that the new provisions "shall apply to all proceedings pending on or commenced after the date of enactment of this Act." S. 2104, 101st Cong., 1st Sess. § 15(a)(4) (1990).

It is entirely possible that Congress inserted the "otherwise specifically provided" language not because it understood the "takes effect" clause to establish a rule of retroactivity to which only two "other specific provisions" would be exceptions, but instead to assure that any specific timing provisions in the Act would prevail over the general "take effect on enactment" command. The drafters of a complicated piece of legislation containing more than 50 separate sections may well have inserted the "except as otherwise provided" language merely to avoid the risk of an inadvertent conflict in the statute. If the introductory clause of § 402(a) was intended to refer specifically to §§ 402(b), 109(c), or both, it is difficult to understand why the drafters chose the word "otherwise" rather than either or both of the appropriate section numbers.

We are also unpersuaded by petitioner's argument that both §§ 402(b) and 109(c) merely duplicate the "take effect upon enactment" command of § 402(a) unless all other provisions, including the damages provisions of § 102, apply to pending cases. That argument depends on the assumption that all those other provisions must be treated uniformly for purposes of their application to pending cases based on preenactment conduct. That thesis, however, is by no means an inevitable one. It is entirely possible—indeed, highly probable—that, because it was unable to resolve the retroactivity issue with the clarity of the 1990 legislation, Congress viewed the matter as an open issue to be resolved by the courts. Our precedents on retroactivity left doubts about what default rule would apply in the absence of congressional guidance, and suggested that some provisions might apply to cases arising before enactment while others might not. Compare Bowen v. Georgetown Univ. Hospital, 488 U.S. 204 (1988) with Bradley v. Richmond School Bd., 416 U.S. 696 (1974). The only matters Congress did not leave to the courts were set out with specificity in §§ 109(c) and 402(b). Congressional doubt concerning judicial retroactivity doctrine, coupled with the likelihood that the routine "take effect upon enactment" language would require courts to fall back upon that doctrine, provide a plausible explanation for both §§ 402(b) and 109(c) that makes neither provision redundant. * * *

The relevant legislative history of the 1991 Act reinforces our conclusion that §§ 402(a), 109(c) and 402(b) cannot bear the weight petitioner places upon them. The 1991 bill as originally introduced in the House contained explicit retroactivity provisions similar to those found in the 1990 bill. However, the Senate substitute that was agreed upon omitted those explicit retroactivity provisions. The legislative history discloses some frankly partisan statements about the meaning of the final effective date language, but those statements cannot plausibly be read as reflecting any general agreement. The history reveals no evidence that Members believed that an agreement had been tacitly struck on the controversial retroactivity issue, and little to suggest that Congress understood or intended the interplay of §§ 402(a), 402(b) and 109(c) to have the decisive effect petitioner assigns them. Instead, the history of the 1991 Act conveys the impression that legislators agreed to disagree about whether and to what extent the Act would apply to preenactment conduct.

* * * In the absence of the kind of unambiguous directive found in § 15 of the 1990 bill, we must look elsewhere for guidance on whether § 102 applies to this case.

It is not uncommon to find "apparent tension" between different canons of statutory construction. As Professor Llewellyn famously illustrated, many of the traditional canons have equal opposites. In order to resolve the question left open by the 1991 Act, federal courts have labored to reconcile two seemingly contradictory statements found in our decisions concerning the effect of intervening changes in the law. Each statement is framed as a generally applicable rule for interpreting statutes that do not specify their temporal reach. The first is the rule that "a court is to apply the law in effect at the time it renders its decision," Bradley, 416 U.S., at 711. The second is the axiom that "[r]etroactivity is not favored in the law," and its interpretive corollary that "congressional enactments and administrative rules will not be construed to have retroactive effect unless their language requires this result." Bowen, 488 U.S., at 208.

We have previously noted the "apparent tension" between those expressions. See Kaiser Aluminum & Chemical Corp. v. Bonjorno, 494 U.S. 827, 837 (1990). We found it unnecessary in *Kaiser* to resolve that seeming conflict "because under either view, where the congressional intent is clear, it governs," and the prejudgment interest statute at issue in that case evinced "clear congressional intent" that it was "not applicable to judgments entered before its effective date." In the case before us today, however, we have concluded that the Civil Rights Act of 1991 does not evince any clear expression of intent on § 102's application to cases arising before the Act's enactment. We must, therefore, focus on the apparent tension between the rules we have espoused for handling similar problems in the absence of an instruction from Congress. * * *

As Justice Scalia has demonstrated, the presumption against retroactive legislation is deeply rooted in our jurisprudence, and embodies a legal doctrine centuries older than our Republic. Elementary considerations of fairness dictate that individuals should have an opportunity to know what the law is and to conform their conduct accordingly; settled expectations should not be lightly disrupted. For that reason, the "principle that the legal effect of conduct should ordinarily be assessed under the law that existed when the conduct took place has timeless and universal appeal." In a free, dynamic society, creativity in both commercial and artistic endeavors is fostered by a rule of law that gives people confidence about the legal consequences of their actions.

It is therefore not surprising that the antiretroactivity principle finds expression in several provisions of our Constitution. [Editor—Discussion of Ex Post Facto, Impairment of Contract Obligations, Takings, Bill of Attainder, and Due Process clauses omitted.] * * *

These provisions demonstrate that retroactive statutes raise particular concerns. The Legislature's unmatched powers allow it to sweep away settled expectations suddenly and without individualized consideration. Its responsivity to political pressures poses a risk that it may be tempted to use retroactive legislation as a means of retribution against unpopular groups or individuals. * * *

The Constitution's restrictions, of course, are of limited scope. Absent a violation of one of those specific provisions, the potential unfairness of retroactive civil legislation is not a sufficient reason for a court to fail to give a statute its intended scope. Retroactivity provisions often serve entirely benign and legitimate purposes, whether to respond to emergencies, to correct mistakes, to prevent circumvention of a new statute in the interval immediately preceding its passage, or simply to give comprehensive effect to a new law Congress considers salutary. However, a requirement that Congress first make its intention clear helps ensure that Congress itself has determined that the benefits of retroactivity outweigh the potential for disruption or unfairness.

While statutory retroactivity has long been disfavored, deciding when a statute operates "retroactively" is not always a simple or mechanical task. Sitting on Circuit, Justice Story offered an influential definition in Society for Propagation of the Gospel v. Wheeler, 22 F.Cas. 756 (CCDNH 1814), a case construing a provision of the

New Hampshire Constitution that broadly prohibits "retrospective" laws both criminal and civil. Justice Story first rejected the notion that the provision bars only explicitly retroactive legislation, i.e., "statutes * * * enacted to take effect from a time anterior to their passage[.]" Such a construction, he concluded, would be "utterly subversive of all the objects" of the prohibition. Instead, the ban on retrospective legislation embraced "all statutes, which, though operating only from their passage, affect vested rights and past transactions." "Upon principle," Justice Story elaborated, "every statute, which takes away or impairs vested rights acquired under existing laws, or creates a new obligation, imposes a new duty, or attaches a new disability, in respect to transactions or considerations already past, must be deemed retrospective * * *." Though the formulas have varied, similar functional conceptions of legislative "retroactivity" have found voice in this Court's decisions and elsewhere.

A statute does not operate "retrospectively" merely because it is applied in a case arising from conduct antedating the statute's enactment, or upsets expectations based in prior law. Rather, the court must ask whether the new provision attaches new legal consequences to events completed before its enactment. The conclusion that a particular rule operates "retroactively" comes at the end of a process of judgment concerning the nature and extent of the change in the law and the degree of connection between the operation of the new rule and a relevant past event. Any test of retroactivity will leave room for disagreement in hard cases, and is unlikely to classify the enormous variety of legal changes with perfect philosophical clarity. However, retroactivity is a matter on which judges tend to have "sound * * * instinct[s]," see Danforth v. Groton Water Co., 178 Mass. 472, 476, 59 N.E. 1033, 1034 (1901)(Holmes, J.), and familiar considerations of fair notice, reasonable reliance, and settled expectations offer sound guidance.

Since the early days of this Court, we have declined to give retroactive effect to statutes burdening private rights unless Congress had made clear its intent. Thus, in United States v. Heth, 3 Cranch 399 (1806), we refused to apply a federal statute reducing the commissions of customs collectors to collections commenced before the statute's enactment because the statute lacked "clear, strong, and imperative" language requiring retroactive application, id. at 413 (opinion of Paterson, J.). The presumption against statutory retroactivity has consistently been explained by reference to the unfairness of imposing new burdens on persons after the fact. Indeed, at common law a contrary rule applied to statutes that merely removed a burden on private rights by repealing a penal provision (whether criminal or civil); such repeals were understood to preclude punishment for acts antedating the repeal. See, e.g., * * * Yeaton v. United States, 5 Cranch 281, 284 (1809). But see 1 U.S. C. § 109 (repealing common-law rule).

The largest category of cases in which we have applied the presumption against statutory retroactivity has involved new provisions affecting contractual or property rights, matters in which predictability and stability are of prime importance. The presumption has not, however, been limited to such cases. * * *

The presumption against statutory retroactivity had special force in the era in which courts tended to view legislative interference with property and contract rights circumspectly. In this century, legislation has come to supply the dominant means of legal ordering, and circumspection has given way to greater deference to legislative judgments. See Usery v. Turner Elkhorn Mining Co., 428 U.S., at 15–16. But while the constitutional impediments to retroactive civil legislation are now modest, prospectivity remains the appropriate default rule. Because it accords with widely held intuitions about how statutes ordinarily operate, a presumption against retroactivity will generally coincide with legislative and public expectations. Requiring clear intent assures that Congress itself has affirmatively considered the potential unfairness of retroactive application and determined that it is an acceptable price to pay for the countervailing benefits. Such a requirement allocates to Congress responsibility for fundamental policy judgments concerning the proper temporal reach of statutes, and has the additional virtue of giving legislators a predictable background rule against which to legislate.

Although we have long embraced a presumption against statutory retroactivity, for just as long we have recognized that, in many situations, a court should "apply the law in effect at the time it renders its decision," Bradley, 416 U.S., at 711, even though that law was enacted after the events that gave rise to the suit. * * *

Changes in procedural rules may often be applied in suits arising before their enactment without raising concerns about retroactivity. For example, in Ex parte Collett, 337 U.S. 55, 71 (1949), we held that 28 U.S.C. § 1404(a) governed the transfer of an action instituted prior to that statute's enactment. We noted the diminished reliance interests in matters of procedure. Because rules of procedure regulate secondary rather than primary conduct, the fact that a new procedural rule was instituted after the conduct giving rise to the suit does not make application of the rule at trial retroactive.

Petitioner relies principally upon Bradley v. Richmond School Bd., 416 U.S. 696 (1974), and Thorpe v. Housing Authority of Durham, 393 U.S. 268 (1969), in support of her argument that our ordinary interpretive rules support application of § 102 to her case. In Thorpe, we held that an agency circular requiring a local housing authority to give notice of reasons and opportunity to respond before evicting a tenant was applicable to an eviction proceeding commenced before the regulation issued. Thorpe shares much with both the "procedural" and "prospective-relief" cases. Thus, we noted in Thorpe that new hearing procedures did not affect either party's obligations under the lease agreement between the housing authority and the petitioner, and, because the tenant had "not yet vacated," we saw no significance in the fact that the housing authority had "decided to evict her before the circular was issued," The Court in Thorpe viewed the new eviction procedures as "essential to remove a serious impediment to the successful protection of constitutional rights."

Our holding in Bradley is similarly compatible with the line of decisions disfavoring "retroactive" application of statutes. In Bradley, the District Court had awarded attorney's fees and costs, upon general equitable principles, to parents who had prevailed in an action seeking to desegregate the public schools of Richmond, Virginia. While the case was pending before the Court of Appeals, Congress enacted § 718 of the Education Amendments of 1972, which authorized federal courts to award the prevailing parties in school desegregation cases a reasonable attorney's fee. The Court of Appeals held that the new fee provision did not authorize the award of fees for services rendered before the effective date of the amendments. This Court reversed. We concluded that the private parties could rely on § 718 to support their claim for attorney's fees, resting our decision "on the principle that a court is to apply the law in effect at the time it renders its decision, unless doing so would result in manifest injustice or there is statutory direction or legislative history to the contrary."

Although that language suggests a categorical presumption in favor of application of all new rules of law, we now make it clear that Bradley did not alter the well-settled presumption against application of the class of new statutes that would have genuinely "retroactive" effect. Like the new hearing requirement in Thorpe, the attorney's fee provision at issue in Bradley did not resemble the cases in which we have invoked the presumption against statutory retroactivity. Attorney's fee determinations, we have observed, are "collateral to the main cause of action" and "uniquely separable from the cause of action to be proved at trial." Moreover, even before the enactment of § 718, federal courts had authority (which the District Court in Bradley had exercised) to award fees based upon equitable principles. As our opinion in Bradley made clear, it would be difficult to imagine a stronger equitable case for an attorney's fee award than a lawsuit in which the plaintiff parents would otherwise have to bear the costs of desegregating their children's public schools. In light of the prior availability of a fee award, and the likelihood that fees would be assessed under pre-existing theories, we concluded that the new fee statute simply "did not impose an additional or unforeseeable obligation" upon the school board. * * *

We now ask whether, given the absence of guiding instructions from Congress, § 102 of the Civil Rights Act of 1991 is the type of provision that should govern cases arising before its enactment.

[T]here is no special reason to think that all the diverse provisions of the Act must be treated uniformly for such purposes. To the contrary, we understand the instruction that the provisions are to "take effect upon enactment" to mean that courts should evaluate each provision of the Act in light of ordinary judicial principles concerning the application of new rules to pending cases and pre-enactment conduct.

Two provisions of § 102 may be readily classified according to these principles. The jury trial right set out in § 102(c)(1) is plainly a procedural change of the sort that would ordinarily govern in trials conducted after its effective date. If § 102 did no more than introduce a right to jury trial in Title VII cases, the provision would presumably apply to cases tried after November 21, 1991, regardless of when the underlying conduct occurred. However, because § 102(c) makes a jury trial available only "[i]f a complaining party seeks compensatory or punitive damages," the jury trial option must stand or fall with the attached damages provisions.

Section 102(b)(1) is clearly on the other side of the line. That subsection authorizes punitive damages if the plaintiff shows that the defendant "engaged in a discriminatory practice or discriminatory practices with malice or with reckless indifference to the federally protected rights of an aggrieved individual." The very labels given "punitive" or "exemplary" damages, as well as the rationales that support them, demonstrate that they share key characteristics of criminal sanctions. Retroactive imposition of punitive damages would raise a serious constitutional question. Before we entertained that question, we would have to be confronted with a statute that explicitly authorized punitive damages for preenactment conduct. The Civil Rights Act of 1991 contains no such explicit command.

The provision of § 102(a)(1) authorizing the recovery of compensatory damages is not easily classified. It does not make unlawful conduct that was lawful when it occurred; [ ] § 102 only reaches discriminatory conduct already prohibited by Title VII. Concerns about a lack of fair notice are further muted by the fact that such discrimination was in many cases (although not this one) already subject to monetary liability in the form of backpay. Nor could anyone seriously contend that the compensatory damages provisions smack of a "retributive" or other suspect legislative purpose. Section 102 reflects Congress' desire to afford victims of discrimination more complete redress for violations of rules established more than a generation ago in the Civil Rights Act of 1964. At least with respect to its compensatory damages provisions, then, § 102 is not in a category in which objections to retroactive application on grounds of fairness have their greatest force.

Nonetheless, the new compensatory damages provision would operate "retrospectively" if it were applied to conduct occurring before November 21, 1991. Unlike certain other forms of relief, compensatory damages are quintessentially backward-looking. Compensatory damages may be intended less to sanction wrong-doers than to make victims whole, but they do so by a mechanism that affects the liabilities of defendants. They do not "compensate" by distributing funds from the public coffers, but by requiring particular employers to pay for harms they caused. The introduction of a right to compensatory damages is also the type of legal change that would have an impact on private parties' planning. In this case, the event to which the new damages provision relates is the discriminatory conduct of respondents' agent John Williams; if applied here, that provision would attach an important new legal burden to that conduct. The new damages remedy in § 102, we conclude, is the kind of provision that does not apply to events antedating its enactment in the absence of clear congressional intent.

In cases like this one, in which prior law afforded no relief, § 102 can be seen as creating a new cause of action, and its impact on parties' rights is especially pronounced. Section 102 confers a new right to monetary relief on persons like petitioner who were victims of a hostile work environment but were not constructively discharged, and the novel prospect of damages liability for their employers. Because Title VII previously authorized recovery of back-pay in some cases, and because compensatory damages under § 102(a) are in addition to any backpay recoverable, the new provision also resembles a statute increasing the amount of dam-ages available under a preestablished cause of action. Even under that view, however, the provision would, if applied in cases arising before the Act's effective date, undoubtedly impose on employers found liable a "new disability" in respect to past events. The extent of a party's liability, in the civil context as well as the criminal, is an important legal consequence that cannot be ignored. Neither in Bradley itself, nor in any case before or since in which Congress had not clearly spoken, have we read a statute substantially increas-ing the monetary liability of a private party to apply to conduct occurring before the statute's enactment.

It will frequently be true, as petitioner and amici forcefully argue here, that retroactive application of a new statute would vindicate its purpose more fully. That consideration, however, is not sufficient to rebut the presumption against retroactivity. Statutes are seldom crafted to pursue a single goal, and compromises necessary to their enactment may require adopting means other than those that would most effectively pursue the main goal. A legislator who supported a prospective statute might reasonably oppose retroactive application of the same statute. Indeed, there is reason to believe that the omission of the 1990 version's express retroactivity provisions was a factor in the passage of the 1991 bill. Section 102 is plainly not the sort of provision that must be understood to operate retroactively because a contrary reading would render it ineffective.

The presumption against statutory retroactivity is founded upon sound considerations of general policy and practice, and accords with long held and widely shared expectations about the usual operation of legislation. We are satisfied that it applies to § 102. Because we have found no clear evidence of congressional intent that § 102 of the Civil Rights Act of 1991 should apply to cases arising before its enactment, we conclude that the judgment of the Court of Appeals must be affirmed.

■ Justice Scalia, with whom Justices Kennedy, and Thomas, join, concurring in the judgment.

I of course agree with the Court that there exists a judicial presumption, of great antiquity, that a legislative enactment affecting substantive rights does not apply retroactively absent clear statement to the contrary. The Court, however, is willing to let that clear statement be supplied, not by the text of the law in question, but by individual legislators who participated in the enactment of the law, and even legislators in an earlier Congress which tried and failed to enact a similar law. For the Court not only combs the floor debate and committee reports of the statute at issue, but also reviews the procedural history of an earlier, unsuccessful, attempt by a different Congress to enact similar legislation, the Civil Rights Act of 1990.

This effectively converts the "clear statement" rule into a "discernible legislative intent" rule—and even that understates the difference. The Court's rejection of the floor statements of certain Senators because they are "frankly partisan" and "cannot plausibly be read as reflecting any general agreement," reads like any other exercise in the soft science of legislative historicizing, undisciplined by any distinctive "clear statement" requirement. If it is a "clear statement" we are seeking, surely it is not enough to insist that the statement can "plausibly be read as reflecting general agreement"; the statement must clearly reflect general agreement. No legislative history can do that, of course, but only the text of the statute itself. That has been the meaning of the "clear statement" retroactivity rule from the earliest times. See, e. g., United States v. Heth, 3 Cranch 399, 408 (1806)(Johnson, J.); id., at 414 (Cushing, J.). I do not deem that clear rule to be changed by the Court's dicta regarding legislative history in the present case. * * *

The Court's opinion begins with an evaluation of petitioner's argument that the text of the statute dictates its retroactive application. The Court's rejection of that argument cannot be as forceful as it ought, so long as it insists upon compromising the clarity of the ancient and constant assumption that legislation is prospective, by attributing a comparable pedigree to the nouveau Bradley presumption in favor of applying the law in effect at the time of decision. See Bradley v. Richmond School Bd., 416 U.S. 696, 711–716 (1974). As I have demonstrated elsewhere and need not repeat here, Bradley and Thorpe v. Housing Authority of Durham, 393 U.S. 268 (1969), simply misread our precedents and invented an utterly new and erroneous rule.

Besides embellishing the pedigree of the Bradley–Thorpe presumption, the Court goes out of its way to reaffirm the holdings of those cases. I see nothing to be gained by overruling them, but neither do I think the indefensible should needlessly be defended. And Thorpe, at least, is really indefensible. The regulation at issue there required that "before instituting an eviction proceeding local housing authorities * * * should inform the tenant * * * of the reasons for the eviction * * *." The Court imposed that requirement on an eviction proceeding instituted eighteen months before the regulation issued. That application was plainly retroactive and was wrong. The result in Bradley presents a closer question; application of an attorney's fees provision to ongoing litigation is arguably not retroactive. If it were retroactive, however, it would surely not be saved (as the Court suggests) by the existence of another theory under which attorney's fees might have been discretionarily awarded.

My last, and most significant, disagreement with the Court's analysis of this case pertains to the meaning of retroactivity. The Court adopts as its own the definition crafted by Justice Story * * *: a law is retroactive only if it "takes away or impairs vested rights acquired under existing laws, or creates a new obligation, imposes a new duty, or attaches a new disability, in respect to transactions or considerations already past."

One might expect from this "vested rights" focus that the Court would hold all changes in rules of procedure (as opposed to matters of substance) to apply retroactively. * * * In fact, however, the Court shrinks from faithfully applying the test that it has announced. It first seemingly defends the procedural-substantive distinction that a "vested rights" theory entails * * *. But it soon acknowledges a broad and ill defined (indeed, utterly undefined) exception: "Whether a new rule of trial procedure applies will generally depend upon the posture of the case in question." Under this exception, "a new rule concerning the filing of complaints would not govern an action in which the complaint had already been filed," and "the promulgation of a new jury trial rule would ordinarily not warrant retrial of cases that had previously been tried to a judge." It is hard to see how either of these refusals to allow retroactive application preserves any "vested right." "'No one has a vested right in any given mode of procedure.'"

The seemingly random exceptions to the Court's "vested rights" (substance-vs.-procedure) criterion must be made, I suggest, because that criterion is fundamentally wrong. * * * [A] procedural change should no more be presumed to be retroactive than a substantive one. The critical issue, I think, is not whether the rule affects "vested rights," or governs substance or procedure, but rather what is the relevant activity that the rule regulates. Absent clear statement otherwise, only such relevant activity which occurs after the effective date of the statute is covered. Most statutes are meant to regulate primary conduct, and hence will not be applied in trials involving conduct that occurred before their effective date. But other statutes have a different purpose and therefore a different relevant retroactivity event. A new rule of evidence governing expert testimony, for example, is aimed at regulating the conduct of trial, and the event relevant to retroactivity of the rule is introduction of the testimony. Even though it is a procedural rule, it would unquestionably not be applied to testimony already taken—reversing a case on appeal, for example, because the new rule had not been applied at a trial which antedated the statute.

The inadequacy of the Court's "vested rights" approach becomes apparent when a change in one of the incidents of trial alters substantive entitlements. The opinion classifies attorney's fees provisions as procedural and permits "retroactive" application (in the sense of application to cases involving pre-enactment conduct). It seems to me, however, that holding a person liable for attorney's fees affects a "substantive right" no less than holding him liable for compensatory or punitive damages, which the Court treats as affecting a vested right. If attorney's fees can be awarded in a suit involving conduct that antedated the fee-authorizing statute, it is because the purpose of the fee award is not to affect that conduct, but to encourage suit for the vindication of certain rights—so that the retroactivity event is the filing of suit [ ]. * * *

I do not maintain that it will always be easy to determine, from the statute's purpose, the relevant event for assessing its retroactivity. As I have suggested, for example, a statutory provision for attorney's fees presents a difficult case. Ordinarily, however, the answer is clear—as it is in both Landgraf and Rivers. Unlike the Court, I do not think that any of the provisions at issue is "not easily classified." They are all directed at the regulation of primary conduct, and the occurrence of the primary conduct is the relevant event.

[Editor—Dissent by Justice Blackmun in this and the following case omitted.]

Rivers v. Roadway Express

511 U.S. 298 (1994).

■ Justice Stevens delivered the opinion of the Court. * * *

[Editor—This case involved a claim of illegal race discrimination under 42 U.S.C. § 1981. The alleged harm predated the Court's decision in Patterson, which held that the statute applied only to discrimination in the formation of the contract, not to discrimination during the performance of the contract. Consequently, charges of employer racial harassment on the job were not covered by § 1981, contrary to what lower courts had held. Section 101 of the Civil Rights Act of 1991, overturned Patterson by defining the term "make and enforce contracts" in § 1981 to include "the making, performance, modification, and termination of contracts, and the enjoyment of all benefits, privileges, terms, and conditions of the contractual relationship." As in Landgraf, the Court still refused to apply the Civil Rights Act of 1991 retroactively.

Consider these questions as you read the case. (1) Should the Court have drawn a distinction based on when the defendant violated the law—whether or not before the decision in Patterson— when the case law was pro-plaintiff? (2) Should it have mattered that Congress reacted immediately to the 1989 Patterson decision; does that deprive the defendants of any claim that they were not on notice of what Congress was likely to do? (3) Should it have mattered that the activity in this case would have violated the old Title VII but no compensatory damages would have been allowed?]

* * * We are persuaded [   ] that the presumption [against retroactivity] is even more clearly applicable to § 101 than to § 102. Section 102 altered the liabilities of employers under Title VII by subjecting them to expanded monetary liability, but it did not alter the normative scope of Title VII's prohibition on workplace discrimination. In contrast, because § 101 amended § 1981 to embrace all aspects of the contractual relationship, including contract terminations, it enlarged the category of conduct that is subject to § 1981 liability.

Moreover, § 1981 (and hence § 101) is not limited to employment; because it covers all contracts, a substantial part of § 101's sweep does not overlap Title VII. In short, § 101 has the effect not only of increasing liability but also of establishing a new standard of conduct. Accordingly, for reasons we stated in Landgraf, the important new legal obligations § 101 imposes bring it within the class of laws that are presumptively prospective.

Petitioners rely heavily on an argument that was not applicable to § 102 of the 1991 Act, the section at issue in Landgraf. They contend that § 101 should apply to their case because it was "restorative" of the understanding of § 1981 that prevailed before our decision in Patterson. * * *

* * * Petitioners maintain that restorative statutes do not implicate fairness concerns relating to retroactivity at least when, as is the case in this litigation, the new statute simply enacts a rule that the parties believed to be the law when they acted. Indeed, amici in support of petitioners contend, fairness concerns positively favor application of § 101 to pending cases because the effect of the Patterson decision was to cut off, after the fact, rights of action

under § 1981 that had been widely recognized in the lower courts, and under which many victims of discrimination had won damage judgments prior to Patterson.

Notwithstanding the equitable appeal of petitioners' argument, we are convinced that it cannot carry the day. * * *

* * * A restorative purpose may be relevant to whether Congress specifically intended a new statute to govern past conduct, but we do not "presume" an intent to act retroactively in such cases. We still require clear evidence of intent to impose the restorative statute "retroactively." Section 101, and the statute of which it is a part, does not contain such evidence.

"The principle that statutes operate only prospectively, while judicial decisions operate retrospectively, is familiar to every law student," and this case illustrates the second half of that principle as well as the first. Even though applicable Sixth Circuit precedents were otherwise when this dispute arose, the District Court properly applied Patterson to this case. The essence of judicial decisionmaking-applying general rules to particular situations-necessarily involves some peril to individual expectations because it is often difficult to predict the precise application of a general rule until it has been distilled in the crucible of litigation.

Patterson did not overrule any prior decision of this Court; rather, it held and therefore established that the prior decisions of the Courts of Appeals which read § 1981 to cover discriminatory contract termination were incorrect. They were not wrong according to some abstract standard of interpretive validity, but by the rules that necessarily govern our hierarchical federal court system. It is this Court's responsibility to say what a statute means, and once the Court has spoken, it is the duty of other courts to respect that understanding of the governing rule of law. A judicial construction of a statute is an authoritative statement of what the statute meant before as well as after the decision of the case giving rise to that construction. Thus, Patterson provides the authoritative interpretation of the phrase "make and enforce contracts" in the Civil Rights Act of 1866 before the 1991 amendment went into effect on November 21, 1991. That interpretation provides the baseline for our conclusion that the 1991 amendment would be "retroactive" if applied to cases arising before that date.

Congress, of course, has the power to amend a statute that it believes we have misconstrued. It may even, within broad constitutional bounds, make such a change retroactive and thereby undo what it perceives to be the undesirable past consequences of a misinterpretation of its work product. No such change, however, has the force of law unless it is implemented through legislation. Even when Congress intends to supersede a rule of law embodied in one of our decisions with what it views as a better rule established in earlier decisions, its intent to reach conduct preceding the "corrective" amendment must clearly appear. We cannot say that such an intent clearly appears with respect to § 101. For this reason, and because it creates liabilities that had no legal existence before the Act was passed, § 101 does not apply to preenactment conduct.

Accordingly, the judgment of the Court of Appeals is affirmed, and the case is remanded for further proceedings consistent with this opinion.

QUESTIONS AND COMMENTS

1. *Tax-funded benefits.* Suppose a statute, silent on the issue of retroactivity, provides (1) unemployment insurance benefits, funded out of taxes on employers, or (2) welfare benefits, funded out of general tax revenues. Would Stevens or Scalia apply the presumption against retroactivity to that statute?

2. *Retroactive legislative override of prior judgment.* The latest sparring over the nature of legislation and adjudication, in the context of retroactive legislation, occurred in Plaut v. Spendthrift Farm, Inc., 115 S.Ct. 1447 (1995). The Court held that the legislature could not retroactively vacate a judgment by a court insofar as it affected parties to the lawsuit. More interesting than the result was the reasoning. Justice Scalia, writing for the Court, relied on Separation of Powers, protecting court judgments from legislative override. Judgments must be protected from retroactive override to preserve the judge's Article III power to say what the law is. Scalia, citing Federalist # 81, noted that the Framers of the Constitution lived among the ruins of intermingled legislative and judicial powers, which they intended to eliminate.

Justice Stevens disagreed with the Court's reasoning, which sharply differentiated between legislation and adjudication. Stevens argued that prior case law announced a rule of law and that later legislation overriding the prior decision should be evaluated under the same principles that governed any retroactive legislation affecting prior law—the Due Process Clause. Stevens therefore merged statutory modification of prior judicial *and* prior legislative lawmaking under the same constitutional analysis, and was potentially more tolerant than the Court of a retroactive legislative override of a prior judgment.

Prospective adjudication? One way to understand the disagreement between Stevens and Scalia is to see it as part of a continuing debate about whether legislation and adjudication are radically different kinds of lawmaking. The traditional assumption about legislation was that it was willful and therefore should be prospective. Adjudication, by contrast, was retroactive. The old (and now obsolete) view was that judges merely discovered the law. The more contemporary view is that adjudication is the unfolding of principle through reasoned elaboration. This avoids the defects of legislation because the gradually evolving reasoning process reduces (perhaps elimi-nates) the role of will, or at least minimizes unfairness and therefore justifies retroactivity.

Both these images of lawmaking may be changing. We have already read Justice Stevens' comments about a change in attitude towards legisla-tion, leading to a softening of the presumption against retroactive statutes. Similarly, the traditional view of judging is now hard to sustain. The political elements in judging seem obvious, leading to a greater willingness to engage in prospective adjudication. The opposition to prospective judging today comes less from advocates of the traditional view that judging does not involve political choices and more from a desire to minimize those choices. After all, if judging is retroactive, judges will be less willing to change the law.

There has been an intense debate within the Supreme Court about prospective adjudication. In 1971, the Court adopted a three-part test in Chevron Oil Co. v. Huson, 404 U.S. 97 (1971), to determine when adjudica-tion would be prospective:

> In our cases dealing with the nonretroactivity question, we have generally considered three separate factors. First, the decision to be applied nonretroactively must establish a new principle of law, either by overruling clear past precedent on which litigants may have relied, or by deciding an issue of first impression whose resolution was not clearly foreshadowed. Second, it has been stressed that "we must * * * weigh the merits and demerits in each case by looking to the prior history of the rule in question, its purpose and effect, and whether retrospective operation will further or retard its operation." Finally, we have weighed the inequity imposed by retroactive application, for "[w]here a decision of this Court could produce substantial inequitable results if applied retroactively, there is ample basis in our cases for avoiding the 'injustice or hardship' by a holding of nonretroactivity."

More recently, the Court has distinguished between pure and modified prospectivity. Under pure prospectivity, a new rule is applied neither to the parties in the case nor to others whose conduct occurred prior to the decision. Under modified (or selective) prospectivity, a court applies a new rule in the case in which it is pronounced, and then returns to the old rule with respect to all others whose conduct occurred prior to the decision. (It might be clearer to call this modified or selective "retroactivity" but that is not the accepted lingo.) Selective prospectivity was used most often in criminal cases, to assure that the accused had an incentive to sue. However, the Court later abandoned selective prospectivity in criminal cases on direct appeal in Griffith v. Kentucky, 479 U.S. 314 (1987). The decision rested in part on the ground that the policy in favor of giving the winning petitioner a special incentive to raise legal issues could not outweigh the policy favoring equal treatment of similarly situated petitioners. (The Court's treatment of criminal cases on *collateral* review, through habeas corpus petitions or other-wise, is beyond the scope of these comments.)

As for civil cases, the Court in Harper v. Virginia Dept. of Taxation, 509 U.S. 86 (1993), continued its critique of prospective adjudication, rejected selective prospectivity, and came close to overruling Chevron.

Harper v. Virginia Dept. of Taxation

509 U.S. 86 (1993).

■ Justice Thomas delivered the opinion of the Court. * * *

* * * When this Court applies a rule of federal law to the parties before it, that rule is the controlling interpretation of federal law and must be given full retroactive effect in all cases still open on direct review and as to all events, regardless of whether such events predate or postdate our announcement of the rule. This rule extends Griffith's ban against "selective application of new rules." Mindful of the "basic norms of constitutional adjudication" that animated our view of retroactivity in the criminal context, we now prohibit the erection of selective temporal barriers to the application of federal law in noncriminal cases. In both civil and criminal cases, we can scarcely permit "the substantive law [to] shift and spring" according to "the particular equities of [individual parties'] claims" of actual reliance on an old rule and of harm from a retroactive application of the new rule. Our approach to retroactivity heeds the admonition that "the Court has no more constitutional authority in civil cases than in criminal cases to disregard current law or to treat similarly situated litigants differently."

The Supreme Court of Virginia "applied the three-pronged Chevron Oil test in deciding the retroactivity issue" presented by this litigation. When this Court does not "reserve the question whether its holding should be applied to the parties before it," however, an opinion announcing a rule of federal law "is properly understood to have followed the normal rule of retroactive application" and must be "read to hold * * * that its rule should apply retroactively to the litigants then before the Court." Furthermore, the legal imperative "to apply a rule of federal law retroactively after the case announcing the rule has already done so" must "prevail over any claim based on a Chevron Oil analysis." * * *

■ Scalia, J., concurring: * * *

What most provokes comment in the dissent * * * is the irony of its invoking stare decisis in defense of prospective decisionmaking at all. Prospective decisionmaking is the handmaid of judicial activism, and the born enemy of stare decisis. It was formulated in the heyday of legal realism and promoted as a "technique of judicial lawmaking" in general, and more specifically as a means of making it easier to overrule prior precedent. Thus, the dissent is saying, in effect, that stare decisis demands the preservation of methods of destroying stare decisis recently invented in violation of stare decisis.

Contrary to the dissent's assertion that Chevron Oil articulated "our traditional retroactivity analysis," the jurisprudence it reflects "came into being," as Justice Harlan observed, less than 30 years ago [   ]. It is so un-ancient that one of the current members of this Court was sitting when it was invented. The true traditional view is that prospective decisionmaking is quite incompatible with the judicial power, and that courts have no authority to engage in the practice. * * *

Four judges disagreed with the majority's general approach to prospective adjudication. Justices Kennedy and White argued "that it is sometimes appropriate in the civil context to give only prospective application to a judicial decision," reaffirming the Chevron Oil test. They would also permit selective prospectivity, because of differences between the civil and criminal contexts. Justice O'Connor and Chief Justice Rehnquist also affirmed that "[w]hen the Court changes its mind, the law changes with it. If the Court decides, in the context of a civil case or controversy, to change the law, it must make [a] determination whether the new law or the old is to apply to conduct occurring before the law-changing decision. Chevron Oil describes our long-established procedure for making this inquiry." O'Connor and Rehnquist noted that the question of pure prospectivity was not at issue in the case.

None of the judges doubted that an otherwise retroactive decision would *not* be applied to cases on which the statute of limitations had run or for which a final judgment had been issued. At least this much selectivity and unequal treatment of litigants in applying new case law was justified.

COMMENTS

1. *State law.* The Supreme Court's approach to retroactive adjudication does not bind state courts deciding state law. Whatever equal treatment concerns disfavor selective prospectivity and whatever Separation of Powers concerns disfavor pure prospectivity do not rise to the level of a federal constitutional mandate; they only affect federal law. In a post-Harper decision, the New Jersey Supreme Court held that its decision adopting a two year statute of limitations for its Law Against Discrimination would be applied on a *purely prospective* basis. Montells v. Haynes, 627 A.2d 654 (N.J.1993).

The plaintiff in Montells filed a sexual harassment complaint when the limitations period for such lawsuits was unclear—some cases had applied a six year, and others, a two year limitations period. The issue was neither settled by precedent nor one of first impression. In that context, the Court held that the law was "sufficiently murky" to justify plaintiff reliance on the longer six year period when the complaint was filed. Moreover, cutting off the plaintiff's claim was inconsistent with the legislature's direction favoring a liberal reading of the anti-discrimination law. Therefore, the decision was not applied "to this case, pending cases, or cases the operative facts of which arose before the date of this decision."

The New Jersey court took explicit note of the Supreme Court's Harper decision and its questioning of "the continuing vitality of Chevron's prospectivity analysis," but stated: "Whatever path that Court may follow, we believe that in an appropriate case a purely prospective application may provide the fairest and most equitable disposition."

2. *Reviving statutes.* Retroactive adjudication raises especially interesting problems when the case overturns a prior decision which had held a statute unconstitutional. The relevant events are: first, passage of a statute; then, case 1 holding the statute unconstitutional; then, case 2 overruling case 1. See W. Treanor & G. Sperling, Prospective Overruling and the Revival of "Unconstitutional" Statutes, 93 Colum. L. Rev. 1902 (1993)(discussion prompted by Planned Parenthood v. Casey, 505 U.S. 833 (1992), which overturned prior cases invalidating certain statutory notice restrictions on abortions). The authors advocate prospective overruling in certain circumstances to prevent revival of prior statutes. They note that the political process often treats overruled earlier cases as nullifying the prior statute, suppressing moves for repeal. Moreover, where liberty interests are involved, they argue against reviving the prior statute, leaving it to the legislature to repass the act. The authors clearly have in mind the possibility that the Supreme Court will reverse Roe v. Wade and hold that the states can make abortion a crime.

What little law there is on this issue is to the contrary. Jawish v. Morlet, 86 A.2d 96 (D.C.Ct.App.1952), involved the 1918 minimum wage statute for women and children, which the Supreme Court held was unconstitutional in 1923 but then (overruling itself) held was constitutional in 1937. The Jawish court decided that the 1918 law revived.

Note the interesting twist on retroactivity raised by Treanor & Sperling. The issue is *not* the usual one of applying a case to events occurring prior to the decision. Indeed, if the Court decides to reverse Roe v. Wade, it would violate Due Process to criminalize events occurring before the decision date, even if the states had left anti-abortion statutes on their books. Although the prohibition of *ex post facto* laws only applies to statutes, retroactive cases "creating" crimes violate Due Process. Marks v. United States, 430 U.S. 188 (1977). Treanor & Sperling would go further and refuse to apply the statute to events occurring *after* the date of the decision, unless the statute was reenacted.

3. *Postponed date.* A prospective decision can be even more like legislation, if its effective date is postponed? The Supreme Court did this when it struck down the federal Bankruptcy law on the ground that it vested the judicial power in non-Article III judges. Northern Pipeline Construction Co. v. Marathon Pipe Line Co., 458 U.S. 50 (1982)(case decided June 28, 1982, but judgment deferred until October 4, 1982, to allow Congress to act to reconstitute the bankruptcy courts).

7.03 TYPE OF DOCUMENT

The most fundamental background consideration affecting interpretation is the type of document the court interprets, because different documents call for different weighting of the relevant interpretive criteria. Textualists might want to deny this on the theory that ordinary usage dominates interpretation regardless of the type of document. The material in this section helps you evaluate this claim. We look at wills, contracts, multi-language texts, statutory grants-in-aid, treaties, initiatives/referendums, and "private lawmaking."

a) PRIVATE DOCUMENTS

i) WILLS

The following case looks beyond the language of a will to the subjective intent of the drafter. Why might the search for subjective intent behind a will be more justified than for a statute?

Engle v. Siegel

377 A.2d 892 (N.J.1977).

■ Mountain, J.

The facts in this will construction case are not in dispute. In September, 1973, Albert and Judith Siegel, together with their two children, lost their lives as the result of a tragic hotel fire in Copenhagen, Denmark. All died within thirty days of one another. Albert's will was dated April 2, 1964 and Judith's was dated September 29, 1964. The instruments were admitted to probate October 3, 1973 and Louis Engle, Judith's father, qualified as executor of both. A common disaster clause appears in each will. The provision in Albert's will read as follows:

> In the event my wife Judith and my children predecease me, or [this is the event which occurred] if we all die as a result of a common accident, or within thirty (30) days from the date of my death, then in that event, I give, devise and bequeath all the rest, residue and remainder of my estate and property of every kind and nature unto my mother, Rose Siegel, and my mother-in-law, Ida Engle, to be divided between them share and share alike.

The corresponding clause in Judith's will was identical except for appropriate alterations as to names and relationships. Rose Siegel, Albert's mother, predeceased her son and daughter-in-law, having died in or about 1967. Judith's mother, Ida Engle, survived and is a party to this action.

The contest has arisen due to the fact that Rose Siegel, named in each will as a residuary legatee, predeceased her son and daughter-in-law. Ida Engle, the other residuary legatee, takes the position that under these circumstances our statute, N.J.S.A. 3A:3–14, becomes operative to cause the entire residuary estate of each decedent to pass to her. This statute reads as follows:

> When a residuary devise or bequest shall be made to 2 or more persons by the will of any testator dying after July 3, 1947, unless a contrary intention shall appear by the will, the share of any such residuary devisees or legatees dying before the testator * * * shall go to and be vested in the remaining residuary devisees or legatees in proportion to their respective shares in said residue. [N.J.S.A. 3A:3–14]

Appellants, Leo H. Siegel and Judith Siegel Baron, are brother and sister of the decedent, Albert Siegel. All three, of course, are also children of the decedent, Rose. It is these appellants' position that the foregoing statute has no relevance here because, by a proper application of the rule of probable intent, the share of each residuary estate set apart for their mother should now pass to them in equal shares. * * *

Traditionally, and perhaps rather monotonously, courts have repeated, as we do here again, that in construing the terms of a will, a court's task is always to determine the intent of the testator. But these words may be given different meanings and the quest for intent can be undertaken and pursued in various ways. The generally accepted method of determining testamentary intent was once described by this Court in these words,

> It is an elementary principle in the construction of wills that the controlling consideration is the effect of the words as actually written rather than the actual intention of the testator independently of the written words. The question is not what the testator actually intended, or what he was minded to say, but rather the meaning of the terms chosen to state the testamentary purpose * * *.

This statement can no longer be said accurately to express the law of our State.

In Fidelity Union Trust Co. v. Robert, 178 A.2d 185 (N.J.1962) this Court, speaking through Justice Jacobs, announced what has come to be known as the doctrine of probable intent. The rule has been stated thus,

> While a court may not, of course, conjure up an interpretation or derive a missing testamentary provision out of the whole cloth, it may on the basis of the entire will, competent extrinsic evidence and common human impulses strive reasonably to

ascertain and carry out what the testator probably intended should be the disposition if the present situation developed.

* * * We are no longer limited simply to searching out the probable meaning intended by the words and phrases in the will. Relevant circumstances, including the testator's own expressions of intent, must also be studied, and their significance assayed. * * *

With these considerations in mind, we turn to the facts of this case. * * * [Editor—The court first concludes that Rose Siegel's death had not been anticipated and its omission from the will was inadvertent.]

We next turn to the relevant and competent extrinsic evidence which bears upon the probable intention of the testators with respect to this unforeseen situation. The attorney who drafted the will, Samuel J. Zucker, Esq., testified as to his conference with Albert and Judith Siegel preceding the drafting of the will. He testified from memory, aided by notes he had made at the conference. The question as to what disposition should be made of their assets in the event of a common disaster was squarely raised. After conferring together, Albert, speaking for his wife and himself, declared that in that event they would like all of their property to be divided equally between their two families. As Albert put it, "split it down the middle so they [the respective families] each get half * * *." Mr. Zucker pointed out that the word "family" was inappropriate as being "a broad term." The problem so posed by the attorney was obviously perceived as one of form or draftsmanship. Certainly, the attorney did not suggest that the Siegels should not provide for the persons constituting their "family." Nor can his advice to his clients be interpreted to mean that the Siegels were being told to designate an individual legatee rather than one standing in a representative capacity for an identifiable group or class of persons. The sense of this exchange between Mr. Zucker and the Siegels is that, if it was their intention to benefit the class of persons constituting their respective families, that designation would have to be accomplished with more definite and precise language. * * *

We have no difficulty in reaching the conclusion that the primary wish of each decedent, given the contingency that occurred, would have been to divide the property included in their residuary estates between the Siegel family and the Engle family. The designation of their respective mothers resulted solely from the scrivener's rejection of the word "family" as a term to describe the recipient of a testamentary benefaction. Each mother was obviously thought of as an appropriate representative of a "family".

To give the assets of both estates entirely to Mrs. Engle would seem to fly directly in the face of all the evidence bearing upon probable intent. * * *

On the other hand, to divide one-half of each residuary estate equally between Leo H. Siegel and Judith Siegel Baron, now obviously the persons constituting the Siegel "family," would seem completely to carry out probable intent. * * *

Is there more or less justification for going beyond the language of a will than a statute? What is the significance of the fact that a will involves one author and is not a political document?

New Jersey is in fact aberrational in applying the "probable intent" approach to wills, although other courts may find surreptitious ways to implement the testator's intent without appearing to violate the text. The more common judicial practice of sticking to the text of a will is still based, however, on background policy considerations, such as discouraging litigation by disgruntled beneficiaries.

ii) CONTRACTS

A contract, unlike a will, is an agreement between parties. Moreover, neither party has sovereign power over the other. Therefore, the subjective intent of one party cannot control the meaning of a contract. The subjective intent of *both* parties to a contract might, however, determine the contract's meaning. Thus, the Restatement of Contracts, 2d, states:

212. Interpretation of Integrated Document * * *

Illustration 4. A and B are engaged in buying and selling shares of stock from each other, and agree orally to conceal the nature of their dealings by using the word "sell" to mean "buy" and using the word "buy" to mean "sell". A sends a written offer to B to "sell" certain shares, and B accepts. The parties are bound in accordance with the oral agreement.

An objective theory of meaning has been proposed for contracts, most vividly in Judge Learned Hand's assertion that the "natural meaning" of the language prevails notwithstanding that the whole House of Bishops might satisfy the court that a different meaning was intended by one or both parties. Eustis Mining Co. v. Beer, Sondheimer & Co., 239 F. 976, 984–985 (D.N.Y.1917). The rationale for an objective approach to interpreting contracts may differ from that applicable to statutes. There may, for example, be a public interest in reducing litigation based on claims about subjective intent and avoiding the uncertainty that would ensue from such litigation.[14]

Does legislative sovereignty suggest that subjective legislative intent is at least as important as the subjective intent of the parties to a contract? Or

14. Whatever the doctrine, subjective intent regarding the meaning of contracts rarely matters, for the following reason. Despite differences in subjective intent, if one party (and only one party) knows (or has reason to know) that the other party has attached a different meaning to the document, the contract has the meaning attached by the other party. Restatement of Contracts, 2d (secs. 20, 201).

does the fact that a statute is a political document suggest that the objective meaning of the text is *more* important for statutes?

The fact that a statute is a political document might suggest another way in which determining the meaning of contracts and statutes should differ. With a political document like a statute, it makes sense to interpret the text's meaning in light of the policy implications, in addition to relying on the statutory text and legislative intent. In the case of a private document like a contract, however, the distinction between meaning and policy considerations may be sharply drawn. In the Restatement of Contracts, for example, Chapter 9, Topic 1, is entitled "The Meaning of Agreements," but the subsequent Topic 2 is entitled "Considerations of Fairness and Public Interest." Topic 2 imposes a duty of good faith and fair dealing (sec. 205) and permits the court not to enforce unconscionable terms (sec. 208). These policies are not read into the contract as an interpretation of the contract's meaning. Similarly, the Restatement places the rule interpreting a document against the draftsman under Topic 2 (Considerations of Fairness and Public Interest), not Topic 1 (Meaning).

How would you categorize discharge of a contract obligation because of impracticality or frustration? Is this an interpretation of the contract or an application of public policy? How does the following excerpt from the Introductory Note to the Restatement of Contracts, Chapter 11, answer this question?

> The rationale behind the doctrines of impracticability and frustration is sometimes said to be that there is an "implied term" of the contract that such extraordinary circumstances will not occur. This Restatement rejects this analysis in favor of that of Uniform Commercial Code 2–615, under which the central inquiry is whether the non-occurrence of the circumstance was a "basic assumption on which the contract was made." In order for the parties to have had such a "basic assumption" it is not necessary for them to have been conscious of alternatives. Where, for example, an artist contracts to paint a painting, it can be said that the death of the artist is an event the non-occurrence of which was a basic assumption on which the contract was made, even though the parties never consciously addressed themselves to that possibility.

> Determining whether the non-occurrence of a particular event was or was not a basic assumption involves a judgment as to which party assumed the risk of its occurrence. In contracting for the manufacture and delivery of goods at a price fixed in the contract, for example, the seller assumes the risk of increased costs within the normal range. If, however, a disaster results in an abrupt tenfold increase in cost to seller, a court might determine that the seller did not assume this risk by concluding that the non-occurrence of the disaster was a "basic assumption" on which the contract was made.

In making such determinations, a court will look at all circumstances, including the terms of the contract. The fact that the event was unforeseeable is significant as suggesting that its non-occurrence was a basic assumption. However, the fact that it was foreseeable, or even foreseen, does not, of itself, argue for a contrary conclusion, since the parties may not have thought it sufficiently important a risk to have made it a subject of their bargaining. Another significant factor may be the relative bargaining positions of the parties and the relative ease with which either party could have included a clause. Another may be the effectiveness of the market in spreading such risks as, for example, where the obligor is a middleman who has an opportunity to adjust his prices to cover them.

Under the rationale of this Restatement, the obligor is relieved of his duty because the contract, having been made on a different "basic assumption," is regarded as not covering the case that has arisen. It is an omitted case, falling within a "gap" in the contract.

b) MULTI-LANGUAGE TEXTS

i) TREATIES

When a treaty has official texts in two or more languages, the plain meaning in one language might differ from plain meaning in another treaty language. There are a variety of approaches courts might take:[15] e.g., rely on the language of the original text in which the treaty was drafted; the principle of minimum common content; binding a party only to the text in his own language; favoring the more precise version. Which interpretive criteria are appropriate if treaties are analogized to contracts?

Some treaties are not like contracts but are more like broad statutes or basic constitutional documents which establish ongoing political rules for the community. As such they may be interpreted in light of "the spirit and the purpose of the provision,"[16] rather any of the specific interpretive rules mentioned above. The Treaty creating the European Economic Community is often said to be more constitution-like.

ii) STATUTES IN MORE THAN ONE LANGUAGE

Many countries, including Canada, South Africa, Belgium, and Switzerland, have official statutory texts in more than one language. For example, the current Official Languages Act in Canada provides that "in construing an enactment, both its versions in the official languages are equally authentic."

15. See Stevens, The Principle of Linguistic Equality in Judicial Proceedings and in the Interpretation of Plurilingual Legal Instruments, 62 Nw. U. L. Rev. 701 (1967)(hereafter "Stevens"); Bederman, Revivalist Canons and Treaty Interpretation, 41 U.C.L.A. L. Rev. 953 (1994).

16. See Stevens, pp. 729–31.

In Re Wolfe and the Queen et al., 137 D.L.R. (3d) 553 (1982), the English text of a Canadian statute permitted the sheriff to enforce a lien "upon all property used in connection with * * * the business of the vendor." The sheriff seized property leased but not owned by the vendor. The French version clearly limited the lien to property owned by the vendor. The narrower French version was used to resolve the uncertainty in the English version. The decision is reminiscent of the approach to treaties which adopts "the minimum common content." But what if the English creditor relied on the broader English language version, consistent with permitting a lien on property leased by the vendor? Are the words in English so obviously unclear that an English creditor would have read (or gotten someone to read) the more precise French version?

The clash of texts in a multi-lingual country makes a court's reliance on legislative purpose more palatable, because verbal uncertainty must be resolved. However, the political implications can be serious. Public reliance and legislative understanding by those familiar with one language might be defeated by adoption of a meaning unfamiliar to those with a different mother tongue, with major political implications.

c) LAWS WHICH MAY BE LIKE CONTRACTS

i) FEDERAL GRANT–IN–AID STATUTES

We suggested earlier that a statute differed from a contract because it was a political document. Perhaps that mischaracterized at least some statutes. A statute could be like a contract because it is a bargain between two or more parties who negotiated over its provisions. Chapter 8 will consider this possibility more fully. A statute might also be a contract in the sense that it sets the ground rules for a contractual arrangement between two political bodies. One example is a federal grant-in-aid statute, which specifies that money will be given to state or local communities on condition that they comply with federal guidelines. These statutes have become very popular for two reasons. First, the federal government is a government of limited powers but it can tax and spend for the "general welfare." Conditioning acceptance of federal money on certain behavior is a method by which the grantor can achieve broad policy objectives. Second, spending through grant-in-aid programs permits the federal government to coax (or force) state or local governments to adopt and administer policies they might otherwise reject.

A grant-in-aid statute can be viewed as an offer to enter into a contract. But it is also a political document, establishing a framework under which the accepting government and individual beneficiaries of the program will be governed. As a political document the statute may be more flexible and open-ended than a contract, permitting change over time in accordance with political norms. As a contract drafted by the richer federal government, however, it might be narrowly construed to protect the state or local government from onerous conditions.

The Court addressed this issue in the following case in which the federal government sued a state for a refund of money improperly spent by the state in violation of Title I of the Elementary and Secondary Education Act of 1965. In Bennett v. Kentucky Dep't. of Educ., 470 U.S. 656 (1985), the Government argued that the Court should simply defer to the Secretary of Education's interpretation of the requirements of Title I, so long as it was a reasonable interpretation. This is the standard usually used for upholding agency rules issued pursuant to a statute. Without disputing the reasonableness of the Secretary's interpretation, the State contended that because the grant program was in the nature of a contract, any ambiguities with respect to the State's obligations must be resolved against the party drafting the contract, which is the federal government. The Court "agree(d) with the State that Title I grant agreements had a contractual aspect" but concluded that

> the program cannot be viewed in the same manner as a bilateral contract governing a discrete transaction. * * * Unlike normal contractual undertakings, federal grant programs originate in and remain governed by statutory provisions expressing the judgment of Congress concerning desirable public policy. Title I, for example, involved multiple levels of government in a cooperative effort to use federal funds to support compensatory education for disadvantaged children. * * * Given the structure of the grant program, the Federal Government simply could not prospectively resolve every possible ambiguity concerning particular applications of the requirements of Title I.

After concluding that the grant-in-aid statute was not the same as a bilateral contract, the Court found "it unnecessary to adopt the Government's suggestion that the Secretary may rely on any reasonable interpretation of the requirements of Title I to determine that previous expenditures violated grant conditions." What the State did in this case "clearly violated existing statutory and regulatory provisions."

ii) TREATIES

The analogy of treaties to contracts might be relevant for interpreting treaties whether or not the texts appear in more than one language. For example, in Trans World Airlines, Inc. v. Franklin Mint Corp., 466 U.S. 243 (1984), the issue was the legality of the limit on liability for lost property imposed on air carriers under the treaty known as the Warsaw Convention, drafted in 1925 and 1929. The Treaty stated the limit in terms of a fixed relationship of currency to a specific quantity of gold. Until 1978, the United States complied with the Treaty through a law establishing a fixed exchange rate between the dollar and an ounce of gold, which translated into a specific dollar liability limit. In that year, however, the United States abandoned the fixed dollar/gold exchange rate and gold's dollar value fluctuated with the market. Despite this fluctuation, the United States Civil Aeronautics Board continue to fix the liability limit at $9.07 per pound of lost property, which was the amount fixed before the dollar/gold exchange rate fluctuated. The Court stated that the treaty was a "contract" among nations, and then proceeded to consider the conduct of the contracting parties in implementing that contract in the first 50 years of its operation (which was an acceptable principle of contract interpretation). That conduct suggested to the Court that it was permissible to adjust the limitation rules after the value of gold fluctuated, so that a predictable liability limit remained in place.

Justice Stevens dissented. He found that going off the gold standard produced a "frustration of purpose" (a contract concept), which should result in rescission, not reformation of the treaty. Justice Stevens apparently did not think the majority interpreted the treaty like a contract. He argued that the majority was applying the maxim *cessante ratione legis, cessat ipsa lex* (when the reason for the rule ceases, the rule ceases). Although he accepted this maxim as applicable to the common law, he rejected it as a guide to interpreting positive law (presumably meaning a treaty or a statute).[17]

d) LEGISLATION BY POPULAR VOTE[18]

About one half the states provide for "popular democracy" in the form of either (1) initiatives (by which proposals with enough voter signatures are placed on the ballot for approval or disapproval); or (2) referendums (where a law passed by the legislature must be presented for voter approval before it becomes law). Frequently, popular democracy is used to amend the state constitution, but it is also used to pass legislation. It can include such controversial issues as expansion of criminal liability, English as an official language, and ceilings on insurance premiums.

This lawmaking process has been criticized as seriously lacking from the standpoint of a deliberative ideal. First, voters do not have good information. Voters often do not read the proposals but instead rely on media coverage for guidance. Sometimes (though not always) there are official government explanations of the proposals prepared for voter review, but these are not always much help. Both the law and the explanation may contain heavy doses of legal jargon. Anticipating the application of the law to facts that might arise in litigation will also be very difficult. Second, the voters' difficulty in understanding the proposals and the dominance of media coverage in shaping debate increase the likelihood that well-organized interests will prevail and that socially-marginalized groups will be hurt.

Some of these same problems also exist in legislatures but may be aggravated in popular elections. The legislative process at least has some experts (usually in committees) who understand complex proposals and their texts. As for unpopular minorities, the legislative process may provide them

---

17. Analogies between a treaty and a contract may also be relevant when the court uses legislative history developed by one signatory country to a treaty to interpret the document. Justice Scalia objected to this practice in United States v. Stuart, 489 U.S. 353, 374 (1989)(Scalia, J., concurring in the judgment), stating that it "is rather like determining the meaning of a bilateral contract between two corporations on the basis of what

the board of directors of one of them thought it meant when authorizing the chief executive officer to conclude it."

18. See Julian Eule, Judicial Review of Direct Democracy, 99 Yale L. J. 1503 (1990); Jane Schacter, The Pursuit of "Popular Intent": Interpretive Dilemmas in Direct Democracy, 105 Yale L. J. 107 (1995) (hereafter "Schacter").

with greater protection through bargaining and debate than popular elections, which are more dominated by the media and temporary passions.

The potential shortcomings in making law through popular democracy has led to suggestions that interpretation take account of these defects. (Judicial review of the constitutionality of laws passed by initiative or referendum is discussed in Chapter 17.) For example, the problem of voter understanding undermines both text and intent as legitimate sources of meaning, which arguably leaves the court somewhat freer to rely on substantive background considerations. And, when there is suspicion that well-organized interests obtain an unfair advantage or minority groups are unfairly disadvantaged, uncertainties in the legislation might be resolved to redress that unfairness.[19]

In light of this discussion, how would you have decided the following case? In Backman v. United States, 516 A.2d 923 (D.C.Ct.App.1986), the court dealt with the definition of "narcotic." In 1981, the Council of the District of Columbia had adopted the Uniform Controlled Substances Act of 1981 (UCSA), which classified substances into narcotics and non-narcotics. The Act replaced older statutes by *removing* cocaine from the earlier statutory listing of "narcotic" substances. Then, on June 7, 1983, District voters passed the Mandatory Minimum Sentencing Initiative of 1981. The initiative adopted several amendments to the UCSA, which imposed a mandatory minimum sentence of not less than four years for certain narcotics crimes but also adopted the "addict exception." The "addict exception" stated that the sentencing court had discretion to exempt a first-time offender of the UCSA from mandatory minimum sentencing if the court determined that the offender was (1) an "addict" at the time of the violation and (2) committed the offense "for the primary purpose of obtaining a narcotic drug which he [or she] required for his [or her] personal use because of his [or her] addiction to such drug."

The defendant relied on the "addict exception" based on a cocaine addiction, but the court disagreed, as follows:

> The voter initiative, which proposed the addict exception, defined an "addict" as "any individual who habitually uses any narcotic drug so as to endanger the public morals, health, safety, or welfare, or who is or has been so far addicted to the use of such narcotic drug as to have lost the power of self-control with reference to his [or her] addiction." D.C. Code § 33–501 (24)(1986 Supp.) Backman challenges his exclusion from the addict exception of the UCSA, arguing that the statutory definition of an addict should be interpreted to include cocaine addicts. He reasons that the meaning of the word "narcotic" is ambiguous because the UCSA amendments were enacted through the voter initiative process, as contrast-

19. Schacter, pp. 152–64.

ed with a bill enacted by the Council. He speculates that the District voters, as distinguished from the Council, intended the dictionary definition of narcotic—which includes cocaine—rather than the statutory definition. * * *

We are unpersuaded by appellant's reasoning. The manner in which the statute was enacted has no bearing on interpreting the statute. We must hold the legislature and the citizenry to the same standards when interpreting the laws they enact. We must treat amendment by initiative the same as amendment by Council legislation, for once the District voters approve an initiative, it becomes an "act of the Council, * * * and thus 'law' through the channel designated for the particular type of act adopted."

When the District voters passed upon the 1981 initiative, they were instructed that the initiative was intended to amend certain portions of the pre-existing UCSA. Thus, they could be expected to use the UCSA as a reference point for any term that was not defined by the initiative itself. We must assume that the District voters relied on the statutory definition of "narcotic" in D.C. Code § 33–501 (15)(1986 Supp.). In this instance, therefore, the plain language of the statute is dispositive.

e) "Private Lawmaking"

We briefly mentioned the American Law Institute ("ALI") and the National Conference of Commissioners on Uniform State Laws ("NCCUSL") at the end of Chapter 2. These private organizations (made up of lawyers, judges, and academics) have a self-image of apolitical expertise and avoiding controversial value choices, which has to some extent survived the Legal Realist attack discussed in Chapter 3. However, recent studies of Article 9 (Secured Transactions) of the Uniform Commercial Code suggest that the apolitical-expert image may be undeserved. These studies label the NCCUSL/ALI product as "private lawmaking" and apply the same scrutiny to its processes that the Public Choice literature applies to legislatures.

Studies of private lawmaking are interesting in their own right for what they tell us about a little-studied corner of the lawmaking process, but they are also important for statutory interpretation. Just as the public choice material in Chapter 4 developed models of the legislative process with implications for how judges determine statutory meaning, so assumptions about the private lawmaking process might influence how judges interpret laws which are adopted after they are drafted by the ALI or NCCUSL.

The following excerpts are from Robert Scott, The Politics of Article 9, 80 Va. L. Rev. 1783 (1994), which looks closely at the institutional origins of Article 9 of the UCC and suggests a model for evaluating lawmaking by such private organizations.[20] The UCC and its updating are a product of the joint

---

20. The model is more fully developed in Schwartz and Scott, The Political Economy of Private Legislatures, 143 U. Pa. L. Rev. 595 (1995).

efforts of the NCCUSL and the ALI, which have established a Permanent Editorial Board for the Code composed of members of both organizations. If the Board and the membership of both organizations agree, the ALI President appoints a study group, after appropriate consultation. Eventually, the study group's product is translated into statutory language by a NCCUSL committee for proposal to the states.

Scott explains the Study Group process used to propose amendments to Article 9, as follows:

> The Article 9 Study Group, typical of U.C.C. projects, was comprised of two academic reporters and sixteen members—three legal academics and thirteen practicing lawyers * * *. [Editor—Scott notes that the Study Group met two or three times a year over nearly a three-year period, considering working papers dealing with topics determined by the reporters and the chair, after consultation with interested parties.]

> The structure and conduct of the Study Group is entirely consistent with the underlying intellectual premise of the ALI and the NCCUSL. If Article 9 rules can be derived from uncontroversial moral premises and constructed with traditional legal skills, then a small group of "experts" can create and propose useful sets of reforms, and larger groups of less informed practitioners and judges, meeting occasionally, can choose the best ones.

> * * *[A]ll expertise is not equally valued. Although academic insights into the structure and social effects of Article 9 are recognized as important, encyclopedic knowledge of how the rules have been interpreted by different courts is valued more highly, and the greatest asset is knowledge of how the rules "really work" in practice. This hierarchy of expertise is not irrational, given the operating assumptions of the ALI and NCCUSL approach.

> On the other hand, the privileged status of "hands on" working knowledge of Article 9 rules has dramatic effects on the dynamics of Study Group deliberations. Most significantly, in-house counsel for banks and finance companies and private commercial lawyers whose practice involves representation of those interests provide the most important source of expertise concerning the nature and effects of proposed revisions to Article 9. Because operational expertise is the relevant criterion, it is unsurprising that eight members of the Study Group (including the chair) were commercial lawyers and house counsel whose practice specialty was the representation of secured creditors. These lawyers are the most knowledgeable concerning the questions the Study Group is asked to resolve, and they properly emerge as the most influential members of the group (other than the academic reporters). * * *

The impact of these structural forces on the deliberations of the Study Group is striking. Efforts by the academic members to place on the agenda a discussion of the broader implications of the proposed changes in Article 9, including their cumulative effects on other societal interests, were uniformly unsuccessful. The several practicing lawyers who were seen as representatives of other interests were similarly marginalized by the focus on the technical task of "fixing" Article 9. Ultimately, these members participated only sporadically in the discussions that led to the final report.

Scott then describes the interests affected by Article 9, in terms of both their knowledge and cohesiveness, which are both salient factors in determining their effectiveness in gaining acceptance for their points of view.

* * * The interests that are most affected by the legal regulation of secured credit, not surprisingly, are specialized asset-based financers (factoring companies and commercial finance companies) and commercial banks that commonly issue secured debt as a part of their portfolio of loans. These groups, because they make such extensive use of Article 9, are well-informed financing insiders. Their repeated occasions to observe the effects of particular regulatory provisions produce a reservoir of private information concerning the actual function of different asset-based financing regimes. Moreover, their interests tend to be cohesive, at least insofar as their views are aligned on the salient features of Article 9.

Unsecured creditors and debtors are also affected by Article 9. These groups have less cohesive interests, however, than do informed secured creditor interests. Many unsecured creditors and debtors and some "occasional" secured creditors are less informed parties; their participation in transactions involving secured credit does not occur with sufficient frequency to justify the costs of becoming fully informed about the effects of the Article 9 regulatory regime. Certain trade creditors and other suppliers, consumer or small business debtors, nonconsensual tort claimants, and warranty claim holders would all fall in this category. * * *

The last group of interested parties are the business lawyers and legal academics for whom Article 9 is an important practice or research specialty. The academics in this group may be distinct from the other lawyers in that they do not necessarily have pecuniary interests that can be affected by changes in Article 9. Nevertheless, the academics might be said to have an interest in the continued existence of the statute, as it serves as the basis for at least a nontrivial proportion of their work, and also as a means for augmenting their reputations.

Business lawyers have both economic and reputational interests at stake. Changes in Article 9 can affect their practice directly. Moreover, success in law reform projects enlarges a lawyer's reputation for good judgment and serves as an important credential, denoting expertise and experience in representing secured creditor interests.

Scott is, however, cautious about inferring "that secured creditor interests are disproportionately able to influence the outcome of the Article 9 revision process. * * * What seems clear [   ] is that the nature of interest group influence on the Article 9 revision process cannot be established either a priori or through impressionistic observations of individual participants." Scott then "sketch[es] an analytic model of the private legislative process that generates the U.C.C. in order to offer a more systematic framework for assessing both the product and the process of any future revisions to Article 9." That framework could, of course, be used to determine what balance of interests produced other "private lawmaking" proposals. Here is some of Scott's discussion. Compare his model of private lawmaking with what you think occurs in the interaction between legislative committees and the entire legislature. What are the similarities and differences?

B.   An Interest Group Model of Private Legislatures

The preceding discussion has suggested that the U.C.C. lawmaking process functions much like a "private legislature" ("PL"). Rules are first proposed in "committees" dominated by members with technical expertise. The initial committee process produces a blueprint for revision that is then delivered to a second "committee" that executes the blueprint in statutory form. The final product is then offered to the larger consultative bodies for their approval.

This suggests that PLs can be studied in the same way that political scientists study legislatures. The action in the law reform game takes place largely at the study group and drafting committee levels, and, to a lesser extent, on the floor where the membership rejects, approves, or suggests modifications to the proposed law. At least in the case of U.C.C. projects, the final stage in which the approved model law is proposed to legislatures for adoption is largely pro forma. Hence, an analyst can treat a study group as a legislative committee and the ALI or NCCUSL as the "legislature."

* * * The currently privileged status of proposed revisions to the U.C.C. in the adopting state legislatures is based upon an implicit and heretofore unexamined assumption: that such private legislative processes yield a product superior to the product of the ordinary legislative process. If that assumption is unwarranted, it follows that the imprimatur of the ALI and NCCUSL should no longer count as an independent factor in favor of any proposed rule.

1.   Baseline Assumptions

* * * I begin by making the following assumptions about the relevant features of a private legislative process such as that which produces the U.C.C.

a.   Logrolling Is Very Difficult [Editor—Discussion omitted]

b. PL Members Act as Individuals and Have No Independent Political Power

Participants in the PL act as individuals; they are not members of "U.C.C. parties" such as those that exist in most legislatures, and that can assert some sort of discipline over their members. * * *

As a consequence of the absence of political parties, PLs have no independent political power and commonly need interest group support, or at least the absence of interest group opposition, to ensure the passage of their proposals by state legislators. Both the ALI and the NCCUSL seek to have their uniform laws adopted, but the evidence of their many failures, and of their strong efforts to enlist interest groups in the law creation process and to yield to them when necessary, also implies the absence of any independent power base.

c. There Are Information Asymmetries Between PL Committees and Study Groups and the Membership at Large

The creators and drafters of the rules are "experts" in that particular field of law. As such, they have information that is too costly for the uninvolved PL "legislator" to discover. The actual membership of a PL consists primarily of either nonexperts or experts in other fields of law. Thus, the median PL member knows little about the subject matter of any particular drafting product.

Moreover, unlike members of a typical legislature, ALI and NCCUSL participants have little incentive to become more educated before voting, thus creating even greater information asymmetries. This assumption is supported by the premise that the typical uninformed PL member seeks to maximize the public good (as she conceives of it) subject to several constraints: (1) that her private interest—for example, her law practice—is not directly impaired; (2) that her reputation for good judgment is not impaired; and (3) that she spends little time on PL business. * * *

d. Members of the Drafting Committees and Study Groups Tend To Have Stronger Preferences for Revision than the Median PL Member.

Study group members have stronger preferences for "reform," because in the usual case, committee members are either academics or interested participants. In general, these members will favor revisions more than the uninformed PL legislator. The preferences of "experts" for revision follow directly from their knowledge of the operational inefficiencies of the status quo, and from their interest in seeking rules that advance the interests of the industry they "represent." Thus, their preferences for targeted changes obviously differ from those of the median member. Academics, who make up the remainder of study groups and drafting committees, also are preference outliers; they have an institutional commitment to reform because most law professors earn reputations by writing articles about how the law can be improved, rather than by defending the status quo.

On the other hand, the constraints that typify the median uninformed PL member, such as information asymmetries and the costs of overcoming ignorance, imply a stronger commitment to the status quo. This suggests that a typical outcome of the PL process will be to reject significant reform, especially where the reform is seen as controversial, unless the median PL member is influenced by the preferences of the members of a particular study group or drafting committee.

2. Preliminary Observations: The Influence of Cohesive Interest Groups

The preceding assumptions suggest that the PL process is susceptible to influence by cohesive interest groups. The effects of interest group activity on the lawmaking process will depend principally on whether a single, dominant group is active or whether interest groups compete with one another.

When only a single, dominant group is active, the preceding assumptions imply that the dominant group will be able to influence the outcome of the PL process whenever their proposals are not inconsistent with the uninformed preferences of the median PL member. This influence increases the likelihood that the interest group will be able to secure revisions that favor its interests. A single, active interest group will be represented by experts who favor the proposed revisions and who have the largest influence on the deliberations of the study groups. As a consequence, interest group representatives will be able to make the most credible representations to uninformed members concerning the effects of reform. Without an organized opposition, PL members will have little reason to vote against a reform proposal so long as the proposal (1) effects only marginal changes in the status quo and (2) is not facially inconsistent with the preferences of most PL participants.

Moreover, the ability of a single, cohesive group to influence the outcome of PL deliberations is likely to be greater than in the case of ordinary legislative bodies. The absence of political parties and clearly defined constituencies reduces the likelihood that alternative views will be presented to the PL member (or that she will have an incentive to seek them out). When considering whether to support the views of a single, active interest group, ordinary legislators must calculate the risk that the unforeseen effects of a proposed rule will cause competing groups to form, and that these new groups will "punish" the legislator for being insufficiently vigilant in protecting the "public" interest. Moreover, ordinary legislators have alternative methods—such as hearings and the like—of becoming informed about the effects of interest group proposals. In a PL, the absence of either party affiliation or constituency removes the threat of subsequent reprisals if an uninformed member supports interest group proposals, whereas the lack of other channels of information increases the cost of becoming informed. [Editor—Later on in the article, Scott argues that the ability of a single group to influence model laws is enhanced for revisions to an existing statute because revisions are seen largely as a matter of technical expertise, correcting minor flaws or updating a statute, with most of the value judgments having already been made.]

On the other hand, when interest groups compete, the analysis suggests quite a different outcome. The inability to enforce trades and to logroll means that competing groups will tend to present contrasting views that require the uninformed participant to make explicit and controversial value choices. In turn, the incentives to do good without doing much work and to protect a reputation for good judgment, coupled with a belief that the PL is engaged in a technical, noncontroversial process, will cause the messages from competing groups to have less influence than in ordinary legislative bodies. If seeking additional information is too costly and if the uninformed preferences of the median members do not clearly favor one proposal over another, the only respectable alternative is to decline to support either proposal. Hence, in the presence of competing groups, the PL will tend to reject reform in favor of the status quo, unless the reform can be presented in a form that disguises the underlying value choices.

f) SUMMARY

This section has suggested that the approach to interpreting a text depends in part on the kind of document and its method of adoption. Is it a political document or a private instrument with few political implications? By what process was the text adopted? At one extreme is the United States Constitution. As Justice Marshall reminded us, "It is a *Constitution* we are expounding." McCulloch v. Maryland, 17 U.S. (4 Wheat.) 316, 407 (1819). This quote has been understood to authorize an expansive open-ended interpretation of our basic political charter. The meaning of such basic documents depends on a complex interplay of writer, text, and judicial reader. The meaning of a will, by contrast, might depend on the writer's intent more than any other document, because it is a private, one-party document.

Many other documents fit between these extremes. Contracts are generally closer to wills, because they are private documents. They are multi-party transactions, however, requiring that greater prominence be given to the specific intent of both parties or to the text. Treaties are bargains, like contracts, but they are also political documents. Some treaties may even be like constitutions, such as the treaty creating the European Economic Community.

Moreover, not all legislation is alike. A grant-in-aid statute might be more like a contract than other legislation. Statutes adopted through elections, rather than the legislative process, might be interpreted differently from routine legislation because of the process of adoption. And "private lawmaking" may or may not fit the self-image of apolitical expertise.

The general point is that characterizing a document is both controversial and relevant to its interpretation. That characterization is a background consideration that must be resolved by a judge and is not mandated by any higher authority (such as the Constitution).

CHAPTER 8

LEGISLATIVE COMPROMISE; DETAILED TEXT

This Chapter looks more closely at a particular kind of external context—the legislative process from which a statute emerged; and at a particular kind of text—a statute with detailed language. Indeed, the two are often related. We want to know how this type of context and text influences statutory interpretation.

8.01   THE LAW AND ECONOMICS (PUBLIC CHOICE) APPROACH

You have already read some of Easterbrook's article, Statutes' Domains, in Chapter 4. Those excerpts are repeated here, along with some additional selections, because they are a clear exposition of why the Law and Economics (Public Choice) approach to statutory interpretation pays special attention to the legislative process (especially compromise) and the detailed text.

Easterbrook, Statutes' Domains
50 U.Chi.L.Rev. 533 (1983).

My suggestion is that unless the statute plainly hands courts the power to create and revise a form of common law, the domain of the statute should be restricted to cases anticipated by its framers and expressly resolved in the legislative process. Unless the party relying on the statute could establish either express resolution or creation of the common law power of revision, the court would hold the matter in question outside the statute's domain. The statute would become irrelevant, the parties (and court) remitted to whatever other sources of law might be applicable. * * *

* * * If [the legislature] enacts some sort of code of rules, the code will be taken as complete (until amended); gaps will go unfilled. If instead it charges the court with a common law function, the court will solve new problems as they arise, but using today's wisdom rather than conjuring up the solutions of a legislature long prorogued.

This is just a slightly different way of making the point that judicial pursuit of the "values" or aims of legislation is a sure way of defeating the original legislative plan. A legislature that seeks to achieve Goal X can do so in one of two ways. First, it can identify the goal and instruct courts or agencies to design rules to achieve the goal. In that event, the subsequent selection of rules implements the actual legislative decision, even if the rules are not what the legislature would have selected itself. The second approach is for the legislature to pick the rules. It pursues Goal X by Rule Y. The selection of Y is a measure of what Goal X was worth to the legislature, of how best to achieve X, and of where to stop in pursuit of X. Like any other rule, Y is bound to be imprecise, to be over— and under—inclusive. This is not a good reason for a court, observing the inevitable imprecision, to add to or subtract from Rule Y on the argument that, by doing so, it can get more of Goal X. The judicial selection of means to pursue X displaces and directly overrides the legislative selection of ways to obtain X. It denies to legislatures the choice of creating or withholding gapfilling authority. The way to preserve the initial choice is for judges to put the statute down once it becomes clear that the legislature has selected rules as well as identified goals.

This approach is faithful to the nature of compromise in private interest legislation. It also gives the legislature a low-cost method to signal its favored judicial approach to public interest legislation. A legislature that tries to approach the line where costs begin to exceed benefits is bound to leave a trail of detailed provisions, which on this approach would preclude judges from attempting to fill gaps. [Editor—Also recall Easterbrook's comments in another article excerpted in Chapter 4, "The Court and the Economic System," 98 Harv. L. Rev. 4 (1984), where he stated: "The more detailed the law, the more evidence of interest-group compromise and therefore the less liberty judges possess" to elaborate purpose.] The approach also is supported by a number of other considerations. First, it recognizes that courts cannot reconstruct an original meaning because there is none to find. Second, it prevents legislatures from extending their lives beyond the terms of their members. Third, it takes a liberal view of the relation between the public and private spheres. Fourth, it takes a realistic view of judges' powers. I elaborate on these below.

1. *Original meaning.* Because legislatures comprise many members, they do not have "intents" or "designs," hidden yet discoverable. Each member may or may not have a design. The body as a whole, however, has only outcomes. It is not only impossible to reason from one statute to another but also impossible to reason from one or more sections of a statute to a problem not resolved.

This follows from the discoveries of public choice theory. Although legislators have individual lists of desires, priorities, and preferences, it turns out to be difficult, sometimes impossible, to aggregate these lists into a coherent collective choice. Every system of voting has flaws. The one used by legislatures is particularly dependent on the order in which decisions are made. Legislatures customarily consider proposals one at a time and then vote them up or down. This method disregards third or fourth options and the intensity with which legislators prefer one option over another. Additional options can be considered only in sequence, and this makes the order of decision vital. It is fairly easy to show that someone with control of the agenda can manipulate the choice so that the legislature adopts proposals that only a minority support. [Editor—Easterbrook is referring to the problem of determining majority choice when three or more voters rank order their preferences in certain ways, previously discussed in Chapter 4.] The existence of agenda control makes it impossible for a court—even one that knows each legislator's complete table of preferences—to say what the whole body would have done with a proposal it did not consider in fact.

2. *Legislatures expire.* Judicial interpolation of legislative gaps would be questionable even if judges could ascertain with certainty how the legislature would have acted. Every legislative body's power is limited by a number of checks, from the demands of its internal procedures to bicameralism to the need to obtain the executive's assent. The foremost of these checks is time. Each session of Congress, for example, lasts but two years, after which the whole House and one-third of the Senate stand for reelection. What each Congress does binds the future until another Congress acts, but what a Congress might have done, had it the time, is simply left unresolved. The unaddressed problem is handled by a new legislature with new instructions from the voters.

If time is classified with the veto as a limit on the power of legislatures, then one customary argument for judicial gap filling— that legislatures lack the time and foresight to resolve every problem—is a reason why judges should *not* attempt to fill statutory gaps. The shortness of time and the want of foresight, like the fear of the veto and the fear of offending constituents, raise the costs of legislation. The cost of addressing one problem includes the inability, for want of time, to address others. If courts routinely construe statutory gaps as authorizing "more in the same vein," they reduce this cost.

[Editor—Easterbrook's argument directly challenges those who say that legislative inertia is a reason *for* judicial activism. His point is that time constraint is desirable and should be integrated into the political philosophy used by the court to interpret statutes.]

In a sense, gap-filling construction has the same effects as extending the term of the legislature *and* allowing that legislature to avoid submitting its plan to the executive for veto. Obviously no court would do this directly. If the members of the Ninety-third

Congress reassembled next month and declared their legislative meaning, the declaration would have absolutely no force. This rump body would get no greater power by claiming that its new "laws" were intimately related to, and just filled gaps in, its old ones. Is there a better reason why the members of the Ninety-third Congress, the Eighty-third, and the Seventy-third, "sitting" in the minds of judges, should continue to be able to resolve new problems "presented" to them? The meta-rule I have suggested reduces the number of times judges must summon up the ghouls of legislatures past. In order to authorize judges (or agencies) to fill statutory gaps, the legislature must deny itself life after death and permit judges or agencies to supply their own conceptions of the public interest.

3. *Liberal principles.* A principle that statutes are inapplicable unless they either plainly supply a rule of decision or delegate the power to create such a rule is consistent with the liberal principles underlying our political order. Those who wrote and approved the Constitution thought that most social relations would be governed by private agreements, customs, and understandings, not resolved in the halls of government. There is still at least a presumption that people's arrangements prevail unless expressly displaced by legal doctrine. All things are permitted unless there is some contrary rule. It is easier for an agency to justify the revocation of rules (or simple nonregulation) than the creation of new rules. A rule declaring statutes inapplicable unless they plainly resolve or delegate the solution of the matter respects this position. It either preserves the private decisions or remits the questions to other statutes through which the legislature may have addressed the problem. A rule of universal construction, in contrast, assumes that statutes supply an answer to all questions. [Editor—What would Easterbrook do if a statute withdrew government power regulating the private sector? If the statute's purpose is to limit government, a narrow limiting interpretation will result in *more* government regulation than a broader interpretation that gives expansive scope to the statute's anti-regulatory purpose. How would he resolve a conflict between his substantive reasons for not looking for an expansive statutory purpose and his view that judges should be restrained in looking for such purposes?]

Perhaps one day the "orgy of statute making" will reach the point at which the preservation of private decisions is the exception, but that point is not yet here and, one hopes, will never arrive. Like nature, regulation abhors a vacuum, and the existence of one law may create problems requiring more laws. Until the legislature supplies the fix or authorizes someone else to do so, there is no reason for judges to rush in.

4. *Judicial Abilities.* Statutory construction is an art. Good statutory construction requires the rarest of skills. The judge must find clues in the structure of the statute, hints in the legislative

history, and combine these with mastery of history, command of psychology, and sensitivity to nuance to divine how deceased legislators would have answered unasked questions.

It is all very well to say that a judge able to understand the temper of 1871 (and 1921), and able to learn the extent of a compromise in 1936, may do well when construing statutes. How many judges meet this description? How many know what clauses and provisos, capable of being enacted in 1923, would have been unthinkable in 1927 because of subtle changes in the composition of the dominant coalitions in Congress? It is hard enough to know this for the immediate past, yet who could deny that legislation that could have been passed in 1982 not only would fail but also could be repealed in 1983? The number of judges living at any time who can, with plausible claim to accuracy, "think [themselves] ... into the minds of the enacting legislators and imagine how they would have wanted the statute applied to the case at bar," may be counted on one hand.

To deny that judges have the skills necessary to construe statutes well—at least when construction involves filling gaps in the statutes rather than settling the rare case that arises from conflicts in the rules actually laid down—is *not* to say that stupid and irresponsible judges can twist any rule. Doubtless the "judge's role should be limited, to protect against willful judges who lack humility and self-restraint." Yet there is a more general reason for limiting the scope of judicial discretion. Few of the best-intentioned, most humble, and most restrained among us have the skills necessary to learn the temper of times before our births, to assume the identity of people we have never met, and to know how 535 disparate characters from regions of great political and economic diversity would have answered questions that never occurred to them. Anyone of reasonable skill could tell that some answers would have been beyond belief in 1866. After putting the impossible to one side, though, a judge must choose from among the possible solutions, and here human ingenuity is bound to fail, often. When it fails, even the best intentioned will find that the imagined dialogues of departed legislators have much in common with their own conceptions of the good.

[Editor—What does Easterbrook's approach suggest about judicial reliance on one of the old chestnuts of statutory interpretation—relying on the preamble (before the enacting clause) or purpose clause (after the enacting language) found at the beginning of a statute? The preamble or purpose clause may be drafted by those who support the bill's general purposes, but not necessarily all of the compromises necessary to obtain its passage.]

COMMENTS

1. *Is legislation really private interest compromise?* Easterbrook does not argue that there is no legislative purpose, but that there is often a particular type of purpose—specifically, private interest compromise (a sort of contract in a public forum). The trouble with purposive interpretation, in Easterbrook's view, is that it is unfaithful to these realities of the legislative process. How accurate is his view of legislation?

First, Easterbrook's view contrasts with the position, implicit in Pound's writings (presented in Chapter 3), that legislation generally reflects public values, whose purpose should inform statutory interpretation. At least some of the political science literature argues that legislators are often motivated by public values and that there are institutional and other pressures on legislators to transform private preferences into public values.

Second, it is very difficult to know whether or not particular legislation is motivated by private interest. Political rhetoric and statutory language often emphasize public values. Moreover, the legislation itself often results from a melding of private interest and public values—for example, the Food Stamps law resulted from a combination of farmer self-interest and redistributionist public values; and Medicaid expansion not only responds to public concerns for the poor but also helps employers, who want to avoid private medical insurance costs for the poor.

Third, suppose a statute is the product of compromise about public values. Would that leave the judge with as little to do (the "beady-eyed" approach) as when the compromise concerned private interests?

2. *Misreading the compromise.* All efforts to identify legislative intent can miss the mark and those adopting the "interest-group compromise" perspective are no exception. Easterbrook may have fallen into the error of finding an interest-group compromise when there was none in Washington Metropolitan Area Transit Authority v. Johnson, 467 U.S. 925 (1984). In this case (WMATA), the Court exempted a general contractor from tort liability to a subcontractor's employee, because the employee was covered by Workers Compensation purchased by the general contractor. Workers Compensation statutes typically provide that, in exchange for purchasing the statutory remedy for workers, the employer is exempt from common law tort recoveries.

Easterbrook asserts that this case demonstrates the "interest-group" approach to statutory interpretation—"[L]ook for and enforce the bargain, but do not elaborate." Easterbrook, Foreword: The Court and the Economic System, 98 Harv. L. Rev. 4, 54 (1984). However, there was a serious question whether the statute applied to the general contractor. The general contractor purchased Workers Compensation benefits, not because the subcontractors refused to buy coverage, but because it could do so more cheaply. The dissent in WMATA argued that the statute did not give a general contractor immunity unless it bought Workers Compensation after the subcontractor refused. It claimed that the majority takes a 1927 statute and reads into it the "modern view" of workers' compensation, whereby both the contractor and the subcontractor receive immunity from tort suits provided somebody secures compensation for injured employees of the subcontractor. In practical terms, the result is undoubtedly good both for the construction industry and for our already congested district courts. The result may even make overall economic sense. But one can hardly pretend that it "adhere[s] closely to what Congress has written." The Court has simply fixed upon what it believes to be good policy and then patched together a rationale as best it could. Believing that it is for Congress, not this Court, to decide whether the [statute] should be updated to reflect current thinking, I dissent.

In other words, in the dissent's view, the court extended the statute to cover a hypothetical bargain not included within the original statutory bargain.

In 1984, Congress wrote the dissent's interpretation into the law. Pub. L. 98–426, § 4, 98 Stat. 1639, 1641 (1984). The Conference Committee stated that the majority in WMATA "changed key components of what had widely been regarded as the proper rules governing contractor and subcontractor liability and immunity under the [Act.]" H.R.Rep. 98–1027, 98th Cong., 2d Sess. 24 (1984).

3. *"Impairing" statutory bargains.* If a statute is like a private contract, why doesn't the Impairment of Contracts Clause of the Constitution (as applied to the federal government through the Fifth Amendment Due Process Clause) prevent repeals or amendments which disadvantage one party? In National R. R. Passenger Corp. v. Atchison, Topeka and Santa Fe Ry. Co., 470 U.S. 451 (1985), Congress had passed an act in 1970 allowing railroads to give up their unprofitable intercity service to Amtrak in exchange for payment by the railroads to Amtrak of a certain sum of money. The statute reserved the right of repeal or amendment at any time. A later statute increased the payments due to Amtrak from the railroads. The Court reiterated a longstanding position that "absent some clear indication that the legislature intends to bind itself contractually, the presumption is that 'a law is not intended to create private contractual or vested rights but merely declares a policy to be pursued until the legislature shall ordain otherwise.'" The Court also observed that this "well-established presumption is grounded in the elementary proposition that the principal function of a legislature is not to make contracts, but to make laws that establish the policy of the state. Policies, unlike contracts, are inherently subject to revision and repeal * * *."

4. *Judicial role.* Even if Easterbrook correctly characterizes the legislative process as a kind of static contract, must courts adopt that view to interpret statutes? Can judges do nothing more than implement the statutory contract? After all, courts presume that a statute is motivated by public purposes when they test a statute for rationality under the Constitution. Why shouldn't they do the same thing to interpret a statute? Is there no continuity between the judicial role in constitutional adjudication and statutory interpretation?

Easterbrook's answers to these questions about judicial role are contained in his points number 2 and 4, which deny judicial power. Number 2 asserts that gap-filling is improper (unless the legislature plainly hands this power to the court) because it implicitly extends the legislature's life, and that would eliminate a check on legislative action analogous to the Presidential veto. Number 4 argues that judges are not good at recreating purpose in light of contemporary facts and, when they make the attempt, they are more likely to be making law inappropriately. Aren't these arguments based on a pre-interpretive conception of good judging, and therefore vulnerable to the criticism that they reflect the judge's own view of the appropriate judicial role, fully as much as the gap-filling or purposive approach reflects a theory of judging? Or would Easterbrook claim that the Separation of Powers principles in the Constitution (previously discussed in Chapter 2) clearly mandates the minimal role he would assign to the judge? Is that view of Separation of Powers and its implications for judging justified by the historical material you read in Chapter 2?

Easterbrook also relies on "liberal" principles (Number 3—most relations governed by private agreements) to limit judicial extension of legislation. Is this image of government more a later 19th Century perspective on government than a view prevalent when the Constitution was adopted? If this image was prevalent at the time of the Founding, was it more applicable to the federal than state government?

8.02   OPEN-ENDED LANGUAGE

a) PLAINLY HAND COURTS A COMMON LAW POWER?

Easterbrook says that a legislature can "plainly hand courts the power to create and revise a form of common law." The model he probably has in mind is the open-ended text of the anti-trust laws. In Standard Oil Co. v. United States, 221 U.S. 1 (1911), the Court stated that the statutory prohibition of combinations "in restraint of trade" in the Anti–Trust Act

> necessarily called for the exercise of judgment which required that some standard should be resorted to for the purpose of determining whether the prohibitions contained in the statute had or had not in any given case been violated. Thus not specifying but indubitably contemplating and requiring a standard, it follows that it was intended that the standard of reason which had been applied at common law * * * was intended to be the measure used for the purpose of determining whether in a given case a particular act had or had not brought about the wrong against which the statute provided.

Judge Hand further described this judicial function in anti-trust cases in United States v. Associated Press, 52 F.Supp. 362 (S.D.N.Y.1943), affirmed, 326 U.S. 1 (1945):

Certainly such a function is ordinarily "legislative"; for in a legislature the conflicting interests find their respective representation, or in any event can make their political power felt, as they cannot upon a court. The resulting compromises so arrived at are likely to achieve stability, and to be acquiesced in: which is justice. But it is a mistake to suppose that courts are never called upon to make similar choices; i.e., to appraise and balance the value of opposed interests and to enforce their preference. The law of torts is for the most part the result of exactly that process, and the law of torts has been judge-made, especially in this very branch. Besides, even though we had more scruples than we do, we have here a legislative warrant, because the Congress has incorporated into the Anti–Trust Acts the changing standards of the common law, and by so doing has delegated to courts the duty of fixing the standard for each case. Congress might have proceeded otherwise; it might have turned the whole matter over to an administrative tribunal, as indeed to a limited extent it has done to the Federal Trade Commission. But, though it has acted, it has left, these particular controversies to the courts, where they have been from very ancient times.

The Anti–Trust laws are a relatively easy case for inferring a judicial common law power. The statutory language was broad and was the same as that previously used by the common law. The common law was therefore the context for a broadly written statute, which was sensibly interpreted to incorporate a judicial common law power. The more difficult question is what other types of legislation "plainly hand courts the power to create and revise a form of common law."

Modern statutes often do not have common law antecedents, but they use open-ended terms like "reasonable," "good faith," "in the public interest," etc. Frequently these statutes delegate power to an agency, which adopts a rule. The legality of the rule then depends on concerns addressed in administrative law courses, such as the regularity of the agency's procedures, its expertise, whether the agency's rules are longstanding and consistently followed, as well as the more conventional criteria of statutory interpretation and general presumptions about the authority of administrative agencies. (See Chapter 11.) Our immediate question in a Legislation course is whether such terms delegate a "common law" power to the judiciary, if they are directed to courts.

This question can be addressed to Easterbrook as follows. Which of two possible theories of statutory interpretation does he adopt? First, does he adopt a theory of statutory language, based on guesses about how legislatures work and on background considerations defining the proper role of courts? As language theory, his approach would look for statutory detail, which confines the judge, or an open-ended text, which delegates a "common law" power. These alternatives could be understood as ends of a spectrum, ranging from extreme detail to open-ended texts, with many statutes falling in between. The court's "common law" power would be a matter of degree, depending on which extreme the statutory text most closely approximated. It might be hard to specify whether a text is more or less detailed or open-ended, but the court would nonetheless take clues primarily from the statute's internal linguistic context.

Second, the court could rely on either the detailed text or the legislative history to restrain the judge. The judge has two strings to the bow, each of which could restrain expansive judicial lawmaking power. If a text is open-ended, the court could still consider what happened in the legislative process. If the judge found that the statute originated in a compromise which restrains the apparent open-ended implications of the text, the statute would not plainly hand the court a broad lawmaking authority. If the legislative history revealed a statute energized by a broad principle, the text's inference of a common law power would be confirmed.

b) DOES LEGISLATIVE COMPROMISE LIMIT OPEN-ENDED LANGUAGE?

Does the following case treat the uncertain statutory text as creating judicial discretion, or does it look at the legislative history to determine whether the judicial power is confined by what happened in the legislative process?

Secretary of the Interior v. California

464 U.S. 312 (1984).

■ Justice O'Connor delivered the opinion of the Court.

This case arises out of the Department of Interior's sale of oil and gas leases on the outer continental shelf [OCS] off the coast of California. We must determine whether the sale is an activity "directly affecting" the coastal zone under § 307(c)(1) of the Coastal Zone Management Act (CZMA). That section provides in its entirety:

"Each Federal agency conducting or supporting activities directly affecting the coastal zone shall conduct or support those activities in a manner which is, to the maximum extent practicable, consistent with approved state management programs." 16 U.S.C. § 1456(c)(1).

We conclude that the Secretary of the Interior's sale of outer continental shelf oil and gas leases is not an activity "directly affecting" the coastal zone within the meaning of the statute. * * *

We are urged to focus first on the plain language of § 307(c)(1). Interior contends that "directly affecting" means "[h]av[ing] a [d]irect, [i]dentifiable [i]mpact on [t]he [c]oastal [z]one." Brief for Federal Petitioners 20. Respondents insist that the phrase means "[i]nitiat[ing] a [s]eries of [e]vents of [c]oastal [m]anagement [c]onsequence." Brief for Respondents State of California, et al. 10. But CZMA nowhere defines or explains which federal activities should be viewed as "directly affecting" the coastal zone, and the alternative verbal formulations proposed by the parties, both of which are superficially plausible, find no support in the Act itself.

We turn therefore to the legislative history. A fairly detailed review is necessary, but that review persuades us that Congress did not intend OCS lease sales to fall within the ambit of CZMA § 307(c)(1).

In the CZMA bills first passed by the House and Senate, § 307(c)(1)'s consistency requirements extended only to federal activities "in" the coastal zone. The "directly affecting" standard appeared nowhere in § 307(c)(1)'s immediate antecedents. It was the House–Senate Conference Committee that replaced "in the coastal zone" with "directly affecting the coastal zone." Both chambers then passed the conference bill without discussing or even mentioning the change.

At first sight, the Conference's adoption of "directly affecting" appears to be a surprising, unexplained, and subsequently unnoticed expansion in the scope of § 307(c)(1), going beyond what was required by either of the versions of § 307(c)(1) sent to conference. But a much more plausible explanation for the change is available.

The explanation lies in the two different definitions of the "coastal zone." The bill the Senate sent to the Conference defined the coastal zone to exclude "lands the use of which is by law subject solely to the discretion of or which is held in trust by the Federal Government, its officers or agents." This exclusion would reach federal parks, military installations, Indian reservations, and other federal lands that would lie within the coastal zone but for the fact of federal ownership. Under the Senate bill, activities on these lands would thus have been entirely exempt from compliance with state management plans. By contrast, the House bill's definition of "coastal zone" included lands under federal jurisdiction; thus federal activities on those lands were to be fully subject to § 307(c)(1)'s consistency requirement. Under *both* bills, however, submerged lands on the OCS were entirely excluded from the coastal zone, and federal agency activities in those areas thus exempt from § 307(c)(1)'s consistency requirement.

Against this background, the Conference Committee's change in § 307(c)(1) has all the markings of a simple compromise. The Conference accepted the Senate's narrower definition of the "coastal zone," but then expanded § 307(c)(1) to cover activities on federal lands not "in" but nevertheless "directly affecting" the zone. By all appearances, the intent was to reach at least some activities conducted in those federal enclaves excluded from the Senate's definition of the "coastal zone."

Though cryptic, the Conference Report's reference to the change in § 307(c)(1) fully supports this explanation. "The Conferees * * * adopted the Senate language * * * which made it clear that Federal lands are not included within a state's coastal zone. *As to the use of such lands which would affect a state's coastal zone, the provisions of section 307(c) would apply.*" H.R.Conf. Rep. No. 92–1544, p. 12 (1972), U.S.Code Cong. & Admin.News 1972, pp. 4776, 4822 (emphasis added). In the entire Conference report, this is the only mention of the definition of the coastal zone chosen by the Conference, and the only hint of an explanation for the change in § 307(c)(1). The "directly affecting" language was not deemed worthy of note by any member of Congress in the subsequent floor debates. The implication seems clear: "directly affecting" was used to strike a balance between two definitions of the "coastal zone." The legislative history thus strongly suggests that OCS leasing, covered by *neither* the House nor the Senate version of § 307(c)(1), was also intended to be outside the coverage of the Conference's compromise.

In 1990 Congress overturned the result in Secretary of the Interior v. California. See 16 U.S.C. § 1456(c)(1)(A). Does that shed any light on the correct interpretation of the statute in 1984?

———

A federal statute gives money to states which have "in effect a policy that assures all handicapped children the right to a free appropriate education." A deaf child requested a sign-language interpreter to enable her to progress as well as children who were not hearing impaired. Does the court have power to give content to the requirement of an "appropriate education" and conclude that "appropriate" means "an opportunity to achieve full potential commensurate with the opportunity provided to other children?" In making its decision, is the court constrained by the legislative history that the statute was only intended to provide the hearing impaired with a meaningful public education, not to develop the child's full potential? Board of Education v. Rowley, 458 U.S. 176 (1982)(limiting judicial discretion and reach of statute based on legislative history).

8.03   DOES DETAILED LANGUAGE CONFINE THE JUDICIAL ROLE?

Easterbrook argues that detailed statutory language should limit the judge's search for legislative purpose. However, the impact of a detailed text on judging is not limited to those with a Law and Economics (Public Choice) perspective on the law. Even judges who are willing to let their search for legislative purpose take them wherever it leads may agree in a particular case that the purpose is not expansive, as suggested by the detailed language. Learned Hand describes the tension between detailed language and legislative purpose in Helvering v. Gregory, 69 F.2d 809, 810–11 (2d Cir.1934), affirmed, 293 U.S. 465 (1935):

* * * It is quite true * * * that as the articulation of a statute increases, the room for interpretation must contract; but the meaning of a sentence may be more than that of the separate words, as a melody is more than the notes, and no degree of particularity can ever obviate recourse to the setting in which all appear, and which all collectively create.

This section considers several situations in which detailed language might confine the judicial role.

a) MEANS AND ENDS

Braunstein v. Commissioner

374 U.S. 65 (1963).

■ Mr. Justice Harlan delivered the opinion of the Court.

[Editor—It will help you understand this case to know something about the tax law problem to which the statute was addressed. The statute tried to prevent a tax avoidance device. The device was the attempt by taxpayers to turn ordinary income into a form of gain which was taxed at lower rates (capital gains rates). A typical example was land subdivided into lots for sale. The taxpayer would put the land into a corporation for development as a subdivision. If the property had not been put into a corporation, its sale would have produced ordinary income, taxed at higher rates. Gain on the sale of corporate stock, however, is usually taxed at lower capital gains rates. Putting the property into a corporation would (it was hoped) result in sale of the stock being taxed at lower rates even though the value of the stock derived from the value of the ordinary income property. The statute was therefore amended to provide that sale of corporate stock would produce ordinary income if the corporation was a "collapsible corporation," a type of entity defined by the statute.

If the taxpayer in this case had not put the property into the corporation, however, sale of the property would *not* have been taxed at higher ordinary income rates. It was property, like stock, eligible for lower capital gains rates. There was therefore no tax avoidance potential from forming the corporation. The language of the statute depriving the taxpayer of lower rates seemed to apply to the taxpayer, however, and the taxpayer asked for an exception.]

As to the language used, § 117(m) defines a collapsible corporation as embracing one formed or availed of principally for the manufacture, construction, or production of property with a view to (1) the sale or exchange of stock prior to the realization by the corporation of a substantial part of the net income from the property and (2) the realization "of gain attributable to such property." * * * If used in their ordinary meaning, the word "gain" * * * simply refers to the excess of proceeds over cost or basis, and the phrase "attributable to" merely confines consideration to that gain caused or generated by the property in question. With these definitions, the section makes eminent sense, since the terms operate to limit its application to cases in which the corporation was availed of with a view to profiting from the constructed property by a sale or exchange of stock soon after completion of construction *and* in which a substantial part of the profit from the sale or exchange of stock in a given year was in fact generated by such property.

There is nothing in the language or structure of the section to demand or even justify reading into these provisions the additional requirement that the taxpayer must in fact have been using the corporate form as a device to convert ordinary income into capital gain. [Editor—Capital gain receives more favorable tax treatment than ordinary income.] * * *

Nor is there anything in the legislative history that would lead us to depart from the plain meaning of the statute as petitioners would have us do. There can of course be no question that the purpose of § 117(m) was, as petitioners contend, to close a loophole that Congress feared could be used to convert ordinary income into capital gain. See H. R. Rep. No. 2319, 81st Cong., 2d Sess.; S. Rep. No. 2375, 81st Cong., 2d Sess. But the crucial point for present purposes is that the method chosen to close this loophole was to establish a carefully and elaborately defined category of transactions in which what might otherwise be a capital gain would have to be treated as ordinary income. There is no indication whatever of any congressional desire to have the Commissioner or the courts make a determination in each case as to whether the use of the corporation was for tax avoidance. Indeed, the drawing of certain arbitrary lines not here involved—such as making the section inapplicable to any shareholder owing 10% or less of the stock or to any gain realized more than three years after the completion of construction—tends to refute any such indication. It is our understanding, in other words, that Congress intended to define what it believed to be a tax avoidance device rather than to leave the presence or absence of tax avoidance elements for decision on a case-to-case basis. [Editor—Does Justice Harlan believe this is the real purpose, or that the detailed language should be interpreted as though it were the purpose?]

COMMENTS

1. Braunstein is an example of a situation in which there might not really be a lack of fit between statutory purpose and the apparent meaning of the text. There can be many statutory purposes, not the least of which is to adopt a method of achieving a statutory purpose that is administrable.

Overbreadth and underbreadth between means and ends do not necessarily indicate a divergence between apparent meaning and purpose. One of the statute's purposes might be to accept some divergence between means and ends to achieve a substantive purpose in an administratively easiest way.

2. Justice Harlan also makes an additional point (not appearing in the prior excerpt from the Braunstein case), which focuses on judicial competence, rather than legislative text and intent. He argues for sticking to the text because it is difficult for the courts to draw lines defining tax avoidance. He gives the example of a corporation with two shareholders, only one of whom would have been taxed at ordinary rates if she had retained and sold the property herself rather than put it into the corporation. Should the other shareholder be tainted by the shareholder who is avoiding taxes? This sounds like an argument that the Court *should* not engage in complicated line-drawing, not simply that detailed texts restrain courts.

3. Justice Stevens gives some additional reasons why textualism might be appropriate in tax cases in the following quotes. How does his argument differ from an argument based on legislative intent, text, or judicial competence? :

> * * * Congress has a special duty to choose its words carefully when it is drafting technical and complex laws; we facilitate our work as well as that of Congress when we adhere closely to the statutory text in cases like this [involving coverage of Unemployment Insurance Tax law]. St. Martin Evangelical Lutheran Church v. South Dakota, 451 U.S. 772, 791 (1981)(Stevens, J., concurring).

> In the final analysis, this case requires us to consider how the law in a highly technical area can be administered most fairly. I firmly believe that the best way to achieve evenhanded administration of our tax laws is to adhere closely to the language used by Congress to define taxpayers' responsibilities. Occasionally there will be clear manifestations of contrary intent that justify a nonliteral reading, but surely this is not such a case. United California Bank v. United States, 439 U.S. 180, 211 (1978)(Stevens, J., dissenting).

b) POLITICAL COMPROMISE AND DETAILED LANGUAGE

The quintessential "public choice" statute is one in which legislative compromise in fact leaves a trail of detailed rules. The detail provides evidence that legislative compromise was at work. Even judges who might otherwise incline towards a more purposive approach to statutory interpretation might be persuaded by evidence of legislative compromise, including statutory detail, to stick closely to the text. Look for evidence of that approach in the following decision.

Mohasco Corp. v. Silver
447 U.S. 807 (1980).

■ Mr. Justice Stevens delivered the opinion of the Court.

The question in this Title VII case is whether Congress intended the word "filed" to have the same meaning in subsection (c) and (e) of § 706 of the Civil Rights Act of 1964, 78 Stat. 260, as amended in 1972, 86 Stat. 104–105, 42 U.S.C. § 2000e–5(c) and (e). The former subsection prohibits the filing of an unfair employment practice charge with the federal Equal Employment Opportunity Commission (EEOC) until after a state fair employment practices agency has had an opportunity to consider it. The latter subsection requires that in all events the charge must be filed with the EEOC within 300 days of the occurrence. We hold that a literal reading of the two subsections gives full effect to the several policies reflected in the statute.

[Editor—§ 706(c) provides that in States which have their own fair employment practice agencies "no charge may be filed * * * by the person aggrieved before the expiration of sixty days after proceedings have been commenced under the State or local law, unless such proceedings have been earlier terminated. * * *" § 706(e) provides, in part: "A charge under this section shall be filed within one hundred and eighty days after the alleged unlawful employment practice occurred * * *, except that (in a state where proceedings are filed with a State agency), such charge shall be filed * * * within three hundred days * * *."]

On August 29, 1975, Mohasco Corp., discharged the respondent from his position as senior marketing economist. On June 15, 1976—291 days later—the EEOC received a letter from respondent asserting that Mohasco had discriminated against him because of his religion. The letter was promptly referred to the New York State Division of Human Rights. The state agency reviewed the matter and, in due course, determined that there was no merit in the charge.

Meanwhile, on August 20, 1976—a date more than 60 days after the respondent's letter had been submitted to the EEOC and 357 days after respondent's discharge—the EEOC notified Mohasco that respondent had filed a charge of employment discrimination.

About a year later, on August 24, 1977, the EEOC issued its determination that "there is not reasonable cause to believe the charge is true," and formally notified respondent that if he wished to pursue the matter further, he had a statutory right to file a private action in a federal district court within 90 days. Respondent commenced this litigation 91 days later in the United States District Court for the Northern District of New York.

The District Court granted Mohasco's motion for summary judgment on the ground that respondent's failure to file a timely charge with the EEOC deprived the court of subject-matter jurisdiction. The court concluded that June 15, 1976 (the 291st day), could not be treated as the date that respondent's charge was "filed" with the EEOC, because § 706(c) provides that in States which have their own fair employment practice agencies—and New York is such a State—"no charge may be filed * * * by the person aggrieved before the expiration of sixty days after proceedings have been commenced under the State or local law, unless such proceedings have been earlier terminated * * *." Since no proceedings had been commenced before the New York agency prior to June 15, 1976, and since the proceedings that were commenced at that time did not terminate within 60 days, the District Court read § 706(c) as precluding any filing with the EEOC until 60 days after June 15, 1976. Because the date was 51 days beyond § 706(e)'s 300–day time limit for filing in so-called "deferral States," the charge was not timely filed. * * *

Over the dissent of Judge Meskill, the Court of Appeals for the Second Circuit reversed. It recognized that the District Court had read the statute literally, but concluded that a literal reading did not give sufficient weight to the overriding purpose of the Act. In the majority's view, in order to be faithful to "the strong federal policy in insuring that employment discrimination is redressed," it was necessary "to conclude that a charge is 'filed' for purposes of § 706(e) when received, and 'filed' as required by § 706(c) when the state deferral period ends." By giving the word "filed" two different meanings, the court concluded that the letter received by the EEOC on June 15, 1976, had been filed within 300 days as required by § 706(e), but had not been filed during the 60–day deferral period for purposes of 706(c).

Judge Meskill believed that a literal reading of the statute was not only consistent with its basic purpose, but was also warranted by the additional purpose of "requir[ing] prompt action on the part of Title VII plaintiffs." 602 F.2d, at 1092. He noted that Congress had imposed a general requirement of filing within 180 days, and that the exceptional period of 300 days for deferral States was merely intended to give the charging party a fair opportunity to invoke his state remedy without jeopardizing his federal rights; the exception was not intended to allow residents of deferral States to proceed with less diligence than was generally required.

Because there is a conflict among the Courts of Appeals on the proper interpretation of the word "filed" in this statute, we granted certiorari. We now reverse.

We first review the plain meaning of the relevant statutory language; we next examine the legislative history of the 1964 Act and the 1972 amendments for evidence that Congress intended the statute to have a different meaning; and finally we consider the policy arguments in favor of a less literal reading of the Act. * * *

[R]espondent urges us to give the word "filed" two different meanings within the same statutory section in order better to effectuate Congress' purpose underlying Title VII. Essentially, his argument is that a rule permitting filings for up to 300 days after the discriminatory occurrence—regardless of the rule against filing during the deferral period—would help further the cause of eliminating discriminatory employment practices. We therefore turn to the legislative history, but in doing so we emphasize that the words of the statute are not ambiguous. Nor does a literal reading of them lead to "absurd or futile results." For time limitations are inevitably arbitrary to some extent; and the limitations at issue here are not so short that a plaintiff's remedy is effectively denied for all practical purposes without an opportunity for a hearing.

It is unquestionably true that the 1964 statute was enacted to implement the congressional policy against discriminatory employment practices, and that that basic policy must inform construction of this remedial legislation. It must also be recognized, however, in light of the tempestuous legislative proceedings that produced the Act, that the ultimate product reflects other, perhaps countervailing, purposes that some Members of Congress sought to achieve. The present language was clearly the result of a compromise. It is our task to give effect to the statute as enacted.

The typical time limitations provision in the numerous proposed civil rights bills required the filing of a charge with the new federal fair employment practices agency within six months of the discriminatory conduct. These initial proposals did not provide for mandatory deferral by the federal agency during comparable state administrative proceedings, though some proposals would have authorized the federal agency to enter agreements of cooperation with state agencies, under which the federal agency would refrain from processing charges in specified cases.

On February 10, 1964, the House of Representatives passed H. R. 7152, its version of the comprehensive Civil Rights Act. Title VII of that bill contained a 6–month limitations provision for the filing of charges with the EEOC, and directed the EEOC to enter into agreements with state agencies providing for suspension of federal enforcement. In the Senate, H. R. 7152 met with exceptionally strong opposition. The principal opposition focused not on the details of the bill, but on its fundamental purpose. During the course of one of the longest filibusters in the history of the Senate, the bipartisan leadership of the Senate carefully forged the compromise substitute (Dirksen compromise) that was ultimately to become in substantial part the Civil Rights Act of 1964. The purpose of the compromise was to attract sufficient support to achieve the two-thirds vote necessary for cloture. This effort was successful. Fifteen days after the Dirksen compromise was offered as an amendment, a cloture motion carried the necessary votes.

Section 706(d) of the compromise provided for a 90 day limitations period [Editor—increased to 180 days in 1972] for filing discrimination claims with the EEOC in nondeferral States, the period ultimately adopted in the 1964 version of the Act. It was the first time the 90–day figure appeared in any proposed bill, and its appearance was unaccompanied by any explanation. Section § 706(b) of the compromise introduced the mandatory deferral concept for the first time, providing that during a 60–day deferral period, "no charge may be filed"—language that figures so prominently in this case. In such deferral States, § 706(d) extended the time for filing with the EEOC to 210 days [Editor—increased to 300 days in 1972].

Since the Senate did not explain why it adopted a time limitation of only half that adopted by the House, one can only speculate. But it seems clear that the 90–day provision to some must have represented a judgment that most genuine claims of discrimination would be promptly asserted and that the costs associated with processing and defending stale or dormant claims outweigh the federal interest in guaranteeing a remedy to every victim of discrimination. To others it must have represented a necessary sacrifice of the rights of some victims of discrimination in order that a civil rights bill could be enacted. Section 706(b) was rather clearly intended to increase the role of States and localities in resolving charges of employment discrimination. And § 706(d)'s longer time of 210 days for filing with the EEOC in deferral States was included to prevent forfeiture of a complainant's federal rights while participating in state proceedings.

But neither this latter provision nor anything else in the legislative history contains any "suggestion that complainants in some States were to be allowed to proceed with less diligence than those in other states." The history identifies only one reason for treating workers in deferral States differently from workers in other States: to give state agencies an opportunity to redress the evil at which the federal legislation was aimed, and to avoid federal intervention unless its need was demonstrated. The statutory plan was not designed to give the worker in a deferral State the option of choosing between his state remedy and his federal remedy, nor indeed simply to allow him additional time in which to obtain state relief. Had that been the plan, a simple statute prescribing a 90–day period in nondeferral States and a 210–day period in deferral States would have served the legislative purpose. Instead, Congress chose to prohibit the filing of any federal charge until after state proceedings had been completed or until 60 days had passed, whichever came sooner. * * *

In sum, the legislative history of the 1964 statute is entirely consistent with the wording of the statute itself. * * *

Finally we consider the additional points advanced in support of respondent's position: (1) that it is unfair to victims of discrimination who often proceed without the assistance of counsel; (2) that it is contrary to the interpretation of the Act by the agency charged with responsibility for its enforcement; and (3) that a less literal reading of the Act would adequately effectuate the policy of deferring to state agencies.

The unfairness argument is based on the assumption that a lay person reading the statute would assume that he had 300 days in which to file his first complaint with either a state or federal agency. We find no merit in this argument. We believe that a lay person would be more apt to regard the general obligation of filing within 180 days as the standard of diligence he must satisfy, and that one who carefully read the entire section would understand it to mean exactly what it says.

We must also reject any suggestion that the EEOC may adopt regulations that are inconsistent with the statutory mandate. As we have held on prior occasions, its "interpretation" of the statute cannot supersede the language chosen by Congress.

Finally, we reject the argument that the timeliness requirements would be adequately served by allowing the EEOC to treat a letter received on the 291st day as "filed" and interpreting the § 706(c) prohibition as merely requiring it to postpone any action on the charge for at least 60 days. There are two reasons why this interpretation is unacceptable.

By choosing what are obviously quite short deadlines, Congress clearly intended to encourage the prompt processing of all charges of employment discrimination. Under a literal reading of the Act, the EEOC has a duty to commence its investigation no later than 300 days after the alleged occurrence; under respondent's "interpretation" of § 706(c), that duty might not arise for 360 days. Perhaps the addition of another 60-day delay in the work of an already seriously overburdened agency is not a matter of critical importance. But in a statutory scheme in which Congress carefully prescribed a series of deadlines measured by numbers of days— rather than months or years—we may not simply interject an additional 60-day period into the procedural scheme. We must respect the compromise embodied in the words chosen by Congress. It is not our place simply to alter the balance struck by Congress in procedural statutes by favoring one side or the other in matters of statutory construction.

In the end, we cannot accept respondent's position without unreasonably giving the word "filed" two different meanings in the same section of the statute. Even if the interests of justice might be served in this particular case by bifurcated construction of that word, in the long run, experience teaches that strict adherence to the procedural requirements specified by the legislature is the best guarantee of evenhanded administration of the law.

Accordingly, the judgment of the Court of Appeals is reversed.

———————

COMMENTS

1. One reason for deferring to plain meaning is to serve a notice function for the public which reads the statute. However, the more detailed the rules, the harder it is to understand what the statute means. For the lay public, "plain meaning" might refer to a few words, not the entire statute. For the lawyer or other specialist reading the statute, "plain meaning" might embrace more words (internal context). In Mohasco, Justice Stevens does not choose approaches.[1] He says that, for a lay person reading the statute, the words imposing the general 180 day obligation would stand out, without being complicated by the rules applicable to claims in deferral states. The specialist "who carefully reads the entire statute," would observe that the rule differed in deferral states, permitting filing with the EEOC after 180 days up to a maximum of 300 days, but in no event before the earlier of 60 days after filing with the state agency or completion of state agency review.

2. Remember Justice Stevens' argument (in Chapter 6) that "prior to December 31" did not mean "prior to December 31." See United States v. Locke, 471 U.S. 84 (1985). He is not reluctant to go behind a text specifying procedural requirements in an appropriate case. What made Mohasco an *in*appropriate case for abandoning strict adherence to the text, compared to Locke?

---

[1]   See also Holywell Corp. v. Smith, 503 U.S. 47, 53 (1992)(word means same in ordinary and legal usage, citing Webster's and Black's Law Dictionary).

CHAPTER 9

CHANGE

In this Chapter we consider the impact of change on the meaning of statutes. Chapter 9.01 contrasts the approach of the common law and statutory interpretation to change. Chapter 9.02 considers the possibility that statutes might become obsolete. We focus on Guido Calabresi's argument that courts should on occasion declare statutes obsolete, just as they would overrule a common law precedent, if the statute is out of touch with the "legal landscape" and if legislative inertia prevents the legislature from updating the law. Chapter 9.03 explores the question of statutory evolution, short of "overruling" the statute. We first consider situations where the statute might incorporate a common law concept. For example, does a statute making it a crime to kill a "person" apply to a fetus; does the "charitable" deduction in the tax law apply to schools which practice race discrimination? We then consider statutory evolution when there is no common law context—for example, whether a civil rights statute providing for equal "rights" applies to relationships between private parties or only to the individual's relationship to the State; whether same-sex couples can adopt. Chapter 9.04 discusses how a textualist might approach change, using a Judge Easterbrook opinion as an example.

This Chapter also elaborates on the earlier discussions of background considerations. Calabresi's conception of "legal landscape" is yet another example of substantive background considerations.

We also deal more specifically in this Chapter with *institutional* background considerations, of which Calabresi's concern about legislative inertia is an example. Institutional background considerations focus attention on which institution ought to decide which questions. Earlier examples of these institutional concerns were the absence of a level legislative playing field (based, for example, on the inability of some interests to organize effectively or to overcome traditional bias); the concern about judicial competence to decide complex legal issues (such as tax and copyright); and the impact of judicial action on the willingness of legislatures to meet their political and statutory drafting responsibilities.

9.01 COMMON LAW VS. STATUTES

The common law is accustomed to dealing with change. When applying a rule from a prior case, the court considers the principles underlying the prior rule, how they apply to contemporary facts, and whether contemporary principles require limitation, extension, or perhaps rejection of the rule. The words of the prior case are not dispositive; they embody relevant principles.

It is tempting to look on this process as mechanical, involving the identification and weighing of principles in the context of new facts. But it is more realistic to acknowledge that principles and facts do not exist in airtight compartments. The application of principles to contemporary facts is a way of understanding what those principles are and should become.

All rules are the result of an equilibrium of policies imparting both thrust and limit to the rule. Uncertainty arises when the interaction of text and facts appears to unsettle the original equilibrium, suggesting that the apparent application of the text to the facts is wrong or that the failure to apply the text makes little sense. Because all rules are what their applications signify, any doubt about whether they apply to new facts is potentially unsettling and requires some rethinking of the rule's meaning in a contemporary setting. The question is how much rethinking a court can do.

The rules in statutes cannot be insulated from the effect of change but it is difficult to figure out how courts should deal with the problem when interpreting legislation. First, the statute's words may not be as malleable as the words of a common law case. Case law language invites distinctions between dictum and holding, which general statutory texts do not. Second, courts need authority to effect change—the legitimacy question. When the original policy comes from statutes, it is unclear where the judicial authority to effect change comes from. Third, statutes are often useful because they are a better method of effecting change than judge-made law. Courts may be no better at adapting statutes to change than in adopting a rule in the first place—the competency question.

9.02 LEGAL EVOLUTION AND OBSOLETE STATUTES

In our earlier discussion of textualism and change in Chapter 5 (especially the discussion of "family"), we have encountered more than a hint of contemporary policy influencing the court's decision. This section directly confronts that issue. In A Common Law for the Age of Statutes (1982), Guido Calabresi explicitly argues that the judge should sometimes rely on contemporary values when dealing with statutes. The particular problem he addresses is the obsolete statute. He suggests that courts have a "common law" power to "overrule" such statutes, just as they could overrule an out-of-date common law precedent. Courts should do this under the following circumstances: the statute does not fit with the "legal landscape;" a representative majority is unlikely to preserve the statute; and legislative inertia prevents reconsideration of the issue.

Calabresi himself is wary of distorting the interpretive process by updating statutes. He prefers an open exercise of a power to declare some statutes obsolete to the practice of pretending that such statutes can be interpreted to make them fit better in a contemporary world. Nonetheless, much of what he says is also relevant to the interpretation of statutes when conditions change. The concepts of a changing legal landscape and legislative inertia specifically address the responsibilities of courts and legislatures to make law, which is an important background consideration in deciding how courts should interpret statutes.

This section will explore Calabresi's ideas and see what his "common law" power to "overrule" statutes implies. Chapter 9.03 will then deal with statutory evolution, short of overruling.

a) CALABRESI

i) LEGAL LANDSCAPE

As you read the discussion of legal landscape, distinguish between two questions—what does the concept mean; and is it legitimate for courts to use that concept in statutory interpretation, as opposed to the common law. One of Calabresi's points is that courts are accustomed to dealing with the legal landscape (whether or not they use the term) in common law cases—indeed, they cannot do without it. For example, what else is a court doing when it rejects charitable immunity in tort law, adopts comparative negligence, or imposes a warranty of habitability on landlord-tenant contracts? But it is still fair to ask whether the legal landscape should be used as vigorously in *statutory interpretation*.

You should also be aware that not everyone is enthusiastic about judicial updating of the *common law*. The Arizona Supreme Court held an employer liable for damages when the discharge of an employee violated state public policy. (The employer had fired a female employee for refusing to publicly indecently expose herself during a staff musical performance.) Wagenseller v. Scottsdale Memorial Hospital, 710 P.2d 1025 (Ariz.1985)(en banc). The Arizona legislature later passed a law (S. 1386, 42d Leg., 2d sess. (1996)) adopting the court's position. However, the legislature stated in sec. 1 of the bill (entitled "intent") that, although "courts interpret the common law," they "are not authorized to establish a cause of action [based on] violation of the public policy of th[e] state."

The statute stated that "[c]ourts are not vested with the authority to create public policy of the state. When courts make pronouncements of public policy on an ad hoc basis, they render it impossible for citizens to know in advance what actions constitute violations of the laws for which they are subject to civil damages." The statute contrasted the legislature, which had "authority to create laws and the public policy of the state," with courts, which "adjudicate cases by applying the laws enacted by the legislature to the facts of those cases." It also stated that "[i]t is the intent of the legislature to establish that the courts cannot create new causes of action. Courts can apply common law causes of action to cases they adjudicate provided that they do not expand, modify or in any manner whatsoever alter the common law causes of action that were adopted by the legislature pursuant to Arizona

Revised Statutes section 1–201." That section is the "boilerplate" provision found in most states, affirming:

> The common law only so far as it is consistent with and adapted to the natural and physical conditions of this state and the necessities of the people thereof, and not repugnant to or inconsistent with the Constitution of the United States or the constitution or laws of this state, or established customs of the people of this state, is adopted and shall be the rule of decision in all courts of this state.

G.   Calabresi, A Common Law for the Age of Statutes
(1982).

> The court's judgment [about whether to exercise a common law power with respect to statutes] must be based primarily on whether the statute fits the legal landscape, because that is what a court is good at discerning and because "fit" is correlated with majoritarian support. The two are far from the same, however, for legislatures can properly want a rule that is out of phase with the topography. The court must therefore do the best it can to avoid following the requirements of the legal landscape when that would conflict with powerful legislative desires. It dares not stray too far from subservience to the landscape, though, because it is unsure of its capacity to gauge majoritarian support. Accordingly it is bound to make some decisions based on the fit of the statute which the legislature will want reversed. The same tension existed at common law. Application of the common law power to statutes, like the greater willingness of legislatures to act in traditionally common law areas, merely means more frequent possibilities of legislative reversals of court judgments. It calls for greater awareness on the part of courts of majoritarian wishes; it does not reduce the responsibility of courts to put subservience to the legal framework first. * * *

> The questions courts should ask themselves [are] ones we have all heard before, for they are strikingly similar to those which at common law determined when old precedents should be discarded.

> Has the common law surrounding the statute so altered that the old [statutory] rule no longer fits in its current form? [Editor—Calabresi argues that this is often true of the common law of comparative negligence, discussed later in this Chapter.] * * *

> Have other statutes been passed which indicate the same type of change in the legal landscape * * *? In this sense a single statute may not have much gravitational force, but, as Landis notes, a collection of statutes in one's own and other jurisdictions surely must create a strong revisionist pressure. [Editor—Statutes concerned with the equal status of women are an example. They include laws creating separate property for married women, provid-

ing that men can receive alimony, and giving divorced women a right to property created jointly during marriage, such as retirement funds.] * * *

Has the constitutional law surrounding the statute so changed that it no longer fits as written? [Editor—The expansion of equal protection principles to apply to women is an example.]

Calabresi next addresses the question of how the statute's age relates to obsolescence. Chronological age is not dispositive. In his view, some statutes age quickly, and some slowly. In general, however, "life expectancy of a statute is relatively low right after birth" because of "inadvertence, overreaction to a particular set of events, or a legislative response to a temporary majority at war with more persistent societal views." Statutory life expectancy "becomes very high after the rule has survived a few years, and then diminishes as it ages." Calabresi then discusses some statutes which might not fit the contemporary legal landscape.

* * * One reason for the shift to statutes [ ] was the legislature's capacity to deal quickly with crises—real or imagined—engendered by rapidly changing technologies and ideologies. It should be obvious that such statutes are likely to age more quickly than other, more organic laws. Such crisis laws are the product of quick changes, and other quick changes can render them anachronistic. Such laws deserve little conservative bias, once the event, the crisis, the technological change, is overcome. They are in fact the very statutes that most justify the use of the doctrine here described.

Examples again are easy: fair trade laws passed during an economic crisis against a background of antitrust laws; emergency rent controls in the context of a still predominantly "free price" society; emergency malpractice laws that place restrictions on recoveries alien to the rest of tort law and that could become dated as a result of relatively minor reorganizations in the medical profession or in the insurance industry. These laws when enacted were all at war with the then prevailing legal fabric. They were justified because majoritarian bodies are there precisely to make new and even *ad hoc* distinctions that do not fit the legal landscape. They may become the source of further common law and statutory change, and serve as landmarks in a whole new topography. Or they may not. Emergency rent control may or may not be the precursor of a regulated price system. Restrictions on malpractice recoveries may or may not represent the beginning of a whole new way of trying to balance safety, accidents, and compensation. Fair trade laws may or may not signal a general move toward protection of competitors.

Even if the principles these laws reflect do not come to prevail generally, there may remain instances in which bodies that are at least majoritarian by representation choose to perpetuate distinctions in favor of special groups. And then it is irrelevant that these distinctions originated in a particular time-limited set of circumstances. But reenactment or reconsideration is required once those time-limited set of circumstances are past. And courts can justifiably force legislatures in such situations to show whether or not they mean to keep in force the distinction which does not fit the law at large and is no longer supported by the circumstances that engendered it.

One should distinguish this kind of time-bound preference from those statutory discriminations that remain supported by the general circumstances existing at the time of enactment. These laws whose lack of fit has stayed constant present the most difficult case for the doctrine. Their justification rests directly in the persistence of the coalition that enacted them, and this becomes increasingly doubtful over time. Yet to determine that the support for these laws has faded, the courts have to make more direct guesses as to legislative support than was traditionally countenanced.

When such laws seem to represent an attempt of a transient majority to write its views in stone, or when they seem to be the last gasp of a dying majority that seeks by legislation to foreclose the future, such statutes create enormous temptations for judicial intervention. Most of the time, if the majority was transient or dying, that intervention will be justified by other visible changes in the landscape. If no such clear changes exist, traditionalists will prefer to stay with a retentionist bias; those who are more comfortable than I with justifications of judicial power based on court capacity to reflect current majorities or disinterested values will permit courts to induce legislatures to reconsider the preferences. * * *

ii) INERTIA

Calabresi does not think that courts should "overrule" all obsolete statutes. Legislative reform is preferable. That is why legislative inertia is a necessary condition, in his view, for "overruling" a statute. He argues that "the courts in exercising the power to induce the updating of statutes should only deal in areas of legislative inertia."

But how does a judge decide when inertia has been overcome? The mere fact that legislation is proposed cannot be sufficient. Bills are often offered when everyone knows they have no chance to be considered. Would the following be sufficient to demonstrate lack of inertia—committee deliberations on an issue; passage of bills in related areas (for example, repeal of some but not all guest statutes making it harder for guests to sue hosts in tort)?

Once the court finds legislative inertia, and determines that the statute does not fit the legal landscape or the likely preferences of the current representative majority, asymmetries in inertia become relevant for deciding whether a statute needs reconsideration. Calabresi discusses *asymmetries* in legislative inertia, as follows.

The force of inertia is frequently not symmetrical in lawmaking and revision. At times reconsideration by a majoritarian or representative body, and hence possible reenactment, can easily be achieved without having to overcome major obstacles if a statute is nullified or cast into doubt. But legislative review of the same statute may require the bypassing of severe, nonmajoritarian obstructions if the statute is left undisturbed or unquestioned by the courts. Conversely, there may be statutes that once nullified can only with great difficulty be reconsidered in a majoritarian way; the same laws, if left in effect, are subject to almost constant review by a representative body. * * *

[T]he chance of a permanent bad result is less great if those on whom the court puts the burden of overcoming the effects of its decision have ready access to legislative reconsideration. * * *

Asymmetries in majoritarian review may be due either to the nature of the law involved or to the nature of the legislature empowered to reconsider the law. As an example of the first, let us assume that some laws require funding by the full legislature every year in order to remain effective. These laws could rather easily be made subject to legislative review even in the absence of court-induced reconsideration. But the same laws, if nullified by courts, might only get reconsidered at the pleasure of a legislative committee. * * * Conversely, the threat to nullify a law that is manifestly needed, but some parts of which are anachronistic, is bound to create a full legislative reconsideration of the law. Leaving the same law undisturbed may, instead, mean that the dubious parts of the statute will only be reviewed if a strong inertial burden is overcome. (Again, to give a rather wild example, if a court believes that some parts of a murder statute no longer fit, a threat of nullification over the whole statute will almost certainly bring about a legislative review; but leaving the statute untouched may make it unlikely that the legislature will ever reconsider the specific parts the court believes to be out of phase.)

The "asymmetries" factor suggests that courts should favor results which are most likely to attract legislative attention. In other words, in close cases, decide for the party with the weaker political clout to provide an incentive for the stronger political group to obtain legislative review. The discussion in Chapter 4 about the difficulties of forming efficacious political groups suggests when asymmetries of political power occur.

––––––––––

Another way to state Calabresi's point about legislative inertia is that a court should sometimes act as a catalyst for legislative behavior. Professor Sax makes this argument in connection with environmental litigation. Joseph Sax, Defending the Environment (1970)(Chapter 6—The Court as Catalyst; Ch 8—Making Democracy Work: Remands to the Legislature). Sax states that "[t]he job of the courts is to raise important policy questions in a context where they can be given the attention they deserve and to restrain essentially irrevocable decisions until those policy questions can be adequately resolved." He gives as an example a Massachusetts state court decision (Robbins v. Department of Public Works, 244 N.E.2d 577 (Mass.1969)), where the court set out the "standard it required as adequate evidence of legislative intent, a standard patently designed to thrust such matters explicitly upon public attention and to require the legislature to put specifically upon the record the [   ] policy it was undertaking."

Another example might be West Virginia Div. of the Izaak Walton League of America, Inc. v. Butz, 522 F.2d 945 (4th Cir.1975). The case involved judicial review of the United States Forestry Service practice of allowing clearcutting of timber. The issue seemed ripe for a court to force attention by the legislature. (1) The governing statute was old (1897). (2) The administering agency had been very tolerant of timber cutting, even though this behavior had grown under increasing attack as environmentally unsound. (3) Signals from Congress suggested criticism of these cutting practices in the form of 1972 guidelines issued by the Senate congressional subcommittee with jurisdiction over this area of law. (4) The timber industry had enough legislative clout to block any legislative change based on the 1972 guidelines, even though environmentalists had more influence in the legislature than in the agency. In this setting, the court held that clearcutting was not allowed. The 1975 decision "stunned" both the agency and the timber industry.[1] Prompted by this decision, Congress revisited and substantially revised the entire statute in 1976, including legislative policy regarding timber cutting.[2]

b) OBSOLETE STATUTES

The power to declare a statute obsolete seemed very important to Calabresi in the following situation. A statute "reformed" the common law many years ago. The common law, if left to its own devices, might provide even more "reform" today, but the statute seemed to have frozen common law development. Interpretation of the statute to provide for a surviving common law power was disingenuous. But the legislature might do very little about updating the law. The following case exemplifies the problem for Calabresi. Is it a good occasion for declaring statutes obsolete? Ask the "Calabresi" questions:

    1. Could the court reasonably interpret the statute to provide a surviving common law power?

    2. Has the legal landscape changed?

    3. Could the court reasonably assume that a legislative majority would want to perpetuate the existing law?

---

1. Dennis LeMaster, Decade of Change, p.56 (1984).

2. See generally Charles Wilkinson and H. Michael Anderson, Land and Resource Planning in the National Forests, pp. 72, 138–47, 155 (1987).

4.   Is there legislative inertia?

5.   Are there political asymmetries regarding legislative inertia and, if so, what are they?

Also note carefully how many judges were willing to revisit and update the common law, despite the old statute.

Vincent v. Pabst Brewing Co.

177 N.W.2d 513 (Wis.1970).

■ Hanley, Justice

Two related questions are presented on this appeal:

(1) Should the doctrine of pure comparative negligence be adopted in Wisconsin; and, if so,

(2) Should such adoption be accomplished by this court rather than by the legislature?

Under the current law in Wisconsin, the appellant can recover nothing from the respondents because his negligence exceeded that of the respondent Nye. Under pure comparative negligence, however, appellant would recover 40 percent of his damages, for pure comparative negligence never bars recovery. Instead, it merely reduces the recoverable amount of one's damages by the percentage of his negligence. In considering the appellant's contention that a doctrine of pure comparative negligence should be adopted, the Wisconsin history of both contributory negligence and comparative negligence should be briefly noted.

The doctrine of contributory negligence as a complete bar to recovery was originally adopted by the English courts in Butterfield v. Forrester (1809), 103 Eng.Rep. 926. This doctrine then spread to this country and was adopted by this court in Chamberlain v. Milwaukee & Mississippi R.R. Co. (1858), 7 Wis. 425, 431, and in Dressler v. Davis (1858), 7 Wis. 527, 531. In order to avoid the harshness of the doctrine of contributory negligence, which had its origin in an era of economic individualism, the Wisconsin legislature [adopted in 1931] * * * sec. 895.045, Stats., [which] reads:

> "Contributory negligence; when bars recovery. Contributory negligence shall not bar recovery in an action by any person or his legal representative to recover damages for negligence resulting in death or in injury to person or property if such negligence was not as great as the negligence of the person against whom recovery is sought, but any damages allowed shall be diminished in the proportion to the amount of negligence attributable to the person recovering."

Noting that contributory negligence is a court-adopted doctrine, the appellant contends that such doctrine has only been partially eliminated by sec. 895.045, Stats. In other words, the appellant contends that the statute eliminates the doctrine where the negligence of the defendant exceeds that of the plaintiff, but that the court-adopted doctrine remains in effect where the negligence of the plaintiff equals or exceeds that of the defendant. Thus, according to the appellant, it is not sec. 895.045, Stats., but the common law doctrine of contributory negligence (to the extent it was left unchanged by the statute) which bars his recovery. If, in fact, such were the case, this court, of course, would have authority to change the common law. * * *

Although considerable disagreement exists as to whether a doctrine of pure comparative negligence should be adopted in Wisconsin, there has been considerable agreement as to the ability or propriety of this court's initiating such adoption. One writer has said that the Wisconsin doctrine of comparative negligence "* * * is a statutory rule and the court is helpless. * * *" The writer continues by stating:

"* * * If the legislature had never developed a comparative negligence doctrine, our supreme court might feel free to act. However, the right of the claimant is now controlled by the 1931 statute. The change should be made, but it will require action by the Wisconsin Legislature."

In support of the contention that this court has authority to adopt pure comparative negligence, it has been argued in the amicus curiae brief of the American Trial Lawyers Association that the legislature, in enacting sec. 895.045, Stats., did not preempt the field of comparative negligence and thereby preclude further development by this court. Analogy is then drawn to this court's decision in Holytz v. Milwaukee (Wis.1962), 115 N.W.2d 618, wherein the common law doctrine of governmental immunity for tort liability was abolished, despite previous legislative activity which had removed immunity in limited circumstances.

This court, however, has consistently interpreted the statute itself as having created the bar to recovery. The statute says: "Contributory negligence shall not bar recovery * * * *if* such (negligence of the party seeking recovery is) not as great as the negligence of the person against whom recovery is sought * * *." The natural inference is that if one's negligence is as great, or greater, than the party against whom recovery is sought recovery is denied. * * *

* * *[I]t should be noted that the legislature in its most recent session has established an interim committee to study problems such as those cited by the respondents. * * *

Such a study could consider respondents' assertions that collateral benefits available to negligent plaintiffs are ample protection for those more negligent than the persons from whom recovery is sought. The collateral benefits to which respondents refer are kept regardless of plaintiff's fault and include such things as medical and hospitalization insurance, automobile insurance and social security.

Since poverty can affect defendants as well as plaintiffs, the possibility that given an ultimate fact verdict, which is necessary in implementing any form of comparative negligence, a defendant will always be found partially negligent should be considered. By adopting pure comparative negligence out of a sense of intellectual fairness one might well be eliminating what has been called an arbitrary rule of no recovery, while at the same time creating an arbitrary rule of partial recovery in *all* cases. If such were the case, pure comparative negligence would render defendants the insurers of any who chose to commence an action.

In short, the legislature should consider whether fairness is preserved by applying the comparative negligence doctrine as we now know it or by applying a doctrine of pure comparative negligence.

Without passing judgment upon the merits of pure comparative negligence as opposed to comparative negligence as it is presently applied in this jurisdiction, we think that the legislature is the body best equipped to adopt the change advocated by the appellant.
* * *

Judgment affirmed. [Editor—Two other judges joined this opinion.]

■ Heffernan, Justice (concurring).

I concur in the result and agree that, in view of the legislature's present study of comparative negligence problems, this court should abstain from considering the question raised by the plaintiff-appellant.

I do not agree, however, that the passage of the comparative negligence act has divested this court of its inherent common-law prerogative of reconsidering matters that stem from judicial decision.

■ Wilkie, Justice (concurring).

I believe there is a need for changing the rule under the Wisconsin comparative negligence system which prohibits a plaintiff from recovering a portion of his damages where his negligence is equal to or greater than the defendant's who is at least partially responsible for his injuries.

Although, in my opinion, the court has the authority to make these changes in the rule, and the legislature has not preempted the entire subject, at this time I would defer to the legislature as the proper body to make a complete study of the subject and to adopt changes it concludes appropriate. Therefore, I concur.

I have been authorized to state that Mr. Justice Beilfuss joins in this concurrence.

■ Hallows, Chief Justice (dissenting).

The doctrine of pure comparative negligence should be adopted and the unjust doctrine of contributory negligence repudiated; this can and should be done by this court exercising its inherent power. * * *

[Editor—The judge's arguments on the merits are omitted. In general, he claims that justice requires recovery from a defendant who is 20% negligent; that collateral benefits for the plaintiff should not diminish a defendant's obligations; and that there is no real danger of a partial recovery in all cases.]

The majority of the court states if there is to be any change it should be done by the legislature. This court has never construed sec. 895.045. Stats., to pre-empt the contributory negligence field of the common law. All this court has done was to decide cases under that section and to interpret what its language meant. This is not the same as holding the section preempted the field by legislative action or by silence. * * *

The history of this statute is clear that it was a reaction against the doctrine of contributory negligence but there is nothing in its history or in its language which evinces any intent to pre-empt this field of common law to the exclusion of this court. I think the argument against pre-emption can be based upon an analogy to our action in Holytz v. Milwaukee (Wis.1962), 115 N.W.2d 618, where we abolished governmental immunity even though there was a statutory enactment allowing recovery in a limited area. I find no preemption based upon a negative inference of what sec. 895.045, Stats., did not do. The doctrine of pre-emption applied to common-law areas should rest only on affirmative action; otherwise, the death of the common law is near at hand. The doctrine of contributory negligence is a child of the common law and the court can and should replace it with the doctrine of pure comparative negligence.

COMMENTS AND QUESTIONS

1. Interpreting statute so common law power survives

(a) *Common law survival.* Calabresi's best guess about the meaning of the 1931 Wisconsin statute was that it covered the entire field regarding comparative negligence. Consequently, the only way to understand the 1970 decision in Vincent v. Pabst is that it assumed a power to declare statutes obsolete. Whether or not Calabresi is correct about the 1931 Wisconsin statute, it is clear that not all statutes dealing with common law subjects eliminate a judicial common law power. Consider whether these three situations are examples of statutes leaving judges a common law power.

(1) A doctor treated a mature-looking 17–year old minor without parental consent. At common law, parental consent was required. Sever-

al statutes permitted treatment of minors without parental consent, including cases of drug abuse and venereal disease. Can the court adopt a "mature minor" exception to the common law parental consent requirement as part of an evolving common law, despite the existing statutes? Cardwell v. Bechtol, 724 S.W.2d 739 (Tenn.1987).

(2) In the 19th Century, wrongful death statutes were adopted permitting survivors to sue after the death of a relative. In one state, the statute permitted a $5,000 recovery by selected family members of deceased railroad *passengers*. Could the court adopt a common law wrongful death action for relatives of deceased railroad *workers* or did the statute freeze the common law? Is there a difference between a court saying that legislative attention to wrongful death should defer judicial adoption of wrongful death recoveries under the common law and saying that the legislature froze the judicial power to adopt wrongful death recoveries?   See Malone, The Genesis of Wrongful Death, 17 Stan. L. Rev. 1043 (1965).

(3) In 1971, the Wisconsin legislature reenacted the old negligence law, altering the contributory negligence bar to recovery by 1%. 1971 Wis., ch. 47. The legislature replaced the language "not as great as" with "no greater than." This meant that the plaintiff could recover if his negligence was equal to (no greater than) the defendant's (50%), but no statutory remedy was provided if the plaintiff's negligence exceeded the defendant's (51%). Would the Justices in Vincent who thought the common law could provide more generous comparative negligence rules than the statute also think that the common law could be more generous than the 1971 statute (for example, if the plaintiff was 51% negligent)? Lupie v. Hartzheim, 195 N.W.2d 461 (Wis.1972).

(b) *Clear elimination of common law power*. Sometimes, though rarely, a statute explicitly freezes the common law as of a particular date, obviously leaving no room for future case law development, unless there is a common law power to declare the statute obsolete. See, e.g., Martin v. Petta, 694 S.W.2d 233, 239 (Tex.App.1985)(a statute stated that the "common law doctrine of res ipsa loquitur shall only apply to health care liability claims against health care providers or physicians in those cases to which it has been applied by the appellate courts of this state as of the effective date of this subchapter.").[3]

(c) *Derogation of common law?* Would it be proper for the court in Vincent v. Pabst to invoke the "derogation of common law" canon to favor a surviving common law power to expand comparative negligence? I think not. The derogation canon makes some sense as a way of asking the legislature whether it really meant to override the substantive values embodied in *prior* common law. In Vincent v. Pabst, the whole point is to allow the court to invoke *contemporary* values which long *postdate* the statute's adoption.

---

3. Sometimes the legislature freezes the law in accordance with preexisting agency interpretations of the law. See, e.g., Revenue Act of 1978, § 132, Pub. L. No. 95–600, 92 Stat. 2763, 2782, freezing the law concerning taxation of deferred compensation in accordance with regulations, rulings, and judicial decisions in effect on February 1, 1978.

2. Updating Techniques

(a) *Warn legislature.* Notice that a judge concerned with statutory obsolescence does not have to declare a statute obsolete. Three of the judges in Vincent v. Pabst warned the legislature that the judges *might* change the law. That often has an effect on the legislature. (Sometimes, this can be done simply by a judge's speech to a bar association.)

(b) *Absurdity.* Would a textualist be helpless in the face of an obsolete statute? How might Justice Scalia decide the following case? A statute made it a crime to pass a car without honking the horn. When the statute was passed, all highways were two lane and honking was meant to warn oncoming drivers. Would the statute apply to passing cars going in the same direction on today's four lane highways? Wouldn't that be an absurd result, given the statute's purpose? Sanders v. Hisaw, 94 So.2d 486 (La.App.1957).

The absurdity approach would have only limited application in helping judges update statutes. For example, it would not allow a judge to update a comparative negligence law which covered only plaintiffs who were less than 50% negligent, as in Vincent v. Pabst.

(c) *Potential unconstitutionality.* Is an obsolete statute potentially unconstitutional? For example, state guest statutes are often considered out of step with contemporary tort law principles. They generally prevent guests in cars from suing the driver for negligence. Some courts hold that these statutes violate the minimum rationality test because there is no reason to distinguish car guests from home or other guests, and because the statute is overbroad in preventing collusive law suits (applying even in the absence of collusion) and underbroad (because there are exceptions permitting guest lawsuits, where collusion is still possible). See, e.g., Bierkamp v. Rogers, 293 N.W.2d 577 (Iowa 1980). Calabresi argues that such decisions distort constitutional decisionmaking and that an explicit power to declare statutes obsolete would be preferable.

Nonetheless, *some* statutes are potentially unconstitutional and obsolescence might properly be considered a factor in deciding that they are unconstitutional, *subject to reconsideration if the legislature repasses the law.* More specifically, a statute might appear to threaten a fundamental interest or impinge on a suspect classification but a judge might be willing to uphold the law if it was more than an obsolete expression of legislative choice, reflecting older prejudices that might not survive today.

This is best understood as a branch of constitutional law requiring "legislative rationality," to which we return in Chapter 17. But it is worth noting here because it is a less controversial way to achieve updating of the law without adopting the most radical version of Calabresi's proposal, which is to declare statutes obsolete without regard to substantive constitutional concerns. Indeed, *Judge* Calabresi (he became a 2d Circuit judge in 1994) applied that approach in Quill v. Vacco, 80 F.3d 716 (2d Cir.1996), cert. granted, 117 S.Ct. 36 (1996). The majority held that New York's statute penalizing a doctor for assisting suicide at the request of a competent terminally-ill patient violated Equal Protection. The unequal treatment arose from the legality of permitting the doctor to respond to requests to terminate life-support systems, but criminalizing other assistance in terminating life.

Judge Calabresi disagreed with this analysis. He concluded that the law impinged on important constitutional rights to privacy (involving the right to die and to control one's body), but refused to hold that these rights necessarily required striking down the statute, *if* New York repassed the law. He observed that the statutes making assistance of suicide a crime dated to 1828, and that later statutes had decriminalized suicide but did not repeal the law making assistance of suicide a crime. After an exhaustive historical review of New York state law, he noted:

> From this historical survey, I conclude that 1) what petitioners seek is nominally still forbidden by New York statutes; 2) the bases of these statutes have been deeply eroded over the last hundred and fifty years; and 3) few of their foundations remain in place today.
>
> Specifically:
>
> The original reason for the statutes—criminalizing conduct that aided or abetted other crimes—is long since gone.
>
> The distinction that has evolved over the years between conduct currently permitted (suicide, and aiding someone who wishes to die to do so by removing hydration, feeding, and life support systems) and conduct still prohibited (giving a competent, terminally ill patient lethal drugs, which he or she can self-administer) is tenuous at best.
>
> The Legislature—for many, many years—has not taken any recognizably affirmative step reaffirming the prohibition of what petitioners seek.
>
> The enforcement of the laws themselves has fallen into virtual desuetude—not so much as to render the case before us nonjusticiable, but enough to cast doubt on whether, in a case like that which the petitioners present, a prosecutor would prosecute or a jury would convict. And this fact by itself inevitably raises doubts about the current support for these laws.

Calabresi therefore concluded as follows:

> I would hold that, on the current legislative record, New York's prohibitions on assisted suicide violate both the Equal Protection and Due Process Clauses of the Fourteenth Amendment of the United States Constitution to the extent that these laws are interpreted to prohibit a physician from prescribing lethal drugs to be self-administered by a mentally competent, terminally ill person in the final stages of that terminal illness. I would, however, take no position on whether such prohibitions, or other more finely drawn ones, might be valid, under either or both clauses of the United States Constitution, were New York to reenact them while articulat-

ing the reasons for the distinctions it makes in the laws, and expressing the grounds for the prohibitions themselves.

Calabresi also argued that a similar approach was the better way to decide cases like Griswold v. Connecticut, 381 U.S. 479 (1965)(constitutional right of privacy violated by Connecticut law prohibiting the sale and use of birth control devices), and Califano v. Goldfarb, 430 U.S. 199 (1977) (statute violated equal protection by providing Social Security automatically to widows but requiring widowers to prove dependence on deceased wife).

(d) *Judge Calabresi as critic.* Judge Calabresi has written critically of at least one example of interpreting a statute to fit the legal landscape. Taber v. Maine, 67 F.3d 1029 (2d Cir.1995), involved a personal injury to an off-duty Navy serviceman (Taber). Taber brought a personal injury action under the Federal Tort Claims Act (FTCA) against the federal government for injuries he sustained in an automobile accident caused by another off-duty Navy serviceman (Maine), who had been drinking on base. The plaintiff, Taber, had been visiting his girl-friend for the weekend. The Federal Torts Claims Act (FTCA) allows civil actions against the government based on the negligent acts or omissions of its employees, including those of members of the Armed Services who are acting "in the line of duty." (The courts equate the FTCA's "line of duty" language with the phrase "scope of employment," as that concept is defined by the respondeat superior law of the jurisdiction in which the accident occurred. Using this standard, the defendant Maine *was* acting within the scope of employment.)

That was not the end of the matter, however. The court had to consider whether the doctrine established by Feres v. United States, 340 U.S. 135 (1950), nonetheless barred the plaintiff's action. Feres had narrowed the application of the FTCA, holding that "the Government is not liable under the Federal Tort Claims Act for injuries to servicemen where the injuries arise out of or in the course of activity incident to service" by the *plaintiff*. It was the Feres doctrine which appeared to Calabresi to be a questionable application of legal landscape analysis to limit the statute's reach. He stated as follows:

> The Feres doctrine started lucidly enough as a rule that barred servicemember's claims under the FTCA for injuries that "arise out of or are [sustained] in the course of activity incident to service." This language, which derived from the words characteristically found in both state and federal workers' compensation statutes, was not chosen accidentally. Indeed, at its inception, the rule in Feres is best understood as an attempt to preclude suits by servicemembers against the government because, as military employees, they received government disability and death benefits—benefits that the Court observed were similar to (and if anything more generous than) most civilian workers' compensation awards.

> Then, as now, civilian workers' compensation statutes typically barred tort suits by employees against their employers for injuries arising out of or in the course of employment. It must have seemed reasonable to the Supreme Court to treat military employees in a

similar manner. After all, treating like cases alike is the great engine of the law.

That such a reading of the FTCA was exceedingly willful, and flew directly in the face of a relatively recent statute's language and legislative history, apparently did not trouble the Court much—intent, as it was, to make the FTCA "fit" the legal landscape of the time. * * *

It may occasionally be desirable for courts to invite legislatures to reconsider outdated statutes so that, unless the legislatures make clear their continued preference for disparate treatment, like cases may be treated alike. See generally, Guido Calabresi, A Common Law for the Age of Statutes (1982). Although apparently this was precisely what the Court was doing in Feres, its willingness to ignore language, history, and the process of incremental law making (not to mention possible ways of dialoguing with Congress to discern the legislature's actual intent) was nevertheless remarkable. In any event, none of these considerations seemed to matter to the Court which seemingly concluded that the federal "systems of simple, certain and uniform compensation for injuries or death in the armed services," should be, like workers' compensation laws, an injured servicemember's sole source of recovery.

Judge Calabresi does not say exactly how the Feres Court could have "dialogued" with Congress. How could you have written an opinion that raised the possible inapplicability of the FTCA to workers whose injuries "arise out of or are [sustained] in the course of activity incident to service," without explicitly adopting that result?

9.03   STATUTORY EVOLUTION

The death of a statute through obsolescence is only one setting in which the issue of statutory evolution arises. In this section, we broaden our discussion to include cases where the statute has not died but may only have evolved. The discussion is divided into two parts: cases where the statute has a common law context and cases where there is no common law context. A statute can have a common law context in either of two senses—either the statute occupies a niche in an area of law over which the court previously had a substantive common lawmaking power, or the statute incorporates a common law principle.

As you decide how to interpret statutes in the following cases, think about whether you are relying on the plain meaning of the text, on how the legislature's purpose might apply to the contemporary case, or on contemporary legal landscape.

a)   COMMON LAW CONTEXT

A statute can have a common law context in one of two senses—(1) the area of law can be one in which courts have a substantive common law power or (2) the statute can incorporate a common law principle. The court's power to update the law is probably greatest when there is a common law context in both senses. Such statutes are more likely to "plainly hand" the court a common law power.

i) BOB JONES

Federal courts do not have a common law power regarding taxation, but the area of income tax law at issue in the following case—the definition of charities—is one which had been the dealt with by the common law long before the modern income tax was adopted.

In Bob Jones University v. United States, 461 U.S. 574 (1983), a section of the tax law provided deductions for contributions to tax exempt "charitable" or "educational" organizations. A school discriminated on the basis of race and the question was whether it could receive deductible charitable contributions as an "educational" organization. The Court had a specific textual problem, in that the statute provided exemption for "charitable" or "educational" institutions in the alternative. Nonetheless, the Court stated that

> [i]t is a well-established canon of statutory construction that a court should go beyond the literal language of a statute if reliance on that language would defeat the plain purpose of the statute * * *.

And, further, that

> entitlement to tax exemption depends on meeting certain common law standards of charity—namely, that an institution seeking tax-exempt status must serve a public purpose and not be contrary to established public policy.

In other words, the statute incorporated underlying common law notions of "charity," even for specifically-designated "educational" institutions.

From there on the case was relatively easy. The common law concept of "charitable" had always evolved over time. Therefore, the fact that racial discrimination in schools was widespread when the tax law was originally passed around the turn of the 19th Century was not dispositive. Contemporary federal statutes, constitutional law, and executive orders established race discrimination to be against public policy and therefore outside a modern conception of "charitable." The Court in effect held that the changing legal landscape gave "charitable" a different meaning today than at the time of the statute's adoption.

Notice how serious a problem the Court had with the text. It was not simply a matter of reading a requirement of a charitable purpose into the text's specification that "educational" organizations were eligible. The statute specifically referred to *charitable* as well "educational" institutions. The resolution of this textual difficulty lies in the different functions of the statutory text "charitable" and the "charitable" purpose the Court read into the law. The statutory text *affirmatively* described a catch-all category of "charitable" organizations eligible for exemption, such as Public Interest Law

Firms. The "charitable" purpose read into the statute served the *negative* function of preventing exempt organizations from violating public policy.

ii) IS A FETUS A "PERSON"

Not all statutes incorporating a substantive common law principle necessarily incorporate legal evolution. The common law crime of murdering a "person" did not include killing a fetus, because a fetus was not a "person." Modern criminal statutes dealing with murder often refer to a "person" and the courts must decide whether they apply to the death of a fetus which can live outside the mother. Can the statutory concept of a "person" evolve?

The relationship of these statutes to their common law antecedents is complex. Most states have abolished common law crimes, so that all crimes are defined by statute. Of course, tax deductions are also defined by statute, and yet the Court in Bob Jones held that the statute incorporated an evolving common law concept of "charitable." The following cases grappled with this problem.

State v. Dickinson

263 N.E.2d 253 (Ohio App.1970), affirmed, 275 N.E.2d 599 (Ohio 1971).

■ Van Nostran, Presiding Judge.

This appeal on questions of law is from a judgment of the Court of Common Pleas of Stark County, Ohio, sentencing the defendant-appellant to one to twenty years in the Ohio Penitentiary for violation of R.C. § 4511.181 which reads as follows:

"No person shall unlawfully and unintentionally cause the death of another while violating Section 4511.19, 4511.20, 4511.201 or 4511.251 of the Revised Code. Any person violating this section is guilty of homicide by vehicle in the first degree."

The evidence before the trial court was in the form of a stipulation between the parties and included a stipulation that in substance the victim of this homicide was a viable but unborn fetus of a seven-month pregnant woman. * * *

Ohio has no common-law crimes. No act is criminal in this state unless it is expressly made so by positive legislative enactment. Although there are no common-law crimes, it is axiomatic that certain words, when used in criminal statutes, are judicially construed to have been used by the Legislature in their common-law sense, in the absence of any express legislative definition to the contrary.

It is well settled that at common law an unborn fetus, viable or otherwise, could not be the subject of homicide. Therefore, since we find no legislative definition of the word "person" in the Ohio criminal homicide statutes, we hold that when the Legislature used the word "person" in a homicide statutes, that word must be understood to mean what it meant in common-law homicide. * * *

For the reasons set out, the judgment of conviction of the Common Pleas Court is reversed and a final judgment of acquittal entered.

Judgment reversed.

■ McLaughlin, Judge.

The controlling question here is whether a seven month viable fetus is a person within the meaning of R.C. § 4511.181, effective November 14, 1967.

In my opinion the words of this statute are clear, plain and unambiguous. * * *

Such a viable fetus, in my opinion, is no less a person entitled to public protection from drunk drivers.

Conditions of modern life, with medical experts and hospitals equipped with the techniques and "know how" to preserve the lives of premature infants, attest to the great concern of the state to protect life before birth.

In my opinion, this viable fetus capable of sustaining life outside the mother's body is a person within the meaning of R.C. § 4511.181.

I would affirm this judgment and sentence.

In Commonwealth v. Cass, 467 N.E.2d 1324 (Mass.1984), however, the court held (prospectively) that a "person" for purposes of the vehicular homicide statute included an eight and one-half month fetus. The court rejected the suggestion that the Legislature intended to crystallize the *preexisting* common law regarding who may be the victim of a homicide. Instead the statute was interpreted as delegating courts a power to adopt an evolving common law definition, which now included a fetus who could survive outside the mother. The original common law rule was justified on the ground that it was impossible to know whether the fetus was alive at the time of the defendant's conduct, but modern technology made that rule obsolete. The court noted that Massachusetts was unlike many other jurisdictions, which had abolished common law crimes and made all crimes statutory (known as "code" states). Massachusetts courts retained a power to define "common law" crimes. Apparently, the fact that the court had a substantive common law power was relevant in interpreting the statutory text incorporating common law language.

Massachusetts has been joined by a few other states in defining a viable fetus as a "person" for the criminal law. See State v. Horne, 319 S.E.2d 703 (S.C.1984)(applying decision prospectively); Hughes v. State, 868 P.2d 730 (Okla.Crim. App.1994)(applying decision prospectively). However, Vermont (which is a "common law" rather than a "code" state) refused to treat the killing of an unborn fetus as murder under a state statute. State v. Oliver, 563 A.2d 1002, 1004 n. 6 (Vt.1989)(summarizing cases).

Missouri has also held that a fetus is a "person" in a vehicular man-slaughter statute. State v. Knapp, 843 S.W.2d 345 (Mo.1992)(six month old fetus was viable). However, the Missouri court relied on a state statute (passed in the same session as the manslaughter statute), which stated:

1. The general assembly of this state finds that:

    (1) The life of each human being begins at conception;

    (2) Unborn children have protectable interests in life, health, and well-being; * * *

    2. Effective January 1, 1988, the laws of this state shall be interpreted and construed to acknowledge on behalf of the unborn child at every stage of development, all the rights, privileges, and immunities available to other persons, citizens, and residents of this state, subject only to the Constitution of the United States, and decisional interpretations thereof by the United States Supreme Court and specific provisions to the contrary in the statutes and constitution of this state.

    3. As used in this section, the term "unborn children" or "unborn child" shall include all unborn child or children or the offspring of human beings from the moment of conception until birth at every stage of biological development.

The prior cases deal with criminal statutes. In contrast to the criminal law, a significant majority of courts find a *civil* wrongful death remedy for death of a fetus. In O'Grady v. Brown, 654 S.W.2d 904 (Mo.1983), overruling State ex rel. Hardin v. Sanders, 538 S.W.2d 336 (Mo.1976), the court held that the death of a viable fetus was covered by the Wrongful Death statute. It noted the relationship of the statute to the common law at several points.

Wrongful death acts do not take away any common law right; they were designed to mend the fabric of the common law, not to weaken it. Remedial acts are not strictly construed although they do change a rule of the common law.

The defendant argued that the definition should be expanded only by the legislature but the court disagreed as follows:

[I]t is significant that the legislature has continued to incorporate common law principles of liability into the statute as the basis of entitlement to an action for wrongful death. This patently indicates that the legislature did not intend to occupy this field of law entirely, leaving no room for judicial development of wrongful death remedies. Instead the drafters expected the statutory cause of action to keep pace with developments in the common law. * * * The issue presented to us is, therefore, properly a matter for judicial decision.

And, in Werling v. Sandy, 476 N.E.2d 1053, 1054 (Ohio 1985), Ohio held that a viable fetus was covered by the Wrongful Death statute. The statute was intended to "alleviate the inequity perceived in the common law." The court relied in part on common law decisions permitting a person born *alive* to sue for injuries suffered while still a fetus. The Ohio decision in Dickinson, supra, denying *criminal* responsibility, was distinguished on the ground that criminal statutes were narrowly construed.

b) STATUTORY EVOLUTION WITHOUT A COMMON LAW CONTEXT

i) "RIGHT" IN AN 1866 STATUTE

Jones v. Alfred H. Mayer Co.
392 U.S. 409 (1968).

■ Mr. Justice Stewart delivered the opinion of the Court.

In this case we are called upon to determine the scope and the constitutionality of an Act of Congress, 42 U.S.C. § 1982, which provides that:

> "All citizens of the United States shall have the same right, in every State and Territory, as is enjoyed by white citizens thereof to inherit, purchase, lease, sell, hold, and convey real and personal property."   * * *

We begin with the language of the statute itself. In plain and unambiguous terms, § 1982 grants to all citizens, without regard to race or color, "the same right" to purchase and lease property "as is enjoyed by white citizens." As the Court of Appeals in this case evidently recognized, that right can be impaired as effectively by "those who place property on the market" as by the State itself. For, even if the State and its agents lend no support to those who wish to exclude persons from their communities on racial grounds, the fact remains that, whenever property "is placed on the market for whites only, whites have a right denied to Negroes." So long as a Negro citizen who wants to buy or rent a home can be turned away simply because he is not white, he cannot be said to enjoy "the *same* right * * * as is enjoyed by white citizens * * * to * * * purchase [and] lease * * * real and personal property." 41 U.S.C. § 1982. (Emphasis added).

On its face, therefore, § 1982 appears to prohibit *all* discrimination against Negroes in the sale or rental of property—discrimination by private owners as well as discrimination by public authorities. Indeed, even the respondents seem to concede that, if § 1982 "means what it says"—to use the words of the respondents' brief— then it must encompass every racially motivated refusal to sell or rent and cannot be confined to officially sanctioned segregation in housing. Stressing what they consider to be the revolutionary implications of so literal a reading of § 1982, the respondents argue that Congress cannot possibly have intended any such result. Our examination of the relevant history, however, persuades us that Congress meant exactly what it said. * * *

[T]he same Congress that wanted to do away with the Black Codes *also* had before it an imposing body of evidence pointing to the mistreatment of Negroes by private individuals and unofficial groups, mistreatment unrelated to any hostile state legislation. * * * The congressional debates are replete with references to private injustices against Negroes—references to white employers who refused to pay their Negro workers, white planters who agreed among themselves not to hire freed slaves without the permission of their former masters, white citizens who assaulted Negroes or who combined to drive them out of their communities.

Indeed, one of the most comprehensive studies then before Congress stressed the prevalence of private hostility toward negroes and the need to protect them from the resulting persecution and discrimination. The report noted the existence of laws virtually prohibiting Negroes from owning or renting property in certain towns, but described such laws as "mere isolated cases," representing "the local outcroppings of a spirit * * * found to prevail everywhere"—a spirit expressed, for example, by lawless acts of brutality directed against Negroes who traveled to areas where they were not wanted. The report concluded that, even if anti-Negro legislation were "repealed in all the States lately in rebellion," equal treatment for the Negro would not yet be secured. * * *

As we said in a somewhat different setting two Terms ago, "We think that history leaves no doubt that, if we are to give [the law] the scope that its origins dictate, we must accord it a sweep as broad as its language." United States v. Price, 383 U.S. 787, 801. "We are not at liberty to seek ingenious analytical instruments," to carve from § 1982 an exception for private conduct—even though its application to such conduct in the present context is without established precedent. And, as the Attorney General of the United States said at the oral argument of this case, "The fact that the statute lay partially dormant for many years cannot be held to diminish its force today." * * *

[Editor—There is a reason the statute lay dormant. An earlier version of the law was passed after the 13th Amendment, abolishing slavery, was adopted. There was doubt about whether the 13th Amendment allowed Congress to pass a law making certain state action denying civil rights illegal. Thereafter, the 14th Amendment was passed, prohibiting states from denying a broader range of rights—including the equal protection of the laws. This led to repassage of the Civil Rights Act of 1866 in the form quoted in the Jones case. The Supreme Court held in the following decades that the 14th Amendment only applied to state action and the statute was correspondingly understood to be so limited. In the modern period, Congress is understood to have the authority to legislate against private discrimination under the 14th Amendment and the

Civil Rights Act of 1866 was interpreted in Jones to have that broader application.]

■ Mr. Justice Harlan, whom Mr. Justice White joins, dissenting.

The decision in this case appears to me to be most ill-considered and ill-advised. * * *

For reasons which follow, I believe that the Court's construction of § 1982 as applying to purely private action is almost surely wrong, and at the least is open to serious doubt. * * *

I shall deal first with the Court's construction of § 1982, which lies at the heart of its opinion. That construction is that the statute applies to purely private as well as to state-authorized discrimination. * * *

Like the Court, I begin analysis of § 1982 by examining its language. In its present form, the section provides:

"All citizens of the United States shall have the same right, in every State and Territory, as is enjoyed by white citizens thereof to inherit, purchase, lease, sell, hold, and convey real and personal property."

The Court finds it "plain and unambiguous," that this language forbids purely private as well as state-authorized discrimination. With all respect, I do not find it so. For me, there is an inherent ambiguity in the term "right," as used in § 1982. The "right" referred to may either be a right to equal status under the law, in which case the statute operates only against state-sanctioned discrimination, or it may be an "absolute" right enforceable against private individuals. To me, the words of the statute, taken alone, suggest the former interpretation, not the latter. * * * [Editor—Justice Harlan then reviews the legislative history to demonstrate that Congress contemplated protecting people from an invasion of rights by the State, not by private parties.]

* * * Another, albeit less tangible, consideration points in the same direction. Many of the legislators who took part in the congressional debates inevitably must have shared the individualistic ethic of their time, which emphasized personal freedom and embodied a distaste for governmental interference which was soon to culminate in the era of laissez-faire. It seems to me that most of these men would have regarded it as a great intrusion on individual liberty for the Government to take from a man the power to refuse for personal reasons to enter into a purely private transaction involving the disposition of property, albeit those personal reasons might reflect racial bias. It should be remembered that racial prejudice was not uncommon in 1866, even outside the South. Although Massachusetts had recently enacted the Nation's first law prohibiting racial discrimination in public accommodations, Negroes could not ride within Philadelphia streetcars or attend public schools with white children in New York City. Only five States accorded equal

voting rights to Negroes, and it appears that Negroes were allowed to serve on juries only in Massachusetts. Residential segregation was the prevailing pattern almost everywhere in the North. There were no state "fair housing" laws in 1866, and it appears that none had ever been proposed. In this historical context, I cannot conceive that a bill thought to prohibit purely private discrimination not only in the sale or rental of housing but in *all* property transactions would not have received a great deal of criticism explicitly directed to this feature. The fact that the 1866 Act received *no* criticism of this kind is for me strong additional evidence that it was not regarded as extending so far.

[Editor—Do not read too much into Harlan's invocation of post-Civil War individualistic substantive values. He is not bringing these values to the statute, the way a judge might invoke a substantive canon. He is relying on external context for the more modest purpose of understanding language. This becomes more essential the older the text. Another example is Saint Francis College v. Al-Khazraji, 481 U.S. 604 (1987), and Shaare Tefila Congregation v. Cobb, 481 U.S. 615 (1987), where the Court held that the "racial discrimination" prohibited by an 1870 Act of Congress included discrimination by Whites against white Jews and Arabs. Although Jews and Arabs might today be considered members of the Caucasian race, the Court noted that the "understanding of 'race' in the 19th century [when the statute was adopted], * * * was different." In the 19th century, race was more akin to ethnicity and that understanding of the text was dispositive.]

In sum, the most which can be said with assurance about the intended impact of the 1866 Civil Rights Act upon purely private discrimination is that the Act probably was envisioned by most members of Congress as prohibiting official, community-sanctioned discrimination in the South, engaged in pursuant to local "customs" which in the recent time of slavery probably were embodied in laws or regulations.* * *

COMMENTS

1. *The meaning of "right".* What is the best argument for an evolving meaning of the statutory word "right" in Jones? Consider this. Justice Harlan argues that after the Civil War most people would have understood "rights" to mean protecting people from the State. Can that statutory concept evolve into a modern concept of rights, which includes the view that private power can also be abused? Many features of the modern welfare state support the idea that a negative "protection from the State" conception of rights is insufficient and that individuals require protection from harms not directly traceable to state action. Private power is now viewed as more of a problem than in 1866, when the frontier was open and economic development seemed boundless. Jones gave a plain contemporary meaning to the evolving statutory text.

2.   *The "Calabresi" questions.* In deciding Jones, consider the "Calabresi" questions. Should the contemporary legal landscape protecting private purchasers from race discrimination count for anything in statutory interpretation? Would a representative majority have supported a statute which did *not* afford relief to a nonwhite purchaser of property? Is there legislative inertia regarding the issue in Jones? Are there asymmetries in legislative inertia, favoring the ability of one side or the other to get congressional attention? Should the answers to any of these questions help decide the case?

Justice Harlan's dissent explicitly refers to the absence of legislative inertia, although he does not relate it to the issue of statutory evolution. He argues that

> the political processes of our own era have, since the date of oral argument in this case, given birth to a civil rights statute embodying "fair housing" provisions which would at the end of this year make available to others, though apparently not to the petitioners themselves, the type of relief which the petitioners now seek. It seems to me that this latter factor so diminishes the public importance of this case that by far the wisest course would be for this Court to refrain from decision and to dismiss the writ as improvidently granted.

3.   *Lawmaking responsibility.* One way to think about inertia as a factor in statutory interpretation is from a lawmaking responsibility perspective. Calabresi's argument is that there is less need for the court to be too aggressive the less "inert" the legislature is. What else determines the allocation of lawmaking responsibility? Suppose the issue is politically controversial. Does that argue for leaving the issue to the legislature, or is a controversial issue likely to raise an important contemporary landscape problem, which the courts should address?

How do the judges determine where lawmaking responsibility lies in the following case? In Sony Corp. of America v. Universal City Studios, Inc., 464 U.S. 417 (1984), the Court considered whether use of a VCR to tape TV programs for watching at another time (time-shifting) violated the copyright law. The Court concluded that it did not, stating:

> From its beginning, the law of copyright has developed in response to significant changes in technology. * * * Repeatedly, as new developments have occurred in this country, it has been the Congress that has fashioned the new rules that new technology made necessary. * * *

> The judiciary's reluctance to expand the protections afforded by the copyright without explicit legislative guidance is a recurring theme. Sound policy, as well as history, supports our consistent deference to Congress when major technological innovations alter the market for copyright materials. Congress has the constitutional authority and the institutional ability to accommodate fully the varied

permutations of competing interests that are inevitably implicated by such new technology.

In a case like this, in which Congress has not plainly marked our course, we must be circumspect in construing the scope of rights created by a legislative enactment which never contemplated such a calculus of interests. * * *

It may well be that Congress will take a fresh look at this new technology, just as it so often has examined other innovations in the past. But it is not our job to apply laws that have not yet been written.

The dissent "hope[d] that these questions ultimately will be considered seriously and in depth by Congress and be resolved there, despite the fact that the Court's decision today provides little incentive for congressional action. Our task in the meantime, however, is to resolve these issues as best we can in the light of ill-fitting existing copyright law." As for the argument that the issue was for Congress, the dissent stated:

It is no answer, of course, to say and stress, as the Court does, this Court's "consistent deference to Congress" whenever "major technological innovations" appear. Perhaps a better and more accurate description is that the Court has tended to evade the hard issues when they are in the area of copyright law. * * *

What exactly does a court mean when it leaves the issue to the legislature? A case involving statutory interpretation always leaves the issue to the legislature in the sense that the legislature can change the judge-made law. Is there a difference between the court, on the one hand, stating that the law is "x," and, on the other hand, stating that it will tolerate a state of the law in which "x" prevails, because it is up to some other institution to say that the law is *not* "x?" For example, is there any difference between (1) saying that the statute means there is no copyright violation and (2) saying that it is up to Congress to say more explicitly that there is a copyright violation, until which time there is none?

If leaving an issue to the legislature defers to the legislature's lawmaking responsibility, is deference permanent? If the legislature never addresses the problem left to it, maybe the judge will *not* leave the issue to the legislature at some later date. For example, in General Motors v. Simmons, 558 S.W.2d 855, 863 (Tex.1977), the court did not adopt comparative negligence in strict liability cases but "respectfully invite[d] further legislative study." The Texas House responded by adopting comparative negligence for strict liability in 1981 but the bill failed in the Senate.[4] Then, in 1984, the court adopted pure comparative negligence in strict liability cases. Duncan v. Cessna Aircraft Co., 665 S.W.2d 414 (Tex.1984). Was this an appropriate case for the court to act after its "invitation" to the legislature had been refused?

---

4. See Sanders & Joyce, "Off to the Races": The 1980s Torts Crisis and the Law Reform Process, 27 Houston L. Rev. 207, 286 (1990).

4. *Defining the statute's audience.* The relationship of statutory interpretation to legal evolution can also be understood as a problem of defining the statute's audience. The textualist's audience is the historical audience at the time of the statute's adoption. The judge must do her best to project herself back in time to recreate how the historical audience would have understood the text, rejecting efforts to project the historical legislature forward in time. In this view, the contemporary audience is mainly eavesdropping on a conversation originally held many years ago. Other judges are more willing to infer that the legislature is speaking to future audiences, who bring their own understanding, including the contemporary legal landscape, to the task of interpretation.

Sometimes the legislature's intent to address future audiences is reasonably clear. Use of open-ended texts, especially those with common law origins, often indicate an intent to write for the future. But legislative intent about the statute's audience is often unclear. It is, by definition, hard for a legislature to understand the future and therefore hard to know whether it wants the understandings of a future audience to determine what the statute means. On the one hand, the statute has future effect and is therefore addressed to future audiences. On the other hand, the text is time-bound, adopted by an author with historical roots. Judges who try to do what Plowden and Hand suggested—holding a pretend-colloquy with the historical legislator to apply the statute to current facts—are necessarily speculating about what a legislature would intend regarding a future it could not possibly know. A conscientious legislator who made the time-travel needed to engage in this conversation might ask the judge so many questions about the environment in which the statute now existed that the only sensible conclusion for the judge would be uncertainty about how to decide the case based solely on the colloquy.

5. *Judicial opinion writing.* Even if you are convinced that statutory evolution helps to explain some judicial decisions, it is quite another matter to write an opinion which updates a statute. You might try your hand at writing an opinion in the Jones case (involving the meaning of the word "right" in a post-Civil War statute) to accommodate the contemporary legal landscape.

6. *Judicial practice; selecting the evolving landscape.* Whatever you think of judicial updating of statutes, it undoubtedly goes on a lot, although judges differ in their willingness to admit it. One example is the pre-emptive effect of the 1925 Federal Arbitration Act (FAA). The Court in Southland Corp. v. Keating, 465 U.S. 1 (1984), held that the federal statute (the FAA) pre-empted state law to require enforcement of an arbitration agreement in state court, not just federal court. The majority stated that this was an honest reading of the original intent of the Act but the dissent argued that Congress originally viewed arbitration laws as procedural and therefore binding only in federal, not state court.

Justice Stevens agreed with the dissent's view of original intent in the 1984 Southland case but stated that "intervening developments in the law compel the conclusion" that the FAA should be applied to actions brought in state court. Presumably, the intervening developments were the Erie decision in 1938 (requiring federal courts to apply state *substantive* law in federal diversity cases) and the later decision that violations of arbitration agreements raised *substantive* not procedural issues under Erie.

In Allied–Bruce Terminix Companies, Inc. v. Dobson, 513 U.S. 265 (1995), Justices Thomas and Scalia wrote a *dissent* arguing that Southland should be reversed because it erroneously interpreted the original intent of the FAA. They noted that it was not until 1959 that any court had suggested that the FAA was binding on state courts. As for the impact of Erie, they stated:

> The distinction between "substance" and "procedure" acquired new meaning after Erie Railroad Co. v. Tompkins, 304 U.S. 64 (1938). Thus, in 1956 we held that for Erie purposes, the question whether a court should stay litigation brought in breach of an arbitration agreement is one of "substantive" law. But this later development could not change the original meaning of the statute that Congress enacted in 1925. Although [the 1956 case] classified portions of the FAA as "substantive" rather than "procedural," it does not mean that they were so understood in 1925 or that Congress extended the FAA's reach beyond the federal courts.

In other words, it was up to Congress to change the law. Judges should not update the rule regarding state court obligations to enforce arbitration agreements.

Moreover, Thomas and Scalia argued that federalism principles favored reversing Southland:

> Even if [there was] uncertainty about the original meaning of the statute, we should resolve the uncertainty in light of core principles of federalism. While "Congress may legislate in areas traditionally regulated by the States" as long as it "is acting within the powers granted it under the Constitution," we assume that "Congress does not exercise [this power] lightly." To the extent that federal statutes are ambiguous, we do not read them to displace state law. Rather, we must be "absolutely certain" that Congress intended such displacement before we give pre-emptive effect to a federal statute. In 1925, the enactment of a "substantive" arbitration statute along the lines envisioned by Southland would have displaced an enormous body of state law: outside of a few States, predispute arbitration agreements either were wholly unenforceable or at least were not subject to specific performance. Far from being "absolutely certain" that Congress swept aside these state rules, I am quite sure that it did not.

Was the dissent relying on federalism principles as they would have been understood in 1925, when the FAA was adopted, or as they would be understood today? Can substantive background considerations evolve to impose "clear statement" requirements on the legislature? If so, why can't other features of the legal landscape evolve to determine statutory meaning?

ii) SAME–SEX ADOPTIONS

Recall the Braschi case, discussed in Chapter 5.02b, dealing with wheth-er a gay couple was a "family." The same changing social attitudes that have created the possibility of a gay family have also given rise to petitions for same-sex adoptions under older statutes. The New York courts followed Braschi with a 4–3 decision allowing a gay or lesbian partner of a biological parent to adopt a child without terminating the rights of the biological parent.

Many of the same interpretive questions we encountered in discussing the Jones case (about how judges should deal with change) recur in the same-sex adoption setting—is there legislative inertia; what is the balance of contemporary political power to effect legislative change; where does law-making responsibility lie; who is the statutory audience?

In the Matter of Jacob

660 N.E.2d 397 (N.Y.1995).

■ Kaye Chief Judge. * * *

Under the New York adoption statute, a single person can adopt a child (Domestic Relations Law § 110). Equally clear is the right of a single homosexual to adopt (see 18 NYCRR 421.16[h][2] [qualified adoption agencies "shall not * * * reject[ ] [adoption petitions] solely on the basis of homosexuality"]). These appeals call upon us to decide if the unmarried partner of a child's biological mother, whether heterosexual or homosexual, who is raising the child together with the biological parent, can become the child's second parent by means of adoption.

Because the two adoptions sought—one by an unmarried heterosexual couple, the other by the lesbian partner of the child's mother—are fully consistent with the adoption statute, we answer this question in the affirmative. To rule otherwise would mean that the thousands of New York children actually being raised in homes headed by two unmarried persons could have only one legal parent, not the two who want them.

Limiting our analysis, as did the courts below, to the [ ] statutory interpretation issues, we conclude that appellants have standing to adopt under Domestic Relations Law § 110 and are not foreclosed from doing so by Domestic Relations Law § 117. There being no statutory preclusion, we now reverse the order of the Appellate Division in each case and remit the matter to Family Court for a factual evaluation and determination as to whether these adoptions would be in the best interest of the children.

The Context of our Statutory Analysis

Two basic themes of overarching significance set the context of our statutory analysis.

First and foremost, since adoption in this State is "solely the creature of * * * statute" the adoption statute must be strictly construed. What is to be construed strictly and applied rigorously in this sensitive area of the law, however, is legislative purpose as well as legislative language. Thus, the adoption statute must be applied in harmony with the humanitarian principle that adoption is a means of securing the best possible home for a child. * * *

A second, related point of overriding significance is that the various sections comprising New York's adoption statute today represent a complex and not entirely reconcilable patchwork. Amended innumerable times since its passage in 1873, the adoption statute was last consolidated nearly 60 years ago, in 1938 (L 1938, ch. 606). Thus, after decades of piecemeal amendment upon amendment, the statute today contains language from the 1870's alongside language from the 1990's.

Though courts surely must, and do, strive to give effect to every word of a statute, our analysis must recognize the difficulty—perhaps unique difficulty—of such an endeavor here. With its long, tortuous history, New York's adoption statute today is a far cry from a "methodical[ ] and meticulous[ ]" expression of legislative judgment. That the questions posed by these appeals are not readily answerable by reference to the words of a particular section of the law, but instead require the traditional and often close and difficult task of statutory interpretation is evident even in the length of today's opinions—whichever result is reached.

Against this backdrop, we turn to the particular provisions at issue.

Domestic Relations Law § 110

Despite ambiguity in other sections, one thing is clear: section 110 allows appellants to become adoptive parents. Domestic Relations Law § 110, entitled "Who May Adopt," provides that an "adult unmarried person or an adult husband and his adult wife together may adopt another person" (Domestic Relations Law § 110). Under this language, both appellant G.M. in Matter of Dana and appellant Stephen T.K. in Matter of Jacob, as adult unmarried persons, have standing to adopt and appellants are correct that the Court's analysis of section 110 could appropriately end here. * * *

The conclusion that appellants have standing to adopt is also supported by the history of section 110. The pattern of amendments since the end of World War II evidences a successive expansion of the categories of persons entitled to adopt regardless of their marital status or sexual orientation. * * * [Editor—One of the examples the court gives is permitting adoption by adults not yet divorced but living apart from their spouses pursuant to separation agreements. Supporting that amendment was New York's "strong policy of assuring that as many children as possible are adopted into suitable family situations." This amendment required prospective adoptive parents to be evaluated on the basis of their ability to provide a permanent home and not on their marital status alone.]

A reading of section 110 granting appellants, as unmarried second parents, standing to adopt is therefore consistent with the words of the statute as well as the spirit behind the modern-day amendments: encouraging the adoption of as many children as possible regardless of the sexual orientation or marital status of the individuals seeking to adopt them.

Domestic Relations Law § 117

Appellants having standing to adopt pursuant to Domestic Relations Law § 110, the other statutory obstacle relied upon by the lower courts in denying the petitions is the provision that "after the making of an order of adoption the natural parents of the adoptive child shall be relieved of all parental duties toward and of all responsibilities for and shall have no rights over such adoptive child or to his property by descent or succession * * *" (Domestic Relations Law § 117[1][a]). Literal application of this language would effectively prevent these adoptions since it would require the termination of the biological mothers' rights upon adoption thereby placing appellants in the "Catch–22" of having to choose one of two co-parents as the child's only legal parent.

As outlined below, however, neither the language nor policy underlying section 117 dictates that result.

The Language of Section 117. Both the title of section 117 ("Effect of Adoption") and its opening phrase ("After the making of an order of adoption") suggest that the section has nothing to do with the standing of an individual to adopt, an issue treated exclusively in section 110. Rather, section 117 addresses the legal effect of an adoption on the parties and their property.

Also plain on the face of section 117 is that it speaks principally of estate law. Words such as "succession," "inheritance," "decedent," "instrument" and "will" permeate the statute. Read contextually, it is clear that the Legislature's chief concern in section 117 was the resolution of property disputes upon the death of an adoptive parent or child. * * *

The Ambiguity Should Be Resolved in the Children's Favor. Finally, even though the language of section 117 still has the effect of terminating a biological parent's rights in the majority of adoptions between strangers—where there is a need to prevent unwanted intrusion by the child's former biological relatives to promote the stability of the new adoptive family—the cases before us are entirely different. * * *

One example of an adoption where the Legislature has explicitly acknowledged that termination is unwarranted is when the child, with the consent of the biological parent, is adopted by a "stepparent" (Domestic Relations Law § 117[1][d]). A second, implicit exception occurs in the adoptions by teenage fathers authorized by the 1951 amendment to section 110. Since minor fathers adopting their own biological children are not "stepparents" under the language of Domestic Relations Law § 117[1][d], they would be prohibited from adopting were section 117's termination language to be mandatory in all cases. The seemingly automatic cut-off language of section 117 could not have been intended to bar these adoptions, however, since they are precisely what the Legislature sought to encourage in the first place. * * *

One conclusion that can be drawn, however, is that section 117 does not invariably require termination in the situation where the biological parent, having consented to the adoption, has agreed to retain parental rights and to raise the child together with the second parent. Despite their varying factual circumstances, each of the adoptions described above—stepparent adoptions [and] adoption by minor fathers [ ]—share such an agreement as a common denominator. Because the facts of the cases before us are directly analogous to these [ ] situations, the half-century old termination language of section 117 should not be read to preclude the adoptions here. Phrased slightly differently, "the desire for consistency in the law should not of itself sever the bonds between the child and the natural relatives."

"When the language of a statute is susceptible of two constructions, the courts will adopt that which avoids injustice, hardship, constitutional doubts or other objectionable results." Given that section 117 is open to two differing interpretations as to whether it automatically terminates parental rights in all cases, a construction of the section that would deny children like Jacob and Dana the opportunity of having their two de facto parents become their legal parents, based solely on their biological mother's sexual orientation or marital status, would not only be unjust under the circumstances, but also might raise constitutional concerns in light of the adoption statute's historically consistent purpose—the best interests of the child. * * *

Conclusion

To be sure, the Legislature that last codified section 117 in 1938 may never have envisioned families that "include[ ] two adult lifetime partners whose relationship * * * is characterized by an emotional and financial commitment and interdependence" (Braschi v. Stahl Assocs. Co., 543 N.E.2d 49). Nonetheless, it is clear that section 117, designed as a shield to protect new adoptive families, was never intended as a sword to prohibit otherwise beneficial intrafamily adoptions by second parents.

The Vermont Supreme Court reached the same conclusion as New York about adoption, based on a similar statute. Adoptions of B.L.V.B. and E.L.V.B., 628 A.2d 1271 (Vt.1993). The court added some explicit comments about change:

> When social mores change, governing statutes must be interpreted to allow for those changes in a manner that does not frustrate the purposes behind their enactment. To deny the children of same-sex partners, as a class, the security of a legally recognized relationship with their second parent serves no legitimate state interest. * * * Social fragmentation and the myriad configurations of modern families have presented us with new problems and complexities that can not be solved by idealizing the past. Today a child who receives proper nutrition, adequate schooling and supportive sustaining shelter is among the fortunate, whatever the source. A child who also receives the love and nurture of even a single parent can be counted among the blessed. Here this Court finds a child who has all of the above benefits and two adults dedicated to his welfare, secure in their loving partnership, and determined to raise him to the very best of their considerable abilities. There is no reason in law, logic or social philosophy to obstruct such a favorable situation. By allowing same-sex adoptions to come within the step-parent exception [ ], we are furthering the purposes of the statute as was originally intended by allowing the children of such unions the benefits and security of a legal relationship with their de facto second parents.

> * * * It is not the courts that have engendered the diverse composition of today's families. It is the advancement of reproductive technologies and society's recognition of alternative lifestyles that have produced families in which a biological, and therefore a legal, connection is no longer the sole organizing principle. But it is the courts that are required to define, declare and protect the rights of children raised in these families, usually upon their dissolution. At that point, courts are left to vindicate the public interest in the children's financial support and emotional well-being by developing theories of parenthood, so that "legal strangers" who are de facto parents may be awarded custody or visitation or reached for support.

How would you respond to the argument that the historical legislature could not possibly have intended to allow same-sex adoptions? Could they possibly have intended to exclude them?

9.04 TEXTUALISM AND CHANGE

a) PURPOSE OF A WORD VS. STATUTORY PURPOSE

A textualist anchors statutory meaning in the historical meaning of the text. Professor Easterbrook's article, discussed in Chapter 8, explained some of the reasons supporting this approach—the absence of a coherent legislative intent; and background considerations, such as the expiration of legislatures, minimalist government, and judicial shortcomings. The textualist usually does not argue, however, that a statute can *only* apply to facts which exist at the time of its adoption. For example, a textualist is unlikely to have trouble deciding that a century old statute permitting government access to "bankers books" in a criminal investigation now permits access to microfilm, invented long after the statute's adoption.[5] The question is whether the new facts describe something serving the same function as a book, determined when the statute was adopted.

But why is the textualist willing to update a statute "functionally?" Why doesn't the textualist say that the historical author/audience did not intend the new facts, about which it knew nothing, to be included within the statutory language, and just put the statute down, as Professor Easterbrook argued in the article excerpted in Chapter 8? Is it because it would be bad government to force the legislature to revisit a statute every time something new comes along? But doesn't the "bad government" question embroil the judge in discretionary judgments about the respective roles of judge and legislature that the textualist wants to avoid?

The textualist's primary goal is to avoid judicial reliance on statutory purpose, in the sense of the mischief or broad purpose at which the statute was aimed. Recall Easterbrook's warning that the attempt to apply historical purpose to current facts is likely to "have much in common with [the judge's] own conceptions of the good." As you read the materials in this section, see whether the distinction between the textualist's limited use of "function" to decide what a word includes can be distinguished from the reliance on statutory purpose against which Easterbrook warns. Does Judge Easterbrook maintain this distinction, asking the "functional" but not the "purpose" question. If you think Judge Easterbrook does not stick to what Professor Easterbrook argued, why might this be so? Is there something in the nature of judging that makes textualism a difficult position to maintain?

b) Is a Haybine a "Mower"?

In this case, Judge Easterbrook agonizes over whether the statutory term "mower" includes a haybine. Although the haybine is a technologically advanced farm implement having much in common with what "mower" meant when the statute was adopted in 1935, it is still a "mower-plus,"capable of doing more than mow (it also "conditions" the hay). Easterbrook tries hard not to consider too much statutory purpose. How well does he succeed? What elements of statutory purpose, if any, does he consider and what does he exclude?

Is there something about being a judge that forces Professor Easterbrook to abandon some of his interpretive theories?

---

5. See Barker v. Wilson, (1980) A.C. 81.

Matter of Erickson

815 F.2d 1090 (7th Cir.1987).

■ Easterbrook, Circuit Judge.

Wis. Stat. § 815.18(6), which makes certain property unavailable to satisfy a civil judgment, allows the judgment debtor to exempt 8 cows, 10 pigs, 50 chickens, 2 horses or 2 mules, 10 sheep, one year's feed for the livestock, and some farm equipment, including: "one wagon, cart or dray, one sleigh, one plow, one drag, one binder, one tractor not to exceed in value the sum of $1,500, one corn binder, one mower, one springtooth harrow, one disc harrow, one seeder, one hay loader, one corn planter," and miscellaneous tools worth as much as $300. Debtors in federal bankruptcy cases sometimes may exempt the property that states protect from civil execution. * * * They may use this exemption for "implements, professional books, or tools, of the trade of the debtor", * * * even though they have given their creditors security interests in the items. In this bankruptcy case, where the parties have agreed that the debtor may keep as an "implement" or "tool of the trade" any asset mentioned in Wis. Stat. § 815.18(6), we must decide whether a baler is a "hay loader" and whether a haybine is a "mower". (We need not and do not decide whether the agreement was provident.)

A baler not only loads hay on a wagon but also ties it in bales; a haybine not only mows hay but also conditions it. Both the bankruptcy judge and the district judge concluded that the extra functions of the machines did not prevent their exemption under § 815.18(6). In an earlier case, however, a different bankruptcy judge held that a baler with thrower is not a "binder", a row corn picker a "corn binder", or a bale elevator a "hay loader" for purposes of § 815.18(6). Dorchester State Bank, which had security interests in the baler (worth $400) and the haybine (worth $1,500), maintains on appeal that it is no more sensible to call a baler a "hay loader" or a haybine a "mower" than it is to call a row corn picker a "corn binder" or a snowmobile a "sleigh" within § 815.18(6). The district court's order, 63 B.R. 632, leaves nothing else to do in this bankruptcy case, so the decision is "final" and appealable under 28 U.S.C. § 158(d).

The problem in this case comes from the fact that technology had done more to change farm implements than the Wisconsin legislature had done to change § 815.18(6). The "mower" and "hay loader" were added to the list in 1935, and § 815.18(6) has been unchanged (with an immaterial exception) since then. The statutory list comprises the equipment that in 1935 would have kept a small farm in operation. But small farms now use a different set of equipment. We concentrate on the haybine, because the same principles influence the treatment of both haybine and baler. The mower, which cuts hay, has been succeeded by the haybine (also called a "mower-conditioner"), which cuts and crushes hay in a single operation so that the hay dries faster. If the statute applies only to farm implements customary in 1935, and therefore omits the haybine, it does not achieve its purpose today; yet if the statute exempts all successors of the listed equipment, technological change may dramatically enlarge the exemption without legislative consideration. One need only think of the technological successor of the statutory "binder"—the self-propelled combine, which may be worth $1 million. Asked at oral argument if a combine would be exempt under § 815.18(6), Erickson's [the debtor's] counsel replied that it would. That cannot be right, yet neither is it appropriate to say that the statute covers only machines called "mowers". * * *

* * * [A] "mower" is not limited to the thing called a mower today, or even the thing called a mower in 1935. A statutory word of description does not designate a particular item * * * but a class of things that share some important feature. Which feature is important depends on the function of the designation and how it will be interpreted by the audience to whom the word is addressed. * * * If someone at a dinner party says: "Pull up a chair to the table", he means a table chair and not an overstuffed easy chair, even though both are called chairs. The word "chair" in an exemption statute, however, might include easy chairs but not Chippendale chairs—because the function of the statute is to leave the person a place to sit rather than to protect an antique valued (and valuable) for its beauty and age rather than its comfort. (There is a standing injunction not to sit on Chippendale chairs because that might destroy their value.) And if a change in language or function should cause a new name to be applied to a place to sit—say, if reclining chairs with stereo speakers built in should come to be called "stereoloungers"—it would be necessary to examine the function of the denotation yet again rather than say that a "stereolounger" is not a "chair" and that is that.

When asked at oral argument whether a mower with a built-in stereo cassette deck would still be a "mower", the Bank's lawyer answered yes, because it would still cut the hay. Yet it would have a second function, entertainment, just as the haybine has a second function, crushing the hay. The Bank's counsel balked at this extension because the crushing function makes the haybine more valuable as a farm implement and thus enlarges the shelter provided by the statutory exemption. Erickson's haybine is worth $1,500, considerably more than a mower. (Erickson also actually owns an old mower, valued at $25.) Yet the tape deck, too, would increase the market value of the mower.

There cannot be an "equal value" principle in § 815.18(6). The "mower" has changed through time. When brought to market in the mid-nineteenth century, the mower was a simple, horse-drawn successor to the reaper.* * * When in 1935 Wisconsin first created an exemption for a mower, many implements called "mowers" were horse drawn. Most mowers designed to be pulled by tractors drew power for the blades from the friction of wheel against ground.* * * The tractor mounted mower, which drew power direct from the drive shaft of the tractor, was not introduced until 1930. After 1935 mowers grew in size, complexity, and efficiency. In 1952 the pitman drive for the blades was replaced by pitmanless cams, which reduced vibration and increased operating speed. Later machines, still called "mowers", grew larger and more sophisticated; some had hydraulic lifts so that they could be maneuvered more accurately. * * * The "mower" that could be found on a farm in 1975 probably had no more parts in common with a horsedrawn 1935–vintage mower than a 1975 haybine had in common with a 1975 mower. The Bank does not deny that a mower made in 1975 would qualify as a "mower", which dooms the argument that an increase in value eliminates the exemption.

Changes in value also cut both ways. The exemption for a tractor is limited to $1,500, for example; in 1935 this might have exempted a small tractor, but now it does not. A true "equal value" principle would interpret "$1,500" as denoting real (inflation-adjusted) rather than nominal dollars, or perhaps it would adjust the exemption to, say, the percentage of the value of the debtor's tractor that $1,500 would have represented in 1935. The Bank does not ask us to increase the value of the exemption for Erickson's tractor; it is no more appropriate to ensure that the exemption for the "mower" is worth now what it was worth in 1935. A legislature can write an exemption with a dollar limit (as it did for tractors and tools) or without; when it chooses the latter course a court may not treat the statute as if it had the missing valuation rule. The exemption for a mower does not depend on value, just as an exemption for an "automobile" would not. A 1986 Audi 5000CS Turbo Quattro and 1976 Volkswagen Rabbit probably have less in common (and surely have a greater difference in value) than a 1975 mower and a 1975 haybine, yet both are cars; so too with farm equipment.

This does not necessarily require a decision in Erickson's favor. Our inability to apply either a "plain meaning" or "same value" approach does not identify with any confidence what a mower is, although it forecloses some ways of identifying what a mower is not. The bankruptcy and district judges concluded that a haybine is a "mower" because it is the "technological successor" to the mower. But the self-propelled combine is the technological successor to the binder, and if you allow enough leeway the Boeing 747 is the technological successor of the chariot. The ability to trace a line of descent is not sufficient—not unless the scope of the statute is entirely liberated from its history and function. A statute designed to allow family farmers to keep the minimum equipment necessary to work the land cannot readily exempt a self-propelled combine, "technological successor" or not. (We needn't consider the possibility that the self-propelled combine is the "successor" to the tractor and so is limited by the $1,500 maximum for tractors.) The role of an exemption in the statutory structure, not the march of technology, is the centerpiece in identifying the meaning of the language.

Alas, § 815.18(6) has no legislative history, and apparently not a single Wisconsin court has construed its language. We are on our own. We cannot determine the meaning of "mower" by using the principle Erickson presses on us: that exemptions are "remedial" statutes and therefore to be "liberally" construed. This tells us the direction to move but does not help us figure out how far to go. "Liberality" may answer the question whether both a direct-drive mower and a friction-drive mower are statutory "mowers"; it does not answer any more complex problem. Finding the meaning of a statute is more like calculating a vector (with direction and length) than it is like identifying which way the underlying "values" or "purposes" point (which has direction alone). * * * Too much "liberality" will undermine the statute as surely as too literal an interpretation would. The statute is designed to give farmers a fresh start. * * * Any fresh-start policy must balance the gains from new beginnings against the costs of making it harder for lenders to collect. The more difficult collection becomes, the fewer assets are available to secure loans, the costlier is credit. Every expansion of the Wisconsin exemption statute makes loans riskier for banks and so raises the interest rate (or makes banks unwilling to lend at all to some people). This effect, which burdens the frugal and the spendthrift alike, can swamp the gains of fresh starts. Identifying the "liberal" function of exemptions does not assist us to determine when the increased cost of credit hurts farmers more than the fresh start helps them.

We must turn to the statute's structure and function. If the function of § 815.18(6) is to enable farmers to keep a minimal set of equipment to work the fields, then a haybine is a "mower". It performs the mowing function of the mower, and its additional drying function used to be performed by rakes and other tools. The haybine and the mower have many features in common; the haybine is a close rather than a distant descendant of the mower. The Bank does not dispute the district court's concluding that the mower is obsolete, and that farmers use mower-conditioner combinations. Nothing in the case suggests that Erickson's haybine is gold-plated or otherwise designed to evade the bankruptcy laws.

No implement could be a mower without having a lot in common with the thing known as a mower in 1935, but the haybine meets this test. It contains the kind of mowing gear that used to be sold as a "mower", plus a bar to bend the hay (so that the butt end flips up when the stalk is cut) and rollers to crush it. Perhaps the change in terminology is itself evidence that a haybine is "enough" separated from the old mower to be a "different" tool, but we hesitate to rely too much on that. The manufacturers' invention of a new name, as opposed to using "enhanced mower" as a handle, may have been a marketing device rather than an attempt to describe the technical differences between the implements. And the alternative name ("mower-conditioner") suggests the close link.

To the extent there is doubt—and there is still substantial doubt, for the age of this statute prevents "literal" application to today's farm equipment, even a piece of equipment called a "mower"—we accept the decision of the bankruptcy and district judges. The views here of judges skilled in the law of the state in which they sit are entitled to respect.* * * The law has need of tie-breakers, and if this case be a tie (it comes close), the nod goes to the district court's construction. This statute needs legislative attention; we cannot provide more than emergency care, and it is wise to avoid switching treatments so quickly.

COMMENTS AND QUESTIONS

1. *"Plain meaning" vs. "plainly hand" court power.* Easterbrook concedes an inability to apply the "plain meaning" approach in this case. He is willing to interpret the word "mower" functionally to include things, like a haybine, which perform "the mowing function of the mower"; "No implement could be a mower without having a lot in common with the thing known as a mower in 1935, but the haybine meets this test." But remember Easterbrook's view that "unless the statute plainly hands courts the power to create and revise a form of common law, the domain of the statute should be restricted to cases anticipated by its framers and expressly resolved in the legislative process." Why doesn't the "plain meaning" approach dictate that a haybine is not a mower? Couldn't Easterbrook have just put the statute down, once it was clear that a haybine was not a mower in a *narrowly* denotative 1935 sense of the term—that is, once the "particular item" did not exist in 1935, when the statutory author passed and statutory audience first read the statute?

Wouldn't the rigorous textualist confine a mower to its 1935 meaning? Why does a text *have* to mean the "function of [its] designation," rather than be limited to the items of which authors and audiences were aware when the text was adopted? Does the word "mower" plainly hand the court the power to interpret the word "functionally" to include a haybine, giving "mower" a *broader* denotative meaning? Do we have a text whose application to the facts falls somewhere between "plain meaning" and "plainly handing" the court a common law power?

2. *"Function" as statutory purpose.* Easterbrook goes further. He does not stop with a broadly denotative functional interpretation of "mower." He also refers to statutory purpose, in the sense of protecting the farmer's minimal set of equipment, although he prefers to call this the "structure and function" of the statute. But then he stops, refusing to consider the statute's broader purpose, in the sense of balancing creditor and debtor interests based on assumptions about the value of the farmer's assets. How does he justify this judicial stopping point?

Actually, he does not quite stop before considering the broader pro-debtor statutory purpose. He seems willing to consider this "liberal-remedial" purpose to decide that "both a direct-drive mower and a friction-drive mower are statutory 'mowers.'" And he also observes that too much "liberality" might *hurt* rather than help farmers. How do those considerations of purpose fit with Professor Easterbrook's theory of judging?

Does contemporary policy have anything to do with how broadly or narrowly the statute is applied? Is there any evidence that contemporary policy influences Easterbrook's decision in Erickson?

How would Easterbrook decide these cases: (1) the Erickson case, if the only mowers in existence in 1935 had been horse drawn; (2) a case like Erickson, involving a $250,000 million contemporary mower whose increase in value resulted (a) solely from its incredible operating speed, or (b) from its speed *plus* the fact that it performed the crushing function of a haybine.

3. *Facts existed when statute adopted.* Courts have trouble deciding whether to apply old statutes to new facts. That much is obvious. But is the question easier to decide if the facts existed when the statute was adopted (that is, if the haybine existed in 1935)?

For example, suppose the issue is whether a 1919 statute which made it a crime to transport stolen "motor vehicles" across state lines applied to airplanes. McBoyle v. United States, 283 U.S. 25, 26 (1931). The statute defined "motor vehicle" to "include an automobile, automobile truck, automobile wagon, motor cycle, or any other self-propelled vehicle not designed for running on rails." Holding that the statute did not apply, the Court stated that "airplanes were well known in 1919, when this statute was passed." Why is that relevant to deciding what the statute means? Is it a statement about the meaning of language, legislative intent, or the respective responsibility of legislatures and courts in making decisions? The Court might be saying that, as long as the facts existed when the statute was adopted, it is reasonable to expect the legislature to resolve any doubts extending the text to those facts. But suppose the facts existed but their policy implications were not well understood. For example, airplane thefts might have been few in number in 1919 because there were few airplanes and pilots.

4. *Inflation-adjusted dollars.* Judge Easterbrook says that statutory dollar figures are static. Is that always true? Suppose inflation renders a dollar figure obsolete. For example, the Kentucky Constitution, in 1949, adopted § 246, establishing dollars ceilings for certain government salaries. Another section of the Constitution stated that officials shall "receive * * * adequate compensation to be fixed by law." The constitutional ceiling for judges was $8,400 but the legislature fixed the salary at $10,800 for 1962. A cost of living inflation adjustment for 1962 would convert the constitution's $8,400 figure to $10,827.60. Is the statute constitutional? Would the result be the same if the *legislature* (not the Constitution) had set dollar ceilings within which an administrative agency could set salaries and the agency provided a salary in excess of the statutory dollar ceiling to account for inflation? Matthews v. Allen, 360 S.W.2d 135 (Ky.1962).

MORE EXAMPLES

There are many other situations which test whether a term will be read (1) in a (a) narrow or (b) broad denotational sense; (2) by considering statutory purpose of varying levels of generality; or (3) by taking account of the contemporary legal landscape. In the following cases, does the court adopt an historical or contemporary reading of the text; if it chooses the historical reading, is it because that is how statutory texts must be interpreted or is it because that reading fits the contemporary legal landscape?

1. *Does "electors" include women?* An 1867 statute provides that jurors are selected from "qualified electors of the respective county." Thereafter the Nineteenth Amendment to the Constitution included women as electors (that is, as voters). Does the 1867 law authorize woman jurors? Specific legislative intent obviously did not include women. Does that matter? Women are, just as obviously, now voters. Does that make the case easy? Are women functionally electors the way a haybine is functionally a mower? If you answer "yes," is that because you considered legislative purpose or contemporary policy? Compare Commonwealth v. Maxwell, 114 A. 825 (Pa.1921) with People v. Barnett, 150 N.E. 290 (Ill.1925).

Of course, it makes good sense to link voting and jury duty, as early 20th Century feminists understood. Amar, The Bill of Rights As a Constitution, 100 Yale L.J. 1131, 1202–03 (1991). But does the text require it? Don't we need an argument about what makes the best sense of the interaction of voting rights and jury duty? Could one argue that voting involves a form of political participation that is much less disruptive of the woman's commitment to the home than jury duty?

2. *Is a bicycle a "carriage"?* The following case holds that bicycles are not "carriages," but why is there any doubt? Surely a bicycle functions much less like a carriage than a haybine like a mower.

Richardson v. Town of Danvers

57 N.E. 688 (Mass.1900).

■ Lathrop, J. The plaintiff, while riding a bicycle on a highway which the defendant was bound to keep in repair, encountered a depression in the way, and fell from her wheel and was injured. * * * The statute in question provides that highways and other ways named shall be kept in repair, at the expense of the town, city, or place where they are situated, "so that the same may be reasonably safe and convenient for travelers, with their horses, teams, and carriages at all seasons of the year." This statute was enacted in 1786, and has been in force ever since. The question, then, is whether a bicycle is a carriage, within the meaning of this term in the statute. We have no doubt that for many purposes a bicycle may be considered a vehicle or a carriage. * * * Under a law permitting the collection of tolls on a turnpike, a bicycle was held to be a carriage. Geiger v. Turnpike Road, 167 Pa. St. 582, 31 Atl. 918, 28 L.R.A. 458. * * * The statute in question was passed long before bicycles were invented, but although, of course, it is not to be confined to the same kind of vehicles then in use, we are of opinion that it should be confined to vehicles ejusdem generis, and that it does not extend to bicycles. * * * A bicycle is more properly a machine than a carriage, and so it is defined in Murray's Dictionary. * * * A bicycle is of but little use in wet weather or on frozen ground. Its great value consists in the pneumatic tire, but this is easily punctured, and no one who uses a wheel thinks of taking a ride of any distance without having his kit of tools with him. A hard rut, a sharp stone, a bit of coal or glass, or a tack in the road may cause the tire to be punctured, and this may cause the rider to fall and sustain an injury. It would impose an intolerable burden upon towns to hold them bound to keep their roads in such a state of repair and smoothness that a bicycle could go over them with assured safety. It is because ordinary roads are not considered suitable for bicycles that cities and towns are given the power * * * to lay out, construct, and maintain paths for bicycles. * * * We are therefore of opinion that a bicycle is not a "carriage," within the meaning of that term in Pub. St. c. 52, § 1. * * *

If a bicycle might be a carriage, can an automobile be a carriage? Does an 1897 statute exempting "one carriage or buggy" from attachment by creditors exempt an automobile? How would Easterbrook answer this question? Parker v. Sweet, 127 S.W. 881 (1910).

Note the dates for many of these decisions involving the statutory term "carriage." Would a modern court be as willing to include new technology, such as bicycles or cars, in a "carriage" statute?

3. *"Farmer" plus?* In National Broiler Marketing Ass'n. v. United States, 436 U.S. 816 (1978), the Court discussed the Capper–Volstead Act, which exempted a person "engaged" as a "farmer" from the Sherman anti-trust law and allowed them to "act together in associations, corporate or otherwise, with or without capital stock, in collectively processing, preparing for market, handling, and marketing in interstate and foreign commerce, such products of persons so engaged." The Court ducked an issue that attracted the following comment in a concurring opinion from Justice Brennan. The issue was whether the exemption applied if someone engaged in farming also owned production further down the distribution chain, including the *processing* of chickens. (Someone who only bred and raised chickens was clearly a

"farmer" under the statute.) Brennan argued against treating the fully integrated producer as a "farmer."

> Definition of the term "farmer" cannot be rendered without reference to Congress' purpose in enacting the Capper–Volstead Act. "When technological change has rendered its literal terms ambiguous, the * * * Act must be construed in light of [its] basic purpose." I seriously question the validity of any definition of "farmer" in [the statute] which does not limit that term to exempt only persons engaged in agricultural production who are in a position to use cooperative associations for collective handling and processing—the very activities for which the exemption was created. At some point along the path of downstream integration, the function of the exemption for its intended purpose is lost, and I seriously doubt that a person engaged in agricultural production beyond that point can be considered to be a farmer, even if he also performs some functions indistinguishable from those performed by persons who are "farmers" under the Act. * * *

> If, because of changes in agriculture not envisioned by it in 1922, Congress' purpose no longer can be achieved, there would be no warrant for judicially extending the exemption, even if otherwise it would fall into desuetude. In construing a specific, narrow exemption to a statute articulating a comprehensive national policy, we must, of course, give full effect to the specific purpose for which the exemption was established. But when that purpose has been frustrated by changed circumstances, the courts should not undertake to rebalance the conflicting interests in order to give it continuing effect. Specific exemptions are the product of rough political accommodations responsive to the time and current conditions. If the passage of time has "antiquated" the premise upon which that compromise was struck, the exemption should not be judicially reincarnated in derogation of the enduring national policy embodied in the Sherman Act. * * *

> The anomaly of allowing the exemption to those who function more as processors * * * points up the danger of judicially extending the exemption to conditions unforeseen by Congress in 1922. The exemption provides a powerful economic weapon for the benefit of one economic interest against another. However desirable the integrated broiler production system may be, and however needful of exemption, judges should not readjust the conflicting interests of growers and integrators; it is for Congress to address the problem of readjusting the power balance between them.

Is Justice Brennan relying solely on his conception of historical statutory purpose or is there some evidence of relying on contemporary legal landscape?

LEGISLATIVE HISTORY

This subpart discusses the role of legislative history in determining statutory meaning. Chapter 10 deals with materials produced as part of the legislative process, prepared at more or less the same time as the relevant legislation (contemporaneous legislative history). Chapter 11 deals with interpretations of statutes by administrative agencies. Some administrative interpretations are similar to conventional legislative history, because they are adopted by administrators who participated in the development of the legislation. But most agency rules do not fit that description. They are adopted after (maybe long after) a statute is passed and may even reverse earlier agency interpretations.

Chapter 12 deals with the effects of legislative action and inaction after passage of a statute—post-enactment legislative history. We first consider statutes and legislative history purporting to interpret prior law. We then discuss reenactment of a statute after an agency or court has interpreted the law, and legislative inaction in the face of such interpretations. This Chapter expands the concept of legislative history beyond its normal meaning to include what happens or does not happen in the legislature after legislation is passed.

The materials in this subpart dwell at greater length than prior chapters on how institutional arrangements for making law should influence statutory interpretation. We are concerned with whether interpretations by certain institutions, such as legislative committees and administrative agencies, should be authoritative. A political theory about who should be making law is therefore a relevant background consideration in deciding whether statements by particular institutions should influence the meaning of a statute. In some sense, that is what statutory interpretation is all about, although the usual focus is on the relevant lawmaking competence of legislatures and courts.

CHAPTER 10

CONTEMPORANEOUS LEGISLATIVE HISTORY

10.01 DEFINING LEGISLATIVE HISTORY

Discussions about legislative history often suffer from lack of clarity about what the discussion is all about. There are a variety of meanings of the term "legislative history" which should be kept in mind as you read the material in this Chapter. This introductory section provides you with some possible meanings. The point is that the dispute about the role of legislative history in determining statutory meaning depends on what kind of history you are considering.

Context vs. legislative materials. In contemporary usage, legislative history usually refers to legislative materials, such as committee reports and floor debates generated as part of the legislative process. But it may also refer to the historical context out of which a statute emerges.

Before U.S. courts began to cite legislative materials towards the end of the 19th Century, a judicial reference to "legislative history" was almost always to the historical context (or public history) from which the statute emerged and which explained the mischief or purpose at which the statute was aimed. This historical context is sometimes revealed in nonlegislative materials, such as newspaper reports or a government commission discussing a problem later addressed by statute. In many instances, it was also known to judges familiar with political activity, especially when statutes were simpler than they are today—correcting the common law or amending a relatively simple prior statute. This Chapter focuses primarily on legislative materials, but you should be alert to references to legislative history in the broader sense of historical context.

Legislative materials as evidence of context or specific intent. Legislative materials may be cited as evidence of (1) context (the mischief or purpose at which the statute was aimed) or (2) specific legislative intent. Holy Trinity is a case where legislative history provided information about the statute's context—specifically, that the statute was aimed at the evil of importing cheap manual labor. Legislative history may also contain statements about specific legislative intent by key players in the legislative process, such as bill sponsors, chairs and members of legislative committees. It is as though a committee report in Holy Trinity referred explicitly to the problem of importing religious pastors rather than discussing in a general way the problem of importing labor.

405

The use of legislative materials to prove context or specific legislative intent raises two familiar problems. (1) *Reliability*. Are the materials reliable evidence of what the legislature wanted? As Dickerson noted in Chapter 6, this problem can arise when legislative history is used to demonstrate context (in the sense of purpose), because statutes may have multiple purposes, producing agreement only about the statutory text. Legislative history may dwell on only one of several purposes, perhaps favoring one side of a compromise. Reliability is also a concern when legislative history is used to demonstrate specific intent. Not infrequently, such legislative history may be created by legislators trying to manipulate a political result for which they cannot gain majority support.

(2) *Legitimacy*. Does legislative history provide evidence which is legitimately used to determine statutory meaning? Even if the materials were reliable evidence of purpose, what role should purpose play in statutory interpretation, along with text and background considerations? Historically, evidence of statutory purpose was an antidote to judicial reliance on background considerations hostile to statutes. For example, in Johnson v. Southern Pac. Co., 196 U.S. 1 (1904), the Court relied on statutory purpose expressed in committee reports to rebuff the argument that the statute should be narrowly construed because it was in derogation of the common law "assumption of risk" doctrine. But, as prior chapters have explained, purposivism draws the judge into the process of lawmaking, which in today's legal environment raises questions about the legitimate judicial role.

When legislative history presents evidence of specific intent, the legitimacy concerns may be even more severe. The materials are a *rival text* addressing a specific problem without the constitutional sanction of being passed by the legislature and signed by the chief executive. They are, moreover, created by only a limited group of legislators, who do not constitute the entire legislature.

The problems of proving and using purpose in statutory interpretation have been discussed previously, so this chapter will pay primary (though not exclusive) attention to using legislative history as evidence of specific intent.

QUESTION

Which use of legislative history is the dispute about in the following quote from United States v. Thompson/Center Arms Co., 504 U.S. 505 (1992). Justice Souter was responding to Justice Scalia's objections to considering legislative history.

> Justice Scalia upbraids us for reliance on legislative history, his "St. Jude of the hagiology of statutory construction." [Editor—St. Jude is the patron of lost causes.] The shrine, however, is well peopled (though it has room for one more) and its congregation has included such noted elders as Mr. Justice Frankfurter: "A statute, like other living organisms, derives significance and sustenance from its environment, from which it cannot be severed without being mutilated. Especially is this true where the statute, like the one before us, is part of a legislative process having a history and a

purpose. The meaning of such a statute cannot be gained by confining inquiry within its four corners. Only the historic process of which such legislation is an incomplete fragment—that to which it gave rise as well as that which gave rise to it—can yield its true meaning." United States v. Monia, 317 U.S. 424, 432 (1943)(dissenting opinion).

Legislative materials as evidence of textual context. Legislative history might also be used as evidence of how authors and audiences understand statutory texts—as evidence of "textual context." Sometimes, this might be unselfconscious, as when a committee report uses language in a particular way, revealing the text's meaning. (For example, a report might say—"Racial discrimination has been especially strong against Eastern Europeans"—indicating that race included ethnicity.) At other times, legislative history about textual context might be more controversial and even manipulative, as when a committee report specifically states which of two meanings is intended—e.g., stating that "intern" includes a resident (see Chapter 5.02a). Is the use of legislative history to prove textual context more reliable or legitimate than using legislative history as evidence of purpose or specific intent?

Drafting context—Language changes during legislative process. There is another kind of legislative history, which is not a statement about context (textual or otherwise) or specific legislative intent, but which consists of legislative materials. A legislature or legislative committee might reject or alter specific language while considering a bill—call it "drafting context." This context might even include drafts considered in earlier legislative sessions. The variety of earlier drafts might be taken as evidence of what the enacted statute was eventually meant to accomplish. Is this more reliable or legitimate as a source of statutory meaning than other kinds of legislative history?

Types of legislative materials. This Chapter deals primarily with contemporaneous legislative history—the legislative materials generated while the statute is produced. The following types of contemporary legislative history are often considered by courts interpreting federal legislation: Committee Reports issued by the House and Senate Committees with jurisdiction to consider proposed legislation; Conference Committee Reports issued after a conference between representatives of House and Senate committees to resolve differences between legislation passed by both houses; testimony at Committee Hearings; statements made by members of Congress, especially if made by a sponsor of the bill or the Chair of the relevant committee.

State legislative history. Legislative history from state sources is generally less useful to a court. Committee hearings and reports are often not transcribed or the material is not very enlightening, although drafting history might be more readily available. This Chapter contains only a brief discussion of state legislative history (Chapter 10.05). My impression is that state judicial opinions are much more prone than federal cases to rely on text and background considerations, perhaps because legislative histories are unavailable.[1]

Our study of legislative history proceeds this way. Chapter 10.02 provides an historical note on the evolution of judicial use of legislative history in the United States. Chapter 10.03 discusses the role of committees in the legislative process and theories justifying judicial reliance on committee reports. Chapter 10.04 then critiques judicial reliance on legislative history in general and committee reports in particular, and considers responses to this critique. After taking a brief look at state legislative history and British practice (Chapters 10.05 and 10.06), we consider the use of legislative debates as legislative history (Chapter 10.07), drafting history (that is, changes in language during the legislative process)(Chapter 10.08), materials from the pre-legislative stage (Chapter 10.09), and presidential legislative history (Chapter 10.10).

QUESTIONS

As you go through the arguments for and against relying on legislative history, think carefully about the following:

1. Do the arguments apply with equal force to using legislative history (a) to prove context *and* specific legislative intent; (b) to prove context in the sense of (i) legislative purpose, (ii) textual context, or (iii) drafting context?

2. Do the arguments apply with equal force whether the statutory text is or is not clear? It is often said that legislative history can be considered by the court if the meaning of the statutory language is unclear, but some reasons for rejecting legislative history may apply whether or not the text is unclear.

3. Do the arguments apply with equal force to all types of legislative history, such as committee reports and floor debates recorded in the congressional record?

10.02 AN HISTORICAL NOTE

We have previously discussed the 1892 Supreme Court decision in Holy Trinity[2] (Chapter 6.04bi) dealing with the interaction of text and purpose. You will recall that a federal statute made it a crime to bring an alien into the country for "labor or service of any kind." The defendant brought in a

---

1. See Popkin, Statutory Interpretation in State Courts—A Study of Indiana Opinions, 24 Ind. L. Rev. 1155 (1991).

2. 143 U.S. 457 (1892).

pastor from England. The text seemed quite clear—this was prohibited activity—but the Court exempted the defendant, relying on the statute's purpose of preventing the importation of "cheap unskilled labor" to compete with domestic labor. Significantly, Holy Trinity was one of the first cases to identify legislative intent by referring to legislative history.

Prior judicial practice had excluded evidence from legislative debates, as the defendant's brief in Holy Trinity explicitly noted.[3] And yet the Court slid into considering committee reports as though it was the most natural thing to do. It quoted the following statement from a report issued by the Senate committee on education and labor, recommending passage of the bill: "Especially would the committee have otherwise recommended amendments, substituting for the expression, 'labor and service,' whenever it occurs in the body of the bill, the words 'manual labor' or 'manual service,' as sufficiently broad to accomplish the purposes of the bill," but that "believing that the bill in its present form will be construed as including only those whose labor or service is manual in character, and being very desirous that the bill become a law before the adjournment, [the committee] have reported the bill without change."[4]

Although resort to legislative materials was (for the most part) a break with the past,[5] it was a natural evolution in response to changing realities in the judicial and legislative process. Judges had always relied on their knowledge of the public history of a statute to help determine meaning. Indeed, the Court in Holy Trinity first makes reference to such public history before it cites committee reports.[6] All the Court did in Holy Trinity was to recognize that it now had a good source of information about the statute's history that could make up for what judges might not know, because they were growing more and more distant from the legislative process (Sedgwick had made this observation when objecting to equitable interpretation—see Chapter 2.04e).[7] As the federal legislature came to operate more and more through committees towards the end of the 19th Century, committee reports told judges what the legislature was doing.

---

3. Brief for Plaintiff in Error in Holy Trinity v. United States, pp. 18–19.

4. 143 U.S. at 464–65.

5. Hans Baade, "Original Intent" in Historical Perspective: Some Critical Glosses, 69 Tex. L. Rev. 1001, 1006–11 (1991)(hereafter "Baade"). But see Killenbeck, A Matter of Mere Approval? The Role of the President in the Creation of Legislative History, 48 Ark. L. Rev. 239, 253, 258 (1995), referring to two pre-Civil War Attorney–General opinions citing committee reports; and three Supreme Court cases in the 1870s, citing drafting history (Blake v. National Banks, 90 U.S. (23 Wall.) 307, 317–20 (1874)), a statement by a bill sponsor (Jennison v. Kirk, 98 U.S. 453, 459–60 (1878)), and a committee report (Collector

of the Port of N.Y. v. Richards, 90 U.S. (23 Wall.) 246, 258–59 (1874)).

6. 143 U.S. at 463.

7. Sedgwick, p. 205 ("But in modern societies, where the division of political attributes is so much more nice and rigorous, where the business of legislation has become multifarious and enormous, and especially in this country where the judiciary is so completely separated from the Legislature, it must be untrue in fact that they can have any personal knowledge sufficient really to instruct them as to the legislative intention; and if untrue in fact, any general theory or loose idea of this kind must be dangerous in practice.").

In fact, a thorough examination of 19th Century *state* cases may reveal somewhat more judicial reliance on legislative history than we generally assume. At the state level, the one type of legislative history with which judges would have been familiar was the report of the commissioners charged with revising the state legislative code. And, it turns out that Massachusetts Chief Judge Shaw relied on such reports. Although most of his references to legislative history were to drafting history (changes made in the text of drafts as they work their way to final legislative passage),[8] some of his references are to statements in commissioner's reports about legislative goals, analogous to modern legislative history found in committee reports: "reasons [ ] stated by the commissioners [ ] in their note to [ ] their report";[9] "report of the revising commissioners, in their comments";[10] "the commissioners, by their note, (*in loco*,) indicate what was their purpose";[11] "fully explained by the report of commissioners for making that revision".[12] And I suspect that a more thorough canvassing of 19th Century decisions might uncover more examples of reliance on the revisers, though much of it is probably drafting history.[13]

In retrospect, the real objections to judicial use of legislative history had been its unreliability as evidence of what the document meant. Most of the concern about legislative history in the early 19th Century centered around the interpretation of the federal constitution and the impropriety of using what the constitutional convention thought it was doing to shed light on what the constitution's authors, the state ratifying conventions, intended. Madison had stated, as a congressman: "[W]hatever veneration might be entertained for the body of men who formed our Constitution, the sense of that body could never be regarded as the oracular guide in expounding the Constitution * * * [since the Constitution] was nothing more than the draft of a plan * * * until life and validity were breathed into it by the voice of the people, speaking through the several State Conventions."[14] Hamilton had criticized Jefferson, in the debate over the constitutionality of the United States Bank, for alluding to what the constitutional framers had intended when they rejected a specific provision empowering Congress to authorize corporations: "[W]hatever may have been the intention of the framers of the constitution, or of a law, that intention is to be sought for in the instrument

---

8. Kidder v. Browne, 63 Mass. 400, 401 (1852); Howard v. Merriam, 59 Mass. 564, 565 (1850); Britton v. Commonwealth, 55 Mass. 302, 305 (1848); Commonwealth v. Mash, 48 Mass. 472, 474 (1844); Williams v. Hadley, 36 Mass. 379, 380 (1837); Tower v. Tower, 35 Mass. 262, 263 (1836).

9. Wright v. Oakley, 46 Mass. 400, 402 (1843).

10. Morrison v. Underwood, 59 Mass. 52, 54 (1849).

11. Marshall v. Crehore, 54 Mass. 462, 466 (1847).

12. Newcomb v. Williams, 50 Mass. 525, 536 (1845).

13. See Wood v. Caldwell, 54 Ind. 276, 281 (drafting history and reviser's note explaining legislative design). Even before Holy Trinity, the Supreme Court had occasionally used drafting history to shed light on what the final text meant. Blake v. National Banks, 90 U.S. (23 Wall.) 307, 317–19 (1874).

14. 4 Annals of Cong. 776 (1796).

itself, according to the usual and established rules of construction."[15] Consequently, although federal convention material may have been off limits because it was one step removed from the constitution's authors, that objection did not apply to material generated by the state ratifying conventions.[16]

Justice Story had also appealed to reliability concerns to reject legislative history regarding legislation, adding as well a constitutional argument.[17] He stated that the "opinions of a few [House] members' expressed neither the views of the House nor of the Senate and President whose views are equally weighty." And: "[L]ittle reliance can be or ought to be placed upon such sources of interpretation of a statute. The questions can be, and rarely are, [ ] debated upon strictly legal grounds, with a full mastery of the subject and of the just rules of interpretation. The arguments are generally of a mixed character, addressed by way of objections, or of support, rather with a view to carry or defeat a bill, than with the strictness of a judicial decision."

Reliability was the key issue. As long as 19th Century legislative procedure had not developed to the point where committees could plausibly speak for the legislature, objections to judicial use of legislative history made sense. Congressional procedure consisted mostly of real debates, where no individual could speak for the entire body. Moreover, 19th Century legislative materials were not always accurate, although matters improved at the federal level with the mid-century adoption of a kind of shorthand (called phonography) to provide approximate verbatim reporting in the Congressional Globe, and, in 1873, congressional authorization for the Government Printing Office to publish the Congressional Record.[18]

Once the legislature began to operate primarily through committees,[19] however, courts turned to congressional committee reports to learn about the public history of the statute (which had always been relevant to statutory interpretation),[20] although unreliable evidence in the form of *debates* remained suspect even after Holy Trinity.[21]

---

15. Hamilton Papers, Vol. VIII, at 110–11. Judicial use of the Federalist Papers to interpret the constitution can be traced to Cohens v. Virginia, 19 U.S. (6 Wheat.) 264, 418 (1821)(citing Federalist Papers). The Federalist Papers could be useful, however, as evidence of contemporaneous understanding, not as evidence of authorial intent. Contemporary understanding is relevant for interpretation as a means of assuring stability in the law, independent of what the authors intended.

16. Baade, pp. 1016–17, 1021–22. State courts were sometimes willing to rely on materials from state constitutional conventions to shed light on the meaning of state constitutions, even though ratification was by vote of the people. Baade, pp. 1055–57.

17. Mitchell v. Great Works Milling & Manufacturing Co., 17 F.Cas. 496, 498–99 (1843).

18. See Elizabeth McPherson, The History of Reporting the Debates and Proceedings of Congress, pp. 201–02, 205 (Ph.D. thesis 1940).

19. Woodrow Wilson, Congressional Government, p. 82 (World Pub. Co.1956).

20. United States v. Union Pacific R.R. Co., 91 U.S. 72, 79 (1875)(public history considered, but not views of individual members of Congress).

21. United States v. Trans–Missouri Freight Ass'n., 166 U.S. 290, 317–18 (1897).

The post-Civil War commentators showed only the slightest tolerance for legislative materials before the Holy Trinity case. Pomeroy's 1874 edition of Sedgwick stated that the "opinion of individual legislators" is entitled to "little weight, if any."[22] Endlich's Maxwell in 1888 rejects legislative history because the opinion of a few are not allowed, although he notes that there is no universal consistency regarding use of committees reports.[23] Sutherland in 1891 states that "[t]here has been occasionally judicial reference to declarations of members of legislative bodies, but such aids are but slightly relied upon, and the general current of authority is opposed to any resort to such aids."[24] Bishop in 1882 was a bit more generous, stating that the materials lack authority but are relevant as "opinion to persuade."[25]

More sensitive to what lay ahead was a comment in a short practitioner-oriented piece in 1881, agreeing with the Supreme Court's view that opinions of individual members were not helpful but urging reliance on "the course of debate [where it] represent[s] the prevailing sentiment" because "no reason exists for excluding [it] from consideration as tending to throw light on the meaning of a statute."[26] The author notes that "[o]f late years [ ] it has become not uncommon for courts to refer to the reports of Congressional committees in construing statutes," although the citations do not support his claim.

Holy Trinity was therefore a sign of the future in its use of legislative materials to discover statutory purpose. By the time of Sutherland's 1904 second edition, the author could state: "The proceedings of the legislature in reference to the passage of an act may be taken into consideration in construing the act."[27] Holy Trinity had used this new evidence in a quite traditional way—to limit the statute's coverage. But, as legislation became more comprehensive and energetic in the 20th Century, purposivist interpreters would need something more than their own guesses about public history to sustain their enthusiastic elaboration of legislative goals and that something was legislative history. By 1937, it could be said that committee reports were "freely used" and that debates were selectively considered when the speaker was a committee chair or member in charge of a bill.[28] This seemed to do no more than implement the New Deal Revolution[29] and the modern theory of government that the legislature expresses popular will.[30]

---

22. Sedgwick, pp. 203–04.

23. Endlich, pp. 42–43, 88 (citing a Pennsylvania court's use of a revising commissioner's report).

24. Sutherland, 1st, p. 384, sec. 300.

25. Bishop, p. 60.

26. Vol. IX, Washington Law Reporter, p. 321 (May 1881).

27. Lewis's Sutherland, Statutes and Statutory Construction, p. 879 (2d edition). Black's 1896 Treatise, however, approves the use of drafting history, but was still quite grudging about relying on opinions of legisla-

tors, even after Holy Trinity. Black, pp. 224–29, secs. 91–92. These opinions were "entitled to but little weight," though the author quotes Bishop to the effect that they can "persuade," citing a case which considered a statement by the chairman of the House Judiciary Committee. Ex parte Farley, 40 Fed. 66 (C.C.W.D.Ark.1889).

28. Note, Legislative Materials to Aid Statutory Interpretation, 50 Harv. L. Rev. 822, 824–25 (1937).

29. Baade, p. 1088.

30. 50 Harv. L. Rev., p. 822.

An important issue in this Chapter is whether modern judicial use of legislative history to determine *specific legislative intent* is less defensible than the earlier judicial practice of using legislative materials to infer statutory purpose.

10.03 COMMITTEE REPORTS

a) THE ROLE OF COMMITTEES

The most important legislative history at the federal level is the committee report. Whether the bill originates with the executive branch, a legislative committee, or a particular legislator, most significant legislation will probably be referred to a committee. Occasionally, a bill or parts of a bill are assigned concurrently or sequentially to more than one committee. House or Senate leadership often influences committee assignments on controversial legislation.

The relevant committee usually seeks comments from appropriate executive agencies and might hold public hearings. Important bills are "marked up" (that is, rewritten) by the committee. At the federal level the committee staff usually drafts a report, which contains a summary of the committee action, a general discussion of the bill's purpose and background, a more detailed explanation of the bill, the supplemental or dissenting views of specific committee members (if any), and statements required by law or the rules of the parent body. Required statements concern the following: cost estimates, inflation impact, findings pursuant to committee oversight responsibility, information concerning new budget authority and tax expenditures, and changes in existing law.

Committee Reports are important as legislative history because they are a record of what is usually the most important aspect of the legislative process. In a famous study of Congress in the late 19th Century, Woodrow Wilson stated: "I know not how better to describe our form of government in a single phrase than by calling it a government by chairmen of the Standing Committees of Congress." W. Wilson, Congressional Government 82 (World Pub. Co.1956).

The role of Congress has changed a great deal since Wilson wrote. Congressional power has diminished relative to the President. The relationship of congressional committees to both the congressional leadership and membership has also altered. The leadership, especially in the House of Representatives, is stronger than when Wilson wrote, though not as strong as it has been at some times in the early 20th century.

The House and Senate membership has also reasserted its power. Senators have always jealously guarded their prerogatives as individual members of a deliberative body against committee and leadership control. Committee products are freely amended on the Senate floor, subject to "unanimous consent" procedures. In the House, there was some movement in the 1970s, which moderated in the 1980s, towards permitting members to propose amendments for floor debate.[31] Nonetheless, committees still play a dominant role in Congress, because they permit the specialization that enables the legislature to rival the Executive in marshaling information and forming coalitions to shape legislative proposals. Significantly, democratization in both the House and Senate primarily takes the form of expanding committees and creating more subcommittees with adequate staffing, so that newer members of the legislature can have greater power. The growing prominence of subcommittees has probably increased judicial citation of *sub*committee reports.[32]

———

A recent study of the Senate confirms the dominant committee role. B. Asbell, The Senate Nobody Knows (paperback ed. 1981).

> On most legislation, even most major and controversial legislation, a Senator must trust the subcommittee that produces a bill. If not the whole subcommittee, at least those members of it with whom a Senator feels generally in tune. He must do that or his job becomes impossible. An individual Senator cannot spend on every major bill the seven years, the hundreds upon hundreds of hours of reading, of hearings, of debate, of haggling, of compromising and resolving that members of the Muskie committee spent on clean air. Each Senator is a member of three major standing committees and of subcommittees under each. On the bills coming before his subcommittees he must become expert, spend the grueling hours, the outstretched years. And other Senators must trust *him*.

> In that sense, a law is not the "work of Congress." That idea is a romantic myth-an impractical delusion. A law is the work of a few men, perhaps three or four or five active participants. It may be the work of only one, whose enthusiasm and insight and will are employed as a driving lash over an ambitious staff. That zealous individual's colleagues on a subcommittee are often carried along by the sheer force of his commitment.

Further on in the book, Asbell quotes as follows from an interview with Senator Muskie:

> A lot of members of the Senate will arrive on the floor, and there's an amendment up that they really haven't had a chance to look at, and they'll just come up and ask, "What's the committee position?" And they'll follow that committee position, meaning the committee majority, which sometimes may be a unanimous position. The majority of a committee that backs a bill is usually bipartisan, or at least crosses party lines. * * *

31. See S. Smith, Call to Order (1989).

32. See, e.g., Lindahl v. Office of Personnel Management, 470 U.S. 768, 783 (1985).

—And the credibility of its chairman is an important part of that. If you've got both the chairman and the ranking member, a Republican, both supporting a committee position, then that's a very powerful influence in the Senate. So it isn't just the four or five men who may be debating a particular bill or who may be managing it. It's the committee. If there's disagreement within the committee, even then the way the committee divides will be determinative of how the rest of the Senate divides most of the time. Nobody's taken any statistics on this, but my observation is that the habit of Senators has not changed much in the eighteen years I've been here, of relying on the committee. Not that the committee's never overturned. It is, on occasion. But the committee position is the first basic piece of information you want.

—In addition, of course, there's the Senator's staff. Rick analyzes every piece of legislation that comes through. There's a one-page or two-page memo for you, so I know what the basic thrust of the legislation is, what amendments can be anticipated so I won't be caught by surprise, and a recommendation based upon his knowledge of my philosophy and of my voting record. He does a very masterful job of digesting and pointing out the strong points, the danger points, and so on. Really, he's very, very good. In my early years I didn't have that kind of very useful service. I sort of had to jump onto the floor, standing there, trying quickly to get the gist of it myself. Very frustrating. This is much better.

When House and Senate Committee reports differ, because different versions of a bill passed each house, the relevant report is the one issued by the committee of the house whose version is eventually adopted. Sometimes a court errs in identifying which version passed. In Buckeye Power, Inc. v. E.P.A., 481 F.2d 162 (6th Cir.1973), the court used the House report because it thought the House rather than the Senate version passed. It based its conclusion on the fact that the number of the bill which was passed was preceded by "H.", which identifies bills originating in the House. In fact, the House bill had been stripped of all its provisions by the Senate and a Senate amendment put in its place. The House bill passed, as amended by the Senate. U.S. Code Cong. & Admin. News, 5356, 5374, 91st Cong., 2d Sess. (1970).

If House and Senate reports differ because they disagree about the same law passed by both houses, there is no authoritative legislative history. Chairman Rostenkowski, of the House Ways and Means Committee, once made the controversial claim that silence of one House constituted disagreement with the legislative history from the other House. See 33 Tax Notes 128 (Oct. 13, 1986).

House and Senate committee reports should be contrasted with the results of Conference Committee action. The Conference Committee process is sufficiently important that it deserves extended comment. There are two primary mechanisms for resolving differences between the House and Senate. First, the bill can go back and forth between the houses, with each house agreeing to the other's action with amendment. If this amending process produces complete agreement, the bill passes. This process is called "amendments between Houses." The vast majority of disagreements are resolved this way, but that is misleading because the procedure is used primarily for minor bills. A conference between the houses is usually convened when there is disagreement over important bills.

Representatives at the conference are usually selected from the House and Senate committees which considered the legislation, based on percentage of party membership in the relevant chamber. They may come from more than one committee within the House or Senate and, for multi-issue bills, some conferees may have authority only for the parts of the bill within their committee's jurisdiction. Regardless of technical rules, the relevant committee chairs and ranking minority members usually make the selection, although the House Speaker has significant influence over House representation. Seniority is important, but so are other factors: loyalty to a committee Chair; cashing in on political favors; support of the bill (especially in the House); and, occasionally, support of a position contrary to what passed in the particular body, especially in the Senate where the leadership may not like floor amendments.

There is a procedure for the House or Senate to "instruct" conferees in advance about what position to take, but it is rarely used, and noncompliance does not necessarily foretell rejection of the conference agreement. The instructions are not binding and they serve mainly as a very modest bargaining chip in the conference. Bargaining power commonly flows from the size of roll call votes in either house, and pledges by conferees to fellow legislators to maintain a position.

To obtain agreement at the conference, a majority of the conference committee members from each Chamber must sign the conference committee report, so there is no advantage to overloading the conference with one chamber's members. The conference committee report contains the agreed-upon statutory language, and is accompanied by a Joint Explanatory Statement, which contains a narrative explanation of the agreement by House and Senate conferees. The Joint Explanatory Statement is like a typical committee report, except that it is often much terser than a House or Senate committee report. Frequently, the Joint Statement is referred to as the conference committee report, although that is technically incorrect. Senate Rule XXVIII(4); House Rule XXVIII(d).[33]

---

33. The difference between the conference "committee report" and the joint explanatory statement was important in National Ass'n. of Greeting Card Publishers v. U.S. Postal Service, 462 U.S. 810, 832 n. 28 (1983). The lower court had given conclusive weight to the House Managers Statement (the predecessor in form to the Joint Explanatory Statement), thinking it was like a typical committee report provided to Congress prior to a vote.

Almost all conference agreements are accepted by Congress. This is the result of several factors. They are privileged business, which means they can come up for floor consideration at any time. House and Senate precedents require that they be accepted or rejected on an all-or-nothing basis. Conference agreements also tend to come up at the end of a session, when obstructing passage would undermine the efforts of many colleagues to obtain acceptable compromise and when attention span is low.

The House or Senate occasionally rejects a conference agreement, more so in recent years. The potential for rejection of a conference is greater in the Senate, where floor amendments may depart from the leadership's position, and be abandoned in conference. In some cases, a Senate floor amendment is understood to be a "show" for constituents, to be bargained away in conference, but not always.

A chamber can reject a conference agreement outright or move to recommit to the conference. Recommittal may result in removal of an offending provision, which is often possible if it is part of a large omnibus act containing many unconnected items. Legislators who dislike part of a bill will, however, usually swallow it all and try in a later session to get the offending part repealed.

The conference itself is not subject to many internal procedural constraints. Since 1975, hearings are supposed to be open ("sunshine" rules), and a point of order technically lies against the results of a conference violating this rule. Still, many of the agreements are concluded in private by key legislators and then ratified at an open meeting. The Tax Reform Act of 1986, a major piece of legislation, was negotiated privately by the Chairs of the House and Senate tax committees to break an impasse. Staff may also do most of the work on minor issues or work out agreement on major issues prior to the conference. Rooms too small for many observers often discourage public attendance. As a practical matter, openness may encourage taking positions to impress lobbyists to whom the legislator is beholden, rather than deliberation in the public interest.

b) THEORIES JUSTIFYING JUDICIAL RELIANCE ON COMMITTEE REPORTS

There are three theories justifying judicial use of legislative history found in committee reports.

1. *Legislative history as "context."* One theory argues that legislative history is useful because it is part of the context in which the legislative debate occurs.[34] It therefore explains what the legislature intends to accomplish. Legislators vote based on what they read in the reports, or at least on

---

In fact, only the committee report (meaning the agreed text of the bill) was provided in advance to Congress, but the House Managers Statement was available only *after* the Senate completed consideration of the conference committee report. On that ground, the Court considered the Managers Statement "significant" but of less weight than a report of a committee in either House.

34. See K. Kofmehl, Professional Staffs of Congress 118–19 (3d ed. 1977).

summaries of the reports, prepared by the legislator's staff or the committee staff. And bill managers refer to committee reports on the floor of Congress. For example, in the case of the Revenue Act of 1978, Congress voted on the Act when it had Committee Reports but not the final version of the bill.[35]

The weakness of this theory lies in the assumption that committee decisions really form the basis for the legislature's vote. The details of a committee report are often of little concern to legislators, whose votes are frequently based only on knowledge of the statute's general purposes, not anything found in committee reports. Occasionally, legislators who do not serve on a committee will (through their staffs) become aware of a particular provision in a committee report, but most legislators are unaware and uninterested in the details.

2. *Committees as agents of the parent chamber.* Another theory justifying judicial use of legislative history assumes that the committee is itself the critical decisionmaker. Its decisions are relevant even if there is no proof that the committee and the legislative majority share a common objective. In the following excerpt, this is called the agency model of legislative intent, and is contrasted with the first theory, which is called the majority model.

MacCallum, Legislative Intent

75 Yale L.J. 754 (1966).

* * * Anyone taking a close look at current judicial and administrative practices must conclude that these practices have only the slightest relationship to [the majority] model. While judges and administrators obviously utilize evidence of the intentions of various individual legislators, they make no serious attempts to discover the actual intentions of the voting majorities; further, our records of legislative proceedings are still not sufficient to support such an enterprise. There are presumptions galore about what, in the light of our records, the legislators must have been aware of and agreed with, but the realities of legislative processes are such that few of these presumptions are thought to be reliable *enough.*

This may persuade some commentators that courts and administrators generally have not been genuinely interested in the intentions of legislatures. But the behavior of judges and administrators vis-a-vis legislative intent would clearly be capricious and irresponsible only if they believed that the majority model set out necessary as well as sufficient conditions for the existence of legislative intent. There is no reason to suppose the judges and administrators believe this * * *.

It is possible that judges and administrators use an agency model of legislative intent. This model recognizes that legislatures delegate certain responsibilities (such as filling in the statutory details) to various persons (legislative draftsmen, committee chair-

---

35. See 7 Tax Notes 484 (1978).

men, judges, administrators), and that this may justify appealing to the intentions of these persons as the intentions of the legislature regarding the aims of statutes or the details thereof. * * *

The strongest case for [adhering to the agency model] could surely be made in the case of legislative reliance upon draftsmen and committee chairmen. In view of the realities of legislative proceedings, it is certainly plausible to say that legislatures go very far in relying on the judgment and discretion of such persons.

A judicial statement of the agency model of legislative intent appeared in S.E.C. v. Robert Collier & Co., 76 F.2d 939 (2d Cir.1935). Judge Learned Hand stated as follows:

It is of course true that members (of Congress) who vote upon a bill do not all know, probably very few of them know, what has taken place in committee. On the most rigid theory possibly we ought to assume that they accept the words just as the words read, without any background of amendment or other evidence as to their meaning. But courts have come to treat the facts more really; they recognize that while members deliberately express their personal position upon the general purposes of the legislation, as to the details of its articulation they accept the work of committees; so much they delegate because legislation could not go on in any other way.

There is still a gap between positing the agency model and justifying its use by courts to rely on legislative history. Why should courts rely on legislative committees as agents of the legislature?

3. *Committees as reflections of parent chamber.* Committees may also reflect majoritarian preferences because their membership is representative of the parent chamber or because the committee members, especially the Chair, work hard to achieve majority support. It was said of Representative Wilbur Mills, the powerful Chair of the House Ways and Means Committee, that he always worked through consensus to report a bill with majority support. His motive was to retain a House leadership position. He may have been helped in this regard by committee membership that was broadly representative of the House. Other committees, however, may consist mostly of "outliers," who are further to the left or right of the chamber's membership or more concerned with favoring interest groups than the parent body. Outliers may, for example, come primarily from regions which can be helped by the committee, such as Agriculture Committee members from farming states, or be ideologically more to the left or right of the House or Senate.[36]

4. *Political, not legal significance of legislative history?* If none of the above theories justifies judicial use of legislative history to determine statutory meaning, what is its function? Perhaps it is simply part of the ongoing push and pull of legislative-executive relations, without *legal* significance. For

---

36. See generally, Krehbiel, Are Congressional Committees Composed of Preference Outliers?, 84 Amer. Pol. Sci. Rev. 149 (1990).

example, executive agencies often follow what an appropriations committee report tells them to do, even if the statute does not explicitly contain the requirement. Such reports are part of the political process of accommodation between Congress and the Executive, but a court of law might not give them legal effect. Similarly, Committee Reports dealing with substantive legislation (not appropriations) might have political but not legally binding effect, as instructions to an administering agency.[37] One study found that, with few exceptions, legislative staff were more concerned with agency than with judicial implementation of the law.[38]

There is a lengthy discussion of the political role of legislative history in International Broth. of Elec. Workers v. N.L.R.B., 814 F.2d 697 (D.C.Cir. 1987). The case dealt with a statute extending the National Labor Relations Act to nonprofit healthcare employees. The extension was the result of a compromise between unions wanting an unrestricted right to organize the employees and hospitals concerned with disrupting healthcare delivery. The two extremes were represented by the Cranston–Javits and Taft bills, which were withdrawn when a compromise was reached. The specific issue in the case was the appropriate number of bargaining units that could be represented. The Act itself, because the issue was so contentious, contained nothing about this problem. Instead both House and Senate Committee Reports contained language "agreed upon" by both sides of the controversy. It stated that "due consideration" would be given to "prevent [ ] proliferation of bargaining units." Senators differed on the import of this language. One Senator voted against reporting the bill out of committee because its language was silent on bargaining units. One Senator stated in the Congressional Record that the Report agreed on "the necessity * * * to reduce and limit the number of bargaining units." Another Senator thought the Report contained only an "admonition" to the administering agency to give "due consideration" to the problem of proliferation of bargaining units. In his concurring opinion, Judge Buckley (a former Senator from New York) had this to say about judicial reliance on the Report and Congressional Record:

> * * * [T]he agreement to include the report language was [not] an empty gesture. To the contrary, there can be little doubt that the two committees expected the [administering agency] to pay attention to their directive—not because it had the force of law, but because agencies are not given to ignoring the commands of potentates who control their budgets and oversee their operations. * * *

> This political reality is well understood by professionals. * * * Thus the inclusion of the admonition in the committee reports could be expected to provide the margin of assurance required to secure the support of at least some of the legislators and lobbyists who were concerned over the prospect of proliferating bargaining units.

37. See Knapp v. Commissioner, 870 F.2d 93 (2d Cir.1989)(legislative history was no more than an admonition to the administering agency, not "law").

38. Katzmann, Bridging the Gulf Between Courts and Congress: A Challenge for Positive Political Theory, 80 Geo. L.J. 653, 663 (1992).

As the admonitory language served a political rather than a legal purpose, each of the key legislators no doubt felt free to "accentuate the positive" by providing his own distinct interpretation on its meaning and effect. This may explain the contrasting glosses [different Senators] placed on the language. * * *

* * * [This] suggests an endemic interplay, in Congress, of political and legislative considerations that makes it necessary for judges to exercise extreme caution before concluding that a statement made in floor debate, or at a hearing, or printed in a committee document may be taken as statutory gospel. Otherwise, they run the risk of reading authentic insight into remarks intended to serve quite different purposes. Furthermore, to the degree that judges are perceived as grasping at any fragment of legislative history for insights in congressional intent, to that degree will legislators be encouraged to salt the legislative record with unilateral interpretations of statutory provisions they were unable to persuade their colleagues to accept * * *.

An additional reason for the exercise of judicial caution is that judges confined to the printed page may not always be able to separate legislative wheat from political chaff, to identify and discard remarks that are designed not so much to inform colleagues as to reach beyond Capitol Hill to audiences ranging from lobbyists who may help a beleaguered legislator achieve his goals, to home state journalists on whose reports the next election may well depend. It is not always easy to distinguish which remarks will fit in which category, especially when read years after the event by judges who have neither the time to review the entire history of a particular bill nor the experience to filter out the political overtones.

10.04 CRITIQUE OF RELIANCE ON COMMITTEE REPORTS

a) RELIANCE OR RATIONALIZATION

Use of legislative history gives courts one more way to justify a result in a case. This may be objectionable, if it allows courts to disguise results with the appearance of principled decisionmaking. The following comment alludes to this problem.

Wald, Some Observations on the Use of Legislative History in the 1981 Supreme Court Term

68 Iowa L.Rev. 195 (1983).

I am left with the sense, expressed by Justice Stevens in a dissent late last Term, that consistent and uniform rules for statutory construction and use of legislative materials are not being followed today. It sometimes seems that citing legislative history is still, as my late colleague Harold Leventhal once observed, akin to "looking over a crowd and picking out your friends." * * *

* * * Frankly, the same Justices who rely on plain language and repudiate thirty years of contrary judicial interpretation in one case say in another that they must look to the broad purposes of the act and not to any cramped phraseology. I certainly do not suggest disingenuousness or opportunism; rather, in the present state of the law, the various approaches to statutory construction are drawn out as needed, much as a golfer selects the proper club when he gauges the distance to the pin and the contours of the course.

Today there appear to be few, if any, restrictions on what judges may look at to discern legislative intent or purpose. Yet, if legislative history is now scanned in every case of statutory construction, rarely is it determinative of the outcome. It competes with presumptions and canons of construction: some old, some newly derived, and many reflecting the policies in our wide-ranging legal and constitutional system that most commend themselves to the majority of judges.

b) PUBLIC AVAILABILITY

Another problem raised by the use of legislative history is its public availability. Not all litigants will have equal access to legislative history, and gaining access is costly and time-consuming.

The problem of public availability can easily be overlooked by those accustomed to using a research library. The privately published Congressional Information Service and the Congressional Index provide well-indexed information about federal legislative hearings, committee reports, and committee prints, and these materials are likely to be available in hard cover or microfiche at a research library. Smaller county law libraries might not have some or all of this material. Westlaw and Lexis services and websites on the Internet may improve access to legislative history, but they do not solve the problem of time and expense for the client.

Moreover, it is not only wealthy clients which have an advantage. Government agencies probably keep elaborate legislative histories, which may not be readily available to others. For example, in Borrell v. U.S. International Communications Agency, 682 F.2d 981, 988 (D.C.Cir.1982), the court cited statements by two Senators in an unpublished mark-up session (where the legislative committee goes over the language of a proposed bill), to support the government's view that a whistleblower did not have a private cause of action against the government for dismissal.

Justice Jackson was very outspoken in asserting the "unavailability" objection to using legislative history. In United States v. Public Utilities Commission, 345 U.S. 295 (1953)(concurring), he stated:

* * * Neither counsel who argued the case for the State Commission nor the Supreme Court of California had access to the [legislative] material used by the Court today. Counsel for the Public Utilities Commission of that State stated at the bar, and confirmed by letter, that he had tried without success over a period of four months to obtain the legislative history of § 20 of Part I of the Federal Power Act. He obtained it only four days before argument, in Washington at the Library of this Court. He stated that the City and County Library of San Francisco, the Library of the University of California, and the library of the largest law office in San Francisco, were unable to supply it. The City and County Library tried to obtain the material by interlibrary loan from the Library of Congress, but the request was refused. Counsel then attempted to obtain the material from the Harvard Law School Library, but it advised that "our rules do not permit this kind of material to be sent out on loan."

The practice of the Federal Government relying on inaccessible law has heretofore been condemned. Some of us remember vividly the argument in Panama Refining Co. v. Ryan, 293, U.S. 388, in which the Government was obliged to admit that the Executive Orders upon which it had proceeded below had been repealed by another Executive Order deposited with the State Department. No regularized system for their publication had been established. Copies could be obtained at nominal cost by writing to the Department. Having discovered the error, the Government brought it to the attention of the Court. At the argument, however, the Court, led by Mr. Justice Brandeis, subjected government counsel to a raking fire of criticism because of the failure of the Government to make Executive Orders available in official form. The Court refused to pass on some aspects of the case, and the result was the establishment of a Federal Register.

In Conroy v. Aniskoff, 507 U.S. 511 (1993), Justice Scalia, in dissent, emphasized the practical problems of researching legislative history:

I confess that I have not personally investigated the entire legislative history * * *. The excerpts I have examined and quoted were unearthed by a hapless law clerk to whom I assigned the task. The other Justices have, in the aggregate, many more law clerks than I, and it is quite possible that if they all were unleashed upon this enterprise they would discover, in the legislative materials dating back to 1917 or earlier, many faces friendly to the Court's holding. Whether they would or not makes no difference to me— and evidently makes no difference to the Court, which gives lipservice to legislative history but does not trouble to set forth and discuss the foregoing material [unearthed by the hapless law clerk and unfavorable to the majority's conclusion] * * *. In my view, that is as it should be, except for the lipservice. The language of the statute is entirely clear, and if that is not what Congress meant then Congress has made a mistake and Congress will have to correct it. We should not pretend to care about legislative intent (as opposed to the meaning of the law), lest we impose upon the practicing bar and their clients obligations that we do not ourselves take seriously.

c) ROLE OF STAFF

No one doubts that committee staff play a very important role in the political process.[39] They arrange hearings, draft legislation, develop compromises, work out the details of legislation, and broaden support by suggesting amendments. Frequently, a legislator learns about a problem only if the staff can not work out solutions agreeable to all parties.

The size of legislative staffs exploded after World War II for several reasons: to allow Congress to develop the expertise it needed for modern legislation, especially as a counterweight to executive specialization; to enable individual members, especially junior legislators, to make their mark; and to manage workload. Ironically, instead of improving the legislator's ability to manage the workload and deliberate about legislation, reliance on staff may have increased the workload and converted legislators into managers of mini-bureaucracies.

_____

The staff's role becomes an important legal issue when courts use Committee Reports as evidence of statutory meaning, because staff prepare these reports. Their drafting role and relationship to committee members is discussed in the following excerpt.

K. Kofmehl, Professional Staffs of Congress

(3d ed. 1977).

Drafting of reports. During the period covered, committee reports to accompany bills were almost entirely a staff product. On a number of committees, the whole staff collaborated in preparing the

_____

39. See generally M. Malbin, Unelected Representatives (1980). The importance of staff is attested to by the Supreme Court's interpretation of the "Speech or Debate" Clause of the Constitution (Art I, § 6, cl. 1) ("[F]or any Speech or Debate in either House [Members of Congress] shall not be questioned in any other Place"). This Clause obviously applies to statements made on the floor of Congress by elected members of Congress, but in Gravel v. United States, 408 U.S. 606 (1972), the Court held that it also applied to legislative acts by Senator Gravel's personal aide, who had been subpoenaed in connection with Senator Gravel's role in publishing the Pentagon Papers about the government's conduct of the Vietnam War. See also Doe v. McMillan, 412 U.S. 306 (1973)(staff preparation of committee reports was protected, but not their dissemination beyond what was needed for legislative purposes).

report on a major measure. Jointly they would draw up the outline for it. Each staff member would write particular portions. Then after the draft of the report was completed, all would participate in revising it. * * *

Before starting to do a report, the staff usually consulted the chairman on what to emphasize in it. Fairly often during the hearings and deliberations on a bill in executive sessions, individual committeemen would state that they wanted certain expository, qualifying, or other passages put in the accompanying report. And, of course, the reactions of the membership throughout the processing of a measure afforded a guide to the staff in deciding what the contents and emphases of the report should be. But for the most part, the staff drafted the reports on bills without much direct supervision from the committee.

Moreover, such reports were reviewed perfunctorily—if at all—by the committee as an entity. Rarely did a committee mark up reports the way it did the bills they accompanied. When a committee did meet to go over a report on a major bill, normally the clerk or staff director merely read eclectically [ ], stressing any portions containing interpretive language. Most of the time, a committee did not collectively consider such a report at all. Instead, the staff would send a copy to each committee member to review individually. Rather often, the staff submitted a draft report to only the chairman and ranking minority member for revision. * * *

Occasionally, members of Congress complained about the lack of opportunity to review reports emanating from their committees. For example, in the 82d Congress, Representative Thomas A. Jenkins (R.-Ohio) charged:

> When the bill [H.R. 7800 (Social Security Act Amendment of 1952)] was reported out, it was accompanied by a beautiful big report. I daresay that nobody on the Ways and Means Committee wrote a line of that report, containing 51 pages of very illustrative tables and figures. And nobody saw that report as far as I know: I know I did not see it.

And Representative Thomas B. Curtis (R.-Mo.) made the following accusations:

> I have constantly been embarrassed in my committee, for example, by refusing to approve a committee report on the ground that the first opportunity I have had to even look at a lengthy report was at the very minute the committee met for the purpose of adopting or rejecting the report. I should not have to state here the obvious fact that it should be routine procedure that lengthy written reports be furnished to the committee members at least a few hours before meeting time in order to give them an opportunity to study the report before the meeting * * *.

However, their strictures were but isolated voices of protests. Most of the members of Congress apparently were satisfied with the existing conditions. For instance, in the 82d Congress, when the staff of the House Education and Labor Committee suggested that it meet to go over a report on a bill, the members replied in astonishment, "Why should we? We never have in the past." With such complacency and the inertia of precedent on the side of current practices, it seemed unlikely that they would be changed on a widespread scale very soon.

In view of the important interpretive function of reports to accompany the bills, the prevailing failure of the committees to review them more carefully was an Achilles heel of the legislative process. Frequently, the staffs had to divine the preferences of the effective majorities of their committees and incorporate those in the reports on bills without the benefit of a confirming check by the principals concerned. This state of affairs again stressed the necessity of having the staffs adhere strictly to their proper role and of holding them immediately responsible to their respective committees.

There is additional anecdotal evidence on both sides. Senator Moynihan wrote a letter to the New York Times dated Sept. 6, 1987, complaining that, although he was a conference committee member, he did not recall any legislator discussing the content of a footnote in a conference committee report on a tax bill; he suspected that staff members wrote the footnote thinking its content was already law and not knowing that a case had decided otherwise. But see Cong. Quart. Weekly Report, March, 24, 1990, p. 917 (some Committee Chairs read committee reports, which are available to committee members).

Justice Scalia has explicitly objected to reliance on committee reports, in part because of the staff's role, in Hirschey v. F.E.R.C., 777 F.2d 1 (D.C.Cir.1985)(concurring):

I frankly doubt that it is ever reasonable to assume that the details, as opposed to the broad outlines of purpose, set forth in a committee report come to the attention of, much less are approved by, the house which enacts the committee's bill. And I think it time for courts to become concerned about the fact that routine deference to the detail of committee reports, and the predictable expansion in that detail which routine deference has produced, are converting a system of judicial construction into a system of committee-staff prescription.

The strongest argument against relying on reports written by staff is that the reports resolve matters of detail that elected officials should decide. Politics should not be just the adoption of principle, leaving details to be worked out by others. A deliberative legislative process requires principles to take on meaning from attention to detail, which politicians too frequently delegate to staff. It is not that staff act in disregard of their employer's point of view. The relationship of trust and the fear of being discharged prevent that. But many significant decisions are still being made by staff, including the writing of legislative history.[40]

There are, however, contrary considerations. The "defect" of staff paying attention to details which are neglected by elected officials is also a strength. Legislatures are very busy and sometimes fail to include the necessary detail in statutes. The ideal of elected officials relating detail to general principle is simply too ambitious. That is why agencies are given so much power. Similarly, staff are often very knowledgeable about how detail relates to the general statutory structure and will do a good job in working out that relationship in committee reports. Relying on legislative history is especially desirable in areas of the law which are very technical. The staff's expertise in resolving such questions of statutory detail is considerable, and judges (who must grapple with the problem if the legislative history is not relied on) are not very good at deciding such issues. Moreover, if the area of the law is one where lawyers pay close attention to legislative history, the problem of surprise to the general public is avoided.[41]

There are two possible qualifications to this argument for relying on legislative history. First, some issues are of such political significance that they should be resolved only by elected officials. In such cases, courts should not rely on committee reports because of the risk that they are primarily staff products. Second, some interest groups may have privileged access to committee staff and be able to obtain favorable one-sided legislative history, even when the issues are not politically controversial and seem merely "technical." Perhaps such access should destroy the usefulness of legislative history for the court.

This discussion suggests that courts might use legislative history selectively, when the advantages outweigh the disadvantages. But can a court effectively balance the strengths and weaknesses of legislative history? Does such "balancing" simply give judges another string to their bow?

QUESTION

Should courts use the following legislative history? Occasionally congressional staff write reports soon *after* a statute is passed. This is true of the so-called "Blue Book," which is authored by the staff of the Joint Committee on Taxation to explain new tax law. These staffers generally participated in the writing of the law and accompanying legislative committee reports. Statements in these documents might clarify an uncertainty in the law, even

40. Concern about the role of staff may also call into question judicial deference to the legislature as a representative body. See Garcia v. San Antonio Metropolitan Transit Authority, 469 U.S. 528, 557 (1985)(Powell, J., dissenting)(distrust of Congress' ability to protect the states, in part because "[f]ederal legislation is drafted primarily by the staffs of the congressional committees").

41. See Livingston, Congress, the Courts, and the Code: Legislative History and the Interpretation of Tax Statutes, 69 Texas L. Rev. 819 (1991).

though no comments on the issue appear in the prior legislative committee reports.[42]

d) MANIPULATION OF COMMITTEE REPORTS

Use of Committee Reports to interpret legislation is often criticized because it permits legislation by subterfuge when a political interest group lacks support to pass explicit legislation. The implication is that legislative history provides a vehicle for sneaking through interpretations that could not be legislated, or would at least be very controversial if they were more openly debated. This seems especially troublesome if it allows strong private interest groups to manipulate the creation of legislative history. Such manipulation is especially likely if, as some suggest, committee members are "outliers," chosen because they can help strong political constituencies without being representative of the parent body. Staff discretion may also contribute to this result, because private interest lobbying often works directly through access to staff.

Ackerman & Hassler, Beyond the New Deal: Coal and the Clean Air Act, 89 Yale L.J. 1466 (1980), discuss this problem in connection with the 1977 Amendments to the Clean Air Act. The ultimate objective of this Act was clean air. For industrial users, this was measured by pounds of emissions related to energy generated—specifically, pounds of sulfur dioxide per MBTU. There were two basic methods to achieve his goal: use of cleaner coal, or use of dirtier coal which had been "scrubbed" to reduce the emissions. Eastern producers of dirty coal formed an alliance with environmentalists to advocate requiring a percentage reduction of the emissions from coal that would otherwise have occurred in the absence of scrubbing treatment. This reduction was to be required for *both* clean and dirty coal. This rule removed the cost advantage that clean coal had over the combination of dirty coal plus scrubbing. The alliance was formed in the House of Representatives as the Clean Air Act worked its way through Congress. This issue was not the most important environmental problem confronting Congress. Automobile emissions attracted much more attention. Ackerman & Hassler commented as follows on the history of this legislation.

> * * * [T]he House staff wondered if it would succeed in using legislative history to inflate its minor changes in statutory language into a scrubbing requirement. Because section 111 [Editor—The section which was the basis of the scrubbing requirement] would no longer float through conference unnoticed, they were not averse to raising their hidden agenda to statutory prominence. Yet, although both sides saw the merit of reworking the language of the House bill, an unambiguous statement of policy would precipitate the confrontation between their principals that all sought to avoid.

42. See generally Livingston, What's Blue and White and Not Quite as Good as a Committee Report: General Explanations and the Role of "Subsequent" Tax Legislative History, 11 Amer. J. Tax Policy 91 (1994).

Senate staffers were successful in making one substantive point. A new subsection (h) made it clear that Congress did not want the Administrator [of the Environmental Protection Agency] to preempt the discharger's choice of the control technology that would best permit him to achieve emission limitations. Thus, unless it is "not feasible" to permit polluters to choose, the subsection denies the Administrator the authority to require a particular "design, equipment, work practice, or operational standard." The new definition of "not feasible," moreover, makes it plain that facilities like power plants cannot be subjected to design or equipment standards.

Yet, while the Senate achieved this substantive prohibition, the House achieved a formal victory that looked in the opposite direction. Henceforth, the statute would require the Administrator to regulate power plants differently from other dischargers. * * * [T]he Administrator must not only require a power plant to discharge no more than X pounds of sulfur oxide per MBTU, but also to reduce the sulfur in the coal by Y percent. By setting the percentage reduction requirement at a level only scrubbers could achieve, eighty-five percent for example, the Administrator could effectively force all coalburners to install scrubbers. But the statute falls far short of mandating such a high percentage. Indeed, it does not even require the Administrator to establish the same percentage for all coalburners. Although each plant must be assigned "a percentage reduction" to achieve, another subsection, unchanged from 1970, expressly authorizes the Administrator "to distinguish among classes, types, and sizes within categories of new sources for the purposes of establishing such [NSPS] standards." Hence, the Administrator has the authority to tell users of low sulfur coal to reduce their sulfur content by Y_1 percent and require high sulfur burners to eliminate Y_2 percent.

Indeed, when viewed within the framework of the section as a whole, the added provision does not even bar the Administrator from establishing a reduction of zero percent for low sulfur coal burners. For the new formal requirements are subject to the old substantive standard that requires the Administrator to consider "the cost of achieving * * * emission reduction[s]" before requiring the use of the "best technological system." The provision explicitly makes cost a consideration before low sulfur users can be required to install scrubbers. * * *

Rather than trying to bring the increasingly complex statutory language under control, the draftsmen turned to their first love: making legislative history. Once again, the House staff gained a victory in the conference report that it utterly failed to achieve on the surface of the statute: "The Senate concurs in the House provision with minor amendments. The agreement * * * preclude[s] use of untreated low sulfur coal alone as a means of compliance." Yet midnight legislative history is a game any number can play. Aides for Senator Domenici were quick to add their own opinion in the next paragraph: "the conferees agreed that the Administrator may, in his discretion, set a range of pollutant reduction that reflects varying fuel characteristics." Given this threat, the House staffers counterattacked with another tack-on: "Any departure from the uniform national percentage reduction requirement, however, must be accompanied by a finding that such a departure does not undermine the basic purposes of the House provision and other provisions of the act, such as maximizing the use of locally available fuels."

These last remarks epitomize the abuses that follow from undisciplined legislative history. The only statutory recognition of Eastern coal interests is to be found in section 125, which does not seek to "maximize" local production but extends a highly qualified protection to areas suffering serious economic dislocation that can be demonstrably linked to pollution regulation. Rather than referring back to the coal lobby rhetoric contained in the old House committee report, an interpretation of the statutory language should refer to the aims of the statute declared in the Act itself-which, apart from section 125, shows no special solicitude for local coal producers. Just as the conference report fantasizes about the Act's basic purposes, its invocation of a *"uniform* national percentage reduction requirement" is, as we have just shown, entirely unsupported by the language and structure of the statutory text. * * *

In short, the draftsmen brewed a mix of statute and legislative history that was worthy of the occasion. Rather than integrating section 111 into the basic structure of the Act, their task was to avoid a potential conference impasse by writing a document whose legal meaning was hopelessly confused. The new section 111 is easier to understand as an exercise in small-group dynamics than as an effort to guide the bureaucratic management of a multibillion dollar problem.

Ackerman and Hassler are led to the following conclusions about statutory interpretation.

* * * It is only by insisting on explicit statutory language that courts can assure themselves that the committee report represents more than a successful effort by a handful of insiders to exploit the overloaded congressional docket. The regular application of this *principle of textual priority* will, over time, bring home to the staff and lobbyists on Capitol Hill that there is only one way to force an agency to do their bidding—and that is to engage in the full debate traditionally associated with explicit statutory amendment. Textual priority is especially important in the interpretation of a large and complex statute like the Clean Air Act. Such statutes have their own distinctive architecture with a few basic principles motivating the often intricate ground plan. * * * [C]ourts should not destroy the

statutory ground plan on the basis of subterranean legislative history.

The present case provides a textbook example of the dangers to democratic principle that flow from the abuse of legislative history. In 1977, the clean air-dirty coal lobby would have vastly preferred a single statutory phrase commanding full scrubbing to a ream of legislative history in praise of "locally available" coal. The reason the lobby settled for less is that it feared it would lose if it went for broke. Moreover, such fears seem perfectly rational when the 45 to 44 Senate victory of section 125 is recalled. Here was a section that *explicitly* authorized the use of scrubbing for the protection of Eastern coal; yet, although it was hedged about with all sorts of checks, it gained the narrowest of victories. This fact speaks louder than ten thousand words of legislative history. If it was so hard to gain the largely symbolic relief for Eastern coal promised by section 125, why should a court presume that Congress "intends" the expenditure of tens of billions of dollars when this intention has not yet achieved clear expression in the text of section 111?

The statute was eventually interpreted in Sierra Club v. Costle, 657 F.2d 298 (D.C.Cir.1981). The E.P.A. Administrator had decided to permit dirty coal, emitting 1.2 pounds of sulfur dioxide, if the user reduced emissions by 90% of what the coal would have emitted before scrubbing, or cleaner coal, emitting .6 pounds, if the emission reduction was at least 70%. The Sierra Club argued against this flexible standard. The court thought that the language of the statute supported the Administrator's flexibility, but it also quoted that portion of the conference committee report inserted by the Senate conferees, supporting the Administrator's discretion, not the portion of the report inserted by the House conferees. The decision is typical of judicial opinions in arguing that both statutory language and legislative history converge, thereby avoiding the result feared by Ackerman & Hassler, that the report would overshadow the language. An interesting question would have arisen if the only legislative history had been that buried in the conference committee report by the House conferees.

The fact that there *was* contrary Senate legislative history might suggest that the problem of manipulation is overstated. When issues are politically controversial, legislators who care may watch out for adverse legislative history and counter with efforts of their own.

QUESTION

Courts often state that the results of a *conference* committee are the most authoritative type of legislative history (see,.e.g., American Jewish Congress v. Kreps, 574 F.2d 624, 629 n. 36 (D.C.Cir.1978)). What does the Ackerman–Hassler discussion suggest about that point of view?

Textual priority? "Textual priority," advocated by Ackerman and Hassler, is supposed to reduce the risk of secret and manipulative legislating, but it might have the opposite effect. The following material discusses a situation, also involving the 1977 Clean Air Act Amendments, in which a committee report was made available to legislators to deflect opposition to complex and controversial legislation. However, the statutory language produced a result different from what the report suggested. The following excerpt explains the legislation. It is followed by a judicial opinion giving "textual priority" to the relevant language. Ask yourself whether the danger of manipulating the legislative process was increased or decreased by textual priority.

A. Maass, Congress and the Common Good

(1982).

The abnormally close relations that developed between the agency [EPA] and the Senate subcommittee tended to exclude from decision making on environmental policy not only the White House but also the full Congress. Indeed, EPA and the subcommittee did not even try to build congressional support in some cases, relying instead on direct relations with each other and on the courts. In this context they used a number of decision-making techniques that required unusually heavy participation by the staffs of the two units. [Senator] Muskie expected EPA to consult with him or his staff on major policy decisions. Muskie's staff, under the leadership of Leon G. Billings, held frequent meetings with EPA officials—assistant administrators, directors of divisions and offices in Washington, regional directors, laboratory chiefs, and lower-level personnel—where important policies were discussed and sometimes negotiated and agreed to.

Under Muskie's direction the committee staff, with the aid of agency personnel, drafted statutory language of extraordinary detail and specificity with the results that the full House and Senate had difficulty comprehending what was being done * * *.

On at least one occasion the staff drafted language that may have been intended to mislead the Congress. In response to overwhelming public, state, and local opposition to EPA's efforts to reduce air pollution in major cities by restricting parking facilities, the House in 1977 undertook to repeal authority for EPA to require such action * * *. [Editor—Such action is known as "indirect source review," or ISR.] The conference report on the 1977 amendments of the Clean Air Act stated that "the administrator would be prohibited outright from requiring indirect source review, either directly or indirectly." But Senate staff members who favored parking restrictions were able to draft the amendment's language so that it failed to shut the door on regulation of independent sources and, therefore, did not match the legislative intent stated in the conference report. [Editor—The following case illustrates how.]

* * * [C]ommittee staff and those within the agency who cooperated closely with them have relied heavily on the eagerness of federal courts, especially the Circuit Court of Appeals for the District of Columbia, to interpret environmental statutes and to issue "action forcing" decisions. As Melnick says: "While Congress as a whole shouted out its opposition to ISR, the court heard only the congressional insiders who wrote—one is compelled to say surreptitiously—the purposely convoluted wording of the statute."

The statute discussed by Maass was interpreted in the following case. The case involved an SIP, which is a State Implementation Plan specifying how the state will comply with federal air pollution requirements. Before the 1977 amendments discussed by Maass, the Environmental Protection Agency (EPA) required that a State SIP incorporate an Indirect Source Review. An Indirect Source Review (ISR) is a pre-construction review of facilities, such as shopping centers, which are likely to attract significant motor traffic, thereby increasing air pollutants. If the State did not comply by a certain date, the EPA would adopt a plan for the state, including ISRs. The ISRs promulgated by the EPA, however, drew heavy criticism because they represented a significant federal intrusion into the traditionally local domain of land use control. As noted by Maass, Congress suspended EPA's authority to require ISRs. The case dealt with a situation in which a state had promulgated its own ISR prior to the 1977 amendments.

Manchester Environmental Coalition v. E.P.A.
612 F.2d 56 (2d Cir.1979).

■ Timbers, Judge. * * *

* * * [The 1977 amendments] created an anomalous situation: federally promulgated ISRs were suspended, while those states which had complied voluntarily with the EPA's requirement to establish an ISR could abolish their ISRs only if they could show that their SIPS were still capable of achieving and maintaining the NAAQS [Editor—National Ambient Air Quality Standards]. To rectify this situation, Congress included in the 1977 amendments to the Clean Air Act a special provision severely limiting the EPA's authority over ISRs, and permitting the states to revise their SIPs "provided that such plan meets the requirements of this section." 42 U.S.C. § 7410(a)(5)(A)(iii)(Supp. I 1977).

Following the enactment of the 1977 amendments and pursuant to the provision referred to above, Connecticut submitted to the Administrator a series of revisions of its ISR, including a proposal to eliminate pre-construction review of all indirect sources except highways and airports. After receiving comments on these proposed revisions, the Administrator approved them on January 26, 1979. The Administrator's approval was premised on his view that § 7410(a)(5)(A)(iii) permitted a state to revise its ISR so long as the state complied with the section's procedural requirements of proper notice and hearing. According to Administrator's construction of the section, it did not require the state to show that its SIP was capable of achieving and maintaining the NAAQS, despite the revocation of the ISR. * * *

The plain meaning of the statutory language would seem to be that a state may revoke its ISR provided that its overall SIP complies with all of the requirements of § 7410—both procedural and substantive. * * *

The EPA, however, has construed the proviso to refer only to the procedural requirements of § 7410, although it concedes that its construction is "difficult to reconcile" with the words of the statute. 43 Fed. Reg. 10709 (1978). Before us the EPA has attempted to support its construction by urging various arguments of policy, legislative intent and possible intra-statutory conflict. We find none to be persuasive. * * *

* * * [N]one of the arguments advanced by the EPA is sufficient to overcome the clear import of the statutory language itself.* * *

The one thing that emerges clearly from the 1977 Amendments is the congressional commitment to the overriding goal of the Clean Air Act, namely, Clean air. H.R.Rep. No. 294, at 3, reprinted in [1977] U.S. Code Cong. & Ad. News 1570. * * *

Accordingly, since we find the EPA's construction of the ISR deletion proviso untenable, the EPA order is vacated and the case is remanded to the EPA for further proceedings consistent with this opinion.

Was the Court's reading of the statutory text faithful to a legislator's likely understanding of the statute, as filtered through the committee report? Recall the committee report language—"the administrator would be prohibited outright from requiring indirect source review, either directly or indirectly."

e) CONSTITUTIONAL THEORY AND THE TEXT

Judge Easterbrook and Justice Scalia have been among the most outspoken critics of relying on legislative history, in part because it may violate constitutional theory.[43]

Matter of Sinclair, 870 F.2d 1340 (7th Cir.1989)(Judge Easterbrook):

[Using legislative history to prove context is different from] the claim that legislative intent is *the* basis of interpretation, that the text of the law is simply evidence of the real rule. In such a regimen

---

43. See also Slawson, Legislative History and the Need to Bring Statutory Interpretation Under the Rule of Law, 44 Stan. L. Rev. 383 (1992); Note, Why Learned Hand Would Never Consult Legislative History Today, 105 Harv. L. Rev. 1005 (1992).

legislative history is not a way to understand the text but is more authentic, because more proximate, expression of legislators' will. One may say in reply that legislative history is a poor guide to legislators' intent because it is written by the staff rather than by members of Congress, because it is often losers' history ("If you can't get your proposal into the bill, at least write the legislative history to make it look as if you'd prevailed"), because it becomes a crutch ("There's no need for us to vote on the amendment if we can write a little legislative history"), because it complicates the task of execution and obedience (neither judges nor those whose conduct is supposed to be influenced by the law can know what to do without delving into legislative recesses, a costly and uncertain process). Often there is so much legislative history that a court can manipulate the meaning of a law by choosing which snippets to emphasize and by putting hypothetical questions—questions to be answered by inferences from speeches rather than by reference to the text, so that great discretion devolves on the (judicial) question-er. Sponsors of opinion polls know that a small change in the text of a question can lead to large differences in the answer. Legislative history offers willful judges an opportunity to pose questions and devise answers, with predictable divergence in results. These and related concerns have lead to skepticism about using legislative history to find legislative intent. These cautionary notes are well taken, but even if none were salient there would still be a hurdle to the sort of argument pressed in our case.

Statutes are law, not evidence of law. References to "intent" in judicial opinions do not imply that legislators' motives and beliefs, as opposed to their public acts, establish the norms to which all others must conform. "Original meaning" rather than "intent" frequently captures the interpretive task more precisely, reminding us that it is the work of the political branches (the "meaning") rather than of the courts that matters, and that their work acquires its meaning when enacted ("originally"). Revisionist history may be revelatory; revisionist judging is simply unfaithful to the enterprise.
* * *

An opinion poll revealing the wishes of Congress would not translate to legal rules. Desires become rules only after clearing procedural hurdles, designed to encourage deliberation and expose proposals (and arguments) to public view and recorded vote. Resort to "intent" as a device to short-circuit these has no more force than the opinion poll—less, because the legislative history is written by the staff of a single committee and not subject to a vote or veto. The Constitution established a complex of procedures, including presidential approval (or support by two-thirds of each house). It would demean the constitutionally prescribed method of legislating to suppose that its elaborate apparatus for deliberation on, amending, and approving a text is just a way to create some *evidence* about the law, while the *real* source of legal rules is the mental processes of legislators. We know from INS v. Chadha, 462 U.S. 919 (1983), that the express disapproval of one house of Congress cannot change the law, largely because it removes the President from the process; it would therefore be surprising if "intents" subject to neither vote nor veto could be sources of law. [Editor—Chadha held that the legislative veto was unconstitutional—see Chapter 17. Chadha certainly means that Committee Reports are not binding law, but does that prevent courts from using legislative history on a selective basis to determine statutory meaning?]

See also Continental Can Co., Inc. v. Chicago Truck Drivers, Helpers and Warehouse Workers Union Pension Fund, 916 F.2d 1154 (7th Cir.1990) ("substantially all" cannot mean 50.1%), where Judge Easterbrook states:

You don't have to be Ludwig Wittgenstein or Hans–Georg Gadamer to know that successful communication depends on meanings shared by interpretive communities. Texts are addressed to readers * * *. Authors' private meanings—meanings subjectively held but not communicated—do not influence the readers' beliefs.

And in Wisconsin Public Intervenor v. Mortier, 501 U.S. 597 (1991), Justice Scalia (concurring in the judgment) stated:

All we know for sure is that the full Senate adopted the text that we have before us here, as did the full House, pursuant to the procedures prescribed by the Constitution; and that that text, having been transmitted to the President and approved by him, again pursuant to the procedures prescribed by the Constitution, became law. On the important question before us today * * * we should try to give the text its fair meaning, whatever various committees might have had to say—thereby affirming the proposition that we are a Government of laws not of committee reports. That is, at least, the way I prefer to proceed.

The Easterbrook/Scalia assault on legislative history must deal with an annoying fact: the tradition of judicial reliance on legislative history. Here are some of their responses.

In Wisconsin Public Intervenor v. Mortier, 501 U.S. 597 (1991), Justice Scalia responded to the majority's claim that judicial reliance on legislative history was an old practice with a long pedigree stretching back to Chief Justice Marshall. In the following quote, he seems to be laying the groundwork for rejecting this practice on the ground that it is a relatively recent phenomenon.

* * * I must reply [ ] to the Court's assertion that the "practice of utilizing legislative history reaches well into [our] past," for which proposition it cites an opinion written by none other than John Marshall himself, Wallace v. Parker, 6 Pet. 680 (1832). What the Court neglects to explain is that what it means by "the practice

of utilizing legislative history" is not the practice of utilizing legislative history for the purpose of giving authoritative cc..tent to the meaning of a statutory text—which is the only practice I object to. * * * As late as 1897, we stated quite clearly that there is "a general acquiescence in the doctrine that debates in Congress are not appropriate sources of information from which to discover the meaning of the language of a statute passed by that body." United States v. Trans–Missouri Freight Assn., 166 U.S. 290, 318. And even as late as 1953, the practice of using legislative history in that fashion was novel enough that Justice Jackson could dismiss it as a "psychoanalysis of Congress," and a "weird endeavor." United States v. Public Utilities Comm'n. 345 U.S. 295, 319 (Jackson, J., concurring). It is, in short, almost entirely a phenomenon of this century—and in its extensive use a very recent phenomenon. See, e.g., Carro & Brann, Use of Legislative Histories by the United States Supreme Court: A Statistical Analysis, 9 J. Legis. 282 (1982); Wald, Some Observations on the Use of Legislative History in the 1981 Supreme Court Term, 68 Iowa L. Rev. 195, 196–197 (1983). [Editor—Recall the earlier historical note about legislative history. Is there a good reason why it is a 20th Century phenomenon.]

In Matter of Sinclair, 870 F.2d 1340 (7th Cir.1989), Judge Easterbrook explained how traditional practice regarding use of legislative history might be justified.

Which prevails in the event of conflict, the statute or its legislative history? * * *

* * * The reports [of Supreme Court cases] teem with statements such as: "When we find the terms of a statute unambiguous, judicial inquiry is complete". * * * Less frequently, yet with equal conviction, the Court writes: "When aid to the construction of the meaning of words, as used in the statute, is available, there certainly can be no 'rule of law' which forbids its use, however clear the words may appear on 'superficial examination.' " Some cases boldly stake out a middle ground, saying, for example: "only the most extraordinary showing of contrary intentions from [the legislative history] would justify a limitation on the 'plain meaning' of the statutory language." This implies that once in a blue moon the legislative history trumps the statute (as opposed to affording a basis for its interpretation) but does not help locate such strange astronomical phenomena. These lines of cases have coexisted for a century, and many cases contain statements associated with two or even all three of them, not recognizing the tension.

What's a court to do? The answer lies in distinguishing among uses of legislative history. An unadorned "plain meaning" approach to interpretation supposes that words have meanings divorced from their contexts—linguistic, structural, functional, social, historical. Language is a process of communication that works only when authors and readers share a set of rules and meanings. In re

Erickson, 815 F.2d 1090 (7th Cir.1987). What "clearly" means one thing to a reader unacquainted with the circumstances of the utterance—including social conventions prevailing at the time of drafting—may mean something else to a reader with a different background. Legislation speaks across the decades, during which legal institutions and linguistic conventions change. To decode words one must frequently reconstruct the legal and political culture of the drafters. Legislative history may be invaluable in revealing the setting of the enactment and the assumptions its authors entertained about how their words would be understood. It may show, too, that words with a denotation "clear" to an outsider are terms of art, with an equally "clear" but different meaning to an insider. It may show too that the words leave gaps, for short phrases cannot address all human experience; understood in context, the words may leave to the executive and judicial branches the task of adding flesh to bones. These we take to be the points of cases * * * holding that judges may learn from the legislative history even when the text is "clear". Clarity depends on context, which legislative history may illuminate. The process is objective; the search is not for the contents of the author's heads but for the rules of the language they used. * * *

* * * To treat the text as conclusive evidence of law is to treat it *as* law—which under the constitutional structure it is. Legislative history then may help a court discover but may not change the original meaning. * * * Legislative history may show the meaning of the texts—may show, indeed, that a text "plain" at first reading has a strikingly different meaning—but may not be used to show an "intent" at variance with the meaning of the text. * * * This approach also supplies the underpinning for the belief that legislative history is "only admissible to solve doubt and not to create it", which punctuates the U.S. Reports. Legislative history helps us learn what Congress meant by what it said, but it is not a source of legal rules competing with those found in the U.S. Code.

[Editor—Easterbrook would, I assume, look kindly on using a statement in legislative history that Congress "was concerned with racial discrimination, especially its impact on Eastern Europeans"— as evidence that "race" meant ethnicity. This statement is the kind of unselfconscious presentation of examples that is both especially reliable evidence of textual meaning and unlikely to be manipulative. Would he also rely on an explicit statement in a committee report that "intern" includes "resident?" Are such explicit statements less reliable evidence of textual meaning? If the courts draw a distinction between explicit statements and unselfconscious examples, won't savvy legislators simply salt legislative history with examples instead of explicit statements about meaning?]

QUESTIONS

1. *Trumping text.* What should a court do when the text is clear but legislative history is to the contrary? Here are some examples.

Example 1. In Commissioner v. Acker, 361 U.S. 87 (1959), the statute imposed tax penalties on a "substantial underestimate of estimated tax" and on failure to file "a declaration of estimated tax." The agency's regulations stated that failure to file was the equivalent of filing a zero declaration, thereby resulting in two penalties on the non-filer. In support of the agency regulation, the government cited the fact that the Senate and Conference Report contained the statement found in the regulation. The Court rejected reliance on the legislative history, as follows:

> * * * Bearing in mind that we are here concerned with an attempt to justify the imposition of a second penalty for the same omission for which Congress has specifically provided a separate and very substantial penalty, we cannot say that the legislative history of the initial enactment is so persuasive as to overcome the [statutory language] which seems clearly to contemplate the filing of an estimate before there can be an underestimate.

Justice Frankfurter, with Justices Harlan and Clark, dissented. Do you agree with their reasoning?

> English courts would decide the case as it is being decided here. They would do so because English courts do not recognize the relevance of legislative explanations of the meaning of a statute made in the course of its enactment. If Parliament desires to put a gloss on the meaning of ordinary language, it must incorporate it in the text of legislation. Quite otherwise has been the process of statutory construction practiced by this Court over the decades in scores and scores of cases. Congress can be the glossator of the words it legislatively uses either by writing its desired meaning, however odd, into the text of its enactment, or by a contemporaneously authoritative explanation accompanying a statute. The most authoritative form of such explanation is a congressional report defining the scope and meaning of proposed legislation. The most authoritative report is a Conference Report acted upon by both Houses and therefore unequivocally representing the will of both Houses as the joint legislative body.
>
> No doubt to find failure to file a declaration of estimated income to be a "substantial underestimate" would be to attribute to Congress a most unlikely meaning for that phrase in § 294(d)(2) simpliciter. But if Congress chooses by appropriate means for expressing its purpose to use language with an unlikely and even odd meaning, it is not for this Court to frustrate its purpose. The Court's task is to construe not English but congressional English. Our problem is not what do ordinary English words mean, but what did Congress mean them to mean. "It is said that when the meaning of language is plain we are not to resort to evidence in order to raise doubts. That is

rather an axiom of experience than a rule of law, and does not preclude consideration of persuasive evidence if it exists." Boston Sand & Gravel v. United States, 278 U.S. 41, 48.

Example 2. In Hearings before the Joint Committee on the Organization of Congress, 103d Cong., 1st Sess. 84–85 (1993), Judge Kozinski discusses 28 U.S.C. § 1491(a)(3), enacted by the Federal Court Improvements Act of 1982. The statutory language was:

> To afford complete relief on any contract claim brought before the contract is awarded, [the United States Claims Court, now renamed the Court of Federal Claims] shall have exclusive jurisdiction to grant declaratory judgments and equitable and extraordinary relief.

Judge Kozinski objects strongly to judicial reliance on legislative history to undermine this text, as follows:

> * * * In discussing this section, the House and Senate Reports explain that exclusive doesn't mean exclusive, but sort of exclusive: This enlarged authority [of the Court of Federal Claims] is exclusive of the Board of Contract Appeals and not to the exclusion of the district courts.
>
> Now, this presents a classic example of what, in my book, is a misuse of legislative history. The Senate and House Judiciary Committees agreed on language that—apparently—did not reflect their intended purpose. Somehow they became aware of the problem but, for unknown reasons, they chose to leave it in the statute and provide a fix by way of legislative history. In such a case, the legislative history does not merely cast light on the statutory language; it recasts the language altogether.
>
> A court faced with this situation is put in a difficult position. Even among judges who rely on legislative history, statutory language usually still comes first. Many are therefore reluctant to look past very clear statutory language only to find equally clear, but utterly contradictory, legislative reports. * * *
>
> Predictably enough, the courts that have interpreted Section 1491(a)(3) have split * * *.
>
> The Judiciary Committee's attempt to preempt this confusion by means of committee reports rather than statutory language just hasn't worked and has had several unfortunate consequences.
>
> One, it has created a split among the Federal circuits that will eventually have to be corrected by the Supreme Court or Congress.
>
> Two, it has caused long-term uncertainty in the law, which in turn wastes time, money, lots of paper and other judicial resources. By my count, there have now been at least 20 published opinions in the Federal courts wrestling with this problem.
>
> Three, there has been shift of authority away from Congress and toward the Federal courts. When Congress speaks with a clear,

purposeful voice, judges seldom ignore it, no matter how much they may disagree with the result—barring unconstitutionality, of course. The more wavering the voice of Congress—as when there is a square conflict between text and legislative history—the more likely it is that policy preferences of the individual judges will prevail.

Four, the confusion surrounding 1491(a)(3) may have legitimized, to some extent, a fuzzy reading of other portions of the same statute. "Look," a judge might say, "it is clear from Section 1491(a)(3) that Congress didn't mean everything it said in the Federal Court Improvements Act of 1982, so I can be just a little bit creative in interpreting other parts of the statute."

2. *Unclear text.* What should a court do (what would Easterbrook and Scalia do) in the following situation: the text is unclear and the legislative history contains a statement about specific legislative intent, which does not shed light on the meaning of the text? In such a case, no plain meaning would be undermined by relying on the legislative history. However, the text of the legislative history has not been passed by Congress and signed by the President. Moreover, the risk of political manipulation is no less present when the statutory text is unclear. Should the court rely on the legislative history?

3. *Intentionalist textualism.* In Matter of Sinclair, supra, Judge Easterbrook is willing to use legislative history for the limited purpose of "learn[ing] what Congress meant by what it said." How does this differ from other uses of legislative history? Does it mean that legislative history can inform us which of several *textual* meanings the legislative author intended—call it "intentionalist textualism"? Does using legislative history to determine textual meaning undermine the limitations which the textualist would impose on the use of legislative history? After all, the court is still looking at language other than the statutory text adopted by the legislature to shed light on statutory meaning. You might argue that knowledgeable statutory audiences will consult the legislative history to find out which of several textual meanings the legislature intended. But haven't knowledgeable audiences relied on legislative history for decades to determine statutory meaning, not limited to what the legislative history tells us about the meaning of the text? Why can the judge look to legislative history for one purpose but not the other?

Which, if any, of the following is an example of intentionalist textualism?

Example 1. Corning Glass Works v. Brennan, 417 U.S. 188 (1974), involved the choice between technical and lay meanings. The Court first affirmed that "where Congress has used technical words or terms of art, 'it (is) proper to explain them by reference to the art or science to which they (are) appropriate.' " It then resorted to legislative history to demonstrate that a technical meaning was intended, stating: "This principle is particularly salutary where, as here, the legislative history reveals that Congress incorporated words having a special meaning within the field regulated by the statute so as to overcome objections by industry representatives that statutory definitions were vague and incomplete." Therefore, although "a layman might well assume that time of day worked reflects one aspect of a job's 'working conditions,' the term has a different and much more specific meaning in the language of industrial relations," which the Court adopted.[44]

Example 2. In Zicherman v. Korean Air Lines Co., Ltd., 116 S.Ct. 629 (1996), the issue was the meaning of the word "damage" in the 1929 Warsaw Convention, a treaty dealing with compensation in lawsuits arising from plane crashes. The treaty's dollar limits on recovery were inapplicable in the circumstances of this case—willful misconduct—but the question remained whether the survivors could recover for "loss of society" damages (loss of love, affection, and companionship). All the treaty said was that "the carrier shall be liable for damage sustained * * *." The treaty's governing official text was French ("damage" was a translation of the French word "dommage"). The Court first concluded that the meaning of "damage" was not limited to what the word meant in French law in 1929. Adopting French law was implausible, the Court said, given knowledge among the contracting states in 1929 that the law on damage recovery varied widely among different jurisdictions. The Court then concluded that the meaning of "damage" was left to the adjudicating courts in each state. To support this conclusion, the Court (per Justice Scalia) referred to legislative history of the Warsaw Convention. In reading the following, consider: (1) whether this is an example of intentionalist textualism or reliance on legislative history to answer a question about specific intent; (2) whether Scalia reaches this conclusion only because this is a treaty, or would his reasoning also apply to statutes?

> Because a treaty ratified by the United States is not only the law of this land, but also an agreement among sovereign powers, we have traditionally considered as aids to its interpretation the negotiating and drafting history (travaux preparatoires) * * *. In the drafting history, the only statements we know of that directly discuss the point were made by the [committee] which did the preparatory work for the two Conferences [ ] that produced the Warsaw Convention. In its report of May 15, 1928, the Committee stated:
>
>> It was asked whether it would not be possible, in this respect, to determine the category of damages subject to reparations.
>>
>> Although this question seemed very interesting, it was not possible to find a satisfactory solution before knowing exactly the legislation of the various countries. It was understood that the question would be studied later on, when the issue of knowing which are the persons, who according to the various national laws, have the right to take action against the carrier, will have been elucidated.
>
> To the same effect is the following passage from the [ ] Report accompanying the 1929 draft:

---

44. See also Director, Office of Workers' Compensation Programs v. Greenwich Collieries, 512 U.S. 267 (1994)(Souter, J., dissenting) (legislative history establishes that Congress intended "burden of proof" to mean "burden of production," not "burden of persuasion".)

> The question was asked of knowing if one could determine who the persons upon whom the action devolves in the case of death are, and what are the damages subject to reparation. It was not possible to find a satisfactory solution to this double problem, and the [Committee] esteemed that this question of private international law should be regulated independently from the present Convention.

Example 3. Suppose a court relied on a statement in the legislative history that "representative" includes an elected judge or that "family" includes a gay couple; or that the phrase "directly affects the coastal zone" does not refer to activities on the Outer Continental Shelf. Are these examples of relying on legislative history to determine textual meaning (which Easterbrook would allow) or intent (about which he is skeptical)?

4. *Legislature intend absurdity?* Justice Scalia is willing to look at legislative history to be sure that Congress did not intend a result which he thinks is absurd and therefore not presumptively within the scope of the statute. Green v. Bock Laundry Machine Co., 490 U.S. 504, 527 (1989) (concurring in the judgment). Is that consistent with Scalia's usual view rejecting use of legislative history?

f) Judicial Alternatives to Relying on Legislative History

The strengths and weaknesses of legislative history do not exist in a decisionmaking vacuum. A judge who does not use legislative history must rely on other criteria of statutory meaning to interpret the statute. Legislative history may turn out, despite its weaknesses, to be preferable. In other words, if not legislative history, then what?

First, the judge might rely on linguistic canons, such as the absence of surplusage and consistent use of language. Some linguistic canons genuinely attempt to identify how texts are understood (for example, ejusdem generis). But many canons are simply rules of thumb that are less concerned with how people understand language (for example, expressio unius est exclusio alterius).

Second, a judge might rely on substantive canons, such as the rule of lenity and refusing to imply a waiver of state sovereign immunity in federal court. These canons are controversial because they have substantive implications.

Which is better—legislative history or reliance on linguistic and substantive canons? Perhaps the textualist's rejection of legislative history is in part motivated by a preference for the interpretive canons, as more or less clear guides to statutory meaning, to reduce judicial lawmaking discretion. Is that an ephemeral hope?

g) Impact on Legislators of Courts Not Relying on Legislative History

A final consideration in deciding what judges should do with legislative history is the effect on the legislative process of limiting judicial use of legislative history. A lot of criticism of legislative history proceeds on the assumption that legislators are shirking their responsibility to decide political issues through explicit legislation, perhaps even trying to manipulate results. If judges reject legislative history, so the argument goes, a better legislative process will occur because legislatures will stop salting the legislative history with statements about legislative intent.

There may, however, be some good reasons why legislators rely on legislative history, rather than amending the statutory text. First, opening up the statutory language for amendment after agreement has been reached on a text may invite filibusters or further amendments, which could delay and even kill a statute, especially near adjournment. Second, detailed statutory drafting may contribute to an unintelligible statute.

Third, there may be genuine doubt about how far to carry a principle on which there is general agreement. Justice Breyer recounts an example in Breyer, On the Uses of Legislative History in Interpreting Statutes, 65 S.Cal.L.Rev. 845 (1992). The issue was whether a provision of federal law pre-empted state law. The bill dealt with federal aid to states for urban mass transit and provided that the Secretary of Labor had to certify that the state had made "fair and equitable arrangements * * * to protect the interests of employees affected" by transit funding. Unambiguous and uncontested legislative history said that the "employee protection" provision did not pre-empt state law. Although the "employee protection" rule was controversial in Congress, the "no pre-emption" legislative history was not. But why not put the pre-emption language into the statutory text? Breyer argues that stating the guiding principle in legislative history leaves room for judicial exceptions as the court encounters specific cases. Moreover, attempts to gain agreement on specific statutory language might doom an entire bill. How far would you carry this argument? If the legislative history concerned an issue central to the bill's purpose or there was evidence that the pre-emption issue was probably controversial, should the judge rely on the legislative history?

10.05   STATE LEGISLATIVE HISTORY

As noted earlier, state legislative history in the form of committee reports, legislative hearings, and records of legislative debates are much less commonly available than at the federal level. Fisher, Guide to State Legislative Materials, periodically updated information about available state legislative history but is now out of date.

a) JUDICIAL GUIDES TO FINDING LEGISLATIVE HISTORY

State legislative history is so hard to find and unfamiliar to many lawyers that one state court took the unusual step of appending instructions on how to locate legislative materials as an Appendix to an opinion. Here are some excerpts from Dillehey v. State, 815 S.W.2d 623 (Tex.Cr.App.1991).   What kinds of legislative history does Texas have?

APPENDIX A

COMPILING TEXAS LEGISLATIVE HISTORY at the Legislative Reference Library State Capitol—Austin, Texas

Unlike U.S. legislation, Texas legislative history is not written and must be compiled by the researcher. The following steps should be taken by the researcher; 1. Determine the bill number and the session which enacted the bill. 2. Examine the original bill file. 3. Listen to the tape recordings of the public hearings of committee meetings and debate in the House and Senate. 4. Examine other documents which may be helpful. * * *

1. DETERMINE THE BILL NUMBER AND THE SESSION WHICH ENACTED THE BILL

A. Locate the desired section or article of the law (the statute) in Vernon's Annotated Texas Statutes * * *.

B. The end of the statute has a history note which lists all the changes made to the statute. Locate the citation to the General and Special Laws of Texas (referred to as the session laws).

Example: Acts 1977, 65th Leg., p. 2411, ch. 571

C. SESSION LAWS—(General and Special Laws of Texas). The session laws are the full text of the final (enrolled) version of all of the bills passed by the Legislature in the order they are signed by the Governor. The bills are called acts and are numbered by chapters. Locate the bill in the session laws by using the citation from the statute to find the volume for the legislative session, the chapter, and/or the page number. Example: The session laws for 1977, from the 65th Legislature, page 2411, chapter 571. Look up the chapter in the session laws, and the bill number is shown directly under the chapter number. Example: Chapter 571 H.B. 2455 number. * * *

2. EXAMINE THE ORIGINAL BILL FILE

A. The bill file typically contains the various versions of the bill, the bill analysis, and the fiscal note. Versions of the bill may include the introduced, committee, engrossed, and the final (enrolled) version.

B. The bill analysis is a brief document which gives a short explanation of the bill, and a summary of each section of the bill. The bill analysis is prepared for the committee version of the bill, not the final version of the bill.

C. The Legislative Reference Library has the bill files on microfilm for bills from the 63rd session (1973) to the present. * * *

3. LISTEN TO THE TAPE RECORDINGS OF THE PUBLIC HEARINGS OF COMMITTEE MEETING AND DEBATE IN THE HOUSE AND SENATE

A. Beginning with the 63rd session (1973), the Legislature began tape recording the public hearings held by committees, and the debate in the House or the Senate. * * * In order to listen to the tapes, you will need the dates of these hearings and debates.

B. Locate the bill's history in the House Bill History volume or the Senate Bill History volume for each session. Note whether the committee is from the House or the Senate (indicated by H or S), the name of the committee, and the date(s) of any public hearing or formal meetings held by that committee. Note the dates of the second and third reading (which is when any debate may have taken place) in both the House and the Senate.

C. You may go to the buildings shown below to listen to the tapes, or you may order copies (prepaid unless you are a State agency) of the tapes. [Editor—Tel. Nos. omitted.] (The time it takes to get your tapes depends on how busy the staff is at that time. Generally, if the Legislature is out of session, it takes only a week, however, waits of up to two months (for Senate tapes) are not unheard of.)

D. The bill history for bills dating before 1973 is given only in the House and Senate Journals for each session. There is a bill history index in the last volume of each of the Journals for each session. No tape recordings are available. Very little information is available for these bills. There may have been an interim study for major legislation.

4. EXAMINE OTHER DOCUMENTS WHICH MAY BE HELPFUL

A. Legislative Interim Committee Reports. Any reports or studies which may have been made by any standing or special legislative committees during the time period between sessions (the interim) are listed in the card catalog of the Legislative Reference Library. These reports are listed in the card catalog by chairman, title, and subject.

B. House Research Organization (HRO) Bill Analysis.

(1) Beginning with the 65th session (1977), the HRO began preparing bill analyses for some bills when the bill reached the 2nd reading in the House. The bill analyses are compiled in Daily Floor Reports.

(2) Locate the bill analysis by noting the date of the 2nd reading in the House, which is given in the bill history. Beginning with the 67th session (1981), the last volume of the Reports also has an index giving the date of the bill analysis.

(3) Then locate the bill analysis in the Daily Floor Report on the date indicated. You may photocopy the bill analysis. Some courts have accepted the HRO bill analysis for proving intent.

* * *

The legislative history information guide in this appendix was provided by the Legislative Reference Library, State Capitol Building, Austin, Texas.

b) State Responses to the Contemporary Debate

When states do have available legislative history, they must decide where they stand in the contemporary debate over the use of legislative materials. In the following case, the majority rejected the dissent's reliance on Scalia's negative view of legislative history. There is as yet no complete survey of the impact at the state level of the current debate about legislative history.

Western Communications Inc. v. Deschutes County

788 P.2d 1013 (Or.App.1990).

■ Riggs, Judge.

* * * The trial court ordered defendant county to disclose to plaintiff, the publisher of the Bend Bulletin [newspaper], the ledger cards on which the county records monthly transient room tax payments from each lodging operator in the unincorporated portions of the county. * * * Because of a change in the applicable law while we have had the case under advisement, we vacate the trial court's decision and remand for further proceedings. * * *

[Editor—The issue in this case was whether the statutory change applied retroactively.]

The legislature intended that [the new law] apply to this case. The bill originated in the Senate, but the crucial action took place in the House Judiciary Committee. Senator Fawbush, whose district included Deschutes County, was the first witness to discuss the bill. In his written testimony, he stated:

"Last year, the Bend Bulletin newspaper sued Deschutes County for access to individual room tax revenue figures, and the Court ruled in favor of the Bulletin. While the court felt that the lodging industry and Deschutes County made a good case for the proprietary nature of such information, it ruled that the existing Public Disclosure Law provides only that the 'public interest' be considered, unless specifically exempt.

"It is extremely important that this information be kept confidential. While it is of no apparent interest to the general public the release of such information could be very damaging to the individual lodging establishments by creating an unfair competitive advantage.

"I believe that it is important to keep this information confidential, as are most other forms of business and personal income. SB 721 would 'fix' the statute to address the court's interpretation, and offer the protection that I believe was and is intended by state and local government." House Committee on the Judiciary, Subcommittee on Civil Law and Judicial Administration, Minutes, May 15, 1989, p 2 and Exhibit A.

After Senator Fawbush's testimony Steven Crew, legal counsel for the Oregon Lodging Association, at whose request Senator Fawbush introduced the bill, testified. The minutes summarize a colloquy with a committee member: "Rep. Mannix: Assumes case is pending?" Crew: It is on appeal. "Rep. Mannix: Wouldn't emergency clause be good in bill, retroactive clause?" Crew: Yes. House Committee on the Judiciary, Subcommittee on Civil Law and Judicial Administration, Minutes, May 15, 1989, p.3. The Committee thereafter added an emergency clause to the bill. Or.Laws 1989, ch. 925, § 2.

Our role in construing a statute is to determine the legislature's intent. ORS 174.020. Deciding the effect that the legislature intended a change in the law to have on events that have already occurred may be a difficult matter. It requires careful attention to the legislative purpose, not the application of so-called rules of statutory construction * * *. In this case we must decide what the legislature intended when it declared that ORS 192.502(16) "takes effect on its passage."

It may well be that in most cases an emergency clause does not express a legislative intent to apply a new law to previous events. There is no doubt, however, that this emergency clause expressed the legislature's intent that the amendment to ORS 192.502 govern this litigation. Senator Fawbush introduced the bill in order to overcome the trial court's decision in this case. Thereafter, another witness told the committee that this case was on appeal. A representative immediately suggested adding an emergency clause to the bill in order to ensure that the change would be retroactive and would thereby control this case. The committee added such a clause, and the bill became law with that change. Although the legislature may not have chosen the best vehicle to achieve its purpose, there is no question of what it intended to accomplish by the vehicle that it did choose. It wanted a different result in this case from the one that the trial court had reached.

We follow the legislature's intent and hold that ORS 192.502(16) governs our decision. It supersedes the exemptions on which defendants previously relied. As a result, most of the information that plaintiff sought now appears to be exempt from disclosure. However, the parties did not try the case with reference to the new criteria for determining what the County must disclose, and we cannot determine from the present record which, if any, requested items may not be exempt. The trial court must decide that issue on remand. * * *

■ Joseph, Chief Judge, dissenting in part; concurring in part.

The majority wins, and permanently retires, the Circulating Award for Most Creative (and Absurd) Use of Legislative History. It says: "The legislature intended that [the amendment of ORS 192.502 by Or.Laws 1989, ch. 925, § 1] apply to this case." If the legislature had expressed itself explicitly, we would not have this dispute. All that the majority is able to cite as proof of legislative intent is the ambiguous testimony of the senator who sponsored the amendment and the apparently confused response by a representative who was a member of the committee. Even on that record, it is notable that the representative referred to an "emergency clause" and a "retroactive clause."

I hope that I will always be able to apply the words that the legislature actually uses and avoid the temptation to read committee testimony involving one witness and one legislator as the intention of 59 other representatives and 30 senators. What the legislature clearly and unambiguously did was to add only an emergency clause. That leaves no room for result-oriented rewriting of the legislation. The legislator on whom the majority relies apparently knew more about the meaning (and non-meaning) of an emergency clause than the majority does. * * *

The majority uses that addition by the committee as a bootstrap to lift itself into a position of being entitled to look for the legislature's intent in doing something or other. What the majority sees as "something or other" is not very clear. What is clear is that, if the majority were to apply what it contemptuously refers to as "so-called rules of statutory construction" [ ] it would find itself in deep, deep trouble. Instead, it enters into paying "careful attention to the legislative purpose." It acknowledges that "in most cases an emergency clause does not express a legislative intent to apply a new law to previous events." To be sure, in no case has the Supreme Court, or this court, ever held that an emergency clause expresses a legislative intent that a new law determine the consequences of completed events. * * *

In other words, an emergency clause declares exactly what the Oregon Constitution says that it does. If the legislature wants a statute to affect past events, it can and should say so. We should not make ourselves look ludicrous in order to do something that the legislature could have done simply but did not do at all.

[Editor—In a footnote, the dissent adopted Scalia's position, stating as follows: As Justice Scalia put it, concurring in INS v. Cardoza–Fonseca, 480 U.S. 421, 453 (1987): "Judges interpret laws rather than reconstruct legislators' intentions. Where the language of those laws is clear, we are not free to replace it with an unenacted legislative intention." In another case, United States v. Taylor, 487 U.S. 326, 345 (1988), Justice Scalia, again concurring, expressed the thought in a way clearly apropos this case: "The text is so unambiguous * * * that it must be assumed that what the

Members of the House and Senators thought they were voting for, and what the President thought he was approving when he signed the bill, was what the text plainly said, rather than what a few Representatives, or even a Committee Report, said it said. Where we are not prepared to be governed by what the legislative history says—to take, as it were, the bad with the good—we should not look to the legislative history at all. This text is eminently clear, and we should leave it at that."]

The majority responded to the dissent, stating that "[t]he dissent seems not to understand how the Oregon legislature functions. Because it generally decides issues in committees rather than on the floor, the dissent's approach would deny the possibility of ever analyzing legislative history to discover the legislative intent. That is not how the [Oregon] Supreme Court views the matter."

The Oregon Supreme Court has since stated how it would proceed to interpret legislation, requiring that the court first look at text and internal context in light of the statutory and case law rules of construction, and if and only if that produces an "unclear" determination of legislative intent, proceed to examine legislative history. Portland General Electric Co. v. Bureau of Labor and Industries, 859 P.2d 1143 (Or.1993). Would the Oregon Supreme Court, following this approach, have examined the legislative history in the Deschutes County case, involving the question of retroactivity?

10.06 BRITISH PRACTICE AND THE RELEVANCE OF INSTITUTIONAL SETTING

Until 1992, the British refused to use legislative history to interpret a statute, with limited exceptions. See Black–Clawson Ltd. v. Papierwerke Waldhof–Aschaffenburg A.G., [1975] 1 All E.R. 810. Legislative materials produced in the process of Parliamentary consideration of a bill were not supposed to be used at all. (These materials are published in Hansard, which is analogous to the United States Congressional Record.) Legislative history, other than legislative materials, could be used (1) only to shed light on the mischief and purpose at which the statute was aimed (2) when the text was unclear—not as evidence of specific legislative intent, and not to trump a clear text.

The legislative history which British courts could use under these limited circumstances consisted of reports issued by various committees, which are not analogous to the legislative standing committees in Congress. First, there is the Law Commission, which is a permanent nonlegislative body created by statute. Its members are leading judges, lawyers, and academics. Most of its work is the study of (supposedly) less politically controversial "law reform" areas of the law (e.g., criminal law). Second, Royal Commissions are appointed by the government to study specific problems. Its membership does not usually include legislators.

There are, in addition, committees specially appointed to deal with a particular problem that may result in proposed legislation and an accompanying report—(1) Parliamentary select committees consisting of legislators; (2) Departmental committees appointed by the Minister in charge of an executive department, which will investigate issues and often propose legislation.[45]

Evaluating the British approach requires making comparisons across legal cultures, which can be tricky.[46] The institutional setting in which the British operate may be so different from ours that it provides little basis for comparison. You can better evaluate the British approach and compare it to the United States if you know something about their system of government. In modern times, the government is controlled by the party with a Parliamentary majority. The members of Parliament are subject to a degree of party discipline that is far greater than anything known in our Congress. In this setting, deference to legislative history might mean excessive power for the majority party. Moreover, British statutes are drafted by a specialized group known as Parliamentary Counsel. They have a long professional tradition and write very detailed statutes. They are readily available to the government to do the kind of work that might be left to legislative history in this country.

On November 26, 1992, British practice changed. The Law Lords (analogous to the U.S. Supreme Court) decided Pepper v. Hart, abandoning their opposition to consulting legislative history under certain circumstances. The text must be ambiguous, obscure, or lead to an absurd result; the legislative history material must consist of one or more statements by a Minister or other promoter of the Bill; and the statements in the legislative history must be clear. Both practical and constitutional concerns about using legislative history, emphasized in earlier English cases, were rejected.

The case is especially interesting because the Law Lords originally concluded by a 5–1 vote that the government should win in a dispute with a taxpayer. Their attention was then drawn to legislative history favoring the taxpayer. There was a rehearing, chaired by Lord Chancellor Mackay, who had been added to the original panel of six judges. The Law Lords then voted 6–1 to consider legislative history, with only Lord Mackay dissenting from that conclusion. All five judges who originally found for the government now held for the taxpayer, based on the legislative history.

The issue involved the taxation of fringe benefits to employees of educational institutions who were allowed to send their children to school at reduced price. The Finance Act of 1976 imposed tax on an amount measured, not by "value," but by the "expense incurred in or in connection with

45. See generally Miers & Page, Legislation (1982).

46. See Jordan, Legislative History and Statutory Interpretation: The Relevance of English Practice, 29 U. San Franc. L. Rev. 1 (1994).

[the fringe benefit's] provision." The question was whether "expense" referred to the marginal costs to the employer (which were small and resulted in no tax), or average cost, which was substantial.

Here is some of what the Law Lords said. As you read the opinions, consider how broadly they would allow for use of legislative history. Do they limit the use of legislative history to what an "intentionalist textualist" would permit—that is, only to clarify the text's meaning; would they allow use of legislative history when a text is unclear, but the legislative history does not clarify textual meaning?

The continued practice of seriatim opinions in England affords us a glimpse of some subtle differences of opinion among the judges. Be alert to differences regarding the practical and constitutional concerns in using legislative history and regarding views about relying on the statutory text and purpose.

Although seriatim opinions remain the norm, the Law Lords now generally rely on one dominant opinion. However, because the order of publication follows seniority (after the Lord Chancellor), you do not reach the dominant opinion in the case—from Lord Browne–Wilkinson—until the fifth opinion.

Pepper v. Hart

[1993] 1 All ER 42, [1992] 3 WLR 1032.

■ **Lord Mackay of Clashfern, LC:** * * *

I believe that practically every question of statutory construction that comes before the courts will involve an argument that the case falls under one or more of [the conditions justifying resort to legislative history]. It follows that the parties' legal advisors will require to study Hansard in practically every such case to see whether or not there is any help to be gained from it. I believe this is an objection of real substance. It is a practical objection not one of principle * * *. Such an approach appears to me to involve the possibility at least of an immense increase in the cost of litigation in which statutory construction is involved. It is of course easy to overestimate such cost but it is I fear equally easy to underestimate it. Your Lordships have no machinery from which any estimate of such cost could be derived. * * *

I do not for my part find the objections in principle to be strong and I would certainly be prepared to agree the rule should no longer be adhered to were it not for the practical consideration to which I have referred * * *.

Lord Bridge of Harwich: [Editor—Lord Bridge originally voted for the government but changed his vote based on the legislative history. As for practical problems he stated as follows.] * * * It should, in my opinion, only be in the rare cases where the very issue of interpretation which the courts are called on to resolve has been addressed in parliamentary debate and where the promoter of the legislation has made a clear statement directed to that very issue, that reference to Hansard should be permitted. Indeed, it is only in such cases that reference to Hansard is likely to be of any assistance to the courts. Provided the relaxation of the previous exclusionary rule is so limited, I find it difficult to suppose that the additional cost of litigation or any other ground of objection can justify the court continuing to wear blinkers which, in such a case as this, conceal the vital clue to the intended meaning of an enactment. I recognize that practitioners will in some cases incur fruitless costs in the search for such a vital clue where none exists. But, on the other hand, where Hansard does provide the answer, it should be so clear to both parties that they will avoid the cost of litigation. * * *

Lord Griffiths: My Lords, I have long thought that the time had come to change the self-imposed judicial rule that forbade any reference to the legislative history of an enactment as an aid to its interpretation. The ever-increasing volume of legislation must inevitably result in ambiguities of statutory language which are not perceived at the time the legislation is enacted. The object of the court in interpreting legislation is to give effect so far as the language permits to the intention of the legislature. If the language proves to be ambiguous I can see no sound reason not to consult Hansard to see if there is a clear statement of the meaning that the words were intended to carry. The days have long passed when the courts adopted a strict constructionist view of interpretation which required them to adopt the literal meaning of the language. The courts now adopt a purposive approach which seeks to give effect to the true purpose of legislation and are prepared to look at much extraneous material that bears on the background against which the legislation was enacted. Why then cut ourselves off from the one source in which may be found an authoritative statement of the intention with which the legislation is placed before Parliament. * * *

I cannot agree with the view that consulting Hansard will add so greatly to the cost of litigation, that on this ground alone we should refuse to do so. Modern technology greatly facilitates the recall and display of material held centrally. I have to confess that on many occasions I have had recourse to Hansard, of course only to check if my interpretation had conflicted with an express parliamentary intention, but I can say that it does not take long to recall and assemble the relevant passages in which the particular section was dealt with in Parliament, nor does it take long to see if anything relevant was said. Furthermore if the search resolves the ambiguity it will in future save all the expense that would otherwise be incurred in fighting the rival interpretations through the courts. * * *

[Editor—Lord Griffiths then notes that he was alone in originally interpreting the law for the taxpayer. He goes on to state that "this case provides a dramatic vindication of the decision to consult Hansard; had your Lordships not agreed to do so the result would have been to place a very heavy burden of taxation on a large number of persons which Parliament never intended to impose."]

Lord Oliver of Aaylmerton: * * * I venture to add a few observations of my own only because I have to confess to having been a somewhat reluctant convert to the notion that the words which Parliament has chosen to use in a statute for the expression of its will may fall to be construed or modified by reference to what individual members of Parliament may have said in the course of debate or discussion preceding the passage of the Bill of law. A statute is, after all, the formal and complete intimation to the citizen of a particular rule of the law which he is enjoined, sometimes under penalty, to obey and by which he is both expected and entitled to regulate his conduct. We must, therefore, I believe, be very cautious in opening the door to the reception of material not readily or ordinarily accessible to the citizen whose rights and duties are to be affected by the words in which the legislature has elected to express its will.

But experience shows that language—and, particularly, language adopted or concurred in under the pressure of a tight parliamentary timetable—is not always a reliable vehicle for the complete or accurate translation of legislative intention; and I have been persuaded * * * that the circumstances of this case demonstrate that there is both the room and the necessity for a limited relaxation of the previously well-settled rule which excludes reference to parliamentary history as an aid to statutory construction.

It is, however, important to stress the limits within which such a relaxation is permissible and which are set out in the speech of my noble and learned friend. It can apply only where the expression of the legislative intention is genuinely ambiguous or obscure or where a literal or prima facie construction leads to a manifest absurdity and where the difficulty can be resolved by a clear statement directed to the matter in issue. Ingenuity can sometimes suggest ambiguity or obscurity where none exists in fact, and if the instant case were to be thought to justify the exercise of combing through reports of parliamentary proceedings in the hope of unearthing some perhaps incautious expression of opinion in support of an improbable secondary meaning, the relaxation of the rule might indeed lead to the fruitless expense and labour which has been prayed in aid in the past as one of the reasons justifying its maintenance. But so long as the three conditions expressed in the speech of my noble and learned friend are understood and observed, I do not, for my part, consider that the relaxation of the rule which he has proposed will lead to any significant increase in the cost of litigation or in the burden of research required to be undertaken by legal advisers.

Lord Browne–Wilkinson: * * * [Editor—Lord Browne–Wilkinson's opinion was the major opinion for the Law Lord's and therefore contains a full discussion of the legislative history. He first notes that "in practice from 1948 to 1975 the Revenue did not seek to extract tax on the basis of the average cost to the employer of providing in-house benefits," highlighting in particular the rules regarding concessionary fares for railroad and airline employees. ("In-house" refers to benefits provided to employees which are also provided to the public.) He then goes on to describe the 1976 legislative history.]

The Finance Bill 1976 sought to make a general revision of the taxation of benefits in kind. The existing legislation on fringe benefits was to be repealed. Clause 52 of the Bill as introduced eventually became § 61 of the 1976 Act and imposed a charge to tax on benefits in kind for higher-paid employees, i.e. those paid more than L5,000 per annum. Clause 54 of the Bill eventually became § 63 of the 1976 Act. As introduced, clause 54(1) provided that the cash equivalent of any benefit was to be an amount equal to "the cost of the benefit". Clause 54(2) provided that, except as provided in later subsections "the cost of a benefit is the amount of any expense incurred in or in connection with its provision". Crucially, clause 54(4) of the Bill sought to tax in-house benefits on a different basis from that applicable to external benefits. It provided that the cost of a benefit consisting of the provision of any service or facility which was also provided to the public (i.e. in-house benefits) should be the price which the public paid for such facility or service. Employees of schools were not excluded from the new charge. [Editor—This provision was withdrawn, however, with the following explanation.] * * *

> * * * I have had many interviews, discussions and meetings on this matter and I have decided to withdraw Clause 54(4). * * * I shall give some reasons which weigh heavily in favour of the withdrawal of this provision. The first is the large difference between the cost of providing some services and the amount of benefit which under the Bill would be held to be received. There are a number of cases of this kind, and I would point out that air and rail journeys are only two of a number of service benefits which have a number of problems attached to them. But there is a large difference between the cost of the benefit to the employer and the value of that benefit as assessed. It could lead to unjustifiable situations resulting in a great number of injustices and I do not think we should continue with it. * * * The second reason for withdrawing Clause 54(4) is that these services would tend to be much less used. * * * The third reason is the difficulty of enforcement and administration which both give rise to certain problems. * * *

The Financial Secretary was then asked to elucidate the impact of this on airline employees. He is reported as saying (at col. 930):

> * * * What we are withdrawing is the arm's length valuation of benefit under Clause 54(4) where an employer is providing services to the employee at a cost which may be very little. The employee earning more than L5,000, or the director will be assessed on the benefit received by him on the basis of the cost to the employer rather than the price that would generally be charged to the public. That is the position that we have now brought in, as opposed to the original one in the Bill where it would be assessed on the cost to a member of the public. That position now is the same as it stands before this legislation is passed.

After being further pressed, the Financial Secretary, (at cols. 931–932) said:

> The position is as I have enunciated it. If a company provides a service to the kind of employee which we have been talking about, and the company subsidizes that service, the benefit assessable on the employee is the cost to the employer of providing that service. This was to have been changed by Clause 54(4) under which the benefit received was to be assessed at the arm's length price which an ordinary member of the public would have paid for that service. Some companies provide services of a kind where the cost to them is very little. For example, an airline ticket, allowing occupation of an empty seat, costs an airline nothing—in fact, in such a case there could be a negative cost, as it might be an advantage to the airline to have an experienced crew member on the flight. The cost to the company, then, would be nothing, but the benefit assessable under Clause 54(4) could be considerable. We are reverting to the existing practice.

He further said (at col. 931):

> If the company provides services to such people at a subsidized rate, the employee will be assessed on the benefit received on the basis of the cost to the employer. That is the position as it was before this Bill and as it will be if the whole of the Bill is passed * * *. It does not produce anything new. * * *

The point was further debated in committee on 22 June 1976. * * *

The very question which is the subject matter of the present appeal was [ ] raised. A member (at cols. 1091–1092) said:

> I should be grateful for the Financial Secretary's guidance on these two points. * * * The second matter applies particularly to private sector, fee-paying schools where, as the Financial Secretary knows, there is often an arrangement for the children of staff in these schools to be taught at less than the

commercial fee in other schools. I take it that because of the deletion of Clause 54(4) that is not now caught. Perhaps these examples will help to clarify the extent to which the Government amendment goes.

The Financial Secretary responded (at col. 1098) to this question as follows:

> He mentioned the children of teachers. The removal of Clause 54(4) will affect the position of a child of one of the teachers at the child's school, because now the benefit will be assessed on the cost to the employer, which would be very small indeed in this case.

Thereafter, clause 54 was not the subject of further debate and passed into law as it now stands as § 63 of the 1976 Act.

The position can therefore be summarized as follows. The 1976 Bill as introduced sought by clause 54(4) to tax in-house benefits on a different basis from other benefits, i.e. not on the cost of the in-house benefit to the employer but on the open market price charged to the public. On the deletion of clause 54(4), in-house benefits were to be taxed on the same basis as external benefits, i.e. on the cost to the employer of providing the benefit. Numerous inquiries were made of the Financial Secretary to elucidate the resulting effect of the Bill on in-house benefits, i.e. concessionary travel for airline, railway and merchant navy employees, on benefits for hotel employees and on concessionary education for the children of teachers. In responding to each of these requests for information (save that relating to teachers), the Financial Secretary stated that the effect of the Bill would be to leave their position unchanged from the previous law. He explained that in each case (including that of teachers) the charge would be on the cost to the employer of providing the services and that in each case that cost would either be nil or very small. After these statements were made by the Financial Secretary the Bill passed into law without further discussion on this aspect of the matter. * * *

[Editor—The opinion then describes current law about judicial use of legislative history.]

Under present law, there is a general rule that references to parliamentary material as an aid to statutory construction is not permissible (the exclusionary rule)(see Davis v Johnson [1979] AC 264; Hadmor Productions Ltd. v. Hamilton [1983] 1 AC 191). This rule did not always apply but was judge-made. Thus, in Ash v. Abdy (1678) 3 Swan 664 Lord Nottingham took judicial notice of his own experience when introducing the Bill in the House of Lords. The exclusionary rule was probably first stated by Willes J in Millar v Taylor (1769) 4 Burr 2303 at 2332. * * *

The exclusionary rule was later extended so as to prohibit the court from looking even at reports made by commissioners on which legislation was based. This rule has now been relaxed so as to permit reports of commissioners, including Law Commissioners, and white papers to be looked at for the purpose solely of ascertaining the mischief which the statute is intended to cure but not for the purpose of discovering the meaning of the words used by Parliament to effect such cure. * * *

[Counsel for the taxpayers] did not urge us to abandon the exclusionary rule completely. His submission was that where the words of a statute were ambiguous or obscure or were capable of giving rise to an absurd conclusion it should be legitimate to look at the parliamentary history, including the debates in Parliament, for the purpose of identifying the intention of Parliament in using the words it did use. He accepted that the function of the court was to construe the actual words enacted by Parliament so that in no circumstances could the court attach to words a meaning that they were incapable of bearing. He further accepted that the court should only attach importance to clear statements showing the intention of the promoter of the Bill, whether a minister or private member: there could be no dredging through conflicting statements of intention with a view to discovering the true intention of Parliament in using the statutory words. * * *

[Counsel for the taxpayers] submitted that the time has come to relax the rule to the extent which I have mentioned. He points out that the courts have departed from the old literal approach of statutory construction and now adopt a purposive approach, seeking to discover the parliamentary intention lying behind the words used and construing the legislation so as to give effect to, rather than thwart, the intentions of Parliament. Where the words used by Parliament are obscure or ambiguous, the parliamentary material may throw considerable light not only on the mischief which the Act was designed to remedy but also on the purpose of the legislation and its anticipated effect. If there are statements by the minister or other promoter of the Bill, these may throw as much light on the "mischief" which the Bill seeks to remedy as do the white papers, reports of official committees and Law Commission reports to which the courts already have regard for that purpose. If a minister clearly states the effect of a provision and there is no subsequent relevant amendment to the Bill or withdrawal of the statement it is reasonable to assume that Parliament passed the Bill on the basis that the provision would have the effect stated. * * * Other common law jurisdictions have abandoned the rule without adverse consequences. Although the practical reasons for the rule (difficulty in getting access to parliamentary materials and the cost and delay in researching it) are not without substance, they can be greatly exaggerated: experience in Commonwealth countries which have abandoned the rule does not suggest that the drawbacks are substantial, provided that the court keeps a tight control on the circumstances in which references to parliamentary material are allowed.

On the other side, the Attorney General submitted that the existing rule had a sound constitutional and practical basis. If statements by ministers as to the intent or effect of an Act were allowed to prevail, this would contravene the constitutional rule that Parliament is "sovereign only in respect of what it expresses by the words used in the legislation it has passed" (see Black–Clawson [1975] AC 591 at 615 per Lord Diplock). It is for the courts alone to construe such legislation. It may be unwise to attach importance to ministerial explanations which are made to satisfy the political requirements of persuasion and debate, often under pressure of time and business. Moreover, in order to establish the significance to be attached to any particular statement, it is necessary both to consider and to understand the context in which it was made. For the courts to have regard to parliamentary material might necessitate changes in parliamentary procedures to ensure that ministerial statements are sufficiently detailed to be taken into account. In addition, there are all the practical difficulties as to the accessibility of parliamentary material, the cost of researching it and the use of court time in analyzing it, which are good reasons for maintaining the rule. * * *

My Lords, I have come to the conclusion that, as a matter of law, there are sound reasons for making a limited modification to the existing rule (subject to strict safeguards) unless there are constitutional or practical reasons which outweigh them. In my judgment, subject to the questions of the privileges of the House of Commons, reference to parliamentary material should be permitted as an aid to the construction of legislation which is ambiguous or obscure or the literal meaning of which leads to an absurdity. Even in such cases references in court to parliamentary material should only be permitted where such material clearly discloses the mischief aimed at or the legislative intention lying behind the ambiguous or obscure words. In the case of statements made in Parliament, as at present advised I cannot foresee that any statement other than the statement of the minister or other promoter of the Bill is likely to meet these criteria.

* * * [M]y main reason for reaching this conclusion is based on principle. Statute law consists of the words that Parliament has enacted. It is for the courts to construe those words and it is the court's duty in so doing to give effect to the intention of Parliament in using those words. It is an inescapable fact that, despite all the care taken in passing legislation, some statutory provisions when applied to the circumstances under consideration in any specific case are found to be ambiguous. One of the reasons for such ambiguity is that the members of the legislature in enacting the statutory provision may have been told what result those words are

intended to achieve. Faced with a given set of words which are capable of conveying that meaning it is not surprising if the words are accepted as having that meaning. Parliament never intends to enact an ambiguity. Contrast with that the position of the courts. The courts are faced simply with a set of words which are in fact capable of bearing two meanings. The courts are ignorant of the underlying parliamentary purpose. Unless something in other parts of the legislation discloses such purpose, the courts are forced to adopt one of the two possible meanings using highly technical rules of construction. In many, I suspect most, cases references to parliamentary materials will not throw any light on the matter. But in a few cases it may emerge that the very question was considered by Parliament in passing the legislation. Why in such a case should the courts blind themselves to a clear indication of what Parliament intended in using those words? The court cannot attach a meaning to words which they cannot bear, but if the words are capable of bearing more than one meaning why should not Parliament's true intention be enforced rather than thwarted?

A number of other factors support this view. As I have said, the courts can now look at white papers and official reports for the purpose of finding the "mischief" sought to be corrected, although not at draft clauses or proposals for the remedying of such mischief. A ministerial statement made in Parliament is an equally authoritative source of such information: why should the courts be cut off from this source of information as to the mischief aimed at? In any event, the distinction between looking at reports to identify the mischief aimed at but not to find the intention of Parliament in enacting the legislation is highly artificial. Take the normal Law Commission report which analyses the problem and then annexes a draft Bill to remedy it. It is now permissible to look at the report to find the mischief and at the draft Bill to see that a provision in the draft was not included in the legislation enacted (see Ex p Factortame [1990] 2 AC 85). There can be no logical distinction between that case and looking at the draft Bill to see that the statute as enacted reproduced, often in the same words, the provision in the Law Commission's draft. Given the purposive approach to construction now adopted by the courts in order to give effect to the true intentions of the legislature, the fine distinctions between looking for the mischief and looking for the intention in using words to provide the remedy are technical and inappropriate. Clear and unambiguous statements made by ministers in Parliament are as much the background to the enactment of legislation as white papers and parliamentary reports. * * *

Textbooks often include reference to explanations of legislation given by a minister in Parliament, as a result of which lawyers advise their clients taking account of such statements and judges when construing the legislation come to know of them. In addition, a number of distinguished judges have admitted to breaching the exclusionary rule and looking at Hansard in order to seek the intention of Parliament. When this happens, the parties do not know and have no opportunity to address the judge on the matter. A vivid example of this occurred in Hadmor [1983] 1 AC 191 where Lord Denning in the Court of Appeal relied on his own researches into Hansard in reaching his conclusions: in the House of Lords, counsel protested that there were other passages to which he would have wished to draw the court's attention had he known that Lord Denning was looking at Hansard (see Hadmor [1983] 1 AC 191 at 233). It cannot be right for such information to be available, by a sidewind, for the court but the parties be prevented from presenting their arguments on such material.

Against these considerations, there have to be weighed the practical and constitutional matters urged by the Attorney General many of which have been relied on in the past in the courts in upholding the exclusionary rule. I will first consider the practical difficulties.

It is said that parliamentary materials are not readily available to, and understandable by, the citizen and his lawyers who should be entitled to rely on the words of Parliament alone to discover his position. It is undoubtedly true that Hansard and particularly records of committee debates are not widely held by libraries outside London and that the lack of satisfactory indexing of committee stages makes it difficult to trace the passage of a clause after it is redrafted or renumbered. But such practical difficulties can easily be overstated. It is possible to obtain parliamentary materials and it is possible to trace the history. The problem is one of expense and effort in doing so, not the availability of the material. In considering the right of the individual to know the law by simply looking at legislation, it is a fallacy to start from the position that all legislation is available in a readily understandable form in any event: the very large number of statutory instruments made every year are not available in an indexed form for well over a year after they have been passed. Yet, the practitioner manages to deal with the problem albeit at considerable expense. * * *

Then it is said that court time will be taken up by considering a mass of parliamentary material and long arguments about its significance, thereby increasing the expense of litigation. In my judgment, though the introduction of further admissible material will inevitably involve some increase in the use of time, this will not be significant as long as courts insist that parliamentary material should only be introduced in the limited cases I have mentioned and where such material contains a clear indication from the minister of the mischief aimed at, or the nature of the cure intended, by the legislation. Attempts to introduce material which does not satisfy those tests should be met by orders for costs made against those who have improperly introduced the material. Experience in the United States of America, where legislative history has for many years been much more generally admissible than I am now suggesting, shows how important it is to maintain strict control over the use of such material. * * *

There is one further practical objection which, in my view, has real substance. If the rule is relaxed legal advisers faced with an ambiguous statutory provision may feel that they have to research the materials to see whether they yield the crock of gold, i.e. a clear indication of Parliament's intentions. In very many cases the crock of gold will not be discovered and the expenditure on the research wasted. This is a real objection to changing the rule. However, again it is easy to overestimate the cost of such research: if a reading of Hansard shows that there is nothing of significance said by the minister in relation to the clause in question, further research will become pointless. * * *

Is there, then, any constitutional objection to a relaxation of the rule? The main constitutional ground urged by the Attorney General is that the use of such material will infringe § 1, art. 9 of the Bill of Rights (1688) as being a questioning in any court of freedom of speech and debates in Parliament. [Editor—The opinion concludes that considering Hansard to determine statutory meaning does not "question" what occurred in Parliament. "In my judgment, the plain meaning of art. 9, viewed against the historical background in which it was enacted, was to ensure that members of Parliament were not subjected to any penalty, civil or criminal for what they said and were able, contrary to the previous assertions of the Stuart monarchy, to discuss what they, as opposed to the monarch, chose to have discussed. Relaxation of the rule will not involve the courts in criticizing what is said in Parliament. The purpose of looking at Hansard will not be to construe the words used by the minister but to give effect to the words used so long as they are clear. Far from questioning the independence of Parliament and its debates, the courts would be giving effect to what is said and done there."] * * *

I therefore reach the conclusion * * * that the exclusionary rule should be relaxed so as to permit reference to parliamentary materials where:

(a) legislation is ambiguous or obscure, or leads to an absurdity;

(b) the material relied on consists of one or more statements by a minister or other promoter of the Bill together if necessary with such other parliamentary material as is necessary to understand such statements and their effect;

(c) the statements relied on are clear.

Further than this, I would not at present go.

[Editor—If these limits on using legislative history were followed in the United States, would courts often rely on legislative history?]

2. Does this case fall within the relaxed rule?

(a) Is § 63 ambiguous?

I have no hesitation in holding that it is. The "expense incurred in or in connection with" the provision of in-house benefits may be either the marginal cost caused by the provision of the benefit in question or a proportion of the total cost incurred in providing the service both for the public and for the employee (the average cost).

In favour of the marginal cost argument, it is submitted by the taxpayers that there has to be a causal link between the benefit in kind taxed under § 61(1) and its "cash equivalent": § 63(1) defines the cash equivalent of the benefit as being an amount equal to the cost of the benefit. Therefore, it is said, one is looking for the actual cost of providing that benefit for the employee. The basic expense of providing and running the school would have been incurred in any event; therefore that expenditure is not caused by the provision of the benefit for the employee. The test is whether the cost would have been incurred but for the provision of the benefit. Therefore, when one comes to § 63(2) one is looking for the additional expense incurred in or in connection with the provision of the benefit.

The taxpayers' contention is supported by certain unfair consequences which could ensue if the cost of the benefit is to be taken as the average cost. Take a railway running at a loss: the average cost of providing concessionary travel would be a sum greater than the fare charged to the public. In the case of a heavily endowed school, the fees charged to the public may be less than sufficient to cover the total cost of running the school, the shortfall being made good by the endowment. On the average cost basis, the taxpayer would be treated as receiving a benefit greater than the amount charged to the public.

On the other side, the Revenue contend that, once one has identified the benefit under § 61, § 63 contains a code for establishing its cash equivalent. Section 63(1) defines the cash equivalent as the cost of the benefit and § 63(2) defines "the cost of a benefit" as being the expense "incurred in or in connection with" its provision. The benefit in this case consists of the enjoyment of the facilities of the school. What is the cost of providing those facilities? It must be the total cost of providing the school. However, the total cost of providing the school is incurred not only in connection with the provision of the benefit to the employee but also in providing the school with fee-paying boys. This provision is expressly covered by the final words of § 63(2) "and includes * * * a proper proportion of any expense relating partly to the benefit and partly to other matters". Therefore, says the Revenue, the cost of the benefit is a proportion of the total cost of providing the services. The Revenue has no answer to the anomalies which arise when the cost of providing a loss-making facility means that the average cost basis results in the taxpayer being treated as receiving a sum by way of benefit greater than the cost of buying that benefit on the open market.

I find these arguments nicely balanced. The statutory words are capable of bearing either meaning. There is an ambiguity or obscurity.

(b) Are the words of the Financial Secretary clear? * * *

The Finance Bill 1976 as introduced proposed to charge in-house benefits on a different basis from that applicable to external benefits i.e. on the open market price charged to the public (see clause 54(4)). Once the government announced its intention to withdraw clause 54(4) a number of members were anxious to elucidate what effect this would have on classes of taxpayers who enjoyed in-house benefits * * *. In answer to these inquiries the Financial Secretary gave similar answers in relation to each class namely * * * that in all cases the amount of the charge would be nil, small or, in the case of the schoolteachers, "very small indeed". In my view these repeated assurances are quite inconsistent with the minister having had, or communicated, any intention other than that the words "the expense incurred in or in connection with" the provision of the benefit would produce a charge to tax on the additional or marginal cost only, not a charge on the average cost of the benefit. * * *

The question then arises whether it is right to attribute to Parliament as a whole the same intention as that repeatedly voiced by the Financial Secretary. In my judgment it is. It is clear from reading Hansard that the committee was repeatedly asking for guidance as to the effect of the legislation once clause 54 was abandoned. That Parliament relied on the ministerial statements is shown by the fact that the matter was never raised again after the discussions in committee, that amendments were consequentially withdrawn and that no relevant amendment was made which could affect the correctness of the minister's statement.

Accordingly, in my judgment we have in this case a clear statement by the responsible minister stating the effect of the ambiguous words used in what became § 63 of the 1976 Act which the parliamentary history shows to have been the basis on which that section was enacted. * * *

Appeal allowed.

After Pepper v. Hart, English courts continue to grapple with whether to consult legislative history in the form of legislative materials. In Director of Public Prosecutions v. Bull, [1994] 4 All E.R. 411, [1994] 3 W.L.R. 1196, the issue was whether a man could commit the crime of being a "common prostitute" under a 1959 statute. The court said "no," relying on the older widely-accepted pre-Pepper v. Hart approach of using a report which was background for the later legislation in order to identify the mischief at which the statute was aimed. The Report of the Committee on Homosexual Offences and Prostitution 1957, which was a departmental report and resulted in the 1959 Act, clearly showed that the mischief which the Act was intended to remedy was a mischief created by women prostitutes.

The court did not decide whether to consult legislative history in the form of Parliamentary debates, but implied that it made little sense not to.

> * * * I have not sought to avail myself of the doctrine in Pepper v. Hart because in my judgment and with the confirmation afforded by the Wolfenden Committee Report, the legislation is neither ambiguous, obscure nor productive of absurdity. However, I must remark that a curious feature of this appeal was [government counsel's] voluntary and frank concession [   ] that if the court was to look at the Parliamentary debates it would become plain that sec. 1(1) of the 1959 Act was intended to be applicable only to women. Had I concluded, as a matter of interpretation, that sec. 1(1) applied to male prostitutes, then a curious situation would have arisen. The judicially ascertained expressed intention of Parliament would have been at variance with what the court had been told was the actual intention of the promoters. The ensuant problems may have to be addressed if concessions of the type made here are repeated on another occasion.

If the court had used Parliamentary debates in this case, would that have been an example of "intentionalist textualism"—looking for evidence of the meaning of a text ("common prostitute") intended by legislative authors—or of using legislative history to prove specific intent?

10.07 LEGISLATIVE DEBATES

Generally, courts prefer committee reports to floor debates as evidence of legislative intent, echoing some of the concerns that were especially prominent during the 19th Century. As the Court said in Zuber v. Allen, 396 U.S. 168 (1969), a committee report is the "considered and collective understanding of those Congressmen involved in drafting and studying proposed legislation. Floor debates reflect at best the understanding of individual Congressmen."

Sometimes, however, floor debates are as good as other kinds of legislative history, especially when the legislative process does not include committee hearings and reports. A bill might bypass the committee process when a hostile committee does not reflect the political make-up of the entire Congress. This has happened with some civil rights legislation, when the issue has aroused such intense concern that normal legislative procedures were circumvented. Amendments to bills might also be offered on the floor of Congress after committee deliberation is complete, so the committee report is silent. This is more likely in the Senate because amendments are more readily permitted than in the House. Legislative debates in the House usually occur pursuant to a closed or modified closed rule, which limits the amendment of bills after they are reported out of Committee.

In the following case, a provision which began as a Senate floor amendment found its way into the law. Notice carefully what there is about the legislative history that might make it good or bad evidence of statutory meaning. Was the material clear? Did it reflect careful thought? Did it express the views of the critical political actors? Does the dissent rely on something that we might call legislative history, even if it is not legislative materials?

a) NORTH HAVEN BD. OF EDUCATION V. BELL, 456 U.S. 512 (1982)

■ Justice Blackmun delivered the opinion of the Court.

At issue here is the validity of regulations promulgated by the Department of Education pursuant to Title IX of the Education Amendments of 1972, Pub. L. 92–318, 86 Stat. 373, 20 U.S.C. § 1681 et seq. These regulations prohibit federally funded education programs from discriminating on the basis of gender with respect to employment.

Title IX proscribes gender discrimination in education programs or activities receiving federal financial assistance. Patterned after Title VI of the Civil Rights Act of 1964, Pub. L. 88–352, 78 Stat. 252, 42 U.S.C. § 2000d et seq. (1976 ed. and Supp. IV), Title IX, as amended, contains two core provisions. The first is a "program-specific" prohibition of gender discrimination:

"No person in the United States shall, on the basis of sex, be excluded from participation in, be denied the benefits of, or be subjected to discrimination under any education program or activity receiving Federal financial assistance * * *." § 901(a).
* * *

The second core provision relates to enforcement. * * * The ultimate sanction for noncompliance is termination of federal funds or denial of future grants. * * *

[Editor—As background, you should keep in mind the different statutory provisions dealing with discrimination, prior to 1972, and what the 1972 amendments accomplished. In 1964, Title VI of the Civil Rights Act prohibited race discrimination (but not sex discrimination) in programs receiving federal funds. It did not apply to employment discrimination except where the primary objective of the federal grant was to provide employment. Title VII of the same Act prohibited employment discrimination by private employers on grounds of race, sex, and other improper criteria, but did not apply to educational institutions. In 1972, the issue of sex discrimination became more important. Title IX of the Education Amendments, at issue in this case, was passed. So was a separate statute adding educational institutions and public employers to the list of employers who were prohibited under Title VII from discriminating on grounds of race, sex, etc. Despite the expansion of Title VII to educational institutions, a Title IX remedy was often preferable to recovery under Title VII, because it permitted a cut-off of federal funds to educational institutions as a sanction.]

Our starting point in determining the scope of Title IX is, of course, the statutory language. Section 901(a)'s broad directive that "no person" may be discriminated against on the basis of gender appears, on its face, to include employees as well as students. Under that provision, employees, like other "persons," may not be "excluded from participation in," "denied the benefits of," or "subjected to discrimination under" education programs receiving federal financial support. * * *

* * * Because § 901(a) neither expressly nor impliedly excludes employees from its reach, we should interpret the provision as covering and protecting these "persons" unless other considerations counsel to the contrary. After all, Congress easily could have substituted "student" or "beneficiary" for the word "person" if it had wished to restrict the scope of § 901(a). * * *

* * * [B]ecause Title IX does not expressly include or exclude employees from its scope, we turn to the Act's legislative history for evidence as to whether Congress meant somehow to limit the expansive language of § 901.

In the early 1970's, several attempts were made to enact legislation banning discrimination against women in the field of education. Although unsuccessful, these efforts included prohibitions against discriminatory employment practices.

In 1972, the provisions ultimately enacted as Title IX were introduced in the Senate by Senator Bayh during debate on the Education Amendments of 1972. In addition to prohibiting gender discrimination in federally funded education programs and threatening termination of federal assistance for noncompliance, the amendment included provisions extending the coverage of Title VII and the Equal Pay Act to educational institutions. Summarizing his proposal, Senator Bayh divided it into two parts—first, the forerunner of § 901(a), and then the extensions of Title VII and the Equal Pay Act:

> "Amendment No. 874 is broad, but basically it closes loopholes in existing legislation relating to general education programs and employment resulting from those programs. * * * [T]he heart of this amendment is a provision banning sex discrimination in educational programs receiving Federal funds. The amendment would cover such crucial aspects as admis-

sions procedures, scholarships, and faculty employment, with limited exceptions. Enforcement powers include fund termination provisions—and appropriate safeguards—parallel to those found in title VI of the 1964 Civil Rights Act. Other important provisions in the amendment would extend the equal employment opportunities provisions of title VII of the 1964 Civil Rights Act to educational institutions, and extend the Equal Pay for Equal Work Act to include executive, administrative and professional women." 118 Cong. Rec. 5803 (1972).

The Senator's description of § 901(a), the "heart" of his amendment, indicates that it, as well as the Title VII and Equal Pay Act provisions, was aimed at discrimination in employment.

Similarly, in a prepared statement summarizing the amendment, Senator Bayh discussed the general prohibition against gender discrimination:

"Central to my amendment are sections 1001–1005, which would prohibit discrimination on the basis of sex in federally funded education programs. * * *

"This portion of the amendment covers discrimination in all areas where abuse has been mentioned—employment practices for faculty and administrators, scholarship aid, admissions, access to programs within the institution such as vocational education classes, and so forth." 118 Cong. Rec. 5807 (1972).

Petitioners observe that the discussion of this portion of the amendment appears under the heading "A. Prohibition of Sex Discrimination in Federally Funded Education Programs," while the provisions involving Title VII and the Equal Pay Act are summarized under the heading "B. Prohibition of Education–Related Employment Discrimination." But we are not willing to ascribe any particular significance to these headings. The Title VII and Equal Pay Act portions of the Bayh amendment are more narrowly focused on employment discrimination than is the general ban on gender discrimination, and the headings reflect that difference. Especially in light of the explicit reference to employment practices in the description of the amendment's general provision, however, the headings do not negate Senator Bayh's intent that employees as well as students be protected by the first portion of his amendment.

The final piece of evidence from the Senate debate on the Bayh amendment appears during a colloquy between Senator Bayh and Senator Pell, chairman of the Senate Subcommittee on Education and floor manager of the education bill. In response to Senator Pell's inquiry about the scope of the sections that in large part became §§ 901(a) and (b), Senator Bayh stated:

"As the Senator knows, we are dealing with three basically different types of discrimination here. We are dealing with discrimination in admission to an institution, discrimination of available services or studies within an institution once students are admitted, and discrimination in employment within an institution, as a member of a faculty or whatever.

"In the area of employment, we permit no exceptions." Id., at 5812.

Although the statements of one legislator made during debate may not be controlling, Senator Bayh's remarks, as those of the sponsor of the language ultimately enacted, are an authoritative guide to the statute's construction. And, because § 901 and § 902 originated as a floor amendment, no committee report discusses the provisions; Senator Bayh's statements—which were made on the same day the amendment was passed, and some of which were prepared rather than spontaneous remarks—are the only authoritative indications of congressional intent regarding the scope of § 901 and § 902. * * *

In our view, the legislative history thus corroborates our reading of the statutory language and verifies the Court of Appeals' conclusion that employment discrimination comes within the prohibition of Title IX.

■ Powell, J., dissenting. * * *

In concluding that the legislative history indicates Title IX was intended to extend to employment discrimination, the Court is forced to rely primarily on the statements of a single Senator. The first statement (quoting 118 Cong. Rec. 5803 (1972)), is ambiguous. Senator Bayh did state that faculty employment would be covered by his amendment after mentioning the sections enacting Title IX but prior to any mention of those amending Title VII and the Equal Pay Act. Immediately thereafter, however, he stated that Title IX's enforcement powers paralleled those in Title VI. Yet Title VI has never provided for fund termination to redress discrimination in employment.

Next, the Court quotes Bayh's statements that (i) he regarded "sections 1001–1005" as "[c]entral to [his] amendment" and (ii) "[t]his portion of the amendment covers discrimination in all areas," including employment (quoting 118 Cong. Rec. 5807 (1972)). But § 1005 of the Bayh amendment is the section amending Title VII and thus §§ 1001–1005 cover employment discrimination regardless of whether Title IX does. * * *

In the third Bayh statement (quoting 118 Cong. Rec. 5812 (1972)), the Senator was responding to a question from Senator Pell regarding Title IX, and the Court assumes that each sentence in that response refers to Title IX. But, as the Court of Appeals for the First Circuit noted [   ]:

"A fair reading both of the colloquy * * *, as well as the discussion immediately preceding and following the above-quoted passage, indicates that Senator Bayh divided his analysis into three sections, two of which were specifically aimed at students (admissions and services), the third at employees (employment). While Senator Bayh's response was more extended than it needed to be for a direct answer to Senator Pell's question, we think HEW's reading [which favored application of Title IX to employment] is strained. We think this particularly in light of the fact that the discussion was an oral one and thus not as precise as a response in written form * * *." 593 F.2d, at 427.

Rather than supporting the Court's view, the legislative history accords with the natural reading of the statute. Title IX prohibits discrimination only against beneficiaries of federally funded programs and activities, not all employment discrimination by recipients of federal funds. Title IX is modeled after Title VI, which is explicitly so limited—and to the extent statements of Senator Bayh can be read to the contrary, they are ambiguous. [Editor—What kind of legislative history is information about the statute which served as the model for the legislation being interpreted—Title VI was the model for Title IX?]

In North Haven, the issues were politically sensitive. Does that argue for judicial caution in relying on legislative history?

b) PROBATIVE VALUE OF CONGRESSIONAL RECORD

The crucial legislative material in North Haven consisted primarily of statements by the bill sponsor, Senator Bayh, and a colloquy between him and another Senator. The usefulness of both types of material can only be evaluated if you know something about the Congressional Record, where such material appears.

The Congressional Record claims only to be a "substantially [ ] verbatim" report of legislative proceedings. 44 U.S.C. § 901. But the practice has departed from any reasonable meaning of the word "substantial." Members of Congress sometimes revise or extend remarks before publication or insert undelivered speeches. In 1978, the Senate and House adopted a "bullet" rule. The insertion of written statements, no part of which was delivered on the floor, was noted with a marker (known as a "bullet"). See Cong. Record, Mar. 28, 1978, p. 7527 (House) and Cong. Record, Mar. 22, 1978, p. 8123 (Senate). The "bullet" could apparently be avoided if the first sentence was spoken or if extemporaneous remarks were elaborated on in a written statement.

In 1985 the House adopted an experiment replacing the "bullet" approach. It required that a substantially verbatim account of remarks actually spoken during House proceedings appear in different typeface from other material inserted under permission to extend remarks. H. Res. 230, 99th Cong., 1st Sess. (1985). This was made permanent in 1986: H. Res. 514, 99th Cong., 2d Sess. (1986), Cong. Record, Aug. 12, 1986, p. H5978.

The phrase "substantially verbatim" allowed for "technical, grammatical, and typographical corrections authorized by the Member making the remarks."

In addition, the House/Senate Joint Committee on Printing specifies that different point-type shall be used, depending on whether the material appearing in the Congressional Record was or was not spoken. Specifically, the rule states:

> 2. *Type and style.* The Public Printer shall print the report of the proceedings and debates of the Senate and House of Represen-tatives, as furnished by the official reporters of the congressional record, in 8–point type; and all matters included in the remarks or speeches of Members of Congress, other than in their own words, and all reports, documents, and other matters authorized to be inserted in the congressional record shall be printed in 7–point type; and all rollcalls shall be printed in 6–point type. See Laws and Rules for Publication of the Congressional Record, 142 Cong. Rec., 104th Cong., 2d sess. (March 8, 1996), unpaginated page before page D166.

A recent lawsuit, claiming that the Congressional Record was "corrupt" because it misrepresented what occurred on the floor of Congress, was dismissed because a remedy would have violated the Speech or Debate Clause—"[F]or any Speech or Debate in either House, [Members of Congress] shall not be questioned in any other Place" (U.S. Constitution, Art. I, § 6, cl. 1). Gregg v. Barrett, 771 F.2d 539 (D.C.Cir.1985).

QUESTIONS AND COMMENTS

1. What difference does it make whether statements in the Congressional Record have been spoken? Even if spoken, they are often not part of a genuine debate. Very few people may be present other than the presiding officer, or the statements are more in the nature of posturing, as anyone who has watched C–SPAN can attest.

2. Material in the congressional record is often in dialogue form (whether spoken or not) constructed by a bill sponsor and another member to support an interpretation of the statute and influence statutory interpretation—referred to as "manufactured legislative history." Such history is often ridiculed as a source of statutory meaning. That may not be justified, however. What do you think of the following argument for relying selectively on manufactured legislative history?

A statement by the floor manager of a bill might be good evidence of an important stage in the legislative process, because it records what the bill sponsor achieved by working out the details of the statute. The Court in North Haven refers favorably to the fact that Senator Bayh's remarks were "prepared," not "spontaneous." The implication is that such evidence was useful because it was thoughtfully prepared at a late stage of the legislative process by someone in a position to know what happened. The fact that it was not part of a genuine legislative debate is irrelevant. North Haven presents one of the strongest cases for relying on such statements because they were made by the bill sponsor, on the day of passage, and no committee report discusses the provisions.

The trouble with many examples of manufactured legislative history is that the speaker is often just one of several important legislative actors and the statement may predate important shifts in legislative viewpoint prior to passage. Moreover, statements and colloquies (as is also true of Committee Reports) may be an attempt by several Members of Congress to obtain authority for a position that is too weak to be included explicitly in the statute itself (that is, it may be "manipulated" legislative history). Finally, it may be inappropriate for some politically controversial issues to be resolved at the level of colloquies between Members of Congress, rather than by the more explicit method of legislative language.

c) UNITED STEELWORKERS OF AMERICA v. WEBER, 443 U.S. 193 (1979)

■ Mr. Justice Brennan delivered the opinion of the Court.

[Editor—This case is unusual in that the Congressional Record reports a real and intense legislative debate. Unlike North Haven, however, the comments are not focused directly on the specific issue in the case, which is whether a private employer can discriminate in favor of a minority group. They provide evidence of context from which the judges attempt to reconstruct a more specific congressional intent. Does this make the legislative history more or less reliable as evidence of statutory meaning?]

Challenged here is the legality of an affirmative action plan—collectively bargained by an employer and a union—that reserves for black employees 50% of the openings in an in-plant craft-training program until the percentage of black craftworkers in the plant is commensurate with the percentage of blacks in the local labor force. The question for decision is whether Congress, in Title VII of the Civil Rights Act of 1964, 78 Stat. 253, as amended, 42 U.S.C. § 2000e et seq., left employers and unions in the private sector free to take such race-conscious steps to eliminate manifest racial imbalances in traditionally segregated job categories. We hold that Title VII does not prohibit such race-conscious affirmative action plans. * * *

The complaint alleged that the filling of craft trainee positions at the Gramercy plant pursuant to an affirmative action program had resulted in junior black employees' receiving training in preference to senior white employees, thus discriminating against respondent and other similarly situated white employees in violation of § 703(a) and (d) of Title VII. * * * [Editor—These sections make it "an unlawful employment practice for an employer" * * * "to discriminate" in certain employment practices on account of race and other prohibited criteria.]

We emphasize at the outset the narrowness of our inquiry. Since the Kaiser–USWA plan does not involve state action, this case does not present an alleged violation of the Equal Protection Clause of the Fourteenth Amendment. Further, since the Kaiser–USWA plan was adopted voluntarily, we are not concerned with what Title VII requires or with what a court might order to remedy a past proved violation of the Act. The only question before us is the narrow statutory issue of whether Title VII forbids private employers and unions from voluntarily agreeing upon bona fide affirmative action plans that accord racial preferences in the manner and for the purpose provided in the Kaiser–USWA plan. * * *

* * * It is a "familiar rule, that a thing may be within the letter of the statute and yet not within the statute, because not within its spirit, nor within the intention of its makers." Holy Trinity Church v. United States, 143 U.S. 457, 459 (1892). The prohibition against racial discrimination in § 703(a) and (d) of Title VII must therefore be read against the background of the legislative history of Title VII and the historical context from which the Act arose. Examination of those sources makes clear that an interpretation of the sections that forbade all race conscious affirmative action would "bring about an end completely at variance with the purpose of the statute" and must be rejected. [Editor—Does the plain language of the statute prohibiting "discrimination" prohibit quotas for a minority? Does "air-conditioning" refer to heating *and* cooling?]

Congress' primary concern in enacting the prohibition against racial discrimination in Title VII of the Civil Rights Act of 1964 was with "the plight of the Negro in our economy." 110 Cong. Rec. 6548 (1964)(remarks of Sen. Humphrey). Before 1964, blacks were largely relegated to "unskilled and semi-skilled jobs." Ibid. (remarks of Sen. Humphrey); id., at 7204 (remarks of Sen. Clark); id., at 7379–7380 (remarks of Sen. Kennedy). Because of automation the number of such jobs was rapidly decreasing. See id., at 6548 (remarks of Humphrey); id., at 7204 (remarks of Sen. Clark). As a consequence, "the relative position of the Negro worker [was] steadily worsening. In 1947 the nonwhite unemployment rate was only 64 percent higher than the white rate; in 1962 it was 124 percent higher.": Id., t 6547 (remarks of Sen. Humphrey). See also id., at 7204 (remarks of Sen. Clark). Congress considered this a serious social problem. As Senator Clark told the Senate:

"The rate of Negro unemployment has gone up consistently as compared with white unemployment for the past 15 years. This is a social malaise and a social situation which we should not tolerate. That is one of the principal reasons why the bill should pass." Id., at 7220.

Congress feared that the goals of the Civil Rights Act—the integration of blacks into the mainstream of American society—could not be achieved unless this trend were reversed. And Congress recognized that that would not be possible unless blacks were able to secure jobs "which have a future." Id., at 7204 (remarks of Sen. Clark). See also id., at 7379–7380 (remarks of Sen. Kennedy). As Senator Humphrey explained to the Senate:

> "What good does it do a Negro to be able to eat in a fine restaurant if he cannot afford to pay the bill? What good does it do him to be accepted in a hotel that is too expensive for his modest income? How can a Negro child be motivated to take full advantage of integrated educational facilities if he has no hope of getting a job where he can use that education?" Id., at 6547.

> "Without a job, one cannot afford public convenience and accommodations. Income from employment may be necessary to further a man's education, or that of his children. If his children have no hope of getting a good job, what will motivate them to take advantage of educational opportunities?" Id., at 6552. * * *

Accordingly, it was clear to Congress that "[t]he crux of the problem [was] to open employment opportunities for Negroes in occupations which have been traditionally closed to them,": 110 Cong. Rec. 6548 (1964) (remarks of Sen. Humphrey), and it was to this problem that Title VII's prohibition against racial discrimination in employment was primarily addressed. * * *

Given this legislative history, we cannot agree with respondent that Congress intended to prohibit the private sector from taking effective steps to accomplish the goal that Congress designed Title VII to achieve. * * * It would be ironic indeed if a law triggered by a Nation's concern over centuries of racial injustice and intended to improve the lot of those who had "been excluded from the American dream for so long," 110 Cong. Rec. 6552 (1964) (remarks of Sen. Humphrey), constituted the first legislative prohibition of all voluntary, private, race-conscious efforts to abolish traditional patterns of racial segregation and hierarchy.

[Editor—The Court further relied on the fact that opponents of the bills were concerned about whether the Act would either require or permit preferential treatment of minorities. In response to these concerns, the Act ended up specifically prohibiting an interpretation requiring preferential treatment, but was silent regarding voluntary programs. When combined with legislative history supporting noninterference with management prerogatives, the silence regarding voluntary preferential treatment was taken as evidence that voluntary programs were not prohibited. The Court concludes that the Kaiser-USWA affirmative action plan is legal because it breaks down old

patterns of racial segregation and hierarchy in occupations traditionally closed to minorities.]

In dissent, Justice Rehnquist was even more exhaustive in exploring the
legislative history. He accused the majority of calling "upon the 'spirit' of the
Act," favoring employment opportunity for minorities, to overcome the
statutory language prohibiting discrimination. He further objected that the
legislative history indicated a different spirit, that of equal opportunity in the
job market, not preferential treatment for minorities. After apologizing that
"the topic hardly makes for light reading," he quoted extensively from the
legislative history to support his view that the bill prohibited discrimination
in favor of workers on account of race, neither requiring nor permitting
racial quotas, and that the purpose of the bill was equality of treatment, not
preferential treatment. He concluded as follows:

> Our task in this case, like any other case involving the construc-
> tion of a statute, is to give effect to the intent of Congress. To divine
> that intent, we traditionally look first to the words of the statute and,
> if they are unclear, then to the statute's legislative history. Finding
> the desired result hopelessly foreclosed by these conventional
> sources, the Court turns to a third source—the "spirit" of the Act.
> But close examination of what the Court proffers as the spirit of the
> act reveals it as the spirit animating the present majority, not the
> 88th Congress. For if the spirit of the Act eludes the cold words of
> the statute itself, it rings out with unmistakable clarity in the words of
> the elected representatives who made the Act law. It is *equality*.
> Senator Dirksen, I think, captured that spirit in a speech delivered
> on the floor of the Senate just moments before the bill was passed:

>> "* * * [T]oday we come to grips finally with a bill that
>> advances the enjoyment of living; but, more than that, it
>> advances the equality of opportunity.

>> "I do not emphasize the word 'equality' standing by itself. It
>> means equality of opportunity in the field of education. It means
>> equality of opportunity in the field of employment. It means
>> equality of opportunity in the field of participation in the affairs
>> of government * * *.

>> "That is it.

>> "Equality of opportunity, if we are going to talk about
>> conscience, is the mass conscience of mankind that speaks in
>> every generation, and it will continue to speak long after we are
>> dead and gone." 110 Cong. Rec. 14510 (1964).

> There is perhaps no device more destructive to the notion of
> equality than the *numerus clausus*—the quota. Whether described
> as "benign discrimination" or "affirmative action," the racial quota is
> nonetheless a creator of castes, a two-edged sword that must
> demean one in order to prefer another. In passing Title VII, Con-
> gress outlawed all racial discrimination, recognizing that no discrimi-
> nation based on race is benign, that no action disadvantaging a

person because of his color is affirmative. With today's holding, the Court introduces into Title VII a tolerance for the very evil that the law was intended to eradicate, without offering even a clue as to what the limits on that tolerance may be. We are told simply that Kaiser's racially discriminatory admission quota "falls on the permissible side of the line." By going not merely *beyond*, but directly *against* Title VII's language and legislative history, the Court has sown the wind. Later courts will face the impossible task of reaping the whirlwind.

COMMENTS AND QUESTIONS

As noted earlier, Weber differs from North Haven in that the legislative history did not focus on the specific issue being litigated. Instead, the legislative history deals with the external context (or purpose) of the legislation, focusing on improving access to jobs and on equality of opportunity. Very little was said, compared to the volume of speeches, to demonstrate specific intent about permitting private employers to provide favorable treatment for minorities.

The problem with using legislative history as evidence of context about such a volatile political issue is that our political and social history is frequently schizophrenic on such important matters. There is no single context. We are committed to equal opportunity and are suspicious of quotas, but we are also concerned with restitution for past wrongs and overcoming obstacles to taking advantage of equal opportunity. It is not surprising that the legislative history mirrored this confusion.

Given this confusion, why do both the majority and dissent spend so much time discussing the legislative debates? What is the alternative to relying on legislative history in this case? Notice that the statute was adopted in 1964, but the decision about affirmative action came much later. Was the Court applying values which probably influenced the 1964 legislature, or more contemporary values about affirmative action which were prevalent in 1979 when the case was decided?

10.08 CHANGES IN LANGUAGE DURING ENACTMENT PROCESS— DRAFTING CONTEXT

This section considers whether changes in the text of a statute as it goes through the legislative process shed light on the meaning of a statute. Drafting context does not pose many of the problems of conventional legislative history. It is not a statement about meaning and is therefore neither a rival text to the statute nor likely to be a self-conscious attempt to manipulate political results. Moreover, it is not a potentially unclear observation about legislative purpose. Language changes are often *unself-conscious* efforts to get the meaning right and may therefore be probative of what the legislature (or at least the drafters) was trying to do. Nonetheless, rejection of one text does not necessarily determine what the adopted text means, as the following excerpt explains.

Report to the Attorney General, Using and Misusing Legislative History: A Re–Evaluation of the Status of Legislative History in Statutory Interpretation (1989).

The rejection of language by a committee, a house, or a conference committee is sometimes interpreted as evidence of an intent to reject the substance of the language. In such instances a court declines to give an interpretation to the enacted statute that would have the same effect as the rejected language. As the Supreme Court has explained, "[i]f we adopted the construction taken below, we would be reading into the Act by implication what the Legislature seemingly rejected." This reasoning has an air of inevitability about it, but it somewhat overstates the case.

Rejecting language and enacting language to the contrary are two distinct legislative acts. The latter is legislation in the constitutional sense, a bicameral act presented to the President. The former, while indisputably an affirmative act, is nevertheless a form of congressional inaction and lacks status as law. Its relevance to interpretation depends entirely upon whether it implies something about the meaning of the language that was ultimately enacted.

The temptation is to view the rejection of proposed language as an "indicat[ion] that the legislature does not intend the bill to include the provisions embodied in the rejected amendment." This view wrongly focuses on the intent of Congress instead of the meaning of the language that was enacted. But even on its own terms, it is a problematic approach. Rejection of proposed language does not necessarily imply an intent to reject its substance. Language may be rejected because it is perceived to be superfluous and potentially damaging to the prospects for passage of the bill. If the perception that it is superfluous is correct, the actual meaning of the statute is the same without the language as it is with it; rejection of that language cannot imply that the enacted statute should be interpreted to mean something different.

Language also may be rejected because members of Congress believe it is poorly drafted and likely to be misinterpreted, or because they want it to be made a part of separate legislation, or because of any number of personal considerations. Rejection is doubtful evidence of the legislative intent, let alone the meaning of the statute as enacted.

In United States v. Chem–Dyne Corp., 572 F.Supp. 802 (D.Ohio 1983), a Senate draft of a bill provided that the liability of CERCLA violators would be joint and several. CERCLA is an environmental statute dealing with the clean-up of hazardous wastes. During debate, the "joint and several" language was deleted. Senator Helms, an opponent of the bill, stated (126 Cong.Rec. S14964 (Nov. 24, 1980)) that this deletion was meant to eliminate joint and several liability, but the Senate bill sponsor had a different explanation.

> We * * * have deleted any reference to joint and several liability, relying on common law principles to determine when parties should be severally liable. * * * The changes were made in recognition of the difficulty in prescribing in statutory terms liability standards which will be applicable in individual cases. * * *

> It is intended that issues of liability not resolved by this act, if any, shall be governed by traditional and evolving principles of common law. An example is joint and several liability. Any reference to these terms has been deleted, and the liability of joint tortfeasors will be determined under common or previous statutory law.

The House sponsor made a similar statement for the Congressional Record. The court held that deletion did not imply rejection of the substantive content of the deleted text.

> Perhaps in other contexts, when Congress deletes certain language it "strongly militates against a judgment that Congress intended a result that it expressly declined to enact." This case, however, presents an exceptional situation. A reading of the entire legislative history in context reveals that the [ ] term joint and several liability w[as] deleted to avoid a mandatory legislative standard applicable in all situations which might produce inequitable results in some cases. The deletion was not intended as a rejection of joint and several liability. Rather, the term was omitted in order to have the scope of liability determined under common law principles, where a court performing a case by case evaluation of the complex factual scenarios associated with multiple-generator waste sites will assess the propriety of applying joint and several liability on an individual basis.

The House sponsor's explanation for rejecting language about joint and several liability sounds a lot like Judge Breyer's explanation (see Chapter 10.04g) for why legislators might put something in legislative history rather than the statutory text—it allows the court to make exceptions to a general principle in specific cases.

––––––––––

The Report to the Attorney General, supra, is a little more enthusiastic about relying on the substitution of different language (rather than deletion of part of a text) as evidence of statutory meaning.

Cases in which there was a simultaneous or nearly simultaneous substitution of different language are somewhat different; there, the interpreter of the statute can at least compare the rejected language with language chosen in its place. While members of Congress may have had many of the same reasons for rejecting the earlier language, independent of any disagreement with its substance, and while the adopted language may actually have substantially the same meaning as the rejected language, a comparison of the rejected language with the enacted language may serve to point out implications of the enacted language that might otherwise go unnoticed. Thus, the interpreter should draw inferences not from the fact of rejection of the proposed language but from the meaning of the statute with the adopted language, as informed by comparison with the rejected language.

Doesn't the textualist who relies on drafting context have a fundamental problem? The meaning of a text depends on what the author and audience share about the use of language. But the audience may not know anything about drafting context. Why might a textualist who is generally hostile to legislative history nonetheless be receptive to considering drafting context?

10.09   PRE-LEGISLATIVE STAGE

Legislative history is sometimes created before the legislative process begins, in the form of reports by people who generate the ideas for legislation. These people may work for the executive branch, or be outside experts appointed by the executive or legislature, or be experts working for legal "think tanks." What weight should be accorded to their statements about statutory meaning?

a)   EXECUTIVE BRANCH

Kosak v. United States
465 U.S. 848 (1984).

■ Mr. Justice Marshall delivered the opinion of the Court. * * *

[Editor—The claimant's property was damaged while in the custody of the United States Customs Service. The Federal Torts Claims Act permits private suits against the United States but exempts claims "arising in respect of * * * the detention of any goods or merchandise by any officer of Customs." 28 U.S.C. § 2680(c). The claimant argued that the withdrawal of permission to sue did not apply to physical damage to property while in custody, but only to damages based on the mere fact of retention, such as spoilage. After starting with the statutory language, the Court turned to the legislative history, which supported the broader exemption.]

[T]he person who almost certainly drafted the language under consideration clearly thought that it covered injury to detained property caused by the negligence of customs officials. It appears that the portion of § 2680(c) pertaining to the detention of goods was first written by Judge Alexander Holtzoff, one of the major figures in the development of the Tort Claims Act. In his Report explicating his proposals, Judge Holtzoff explained:

> "[The proposed provision would exempt from the coverage of the Act] [c]laims arising in respect of the assessment or collection of any tax or customs duty. This exception appears in all previous drafts. It is expanded, however, so as to include immunity from liability in respect of loss in connection with the detention of goods or merchandise by any officer of customs or excise. The additional proviso has special reference to the detention of imported goods in appraisers' warehouses or customs houses, as well as seizures by law enforcement officials, internal revenue officers, and the like." A. Holtzoff, Report on Proposed Federal Tort Claims Bill 16 (1931)(Holtzoff Report).

Though it cannot be definitively established that Congress relied upon Judge Holtzoff's report, it is significant that the apparent draftsman of the crucial portion of § 2680(c) believed that it would bar a suit of the sort brought by petitioner.

In footnote 13 to the opinion the Court explained more fully the circumstances underlying the writing and circulation of the report.

Mr. Holtzoff wrote his report while serving as Special Assistant to the Attorney General. He had been "assigned by Attorney General Mitchell to the special task of co-ordinating the views of the Government departments" regarding the proper scope of a tort claims statute. See Borchard, The Federal Tort Claims Bill, 1 U.Chi. L.Rev. 1, n.2 (1933). Holtzoff submitted his report, in which his draft bill was contained, to Assistant Attorney General Rugg, who in turn transmitted it to the General Accounting Office of the Comptroller General. Insofar as Holtzoff's report embodied the views of the Executive Department at the stage of the debates over the tort claims bill, it is likely that, at some point, the report was brought to the attention of the Congressmen considering the bill. We agree with the dissent that, because the report was never introduced into the public record, the ideas expressed therein should not be given great weight in determining the intent of the legislature. But, in the absence of any direct evidence regarding how members of Congress understood the provision that became § 2680(c), it seems to us senseless to ignore entirely the views of its draftsman.

Justice Stevens, in dissent, "would eschew any reliance on the intent of the lobbyist whose opinion on the question before us was not on the public record." Can the drafter in the executive department be considered only a "lobbyist?"

QUESTIONS

1. Does the Court give some weight to the Report because it was drafted by a knowledgeable member of the executive branch? If so, is that wrong because the drafter is (as Stevens says) like a lobbyist?

2. Is the Court right to assume legislative awareness of the Report? Even if there was awareness, what supports a judgment that the legislature approved of its contents?

3. If the Report was not "on the public record," presumably those affected by the statute were unaware of its contents. Does that make it unfair to give an expansive reading of an exemption from government liability based on the Report?

b) "NONPOLITICAL EXPERTS"

The Executive branch is not the only source of pre-legislative materials. Various commissions established by law (roughly analogous to the English Law Commission and Royal Commissions) and several private groups may study an issue and make proposals for legislation. Consider whether it is a plus or minus for judicial reliance on the legislative history generated by these commissions and groups that membership consists of politicians or nonpolitical "experts."

Legislative study commissions. Standing committees in state legislatures are often less thorough in studying an issue than congressional committees. Moreover, they frequently do not issue committee reports. When they do, they often contain only recommendations about passage of proposed legislation, without elaboration. Various bodies therefore exist as alternatives or supplements to standing legislative committees. These bodies differ from standing committees in one important respect. Instead of evaluating a proposed bill introduced in the legislature, they evaluate a problem and propose legislation with accompanying commentary. The legislature may or may not make changes when it adopts the recommended legislation.

A majority of states have permanent Law Revision Commissions or Legislative Councils. They are primarily concerned with managing legislative business between sessions, but they may also take responsibility for analyzing problems and proposing legislative solutions. Their membership is often political, made up either of legislators or gubernatorial appointees, but their staffs and subordinate committees will often consist of nonlegislative "experts."

Special ad hoc commissions may also be established by the state legislature to study specific problems. Their membership might not include elected politicians. Or a nonpolitical expert (often a law professor) might be asked to study an issue.

"*Private lawmaking.*" Chapters 2 and 7 alluded to private national organizations which study problems and propose legislation for passage by state legislatures after a thorough and open evaluation of the relevant issues and comments by interested parties—such as the National Conference of Commissioners on Uniform State Laws (NCCUSL) and the American Law Institute (ALI). These organizations are supposed to be expert and apolitical, but studies of the history of Article 9 of the Uniform Commercial Code (discussed in Chapter 7) suggest that this might not be the case.

This raises questions about the usefulness of the "legislative history" which emerges from these "private lawmaking" endeavors. One example is the commentary written by the Reporter for the UCC (and other ALI projects), which is attached to proposals for legislative action. Building on the UCC study discussed in Chapter 7, Laurens Walker questions whether courts should rely on such commentary.[47] He notes that some earlier UCC drafts explicitly allowed courts to consult commentary to the UCC, but that this provision was eventually deleted, probably in response to a statement by the New York Law Revision Commission that they were "unnecessary and could lead to unprecedented use of the Comments to expand and qualify the text." Despite this deletion, Walker observes that courts still consult the commentary, taking to them "like ducks to water." This is true even when the commentary on which courts rely has been changed, although the statutory text remains the same. Walker suggests that "expert" commentary is one way for private interests to exert influence.

Should commentary attached to laws proposed by the NCCUSL and the ALI be weighty evidence of statutory meaning on the ground that it promotes uniformity among states? Can a court distinguish between situations in which the commentary is "technical" or "apolitical," or at least was not the product of interest group pressure that unfairly skewed the lawmaking process?

Would it be a good idea to rely on such commentary, simply because the statute's audience routinely relies on it? Why do courts cite treatises? Is there any requirement that the treatise writer be aware of or part of the legislative drafting process?

Some cases. In practice, reports and commentary from the sources discussed above stand the best chance of being relied by a court if a standing legislative committee explicitly states that the comments by drafters reflect the committee's view. Kaplan v. Superior Court of Orange County, 491 P.2d 1, 5 n. 4 (Cal.1971)(two legislative committees state that the official comments by the State's Law Revision Commission reflect legislative intent). See also Sheffield–Briggs Steel Products, Inc. v. Ace Concrete Service Co., 63 So.2d 924, 926 (Fla.1953)(legislative approval for commentary accompanying a Uniform State Law is inferred when the commentary was public for two years and available to the legislature before passage of the statute).

47. Laurens Walker, Writings on the Margin of American Law: Committee Notes, Comments, and Commentary, 29 Georgia L. Rev. 993 (1995).

However, Twentieth Century Furniture, Inc. v. Labor & Indus. Relations Appeal Bd., 482 P.2d 151, 153 (Hawaii 1971), did not rely on a report by a professor who had conducted a study of Workers Compensation laws for the legislature. The issue was whether the rule for computing permanent total disability benefits applied to temporary disability. The professor's report said that it did not. The court was reluctant to use the report because it was difficult to be sure that a nonlegislator's ideas could be equated with legislative will. Does the fact that only one professor conducted the study distinguish this report from the reports of national bodies or Legislative Commissions? In Institute of Living v. Town & City of Hartford, 50 A.2d 822, 825 (Conn.1946), the report of a special ad hoc committee established by the legislature was not accorded weight concerning whether hospitals were exempt from property tax, because the legislature made many changes in the committee's proposal. The legislature apparently built on but did not adopt the committee's work.

10.10 PRESIDENTIAL INTERPRETATIONS

In contemporary practice, the President issues a signing statement accompanying the signing of a bill. Most signing statements contain empty generalities praising or criticizing the bill, or objections to portions which are allegedly unconstitutional, usually regarding the President's appointment[48] or foreign relations power. Before 1986, there were sporadic instances of signing statements which interpreted a statute. Presidents Jackson and Tyler each did so once in the first half of the 19th century, when any aggressive Presidential legislative role (even use of the veto) was controversial. President Truman twice construed an act he was signing in the late 1940s.[49] President Carter issued six, apparently uncontroversial interpretations.[50]

In 1986, however, President Reagan began to add interpretive comments to these signing statements with some frequency.[51] Some of these were very controversial, either contradicting other strong evidence of statutory meaning or asserting positions on politically sensitive issues about which there was no apparent legislative agreement. One statement asserted that illegal discrimination against aliens could only be established by proving

---

48. Federal legislation can be administered only by officials appointed by the President. When legislation purports to grant enforcement power to others, the President's signing statement usually says that the statutory authority will be construed as merely advisory.

49. See J. Sundquist, The Decline and Resurgence of Congress 24 (1981); Corwin, The President: Office and Powers 319 (5th ed. 1984); Zinn, The Veto Power of the President, 12 F.R.D. 207, 230–31 (1952).

50. 14 Weekly Comp. Pres. Doc. 1794; 15 id. 1435; 16 id. 466, 1334, 1521, 2231.

51. See generally Garber & Wimmer, Presidential Signing Statements as Interpretations of Legislative Intent: An Executive Aggrandizement of Power, 24 Harv. J. Leg. 363 (1987); Popkin, Judicial Use of Presidential Legislative History: A Critique, 66 Ind. L. J. 699 (1991); Killenbeck, A Matter of Mere Approval? The Role of the President in the Creation of Legislative History, 48 Ark. L. Rev. 239 (1995).

discriminatory intent, not discriminatory impact.[52] Another claimed that federal enforcement of the Safe Drinking Water Act was more discretionary than the statute and some other legislative history suggested.[53] A third statement took sides in a Senate–House controversy over the effective date and judicial discretion under the Sentencing Act of 1987.[54] A fourth statement asserted a weaker standard for deciding whether the government had to pay a prevailing party's attorney's fees than a standard appearing in a House Report.[55] Some signing statements were less controversial; they claimed to record an agreement with legislative leaders about what the statute means, rather than to assert an independent Presidential interpretation.[56]

President Reagan was clearly trying to have a significant impact with many of these statements. Instead of just allowing them to be published in the official Weekly Compilation of Presidential Documents (where all such statements routinely began to appear in 1966), his Attorney General persuaded the privately published United States Code Congressional and Administrative News (USCCAN) to include them in its "Legislative History" section, beginning in 1986. USCCAN is typically purchased by lawyers throughout the country, who do not always have easy access to official legislative history.

COMMENTS AND QUESTIONS

1. Should the President's signing statements carry the same weight as legislative history emerging from Congress? One argument for giving the President equal power with the legislature to create legislative history is his legislative role, specified in Article I of the Constitution. He must concur in legislation, unless his veto is overridden by a two-thirds vote of each House of Congress. But the President's veto power is normally understood to be only a negative power. It does not give the President an affirmative legislative role, justifying judicial reliance on his interpretation of the law. The President does not even have to sign a bill for it to become a law. Failure to sign will still result in the bill becoming law, except in the special case of a pocket veto. At one time there was even doubt whether Presidential signature after congressional adjournment could make a law, but the Supreme Court held that it could.[57]

52. Statement accompanying signing of Pub.L.No. 99–603, 22 Weekly Comp. Pres. Doc. 1534 (Nov. 6, 1986).

53. Statement accompanying signing of Pub.L.No. 99–339, 22 Weekly Comp. Pres. Doc. 831 (June 23, 1986).

54. Statement accompanying signing of Pub.L.No. 100–182, 23 Weekly Comp. Pres. Doc. 1452 (Dec. 7, 1987).

55. Statement accompanying signing of Pub.L.No. 99–80, 21 Weekly Comp. Pres. Doc. 966 (Aug. 5, 1985).

56. Statements accompanying signing of Pub.L.Nos. 99–349, 99–396, and 100–2, 22 Weekly Comp. Pres. Doc. 893 (July 7, 1986), 1125 (Sept. 1, 1986), and 23 id. 87 (Jan. 28, 1987).

57. Edwards v. United States, 286 U.S. 482, 490–91 (1932).

Another argument for a Presidential power to interpret laws through signing statements relies on the grant of executive power to the chief executive and the President's duty to "take care that the laws be faithfully executed." (Article II, § 1, cl. 1 and § 3 of the Constitution). The idea is that "execution" of the laws necessarily includes an interpretive power.[58] One weakness of this argument is that it would apply only if the law requires execution by the federal executive branch.

A more basic objection is that an executive official, including the President, cannot exercise rulemaking power (including a power of interpretation), which interferes with the grant a rulemaking by the governing statute.[59] Unless the legislation grants a rulemaking power to the President directly, the most that a President can do is participate in rulemaking with those whom Congress has charged with administering the law, perhaps to coordinate federal policy. Any greater Presidential power would allow him not only to undermine a substantive grant of authority by Congress to a particular agency, but also to bypass rulemaking procedures (such as the opportunity for public comment), which are either explicitly required by the Administrative Procedure Act or are adopted in practice by the agency.

The possibility of an independent Presidential power to create legislative history must also be evaluated in light of disputes about the line item veto and impoundment power. See Chapter 18. Creating legislative history is part of the broader claim of Presidential power to play a legislative role beyond initiating legislative proposals and becoming involved in the legislative bargaining process. In fact, an interpretive power might be used as a substitute for a line item veto or impoundment power in some situations, beyond whatever power the President already has.

2.   Should Presidential legislative history be accorded some weight when the President participated in the negotiations over details of the final bill which is discussed in the signing statement? See, e.g., U.S. v. Story, 891 F.2d 988, 994 (2d Cir.1989)(President's views on Sentencing Act are significant because he participated in negotiation over compromise legislation). In such cases the President can at least lay claim to knowing about the legislative compromise. However, Presidential legislative history comes after a bill has been passed, when no one can respond as part of the normal give and take of legislative debate. It therefore has the potential to manipulate results in the manner of a conference committee report issued in the rush to legislative adjournment.

3.   Should Presidential legislative history be accorded some weight if it records a real agreement with legislative leaders on an issue which is not politically sensitive, as is often the case with more conventional legislative history?

4.   Suppose the President vetoes a bill because of objections to the legislative history in legislative materials, but Congress overrides the veto? Does the veto undermine the weight of the legislative materials, even if Presidential statements are not weighty evidence of statutory meaning?

---

58. See Myers v. United States, 272 U.S. 52, 135 (1926).

59. See Chrysler Corp. v. Brown, 441 U.S. 281, 304–08 (1979).

Here is an example which the courts may confront in the future. The Private Securities Litigation Reform Act of 1995 (Pub. L. 104–67, 104th Cong., 1st Sess. (1995)) dealt with proof of securities fraud, ratcheting up the pleadings requirements for plaintiffs. The statute stated that, to prove a defendant's fraudulent state of mind, the plaintiff had to plead "with particularity facts giving rise to a strong inference that the defendant acted with [fraud]." This provision tightened the pleading requirements compared to prior law so that a plaintiff could not simply make a *general allegation* of fraud (this had been the 9th Circuit's approach under prior law). Most experts in the field saw the new statutory text as the product of a compromise which adopted the Second Circuit's approach—which had required offering proof of specific facts giving rise to an inference of fraud or motive. However, the H.R. Conf. Rep. 104–369 stated: "Because the Conference Committee intends to strengthen existing pleading requirements, it does not intend to codify the Second Circuit's case law interpreting this pleading standard," implying that pleading requirements were even stricter than the Second Circuit standard. President Clinton vetoed the bill containing this language but the veto was overridden.

The popular press reported that one reason for the veto was the President's view that the legislative history improperly interpreted the statutory text to be too disadvantageous to plaintiffs—even tougher than the Second Circuit approach. In future litigation, the President's overridden veto might be cited as evidence that the legislative history in the committee report lacked the weight it might otherwise enjoy.

––––––––––

There are very few cases dealing with Presidential interpretations. Several cases from the Reagan era cited Presidential signing statements: (1) Equal Access to Justice Act: Taylor v. Heckler, 835 F.2d 1037, 1044 n. 17 (3d Cir.1987)(court refused to decide what authority the statement had, because the court followed prior precedent); Hadden v. Bowen, 657 F.Supp. 679, 684 n. 2 (D.Utah 1986)(did not follow the President's interpretation); Miles v. Bowen, 632 F.Supp. 282, 285 (D.Ala.1986) (citing the President's statement as partial authority for its conclusion); and (2) Sentencing Act: United States v. Charleus, 871 F.2d 265 (2d Cir.1989)(citing the signing statement, but there was no dispute over the issue addressed by the statement); U.S. v. Story, 891 F.2d 988, 994 (2d Cir.1989)(President's views on Sentencing Act are significant because he participated in negotiation over compromise legislation).[60]

Several cases discussed President Bush's signing statement that the Civil Rights Act of 1991 was prospective. Petitti v. New England Telephone and Telegraph Co., 1992 WL 359643 (D.Mass.1992), stated that there was no

60. See also City of Burbank v. Lockheed Air Terminal Inc., 411 U.S. 624, 637–38 (1973)(Presidential signing statement was considered relevant to a decision whether a federal statute pre-empted local control of air traffic noise); Waterman S. S. Corp. v. United States, 381 U.S. 252, 268–69 (1965)(President's veto of a bill interpreting prior law deprives legislative interpretation of any weight because the President who vetoed the bill was also the President who signed the bill being interpreted).

reason to treat the statement as "anything other than a [   ] statement of intent that was unable to be stated explicitly in the legislation, due to countervailing intent." Crumley v. Delaware State College, 797 F.Supp. 341 (D.Del.1992), treated the signing statement as carrying no more interpretative weight than the EEOC policy statement, on which the court refused to place any weight. But Illinois District Courts treated both the EEOC policy statement and the Presidential signing statement as relevant legislative history. Ribando v. United Airlines, Inc., 787 F.Supp. 827 (D.Ill.1992); Sofferin v. American Airlines, Inc., 785 F.Supp. 780 (D.Ill.1992).

There are also occasional references to a state Governor's statement about legislative intent in determining the meaning of a state statute. State v. Brasel, 623 P.2d 696, 699 (Wash.App.1981); State v. Strong Oil Co., 433 N.Y.Supp.2d 345, 350 (N.Y.Sup.1980).

The executive's legislative authority is also relevant when Congress passes two bills in one order but they are signed by the President in a different order. For example, assume that two bills contain tax penalty provisions—one for 20% of the tax due (Bill–20%), the other for 25% (Bill–25%). Bill–20% passes the legislature first but transmittal to the President is delayed until after Bill–25% is sent to the President and signed. Thus, Bill–20% is first passed, but last signed. Generally, the latest bill to become law is the law. But what is the latest bill—the last one passed by Congress or the last one signed by the President? In Pallottini v. Commissioner, 90 T.C. 498 (1988), the court held that the issue was one of legislative intent. Therefore, the second bill passed by the legislature prevailed (Bill–25%), even though signed first.

One judge concurred on the grounds that the latest bill passed by Congress was the "law," regardless of legislative "intent." The latest-passed-is-law approach can be justified on the ground that Presidential signature is not usually required for a bill to become law? Normally, a bill can become law without Presidential signature. Article I of the U.S. Constitution provides that the President, "[i]f he approve[s a bill] he shall sign it, but if not he shall return it, with his Objections * * *." This allows a two-thirds majority of Congress to override a veto. But a signature is not usually necessary. The Constitution continues: "If any Bill shall not be returned by the President within ten Days (Sundays excepted) after it shall have been presented to [the President], the Same shall be a Law, in like Manner as if he had signed it * * *." However, if "Congress by their Adjournment prevent [the bill's] Return, [the bill] shall not be a Law." Congressional adjournment during the ten-day period after presentment to the President allows the President to do what is called "pocket veto" the bill, by not signing it, if Congress has so adjourned. In this narrow circumstance (of congressional adjournment after presentment), Presidential signature is necessary for a bill to become law. Would the concurring judge decide that a first-passed-but-later-signed bill was the law, if the President's signature was necessary for the bill to become a statute because Congress had adjourned after passage and presentment to the President?

CHAPTER 11

ADMINISTRATIVE INTERPRETATION

11.01 INTRODUCTION

In Chapter 10 we discussed judicial reliance on contemporaneous legislative history as evidence of statutory meaning. In this Chapter, we consider judicial deference to administrative interpretations of statutes. In the modern state, a vast majority of law (maybe most law) is made at the administrative level. In a legislation course, we can only briefly consider the relationship between legislature, courts, and administrative agencies, leaving a more complete analysis to administrative law courses. We can, however, place the problem of judicial deference to agency interpretation in the broader setting of statutory interpretation.

Deference to the agency is a direct challenge to the court's traditional role of interpreting statutes. Courts which were so jealous of their power that they narrowly interpreted statutes in derogation of the common law could hardly be expected to look more kindly on administrative agencies, which lacked even the democratic lineage that statutes possessed. Administrative rules have always had an uneasy place in our system, because they are not issued by elected officials and their rulemaking procedures do not always afford the kind of public participation that might legitimate agency action.

This tension has suggested two models regarding judicial reliance on agency interpretations, referred to as the "independent judgment" and "deferential" model by Farina, Statutory Interpretation and the Balance of Power in the Administrative State, 89 Colum. L.Rev. 452 (1989). In the *independent judgment* model, the court exercises its traditional independent judgment to interpret the statute, but relies on help from the agency to identify legislative intent. The *deferential* model requires the court to accept constructions offered by the agency when legislative intent is unclear.

The *deferential* model itself has a number of variations. One variation requires deference to the agency, guided by considerations of *institutional competence*. It leaves room for some independent judicial judgment, but leans towards deference to the agency's rules when the agency is competent to make decisions. A second variation is the *super-deferential* approach, arguably adopted by Chevron, U.S.A., Inc. v. Natural Resources Defense Council, 467 U.S. 837 (1984). A super-deferential approach relies on an agency's reasonable interpretation whenever the statute is unclear, without regard to institutional competence.

Finally, the *super-deferential* approach itself contains an ambiguity. What determines when the statute is unclear? In one view, the issue is *textual.*

Whenever the text is unclear, the court defers to a reasonable agency interpretation. In another view, lack of statutory clarity is a function of legislative intent, determined by *"traditional tools of interpretation"*, which could include text, purpose, legislative history, and substantive background considerations. Under the "legislative intent-traditional tools" approach, textual uncertainty is not sufficient to force deference to an agency's interpretation, and textual clarity is not sufficient to prevent deference.

This framework for judicial use of agency interpretations can be outlined as follows:

1. Independent judgment model
2. Deferential model, based on

    a) Agency institutional competence

    b) Super-deferential approach, invoked if

        i) Textual uncertainty in statute, or

        ii) Legislative intent uncertain, based on traditional tools of interpretation

Chapter 11.02 discusses the "independent judgment" model. Chapter 11.03 analyzes deference based on institutional competence. Chapter 11.04 focuses on the super-deferential approach in general and, more particularly, on the Chevron case, which is allegedly the source of that approach. We want to know just how deferential the Chevron case requires courts to be and under what circumstances. Chapter 11.05 compares judicial deference to agencies and reliance on legislative history.

11.02 INDEPENDENT JUDICIAL JUDGMENT

The easiest way to reconcile agency rules with a court's interpretive role is to pretend that the agency can help the court identify the intent of the enacting legislature. To that end, courts developed the notion that agency rules adopted contemporaneously with the passage of a statute were more entitled to judicial deference. The theory was that contemporaneous rules were likely to reflect what the legislature wanted because they were issued close to the time of enactment by an agency which knew the legislature's intent.

There are obvious difficulties with this approach. First, agencies may be responsive to different political pressures than the legislature. Second, when the agency follows the "legislature," it is usually legislative committees which lead the way. See, e.g., Consolidated Rail Corp. v. Darrone, 465 U.S. 624, 634 (1984)(congressional committees participated in formation of regulations). The agency interpretation can therefore claim no greater weight than a committee report. Indeed, one of the problems with the political process is the so-called iron triangle of agency, legislative committee, and special interest groups subject to government regulation. Deferring to an agency interpretation might therefore ratify the results of that confluence of political forces.

The cases do not reveal any " 'consistent application' of the 'contemporaneousness' " approach. Justice Steven's dissent in Adamo Wrecking Co. v. United States, 434 U.S. 275, 302 (1978), is typical, citing Justice Cardozo for the principle

> that an administrative "practice has peculiar weight when it involves a contemporaneous construction of a statute by the men charged with the responsibility of setting its machinery in motion, of making the parts work efficiently and smoothly while they are yet untried and new."

Justice Blackmun also appealed to contemporaneousness in Aluminum Co. v. Central Lincoln Peoples' Utility Dist., 467 U.S. 380, 390 (1984):

> [The agency] * * * was intimately involved in the drafting and consideration of the statute by Congress. Following enactment of the statute, the agency immediately interpreted the statute in the manner now under challenge. Thus, [the agency's] interpretation represents "a contemporaneous construction of a statute by the men charged with the responsibility of setting its machinery in motion, of making the parts work efficiently and smoothly while they are yet untried and new."

Despite these references, "contemporaneousness" as evidence of legislative intent is a weak principle, probably cited to give the agency rules a democratic pedigree. Indeed, in the Aluminum Co. case just cited, Justice Blackmun's statement follows immediately after his observation that the issue is "technical and complex," and the agency has "longstanding expertise," both of which relate to the agency's institutional competence (discussed *infra*), not its knowledge of legislative intent.

The weakness of the contemporaneousness principle shows up clearly when the court upholds a *non*contemporaneous agency rule. For example, in National Muffler Dealers Ass'n, Inc. v. United States, 440 U.S. 472 (1979), the Court dealt with a 1929 tax Regulation reversing a 1919 regulation defining a tax exempt business league. Justice Blackmun stated:

> Contemporaneity, however, is only one of the many considerations that counsel courts to defer to the administrative interpretation of a statute. It need not control here. Nothing in the regulations or case law, directly explains the [agency's] shift. We do know, however, that the change in 1929 incorporated an interpretation thought necessary to match the statute's construction to the original congressional intent. We would be reluctant to adopt the rigid view that an agency may not alter its interpretation in light of administrative experience.

But see Rowan Companies, Inc. v. United States, 452 U.S. 247 (1981) (agency cannot change its view, originally embodied in contemporaneous regulations, that "wages" for social security and unemployment tax did *not* include meals provided to an employee for the employer's convenience).

11.03   DEFERENCE BASED ON INSTITUTIONAL COMPETENCE

Another approach to deciding whether a court should defer to an agency rule is to rely on the agency's institutional competence. There are multiple criteria for determining agency competence and application of this approach requires the court to make very complex judgments.

1. *Political responsiveness of the agency.* Some agencies pay close attention to what elected officials want, giving their decisions at least the appearance of a democratic source. But which source of post-enactment political influence should prevail in case of a conflict—congressional oversight or Presidential leadership?

2. *Public participation in agency proceedings.* The agency may develop a democratic pedigree of its own through procedures permitting public notice and comment prior to adoption of agency rules. Agency rules adopted after public participation may earn judicial deference.

3. *The rationality of the agency's reasoning process.* In Adamo Wrecking Co. v. United States, 434 U.S. 275, 289 n. 5 (1978), the Court held the agency to a very high level of rationality. The issue was whether the statutory authority to promulgate "emission standards" included the authority to specify that a certain "work practice" be followed while demolishing a building containing asbestos, when the agency did not explicitly limit asbestos emissions during demolition.

> Our Brother Stevens quite correctly points out, that an administrative "contemporaneous construction" of a statute is entitled to considerable weight, and it is true that the originally proposed regulations contain, with respect to some uses of asbestos, the sort of provisions which the Administrator and the Congress later designated as "work practice standards." It bears noting, however, that these regulations can only be said to define by implication the meaning of the term "emission standard." The Administrator * * * denominated [them] "emission standards"; and it is undoubtedly a fair inference that the Administrator thought [them] to be an "emission standard." But neither the regulations themselves nor the comments accompanying them give any indication of the Administrator's reasons for concluding that Congress, in authorizing him to promulgate "emission standards," intended to include "work practice standards" within the meaning of that term. See 38 Fed. Reg. 8820–8822, 8829–8830 (1973); 36 Fed. Reg. 23239–23240, 23242 (1971).
>
> This lack of specific attention to the statutory authorization is especially important in light of this Court's pronouncement in Skidmore v. Swift & Co., 323 U.S. 134, 140 (1944), that one factor to be considered in giving weight to an administrative ruling is "the thoroughness evident in its consideration, the validity of its reason-

ing, its consistency with earlier and later pronouncements, and all those factors which give it power to persuade, if lacking power to control." The Administrator's remarks with regard to these regulations clearly demonstrate that he carefully considered available techniques and methods for controlling asbestos emissions, but they give no indication of "the validity of [his] reasoning" in concluding that he was authorized to promulgate these techniques as an "emission standard," within the statutory definition. Since this Court can only speculate as to his reasons for reaching that conclusion, the mere promulgation of a regulation, without a concomitant exegesis of the statutory authority for doing so, obviously lacks "power to persuade" as to the existence of such authority.

4. *Agency expertise in dealing with technical problems.* The agency may be an expert in resolving technically complex problems. In Aluminum Co. of America v. Central Lincoln Peoples' Utility Dist., 467 U.S. 380, 390 (1984), for example, Justice Blackmun states:

> These principles of deference [to the agency] have particular force in the context of this case. The subject under regulation is technical and complex. [The agency] has longstanding expertise in the area * * *.

5. *Agency "bias".* Some issues might not be trusted to the agency because the agency's own interest might distort its judgment. The boundary between "bias" and expertise is fuzzy, however. Should courts be more reluctant to defer to agency decisions about taking jurisdiction or refusing to regulate, because the agency's decisions about its own power are likely to be influenced by improper standards? Or do decisions about exercising power implicate the kinds of policy judgments which should be entrusted to the agency?

6. *The importance of obtaining a legislative (rather than an agency) decision on certain issues.* Courts may decide that certain issues should be resolved by a legislature rather than an agency. Some political decisions, despite the agency's expertise, require a clear legislative statement.

7. *The importance of protecting persons from serious harms.* Some harms should not be imposed without a clear legislative statement. When Justice Stevens argued that filing with an agency "before December 31" meant "on or before December 31" (Locke v. United States, Chapter 6.04biv), he was concerned that the agency was depriving the claimant of his livelihood. In other cases, the agency's interpretation may have free speech implications or harm social insurance or welfare claimants. This criterion requires courts to decide what "harms" are serious, even when there are no constitutional implications.

8. *Longstanding rules.* Courts frequently place greater weight on longstanding rules, without explaining why. When a rule has existed for a long time, that may imply that it has withstood the political test of time, suggesting that the agency's political savvy justifies deference. Another justification is that people rely on a longstanding rule. Concern about rejecting such a rule

is therefore a special case of preventing harm. However, prospective rejection of the agency rule would protect reliance interests, if future and retroactive effects can be sorted out.

11.04   SUPER–DEFERENCE

a) INTRODUCTION

Rather than rely on the agency's help in identifying legislative intent or defer to the agency on institutional competence grounds, the court might defer to the agency whenever the statute appears to leave an issue unresolved and the agency's resolution is "reasonable." This has been referred to as the super-deferential approach and is usually traced to Chevron, U.S.A., Inc. v. Natural Resources Defense Council, 467 U.S. 837 (1984).

In effect, the super-deferential approach completely reverses the traditional judicial suspicion of agencies. Rather than be suspicious of the agency, the dominant institutional background consideration is that legislatures and agencies should be left to work out the answers to political questions, with the courts playing the more modest role of identifying whether there is an issue left unresolved by the legislature and, if so, whether the agency rule is "reasonable." When those conditions are met, the statute is presumed to authorize the agency rule.

It will help you evaluate the application of the Chevron case to keep in mind the political implications of a super-deferential approach. Deference to agencies was originally favored by the political Left, because agencies were created to reform and regulate the economy and redistribute wealth. Two contemporary developments have undermined the "Left's" enthusiasm for judicial deference to agencies. The first is private interest group influence over many (though by no means all) agency decisions. The second is that agencies have, in at least some instances, shifted to the right. In the economic sphere, this shift is apparent in the move towards deregulation. In the social sphere, prohibiting recipients of federal funds from providing abortion counseling is an example.

When agencies reverse earlier "liberal" rules, a super-deferential court permits the new agency rule to stand. Efforts by Congress to reverse the agency rule may be unavailing, because Congress lacks the ⅔ds majority to override a Presidential veto, exercised to protect the agency rule. This is what happened in Rust v. Sullivan, 500 U.S. 173 (1991). The Court permitted the agency to change course and adopt regulations forbidding use of federal funds to provide abortion counseling, relying on Chevron. Congress voted to override Rust in an appropriations bill for the Departments of Labor and Health and Human Services, but could not override President Bush's veto. 137 Cong. Rec. H10508 (Nov. 19, 1991).

Judicial deference to agencies under Chevron also combines with several other legal rules to enhance executive power. Congress can delegate broad rulemaking powers to an agency (Mistretta v. United States, 488 U.S. 361 (1989)), and the legislative veto is unconstitutional (Immigration and Naturalization Service v. Chadha, 462 U.S. 919 (1983)(see Chapter 18.04b, dealing with the legislative veto)).

In the remainder of this section, we read the Chevron case itself and consider what it really means.[1] How does the court determine whether the statute is unclear, thus prompting deference to the agency? Does Chevron always rule out considerations of institutional competence?

b) Chevron, U.S.A., Inc. v. Natural Resources Defense Council, 467 U.S. 837 (1984)

■ Justice Stevens delivered the opinion of the Court.

In the Clean Air Act Amendments of 1977, Pub.L. 95–95, 91 Stat. 685, Congress enacted certain requirements applicable to States that had not achieved the national air quality standards established by the Environmental Protection Agency (EPA) pursuant to earlier legislation. The amended Clean Air Act required these "nonattainment" States to establish a permit program regulating "new or modified major stationary sources" of air pollution. Generally, a permit may not be issued for a new or modified major stationary source unless several stringent conditions are met. The EPA regulation promulgated to implement this permit requirement allows a State to adopt a plantwide definition of the term "stationary source". Under this definition, an existing plant that contains several pollution-emitting devices may install or modify one piece of equipment without meeting the permit conditions if the alteration will not increase the total emissions from the plant. The question presented by this case is whether EPA's decision to allow States to treat all of the pollution-emitting devices within the same industrial grouping as though they were encased within a single "bubble" is based on a reasonable construction of the statutory term "stationary source."

The EPA regulations containing the plantwide definition of the term stationary source were promulgated on October 14, 1981. 46 Fed. Reg. 50766. * * *

The [Court of Appeals] observed that the relevant part of the amended Clean Air Act, "does not explicitly define what Congress envisioned as a 'stationary source', to which the permit program * * * should apply," and further stated that the precise issue was not "squarely addressed in the legislative history." * * *

When a Court reviews an agency's construction of the statute which it administers, it is confronted with two questions. First,

---

1. Cass Sunstein asserts that Chevron defines "a cluster of ideas about who is entrusted with interpreting ambiguous statutes and, less obviously, about what legal interpretation actually is." Sunstein, Law and Administration After Chevron, 90 Colum. L. Rev. 2071 (1990)

always, is the question whether Congress has directly spoken to the precise question at issue. If the intent of Congress is clear, that is the end of the matter; for the court, as well as the agency, must give effect to the unambiguously expressed intent of Congress. [Editor—At this point, the Court states the "traditional tools of statutory construction" test in a footnote, as follows: "The judiciary is the final authority on issues of statutory construction and must reject administrative constructions which are contrary to clear congressional intent. If a court, employing traditional tools of statutory construction, ascertains that Congress had an intention on the precise question at issue, that intention is the law and must be given effect."] If, however, the court determines Congress has not directly addressed the precise question at issue, the court does not simply impose its own construction on the statute, as would be necessary in the absence of an administrative interpretation. Rather, if the statute is silent or ambiguous with respect to the specific issue, the question for the court is whether the agency's answer is based on a permissible construction of the statute.

"The power of an administrative agency to administer a congressionally created * * * program necessarily requires the formulation of policy and the making of rules to fill any gap left, implicitly or explicitly, by Congress." Morton v. Ruiz, 415 U.S. 199, 231(1974). If Congress has explicitly left a gap for the agency to fill, there is an express delegation of authority to the agency to elucidate a specific provision of the statute by regulation. Such legislative regulations are given controlling weight unless they are arbitrary, capricious, or manifestly contrary to the statute. Sometimes the legislative delegation to an agency on a particular question is implicit rather than explicit. In such a case, a court may not substitute its own construction of a statutory provision for a reasonable interpretation made by the administrator of an agency.

We have long recognized that considerable weight should be accorded to an executive department's construction of a statutory scheme it is entrusted to administer, and the principle of deference to administrative interpretations

"has been consistently followed by this Court whenever decision as to the meaning or reach of a statute has involved reconciling conflicting policies, and a full understanding of the force of the statutory policy in the given situation has depended upon more than ordinary knowledge respecting the matters subjected to agency regulations.

"* * * If this choice represents a reasonable accommodation of conflicting policies that were committed to the agency's care by the statute, we should not disturb it unless it appears from the statute or its legislative history that the accommodation is not one that Congress would have sanctioned." United States v. Shimer, 367 U.S. 374, 382, 383 (1961).

In light of these well-settled principles it is clear that the Court of Appeals misconceived the nature of its role in reviewing the regulations at issue. Once it determined, after its own examination of the legislation, that Congress did not actually have an intent regarding the applicability of the bubble concept to the permit program, the question before it was not whether in its view the concept is "inappropriate" in the general context of a program designed to improve air quality, but whether the Administrator's view that it is appropriate in the context of this particular program is a reasonable one. Based on the examination of the legislation and its history which follows, we agree with the Court of Appeals that Congress did not have a specific intention on the applicability of the bubble concept in these cases, and conclude that the EPA's use of that concept here is a reasonable policy choice for the agency to make.

[Editor—The Court then explains the history of the agency Regulations. Before 1977, when the Clean Air Act Amendments were adopted, EPA had adhered to a plantwide definition of "source." After the 1977 amendments, the agency considered the definition three times. In January, 1979, the agency rejected a plantwide definition if there was no Statewide Implementation Plan (SIP) in effect by July, 1979. In certain circumstances, however, an approved SIP in effect by that date could adopt a plantwide definition. In 1980, the Regulations were changed to follow two Courts of Appeals cases. The Regulations distinguished areas which had not attained national air quality standards from those areas which were maintaining such standards. A plantwide definition was permitted in maintenance but not nonattainment areas. Then in 1981, a new administration permitted a plantwide definition whether the area was a nonattainment or maintenance area. The issue was whether the statute permitted the agency to adopt the 1981 Regulation.]

* * * [R]espondents argue that the legislative history and policies of the Act foreclose the plantwide definition, and that the EPA's interpretation is not entitled to deference because it represents a sharp break with prior interpretations of the Act.

Based on our examination of the legislative history, we agree with the Court of Appeals that it is unilluminating. * * *

Our review of the EPA's varying interpretations of the word "source"—both before and after the 1977 Amendments—convince us that the agency primarily responsible for administering this important legislation has consistently interpreted it flexibly—not in a sterile textual vacuum, but in the context of implementing policy decisions in a technical and complex arena. The fact that the agency has from time to time changed its interpretation of the term source does not, as respondents argue, lead us to conclude that no deference should be accorded the agency's interpretation of the statute. An initial agency interpretation is not instantly carved in stone. On the contrary, the agency, to engage in informed rulemaking, must consider varying interpretations and the wisdom of its policy on a continuing basis. Moreover, the fact that the agency has adopted different definitions in different contexts adds force to the argument that the definition itself is flexible, particularly since Congress has never indicated any disapproval of a flexible reading of the statute.

Significantly, it was not the agency in 1980, but rather the Court of Appeals that read the statute inflexibly to command a plantwide definition for programs designed to maintain clean air and to forbid such a definition for programs designed to improve air quality. The distinction the court drew may well be a sensible one, but our labored review of the problem has surely disclosed that it is not a distinction that Congress ever articulated itself, or one that the EPA found in the statute before the courts began to review the legislative work product. We conclude that it was the Court of Appeals, rather than Congress or any of the decisionmakers who are authorized by Congress to administer this legislation, that was primarily responsible for the 1980 position taken by the agency.

* * *

The arguments over policy that are advanced in the parties' brief create the impression that respondents are now waging in a judicial forum a specific policy battle which they ultimately lost in the agency and in the 32 jurisdictions opting for the bubble concept, but one which was never waged in the Congress. Such policy arguments are more properly addressed to legislators or administrators, not to judges.

In this case, the Administrator's interpretation represents a reasonable accommodation of manifestly competing interests and is entitled to deference: the regulatory scheme is technical and complex, the agency considered the matter in a detailed and reasoned fashion, and the decision involves reconciling conflicting policies. Congress intended to accommodate both interests, but did not do so itself on the level of specificity presented by this case. Perhaps that body consciously desired the Administrator to strike the balance at this level, thinking that those with great expertise and charged with responsibility for administering the provision would be in a better position to do so; perhaps it simply did not consider the question at this level; and perhaps Congress was unable to forge a coalition on either side of the question, and those on each side decided to take their chances with the scheme devised by the agency. For judicial purposes, it matters not which of these things occurred.

Judges are not experts in the field, and are not part of either political branch of the Government. Courts must, in some cases, reconcile competing political interests, but not on the basis of the judges' personal policy preferences. In contrast, an agency to which

Congress has delegated policymaking responsibilities may, within the limits of that delegation, properly rely upon the incumbent administration's views of wise policy to inform its judgments. While agencies are not directly accountable to the people, the Chief Executive is, and it is entirely appropriate for this political branch of the Government to make such policy choices—resolving the competing interests which Congress itself either inadvertently did not resolve, or intentionally left to be resolved by the agency charged with the administration of the statute in light of everyday realities.

When a challenge to an agency construction of a statutory provision, fairly conceptualized, really centers on the wisdom of the agency's policy, rather than whether it is a reasonable choice within a gap left open by Congress, the challenge must fail. In such a case, federal judges—who have no constituency—have a duty to respect legitimate policy choices made by those who do. The responsibilities for assessing the wisdom of such policy choices and resolving the struggle between competing views of the public interest are not judicial ones: "Our Constitution vests such responsibilities in the political branches." TVA v. Hill, 437 U.S. 153, 195 (1978).

In Rust v. Sullivan, 500 U.S. 173 (1991), the Court also invoked Chevron to defer to agency rules which reversed longstanding agency policy. The new Regulations prohibited use of federal money for counseling regarding abortion as a method of family planning. The statute stated that "[n]one of the funds appropriated under this subchapter shall be used in programs where abortion is a method of family planning." The Court held that the text and legislative history were ambiguous regarding counseling, and that Chevron permits an agency to break sharply with the past. It added that the new rule was accompanied by "reasoned analysis," was justified by client experience under the prior policy, and was supported by a shift in attitude against abortion.

The Court rejected the dissenters' view that the regulations were invalid because they raised serious constitutional issues about imposing viewpoint-based restrictions on protected speech. It concluded that the regulations "do not raise the sort of 'grave and doubtful constitutional questions' that would lead us to assume Congress did not intend to authorize their issuance."

Justice Stevens added a separate dissent, arguing that "[i]n a society that abhors censorship and in which policymakers have traditionally placed the highest value on the freedom to communicate, it is unrealistic to conclude that statutory authority to regulate conduct implicitly authorized the Executive to regulate speech."

c) Determining Whether the Statute Is Uncertain—Legislative Intent vs. Textualism

Chevron recognizes limits to super-deference. It asks whether "Congress has [   ] directly addressed the precise question at issue," whether "Congress has explicitly left a gap for the agency to fill" (recognizing that "legislative delegation to an agency on a particular question [can be] implicit rather than explicit"), and whether "the statute is silent or ambiguous with respect to the specific issue." But how does a court determine whether those conditions exist? Does it depend on textual uncertainties or on broader criteria of legislative intent?

i) LEGISLATIVE INTENT—"TRADITIONAL TOOLS OF INTERPRETATION"

As noted earlier, there is an ambiguity in the super-deferential approach, concerning whether the boundaries of the governing statute are unclear. One version of the super-deferential approach looks only to the statutory language. If it is unclear, the agency has interpretive power to reach a reasonable conclusion to which courts must defer. If the text is clear, however, the agency's rule cannot defeat the text. Another version relies on "legislative intent," rather than the text. Its source is footnote 9 of the Chevron opinion, as follows:

> The judiciary is the final authority on issues of statutory construction and must reject administrative constructions which are contrary to clear congressional intent. If a court, employing traditional tools of statutory construction, ascertains that Congress had an intention on the precise question at issue, that intention is the law and must be given effect.

"Traditional tools of interpretation" for determining legislative intent include not only the text, but also purpose beyond that which sheds light on textual meaning, legislative history, and substantive background considerations. The same dispute between relying on textualism and legislative intent, encountered throughout this course, now reemerges to decide whether to defer to agency rules.

Justice Stevens, the author of Chevron, has disagreed with Justice Scalia regarding some applications of Chevron, precisely because he applies the "traditional tools," rather than a textualist approach. For example, in INS v. Cardoza–Fonseca, 480 U.S. 421 (1987), the statute authorized a grant of asylum to an alien unable or unwilling to return home "because of * * * a well-founded fear of persecution." The government argued that the "well-founded fear" standard was equivalent to a "clear probability" standard. Justice Stevens, writing for the Court, rejected the claim that the government's view was entitled to deference, as follows:

> The question whether Congress intended the two standards to be identical is a pure question of statutory construction for the courts to decide. * * *
>
> In Chevron, we explained:
>
>> "The judiciary is the final authority on issues of statutory construction and must reject administrative constructions which are contrary to clear congressional intent. If a court, employing traditional tools of statutory construction, ascertains that Con-

gress had an intention on the precise question at issue, that intention is the law and must be given effect." 467 U.S. at 843 n.9.

The narrow legal question whether the two standards are the same is, of course, quite different from the question of interpretation that arises in each case in which the agency is required to apply either or both standards to a particular set of facts. There is obviously some ambiguity in a term like "well-founded fear" which can only be given concrete meaning through a process of case-by-case adjudication. In that process of filling " 'any gap left, implicitly or explicitly, by Congress,' " the courts must respect the interpretation of the agency to which Congress has delegated the responsibility for administering the statutory program. But our task today is much narrower, and is well within the province of the judiciary. We do not attempt to set forth a detailed description of how the "well-founded fear" test should be applied. Instead, we merely hold that [it is error to conclude] that the two standards are identical.

Justice Scalia, however, refused to accept Justice Stevens interpretation of Chevron. In a concurring opinion in Cardoza–Fonseca, Justice Scalia stated:

I am far more troubled, however, by the Court's discussion of the question whether the [agency's] interpretation of "well founded fear" is entitled to deference. Since the Court quite rightly concludes that the [agency's] interpretation is clearly inconsistent with the plain meaning of that phrase and the structure of the Act, there is simply no need and thus no justification for a discussion of whether the interpretation is entitled to deference. Even more unjustifiable, however, is the Court's use of this superfluous discussion as the occasion to express controversial, and I believe erroneous, views on the meaning of this Court's decision in Chevron. Chevron stated that where there is no "unambiguously expressed intent of Congress, a court may not substitute its own construction of a statutory provision for a reasonable interpretation made by the administrator of an agency." This Court has consistently interpreted Chevron * * * as holding that courts must give effect to a reasonable agency interpretation of a statute unless that interpretation is inconsistent with a clearly expressed congressional intent. The Court's discussion is flatly inconsistent with this well established interpretation. The Court first implies that courts may substitute their interpretation of a statute for that of an agency whenever "[e]mploying traditional tools of statutory construction," they are able to reach a conclusion as to the proper interpretation of the statute. But this approach would make deference a doctrine of desperation, authorizing courts to defer only if they would otherwise be unable to construe the enactment at issue. This is not an interpretation, but an evisceration of Chevron.

The Court also implies that courts may substitute their interpretation of a statute for that of an agency whenever they face "a pure question of statutory construction for the courts to decide," rather than a "question of interpretation [in which] the agency is required to apply [a legal standard] to a particular set of facts." No support is advanced for this proposition, which is contradicted by the case the Court purports to be interpreting, since in Chevron the Court deferred to the Environmental Protection Agency's abstract interpretation of the phrase "stationary source."

ii) FINDING TEXTUAL UNCERTAINTY

If textual uncertainty is the test, it is still difficult to decide when the text is unclear. Do you agree with the Court's judgment in the following cases that the text is unclear?

In Sullivan v. Everhart, 494 U.S. 83 (1990), Justice Scalia concluded that the Social Security Act provision dealing with recovery of overpayments was ambiguous, thus calling into play Chevron's deference to the agency's construction. The statute stated that when

> the Secretary finds that more or less than the correct amount of payment has been made to any person * * * proper adjustment or recovery shall be made, under regulations prescribed by the Secretary * * *.

The statute also waived recovery of overpayments, specifying that:

> [i]n any case in which more than the correct amount of payment has been made, there shall be no adjustment of payments to, or recovery by the United States from, any person who is without fault if such adjustment would defeat the purpose of this subchapter or would be against equity and good conscience.

The Secretary determined that an overpayment subject to waiver was the netted difference between past under- and overpayments. For example, if a recipient was entitled to $100 in two different months, but was erroneously paid $150 in one month and $80 in another, there would be a $30 overpayment, to which the waiver provisions applied. The claimant argued that she was entitled to receive the $20 underpayment and to seek a waiver of the $50 overpayment for the other month.

The Court held that the "correct amount" subject to the waiver rules could refer either to the amount "for a given month" or to a netted amount. Justice Scalia noted that the statute refers to "the correct amount of payment," not "any" payment. In his view, the latter is the "more natural" way to specify shortfalls in individual monthly payments. In any event, the statute was ambiguous, requiring deference to the agency under Chevron.

Justice Stevens dissented:

> The kingly power to rewrite history has not been delegated to the Secretary of Health and Human Services. * * * Because I believe [the netting approach] is inconsistent with both common sense and the plain terms of the statute, I respectfully dissent.

Justice Stevens relied on a very different hypothetical fact situation to illustrate the impact of the majority's interpretation of the statute. Justice Scalia had given an example of under- and overpayments encompassing two months in the same year. Justice Stevens observed that the majority would allow an overpayment ten years earlier to be balanced against an underpayment the month before an adjustment would be made, leaving the claimant in dire financial straits. He also argued that the majority's decision encouraged the Secretary to "await underpayments before recognizing overpayments" so as to avoid the hearing procedures available in connection with the waiver of overpayment process. As for the possibility that "*any* payment" is the more natural way to specify shortfalls in individual monthly payments, he stated:

> Perhaps that is so. But it is entirely possible that Congress clearly intended to prohibit any netting that diminishes waiver rights, but nonetheless did not have the netting problem in mind when drafting language relevant to overpayments and underpayments. The netting procedure here is so inconsistent with the mandatory character of the waiver provision * * * that Congress might simply have thought it unnecessary to add further language ruling out specifically any such program. * * * [We] do not sit to insist that Congress express its intent as precisely as would be possible. Our duty is to ask what Congress intended, and not to assay whether Congress might have stated that intent more naturally, more artfully, or more pithily.

Young v. Community Nutrition Institute

476 U.S. 974 (1986).

■ Justice O'Connor delivered the opinion of the Court.

[Editor—The Food and Drug Administration (FDA) enforces a law banning adulterated food from interstate commerce. 21 U.S.C. § 331(a). Section 342(a) deems food to be "adulterated" under certain situations. One situation is food which contains "any added poisonous or added deleterious substance * * * which is unsafe within the meaning of section 346(a)." The issue in this case was the definition of "unsafe" in § 346.]

Section 346 states:

> "Any poisonous or deleterious substance added to any food, except where such substance is required in the production thereof or cannot be avoided by good manufacturing practice shall be deemed to be unsafe for purposes of the application of clause (2)(A) of section 342(a) of this title; but when such substance is so required or cannot be so avoided, the Secretary shall promulgate regulations limiting the quantity therein or thereon to such extent as he finds necessary for the

protection of public health, and any quantity exceeding the limits so fixed shall be deemed to be unsafe for purposes of the application of clause (2)(A) of section 342(a) of this title. While such a regulation is in effect * * * food shall not, by reason of bearing or containing any added amount of such substance, be considered to be adulterated. * * *"

* * *

The parties do not dispute that, since the enactment of the Act in 1938, the FDA has interpreted this provision to give it the discretion to decide whether to promulgate a § 346 regulation, which is known in the administrative vernacular as a "tolerance level." * * *

The substance at issue in this case is aflatoxin, a bacterial mold that grows in some foods. Aflatoxin, a potent carcinogen, is undisputedly "poisonous" or "deleterious" under §§ 342 and 346. The parties also agree that, although aflatoxin is naturally and unavoidably present in some foods, it is to be treated as "added" to food under § 346. As a "poisonous or deleterious substance added to any food," then, aflatoxin is a substance falling under the aegis of § 346, and therefore is at least potentially the subject of a tolerance level.

The FDA has not, however, set a § 346 tolerance level for aflatoxin. * * *

The FDA's longstanding interpretation of the statute that it administers is that the phrase "to such extent as he finds necessary for the protection of public health" in § 346 modifies the word "shall." The FDA therefore interprets the statute to state that the FDA shall promulgate regulations to the extent that it believes the regulations necessary to protect the public health. Whether regulations are necessary to protect the public health is, under this interpretation, a determination to be made by the FDA.

Respondents, in contrast, argue that the phrase "to such extent" modifies the phrase "the quantity therein or thereon" in § 346, not the word "shall." Since respondents therefore view the word "shall" as unqualified, they interpret § 346 to require the promulgation of tolerance levels for added, but unavoidable, harmful substances. The FDA under this interpretation of § 346 has discretion in setting the particular intolerance level, but not in deciding whether to set a tolerance level at all.

Our analysis must begin with Chevron U.S.A. Inc. v. Natural Resources Defense Council, Inc., 467 U.S. 837 (1984). * * *

While we agree [ ] that Congress in § 346 was speaking directly to the precise question at issue in this case, we cannot agree [ ] that Congress unambiguously expressed its intent through its choice of statutory language. * * * [T]he phrasing of § 346 admits of either respondents' or petitioner's reading of the statute. As enemies of the dangling participle well know, the English language does not always force a writer to specify which of two possible objects is the one to which a modifying phrase relates. A Congress more precise or more prescient than the one that enacted § 346 might, if it wished petitioner's position to prevail, have placed "to such extent as he finds necessary for the protection of public health" as an appositive phrase immediately after "shall" rather than as a free-floating phrase after "the quantity therein or thereon." A Congress equally fastidious and foresighted, but intending respondents' position to prevail, might have substituted the phrase "to the quantity" for the phrase "to such extent as." But the Congress that actually enacted § 346 took neither tack. In the absence of such improvements, the wording of § 346 must remain ambiguous.

The FDA has therefore advanced an interpretation of an ambiguous statutory provision. * * *

[Editor—The Court then explains that the FDA's reading is not "absurd" and that the legislative history provides no single view about whether tolerance levels were mandatory or permissive.]

■ Justice Stevens, dissenting. * * *

The Court's [ ] conclusion reflects an absence of judgment and of judging. * * *

The Court's finding of ambiguity is simply untenable. The antecedent of the qualifying language is quite clearly the phrase "limiting the quantity therein or thereon," which immediately precedes it, rather than the word "shall," which appears eight words before it. Thus, the Commissioner is to "limi[t] the quantity [of an added, unavoidable poisonous or deleterious substance] therein or thereon to such extent as he finds necessary for the protection of public health." By instead reading the section to mean that "the Secretary shall promulgate regulations * * * to such extent as he finds necessary," the Court ignores the import of the words immediately following, which specify the effect of the "limits so fixed"—i.e., fixed by "limiting the quantity [of the poisonous substance] therein or thereon to such extent as he finds necessary for the protection of public health"—which can only mean that the qualification modifies the *limits* set by regulation rather than the *duty* to regulate. In addition, the Court's construction, by skipping over the words "limiting the quantity therein or thereon," renders them superfluous and of no operative force or effect. * * *

The task of interpreting a statute requires more than merely inventing an ambiguity and invoking administrative deference. * * * Thus, to say that the statute is susceptible of two meanings, as does the Court, is not to say that either is acceptable. * * * The Court, correctly self-conscious of the limits of the judicial role, employs a reasoning so formulaic that it trivializes the art of judging.

These cases suggest that the Court is leaning towards finding enough uncertainty in the text to defer to the agency under Chevron, but that may not be true. In Pierce, The Supreme Court's New Hypertextualism, 95 Colum. L. Rev. 749 (1995), the author argues that the Supreme Court has often invoked "hypertextualism" under the first branch of the Chevron test to *limit* agency discretion. This means that, contrary to what had originally been anticipated, Chevron *decreased* agency discretion. This hypertextualism takes the form of wrenching words out of their statutory context and finding plain meaning when there arguably is none.

Pierce gives as an example of hypertextualism Justice Scalia's majority opinion in MCI Telecommunications Corp. v. American Telephone and Telegraph Co., 512 U.S. 218 (1994). The statute allowed the agency to "modify any requirement," one of which was filing telephone rate tariffs. The Court interpreted the statutory word "modify" to deny the agency discretion to make tariff filing optional for nondominant long distance carriers (everyone but AT&T). Such a "detariffing" policy was too basic and fundamental to be a "modification."

The dispute between the parties turns on the meaning of the phrase "modify any requirement" in § 203(b)(2). Petitioners argue that it gives the Commission authority to make even basic and fundamental changes in the scheme created by that section. We disagree. The word "modify"—like a number of other English words employing the root "mod-" (deriving from the Latin word for "measure"), such as "moderate," "modulate," "modest," and "modicum,"—has a connotation of increment or limitation. Virtually every dictionary we are aware of says that "to modify" means to change moderately or in minor fashion. See, e.g., Random House Dictionary of the English Language 1236 (2d ed. 1987)("to change somewhat the form or qualities of; alter partially; amend"); Webster's Third New International Dictionary 1452 (1976)("to make minor changes in the form or structure of: alter without transforming"); 9 Oxford English Dictionary 952 (2d ed. 1989)("to make partial changes in; to change (an object) in respect of some of its qualities; to alter or vary without radical transformation"); Black's Law Dictionary 1004 (6th ed. 1990)("to alter; to change in incidental or subordinate features; enlarge; extend; amend; limit; reduce").

In support of their position, petitioners cite dictionary definitions contained in or derived from a single source, Webster's Third New International Dictionary 1452 (1976)("Webster's Third"), which includes among the meanings of "modify," "to make a basic or important change in." Petitioners contend that this establishes sufficient ambiguity to entitle the Commission to deference in its acceptance of the broader meaning, which in turn requires approval of its permissive detariffing policy. See Chevron U.S.A. Inc. v. Natural Resources Defense Council, Inc., 467 U.S. 837, 843 (1984). In short, they contend that the courts must defer to the agency's choice among available dictionary definitions, citing National Railroad Passenger Corp. v. Boston and Maine Corp., 503 U.S. 407 (1992).

But Boston and Maine does not stand for that proposition. * * * [W]hen the Boston and Maine opinion spoke of "alternative dictionary definitions," it did not refer to what we have here: one dictionary whose suggested meaning contradicts virtually all others. It referred to alternative definitions within the dictionary cited (Webster's Third, as it happens), which was not represented to be the only dictionary giving those alternatives. * * *

Most cases of verbal ambiguity in statutes involve, as Boston and Maine did, a selection between accepted alternative meanings shown as such by many dictionaries. One can envision (though a court case does not immediately come to mind) having to choose between accepted alternative meanings, one of which is so newly accepted that it has only been recorded by a single lexicographer. * * * But what petitioners demand that we accept as creating an ambiguity here is a rarity even rarer than that: a meaning set forth in a single dictionary (and, as we say, its progeny) which not only supplements the meaning contained in all other dictionaries, but contradicts one of the meanings contained in virtually all other dictionaries. Indeed, contradicts one of the alternative meanings contained in the out-of-step dictionary itself—for as we have observed, Webster's Third itself defines "modify" to connote both (specifically) major change and (specifically) minor change. It is hard to see how that can be. When the word "modify" has come to mean both "to change in some respects" and "to change fundamentally" it will in fact mean neither of those things. It will simply mean "to change," and some adverb will have to be called into service to indicate the great or small degree of the change.

If that is what the peculiar Webster's Third definition means to suggest has happened—and what petitioners suggest by appealing to Webster's Third—we simply disagree. "Modify," in our view, connotes moderate change. It might be good English to say that the French Revolution "modified" the status of the French nobility—but only because there is a figure of speech called understatement and a literary device known as sarcasm. And it might be unsurprising to discover a 1972 White House press release saying that "the Administration is modifying its position with regard to prosecution of the war in Vietnam"—but only because press agents tend to impart what is nowadays called "spin." Such intentional distortions, or simply careless or ignorant misuse, must have formed the basis for the usage that Webster's Third, and Webster's Third alone, reported. [Editor—At this point in the opinion, footnote 3 states: That is not an unlikely hypothesis. Upon its long-awaited appearance in 1961, Webster's Third was widely criticized for its portrayal of common error as proper usage. An example is its approval (without qualification) of the use of "infer" to mean "imply" * * *.] It is perhaps gilding the lily to add this: In 1934, when the Communications Act became law—the most relevant time for determining a statutory term's meaning—Webster's Third was not yet even contemplated. To our knowledge all English dictionaries provided the narrow definition of "modify," including those published by G. & C. Merriam Company. See Webster's New International Dictionary 1577 (2d ed. 1934); Webster's Collegiate Dictionary 628 (4th ed. 1934). We have not the slightest doubt that is the meaning the statute intended.

Justice Stevens' dissent argues that "dictionaries can be useful aides in statutory interpretation, but they are no substitute for close analysis of what words mean as used in a particular statutory context. Cabell v. Markham, 148 F.2d 737, 739 (2d Cir.1945)(Hand, J.). Even if the sole possible meaning of 'modify' were to make 'minor' changes, further elaboration is needed to show why the detariffing policy should fail."

Pierce is unsure why there has been a shift away from deference to the agency. It may reflect a general concern with excessive delegation to agencies or a specific concern with the liberalism inherent in some agency rulemaking. In any event, it is clear that generalizations about judicial allocation of lawmaking authority are hard to sustain at any one point in time and certainly over any significant period of time. If that is true of how judges view agency rulemaking, why shouldn't it also be true of the allocation of lawmaking power implicit in statutory interpretation?

d) LINGERING "INSTITUTIONAL COMPETENCE" STANDARDS?

Do some aspects of the institutional competence approach linger on in post-Chevron decisions?

i) LITIGATING POSITION

Bowen v. Georgetown University Hosp.
488 U.S. 204 (1988).

■ Justice Kennedy delivered the opinion of the Court. * * *

Under the Medicare program, health care providers are reimbursed by the Government for expenses incurred in providing medical services to Medicare beneficiaries. Congress has authorized the Secretary of Health and Human Services to promulgate regulations setting limits on the levels of Medicare costs that will be reimbursed. The question presented here is whether the Secretary may exercise this rulemaking authority to promulgate cost limits that are retroactive. [Editor—The specific cost-limit rule concerned the method for calculating the wage-index used to reflect salary levels for hospital employees on which reimbursement was based.] * * *

It is axiomatic that an administrative agency's power to promulgate legislative regulations is limited to the authority delegated by Congress. In determining the validity of the Secretary's retroactive cost-limit rule, the threshold question is whether the Medicare Act authorizes retroactive rulemaking.

Retroactivity is not favored in the law. Thus, congressional enactments and administrative rules will not be construed to have retroactive effect unless their language requires this result. By the same principle, a statutory grant of legislative rulemaking authority will not, as a general matter, be understood to encompass the power to promulgate retroactive rules unless the power is conveyed by Congress in express terms. Even where some substantial justification for retroactive rulemaking is presented, courts should be reluctant to find such authority absent an express statutory grant. * * *

The authority to promulgate cost reimbursement regulations is set forth in § 1395x(v)(1)(A). That subparagraph also provides that:

"Such regulations shall * * * (ii) provide for the making of suitable retroactive corrective adjustments where, for a provider of services for any fiscal period, the aggregate reimbursement produced by the methods of determining costs proves to be either inadequate or excessive."

This provision on its face permits some form of retroactive action. We cannot accept the Secretary's argument, however, that it provides authority for the retroactive promulgation of cost-limit rules. To the contrary, we agree with the Court of Appeals that clause (ii) directs the Secretary to establish a procedure for making case-by-case adjustments to reimbursement payments where the regulations prescribing computation methods do not reach the correct result in individual cases. The structure and language of the statute require the conclusion that the retroactivity provision applies only to case-by-case adjudication, not to rulemaking. * * *

Despite the novelty of this interpretation, the Secretary contends that it is entitled to deference under Young v. Community Nutrition Institute, 476 U.S. 974, 980–981 (1986), and Chevron U.S.A. Inc. v. Natural Resources Defense Council, Inc., 467 U.S. 837, 842–844 (1984). We have never applied the principle of those cases to agency litigating positions that are wholly unsupported by regulations, rulings, or administrative practice. To the contrary, we have declined to give deference to an agency counsel's interpretation of a statute where the agency itself has articulated no position on the question, on the ground that "Congress has delegated to the administrative official and not to appellate counsel the responsibility for elaborating and enforcing statutory commands." * * * Even if we were to sanction departure from this principle in some cases, we would not do so here. Far from being a reasoned and consistent view of the scope of clause (ii), the Secretary's current interpretation of clause (ii) is contrary to the narrow view of that provision advocated in past cases * * *.

COMMENT

The Court's observations about deferring to the agency's litigating position invite comparison between judicial deference to the agency under Chevron and the standards for deferring to Congress in constitutional adjudication challenging legislation. Justice Stevens' plurality opinion in Bowen v. American Hosp. Ass'n, 476 U.S. 610 (1986), asserted a difference:

> Agency deference has not come so far that we will uphold regulations whenever it is possible to "conceive a basis" for administrative action. To the contrary, the "presumption of regularity afforded an agency in fulfilling its statutory mandate" is not equivalent to "the minimum rationality a statute must bear in order to withstand analysis under the Due Process Clause."

And Justice Blackmun was even more forceful in denigrating reliance on agency litigating positions in Securities Industry Ass'n v. Board of Governors of Federal Reserve System, 468 U.S. 137 (1984), stating

> that post hoc rationalizations by counsel for agency action are entitled to little deference: "It is the administrative official and not appellate counsel who possesses the expertise that can enlighten and rationalize the search for the meaning and intent of Congress." As a result, the Board's presentation here of the policies behind the Act as they apply to this case is of less significance than it would be if it had occurred at the administrative level.

By contrast, as you may recall from your constitutional law class, the Court will often accept post hoc rationalizations presented as litigating positions to justify a *statute's* constitutionality. We return to this issue in Chapter 17.03, concerning legislative rationality.

ii) NO PUBLIC NOTICE AND COMMENT

Suppose that the agency position is something more than a litigating position advanced by the agency's counsel, but has not gone through a public notice and comment procedure prior to adoption. Do such procedural concerns still matter after Chevron? How do the following cases answer this question?

Doe v. Reivitz

842 F.2d 194 (7th Cir.1988).

■ Cudahy, Circuit Judge. * * *

In reviewing [Health and Human Services'] interpretation of the eligibility requirements under AFDC–UP [Editor—an AFDC welfare program which covers otherwise qualified participants with an un-employed second parent in the household], the first issue we must address is the degree of deference owed the agency's interpretation by a reviewing court. [Editor-HHS said that illegal aliens could not qualify as an unemployed second parent.] HHS argues that the very deferential standard of review enunciated by the Supreme Court in Chevron, should apply in this case. In Chevron, the Court held that, unless Congress has clearly expressed its opinion on an issue of statutory interpretation, the only question remaining for a reviewing court is "whether the agency's answer is based on a permissible construction of the statute." We do not agree with HHS that Chevron provides the appropriate standard of review in this case. In Chevron, the court was reviewing a regulation that was issued by the EPA through notice-and-comment rule making procedures pur-suant to an implicit delegation of power by Congress. The regulation there is most appropriately characterized as a "legislative rule" because it was issued by an agency acting pursuant to a delegation of authority by Congress. A "legislative rule" that is "reasonably related to the purposes of the legislation, promulgated through proper procedures and not arbitrary or capricious" has the force of law and is controlling on the courts. The documents at issue in this case are interpretative rather than legislative in nature, and under longstanding principles, agency interpretations are not entitled to the same degree of deference commanded by the high-powered regulations reviewed in Chevron. The Court in Chevron did not purport to alter the scope of review traditionally accorded interpreta-tive documents. There are good reasons why the HHS statements in question here should be viewed as interpretative and accorded less deference than force-of-law regulations.

[Editor—The court's reference to "interpretive" and "substan-tive" rules is confusing. A "substantive" rule is one issued pursuant to an explicit grant of rulemaking authority in the governing statute. An "interpretive" rule gives the agency's interpretation of the statute, even if there is no specific grant of rulemaking authority. Under the federal Administrative Procedure Act, most substantive rules must be issued only after notice to the public and an opportunity to comment. Interpretive rules are not subject to notice and comment requirements, although some agencies usually follow notice and comment procedures for interpretive rules (for example, the Trea-sury for tax regulations). The real issue in this case is whether Chevron accords an interpretive rule the kind of deference normally given to substantive rules, even though it is adopted *without* follow-ing a notice and comment procedure. Labeling the rule "interpre-tive" does not answer that question. Presumably, the court would have had no trouble deferring to an interpretive regulation if it had been issued after public notice and comment.]

The AFDC–UP eligibility requirement at issue here was first enunciated in a letter written by an HHS regional administrator to the Wisconsin DHSS, the Downing letter. Subsequent to the initiation of the present litigation in district court, the associate commissioner and the deputy associate commissioner of the Office of Family Assistance, the office within HHS responsible for administering AFDC, prepared a memorandum and declaration, respectively, in which they endorsed the policy expressed in the Downing letter; these documents were prepared specifically in response to this suit. Although Congress [in § 607(a)] has given the Secretary of HHS the power to define the term "unemployment" for purposes of AFDC–UP eligibility, neither the Downing letter nor the documents subsequently prepared by the Office of Family Assistance suggest that the policy in question was promulgated pursuant to the delegation of authority in section 607(a).

HHS' AFDC–UP eligibility policy is also more appropriately classified as interpretative in view of the informal and non-authoritative manner of its announcement. The deference due a substantive force-of-law rule is attributable in part to the way such rules are promulgated through notice-and-comment rule making pursuant to section 553 of the Administrative Procedure Act. HHS did not engage in notice-and-comment rule making in issuing its AFDC–UP eligibility policy. The agency cannot now contend that courts must accord to this policy the deference due a legislative rule when the agency has not followed the normal procedures associated with force-of-law rule making.

Not only has the policy not been subject to notice and comment, but the Secretary's interpretation has also not been widely disseminated. At oral argument, the attorney for HHS stated that the Secretary's interpretation represents a policy uniformly applied across the country; however, the states apparently are not informed of this policy until the federal government discovers that a state is providing AFDC–UP benefits to families headed by unemployed illegal aliens. The agency has not pointed us to any policy statement that is accessible to all the state agencies charged with administering the AFDC–UP program, and HHS has not indicated whether it has had occasion to enforce this policy against any other state than Wisconsin. Indeed, Wisconsin may be the only state aware of HHS' policy on this issue. For the foregoing reasons, the HHS policy should be subjected only to the scope of review appropriate to agency interpretations.

Wagner Seed Co. v. Bush

946 F.2d 918 (D.C.Cir.1991).

■ D. H. Ginsburg, Circuit Judge. * * *

[Editor—The issue was whether a federal statute providing Superfund clean-up cost reimbursement was retroactive. Retroactivity helped the petitioner, Wagner Seed. The agency rejected Wagner Seed's reimbursement claim in a letter holding that the reimbursement provision applied only to clean-up orders received *after* Congress adopted that provision. The court dealt with the Chevron issue as follows.]

* * * Wagner argues that Chevron deference is not in order because the EPA issued its prospective-only interpretation of § 106(b)(2) in a decision letter, "without a hearing, without the use of an administrative law judge, without briefing, and, indeed, without demonstrating any consideration or analysis of the issues raised by Wagner['s] claim." "Such a blind process," we are told, "makes the EPA's position merely 'interpretive,' and not entitled to the deference accorded 'legislative' rulemaking."

At the outset, we wish to be clear that we do not accept Wagner's premises that the agency's decision process was defective and that it gave no consideration to the issues involved, a claim that is at best hyperbolic. It may well be that the greater the procedural trappings that attend an agency's interpretive moment, the less reason for judicial concern that the interpretation was offhanded or opportunistic, susceptible to discard tomorrow when another permissible interpretation better suits the agency's needs of the day. Likewise, the opinion of a low-level bureaucrat, given in a non-adversarial or informal context, may or may not be deemed sufficiently relevant to the agency's administration of the law to warrant deference under Chevron; but that is not at all the case before us.

The EPA's interpretation of § 106(b)(2) was given after due consideration in order to resolve an important and recurring matter before it. The decision letter under review poses the question whether retroactive application to Wagner is authorized or appropriate, considers the legislative history of the statute, and upon analysis describes its purpose as the creation of an incentive to comply with agency clean-up orders. Furthermore, the agency has applied this interpretation consistently.

In any event, it simply is not the law of this circuit that an interpretive regulation does not receive the Chevron deference accorded a legislative regulation.

Seeking post Chevron authority for its position, Wagner relies principally upon Doe v. Reivitz, 830 F.2d 1441 (7th Cir.1987), amended, 842 F.2d 194 (7th Cir.1988), which held that a lesser degree of deference is owed to an "agency interpretation" than to the "high-powered" legislative type of regulation to which the Court deferred in Chevron. The vitality of Reivitz is unclear, however— except in the present context. For when the Seventh Circuit considered the very EPA interpretation now before us, it deferred pursuant to Chevron, rejecting the argument that the courts should give less deference to an "interpretive ruling" than to a "legislative ruling," Bethlehem Steel, 918 F.2d at 1327 n. 3. Thus, whatever Reivitz means, the Seventh Circuit itself does not believe that it means that the EPA's interpretation of the statute in this case should receive less than the usual deference due under Chevron.

In Reno v. Koray, 115 S.Ct. 2021 (1995), the Court made the following statement about Chevron-deference, which accords "some deference" to interpretive rules issued without notice and comment.

It is true that the Bureau's interpretation appears only in a "Program Statement"—an internal agency guideline—rather than in "published regulations subject to the rigors of the Administrative Procedure Act, including public notice and comment." But [the Bureau's] internal agency guideline, which is akin to an "interpretive rule" that "does not require notice-and-comment," is still entitled to some deference, since it is a "permissible construction of the statute" [citing Chevron].

This decision has been relied on by the Third Circuit in a later case, to uphold interpretive rules issued by the Department of Health and Human Services, which prevented the states from unduly interfering with Medicaid-funded abortions. Medicaid is a federal grant-in-aid program, in which federal funds are provided to the states on condition that they comply with certain federal rules. Elizabeth Blackwell Health Center for Women v. Catherine Baker Knoll, 61 F.3d 170 (3d Cir.1995), involved a dispute over the Hyde amendment, which is periodically attached to federal appropriations legislation and states that federal funds are available for abortions only under limited circumstances. These circumstances change periodically because the amendment has to be renewed with each annual Medicaid appropriation. The version of the Hyde Amendment in effect in this case allowed federal funding for abortions in cases of rape or incest, as well as when the mother's life was endangered.

The Secretary of Health and Human Services delegated her authority to oversee and enforce the Medicaid program to the Health Care Financing Administration ("HCFA"). On December 28, 1993, HCFA issued a directive to state Medicaid directors, one provision of which stated:

States may impose reasonable reporting or documentation requirements on recipients or providers, as may be necessary to assure themselves that an abortion was for the purpose of terminating a pregnancy caused by an act of rape or incest. States may not impose reporting or documentation requirements that deny or impede coverage for abortions where pregnancies result from rape or incest. To insure that reporting requirements do not prevent or impede coverage for covered abortions, any such reporting requirement must be waived and the procedure considered to be reimbursable if the treating physician certifies that in his or her professional opinion, the patient was unable, for physical or psychological reasons, to comply with the requirement.

The issue in the case concerned Pennsylvania's refusal to provide the waiver of reporting requirements specified in the above directive.

The court concluded that the Medicaid statute contained two competing principles—making sure that the woman's report of rape or incest was true and making sure that state rules were not more restrictive than the criteria established by Congress. In resolving these competing principles, the court placed considerable weight on the Directive. Here is what it said about the Chevron issue and the fact that the Directive was not promulgated after public notice and comment.

> The Secretary of HHS bears the responsibility of reconciling these competing interests in the statute. The Supreme Court has noted that "perhaps appreciating the complexity of what it had wrought, Congress conferred on the Secretary exceptionally broad authority to prescribe standards for applying certain sections of the [Medicaid] Act." * * *

> * * * If [the agency's] choice represents a reasonable accommodation of conflicting policies that were committed to the agency's care by the statute, we should not disturb it unless it appears from the statute or its legislative history that the accommodation is not one that Congress would have sanctioned [citing Chevron]. Such deference is appropriate here even though the Secretary's interpretation is not contained in a "legislative rule." See, e.g., Health Insurance Ass'n of America v. Shalala, 23 F.3d 412, 424 (D.C.Cir. 1994); Hicks v. Cantrell, 803 F.2d 789, 791–92 (4th Cir.1986). Indeed, the Supreme Court recently reversed our decision in Koray v. Sizer, 21 F.3d 558, 562–65 (3d Cir.1994), where we had declined to defer to the Bureau of Prisons' interpretation of 18 U.S.C. § 3585(b). * * *

> The Secretary's reconciliation of the competing interests in the Medicaid statute and Hyde Amendment is reasonable. Because the Secretary's consistent and contemporaneously expressed construction of the Medicaid statute as amended by the Hyde Amendment is a reasonable one, it is accorded considerable weight under principles announced in Chevron.

> Accordingly, we will defer to the Secretary's interpretation of the Hyde Amendment, and hold that because the Pennsylvania reporting requirements lack a waiver procedure and therefore may deprive eligible women of the benefits which Congress has made available to them, they are to this extent in conflict with federal law and are invalid. Thus, until Pennsylvania, pursuant to state law, adopts a waiver provision in accordance with the Secretary's directive, the Commonwealth is enjoined from enforcing its rape and incest reporting requirements.

e) State Law

States are, of course, free to follow their own approach to interpreting statutes which involve an administering agency. Which approach does the following case adopt towards statutory interpretation and deference to agency rules?

In Gugin v. Sonico, Inc., 846 P.2d 571, 574 (Wash. App.1993), the statute prohibited discrimination based specifically on race, creed, color, national origin, sex, marital status, age, or handicap and authorized the state Human Rights Commission "[t]o adopt, promulgate, amend, and rescind suitable rules and regulations * * *" to carry out the anti-discrimination law. The Human Rights Commission then declared that an employment practice which automatically excludes a person with a prior criminal conviction has the potential for illegal discrimination. The regulation stated in part:

> To the extent that an employment practice automatically excludes persons with convictions, it has the potential for discrimination because of race and ethnic origin. This is because minority groups in our society have experienced unequal law enforcement.

The court rejected the Commission's regulation on the ground that the agency had created a new protected class, and that this "exceed[ed] the Legislature's grant of authority to the Human Rights Commission."

11.05 Deference to Agencies and Relying on Legislative History

Chevron may have implications for judicial reliance on legislative history, discussed in Chapter 10. The argument for relying on legislative history is often couched in the rhetoric of legislative intent. Counter arguments correctly observe that legislative history probably does not express the "intent" of most legislators.

However, we also noted an institutional competence argument for judicial reliance on legislative history. Some issues are so technical that legislative history might be a good way to resolve them, especially if a specialized bar routinely examined that history. There are, of course, institutional competence arguments *against* relying on legislative history. It is often secret and manipulative; the role of staff in drafting committee reports is controversial; and powerful interests groups may influence its content.

The material in this chapter suggests that "institutional competence" may be a broad principle of statutory construction. If agency rules, which are not themselves legislation, can be valid on institutional competence grounds, perhaps legislative history can also be a valid source of law, even though it is not legislation.

The institutional competence perspective also suggests that legislative history might *not* fare so well against administrative interpretations. Once legislative history is uncoupled from legislative intent, it loses any privileged status it might have in competition with administrative rules. For example, in United States v. Shreveport Grain & Elevator Co., 287 U.S. 77 (1932), the Court indicated a preference for agency Regulations, as follows:

> * * * If the meaning of the statutory words was doubtful, so as to call for a resort to extrinsic aids in an effort to reach a proper construction of them, we should hesitate to accept the committee reports in preference to this contemporaneous and long continued practical construction of the act on the part of those charged with its administration.

Legislative Action and Inaction After Passage of Legislation

"Legislative history" after a statute's passage seems like an oxymoron to some, but subsequent events are history to the judge looking back from the time of interpretation. If you think the only relevant moment for a statute is the time of creation, then anything which happens later cannot be history. But if the meaning of statute is the result of a collaborative effort between the legislature and court, a statute's history does not stop when the law is passed. This Chapter asks whether meaning can evolve as a result of events occurring after adoption of a statute. It is therefore a further elaboration of the themes considered in Chapter 9, dealing with change in statutory meaning.

Chapter 12.01 discusses the impact of later statutes on the meaning of prior law. Chapter 12.02 evaluates later legislative history. Chapters 12.03 through 12.05 discuss the relevance of reenacting a statute and legislative inaction after an intervening interpretation by a court or agency.

12.01   Later Legislation

a)   Interpreting Prior Statute

Assume statute 1 is passed in 1980. In 1985, the legislature wants to make sure that statute 1 achieves a certain result. It can do one of two things. First, it can pass statute 2, retroactively amending statute 1. Second, it can pass a declaratory statute 2, stating that statute 1 always meant the result the legislature wants to achieve.

Why might a legislature adopt declaratory legislation, rather than amend a statute retroactively? As Chapter 7 noted, there is suspicion of retroactive statutes, which results in either a presumption against retroactivity or a finding that the law is unconstitutional. Declaratory statutes, stating what prior law was intended to be, might appear to avoid these problems.

Here is an example of a decision which seems to take seriously the legislature's claim that it was interpreting prior law. In Federal Housing Administration v. The Darlington, Inc., 358 U.S. 84 (1958), the question was whether a housing mortgagor eligible for federal mortgage insurance was allowed to rent to transients under a pre–1954 law. The Court observed that "[t]he aim of the [original] Act as stated in § 608(b)(2) is to provide housing for veterans of World War II and their immediate families" and that the agency had interpreted the statute to preclude rental to transients. Although "there is no express provision" in the statute "one way or the other," the prohibition of transients is "fairly implied." To support that implication, the Court called attention to the following 1954 law:

> The Congress hereby declares that it has been its intent since the enactment of the National Housing Act that housing built with the aid of mortgages insured under that Act is to be used principally for residential use; and that this intent excludes the use of such housing for transient or hotel purposes while such insurance on the mortgage remains outstanding.

It then made the following observation about the 1954 statute:

> When Congress passed the 1954 Amendment, it accepted the construction of the prior Act which bars rentals to transients. Subsequent legislation which declares the intent of an earlier law is not, of course, conclusive in determining what the previous Congress meant. But the later law is entitled to weight when it comes to the problem of construction. The purpose of the Act, its administrative construction, and the meaning which a later Congress ascribed to it all point to the conclusion that the housing business to be benefited by FHA insurance did not include rental to transients.

Why give later legislation *any* weight as evidence of prior meaning? How reliable are such congressional statements? Isn't current politics more likely to explain current legislation than an effort to shed light on prior meaning?

———

Historically, declaratory statutes frequently encountered a hostile judicial reaction on the ground that they impinged unconstitutionally on the court's power to interpret statutes. Separation of Powers concerns were implicated. It is unusual to find such statements today.[1] When a court does refer to Separation of Powers, a close reading of the case usually reveals that something else was wrong with the statute besides interpreting prior law. See, e.g., Federal Express Corp. v. Skelton, 578 S.W.2d 1 (Ark.1979)(a statute stated that it had never been the legislature's intent in an earlier act to impose property tax on certain corporations, even though a prior case had interpreted the earlier statute to impose the tax; the State Constitution

---

1. But see Pierce v. Underwood, 487 U.S. 552, 566 (1988)(Scalia, J.) ("it is the function of the courts and not the Legislature * * * to say what an enacted statute means").

prohibited releasing a corporation from indebtedness to the State and prohibited "special" legislation, helping only a few persons). Modern courts usually recognize that the real problem with declaratory statutes is their potential retroactive impact and analyze them as potentially retroactive legislation.[2] This is less hostile to legislation because Separation of Powers analysis destroys the entire statutory provision, but objections to retroactivity leave the law in tact for future application.

b) LATER PROSPECTIVE STATUTES ON SAME ISSUE AS PRIOR LAW

So far we have discussed statutes which try to affect the interpretation of prior law retroactively. What if a statute deals prospectively with the same issue as a prior statute. Does the later law imply anything about the meaning of prior law?

Evaluate the following argument. If the prior law was the same as the new law, the new law would have been unnecessary. Therefore, the old law is different from the new law. Courts sometimes use later statutes to interpret prior law this way,[3] but that is a very questionable approach. Legislatures, like people, often specify how things should be in the future, without prejudging the answer for the past. The problem is the same as that raised by the canon *expressio unius est exclusio alterius* (reference to one thing excludes similar treatment of another thing). In fact, reference to one thing often tells us nothing about how to treat unmentioned items. Similarly, specifying a result for the future does not necessarily exclude the same result for the past.[4]

Courts often conclude that later law leaves open the proper interpretation of prior law. In McCabe v. Commissioner, 54 T.C. 1745, 1747 (1970), the taxpayers argued that insurance proceeds to cover extra living expenses incurred after their residence was damaged were not taxable. The tax statute had been prospectively amended to exclude at least some of these payments but a prior Tax Court decision had included the recoveries in income. In the McCabe case, the court stated: "Mindful of the adverse legislative response to our (earlier) opinion, * * * we have carefully considered the petitioners' position. We do not agree with [the government] that the prospective effect of [the statutory amendment] necessarily forecloses reexamination of the prior case law."

Sometimes a later statute will be accompanied by legislative history stating that the new statute *changes* the law.[5] In that case, the new statute is not itself evidence that the law is changed. It is the subsequent legislative

---

2. See generally Note, Declaratory Legislation, 49 Harv. L. Rev. 137 (1935).

3. See Wilson v. Harris Trust & Sav. Bank, 777 F.2d 1246, 1249 (7th Cir.1985).

4. Sometimes a Committee Report explicitly states that a new law should not affect interpretation of prior law. See. e.g., Holladay v. Commissioner, 72 T.C. 571, 586 n. 7 (1979), affirmed, 649 F.2d 1176 (5th Cir.1981)(citing S.Rept. 94–938 (1976)).

5. See United States v. Plesha, 352 U.S. 202, 208 n. 15 (1957).

history that is probative of prior law, subject to all the infirmities associated with such evidence. Later legislative history is discussed in the next section.

12.02　Later Legislative History—Institutional Competence

a) Critique

In Chapter 10 we considered various types of legislative history written when the statute was adopted. Several judges had serious reservations about relying on such statements because the only constitutionally authoritative text is the statute, and because of the dubious political origins of such texts (for example—staff authorship; potential manipulation by Members of Congress, especially regarding politically sensitive issues; and interest group influence). The penchant for judicial references to legislative history in this country is difficult to restrain, however, and has extended even to statements made *after* the statute was passed. As to these statements, there is not even a semblance of an argument that they were part of the historical context for members of Congress voting on the adopted text.[6]

Of course, the "legislative history as context" argument was never very realistic in the first place because the detail in legislative history is not known by most voting legislators. Nonetheless, we suggested in Chapter 10 that courts might use legislative history because decision making at that level was sometimes acceptable—because it was "institutionally competent"—not because it reflected legislative intent. If that argument is justified, perhaps it can be applied to later legislative history as well.

Here are three cases in which the court discusses later legislative history as evidence of prior intent. One of the observations you may make is that the legislative materials are likely to be evidence of contemporary politics rather than prior legislative intent. If that is true, is it necessarily fatal to judicial use of such materials? Can the material nonetheless be "institutionally competent" as evidence of statutory meaning? In this connection, consider these questions:

(1) Do the statements resolve questions of statutory detail, on matters which are not politically sensitive?

(2) Is there sufficient notice to legislators (through their staffs) that later legislative history is being created?

(3) Is such legislative history likely to be the product of special interest group pressure?

(4) Are potential litigants or their counsel likely to have access to such legislative history and to consult it?

---

6. See generally Brudney, Congressional Commentary on Judicial Interpretations of Statutes: Idle Chatter or Telling Response?, 93 Mich. L. Rev. 1 (1994)

b) CASES

Walt Disney Productions v. United States

480 F.2d 66 (9th Cir.1973).

■ Alfred T. Goodwin, C. Judge. * * *

[Editor—The taxpayer invested in movie and television films. The statute provided favorable tax treatment, in the form of an investment tax credit, for investment in "tangible personal property." Copyrights are intangible but the film itself is tangible, and the question was whether the taxpayer's investment was eligible for the credit. The investment occurred in 1962, when the investment credit was first adopted. A government regulation denied the credit. The credit had been repealed but was reinstated in 1971. The legislative history in this case was written incident to the 1971 reinstatement, which again applied to "tangible personal property," but with some modifications in the definition of eligible property (for example, to include some property used outside the United States).]

It is evident from a reading of the legislative history of the investment credit that Congress intended the credit to be allowed to those in Disney's position. Exhibit statements of legislative intent that films can qualify as tangible depreciable property are found: in the Senate Finance Committee report on the 1971 restoration of the investment credit; in the discussion in the House on the 1971 Act in a statement by Chairman Mills of the House Committee on Ways and Means in response to a specific question from the floor, 117 Cong.Rec. 34894 (1971); and in the House debates on the 1971 Act conference report, again in a statement by Chairman Mills on the House floor in response to a specific question, 117 Cong. Rec. H–12127 (daily ed. Dec. 9, 1971).

* * * Representative Mills was Chairman of the House Committee on Ways and Means in 1962 and 1971, and many members of the Senate Finance Committee served in both years. The statements by the Finance Committee and by Chairman Mills demonstrate that the Commissioner's regulation was contrary to the Congressional intent. We hold it invalid insofar as it denied an investment credit on the films in question.

[Editor—Whether a film is eligible for an investment tax credit is not a controversial political question, but is of intense concern to the movie industry. That industry might have been a major contributor to the reelection campaign of tax committee members. Should these considerations prevent reliance on the legislative history in Walt Disney?]

Commonwealth of Pennsylvania v. Lynn

501 F.2d 848 (D.C.Cir.1974).

■ McGowan, Circuit Judge. * * *

[Editor—This case involved the suspension by the Secretary of Housing and Urban Development of certain contract authority to construct housing, given to the Secretary by 1965 and 1968 legislation. The issue was whether the legislation gave the Secretary discretion to determine whether the legislative purpose would be frustrated by continuing to exercise the contract authority and, if it would be, to suspend its exercise. It was undisputed that the suspension was for "program-related" reasons and not for reasons of fiscal policy, extrinsic to the operation of the program. The court said that the legal issue was one of congressional intent. In deciding whether the statute granted discretion to the Secretary, the Court stated as follows.]

2. The Congressional response.

The legislative history of the 1965 and 1968 Acts is, not surprisingly, unenlightening on the precise question before us. When Congress establishes a new program, however novel or untested, it does not normally express itself on the question of what the executive officer charged with its administration should do if and when he has reason to believe that it is frustrating the policies he is obliged to serve. In such unanticipated circumstances, it becomes the duty of a court to construe the relevant statutes in a manner that most fully effectuates the policies to which Congress was committed. We are not, however, entirely without congressional guidance, beyond the inferences to be drawn from the statutes themselves, in the unusual circumstances of this case. * * *

On January 29, 1973, the President submitted his 1974 budget proposals to Congress, and urged enactment of new legislation emphasizing an alternative approach to achieving the national housing goal. No funds were requested for the suspended programs. In March the Housing subcommittee of the House Committee on Banking and Currency held a hearing on the suspension at which Secretary Lynn and Under Secretary Hyde explained the basis for the action. During the course of that hearing a few members questioned the degree to which mismanagement accounted for the situation giving rise to the suspension but, significantly, not a single member drew in question its legality, even inferentially.

The Housing Subcommittee did not recommend special legislation to order resumption of the programs, but two items relevant to the programs were soon to come before the Congress: extension of the insuring authority of the Federal Housing Administration, including its authority for Sections 235 and 236, which was due to expire at the end of the fiscal year; and the HUD appropriation for 1974.

a.   The House

The House approved a one-year extension of insuring authority by House Joint Resolution 512 on May 21. The report of the Committee on Banking and Currency, Temporary Extension of Certain Housing and Urban Development Laws and Authorities, H.Rep. No.93–206, 93d Cong.,1st Sess. 2 (1973), explained Section 1 of the resolution:

> This section includes extension of authority for the sections 235 (homeownership) and 236 (rental) housing programs which have been temporarily suspended by the President. Approximately $400 million in contract authority is available for use by the Administration, pending its review and evaluation of Federal housing subsidy programs.
>
> * * * Extension of these programs for one year will enable the President to reactivate these programs during the Fiscal Year 1974 * * *.

Two members of the Committee expressed their separate view "that enactment of this bill should in no way imply an acquiescence" in the housing subsidy moratorium. But the "acquiescent" tenor of the passage quoted first, and endorsed by the other thirty-eight Committee members, takes on added significance in light of the Committee's other recommendations. For example, the President had purported to terminate the open space land program on January 5, and in his Budget proposed to terminate other community development programs as of June 30, and to replace them with a special revenue sharing act (the "Better Communities Act"). The Committee, however, citing transitional problems that local governments would experience by a funding hiatus between June 30 and eventual enactment of a new program, recommended appropriation of new monies for four of the programs, including the open space land program. Its intention that this money be spent to alleviate the problems it described could not have been clearer, nor more in contrast with its handling of the Section 235 and 236 programs. * * *

The point here is not that the House committee with responsibility for oversight of the suspended housing programs failed to inveigh against the suspension, much less insist upon their resumption. Rather, the point is that, with its intimate knowledge of the Acts creating the programs, it did not view the suspension as being beyond the Executive's power under the statutes. The Committee did not necessarily "acquiesce" in the sense of accepting the suspension as necessary or desirable, but it certainly appears to have accepted its legality. * * *

b.   The Senate.

The Senate was clear in expressing its disagreement with the Executive over the *wisdom* of the housing suspension, but did not question its *legality*. The Senate Committee on Banking, Housing and Urban Affairs reported out House Joint Resolution 512 with amendments, accepted by the Senate, to increase the Secretary's contract authority under Section 236, and to require the Secretary "to utilize the [*new*] contract authority or other funds appropriated during the fiscal year" for a number of suspended programs including Sections 235, 236 and 101. The HUD appropriations bill, H.R. 8825, was also amended in committee to require obligation of *new* contract authority only. As to the prior unused authority involved in this suit the Committee merely urged HUD, "[i]f the study presently being conducted by [HUD] * * * indicates that it would be feasible to restore the rent supplement program," to do so as soon as possible and "not necessarily wait for completion of the aforesaid study." The same course was urged respecting Sections 235 and 236. Obviously, this approach suggests not that the suspension was unlawful, but rather that the Committee proposed to make further non-expenditure prospectively unauthorized. * * *

We emphasize that Congress's failure to enact mandatory spending legislation in response to the Executive's decision to withhold authorized funds is not and cannot be the basis, in any degree, for an inference that it did not intend in the first instance to preclude executive discretion to suspend the programs. Congress may make its adherence to an original intent unmistakable by further legislation, or by overriding a presidential veto, see City of New York v. Train, 161 U.S.App.D.C. 114, 494 F.2d 1033, cert. granted, 416 U.S. 969 (1974), but it cannot be put to the necessity of acting twice before it is taken to mean what it said in duly enacted legislation. We have examined Congress's response to the executive action here challenged only for the light it might shed on its original intent in establishing these three housing programs.

That response is corroborative of the inference of discretion in the Secretary reasonably to be drawn from the statutes and their contexts; and we hold that, in the circumstances revealed by this record, the Secretary is not without authority to suspend the Section 235, 236 and 101 programs.

In New York State Dept. of Social Services v. Dublino, 413 U.S. 405 (1973), the Court had to interpret a provision of the AFDC program adopted in 1967. The federal government provided grants to the states with AFDC programs that complied with federal requirements. The federal rules required the states to adopt federally approved work incentive programs (known as WIN) in certain areas of the state, to encourage welfare recipients to obtain work. If an applicant or recipient refused to participate in the program, their benefits could be reduced or denied. New York did more than comply with the federal requirements. It also adopted additional work incentive programs in areas not covered by the federally approved program. The Court held that these additional programs were permitted under the federal statute and cited the following 1972 colloquy in the Congressional Record concerning the meaning of the Act in support of its conclusion:

Perhaps the most revealing legislative expressions confirm, subsequent to enactment, a congressional desire to preserve supplementary state work programs, not to supersede them. In the wake of the invalidation of the New York Work Rules by the three-judge District Court, members of the New York congressional delegation became concerned that the court had misconstrued the intent of Congress. The following colloquy occurred between Senator Buckley of New York and Senator Long of Louisiana, Chairman of the Finance Committee which considered WIN prior to approval by the Senate:

"Mr. Buckley. Was it ever the intention of Congress at that time to have the provisions of the WIN statutes preempt the field of employment and training for ADC recipients?

"Mr. Long. I did not have that in mind. * * *

"Mr. Buckley. * * * So far as the distinguished chairman is concerned, was it ever the intention of at least this body to have a preemption in this field?

"Mr. Long. It was never our intention to prevent a State from requiring recipients to do something for their money if they were employable * * *." 118 Cong. Rec. 36819 (1972).

In the House of Representatives, a similar dialogue took place between Congressman Carey of New York and Congressman Mills, Chairman of the house Ways and Means Committee, which considered the WIN program:

"Mr. Carey of New York * * *. My specific question for the chairman has to do with the intent of the Congress in authorizing the WIN program in 1967 and in amendments to that program in subsequent years. It is my understanding that Congress intended, through the WIN program, merely to assist the States in the critical area of guiding able-bodied welfare recipients toward self-sufficiency—and not to supersede individual State programs designed to achieve the same end. Under this interpretation, New York and other States could operate their own programs as supplementary to the Federal WIN program. Is my understanding of the congressional intent in this area correct?

"Mr. Mills of Arkansas. I agree with the interpretation of my friend, the gentleman from New York, on the matter, so long as the State program does not contravene the provisions of Federal law." 118 Cong. Rec. 36931 (1972).

The above colloquy with Senator Buckley was presumably one experience which helped Judge Buckley learn about the political rather than legal significance of legislative history, noted in Chapter 10.

c) COMMENTS AND QUESTIONS

1. *Linking legislative history to legislation?* In Pierce v. Underwood, 487 U.S. 552 (1988), Justice Scalia argues against relying on later (1985) legislative history related to reenactment of an earlier 1980 statute. He states that the 1985 committee report cannot reasonably be considered an authoritative expression of what the later legislature intends

> because it is not an explanation of any language that the Committee drafted, because on its face it accepts the 1980 meaning of the terms as subsisting, and because there is no indication whatever in the text or even in the legislative history of the 1985 reenactment that Congress thought it was doing anything insofar as the present issue is concerned except reenacting and making permanent the 1980 legislation.

In other words, there is no legislation to speak of in 1985 *about the issue being litigated*, because the text was simply reenacted, without focusing on the subject in dispute. Consequently, the legislative history was not an effort to explain anything the legislature (as opposed to the committee) did in 1985.

But isn't it a fiction in the first place to assume that the legislature carefully focused on the content of legislative history? Why must legislative history be attached to legislation at all? Maybe the right question to ask is what function is served by linking legislative history to legislation? Could it be this? Legislative history should be useful in determining statutory meaning only if it is a part of a legislative process in which legislators have a reasonable opportunity to be aware of and respond to the legislative history. That is why there must be some evidence that the legislature was at least concerned with the issue which was the subject of legislative history. Based on that standard, do you think any of the following legislative history would be useful: a committee report attached to a bill that passed only one House; that passed both Houses but was not sent to the President or was vetoed by the President; was unattached to any pending legislation?

2. *Legislators' affidavits in litigation?* Is it ever appropriate for courts to rely on affidavits prepared for litigation by legislators about the meaning of a statute? At least committee reports and colloquies in the congressional record reflect political dialogue in a setting where politicians know political decisions are made. There will usually be an opportunity for legislators to have access to creators of these traditional forms of legislative history, if their staffs are alert. Can affidavits satisfy even these rudimentary procedural requirements for legislative participation?

Does the fact that an affidavit involves legislators in specific adjudication, rather than rulemaking, make these post-enactment statements even more suspect?

In Bread Political Action Committee v. Federal Election Commission, 455 U.S. 577 (1982), the Court stated in footnote 3:

> Perhaps because Senator Buckley's intent as expressed in the legislative history remains uncertain, the appellants have submitted to this Court affidavits from Senator Buckley and David A. Keene, the Executive Assistant to the Senator who prepared the original draft of § 437h, expressing the belief that the amendment was not intended to exclude organizations from challenging the constitutionality of the Act. See Affidavit of James Buckley (Nov. 11, 1977); Affidavit of David A. Keene (Oct. 21, 1977). We cannot give probative weight to these affidavits, however, because "[s]uch statements 'represent only the personal views of th[is] legislato[r], since the statements were [made] after passage of the Act.'" Regional Rail Reorganization Act Cases, 419 U.S. 102, 132 (1974), quoting National Woodwork Manufacturers Assn. v. NLRB, 386 U.S. 612, 639, n. 34 (1967). See Also Quern v. Mandley, 436 U.S. 725, 736, n. 10 (1978), in which we noted that *"post hoc observations by a single member of Congress carry little if any weight."*

See also City of Spokane v. State, 89 P.2d 826, 828–29 (Wash.1939) (depositions of the governor, committee chairs, and Speaker of the House about what they thought the act meant when they exercised their legislative functions are inadmissible). But see Stewart v. Bd. of Medical Quality Assur., 143 Cal.Rptr. 641, 647 (Ct.App.1978)(statements of individual legislators are admissible; court must determine their weight).

3. *The President's role?* One of the objections to relying on legislative history is that the President agrees only to the text of the law, not legislative history. What if the President positively rejects later legislative history, as in the following case where he vetoes a later law which is accompanied by legislative history stating that it simply clarified the meaning of a prior statute? Does the veto completely destroy the usefulness of the later legislative history?

Waterman S. S. Corp. v. United States
381 U.S. 252 (1965).

■ Mr. Justice Goldberg delivered the opinion of the Court.
* * *

[Editor—The taxpayer claimed very favorable tax treatment for tax years 1947–50 under a 1946 Act and claimed that the legislative history of a 1950 amendment supported the taxpayer's interpretation of the earlier legislation.]

Finally, petitioner argues that the congressional history subsequent to the enactment of the 1946 statute supports its interpretation of the Act. In 1950 Congress passed an amendment to the 1946 Act, designed to provide precisely the tax result here contended for by petitioner. This amendment, however, was vetoed by President Truman. While both House and Senate Committee Reports contain statements that this amendment was deemed simply a clarifying one which expressed the intent of the original Act, see H. R. Rep. No. 1342, 81st Cong., 1st Sess., 1; S. Rep. No. 1915, 81st Cong., 2d Sess., 1, it was vetoed by President Truman on the ground that, on the contrary, he considered it to vitiate the intent of Congress in enacting the 1946 Act. * * *

Thus, it is apparent that the President and Congress disagreed over the meaning of a law passed by a prior Congress, and that the President, deeming the amendment to depart from the purpose of the original statute, refused to approve it so that the amendment was not enacted into law. This Court has pointed out on previous occasions that "the views of a subsequent Congress form a hazardous basis for inferring the intent of an earlier one." This is particularly true where a President (the same President who signed the original Act) vetoes a "clarifying" amendment on the grounds that, in his view, it does not clarify but rather vitiates the intent of the Congress that passed the original Act. * * *

Does this case indirectly affirm the potential authority of legislative history from legislative sources, even though it is not attached to legislation which becomes law, by emphasizing the President's *explicit* disagreement as a reason for not relying on the 1950 legislative history? After all, no law was passed in 1950 because of the veto.

The case also notes that the 1950 veto was by the same President who had signed the 1946 law, which was being interpreted. Does that imply that the President has power to create legislative history through signing statements (see Chapter 10.10)?

4.   *Legislative history vs. administrative interpretations?* The traditional approach to analyzing later legislative history—whether it is probative of prior "legislative intent"—might mislead a court. As evidence of prior legislative intent, later legislative history might seem superior to administrative interpretations, because evidence of original legislative intent might trump agency rules, especially noncontemporaneous agency rules. For example, in the Walt Disney case, a Treasury Regulation was shunted aside, in favor of post-enactment statements by a Committee Chair. Which should prevail—later legislative history or a Regulation? Which statement of law emerges from a better political process (one that is more open, reflective, not captured by special interests, or any other criteria of institutional competence that you consider important)?

5.   *Treatises?* What about another probative source of law which appears after a statute is adopted—the treatise? If the author had nothing to do with the statute's passage, and there is no evidence that the treatise was part of legislative context, there is no way to link the treatise with legislative intent. And yet treatises are often cited—for example: Bittker et al., on the Income and Corporate Tax; White & Summers on the UCC. Should the "expert's" interpretation of a statute be useful to the court? On what theory? Is it better than later legislative history from legislative sources? Is the treatise-writing expert more or less vulnerable to the interest group pressure that affects more conventional legislative history?

12.03   LEGISLATIVE REENACTMENT

In prior sections, we considered statements interpreting prior law by the legislature, legislative committees, and others connected with the legislative process. We now consider another situation in which legislative action after a statute is passed is sometimes treated as evidence of statutory meaning. The situation is one in which a legislature reenacts a statute after a court or agency has interpreted the law. Reenactment seems to resolve one problem that plagues the use of legislative history—there is a legislative event which deserves to be called law.[7] A text (the reenacted statute) is passed by the legislature and signed by the executive. The difficult question remains whether reenactment properly leads to the inference that the intervening interpretation has been approved by the legislature. In the conventional language of statutory interpretation, the intervening interpretation potentially provides the context for the later reenactment, but (as with all context claims) it is often unclear what context is genuinely incorporated into a law.

a) INTERVENING INTERPRETATION AS CONTEXT FOR REENACTED STATUTE

Courts sometimes cite the mere fact of reenactment as incorporating the intervening interpretation, as a matter of legislative intent. This use of legislative reenactment has been severely criticized on the ground that reenactment itself suggests nothing about legislative intent regarding a prior interpretation.

What must be true before reenactment could really amount to intentional ratification of an intervening case or agency interpretation of a statute? The prior interpretation must be a genuine part of the statute's context, which implies the following. First, the legislature must be aware of the intervening interpretation. Second, it must approve of it. The cases in this section discuss the circumstances in which these conditions might be present.

i) AWARENESS

In the following case, the court criticizes the conventional use of reenactment as evidence of legislative intent. What does the court require before the reenactment doctrine can be applied? Is legislative awareness or approval missing in the case?

Fishgold v. Sullivan Drydock & Repair Corp.

154 F.2d 785 (2d Cir.1946), affirmed, 328 U.S. 275 (1946).

■ Learned Hand, Judge. * * *

[Editor—The claimant was a veteran employed as a welder. He was laid off by his employer during a period when nonveterans

---

7. See Tribe, Toward a Syntax of the Unsaid, 57 Ind. L.J. 515 (1982).

were hired. The issue was whether the priority granted to veterans by § 8(b) of the Selective Training and Service Act of 1940 prohibited such layoffs. The Act stated: "Such employer shall restore such person to such position or to a position of like seniority, status and pay unless the employer's circumstances have so changed as to make it impossible or unreasonable to do so." The defendant argued that the Act only required restoring veterans to the same place in the job hierarchy that they would have enjoyed if they had been on leave instead of in the Armed Services, not to a position of seniority over nonveterans. The Director of Selective Service issued a rule which supported the claimant. After this rule was issued, the Act was amended in 1944.]

There remains the question whether the amendment of § 8 in December, 1944, and the extension of the whole act until May 15, 1946, is to be taken as embodying the Director's position. The amendment, taken alone, only extended the time within which a veteran might apply for reinstatement from forty days to ninety days, and made that period begin from the termination of "hospitalization continuing after discharge for a period of not more than one year," if he was in a hospital. Of itself this indicated no other change in intent; but the Director's ruling had been made for over six months in December, 1944. Moreover, Colonel Keesling, of the Director's office, in one part of his testimony before the subcommittee of the Committee on Military Affairs, stated the Director's position. * * *

* * * [W]e cannot * * * assimilate the situation to that to which courts so frequently resort in aid of the interpretation of ambiguous language; i.e., reenactment without change after administrative interpretation. The rationale of that canon must be, either that those in charge of the amendment are familiar with existing rulings, or that they mean to incorporate them, whatever they may be. The second would hardly be tenable; we should hesitate to say that Congress might enact as law regulatory provisions with which it concededly had no acquaintance. On the other hand, if we are to suppose, in the absence of evidence to the contrary, that Congress is familiar with all existing administrative interpretations, and is content to accept them when it makes no change, it would seem that the force of that assumption should vary with the circumstances. For example, successive recessions of the Internal Revenue Act are the result of detailed conferences between the Treasury and the committees of Congress; and there is good reason to assume that, in so far as the statute is not changed, existing regulations and even less formal interpretations are expressly affirmed. That may well be a proper inference in the case of all general recessions, accompanied as these ordinarily are by continuous and intimate consultation with administrative officers. But it would seem hazardous to carry such a conclusion to the situation

here at bar. So far as concerns any actual information conveyed to Congress, it was at most confined to the occasion which we have discussed, for it would be gratuitous to suppose that the same information ever reached the Senate Committee of Military Affairs. * * * We should be clutching at straws and relying on phantoms, if we were to suppose that the re-enactment of this section with its very specific amendment was intended to effect so vital a change in industrial relations. Certainly we should be unwarranted in believing that Congress would have made so far reaching a change without notice to those who had an interest equal with the veterans themselves—the unions. * * *

We cannot conclude without expressing the hope, though it may not be realized, that our decision may not be taken as indicating any indifference to the claims of those who stood by the nation in the hour of its need at the hazard, and so often with the loss, of all that life holds dear.

Judgment reversed; complaint dismissed.

QUESTIONS AND COMMENTS

1. Why wasn't there sufficient legislative awareness in this case? Is it because it occurred in *subcommittee* hearings? Is it because it occurred in subcommittee *hearings*; who attends hearings?

2. What does the court mean when it states: "Certainly we should be unwarranted in believing that Congress would have made so far reaching a change without notice to those who had an interest equal with the veterans themselves—the unions." Is the statement concerned with legislative intent or something else, such as "legislative due process?"

3. What do you think of the suggestion in Fishgold that reenactment might ratify a prior interpretation if Congress continuously revisits and reworks a statute, especially with the cooperation of an executive agency? Does such revisiting demonstrate awareness; approval; something else?

4. Why not presume ratification by reenactment unless the statute or legislative history includes a statement *denying* any implication of approval from reenactment? See e.g. American Law Institute, Proposed Official Draft, Federal Securities Code, § 2010(b)(1978): "Enactment of this Code is not a legislative ratification of prior judicial or administrative precedents."

ii) APPROVAL

Awareness of an intervening interpretation at the time of reenactment is, obviously, not sufficient to demonstrate legislative approval of the interpretation. How is approval demonstrated? Is the following case an example?

In Snyder v. Harris, 394 U.S. 332 (1969), the Court was asked to interpret the requirement of the federal jurisdiction statute that there be a minimum $10,000 amount in controversy (since repealed), so that a group of plaintiffs could aggregate their claims. In the following excerpt, what justifies the Court's decision that reenactment incorporates prior judicial decisions denying aggregation? Were those decisions genuinely part of the statute's context, of which Congress approved?

* * * It is argued in behalf of this position that (1) the determination of whether claims are "separate and distinct" is a troublesome question that breeds uncertainty and needless litigation, and (2) the inability of parties to aggregate numerous small claims will prevent some important questions from being litigated in federal courts. And both of these factors, it is argued, will tend to undercut the attempt of the Judicial Conference to promulgate efficient and modernized class action procedures. We think that whatever the merit of these contentions, they are not sufficient to justify our abandonment of a judicial interpretation of congressional language that has stood for more than a century and a half.

It is linguistically possible, of course, to interpret the old congressional phrase "matter in controversy" as including all claims that can be joined or brought in a single suit through the class action device. But, beginning with the first Judiciary Act in 1789 Congress has placed a jurisdictional amount requirement on access to the federal courts in certain classes of cases, including diversity actions. The initial requirement was $500 and a series of increases have, as pointed out above, finally placed the amount at $10,000. Congress has thus consistently amended the amount-in-controversy section and re-enacted the "matter-in-controversy" language without change of its jurisdictional effect against a background of judicial interpretation that has consistently interpreted that congressionally enacted phrase as not encompassing the aggregation of separate and distinct claims. This judicial interpretation has been uniform since at least the 1832 decision of this Court in Oliver v. Alexander, 6 Pet. 143. There are no doubt hazards and pitfalls involved in assuming that re-enactment of certain language by Congress always freezes the existing judicial interpretation of the statutes involved. Here, however, the settled judicial interpretation of "amount in controversy" was implicitly taken into account by the relevant congressional committees in determining, in 1958, the extent to which the jurisdictional amount should be raised. It is quite possible, if not probable, that Congress chose the increase to $10,000 rather than the proposed increases to $7,500 or $15,000 on the basis of workload estimates which clearly relied on the settled doctrine that separate and distinct claims could not be aggregated. Where Congress has consistently re-enacted its prior statutory language for more than a century and a half in the face of a settled interpretation of that language, it is perhaps not entirely realistic to designate the resulting rule a "judge-made formula."

To overrule the aggregation doctrine at this late date would run counter to the congressional purpose in steadily increasing through the years the jurisdictional amount requirement. * * *

The dissenting opinion took a different view about whether reenactment incorporated prior judicial decisions:

> The hearings and reports on the 1958 statute raising the jurisdictional amount from $3,000 to $10,000—which the majority fastens on as the adopting re-enactment—include not one word about the whole complex body of rules by which courts determine when the amount is at issue, much less any reference to the particular problem of aggregation of claims in class action cases. * * * If we are to attribute to Congress any thoughts on this highly technical and specialized matter, it seems to me far more reasonable to assume that Congress was aware that the courts had been developing the interpretation of the jurisdictional amount requirement in class actions and would continue to do so after the 1958 amendments.

The following case deals with § 5 of the Voting Rights Act. The Act specified that changes in voting rules, under certain circumstances, required approval by the Attorney General. An Alabama city, Sheffield, wanted to change from a Commission form of government to a mayoral form. The Attorney General approved the change but balked at the city's use of at-large elections for city councilmen. The issue in the case was whether § 5 applied to Sheffield. If it did not, the Attorney General's approval was not needed. Although Alabama was a state covered by the statute, Sheffield itself was not a political unit that registered voters. The argument on behalf of the city was that the statute applied only to political units that registered voters.

The Court concluded that the Act's coverage did not depend on registering voters, relying heavily on statutory reenactment after an intervening Attorney General interpretation adopting this view. As you read the case, identify precisely the evidence of legislative awareness and approval which supported this conclusion.

United States v. Board of Com'rs of Sheffield, Ala.

435 U.S. 110 (1978).

■ Mr. Justice Brennan delivered the opinion of the Court. * * *

We first consider whether Congress intended to exclude from § 5 coverage political units, like Sheffield, which have never conducted voter registration. In concluding that Congress did, the District Court noted that § 5 applies to "a [designated] state or a [designated] *political subdivision*" and construed § 5 to provide that, where a State in its entirety has been designated for coverage, the only political units within it that are subject to § 5 are those that are "political subdivisions" within the meaning of § 14(c)(2). Because § 14(c)(2) refers only to counties and to the units of state government that register voters, the District Court held that political

units like the City are not subject to the duties imposed by § 5.
* * *

Although this Court has described the workings of the Voting Rights Act in prior cases, it is appropriate again to summarize its purposes and structure and the special function of § 5. Congress adopted the Act in 1965 to implement the Fifteenth Amendment and erase the blight of racial discrimination in voting. The core of the Act "is a complex scheme of stringent remedies aimed at areas where voting discrimination has been the most flagrant." Congress resorted to these stern measures because experience had shown them to be necessary to eradicate the "insidious and pervasive evil of [racial discrimination in voting] that had been perpetuated in certain parts of our country." [Editor—This quote and others in this paragraph are from South Carolina v. Katzenbach, 383 U.S. 301 (1966).] Earlier efforts to end this discrimination by facilitating case-by-case litigation had proved ineffective in large part because voting suits had been "unusually onerous to prepare" and "exceedingly slow" to produce results. And even when favorable decisions had been obtained, the affected jurisdictions often "merely switched to discriminatory devices not covered by the federal decrees." * * *

* * * Where, as here, a State has been designated for coverage, the meaning of the term "political subdivision" has no operative significance in determining the reach of § 5: the only question is the meaning of "[designated] State."

* * * [T]he Attorney General has, since the Act was adopted in 1965, interpreted § 5 as requiring all political units in designated jurisdictions to preclear proposed voting changes. * * * Moreover, the Attorney General's longstanding construction of § 5 was reported to Congress by Justice Department officials in connection with the 1975 extension of the Act.

And the legislative history of the 1970 and 1975 re-enactments compellingly supports the conclusion that Congress shared the Attorney General's view. In 1970, Congress was clearly fully aware of this Court's interpretation of § 5 as reaching voter changes other than those affecting the registration process and plainly contemplated that the Act would continue to be so construed. See, e.g., Hearings on H. R. 4249 et al. before Subcommittee No. 5 of the House Committee on the Judiciary, 91st Cong., 1st Sess., 1, 4, 18, 83, 130–131, 133, 147–149, 154–155, 182–184, 402–454 (1969); Hearings on S. 818 et al. before the Subcommittee on Constitutional Rights of the Senate Committee on the Judiciary, 91st Cong., 1st and 2d Sess., 48, 195–196, 369–370, 397–398, 426–427, 469 (1970). [Editor—Notice that the Court here cites awareness by a *subcommittee*.] The history further suggests that Congress assumed that, just as § 5 applies to changes that affect aspects of voting other than registration, so it also applies to entities other than those which conduct voter registration. One of the principal factual arguments

advanced in favor of the renewal of § 5 was that Anniston, Ala.—
which, like Sheffield, has never conducted voter registration—had
failed to obtain preclearance of some highly significant voting
changes. See Joint View of 10 Members of the Senate Judiciary
Committee Relating to the Extension of the Voting Rights Act of
1965, 116 Cong. Rec. 5521 (1970).

The congressional history is even clearer with respect to the
1975 extension, which, of course, is the legislation that controls the
case at bar. Both the House and Senate Hearings on the bill reflect
the assumption that the coverage of § 5 was unlimited was widely
shared and unchallenged. In addition to the aforementioned testimony of the then Assistant Attorney General, which of course has
special significance, numerous witnesses expressed this view, either
directly or indirectly. More significantly, both the House and Senate
Committee Reports preclude the conclusion that § 5 was not understood to operate territorially. Not only do the reports state that § 5
applies "*[i]n* [designated] jurisdictions," see S. Rep. No. 94–295, p.
12 (1975)(1975 Senate Report); H. R. Rep. No. 94–196, p. 5
(1975)(1975 House Report)(emphasis supplied), they also announce
that one benefit of the proposed extension of the Act to portions of
Texas would be that Texas cities and school districts—neither of
which has ever registered voters—would be subject to the preclearance requirement. 1975 Senate Report 27–28; 1975 House Report
19–20. * * *

Whatever one might think of the other arguments advanced, the
legislative background of the 1975 re-enactment is conclusive of the
question before us. When a Congress that re-enacts a statute voices
its approval of an administrative or other interpretation thereof,
Congress is treated as having adopted that interpretation, and this
Court is bound thereby. While we have no quarrel with our Brother
Stevens' view that it is impermissible to draw inferences of approval
from the unexplained inaction of Congress, citing Hodgson v. Lodge
851, Int'l Assn. of Mach. & Aerospace Workers, 454 F.2d 545, 562
(C.A.7 1971)(Stevens, J., dissenting), that principle has no applicability to this case. Here, the "slumbering army" of Congress was
twice "aroused," and on each occasion it re-enacted the Voting
Rights Act and manifested its view that § 5 covers all cities in
designated jurisdictions.

In short, the legislative background of the enactment and re-
enactments compels the conclusion that, as the purposes of the Act
and its terms suggest, § 5 of the Act covers all political units within
designated jurisdictions like Alabama. Accordingly, we hold that the
District Court erred in concluding that § 5 does not apply to
Sheffield.

Justice Stevens filed a dissent in Sheffield in which he argued that the
Court was relying on legislative *inaction*. At first, that is a somewhat puzzling
claim. The statute was obviously reenacted in 1975. Here is what he said:

[T]he subsequent amendments of the Act in 1970 and 1975 [are not] reliable guides to what Congress intended in 1965 when it drafted the relevant statutory language. The 1970 and 1975 extensions of the Act did not change the operative language in § 5 or alter the definition of the term "political subdivision." As I suggested a few years ago, "[a]n interpretation of a provision in [a] controversial and integrated statute * * * cannot fairly be predicated on unexplained inaction by different Congresses in subsequent years." Hodgson v. Lodge 851, Int'l Assn. of Mach. & Aerospace Workers, 454 F.2d 545, 562 (C.A.7 1971)(dissenting opinion).

In sum, I am persuaded that the result the Court reaches today is not a faithful reflection of the actual intent of the Congress that enacted the statute. I therefore respectfully dissent.

In footnote 12, Stevens responds to an argument made by the Court that the 1975 reenactment was not like legislative inaction.

* * * [T]he court has suggested that * * * I have sought an answer to the wrong question because we are construing the 1975, rather than the 1965, Act. However, the question whether the Act was "re-enacted" in 1975 is of only technical significance. Section 5 would have continued in operation beyond 1975 for States such as Alabama even without the 1975 extension. See comments of Senator Tunney, 121 Cong. Rec. 24706 (1975). More importantly, the 1975 Congress made no change in the definition of "political subdivision" and no one called its attention to any aspect of the issue decided today. The question I have tried to answer is what Congress actually intended to accomplish by its definition of the term "political subdivision." That definition was, perhaps, the product of a legislative compromise, and the resulting statutory language may be "crippling" to the Court's reading of the full remedial purposes of the statute. But we have an obligation to respect the product of legislative compromise as well as policy decisions we wholeheartedly endorse.

QUESTIONS

1. Is Justice Stevens making the same point Justice Scalia did in Pierce v. Underwood, *supra*, when he objected to relying on legislative history attached to a statutory text that was perfunctorily reenacted? In other words, does legislative approval require something more than awareness in congressional hearings and statements in committee reports?

2. How do you make sense of Stevens' claim that "Congress made no change in the definition of 'political subdivision?' " Whenever a statute is reenacted, the specific statutory language being interpreted is *not* changed. If it were, that language would not be reenacted. Perhaps Stevens means the following. Mechanical reenactment of a text may be insufficient to justify an inference that Congress was aware of and approved the intervening interpretation. But suppose the statute reenacts the language being interpreted, and changes other related parts of the text. For example, suppose in Sheffield, the statutory text in § 5 had been amended by redefining "political subdivision?" That might provide some evidence that Congress focused on the problem of which political units were covered by § 5 of the Voting Rights Act, reworked some of the law regarding covered units, but left untouched the intervening interpretation (of which it was aware) that State designation was sufficient without regard to whether a political subdivision registered voters. In that setting, it might be reasonable to assume that the intervening interpretation was implicitly approved. But this still invites the following question: How related must the changed text be to the reenacted text to support the inference that reenactment incorporates an intervening interpretation?

3. What does Stevens mean when he says that "no one called [Congress'] attention to any aspect of the issue decided today"? How can that statement be reconciled with the majority's observations about what occurred in legislative hearings and the statements in committee reports, including the examples of jurisdictions which did not register voters?

4. Stevens was very concerned with voting rights and racial discrimination in Chisom v. Roemer. What explains his diminished willingness to interpret this statute to protect the civil rights claimant?

b) CHANGING LAW DESPITE REENACTMENT

In some cases the courts reconsider prior interpretations after reenactment of the statute, even when there is a strong argument that the prior interpretation was incorporated into the reenacted statute. For example, Girouard v. United States, 328 U.S. 61 (1946), held that a statutory oath to support and defend the Constitution and laws of the United States did *not* require bearing arms. Three cases, the last of which was decided in 1931, had interpreted the statute differently; they interpreted the statute to require bearing arms. The Girouard majority first noted an argument based on reenactment:

> Many efforts were made to amend the law so as to change the rule announced by those cases; but in every instance the bill died in committee. Moreover, when the Nationality Act of 1940 was passed, Congress reenacted the oath in its pre-existing form, though at the same time it made extensive changes in the requirements and procedure for naturalization. From this it is argued that Congress adopted and reenacted the rule of the [three prior] cases.

The Court then rejected this argument, stating:

> We stated in Helvering v. Hallock, 309 U.S. 106, 119, that "It would require very persuasive circumstances enveloping Congressional silence to debar this Court from reexamining its own doctrines." It is at best treacherous to find in congressional silence alone the adoption of a controlling rule of law. We do not think under the circumstances of this legislative history that we can properly place on the shoulders of Congress the burden of the

Court's own error. The history of the 1940 Act is at most equivocal. It contains no affirmative recognition of the rule of the [the prior three] cases. The silence of Congress and its inaction are as consistent with a desire to leave the problem fluid as they are with an adoption by silence of the rule of those cases. * * *

———

And in James v. United States, 366 U.S. 213 (1961), the Court reversed an earlier decision (Wilcox) which had *not* taxed embezzlement income. The taxpayer advanced the reenactment argument and the Court responded as follows.

Petitioner contends that the Wilcox rule has been in existence since 1946; that if Congress had intended to change the rule, it would have done so; that there was a general revision of the income tax laws in 1954 without mention of the rule; that a bill to change it was introduced in the Eighty-sixth Congress but was not acted upon; that, therefore, we may not change the rule now. But the fact that Congress has remained silent or has re-enacted a statute which we have construed, or that congressional attempts to amend a rule announced by this Court have failed, does not necessarily debar us from re-examining and correcting the Court's own errors. Girouard v. United States. There may have been any number of reasons why Congress acted as it did. One of the reasons could well be our subsequent decision in [another case] which has been thought by many to have repudiated Wilcox. Particularly might this be true in light of the decisions of the Courts of Appeals which have been riding a narrow rail between the two cases and further distinguishing them to the disparagement of Wilcox.

We believe that Wilcox was wrongly decided and we find nothing in congressional history since then to persuade us that Congress intended to legislate the rule. Thus, we believe that we should now correct the error and the confusion resulting from it, certainly if we do so in a manner that will not prejudice those who might have relied on it. [Editor—The Court applied the new rule prospectively.] We should not continue to confound confusion, particularly when the result would be to perpetuate the injustice of relieving embezzlers of the duty of paying income taxes on the money they enrich themselves with through theft while honest people pay their taxes on every conceivable type of income.

———

There are also many cases where the courts allow an administrative agency to change its interpretation despite an intervening reenactment. The following case explains why.

Helvering v. Wilshire Oil Co.

308 U.S. 90 (1939).

■ Mr. Justice Douglas delivered the opinion of the Court. * * *

* * * The oft-repeated statement that administrative construction receives legislative approval by reenactment of a statutory provision, without material change covers the situation where the validity of administrative action standing by itself may be dubious or where ambiguities in a statute or rules are resolved by reference to administrative practice prior to reenactment of a statute; and where it does not appear that the rule or practice has been changed by the administrative agency through exercise of its continuing rule-making power. It does not mean that a regulation interpreting a provision of one act becomes frozen into another act merely by reenactment of that provision, so that that administrative interpretation cannot be changed prospectively through exercise of appropriate rule-making powers. The contrary conclusion would not only drastically curtail the scope and materially impair the flexibility of administrative action; it would produce a most awkward situation. Outstanding regulations which had survived one Act could be changed only after a pre-view by the Congress. In preparation for a new revenue Act the Commissioner would have to prepare in advance new regulations covering old provisions. Their effectiveness would have to await Congressional approval of the new Act. The effect of such procedure, so far as time is concerned, would be precisely the same as if these new regulations were submitted to the Congress for approval. Such dilution of administrative powers would deprive the administrative process of some of its most valuable qualities—ease of adjustment to change, flexibility in light of experience, swiftness in meeting new or emergency situations. It would make the administrative process under these circumstances cumbersome and slow. Known inequities in existing regulations would have to await the advent of a new revenue act. Paralysis in effort to keep abreast of changes in business practices and new conditions would redound at times to the detriment of the revenue; at times to the disadvantage of the taxpayer. Likewise the result would be to read into the grant of express administrative powers an implied condition that they were not to be exercised unless, in effect, the Congress had consented. We do not believe that such impairment of the administrative process is consistent with the statutory scheme which the Congress has designed.

These cases pose something of a puzzle for the reenactment doctrine. Arguably, we might assume that the appropriate circumstances for applying the reenactment doctrine were absent. But the case for its application was about as strong as it will ever be—in Girouard, obvious congressional awareness and tinkering with related statutory language; in James and Wilshire Oil Co, the congressional awareness of tax cases that comes with the periodic congressional revision of the income tax law at that time (although, in James, the case law prior to reenactment might have been in a state of flux). The inference is that, notwithstanding reenactment, the court or agency can change its earlier interpretation. But how can that be? If reenactment ratifies a prior interpretation of a statute, how can the interpreter change its mind after the reenactment? Isn't the whole point of relying on reenactment that the legislature intended to incorporate into law the prior interpretation?

The implication of these comments is that the reenactment doctrine cannot really be concerned with legislative intent, but with something else. Chapter 12.05 will speculate on what that something else might be, after we look at the "inaction" doctrine.

12.04   LEGISLATIVE INACTION

a) CRITIQUE

Some judges would not be bothered by the fact that reenactment might be the equivalent of legislative inaction. They cite legislative inaction in the face of an intervening interpretation as evidence that the legislature intended the interpretation to be law, even if the statute is not reenacted.

The "inaction" doctrine, however, has few defenders. First, there is the fundamental constitutional problem that inaction is, by definition, not associated with any legislative event. At least defenders of the reenactment doctrine could point to a reenacted statute, even though reenactment is often the functional equivalent of inaction.

Second, on a more political note, there are three reasons why legislative inaction is not much of a guide to identifying legislative intent regarding an intervening interpretation.

1. *Inertia*. Legislative inertia is a powerful force. Congress may have other more pressing business or simply want to adjourn, rather than reject a court or agency interpretation. Inertia is, after all, a central fact of legislative life.

> [O]ne must ignore rudimentary principles of political science to draw any conclusions regarding that intent from the failure to enact legislation. The "complicated check on legislation," The Federalist No. 62, p. 378 (C. Rossiter ed. 1961), erected by our Constitution creates an inertia that makes it impossible to assert with any degree of assurance that congressional failure to act represents (1) approval of the status quo, as opposed to (2) inability to agree upon how to alter the status quo, (3) unawareness of the status quo, (4) indifference to the status quo, or even (5) political cowardice.

Johnson v. Transportation Agency, Santa Clara County, 480 U.S. 616, 671–72 (1987)(Scalia, J., dissenting).

2. *Blocking legislation.* There are many ways for political minorities to block legislation. In the Senate the filibuster is the most obvious method, but there are others. Particular voting blocks may defer to strong minority preferences to avoid giving offense and gain future political allies. Committees, which act as gatekeepers for legislation, may be dominated by minority viewpoints. Silence in the face of an existing interpretation may therefore indicate, at most, minority approval, not majority support. Of course, minority control of the legislative agenda may or may not be bad, and it may or may not reflect strong legislative preferences, but the inaction it produces should not be casually confused with legislative approval of prior interpretations.

3. *Public choice theory.* Public choice theory suggests another reason why legislative inaction is a poor guide to original legislative intent. Justice Scalia explained this in the following excerpt from his dissent in Johnson v. Transportation Agency Santa Clara County, 480 U.S. 616, 671 (1987).

* * * [Legislative inaction] assays the current Congress' desires *with respect to the particular provision in isolation*, rather than (the way the provision was originally enacted) as part of a total legislative package containing many *quids pro quo*. Whereas the statute as originally proposed may have presented to the enacting Congress a question such as "Should hospitals be required to provide medical care for indigent patients, with federal subsidies to offset the cost?," the question theoretically asked of the later Congress, in order to establish the "correctness" of a judicial interpretation that the statute provides no subsidies, is simply "Should the medical care that hospitals are required to provide for indigent patients be federally subsidized?" Hardly the same question—and many of those legislators who accepted the subsidy provisions in order to gain the votes necessary for enactment of the care requirement would not vote for the subsidy in isolation, now that an unsubsidized care requirement is, thanks to the judicial opinion, safely on the books. * * *

b) TWO CASES CITING LEGISLATIVE INACTION

The following two cases are probably the best known examples of the Court's reliance on legislative inaction. Does inaction in these cases really indicate legislative approval? If not, ask (as you did with the reenactment doctrine) what other theory might explain the decision.

Bob Jones University v. United States
461 U.S. 574 (1983).

■ Chief Justice Burger delivered the opinion of the Court. * * *

[Editor—In 1970 and 1971 rulings the IRS denied tax exemption to schools whose practices discriminated on racial grounds. The statute's text granted exemption to "educational" or "charitable" institutions. The underlying concept of a "charity" had evolved to exclude institutions which practiced race discrimination, but the taxpayer argued that the statute literally allowed exemption because either "educational" *or* "charitable" organizations were exempt. The Court held that a "charitable" purpose was a necessary condition for all tax exempt organizations, including those engaged in educational activities. This aspect of the decision, interpreting the statute to incorporate a common law power to define "charitable," was discussed in Chapter 9, dealing with change. In addition, the opinion also considered legislative inaction after the agency adopted its rulings.]

The actions of Congress since 1970 leave no doubt that the IRS reached the correct conclusion in exercising its authority. It is, of course, not unknown for independent agencies or the Executive Branch to misconstrue the intent of a statute; Congress can and often does correct such misconceptions, if the courts have not done so. Yet for a dozen years Congress has been made aware—acutely aware—of the IRS rulings of 1970 and 1971. As we noted earlier, few issues have been the subject of more vigorous and widespread debate and discussion in and out of Congress than those related to racial segregation in education. Sincere adherents advocating contrary views have ventilated the subject for well over three decades. Failure of Congress to modify the IRS rulings of 1970 and 1971, of which Congress was, by its own studies and by public discourse, constantly reminded; and Congress' awareness of the denial of tax-exempt status for racially discriminatory schools when enacting other and related legislation make out an unusually strong case of legislative acquiescence in and ratification by implication of the 1970 and 1971 rulings.

Ordinarily, and quite appropriately, courts are slow to attribute significance to the failure of Congress to act on particular legislation. See, e.g., Aaron v. SEC, 446 U.S. 680, 694 n. 11 (1980). We have observed that "unsuccessful attempts at legislation are not the best of guides to legislative intent," Red Lion Broadcasting Co. v. FCC, 395 U.S. 367, 381–382 n. 11 (1969). Here, however, we do not have an ordinary claim of legislative acquiescence. Only one month after the IRS announced its position in 1970, Congress held its first hearings on this precise issue. Equal Educational Opportunity: Hearings Before the Senate Select Comm. on Equal Educational Opportunity, 91st Cong., 2d Sess. 1991 (1970). Exhaustive hearings have been held on the issue at various times since then. These include hearings in February 1982, after we granted review in this case.

Non-action by Congress is not often a useful guide, but the non-action here is significant. During the past 12 years there have been no fewer than 13 bills introduced to overturn the IRS interpretation of § 501(c)(3). Not one of these bills has emerged from any committee, although Congress has enacted numerous other amendments to § 501 during this same period, including an amendment to § 501(c)(3) itself. Tax Reform Act of 1976, Pub.L. 94–455, 1313(a), 90 Stat. 1520, 1730 (1976). It is hardly conceivable that Congress—and in this setting, any Member of Congress—was not abundantly aware of what was going on. In view of its prolonged and acute awareness of so important an issue, Congress' failure to act on the bills proposed on this subject provides added support for concluding that Congress acquiesced in the IRS rulings of 1970 and 1971.

The evidence of Congressional approval of the [IRS] policy * * * goes well beyond the failure of Congress to act on legislative proposals. Congress affirmatively manifested its acquiescence in the IRS policy when it enacted the present § 501(I) of the Code, Act of October 20, 1976, Pub.L. 94–568, 90 Stat. 2697 (1976). That provision denies tax-exempt status to social clubs whose charters or policy statements provide for "discrimination against any person on the basis of race, color, or religion." Both the House and Senate committee reports on that bill articulated the national policy against granting tax exemptions to racially discriminatory private clubs. [Editor—If Congress was so approving of the IRS policy, why didn't it also amend the law to require a nondiscrimination policy for schools?]

Even more significant is the fact that both reports focus on this Court's affirmance of [a 1971] case, as having established that "discrimination on account of race is inconsistent with an *educational institution's* tax exempt status." S.Rep. No. 1318, supra, at 7–8 and n.5; H.R. Rep. No. 1353, supra, at 8 and n. 5 (emphasis added), U.S.Code Cong. & Admin. News, p. 6058. These references in Congressional committee reports on an enactment denying tax exemptions to racially discriminatory private social clubs cannot be read other than as indicating approval of the standards applied to racially discriminatory private schools by the IRS subsequent to 1970, and specifically of Revenue Ruling 71–447.

In Flood v. Kuhn , 407 U.S. 258 (1972), the Court refused to overrule a 1922 case in which the Supreme Court did not apply the anti-trust laws to baseball on the ground that baseball was not a business in interstate commerce. The Court stated:

1.   Professional baseball is a business and it is engaged in interstate commerce.

2.   With its reserve system enjoying exemption from the federal antitrust laws, baseball is, in a very distinct sense, an exception and an anomaly. Federal Baseball and Toolson have become an aberration confined to baseball. [Editor—Federal Baseball was the 1922 decision and Toolson was a later case following the Federal Baseball decision.]

3.   Even though others might regard this as "unrealistic, inconsistent, or illogical," the aberration is an established one. * * * It is an aberration that has been with us now for half a century, one heretofore deemed fully entitled to the benefit of *stare decisis*, and one that has survived the Court's expanding concept of interstate commerce. It rests on a recognition and an acceptance of baseball's unique characteristics and needs.

4.   Other professional sports operating interstate—football, boxing, basketball, and presumably, hockey and golf—are not so exempt. * * *

6.   The Court has emphasized that since 1922 baseball, with full and continuing congressional awareness, has been allowed to develop and to expand unhindered by federal legislative action. Remedial legislation has been introduced repeatedly in Congress but none has ever been enacted. The Court, accordingly, has concluded that Congress as yet has had no intention to subject baseball's reserve system to the reach of the antitrust statutes. This, obviously, has been deemed to be something other than mere congressional silence and passivity.

7.   The Court has expressed concern about the confusion and the retroactivity problems that inevitably would result with a judicial overturning of Federal Baseball. It has voiced a preference that if any change is to be made, it come by legislative action, that by its nature, is only prospective in operation. * * *

* * * We continue to be loath, 50 years after Federal Baseball and almost two decades after Toolson, to overturn those cases judicially when Congress, by its positive inaction, has allowed those decisions to stand for so long and, far beyond mere inference and implication, has clearly evinced a desire not to disapprove them legislatively. [Editor—What does "positive inaction" mean?]

12.05   REINTERPRETING REENACTMENT AND INACTION CASES

Reenactment and inaction are often such flimsy evidence of legislative intent to ratify an intervening interpretation that commentators have looked for other explanations for decisions invoking these doctrines. One explanation is that they give a legislative pedigree for a prior interpretation that might not stand on its own. Undoubtedly, many cases can be cynically explained that way, but there may be other ways to explain at least some decisions invoking the reenactment and inaction doctrines.

a) DEFERENCE TO THE AGENCY

When the intervening interpretation is by an agency, some cases invoking the reenactment or inaction doctrines may be explicable as deferring to agency discretion without saying so. We saw in Chapter 11 that the conditions for deference to agency rules are contested and it might seem convenient to the court not to get into a dispute about whether those conditions are met. For example, in Bob Jones the agency interpretation was in the form of a Revenue Ruling, which is a published statement by the Internal Revenue Service of its view of the law, not issued after public notice and comment. It may seem easier to the court to assert that the legislature approved the agency decision by reenactment or inaction, without getting into a discussion of how much support the agency ruling should enjoy on its own under the Chevron doctrine (Chapter 11.04).

b) SUPER-STRONG STARE DECISIS FOR CASES INTERPRETING STATUTES

Some cases relying on legislative reenactment or inaction after a case interprets a statute might implicitly adopt the doctrine that cases interpreting statutes are *more* binding under *stare decisis* principles than cases based on the common law. Eskridge calls this the "super-strong presumption" for *stare decisis* in statutory interpretation cases.[8] For example:

> If a statute is to be amended after it has been authoritatively construed by this Court, that task should almost always be performed by Congress. Guardians Ass'n v. Civil Service Com'n of City of New York, 463 U.S. 582, 641 (1983)(Stevens, J.).

Professor Horack stated the super-strong presumption even more decisively: "After the decision [interpreting the statute], whether the Court correctly or incorrectly interpreted the statute, the law consists of the statute *plus* the decision of the Court." Reversal of the prior decision is a "legislative" activity, impinging on the right of Congress to decide what is and is not "inconsistent with the intent of Congress." Horack, Congressional Silence: A Tool of Judicial Supremacy, 25 Tex. L. Rev. 247, 251–52 (1946).

Many decisions upholding prior judicial interpretations because of later reenactment or inaction might be reanalyzed as applications of the super-strong stare decisis presumption. But *should* there be a super-strong presumption for statutory interpretation cases?

---

8. See Eskridge, Overruling Statutory Precedents, 76 Geo. L. Rev. 1361 (1988). Inferences about super-strong *stare decisis* for *federal* statutory interpretation cases are clouded by the difficulty of finding appropriate comparisons. A finding of super-strong *stare decisis* depends on comparison with the legislature's approach to common law cases, and there is not much federal common law.

1.   Is the legislature more likely to be aware of cases interpreting statutes than other cases?

2.   Is the legislature more likely to enact laws about cases interpreting statutes? If so, that might support super-strong *stare decisis* on the theory that the less legislative inertia, the less reason there is for the court to revisit a prior decision.

3.   Are statutes more likely to deal with areas of law on which the public relies, more so than under the common law? Overruling statutory interpretation cases would, on this theory, be more likely to undercut reliance interests.

4.   Perhaps the super-strong presumption derives support from a formalistic distinction between legislation and adjudication. For example, in Zimmerman v. Wisconsin Elec. Power Co., 157 N.W.2d 648, 651 (1968), the court stated:

> * * * Where a law passed by the legislature has been construed by the courts, legislative acquiescence in or refusal to pass a measure that would defeat the courts' construction is not an equivocal act. The legislature is presumed to know that in absence of its changing the law, the construction put upon it by the courts will remain unchanged; for a principle of the courts' decision—legislative intent—is a historical fact and, hence, unchanging. Thus, when the legislature acquiesces or refuses to change the law, it has acknowledged that the courts' interpretation of legislative intent is correct. This being so, however, the courts are henceforth constrained not to alter their construction; having correctly determined legislative intent, they have fulfilled their function.

Legislative intent, identified by the prior case, is an historical fact and overruling a precedent would be rewriting history. This assumption is consistent with the common practice of finding an error in identifying legislative intent as the major reason for overruling statutory interpretation precedent. By contrast, common law decisions are acts of judicially creative lawmaking and can therefore be changed by the court as the law evolves. In other words, even though we no longer think courts discover the common law, they still discover statutory meaning. Greater deference to decisions interpreting statutes would be a symptom of a jurisprudence which distinguishes sharply between judge-made law and statutes.

5.   Congress has a greater *responsibility* to pay attention to cases interpreting statutes and a super-strong *stare decisis* approach would encourage Congress to meet its responsibilities.

Here is a recent typical statement about why *stare decisis* in statutory interpretation cases is especially appropriate. Neal v. United States, 116 S.Ct. 763 (1996). Which of the five rationales for this approach, if any, does the Court seem to adopt?

Our reluctance to overturn precedents derives in part from institutional concerns about the relationship of the judiciary to Congress. One reason that we give great weight to stare decisis in the area of statutory construction is that "Congress is free to change this Court's interpretation of its legislation." [Editor—Isn't a legislature free to overturn a common law decision as well?] We have overruled our precedents when the intervening development of the law has "removed or weakened the conceptual underpinnings from the prior decision, or where the later law has rendered the decision irreconcilable with competing legal doctrines or policies." [Editor—Is a "development of the law" which has "removed or weakened the conceptual underpinnings from [a] prior decision" a change in the legal landscape?] Absent those changes or compelling evidence bearing on Congress' original intent, our system demands that we adhere to our prior interpretations of statutes. * * * Entrusted within its sphere to make policy judgments, [an agency] may abandon its old [rule] in favor of what it has deemed a more desirable [rule.] We, however, do not have the same latitude to forsake prior interpretations of a statute. * * * [ ] Congress, not this Court, has the responsibility for revising its statutes. Were we to alter our statutory interpretations from case to case, Congress would have less reason to exercise its responsibility to correct statutes that are thought to be unwise or unfair.

Is there an argument favoring *more* judicial flexibility regarding statutory interpretation decisions than the common law? After all, statutory law originates with the legislature, not the courts. For that reason, judicial opinions interpreting a statute might deserve less weight than common law decisions. See, e.g., Windust v. Department of Labor & Industries, 323 P.2d 241, 244 (Wash.1958).

Whatever the merits of the super-strong presumption favoring stare decisis for statutory interpretation cases, the presumption may exert some pull on courts. Eskridge, in the article cited above, notes that the Supreme Court has overruled many cases interpreting statutes in recent years, but finds that the super-strong presumption still has some attraction for the Court. That attraction may in turn manifest itself as the hidden principle in cases supporting a prior statutory interpretation on reenactment or inaction grounds.

c) LEGAL LANDSCAPE ANALYSIS

In Chapter 9, we discussed Calabresi's idea of a contemporary legal landscape and the fact that a legislature might prefer a particular result even though it was out of step with the broader legal landscape. No one pretends that these ideas are easy to apply, but there is evidence that courts are concerned with these issues in some reenactment and inaction cases.

1. Recall the Bob Jones case, *supra*, where the Court accepted the agency's view that a university which discriminated on the basis of race was not tax exempt, in part because of legislative inaction with obvious knowledge of the agency rule. This case might be a good example of keeping the law in touch with the contemporary legal landscape dealing with race discrimination. A legislative committee not only blocked bills overruling the revenue rulings prohibiting race discrimination (which resulted in legislative inaction), but also reported out successful legislation preventing exemption for social clubs with racially discriminatory policies. Anyone concerned with coherence in the law governing tax exempt institutions might find it difficult to justify the legislature prohibiting tax exempt social clubs from discriminating but allowing schools that freedom, when the legislature knew that the agency had already denied exemption to discriminating schools.

There is a contrary argument, however. The "social club" provision (26 U.S.C. § 501(i)) withdraws exemption only for written discrimination policies, not discriminatory action. This might be an example of Congress having it both ways—legislating what appears to be a broad public policy without much teeth. In that view, the statute did not unequivocally express a policy against discriminatory *action*.

2. Flood v. Kuhn, *supra*, involving baseball's exemption from anti-trust laws might be an example of a decision which the legislature would support, notwithstanding its departure from the contemporary anti-trust legal landscape. If ever there was a case where the legislature might not want to tamper with departures from the legal landscape, baseball might be it,[9] at least until recent strikes by players might have changed the public mood.

d) LEGISLATIVE RESPONSIBILITY TO REJECT THE INTERVENING INTERPRETATION

There is another way to make sense out of at least some reenactment and inaction cases. Some decisions might apply a principle that the intervening interpretation should stand unless the legislature exercises its responsibility to reject it. When you look at judicial opinions relying on reenactment and inaction, it is surprising how often you find statements, almost offhand, about legislative responsibility to reject the intervening interpretation. Many of the opinions stress one of two reasons for legislative rather than judicial responsibility: the area of law is technical; or it involves politically sensitive issues. At least that is my reading.[10]

---

9. See Eskridge, Overriding Supreme Court Statutory Interpretation Decisions, 101 Yale L.J. 331, 401 nn.229–30 (1991).

10. Also recall the Supreme Court's statement in Neal v. U.S., *supra*, dealing with super *stare decisis*, that "Congress would have

less reason to exercise its responsibility to correct statutes that are thought to be unwise or unfair," if the Court revisited earlier statutory interpretation cases.

Girouard v. United States

328 U.S. 61 (1946)(dissenting opinion of Chief Justice Stone).

[Editor—The Court's majority opinion in this case was discussed earlier in Chapter 12. It overruled prior cases and held that Congress had not required bearing arms as a condition to naturalization. Chief Justice Stone's dissent in this case, excerpted *infra*, favored application of the reenactment doctrine to prevent overruling of prior cases.]

Any doubts that [ ] the purpose and will of Congress [supported application of prior decisions] would seem to have been dissipated by the reenactment by Congress in 1940 of Paragraphs "Third" and "Fourth" of § 4 of the Naturalization Act of 1906, and by the incorporation in the Act of 1940 of the very form of oath which had been administratively prescribed for the applicants in the Schwimmer, Macintosh and Bland cases. See Rule 8(c), Naturalization Regulations of July 1, 1929.

The Nationality Act of 1940 was a comprehensive, slowly matured and carefully considered revision of the naturalization laws. The preparation of this measure was not only delegated to a Congressional Committee, but was considered by a committee of Cabinet members, one of whom was the Attorney General. Both were aware of our decisions in the Schwimmer and related cases and that no other question pertinent to the naturalization laws had been as persistently and continuously before Congress in the ten years following the decision in the Schwimmer case. The modifications in the provisions of Paragraphs "Third" and "Fourth" of § 4 of the 1906 Act show conclusively the careful attention which was given to them.

In the face of this legislative history the "failure of Congress to alter the Act after it had been judicially construed, and the enactment by Congress of legislation which implicitly recognizes the judicial construction as effective, is persuasive of legislative recognition that the judicial construction is the correct one. This is the more so where, as here, the application of the statute * * * has brought forth sharply conflicting views both on the Court and in Congress, and where after the matter has been fully brought to the attention of the public and the Congress, the latter has not seen fit to change the statute." Apex Hosiery Co. v. Leader, 310 U.S. 469, 488–9. It is the responsibility of Congress, in reenacting a statute, to make known its purpose in a controversial matter of interpretation of its former language, at least when the matter has, for over a decade, been persistently brought to its attention. In the light of this legislative history, it is abundantly clear that Congress has performed that duty. In any case it is not lightly to be implied that Congress has failed to perform it and has delegated to this Court the responsibility of giving new content to language deliberately readopted after this Court has construed it. * * *

How would you write an opinion on behalf of the majority in Girouard, arguing for overruling the prior cases, because it was the *court's* responsibility?

James v. United States

366 U.S. 213 (1961)(opinion of Justice Black dissenting from overruling Wilcox).

[Editor—The majority opinion in James was also discussed earlier in this Chapter. It overruled the Wilcox case, which had excluded embezzled funds from taxable income. Justice Black's dissent explains why he would let Wilcox stand.]

The Wilcox case was decided fifteen years ago. Congress has met every year since then. All of us know that the House and Senate Committees responsible for our tax laws keep a close watch on judicial rulings interpreting the Internal Revenue Code. Each committee has one or more experts at its constant disposal. It cannot possibly be denied that these committees and these experts are, and have been, fully familiar with the Wilcox holding. When Congress is dissatisfied with a tax decision of this Court, it can and frequently does act very quickly to overturn it. On one occasion such an overruling enactment was passed by both the House and Senate and signed by the President all within one day after the decision was rendered by this Court. In 1954 Congress, after extended study, completely overhauled and recodified the Internal Revenue Code. The Wilcox holding was left intact. In the Eighty-sixth Congress and in the present Eighty-seventh Congress bills have been introduced to subject embezzled funds to income taxation. They have not been passed. This is not an instance when we can say that Congress may have neglected to change the law because it did not know what was going on in the courts. * * * What we have here instead is a case in which Congress has not passed bills that have been introduced to make embezzled funds taxable and thereby make failure to report them as income a federal crime.

In American Automobile Association v. United States, 367 U.S. 687 (1961), the Commissioner of Internal Revenue refused to allow the taxpayer to use a method of accounting which deferred tax on prepaid membership dues. The Court upheld the agency's decision, noting that

it appears Congress has long been aware of the problem this case presents. * * * At the very least, this background indicates congressional recognition of the complications inherent in the problem and its seriousness to the general revenue. We must leave to the Congress the fashioning of a rule which, in any event, must have wide ramifications. The Committees of Congress have standing committees expertly grounded in tax problems.

―――――――――

In United States v. Rutherford, 442 U.S. 544, 554 (1979), terminally ill patients claimed an exception to a Food and Drug Administration rule prohibiting the sale of certain drugs, including laetrile, which the patients wanted to use. The Court deferred to the agency's rule, as follows:

> * * * Such deference is particularly appropriate where, as here, an agency's interpretation involves issues of considerable public controversy, and Congress has not acted to correct any misperception of its statutory objectives.

There was evidence of legislative awareness contained in a Subcommittee hearing.[11]

―――――――――

If judicial deference to legislative responsibility is an operative principle, there might be differences between specialized and generalist courts in applying this approach. We often compare courts and legislatures as lawmaking institutions on the assumption that all courts are alike, but that might not be true. A specialist court might be more willing to grapple with an issue which it feels competent to resolve, rather than defer to a legislature. That is at least an hypothesis which could test the empirical validity of the "legislative responsibility" model.

―――――――――

Critique of "legislative responsibility" approach. When a court defers to the legislature, whether through reenactment, inaction or any other doctrine, it remands the losing litigant to another forum for relief. In effect, it deems the legislature more competent than the court to resolve the issue. Whenever a court allocates power to the legislature, however, it must confront some troublesome questions.

First, what are the prospects that the legislature will take up the losing litigant's complaint? Will the issue get on the legislative agenda and what are the chances of the loser prevailing? If the losing litigant is in a very weak political position, a remand to the legislature may be politically meaningless. What passes for "legislative awareness" often pays no attention to whether issues are really on the legislative agenda. Legislative hearings and introducing bills on a subject may be pro forma posturing, because no legislator expects anything to happen. Sometimes, however, legislative hearings are serious business and a committee mark-up of a bill and committee report are

―――――――――

11. See also CBS, Inc. v. F.C.C., 453 U.S. 367, 382 (1981)(citing the above quote from Rutherford and upholding regulations dealing with access to broadcast stations).

good evidence that an issue is on the legislative agenda. When an issue is seriously considered by the legislature, deference to legislative responsibility at least remands an issue to an institution that is paying some attention.

Even if an issue receives serious legislative attention, however, an imbalance in political forces may destroy any chance of getting results. For example, baseball owners may be much more likely to organize effectively to lobby for an anti-trust exemption than baseball players, whose interests vary among superstars, journeyman, beginners, etc. Moreover, if exemption from anti-trust laws permits price fixing, consumers are unlikely to organize to oppose higher prices. You might reject this analysis, and conclude that political imbalance is irrelevant. After all, there are always political losers and the likelihood of a political loss should not influence the court's decision to defer to the legislature. But you might also conclude that deference to legislative responsibility should be an operative principle only when political forces operate on a more or less level playing field. Political losses are often attributable to superior organizational and financing capability, rather than open deliberation about public concerns, and these political advantages should not be compounded by a single-minded and unvarying judicial deference to legislative responsibility.

Second, deferring to legislative responsibility may have undesirable substantive implications. Deference to the legislature lets the winner in the earlier political/legal battle before an agency or court carry the day, and forces the loser in that battle to get the result overturned by the legislature. These substantive consequences may be too much to accept. Judicial concern for the substance of statutory interpretation has recurred throughout this course—for example, in "plain statement" requirements, identifying "absurd" consequences, and in Marshall's 19th Century distinction between fundamental values vs. inconvenient results. Substantive concerns might also prevent judicial deference to the legislature through reliance on the reenactment and inaction doctrines.

Many cases in which the court "defers" to the legislature involve politically innocuous issues, often of a technical nature, where a court might be tempted to let the legislature work out the solution regardless of the impact on litigants. But when the issues are politically sensitive, the courts are pulled in two directions. It is tempting to let a politically sensitive issue be settled by the legislature, as the Court stated in the "laetrile" case. United States v. Rutherford, 442 U.S. 544 (1979). However, a politically controversial issue is also likely to attract strong views among some judges, who will object to the result in the prior interpretation. They will insist on a "plain statement" from the legislature that the loser under the prior interpretation was in fact meant to lose. A sense of judicial responsibility conflicts with a belief (or hope) that the legislature will discharge its responsibility. This suggests that courts may be quite selective in deciding when to leave an issue to a "responsible" legislature and raises the question of what substantive values should be favored.[12] In the following case, what substantive concerns prevented the court from leaving it to Congress to reject an agency rule?

---

12. Selective deferral to the legislature sounds something like judicial agenda-setting   through application of gatekeeping rules, such as standing, ripeness, and political question

In S.E.C. v. Sloan, 436 U.S. 103 (1978), an agency rule claimed broad discretion to suspend trading in a stock for a continuous series of ten day periods. In response to the agency's claim that congressional reenactment ratified the agency's rule, the Court stated as follows:

> Finally, the Commission argues that for a variety of reasons Congress should be considered to have approved the Commission's construction of the statute as correct. Not only has Congress re-enacted the summary suspension power without disapproving the Commission's construction, but the Commission participated in the drafting of much of this legislation and on at least one occasion made its views known to Congress in Committee hearings. Furthermore, at least one Committee indicated on one occasion that it understood and approved of the Commission's practice.

> While we of course recognize the validity of the general principle illustrated by the cases upon which the Commission relies, we do not believe it to be applicable here. In Zuber v. Allen, 396 U.S. at 192, 90 S.Ct. at 328, the Court stated that a contemporaneous administrative construction of an agency's own enabling legislation "is only one input in the interpretational equation. Its impact carries most weight when the administrators participated in drafting and directly made known their views to Congress in committee hearings." Here the administrators, so far as we are advised, made no reference at all to their present construction of § 12(k) to the Congress which drafted the "enabling legislation" here in question—the Securities Exchange Act of 1934. They made known to at least one committee their subsequent construction of that section 29 years later, at a time when the attention of the Committee and of the Congress was focused on issues not directly related to the one presently before the Court. [Editor—The specific legislative change to which Congress directed its attention was whether to extend the statute to over-the-counter trading.] Although the section in question was re-enacted in 1964, and while it appears that the Committee Report did recognize and approve of the Commission's practice, this is scarcely the sort of congressional approval referred to in Zuber, supra.

> We are extremely hesitant to presume general congressional awareness of the Commission's construction based only upon a few isolated statements in the thousands of pages of legislative documents. That language in a Committee Report, without additional indication of more widespread congressional awareness, is simply not sufficient to invoke the presumption in a case such as this. For

doctrine. Selective use of gatekeeping doctrines to control the courts' substantive agenda has been criticized on the ground that these doctrines are based on important policies and should not be distorted by substantive considerations. Gunther, The Subtle Vices of the 'Passive 'Virtues', 64 Colum. L. Rev. 1 (1984). Can the courts articulate clear criteria explaining why an issue should or should not be left to the legislature?

here its invocation would result in a construction of the statute which not only is at odds with the language of the section in question and the pattern of the statute taken as a whole, but also is extremely far reaching in terms of the virtually untrammeled and unreviewable power it would vest in a regulatory agency. * * *

In sum, had Congress intended the Commission to have the power to summarily suspend trading virtually indefinitely we expect that it could and would have authorized it more clearly than it did in § 12(k). The sweeping nature of that power supports this expectation. * * *

Does the Court sound like Judge Hand in Fishgold, where he stated: "Certainly we should be unwarranted in believing that Congress would have made so far reaching a change [in the seniority rules for employees] without notice to those who had an interest equal with the veterans themselves—the unions." In other words, some "far reaching" judgments must be reached only by the legislature.

But can a court identify what is "far reaching" without some exercise of substantive judgment? In Sloan, the concern was about administrators making far reaching decisions affecting business activity—reminiscent of Justice Stevens' concern in his dissent in the Locke case, about the impact of the agency insisting on filing *before* December 31 to avoid forfeiture of mining claims.

STATUTES AS A SOURCE OF LAW

Early 20th century commentators, such as Pound, foresaw a time when the policies underlying statutes would establish principles from which the court would develop the common law. The search for such principles also underlies Calabresi's notion of a legal landscape. Public choice theory, by contrast, is reluctant to find such principles in legislation; a statute's domain is limited, as Easterbrook suggests.

This Subpart II–C considers various settings in which statutes may be a source of law. Chapter 13 considers extending statutes, both when the courts have a substantive common lawmaking power and when they do not. Chapter 14 addresses a particular version of that problem—inferring private causes of action and remedies from statutes whose language does not explicitly provide them.

Chapter 15 deals with the relationship between two or more statutes. When statutes appear to conflict, either directly or by implication, what should a court do? Should the later law prevail; or should the prior law be presumed to survive, unless repeal of the prior law is explicit? Can two or more statutes reinforce each other, shaping the legal landscape in ways that influence statutory interpretation?

The issues in this Subpart explore the boundaries of the judicial role in statutory interpretation. There have always been two rival conceptions of how legislation fits into the law. First, legislation is the paramount form of lawmaking and courts simply determine, more or less passively, what the statute means. Second, legislation, like all law, is part of a broader legal landscape, and courts must play an active role in determining how statutes fit into that landscape.

Until the 20th Century, this second conception worked to the disadvantage of legislation, as courts narrowly interpreted statutes in derogation of the common law. Today, statutes are not an inferior form of lawmaking. The modern question is how courts can play a more or less active role in fitting statutes into the broader fabric of the law, without reverting to a pre–20th Century negative presumption against legislation. The material in this Subpart II–C about "statutes as a source of law" forces you to think about these issues.

CHAPTER 13

Extending Statutes

13.01 Statutes Influencing the Common Law

When courts have a common law power, they must identify sources of common law principles. Courts which were hostile to legislation or denigrated legislative lawmaking would not have found such principles in legislation. But, as Pound argued, modern courts are likely to find evidence of the legal landscape in patterns of legislation. This section provides some examples. Remember that we have still not reached the hard cases—those in which the court is not exercising a substantive common law power but nonetheless relies on statutory patterns to determine the law.

a) Admiralty Law

i) MORAGNE v. STATES MARINE LINES, 398 U.S. 375 (1970)

■ Mr. Justice Harlan delivered the opinion of the Court.

[Editor—This case involved a suit for wrongful death by a longshoreman under federal maritime law, which is federal common law. The suit was based on the vessel's unseaworthiness, which is easier to prove than negligence. The relevant events occurred in a state's *territorial* waters, not on the high seas. The Harrisburg case, referred to in the opinion, held that there was no cause of action for wrongful death under federal maritime law. How does the Court use legislation to create new federal common law?]

We brought this case here to consider whether The Harrisburg, 119 U.S. 199, in which this Court held in 1886 that maritime law does not afford a cause of action for wrongful death, should any longer be regarded as acceptable law. * * *

We need not * * * pronounce a verdict on whether The Harrisburg, when decided, was a correct extrapolation of the principles of decisional law then in existence. A development of major significance has intervened, making clear that the rule against recovery for wrongful death is sharply out of keeping with the policies of modern American maritime law. This development is the wholesale abandonment of the rule in most of the areas where it once held sway, quite evidently prompted by the same sense of the rule's injustice that generated so much criticism of its original promulgation.

To some extent this rejection has been judicial. The English House of Lords in 1937 emasculated the rule without expressly overruling it. * * *

In the United States, every State today has enacted a wrongful-death statute. The Congress has created actions for wrongful deaths of railroad employees, Federal Employers' Liability Act, 45 U.S.C. § 51–59; of merchant seamen, Jones Act, 46 U.S.C. § 688; and of persons on the high seas, Death on the High Seas Act, 46 U.S.C. §§ 761, 762. Congress has also, in the Federal Tort Claims Act, 28 U.S.C. § 1346(b), made the United States subject to liability in certain circumstances for negligently caused wrongful death to the same extent as a private person.

These numerous and broadly applicable statutes, taken as a whole, make it clear that there is no present public policy against allowing recovery for wrongful death. The statutes evidence a wide rejection by the legislatures of whatever justifications may once have existed for a general refusal to allow such recovery. This legislative establishment of policy carries significance beyond the particular scope of each of the statutes involved. The policy thus established has become itself a part of our law, to be given its appropriate weight not only in matters of statutory construction but also in those of decisional law. See Landis, Statutes and the Sources of Law, in Harvard Legal Essays 213, 226–227 (1934). * * *

This appreciation of the broader role played by legislation in the development of the law reflects the practices of common-law courts from the most ancient times. As Professor Landis has said, "much of what is ordinarily regarded as 'common law' finds its source in legislative enactment." It has always been the duty of the common-law court to perceive the impact of major legislative innovations and to interweave the new legislative policies with the inherited body of common-law principles—many of them deriving from earlier legislative exertions.

The legislature does not, of course, merely enact general policies. By the terms of a statute, it also indicates its conception of the sphere within which the policy is to have effect. In many cases the scope of a statute may reflect nothing more than the dimensions of the particular problem that came to the attention of the legislature, inviting the conclusion that the legislative policy is equally applicable to other situations in which the mischief is identical. This conclusion is reinforced where there exists not one enactment but a course of legislation dealing with a series of situations, and where the generality of the underlying principle is attested by the legislation of other jurisdictions. On the other hand, the legislature may, in order to promote other, conflicting interests, prescribe with particularity the compass of the legislative aim, erecting a strong inference that territories beyond the boundaries so drawn are not to feel the impact of the new legislative dispensation. We must, therefore, analyze with care the congressional enactments that have abrogated the common-law rule in the maritime field, to determine the impact of the fact that none applies in terms to the situation of this case. However, it is sufficient at this point to conclude, as Mr. Justice Holmes did 45 years ago, that the work of the legislatures has made the allowance of recovery for wrongful death the general rule of American law, and its denial the exception. Where death is caused by the breach of a duty imposed by federal maritime law, Congress has established a policy favoring recovery in the absence of a legislative direction to except a particular class of cases.

Our undertaking, therefore, is to determine whether Congress has given such a direction in its legislation granting remedies for wrongful deaths in portions of the maritime domain. We find that Congress has given no affirmative indication of an intent to preclude the judicial allowance of a remedy for wrongful death to persons in the situation of this petitioner.

From the date of The Harrisburg until 1920, there was no remedy for death on the high seas caused by breach of one of the duties imposed by federal maritime law. For deaths within state territorial waters, the federal law accommodated the humane policies of state wrongful death statutes by allowing recovery whenever an applicable state statute favored such recovery. Congress acted in 1920 to furnish the remedy denied by the courts for deaths beyond the jurisdiction of any State, by passing two landmark statutes. The first of these was the Death on the High Seas Act, 41 Stat. 537, 46 U.S.C. § 761 et seq. Section 1 of that Act provides that:

> "Whenever the death of a person shall be caused by wrongful act, neglect, or default occurring on the high seas beyond a marine league from the shore of any State, * * * the personal representative of the decedent may maintain a suit for damages in the district courts of the United States, in admiralty, for the exclusive benefit of the decedent's wife, husband, parent, child, or dependent relative against the vessel, person, or corporation which would have been liable if death had not ensued."

Section 7 of the Act further provides:

> "The provisions of any State statute giving or regulating rights of action or remedies for death shall not be affected by this [Act]. Nor shall this [Act] apply to the Great Lakes or to any waters within the territorial limits of any State * * *."

[Editor—The second statute was the Jones Act, which gave *seamen* a remedy for injury or death, but only for negligence.]

* * * There should be no presumption that Congress has removed this Court's traditional responsibility to vindicate the policies of maritime law by ceding that function exclusively to the

States. However, respondents argue that an intent to do just that is manifested by the portions of the Death on the High Seas Act quoted above.

The legislative history of the Act suggests that respondents misconceive the thrust of the congressional concern. Both the Senate and House Reports consist primarily of quoted remarks by supporters of the proposed Act. Those supporters stated that the rule of The Harrisburg, which had been rejected by "[e]very country of western Europe," was "a disgrace to a civilized people." "There is no reason why the admiralty law of the United States should longer depend on the statute laws of the States. * * * Congress can now bring our maritime law into line with the laws of those enlightened nations which confer a right of action for death at sea." The Act would accomplish that result "for deaths on the high seas, leaving unimpaired the rights under State statutes as to deaths on waters within the territorial jurisdiction of the States. * * * This is for the purpose of uniformity, as the States cannot properly legislate for the high Seas." S.Rep. No. 216, 66th Cong., 1st Sess., 3, 4 (1919); H.R. Rep. no. 674, 66th Cong., 2d Sess. 3, 4, (1920). The discussion of the bill on the floor of the House evidenced the same concern that a cause of action be provided "in cases where there is now no remedy," 59 Cong. Rec. 4486, and at the same time that "the power of the States to create actions for wrongful death in no way be affected by enactment of the federal law."

Read in light of the state of maritime law in 1920, we believe this legislative history indicates that Congress intended to ensure the continued availability of a remedy, historically provided by the States, for deaths in territorial waters; its failure to extend the Act to cover such deaths primarily reflected the lack of necessity for coverage by a federal statute, rather than an affirmative desire to insulate such deaths from the benefits of any federal remedy that might be available independently of the Act. The void that existed in maritime law up until 1920 was the absence of any remedy for wrongful death on the high seas. Congress, in acting to fill that void, legislated only to the three-mile limit because that was the extent of the problem. The express provision that state remedies in territorial waters were not disturbed by the Act ensured that Congress' solution of one problem would not create another by inviting the courts to find that the Act pre-empted the entire field, destroying the state remedies that had previously existed.

The beneficiaries of persons meeting death on territorial waters did not suffer at that time from being excluded from the coverage of the Act. To the contrary, the state remedies that were left undisturbed not only were familiar but also may actually have been more generous than the remedy provided by the new Act. On the one hand, the primary basis of recovery under state wrongful-death statutes was negligence. On the other hand, the substantive duties imposed at that time by general maritime law were vastly different from those that presently exist. "[T]he seaman's right to recover damages for injuries caused by unseaworthiness of the ship was an obscure and relatively little used remedy," perhaps largely because prior to this Court's decision in Mahnich v. Southern S.S. Co., 321 U.S. 96 (1944), the shipowner's duty was only to use due diligence to provide a seaworthy ship. * * * Congress in 1920 thus legislated against a backdrop of state laws that imposed a standard of behavior generally the same as—and in some respects perhaps more favorable than—that imposed by federal maritime law.

Since that time the equation has changed drastically, through this Court's transformation of the shipowner's duty to provide a seaworthy ship into an absolute duty not satisfied by due diligence. The unseaworthiness doctrine has become the principal vehicle for recovery by seamen for injury or death, overshadowing the negligence action made available by the Jones Act; and it has achieved equal importance for longshoremen and other harbor workers to whom the duty of seaworthiness was extended because they perform work on the vessel traditionally done by seamen. [Editor—"Unseaworthiness" is a federal common law doctrine, not of statutory origin.] The resulting discrepancy between the remedies for deaths covered by the Death on the High Seas Act and for deaths that happen to fall within a state wrongful-death statute not encompassing unseaworthiness could not have been foreseen by Congress. Congress merely declined to disturb state remedies at a time when they appeared adequate to effectuate the substantive duties imposed by general maritime law. That action cannot be read as an instruction to the federal courts that deaths in territorial waters, caused by breaches of the evolving duty of seaworthiness, must be *damnum absque injuria* unless the States expand their remedies to match the scope of the federal duty.

To put it another way, the message of the Act is that it does not by its own force abrogate available state remedies; no intention appears that the Act have the effect of foreclosing any nonstatutory federal remedies that might be found appropriate to effectuate the policies of general maritime law. * * *

We conclude that the Death on the High Seas Act was not intended to preclude the availability of a remedy for wrongful death under general maritime law in situations not covered by the Act. Because the refusal of maritime law to provide such a remedy appears to be jurisprudentially unsound and to have produced serious confusion and hardship, that refusal should cease unless there are substantial countervailing factors that dictate adherence to The Harrisburg simply as a matter of *stare decisis*. [Editor—The Court goes on to overrule The Harrisburg.]

ii) LOSS OF SOCIETY DAMAGES

After Moragne the Court continued to develop federal common law for wrongful death based on unseaworthiness in *territorial* waters. In Sea–Land Services, Inc. v. Gaudet, 414 U.S. 573 (1974), the Court allowed a longshoreman's widow to recover for loss of society damages (love, affection, care, etc.). The Court took a different approach four years later, however, in Mobil Oil Corp. v. Higginbotham, 436 U.S. 618 (1978). Higginbotham involved a death *on the high seas,* not in territorial waters. The 1920 Death on the High Seas Act (referred to in Moragne) specifies that "recovery * * * shall be * * * for the pecuniary loss sustained by the persons for whose benefit the suit is brought." The plaintiffs sought damages for "loss of society," not just pecuniary loss, but the Court refused. The claimants argued that "Congress does not have the last word" because "admiralty courts have traditionally undertaken to supplement maritime statutes" and that "such a step is necessary in this case to preserve the uniformity of maritime law" (by providing the same relief as in territorial waters). The Court responded that "a desire for uniformity cannot override the statute." The federal statute dealing with death *on the high seas* "announced Congress' considered judgment on the subject. * * * There is a basic difference between filling a gap left by Congress' silence and rewriting rules that Congress has affirmatively and specifically enacted."

How did the Court know there was no gap regarding damages for wrongful death on the high seas? Is the affirmative provision of damages for pecuniary loss like providing statutory recovery for comparative negligence to someone who is not more than 50% negligent, excluding whatever is not explicitly provided? Of the judges who voted in both Gaudet and Higginbotham, all of the majority in the first case were in the minority in the second case, and vice-versa, except Justice White, who voted for loss of society damages in Gaudet and against recovery of such damages in the later Higginbotham case.

What happened in Higginbotham? Was the statute (Death on the High Seas Act) genuinely more pervasive in effect than in Moragne? Was the Court moving away from creating common law in areas which Congress had addressed by statute? Had the pro-claimant legal landscape changed in 1978 when Higginbotham was decided?

In Miles v. Apex Marine Corp., 498 U.S. 19 (1990), the Court returned to loss of society damages in a Wrongful Death action based on a common law claim of unseaworthiness arising in *territorial* waters, except now the injury was to a *seaman,* not (as in Moragne and Gaudet) a longshoreman. The Court noted that the Jones Act, a *statute* which covered injury to *seamen* arising from negligence (not unseaworthiness) both on the high seas and territorial waters, had been interpreted not to allow damages for loss of society. It concluded that the Jones Act precluded recovery for loss of society damages in federal *common law* actions by seamen (not longshoremen) for unseaworthiness in territorial waters.

The preclusive effect of the Jones Act statute in Miles regarding loss of society damages was even more questionable as a matter of legislative intent than the preclusive effect of the 1920 federal law (Death on the High Seas Act) in Higginbotham. Farber & Frickey, In the Shadow of the Legislature: The Common Law in the Age of the New Public Law, 89 Mich. L. Rev. 875, 903–04 (1991), explain why:

> The Jones Act itself contains no limitation on the types of damages recoverable. It borrowed its language from the FELA [Federal Employers Liability Act], which provided a federal remedy for injuries to railroad workers. The FELA also contained no express limitation on damages, but the Supreme Court read such a limitation into the FELA in 1913. It was this decision that formed the basis for the ruling in Miles. Since Congress said nothing to the contrary, according to the Miles Court, it "must have intended" to incorporate this judicial gloss when it passed the Jones Act [in 1920]. In short, what the Court proclaims as judicial deference to the legislature, turns out really to be the 1990 Court's deference to a decision by the 1913 Court under a different statute. Congress is "assumed" to have agreed with the 1913 Court, so the current Court would be exceeding its constitutional role were it to adopt a different rule—not under the FELA, which was the subject on the 1913 decision, nor under the Jones Act, which is presumed to have endorsed the 1913 decision, but under the federal common law created by Moragne, which neither the two earlier statutes nor the 1913 decision had foreseen. This conclusion was especially ironic because Moragne was based on a rejection of the grudging attitude toward wrongful death actions encompassed in the 1913 decision itself.

Can Miles nonetheless be explained in either of the following two ways? First, the Court is retreating from a common lawmaking role because there is no legislative inertia. The Court in Miles stated:

> We no longer live in an era when seamen and their loved ones must look primarily to the courts as a source of substantive legal protection from injury and death; Congress and the States have legislated extensively in this area.

Second, the Court was trying its best to provide uniform remedies to injured workers. The uniformity problem in 1990, when Miles was decided, was this. In 1972, Congress by statute *withdrew* common law unseaworthiness-based claims for longshoremen against shipowners. This overruled the result in Gaudet (as well as Moragne), which had arisen under pre–1972 law. Therefore, longshoremen could no longer recover for loss of society damages in territorial waters based on unseaworthiness. Higginbotham had denied loss of society damages for death on the high seas. The Jones Act had been interpreted to preclude loss of society damages for seamen in negligence cases. Miles (in 1990) held that seamen could not recover for loss of society damages based on unseaworthiness in territorial waters. All the talk about the preclusive effect of the Jones Act really masks judicial use of the evolving legal landscape to *deny* loss of society damages.

b) LEGAL LANDSCAPE

Compare the Court's approach in Moragne to the way the court uses statutes to influence the common law in the following case. What is the difference?

Jersey Shore Medical Center–Fitkin Hospital v. Baum's Estate
417 A.2d 1003 (N.J.1980).

■ Pollock, J. * * *

The hospital sued Mrs. Baum and the estate of Mr. Baum for the balance due on Mr. Baum's bill, contending that the common law rule that imposed liability on a husband for the necessaries furnished to his wife should be extended so that a wife would be liable for the necessaries, such as expenses of a last illness, of her husband. That contention is based on the increasing independence of women, the emerging concept of marriage as a partnership, and the belief that husbands and wives should be treated equally.

We conclude that the common law rule must yield to the evolving interdependence of married men and women and to the reality that a marriage is a partnership. Consequently, we declare that both spouses are liable for necessary expenses incurred by either spouse in the course of the marriage. As long as the marriage subsists, the financial resources of both spouses should be available to pay a creditor who provides necessary goods and services to either spouse. That conclusion comports with our belief that in most marriages a husband and wife consider themselves as a financial unit in paying necessary expenses incurred by either marital partner. However, a judgement creditor must first seek satisfaction from the income and other property of the spouse who incurred the debt. If those financial resources are insufficient, the creditor may then seek satisfaction from the income and property of the other spouse.

The common law rule imposing liability on a husband for his wife's necessaries derived from the husband's obligation to support his wife. That duty arises not from principles of contract law, but from the marriage relation and the public policy of the State. The husband's duty developed in an era when a wife depended on her husband for support and, in exchange, provided him with her services and society. A wife had no duty at common law to support her husband.

The husband's duty to support his wife led to the imposition of liability on him for necessaries furnished to her. The basis of liability for expenses incurred by the wife was the husband's presumed failure to provide adequate support. There is no doubt that the cost of hospital and medical care qualifies as a necessary expense. Accordingly, in the converse of the present case, a widower was found liable for the payment of the expenses of the last illness of his wife. However, a wife was not bound to pay the expense of the last illness of her husband unless she assumed that obligation.

Statutes have modified the rights and duties of husband and wife in dealing with each other and with creditors, but not regarding necessary expenses. For example, N.J.S.A. 2A:34–23 imposes the same duties of alimony or support on both spouses in matrimonial actions and provides for the equitable distribution of property on divorce. However, that statute does not apply to the liability of one spouse to a creditor for necessaries acquired by the other spouse.

Similarly, the Married Woman's Act declares that the separate property of a married woman shall not be liable for her husband's debts. N.J.S.A. 37:2–15. A corresponding provision states that a husband shall not be liable for the debts of his wife contracted in her own name. N.J.S.A. 37:2–10. However, the Married Woman's Act did not alter the husband's duty to pay for the necessary expenses of his wife. A husband has an independent duty arising out of the marital relationship to pay for the necessary expenses of his wife. In effect, a wife's necessaries are her husband's debts. Consequently, the Married Woman's Act, which protects a husband from the debts of his wife, does not affect his independent liability. * * *

* * * [T]he common law has an inherent capacity to adapt to changes such as the movement of married women toward economic equality. See, e.g., Immer v. Risko, 267 A.2d 481 (N.J.1970)(abolishing interspousal immunity for torts arising out of negligent operation of automobile). At one time, the status of married women might have justified placing on a husband the duty to pay for his wife's necessary expenses without a correlative duty on her part. As previously discussed, the imposition of that duty no longer comports with the role of a contemporary wife and concepts of a modern marriage. The common law must adapt to the progress of women in achieving economic equality and to the mutual sharing of all obligations by husbands and wives.

There are various alternatives available in establishing a gender-neutral rule for the payment of necessary expenses incurred by either spouse. One alternative is to read literally the Married Woman's Act, N.J.S.A. 37:2–10 and 15. That act forms a gender neutral scheme under which each spouse is independent of the other. However, literal application of the act would leave creditors of a dependent spouse without recourse to the only realistic source of payment, the financially independent spouse. The act tends to ignore that in a modern marriage husbands and wives, whether they contribute income or domestic services, are a financial unit. A necessary expense incurred by one spouse benefits both. In a viable marriage, husbands and wives ordinarily do not distinguish their financial obligations on the basis of which one incurred the debt. Consequently, literal application of the Married Woman's Act would not comport with the expectations of husbands, wives, or their creditors.

Another alternative is to extend the common law rule and hold each spouse completely liable for the other's debts. Although that rule would treat spouses equally, it would be equality with a vengeance. The rule would result in the immediate exposure of the property of one spouse for a debt incurred by the other spouse. A creditor would receive the same benefits as if both spouses had agreed to joint liability. Neither equity nor reality justifies imposing unqualified liability on one spouse for the debts of the other or exempting one spouse from liability for the necessary expenses of the other. * * *

The appropriate result concerning the liability for necessaries follows from our view that "marriage is a shared enterprise, a joint undertaking, that in many ways * * * is akin to a partnership." Rothman v. Rothman, 320 A.2d 496 (N.J.1974). We hold that both spouses are liable for the necessary expenses incurred by either spouse. In a viable marriage, the marital partners can decide between themselves how to pay their debts. A creditor providing necessaries to one spouse can assume that the financial resources of both spouses are available for payment. However, in the absence of an agreement, the income and property of one spouse should not be exposed to satisfy a debt incurred by the other spouse unless the assets of the spouse who incurred the debt are insufficient.

13.02 STATUTES AS A SOURCE OF LAW WHEN THERE IS NO COMMON LAW

If there is no common law power, can courts extend statutes or otherwise use legislation as a source of principles from which to shape the law? This is obviously a more controversial exercise of judicial power than when courts have an underlying common law authority. (Recall that it would not have always seemed controversial. Equitable interpretation, discussed in Chapter 2, permitted extension of statutory coverage to like cases—that is, extension to a *casus omissus*.)

As you read the cases, notice that it is not always easy to be sure that the court is extending a statute. Be alert to the possibility that the text itself may provide interpretive leeway or plainly hand the court a "common law" power.

The cases are divided into older and newer decisions. This division should make you reflect on whether interpretive approaches have changed. Was it easier or harder to extend older than newer statutes?

a) OLDER CASES

i) JOHNSON v. UNITED STATES, 163 F. 30 (1st Cir.1908)(Justice Holmes)

In this case, the defendant was indicted for concealing property from the trustee of his estate in bankruptcy. The Government offered in evidence the schedule of assets filed by the bankrupt in district court. The defendant objected to the use of this evidence, based on the following statute.

No pleading of a party, nor any discovery or evidence obtained from a party or witness by means of a judicial proceeding in this or any foreign country, shall be given in evidence, or in any manner used against him for his property or estate, in any court of the United States, in any criminal proceeding, or for the enforcement of any penalty or forfeiture: Provided, that this section shall not exempt any party or witness from prosecution and punishment for perjury committed in discovering or testifying as aforesaid.

The Government argued that the schedule was not "pleading, discovery, or evidence" and that therefore the statute did not apply. Holmes rejected the Government's argument, as follows:

* * * We quite agree that vague arguments as to the spirit of a constitution or statute have little worth. We recognize that courts have been disinclined to extend statutes modifying the common law beyond the direct operation of the words used, and that at times this disinclination has been carried very far. But it seems to us that there may be statutes that need a different treatment. A statute may indicate or require as its justification a change in the policy of the law, although it expresses that change only in the specific cases most likely to occur to the mind. The Legislature has the power to decide what the policy of the law shall be, and if it has intimated its will, however indirectly, that will should be recognized and obeyed. The major premise of the conclusion expressed in a statute, the change of policy that induces the enactment, may not be set out in terms, but it is not an adequate discharge of duty for courts to say: We see what you are driving at, but you have not said it, and therefore we shall go on as before. [Editor—Why wasn't the legislature driving at the limits of the statute rather than the underlying principle?]

This section of the Revised Statutes goes beyond and outside of the Fifth Amendment. It applies, even to a sworn bill or answer in chancery, what is said to be the rule of common law, that pleadings are not evidence against the party concerned. It makes this a general provision, and its object seems to us clear. We think that object was to prevent the required steps of the written procedure in court preliminary to trial from being used against the party for whom they were filed. * * * On the same principle we think that schedules in bankruptcy are protected. We can see no reason that would apply to an answer in equity that does not apply to them. They are required by the law. They are a regular step in the written procedure preliminary to the proof of facts. If necessary, it might be argued that they are pleadings within the meaning of the act. Bankruptcy is a proceeding in rem. The schedules indicate those who are to be made parties in the proceeding, the extent of their supposed claims, and the subject-matter of the distribution. They have such characteristics of pleadings as are possible at that stage of a proceeding of this kind against all the world. * * *

What exactly is meant by seeing what the legislature is "driving at?" Does it mean that the court puts itself in the legislature's shoes to see how the legislature would have dealt with a situation that was not anticipated or was overlooked when the statute was adopted; or does it mean something else?

ii) BAKER v. JACOBS, 23 A. 588 (Vt.1891)

In this case, a statute provided that

if a party obtaining a verdict in his favor shall, during the term of the court in which such verdict is obtained, give to any of the jurors in the cause, knowing him to be such, any victuals or drink, or procure the same to be done, by way of treat, either before or after such verdict, on proof thereof being made the verdict shall be set aside and a new trial granted.

A winning plaintiff treated the jury to free cigars. The court stated:

* * * In construing a statute of this kind * * * we are to "look to the whole, * * * to the subject, to the effects and consequences, and to the reason and spirit of the law, and thus ascertain the true meaning of the legislature, though the meaning so ascertained conflict with the literal sense of the word." * * *

* * * The evil against which the legislature has sought to guard and has intended to suppress, from its earliest enactment on this subject to the present time, has been to prevent jurors from being biased by being treated by a party to the suit before rendering their verdict, or by the hope or expectation of being treated after they should render it, and to prevent a suitor from directly or indirectly seeking to influence a verdict in his favor by such means. This has been the policy of our law for a century, and we think the furnishing a juror with a cigar by way of treat is as much within the true intent and spirit of the statute as the treating him with a glass of whisky. Indeed, among a large class of people, in treating, cigars are now given and received instead of intoxicating liquors. * * *

Is this a harder or easier case than Johnson (involving a schedule of assets in bankruptcy)? (1) What facts about the year of the statute's passage and about cigars would help you answer this question? (2) Is the text more obviously disregarded by the decision in Baker v. Jacobs than Johnson?

iii) UNITED STATES v. PERRYMAN, 100 U.S. 235 (1879)

■ Mr. Chief Justice Waite delivered the opinion of the court.

This suit was brought to enforce an alleged liability of the United States, under sects. 2154 and 2155 of the Revised Statutes, to pay the value of twenty-three head of beef cattle, stolen from the claimant, a friendly Indian, within the Indian country.

These sections are as follows:—

"Sect. 2154. Whenever, in the commission, by a white person, of any crime, offence, or misdemeanor within the Indian country, the property of any friendly Indian is taken, injured, or destroyed, and a conviction is had for such crime, offense, or misdemeanor, the person so convicted shall be sentenced to pay to such friendly Indian to whom the property may belong, or whose person may be injured, a sum equal to twice the just value of the property so taken, injured, or destroyed.

"Sect. 2155. If such offender shall be unable to pay a sum at least equal to the just value or amount, whatever such payment shall fall short of the same shall be paid out of the treasury of the United States. If such offender cannot be apprehended and brought to trial, the amount of such property shall be paid out of the treasury. But no Indian shall be entitled to any payment out of the treasury of the United States, for any such property, if he, or any of the nation to which he belongs, have sought private revenge, or have attempted to obtain satisfaction by any force or violence." * * *

The facts are briefly these: On the 18th of December, 1874, Henry Carter, a negro, and not an Indian, and John Conner, a white man, stole from the claimant, a friendly Creek Indian, in the Indian country, the cattle sued for. At the May Term, 1875, of the District Court of the United States for the Western District of Arkansas, both Carter and Conner were indicted for the larceny. Afterwards, a nolle prosequi was entered as to Conner, and he was discharged; but Carter was tried, found guilty, and sentenced to pay to the claimant double the value of the cattle stolen, and be imprisoned in the penitentiary. He being unable to pay the judgment, this suit was brought. The Court of Claims was divided on the question whether the United States were liable in such a case for a theft committed by a negro, and, in order to allow an appeal, gave judgment pro forma for the claimant. From this judgement the United States appealed.

The single question we have to consider is, whether the United States are liable under the statute to the claimant, since the only offender who has been convicted and sentenced to pay for the property stolen was a negro, and not a white person. The term "white person," in the Revised Statutes, must be given the same meaning it had in the original act of 1834. Congress has nowhere manifested an intention of using it in a different sense. While the negro, under the operation of the constitutional amendments, has been endowed with certain civil and political rights which he did not have in 1834, he is no more, in fact, a white person now than he was then. He is a citizen of the United States, and free. No State can abridge his privileges and immunities as a citizen, or deny him the equal protection of the laws; but his race and color are the same, and he is no more included now within the descriptive term of a white person, than he always has been. If, then, this term was used in the act of 1834 to exclude the liability of the United States for the depredations of the negroes in the Indian country, it must be considered as having been so used in the Revised Statutes. There may be no good reason for restricting any longer this liability to acts of whites; but until Congress sees fit to change the statute in this particular, the courts are not at liberty to disregard the law as it is left to stand. The question is not as to the effect of the constitutional amendments on an existing statute affecting the civil or political rights of the negro himself, but as to the meaning of the words "white person," when used as words of description in a statute making the United States liable for the acts of the persons described. No rights of the negro himself, as a citizen, or otherwise, are in any way involved.

It is contended, however, that the term "white person," as here used, means no more than "not an Indian;" in other words, that the intention of Congress was to make the United States liable in the way indicated for all injuries to the property of friendly Indians by persons engaged in crime within the Indian Territory who were not themselves Indians. Such, we think, is not the true construction of the statute. The act of 1834 was not the first statute upon this subject. On the 19th of May, 1796, an act was passed "to regulate trade and intercourse with the Indian tribes and to preserve peace on the frontiers." 1 Stat. 469. In this statute various provisions were made in respect to "any citizen of, or other person resident in, the United States or either of the territorial districts of the United States;" and the liability of the United States for depredations, & c., was extended to certain specified acts of all such persons. This statute expired by its own limitation in 1799, and on the 3d of March of that year another was passed with similar provisions, which continued in force for three years. Id. 743. On the 30th of March, 1802, a permanent statute on the same subject was passed (2 id. 139), making much the same general provisions. In this also various penalties were prescribed for certain acts by "any citizen of, or other person resident in, the United States, or either of the territorial districts of the United States." The liability of the United States for injuries to the property of friendly Indians was extended to the enumerated acts of all "such citizens or other persons," the same as in the statute of 1796. This continued in force until that of 1834, supra, was passed. In the statute of 1834 the phrase "any citizen or other person residing within the United States or the territory thereof" is retained in all the provisions for penalties, & c., except in sect. 16, which was evidently intended to take the place of sect. 4 in the statute of 1802, providing for the liability of the United States for injuries by certain persons to the property of friendly Indians. In that section (16) the words "a white person" were substituted for "any such citizen or other person;" that is to say, "any citizen or other person resident of the United States," & c. It is impossible to believe that this was not done for a purpose. Had the phraseology throughout the entire statute been correspondingly changed, the question might have been different; but, confined as the change was to this particular section, we cannot but think that Congress meant just what the language used conveys to the popular mind. The Cherokee nation, which had given the State of Georgia so much trouble, was about to remove to its new home west of the Mississippi. It was, no doubt, thought if the United States made themselves liable only for such depredations as were committed by the whites, these and other Indians would be less likely to tolerate fugitive blacks in their country. Hence, as a means of preventing the escape of slaves, the change in the law was made. Although the reason of the change no longer exists, Congress has seen fit to keep the law as it was. As the right is statutory, the claimant cannot recover unless he brings himself within the terms of the statute. That he has not done.

The judgment of the Court of Claims will be reversed, and the cause remanded with instructions to dismiss the petition; and it is [s]o ordered.

QUESTIONS

1. Does the Court hold that "White" simply means "White?" If that were true, how would the opinion read?

2. Is there a reason why cigars can be treated like "victuals or drink" in Baker v. Jacobs, but Blacks cannot be within the statute in Perryman? Criticize the following argument for distinguishing the two cases. The definition of "White" was the focus of legislative attention, but no one in the legislature worried much about whether winning litigants would give cigars to a jury. Even judges who interpret statutes freely are unwilling to extend a statute when the legislature worried about the specific definitional issue raised in a later case.

3. How would Perryman be decided today? Would the Court agree with the statement in Perryman that "no rights of the Negro himself, as a citizen, or otherwise, are in any way involved?"[1]

---

1. See Wilson v. Omaha Indian Tribe, 442 U.S. 653, 679 (1979)(Blackmun, J., concurring)(another section of the pre-Civil War statute discussed in Perryman placed the burden of proof on a "white person" in suits with Indians; Justice Blackmun, in part to avoid a constitutional issue, defined "white" to mean "non-Indian").

b) NEWER CASES

i) KENOSHA COUNTY DEP'T. OF SOCIAL SERVICES v. NELSEN, 305 N.W.2d 924 (Wis.1981)

■ Heffernan, Justice. * * *

[Editor—The state law provided that welfare payments (AFDC) had to be repaid by a former recipient out of certain lump sum acquisitions by a welfare father or step-father. The step-father in this case had won a lottery and the question was whether he had to repay welfare benefits previously received by his family. As you read the opinion, consider whether extending a statute is likely to have a liberal or conservative political effect.]

Sec. 49.195(1), Stats., itemizes the modes of acquisition which trigger liability for reimbursement under the statute. They are acquisition by gift, inheritance, sale of assets, court judgment or settlement of any damage claim.

The itemization is of the means or the methods of acquisition. It is apparent it is not exhaustive. Had it been the legislative intent to predicate reimbursement on the ability to pay, other forms of acquisition or sources of income or property would have been included. The county, however, makes the argument that the public treasury is not bottomless, and because it is in the interest of the public fisc that aid-payments of whatever nature should be repaid, the statute should be interpreted with that in mind.

It is clear, however, that this generalized public purpose could not have been in the mind of the legislature when it approved this statute. Had that been true, ordinary earned income would have been included, as well as interest on investments or savings. Not even all forms of windfall increments to assets as income are included, e.g., fortuitous findings—treasure trove, rewards, or employees' bonuses are not included. There is no indication that the statute was intended to sweep broadly on the premise that reimbursement should depend on ability to pay. Nor was the scope of the statute made subject to expanded interpretation by any catch-all phrase which would trigger application of the *ejusdem generis* rule of statutory construction.

We assume that the legislature knew what it was doing when it enacted this statute. Were the statute subject to the unduly broad interpretation urged by the county, it might well be subject to attack on the ground that it failed to give notice of what types of acquisitions it attempted to encompass.

The hazards of open-ended, vague legislation of that type or legislation subject to the county's urged interpretation are illustrated by the facts of this case. Nels Nelsen, prior to his marriage to Judith, knew that the father of Judith's children was delinquent in his support payments. He knew that his lottery winnings would be paid for years to come. Hence, Judith and Nels specifically sought the counsel of an employee of Kenosha county for advice in respect to his liability for support because of his lottery winnings. He testified that he was told that the provisions of the statute did not subject those winnings to liability. His conduct shows that he was aware of the statute and concluded, upon the advice of others, that his situation was not within the purview of the statute. His conclusion was correct. He had notice of the sweep of the statute and acted accordingly. The legislature may well have considered the problems that would ensue if the statute were made indefinite or of too broad or vague a sweep. The legislature acted wisely in its determination to enact a reimbursement statute that precisely defined the liability of those who might come within its scope and thus gave precise notice of potential liability. [Editor—Could a later decision distinguish this case as an estoppel case?]

The defendant has properly pointed out that the primary support responsibility rests upon the natural father. No provision of the common law has been cited which would place that obligation on a stepparent. The statute makes some alterations in the common law obligation of support, but, because it is in derogation of the common law, it must be given its plain meaning according to its terms. A broader interpretation could only be given under circumstances where it is apparent that such was the intent of the legislature. The legislature could well have concluded that the reimbursement statute should be given broader scope, but it did not. This court, not finding any legislative intent to broaden the liability beyond the enumerated transactions cannot expand upon it.

The statute is plain on its face. It is unambiguous and not subject to interpretation or construction.

Is it possible to distinguish Baker v. Jacobs (involving cigars) and Kenosha? Don't they both involve (a) small steps extending the statute (b) to situations which the legislature overlooked?

ii) MACMILLAN v. DIRECTOR, DIVISION OF TAXATION, 445 A.2d 397 (N.J.1982)

In this case, the court dealt with a statute that granted tax rebates to persons who owned a proprietary interest, which the statute expressly defined as "legal or beneficial ownership; a tenancy for life or for 99 years or more; possession and entitlement thereto under an executory contract or under an agreement with a lending institution which holds title as security, or as resident shareholdership in a cooperative or mutual housing corporation." The taxpayers were retirement community "life-care" residents who almost invariably had sold their homes and invested their savings in a capital fee paid to the retirement community. The following opinion is from the lower court, 434 A.2d 620, 621–22 (N.J.Super.1981), whose reasoning was adopted on appeal in 445 A.2d 397 (N.J.1982). It denied a tax rebate to life-care residents. It is followed by a dissent.

■ Fritz, P.J.A.D.

Never more than here did an appeal tend to demonstrate the capacity of hard facts to make bad law. The sole question involved is the eligibility of retirement community residents for tax rebates under the Homestead Rebate Act., N.J.S.A. 54:4–3.80 et seq. * * *

We respect the demonstrated humanity of the tax court judge. We are not sufficiently insensitive to demean his concern for "common sense" or his reach for the "equity of the statute" principle. We are not sufficiently bold to gainsay stubbornly his conviction that "if the Legislature were [today] to consider squarely the status of retirement community residents it would treat them for purposes of the act the same as 'tenants for life' and accordingly as eligible for the rebate."

But we remain judges and as such cannot succumb to the humanistic pressures or substitute our concern in place of the legislative design. Indeed, we may not even permit ourselves the luxury of liberal construction—or, as a matter of fact, any construction—if the words of the statute plainly convey the legislative intent, as we are persuaded they do here. * * *

Restraint is particularly essential in tax matters. * * *

Implementation of these principles and application of these standards are demonstrated by the fact that when statutory construction is necessary or permitted, tax preference provisions are strictly construed against those claiming exemption. This is so with regard to local property taxes. * * *

Nor should we lose sight of the fact that answers so clear and necessary in our view that they tempt us to embellish must be equally clear to the many fine minds in the Legislature, the body charged with determining the necessity in any event. We may, of course, draw the attention of the Legislature, the body charged with determining the necessity in any event. We may, of course, draw the attention of the Legislature to the result and this seems to be an entirely appropriate situation in which to do that. * * *

But the fact remains that the statute is outspoken and unambiguous. The statutory scheme is clear. The legislation requires a proprietary interest * * *. The tax court judge recognized, as is the fact, that the "life-care" residents do not have a proprietary interest in their place of residence. Satisfied that "[a]lthough plaintiffs do not possess an ownership interest in Meadow Lakes, the spirit of the Homestead Rebate Act indicates * * * they should be treated as owners for purposes of the act," and that "[e]quity and common sense require this result," he then rejected the clear statutory prerequisite and added life-care residents to the list of those eligible for rebate. We do not lack sympathy or appreciation for his concern. We simply do not agree with his judgment for we are convinced that neither he nor we may thus pre-empt the legislative function.

■ Pashman, J., dissenting: * * *

I agree that where the plain language of a statute suggests a certain result and there are no indications of legislative intent to the contrary, the Court's job is clear. However that is not the case. Words take meaning from their context. Failure to consider relevant statutory policies and statutory history may cause courts to frustrate rather than implement the legislative will. The plain meaning rule does not compel us to view the statutory language out of context. Nor does it require us to ignore the history of the statute, its scope and its relation to other legislative enactments. * * *

Judges invented the rule that tax exemptions are strictly construed because they presumed that legislatures intend all citizens to pay their fair share of taxes. We use the rule because, as a general matter, it is probably a good statement of what the Legislature wants us to do. However the rule is merely a presumption; the ultimate inquiry remains legislative intent. When other indications show that the Legislature intended a broad interpretation of a tax exemption, it is not our role to thwart the legislative purpose by mechanically applying traditional rules of construction.

In this case, there is ample evidence that the Legislature intended the property rebate to be liberally construed to include "life-care" residents. As the Tax Court noted, the Legislature has made property tax relief available on a broad scale to comply with the constitutional mandate to use the income tax to grant property tax relief. It has also amended the statute several times, progressively broadening the categories of persons benefitted by the rebate. Moreover, in recent years the Legislature has given special attention to the needs of the State's senior citizens. It has repeatedly granted them special tax benefits. This is a further indication of a legislative desire to include plaintiffs within the scope of the statute.

As a practical matter, plaintiffs have de facto life tenancies. Virtually all make large down payments. The overwhelming majority of residents stay for the remainder of their lives. During the 14-year history of Meadow Lakes, for example, the corporation has attempted to terminate the residency of only two persons out of a total of approximately 900. The small technical differences between life-care contracts and life tenancies as such do not suggest any reason for granting rebates only to the latter.

All the residents of life-care facilities are elderly. They enter these communities for companionship, care and peace of mind. The unique contractual and property interests involved are designed to satisfy those needs. I do not believe the Legislature intended to exclude life-care residents from the property tax rebate merely because they had the good sense to avail themselves of an innovative living arrangement. The special needs that impel the elderly to enter life-care communities should not be frustrated by special burdens.

Finally, I respectfully reject the Appellate Division assertion that in construing statutes, judges must not "succumb to the humanistic pressures * * *." We should presume that the Legislature acts with such considerations in mind. There is simply no good reason to believe the Legislature intended the harsh and inequitable result of excluding the elderly residents of life-care communities from the statute's coverage.

QUESTIONS

1. Comment on the following parallelism: the life care arrangement in MacMillan bears the same relationship to the property interests eligible for property tax rebates as the copyhold interest in Heydon's Case (Chapter 2) bears to the property interests which could not be conveyed to avoid Henry VIII's seizure of Church property.

2. Can the elderly take care of themselves in the legislature? If so, does that justify the majority's decision?

13.03   Federal "Common Law"

a) Introduction

The prior discussion has not focused on the special problems encountered by federal courts treating statutes as a source of law. Except in limited situations (such as admiralty), federal courts do not have an independent common lawmaking power. Consequently, when federal courts "extend" a statute, they usually cannot rely on an underlying common law authority.

i) LIMITS ON FEDERAL COMMON LAW

There are two potential limits on the *federal* judiciary's common law power. First, the federal government (courts, executive *and* legislature) has only limited powers. These limits were an important constraint on the federal judiciary in the early 19th Century, because an independent federal common law power would have given the federal government lawmaking authority not granted to Congress by Article I of the Constitution. These concerns contributed to the decision in United States v. Hudson & Goodwin, 11 U.S. (7 Cranch) 32 (1812), that there was no federal common law of crimes;[2] and to the following statement in Wheaton v. Peters, 33 U.S. (8 Pet.) 591 (1834) (copyright dispute) that

---

2. See generally Rowe, The Sound of Silence: United States v. Hudson & Goodwin, the Jeffersonian Ascendancy, and the Aboli-tion of Federal Common Law Crimes, 101 Yale L.J. 919 (1992).

[i]t is clear, there can be no common law of the United States. * * *
The common law could be made a part of our federal system only
by legislative adoption.

Not too much should be made of this limitation today, however. Since the
late 1930s, the Constitution has been expansively interpreted to allow
Congress broad power to act regarding interstate commerce and to tax and
spend for the general welfare.

Second, the power of federal *courts* to create law is limited by the federal
constitutional scheme, which is concerned with separation of legislative and
judicial powers and electoral accountability. Even if the federal government
has power, it resides primarily in the elected Congress, not the courts.

Constitutional concerns about federalism and separation of powers
merge in the Rules of Decision Act (28 U.S.C. § 1652). That Act specifies
that

(t)he laws of the several states, except where the Constitution,
treaties, or statutes of the United States otherwise require or provide, shall be regarded as rules of decision in trials at common law,
in the courts of the United States, in cases where they apply.

The Rules of Decision Act is declarative of the constitutional rules governing
federal courts, even if the Act had not been passed. Guaranty Trust Co. of
New York v. York, 326 U.S. 99 (1945)(no federal common law in suits in
equity as well as actions at law).

This constitutional and statutory scheme prevents federal courts from
creating common law in diversity cases between citizens of different states.
Erie Railroad Co. v. Tompkins, 304 U.S. 64 (1938)(overruling Swift v. Tyson,
41 U.S. (16 Pet.) 1 (1842), in which federal courts had exercised a power to
fashion "general commercial law"). But Erie has broader implications. Even
when a federal court implements a federal statute, state law applies unless
the federal statute otherwise "requires" or "provides."[3]

There is a further complexity that you must consider when thinking
about the question of federal common law in the context of statutory
interpretation. The "common law" we have been discussing is substantive
law. But federal courts have implied powers, as the Supreme Court noted
when it rejected federal power to create substantive common law crimes in
United States v. Hudson & Goodwin, 11 U.S. (7 Cranch) 32 (1812):

Certain implied powers must necessarily result to our Courts of
justice from the nature of their institution. * * * To fine for contempt,
* * * inforce the observation of order, etc. are powers which cannot
be dispensed with in a Court, because they are necessary to the
exercise of all others; and so far our Courts no doubt possess
powers not immediately derived from statute * * *.

---

3. See generally, Merrill, The Common
Law Powers of Federal Courts, 52 U. Chi. L.
Rev. 1 (1985); Jay, Origins of Federal Common Law: Part Two, 133 U. Pa. L. Rev. 1231
(1985).

One of these "necessary" implied judicial powers is a common law power of statutory interpretation, which (as Chapter 2 explained) is given to federal judges by the grant of Judicial Power to federal courts by Article III, sec. 1, of the U.S. Constitution. Indeed, when the U.S. Constitution was adopted, this interpretive power probably included what we would describe today as a substantial amount of lawmaking authority.

ii) SCOPE OF FEDERAL COMMON LAW

The scope of federal common law is described somewhat narrowly in Texas Industries, Inc. v. Radcliff Materials, Inc., 451 U.S. 630 (1981):

> There is, of course, "no federal general common law." Erie R.Co. v. Tompkins. Nevertheless, the Court has recognized the need and authority in some limited areas to formulate what has come to be known as "federal common law." These instances are "few and restricted," and fall into essentially two categories: those in which a federal rule of decision is "necessary to protect uniquely federal interest," and those in which the Congress has given the courts the power to develop substantive law.
>
> The vesting of jurisdiction in the federal courts does not in and of itself give rise to authority to formulate federal common law, nor does the existence of congressional authority under Article I mean that federal courts are free to develop a common law to govern those areas until Congress acts. Rather, absent some congressional authorization to formulate substantive rules of decision, federal common law exists only in such narrow areas as those concerned with the rights and obligations of the United States, interstate and international disputes implicating the conflicting rights of States or our relations with foreign nations, and admiralty cases. In these instances, our federal system does not permit the controversy to be resolved under state law, either because the authority and duties of the United States as sovereign are intimately involved or because the interstate or international nature of the controversy makes it inappropriate for state law to control.

The second of the Texas Industries categories of federal common law— cases in which Congress has given courts the power to develop substantive law—requires further comment. One way Congress can grant this authority is to "plainly hand courts a common law power" (see Easterbrook's discussion in Chapter 8). We have already discussed the most obvious example— the anti-trust law prohibition of "restraint of trade." This is a classic case of "plainly handing courts a common law power" in two senses. First, the statute's text is open-ended. Second the language of the statute incorporates a common law standard—"restraint of trade."

The federal courts' common law power cannot be so narrowly confined, however. As we have seen repeatedly throughout this course, interpretation of statutes involves judgment about a complex mix of text, statutory purpose, and background considerations. Interpretation deserves to be called a "power to develop substantive law," as long as we keep in mind differences in degree between an open-ended common law authority and the narrower authority to interpret. The reference in the Rules of Decision Act to what a federal statute "require[s] or provide[s]" includes what a federal court infers from the statute in the exercise of an interpretive power. Indeed, the original conception of statutory interpretation as a "common law" power (see Chapter 2) implies that all statutes give federal courts *some* power to develop substantive law.

The remainder of this section considers two issues. First, we discuss federal "common law" when there is a "unique federal interest." Second, we consider the federal court's "power to develop substantive law," in the sense of interpreting what the statute "requires or provides."

b) UNIQUE FEDERAL INTEREST

i) EASY CASES

The first category of federal common law in Texas Industries is a "unique federal interest." No legislation is needed to support a federal common law power in this category. The federal interest itself is sufficient. Obviously a great deal turns on what is meant by "unique federal interest." The easiest cases involve foreign relations. See Banco Nacional de Cuba v. Sabbatino, 376 U.S. 398 (1964)("act of state" doctrine proscribes challenge to validity of Cuban expropriation decree).

Federal common law also exists when the federal government is a party to a contract. See, e.g., Clearfield Trust Co. v. United States, 318 U.S. 363 (1943)(federal government's obligations under commercial paper issued by the government is determined by federal law because a uniform national law is desirable); Priebe & Sons v. United States, 332 U.S. 407 (1947) ("general contract law" applied to a government contract); West Virginia v. United States, 479 U.S. 305 (1987)(interest on delayed payment of contractual obligations to the United States was determined by federal common law).

ii) ADMIRALTY; JURISDICTIONAL GRANTS

There is also a federal common law of admiralty, as the Moragne case indicates. This common law power has an unusual origin, because it is inferred from the Constitution's extension of federal court jurisdiction to cases of admiralty and maritime law. Romero v. International Terminal Operating Co., 358 U.S. 354 (1959)(Art. III, § 2, cl. 1 "empowered the federal courts in their exercise of the admiralty and maritime jurisdiction which had been conferred on them, to draw on the substantive law 'inherent in the admiralty and maritime jurisdiction.'"); Knickerbocker Ice Co. v. Stewart, 253 U.S. 149 (1920)("Since the beginning, federal courts have recognized and applied the rules and principles of maritime law as something distinct from laws of the several states.").[4] Usually, federal court jurisdiction does not by itself support a federal common law power. If it did,

---

4. See generally, Currie, Federalism and the Admiralty: "The Devil's Own Mess," 1960   S.Ct. Rev. 158.

the Constitution's Article III grant of diversity jurisdiction to federal courts would give them power to create substantive common law in diversity cases, contrary to Erie.[5]

iii) INFERRING FEDERAL DEFENSE TO STATE TORT CLAIM

How does the Court justify a "unique federal interest" in the next case? Is federal legislation at all relevant? In Boyle v. United Technologies Corp., 487 U.S. 500 (1988), the Court (per Justice Scalia) dealt with a state law tort claim against a federal defense contractor based on an allegation of defective design of a helicopter's emergency escape-hatch system. The question was whether a "unique federal interest" pre-empted state law to immunize the government-contractor defendant from tort liability. The Court held that, although the case involved a tort suit between private parties, it bordered on two areas where a "unique federal interest" had been found: the rights of the United States under contracts to which it is a party, and the civil liability of federal officials for actions taken in the course of their duty under the Federal Tort Claims Act. The Court then went on to consider whether a

"significant conflict" exists between an identifiable "federal policy or interest and the [operation] of state law," or the application of state law would "frustrate specific objectives" of federal legislation. The conflict with federal policy need not be as sharp as that which must exist for ordinary pre-emption when Congress legislates "in a field which the States have traditionally occupied." Or to put the point differently, the fact that the area in question *is* one of unique federal concern changes what would otherwise be a conflict that cannot produce pre-emption into one that can.

The Court found a potential for significant conflict in the Federal Tort Claims Act's exemption from government liability for acts of officials, when the claim is based on the "exercise or performance or the failure to exercise or perform a discretionary function." The selection of an appropriate design for military equipment was a discretionary function, requiring "not merely engineering analysis but judgment as to the balancing of many technical, military, and even social considerations, including specifically the trade-off between greater safety and greater combat efficiency." Permitting "second-guessing" of these discretionary judgments through state tort suits would have the same effect that the Federal Tort Claims Act exemption was meant to avoid, because the burden of any judgment would be passed through to the government through price increases.

---

5. Occasionally, a legislative grant of jurisdiction to federal courts is interpreted (controversially) to support a federal common law power, despite what Texas Industries says. For example, in Textile Workers Union v. Lincoln Mills, 353 U.S. 448 (1957), the Court inferred a federal common law power from a provision in a federal labor statute giving jurisdiction to the federal courts. The Court treated the grant of jurisdiction as authoriza- tion for "federal courts to fashion a body of federal law for the enforcement of * * * collective bargaining agreements" between unions and employers. In United Ass'n of Journeymen v. Local 334, 452 U.S. 615 (1981), the Court extended Lincoln Mills to cases involving disputes between local labor unions who were governed by a contract embodied in the constitution of an international union to which they belonged.

The case limited pre-emption of state tort law based on a unique federal interest to cases where (1) the helicopter's "reasonably precise [design] specifications" had been approved by the United States, and (2) the supplier had warned the United States about dangers in its use. The first requirement assured that the lawsuit would frustrate the government's exercise of a discretionary function. The second requirement assured that the contractor would not have an incentive to withhold information from federal officials.

Is the Court's decision in Boyle really based on a "unique federal interest," or on federal legislation, or both?

The dissent noted that Congress has "resisted a sustained campaign by Government contractors to legislate for them some defense," either by limiting liability or obtaining indemnity from the Government. The evidence of a "sustained campaign" was a citation of six bills which did not pass—a House and Senate bill in 1986, and House bills in 1979, 1981, 1984, and 1987. No hearings or committee reports are cited. Does this citation support the claim of a sustained campaign?

In Jackson v. Johns–Manville Sales Corp., 750 F.2d 1314 (5th Cir.1985), the court rejected the defendant's claim that there should be federal common law to prevent the multitude of tort claims arising out of asbestos-related injuries. Does the court's reasoning adequately distinguish this case from Boyle?

The defendant argued that the potential conflict among plaintiffs for the limited resources of the asbestos companies is analogous to interstate conflicts over water rights and pollution, which involve "uniquely federal interests." The court disagreed, distinguishing the water rights cases as involving a conflict between states as quasi-sovereign bodies over shared resources. The defendants also argued that there was a uniquely federal interest in assuring compensation to injured persons and maintaining government asbestos suppliers, which would be served by the creation of federal rules restricting the types of damages recoverable in asbestos suits. The court stated that "uniquely federal interests" were not merely national interests; that the existence of national interests, no matter their significance, cannot by themselves give federal courts the authority to supersede state policy. To be "uniquely federal" and thus a sufficient predicate for the imposition of a federal substantive rule, an interest must relate to an articulated congressional policy or directly implicate the authority and duties of the United States as sovereign.

c) FEDERAL STATUTE GIVING COURTS POWER TO DEVELOP SUBSTANTIVE LAW

i) INTRODUCTION

Federal "common law" also exists when "Congress has given the courts the power to develop substantive law." As noted earlier, this authority is not limited to cases in which the statute plainly hands courts a common law power. The statute's text, purpose, and substantive background require interpretation, which includes a power to develop substantive law.[6]

The following cases illustrate how federal courts develop federal law, where there is no obvious creation of an open-ended common law power and the court must decide about the scope of federal policy and its interaction with state law. We discuss pre-emption doctrine and filling statutory "gaps."

ii) "ORDINARY" FEDERAL PRE–EMPTION

One setting in which federal courts must work out the implications of a federal statute involves "ordinary pre-emption" of state law. Pre-emption is "ordinary" because there is no "unique federal interest" to influence the decision.[7]

The framework for deciding ordinary federal pre-emption cases is set forth in Gade v. National Solid Wastes Management Assn., 505 U.S. 88 (1992). The Court refers to *express* pre-emption, *implied-field* pre-emption, and *implied-conflict* pre-emption.

> Pre-emption may be either expressed or implied, and "is compelled whether Congress' command is explicitly stated in the statute's language or implicitly contained in its structure and purpose." Absent explicit pre-emptive language, we have recognized at least two types of implied pre-emption: field pre-emption, where the scheme of federal regulation is "so pervasive as to make reasonable the inference that Congress left no room for the States to supplement it," and conflict pre-emption, where "compliance with both federal and state regulations is a physical impossibility," or where state law "stands as an obstacle to the accomplishment and execution of the full purposes and objectives of Congress."

6. Even if federal courts do not create common law based on a federal statute, a state court might incorporate federal statutory policy into state common law. See, e.g., In re Agent Orange Product Liability Litigation, 580 F.Supp. 690 (E.D.N.Y.1984)(although there was no federal common law regarding veterans' claims for Agent Orange injury in Vietnam, a federal court in a diversity case determined that a state court would incorporate federal standards into state common law to create a state cause of action); Merrell Dow Pharmaceuticals Inc. v. Thompson, 478 U.S. 804 (1986)(state law incorporates standards of federal statute for determining state law negligence; no federal question jurisdiction).

7. As the Boyle case suggested, the distinction between ordinary pre-emption and pre-emption based on a unique federal interest is not airtight. Sometimes federal statutes reinforce a not-so-strong case of a "unique federal interest" to affirm federal pre-emption. United States v. Little Lake Misere Land Co., 412 U.S. 580 (1973), involved the respective rights of the federal government to land taken for a wildlife refuge and of the former owner who was claiming certain retained rights. The Court noted that even the United States might be governed by state law in its ordinary proprietary dealings. Ultimately, a federal common law governed, however, because the land acquisition arose from and bore heavily on federal statutory programs involving wildlife refuges.

An additional factor, arguing against federal pre-emption, is whether the federal statute operates in "areas traditionally regulated by the States." See, e.g., California v. ARC America Corp., 490 U.S. 93 (1989) (federal anti-trust law does not pre-empt lawsuit under state law by indirect purchasers—defined as those who buy products from those directly purchasing price-fixed goods—because of the long history of state common law and statutory remedies against monopolies and unfair business practices).

QUESTIONS

Here are some questions to consider as you read the following pre-emption cases.

1. How do text, statutory purpose, and substantive background considerations interact to resolve what a federal court should do? Which factors are most persuasive for which judges?

2. In Chapter 7 we discussed the substantive canon of interpretation which required a plain statutory statement before the law would be interpreted to burden States. Are judges who are enthusiastic about that canon likely to find "*implied* pre-emption" of state law?

3. Would you expect a textualist to rely on "implied pre-emption;" to treat the "ultimate question [as] one of Congress's intent, as revealed in the text, structure, purpose, and subject matter of the statutes involved?" Cipollone v. Liggett Group, Inc., 505 U.S. 504 (1992)(Scalia, J., concurring in the judgment and dissenting in part).

(A) **Implied pre-emption?**

Gade v. National Solid Wastes Management Assn.

505 U.S. 88 (1992).

■ Justice O'Connor announced the judgment of the Court and delivered [a plurality opinion,] joined by the Chief Justice, Justice White, and Justice Scalia.

In 1988, the Illinois General Assembly enacted the Hazardous Waste Crane and Hoisting Equipment Operators Licensing Act, and the Hazardous Waste Laborers Licensing Act. The stated purpose of the acts is both "to promote job safety" and "to protect life, limb and property." In this case, we consider whether these "dual impact" statutes, which protect both workers and the general public, are pre-empted by the federal Occupational Safety and Health Act of 1970, 84 Stat. 1590, 29 U.S.C. § 651 et seq. (OSH Act), and the standards promulgated thereunder by the Occupational Safety and Health Administration (OSHA). * * *

In response to [a] congressional directive, OSHA * * * promulgated regulations on "Hazardous Waste Operations and Emergency Response," including detailed regulations on worker training requirements. The OSHA regulations require, among other things, that workers engaged in an activity that may expose them to hazardous wastes receive a minimum of 40 hours of instruction off the site, and a minimum of three days actual field experience under the supervision of a trained supervisor. Workers who are on the site only occasionally or who are working in areas that have been determined to be under the permissible exposure limits must complete at least 24 hours of off-site instruction and one day of actual field experience. On-site managers and supervisors directly responsible for hazardous waste operations must receive the same initial training as general employees, plus at least eight additional hours of specialized training on various health and safety programs. Employees and supervisors are required to receive eight hours of refresher training annually. Those who have satisfied the training and field experience requirement receive a written certification; uncertified workers are prohibited from engaging in hazardous waste operations.

In 1988, while OSHA's interim hazardous waste regulations were in effect, the State of Illinois enacted the licensing acts at issue here. The laws are designated as acts "in relation to environmental protection," and their stated aim is to protect both employees and the general public by licensing hazardous waste equipment operators and laborers working at certain facilities. Both acts require a license applicant to provide a certified record of at least 40 hours of training under an approved program conducted within Illinois, to pass a written examination, and to complete an annual refresher course of at least eight hours of instruction. In addition, applicants for a hazardous waste crane operator's license must submit "a certified record showing operation of equipment used in hazardous waste handling for a minimum of 4,000 hours." Employees who work without the proper license, and employers who knowingly permit an unlicensed employee to work, are subject to escalating fines for each offense.

The respondent in this case, National Solid Waste Management Association (the Association), is a national trade association of businesses that remove, transport, dispose, and handle waste material, including hazardous waste. The Association's members are subject to the OSH Act and OSHA regulations, and are therefore required to train, qualify, and certify their hazardous waste remediation workers. For hazardous waste operations conducted in Illinois, certain of the workers employed by the Association's members are also required to obtain licenses pursuant to the Illinois licensing acts. Thus, for example, some of the Association's members must ensure that their employees receive not only the three days of field experience required for certification under the OSHA regulations, but also the 500 days of experience (4,000 hours) required for licensing under the state statutes.

* * * The Association sought to enjoin IEPA from enforcing the Illinois licensing acts, claiming that the acts were pre-empted by the OSH Act and OSHA regulations and that they violated the Commerce Clause of the United States Constitution. * * *

In the OSH Act, Congress endeavored "to assure so far as possible every working man and woman in the Nation safe and healthful working conditions." To that end, Congress authorized the Secretary of Labor to set mandatory occupational safety and health standards applicable to all businesses affecting interstate commerce, and thereby brought the Federal Government into a field that traditionally had been occupied by the States. Federal regulation of the workplace was not intended to be all-encompassing, however. First, Congress expressly saved two areas from federal pre-emption. Section 4(b)(4) of the OSH Act states that the Act does not "supersede or in any manner affect any workmen's compensation law or * * * enlarge or diminish or affect in any other manner the common law or statutory rights, duties, or liabilities of employers and employees under any law with respect to injuries, diseases, or death of employees arising out of, or in the course of, employment." Section 18(a) provides that the Act does not "prevent any State agency or court from asserting jurisdiction under State law over any occupational safety or health issue with respect to which no [federal] standard is in effect."

Congress not only reserved certain areas to state regulation, but it also, in § 18(b) of the Act, gave the States the option of pre-empting federal regulation entirely. That section provides:

"Submission of State plan for development and enforcement of State standards to pre-empt applicable Federal standards.

"Any State which, at any time, desires to assume responsibility for development and enforcement therein of occupational safety and health standards relating to any occupational safety or health issue with respect to which a Federal standard has been promulgated [by the Secretary under the OSH Act] shall submit a State plan for the development of such standards and their enforcement."

* * *

Our ultimate task in any pre-emption case is to determine whether state regulation is consistent with the structure and purpose of the statute as a whole. Looking to "the provisions of the whole law, and to its object and policy," we hold that nonapproved state regulation of occupational safety and health issues for which a federal standard is in effect is impliedly pre-empted as in conflict with the full purposes and objectives of the OSH Act. The design of the statute persuades us that Congress intended to subject employers and employees to only one set of regulations, be it federal or state, and that the only way a State may regulate an OSHA-regulated occupational safety and health issue is pursuant to an approved state plan that displaces the federal standards.

The principal indication that Congress intended to pre-empt state law is § 18(b)'s statement that a State "shall" submit a plan if it wishes to "assume responsibility" for "development and enforcement * * * of occupational safety and health standards relating to any occupational safety or health issue with respect to which a Federal standard has been promulgated." The unavoidable implication of this provision is that a State may not enforce its own occupational safety and health standards without obtaining the Secretary's approval, and petitioner concedes that § 18(b) would require an approved plan if Illinois wanted to "assume responsibility" for the regulation of occupational safety and health within the State. Petitioner contends, however, that an approved plan is necessary only if the State wishes completely to replace the federal regulations, not merely to supplement them. She argues that the correct interpretation of § 18(b) is that posited by Judge Easterbrook below: i.e., a State may either "oust" the federal standard by submitting a state plan to the Secretary for approval or "add to" the federal standard without seeking the Secretary's approval.

Petitioner's interpretation of § 18(b) might be plausible were we to interpret that provision in isolation, but it simply is not tenable in light of the OSH Act's surrounding provisions. "[W]e must not be guided by a single sentence or member of a sentence, but look to the provisions of the whole law." The OSH Act as a whole evidences Congress' intent to avoid subjecting workers and employers to duplicative regulation; a State may develop an occupational safety and health program tailored to its own needs, but only if it is willing completely to displace the applicable federal regulations.

Cutting against petitioner's interpretation of § 18(b) is the language of § 18(a), which saves from pre-emption any state law regulating an occupational safety and health issue with respect to which no federal standard is in effect. Although this is a saving clause, not a pre-emption clause, the natural implication of this provision is that state laws regulating the same issue as federal laws are not saved, even if they merely supplement the federal standard. Moreover, if petitioner's reading of § 18(b) were correct, and if a State were free to enact nonconflicting safety and health regulations, then § 18(a) would be superfluous: there is no possibility of conflict where there is no federal regulation. Because "[i]t is our duty 'to give effect, if possible, to every clause and word of a statute,'" we conclude that § 18(a)'s preservation of state authority in the absence of a federal standard presupposes a background pre-emption of all state occupational safety and health standards whenever a federal standard governing the same issue is in effect. * * *

Looking at the provisions of § 18 as a whole, we conclude that the OSH Act precludes any state regulation of an occupational safety or health issue with respect to which a federal standard has been established, unless a state plan has been submitted and approved pursuant to § 18(b). Our review of the Act persuades us that Congress sought to promote occupational safety and health while at the same time avoiding duplicative, and possibly counter-productive, regulation. It thus established a system of uniform federal occupational health and safety standards, but gave States the option of pre-empting federal regulations by developing their own occupational safety and health programs. In addition, Congress offered the States substantial federal grant monies to assist them in developing their own programs. To allow a State selectively to "supplement" certain federal regulations with ostensibly nonconflict-ing standards would be inconsistent with this federal scheme of establishing uniform federal standards, on the one hand, and en-couraging States to assume full responsibility for development and enforcement of their own OSH programs, on the other.

We cannot accept petitioner's argument that the OSH Act does not pre-empt nonconflicting state laws because those laws, like the Act, are designed to promote worker safety. In determining whether state law "stands as an obstacle" to the full implementation of a federal law, "it is not enough to say that the ultimate goal of both federal and state law" is the same. "A state law also is pre-empted if it interferes with the methods by which the federal statute was designed to reach th[at] goal." The OSH Act does not foreclose a State from enacting its own laws to advance the goal of worker safety, but it does restrict the ways in which it can do so. If a State wishes to regulate an issue of worker safety for which a federal standard is in effect, its only option is to obtain the prior approval of the Secretary of Labor, as described in § 18 of the Act. * * *

[Editor—The Court then holds that the state statute's dual purpose of protecting both workers and the public does not prevent pre-emption, stating that "we have refused to rely solely on the legislature's professed purpose and have looked as well to the effects of the law." It distinguished "state laws of general applicabili-ty (such as laws regarding traffic safety or fire safety) that do not conflict with OSHA standards and that regulate the conduct of workers and non-workers alike[, which] would generally not be pre-empted. Although some laws of general applicability may have a 'direct and substantial' effect on worker safety, they cannot fairly be characterized as 'occupational' standards, because they regulate workers simply as members of the general public. * * * [W]e agree with the court below that a law directed at workplace safety is not saved from pre-emption simply because the State can demonstrate some additional effect outside of the workplace."]

■ Justice Kennedy, concurring in part and concurring in the judgment.

Though I concur in the Court's judgment and with the ultimate conclusion that the state law is pre-empted, I would find express pre-emption from the terms of the federal statute. I cannot agree that we should denominate this case as one of implied pre-emption. The contrary view of the plurality is based on an undue expansion of our implied pre-emption jurisprudence which, in my view, is neither wise nor necessary. * * *

Our decisions establish that a high threshold must be met if a state law is to be pre-empted for conflicting with the purposes of a federal Act. Any conflict must be "irreconcilable * * *. The existence of a hypothetical or potential conflict is insufficient to warrant the pre-emption of the state statute." In my view, this type of pre-emption should be limited to state laws which impose prohibitions or obligations which are in direct contradiction to Congress' primary objectives, as conveyed with clarity in the federal legislation.

I do not believe that supplementary state regulation of an occupational safety and health issue can be said to create the sort of actual conflict required by our decisions. The purpose of state supplementary regulation, like the federal standards promulgated by the Occupational Safety and Health Administration (OSHA) is to protect worker safety and health. Any potential tension between a scheme of federal regulation of the workplace and a concurrent, supplementary state scheme would not, in my view, rise to the level of "actual conflict" described in our pre-emption cases. Absent the express provisions of § 18 of the Occupational Safety and Health Act of 1970, I would not say that state supplementary regulation conflicts with the purposes of the OSH Act, or that it "interferes with the methods by which the federal statute was designed to reach [its] goal."

The plurality's broad view of actual conflict pre-emption is contrary to two basic principles of our pre-emption jurisprudence. First, we begin "with the assumption that the historic police powers of the States [are] not to be superseded * * * unless that was the clear and manifest purpose of Congress," Second, "the purpose of Congress is the ultimate touchstone" in all pre-emption cases. A free-wheeling judicial inquiry into whether a state statute is in tension with federal objectives would undercut the principle that it is Congress rather than the courts that pre-empts state law.

Nonetheless, I agree with the Court that "the OSH Act pre-empts all state 'occupational safety and health standards relating to any occupational safety or health issue with respect to which a Federal standard has been promulgated.'" I believe, however, that this result is mandated by the express terms of § 18(b) of the OSH Act. It follows from this that the pre-emptive scope of the Act is also limited to the language of the statute. When the existence of pre-emption is evident from the statutory text, our inquiry must begin and end with the statutory framework itself.

A finding of express pre-emption in this case is not contrary to our longstanding rule that we will not infer pre-emption of the States' historic police powers absent a clear statement of intent by Congress. Though most statutes creating express pre-emption contain an explicit statement to that effect, a statement admittedly lacking in § 18(b), we have never required any particular magic words in our express pre-emption cases. Our task in all pre-emption cases is to enforce the "clear and manifest purpose of Congress." We have held, in express pre-emption cases, that Congress' intent must be divined from the language, structure, and purposes of the statute as a whole. The language of the OSH statute sets forth a scheme in light of which the provisions of § 18 must be interpreted, and from which the express pre-emption that displaces state law follows.

[Editor—Justice Kennedy goes on to say very much what the majority says about §§ 18(a), (b), but labeling the analysis "express pre-emption." The majority responded to his argument, stating that "[w]e cannot agree that the negative implications of the text, although ultimately dispositive to our own analysis, expressly address the issue of federal pre-emption of state law. We therefore prefer to place this case in the category of implied pre-emption. Although we have chosen to use the term 'conflict' pre-emption, we could as easily have stated that the promulgation of a federal safety and health standard 'pre-empts the field' for any nonapproved state law regulating the same safety and health issue."]

■ Justice Souter, with whom Justice Blackmun, Justice Stevens, and Justice Thomas join, dissenting. * * *

Analysis begins with the presumption that "Congress did not intend to displace state law." "Where, as here, the field which Congress is said to have pre-empted has been traditionally occupied by the States, 'we start with the assumption that the historic police powers of the States were not to be superseded by the Federal Act unless that was the clear and manifest purpose of Congress.' This assumption provides assurance that the 'federal-state balance,' will not be disturbed unintentionally by Congress or unnecessarily by the courts. But when Congress has 'unmistakably * * * ordained' that its enactments alone are to regulate a part of commerce, state laws regulating that aspect of commerce must fall." Subject to this principle, the enquiry into the possibly pre-emptive effect of federal legislation is an exercise of statutory construction. If the statute's terms can be read sensibly not to have a pre-emptive effect, the presumption controls and no pre-emption may be inferred. * * *

[Editor—The dissenters then discuss the negative implication of § 18(a):

"Nothing in this chapter shall prevent any State agency or court from asserting jurisdiction under State law over any occupational safety or health issue with respect to which no standard is in effect under section 655 of this title.''

They argue that this section negatives *field* pre-emption in the absence of a federal standard, leaving open the question of whether state law *conflicts* with federal standards. They also argue that § 18(b), regarding the Secretary's approval of a State plan to pre-empt federal rules, merely specifies the conditions for a State to assume full responsibility for health or safety issues, implying nothing about specific state law in a field addressed by an OSHA standard.]

In sum, our rule is that the traditional police powers of the State survive unless Congress has made a purpose to pre-empt them clear. * * * Each provision can be read consistently with the others without any implication of pre-emptive intent. They are in fact just as consistent with a purpose and objective to permit overlapping state and federal regulation as with one to guarantee that employers and employees would be subjected to only one regulatory regime. Restriction to one such regime by precluding supplemental state regulation might or might not be desirable. But in the absence of any clear expression of congressional intent to pre-empt, I can only conclude that, as long as compliance with federally promulgated standards does not render obedience to Illinois' regulations impossible, the enforcement of the state law is not prohibited by the Supremacy Clause. I respectfully dissent.

(B) **Express pre-emption?**

American Airlines, Inc. v. Wolens

513 U.S. 219 (1995).

■ Justice Ginsburg delivered the opinion of the Court.

[Editor—The facts, as stated later in the opinion, were these: Plaintiffs in both actions (respondents here) are participants in American Airlines' frequent flyer program, AAdvantage. AAdvantage enrollees earn mileage credits when they fly on American. They can exchange those credits for flight tickets or class-of-service upgrades. Plaintiffs complained that AAdvantage program modifications, instituted by American in 1988, devalued credits AAdvantage members had already earned. Plaintiffs featured American's imposition of capacity controls (limits on seats available to passengers obtaining tickets with AAdvantage credits) and blackout dates (restrictions on dates credits could be used). Conceding that American had reserved the right to change AAdvantage terms and conditions, plaintiffs challenged only the retroactive application of modifications, i.e., cutbacks on the utility of credits previously accumulated. These cutbacks, plaintiffs maintained, violated the Illinois Consumer Fraud and Deceptive Business Practices Act and constituted a breach of contract. Plaintiffs currently seek only monetary relief.

As you read the opinions, notice the relevance for pre-emption of the debate over the Legal Realist's view of the common law—as reflecting governmental policy choices—previously discussed in Chapter 3.]

The Airline Deregulation Act of 1978 (ADA) prohibits States from "enact[ing] or enforc[ing] any law * * * relating to [air carrier] rates, routes, or services." This case concerns the scope of that preemptive provision, specifically, its application to a state-court suit, brought by participants in an airline's frequent flyer program, challenging the airline's retroactive changes in terms and conditions of the program. We hold that the ADA's preemption prescription bars state-imposed regulation of air carriers, but allows room for court enforcement of contract terms set by the parties themselves. * * *

This case is our second encounter with the ADA's preemption clause. In 1992, in Morales, we confronted detailed Travel Industry Enforcement Guidelines, composed by the National Association of Attorneys General (NAAG). The NAAG guidelines purported to govern, inter alia, the content and format of airline fare advertising. See Morales, 112 S.Ct. at 2041–2054. Several States had endeavored to enforce the NAAG guidelines, under the States' general consumer protection laws, to stop allegedly deceptive airline advertisements. The States' initiative, we determined, " 'relat[ed] to [airline] rates, routes, or services,' " id., at 112 S.Ct., at 2055; consequently, we held, the fare advertising provisions of the NAAG guidelines were preempted by the ADA.

For aid in construing the ADA words "relating to rates, routes, or services of any air carrier," the Court in Morales referred to the Employee Retirement Income Security Act of 1974 (ERISA), which provides for preemption of state laws "insofar as they * * * relate to any employee benefit plan." Under the ERISA, we had ruled, a state law "relates to" an employee benefit plan "if it has a connection with or reference to such a plan." Morales analogously defined the "relating to" language in the ADA preemption clause as "having a connection with or reference to airline 'rates, routes, or services.'" [Editor—The dissent in Morales (by Justice Stevens, joined by Rehnquist and Blackmun) argued that ERISA was unique. It relied instead on the "history and structure of the [Airline Deregulation Act]," rather "than a narrow focus on the words 'relating to.' "]
* * *

* * * Plaintiffs' claims relate to "rates," i.e., American's charges in the form of mileage credits for free tickets and upgrades, and to "services," i.e., access to flights and class-of-service upgrades unlimited by retrospectively applied capacity controls and blackout dates. But the ADA's preemption clause contains other words in need of interpretation, specifically, the words "enact or enforce any

law" in the instruction: "[N]o state * * * shall enact or enforce any law * * * relating to [air carrier] rates, routes, or services." 49 U.S.C.App. § 1305(a)(1). Taking into account all the words Congress placed in § 1305(a)(1), we first consider whether plaintiffs' claims under the Illinois Consumer Fraud Act are preempted, and then turn to plaintiffs' breach of contract claims.

The Illinois Consumer Fraud Act declares unlawful "[u]nfair methods of competition and unfair or deceptive acts or practices, including but not limited to the use or employment of any deception, fraud, false pretense, false promise, misrepresentation or the concealment, suppression or omission of any material fact, with intent that others rely upon the concealment, suppression or omission of such material fact, or the use or employment of any practice described in Section 2 of the 'Uniform Deceptive Trade Practices Act' * * * in the conduct of any trade or commerce * * * whether any person has in fact been misled, deceived or damaged thereby." The Act is prescriptive; it controls the primary conduct of those falling within its governance. This Illinois law, in fact, is paradigmatic of the consumer protection legislation underpinning the NAAG guidelines. The NAAG Task Force on the Air Travel Industry, on which the Attorneys General of California, Illinois, Texas, and Washington served, reported that the guidelines created no "new laws or regulations regarding the advertising practices or other business practices of the airline industry. They merely explain in detail how existing state laws apply to air fare advertising and frequent flyer programs."

The NAAG guidelines highlight the potential for intrusive regulation of airline business practices inherent in state consumer protection legislation typified by the Illinois Consumer Fraud Act. For example, the guidelines enforcing the legislation instruct airlines on language appropriate to reserve rights to alter frequent flyer programs, and they include transition rules for the fair institution of capacity controls.

As the NAAG guidelines illustrate, the Illinois Consumer Fraud Act serves as a means to guide and police the marketing practices of the airlines; the Act does not simply give effect to bargains offered by the airlines and accepted by airline customers. In light of the full text of the preemption clause, and of the ADA's purpose to leave largely to the airlines themselves, and not at all to States, the selection and design of marketing mechanisms appropriate to the furnishing of air transportation services, we conclude that § 1305(a)(1) preempts plaintiffs' claims under the Illinois Consumer Fraud Act.

* * * We do not read the ADA's preemption clause, however, to shelter airlines from suits alleging no violation of state-imposed obligations, but seeking recovery solely for the airline's alleged breach of its own, self-imposed undertakings. As persuasively ar-

gued by the United States, terms and conditions airlines offer and passengers accept are privately ordered obligations "and thus do not amount to a State's 'enact[ment] or enforce[ment] [of] any law, rule, regulation, standard, or other provision having the force and effect of law' within the meaning of § 1305(a)(1)." [Editor—At this point, the Court states in a footnote: The United States recognizes that § 1305(a)(1), because it contains the word "enforce" as well as "enact," "could perhaps be read to preempt even state-court enforcement of private contracts." But the word series "law, rule, regulation, standard, or other provision," as the United States suggests, "connotes official, government-imposed policies, not the terms of a private contract." Similarly, the phrase "having the force and effect of law" is most naturally read to "refe[r] to binding standards of conduct that operate irrespective of any private agreement." Finally, the ban on enacting or enforcing any law "relating to rates, routes, or services" is most sensibly read, in light of the ADA's overarching deregulatory purpose, to mean "States may not seek to impose their own public policies or theories of competition or regulation on the operations of an air carrier."] A remedy confined to a contract's terms simply holds parties to their agreements—in this instance, to business judgments an airline made public about its rates and services. * * *

[Editor—The Court then notes and reject's American's argument that DOT is "the exclusively competent monitor of the airline's undertakings." It adopts the United States' view that the Department "has neither the authority nor the apparatus required to superintend a contract dispute resolution regime," and, further, that "[w]hen Congress dismantled [airline regulation] the lawmakers indicated no intention to establish, simultaneously, a new administrative process for DOT adjudication of private contract disputes." Moreover, the Court states: "Nor is it plausible that Congress meant to channel into federal courts the business of resolving, pursuant to judicially fashioned federal common law, the range of contract claims relating to airline rates, routes, or services. The ADA contains no hint of such a role for the federal courts."]

American ultimately argues that even under the position on preemption advanced by the United States—the one we adopt— plaintiffs' claims must fail because they "inescapably depend on state policies that are independent of the intent of the parties." "The state court cannot reach the merits," American contends, "unless it first invalidates or limits [American's] express reservation of the right to change AAdvantage Program rules contained in AAdvantage contracts."

American's argument is unpersuasive, for it assumes the answer to the very contract construction issue on which plaintiffs' claims turn: Did American, by contract, reserve the right to change the value of already accumulated mileage credits, or only to change the rules governing credits earned from and after the date of the change? * * * That question of contract interpretation has not yet had a full airing, and we intimate no view on its resolution.

Responding to our colleagues' diverse opinions dissenting in part, we add a final note. * * * Justice Stevens reads our Morales decision to demand only minimal preemption; in contrast, Justice O'Connor reads the same case to mandate total preemption. The middle course we adopt seems to us best calculated to carry out the congressional design; it also bears the approval of the statute's experienced administrator, the DOT.

■ Justice Stevens, concurring in part and dissenting in part.

Although I agree with the majority that the Airline Deregulation Act of 1978 (ADA) does not pre-empt respondents' breach-of-contract claims, I do not agree with the Court's disposition of their consumer-fraud claims. In my opinion, private tort actions based on common-law negligence or fraud, or on a statutory prohibition against fraud, are not pre-empted. * * *

Unlike the National Association of Attorneys General (NAAG) guidelines reviewed in Morales, the Illinois Consumer Fraud and Deceptive Business Practices Act (Consumer Fraud Act) does not instruct the airlines about how they can market their services. Instead, it merely requires all commercial enterprises—airlines included—to refrain from defrauding their customers. The Morales opinion said nothing about pre-empting general state laws prohibiting fraud. The majority's extension of the ADA's pre-emptive reach from airline-specific advertising standards to a general background rule of private conduct represents an alarming enlargement of Morales' holding.

I see no reason why a state law requiring an airline to honor its contractual commitments is any less a law relating to its rates and services than is a state law imposing a "duty not to make false statements of material fact or to conceal such facts." In this case, the two claims are grounded upon the exact same conduct and would presumably have an identical impact upon American's rates, routes, and services. The majority correctly finds that Congress did not intend to pre-empt a claim that an airline breached a private agreement. I see no reason why the ADA should pre-empt a claim that the airline defrauded its customers in the making and performance of that very same agreement.

I would analogize the Consumer Fraud Act to a codification of common-law negligence rules. Under ordinary tort principles, every person has a duty to exercise reasonable care toward all other persons with whom he comes into contact. Presumably, if an airline were negligent in a way that somehow affected its rates, routes, or services, and the victim of the airline's negligence were to sue in state court, the majority would not hold all common-law negligence rules to be pre-empted by the ADA. Like contract principles, the standard of ordinary care is a general background rule against which all individuals order their affairs. Surely Congress did not intend to give airlines free rein to commit negligent acts subject only to the supervision of the Department of Transportation, any more than it meant to allow airlines to breach contracts with impunity. And, if judge-made duties are not pre-empted, it would make little sense to find pre-emption of identical rules codified by the state legislature. The duty imposed by the Illinois Consumer Fraud Act is to refrain from committing fraud in commercial dealings—it is "the duty not to deceive." This is neither a novel nor a controversial proscription. It falls no more heavily upon airlines than upon any other business. It is no more or less a state-imposed "public policy" than a negligence rule. In sum, I see no difference between the duty to refrain from deception and the duty of reasonable care, and I see no meaningful difference between the enforcement of either duty and the enforcement of a private agreement.

The majority's extension of Morales is particularly untenable in light of the interpretive presumption against pre-emption. * * *

■ Justice O'Connor with whom Justice Thomas joins [   ], concurring in the judgment in part and dissenting in part.

In permitting respondents' contract action to go forward, the Court arrives at what might be a reasonable policy judgment as to when state law actions against airlines should be preempted if we were free to legislate it. It is not, however, consistent with our controlling precedents, and it requires some questionable assumptions about the nature of contract law. I would hold that none of respondents' actions may proceed. * * *

* * * I cannot distinguish this case from Morales. In both, the subject matter of the action (the guidelines in Morales, the contract here) relates to airline rates and services. In both, that subject matter has no legal force, except insofar as a generally applicable state law (a consumer fraud law in Morales), state contract law here permits an aggrieved party to invoke the State's coercive power against someone refusing to comply with the subject matter's terms (the requirements of the guidelines in Morales, the terms of the contract here). Morales' conclusion that § 1305 preempts such an invocation is dispositive here, both of respondents' consumer fraud claims, and of their contract claims. * * *

The Court argues that the words "law, rule, regulation, standard, or other provision" in § 1305 refer only to " 'official, government-imposed policies, not the terms of a private contract.' " To be sure, the terms of private contracts are not "laws," any more than the guidelines at issue in Morales were "laws." But contract law, and generally applicable consumer fraud statutes, are laws, and Morales held that § 1305 prevents enforcement of "any [state] law" against the airlines when the subject matter of the action "relates" to airline rates, routes, or services. Thus, where the terms of a private contract relate to airline rates and services, and those terms can only be enforced through state law, Morales is indistinguishable. As Justice Stevens persuasively argues, there is "no reason why a state law requiring an airline to honor its contractual commitments is any less a law relating to its rates and services than is a state law imposing a 'duty not to make false statements of material fact or to conceal such facts.' "

In addition [   ] I disagree with the Court's view that courts can realistically be confined, "in breach of contract actions, to the parties' bargain, with no enlargement or enhancement based on state laws or policies external to the agreement." When they are so confined, the Court says, courts are "simply hold[ing] parties to their agreements," and are not "enforcing" any "law." The Court also says that " '[s]ome state-law principles of contract law * * * might well be preempted to the extent they seek to effectuate the State's public policies, rather than the intent of the parties.' "

The doctrinal underpinnings of the notion that judicial enforcement of the "intent of the parties" can be divorced from a State's "public policy" have been in serious question for many years. As one author wrote some time ago: "A contract, therefore, between two or more individuals cannot be said to be generally devoid of all public interest. If it be of no interest, why enforce it? For note that in enforcing contracts, the government does not merely allow two individuals to do what they have found pleasant in their eyes. Enforcement, in fact, puts the machinery of the law in the service of one party against the other. When that is worthwhile and how that should be done are important questions of public policy * * *. [T]he notion that in enforcing contracts the state is only giving effect to the will of the parties rests upon an * * * untenable theory as to what the enforcement of contracts involves." Cohen, The Basis of Contract, 46 Harv.L.Rev. 553, 562 (1933). More recent authors have expressed similar views. See, e.g., Braucher, Contract Versus Contractarianism: The Regulatory Role of Contract Law, 47 Wash. & Lee L.Rev. 697, 699 (1990)("Mediating between private ordering and social concerns, contract is a socioeconomic institution that requires an array of normative choices * * *. The questions addressed by contract law concern what social norms to use in the enforcement of contracts, not whether social norms will be used at all"). Contract law is a set of policy judgments concerning how to decide the meaning of private agreements, which private agreements should be legally enforceable, and what remedy to afford for their breach. The Court fails to recognize that when a State decides to force parties to comply with a contract, it does so only because it is satisfied that state policy, as expressed in its contract law, will be advanced by that decision.

Thus, the Court's allowance that " '[s]ome state-law principles of contract law * * * might well be preempted to the extent they seek to effectuate the State's public policies, rather than the intent of the parties,' " n. 8 (quoting Brief for United States as *Amicus Curiae*), threatens to swallow all of contract law. For example, the Court observes that on remand, the state court will be required to decide whether petitioner reserved the right to alter the terms of its frequent flyer program retroactively, or instead only prospectively. The court will presumably decide that question by looking to the usual "rules" of contract interpretation to decide what the contract's language means. If the court finds the language to be ambiguous, it might invoke the familiar rule that the contract should be construed against its drafter, and thus that respondents should receive the benefit of the doubt. That rule of contract construction is not essential to a functional contract system. It is a policy choice that our contract system has made. Other such policy choices are that courts should not enforce agreements unsupported by consideration; that courts should supply "reasonable" terms to fill "gaps" in incomplete contracts; the method by which courts should decide what terms to supply; and that a breach of contract entitles the aggrieved party to expectation damages most of the time, but specific performance only rarely. If courts are not permitted to look to these aspects of contract law in airline-related actions, they will find the cases difficult to decide.

Even the doctrine of unconscionability, which the United States suggests as an aspect of contract law that "might well be preempted" because it "seek[s] to effectuate the State's public policies, rather than the intent of the parties," cannot be so neatly categorized. On the one hand, refusing to enforce a contract because it is "unfair" seems quintessentially policy-oriented. But on the other, "[p]rocedural unconscionability is broadly conceived to encompass not only the employment of sharp practices and the use of fine print and convoluted language, but a lack of understanding and an inequality of bargaining power." In other words, a determination that a contract is "unconscionable" may in fact be a determination that one party did not intend to agree to the terms of the contract. Thus, the unconscionability doctrine, far from being a purely "policy-oriented" doctrine that courts impose over the will of the parties, instead demonstrates that state public policy cannot easily be separated from the methods by which courts are to decide what the parties "intended."

"[T]he law itself imposes contractual liability on the basis of a complex of moral, political, and social judgments." The rules laid down by contract law for determining what the parties intended an agreement to mean, whether that agreement is legally enforceable, and what relief an aggrieved party should receive, are the end result of those judgments. Our legal system has decided to allow private parties to invoke the coercive power of the State in the effort to enforce those (and only those) private agreements that conform to rules set by those state policies known collectively as "contract law." Courts cannot enforce private agreements without reference to those policies, because those policies define the role of courts in deciding disputes concerning private agreements.

For these reasons, I would reverse the judgment of the Illinois Supreme Court.

Public choice and pre-emption. What is the "public choice" perspective on pre-emption? In Easterbrook, Foreword: The Court and the Economic System, 98 Harv. L. Rev. 4 (1984), the author comments on the pre-emptive effect of federal statutes and agency regulations in the area of nuclear power on a state's ability to award punitive tort damages for violation of federal safety standards. In Silkwood v. Kerr–McGee Corp., 464 U.S. 238 (1984), the Court allowed a state jury to award punitive damages which were over 100 times the highest fine the statute authorized the federal agency to impose. Easterbrook argues that the result can be defended if

> the federal statutes are private-interest laws, compromises to be read no more broadly than the scope of the deal struck by the participants. They did not strike a deal to pre-empt state tort law * * *. The complex package of statutes prevented states from establishing regulatory commissions, which might promulgate inconsistent regulations. Punitive damages awarded by juries are more like lightning. Large firms can tolerate risk and pay the awards more readily than they can survive enforceable orders to conduct the business in undesirable ways. The awards of juries may be good or they may be bad, but if the parties' deal did not cover them, Kerr–McGee has no case. The private-interest reading of the statute leads to a ruling against the nuclear power industry.

He notes that the "majority (Justices Brennan, White, Rehnquist, Stevens, and O'Connor) trudged through the history of the Atomic Energy Act looking for the critical bargain [favoring pre-emption]. They did not find it."

QUESTIONS

1. Can we really expect everything regarding the legislative bargaining process to be in the legislative history? Is the search for the contents of a bargain in legislative history inconsistent with the more usual position of textualists like Easterbrook, that legislative history is unreliable?

2. Would the Silkwood case be better decided by balancing the federal interest in pre-empting state law affecting nuclear accidents with "federalism" concerns, which would leave states free to provide damages not explicitly pre-empted?

3. Does the fact that a defendant's statutory fine was limited to a specific amount imply that the larger award of punitive damages was excluded as an appropriate remedy?

iii) "GAPS"

Federal statutes might not deal with all aspects of a problem. They might, for example, fail (1) to resolve whether defendants are jointly and severally liable when they violate a federal statutory obligation, or (2) to identify the statute of limitations. Is a federal court free to fill in these "gaps" as federal common law (perhaps choosing state law) or does state law *necessarily* apply?

One way to resolve this issue is to observe that federal courts have traditionally filled in at least some of these gaps and assume that, as part of statutory context, Congress expected federal courts to exercise this power. But this may assume too much. Before Erie, federal courts assumed a federal common law power to decide general commercial law questions and that turned out to be improper. Assumptions about statutory gap-filling might similarly be based on an obsolete conception of federal-state relations. Hence, the opposite assumption might prevail—assume state law governs absent strong evidence that it would undermine federal policy. This is just another way of saying that the existence of a gap to be filled by federal courts is a question of statutory interpretation, which might be influenced by background considerations regarding the respective roles of the federal and state governments and the lawmaking role of federal courts.

(A) **Introduction—Federal or State law?**

When the court applies state law to fill statutory gaps, it is not always clear whether the court *chooses* state law as a matter of federal law or whether it adopts state law because it has to, under Erie. Often, the court refuses to tell you which theory it applies. See, e.g., United States v. Yazell, 382 U.S. 341 (1966)("Although it is unnecessary to decide whether the Texas law [   ] should apply *ex proprio vigore* * * * or by 'adoption' as a federal principle, it is clear that the state rule should govern.") The distinction is important because experience with choosing state law might demonstrate that a different federal rule is desirable, which the court could adopt only if state law was not mandatory under Erie and the court had the power to choose which law to apply.

Sometimes, the court is very clear that federal law chooses state law to fill gaps. For example, in Kamen v. Kemper Financial Services, 500 U.S. 90 (1991), the issue was whether a shareholder who brought a derivative action to enforce a corporation's claim first had to make a demand on the corporation's board of directors. The Court adopted the law of the state of incorporation, which excused a demand when it would be "futile," reversing the Court of Appeals (908 F.2d 1338 (7th Cir.1990)(Judge Easterbrook)), which had adopted a uniform federal rule that a demand had to be made in all cases. The Court stated that "[i]t is clear that the contours of the demand requirement [   ] are governed by *federal* law. Because the [statute] is a federal statute, any common law rule necessary to effectuate a private cause of action under that statute is necessarily federal in character." But that was not all.

> It does not follow [ ] that the content of such a rule must be wholly the product of a federal court's own devising. Our cases indicate that a court should endeavor to fill the interstices of federal remedial schemes with uniform federal rules only when the scheme in question evidences a distinct need for nationwide legal standards, or when express provisions in analogous statutory schemes embody congressional policy choices readily applicable to the matter at hand. Otherwise, we have indicated that federal courts should "incorporate [state law] as the federal rule of decision," unless "application of [the particular] state law [in question] would frustrate specific objectives of the federal programs."

This issue of how federal courts fill gaps has often been contested in the context of statutes of limitations, whenever the federal statute does not specifically provide a limitations period. The courts sometimes say that the practice of adopting state law has "enjoyed sufficient longevity that we may presume that * * * Congress ordinarily 'intends by its silence that we borrow state law,'" an approach which traces adoption of state law to the federal statute. Lampf, Pleva, Lipkind, Prupis & Petigrow v. Gilbertson, 501 U.S. 350 (1991). But some judges are just as adamant that the state statute of limitations applies of its own force under Erie, absent some indication that federal law should pre-empt state law. For example, in Lampf, Justice Stevens' dissent argued for borrowing the state time limit, on the ground that "Congress, rather than the federal judiciary, has the responsibility for making the [necessary] policy determinations," and on the ground that using state statutes of limitations is required by the Rules of Decision Act. And in Agency Holding Corp. v. Malley–Duff & Associates, Inc., 483 U.S. 143 (1987), Justice Scalia concludes that, absent pre-emption, state law applies of its own force. Federal courts do not "borrow" state law. Justice Scalia, however, admits that courts have referred for years to federal borrowing of state statutes of limitations and that "it is reasonable to say that such a result is what Congress must expect, and hence intend, by its silence."

In *some* cases, the courts decided that federal interests in uniformity, predictability, and judicial economy required a uniform statute of limitations. In such instances, the courts usually selected a single federal rule, borrowing the time limit from the most analogous federal statute. See Agency Holding Corp. v. Malley–Duff & Associates, 483 U.S. 143 (1987)(anti-trust Clayton Act statute of limitations applies to RICO civil action because RICO was patterned on the Clayton Act and both statutes are designed to remedy economic injury by providing recovery for treble damages, costs, and attorney's fees; there is no satisfactory alternative state analogue to RICO).

Is the statute of limitations issue different from the issue in Kamen, *supra*, where the Court was clear that federal law *borrowed* state law. Kamen involved the contours of the requirement that shareholders make a demand on the corporate board of directors as a prerequisite to bringing a derivative cause of action? Is the issue in Kamen more central to the substance of the cause of action than a statute of limitations?

The specific question of what statute of limitations to apply has been mooted for statutes adopted after December 1, 1990, by federal statute,[8] which provides:

> Except as otherwise provided by law, a civil action arising under an Act of Congress enacted after the date of the enactment of this section may not be commenced later than 4 years after the cause of action arises. 28 U.S.C. § 1658.

However, the approach taken by courts in the older statute of limitations cases is still relevant for deciding how and when federal courts should fill statutory gaps with state law.

(B) Joint and several liability

Another potential gap is whether defendants are jointly and severally liable. The courts have addressed this problem in connection with the federal statute known as CERCLA (Comprehensive Environmental Response, Compensation and Liability Act). CERCLA funds environmental clean up by excise taxes on petroleum and certain chemicals and, to a lesser extent, by general revenues (the Superfund). The Superfund provides for a right of reimbursement from people who are "liable," and lists classes of people who are potentially liable, including owners and operators of the property at which hazardous substances were disposed of, and any person who arranged for disposal, treatment or transportation of hazardous substances. 42 U.S.C. § 9607. The statute is silent on whether defendants are jointly and severally liable. Here is how the courts resolved that question in United States v. Chem–Dyne Corp., 572 F.Supp. 802 (D.Ohio 1983). The court first determined that the "State law as a rule of decision is not mandated under the Erie doctrine in this case because it falls within the exception provided for federal laws," stating as follows:

> The improper disposal or release of hazardous substances is an enormous and complex problem of national magnitude involving uniquely federal interests. Typically, an abandoned waste site will consist of waste produced by companies in several states within the area or region. The pollution of land, groundwater, surface water and air as a consequence of this dumping presents potentially interstate problems. A driving force toward the development of CERCLA was the recognition that a response to this pervasive condition at the state level was generally inadequate. The subject

---

8. Justice Scalia did his best to encourage a federal legislative solution in his opinion in Agency Holding Corp. v. Malley–Duff & Associates, Inc., 483 U.S. 143 (1987), where he argued that, if federal pre-emption rejects the state statute of limitations, there is *no* limitations period. That, in his view, was better than "prowling hungrily through the Statutes at Large for an appetizing federal limitations period." It would also, in his view, "prompt Congress to enact a limitations period that it believes 'appropriate.'"

Apparently, Congress' adoption of a prospective four-year fall-back statute of limitations was not a response to Justice Scalia's prodding but to a proposal in the Report of the Federal Courts Study Committee. See H. Rep. No. 101–734, 101st Cong., 2d Sess. p. 24 (1990).

matter dealt with in CERCLA is easily distinguished from areas of primarily state concern, such as domestic relations or real property rights, where state law was applied and there was no overriding interest in nationwide uniformity. Additionally, the superfund monies expended, for which the United States seeks reimbursement, are funded by general revenues and excise taxes. The degree to which the United States will be able to protect its financial interest [   ] is directly related to the scope of liability under CERCLA and is in no way dependent upon the laws of any state. When the United States derives its authority for reimbursement from the specific Act of Congress passed in the exercise of a constitutional function or power, its rights should also derive from federal common law. In conclusion, the rights, liabilities and responsibilities of the United States under 42 U.S.C. § 9607 are governed by a federal rule of decision.

The court then addressed whether federal law should or should not adopt state common law about joint and several liability.

The question now becomes whether the scope of liability should be interpreted according to the incorporated state law of the forum state or a federally created uniform law. This determination is a matter of judicial policy dependent upon a variety of considerations relevant to the nature of the specific governmental interests and to the effects upon them of applying state law. Federal programs that by their nature are and must be uniform in character throughout the nation necessitate the formulation of federal rules of decision. * * * A liability standard which varies in the different forum states would undermine the policies of the statute by encouraging illegal dumping in states with lax liability laws. There is no good reason why the United States' right to reimbursement should be subjected to needless uncertainty and subsequent delay occasioned by diversified local disposition when this matter is appropriate for uniform national treatment.

Finding, then, that the delineation of a uniform federal rule of decision is consistent with the legislative history and policies of CERCLA and finding further that no compelling local interests mandate the incorporation of state law, a determination of the content of the federal rule is the final step in the analysis. * * *

Typically, as in this case, there will be numerous hazardous substance generators or transporters who have disposed of wastes at a particular site. * * * An examination of the common law reveals that when two or more persons acting independently caused a distinct or single harm for which there is a reasonable basis for division according to the contribution of each, each is subject to liability only for the portion of the total harm that he has himself caused. But where two or more persons cause a single and indivisible harm, each is subject to liability for the entire harm. Furthermore, where the conduct of two or more persons liable under § 9607 has combined to violate the statute, and one or more of the defendants seeks to limit his liability on the ground that the entire harm is capable of apportionment, the burden of proof as to apportionment is upon each defendant. These rules clearly enumerate the analysis to be undertaken when applying 42 U.S.C. § 9607 and are most likely to advance the legislative policies and objectives of the Act.

The uniform federal common law adopted by the court was the Restatement rule, producing joint and several liability if the harm was indivisible, several liability if the harm was divisible, and placing the burden of proof regarding divisibility on the defendant. A few courts have exercised their federal common law power to permit only several liability (permitting apportionment), despite indivisibility, depending on the amount of waste involved, its toxicity, the involvement and care of the defendants, and their cooperation with the government. This "several liability" standard had passed the House but failed in the Senate when CERCLA was adopted.[9]

(C) Comments and Questions

1. *Torts and taxes.* Federal law creates a cause of action for a railroad employee's wrongful death. Part of the recovery includes the replacement of future wages, which are tax-free under the federal income tax. Does federal law determine whether a jury is told that the tort recovery is tax free? Suppose such a jury instruction would not be allowed if the tort arose under state law? See Norfolk & Western Ry. Co. v. Liepelt, 444 U.S. 490 (1980).

2. *Attorney's fees.* The American Rule requires parties to pay their own attorney's fees, unless a statute alters the rule or a losing party has acted in bad faith. Federal courts follow this approach. Alyeska Pipeline Service Co. v. Wilderness Soc., 421 U.S. 240 (1975); Chambers v. NASCO, Inc., 501 U.S. 32 (1991). Do federal courts do this because that is state law, which federal courts must follow; or are attorney's fees issues inherently matters of federal common law?

Does a federal court's power to shift attorney's fees depend on whether the argument for shifting rests on any of the following: to encourage one party to bring a lawsuit as a private attorney-general; or to punish a party for bad faith litigation tactics? Does your answer vary depending on whether the case in federal court involves a claim arising under a federal statute or a state claim in federal court under diversity jurisdiction?

13.04 EXTENDING STATUTES WHICH VIOLATE EQUAL PROTECTION

When an underinclusive statute violates equal protection, the court can either extend or nullify the statute to prevent unequal treatment. For

---

9. See, e.g., Allied Corp. v. Acme Solvents Reclaiming, Inc., 691 F.Supp. 1100, 1117 (D.Ill.1988).

example, when X is benefited by a statute, the inequity of omitting Y is cured either by giving Y the same benefit or by taking the benefit away from X. Welsh v. United States, 398 U.S. 333 (1970)(Harlan, J., concurring). The judicial rhetoric for resolving this issue dwells on legislative intent, but the legislature is unlikely to have any intent about what should happen if the statute violates the Constitution. Nonetheless, the federal court's power to extend a statute which violates equal protection is apparently unquestioned, despite the lack of a substantive common lawmaking power. As Justice Harlan states in Welsh:

> If an important congressional policy is to be perpetuated by recasting unconstitutional legislation * * *, the analytically sound approach is to accept responsibility for decision. Its justification cannot be by resort to legislative intent, as that term is usually employed, but by a different kind of legislative intent, namely the presumed grant of power to the courts to decide whether it more nearly accords with Congress' wishes to eliminate its policy altogether or extend it in order to render what Congress plainly did intend, constitutional.

Occasionally, a statute will state that a violation of equal treatment cannot be remedied by extending the statutory benefits, but that is unusual. Heckler v. Mathews, 465 U.S. 728 (1984)(non-extension provision does not deny standing to object to unequal treatment by omitted group).

The following case illustrates how difficult the decision about extension can be.

Califano v. Westcott

443 U.S. 76 (1979).

■ Mr. Justice Blackmun delivered the opinion of the Court.
* * *

[Editor—This case involved the Aid to Families with Dependent Children statute. One portion of this statute, § 407, provided welfare to families with both a mother and an unemployed father. Families with a father and unemployed mother were not covered. "Unemployed" was a term of art, referring to persons not now working, but with a prior job record, as defined in the statute. The Court held that the discrimination between households with unemployed fathers and unemployed mothers was unconstitutional and then turned to the remedy question.]

"Where a statute is defective because of under-inclusion," Mr. Justice Harlan noted, "there exist two remedial alternatives: a court may either declare [the statute] a nullity and order that its benefits not extend to the class that the legislature intended to benefit, or it may extend the coverage of the statute to include those who are aggrieved by the exclusion." Welsh v. United States, 398 U.S. 333, 361 (1970)(concurring result). In previous cases involving equal protection challenges to underinclusive federal benefits statutes, this Court has suggested that extension, rather than nullification, is the proper course. Indeed, this Court regularly has affirmed District Court judgments ordering that welfare benefits be paid to members of an unconstitutionally excluded class.

The District Court ordered extension rather than invalidation by way of remedy here, and equitable considerations surely support its choice. Approximately 300,000 needy children currently receive AFDC–UF benefits, see 42 Soc. Sec. Bull. 78 (Jan. 1979), and an injunction suspending the program's operation would impose hardship on beneficiaries whom Congress plainly meant to protect. The presence in the Social Security Act of a strong severability clause, 42 U.S.C. § 1303, likewise counsels against nullification, for it evidences a congressional intent to minimize the burdens imposed by a declaration of unconstitutionality upon innocent recipients of government largesse.

There is no need, however, to elaborate here the conditions under which invalidation rather than extension of an under-inclusive federal benefits statute should be ordered, for no party has presented that issue for review. All parties before the District Court agreed that extension was the appropriate remedy. Appellees support that remedy here, and the Secretary, while arguing in favor of § 407's constitutionality, urges that, if the statute is invalidated, the District Court's remedy should be affirmed. The Commissioner likewise argues that extension, rather than nullification, is proper; indeed, the Commissioner did not appeal from the District Court's April 20 extension order, but only from its August 9 refusal to limit extension along "principal wage-earner" lines. Since no party has presented the issue of extension versus nullification for review, we would be inclined to consider it only if the power to order extension were clearly beyond the constitutional competence of a federal district court. This Court's previous decisions, however, which routinely have affirmed District Court judgments ordering extension of federal welfare programs, suggest strongly that no such remedial incapacity exists.

The narrower question presented by the Commissioner's appeal concerns not the merits of extension versus nullification, but rather the form that extension should take. The District Court ordered that benefits be paid to families if either the mother or the father is unemployed within the meaning of the Act. The Commissioner agrees that either the mother's or the father's unemployment should be able to qualify the needy family for benefits, but proposes to award them only if the parent in question can show that he or she is both unemployed and the family's "principal wage-earner." Citing the legislative history of the AFDC–UF program, the Commissioner argues that his proposed remedy comports with Congress' intent to aid families made needy by their breadwinner's unemployment.

This argument, as the preceding portions of this opinion show, is not without force. We may assume arguendo that, if Congress knew in 1968 what it knows now, it might well have adopted the "principal wage-earner" model suggested by the Commissioner. But this does not mean that the AFDC–UF program should be restructured along these lines by a federal court.

First, the Commissioner's proposed remedy would have the effect of terminating benefits to many families currently receiving them. Under the Act and implementing regulations, benefits are paid to needy families of all unemployed fathers, whether or not the father is actually the "principal wage-earner." See 42 U.S.C. § 607(a); 45 CFR § 233.100(a)(1) (1978). No one contends that the Act and regulations, insofar as they provide benefits to families of all unemployed fathers, are invalid. Absent some such showing of invalidity, we would hesitate to terminate needy families' entitlement to statutory benefits merely because the unemployed father cannot prove "breadwinner" status.

Second, the Commissioner's proposed remedy would involve a restructuring of the Act that a court should not undertake lightly. Whenever a court extends a benefits program to redress unconstitutional underinclusiveness, it risks infringing legislative prerogatives. The extension ordered by the District Court possesses at least the virtue of simplicity: by ordering that "father" be replaced by its gender-neutral equivalent, the court avoided disruption of the AFDC–UF program, for benefits simply will be paid to families with an unemployed parent on the same terms that benefits have long been paid to families with an unemployed father. The "principal wage-earner" solution, by contrast, would introduce a term novel in the AFDC scheme, and would pose definitional and policy questions best suited to legislative or administrative elaboration. The Commissioner, with his "principal wage-earner" gloss on parental unemployment, in essence asks this Court to redefine "unemployment" within the meaning of the Act. Yet "Congress in § 407(a) expressly delegated to the Secretary the power to prescribe standards for determining eligibility. In a situation of this kind, Congress entrusts to the Secretary, rather than to the courts, the primary responsibility for interpreting the statutory term."

The remedy the Commissioner proposes, of course, undeniably would be cheaper than the remedy the District Court decreed, in part because it would terminate some current recipients' eligibility. Although cost may prove a dispositive factor in the other contexts, we do not regard it as controlling here. The United States, which will bear the main burden of added coverage through federal matching grants, urges that the District Court's remedy be affirmed. The AFDC–UF program, furthermore, is optional with the States, and any State is free to drop out of it if dissatisfied with the added expense. This Court, in any event, is ill-equipped both to estimate the relative costs of various types of coverage, and to gauge the effect that different levels of expenditures would have upon the alleviation of human suffering. Under these circumstances, any fine-tuning of AFDC coverage along "principal wage-earner" lines is properly left to the democratic branches of the Government. In sum, we believe the District Court, in an effort to render the AFDC–UF program gender neutral, adopted the simplest and most equitable extension possible.

■ Mr. Justice Powell, with whom The Chief Justice, Mr. Justice Stewart, and Mr. Justice Rehnquist join, concurring in part and dissenting in part.

I agree with the Court that § 407 violates the equal protection component of the Fifth Amendment. In my view, however, the court below erred when it ordered the extension of benefits to all families in which a mother has become unemployed. This extension reinstates a system of distributing benefits that Congress rejected when it amended § 407 in 1968. Rather than frustrate the clear intent of Congress, the court simply should have enjoined any further payment of benefits under the provision found to be unconstitutional. * * *

* * * In choosing between [extension and enjoining benefits], a court should attempt to accommodate as fully as possible the policies and arguments expressed in the statutory scheme as a whole. It should not use its remedial powers to circumvent the intent of the legislature.

The Court correctly observes that "the gender qualification [of § 407] was part of the general objective of the 1968 amendments to tighten standards for eligibility and reduce program costs." It is clear that Congress intended to proscribe the payment of benefits to families where only one parent was unemployed and where the principal wage earner continued to work.

> "From all that appears, Congress, with an image of the 'traditional family' in mind, simply assumed that the father would be the family breadwinner, and that the mother's employment role, if any, would be secondary."

Yet the result of the Court's decision affirming the District Court's relief is to compel exactly the extension of benefits Congress wished to prevent.

Rather than thus rewriting § 407, we should leave this task to Congress. Now that we have held that this statute constitutes impermissible gender-based discrimination, it is the duty and function of the Legislative Branch to review its AFDC–UF program in light of our decision and make such changes therein as it deems appropriate. Leaving the resolution to Congress is especially desirable in cases such as this one, where the allocation and distribution of welfare funds are peculiarly within the province of the Legislative Branch.

We cannot predict what Congress will think to be in the best interest of its total welfare program. The extension of AFDC benefits to families suffering only from unemployment was a relatively recent development in the history of the program, a development that Congress made permanent only on the understanding that payments could be limited to cases where the principal wage earner was out of work. We cannot assume that Congress in 1968 would have approved this extension if it had known that ultimately payments would be made whenever either parent became unemployed. Nor can we assume that Congress now would adopt such a system in light of the Court's ruling that § 407 is invalid.

The Court emphasizes the hardships that may be caused by enjoining the program until Congress can act. There is the possibility, not mentioned by the Court, that other hardships might be occasioned in the allocating of limited funds as a result of court-ordered extension of these particular benefits. In any event, Congress has the option to mitigate hardships by providing promptly for retroactive payments. An injunction prohibiting further payments at least will conserve the funds appropriated until Congress determines which group, if any, it does want to assist. The relief ordered by the Court today, in contrast, ensures the irretrievable payment of funds to a class of recipients Congress did not wish to benefit.

Because it is clear that Congress intended to prevent the result mandated today, and that the re-examination of § 407 required under our decision properly should be made by Congress, I dissent.

QUESTIONS

1. What criteria do the majority and minority judges consider in deciding on the remedy for the statute violating Equal Protection? Are they trying to be faithful to the historical legislature, or contemporary policy?

2. After this decision, Congress changed the statute to provide coverage when the "principal earner" was unemployed. Pub. L. 97–35, § 2313(a)(2), 95 Stat. 853 (1981). Was the Court correct in assuming that it could not or should not order this result on its own?

CHAPTER 14

INFERRING PRIVATE CAUSES OF ACTION FROM STATUTES

14.01 HISTORICAL AND EVOLVING BACKGROUND CONSIDERATIONS

a) INTRODUCTION

Should a court infer a private cause of action from statutes which do not explicitly provide them? This is a special case of the issue discussed in Chapter 13—the extension of a statute beyond its text. The question deserves separate treatment, however, because of the variety of settings in which it arises, and the intense concern it has aroused in Supreme Court cases. It is also an example of how evolving background considerations have led the Court to change its approach to interpreting statutes.

There is a long tradition of common law courts relying on criminal statutes to establish standards of negligence in tort cases, often in cases involving worker and product safety and the behavior of automobile drivers. At this point in the course, you should recognize that this issue does not raise any significant questions of power for a common law court, only matters of good judgment. If the court has a common law power to determine negligence, it is free to infer standards of behavior from various sources, including criminal statutes, just as the federal common law power in admiralty permitted the Court in Moragne to infer a wrongful death action from analogous statutory developments.[1]

The issue addressed by this Chapter concerns inferring a private cause of action when a court does *not* have a substantive common lawmaking power. We focus primarily on federal statutes dealing with civil rights, the environment, and securities transactions.[2]

---

1. Whether negligence *should* be inferred from a criminal statute is debatable. You might think that a criminal penalty is necessarily worse than civil liability and that therefore criminal behavior must be tortious. That is much too simple a view of the law, however, especially in today's world of criminal statutes regulating economic behavior. Prosecutorial discretion and fixed dollar fines, combined with a mild stigma, might make the modern criminal statute *less* burdensome than widespread tort liability, enforceable by plaintiffs with access to jury awards throughout the country.

2. Remember that state courts with common law powers can use policies underlying federal statutes to create state causes of action. See Hofbauer v. Northwestern Nat. Bank of Rochester, 700 F.2d 1197 (8th Cir.1983)(no federal cause of action but case remanded to determine whether there was a state cause of action for negligence based on the federal

A complicating factor in cases involving implied federal causes of action is the institutional setting in which the federal statute operates, which provides a variety of alternative remedies to a private cause of action. These alternatives might suggest the absence of an additional remedy in the form of a private cause of action (expressio unius est exclusio alterius). First, some statutes establish grant-in-aid programs, in which the federal government gives money to the states or other recipients on condition that they do certain things, like adopt welfare, medical, or educational programs. A grant-in-aid program could be enforced solely by federal withdrawal of funds, restitution by the recipient of the funds, or specific enforcement by the federal government. Or, the individual beneficiaries of the program might also have a private cause of action against the recipient of the grant for violation of federal requirements. Second, some statutes establish federal administrative agencies, as in environmental and securities law, with broad enforcement powers. In such cases, can private parties injured by violation of federal standards sue to enforce federal rules, or is administrative enforcement the only remedy?

One possible solution to the question of inferring a private cause of action from federal statutes is to rely on the statutory text. Because the text is silent, a court without a substantive common law power cannot infer a private cause of action. Textualism is not completely persuasive in this setting, however, because there is a long background tradition of inferring a private cause of action from statutes which set legal standards. This tradition is often described as creating a "common law" judicial power, although it should not be confused with a substantive lawmaking power to define an underlying obligation (as in negligence cases). The tradition of inferring a private cause of action is part of the context in which Congress legislates and congressional silence might therefore include an assumption that a private cause of action exists or at least that courts will continue to decide whether or not to infer a cause of action. For example, in California v. Sierra Club, 451 U.S. 287 (1981), Justice Stevens' concurrence made the following point:

> At the time the statute was enacted, I believe the lawyers in Congress simply assumed that private parties * * * would have a remedy for any injury suffered by reason of a violation of the new federal statute. For at that time the implication of private causes of action was a well-known practice at common law and in American courts. Therefore, in my view, the Members of Congress merely assumed that the federal courts would follow the ancient maxim "ubi jus, ibi remedium" and imply a private right of action.

From earlier discussions, however, you know that background considerations which are part of a statute's context can change. They might even evolve *after* a statute's adoption so that a modern interpretation might differ from that which would have prevailed when the statute was adopted.

statute). But see R.B.J. Apartments, Inc. v. Gate City Sav. & Loan Ass'n, 315 N.W.2d 284 (N.D.1982)(the state court held that separation of powers and federalism considerations militated against using a federal statute to infer a state law cause of action for negligence).

In California v. Sierra Club, *supra*, for example, the Court denied private parties the right to sue under the Rivers and Harbors Appropriation Act of 1899 to enjoin the construction and operation of water diversion facilities which are part of the California Water Project. § 10 of the Act prohibited "[t]he creation of any obstruction not affirmatively authorized by Congress, to the navigable capacity of any of the waters of the United States," but did not explicitly create a private cause of action. Justice Stevens' concurrence in this 1981 case did not rely on the historical context to which he explicitly alluded, *supra*, and instead adhered to a more modern evolving doctrinal approach to decide whether there is a private cause of action, found in the 1975 Cort v. Ash case, excerpted below. He thought it was more important "to adhere to the analytical approach the Court has adopted than to base my vote on my own opinion about what Congress probably assumed [when the statute was adopted]."

b) Cort v. Ash

In Cort v. Ash, 422 U.S. 66 (1975), the Court began the modern approach to inferring private causes of action from federal statutes. Subsequent cases have argued over what Cort v. Ash means, but there is general agreement that it was more restrictive than the traditional common law approach. The case involved a federal statute prohibiting corporate expenditures in federal electoral campaigns. A corporate stockholder sought damages and an injunction in the corporation's behalf based on violation of the statute. In denying a private cause of action, the Court set forth the following four criteria for inferring a private cause of action:

> First, is the plaintiff "one of the class for whose *especial* benefit the statute was enacted,"—that is, does the statute create a federal right in favor of the plaintiff?

> Second, is there any indication of legislative intent, explicit or implicit, either to create such a remedy or to deny one?

> Third, is it consistent with the underlying purposes of the legislative scheme to imply such a remedy for the plaintiff?

> And finally, is the cause of action one traditionally relegated to state law, in an area basically the concern of the States, so that it would be inappropriate to infer a cause of action based solely on federal law?

c) The "Conservative" Reaction

For many judges, the Cort v. Ash rules are still too expansive in inferring a private cause of action. Those relying on public choice theory, textualism, and constitutional principle (Separation of Powers) would deny a private cause of action unless the statute explicitly so provides.

1. *Public choice.* An implied cause of action is inconsistent with the view of statutes as essentially matters of compromise. The presence or absence of

a remedy is presumed part of that compromise. Thus, one side of the legislative bargain might accept more burdensome substantive rules on condition that enforcement is limited. Easterbrook puts it this way in The Court and the Economic System, 98 Harv. L. Rev. 4 (1984):

> If legislation grows out of compromises among special interests, [ ] a court cannot add enforcement to get more of what Congress wanted. What Congress wanted was the compromise, not the objectives of the contending interests. The statute has no purpose.

This is contrasted with the purposive approach:

> * * * Once Congress has marked the golden path, judges may take additional steps in the same direction. Private actions and more effective remedies move in the right direction. * * * This view provides the justification for easy inference of private rights of action from silent statutes * * * and for judicial discretion in the design of remedies.

2. *Textualism.* The renewed interest in textualism in statutory interpretation rejects implying something about which the statute is silent. A statute which is silent about private causes of action simply does not provide any.

Justice Scalia states this view in his concurrence in Thompson v. Thompson, 484 U.S. 174 (1988):

> It is, to be sure, not beyond imagination that in a particular case Congress may intend to create a private cause of action, but chooses to do so by implication. One must wonder, however, whether the good produced by a judicial rule that accommodates this remote possibility is outweighed by its adverse effects. An enactment by implication cannot realistically be regarded as the product of the difficult lawmaking process our Constitution has prescribed. Committee Reports, floor speeches, and even colloquies between Congressmen, are frail substitutes for bicameral vote upon the text of a law and its presentment to the President. It is at best dangerous to assume that all the necessary participants in the law-enacting process are acting upon the same unexpressed assumptions. And likewise dangerous to assume that, even with the utmost self-discipline, judges can prevent the implications they see from mirroring the policies they favor. * * *
>
> If we were to announce a flat rule that private rights of action will not be implied in statutes hereafter enacted, the risk that that course would occasionally frustrate genuine legislative intent would decrease from its current level of minimal to virtually zero. * * * I believe, moreover, that Congress would welcome the certainty that such a rule would produce. Surely conscientious legislators cannot relish the current situation, in which the existence or nonexistence of a private right of action depends upon which of the opposing legislative forces may have guessed right as to the implications the statute will be found to contain.

As Scalia observes, one argument for relying on the text alone is that this will encourage the legislature to pay attention to important political issues, rather than leaving them for judicial resolution. In this connection, the following excerpt from B. Asbell, The Senate Nobody Knows 224 (paperback ed. 1981), is edifying. It reports a conversation at a subcommittee hearing on environmental legislation, suggesting disdain for Senatorial consideration of such mundane matters.

> At about twelve-thirty today, when already bones are weary and minds fuzzy, the committee turns to a new question: since the bill authorizes each state to set certain air standards of its own, provided they are no lower than minimum federal standards, what if a state refuses to enforce its own standards? Who may sue the state to force its enforcement? The EPA? A citizen's suit? The committee, almost all lawyers, haggle and bicker and bicker and haggle. Finally [Senator] Gary Hart, sitting as silently as [Senator] Muskie but looking more bored, bursts out, "Can't it be one or the other or both? Is this a thing that a group of Senators should be spending a Saturday afternoon deciding?"

3. *Constitutional theory.* Some judges have questioned the constitutional legitimacy of a federal court inferring private causes of action on the ground that this is lawmaking beyond the federal judicial power. For example, in Lampf, Pleva, Lipkind, Prupis & Petigrow v. Gilbertson, 501 U.S. 350 (1991), Justice Scalia stated:

> Raising up causes of action where a statute has not created them may be a proper function for common-law courts, but not for federal tribunals.

Justice Powell, as we will see in several cases in Chapter 14.02b, shared this point of view.

d) IT ALL DEPENDS

Another contemporary approach accepts the view that background considerations can support an implied cause of action, but rejects the traditional casual implication of an implied cause of action and the oversimplified approach of Cort v. Ash. It all depends on a complex analysis of the values advanced by private enforcement and how such enforcement fits the statutory scheme. Stewart and Sunstein, Public Programs and Private Rights, 95 Harv.L.Rev. 1193 (1982), argue that

> [w]hen courts apply or interpret a statute, they must look to general background understandings as a basis for identifying the norms— sometimes hypostatized as "legislative intent"—that underlie the statute. But the identification of such background understandings is no simple task. The more general and powerful the background understanding, the less likely it is to have been stated explicitly by the legislature, even if the legislature in fact shares that understanding. Moreover, because background understandings derive from an evolving political and social context, they must also change over

time. Finally, because they provide the context that gives meaning to a large variety of statutes, the understandings among legislature, agency and judge necessarily remain fluid.

The authors identify three relevant background considerations, each of which might produce different conclusions about inferring a private cause of action: (1) a *public values* perspective views institutions as a setting for public participation in determining public values; (2) a *production* perspective tries to maximize wealth by correcting market failures; and (3) an *entitlement* perspective emphasizes protection of personal rights. They argue that reliance on these background considerations inevitably guide judicial decisions and are therefore "an established and legitimate device of lawmaking through statutory construction rather than a controversial intrusion on legislative prerogatives."

Here is some of what they say about each perspective.

Public Values. Stewart and Sunstein find that courts have appropriately failed to rely on the public values conception to infer a private cause of action.

> There is paradox in the notion that the private right of action could serve as a crucible for the advancement of public values; the very origins of administrative agencies lay in dissatisfaction with private litigation as an undemocratic mechanism for social choice and control.   Nonetheless, one could base a public values justification for private rights of action on a theory of the regulatory process that focuses on transaction cost barriers to organized advocacy by regulatory beneficiaries. In the implementation process, administrative bureaucracies sometimes tend to sacrifice the diffused interests of widely scattered beneficiaries in favor of the interest of more cohesive and better-organized groups, such as regulated firms and the bureaucrats themselves. This tendency could block the full realization of the public values embodied in regulatory programs.

> On such a theory, private rights of action might be justified as an open, nonbureaucratic means of asserting public values, ensuring their enforcement, and reestablishing the balance struck in the regulatory statute. The courtroom might also serve as a stage for dramatizing these social values and for awakening the concern of the media, the public, and the legislature.

> Nevertheless, courts have generally not adopted a public values rationale in private right of action cases. * * * Moreover, the rhetoric employed in creating private rights of action includes no reference to the values of beneficiary participation and public education.

> Judicial rejection of the public values conception in this setting is quite understandable. Litigation between private parties is an unlikely forum for achieving community self-determination, and there is little evidence that such litigation has awakened public or congressional concern over regulatory policies. Furthermore, the premise that unorganized beneficiary interests are systematically under-

represented is not easily verified; one person's "implementation slippage" is another's safeguard against excesses of regulatory zeal. Even if the premise of transaction-cost barriers were accepted, private rights of initiation are a superior remedy from a public values perspective because they seek to invigorate administrative and political processes. [Editor—A private right of initiation allows private parties to obtain judicial review of agency inaction, seeking to force agency consideration of an issue.]

Production. The authors argue that a production rationale is a more promising background consideration for inferring a private cause of action, both normatively and descriptively, although it is very complex.

* * * Under the production conception, the creation of private rights of action would be justified when two conditions are met. First, the regulatory agency must have devoted inadequate resources to enforcement or must lack the sanctions needed to obtain an economically appropriate level of compliance from regulated firms. Second, private enforcement must promote a higher level of compliance without costing more than its incremental benefits.

In order to make these determinations in particular cases, judges would have to measure and weigh numerous variables that are usually inaccessible to courts—including the relative costs of, incentives for, and effectiveness of public and private enforcement. To perform such a calculus in each case would be absurd: decisional costs would be high and the risk of error substantial. Rules of thumb are required that can be applied to decide individual cases. The following issues must be addressed in developing such rough guidelines:

[Editor—The authors list six criteria: (1) whether the statutory norm promotes efficiency; (2) whether additional compliance with the norm is efficient; (3) whether enforcement costs exceed benefits of additional compliance; (4) whether private enforcement produces serious problems of over inclusiveness, resulting from the fact that statutory standards are often over inclusive; (5) whether nonuniform enforcement resulting from private remedies is undesirable; and (6) whether costly private enforcement is still cheaper than public enforcement. They conclude that the six criteria can more easily justify inferring a private cause of action from criminal than regulatory statutes.]

Victim Compensation Remedies for Criminal Violations.—The classic example of a judicially created private right of action is a common law decision to extend civil damage remedies to a person injured by the violation of a criminal statute designed to protect a class of which he is a member. In this context, the argument that the legislature has made careful calibrations to ensure a particular level of compliance is unpersuasive, both because of the enormous discretion afforded in the criminal enforcement process and because the prosecutor enforces hundreds of statutes for which he generally receives funding on a lump-sum basis.

Moreover, the six efficiency-related criteria all normally point in favor of private rights of action for victim compensation. Traditional criminal prohibitions parallel common law entitlements; increased compliance with these prohibitions tends to advance production. The remedy is available only to a limited beneficiary class for whom the costs of identifying and proving harm will be comparatively low. Constitutional strictures of overbroad criminal statutes reduce the danger of overinclusiveness; similarly, procedural safeguards and over-breadth doctrines mitigate the need for coordinated enforcement by reducing the likelihood of inconsistent application. And the victim compensation hedge serves to limit overdeterrence and excessive enforcement costs. [Editor—The victim compensation hedge arises from requiring plaintiffs to bear their own litigation expenses.]

Victim Compensation Actions Under Regulatory Statutes.—After the creation of regulatory agencies, litigants often sought victim compensation remedies for violations of regulatory prohibitions. Under the production conception, however, this extension is not always desirable; private enforcement of regulatory statutes is less likely to be efficient than is private enforcement of criminal statutes. Because the stigma associated with regulatory violations is less than that associated with crimes, society is willing to tolerate over inclusive regulatory standards. Moreover, overbreadth is inevitable when agencies are given responsibility to supervise an entire sector of the economy under changing conditions. Finally, unlike the criminal law, regulation is often prompted by the need for coordinated and centralized enforcement; decentralized private enforcement undercuts that goal.

Courts have been sensitive to these problems. They tend to refuse to create private rights of action when broadly phrased regulatory statutes delegate "planning" responsibility, require specialized experience and resources for implementation, or necessitate coordinated enforcement. * * *

Stewart and Sunstein note and generally dismiss the objection that inferring a private cause of action may disrupt legislative fine-tuning of a regulatory program. They doubt that the legislature has made a finely-tuned decision in the common case of a general or ambiguous statutory text. They do, however, give credence to another objection.

Private rights of action circumvent administrative responsibility for regulatory policy. Litigants asserting such rights can force courts to define the content of necessarily overbroad regulatory statutes, thereby undermining the advantages of political accountability, specialization, and centralization that administrative regulation was designed to provide. Private rights of action may also impair an agency's ability to harmonize potentially conflicting statutory provisions and to negotiate with regulated firms and other affected interests in order to establish a workable and consistent regulatory system.

    * * * [W]hen the governing statute is vague or ambiguous and when centralized and coordinated enforcement appears to be critical to the regulatory scheme, judicial creation of private rights of action should be discouraged.

The authors note that the lower federal courts have greatly expanded the availability of private rights of action under regulatory statutes over the past fifteen years, but that the Supreme Court has begun to severely restrict the availability of private remedies in a wide variety of regulatory contexts. They state that these "decisions apparently reflect a general perception that the expansion of private rights of action, in association with the proliferation of regulation during the past fifteen years, has resulted in overdeterrence and excessive enforcement costs."

Entitlement. Stewart and Sunstein find that

[t]he Supreme Court and the lower federal courts have [ ] continued to recognize private rights of action when litigants have challenged discrimination (against minority group members, women, or the handicapped), protested the failure to pay minimum wages or to provide adequate working conditions, or sought to redress restriction of voting rights. These decisions do not seek to enhance production, for they involve norms whose enforcement often does not promote efficiency; moreover, they present potentially severe problems of overinclusiveness and overdeterrence. The decisions instead reflect a conception of entitlement that still has tenacious hold in the area of "personal rights."

They note an important difference between welfare entitlements and rights derived from regulatory programs. Welfare involves bilateral relationships (the government and the claimant), but regulatory programs involve a trilateral relation among government, regulatory beneficiary, and regulated entity. They conclude that the entitlement conception justifies a private right of action when the statute grants protection to an identifiable beneficiary class and the legislature has not expressly precluded private rights of action. They further conclude that a few rights, such as the freedom from racial discrimination, may justify inferring personal entitlements from a statute in all events.

14.02 FEDERAL STATUTES

a) ANALYTICAL FRAMEWORK

As Stewart and Sunstein note, the Supreme Court is becoming more reluctant to infer a private cause of action. At this point in the course, you should not find this surprising. With the growth of statute lawmaking, courts no longer casually assume a "common law" power to supplement statutes. We saw this evolution in the Court's attitude towards admiralty law in Chapter 13. However, the analytical framework for changing the judicial approach is very controversial.

First, in the case of older statutes adopted when courts generously inferred a private cause of action, *denying* a cause of action requires applying background considerations which *postdate* the statute's adoption. This is not a problem for judges who believe that statutes can evolve along with background considerations. But it is not an easy task for a "conservative" judge, who prefers to anchor interpretation in the statute's historical setting, rather than post-passage evolution. What is the "conservative" judge's likely response to this concern?

Second, the Court's pronouncements have clearly changed the background against which statutes are adopted. A context-oriented interpreter can no longer assume that a newer statute incorporates judicial power to infer a private cause of action. At the very least, Cort v. Ash is the context for post–1975 statutes, except for those mechanically reenacted. Certainly, a contemporary legislator who paid any attention to what the Court has done might predict that the "conservative" judicial position would prevail and would include an explicit provision for a private cause of action, if that were truly intended. The context-oriented interpreter is therefore less able to assume that congressional silence supports inferring a private cause of action in more recent statutes.

Third, assuming that the approach to inferring a private cause of action should evolve, what are its limits? Should the Court stop with Cort v. Ash; adopt Justice Scalia's rejection of an implied cause of action if the text is silent; or follow the complex "it all depends" approach advocated by Stewart and Sunstein; or something else?

These complex strands of analysis come together in the following judicial opinions. Which analysis do the judges adopt?

b) SUPREME COURT CASES

i) CIVIL RIGHTS

Cannon v. University of Chicago

441 U.S. 677 (1979).

■ Mr. Justice Stevens delivered the opinion of the Court. * * *

Only two facts alleged in the complaints are relevant to our decision. First, petitioner was excluded from participation in the respondents' medical education programs because of her sex. Second, these education programs were receiving federal financial assistance at the time of her exclusion. These facts, admitted *arguendo* by respondents' motion to dismiss the complaints, establish a violation of § 901(a) of Title IX of the Education Amendments of 1972 (hereinafter Title IX).

That section, in relevant part, provides:

> "No person in the United States shall, on the basis of sex, be excluded from participation in, be denied the benefits of, or be subjected to discrimination under any education program or activity receiving Federal financial assistance * * *."

The statute does not, however, expressly authorize a private right of action by a person injured by a violation of § 901. For that reason, and because it concluded that no private remedy should be inferred, the District Court granted the respondents' motions to dismiss.

The Court of Appeals agreed that the statute did not contain an implied private remedy. * * *

The Court of Appeals quite properly devoted careful attention to this question of statutory construction. As our recent cases—particularly Cort v. Ash—demonstrate, the fact that a federal statute has been violated and some person harmed does not automatically give rise to a private cause of action in favor of that person. Instead, before concluding that Congress intended to make a remedy available to a special class of litigants, a court must carefully analyze the four factors that Cort identifies as indicative of such an intent. Our review of those factors persuades us, however, that the Court of Appeals reached the wrong conclusion and that petitioner does have a statutory right to pursue her claim that respondents rejected her application on the basis of her sex. After commenting on each of the four factors, we shall explain why they are not overcome by respondents' countervailing arguments.

First, the threshold question under Cort is whether the statute was enacted for the benefit of a special class of which the plaintiff is a member. That question is answered by looking to the language of the statute itself. * * *

* * * [I]t was statutory language describing the special class to be benefited by § 5 of the Voting Rights Act of 1965 that persuaded the Court that private parties within that class were implicitly authorized to seek a declaratory judgment against a covered State. The dispositive language in that statute—"no person shall be denied the right to vote for failure to comply with [a new state enactment covered by, but not approved under, § 5]"—is remarkably similar to the language used by Congress in Title IX.

The language in these statutes—which expressly identifies the class Congress intended to benefit—contrasts sharply with statutory language customarily found in criminal statutes, such as that construed in Cort, supra, and other laws enacted for the protection of the general public. There would be far less reason to infer a private remedy in favor of individual persons if Congress, instead of drafting

Title IX with an unmistakable focus on the benefited class, had written it simply as a ban on discriminatory conduct by recipients of federal funds or as a prohibition against the disbursement of public funds to educational institutions engaged in discriminatory practices.

Unquestionably, therefore, the first of the four factors identified in Cort favors the implication of a private cause of action. Title IX explicitly confers a benefit on persons discriminated against on the basis of sex, and petitioner is clearly a member of that class for whose special benefit the statute was enacted.

Second, the Cort analysis requires consideration of legislative history. We must recognize, however, that the legislative history of a statute that does not expressly create or deny a private remedy will typically be equally silent or ambiguous on the question. Therefore, in situations such as the present one "in which it is clear that federal law has granted a class of persons certain rights, it is not necessary to show an intention to *create* a private cause of action, although an explicit purpose to *deny* such cause of action would be controlling." But this is not the typical case. Far from evidencing any purpose to *deny* a private cause of action, the history of Title IX rather plainly indicates that Congress intended to create such a remedy. [Editor— Discussion of legislative history omitted.] * * *

Third, under Cort, a private remedy should not be implied if it would frustrate the underlying purpose of the legislative scheme. On the other hand, when that remedy is necessary or at least helpful to the accomplishment of the statutory purpose, the Court is decidedly receptive to its implication under the statute.

Title IX, like its model Title VI, sought to accomplish two related, but nevertheless somewhat different, objectives. First, Congress wanted to avoid the use of federal resources to support discriminatory practices; second, it wanted to provide individual citizens effective protection against those practices. Both of these purposes were repeatedly identified in the debates on the two statutes.

The first purpose is generally served by the statutory procedure for the termination of federal financial support for institutions engaged in discriminatory practices. That remedy is, however, severe and often may not provide an appropriate means of accomplishing the second purpose if merely an isolated violation has occurred. In that situation, the violation might be remedied more efficiently by an order requiring an institution to accept an applicant who had been improperly excluded. Moreover, in that kind of situation it makes little sense to impose on an individual, whose only interest is in obtaining a benefit for herself, or on HEW, the burden of demonstrating that an institution's practices are so pervasively discriminatory that a complete cutoff of federal funding is appropriate. The award of individual relief to a private litigant who has prosecuted her own suit is not only sensible but is also fully consistent with—and in some cases even necessary to—the orderly enforcement of the statute. * * *

Fourth, the final inquiry suggested by Cort is whether implying a federal remedy is inappropriate because the subject matter involves an area basically of concern to the States. No such problem is raised by a prohibition against invidious discrimination of any sort, including that on the basis of sex. Since the Civil War, the Federal Government and the federal courts have been the " '*primary* and powerful reliances' " in protecting citizens against such discrimination. Moreover, it is the expenditure of federal funds that provide the justification for this particular statutory prohibition. There can be no question but that this aspect of the Cort analysis supports the implication of a private federal remedy.

In sum, there is no need in this case to weigh the four Cort factors; all of them support the same result. Not only the words and history of Title IX, but also its subject matter and underlying purposes, counsel implication of a cause of action in favor of private victims of discrimination. * * *

When Congress intends private litigants to have a cause of action to support their statutory rights, the far better course is for it to specify as much when it creates those rights. But the Court has long recognized that under certain limited circumstances the failure of Congress to do so is not inconsistent with an intent on its part to have such a remedy available to the persons benefited by its legislation. Title IX presents the atypical situation in which *all* of the circumstances that the Court has previously identified as supportive of an implied remedy are present. We therefore conclude that petitioner may maintain her lawsuit, despite the absence of any express authorization for it in the statute.

■ Mr. Justice Powell, dissenting.

* * * The time has come to reappraise our standards for the judicial implication of private causes of action.

Under Art. III, Congress alone has the responsibility for determining the jurisdiction of the lower federal courts. As the Legislative Branch, Congress also should determine when private parties are to be given causes of action under legislation it adopts. As countless statutes demonstrate, including Titles of the Civil Rights Act of 1964, Congress recognizes that the creation of private actions is a legislative function and frequently exercises it. When Congress chooses not to provide a private civil remedy, federal courts should not assume the legislative role of creating such a remedy and thereby enlarge their jurisdiction.

The facts of this case illustrate the undesirability of this assumption by the Judicial Branch of the legislative function. Whether every disappointed applicant for admission to a college or university receiving federal funds has the right to a civil-court remedy under

Title IX is likely to be a matter of interest to many of the thousands of rejected applicants. It certainly is a question of vast importance to the entire higher educational community of this country. But quite apart from the interests of the persons and institutions affected, respect for our constitutional system dictates that the issue should have been resolved by the elected representatives in Congress after public hearings, debate, and legislative decision. It is not a question properly to be decided by relatively uninformed federal judges who are isolated from the political process.

In recent history, the Court has tended to stray from the Art. III and separation-of-powers principle of limited jurisdiction. This, I believe, is evident from a review of the more or less haphazard line of cases that led to our decision in Cort v. Ash. The "four factor" analysis of that case is an open invitation to federal courts to legislate causes of action not authorized by Congress. It is an analysis not faithful to constitutional principles and should be rejected. Absent the most compelling evidence of affirmative congressional intent, a federal court should not infer a private cause of action.

The implying of a private action from a federal regulatory statute has been an exceptional occurrence in the past history of this Court. A review of those few decisions where such a step has been taken reveals in almost every case special historical circumstances that explain the result, if not the Court's analysis. These decisions suggest that the doctrine of implication applied by the Court today not only represents judicial assumption of the legislative function, but also lacks a principled precedential basis.

The origin of implied private causes of actions in the federal courts is said to date back to Texas & Pacific Ry. Co. v. Rigsby, 241 U.S. 33 (1916). A close look at the facts of that case and the contemporary state of the law indicates, however, that Rigsby's reference to the "inference of a private right of action," carried a far different connotation than the isolated passage quoted by the Court, might suggest. The narrow question presented for decision was whether the standards of care defined by the Federal Safety Appliance Act's penal provisions applied to a tort action brought against an interstate railroad by an employee not engaged in interstate commerce at the time of his injury. * * * The practice of judicial reference to legislatively determined standards of care was a common expedient to establish the existence of negligence. Rigsby did nothing more than follow this practice, and cannot be taken as authority for the judicial creation of a cause of action not legislated by Congress. * * *

During [the 50 year period after Rigsby], the Court frequently turned back private plaintiffs seeking to imply causes of action from federal statutes. * * *

A break in this pattern occurred in J. I. Case Co. v. Borak, 377 U.S. 426 (1964). There the Court held that a private party could maintain a cause of action under § 14(a) of the Securities Exchange Act of 1934, in spite of Congress' express creation of an administrative mechanism for enforcing that statute. I find this decision both unprecedented and incomprehensible as a matter of public policy. The decision's rationale, which lies ultimately in the judgment that "[p]rivate enforcement of the proxy rules provides a necessary supplement to Commission action," ignores the fact that Congress, in determining the degree of regulation to be imposed on companies covered by the Securities Exchange Act, already had decided that private enforcement was unnecessary. More significant for present purposes, however, is the fact that Borak, rather than signaling the start of a trend in this Court, constitutes a singular and, I believe, aberrant interpretation of a federal regulatory statute. * * *

[Editor—Justice Stevens, in Merrill Lynch, Pierce, Fenner & Smith, Inc. v. Curran, 456 U.S. 353, 376–77 (1982), took a different view of the post-Rigsby history. "During the years prior to 1975, the Court occasionally refused to recognize an implied remedy, either because the statute in question was a general regulatory prohibition enacted for the benefit of the public at large, or because there was evidence that Congress intended an express remedy to provide the exclusive method of enforcement. While the Rigsby approach prevailed, however, congressional silence or ambiguity was an insufficient reason for the denial of remedy for a member of the class a statute was enacted to protect."]

These few cases applying Borak must be contrasted with the subsequent decisions where the Court refused to imply private actions. * * *

It was against this background of almost invariable refusal to imply private actions, absent a complete failure of alternative enforcement mechanisms and a clear expression of legislative intent to create such a remedy, that Cort v. Ash was decided. In holding that no private action could be brought to enforce 18 U.S.C. § 610, a criminal statute, the Court referred to four factors said to be relevant to determining generally whether private actions could be implied. As Mr. Justice White suggests, these factors were meant only as guideposts for answering a single question, namely whether Congress intended to provide a private cause of action. The conclusion in that particular case was obvious. But, as the opinion of the Court today demonstrates, the Cort analysis too easily may be used to deflect inquiry away from the intent of Congress, and to permit a court instead to substitute its own views as to the desirability of private enforcement.

Of the four factors mentioned in Cort, only one refers expressly to legislative intent. The other three invite independent judicial lawmaking. Asking whether a statute creates a right in favor of a private party, for example, begs the question at issue. What is involved is not the mere existence of a legal right, but a particular person's right to invoke the power of the courts to enforce that right. Determining whether a private action would be consistent with the "underlying purposes" of a legislative scheme permits a court to decide for itself what the goals of a scheme should be, and how those goals should be advanced. Finally, looking to state law for parallels to the federal right simply focuses inquiry on a particular policy consideration that Congress already may have weighed in deciding not to create a private action. * * *

In my view, the implication doctrine articulated in Cort and applied by the Court today engenders incomparably greater problems than the possibility of occasionally failing to divine an unexpressed congressional intent. If only a matter of statutory construction were involved, our obligation might be to develop more refined criteria which more accurately reflect congressional intent. "But the unconstitutionality of the course pursued has now been made clear" and compels us to abandon the implication doctrine of Cort. Erie R. Co. v. Tompkins, 304 U.S. 64, 77–78 (1938).

* * * Cort allows the Judicial Branch to assume policymaking authority vested by the Constitution in the Legislative Branch. It also invites Congress to avoid resolution of the often controversial question whether a new regulatory statute should be enforced through private litigation. Rather than confronting the hard political choices involved, Congress is encouraged to shirk its constitutional obligation and leave the issue to the courts to decide. When this happens, the legislative process with its public scrutiny and participation has been bypassed, with attendant prejudice to everyone concerned. Because the courts are free to reach a result different from that which the normal play of political forces would have produced, the intended beneficiaries of the legislation are unable to ensure the full measure of protection their needs may warrant. For the same reason, those subject to the legislative constraints are denied the opportunity to forestall through the political process potentially unnecessary and disruptive litigation. Moreover, the public generally is denied the benefits that are derived from the making of important societal choices through the open debate of the democratic process.

The Court's implication doctrine encourages, as a corollary to the political default by Congress, an increase in the governmental power exercised by the federal judiciary. The dangers posed by judicial arrogation of the right to resolve general societal conflicts have been manifest to this Court throughout its history. * * *

Congress already has created a mechanism for enforcing the mandate found in Title IX against gender-based discrimination. At least in the view of Congress, the fund-termination power conferred on HEW is adequate to ensure that discrimination in federally funded colleges and universities will not be countenanced. The current position of the Government notwithstanding, overlapping judicial and administrative enforcement of these policies inevitably will lead to conflicts and confusion; our national goal of equal opportunity for men and women, as well as the academic community, may suffer. A federal court should resolve all doubts against this kind of self-aggrandizement, regardless of the temptation to lend its assistance to the furtherance of some remedial end deemed attractive.

ii) ENVIRONMENTAL LAW

Middlesex County Sewerage Authority v. National Sea Clammers

453 U.S. 1 (1981).

■ Justice Powell delivered the opinion of the Court.

In these cases, involving alleged damage to fishing grounds caused by discharges and ocean dumping of sewage and other waste, we are faced with questions concerning the availability of a damages remedy, based * * * on the provisions of two Acts—the Federal Water Pollution Control Act (FWPCA), 86 Stat. 816, as amended, 33 U.S.C. § 1251 et seq. (1976 ed. and Supp. III), and the Marine Protection, Research, and Sanctuaries Act of 1972 (MPRSA), 86 Stat. 1052, as amended, 33 U.S.C. § 1401 et seq. (1976 ed. and Supp. III). * * *

It is unnecessary to discuss at length the principles set out in recent decisions concerning the recurring question whether Congress intended to create a private right of action under a federal statute without saying so explicitly. The key to the inquiry is the intent of the Legislature. We look first, of course, to the statutory language, particularly to the provisions made therein for enforcement and relief. Then we review the legislative history and other traditional aids of statutory interpretation to determine congressional intent.

These Acts contain unusually elaborate enforcement provisions, conferring authority to sue for this purpose both on government officials and private citizens. The FWPCA, for example, authorizes the EPA Administrator to respond to violations of the Act with compliance orders and civil suits. § 309, 33 U.S.C. § 1319. He may seek a civil penalty of up to $10,000 per day, § 309(d), 33 U.S.C. § 1319(d), and criminal penalties also are available, § 309(c), 33 U.S.C. § 1319(c). States desiring to administer their own permit programs must demonstrate that state officials possess adequate authority to abate violations through civil or criminal penalties or other means of enforcement. § 402 (b)(7), 33 U.S.C. § 1342 (b)(7). In addition, under § 509(b), 33 U.S.C. § 1369(b), "any interested person" may seek judicial review in the United States courts of appeals of various particular actions by the Administrator, including establishment of effluent standards and issuance of permits for discharge of pollutants. Where review could have been obtained under this provision, the action at issue may not be challenged in any subsequent civil or criminal proceeding for enforcement. § 1369(b)(2).

These enforcement mechanisms, most of which have their counterpart under the MPRSA, are supplemented by the express citizen-suit provisions in § 505(a) of the FWPCA, 33 U.S.C. § 1365(a), and § 105(g) of the MPRSA, 33 U.S.C. § 1415(g). These citizen-suit provisions authorize private persons to sue for injunctions to enforce these statutes. Plaintiffs invoking these provisions first must comply with specified procedures—which respondents here ignored—including in most cases 60 days' prior notice to potential defendants.

In view of these elaborate enforcement provisions it cannot be assumed that Congress intended to authorize by implication additional judicial remedies for private citizens suing under MPRSA and FWPCA. * * * In the absence of strong indicia of a contrary congressional intent, we are compelled to conclude that Congress provided precisely the remedies it considered appropriate. * * *

■ Justice Stevens, with whom Justice Blackmun joins, concurring in the judgment in part and dissenting in part.

When should a person injured by a violation of federal law be allowed to recover his damages in a federal court? This seemingly simple question has recently presented the Court with more difficulty than most substantive questions that come before us. During most of our history, however, a simple presumption usually provided the answer. Although criminal laws and legislation enacted for the benefit of the public at large were expected to be enforced by public officials, a statute enacted for the benefit of a special class presumptively afforded a remedy for members of that class injured by violations of the statute. Applying the presumption, our truly conservative federal judges—men like Justice Harlan, Justice Clark, Justice Frankfurter, and Judge Kirkpatrick—readily concluded that it was appropriate to allow private parties who had been injured by a violation of a statute enacted for their special benefit to obtain judicial relief. For rules are meant to be obeyed, and those who violate them should be held responsible for their misdeeds. Since the earliest days of the common law, it has been the business of courts to fashion remedies for wrongs.

In recent years, however, a Court that is properly concerned about the burdens imposed upon the federal judiciary, the quality of the work product of Congress, and the sheer bulk of new federal legislation, has been more and more reluctant to open the courthouse door to the injured citizen. In 1975, in Cort v. Ash, 422 U.S. 66, the Court cut back on the simple common-law presumption by fashioning a four-factor formula that led to the denial of relief in that case. Although multifactor balancing tests generally tend to produce negative answers, more recently some Members of the Court have been inclined to deny relief with little more than a perfunctory nod to the Cort v. Ash factors. The touchstone now is congressional intent. Because legislative history is unlikely to reveal affirmative evidence of a congressional intent to authorize a specific procedure that the statute itself fails to mention, that touchstone will further restrict the availability of private remedies.

Although I agree with the Court's disposition of the implied-private-right-of-action question in these cases, I write separately to emphasize that the Court's current approach to the judicial task of fashioning appropriate remedies for violations of federal statutes is out of step with the Court's own history and tradition. * * *

* * * I agree with the Court's holding that neither [FWPCA or MPRSA] implicitly authorizes a private damages remedy, [but] I reach that conclusion by a different route. Under the traditional common-law analysis, the primary question is whether the statute was enacted for the special benefit of a particular class of which the plaintiff is a member. As we have held in the past, "[t]hat question is answered by looking to the language of the statute itself." Cannon v. University of Chicago, 441 U.S. 677, 689.

The language of neither [statute] defines any such special class. Both the substantive provisions of these statutes and the breadth of their authorizations of citizen suits indicate that they were "enacted for the protection of the general public." Thus, even under the more liberal approach to implied rights of action * * *, respondents cannot invoke implied private remedies under these statutes. [Editor—FWPCA made it "unlawful for any person to discharge a pollutant without obtaining a permit * * *;" MPRSA requires a permit for dumping into ocean waters.]

QUESTIONS

1. What does Justice Stevens mean when he says that a "congressional intent" test has replaced reliance on Cort v. Ash? What is the difference between focusing on congressional intent and relying on the Cort v. Ash criteria?

2. How might Stewart and Sunstein analyze the issue in Middlesex? Would they use a production or entitlement rationale?

iii) SECURITIES LAW

Merrill Lynch, Pierce, Fenner & Smith, Inc. v. Curran
456 U.S. 353 (1982).

■ Mr. Justice Stevens delivered the opinion of the Court. * * *

[Editor—For over 60 years, Congress had regulated commodity futures exchanges. The original statute was passed in 1921 and was then rewritten to deal with objections to its constitutionality. Changes were made in 1936, 1968 and 1974. The basic statute is the Commodities Exchange Act (CEA). The issue in the case was whether the Act created an implied right of action for fraud in favor of a customer against his broker. The relevant statutory language was adopted in 1936, stating: "It shall be unlawful (1) for any member of a contract market (and certain others) * * * to make * * * any contract of sale of any commodity * * * for or on behalf of any other person * * * (A) to cheat or defraud * * * such other person * * *."

Does Justice Stevens accept the "congressional intent" approach in the following opinion, implicitly abandoning Cort v. Ash? If so, (1) why, and (2) do his reasons differ from Justice Powell's?]

In 1974, after extensive hearings and deliberation, Congress enacted the Commodity Futures Trading Commission Act of 1974. 88 Stat. 1389. Like the 1936 and the 1968 legislation, the 1974 enactment was an amendment to the existing statute that broadened its coverage and increased the penalties for violation of its provisions. The Commission was authorized to seek injunctive relief, to alter or supplement a contract market's rules, and to direct a contract market to take whatever action deemed necessary by the Commission in an emergency. The 1974 legislation retained the basic statutory prohibitions against fraudulent practices and price manipulation, as well as the authority to prescribe trading limits. The 1974 amendments, however, did make substantial changes in the statutory scheme; Congress authorized a newly created Commodities Futures Trading Commission to assume the powers previously exercised by the Secretary of Agriculture, as well as certain additional powers. The enactment also added two new remedial provisions for the protection of individual traders. The newly enacted § 5a(11) required every contract market to provide an arbitration procedure for the settlement of traders' claims of no more than $15,000. And the newly enacted § 14 authorized the Commission to grant reparations to any person complaining of any violation of the CEA, or its implementing regulations, committed by any futures commission merchant or any associate thereof, floor broker, commodity trading adviser, or commodity pool operator. This section authorized the Commission to investigate complaints and, "if in its opinion the facts warrant such action," to afford a hearing before an administrative law judge. Reparations orders entered by the Commission are subject to judicial review.

The latest amendments to the CEA, the Futures Trading Act of 1978, 92 Stat. 865, again increased the penalties for violations of the statute. The enactment also authorized the States to bring *parens patriae* actions, seeking injunctive or monetary relief for certain violations of the CEA, implementing regulations, or Commission orders.

Like the previous enactments, as well as the 1978 amendments, the Commodity Futures Trading Commission Act of 1974 is silent on the subject of private judicial remedies for persons injured by a violation of the CEA. * * *

* * * For the purpose of considering the question whether respondents may assert an implied cause of action for damages, it is assumed that each of the petitioners has violated the statute and thereby caused respondents' alleged injuries. * * *

Our approach to the task of determining whether Congress intended to authorize a private cause of action has changed significantly, much as the quality and quantity of federal legislation has undergone significant change. When federal statutes were less comprehensive, the Court applied a relatively simple test to determine the availability of an implied private remedy. If a statute was enacted for the benefit of a special class, the judiciary normally recognized a remedy for members of that class. Under this approach, federal courts, following a common-law tradition, regarded the denial of a remedy as the exception rather than the rule.

Because the Rigsby approach prevailed throughout most of our history, there is no merit to the argument advanced by petitioners that the judicial recognition of an implied private remedy violates the separation-of-powers doctrine. * * *

In 1975 the Court unanimously decided to modify its approach to the question whether a federal statute includes a private right of action [in Cort v. Ash]. * * * The increased complexity of federal legislation and the increased volume of federal litigation strongly supported the desirability of a more careful scrutiny of legislative intent than Rigsby had required. Our cases subsequent to Cort v. Ash have plainly stated that our focus must be on "the intent of Congress." "The key to the inquiry is the intent of the Legislature." Middlesex County Sewerage Auth. v. National Sea Clammers Assn., 453 U.S. 1, 13 (1981). The key to these cases is our understanding of the intent of Congress in 1974 when it comprehensively reexamined and strengthened the federal regulation of futures trading. * * *

Prior to the comprehensive amendments to the CEA enacted in 1974, the federal courts routinely and consistently had recognized an implied private cause of action on behalf of plaintiffs seeking to enforce and to collect damages for violation of provisions of the CEA or rules and regulations promulgated pursuant to the statute. * * *

In view of the absence of any dispute about the proposition prior to the decision of Cort v. Ash in 1975, it is abundantly clear that an implied cause of action under the CEA was a part of the "contemporary legal context" in which Congress legislated in 1974. In that context, the fact that a comprehensive reexamination and significant amendment of the CEA left intact the statutory provisions under which the federal courts had implied a cause of action is itself evidence that Congress affirmatively intended to preserve that remedy. * * *

In view of our construction of the intent of the Legislature there is no need for us to "trudge through all four of the factors when the dispositive question of legislative intent has been resolved." We hold that the private cause of action under the CEA that was previously available to investors survived the 1974 amendments.

Justice Powell dissented. He objected to the Court's use of lower court decisions as pre–1974 context because this would force Congress to respond to lower court opinions. He read the 1974 amendments to the Commodity Exchange Act as a congressional effort to prescribe precisely what remedies were available.

c) Post–Cort v. Ash Statutes

In Karahalios v. National Federation of Federal Employees, 489 U.S. 527 (1989), the Court held unanimously that a 1978 statute did *not* create a cause of action for federal employees who objected to a union's breach of the statutory duty of fair representation towards a nonunion member. The statute states that the union "is responsible for representing the interests of all employees in the unit it represents without regard to labor organization membership." The statute created administrative remedies before the Federal Labor Relations Authority and the Court stated that "courts must be especially reluctant to provide additional remedies," citing Middlesex. Moreover, the statute codified an Executive Order under which courts had played no pre-existing role, so there was no pattern of judicial enforcement which Congress might arguably have preserved. The Court reiterated the "legislative intent" standard but came close to adopting a "plain statement" requirement for creating a private cause of action for post-Cort v. Ash statutes.

* * * Congress undoubtedly was aware from our cases such as Cort v. Ash, 422 U.S. 66 (1975), that the Court had departed from its prior standard for resolving a claim urging that an implied statutory cause of action should be recognized, and that such issues were being resolved by a straightforward inquiry into whether Congress intended to provide a private cause of action. Had Congress intended the courts to enforce a federal employees union's duty of fair representation, we would expect to find some evidence of that intent in the statute or its legislative history. We find none.

See also Thompson v. Thompson, 484 U.S. 174, 189 (1988)(Scalia, J., concurring in the judgment):

* * * It could not be plainer that we effectively overruled the Cort v. Ash analysis in [earlier cases], converting one of its four

factors (congressional intent) into *the determinative factor*, with the other three merely indicative of its presence of absence.

In Thompson, the Court's majority had claimed that there was still life in the Cort v. Ash test, stating:

As guides to discerning [legislative] intent, we have relied on the four factors set out in Cort v. Ash, along with other tools of interpretation. Our focus on congressional intent does not mean that we require evidence that Members of Congress, in enacting the statute, actually had in mind the creation of a private cause of action. The implied cause of action doctrine would be a virtual dead letter were it limited to correcting drafting errors when Congress simply forgot to codify its evident intention to provide a cause of action. Rather, as an *implied* cause of action doctrine suggests, "the legislative history of a statute that does not expressly create or deny a private remedy will typically be equally silent or ambiguous on the question." We therefore have recognized that Congress' "intent may appear implicitly in the language or structure of the statute, or in the circumstance of its enactment."

Justice Scalia objected to the majority's opinion in Thompson on the ground that it was a "Delphic pronouncement that intent is required but need not really exist." Elsewhere in his Thompson opinion, Scalia advocated "a flat rule that private rights of action will not be implied in statutes hereafter enacted."

In the following case, the majority refuses to infer a private cause of action for *aiding and abetting* a violation of the Securities laws, purporting to apply the accepted methodology for inferring private remedies from statutes. Justice Stevens in dissent argues that the Court is applying the new methodology (which should be applicable only to recent legislation) to an older statute.

Central Bank of Denver v. First Interstate Bank of Denver

511 U.S. 164 (1994).

■ Justice Kennedy delivered the opinion of the Court.

As we have interpreted it, § 10(b) of the Securities Exchange Act of 1934 imposes private civil liability on those who commit a manipulative or deceptive act in connection with the purchase or sale of securities. In this case, we must answer a question reserved in two earlier decisions: whether private civil liability under § 10(b) extends as well to those who do not engage in the manipulative or deceptive practice but who aid and abet the violation. * * *

In our cases addressing § 10(b) and Rule 10b–5, we have confronted two main issues. First, we have determined the scope of conduct prohibited by § 10(b). Second, in cases where the defendant has committed a violation of § 10(b), we have decided questions about the elements of the 10b–5 private liability scheme: for example, whether there is a right to contribution, what the statute of limitations is, whether there is a reliance requirement, and whether there is an in pari delicto defense.

The latter issue, determining the elements of the 10b–5 private liability scheme, has posed difficulty because Congress did not create a private § 10(b) cause of action and had no occasion to provide guidance about the elements of a private liability scheme. We thus have had "to infer how the 1934 Congress would have addressed the issue[s] had the 10b–5 action been included as an express provision in the 1934 Act."

With respect, however, to the first issue, the scope of conduct prohibited by § 10(b), the text of the statute controls our decision. In § 10(b), Congress prohibited manipulative or deceptive acts in connection with the purchase or sale of securities. It envisioned that the SEC would enforce the statutory prohibition through administrative and injunctive actions. Of course, a private plaintiff now may bring suit against violators of § 10(b). But the private plaintiff may not bring a 10b–5 suit against a defendant for acts not prohibited by the text of § 10(b). To the contrary, our cases considering the scope of conduct prohibited by § 10(b) in private suits have emphasized adherence to the statutory language, " '[t]he starting point in every case involving construction of a statute.' " We have refused to allow 10b–5 challenges to conduct not prohibited by the text of the statute. [Editor—Discussion of securities cases omitted.] * * *

Our consideration of statutory duties, especially in cases interpreting § 10(b), establishes that the statutory text controls the definition of conduct covered by § 10(b). That bodes ill for respondents, for "the language of Section 10(b) does not in terms mention aiding and abetting." Brief for SEC as Amicus Curiae 8 (hereinafter Brief for SEC). To overcome this problem, respondents and the SEC suggest (or hint at) the novel argument that the use of the phrase "directly or indirectly" in the text of § 10(b) covers aiding and abetting.

The federal courts have not relied on the "directly or indirectly" language when imposing aiding and abetting liability under § 10(b), and with good reason. There is a basic flaw with this interpretation. According to respondents and the SEC, the "directly or indirectly" language shows that "Congress * * * intended to reach all persons who engage, even if only indirectly, in proscribed activities connected with securities transactions." The problem, of course, is that aiding and abetting liability extends beyond persons who engage, even indirectly, in a proscribed activity; aiding and abetting liability reaches persons who do not engage in the proscribed activities at all, but who give a degree of aid to those who do. A further problem with respondents' interpretation of the "directly or indirectly" language is posed by the numerous provisions of the 1934 Act that use the term in a way that does not impose aiding and abetting liability. In short, respondents' interpretation of the "directly or indirectly" language fails to support their suggestion that the text of § 10(b) itself prohibits aiding and abetting.

Congress knew how to impose aiding and abetting liability when it chose to do so. See, e.g., Act of Mar. 4, 1909, § 332, 35 Stat. 1152, as amended, 18 U.S.C. § 2 (general criminal aiding and abetting statute); Packers and Stockyards Act, 1921, ch. 64, § 202, 42 Stat. 161, as amended, 7 U.S.C. § 192(g)(civil aiding and abetting provision). If, as respondents seem to say, Congress intended to impose aiding and abetting liability, we presume it would have used the words "aid" and "abet" in the statutory text. But it did not.

We reach the uncontroversial conclusion, accepted even by those courts recognizing a § 10(b) aiding and abetting cause of action, that the text of the 1934 Act does not itself reach those who aid and abet a § 10(b) violation. Unlike those courts, however, we think that conclusion resolves the case. It is inconsistent with settled methodology in § 10(b) cases to extend liability beyond the scope of conduct prohibited by the statutory text. To be sure, aiding and abetting a wrongdoer ought to be actionable in certain instances. Cf. Restatement (Second) of Torts s 876(b)(1977). The issue, however, is not whether imposing private civil liability on aiders and abettors is good policy but whether aiding and abetting is covered by the statute.

As in earlier cases considering conduct prohibited by § 10(b), we again conclude that the statute prohibits only the making of a material misstatement (or omission) or the commission of a manipulative act. The proscription does not include giving aid to a person who commits a manipulative or deceptive act. We cannot amend the statute to create liability for acts that are not themselves manipulative or deceptive within the meaning of the statute. * * *

Reversed.

■ Justice Stevens, with whom Justices Blackmun, Souter and Ginsburg join, dissenting. * * *

In hundreds of judicial and administrative proceedings in every circuit in the federal system, the courts and the SEC have concluded that aiders and abettors are subject to liability under § 10(b) and Rule 10b–5. While we have reserved decision on the legitimacy of the theory in two cases that did not present it, all 11 Courts of Appeals to have considered the question have recognized a private cause of action against aiders and abettors under § 10(b) and Rule 10b–5. The early aiding and abetting decisions relied upon principles borrowed from tort law; in those cases, judges closer to the times and climate of the 73d Congress than we concluded that holding aiders and abettors liable was consonant with the 1934 Act's purpose to strengthen the antifraud remedies of the common law. * * *

Many of the observations in the majority's opinion would be persuasive if we were considering whether to recognize a private right of action based upon a securities statute enacted recently. Our approach to implied causes of action, as to other matters of statutory construction, has changed markedly since the Exchange Act's passage in 1934. At that time, and indeed until quite recently, courts regularly assumed, in accord with the traditional common law presumption, that a statute enacted for the benefit of a particular class conferred on members of that class the right to sue violators of that statute. Moreover, shortly before the Exchange Act was passed, this Court instructed that such "remedial" legislation should receive "a broader and more liberal interpretation than that to be drawn from mere dictionary definitions of the words employed by Congress." Piedmont & Northern R. Co. v. ICC, 286 U.S. 299, 311 (1932). There is a risk of anachronistic error in applying our current approach to implied causes of action, to a statute enacted when courts commonly read statutes of this kind broadly to accord with their remedial purposes and regularly approved rights to sue despite statutory silence. * * *

d) CAUSE OF ACTION AND REMEDY

One of the ambiguities in this area of law is the distinction between implying a cause of action and determining what specific remedy (for example, injunction, back pay, monetary damages) a plaintiff can recover. In the following 1992 case, the Court decided that monetary damages are available *once a cause of action is inferred*, "absent clear direction to the contrary by Congress." Franklin v. Gwinnett County Public Schools, 503 U.S. 60 (1992). The case involved the implied cause of action under Title IX established by Cannon, *supra*, against a school which had failed to halt sexually-oriented conversation and forcible sexual contact by a teacher/coach and had discouraged the plaintiff's complaint. The Court held that

the question of what remedies are available under a statute that provides a private right of action is "analytically distinct" from the issue of whether such a right exists in the first place. Thus, although we examine the text and history of a statute to determine whether Congress intended to create a right of action, we presume the availability of all appropriate remedies unless Congress has expressly indicated otherwise. This principle has deep roots in our jurisprudence.

The Court identified those roots, as follows:

In Marbury v. Madison, 5 U.S. 137, 163 (1803), for example, Chief Justice Marshall observed that our government "has been emphatically termed a government of laws, and not of men. It will certainly cease to deserve this high appellation, if the laws furnish no remedy for the violation of a vested legal right." This principle originated in the English common law, and Blackstone described "it as a general and indisputable rule, that where there is a legal right, there is also a legal remedy, by suit or action at law, whenever that right is invaded."

The Court concluded that this tradition had not weakened in recent cases, distinguishing the question of inferring a cause of action from the right to monetary damages once a cause of action is implied. "The general rule, [ ] is that absent clear direction to the contrary by Congress, the federal courts have the power to award any appropriate relief in a cognizable cause of action brought pursuant to a federal statute."

The Court then finds no clear direction precluding monetary damages. Congressional silence did not argue against a damage remedy because "it is hardly surprising that Congress [ ] said nothing about the applicable remedies for an implied right of action."

Justice Scalia concurred in the judgment on the ground that a 1986 law abrogating State sovereign immunity in Title IX cases affirmed the existence of relief for monetary damages, but objected to the Court's analysis.

> In my view, when rights of action are judicially "implied," categorical limitations upon their remedial scope may be judicially implied as well. Although we have abandoned the expansive rights-creating approach exemplified by Cannon, and perhaps ought to abandon the notion of implied causes of action entirely, see Thompson v. Thompson, 484 U.S. 174, 191 (1988)(Scalia, J., concurring in judgment)—causes of action that came into existence under the ancien regime should be limited by the same logic that gave them birth. To require, with respect to a right that is not consciously and intentionally created, that any limitation of remedies must be express, is to provide, in effect, that the most questionable of private rights will also be the most expansively remediable.

QUESTIONS

1. How can you reconcile the Court's mechanical presumption that monetary damages are available, once the cause of action is implied, with its greater reluctance to infer a cause of action in the first place?

2. Do the factors favoring a cause of action automatically favor monetary damages? Perhaps they do for civil rights claims, such as those in Cannon and Franklin, but is that true in other areas of the law, such as environmental and securities law, discussed earlier? Aren't the problems of overdeterrence and consistency with the legislative scheme as relevant for deciding whether monetary damages are appropriate as for determining whether there is a cause of action in the first place?

3. Has the Court simply reached the outer limits of its ability to speculate about what should be implied from the statute, so it reverts to a clear presumption favoring monetary damages, once it has made the difficult decision to infer a cause of action?

e) ANALOGOUS SITUATIONS

Similar questions about whether to infer rights and remedies recur in other situations besides those discussed in this chapter but there is as yet no comprehensive approach integrating the rules in the various legal niches. Indeed, it is fair to say that the law is confused and the courts have not come close to resolving the tensions between creating legal obligations and designing appropriate enforcement techniques.

First, federal courts have created a money damage remedy for constitutional torts (under Bivens v. Six Unknown Federal Narcotics Agents, 403 U.S. 388 (1971)), arising when a *federal* government official violates *constitutional* rights. However, this damage remedy will not be inferred when Congress has provided what it considers adequate remedies, even if those remedies do not provide complete relief. Schweiker v. Chilicky, 487 U.S. 412 (1988).

Second, violations of *constitutional* rights by *state* government officials may give rise to a remedy in the form of an injunction against the official even if the state itself enjoys sovereign immunity. A recent Supreme Court case, however, held that the existence of other adequate remedies forecloses injunctive relief against a state official, citing the Schweiker v. Chilicky case. Seminole Tribe of Florida v. Florida, ___ U.S. ___, ___, 116 S.Ct. 1114, 1132 (1996).

Third, 42 U.S.C. § 1983 creates civil and injunction relief for a person subject "to the deprivation of any rights, privileges, or immunities secured by the Constitution and laws" by another person acting under color of any *state* law. The reference to "laws" in § 1983 invites the question whether there is a right created by another federal statute for which § 1983 provides a remedy. That can be important because attorney's fees can be recovered by a litigant in a § 1983 action and the remedies provided by the underlying statute may be less complete than under § 1983. The latest Supreme Court case is Suter v. Artist M., 503 U.S. 347 (1992), which appeared to cut back on a prior presumption in favor of a § 1983 cause of action.

The pre-Suter test under § 1983 had two prongs—(1) whether the other federal statute creates an enforceable right, and (2) whether the other federal statute foreclosed enforcement. The first prong of the pre-Suter test was applied very much like the first prong of Cort v. Ash—"whether the provision in question was intend[ed] to benefit" the plaintiff—subject to denial only if the provision expressed merely a congressional preference for conduct rather than a binding legal obligation, or the plaintiff's interest was "too vague or amorphous." The second prong sounds a lot like the emphasis on alternative enforcement procedures which has been relied on to identify congressional intent under Cort v. Ash.

In Suter, however, the Court held that the Adoption Assistance and Child Welfare Act of 1980 did not create a § 1983 cause of action. The decision rested on the first prong of the § 1983 analysis—no right was created by the Adoption Assistance and Child Welfare Act of 1980. That statute provided funds to the states on condition that they take reasonable efforts to prevent removal of children from their homes and facilitate reunification of families if removal occurred. The plaintiffs sought an injunction against state officials, based on their failure to make "reasonable efforts." The standard the Court used to deny that there was a § 1983 cause of action was as follows:

> Did Congress * * * unambiguously confer upon the child beneficiaries of the Act a right to enforce the requirement that the State make "reasonable efforts" to prevent a child from being removed from his home, and once removed to reunify the child with his family?

A prior case upholding a § 1983 cause of action was distinguished, on the ground that the "reasonable efforts" required from the State were set forth "in some detail."

Justice Stevens' dissent in Suter argued that the Court's § 1983 analysis had "changed the rules of the game without offering even minimal justification."

Lower courts have continued to struggle with the uncertainty created by these cases,[3] as well as trying to reconcile Suter with yet another case—Livadas v. Bradshaw, 512 U.S. 107, 115 (1994)—in which the Court stated: "§ 1983 remains a generally and presumptively available remedy for claimed violations of federal law."

14.03 JUDICIAL-LEGISLATIVE DIALOGUE

Methods of enforcement, such as a private cause of action, are among the many issues to which Congress could pay more careful attention when it adopts legislation. By this point in the course, you have seen many such examples, arising from the following:

(1) legislative carelessness, either in (a) drafting, (b) failing to consider the interaction between text, purpose, and specific fact situations, or (3) failing to address matters of detail (such as enforcement through private causes of action), and

(2) legislative failure to address problems of change.

In recent years, there have been several proposals to heighten congressional awareness and bring about legislative changes to fill gaps and correct

---

3. See case note on Freestone v. Cowan, 68 F.3d 1141 (9th Cir.1995), 109 Harv. L. Rev. 1451 (1996).

errors through improved judicial-legislative dialogue. These proposals, described below, are distantly related to earlier suggestions for a government body which would pay attention to what Judge Friendly referred to as problems which legislators won't address and judges can't resolve. Friendly, The Gap in Lawmaking—Judges Who Can't and Legislators Who Won't, 63 Colum. L. Rev. 787, 799–802, 805 (1963). Friendly noted that

> [t]he problem is not always a defect in a statute, be this ambiguity, the *casus omissus*, the case included that ought not to have been, or the statute that time has proved to be a poor solution to a problem. Often the difficulty is a veritable rash of doctrine, some made by judges, some by legislators, all perhaps well-conceived at the outset, but ending in what can only be described, to plagiarize from a former law clerk, as "the Devil's own mess."

He gives as an example of the Devil's own mess the law governing liability for injury to workers in various forms of transportation, such as truck drivers, railroad workers, longshoremen, and seamen. He then asks:

> What is the reason for the failure of Congress to perform its legislative task in these areas? The examples I have chosen [ ] are not in those highly controversial areas in which lack of action may reflect not lack of interest or activity but equivalence of conflicting pressures—in which the chessmen have been moved and moved but the game has been a draw. The instances i have put before you, as countless others could have been, are rather what Dean Pound once called "the petty tinkering of the legal system which is necessary to keep it in running order." No Congressman would lose a vote if orders of the Interstate Commerce Commission were made reviewable by courts of appeals rather than by a district court of three judges, a proposal made by Chief Justice Stone over twenty years ago and recently revived by the Administrative Conference. [Editor—Is Friendly too sanguine about the potential for political controversy from "petty tinkering?"] Neither can the inertia be explained by the stereotype that most Congressmen are indolent and unintelligent creatures. I doubt that ever was true; I know it has not been during the thirty-five years as to which I can give testimony. The difficulty is rather that Congressmen are too driven to be able to attend to such matters, save occasionally, and then under the pressure of a special force. * * *

> What is strange is that although the ailment and the cure have been known for well over a century, the patient, at least on the federal scene, has gone without remedy. In this country, the diagnosis and the prescription were written out at least as early as Dean Pound's address to the delegates of the American Bar Association at Saratoga in 1917. "Our legislative organization and legislative methods," he said, "are devised for appropriations and political legislation, not for legislation on legal matters"; what is needed is "a ministry of justice, charged with the responsibility of making the legal system an effective instrument of justice." Even then the idea

was old—it goes back to Lord Brougham's speech of 1828 on law reform, to Bentham's provision for a ministry of justice in his draft of a constitutional code, and to the resolution, offered in the House of Commons in 1856, that "provision should be made for an efficient and responsible Department of Public Justice with a view to secure the skillful preparation and proper structure of Parliamentary Bills and promote the progressive amendment of the Laws of the United Kingdom." * * * [Editor—You can also hear an echo here of the early 19th Century willingness in the United States to revise state statutes to update and correct older legislation.]

Ideas as to the membership of such an agency will differ. Let me send up a trial balloon. The agency should include the chairman and the ranking minority member of the Judiciary Committees of the Senate and the House, with each having the right to appoint another committee member of his own party as his standing alternate. Its chairman should be a federal judge, selected by the Chief Justice from judges who have availed themselves of the privilege of retirement from active service.

* * * I would add another four or six part time members, appointed by the President, with the advice and consent of the Senate, for terms of say six years—with the caveat that the "part" should be a large part, of the order of fifty percent. They should be drawn from the ranks of legal scholars, retired judges, and lawyers who have attained the age when such public service is more attractive than continued professional success. The permanent staff would be small; but the agency should have an appropriation sufficient to enable it to call on the outside resources most useful for whatever task is at hand. It should work closely with the law schools and the American Law Institute, and use the aid now available in the American Bar Foundation * * *.

Some contemporary suggestions for dealing with problems in existing legislation include the following. How effective do you think they are likely to be? Are the shortcomings institutional, capable of being overcome by better design of government institutions, or are there deeper political problems, which are relatively immune to correction?

1.   The Report of the Federal Courts Study Committee, Judicial Conference of the United States, 89–93 (1990), proposed establishing an Office of Judicial Impact Assessment within the Judiciary, which would provide legislative committee staffs and statutory drafters with a checklist of subjects creating interpretation problems, including whether to infer a private cause of action. The Committee included the following on the checklist:

the statute of limitations;

whether a private cause of action is intended;

whether pre-emption of state law is intended;

the definition of key terms;

the mens rea requirement in criminal statutes;

severability;

whether a proposed bill would repeal or otherwise circumscribe, displace, impair, or change the meaning of existing federal legislation;

whether retroactivity is intended.

The purpose of judicial contacts with the legislature is, of course, to get Congress to listen. To that end, several members of the Federal Courts Study Committee expressed the view that the "committee has missed a golden opportunity to recommend institutional reforms in both branches." They wanted more than a one-way Judiciary-to-Congress communication. They advocated an entity within Congress which would call Congress' attention to judicial and administrative decisions with important consequences.

2.   The District of Columbia Circuit already has contact with Congress to improve legislation. Katzmann, Bridging the Gulf Between Courts and Congress: A Challenge for Positive Political Theory, 80 Geo. L.J. 653 (1992), describes an ongoing project in which the D. C. Circuit's chief staff counsel sends complete Court of Appeals opinions without comment to the Speaker of the House, the minority leader, the Parliamentarian, the general counsel to the Clerk, and the House Legislative Counsel. The Legislative Counsel is expected to contact relevant committee personnel. Katzmann identifies four major problems which call for congressional attention: statutory "gaps" (such as pre-emption and retroactivity); ambiguity; grammatical problems; substantive issues which courts identify as requiring legislative attention.

3.   Ginsburg & Huber, The Intercircuit Committee, 100 Harv. L. Rev. 1417, 1429–34 (1987), have proposed beefing up the Office of Law Revision Counsel in the House of Representatives (whose major responsibility is to prepare and publish the U.S. Code), so that it can take advantage of its statutory authority to "remove ambiguities, contradictions, and other imperfections both of substance and form." 2 U.S.C. § 285b(1). The authors view this as a less sweeping version of proposals by Friendly (discussed *supra*) for something like a Law Revision Commission to fill gaps in lawmaking and engage in "petty tinkering" to fix up the law.

4.   Nagle, Corrections Day, 43 U.C.L.A. L. Rev. 1267, 1282–85, 1294–1303, 1315 (1996), discusses the adoption by the House of Representatives in 1995 of a procedure known as "Corrections Day." This is another procedure which might address legislative failures.[4] The idea is to bring up for consideration statutory amendments which will fix prior legislative and agency mistakes, probably once or twice a month. There is no effort to define a "mistake," but informal guidelines require that a corrections bill address laws and regulations which are "ambiguous, arbitrary, or ludicrous," should deal with noncontroversial issues, and should have broad bipartisan support. In response to fears that a correction bill would not receive sufficient

---

4. In addition, it provides a way for Congress to correct judicial statutory interpre- tation with which it disagrees.

deliberation and would be a vehicle for special interests to undo prior compromises, a correction bill must receive committee review and be passed by a 60% majority vote. Only the House Speaker can place a bill on the Corrections Calendar, but he acts in consultation with the minority leader and with the advice of an Advisory Committee (7 Republicans and 5 Democrats in the current House).

Nagle observes that existing legislative occasions for making corrections have serious shortcomings. Statutory reauthorizations occur only when and if a law expires and often contain controversial provisions, which prevent or postpone passage of uncontroversial corrective legislation. Riders to appropriations bills often bypass committee deliberations and are hastily considered. Later legislative history has serious problems, which we discussed in Chapter 12.

Nagle's description of the first seven Corrections Days gives an idea of the "mistakes" Congress might address. None (at least so far) involve the kind of collateral issues which Congress might have overlooked (such as a private cause of action, pre-emption, retroactivity, and severability); and none involve drafting errors. The matters considered included the following:

> an exception from the Clean Water Act's secondary treatment requirements for San Diego's municipal sewerage discharged into the Pacific;

> reducing the regulatory burdens on vegetable oil imposed by a statute regulating vessels carrying "oil" after the Exxon Valdez Alaskan oil spill;

> allowing eviction of public housing residents who threatened elderly residents;

> updating a law regulating safety rules which were obsolete due to technological advances;

> eliminating obsolete obligations for agencies to make reports to Congress;

> ending an earlier pacemaker registration requirement made redundant by 1990 Food, Drug, and Cosmetic Act reporting rules; and ending a store-posting requirement for saccharin after package-warnings had been required.

QUESTIONS

1. What is likely to occur from these judicial-legislative contacts? It may depend on the issue about which dialogue occurs. Legislative attention may be likely on those issues which fall somewhere between "politically too controversial" and "too busy to care"—for example, statutes of limitations. As noted in Chapter 13, Congress has prospectively adopted a general four year statute of limitations when the federal statute is otherwise silent. Is Congress likely to adopt general federal legislation about implying private causes of action or about retroactivity; or to respond to judicial requests to resolve either of these issues in a specific federal statute?

2.   Is Congress likely to respond when courts identify textual and other uncertainties that need attention? Remember that the problem of clarification comes to the legislature after someone has won a case, and legislative change must overcome the forces of inertia and political pressure by the winning litigant to preserve the status quo. When might the political pressure favor legislative revisiting of the statutory text—a strong private interest lobby; an executive agency which closely monitors legal developments? What will happen if these sources of political pressure are evenly balanced?

3.   Is congressional review of statutory interpretation cases already likely, but on political terms set by Congress? Eskridge finds that almost half of the Supreme Court's statutory interpretation decisions were the subject of legislative hearings, and that about 5% of them were overridden during the 1980's.[5] Eskridge also reports that Congress often reviews and overrules lower court tax cases.[6] Is there some reason why tax cases are likely to attract Congress' attention, that also applies to other areas of law?

4.   What effect should the existence of congressional review, such as the Corrections Day calendar, have on the judicial role in statutory interpretation? Nagle argues[7] that judges should be less willing to correct "mistakes," to the extent that this willingness was based on congressional failure to do the job itself. It should, he claims, dampen the enthusiasm of a Calabresian judge for updating statutes, because legislative inertia would be less of a problem. And it justifies the reenactment and inaction doctrines and super stare decisis (discussed in Chapter 12.03–.05), because Congress is more willing and able to address intervening interpretations of which it disapproves. Is there anything in the Corrections Day procedure to overcome the problem of asymmetries in legislative inertia—the ability of only certain groups to bend the legislature's ear?

5.   Eskridge, Overriding Supreme Court Statutory Interpretation Decisions, 101 Yale L.J. 331, 336 & 377 (1991)(hereafter "Eskridge, Overriding").

6.   "Eskridge, Overriding" at 424–41, Appendix i.

7.   Nagle, Corrections Day, 43 U.C.L.A. L. Rev. at 1315–18.

CHAPTER 15

Statutory Patterns

In this Chapter we consider how two or more statutes create a pattern which must be worked out by the court. Interaction between multiple sources of law is nothing new. Chapter 3 considered the interaction of prior common law and later statute law (and the controversial "derogation of common law" canon). Now we want to know how several statutes interrelate.

First, an earlier statute may try to control how later statutes are made— for example, by requiring specific language to change prior law, or by requiring action within a certain time. Efforts by the past to control the future are discussed in Chapter 15.02. Second, a later statute might conflict with a prior statute. This conflict can be explicit in the text, or the conflict can be implied, as when later statutes appropriate money for activities not previously authorized. Courts often preserve the earlier statute by invoking the doctrine that a later statute will not repeal an earlier statute by implication. Conflicting statutes are discussed in Chapter 15.03.

Third, the interaction among several statutes might be supportive, creating a legal landscape relevant for interpreting specific statutes. Or, the statutes might interact negatively—what is specified in one statute is presumed omitted from another. Or, each statute can stand completely on its own. Chapter 15.04 considers the possibility of supportive, negative, and independent relationships. Chapter 15.05 focuses on a specific issue of statutory interaction—whether statutory patterns can create a momentum that favors extensive statutory interpretation to achieve equal treatment of equals.

Before we look at specific examples, Chapter 15.01 suggests several frameworks for analyzing statutory patterns.

15.01 ANALYTICAL FRAMEWORKS

The basic question, as usual, is what the judicial role should be. As legislation becomes the dominant form of law, judges must inevitably decide how to work out the relationship between multiple statutes. And, in doing this, they can adopt either a more or less reticent lawmaking role.

As you read the material in this chapter, consider which of the following analytical frameworks the courts adopt and what conception of the judicial role it reflects. Which approach minimizes judicial lawmaking discretion, which maximizes it? Does the particular interpretive approach to multiple

642

statutes reduce discretion only to a limited extent, by limiting the judge's substantive concerns to preventing an "absurd" result (as in the Golden Rule)?

a) SUPER-TEXT

The court might treat the entire body of statute law or at least some groups of statutes as one large super-text, whose internal textual coherence should be preserved. One version of the super-text approach applies the linguistic canons of construction (often used to interpret a single statute) to groups of statutes. Thus, a court might presume the consistent use of language in different statutes; or that there is a negative inference from the omission in one statute of what is explicit in another.

A textualist might cite several advantages to the super-text approach. It severs analysis of a statute's meaning from considerations of statutory purpose. It might also encourage greater legislative drafting responsibility, although its efficacy in this regard is doubtful. Finally, in *some* areas of the law, lawyers might actually read multiple statutory texts as an integrated document, in which case interpreting the statutes as a single text might conform to how the statutory audience reads the law.

There is an important difference between a super-text approach and conventional reliance on the "internal context" of a statute. "Internal context" refers to language drafted purposely as part of an integrated text (see Chapter 5). Like all conventional textualist readings, reliance on internal context should refer to the meaning shared in common between author and audience. The super-text approach does not always meet this "common understanding" standard because of the way statutes are drafted and codified.

First, at the federal level, a Public Law may deal with many subjects; there is no single-subject rule for federal statutes. (Chapter 18 discusses single subject requirements, which are typical in state constitutions.) Consequently, different portions of the legislation might not be drafted by the same legislators. It may therefore be difficult to assume that the same language in different parts of a Public Law was purposely drafted to have the same meaning. Moreover, whatever the drafter's intent, the provisions may be codified in different places and therefore not be read together by the typical audience.

Second, provisions which appear in one place in a codified text (such as the United States Code), are not necessarily drafted with the surrounding parts of the codified law in mind. Parts of the codified material may have been written at different times and the drafter may not take care to read the surrounding language into which a Public Law provision is codified. In such cases, the legislative author might not view the text as an integrated whole, even if the statute's audience would.

The super-textualist might not care whether the author and audience treat the words as part of an integrated document. As noted above, this may serve the textualist's purposes of reducing judicial discretion, forcing better drafting, or deferring to the audience's perspective (if the audience treats the texts as integrated), but it is not an application of the conventional "common understanding" approach to understanding language.

A recent case (Association of American Physicians & Surgeons, Inc. v. Clinton, 997 F.2d 898 (D.C.Cir.1993)), paid some attention to the problem of two statutory provisions passed at different times but codified in the same place. The case dealt with the Federal Advisory Committee Act (FACA), which was codified as an Appendix to Title 5 of the U.S. Code. FACA imposed some onerous requirements on federal advisory committees, including open meetings. These requirements do not apply, however, to an advisory committee "which is composed wholly of full-time officers or employees of the Federal Government." The question was whether the President's Task Force on National Health Care Reform was covered by FACA. All of its members were government employees, except (perhaps) its chair, Mrs. Clinton (the President's wife).

The court held that she was a de facto officer or employee, as First Lady, but had to deal with the fact that Title 5 of the U.S.Code, §§ 2104, 2105, defined officer and employee in a way that excluded Mrs. Clinton. Under those sections, an officer or employee must be: (i) appointed to the civil service; (ii) engaged in the performance of a federal function; and (iii) subject to supervision by a higher elected or appointed official. Mrs. Clinton had not been appointed to the civil service.

To overcome the Title 5 definition, the court noted:

> FACA is not part of Title 5, which was enacted six years before FACA's passage, see Pub.L. No. 89–554, 80 Stat. 378 (1966), but, instead is only temporarily housed there as an appendix. Typically, when Congress wishes to add a statute to Title 5, it amends the Title. See, e.g., Government in the Sunshine Act, § 3(a), Pub.L. No. 94–409, 90 Stat. 1241 (1976); Privacy Act of 1974, Pub.L. No. 93–579, 88 Stat. 1896 (1974).

Judge Buckley (concurring) gave short shrift to this effort by the majority to sever Title 5 definitions from the Appendix containing FACA. He stated that

> Congress surely knew that FACA would be codified under Title 5. The same statute that adopted sections 2104 and 2105 also stipulated that Title 5 be captioned: "Government Organization and Employees." Pub. L. No. 89–554, 80 Stat. 378, 408–09 (1966).

He explained the location of FACA in Title 5's appendix on the following grounds.

> The United States Code is published pursuant to 1 U.S.C. §§ 201–13 (1988). That law requires the codification of new laws in annual Code supplements and permits the publication of an entirely new Code every five years. See id. § 202. Thus, the current United

States Code and supplement contain all laws of the United States that are "general and permanent in their nature." Id. § 204(a). As of 1988, ten of the fifty U.S.C. titles contained an appendix. See 5, 10, 11, 18, 26, 28, 40, 46, 49, 50 U.S.C. (1988). Some statutes have been placed in appendices because, while considered more than temporary, they are viewed as less than permanent additions to the Code. See 40 U.S.C.App. (Appalachian Regional Development Act of 1965). Other statutes have been relegated to appendices because they were not enacted directly by Congress. See 11 U.S.C.App. (Bankruptcy Rules and Official Forms as promulgated by Supreme Court pursuant to 28 U.S.C. § 2075). With respect to Title 5, Congress has divided it into three parts: "The Agencies Generally" (Part I), "Civil Service Functions and Responsibilities" (Part II), and "Employees" (Part III). See Pub.L. No. 89–554, 80 Stat. 378 (1966), as amended by Pub.L. No. 96–54, § 2(a)(1), 93 Stat. 381 (1979). An appendix to Title 5, then, is the natural place to codify statutes that relate to "Government Organization and Employees" but do not pertain to "The Agencies Generally," "Civil Service Functions and Responsibilities," or "Employees."

b) CONTEXT–TEXT; 3 VARIATIONS

Statutory patterns might also be analyzed within the context-text framework, with all of the uncertainties that such analysis entails. In our discussion of external context—Chapters 6 and 7, dealing with purpose and substantive background considerations—we noted that context *might* be good evidence of what the legislature would want. Sometimes there was good evidence that the legislature actually considered the context (usually regarding purpose); in other instances, we could be quite confident that the legislature would want something if it had thought about it (usually with substantive background considerations). But, in many cases, context served a different or, at least, supplemental role—embodying policies which *deserved* implementation. This was apparent when judges exercised discretion to elaborate certain purposes or imposed plain statement rules regarding certain substantive background considerations.

The same ambiguity exists when judges work out the interaction of multiple statutes. Sometimes we can be pretty sure that the legislature either did consider prior statutes or would have wanted the judge to take account of prior statutes that the legislature did not specifically consider. But sometimes the interaction of multiple statutes leaves the court guessing about actual or likely legislative intent, much as it did when dealing with purpose or substantive background considerations. In such cases, the relationship of multiple statutes might take on a life of its own, not as a super-text, but as an expression of coherent policy. For example, similar texts would be interpreted in the same way only if the statutes dealt with similar policy concerns (that is, if the statutes were *in pari materia*).

The fine line between the court treating prior law as evidence of actual or likely legislative intent and trying to make policy sense out of statutory interactions is evident in the following quote from Radzanower v. Touche Ross & Co., 426 U.S. 148 (1976), where Justice Stevens describes the doctrine against implied repeal of an earlier statute as merely a guideline to determine the

> real intent of the legislature. When we are dealing with a *well-established and clearly defined old rule*, it is usually reasonable to suppose that the legislative intent to change such a rule would be unambiguously expressed (emphasis added). Or if we are dealing with an *old rule that is an established and important part of our national policy*, we must be sure that it is not changed merely by inadvertent use of broad language (emphasis added). * * * But if neither the existence of, nor the reason for, the old rule is clear at the time of the later enactment, there is no special reason for questioning the legislative intent to have the later statute mean exactly what it says.

There is a third possibility—in addition to (1) context as evidence of actual or likely legislative intent; and (2) context as an element in judicial "policy coherence" analysis. The third possibility is that a prior statute has a privileged status, without regard to actual or likely legislative intent or the strength of the policy it embodies. The application of the interpretive canon against implied legislative repeals of prior statutes may be an example of this approach. In other words, there may be a kind of "narrow interpretation of statutes in derogation of prior *statute* law" doctrine, which gives retention of prior law a privileged status. If there is such a derogation canon, it raises the following question. When a court applied the derogation canon regarding the common law, that rested on a substantive commitment to the common law. What would justify a similar canon regarding prior *statutes*?

One way to answer that question is to note that, in the 20th Century, legislation has a claim that it did not enjoy at an earlier time. Its democratic pedigree entitles prior legislation to a permanence that prior common law no longer enjoys. I am not suggesting that a prior legislature can prevent repeal of a statute. (The technical term for legislatively self-imposed prohibitions on statutory repeal is "entrenchment" of prior law.) I am suggesting only that there might be a fundamental background consideration which entitles legislative lawmaking to a presumption of continuance. See Julian Eule, Temporal Limits on the Legislative Mandate: Entrenchment and Retroactivity, 1987 Amer. Bar Found. Res. Jl. 379.

As you read the following material, see whether any of the above analytical frameworks explains the decision: super-text; context-text (actual or likely legislative intent); context-text (policy coherence); or context-text (privileging prior statute law).

15.02 PRIOR STATUTES CONSTRAINING FUTURE LAW

There is an ancient principle of legislation going back to Roman Law and repeated by Blackstone, which is that later law prevails; prior legislatures cannot entrench prior law. Blackstone, Commentaries on the Law of England, Vol. I, at 49, 90–91 (1978). Popular sovereignty is always complete and cannot be limited, except by a constitutional rule which is superior to the statute. A modern policy supporting this principle is that a new generation should not be tied to tradition if it wants to change the law. Notwithstanding the principle that later law prevails, the legislature might try to make it harder to repeal prior law in several ways.

a) REQUIRING FUTURE TEXT

An earlier legislature might try to control the text by which later legislation is enacted. For example, the Anti–Injunction Act states: "A court of the United States may not grant an injunction to stay proceedings in a State court except as expressly authorized by Act of Congress * * *." 28 U.S.C. § 2283.[1] But what does "expressly" mean?

Vendo Co. v. Lektro–Vend Corp., 433 U.S. 623 (1977) involved a later statute authorizing injunctions to enforce the Clayton Act, an anti-trust statute. The Clayton Act said:

> [A]ny person * * * shall be entitled to sue for and have injunctive relief * * * against threatened loss or damage by violation of the antitrust laws * * * when and under the same conditions and principles as injunction relief against threatened conduct that will cause loss or damage is granted by courts of equity.

All of the judges agreed that a statute can authorize an injunction against state court proceedings without specifically mentioning either the Anti–Injunction Act or state court proceedings. They also agreed with the test stated by the three-judge plurality opinion—determining whether a later statute authorizes an injunction depends on whether an Act of Congress can be given its intended scope only by a stay of state court proceedings. That was about all the judges could agree on. Look for evidence of a "policy coherence" approach in the following explanations of the opinions.

Three judges found no express authorization to enjoin state court proceedings in the Clayton Act, noting the fact (though it was not dispositive) that the later statute did not expressly mention the Anti–Injunction Act or an injunction against state court proceedings; and, further, appealing to the

---

1. See also: "[A] subsequent statute may not be held to supersede or modify this subchapter * * * except to the extent that it does so expressly." 5 U.S.C. § 559 (Administrative Procedure Act).

"fundamental principle of a dual system of courts." They distinguished an earlier case permitting an injunction, which involved a federal civil rights statute, where the legislative history affirmed the importance of federal court availability to protect civil rights against unconstitutional state court action. Four judges stated that the Clayton Act included a power to enjoin state court proceedings so that "a man does not have to wait until he is ruined in his business before he has his remedy," referring to the anti-trust law as "that basic charter of economic freedom." Two judges held that the Clayton Act expressly authorized injunctive relief, but not on the facts of this case. Thus, six judges held that the Clayton Act expressly authorized injunctions, but a majority agreed that no injunction should issue in this case.

Occasionally, a statute specifies that its repeal can only be accomplished by explicit reference to the prior statute. For example—"No law enacted after September 14, 1976 shall supersede this subchapter unless it does so in specific terms, referring to this subchapter and declaring that the new law supersedes the provisions of this subchapter." 50 U.S.C. § 1621(b). Does this statute bind later legislatures and, if so, on what theory; does it have considerable weight in determining the meaning of later legislation?

b) REQUIRING LEGISLATIVE PROCEDURES

Although most procedures for passing statutes at the federal level are adopted by each house of Congress by simple resolution, an earlier statute sometimes specifies procedures for adopting later law—e.g., stating the committee to which a bill must be referred. However, the statutory rules are adopted pursuant to the legislature's power to adopt its own internal procedures, and can be disregarded (like any internal procedural rule) by the legislature enacting later law. Metzenbaum v. Federal Energy Regulatory Comm'n, 675 F.2d 1282 (D.C.Cir.1982). Statutes about legislative procedures are therefore not constraints on future legislation. Should they be?

c) REQUIRING LEGISLATION WITHIN A TIME PERIOD

A statute might state that future action must be taken within a specific time. For example, a law states that congressional salary raises proposed by a Presidential commission will go into effect within 30 days of Presidential approval unless Congress passes a joint resolution rejecting the raises. In 1987, Congress adopted a disapproving joint resolution, Pub. L. 100–6, § 3, 101 Stat. 94 (1987), but the House had acted on this resolution *after* the 30–day period specified by prior law. The tardy text was as follows:

> The recommendations of the President relating to rates of pay for offices and positions * * * as included * * * in the budget transmitted to the Congress for fiscal year 1988, are disapproved.

Most people, including the President (23 Weekly Comp. Pres. Doc. 148 (Feb. 16, 1987)), assumed that the disapproval was *in*effective. Why? A later law disapproving the raises would prevent the raises (except for any constitutional problems with retroactive deprivation of vested pay increases). Was Congress actually aware of the prior law establishing the time limit for disapproval, rendering tardy disapproval an expression of legislative objection without the force of law (like a committee report)?

Your answer to this question may depend on knowing the following history.[2] On January 5, 1987, The President had recommended a congressional pay raise. The Senate and House leadership had an informal agreement that the Senate would pass a free standing resolution disapproving the raises and the House would let the resolution die, permitting the raises to go into effect. The Senate honored this commitment by not appending its disapproval to a popular resolution dealing with clean water, but Senatorial opposition to the raises was intense. Consequently, the Senate disapproved the raises on January 29, 1987, not only by passing a free standing joint resolution, S.J. Res. 34, 100th Cong., 1st Sess.; 133 Cong. Rec. S1345 (daily ed. Jan. 29, 1987), but also by adding language disapproving the raises to a popular joint resolution aiding the homeless, which had earlier passed the House. The House was politically unable to oppose the homeless aid joint resolution. It therefore delayed its vote on the homeless aid joint resolution until February 4, having voted overwhelmingly to adjourn on February 3 to block an earlier decision. February 4 was one day after expiration of the 30–day disapproval period for rejecting salary raises.

This history demonstrates clear awareness by Congress of the time limit law. Everyone knew about it and wanted to miss the deadline. Does that mean that the later law was ineffective, despite the text? Is this any way to legislate, allowing legislators to say one thing (disapproving the pay raise) and mean another *on purpose*? Why not hold legislators to the "disapproval" language, to discourage this kind of legislation? Does anyone have standing to object to the pay raise?[3]

d) Is Controlling the Future Constitutional?

The conclusion that earlier law might constrain future lawmaking runs counter to the principle that later law prevails. Paul Kahn has suggested that the priority of later law may be constitutionally mandated.[4] The argument is that future legislatures cannot be constrained by prior law unless the prior law is formally superior, such as a constitutional rule about how a statute is made. Kahn makes this argument as an objection to the Gramm–Rudman law (Pub. L. 99–177, 99 Stat. 1037 (1986)), which was an earlier law requiring reduction of *future* appropriations in accordance with a more-or-less across-the-board formula, if total spending exceeded a certain target. A

2. This history is reported in the following pages of the Congressional Quart. Weekly Report. See 1987 Cong. Quart. Weekly Rep. 135; 1987 Cong. Quart. Weekly Rep. 219; 1987 Cong. Quart. Weekly Rep. 220; 1987 Cong. Quart. Weekly Rep. 186; 1987 Cong. Quart. Weekly Rep. 220.

3. Humphrey v. Baker, 665 F.Supp. 23 (D.D.C.1987)(members of Congress have standing to challenge pay raise and court will

not exercise equitable discretion to avoid deciding the issue), reversed, 848 F.2d 211 (D.C.Cir.1988)(equitable discretion exercised to deny hearing case because internal congressional remedy available). "Equitable discretion" doctrine is discussed in Chapter 18.

4. Kahn, Gramm–Rudman and the Capacity of Congress to Control the Future, 13 Hastings Const. L. Quart. 185 (1986).

future appropriations law could avoid this effect if the law explicitly exempted itself from Gramm–Rudman, but that required sufficient political will to pass the exemption as well as the appropriation bill itself.

Whether or not the constitutional argument has any validity, the argument is potentially a powerful background consideration which could influence interpretation of statutes adopted in the shadow of prior law specifying the language, procedure, or timing required for later law. The stronger the argument favoring freedom to make later law, the less likely prior law can constrain how future law is made.

In deciding whether there should be a presumption against past legislatures controlling future legislation, consider that earlier legislatures already influence later legislation by various methods other than determining how law can be made. First, many statutes constrain their own repeal by creating interest groups that cluster around them. Second, statutes defining electoral districts, ballot access, and campaign financing severely affect future lawmaking by shaping the electorate and the composition of the legislature (discussed in Chapter 16).

e) DICTIONARY ACTS

Another way the past can try to control the future is by a statute defining specific terms—often called Dictionary Acts. These Acts often appear at the beginning of the jurisdiction's statutory code. One example is 1 U.S.C. § 1, originally adopted in 1871. It contained what many would view as routine codifications of common usage, such as: "words importing the singular number may extend and be applied to several persons or things;" and "the masculine gender may be applied to females." (Was it so clear in 1871 that the masculine included the feminine? Suppose the statute dealt with qualifications for bar membership?)

Some provisions of 1 U.S.C. § 1 might stretch common usage—such as, "the word 'person' * * * include[s] corporations, companies, associations, firms, partnerships, societies, and joint stock companies, as well as individuals." This quote reflects a 1948 amendment to the Dictionary Act, which expanded "person" to include associations as well as individuals. The Dictionary Act also specifies that it applies "unless the context indicates otherwise."

The "context" escape hatch may seem to eliminate the problem of deciding whether the prior Dictionary Act has a mandatory effect on later law, but that is not necessarily true. If "context" includes everything that a court would consider when interpreting a later statute containing a previously defined term, then there is no need to decide whether the Dictionary Act is mandatory. All evidence of the later statute's meaning is relevant, either independently, or because it is authorized by the "context" escape hatch in the earlier Dictionary Act. But there is an argument that "context" means only *internal* context, excluding legislative history materials and evidence of statutory purpose. If so, then a *mandatory* Dictionary Act limits what a court can consider when interpreting a later statute using the word defined in the Dictionary Act.

The Supreme Court, in Rowland v. California Men's Colony, 506 U.S. 194 (1993), treated the Dictionary Act as mandatory and held that the word "context" in the Dictionary Act "means the text of the Act of Congress surrounding the word at issue, or the texts of other related congressional Acts * * *"—in other words, internal context, defined to include related statutes. The Court acknowledged that "context" could have a "secondary meaning of '[a]ssociated surroundings * * * ,'" but doubted that this broader sense applied to the Dictionary Act *because* the purpose of determining the meaning of a statute "suggest[ed] the primary sense." See also Hubbard v. United States, 115 S.Ct. 1754 (1995)(following Rowland—context does not mean "congressional intent" and the Dictionary Act is binding).

The specific issue in Rowland was whether the word "person" in a 1959 statute permitting "persons" to proceed *in forma pauperis* meant only natural persons, not artificial entities. The case involved a suit by an association of prisoners objecting to the prison's no smoking policy. The Court held that "person" in the 1959 law was limited to natural persons, notwithstanding the broader Dictionary Act definition to include "associations." The Court's decision is puzzling because it relied in part on the practical concerns posed by including artificial entities as "persons" eligible for *in forma pauperis* status. The Court noted that an affiant must certify the person's poverty and that there are serious problems identifying whether the affiant has authority to speak for an entity and imposing effective penalties on an entity to deter perjury. In addition, applying the "inability to pay" standard to determine whether artificial entities were poor was very difficult, both regarding the choice of insolvency definitions and deciding when to pierce the entity's veil to consider the owners' or members' economic condition.

The appeal to practicality would, of course, make sense on one of two theories: either "context" has a more expansive meaning in the Dictionary Act than internal context; or the Dictionary Act is not mandatory. But the Court previously rejected both theories, holding that "context" means "internal context" and that the Dictionary Act was mandatory. Perhaps the Court was trying to have it both ways by stating that the prior Dictionary Act was binding but then in fact interpreting a later act on the basis of criteria not authorized by the Dictionary Act.

Justices Thomas, Blackmun, Stevens, and Kennedy dissented on the ground that the Court had given the phrase "unless the context indicates otherwise" an "impermissibly broad reading." Justice Scalia voted with the majority.

QUESTIONS

1. Should prior Dictionary Acts be mandatory? If they are not mandatory, do they have "weight," and, if so, on what theory of statutory interpretation can a prior Act have less than mandatory "weight?"

2. Why should "context" have the narrow meaning of internal context, just because (as the Court says) the Dictionary Act is concerned with statutory meaning?

3.   Perhaps the Court means that "context" in 1871 meant internal context, nothing more. Blackstone's use of the word "context" was probably so limited (see the material in Chapter 2). But couldn't the word "context" in an 1871 statute evolve to mean something broader today?

4.   The Court makes a point of the fact that, under the Dictionary Act, "context" need only "indicate" a different meaning, not "require" it. Does that leave enough leeway to decide that the internal context prevents "person" from applying to an association, in a statute permitting petitioners to proceed *in forma pauperis*, based on the practical problems of certifying an association's poverty?

15.03   CONFLICT BETWEEN PRIOR AND LATER STATUTES—THE "NO REPEAL BY IMPLICATION" DOCTRINE

As noted earlier, courts frequently invoke a "no repeal by implication" doctrine to preserve prior legislation, or reach that result without explicitly invoking the doctrine. Does this judicial approach operate in the following cases to identify likely legislative intent or is it sufficiently malleable that it allows the court to adopt a policy coherence approach? Is the court's concern with policy limited to preventing an "absurd" result?

a) SUBSTANTIVE STATUTES

Sorenson v. Secretary of Treasury
475 U.S. 851 (1986).

■ Justice Blackmun delivered the opinion of the Court. * * *

[Editor—The critical facts were these:

1.   Beginning in 1975, applicants for welfare (AFDC) had to assign any right to child-support to the State to repay welfare benefits. Stanley Sorenson's former wife made this assignment when she applied for AFDC for herself and Stanley's child.

2.   In 1975, the income tax law was amended to provide an earned income credit. The credit reduced taxes on low income workers. If the credit exceeded the tax due, the excess was "considered an overpayment of tax" under § 6401(b) of the Internal Revenue Code. § 6402(a) provides for a refund of a "any overpayment," including that created by an earned income credit.

3.   In 1981 the Omnibus Budget Reconciliation Act of 1981 (OBRA) adopted an intercept rule, whereby the State notified the Secretary of the United States Treasury of persons owing past-due child support assigned to it. The Treasury then intercepted tax refunds otherwise payable to child support debtors. OBRA explicitly added a new § 6402(c) to the Internal Revenue Code, as follows:

"The amount of any overpayment to be refunded to the person making the overpayment shall be reduced by the amount of any past-due support * * * owed by that person of which the Secretary has been notified by a State * * *. The Secretary shall remit the amount by which the overpayment is so reduced to the State to which such support has been assigned and notify the person making the overpayment that so much of the overpayment as was necessary to satisfy his obligation for past-due support has been paid to the State. * * *"

4. In 1981, Stanley Sorenson had remarried and was entitled to a "refund" based on the excess earned income credit over tax due. The issue was whether this refund could be intercepted. The petitioner was Stanley's wife in 1981.]

Petitioner advances two arguments to support her claim that an excess earned-income credit cannot be intercepted. First she claims that the language and structure of the interlocking statutory provisions that make up the intercept law exclude an earned-income credit from its reach: excess earned-income credits are neither "over-payments" nor "refunds of Federal taxes paid," and only those items are subject to interception. Second, she claims that permitting interception of an earned-income credit would frustrate Congress' aims in providing the credit, and thus that Congress could not have intended the intercept law to reach earned-income credits. We find neither argument persuasive.

The Internal Revenue Code's treatment of earned-income credits supports the Government's position. An individual can receive the amount by which his entitlement to an earned-income credit exceeds his tax liability only because § 6401(b) of the Code defines that amount as an "over-payment," and § 6402 provides a mechanism for disbursing overpayments, namely, the income tax refund process. The refundability of the earned-income credit is thus inseparable from its classification as an overpayment of tax. Petitioner therefore acknowledges that the excess earned-income credit is an "overpayment" for purposes of § 6402(a), the general provision that authorizes all tax refunds. If it were not, the Secretary would lack authorization for refunding it to her. She claims, however, that while an excess earned-income credit is an "overpayment" for purposes of § 6402(a), it is not an "overpayment" for purposes of § 6402(c), which requires that the "amount of any overpayment * * * shall be reduced by the amount of any past-due support" assigned to the State.

The normal rule of statutory construction assumes that " 'identical words used in different parts of the same act are intended to have the same meaning.' " That the Internal Revenue Code includes an explicit definition of "overpayment" in the same subchapter strengthens the presumption. And that both subsections concern

the tax-refund treatment of "overpayment[s]" is especially damaging to any claim "that the words, though in the same act, are found in such dissimilar connections as to warrant the conclusion that they were employed in the different parts of the act with different intent."
* * *

Nor do we agree with petitioner's claim that Congress did not intend the intercept program to reach excess earned-income credits. Petitioner and the Government agree that Congress never mentioned the earned-income credit in enacting OBRA. But it defies belief that Congress was unaware, when it provided in § 6402(c) that "any overpayment to be refunded * * * shall be reduced by the amount of any past-due support", that this would include refunds attributable to excess earned-income credits. Congress had previously expressly defined an excess earned-income credit as an "overpayment," in § 6401(b) of the Internal Revenue Code—the section immediately preceding the section to which Congress added the intercept provision.

What petitioner * * * [is] claiming is that the intercept law should be read narrowly to avoid frustrating the goals of the earned-income credit program. The earned-income credit was enacted to reduce the disincentive to work caused by the imposition of social security taxes on earned income (welfare payments are not similarly taxed), to stimulate the economy by funneling funds to persons likely to spend the money immediately, and to provide relief for low-income families hurt by rising food and energy prices. Each is an undeniably important objective. It is impossible, however, for us to say that these goals out-weigh the goals served by the subsequently enacted tax-intercept program—securing child support from absent parents whenever possible and reducing the number of families on welfare. Congress of course could conclude that families eligible for earned-income credits have a more compelling claim to the funds involved than do either the States or non-AFDC families. But it is equally clear that Congress could have decided that the more pressing need was to alleviate the "devastating consequences for children and the taxpayers" of the epidemic of nonsupport. See Hearings before the Senate Committee on Finance on Spending Reduction Proposals, 97th Cong., 1st Sess., pt. 1, p. 34 (1981)(statement of Secretary Schweiker).

The ordering of competing social policies is a quintessentially legislative function. In light of Congress' decision to direct the interception of any overpayment otherwise refundable to a taxpayer, the Ninth Circuit correctly refused to "speculate that Congress intended otherwise." Its judgment, accordingly, is affirmed.

■ Justice Stevens, dissenting.

The class of persons that Congress intended to benefit by creating the "Earned Income Credit" Program in 1975 is composed entirely of low-income families. * * *

The mechanism by which Congress funneled the funds to those persons was to treat the credits as though their recipients had overpaid their taxes, giving them a right to a "refund" of a hypothetical overpayment. This relatively obscure provision of the Internal Revenue Code gave rise to no particular difficulties for the ensuing six years.

The principal beneficiaries of the Intercept Program enacted by Congress as part of what is appropriately called the Omnibus Budget Reconciliation Act of 1981 were state governments which had claims for recoupment of welfare payments made to families that were unable to enforce a departed parent's child-support obligations. Thus, the real adversaries in this case are the Sorensons— a low-income family—on the one hand, and the State of Washington, on the other, which will ultimately receive the intercepted "refund" under the Court's holding. The question is whether congress in 1981 intended to divert these federal funds from the original beneficiaries of the Earned Income Credit Program to the treasuries of state governments. Notwithstanding the Court's careful and admittedly accurate parsing of the language of the statute, I am not persuaded that Congress had any such intent.

The Court confidently asserts that "it defies belief that congress was unaware" of the impact of its Intercept Program upon the Earned Income Credit Program when it enacted OBRA in 1981. The Court does not pause to tell us why, if that be so, Congress did not even mention this important change at any point in the legislative history of OBRA. With all due respect to the Court and to our hard working neighbors in the Congress, I think "it defies belief" to assume that a substantial number of legislators were sufficiently familiar with OBRA to realize that somewhere in that vast piece of hurriedly enacted legislation there was a provision that changed the 6-year-old Earned Income Credit Program.

I agree that the Court's reading of the statutory language is faithful to its grammar. I am not persuaded, however, that it actually reflects the intent of the Congress that enacted OBRA. I therefore would accept the construction of the relevant statutes adopted by the Court of Appeals for the Second and Tenth Circuits.

[Editor—Recall that Justice Stevens held that "filed" meant the same thing in two different sections of a Civil Rights law, in the Mohasco case. Why the different result here, holding that overpayment has different meanings in two different sections?]

How can you distinguish Sorenson from the following Watt case, where the Court did *not* find repeal by implication?

Watt v. Alaska

451 U.S. 259 (1981).

■ Justice Powell delivered the opinion of the Court.

The narrow issue presented by these cases is which of two federal statutes provides the formula for distribution of revenues received from oil and gas leases on national wildlife refuges reserved from public lands. * * *

[Editor—The older of the two statutes was § 35 of the Mineral Leasing Act of 1920. It provides that 90% of the revenues from mineral leases on wildlife refuges withdrawn (that is, reserved) from public lands be paid to Alaska and 10% to the United States. The land at issue was the Kenai National Moose Range, which was created in 1941 by the withdrawal of nearly two million acres from public lands on the Kenai Peninsula in Alaska. The revenues were derived from oil and gas leases beginning in the mid–1950's. Prior to 1964, § 35 of the Mineral Leasing Act of 1920 governed distribution of revenues from mineral leases on wildlife refuges withdrawn from public lands.

A problem arose when Congress amended § 401(a) of the Wildlife Refuge Revenue Sharing Act in 1964. The amendment added the word "minerals" to the list of refuge resources, the revenues from which were to be distributed under § 401(c) of the Act, as amended in 1964. "Minerals" include oil and gas. The Act explicitly applied to land "acquired or reserved" for conservation and protection of certain fish and wildlife. The Act's distribution formula gave 25% to the county where the refuge lies and 75% to the U.S. Department of the Interior for public purposes.]

The Secretary [of the Interior] and the Kenai Borough rely primarily on the "plain language" of § 401(a) of the Wildlife Refuge Revenue Sharing Act [as amended in 1964]. They contend that it provides without ambiguity that mineral resources from all national wildlife refuges be distributed according to the formula described in § 401(a) of the Act. * * *

The provision defines the wildlife refuge system to include lands "acquired or reserved" for conservation and protection of certain fish and wildlife. No restriction is placed upon the common meaning of "minerals." Given this clarity, it is argued, resort to the legislative history is unnecessary or improper. * * *

Congress gave extensive consideration to the purpose and probable effect of the 1964 amendments to the Wildlife Refuge Revenue Sharing Act. Pub. L. 88–523, 78 Stat. 701. Nonetheless, and we think it significant, there is no explanation in the legislative history for the addition of the single word "minerals" to the list of refuge resources subject to the Act. Our study of the few legislative materials pertinent to the insertion of "minerals" persuades us that

Congress intended to work no change in the pre-existing formula for distribution of mineral revenues from federal wildlife refuges. * * *

* * * The impetus for proposals leading to the passage of the [1964] amendments was the difficulty the Department had experienced in acquiring new refuge lands. Localities resisted having land removed from local tax rolls. The purpose of the amendments was to "provide a more equitable formula for payments to counties as compensation for loss of taxable properties that have been acquired by the Federal wildlife refuge system." Public Law 88–523 met this problem by changing the formula for distribution of revenues from refuges consisting of acquired lands. § 401(c)(1), 78 Stat. 701. * * * Congress intended the Department to pay more to counties under the new law than it had under the old. * * *

During deliberations on the amendments, the Fish and Wildlife Service presented to Senate and House Committees tables showing present payments to counties containing refuges, and payments estimated under the proposed amendments. The relevant table shows no change in the expected payments to the Borough of Kenai Peninsula. This table assumed that oil and gas revenues were governed by the Mineral Leasing Act of 1920 both before and after the amendments.

The inference seems inescapable that Congress in 1964 did not intend by the insertion of "minerals" in § 401(a) of the Wildlife Refuge Revenue Sharing Act to subject revenues from oil leases on reserved refuge lands to its distribution formula. * * *

* * * We hold that Congress inserted "minerals" in the amended § 401(a) to make clear that the amended distribution formula applied to mineral revenues from acquired lands. This conclusion draws support from the evident fact that Congress was concerned almost exclusively with problems related to acquired refuge lands in adopting the 1964 amendments. * * *

In summary, we hold that revenues generated by oil and gas leases on federal wildlife refuges consisting of reserved public lands must be distributed according to the formula provided in § 35 of the Mineral Leasing Act of 1920. Finding no "clearly expressed congressional intention" to repeal this provision by implication, we conclude that the term "minerals" in § 401(a) of the Wildlife Refuge Revenue Sharing Act applies only to minerals on acquired refuge lands. Accordingly, the judgment of the Court of Appeals is affirmed.

The dissent in Watt refused to apply the "no repeal by implication" doctrine, on the ground that it applies only when a general statute, wholly occupying a field, appears to eviscerate an earlier and more specific enactment of limited coverage.

Evolving legal landscape. Here is one more case, in which the Court held in favor of an implied repeal. The situation is a little different from the prior two cases. Here, statutes in a particular area of law seem to be evolving in a particular direction—Calabresi might say that there is evidence of a developing legal landscape. The last statute in the chain, however, does not explicitly achieve a certain result, but does so (according to the Court) only by impliedly repealing a provision in a prior statute. As you will see, a dissent thought this was a pretty radical step for the Court to take.

In United States v. Hutcheson, 312 U.S. 219 (1941), Justice Frankfurter (writing for the Court), held that a later anti-injunction statute repealed an earlier criminal law *by implication.* Specifically, the 1890 Sherman Act made certain labor union activities criminal. A later 1914 statute prohibited an injunction *and* criminal prosecution of union activities, but the courts limited the prohibition to union activities against employers. Inter-union rivalry activities, at issue in the Hutcheson case, could still be illegal. Then, in 1932, the Norris–LaGuardia Act explicitly prohibited injunctions against *inter-union* rivalry activities as well. Frankfurter held that the 1932 Act also *decriminalized* the behavior against which injunctions were prohibited, stating:

> * * * It would be strange indeed that although neither the Government nor [the employer] could have sought an injunction against the acts here challenged, the elaborate efforts to permit such conduct failed to prevent criminal liability punishable with imprisonment and heavy fines. That is not the way to read the will of Congress, particularly when expressed by a statute which, as we have already indicated, is practically and historically one of a series of enactments touching one of the most sensitive national problems. Such legislation must not be read in a spirit of mutilating narrowness. On matters far less vital and far less interrelated we have had occasion to point out the importance of giving "hospitable scope" to Congressional purpose even when meticulous words are lacking. Keifer & Keifer v. Reconstruction Finance Corp., 306 U.S. 381, 391, and authorities there cited. The appropriate way to read legislation in a situation like the one before us, was indicated by Mr. Justice Holmes on circuit: "A statute may indicate or require as its justification a change in the policy of the law, although it expresses that change only in the specific cases most likely to occur in the mind. The Legislature has the power to decide what the policy of the law shall be, and if it has intimated its will, however indirectly, that will should be recognized and obeyed. The major premise of the conclusion expressed in a statute, the change of policy that induces the enactment, may not be set out in terms, but it is not an adequate discharge of duty for the courts to say: We see what you are driving at, but you have not said it, and therefore we shall go on as before." Johnson v. United States, 163 F. 30, 32.
>
> The relation of the Norris–LaGuardia Act to the Clayton Act is not that of a tightly drawn amendment to a technically phrased tax provision. The underlying aim of the Norris–LaGuardia Act was to

restore the broad purpose which Congress thought it had formulated in the Clayton Act but which was frustrated, so Congress believed, by unduly restrictive judicial construction. * * * The Norris–LaGuardia Act reasserted the original purpose of the Clayton Act by infusing into it the immunized trade union activities as redefined by the later Act. In this light § 20 removes all such allowable conduct from the taint of being a "violation of any law of the United States," including the Sherman Law.

The dissent was aghast at Frankfurter's approach to interpretation, stating:

> By a process of construction never, as I think, heretofore indulged by this court, it is now found that, because Congress forbade the issuing of injunctions to restrain certain conduct, it intended to repeal the provisions of the Sherman Act authorizing actions at law and criminal prosecutions for the commission of torts and crimes defined by the anti-trust laws. The doctrine now announced seems to be that an indication of a change of policy in an Act as respects one specific item in a general field of the law, covered by an earlier act, justifies this court in spelling out an implied repeal of the whole of the earlier statute as applied to conduct of the sort here involved. I venture to say that no court has ever undertaken so radically to legislate where Congress has refused so to do.

> The construction of the act now adopted is the more clearly inadmissible when we remember that the scope of proposed amendments and repeals of the anti-trust laws in respect of labor organizations has been the subject of constant controversy and consideration in Congress. In the light of this history, to attribute to Congress an intent to repeal legislation which has had a definite and well understood scope and effect for decades past * * * seems to me a usurpation by the courts of the function of the Congress not only novel but fraught, as well, with the most serious dangers to our constitutional system of division of powers.

b) APPROPRIATIONS ACTS

i) FEDERAL APPROPRIATIONS PROCESS AND SUBSTANTIVE LEGISLATION

Special considerations apply when the later statute which arguably repeals an earlier law is a federal appropriations statute. The "no repeal by implication" doctrine applies with greater force than in other situations. Why is that so? Is the policy or practice against substantive legislation in appropriations legislation so strong that the "no repeal by implication" doctrine indicates likely legislative intent? To answer that question, consider the following discussion about the rules and realities of the appropriations process.

The House and Senate have rules discouraging appropriation of unauthorized expenditures and substantive legislation in an appropriations bill. As of 1996, House Rule XXI(2) provides:

(a) No appropriation shall be reported in any general appropriation bill, or be in order as an amendment thereto, for any expenditure not previously authorized by law, except to continue appropriations for such public works and objects as are already in progress.

(b) No provision changing existing law shall be reported in any general appropriation bill except germane provisions which retrench expenditures by the reduction of amounts of money covered by the bill * * *.

(c) No amendment to a general appropriation bill shall be in order if changing existing law. * * *

The Senate rules are more complex. Senate Rule XVI provides:

1.   * * * [N]o amendments shall be received to any general appropriations bill the effect of which will be * * * to add a new item of appropriation, unless it be made to carry out the provisions of some * * * act or resolution previously passed by the Senate during that session; or unless the same shall be moved by direction of the Committee on Appropriations or of a committee of the Senate having legislative jurisdiction of the subject matter, or proposed in pursuance of an estimate submitted in accordance with law.

2.   The Committee on Appropriations shall not report an appropriation bill containing amendments to such bill proposing new or general legislation * * *.

4.   [N]o amendment offered by any other Senator which proposes general legislation shall be received to any general appropriation bill * * *.

The typical pattern today is for Congress to follow these rules and to authorize spending in one law and appropriate funds in another statute, or to adopt a substantive program in one law and appropriate funds in another. The radical separation of appropriations from other legislation was not always observed. In the last half of the 19th century, detailed line-item appropriations were a common method of authorizing federal programs, used in about half the statutes adopted by Congress. Our image of modern legislation—separating authorization and appropriation—is a product of the modern state, which typically involves broad program authorizations in one law followed by specific appropriations in another law.

Moreover, even today, there are many ways to blur the line between, on the one hand, appropriations laws, and, on the other hand, authorization of spending for programs and substantive legislation.

1.   In the House, the "Holman" rule permits legislation changing existing law in an appropriations bill if it results in a reduction

("retrenchment") of expenditures (such as by canceling a program calling for expenditure of a specific amount of money).

2.   Continuing resolutions are not subject to the prohibitions applicable to general appropriations bills. A continuing resolution is used to provide funds at prior levels when regular appropriations expire at the end of a fiscal year and no new regular appropriations have been passed. Budget crises at the end of legislative sessions have made continuing resolutions more common in recent years.

3.   A limitation on the expenditure of funds is not considered improper in an appropriations law, as long as it does not impose newly enacted additional duties or discretionary judgments. For example, in the late 1970's, Congress prohibited the IRS from spending money to enforce a ruling requiring affirmative action by schools to qualify for tax exemption. These so-called "limitation" riders expire, however, once the appropriations bill with the rider expires.

House floor amendments offering limitation riders proliferated in the 1970's as an end run around substantive committees and House leadership. The House rules were therefore changed in 1983 to make such floor amendments very difficult. See House Rules XXI(2)(c-d). Only very popular floor amendments with limitation riders can pass, such as those on abortion funding.

4.   No question of following the House and Senate rules arises if a point of order is not raised by a member of Congress. In the House, a "special rule" proposed by the Rules Committee and adopted by the House can prohibit a point of order against a bill, even though it contains provisions in an appropriations bill that would violate House rules. In the Senate, the same result can be achieved by a Unanimous Consent Agreement (UCA). Even if a point of order is raised, the definition of "unauthorized" spending or substantive legislation in an appropriations bill may be unclear. In the Senate, where points of order are much more common than in the House, floor votes are often based on political considerations rather than judgments about procedural niceties. Remember also that raising a point of order may be considered an unfriendly act, creating enemies among colleagues whose good favor is needed in the future.

The blurring of lines between appropriations and other types of legislation is also achieved by using the authorization process to control appropriations. Some authorization statutes, for example, leave no room for expenditure control. This is true of many entitlement programs like Social Security. Authorization statutes can also impose a very short authorization period. Many Defense authorizations are of this type. This means that periodic review of a program, often the province of appropriations committees, is in fact undertaken by the authorization committees.

Authorization statutes might also contain various techniques for constraining the appropriations process. They might adopt appropriation-forcing language, such as funds "shall be available," or funds shall "not be less than" some amount. The appropriations committees sometimes object to such legislation as improper in authorization legislation. Another technique is for an authorization statute to specify that, if total funding is less than the total authorized, the authorized funding for each program is proportionately reduced, or that authorization for one program depends on a certain level of appropriations for one or more other programs.

Federal legislation can also authorize federal borrowing, federal contracts, and tax breaks ("tax expenditures"), without going through the appropriations process.

Finally, there is a recent tendency towards using federal appropriations legislation for passage of substantive law, because the party split between the Presidency and Congress and the drying up of revenue for innovative programs has made free-standing substantive law hard to pass. Appropriations laws must, however, be passed every year and they have become convenient vehicles for substantive legislation. Another reason is that the federal budget process (see Chapter 18.02ci) requires annual "reconciliation" legislation to match appropriations with congressional budget targets and this legislation is not subject to a Senate filibuster.

Whatever the legislative practice, there is nothing illegal about using a federal appropriations statute to authorize expenditures or to change substantive law. In this respect, federal legislation differs from state law; state constitutions usually prohibit substantive legislation in appropriations laws—see Chapter 18. For example, in City of Los Angeles v. Adams, 556 F.2d 40 (D.C.Cir.1977), the court stated:

> According to its own rules, Congress is not supposed to use appropriations measures as vehicles for the amendment of general laws, including revision of expenditure authorization. * * * Where Congress chooses to do so, however, we are bound to follow Congress's last word on the matter even in an appropriations law.

In United States v. Dickerson, 310 U.S. 554 (1940), the Court held that repeated yearly enactment of an appropriations law, denying funds for payment of reenlistment allowances, had the effect of suspending the right to the allowances during the affected year. You may have difficulty imagining how legal rights could have survived failure to appropriate money in the first place. First, absence of appropriations prevents a federal official from making a disbursement, but the underlying right might still survive and be enforced by injunction. Second, a money remedy from the government might even be available in the United States Claims Court if the statute created a cause of action for money against the United States and a remedy was provided for violation of the statute in the Claims Court, for which there is a general appropriation. See United States v. Langston, 118 U.S. 389

(1886)(statute authorized $7,500 salary and later appropriations statute did not state that the lesser appropriation of $5,000 was "full" compensation); New York Airways, Inc. v. United States, 369 F.2d 743 (Ct.Cl.1966)(inadequate appropriation did not modify amounts due under contract for carrying mail).[5]

Although there is nothing illegal about substantive legislation in federal appropriations statutes, courts sometimes take note of "a general principle that Congress cannot and does not legislate through the appropriations process." Atchison, Topeka & Santa Fe Ry. Co. v. Callaway, 382 F.Supp. 610 (1974). This general principle affected the Court's decision in Andrus v. Sierra Club, 442 U.S. 347 (1979). A statute required an Environmental Impact Statement to accompany an agency's "proposals for legislation." The Court held that an agency's appropriations request was not a proposal for legislation and, therefore, did not require an Impact Statement.

QUESTION

In the following cases involving legislation providing and denying appropriations, the courts reach different results. In one case, providing money does *not* override prior substantive law; in the other, denying funds changes prior substantive law. What explains the difference? Is there a difference regarding likely legislative intent; policy coherence; anything else?

ii) PROVIDING MONEY

Tennessee Valley Authority v. Hill

437 U.S. 153 (1978).

■ Mr. Justice Burger delivered the opinion of the Court. * * *

[Editor—This case involved the Endangered Species Act of 1973. The Court interpreted this statute to prohibit the construction of a dam which endangered the snail darter. An injunction was sought when the construction was virtually complete. The question was whether later appropriations, which included money to build the dam, had any effect on the 1973 Act.

The year after this case granted the injunction against finishing dam construction Congress "authorized and directed completion" of the dam in Public Law 96–69, Title IV, 93 Stat. 449 (1979). Does this mean that the decision was wrong?]

---

5. See also Office of Personnel Management v. Richmond, 496 U.S. 414 (1990)(estoppel cannot be applied to force government to pay money claim because that would violate the prohibition against spending unappropri- ated funds; improper government behavior is dealt with only by private bills passed by the legislature and general appropriations to fund payments under statutes enforced by Claims Court judgments).

Notwithstanding Congress' expression of intent in [the Endangered Species Act of] 1973, we are urged to find that the continuing appropriations for Tellico Dam constitute an implied repeal of the 1973 Act, at least insofar as it applies to the Tellico Project. In support of this view, TVA points to the statements found in various House and Senate Appropriations Committees' Reports; those Reports generally reflected the attitude of the *Committees* either that the Act did not apply to Tellico or that the dam should be completed regardless of the provisions of the Act. Since we are unwilling to assume that these later Committee statements constituted advice to ignore the provisions of a duly enacted law, we assume that these Committees believed that the Act simply was not applicable in this situation. But even under this interpretation of the Committees' actions, we are unable to conclude that the Act has been in any respect amended or repealed. [Editor—In the material dealing with legislative history in Chapter 13, courts often deferred to committee reports. Why don't they do so here?]

There is nothing in the appropriations measures, as passed, which states that the Tellico Project was to be completed irrespective of the requirements of the Endangered Species Act. These appropriations, in fact, represented relatively minor components of the lump-sum amounts for the *entire* TVA budget. [Editor—The Court also noted in footnote 35: "The Appropriations Acts did not themselves identify the projects for which the sums had been appropriated; identification of these projects requires reference to the legislative history. Thus, unless a Member scrutinized in detail the Committee proceedings concerning the appropriations, he would have no knowledge of the possible conflict between the continued funding and the Endangered Species Act." In other words, the Appropriations Acts provided a lump-sum and the TVA Authority determined which specific projects to implement.] To find a repeal of the Endangered Species Act under these circumstances would surely do violence to the " 'cardinal rule * * * that repeals by implication are not favored.' " Morton v. Mancari, 417 U.S. 535, 549 (1974), quoting Posadas v. National City Bank, 296 U.S. 497, 503 (1936). In Posadas this Court held, in no uncertain terms, that "the intention of the legislature to repeal must be clear and manifest." In practical terms, this "cardinal rule" means that "[i]n the absence of some affirmative showing of an intention to repeal, the only permissible justification for a repeal by implication is when the earlier and later statutes are irreconcilable." Mancari, supra.

The doctrine disfavoring repeals by implication "applies with full vigor when * * * the subsequent legislation is an *appropriations* measure." This is perhaps an understatement since it would be more accurate to say that the policy applies with even *greater* force when the claimed repeal rests solely on an Appropriations Act. We recognize that both substantive enactments and appropriations measures are "Acts of Congress," but the latter have the limited and specific purpose of providing funds for authorized programs. When voting on appropriations measures, legislators are entitled to operate under the assumption that the funds will be devoted to purposes which are lawful and not for any purpose forbidden. Without such an assurance, every appropriations measure would be pregnant with prospects of altering substantive legislation, repealing by implication any prior statute which might prohibit the expenditure. Not only would this lead to the absurd result of requiring Members to review exhaustively the background of every authorization before voting on an appropriation, but it would flout the very rules the Congress carefully adopted to avoid this need. House Rule XXI(2), for instance, specifically provides:

> "No appropriation shall be reported in any general appropriation bill, or be in order as an amendment thereto, for any expenditure not previously authorized by law, unless in continuation of appropriations for such public works as are already in progress. *Nor shall any provision in any such bill or amendment thereto changing existing law be in order.*" (Emphasis added.)

See also Standing Rules of the Senate, Rule 16.4. Thus, to sustain petitioner's position, we would be obliged to assume that Congress meant to repeal pro tanto § 7 of the Act by means of a procedure expressly prohibited under the rules of Congress.

iii) DENYING MONEY

Preterm, Inc. v. Dukakis
591 F.2d 121 (1st Cir.1979)

■ Coffin, Chief Judge.

[Editor—Medicaid is a federal grant-in-aid program, which gives money to the states on condition that the states provide certain medical care to the poor. The federal appropriations law was amended (the Hyde Amendment) to prohibit use of federal money for abortions, except in limited circumstances, including cases of rape and incest, and to preserve the mother's life. The appropriations law did not explicitly change the conditions imposed on the states to get federal money. Plaintiff argued and the court agreed that state acceptance of federal money carried with it an obligation to provide abortions to protect the mother's health under all circumstances, wholly out of state funds, *unless* the Hyde Amendment had changed the substantive law. The court concluded that the Hyde Amendment changed the law.]

In this case we are called upon to assess the validity, in terms of compliance with the federal Medicaid Act, of Chapter 367, § 2, Item 4402–5000 of the Massachusetts Acts of 1978. Chapter 367 is an appropriations provision, limiting the expenditure of state funds for abortions to those abortions "which are necessary to prevent the death of the mother" and to those procedures "necessary for the proper treatment of the victims of forced rape or incest" if the incident is properly reported within thirty days.

At issue, as well, is the impact on the Medicaid Act and state plan thereunder of the Hyde Amendment, Section 101 of Pub. L. 95–205; 91 Stat. 1460 (Dec. 9, 1977), first enacted as a rider to the FY 1977 Health, Education and Welfare appropriations bill. The Hyde Amendment for FY 1978 prohibits federal funding for abortions except "where the life of the mother would be endangered", when the woman is a "victim of rape or incest" and reports the incident "promptly" and in instances where "severe and long-lasting physical health damage to the mother would result if the pregnancy were carried to term when so determined by two physicians." * * *

Plaintiffs contend that the Hyde Amendment must be construed according to its literal terms as authorizing federal funds for certain limited categories of abortions and thus shifting the total cost to the states of providing those abortion services not funded by the Hyde Amendment but nonetheless required by the Medicaid Act. They maintain that the Hyde Amendment has no impact on a state's obligations to provide services required by the Act.

The state, on the other hand, argues that * * * the Hyde Amendment is to be viewed as a policy decision concerning a state's obligations to provide publicly funded abortions and not as merely a shifting of the costs of non-Hyde Amendment abortions to the states. In support of its position, the state points to the congressional debates which preceded passage of the Amendment as well as the basic structure of the Act, namely joint federal and state participation in providing medical assistance to the needy. * * *

Our inquiry begins with the words of the statute itself, which if clear, ordinarily obviate the need to resort to extrinsic aids of statutory construction. The language of the Hyde Amendment, on its face, supports the plaintiffs' position. The Amendment states that "none of the funds provided for in this paragraph shall be used" to perform abortions, unless they fall within specified categories, and thus reads as a mere withdrawal of federal funds for certain services. No mention is made in the provision of any impact on the state's obligations. However, when the plain meaning of a statute produces a result " 'plainly at variance with the policy of the legislation as a whole' " and "aid to construction of the meaning of words, as used in the statute, is available, there certainly can be no 'rule of law' which forbids its use, however clear the words may appear on 'superficial examination.' " The construction urged by the plaintiffs would result in imposing an obligation on the states to fund the total cost of nonHyde Amendment therapeutic abortions, a result not consonant with the basic policy of the Medicaid system under which the federal government participates in the funding of medical services provided by the states. We therefore think it necessary to consider the legislative history of the Hyde Amendment.

The Legislative History

Congressional consideration of the Hyde Amendment began in the House of Representatives on June 17, 1977 and ended with a Senate debate and vote on a compromise measure on December 7, 1977. During this six month period some ten different versions were passed in one of the chambers, and no fewer than 25 roll call votes had been taken in the House and Senate. Congressional Quarterly, Weekly Report, Vol. XXXVI No. 5 at 258 (Feb. 4, 1978). There are neither conference reports nor committee reports; all we have are the debates and insertions in the Congressional Record. These, however, if considered as a whole, are illuminating. The leaders of both sides in the debate spoke often and long enough and clearly enough so that there is no doubt about what the Congress wanted to do and thought it was doing. * * *

* * * [T]he record is clear that both houses of Congress were acutely conscious that they were engaging in substantive legislation. The very first event which took place in the House of Representatives was the making of two points of order, the sustaining of the same, and an amendment by sponsor Hyde simply confining his Amendment to a ban on spending federal funds for abortions, any abortions. Congressman Hyde then expressed his regret that the points of order forced him to exclude mother's-lifesaving therapeutic abortions from his Amendment, adding that he agreed with those who had said it was unfortunate to burden appropriation bills with complex issues such as busing and abortion but that "The problem is that there is no other vehicle that reaches this floor in which these complex issues can be involved. Constitutional amendments which prohibit abortions stay languishing in subcommittee, much less committee, and so the only vehicle where the Members may work their will, unfortunately, is an appropriation bill." 123 Cong.Rec.H. 6083 (June 17, 1977). Subsequently, on August 2, after a candid explanation by Congressman Flood that the only way to enable the Amendment to exclude from its proscriptions abortions in cases of life endangering pregnancies was to restore the original language, such language was restored and no further points of order were made. 123 Cong. Rec.H. 8348–49 (Aug. 2, 1977). * * *

[Editor—The problem the House confronted was that limitation riders requiring the exercise of judgment not already permitted by law violate House rules.]

[In the Senate,] Senator Magnuson, a proponent of fewer restrictions, expressed his unhappiness, saying pithily, "I have said many, many times, as sort of a voice in the wilderness, that this does not belong on the HEW bill. It is legislation of the rawest nature on an appropriations-money-bill." 123 Cong. Rec. S. 19440 (Dec. 7, 1977). * * * [Editor—However, a point of order against the Senate version of the appropriation rider was defeated by a 74–21 vote in favor of its germaneness. Ultimately, Congress agreed on the language of the Hyde amendment even though it required the exercise of judgment by grant recipients.]

Perhaps the message of the legislation was conveyed most clearly by those who were opposed to restrictions on publicly funded abortions. Their litany of opposition stressed the harshness of depriving the poor of abortions which the more affluent could afford. The universal assumption in debate was that if the Amendment passed there would be no requirement that states carry on the service. [Editor—Courts will often disregard statements about a law's meaning by its opponents, on the theory that they will exaggerate the disadvantages of the legislation. Why did the court pay attention to what opponents said in this case?] * * *

Finally, the total absence in the debate of any suggestion that massive financial burdens were being shifted to the state further belies plaintiffs' contention that states were to continue to fund abortions beyond those qualifying under the Hyde Amendment. Indeed, were a state to undertake to pick up the burden dropped by the federal government and divert funds from other medical services, the functioning of its entire plan would be crippled.

From this sampling—which we think is a fair representation of the entire Congressional debate—we are persuaded that Congress realized that it was using the unusual and frowned upon device of legislating via an appropriations measure to accomplish a substantive result. That result was, it believed, far more significant than the proscription of federal funding of a program mandated by Medicaid to continue even if only with state funding.

Repeal by Implication

Plaintiffs contend that this reading of the Hyde Amendment brings it into conflict with the Medicaid Act and thus violates both the principle that we should endeavor so to construe two statutes that they may be capable of coexistence, "absent a clearly expressed congressional intention to the contrary", Morton v. Mancari, 417 U.S. 535, 551 (1974), and the equally prominent principle disfavoring repeals by implication, especially repeals via appropriations measures, Tennessee Valley Authority v. Hill, 98 S.Ct. 2279, 2299–2300 (1978). * * *

* * * Although [the plaintiff's] reading may permit the Hyde Amendment and the Medicaid Act to co-exist facially by effecting no change in the Act's requirements for state plans, it requires us to do violence to the Medicaid Act on a more pervasive and fundamental level than would result from reading the Amendment as a substantive alteration of those requirements. The Medicaid program is one of federal and state cooperation in funding medical assistance; a complete withdrawal of the federal prop in the system with the intent to drop the total cost of providing the service upon the states, runs directly counter to the basic structure of the program and could

seriously cripple a state's attempts to provide other necessary medical services embraced by its plan.

Moreover, the principle that two statutes should if possible be found capable of co-existence does not suggest that we should approach the statute with blinders and reconcile them at all costs, even when the second enactment is an appropriations measure. Tennessee Valley Authority v. Hill, supra, which plaintiffs have so vigorously invoked as indicating that either express or implied repeal of Medicaid is unthinkable, is not authority to the contrary. Indeed, our analysis of the factors which distinguish that case from the one at bar indicates that our construction of Congressional intent is proper. Tennessee Valley Authority v. Hill, supra, involved an unsuccessful argument that the continued appropriating of funds for the Tellico Dam repealed by implication the Endangered Species Act insofar as that Act would otherwise have required construction of the dam to be held up because of the fact that the snail darter and its habitat would be placed in jeopardy. The elements in that case were (1) brief statements of opinion of committee members in a lengthy report, that (2) monies in a very large appropriation act should be used to complete a dam, (3) although the act itself did not identify the approved objects of expenditure, and (4) the act supposedly repealed pro tanto lay in the jurisdiction of another committee. The Court had no difficulty in observing that since legislators are entitled to assume that appropriated funds are to be "devoted to purposes which are lawful", 98 S.Ct. at 2300, there was no basis to suppose that they felt any conflict between funding the dam and the Endangered Species Act. It also noted that there was "no indication that Congress as a whole was aware of [the committees'] views", that "the appropriations committees had no jurisdiction over the subject of endangered species", id., and that the "appropriations Acts did not themselves identify the projects for which the sums had been appropriated."

Here, in contrast, the objective was a solitary, specific proscription, not a hidden permitted purpose among a multitude; and the appropriation related completely to the subject matter of the affected substantive legislation. In United States v. Dickerson, 310 U.S. 554 (1940), the Court faced a situation more apposite to that at bar. Congress had enacted a proviso, appended to an appropriations bill, that none of the funds appropriated therein were to be used for payment "of any enlistment allowance for 'reenlistments made during the fiscal year ending June 30, 1939, notwithstanding the applicable portions of sections 9 and 10' of the Act of June 10, 1922." The Court concluded that Congress had intended to suspend the enlistment allowance authorized by § 9 and not merely to restrict the use of federal funds for that purpose. It refused to limit its analysis to the "plain and unambiguous" language of that statute and turned to the legislative history which clearly showed Congressional intent to legislate by an appropriations bill.

Furthermore, the legislative history which we have turned to in resolving this case does not suffer from the defects noted by the Tennessee Valley Authority v. Hill Court. The statement of Congressional intent upon which we rely is not embodied in appropriations committee reports, which represent merely the views of its members and may never have come to the attention of Congress as a whole. The heated and lengthy debates that led to passage of the numerous versions of the Hyde Amendment took place on the floor of each house, and the views expressed were those of a wide spectrum of its members. [Editor—Why were debates, usually weaker legislative history than Reports, given so much weight here?]

We recognize the force of our brother's dissent, that a court should not infer lightly that Congress has legislated in an appropriations measure so as to repeal a prior enactment, a legislative process that contravenes its rules, and that Congress has not, in so many words, stated that the Hyde Amendment repeals portions of the Medicaid Act. But we are unable to view this six month intensive debate—albeit an emotional one—as a mere exercise in cost-shifting. To so conclude ignores statement after statement by proponents and opponents of the Amendment that its passage would allow states to choose whether to fund more abortions than those specified therein and that it would affect drastically the lives of poor women by closing off their access to these services. Such a conclusion ignores as well the unquestionably explicit awareness by the legislators that they were using the disfavored vehicle of an appropriations measure to legislate this result and that they were setting aside their rules to do so. Indeed, were these expressions of Congressional intent held to be insufficient in quantity or quality to legislate substantively, we would in candor be forced to admit that legislation in appropriations acts was, as a practical matter, out of the question. Such a determination, regardless of our view of the wisdom of the course chosen by the legislature, is clearly beyond the proper scope of this court. * * *

■ Bownes, Circuit Judge (dissenting).

I respectfully dissent.

While I have no problem with my brethren's analysis as to the requirements that the Medicaid Act imposes on a participating state, I cannot agree that the Hyde Amendment has worked a substantive change in those requirements. * * *

Although my brethren recognize that the language of the Hyde Amendment speaks only to the use of federal funds, they feel that an extensive excursion into legislative history is necessary because its plain meaning produces a result at variance with the policy of the legislation as a whole. This is a bootstrap approach to statutory construction; it allows a court to ignore the plain language of a statute and rewrite it by drawing upon its legislative history. While congressional debates and committee reports can be a helpful guide to the intent of an ambiguously worded statute, they should not be used to defeat the clearly expressed statutory language. * * *

We have here a statute whose plain meaning is clear and whose congressional history can be construed to mean that a number of congressmen felt that, contrary to what the statute said, it would effect a substantial change in the Medicaid Act. If this were merely a matter of balancing the words of the statute against the words of the debate, this would be a close case, but the principle disfavoring repeal by implication and Congress' own procedural rules expressly prohibiting changing existing law via an appropriations bill, apply with particular pertinence here and compel a finding that there was no substantive amendment of the Medicaid Act.

The majority's attempt to distinguish this case from TVA v. Hill, supra, rests on the grounds that full-fledged and lengthy congressional debate is a better gauge of congressional intent than a committee report. As I noted before, however, the subject matter of the debate is an important factor to consider. It would not be inaccurate to say that the more emotional the subject, the less sure we can be that the words used reflect considered thought rather than expressing deeply ingrained feelings. [Editor—Why should "considered thought" receive priority over expressed feelings?] * * *

Another factor militating against the result reached by the majority is Congress' own rules. As pointed out in TVA v. Hill, supra, both houses of Congress have a rule that expressly prohibits changing existing law by an amendment to an appropriation bill. There is scant mention in the congressional debate of these rules or the fact that both houses intended to flout them. Are we to assume that Congress deliberately evaded and ignored its own procedural rules, or forgot about them, or was entirely ignorant of them? The only logical conclusion that gives due deference to Congress' knowledge and respect for its own procedural requirements is that the Hyde Amendment was limited to the use of federal funds only.

15.04 SUPPORTIVE, NEGATIVE, OR INDEPENDENT RELATIONSHIPS AMONG STATUTES

Several statutes often contain similar or divergent texts about particular problems, such as whether a winning litigant is entitled to recover attorney's fees and other costs from the loser. The question is whether these statutes are part of a pattern *or* should instead be interpreted as independent pronouncements. If there is a pattern, is it determined by the text—the same interpretation of similar language; different interpretation when the texts differ? Or should the existence of a pattern be determined by policy implications—a common interpretation if policies underlying the statutes are similar (the *pari materia* doctrine), but a different interpretation if the underlying statutory policies differ?

a) SAME TEXT

If two statutes contain the same language, does that suggest that the words have the same meaning? We have earlier discussed a linguistic canon that words should have similar meanings when used within the same statute, though we noted exceptions. Not surprisingly, the similarity of meaning of language across statutes is even more problematic. The similarity of meaning usually depends on whether the statutes deal with the same subject matter (*pari materia*). Of course, it is not always easy to decide whether the subject matter is similar enough—whether the policy implications are similar enough—to justify an inference that the textual meanings are similar.

The fundamental issue is the extent to which a text's home in a particular statute gives it a meaning different from what the same term might have in another textual setting. This is simply another version of the more general problem of deciding how much context to consider and what that context suggests about the meaning of language (recall Chisom v. Roemer—does "representatives" include elected judges). How do the judges answer these questions in the following cases?

Ruckelshaus v. Sierra Club

463 U.S. 680 (1983).

■ Mr. Justice Rehnquist delivered the opinion of the Court.

* * *

[Editor—The issue in this case was whether attorney's fees could be recovered from a party who had won every issue litigated. Sec. 307(f) of the Clean Air Act provided for recovery of attorney's fees from another party "whenever (the court) determines that such an award is appropriate." The Court refused to hold that an award could be "appropriate" if a party lost on all issues. It supported its conclusion by reference to the general American Rule against recoveries of attorney's fees from other litigants. It also relied on the relationship of § 307(f) to another provision of the statute, § 304(d).]

* * * [T]he relation between § 304(d) and § 307(f) is instructive. Like § 307(f), § 304(d) provides that a court may award fees when "appropriate." Importantly, however, suits may be brought under § 304 against *private* parties alleged to be in violation of the requirements of the Clean Air Act. It is clear, as explained below, that, whatever general standard may apply under § 307(f), a similar standard applies under § 304(d). In Northcross v. Memphis Bd. of Ed., 412 U.S. 427, 93 S.Ct. 2201, 37 L.Ed.2d 48 (1973), we held that similar attorney's fee provisions should be interpreted pari passu, and read the "prevailing party" standard in 20 U.S.C. § 1617 as identical to that in 42 U.S.C. § 2000a–3(b). * * * Thus, it is clear, at least as a general principle, that awards of attorney's fees under § 304(d) will be "appropriate" in circumstances similar to those that are "appropriate" under § 307(f).

Given the foregoing, respondents' argument that fee awards are available even to unsuccessful plaintiffs encounters yet further difficulties. Section 304 suits may be brought against private businesses by any private citizen. Such suits frequently involve novel legal theories, theories that the EPA has rejected. After protracted litigation requiring payment of expensive legal fees and associated costs in both money and manpower, the private defendant may well succeed in refuting each charge against it—proving it was in complete compliance with every detail of the Clean Air Act. Yet, under respondents' view of the Act, the defendant's reward could be a second lawyer's bill—this one payable to those who wrongly accused it of violating the law. We simply do not believe that Congress would have intended such a result without clearly saying so. * * *

We conclude, therefore, that the language and legislative history of § 307(f) do not support respondents' argument that the section was intended as a radical departure from established principles requiring that a fee claimant attain some success on the merits before it may receive an award of fees. Instead, we are persuaded that if Congress intended such a novel result—which would require federal courts to make sensitive, difficult, and ultimately highly subjective determinations—it would have said so in far plainer language than that employed here. Hence, we hold that, absent some degree of success on the merits by the claimant, it is not "appropriate" for a federal court to award attorney's fees under § 307(f). Accordingly, the judgment of the Court of Appeals is Reversed.

Justice Stevens' dissent commented as follows about whether the word "appropriate" had the same meaning in §§ 304 and 307.

The word "appropriate," however, may well have different meanings in § 304 suits, which serve the primary function of aiding in the abatement of air pollution by stimulating *enforcement* of standards and regulations under the Clean Air Act, and in § 307 suits, which challenge the *validity* of air pollution standards promulgated by the agency. The reference in the 1970 legislative history to abatement of a violation before judgment in litigation, for example, has no direct applicability to § 307 actions seeking judicial review. In addition, private parties may be defendants in § 304 actions but not in § 307 judicial review proceedings. I do not believe it would be appropriate for a court to require a *private* defendant to pay the attorney's fees of an unsuccessful plaintiff in a § 304 suit, and of course, the possibility would never arise in a § 307 action. Thus, the

Court's discussion has the same heroic quality as Don Quixote's defense against the charge of the windmills.

Fogerty v. Fantasy, Inc.

510 U.S. 517 (1994).

■ Chief Justice Rehnquist delivered the opinion of the Court.

The Copyright Act of 1976, 17 U.S.C. § 505, provides in relevant part that in any copyright infringement action "the court may * * * award a reasonable attorney's fee to the prevailing party as part of the costs." The question presented in this case is what standards should inform a court's decision to award attorney's fees to a prevailing defendant in a copyright infringement action—a question that has produced conflicting views in the Courts of Appeals. * * *

[Editor—17 U.S.C. § 505 states: "In any civil action under this title, the court in its discretion may allow the recovery of full costs by or against any party other than the United States or an officer thereof. Except as otherwise provided by this title, the court may also award a reasonable attorney's fee to the prevailing party as part of the costs." In this case, the plaintiff-respondent lost and argued that defendant's right to attorney's fees should be determined by the same "non-even-handed" approach used in civil rights states, which gave prevailing plaintiffs a better chance of recovering attorney's fees than a prevailing defendant.]

The statutory language—"the court may also award a reasonable attorney's fee to the prevailing party as part of the costs"—gives no hint that successful plaintiffs are to be treated differently than successful defendants. But respondent contends that our decision in Christiansburg Garment Co. v. EEOC, 434 U.S. 412 (1978), in which we construed virtually identical language, supports a differentiation in treatment between plaintiffs and defendants.

Christiansburg construed the language of Title VII of the Civil Rights Act of 1964, which in relevant part provided that the court "in its discretion, may allow the prevailing party * * * a reasonable attorney's fee as part of the costs * * *." 42 U.S.C. § 2000e–5(k). We had earlier held, interpreting the cognate provision of Title II of that Act, 42 U.S.C. § 2000a–3(b), that a prevailing plaintiff "should ordinarily recover an attorney's fee unless some special circumstances would render such an award unjust." Newman v. Piggie Park Enterprises, Inc., 390 U.S. 400, 402 (1968). This decision was based on what we found to be the important policy objectives of the Civil Rights statutes, and the intent of Congress to achieve such objectives through the use of plaintiffs as " 'private attorneys general.' " In Christiansburg, we determined that the same policy considerations were not at work in the case of a prevailing civil rights defendant. We noted that a Title VII plaintiff, like a Title II plaintiff in Piggie Park, is "the chosen instrument of Congress to vindicate 'a policy that Congress considered of the highest priority.' " We also relied on the admittedly sparse legislative history to indicate that different standards were to be applied to successful plaintiffs than to successful defendants.

Respondent points to our language in Flight Attendants v. Zipes, 491 U.S. 754, 758, n. 2 (1989), that "fee-shifting statutes' similar language is a 'strong indication' that they are to be interpreted alike." But here we think this normal indication is overborne by the factors relied upon in our Christiansburg opinion which are absent in the case of the Copyright Act. * * *

The goals and objectives of the [Civil Rights and Copyright] Acts are [ ] not completely similar. Oftentimes, in the civil rights context, impecunious "private attorney general" plaintiffs can ill afford to litigate their claims against defendants with more resources. Congress sought to redress this balance in part, and to provide incentives for the bringing of meritorious lawsuits, by treating successful plaintiffs more favorably than successful defendants in terms of the award of attorney's fees. The primary objective of the Copyright Act is to encourage the production of original literary, artistic, and musical expression for the good of the public. In the copyright context, it has been noted that "entities which sue for copyright infringement as plaintiffs can run the gamut from corporate behemoths to starving artists; the same is true of prospective copyright infringement defendants."

We thus conclude that respondent's argument based on our fee-shifting decisions under the Civil Rights Act must fail.

b) DIFFERENT TEXTS

When statutes have different texts, does that necessarily imply that the meanings are different, or are there still policy coherence questions. Just as similar texts might have different meanings, so different texts might have similar meanings.

One way to approach the textual differences is to adopt a super-text approach and assume that textual differences imply different meanings. A somewhat more refined approach, still focused on the text, is to ask about drafting realities. After all, if texts have meaning shared by authors and audiences, different texts might *not* have different meanings, if the authors are different. Finally, the textual differences might be approached from a policy coherence perspective, which might suggest a similar meaning for statutes with different texts in different statutory settings. Which of these approaches is taken by the judges in the following cases?

West Virginia University Hospitals, Inc. v. Casey

499 U.S. 83 (1991).

■ Justice Scalia delivered the opinion of the Court.

This case presents the question whether fees for services rendered by experts in civil rights litigation may be shifted to the losing party pursuant to 42 U.S.C. § 1988, which permits the award of "a reasonable attorney's fee."

Petitioner West Virginia University Hospitals, Inc. (WVUH), operates a hospital in Morgantown, W.Va., near the Pennsylvania border. The hospital is often used by medicaid recipients living in southwestern Pennsylvania. In January 1986, Pennsylvania's Department of Public Welfare notified WVUH of new medicaid reimbursement schedules for services provided to Pennsylvania residents by the Morgantown hospital. In administrative proceedings, WVUH unsuccessfully objected to the new reimbursement rates on both federal statutory and federal constitutional grounds. After exhausting administrative remedies, WVUH filed suit in Federal District Court under 42 U.S.C. § 1983. Named as defendants (respondents here) were Pennsylvania Governor Robert Casey and various other Pennsylvania officials.

Counsel for WVUH employed Coopers & Lybrand, a national accounting firm, and three doctors specializing in hospital finance to assist in the preparation of the lawsuit and to testify at trial. WVUH prevailed at trial in May 1988. The District Court subsequently awarded fees pursuant to 42 U.S.C. § 1988, including over $100,-000 in fees attributable to expert services. The District Court found these services to have been "essential" to presentation of the case—a finding not disputed by respondents. * * *

The record of statutory usage demonstrates convincingly that attorney's fees and expert fees are regarded as separate elements of litigation cost. While some fee-shifting provisions, like § 1988, refer only to "attorney's fees," see, e.g., Civil Rights Act of 1964, 42 U.S.C. § 2000e–5(k), many others explicitly shift expert witness fees as well as attorney's fees. In 1976, just over a week prior to the enactment of § 1988, Congress passed those provisions of the Toxic Substances Control Act, 15 U.S.C. §§ 2618(d), 2619(c)(2), which provide that a prevailing party may recover "the costs of suit and reasonable fees for attorneys *and expert witnesses*." (Emphasis added.) Also in 1976, Congress amended the Consumer Product Safety Act, 15 U.S.C. §§ 2060(c), 2072(a), 2073, which as originally enacted in 1972 shifted to the losing party "costs of suit, including a reasonable attorney's fee," see 86 Stat. 1226. In the 1976 amendment, Congress altered the fee shifting provisions to their present form by adding a phrase shifting expert witness fees in addition to attorney's fees. See Pub. L. 94–284, § 10, 90 Stat. 506, 507. Two other significant acts passed in 1976 contain similar phrasing: The

Resource Conservation and Recovery Act of 1976, 42 U.S.C. § 6972(e) ("costs of litigation (including reasonable attorney and expert witness fees)"), and the Natural Gas Pipeline Safety Act Amendments of 1976, 49 U.S.C. App. § 1686(e)("costs of suit, including reasonable attorney's fees and reasonable expert witnesses fees").

Congress enacted similarly phrased fee-shifting provisions in numerous statutes both before 1976, see, e.g., Endangered Species Act of 1973, 16 U.S.C. § 1540(g)(4)("costs of litigation (including reasonable attorney and expert witness fees)"), and afterwards, see, e.g., Public Utility Regulatory Policies Act of 1978, 16 U.S.C. § 2632(a)(1)("reasonable attorneys' fees, expert witness fees, and other reasonable costs incurred in preparation and advocacy of [the litigant's] position"). These statutes encompass diverse categories of legislation, including tax, administrative procedure, environmental protection, consumer protection, admiralty and navigation, utilities regulation, and, significantly, civil rights: The Equal Access to Justice Act (EAJA), the counterpart to § 1988 for violation of federal rights by federal employees, states that " 'fees and other expenses' [as shifted by § 2412(d)(1)(A)] includes the reasonable expenses of expert witnesses * * * and reasonable attorney fees." 28 U.S.C. § 2412(d)(2)(A). At least 34 statutes in 10 different titles of the U.S. Code explicitly shift attorney's fees and expert witness fees.

The laws that refer to fees for nontestimonial expert services are less common, but they establish a similar usage both before and after 1976: Such fees are referred to *in addition* to attorney's fees when a shift is intended. [Editor—Discussion of laws referring to the services of nontestimonial experts omitted.] * * *

We think this statutory usage shows beyond question that attorney's fees and expert fees are distinct items of expense. If, as WVUH argues, the one includes the other, dozens of statutes referring to the two separately become an inexplicable exercise in redundancy. * * *

[Editor—The Court then argues that *judicial* usage of the phrase "attorney's fees" did not include expert's fees. Federal courts shifted expert's fees to losing parties pursuant to equitable discretion but not as an element of attorney's fees. The Court then discussed the context and legislative history underlying the statute interpreted in this case.]

WVUH suggests that a distinctive meaning of "attorney's fees" should be adopted with respect to § 1988 because this statute was meant to overrule our decision in Alyeska Pipeline Service Co. v. Wilderness Society, 421 U.S. 240 (1975). As mentioned above, prior to 1975 many courts awarded expert fees and attorney's fees in certain circumstances pursuant to their equitable discretion. In Alyeska, we held that this discretion did not extend beyond a few exceptional circumstances long recognized by common law. Specifically, we rejected the so-called "private attorney general" doctrine recently created by some lower federal courts, which allowed equitable fee shifting to plaintiffs in certain types of civil rights litigation. WVUH argues that § 1988 was intended to restore the pre-Alyeska regime—and that, since expert fees were shifted then, they should be shifted now.

Both chronology and the remarks of sponsors of the bill that became § 1988 suggest that at least some members of Congress viewed it as a response to Alyeska. It is a considerable step, however, from this proposition to the conclusion the hospital would have us draw, namely, that § 1988 should be read as a reversal of Alyeska in all respects.

By its plain language and as unanimously construed in the courts, § 1988 is both broader and narrower than the pre-Alyeska regime. Before Alyeska, civil rights plaintiffs could recover fees pursuant to the private attorney general doctrine only if private enforcement was necessary to defend important rights benefiting large numbers of people, and cost barriers might otherwise preclude private suits. Section 1988 contains no similar limitation—so that in the present suit there is no question as to the propriety of shifting WVUH's attorney's fees, even though it is highly doubtful they could have been awarded under pre-Alyeska equitable theories. In other respects, however, § 1988 is not as broad as the former regime. It is limited, for example, to violations of specified civil rights statutes—which means that it would not have reversed the outcome of Alyeska itself, which involved not a civil rights statute but the National Environmental Policy Act of 1969, 42 U.S.C. § 4321 et seq. Since it is clear that, in many respects, § 1988 was not meant to return us precisely to the pre-Alyeska regime, the objective of achieving such a return is no reason to depart from the normal import of the text.

WVUH further argues that the congressional purpose in enacting § 1988 must prevail over the ordinary meaning of the statutory terms. * * * As we have observed before, however, the purpose of a statute includes not only what it sets out to change, but also what it resolves to leave alone. The best evidence of that purpose is the statutory text adopted by both Houses of Congress and submitted to the President. Where that contains a phrase that is unambiguous—that has a clearly accepted meaning in both legislative and judicial practice—we do not permit it to be expanded or contracted by the statements of individual legislators or committees during the course of the enactment process. Congress could easily have shifted "attorney's fees and expert witness fees," or "reasonable litigation expenses," as it did in contemporaneous statutes; it chose instead to enact more restrictive language, and we are bound by that restriction. * * *

WVUH's last contention is that, even if Congress plainly did not include expert fees in the fee-shifting provisions of § 1988, it would have done so had it thought about it. Most of the pre–§ 1988 statutes that explicitly shifted expert fees dealt with environmental litigation, where the necessity of expert advice was readily apparent; and when Congress later enacted the EAJA, the federal counterpart of § 1988, it explicitly included expert fees. Thus, the argument runs, the 94th Congress simply forgot; it is our duty to ask how they would have decided had they actually considered the question.

This argument profoundly mistakes our role. Where a statutory term presented to us for the first time is ambiguous, we construe it to contain that permissible meaning which fits most logically and comfortably into the body of both previously and subsequently enacted law. We do so not because that precise accommodative meaning is what the lawmakers must have had in mind (how could an earlier Congress know what a later Congress would enact?) but because it is our role to make sense rather than nonsense out of the corpus juris. [Editor—This is about as strong a statement of the "policy coherence" approach as you will find. Notice that it come from Justice Scalia. Notice also, in the remainder of this paragraph, that he would severely limits its application.] But where, as here, the meaning of the term prevents such accommodation, it is not our function to eliminate clearly expressed inconsistency of policy, and to treat alike subjects that different Congresses have chosen to treat differently. The facile attribution of congressional "forgetfulness" cannot justify such a usurpation. Where what is at issue is not a contradictory disposition within the same enactment, but merely a difference between the more parsimonious policy of an earlier enactment and the more generous policy of a later one, there is no more basis for saying that the earlier Congress forgot than for saying that the earlier Congress felt differently. In such circumstances, the attribution of forgetfulness rests in reality upon the judge's assessment that the later statute contains the better disposition. But that is not for judges to prescribe. * * *

■ Justice Stevens, with whom Justice Marshall and Justice Blackmun join, dissenting. * * *

In the early 1970s, Congress began to focus on the importance of public interest litigation, and since that time, it has enacted numerous fee-shifting statutes. In many of these statutes, which the majority cites at length, Congress has expressly authorized the recovery of expert witness fees as part of the costs of litigation. The question in this case is whether, notwithstanding the omission of such an express authorization in 42 U.S.C. § 1988, Congress intended to authorize such recovery when it provided for "a reasonable attorney's fee as part of the costs." * * *

The Senate Report on the Civil Rights Attorneys' Fees Awards Act explained that the purpose of the proposed amendment to 42

U.S.C. § 1988 was "to remedy anomalous gaps in our civil rights laws created by the United States Supreme Court's recent decision in Alyeska, and to achieve consistency in our civil rights laws." S. Rep. No. 94–1011, p. 1 (1976). The Senate Committee on the Judiciary wanted to level the playing field so that private citizens, who might have little or no money, could still serve as "private attorneys general" and afford to bring actions, even against state or local bodies, to enforce the civil rights laws. * * *

To underscore its intention to return the courts to their pre-Alyeska practice of shifting fees in civil rights cases, the Senate Committee's Report cited with approval not only several cases in which fees had been shifted, but also all of the cases contained in Legal Fees, Hearings before the Subcommittee on Representation of Citizen Interests of the Senate Committee on the Judiciary, 93rd Cong., 1st Sess., pt. 3, pp. 888–1024, 1060–1062 (1973)(hereinafter Senate Hearings). See S. Rep. No. 94–1011, p. 4, n. 3 (1976). The cases collected in the 1973 Senate Hearings included many in which courts had permitted the shifting of costs, including expert witness fees. At the time when the Committee referred to these cases, though several were later reversed, it used them to make the point that prior to Alyeska, courts awarded attorney's fees and costs, including expert witness fees, in civil rights cases, and that they did so in order to encourage private citizens to bring such suits. It was to this pre-Alyeska regime, in which courts could award expert witness fees along with attorney's fees, that the Senate Committee intended to return through the passage of the fee-shifting amendment to § 1988.

The House Report expressed concerns similar to those raised by the Senate Report. * * *

This Court's determination today that petitioner must assume the cost of $104,133.00 in expert witness fees is at war with the congressional purpose of making the prevailing party whole. * * *

Evolving legal landscape. Justice Stevens concludes his dissent with some broad comments about statutory interpretation. He notes that "the Court has vacillated between a purely literal approach to the task of statutory interpretation and an approach that seeks guidance from historical context, legislative history, and prior cases identifying the purpose that motivated the legislation." He then observes that "when the Court has put on its thick grammarian's spectacles and ignored the available evidence of congressional purpose," Congress has enacted statutes reversing the Court's decision.[6] He concludes:

---

6. Congress overrode Casey itself as it applied to expert's fees in *employment discrimi-* *nation* cases. Civil Rights Act of 1991, § 113, Pub. L. 102–166, 105 Stat. 1071 (1991).

In the domain of statutory interpretation, Congress is the master. It obviously has the power to correct our mistakes, but we do the country a disservice when we needlessly ignore persuasive evidence of Congress' actual purpose and require it "to take the time to revisit the matter" and to restate its purpose in more precise English whenever its work product suffers from an omission or inadvertent error. * * *

The Court concludes its opinion with the suggestion that disagreement with its textual analysis could only be based on the dissenter's preference for a "better" statute. It overlooks the possibility that a different view may be more faithful to Congress' command. The fact that Congress has consistently provided for the inclusion of expert witness fees in fee-shifting statutes when it considered the matter is a weak reed on which to rest the conclusion that the omission of such a provision represents a deliberate decision to forbid such awards. Only time will tell whether the Court, with its literal reading of § 1988, has correctly interpreted the will of Congress with respect to the issue it has resolved today.

Justice Scalia responds to Justice Stevens comments as follows:

WVUH at least asks us to guess the preferences of the enacting Congress. Justice Stevens apparently believes our role is to guess the desires of the present Congress, or of Congresses yet to be. "Only time will tell," he says, "whether the Court, with its literal reading of § 1988, has correctly interpreted the will of Congress." The implication is that today's holding will be proved wrong if Congress amends the law to conform with his dissent. We think not. The "will of Congress" we look to is not a will evolving from Session to Session, but a will expressed and fixed in a particular enactment. Otherwise, we would speak not of "interpreting" the law but of "intuiting" or "predicting" it. Our role is to say what the law, as hitherto enacted, is; not to forecast what the law, as amended, will be.

COMMENTS AND QUESTIONS

1. *Judge Posner.* Compare the Court's approach in Casey with Judge Posner's opinion in Matter of Wagner, 808 F.2d 542 (7th Cir.1986). The issue was the definition of "gross income" in the Bankruptcy Act. This mattered because a farmer with more than 80% gross income from farming in the prior taxable year could not be forced into bankruptcy. Judge Posner held that "gross income" in the Bankruptcy Act had the same meaning as in the Internal Revenue Code. He rejected any contrary implication from the fact that many provisions of the United States Code (but not the Bankruptcy Act) explicitly stated that "gross income" had the same meaning as under the Internal Revenue Code. In Posner's view, failure to *explicitly* affirm a common tax and bankruptcy definition was irrelevant because "the United States

Code is not the work of a single omniscient intellect." Judge Posner goes on to adopt a common definition of "gross income" in the income tax and bankruptcy laws, because it would implement the underlying policy of the Bankruptcy Act favoring mechanical simplicity and certainty.[7]

2. *Justice Frankfurter.* In the following case, the majority appears to adopt a super-text approach. Why does Frankfurter's dissent reject that approach—is it the reality of legislative drafting; policy coherence?

United States v. Monia

317 U.S. 424 (1943).

■ Mr. Justice Roberts delivered the opinion of the Court. * * *

* * * The question is whether one who, in obedience to a subpoena, appears before a grand jury inquiring into an alleged violation of the Sherman Act, and gives testimony under oath substantially touching the alleged offense, obtains immunity from prosecution for that offense, pursuant to the terms of the Sherman Act, although he does not claim his privilege against self-incrimination. [Editor—The Government argued that the witness must claim the privilege to enjoy immunity.]

The Sherman Act provides in part:

"* * * no person shall be prosecuted or be subjected to any penalty or forfeiture for or on account of any transaction, matter, or thing concerning which he may testify or produce evidence, documentary or otherwise, in any proceeding, suit, or prosecution under said Acts [the Interstate Commerce Act, the Sherman Antitrust Act, and other acts]; Provided further, that no person so testifying shall be exempt from prosecution or punishment for perjury committed in so testifying."

That statute was supplemented by the Act of June 30, 1906, which, so far as material, is

"* * * under the immunity provisions [of the Sherman Act and other acts] immunity shall extend only to a natural person who, in obedience to a subpoena, gives testimony under oath or produces evidence, documentary or otherwise, under oath."
* * *

Not until 1933 did Congress evidence an intent that if the witness desired immunity he must, in addition, assert his constitutional privilege. In a series of acts adopted between 1934 and 1940 an additional provision was inserted adding this requirement. These

---

7. But cf. Lukhard v. Reed, 481 U.S. 368 (1987)(Justice Scalia)(personal injury awards are income in AFDC welfare program; the fact that Congress was silent in the AFDC statute but explicitly excluded personal injury awards from income under the income tax and Food Stamps laws tends to refute rather than support a legislative intent to exclude personal injury awards from AFDC computations).

acts indicate how simple it would have been to add a similar provision applicable to the Interstate Commerce Act, the Sherman Act, and others which have been allowed to stand as originally enacted save for the amending Act of 1906.

The legislation involved in the instant case is plain in its terms and, on its face, means to the layman that if he is subpoenaed, and sworn, and testifies, he is to have immunity. [Editor—Notice the Court's concern here for the layman's understanding of the statutory text. Whose understanding of the text does Justice Frankfurter's dissent, *infra*, emphasize?] * * * Congress evidently intended to afford Government officials the choice of subpoenaing a witness and putting him under oath, with the knowledge that he would have complete immunity from prosecution respecting any matter substantially connected with the transactions in respect of which he testified, or retaining the right to prosecute by foregoing the opportunity to examine him. That Congress did not intend, or by the statutes in issue provide, that, in addition, the witness must claim his privilege, seems clear. It is not for us to add to the legislation what Congress pretermitted. * * *

■ Mr. Justice Frankfurter, dissenting:

It is beyond dispute that the Constitution does not compel Congress to afford immunity from prosecution to those who testify without invoking the constitutional privilege against self-incrimination. The question for decision here is whether, by the Act of June 30, 1906, 34 Stat. 798, Congress granted more than the Constitution requires * * * by conferring immunity to persons who testify without claiming the protection of the privilege against self-incrimination and who in no way indicate that their testimony is being given in return for the statutory immunity. * * *

This question cannot be answered by closing our eyes to everything except the naked words of the Act of June 30, 1906. The notion that because the words of a statute are plain, its meaning is also plain, is merely pernicious oversimplification. It is a wooden English doctrine of rather recent vintage, to which lip service has on occasion been given here, but which since the days of Marshall this Court has rejected, especially in practice. A statute, like other living organisms, derives significance and sustenance from its environment, from which it cannot be severed without being mutilated. Especially is this true where the statute, like the one before us, is part of a legislative process having a history and a purpose. The meaning of such a statute cannot be gained by confining inquiry within its four corners. Only the historic process of which such legislation is an incomplete fragment—that to which it gave rise as well as that which gave rise to it—can yield its true meaning. * * *

[Editor—Justice Frankfurter then reviews the history of the 1906 immunity legislation and concludes that it was intended to permit a witness to obtain immunity only to the extent required by the

Constitution, which applies only if the witness claims the privilege against self-incrimination. He traces the text of the 1906 Act to the specific need to correct a misapprehension created by a lower court decision that the immunity might be available to corporations and to witnesses who were not subpoenaed—hence, the specific reference in the 1906 Act to "natural person" and "obedience to a subpoena." Justice Frankfurter then explains why no negative inference should be drawn from the fact that, beginning in 1933, some but not all immunity provisions affirmatively required the witness to invoke the constitutional privilege.]

Beginning with the Securities Act of 1933, 48 Stat. 87, Congress has enacted no less than seventeen regulatory measures which contain provisions for immunity from prosecution in exchange for self-incriminating testimony. Of these, fourteen, including inter alia the Securities Exchange Act, 49 Stat. 832, the Federal Power Act, 49 Stat. 858, and the Civil Aeronautics Act of 1938, 52 Stat. 1022, confer immunity when a person testifies under compulsion "after having claimed his privilege against self-incrimination." Three of these statutes, however, the Motor Carrier Act of 1935, 49 Stat. 550, the Industrial Alcohol Act, 49 Stat. 875, and the Fair Labor Standards Act of 1938, 52 Stat. 1065, do not contain this additional clause—they merely follow the old form customarily used by Congress prior to the Securities Act of 1933. Of course, there is a difference in the language of these statutory provisions. But the process of construing a statute cannot end with noting literary differences. The task is one of finding meaning; and a difference in words is not necessarily a difference in the meaning they carry. The question is not whether these provisions are different, but whether there is significance in the difference. If the difference in language reflected a difference in the scope of the immunity given, or in the nature of the considerations that moved Congress to make a differentiation, there would surely be some indication, however faint, somewhere in the legislative history of these enactments that some legislator was aware that the difference in language had significance. But there is none.

* * * It is only fair to Congress to assume that if there was a purpose to make a difference in the demands upon citizens when they appear as witnesses under one statute rather than the other, that purpose would have been stated somewhere in the course of the legislative history. But there is a total absence of any indication anywhere that any Congressman had any notion that the enforcement of the Motor Carrier Act of 1935, the Industrial Alcohol Act, or the Fair Labor Standards Act of 1938, called for a different treatment of witnesses in proceedings under these Acts than in enforcement proceedings under the other fourteen Acts. The explanation seems obvious. There are no expressions in the legislative materials to indicate that the legislative purpose varied in this respect between these Acts because there was no difference in purpose.

But the variations in the phraseology employed in the Acts are not to be explained away as just caprices of a single draftsman. The explanation is likely to be found in the manner in which Congress usually acts in adopting regulatory legislation. If a single draftsman had drafted each of these provisions in all seventeen statutes, there might be some reason for believing that the difference in language reflected a difference in meaning. But it is common knowledge that these measures are frequently drawn, at least in the first instance, by specialists (perhaps connected with interested government departments) in the various fields. Provisions in different measures dealing with the same procedural problem not unnaturally, therefore, lack uniformity of phrasing.

We do not have to look very far in order to see how Congress happened to use one form of immunity provision in some of these statutes and another form in others. Consider the evolution of the three statutes which followed the old, pre–1933 form. The Motor Carrier Act of 1935 was enacted as an amendment to the Interstate Commerce Act. What was more natural than that the enforcement provisions of the old Act should be incorporated by reference in providing for the new powers of the Commission. And the Industrial Alcohol Act of 1935, so far as its enforcement provisions were concerned, was patterned upon its predecessor, the National Prohibition Act of 1919, 41 Stat. 317, and the draftsman naturally took the immunity provision from that statute. * * *

To attribute caprice to Congress is not to respect its rational purpose when, as here, we find a uniform policy deeply rooted in history even though variously phrased but always directed to the same end of meeting the same constitutional requirement.

I am therefore of opinion that an appearance in response to a subpoena does not of itself confer immunity from prosecution for anything that a witness so responding may testify. There must be conscious surrender of the privilege of silence in the course of a testimonial inquiry. * * *

Justice Frankfurter's dissent in Monia is similar to his approach in his majority opinion in Keifer & Keifer v. Reconstruction Finance Corp., 306 U.S. 381 (1939). The issue was whether a federal statute implicitly granted a government corporation sovereign immunity. Statutes governing at least forty government corporations created during the 1920s and 1930s had explicitly waived government immunity. Justice Frankfurter stated:

> * * * Such a firm practice is partly an indication of the present climate of opinion which has brought governmental immunity from suit into disfavor, partly it reveals a definite attitude on the part of Congress which should be given hospitable scope.

He had the following to say about the statute's language, which was silent on the question of sovereign immunity:

> * * * It is not a textual problem; for Congress has not expressed its will in words. Congress may not even have had a consciousness of intention. The Congressional will must be divined, and by a process of interpretation which, in effect, is the ascertainment of policy, immanent not merely in the single statute from which flow the rights and responsibilities of (the government corporation), but in a series of statutes utilizing corporations for governmental purposes and drawing significance from dominant contemporaneous opinion regarding the immunity of governmental agencies from suit.

Justice Frankfurter goes on to infer a waiver of sovereign immunity, refusing to "impute to Congress a desire for incoherence in a body of affiliated enactments and for drastic legal differentiation when policy justifies none."

15.05   EQUAL TREATMENT

When we discussed injured maritime workers in Chapter 13, we focused on the common law of admiralty. Who was entitled to recover at common law for unseaworthiness (Wrongful Death actions in territorial waters—Moragne) and what damages were recoverable in unseaworthiness cases (loss of society—Higginbotham, Gaudet, and Miles)? (Unseaworthiness was a common law claim against the shipowner which changed in the 1940s from "an obscure and relatively little used" liability standard—because the shipowner's duty was only to use "due diligence" to provide a seaworthy ship—into an absolute no-fault liability remedy against shipowners to "furnish a vessel [ ] reasonably fit for [ ] use."[8]) We also alluded to two 1920 statutes—the Death on the High Seas Act and the Jones Act—but only as elements in an expansive legal landscape (to create Wrongful Death actions at common law) and as implicit limitations on recovery for loss of society damages. In this section we look closely at the statutory pattern for injured sea-based workers in territorial waters and for land-based maritime workers.

On the one hand, the courts may have more interpretive power in this area of the law because of its common law background. On the other hand, legislation may have taken over the field to such an extent that courts are now reluctant to adopt a more aggressive lawmaking role.

a) JONES ACT—1920

Implied federal pre-emption of state law. Just prior to 1920, someone worried about injured workers would think of both Workers Compensation statutes and common law causes of action. For injuries in territorial waters,

---

8. Yamaha Motor Corp,. U.S.A. v. Calhoun, 116 S.Ct. 619, 624 (1996). See also   Mahnich v. Southern S.S. Co., 321 U.S. 96 (1944).

however, their thoughts would be confined to federal law. State law was generally unavailing. Federal maritime jurisdiction was exclusive, except for "maritime but local" employment;[9] moreover, Congress could not even give states power to provide workers compensation benefits to injured longshoremen and seamen in territorial waters.[10] Federal law was not much help either. The general common law negligence action against employers was hedged about with common law defenses, such as assumption of risk and the fellow servant rule; and there was no federal workers compensation statute for these workers.

Seamen—statutory negligence actions. In 1920, Congress passed the Jones Act, permitting common law negligence actions against *employers* by "seamen" injured in the course of employment in territorial waters or on the high seas,[11] and stripped employers of the special common law defenses, such as assumption of risk and the fellow servant rule. This nonetheless seemed to leave a gap in the law regarding *longshoremen* (sometimes referred to as stevedores), who worked in territorial waters. (1) There was no federal Workers Compensation statute applicable to longshoremen. (2) The federal common law of unseaworthiness was not extended to longshoremen until the 1940s,[12] when (as noted above) it turned into a no-fault liability remedy against *shipowners*. (3) The states still could not provide relief. In 1922 Congress tried again to give states power to provide workers compensation benefits, this time for longshoremen only, but the Court again held that federal jurisdiction was exclusive.[13]

There was one way federal law might give longshoremen effective relief—they might be "seamen" under the Jones Act. In 1926, the Court said they were.

International Stevedoring Co. v. Haverty

272 U.S. 50 (1926).

■ Mr. Justice Holmes delivered the opinion of the Court.

This is an action brought in a State Court seeking a common law remedy for personal injuries sustained by the plaintiff, the

---

9. Southern Pac. Co. v. Jensen, 244 U.S. 205 (1917); Chelentis v. Luckenbach S.S. Co., 247 U.S. 372 (1918). Justice Holmes' dissent in Jensen objected to the pre-emptive effect of the *silent* federal maritime common law, and contains one of the most famous quotes in the legal literature—"The common law is not a brooding omnipresence in the sky but the articulate voice of some sovereign or quasi-sovereign that can be identified."

The "maritime-but-local" exception appeared in Western Fuel Co. v. Garcia, 257 U.S. 233 (1921).

10. Knickerbocker Ice Co. v. Stewart, 253 U.S. 149 (1920)(dealing with 1917 federal statute which tried to preserve state workers compensation remedies for longshoremen and seamen).

11. After some uncertainty, the Jones Act was applied to seaman injured not only in territorial waters but also on land. O'Donnell v. Great Lakes Dredge & Dock Co., 318 U.S. 36 (1943).

12. Seas Shipping Co. v. Sieracki, 328 U.S. 85 (1946).

13. State of Washington v. W.C. Dawson & Co., 264 U.S. 219 (1924).

respondent here, upon a vessel at dock in the harbor of Seattle. The plaintiff was a longshoreman engaged in stowing freight in the hold. Through the negligence of the hatch tender no warning was given that a load of freight was about to be lowered, and when the load came down the plaintiff was badly hurt. The plaintiff and the hatch tender both were employed by the defendant [ ], the petitioner here, and the defendant asked for a ruling that they were fellow servants and that therefore the plaintiff could not recover. * * *

The petitioner argues that the case is governed by the admiralty law; that the admiralty law has taken up the common law doctrine as to fellow servants, and that by the common law the plaintiff would have no case. Whether this last proposition is true we do not decide. * * * It is open to Congress, however, to change the rule and in our opinion it has done so. By the [Jones] Act:

> "Any seaman who shall suffer personal injury in the course of his employment may, at his election, maintain an action for damages at law, with the right of trial by jury, and in such action all statutes of the United States modifying or extending the common-law right or remedy in cases of personal injury to railway employees shall apply."

It is not disputed that the statutes do away with the fellow servant rule in the case of personal injuries to railway employees. The question therefore is how far the Act of 1920 should be taken to extend.

It is true that for most purposes, as the word is commonly used, stevedores are not "seamen." But words are flexible. The work upon which the plaintiff was engaged was a maritime service formerly rendered by the ship's crew. We cannot believe that Congress willingly would have allowed the protection to men engaged upon the same maritime duties to vary with the accident of their being employed by a stevedore rather than by the ship. The policy of the statute is directed to the safety of the men and to treating compensation for injuries to them as properly part of the cost of the business. If they should be protected in the one case they should be in the other. In view of the broad field in which Congress has disapproved and changed the rule introduced into the common law within less than a century, we are of opinion that a wider scope should be given to the words of the act, and that in this statute "seamen" is to be taken to include stevedores employed in maritime work on navigable waters as the plaintiff was, whatever it might mean in laws of a different kind.

QUESTIONS

1. Is this case an example of extensive equitable interpretation, even though the Court does not say so? The decision appears to extend application of the word "seamen" to include longshoremen.

2. Why can't Holmes believe Congress would have distinguished between people engaged in similar maritime duties? Was it because of Congress' prior unsuccessful attempts to give states power to provide remedies to injured maritime workers?

3. Holmes had dissented from the previously mentioned decisions denying states the power to provide remedies to injured maritime workers, but wrote for a unanimous Court in Haverty that the Jones Act covered longshoremen. How can you explain the *unanimous* decision?

b) LHWCA—1927

Longshoremen—workers compensation remedies. In 1927 Congress responded to the Haverty decision by treating longshoremen differently from seamen. It adopted the Longshoremen's and Harbor Workers' Compensation Act (LHWCA), creating a federal Workers Compensation scheme for longshoremen and other maritime workers (except "a master or member of a crew of any vessel"—that is, a seaman) in territorial waters. Somewhat belatedly, in 1946, the Court recognized that LHWCA and the Jones Act were mutually exclusive.[14] They had more difficulty drawing the line between LHWCA and state law coverage.

LHWCA vs. state law. LHWCA provided benefits only if "recovery * * * through workmen's compensation proceedings may not validly be provided by State law." This seemed to draw a line between federal LHWCA benefits and state benefits for "maritime but local" employment, which the Court had permitted states to provide in prior decisions. The "maritime but local" standard was very hard to apply, however, and workers who guessed wrong incurred not only expense but also the risk that the statute of limitations might expire on the alternative remedy. Eventually, the Court interpreted LHWCA to include a twilight zone of concurrent state and federal coverage,[15] which, eventually, applied to all covered workers injured on navigable waters, without regard to the "maritime but local" standard.[16] This approach to interpreting a federal statute extended federal coverage to avoid benefit gaps for injured maritime workers, at least when there was a serious risk that the worker might guess wrong.

LHWCA vs. common law unseaworthiness claims for longshoremen. There was also a potential for overlap between statutory LHWCA and federal common law unseaworthiness claims for longshoremen. In 1946 the Court held that

---

14. Swanson v. Marra Bros., 328 U.S. 1 (1946); McDermott International, Inc. v. Wilander, 498 U.S. 337 (1991). The phrase "master or member of a crew" in LHWCA was treated as a refinement of the term "seaman" in the Jones Act. In McDermott, the Court found it "odd but true that the key require-ment for Jones Act coverage now appears in another statute [LHWCA]."

15. Davis v. Department of Labor & Industries, 317 U.S. 249 (1942).

16. Calbeck v. Travelers Ins. Co., 370 U.S. 114 (1962). Calbeck did not, however, eliminate state jurisdiction over "maritime but

LHWCA did not negate the common law remedy.[17] Seamen had retained the common law cause of action for unseaworthiness, despite the Jones Act,[18] and the Court appealed to the spirit of Haverty to justify equal treatment for seamen and longshoremen.

> Running through [Haverty] is a [ ] core of policy which has been controlling, although the specific issue has varied from a question of admiralty jurisdiction to one of coverage under statutory liability within the admiralty field. It is that for injuries incurred while working on board the ship in navigable waters the stevedore is entitled to the seaman's traditional and statutory protections * * *.[19]

Even though the 1927 LHWCA statute overrode the specific holding of Haverty (which had treated longshoremen and seamen alike), the Court's equal treatment approach survived to provide both longshoremen and seamen a common law unseaworthiness cause of action.

Obsolete statutes? The impact of allowing longshoremen an unseaworthiness claim in effect undermined the employer's limited liability under the LHWCA workers compensation statute, because shipowners liable for unseaworthiness could sue the employers for indemnity.[20] In G. Gilmore & C. Black, Law of Admiralty 446–48 (2d ed. 1975), the authors characterize the Court's approach to unseaworthiness as an example of "statutory nullification," justifiable (if at all) on the ground that the 1927 LHWCA remedies had become obsolete and Congress had shown no interest in "remedying a scandalous situation." They conclude by suggesting that judicial nullification of a statute "may not seem, to the legal mind of the 1990's, as shocking as it did to the legal mind of the 1960's." Do you agree with Gilmore and Black's conclusion, which influenced Calabresi's book, A Common Law for the Age of Statutes, discussed in Chapter 9?

c) LHWCA—1972

Land-based workers. So much for injured workers in territorial waters. There soon emerged another serious problem of unequal coverage. Long-shoremen worked not only on ships but also on land, in maritime related jobs. The law applicable to their injuries changed as they walked across the shoreline from territorial waters to state jurisdiction. This was significant because federal LHWCA remedies had outstripped less generous state law benefits for land-based workers. The 1972 amendments to LHWCA extended LHWCA to land-based workers around piers, etc. (a situs test), who engaged in "maritime employment" (a status test). The exact scope of the "maritime employment" language is the subject of the Herb's Welding case,

local" workers. Sun Ship, Inc. v. Pennsylvania, 447 U.S. 715 (1980).

17. Seas Shipping Co. v. Sieracki, 328 U.S. 85 (1946).

18. Panama R. Co. v. Johnson, 264 U.S. 375 (1923); Cortes v. Baltimore Insular Line, 287 U.S. 367 (1932).

19. Sea Shipping, 328 U.S., at 99.

20. Ryan Stevedoring Co. v. Pan–Atlantic Steamship Corp., 350 U.S. 124 (1956).

discussed below. The status test was adopted so that the 1972 LHWCA amendments would not introduce a new inequity, by giving federal benefits to workers at the designated situs whenever they showed up at the situs (for example, truck drivers delivering goods to the pier).

The legislative bargain. The 1972 law also did two other important things. First, LHWCA benefits were increased. Second, as part of the legislative bargain for extending and raising federal workers compensation benefits, the unseaworthiness claim for longshoremen against shipowners was eliminated. Employers cared about the unseaworthiness claim because liable shipowners were entitled to indemnity from employers. The 1972 amendments drew a line, like the original 1927 law, distinguishing longshoremen from seamen, for whom the unseaworthiness claim survived.[21]

Applicability of "status" requirement to sea-based workers. The 1972 amendments, requiring "maritime employment" (the "status" test), raised a question regarding the coverage of workers in territorial waters. Did the "maritime employment" test apply in territorial waters or only to land-based injuries? The Court held in Perini[22] that the main purpose of the 1972 law was to extend LHWCA landward, not to restrict recoveries in *territorial waters*. The pre–1972 LHWCA case law had developed to cover all workers in territorial waters (except "seamen"), without excluding "maritime but local" workers, and the "maritime employment" test was simply a different way to articulate the coverage distinction previously achieved by the "maritime but local" standard. Perini therefore allowed post–1972 LHWCA coverage to an injured marine construction worker, who would have been covered by LHWCA before 1972, without regard to the "maritime employment" statutory test. The Court's decision was influenced by a reluctance to reintroduce the worker's dilemma of not knowing whether a federal remedy was available and incurring the risks of a wrong guess.[23]

"Liberal" interpretation and statutory bargains. The Court's Perini decision, that LHWCA applied to all workers injured in territorial waters, relied in part on the principle that LHWCA should be liberally construed. Is that reliance misplaced, because statutory deals should not be extended to help one side of the bargain? The 1972 LHWCA amendments suggest how difficult it is to draw inferences about statutory bargains. The conventional view of workers compensation is that employers guarantee benefits for employees, but bargain for liability limits in exchange. "Liberal construction" for employees would be unfaithful to the limits for which the employer bargained. This "bargaining" perspective influenced Justice Stevens' dissent

---

21. Longshoremen were not, however, completely deprived of a common law claim. Under the 1972 amendments, they still retained a common law negligence action against the shipowner, but without shipowner indemnity from the employer. LHWCA, 33 U.S.C. § 905(b).

22. Director v. Perini North River Associates, 459 U.S. 297 (1983).

23. The same concern about whipsawing injured workers supported the decision in Sun Ship, Inc. v. Pennsylvania, 447 U.S. 715 (1980), that the land-based coverage of LHWCA could overlap with state workers compensation.

in the Perini decision, where he argued that the burden on the employer of increased employee benefits, provided by the 1972 LHWCA amendments, was offset by the "maritime employment" status limitation.

The legislative history suggests, however, that employers might have gotten something else in exchange for agreeing to expanded benefits—the elimination of the longshoreman's unseaworthiness claim. Perhaps that is what employers received in the statutory bargain, in exchange for which employees got expanded benefits, sweetened by "liberal interpretation." Indeed, maybe employers got something else from employees when bargaining over *other* legislation; some legislative bargains are "on the side." How does a court know the terms of the legislative bargain?

d) "MARITIME EMPLOYMENT"

What does "maritime employment" mean for workers *not injured on territorial waters*? In the 1985 Herb's Welding case, set forth below, the Court held (by a 5–4 margin) that welders on fixed oil platforms in territorial waters did not engage in "maritime employment."[24] What happened in this case to the Court's approach which characterized so many of its decisions involving maritime personal injury law: (1) "liberal interpretation" for the worker; (2) equal treatment; and (3) concern about inadequate state benefits? Has the Court simply abandoned these concerns? Is there something special about Herb's Welding and its legislative history that explains why coverage was denied?

The Court has not been entirely unwilling to interpret LHWCA expansively to apply to land-based workers. In Chesapeake & Ohio Ry. Co. v. Schwalb, 493 U.S. 40 (1989), the Court held (after Herb's Welding) that "maritime employment" was not limited to physical loading and unloading of cargo, but also applied to a railroad worker who was repairing and maintaining equipment essential to loading and unloading at the shoreside situs. Justice Stevens (who voted with the majority denying benefits in Herb's Welding) concurred in Schwalb, abandoning his view (forcefully advanced in his Perini dissent) that LHWCA applies only to "amphibious workers."

Herb's Welding, Inc. v. Gray
470 U.S. 414 (1985).

■ Justice White delivered the opinion of the Court.

The Longshoremen's and Harbor Workers' Compensation Act (LHWCA or Act), 44 Stat. 1424, as amended, 33 U.S.C. § 901 et seq., provides compensation for the death or disability of any person engaged in "maritime employment," § 902(3), if the disability or death results from an injury incurred upon the navigable waters of the United States or any adjoining pier or other area customarily

---

24. Herb's Welding, Inc. v. Gray, 470 U.S. 414 (1985).

used by an employer in loading, unloading, repairing, or building a vessel, § 903(a). Thus, a worker claiming under the Act must satisfy both a "status" and a "situs" test. The court below held that respondent Robert Gray, a welder working on a fixed offshore oil-drilling platform in state territorial waters, was entitled to benefits under the Act. We reverse for the reason that Gray was not engaged in maritime employment.

[Editor—The statute provided as follows:

Section 2(3) of the Act, 86 Stat. 1251, 33 U.S.C. § 902(3), provides:

The term "employee" means any person engaged in maritime employment, including any longshoreman or other person engaged in longshoring operations, and any harborworker including a ship repairmen, shipbuilder, and shipbreaker, but such term does not include a master or member of a crew of any vessel, or any persons engaged by the master to load or unload or repair any small vessel under eighteen tons net.

Section 3(a) of the Act, 33 U.S.C. § 903(a), provides in part:

Compensation shall be payable * * * if the disability or death results from an injury occurring upon the navigable waters of the United States (including any adjoining pier, wharf, dry dock, terminal, building way, marine railway, or other adjoining area customarily used by an employer in loading, unloading, repairing, or building a vessel).]

Respondent worked for Herb's Welding, Inc., in the Bay Marchand oil and gas field off the Louisiana coast. Herb's Welding provided welding services to the owners of drilling platforms. The field was located partly in Louisiana territorial waters, i.e., within three miles of the shore, and partly on the Outer Continental Shelf. Gray ate and slept on a platform situated in Louisiana waters. He spent roughly three-quarters of his working time on platforms in state waters and the rest on platforms on the Outer Continental Shelf. He worked exclusively as a welder, building and replacing pipelines and doing general maintenance work on the platforms.

On July 11, 1975, Gray was welding a gas flow line on a fixed platform located in Louisiana waters. [Editor—A footnote explained that offshore oil rigs are of two general sorts: fixed and floating. Floating structures have been treated as vessels by the lower courts. Workers on them, unlike workers on fixed platforms, enjoy the same remedies as workers on ships. If permanently attached to the vessel as crewmembers, they are regarded as seamen; if not, they are covered by the LHWCA because they are employed on navigable waters. Gray is not in a position to take advantage of this line of cases. All, or almost all, the platforms in the field were fixed production platforms rather than floating rigs. There has never been any dispute that Gray was injured on a fixed platform, nor any contention that he should be considered to have been on a vessel at the time of his injury. The only question, therefore, is whether Gray is limited to state workers' compensation remedies or may also recover under the LHWCA.] [Gray] burnt through the bottom of the line and an explosion occurred. Gray ran from the area, and in doing so hurt his knee. He sought benefits under the LHWCA for lost wages, disability, and medical expenses. When petitioner United States Fidelity & Guaranty Co., the workers' compensation carrier for Herb's Welding, denied LHWCA benefits, Gray filed a complaint with the Department of Labor. * * *

The Benefits Review Board * * * concluded that irrespective of the nature of his employment, Gray could recover by virtue of a provision of the Outer Continental Shelf Lands Act, 67 Stat. 462, 43 U.S.C. § 2442 et seq. (Lands Act), that grants LHWCA benefits to offshore oil workers injured on the Outer Continental Shelf. Although Gray had been injured in state waters, the Board felt that his injury nonetheless could be said to have occurred, in the words of the statute, "as a result of" operations on the outer shelf. It considered his work "integrally related" to such operations. * * *

* * * [P]etitioners sought review in the Court of Appeals for the Fifth Circuit. The court affirmed, relying directly on the LHWCA rather than on the Lands Act. * * * [S]ince workers injured on movable barges, on fixed platforms on the Outer Continental Shelf, or en route to fixed platforms, are all covered, there would be a "curious hole" in coverage if someone in Gray's position were not. * * *

When extractive operations first moved offshore, all claims for injuries on fixed platforms proceeded under state workers' compensation schemes. With the 1953 passage of the Lands Act, Congress extended LHWCA coverage to oil workers more than three miles offshore. Because until 1972 the LHWCA itself extended coverage only to accidents occurring on navigable waters, 33 U.S.C. § 903 (1970 ed.), and because stationary rigs were considered to be islands, oil rig workers inside the 3–mile limit were left to recover under state schemes. * * *

So matters stood when Congress amended the LHWCA in 1972. What is known about the congressional intent behind that legislation has been amply described in our prior opinions. The most important of Congress' concerns, for present purposes, was the desire to extend coverage to longshoremen, harborworkers, and others who were injured while on piers, docks, and other areas customarily used to load and unload ships or to repair or build ships, rather than while actually afloat. Whereas prior to 1972 the Act reached only accidents occurring on navigable waters, the amended 33 U.S.C. § 903 expressly extended coverage to "adjoining area[s]." At the same time, the amended definition of an "employee" limited coverage to employees engaged in "maritime employment."

The Act, as amended, does not mention offshore drilling rigs or the workers thereon. The legislative history of the amendment is also silent * * *. [Editor—The Court notes that a 1972 bill to extend LHWCA to *all* offshore oil workers, including seamen as well as people like Gray, died in committee. The bill's primary purpose, however, was to limit remedies of those who could qualify as seamen, and its defeat shed no light on whether LHWCA extended to fixed oil platform workers.]

* * * Congress did not seek to cover all those who breathe salt air. Its purpose was to cover those workers on the situs who are involved in the essential elements of loading and unloading; it is "clear that persons who are on the situs but not engaged in the overall process of loading or unloading vessels are not covered." Northeast Marine Terminal Co. v. Caputo, 432 U.S., at 267. While "maritime employment" is not limited to the occupations specifically mentioned in § 2(3), neither can it be read to eliminate any requirement of a connection with the loading or construction of ships. [Editor—A footnote stated that the LHWCA covers "any person engaged in maritime employment, including any longshoreman or other person engaged in longshoring operations, and any harbor worker including a ship repairman, shipbuilder, and shipbreaker." By the use of the term "including," Congress indicated that the specifically mentioned occupations are not exclusive.] As we have said, the "maritime employment" requirement is "an occupational test that focuses on loading and unloading." The Amendments were not meant "to cover employees who are not engaged in loading, unloading, repairing, or building a vessel, just because they are injured in an area adjoining navigable waters used for such activity." H.R.Rep. No. 92–1441, p. 11 (1972); S.Rep. No. 92–1125, p. 13 (1972), U.S. Code Cong. & Admin. News 1972, p. 4708. We have never read "maritime employment" to extend so far beyond those actually involved in moving cargo between ship and land transportation. * * * [Editor—The Court distinguished Perini's expansive interpretation of "maritime employment" dealing with injuries in territorial waters, on the ground that "[Perini was] limited to workers covered prior to 1972, a group to which Gray does not belong."]

Gray was a welder. His work had nothing to do with the loading or unloading process, nor is there any indication that he was even employed in the maintenance of equipment used in such tasks. Gray's welding work was far removed from traditional LHWCA activities, notwithstanding the fact that he unloaded his own gear upon arriving at a platform by boat. He built and maintained pipelines and the platforms themselves. There is nothing inherently maritime about those tasks. They are also performed on land, and their nature is not significantly altered by the marine environment, particularly since exploration and development of the Continental Shelf are not themselves maritime commerce.

The dissent emphasizes that Gray was generally on or near the water and faced maritime hazards. To the extent this is so, it is relevant to "situs," not "status." To hold that Gray was necessarily engaged in maritime employment because he was on a drilling platform would ignore Congress' admonition that not everyone on a covered situs automatically satisfies the status test. See S.Rep. No. 92–1125, p. 13 (1972). The dissent considers "[t]he maritime nature of the occupation * * * apparent from examining its location in terms of the expanded situs coverage of the 1972 Amendments." We recognize that the nature of a particular job is defined in part by its location. But to classify Gray's employment as maritime because he was on a covered situs, or in a "maritime environment," would blur together requirements Congress intended to be distinct. We cannot thus read the status requirement out of the statute.

Respondents, and the dissenters, object that denying coverage to someone in Gray's position will result in exactly the sort of inconsistent, checkered coverage that Congress sought to eliminate in 1972. In the words of the court below, it creates a "curious hole" in coverage, because Gray would have been covered had he been injured on navigable waters or on the outer shelf.

We do not find the argument compelling. First, this submission goes far beyond Congress' undoubted desire to treat equally all workers engaged in loading or unloading a ship, whether they were injured on the ship or on an adjoining pier or dock. The former were covered prior to 1972; the latter were not. Both are covered under the 1972 amendments. Second, there will always be a boundary to coverage, and there will always be people who cross it during their employment. If that phenomenon was enough to require coverage, the Act would have to reach much further than anyone argues that it does or should. Third, the inconsistent coverage here results primarily from the explicit geographic limitation to the Lands Act's incorporation of the LHWCA [Editor—so that the Lands Act applied only to the Outer Continental Shelf]. Gray would indeed have been covered for a significant portion of his work-time, but because of the Lands Act, not because he fell within the terms of the LHWCA. Congress' desire to make LHWCA coverage uniform reveals little about the position of those for whom partial coverage results from a separate statute. This is especially true because that statute draws a clear geographical boundary that will predictably result in workers moving in and out of coverage.

As we have said before in this area, if Congress' coverage decisions are mistaken as a matter of policy, it is for Congress to change them. We should not legislate for them.

Because Gray's employment was not "maritime," he does not qualify for benefits under the LHWCA. We need not determine whether he satisfied the Act's situs requirement. * * *

It is so ordered.

■ Justice Marshall, with whom Justice Brennan, Justice Blackmun, and Justice O'Connor join, dissenting.

Today the Court holds that a marine petroleum worker is not covered by the Longshoremen's and Harborworkers' Compensation Act (LHWCA or Act), 44 Stat. 1424, as amended, 33 U.S.C. § 901 et seq., when pursuing his occupation on a fixed offshore rig within the three-mile limit of a state's territorial waters. Although such an individual routinely travels over water as an essential part of his job and performs the rest of his job adjacent to and surrounded by water, he is not covered because, in the Court's view, his occupation is not "maritime employment." See § 2(3), 33 U.S.C. § 902(3). The Court reaches this conclusion even though a worker of the same occupation, working in the same industry, and performing the same tasks on a rig located in the same place, would be covered if that rig were one that was capable of floating. Neither the Court, nor any of the parties have identified any reason why Congress might have desired this distinction. To the contrary, a principal congressional goal behind the 1972 Amendments was to rid the Act of just such arbitrary distinctions derived from traditional admiralty jurisprudence. Because the coverage pattern that the Court adopts is at odds with the Act's 1972 Amendments, and because the accident here meets the Amendments' status and situs tests, I respectfully dissent.

At the outset, it is useful to examine the LHWCA's general coverage pattern, and, in particular, the purposes of its 1972 Amendments. Before 1972, LHWCA coverage was determined largely by the traditional "locality" test of maritime tort jurisdiction. Under that test, if an accident occurred on the navigable waters (which usually meant on a vessel) the worker was covered, no matter how close the accident may have been to the adjoining land or pier; in contrast, if an accident occurred on adjoining land, pier, or wharf there was only state coverage, no matter how close the accident may have been to the water's edge. A longshoreman moving cargo from ship to pier was thus covered for injuries incurred onboard the ship, but not for any injuries incurred after stepping onto the pier.

Behind this system of "checkered coverage" stood the reality that federal and state workers' compensation schemes usually had very different benefit levels, the state benefit levels often being inadequate. Thus, those workers whose professional lives might require that they move back and forth between water and adjoining land—"amphibious workers"—and whose protection was the principal goal of the LHWCA, had to rely for workers' compensation on an imperfect amalgam of federal and state workers' compensation laws. As critics noted, the system's adequacy in any given case was a function of the pure fortuity of a work related accident's exact location. * * *

[Editor—The dissent then recounts the history of the 1972 amendments, setting forth the statutory text defining the land-based situs, and explains why the "maritime employment" status limitation was needed.]

But if only the situs of coverage had been altered, a new problem would have been created. Expanding the situs landward would not only have brought uniform coverage to those occupations previously covered in part, it would also have brought within the covered situs large numbers of occupations whose members had never before been covered at all. Workers such as truck drivers or clericals, though present on a pier at certain times as part of their employment, are engaging in purely landbound, rather than amphibious, occupations. To expand coverage to these workers, whose work lives take them back and forth between newly covered "adjoining area[s]" and uncovered inland locations, would create a serious demarcation line problem, and would also obviously recreate, and even enlarge the problem of "checkered coverage" based on the fortuity of the exact location of a particular injury. Thus, Congress adopted a "status" test for coverage to exclude members of these land bound occupations. "The 1972 Amendments thus changed what had been essentially only a 'situs' test of eligibility for compensation to one looking to both the 'situs' of the injury and the 'status' of the injured." * * *

Both changes together were part of an effort to rationalize the Act's coverage pattern. Congress wanted a system that did not depend on the "fortuitous circumstance of whether the injury occurred on land or over water," S.Rep. 13; H.R.Rep. 10–11, U.S.Code Cong. & Admin. News 1976, p. 4708, and it wanted a "uniform compensation system to apply to employees who would otherwise be covered * * * for part of their activity." Analyzing this case in terms of Congress' stated goals and in terms of this Court's prior efforts to give meaning to the 1972 Amendments makes clear that the Act applies to marine petroleum workers such as Gray.

Workers on fixed offshore rigs are "amphibious workers" who spend almost their entire work life either traveling on the navigable waters or laboring on statutorily covered pier-like areas immediately adjacent thereto. They are exposed on a daily basis to hazards associated with maritime employment. And most important, given the fact that workers on floating rigs are covered by the Act, the Court's result recreates exactly the type of "incongruous" coverage distinctions that Congress specifically sought to eliminate in 1972. * * *

* * * Other than the fact that their rigs were a traditional admiralty situs, there is little to distinguish the job or location of a worker on a floating rig from those of a worker on a fixed rig. Physically, the structures may be quite similar. For example, they are similarly small, relatively isolated, and totally surrounded by the sea. The two types of structures are parts of similar enterprises and operations that are carried out in the same marine environment. Indeed, other than for the type of structure, the locations of the work are the same. Moreover, the work tasks are quite similar, as are the working conditions, and hazards. I can therefore see no reason to believe that Congress, in passing a measure designed to rationalize coverage patterns through an occupational test for coverage, would have worked to treat these workers as belonging to two different occupations, one maritime and the other non-maritime. * * *

The maritime nature of the occupation is even more apparent from examining its location in terms of the expanded situs coverage of the 1972 amendments. Assuming that a fixed offshore platform is a covered situs under § 3(a), then fixed platform workers could not simply be termed "land-based" workers. Unlike typical "land-based" workers, they would spend virtually their entire work lives within the statute's covered "maritime situs"—that is, either on or immediately adjacent to the actual navigable waters. This is in fact the situation here, for a fixed offshore oil rig easily fits into § 3(a)'s situs test. * * *

Fixed rigs are also physically quite analogous to piers or wharves. They are of limited size, so a worker almost anywhere on the deck would be aware of his close proximity to the water. Similarly, the decks are elevated over the water, built to provide access to the water, and situated so that working conditions are influenced by the surrounding marine environment. Given these factors, I have little problem classifying the whole of the platform as a covered situs, either because it is an "other adjoining area customarily used by an employer in loading [or] unloading" or because it is analogous to a pier of wharf facility.

Given this determination, a fixed platform worker is quite distinct from the truckdriver or clerical worker who in the legislative history exemplifies the non- maritime worker. Truckdrivers or clericals are land-bound workers whose work never takes them on the actual navigable waters, and only sporadically takes them on the pier-like areas brought under the LHWCA's coverage by the 1972 Amendments. The greatest part of their work is done in inland locales that are clearly beyond the coverage of the Act. Therefore, coverage of these workers under the Act could at most be "checkered" and "fortuitous." Avoiding such widespread "checkered coverage" was an envisioned function of the status test. Fixed rig workers, in contrast, are in a position to benefit from uniform coverage if classified as "maritime," for they are on a covered situs for the overwhelming part of their work. Classifying them as "maritime" in light of their constant and required presence on a covered situs conforms to Congress' desire for uniform coverage of those workers who would otherwise be partially covered. Under the Court's approach, they remain only partially covered.

A last reason for classifying these workers as maritime is that they face working conditions and hazards associated with their maritime location. This was clearly stated in the testimony of a high official of an offshore drilling company before a recent congressional hearing on offshore worker safety:

> "Offshore work has a special set of concerns because we are a hybrid industry. In one sense, we are an onshore industry that initially crept out over the water. But it is equally fair to characterize us as a maritime industry, the same as the merchant marine or any other.

> "In point of fact we share all of the concerns of both the drilling and maritime industries, plus a few uniquely ours."
> * * *

For the reasons discussed above, respondent Gray was "engaged in maritime employment" within the meaning of § 2(3) of the Act. It is also clear that a fixed offshore petroleum platform is a covered situs within the meaning of § 3(a) of the Act. I would thus affirm the Court of Appeals.

COMMENT AND QUESTION

1. The majority and dissent in Herb's Welding mirror the fundamental approaches to judicial power and responsibility which this course has addressed. The Herb's Welding majority sounds a lot like Easterbrook (all statutes have boundaries) and the dissent sounds like Frankfurter (or maybe Calabresi or Pound), trying to discern a consistent statutory pattern.

2. Would Justice Holmes (who wrote the Haverty decision defining "seamen" to include longshoremen) agree with the dissent, because he saw what the legislature was driving at?

PART III

LAW AND THE POLITICAL PROCESS

The law is concerned with the political process not only indirectly, through statutory interpretation, but also directly, through the rules applicable to elections, legislation, and executive-legislative relations.

We have examined various empirical and normative models of the political process in Chapter 4—the Law and Economics (Public Choice) and Republican conceptions of how legislation is and should be made. As you read the materials in subsequent chapters, consider what empirical and normative model of politics underlies the legal requirements, and whether they are related to the models already discussed. Consider also what judicial role the courts are willing to play. We want to know where the judge's conception of the political process and of the judicial role comes from. It will turn out that different judges have different conceptions, not clearly mandated by anything in the Constitution, just as they did when interpreting statutes.

Chapter 16 considers the electoral process. In our society, we are willing to accept expressions of popular and legislative will as legitimate forms of political action, in large part because the electoral process conforms to certain ground rules which we consider fair. Chapter 16 is about that concept of fairness.

Even if the electoral process works well, however, the legislative process itself might be flawed. Chapter 17 discusses rules governing legislative behavior. Chapter 18 deals with the relationship between the executive and the legislature.

CHAPTER 16

ELECTORAL PROCESS

16.01 INTRODUCTION

The Supreme Court is very concerned with voting requirements. A primary area of concern has been the electoral ground rules governing representation. In a famous group of cases in the 1960's, the court imposed the one-person one-vote rule, requiring the same number of voters in each electoral district,[1] although the state can now depart from these rigid numerical requirements under certain circumstances. The basic impact of these decisions was to force states to redesign old electoral districts so that thinly populated rural areas were not vastly overrepresented.

A second area of concern has been voting eligibility requirements, especially wealth requirements. In Harper v. Virginia State Board of Elections, 383 U.S. 663 (1966), the Court struck down a poll tax, as it applied to all voters, not just the poor: payment of a tax could not be exacted as a condition for voting. Later cases elaborated on Harper to limit the imposition of property ownership qualifications for voting. In Kramer v. Union Free School District, 395 U.S. 621 (1969), the Court struck down property ownership requirements for school board elections. Property ownership qualifications were also struck down when the vote concerned the issuance of general obligation bonds to fund public activities, such as parks, police, and sewers, not just the election of officials. Phoenix v. Kolodziejski, 399 U.S. 204 (1970). The Court disallowed the property requirement, even though property owners had to finance payment of the bonds. The opinion reasoned that the *beneficiaries* of the expenditures were as interested in the election's outcome as those who financed the bonds and that it was therefore unconstitutional to exclude those beneficiaries from the electoral process.

Chapters 16.02 and 16.03 explore the implications of these decisions—dealing with voting qualification and electoral ground rules. The most striking thing about the cases is that, whatever the judicial rhetoric, the Court does not simply treat voting as a fundamental right which can be interfered with only on the basis of a compelling state interest. Rather, the Court has a conception of the political community and the role of voters, interest groups, and political parties which guides its decisions. Voting is not an abstract right that must be balanced against an alleged state interest. Instead, the right comes already burdened with limitations governing what

---

1. Gray v. Sanders, 372 U.S. 368 (1963)(state executive offices); Wesberry v. Sanders, 376 U.S. 1 (1964)(congressional dis- tricts); Reynolds v. Sims, 377 U.S. 533 (1964)(state legislative offices).

the state can and cannot do to influence the political process. These limitations are an essential part of the judicial theory of political community. As you read the cases, try to articulate that theory. Is the court trying to provide adequate representation for political interests, to assure a deliberative process, to further public values, to do some or all of the above, or to achieve something else?

We first deal with limits on voter eligibility, such as property qualifications. We next turn to electoral ground rules dealing with such issues as filing fees to be a candidate, favoring the two-party system, providing access by independent candidates, election financing, multimember districts, gerrymanders, and supramajorities. Our purpose is not to repeat material you study in a constitutional or civil rights course. We therefore do not focus on the important problem of discrimination against minorities in the electoral process, but instead deal primarily with the constitutionality of efforts to control the electoral process.

Chapter 16.04 concludes with a discussion of money and politics.

16.02   VOTING QUALIFICATIONS

a) WEALTH

Harper v. Virginia State Board of Elections
383 U.S. 663 (1966).

■ Mr. Justice Harlan, *dissenting.* * * *

[Editor—In this case the Court struck down the requirement that a voter pay a $1.50 poll tax as a condition of voting on the ground that it violated the Equal Protection Clause of the U.S. Constitution. The majority stated that "wealth, like race, creed, or color, is not germane to one's ability to participate intelligently in the electoral process. Lines drawn on the basis of wealth or property, like those of race, are traditionally disfavored." (Where did the Court get the idea that "intelligent" participation is *the* criterion for judging the legitimacy of voting restrictions?)   The Court also relied on other cases stating that "the political franchise of voting" is a "fundamental political right, because preservative of all rights."

The deeper significance of the case lies in the Court's willingness to adopt a theory of access to the ballot, which prompted Justice Harlan to make the following comments in his *dissenting* opinion. Is Harlan objecting to the majority's view about the role of tradition in constitutional adjudication; about the role of the courts in creating law; about the correct theory of representation?]

Property qualifications and poll taxes have been a traditional part of our political structure. In the Colonies the franchise was generally a restricted one. Over the years these and other restrictions were gradually lifted, primarily because popular theories of political representation had changed. Often restrictions were lifted only after wide public debate. The issue of woman suffrage, for example, raised questions of family relationships, of participation in public affairs, of the very nature of the type of society in which Americans wished to live; eventually a consensus was reached, which culminated in the Nineteenth Amendment no more than 45 years ago.

Similarly with property qualifications, it is only by fiat that it can be said, especially in the context of American history, that there can be no rational debate as to their advisability. Most of the early Colonies had them; many of the States have had them during much of their histories; and, whether one agrees or not, arguments have been and still can be made in favor of them. For example, it is certainly a rational argument that payment of some minimal poll tax promotes civic responsibility, weeding out those who do not care enough about public affairs to pay $1.50 or thereabouts a year for the exercise of the franchise. It is also arguable, indeed it was probably accepted as sound political theory by a large percentage of Americans through most of our history, that people with some property have a deeper stake in community affairs, and are consequently more responsible, more educated, more knowledgeable, more worthy of confidence, than those without means, and that the community and Nation would be better managed if the franchise were restricted to such citizens. Nondiscriminatory and fairly applied literacy tests, upheld by this Court in Lassiter v. Northampton County Bd. of Elections, 360 U.S. 45, find justification on very similar grounds.

These viewpoints, to be sure, ring hollow on most contemporary ears. Their lack of acceptance today is evidenced by the fact that nearly all of the States, left to their own devices, have eliminated property or poll-tax qualification; by the cognate fact that Congress and three-quarters of the States quickly ratified the Twenty–Fourth Amendment [Editor—prohibiting a poll tax in elections for federal officials]; and by the fact that rules such as the "pauper exclusion" in Virginia law, Va. Const. 23, Va. Code § 24–18, have never been enforced.

Property and poll-tax qualifications, very simply, are not in accord with current egalitarian notions of how a modern democracy should be organized. It is of course entirely fitting that legislatures should modify the law to reflect such changes in popular attitudes. However, it is all wrong, in my view, for the Court to adopt the political doctrines popularly accepted at a particular moment of our history and to declare all others to be irrational and invidious, barring them from the range of choice by reasonably minded people acting through the political process. It was not too long ago that Mr.

Justice Holmes felt impelled to remind the Court that the Due Process Clause of the Fourteenth Amendment does not enact the *laissez-faire* theory of society, Lochner v. New York, 198 U.S. 45, 75–76. The times have changed, and perhaps it is appropriate to observe that neither does the Equal Protection Clause of that Amendment rigidly impose upon America an ideology of unrestrained egalitarianism.

b) RESIDENCE, AGE, AND LITERACY

Before and after Harper, the Court permitted many restrictions on voting, although it looked carefully to make sure that the restrictions did not exceed those necessary to serve the underlying state policy. State requirements that voters take up residence within a certain time before they voted were upheld as long as the period was related to the need to prepare voting rolls for the upcoming elections. Dunn v. Blumstein, 405 U.S. 330 (1972)(3 month residence requirement in county is too long); Marston v. Lewis, 410 U.S. 679 (1973)(50 day residence requirement is not too long).

Before adoption of the 26th Amendment guaranteeing 18–year olds the right to vote in both federal and nonfederal elections, state age requirements for state elections did *not* violate the Constitution. Indeed, Congress could not even mandate an 18–year old voting age for state elections, although it could do so for federal elections. See Oregon v. Mitchell, 400 U.S. 112 (1970)(four judges thought Congress had authority to mandate federal *and* state election age requirements to enforce the Equal Protection Clause; four judges thought Congress could not mandate age requirements in federal *or* state elections; a fifth judge thought the Equal Protection Clause did not authorize Congress to mandate age requirements for state elections, but found constitutional authority for Congress to mandate federal election age rules).

Congress has greater power, however, in controlling literacy tests than age requirements. To some extent, this power derives from concern about race discrimination. For example, in Oregon v. Mitchell, 400 U.S. 112 (1970), the Court upheld a congressional ban on state literacy tests because Congress had evidence of a "long history of discriminatory use of literacy tests to disenfranchise voters on account of their race." In Katzenbach v. Morgan, 384 U.S. 641 (1966), however, the Court went further in upholding a congressional ban on state literacy tests in both federal and nonfederal elections. The case dealt with a federal statute (sec. 4(e)) which prohibited use of English literacy tests for persons educated in American-flag schools in which English was not the predominant language—that is, Puerto Rico. The Court found congressional authority for the ban in the Equal Protection Clause of the U.S. Constitution, stating:

> * * * The practical effect of § 4(e) is to prohibit New York from denying the right to vote to large segments of its Puerto Rican community. Congress has thus prohibited the State from denying to that community the right that is "preservative of all rights." This

enhanced political power will be helpful in gaining nondiscriminatory treatment in public services for the entire Puerto Rican community. Section § 4(e) thereby enables the Puerto Rican minority better to obtain "perfect equality of civil rights and the equal protection of the laws." It was well within congressional authority to say that this need of the Puerto Rican minority for the vote warranted federal intrusion upon any state interests served by the English literacy requirement.
* * *

The result is no different if we confine our inquiry to the question whether § 4(e) was merely legislation aimed at the elimination of an invidious discrimination in establishing voter qualifications. We are told that New York's English literacy requirement originated in the desire to provide an incentive for non-English speaking immigrants to learn the English language and in order to assure the intelligent exercise of the franchise. Yet Congress might well have questioned, in light of the many exemptions provided, and some evidence suggesting that prejudice played a prominent role in the enactment of the requirement, whether these were actually the interests being served. Congress might have also questioned whether denial of a right deemed so precious and fundamental in our society was a necessary or appropriate means of encouraging persons to learn English, or of furthering the goal of an intelligent exercise of the franchise. Finally, Congress might well have concluded that as a means of furthering the intelligent exercise of the franchise, an ability to read or understand Spanish is as effective as ability to read English for those to whom Spanish-language newspapers and Spanish-language radio and television programs are available to inform them of election issues and governmental affairs. Since Congress undertook to legislate so as to preclude the enforcement of the state law, and did so in the context of a general appraisal of literacy requirements for voting, to which it brought a specially informed legislative competence, it was Congress' prerogative to weigh these competing considerations. Here again, it is enough that we perceive a basis upon which Congress might predicate a judgment that the application of New York's English literacy requirement to deny the right to vote to a person with a sixth grade education in Puerto Rican schools in which the language of instruction was other than English constituted an invidious discrimination in violation of the Equal Protection Clause.

English literacy tests appear to fall between poll taxes, which a state cannot impose, and age requirements, which Congress could not prohibit states from imposing in nonfederal elections (before a specific constitutional amendment allowed 18–year olds to vote in both state and federal elections). Congress can apparently impose its vision of political community on the states respecting the use of English literacy tests in both federal and nonfederal elections, even though there is no evidence of racial or ethnic prejudice in the state's use of these tests.

In the absence of a federal legislative prohibition, a state has been allowed to limit the exercise of a right "preservative of all rights" to those citizens who are literate in English.[2] What would justify such a state law: intelligent exercise of the franchise; preventing exploitation of voters; enabling the voter to understand propositions on the ballot; encouraging learning English; affirming cultural values; fostering a unilingual society?

Some states have declared English as the official language, although the impact of the declaration is uncertain. In Yniguez v. Arizonans, 69 F.3d 920 (9th Cir.1995), cert. granted, 116 S.Ct. 1316 (1996), the court struck down Arizona's official English provision (XXVIII of the Arizona Constitution), which stated "that English is the official language of the state of Arizona, and that the state and its political subdivisions—including all government officials and employees performing government business—must 'act' only in English." The court was especially troubled by the "severe consequences [of the constitutional provision] not only for its public officials and employees, but for the many thousands of Arizonans who would be precluded from receiving essential information from their state and local governments if the drastic prohibition contained in the provision were to be implemented." It concluded that "Article XXVIII constitutes a prohibited means of promoting the English language and affirm[ed] the district court's ruling that it violates the First Amendment." Does this imply that conducting politics in a language other than English is a protected right? Does it follow that the franchise cannot be limited to those literate in English?

c) PUBLIC VS. PRIVATE

So far we have focused on what limits can be placed on participation in electoral politics. The following case deals with what activities must be subject to the rules applicable to political elections. This is an unusual question to ask. Attention is usually paid to the impact of private interests on the political process, rather than with how far into the private sector the electoral process can intrude. We are, in effect, asking what amounts to "state action" for purposes of the rules monitoring the electoral process.

Ball v. James

451 U.S. 355 (1981).

■ Mr. Justice Stewart delivered the opinion of the Court.

This appeal concerns the constitutionality of the system for electing the directors of a large water reclamation district in Arizona, a system which, in essence, limits voting eligibility to landowners and apportions voting power according to the amount of land a voter owns. The case requires us to consider whether the peculiarly

---

2. The Court has held that states can require voters to pass English literacy tests, as long as they are not administered to discriminate against minorities. Lassiter v. Northampton County Elections Board, 360 U.S. 45 (1959); Louisiana v. United States, 380 U.S. 145 (1965).

narrow function of this local governmental body and the special relationship of one class of citizens to that body releases it from the strict demands of the one-person, one-vote principle of the Equal Protection Clause of the Fourteenth Amendment.

I

The public entity at issue here is the Salt River Project Agricultural Improvement and Power District, which stores and delivers untreated water to the owners of land comprising 236,000 acres in central Arizona. The District, formed as a governmental entity in 1937, subsidizes its water operations by selling electricit., and has become the supplier of electric power for hundreds of thousands of people in an area including a large part of metropolitan Phoenix. Nevertheless, the history of the District began in the efforts of Arizona farmers in the 19th century to irrigate the arid lands of the Salt River Valley, and, as the parties have stipulated, the primary purposes of the District have always been the storage, delivery, and conservation of water.

As early as 1867, farmers in the Salt River Valley attempted to irrigate their lands with water from the Salt River. In 1895, concerned with the erratic and unreliable flow of the river, they formed a "Farmers Protective Association," which helped persuade Congress to pass the Reclamation Act of 1902, 32 Stat. 388, 43 U.S.C. § 371 et seq. Under that Act, the United States gave interest-free loans to help landowners build reclamation projects. The Salt River Project, from which the District developed, was created in 1903 as a result of this legislation. In 1906, Congress authorized projects created under the Act to generate and sell hydroelectric power, 43 U.S.C. § 522, and the Salt River Project has supported its water operations by this means almost since its creation. The 1902 Act provided that the water users who benefited from the reclamation project had to agree to repay to the United States the costs of constructing the project, and the Salt River Valley Water Users Association was organized as an Arizona corporation in 1903 to serve as the contracting agent for the landowners. The Association's Articles, drafted in cooperation with the Federal Reclamation Service, gave subscribing landowners the right to reclamation water and the power to vote in Association decisions in proportion to the number of acres the subscribers owned. The Articles also authorized acreage-proportionate stock assessments to raise income for the Association, the assessments becoming a lien on the subscribing owners' land until paid. For almost 15 years, the Federal Reclamation Service operated and maintained the project's irrigation system for the landowners; under a 1917 contract with the United States, however, the Association itself took on these tasks, proceeding to manage the project for the next 20 years.

The Association faced serious financial difficulties during the Depression as it built new dams and other works for the project, and it sought a means of borrowing money that would not overly encumber the subscribers' lands. The means seemed to be available in Arizona's Agricultural Improvement District Act of 1922, which authorized the creation of special public water districts within federal reclamation projects. Ariz. Rev. Code of 1928, § 3467 et seq. Such districts, as political subdivisions of the State, could issue bonds exempt from federal income tax.

Nevertheless, many Association members opposed creating a special district for the project, in part because the state statute would have required that voting power in elections for directors of the district be distributed per capita among landowners, and not according to the acreage formula for stock assessments and water rights. In 1936, in response to a request from the Association, the state legislature amended the 1922 statute. Under the new statutory scheme, which is essentially the one at issue in this case, the legislature allowed the district to limit voting for its directors to voters, otherwise regularly qualified under state law, who own land within the district, and to apportion voting power among those landowners according to the number of acres owned. Ariz. Rev. Stat. Ann. §§ 45–909, 45–983 (Supp. 1980–1981). The Salt River Project Agricultural Improvement and Power District was then formed in 1937, its boundaries essentially the same as the Association's. Under the 1937 agreement, the Association made the District its contracting agent, and transferred to the District all its property, and the Association in turn agreed to continue to operate and maintain the Salt River Project. Under the current agreement, the District itself manages the power and water storage work of the project, and the Association, as agent for the District, manages water delivery. As for financing, the statute now permits the special districts to raise money through an acreage-proportionate taxing power that mirrors the Association's stock assessment scheme, Ariz. Rev. Stat. Ann. §§ 45–1014, 45–1015 (1956), or through bonds secured by liens on the real property within the District, though the bonds can simultaneously be secured by District revenues, Ariz. Rev. Stat. Ann. § 45–936 (Supp. 1980–1981).

II

This lawsuit was brought by a class of registered voters who live within the geographic boundaries of the District, and who own either no land or less than an acre of land within the District. The complaint alleged that the District enjoys such governmental powers as the power to condemn land, to sell tax-exempt bonds, and to levy taxes on real property. It also alleged that because the District sells electricity to virtually half the population of Arizona, and because, through its water operations, it can exercise significant influence on flood control and environmental management within its boundaries, the District's policies and actions have a substantial effect on all people who live within the District, regardless of property ownership. Seeking declaratory and injunctive relief, the appellees claimed that the acreage-based scheme for electing directors of the District violates the Equal Protection Clause of the Fourteenth Amendment. * * *

III

Reynolds v. Sims, supra, held that the Equal Protection Clause requires adherence to the principle of one-person, one-vote in elections of state legislators. Avery v. Midland County, 390 U.S. 474, extended the Reynolds rule to the election of officials of a county government, holding that the elected officials exercised "general governmental powers over the entire geographic area served by the body." [Editor—Among the duties of the County Commissioners Court in Avery were establishing courthouses and jails, appointing health officials, building roads and bridges, administering welfare, setting the county tax rate, adopting the county budget, and equalizing tax assessments.] The Court, however, reserved any decision on the application of Reynolds to "a special-purpose unit of government assigned the performance of functions affecting definable groups of constituents more than other constituents." In Hadley v. Junior College District, 397 U.S. 50, the Court extended Reynolds to the election of trustees of a community college district because those trustees "exercised general governmental powers" and "perform[ed] important governmental functions that had significant effect on all citizens residing within the district." But in that case the Court stated: "It is of course possible that there might be some cases in which a State elects certain functionaries whose duties are so far removed from normal governmental activities and so disproportionately affect different groups that a popular election in compliance with Reynolds * * * might not be required * * *." [Editor—The Court held that the Junior College District in Hadley did not fall within its exception because "[e]ducation has traditionally been a vital governmental function, and these * * * are governmental officials in every relevant sense of that term."]

The Court found such a case in Salyer. The Tulare Lake Basin Water Storage District involved there encompassed 193,000 acres, 85% of which were farmed by one or another of four corporations. Salyer Land Co. v. Tulare Lake Basin Water Storage District. Under California law, public water districts could acquire, store, conserve, and distribute water, and though the Tulare Lake Basin Water Storage District had never chosen to do so, could generate and sell any form of power it saw fit to support its water operations. The costs of the project were assessed against each landowner according to the water benefits the landowner received. At issue in the case was the constitutionality of the scheme for electing the directors of the district, under which only landowners could vote, and voting power was apportioned according to the assessed valuation of the voting landowner's property. The court recognized that the Tulare Lake Basin Water Storage District did exercise "some typical governmental powers," including the power to hire and fire workers, contract for construction of projects, condemn private property, and issue general obligation bonds. Nevertheless, the Court concluded that the district had "relatively limited authority," because "its primary purpose, indeed the reason for its existence, is to provide for the acquisition, storage, and distribution of water for farming in the Tulare Lake Basin." The Court also noted that the financial burdens of the district could not but fall on the landowners, in proportion to the benefits they received from the district, and that the district's actions therefore disproportionately affected the voting landowners. The Salyer Court thus held that the strictures of Reynolds did not apply to the Tulare District, and proceeded to inquire simply whether the statutory voting scheme based on land valuation at least bore some relevancy to the statute's objectives. The Court concluded that the California Legislature could have reasonably assumed that without voting power apportioned according to the value of their land, the landowners might not have been willing to subject their lands to the lien of the very assessments which made the creation of the district possible.

As noted by the Court of Appeals, the services currently provided by the Salt River District are more diverse and affect far more people than those of the Tulare Lake Basin Water Storage District. Whereas the Tulare District included an area entirely devoted to agriculture and populated by only 77 persons, the Salt River District includes almost half the population of the State, including large parts of Phoenix and other cities. Moreover, the Salt River District, unlike the Tulare District, has exercised its statutory power to generate and sell electric power, and had become one of the largest suppliers of such power in the State. Further, whereas all the water delivered by the Tulare District went for agriculture, roughly 40% of the water delivered by the Salt River District goes to urban areas or is used for nonagricultural purposes in farming areas. Finally whereas all operating costs of the Tulare District were born by the voting landowners through assessments apportioned according to land value, most of the capital and operating costs of the Salt River District have been met through the revenues generated by the selling of electric power. Nevertheless, a careful examination of the Salt River District reveals that, under the principles of the Avery, Hadley, and Salyer cases, these distinctions do not amount to a constitutional difference.

First, the District simply does not exercise the sort of governmental powers that invoke the strict demands of Reynolds. The District cannot impose ad valorem property taxes or sales taxes. It cannot enact any laws governing the conduct of citizens, nor does it administer such normal functions of government as the maintenance of streets, the operation of schools, or sanitation, health, or welfare services.

[Editor—The Court then observed in a footnote:

In Salyer, we recognized that the powers to contract for and staff projects, to condemn property, and to issue bonds do not amount to such general governmental authority. And as recognized by the dissenting opinion in the companion case to Salyer, the power to levy and collect special assessments also does not create such general governmental authority.

In other cases, the Court has found invalid state laws tying voting eligibility to property ownership in elections to approve issuance of bonds to finance a city library, Hill v. Stone, 421 U.S. 289, and a municipal utility, Cipriano v. City of Houma, 395 U.S. 701 (per curiam), and to issue general obligation bonds secured by a lien on real property, Phoenix v. Kolodziejski, 399 U.S. 204. In those cases, however, the elections concerned the operations of traditional municipalities exercising the full range of normal governmental powers, and so the cases do not bear on the question of a special-purpose governmental entity like the Salt River District.]

Second, though they were characterized broadly by the Court of Appeals, even the District's water functions, which constitute the primary and originating purpose of the District, are relatively narrow. The District and Association do not own, sell, or buy water, nor do they control the use of any water they have delivered. The District simply stores water behind its dams, conserves it from loss, and delivers it through project canals. It is true, as the Court of Appeals noted, that as much as 40% of the water delivered by the District goes for nonagricultural purposes. But the distinction between agricultural and urban land is of no special constitutional significance in this context. The constitutionally relevant fact is that all water delivered by the Salt River District, like the water delivered by the Tulare Lake Basin Water Storage District, is distributed according to land ownership and the District does not and cannot control the use to which the landowners who are entitled to the water choose to put it. As repeatedly recognized by the Arizona courts, though the state legislature has allowed water districts to become nominal public entities in order to obtain inexpensive bond financing, the districts remain essentially business enterprises, created by and chiefly benefiting a specific group of landowners. As in Salyer, the nominal public character of such an entity cannot transform it into the type of governmental body for which the Fourteenth Amendment demands a one-person, one-vote system of election.

Finally, neither the existence nor size of the district's power business affects the legality of its property-based voting scheme. As this Court has noted in a different context, the provision of electricity is not a traditional element of governmental sovereignty, Jackson v.

Metropolitan Edison Co., 419 U.S. 345, 353, and so is not in itself the sort of general or important governmental function that would make the government provider subject to the doctrine of the Reynolds case. In any event, since the electric power functions were stipulated to be incidental to the water functions which are the District's primary purpose, they cannot change the character of that enterprise. * * *

The appellees claim, and the Court of Appeals agreed, that the sheer size of the power operations and the great number of people they affect serve to transform the district into an entity of general governmental power. But no matter how great the number of nonvoting residents buying electricity from the District, the relationship between them and the District's power operations is essentially that between consumers and a business enterprise from which they buy. Nothing in the Avery, Hadley, or Salyer cases suggests that the volume of business or the breadth of economic effect of a venture undertaken by a government entity as an incident of its narrow and primary governmental public function can, of its own weight, subject the entity to the one-person, one-vote requirements of the Reynolds case.

The functions of the Salt River District are therefore of the narrow, special sort which justifies a departure from the popular-election requirement of the Reynolds case. And as in Salyer, an aspect of that limited purpose is the disproportionate relationship the District's functions bear to the specific class of people whom the system makes eligible to vote. The voting landowners are the only residents of the District whose lands are subject to liens to secure District bonds. Only these landowners are subject to the acreage-based taxing power of the District, and voting landowners are the only residents who have ever committed capital to the District through stock assessments charged by the Association. The Salyer opinion did not say that the selected class of voters for a special public entity must be the only parties at all affected by the operations of the entity, or that their entire economic well-being must depend on that entity. Rather the question was whether the effect of the entity's operations on them was disproportionately greater than the effect on those seeking the vote.

As in the Salyer case, we conclude that the voting scheme for the District is constitutional because it bears a reasonable relationship to its statutory objectives. Here, according to the stipulation of the parties, the subscriptions of land which made the Association and then the District possible might well have never occurred had not the subscribing landowners been assured a special voice in the conduct of the District's business. Therefore, as in Salyer, the State could rationally limit the vote to landowners. Moreover, Arizona could rationally make the weight of their vote dependent upon the number of acres they own, since that number reasonably reflects the relative risks they incurred as landowners and the distribution of the benefits and the burdens of the District's water operations.

The judgment of the Court of Appeals is reversed, and the case is remanded for further proceedings consistent with this opinion. It is so ordered.

■ Justice White, with whom Justice Brennan, Justice Marshall, and Justice Blackmun join, dissenting.

[Editor—The dissent lists what it considers the District's indicia of governmental powers, including issuing of tax exempt bonds, exemption from property tax, and eminent domain power. In addition, unlike private utilities, the District could set rates free of public regulation. It then goes on to compare the impact of the District's activities on landowners and those who cannot vote.]

In terms of the relative impact of the Salt River District's operations on the favored landowner voters and those who may not vote for the officers of this municipal corporation, the contrast with the Water District in Salyer is even more pronounced. A bird's-eye view of the District's operations will be helpful. Historically, the Salt River District was concerned only with storing water and delivering it for agricultural uses within the District. This was a crucial service, but it proved too expensive for a wholly private concern to maintain. It needed public help, which it received. It became a municipal corporation, a transformation which rendered its bonds and property tax exempt. It also needed a public subsidy, which was provided by authorizing it to engage in the generation and sale of electricity. It was also authorized to supply water for municipal and other nonagricultural uses.

The area within the District, once primarily rural, now encompasses eight municipalities and a major part of the city of Phoenix. Its original purpose, the supply of irrigation water, now provides only a tiny fraction of its gross income. For the fiscal year ending April 30, 1980, the District had a total operating income of approximately $450 million, 98% of which was derived from the generation of electricity and its sale to approximately 240,000 consumers. See Salt River Project, 1979–1980 Annual Report, p. 25 The District is now the second largest utility in Arizona. Furthermore, as of April 30, 1980, the District had outstanding long-term debt of slightly over $2 billion. Approximately $1.78 billion, or about 88%, of that debt are in the form of revenue bonds secured solely by the revenues from the District's electrical operations. All of the District's capital improvements since 1972 have been financed by revenue bonds, and the general obligation bonds, now representing a small fraction of the District's long-term debt, are being steadily retired from the District's general revenues. It must also be noted that at the present time, 40% of the water delivered by the District is used for nonagricultural purposes—25% for municipal purposes and 15% to schools, playgrounds, parks, and the like.

With these facts in mind, it is indeed curious that the Court would attempt to characterize the District's electrical operations as "incidental" to water operations, or would consider the power operations to be irrelevant to the legality of the voting scheme. The facts are that in Salyer the burdens of the Water District fell entirely on the landowners who were served by the District. Here the landowners could not themselves afford to finance their own project and turned to a public agency to help them. That agency now subsidizes the storage and delivery to the public at prices that neither the voters nor any representative public agency has any right to control. Unlike the situation in Salyer, the financial burden of supplying irrigation water has been shifted from the landowners to the consumers of electricity. At the very least, the structure of the District's indebtedness together with the history of the District's operations compels a finding that the burdens placed upon the lands within the District are so minimal that they cannot possibly serve as a basis for limiting the franchise to property owners. * * *

Simply put, the District is an integral governmental actor providing important governmental services to residents of the District. To conclude otherwise is to ignore the urban reality of the District's operations.

Underlying the Court's conclusion in this case is the view that the provision of electricity and water is essentially private enterprise and not sufficiently governmental—that the District "simply does not exercise the sort of governmental powers that invoke the strict demands" of the Fourteenth Amendment because it does not administer "such normal functions of government as the maintenance of streets, the operation of schools, or sanitation, health, or welfare services." This is a distinctly odd view of the reach of municipal services in this day and age. Supplying water for domestic and industrial uses is almost everywhere the responsibility of local government, and this function is intimately connected with sanitation and health. Nor is it any more accurate to consider the supplying of electricity as essentially a private function. The United States Government and its agencies generate and sell substantial amounts of power; and in view of the widespread existence of municipal utility systems, it is facetious to suggest that the operation of such utility systems should be considered as an incidental aspect of municipal government. Nor will it do, it seems to me, to return to the proprietary-governmental dichotomy in order to deliver into wholly private hands the control of a major municipal activity which acts to subsidize a limited number of landowners. * * *

QUESTIONS

Which of the following factors is influential in the Ball v. James opinions? After thinking about each factor, see whether there is some particular combination of factors that the majority and dissent consider crucial, even if no one factor is dispositive.

1. *Who bears the financial risk?* The landowners were ultimately responsible for financing the venture, if electricity revenue was inadequate. But remember that financing responsibility also rests with property owners whenever general obligation bonds are issued and voting on such bonds cannot be limited to property owners for that reason alone. See Phoenix v. Kolodziejski, 399 U.S. 204 (1970). Was it important that the landowners took the initial financial risk?

2. *Benefits from the activity.* Both the majority and dissent take note of the widespread distribution of electricity to paying customers and the fact that a lot of the water was distributed to urban users. What is the difference of opinion between the majority and dissent about the legal relevance of benefit distribution?

3. *Government powers.* The dissent emphasizes the entity's power to issue tax exempt bonds, its tax exemption, and its freedom from rate regulation because of its governmental status. How does the majority treat these factors?

In Ball v. James, the question was whether "private" activity should be subject to public electoral control. In Flagg Bros., Inc. v. Brooks, 436 U.S. 149 (1978), the issue was whether certain "private" activity was subject to the "prior hearing" requirement that is often applied to public action. For example, the government cannot withdraw welfare benefits without a prior hearing, if withdrawal depends on contested facts. The specific issue in Flagg was whether a creditor could seize the debtor's property for nonpayment of storage costs under UCC § 7–210, without the debtor first obtaining a hearing on the merits of the claim. The creditor exercised self-help without the explicit aid of a government official.

The Court held that there was no state action and therefore no procedural due process right to a hearing prior to the seizure. The debtor argued that the state had delegated to the creditor a power "traditionally exclusively reserved to the State"—specifically, the resolution of private disputes. Justice Rehnquist said that only very few functions fit that description—for example, elections and the control of streets by a company town. These functions had the common feature of exclusivity. Debtor-creditor disputes, by contrast, were private disputes which could be resolved in many ways (including obtaining a waiver of the creditor's right to sell when the goods were stored; and a damage or replevin action by the debtor).

In dissent, Mr. Justice Stevens took a different view of "public" responsibility. He stated:

> * * * [W]e expect government "to provide a reasonable and fair framework of rules which facilitate commercial transactions * * *." This "framework of rules" is premised on the assumption that the State will control nonconsensual deprivations of property

and that the State's control will, in turn, be subject to the restrictions of the Due Process Clause. The power to order legally binding surrenders of property and the constitutional restrictions on that power are necessary correlatives in our system. In effect, today's decision allows the State to divorce these two elements by the simple expedient of transferring the implementation of its policy to private parties.

16.03 ELECTORAL GROUND RULES

In this section we consider electoral ground rules in two broad categories: the rules which discourage third party and independent candidates, and the rules which make it difficult for political groups to be represented. The first category includes filing deadlines, signature requirements, and public financing of elections. The second category includes multimember districts and partisan gerrymandering. You should try to identify what political vision, if any, underlies the court's decision. Is it the following: a preference for two-party interest-group pluralism, where interest groups can bargain within the two party structure, and no single interest group is frozen in or out of the political system? Are there some interest groups the government must not exclude, some they can prefer? How are they defined?

a) THE BALANCE BETWEEN THE TWO PARTY SYSTEM AND CHALLENGERS

i) INTRODUCTION

The state can discourage unlimited access to the ballot. The Court put it this way in Lubin v. Panish, 415 U.S. 709 (1974):

Historically, since the Progressive movement of the early 20th century, there has been a steady trend toward limiting the size of the ballot in order to "concentrate the attention of the electorate on the selection of a much smaller number of officials and so afford to the voters the opportunity of exercising more discrimination in their use of the franchise." This desire to limit the size of the ballot has been variously phrased as a desire to minimize voter confusion, to limit the number of runoff elections, to curb "ballot flooding," and to prevent the overwhelming of voting machines—the modern counterpart of ballot flooding.

* * * [I]nviting or permitting every citizen to present himself to the voters on the ballot without some means of measuring the seriousness of the candidate's desire and motivation would make rational voter choices more difficult because of the size of the ballot and hence would tend to impede the electoral process. * * *

That "laundry list" ballots discourage voter participation and confuse and frustrate those who do participate is too obvious to call for extended discussion. The means of testing the seriousness of a given candidacy may be open to debate; the fundamental importance of ballots of reasonable size limited to serious candidates with some prospects of public support is not. Rational results within the framework of our system are not likely to be reached if the ballot for a single office must list a dozen or more aspirants who are relatively unknown or have no prospects of success.

The Court concedes, however, that limiting the size of the ballot can conflict with the modern pressure to expand political opportunity. These conflicting concerns are balanced in several settings, discussed below, including ballot access and financing elections.

ii) BALLOT ACCESS

The clash between ballot access and preserving the two party system is sharply presented when the state imposes obstacles to a third party or independent candidate. How does the Court balance the relevant interests in the following cases dealing with filing deadlines and signature requirements?

Anderson v. Celebrezze
460 U.S. 780 (1983).

■ Mr. Justice Stevens delivered the opinion of the Court. * * *

[Editor–An independent Presidential candidate was required to file by March 20, 1980 in order to be on the Ohio ballot. Major party candidates were automatically placed on the ballot when nominated in the summer at their national conventions. The petitioner challenged the legality of this early filing date.]

Although the Court of Appeals did not discuss the State's interest in political stability, that was the primary justification advanced by respondent in the District Court, and it is again asserted in this Court. The State's brief explains that the State has a substantial interest in protecting the two major political parties from "damaging intraparty feuding." Brief for Respondent 41. According to the State, a candidate's decision to abandon efforts to win the party primary and to run as an independent "can be very damaging to state political party structures." Anderson's decision to run as an independent, the State argues, threatened to "splinter" the Ohio Republican party "by drawing away its activists to work in his 'independent' campaign."

Ohio's asserted interest in political stability amounts to a desire to protect existing political parties from competition—competition for campaign workers, voter support, and other campaign resources—generated by independent candidates who have previously been affiliated with the party. * * *

* * * [I]n Storer v. Brown we upheld two California statutory provisions that restricted access by independent candidates to the

general election ballot. Under California law, a person could not run as an independent in November if he had been defeated in a party primary that year or if he had been registered with a political party within one year prior to that year's primary election. We stated that "California apparently believes with the Founding Fathers that splintered parties and unrestrained factionalism may do significant damage to the fabric of government," and that destruction of the "political stability of the system of the State" could have "profound consequences for the entire citizenry." Further, we approved the State's goals of discouraging "independent candidacies prompted by short-range political goals, pique, or personal quarrel."

Thus in Storer we recognized the legitimacy of the State's interest in preventing "splintered parties and unrestrained factionalism." But we did not suggest that a political party could invoke the powers of the State to assure monolithic control over its own members and supporters. Political competition that draws resources away from the major parties cannot, for that reason alone, be condemned as "unrestrained factionalism." Instead, in Storer we examined the two challenged provisions in the context of California's electoral system. By requiring a candidate to remain in the intraparty competition once the disaffiliation deadline had passed, and by giving conclusive effect to the winnowing process performed by party members in the primary election, the challenged provisions were an essential part of "a general state policy aimed at maintaining the integrity of the various routes to the ballot." Moreover, we pointed out that the policy "involves no discrimination against independents."

Ohio's challenged restriction is substantially different from the California provisions upheld in Storer. As we have noted, the early filing deadline does discriminate against independents. And the deadline is neither a "sore loser" provision nor a disaffiliation statute. Furthermore, it is important to recognize that Storer upheld the State's interest in avoiding political fragmentation in the context of elections wholly within the boundaries of California. The State's interest in regulating a nationwide Presidential election is not nearly as strong; no State could singlehandedly assure "political stability" in the Presidential context. The Ohio deadline does not serve any state interest in "maintaining the integrity of the various routes to the ballot" for the Presidency, because Ohio's Presidential preference primary does not serve to narrow the field for the general election. A major party candidate who loses the Ohio primary, or who does not even run in Ohio, may nonetheless appear on the November general election ballot as the party's nominee. In addition, the national scope of the competition for delegates at the Presidential nominating conventions assures that "intraparty feuding" will continue until August.

More generally, the early filing deadline is not precisely drawn to protect the parties from "intraparty feuding," whatever legitimacy that state goal may have in a Presidential election. If the deadline is designed to keep intraparty competition within the party structure, its coverage is both too broad and too narrow. It is true that in this case [the filing requirement] was applied to a candidate who had previously competed in party primaries and then sought to run as an independent. But the early deadline applies broadly to independent candidates who have not been affiliated in the recent past with any political party. On the other hand, as long as the decision to run is made before the March deadline, Ohio does not prohibit independent candidacies by persons formerly affiliated with a political party, or currently participating in intraparty competition in other States—regardless of the effect on the political party structure. * * *

We conclude that Ohio's March filing deadline for independent candidates for the office of President of the United States cannot be justified by the State's asserted interest in protecting political stability.

Norman v. Reed

502 U.S. 279 (1992).

■ Justice Souter delivered the opinion of the Court. * * *

In these consolidated cases, we review a decision of the Supreme Court of Illinois barring petitioners from appearing under the name of the Harold Washington Party on the November 1990 ballot for Cook County offices. * * *

Under Illinois law, citizens organizing a new political party must canvass the electoral area in which they wish to field candidates and persuade voters to sign their nominating petitions. Organizers seeking to field candidates for statewide office must collect the signatures of 25,000 eligible voters, Ill. Rev. Stat., ch. 46, § 10-2 (1989), and, if they wish to run candidates solely for offices within a large "political subdivision" like Cook County, they need 25,000 signatures from the subdivision. If, however, the subdivision itself comprises large separate districts from which some of its officers are elected, party organizers seeking to fill such offices must collect 25,000 signatures from each district. [Editor—More precisely, party organizers must obtain signatures of the lesser of 5% of the voters in the prior election, or 25,000. For units the size of Cook County, 25,000 was the operative figure.] * * *

Cook County comprises two electoral districts: the area corresponding to the city of Chicago (city district) and the rest of the county (suburban district). Although some county officials are elected at large by citizens of the entire county, members of the County

Board of Commissioners are elected separately by the citizens of each district to fill county board seats specifically designated for that district. While certain petitioners wished to run for offices filled by election at large, others sought to capture the county board seats representing the city and suburban districts of Cook County.

[S]ince petitioners wished to field candidates for the county board seats allocated to the separate districts, they [ ] had to collect 25,000 signatures from each district. Petitioners gathered 44,000 signatures on the city-district component of their petition, but only 7,800 on the suburban component. * * *

[Editor—The Illinois Supreme Court interpreted the law to mean that a party which did not obtain the required signatures to run in the suburban district was disqualified from running candidates in the city and county-wide elections.]

* * * In Illinois Elections Bd. v. Socialist Workers Party, 440 U.S. 173 (1979), we examined Illinois's earlier ballot-access scheme, under which party organizers seeking to field candidates in state-wide elections were (as they still are) effectively required to gather 25,000 signatures. At that time, the statute separately required those organizing new parties in political subdivisions to collect signatures totalling at least 5% of the number of people voting at the previous election for offices of that subdivision. In the city of Chicago, the subdivision at issue in Socialist Workers Party, the effect of that provision was to require many more than 25,000 signatures. Although this Court recognized the State's interest in restricting the ballot to parties with demonstrated public support, the Court took the requirement for statewide contests as an indication that the more onerous standard for local contests was not the least restrictive means of advancing that interest.

The Illinois Legislature responded to this ruling by amending its statute to cap the 5% requirement for "any district or political subdivision" at 25,000 signatures. Thus, if organizers of a new party wish to field candidates in a large county without separate districts, and if 5% of the number of voters at the previous county election exceeds 25,000, the party now needs to gather only 25,000 signatures.

Under the interpretation of s 10–2 rendered below, however, Illinois law retains the constitutional flaw at issue in Socialist Workers by effectively increasing the signature requirement applicable to elections for at least some offices in subdivisions with separate districts. Under that interpretation, the failure of a party's organizers to obtain 25,000 signatures for each district in which they run candidates disqualifies the party's candidates in all races within the subdivision. Thus, a prerequisite to establishing a new political party in such multi-district subdivisions is some multiple of the number of signatures required of new statewide parties. * * * The State may not do this in the face of Socialist Workers, which forbids it to require petitioners to gather twice as many signatures to field candidates in Cook County as they would need statewide.

Reed nonetheless tries to skirt Socialist Workers by advancing what she claims to be a state interest, not addressed by the earlier case, in ensuring that the electoral support for new parties in a multidistrict political subdivision extends to every district. Accepting the legitimacy of the interest claimed would not, however, excuse the requirement's unconstitutional breadth. Illinois might have compelled the organizers of a new party to demonstrate a distribution of support throughout Cook County without at the same time raising the overall quantum of needed support above what the State expects of new parties fielding candidates only for statewide office. The State might, for example, have required some minimum number of signatures from each of the component districts while maintaining the total signature requirement at 25,000. While we express no opinion as to the constitutionality of any such requirement, what we have said demonstrates that Illinois has not chosen the most narrowly tailored means of advancing even the interest that Reed suggests.

Nor is that the only weakness of Reed's rationale. Illinois does not require a new party fielding candidates solely for statewide office to apportion its nominating signatures among the various counties or other political subdivisions of the State. Organizers of a new party could therefore win access to the statewide ballot, but not the Cook County ballot, by collecting all 25,000 signatures from the county's city district. But if the State deems it unimportant to ensure that new statewide parties enjoy any distribution of support, it requires elusive logic to demonstrate a serious state interest in demanding such a distribution for new local parties. * * * Reed has adduced no justification for the disparity here. * * *

The judgment of the State Supreme Court is * * * reversed in part, and the case is remanded for further proceedings not inconsistent with this opinion.

Party control of nominees. In the cases discussed above, someone seeks access to the ballot outside of the two-party system. How free is a party to determine how its nominees shall be determined? The following cases protect the party's decision on freedom of political association grounds.

In Eu v. San Francisco County Democratic Central Committee, 489 U.S. 214 (1989), the Court held that the State could not prevent a party from endorsing one of several primary candidates. And, in Democratic Party of U.S. v. Wisconsin, 450 U.S. 107 (1981), the State was not allowed to require an open primary to determine delegates to the Presidential National Convention; in an open primary, voters not registered with the party can vote.

These two cases seem uncontroversial, but what about Tashjian v. Republican Party of Connecticut, 479 U.S. 208 (1986)? The State mandated a closed primary by forbidding independents from voting in a party primary, even though the party wanted an open primary. The Court struck down the State's decision, but Justice Scalia *dissented* as follows:

> * * * [E]ven if it were the fact that the majority of the Party's members wanted its candidates to be determined by outsiders, there is no reason why the State is bound to honor that desire—any more than it would be bound to honor a party's democratically expressed desire that its candidates henceforth be selected by convention rather than by primary, or by the party's executive committee in a smoke-filled room. In other words, the validity of the state-imposed primary requirement itself, which we have hitherto considered "too plain for argument," presupposes that the State has the right "to protect the Party against the Party itself." Connecticut may lawfully require that significant elements of the democratic election process be democratic—whether the Party wants that or not. It is beyond my understanding why the Republican Party's delegation of its democratic choice to a Republican Convention can be proscribed, but its delegation of that choice to nonmembers of the Party cannot.

Minor and major party with same nominee. The Supreme Court has agreed to review a case combining the issues of a party's freedom of association and the impact of minor parties on the two-party system. In Twin Cities Area New Party v. McKenna, 73 F.3d 196 (8th Cir.1996), cert. granted, 116 S.Ct. 1846 (1996), the court dealt with a Minnesota law prohibiting a minor party from nominating candidates already nominated by a major party. Such prohibitions appear in about forty states. Minnesota's law applies even though the candidate consents to the minor party's nomination and the major party does not object. The court held the law unconstitutional on the ground that it burdened the minor party's core associational rights severely "because [it] keep[s] the [minor party] from developing consensual political alliances and thus broadening the base of public participation in and support for its activities." It noted that

> [h]istory shows that minor parties have played a significant role in the electoral system where multiple party nomination is legal, but have no meaningful influence where multiple party nomination is banned. This is so because a party's ability to establish itself as a durable, influential player in the political arena depends on the ability to elect candidates to office. And the ability of minor parties to elect candidates depends on the parties' ability to form political alliances. When a minor party and a major party nominate the same candidate and the candidate is elected because of the votes cast on the minor party line, the minor party voters have sent an important

message to the candidate and the major party, which gets attention for the minor party's platform. By foreclosing a consensual multiple party nomination, Minnesota's statutes force the [minor party] to make a no-win choice. [The minor party] members must either cast their votes for candidates with no realistic chance of winning, defect from their party and vote for a major party candidate who does, or decline to vote at all.

The court took account of the state's interest in preventing a minor party from riding the coattails of a major party, thereby disrupting the two-party system, but held that this problem was avoided by requiring the consent of the candidate and both parties before the minor party could nominate a candidate. The court also held that the prohibition could not be justified as preventing voter confusion, because it was easy to provide simple explanations in the ballot directions to cast the ballot for the candidate on one party line or the other. Moreover, the court said, "a consensual multiple party nomination informs voters rather than misleads them. If a major party and a minor party believe the same person is the best candidate and would best deliver on their platforms, multiple party nomination brings their political alliance into the open and helps the voters understand what the candidate stands for."

———————

Write-ins. Is the opportunity to write in a candidate's name a protected constitutional right? Burdick v. Takushi, 504 U.S. 428 (1992) applied the following standard to deal with this issue:

It is beyond cavil that "voting is of the most fundamental significance under our constitutional structure." It does not follow, however, that the right to vote in any manner and the right to associate for political purposes through the ballot are absolute. The Constitution provides that States may prescribe "[t]he Times, Places and Manner of holding Election for Senators and Representatives." Common sense, as well as constitutional law, compels the conclusion that government must play an active role in structuring elections; "as a practical matter, there must be a substantial regulation of elections if they are to be fair and honest and if some sort of order, rather than chaos, is to accompany the democratic processes."

Election laws will invariably impose some burden upon individual voters. * * * Consequently, to subject every voting regulation to strict scrutiny and to require that the regulation be narrowly tailored to advance a compelling state interest [ ] would tie the hands of States seeking to assure that elections are operated equitably and efficiently. * * *

* * * A court considering a challenge to a state election law must weigh "the character and magnitude of the asserted injury to the rights protected by the First and Fourteenth Amendments that

the plaintiff seeks to vindicate" against "the precise interests put forward by the State as justifications for the burden imposed by its rule," taking into consideration "the extent to which those interests make it necessary to burden the plaintiff's rights."

Based on this standard, the Court upheld prohibition of write-ins in a primary election. First, the burden on the voter was not great because it took only 15 to 25 signatures to get a nonparty candidate on the primary ballot, and the nonparty candidate could advance to the general election with the lower of 10% of the primary vote or the vote needed to advance a party candidate. In response to the argument that this was a voting rights case, not a ballot access case, and therefore subject to higher judicial scrutiny, the Court stated:

> [We have] minimized the extent to which voting rights cases are distinguishable from ballot access cases * * *. [T]he function of the election process is "to winnow out and finally reject all but the chosen candidates," not to provide a means of giving vent to "short-range political goals, pique, or personal quarrel[s]." Attributing to elections a more generalized expressive function would undermine the ability of States to operate elections fairly and efficiently.

Second, having minimized the voter's interest in write-ins, the Court deferred to the State's judgment that prohibiting write-ins would discourage "unrestrained factionalism," thereby preventing divisive sore-loser candidacies and focusing voter attention on contested races. It concluded that

> when the State's ballot access laws pass constitutional muster * * * a prohibition on write-in voting will be presumptively valid, since any burden on the right to vote for the candidate of one's choice will be light and normally will be counterbalanced by the very state interests supporting the ballot access scheme.

This last quote goes very far in admitting that voting rights come to constitutional analysis already burdened by a conception of political community embodied in the rules applicable to ballot access.

iii) FINANCING ELECTIONS

Buckley v. Valeo

424 U.S. 1 (1976).

Per Curiam. * * *

III. PUBLIC FINANCING OF PRESIDENTIAL ELECTION CAMPAIGNS

Section 9006 establishes a Presidential Election Campaign Fund (Fund), financed from general revenues in the aggregate amount designated by individual taxpayers, under § 6096, who on their income tax returns may authorize payment to the Fund of one dollar of their tax liability in the case of an individual return or two dollars in the case of a joint return.

Chapter 95 of Title 26, * * * distinguishes among "major," "minor," and "new" parties. A major party is defined as a party whose candidate for President in the most recent election received 25% or more of the popular vote. § 9002 (6). A minor party is defined as a party whose candidate received at least 5% but less than 25% of the vote at the most recent election. § 9002 (7). All other parties are new parties, § 9002 (8), including both newly created parties and those receiving less than 5% of the vote in the last election. * * *

For expenses in the general election campaign, § 9004 (a)(1) entitles each major-party candidate to $20,000,000. This amount is also adjusted for inflation. See § 9004 (a)(1). To be eligible for funds the candidate must pledge not to incur expenses in excess of the entitlement under § 9004 (a)(1) and not to accept private contributions except to the extent that the fund is insufficient to provide the full entitlement. § 9003 (b). Minor-party candidates are also entitled to funding, again based on the ratio of the vote received by the party's candidate in the preceding election to the average of the major party candidates. § 9004 (a)(2). Minor-party candidates must certify that they will not incur campaign expenses in excess of the major-party entitlement and that they will accept private contributions only to the extent needed to make up the difference between that amount and the public funding grant. § 9003 (c). New-party candidates receive no money prior to the general election, but any candidate receiving 5% or more of the popular vote in the election is entitled to post-election payments according to the formula applicable to minor-party candidates. § 9004(a)(3). Similarly, minor-party candidates are entitled to post-election funds if they receive a greater percentage of the average major-party vote than their party's candidate did in the preceding election; the amount of such payments is the difference between the entitlement based on the preceding election and that based on the actual vote in the current election. § 9004(a)(3). A further eligibility requirement for minor- and new-party candidates is that the candidate's name must appear on the ballot, or electors pledged to the candidate must be on the ballot, in at least 10 states. § 9002 (2)(B). * * *

* * * In several situations concerning the electoral process, the principle has been developed that restrictions on access to the electoral process must survive exacting scrutiny. The restriction can be sustained only if it furthers a "vital" governmental interest, that is "achieved by a means that does not unfairly or unnecessarily burden either a minority party's or an individual candidate's equally important interest in the continued availability of political opportunity." These cases, however, dealt primarily with state laws requiring a candidate to satisfy certain requirements in order to have his name

appear on the ballot. These were, of course, direct burdens not only on the candidate's ability to run for office but also on the voter's ability to voice preferences regarding representative government and contemporary issues. * * * [Editor—The Court states that denial of public financing does not prevent a candidate from getting on the ballot, does not make private financing any harder for the minor-party candidate, and removes some competition for private funding by eliminating private contributions to major-party candidates who accept public financing.]

It cannot be gainsaid that public financing as a means of eliminating the improper influence of large private contributions furthers a significant governmental interest. * * * Congress properly regarded public financing as an appropriate means of relieving major-party Presidential candidates from the rigors of soliciting private contributions. The States have also been held to have important interests in limiting places on the ballot to those candidates who demonstrate substantial popular support. Congress' interest in not funding hopeless candidacies with large sums of public money necessarily justifies the withholding of public assistance from candidates without significant public support. * * *

> Appellants insist that Chapter 95 falls short of the constitutional requirement in that its provisions supply larger, and equal, sums to candidates of major parties, use prior vote levels as the sole criterion for pre-election funding, limit new-party candidates to post-election funds, and deny any funds to candidates of parties receiving less than 5% of the vote. These provisions, it is argued, are fatal to the validity of the scheme, because they work invidious discrimination against minor and new parties in violation of the Fifth Amendment. We disagree.

As conceded by appellants, the Constitution does not require Congress to treat all declared candidates the same for public financing purposes. As we said in Jenness v. Fortson, "there are obvious differences in kind between the needs and potentials of a political party with historically established broad support, on the other hand, and a new or small political organization on the other * * *. Sometimes the grossest discrimination can lie in treating things that are different as though they were exactly alike * * *." Since the Presidential elections of 1856 and 1860, when the Whigs were replaced as a major party by the Republicans, no third party has posed a credible threat to the two major parties in Presidential elections. [Editor—In a footnote, the Court observed that Theodore Roosevelt ran in 1912 as the candidate of the Progressive Party, which had split from the Republican Party, and that he received more votes than Taft, the Republican candidate, but that this third-party "threat" was short-lived; in 1916 the Progressives came back into the Republican Party when the party nominated Charles Evans Hughes as its candidate for the Presidency.] Third parties have been completely incapable of matching the major parties' ability to raise money and win elections. Congress was, of course, aware of this fact of American life, and thus was justified in providing both major parties full funding and all other parties only a percentage of the major-party entitlement. Identical treatment of all parties, on the other hand, "would only make it easy to raid the United States Treasury, it would also artificially foster the proliferation of splinter parties." The Constitution does not require the Government to "finance the efforts of every nascent political group," merely because Congress chose to finance the efforts of the major parties.

Furthermore, appellants have made no showing that the election funding plan disadvantages nonmajor parties by operating to reduce their strength below that attained without any public financing. * * *

Appellants challenge reliance on the vote in past elections as the basis for determining eligibility. That challenge is foreclosed, however, by our holding in Jenness v. Fortson, 403 U.S., at 439–440, that popular vote totals in the last election are a proper measure of public support. And Congress was not obliged to select instead from among appellants' suggested alternatives. Congress could properly regard the means chosen as preferable, since the alternative of petition drives presents cost and administrative problems in validating signatures, and the alternative of opinion polls might be thought inappropriate since it would involve a Government agency in the business of certifying polls or conducting its own investigation of support for various candidates, in addition to serious problems with reliability. * * *

Is the Court in Buckley permitting the government to lock in existing political power structures? If so, how does that contrast with its one-person one-vote decision, which destroyed the preexisting electoral balance favoring farm interests? Does the fact that one decision is about political parties and the other about voting explain the distinction?

b) PROTECTING POLITICAL GROUPS FROM EXCLUSION

i) WHO IS PROTECTED AND HOW?

The rules about electoral districts can have a significant effect on who is represented in a legislature. We earlier noted the Court's imposition of a one-person one-vote rule, requiring the same number of voters in each electoral district. Subsequent cases have allowed departures from that standard under certain circumstances? For example, in Mahan v. Howell, 410 U.S. 315 (1973), the Court distinguished between congressional districting and *state* legislative reapportionments. It allowed some "divergences from a strict population standard[   ] based on legitimate considerations incident to the effectuation of a rational state policy" for drawing *state* electoral districts. The Court accepted the State's justification for divergences to "maintain[   ] the integrity of political subdivision lines." The Court also seems to have accepted small deviations from one-person one-vote for federal congressional elections. In Anne Arundel County Republican Cent. Committee v. State Administrative Bd. of Election Laws, 781 F.Supp. 394 (D.Md.1991), affirmed without opinion, 504 U.S. 938 (1992), a deviation from equality of an average variance of 2.75 people was justified to keep major regions of the state in tact, create a minority voting district, and preserve incumbent representation in the House of Representatives.

Nonetheless, the Court continues to scrutinize efforts to block access to the political process and this scrutiny is not limited to determining whether or not the state has violated the one-person one-vote standard. Special attention is given to the use of multimember districts. Identifiable groups which could elect someone from a single member district can be frustrated by multimember districts, in which several candidates are elected in a winner-take-all election. For example, assume four people are elected from a large district with 1,000,000 voters. 750,000 voters prefer the four Republican candidates and can outvote those who favor the Democratic candidates for all four positions. If the electoral district were broken down into four equal smaller districts, with Democrats in a majority in one district, at least one Democratic candidate would be elected. The Court acknowledges this problem by preferring single-member districts for *court-ordered* reapportionment plans but refuses to reject state-adopted multimember districts automatically. Chapman v. Meier, 420 U.S. 1 (1975)(state can justify multimember districts by showing that certain interests such as city- or region-wide views are represented).

Another way in which a political group can be disadvantaged, despite satisfying the one-person one-vote rule, is by splitting the group among several single-member districts to dilute their vote.

Sensitive to these realities, the Court does more than impose a one-person one-vote requirement. It recognizes that politics operates through groups. Most of the litigation is about attempts to dilute the voting strength of racial and ethnic minorities, where the Court has developed the following *constitutional* standard: the constitution is violated if there is an intent and effect to cancel out the voting strength of a racial group. Mobile v. Bolden, 446 U.S. 55 (1980). See also White v. Regester, 412 U.S. 755 (1973)(ethnic groups). A large body of law has since developed about how to identify a cohesive minority group and whether the state has impaired its ability to influence elections.[3]

Although this course is not concerned with discrimination on racial or ethnic grounds, but with efforts by the state to favor or disadvantage any political group, the underlying constitutional doctrine is the same—the state cannot intentionally disadvantage *any* political group by "minimiz[ing] or cancel[ing] out the voting strength of racial or *political* elements of the voting

---

3. Thornburg v. Gingles, 478 U.S. 30 (1986); Armour v. State of Ohio, 775 F.Supp. 1044 (D.Ohio 1991).

population (emphasis added)." Whitcomb v. Chavis, 403 U.S. 124 (1971). Can you identify a political group which might be protected?

———————

Two such groups might be the poor and gays. One can imagine a legislature breaking up a geographically concentrated residential group of poor or gays so that they are transformed from a majority in one electoral district to a small minority in several other districts; or concentrating them in one district where they can influence only one election rather than being swing votes in several districts; or placing them in a multimember district whether they cannot elect a representative.

A recent decision involving gays (Romer v. Evans, 116 S.Ct. 1620 (1996), affirming, Evans v. Romer, 854 P.2d 1270 (Colo.1993) and 882 P.2d 1335 (Colo.1994)), might shed some light on whether gays will receive judicial protection in the electoral process. The case involved a referendum amending the Colorado constitution which stated:

> No Protected Status Based on Homosexual, Lesbian, or Bisexual Orientation. Neither the State of Colorado, through any of its branches or departments, nor any of its agencies, political subdivisions, municipalities or school districts, shall enact, adopt or enforce any statute, regulation, ordinance or policy whereby homosexual, lesbian or bisexual orientation, conduct, practices or relationships shall constitute or otherwise be the basis of or entitle any person or class of persons to have or claim any minority status quota preferences, protected status or claim of discrimination.

The amendment passed 53.4% to 46.6% and was struck down by both the Colorado and United States Supreme Courts. The Colorado court analyzed the case as involving a fundamental right to participate in the political process and applied strict scrutiny, stating (854 P.2d at 1276, 1285):

> The value placed on the ability of individuals to participate in the political process has manifested itself in numerous equal protection cases decided by the Supreme Court over the last thirty years. These include the reapportionment cases, see, e.g., Reynolds v. Sims, 377 U.S. 533 (1964); Wesberry v. Sanders, 376 U.S. 1 (1964), cases concerning minority party rights, see, e.g., Williams v. Rhodes, 393 U.S. 23 (1968), cases involving direct restrictions on the exercise of the franchise, see, e.g., Dunn v. Blumstein, 405 U.S. 330 (1972); Kramer v. Union Free Sch. Dist. No. 15, 395 U.S. 621 (1969); Harper v. Virginia Bd. of Elections, 383 U.S. 663 (1966), and cases involving attempts to limit the ability of certain groups to have desired legislation implemented through the normal political processes, see, e.g., Gordon v. Lance, 403 U.S. 1 (1971); and Hunter v. Erickson, 393 U.S. 385 (1969). When considered together, these cases demonstrate that the Equal Protection Clause guarantees the fundamental right to participate equally in the political process and

that any attempt to infringe on an independently identifiable group's ability to exercise that right is subject to strict judicial scrutiny. * * *

The right to participate equally in the political process is clearly affected by Amendment 2, because it bars gay men, lesbians, and bisexuals from having an effective voice in governmental affairs insofar as those persons deem it beneficial to seek legislation that would protect them from discrimination based on their sexual orientation. Amendment 2 alters the political process so that a targeted class is prohibited from obtaining legislative, executive, and judicial protection or redress from discrimination absent the consent of a majority of the electorate through the adoption of a constitutional amendment. Rather than attempting to withdraw antidiscrimination issues as a whole from state and local control, Amendment 2 singles out one form of discrimination and removes its redress from consideration by the normal political processes.

The Colorado Supreme Court opinion rejected the State's claim that "Amendment 2 'serves to deter factionalism through ensuring that decisions regarding special protections for homosexuals and bisexuals are made at the highest level of government.' More specifically, [the State] argue[s] that 'Amendment 2 is intended, not to restrain the competition of ideas,' but 'seeks to ensure that the deeply divisive issue of homosexuality's place in our society does not serve to fragment Colorado's body politic.' Amendment 2 accomplishes this end by eliminating 'city-by-city and county-by-county battles over this issue.' " The Court rejected that argument as follows:

We reject the argument that the interest in deterring factionalism, as defined by defendants, is compelling. Political debate, even if characterized as "factionalism," is not an evil which the state has a legitimate interest in deterring but rather, constitutes the foundation of democracy. "There is no significant state or public interest in curtailing debate or discussion of a ballot measure." We fail to see how the state, which is charged with serving the will of the people, can have any legitimate interest in preventing one side of a controversial debate from pressing its case before governmental bodies simply because it would prefer to avoid political controversy or "factionalism."

In support of the asserted compelling interest in deterring factionalism, defendants rely on Storer v. Brown, 415 U.S. 724 (1974). Storer involved a state requirement that proponents of any viewpoint resign from political parties and not run in those parties' primaries if the proponents intend to run as independent candidates. The purpose of this neutral election procedure was to insure that independent candidates were more than merely sore losers who, having lost one primary, ran as "independents" to satisfy "short-range political goals, pique, or personal quarrel."

Neither Storer, nor any other case we are aware of supports the proposition that there is a compelling governmental interest in preventing divisive issues from being debated at all levels of government by prohibiting one side of the debate from seeking desirable legislation in those fora. We conclude that the interest in deterring "factionalism" is not a compelling state interest.

The Colorado court is surely correct in rejecting the state's interest in preventing "factionalism" in the context of this case. We have seen the "factionalism" argument earlier, in the context of ballot access cases, where it was given considerable weight in discouraging multiple parties and sore losers from getting on the ballot. But it is quite another matter to shut down debate on a particular issue just because it is divisive.

There is, however, a deeper problem with the Colorado decision. The Amendment was not really aimed at suppressing factionalism. It took a specific substantive stance. In doing this, moreover, it did not completely fence out access to the political process; all it did was make it harder to pass laws to achieve a particular substantive result. In this respect, the Amendment sounds like a supramajority rule, which makes it more difficult to pass a law favoring a particular substantive value. As we will see later (Chapter 16.03biii—discussing Gordon v. Lance, 403 U.S. 1 (1971)), the Supreme Court has been very tolerant of supramajority requirements, allowing approval by 60% of the voters in a referendum election to incur bonded indebtedness or increase tax rates beyond those established by the Constitution.

The only difference between the Colorado Amendment and more common supramajority rules—from the perspective of rules affecting the political process—is that the Amendment disadvantaging gay rights could be overturned only by the more difficult process of constitutional amendment. Does this mean that inserting value judgments into the state constitution is constitutionally more vulnerable than other supramajority requirements? Perhaps that is what the Colorado court meant when it stated—"Amendment 2 singles out one form of discrimination and removes its redress from consideration by the *normal* political processes (emphasis added)."

We return to this case and the problems of justifying the result in a later section when we read the United States Supreme Court's affirmance. The United States Supreme Court applied the less stringent "rationality" test and still determined that the Colorado constitutional amendment violated the United States Constitution. For that reason, the Supreme Court's opinion is set out in a later section, dealing with rationality in the lawmaking process, with special attention to direct democracy (referendums and initiatives). See Chapter 17.03b. You may conclude at that time that the result in Romer v. Evans can only be justified by one or more of the following rationales, perhaps in combination with concerns about fencing out gay rights from the "normal political processes:" (1) laws disadvantaging those with a particular sexual preference impinge on a suspect classification or fundamental interest; (2) decisions made by direct democracy, such as the initiative in the Colorado case, are more closely scrutinized than other forms of lawmaking; (3) the Colorado provision imposes greater disadvantages on gay citizens than just interfering with access to "normal political processes."

Remember at this point why we are reading Romer v. Evans. We wanted to know whether there were groups, other than racial or ethnic minorities, who could successfully complain of the way electoral districts were drawn to disadvantage them. We can certainly conclude that a court with Colorado's perspective would be inclined to squint hard at any effort to draw electoral boundaries to disadvantage gay voters.

One problem lurking near the surface of cases protecting access to the electoral process is proportional representation. After the Court held in Mobile v. Bolden, supra, that the constitutional standard required an intent to discriminate, Congress passed the Voting Rights Amendments of 1982. This statute prohibits a state practice "which results in a denial or abridgement of the right of any citizen of the United States to vote on account of race or color." A violation is established if the protected class has "less opportunity than other members of the electorate to participate in the political process and to elect representatives of their choice." 42 U.S.C. § 1973. The statute tries to walk a tightrope between protecting group access to the political process and requiring proportional representation by adding that "nothing in this section establishes a right to have members of a protected class elected in numbers equal to their proportion in the population." 42 U.S.C. § 1973(b).

Although our focus is not on voting rights law dealing with racial and ethnic minorities, a Supreme Court case dealing with race-based gerrymandering may suggest how the Court would approach a case in which there was a claim of political exclusion *without* racial or ethnic overtones. In Shaw v. Reno, 509 U.S. 630 (1993), white voters objected to the creation of district boundaries with dramatically irregular shape, which created a district with Black representation. The issue was whether it was constitutional to pass "redistricting legislation that is so extremely irregular on its face that it rationally can be viewed only as an effort to segregate the races for purposes of voting." The Court noted that all race classifications are odious, even when remedial, because they stigmatize, stimulate racial hostility and race-consciousness, and suggest the utility of basing decisions on a factor that ideally bears no relationship to an individual's worth.

The Court then held that a plan which places people together who are widely separated by geographical and political boundaries and have little in common except race looks like political apartheid, reinforcing a view which stereotypes racial groups as thinking alike and sharing the same political interests. This undermined our system of representative democracy by signaling to elected officials that they represent a particular racial group rather than a constituency as a whole. Therefore, the racial district was unconstitutional even without a showing that the white voters' interest was diluted by the gerrymander.

This last point may have broad implications for when courts will protect political groups. It suggests that it will be more difficult to claim membership in a group deserving protection in a separate political unit, because ideally officials should represent the entire constituency. Given this ideal (that a minority of voters can have influence within a district), the Court may be more willing to find that in fact such influence exists to counter claims for separate representation.

ii) TWO PARTY GERRYMANDERING

There has been litigation over efforts by the two major parties to gain an advantage by gerrymandering the state. In Gaffney v. Cummings, 412 U.S. 735 (1973), state election district lines were drawn to replicate overall voting strength for the two major parties in the legislature. To do this, some districts attained a peculiar shape. The result was that some Democratic voters were placed in safe Republican districts, and vice-versa. The Court admitted that state legislative districts may be equal or substantially equal in population and still be vulnerable under the Fourteenth Amendment, if they fence out a racial or political group. But it upheld this gerrymander, stating:

> * * * Politics and political considerations are inseparable from districting and apportionment. The political profile of a State, its party registration, and voting records are available precinct by precinct, ward by ward. These subdivisions may not be identical with census tracts, but, when overlaid on a census map, it requires no special genius to recognize the political consequences of drawing a district line along one street rather than another. It is not only obvious, but absolutely unavoidable, that the location and shape of districts may well determine the political complexion of the area. District lines are rarely neutral phenomena. They can well determine what district will be predominantly Democratic or predominantly Republican, or make a close race likely. Redistricting may pit incumbents against one another or make very difficult the election of the most experienced legislator. The reality is that districting inevitably has and is intended to have substantial political consequences.

In Karcher v. Daggett, 462 U.S. 725 (1983), a state had constructed population districts for federal congressional elections that diverged from equal population per district (one-person one-vote) by less than 1% but the lines had been drawn by Democrats to disfavor Republicans. The majority latched on to the population disparity to strike down the plan because it did not represent a good faith effort to achieve a legitimate state objective. The Court stated that minor population deviations for federal congressional elections might be permitted to "achieve some legitimate state objective," but the state had not proven that the deviations served such purposes.

The Court returned to the problem of two-party state gerrymandering in Davis v. Bandemer, 478 U.S. 109 (1986), involving the gerrymandering of Indiana state legislature districts by Republicans to disadvantage Democrats. The majority opinion reports the facts and history of the case, as follows:

In early 1981, the General Assembly initiated the process of reapportioning the State's legislative districts pursuant to the 1980 census. At this time, there were Republican majorities in both the House and the Senate, and the Governor was Republican. Bills were introduced in both Houses, and a reapportionment plan was duly passed and approved by the Governor. This plan provided 50 single-member districts for the Senate; for the House, it provided 7 triple-member, 9 double-member, and 61 single-member districts. In the Senate plan, the population deviation between districts was 1.15%; in the House plan, the deviation was 1.05%. The multimember districts generally included the more metropolitan areas of the State, although not every metropolitan area was in a multimember district. Marion County, which includes Indianapolis, was combined with portions of its neighboring counties to form five triple-member districts. Fort Wayne was divided into two parts, and each part was combined with portions of the surrounding county or counties to make two triple-member districts. On the other hand, South Bend was divided and put partly into a double-member district and partly into a single-member district (each part combined with part of the surrounding county or counties). Although county and city lines were not consistently followed, township lines generally were. The two plans, the Senate and the House, were not nested; that is, each Senate district was not divided exactly into two House districts. There appears to have been little relation between the lines drawn in the two plans. * * *

In November 1982, before the case went to trial, elections were held under the new districting plan. All of the House seats and half of the Senate seats were up for election. Over all the House races statewide, Democratic candidates received 51.9% of the vote. Only 43 Democrats, however, were elected to the House. Over all the Senate races statewide, Democratic candidates received 53.1% of the vote. Thirteen (of 25) Democrats were elected. In Marion and Allen Counties, both divided into multimember House districts, Democratic candidates drew 46.6% of the vote, but only 3 of the 21 House seats were filled by Democrats.

On December 13, 1984, a divided District Court issued a decision declaring the reapportionment to be unconstitutional, enjoining the appellants from holding elections pursuant to the 1981 redistricting, ordering the General Assembly to prepare a new plan, and retaining jurisdiction over the case.

To the District Court majority, the results of the 1982 elections seemed "to support an argument that there is a built-in bias favoring the majority party, the Republicans, which instituted the reapportionment plan." Although the court thought that these figures were unreliable predictors of future elections, it concluded that they warranted further examination of the circumstances surrounding the passage of the reapportionment statute. In the course of this further examination, the court noted the irregular shape of some district lines, the peculiar mix of single-member and multimember districts, and the failure of the district lines to adhere consistently to political subdivision boundaries to define communities of interest. * * * These factors, concluded the court, evidenced an intentional effort to favor Republican incumbents and candidates and to disadvantage Democratic voters. This was achieved by "stacking" Democrats into districts with large Democratic majorities and "splitting" them in other districts so as to give Republicans safe but not excessive majorities in those districts. Because the 1982 elections indicated that the plan also had a discriminatory effect in that the proportionate voting influence of Democratic voters had been adversely affected and because any scheme "which purposely inhibit[s] or prevent[s] proportional representation cannot be tolerated," the District Court invalidated the statute. * * *

Six of the Justices concluded that the issue was *not* a political question and was therefore justiciable. Three Justices (O'Connor, Rehnquist, and Burger) argued that the issue was not justiciable. They distinguished earlier "one-person one-vote" cases on the ground that they preserved the *individual's* right to vote, *not* the rights of a *group*, as was asserted in the Indiana case. They also distinguished race discrimination cases as involving a suspect classification.

The six Justices who reached the merits did not, however, agree on how to decide the case. Four of them refused to strike down the Indiana gerrymander. With the three Justices who considered the issue nonjusticiable, this produced a majority to dismiss the complaint. Two Justices (Powell and Stevens) found the Indiana gerrymander unconstitutional.

The four-judge plurality upholding the gerrymander stated as follows:

[We] also agree with the District Court that in order to succeed the Bandemer plaintiffs were required to prove both intentional discrimination against an identifiable political group and an actual discriminatory effect on that group. See, e.g., Mobile v. Bolden, 446 U.S., at 67–68. Further, we are confident that if the law challenged here had discriminatory effects on Democrats, this record would support a finding that the discrimination was intentional. Thus, we decline to overturn the District Court's finding of discriminatory intent as clearly erroneous. * * *

We do not accept, however, the District Court's legal and factual bases for concluding that the 1981 Act visited a sufficiently adverse effect on the appellees' constitutionally protected rights to make out a violation of the Equal Protection Clause. The District Court held that because any apportionment scheme that purposely prevents proportional representation is unconstitutional, Democratic voters need only show that their proportionate voting influence has been adversely affected. Our cases, however, clearly foreclose any claim that the Constitution requires proportional representation or that legislatures in reapportioning must draw district lines to come as near as possible to allocating seats to the contending parties in proportion to what their anticipated statewide vote will be. * * *

To draw district lines to maximize the representation of each major party would require creating as many safe seats for each party as the demographic and predicted political characteristics of the State would permit. This in turn would leave the minority in each safe district without a representative of its choice. We upheld this "political fairness" approach in Gaffney v. Cummings, despite its tendency to deny safe district minorities any realistic chance to elect their own representatives. But Gaffney in no way suggested that the Constitution requires the approach that Connecticut had adopted in that case. * * *

* * * [T]he mere fact that a particular apportionment scheme makes it more difficult for a particular group in a particular district to elect the representatives of its choice does not render that scheme constitutionally infirm. This conviction, in turn, stems from a perception that the power to influence the political process is not limited to winning elections. An individual or a group of individuals who votes for a losing candidate is usually deemed to be adequately represented by the winning candidate and to have as much opportunity to influence that candidate as other voters in the district. We cannot presume in such a situation, without actual proof to the contrary, that the candidate elected will entirely ignore the interests of those voters. This is true even in a safe district where the losing group loses election after election. Thus, a group's electoral power is not unconstitutionally diminished by the simple fact of an apportionment scheme that makes winning elections more difficult, and a failure of proportional representation alone does not constitute impermissible discrimination under the Equal Protection Clause. * * *

* * * [U]nconstitutional discrimination occurs only when the electoral system is arranged in a manner that will consistently degrade a voter's or a group of voters' influence on the political process as a whole.

Although this is a somewhat different formulation than we have previously used in describing unconstitutional vote dilution in an individual district, the focus of both of these inquiries is essentially the same. In both contexts, the question is whether a particular group has been unconstitutionally denied its chance to effectively influence the political process. In a challenge to an individual district, this inquiry focuses on the opportunity of members of the group to participate in party deliberations in the slating and nomination of candidates, their opportunity to register and vote, and hence their chance to directly influence the election returns and to secure the attention of the winning candidate. Statewide, however, the inquiry centers on the voters' direct or indirect influence on the elections of the state legislature as a whole. And, as in individual district cases, an equal protection violation may be found only where the electoral system substantially disadvantages certain voters in their opportunity to influence the political process effectively. In this context, such a finding of unconstitutionality must be supported by evidence of continued frustration of the will of a majority of the voters or effective denial to a minority of voters of a fair chance to influence the political process.

Based on these views, we would reject the District Court's apparent holding that any interference with an opportunity to elect a representative of one's choice would be sufficient to allege or make out an equal protection violation, unless justified by some acceptable state interest that the State would be required to demonstrate. In addition to being contrary to the above-described conception of an unconstitutional political gerrymander, such a low threshold for legal action would invite attack on all or almost all reapportionment statutes. District-based elections hardly ever produce a perfect fit between votes and representation. * * * Inviting attack on minor departures from some supposed norm would too much embroil the judiciary in second-guessing what has consistently been referred to as a political task for the legislature * * *. We decline to take a major step toward that end, which would be so much at odds with our history and experience. * * *

Relying on a single election to prove unconstitutional discrimination is unsatisfactory. The District Court observed, and the parties do not disagree, that Indiana is a swing State. Voters sometimes prefer Democratic candidates, and sometimes Republican. The District Court did not find that because of the 1981 Act the Democrats could not in one of the next few elections secure a sufficient vote to take control of the assembly. Indeed, the District Court declined to hold that the 1982 election results were the predictable consequences of the 1981 Act and expressly refused to hold that those results were a reliable prediction of future ones. The District Court did not ask by what percentage the statewide Democratic vote would have had to increase to control either the House or the Senate. The appellants argue here, without a persuasive response from appellees, that had the Democratic candidates received an additional few percentage points of the votes cast statewide, they would have obtained a majority of the seats in both houses. Nor was there any finding that the 1981 reapportionment would consign the Democrats to a minority status in the Assembly throughout the 1980's or that the Democrats would have no hope of doing any better in the reapportionment that would occur after the 1990 census. Without findings of this nature, the District Court erred in concluding that the 1981 Act violated the Equal Protection Clause.
* * *

Justice Powell's dissenting opinion relied on objective factors, such as the weird shape of voting districts and lack of adherence to established political subdivision boundaries. Another criterion was the legislative procedure used by the majority party. In this case the "legislative process consisted of nothing more than the majority party's private application of computer technology to mapmaking." No member of the Democratic party or the public was provided with any information used in or generated by the computer program.

QUESTION

How can a voter show that gerrymandering of electoral districts to favor one party "consistently degrade[s] a voter's or a group of voters' influence on the political process as a whole?" After all, parties and political groups are not identical categories. Many groups influence both parties, which is what the Court probably means when it says that an "individual or a group of individuals who votes for a losing candidate is usually deemed to be adequately represented by the winning candidate and to have as much opportunity to influence that candidate as other voters in the district."

iii) SUPRAMAJORITIES

Gordon v. Lance

403 U.S. 1 (1971).

■ Mr. Chief Justice Burger delivered the opinion of the Court.

We granted certiorari to review a challenge to a 60% vote requirement to incur public debt as violative of the Fourteenth Amendment.

The Constitution of West Virginia and certain West Virginia statutes provide that political subdivisions of the State may not incur bonded indebtedness or increase tax rates beyond those established by the Constitution without the approval of 60% of the voters in a referendum election.

On April 29, 1968, the Board of Education of Roane County, West Virginia, submitted to the voters of Roane County a proposal calling for the issuance of general obligation bonds in the amount of $1,830,000 for the purpose of constructing new school buildings and improving existing educational facilities. At the same election, by separate ballot, the voters were asked to authorize the Board of Education to levy additional taxes to support current expenditures and capital improvements. Of the total votes cast, 51.55% favored the bond issues and 51.51% favored the tax levy. Having failed to obtain the requisite 60% affirmative vote, the proposals were declared defeated.

Following the election, respondents appeared before the Board of Education on behalf of themselves and other persons who had voted in favor of the proposals and demanded that the Board authorize the bonds and the additional taxes. The Board refused.

Respondents then brought this action, seeking a declaratory judgment that the 60% requirements were unconstitutional as violative of the Fourteenth Amendment. * * *

Unlike the restrictions in our previous cases, the West Virginia Constitution singles out no "discrete and insular minority" for special treatment. The three-fifths requirement applies equally to all bond issues for any purpose, whether for schools, sewers, or highways. * * *

Although West Virginia has not denied any group access to the ballot, it has indeed made it more difficult for some kinds of governmental actions to be taken. Certainly any departure from strict majority rule gives disproportionate power to the minority. But there is nothing in the language of the Constitution, our history, or our cases that requires that a majority always prevail on every issue. On the contrary, while we have recognized that state officials are normally chosen by a vote of the majority of the electorate, we have found no constitutional barrier to the selection of a Governor by a state legislature, after no candidate received a majority of the popular vote.

The Federal Constitution itself provides that a simple majority vote is insufficient on some issues; the provisions on impeachment and ratification of treaties are but two examples. Moreover, the Bill of Rights removes entire areas of legislation from the concept of majoritarian supremacy. The constitutions of many States prohibit or severely limit the power of the legislature to levy new taxes or to create or increase bonded indebtedness, thereby insulating entire areas from majority control. Whether these matters of finance and taxation are to be considered as less "important" than matters of treaties, foreign policy, or impeachment of public officers is more properly left to the determination by the States and the people than to the courts operating under the broad mandate of the Fourteenth Amendment. It must be remembered that in voting to issue bonds voters are committing, in part, the credit of infants and of generations yet unborn, and some restriction on such commitment is not an unreasonable demand. That the bond issue may have the desirable objective of providing better education for future generations goes to the wisdom of an indebtedness limitation: it does not alter the basic fact that the balancing of interests is one for the State to resolve.

Wisely or not, the people of the State of West Virginia have long since resolved to remove from a simple majority vote the choice on certain decisions as to what indebtedness may be incurred and what taxes their children will bear.

We conclude that so long as such provisions do not discriminate against or authorize discrimination against any identifiable class they do not violate the Equal Protection Clause. We see no meaningful distinction between such absolute provisions on debt, changeable only by constitutional amendment, and provisions that legislative decisions on the same issues require more than a majority vote in the legislature. On the contrary, these latter provisions may, in practice, be less burdensome than the amendment process. Moreover, the same considerations apply when the ultimate power, rather than being delegated to the legislature, remains with the people, by way of a referendum. Indeed, we see no constitutional distinction between the 60% requirement in the present case and a state requirement that a given issue be approved by a majority of all registered voters.

That West Virginia has adopted a rule of decision, applicable to all bond referenda, by which the strong consensus of three-fifths is required before indebtedness is authorized, does not violate the Equal Protection Clause or any other provision of the Constitution.

[Editor—The Court left itself an escape hatch, however, in a footnote: "We intimate no view on the constitutionality of a provision requiring unanimity or giving a veto power to a very small group. Nor do we decide whether a State may, consistently with the Constitution, require extraordinary majorities for the election of public officers."]

Recall Justice Harlan's comments in Harper, involving the poll tax, where he objected to constitutionalizing egalitarianism. In Whitcomb v. Chavis, 403 U.S. 124 (1971), he wrote a separate opinion noting that Gordon v. Lance gives opponents of school bond issues half again the voting power of proponents. More broadly, he noted that the Court permitted departures from one-person one-vote in state elections, to permit representation from preexisting political subdivisions. He hoped that the Court would "frankly recognize the error of its ways in ever having undertaken to restructure state electoral processes."

Do you agree with Justice Harlan that the courts should get out of the business of monitoring manipulation of electoral districts? Should the Court take the smaller step suggested by Justice O'Connor of limiting concern (1) to individual rights (enforced under the one-person one-vote standard) and (2) to prohibition of discrimination against a suspect classification?

The problem with O'Connor's suggestion is that individual rights may not have had much to do with the rationale for the original one-person one-vote standard in the first place. Wasn't the real point of the one-person one-vote decision that certain groups—residents of rural areas—should not be entitled to the advantage they enjoyed from failure to redraw electoral districts for decades? Moreover, didn't the Court abandon the argument that the one-person one-vote rule protects individual rights when it allowed departure from that standard under certain circumstances?

In sum, hasn't the Court adopted a group-focused analysis of voting rights: (1) allowing some groups to protect their political clout (e.g., the party which dominates the legislature at the time of redistricting; existing political units, such as cities; regions of the state); and (2) insisting that some groups be let in (racial, ethnic, and "some" undefined category of political groups)? Can the Court develop a constitutionally enforceable theory of group political representation?

Does concern with the one-person one-vote rule look trivial in light of census undercounts of certain groups? If so, does that suggest that the Court should stop adjudicating one-person one-vote claims? In Wisconsin v. City of New York, 116 S.Ct. 1091 (1996), the Court held that the Secretary of Commerce had wide discretion not to make certain statistical adjustments to deal with the problem of undercounting minority groups.

16.04   CONTROLLING THE INFLUENCE OF MONEY ON POLITICS

There is general unease about the impact of money on politics.[4] (The reference to "money" includes anything of value to the recipient—a job, sexual favors, etc.).

The most obvious problem is when money distorts the political process by purchasing a vote. Our ideal of politics is deliberation about the public good. Although we know that ideal is often not achieved, we object when a political actor takes himself or herself out of the deliberative process from the outset. Statutes making bribery a crime embody that policy. They prohibit a quid pro quo for a political commitment.

We also have rules which try to minimize the chances that money will influence the political actor, even if we are unable to prove anything as direct as bribery. In this category are rules concerned with outside income—such as gifts, travel, entertainment, honorariums, employment with those dealing with the government (and other potential conflicts of interest), and disclosure of financial information.

Finally, there are rules which limit or prohibit campaign contributions and independent political expenditures under certain circumstances. These rules are, in part, designed to back up the rules about bribery and outside income, but they have other purposes as well. Consider whether these rules are aimed at any of the following concerns:

1.   Appearance of corruption;

---

4. See generally Lowenstein, Political Bribery and the Intermediate Theory of Politics, 32 U.C.L.A. L. Rev. 784 (1985); Clarisa Long, Shouting Down the Voice of the Peo- ple: Political Parties, Powerful PACs, and Concerns About Corruption, 46 Stan. L. Rev. 1161 (1994).

2. Special access to legislators;

3. Undue influence on the public through the media;

4. Fund raising takes too much time away from political work.

We look briefly at the rules about bribery and outside income and then focus our primary attention on limits imposed on campaign contributions and independent political expenditures.

a) BRIBERY, ETC.

Payments to legislators. A number of laws criminalize behavior involving the receipt of money (or something else of value) by a legislator in exchange, acknowledgment, or contemplation of a political act.[5] Among federal statutes, three are particularly important—dealing with bribery, extortion, and the receipt of an improper gratuity. Here is the statutory language, which is not a model of clarity.

Bribery occurs when a public official "directly or indirectly, corruptly demands, seeks, receives, accepts, or agrees to receive or accept anything of value personally or for any other person or entity, in return for * * * (A) being influenced in performance of any official act." 18 U.S.C. § 201(b)(2). Bribery violations include providing value to influence a legislator's future behavior.

Extortion "means the obtaining of property from another with his consent, induced by the wrongful use of actual or threatened force, violence, or fear, or under color of official right." 18 U.S.C. § 1951. McCormick v. United States, 500 U.S. 257 (1991), held that extortion of a campaign contribution required a quid pro quo, in the form of an explicit promise or undertaking to perform or not to perform an official act. The case reminds us that the money does not have to be for the politician's private benefit (it can be for a political campaign), although it usually is for private benefit.[6] Evans v. United States, 504 U.S. 255 (1992), held that "under color of official right" did not require a demand or request from the public official; and that it was sufficient that the public official obtained payment knowing that it was made in return for official action, without proof that the action actually occurred.

A *gratuity* violation occurs when the public official accepts something "for or because of any official act performed or to be performed." 18 U.S.C. § 201(c)(1)(B). A gratuity violation can include receiving value for past acts, where the *quid pro quo* for the gratuity is not explicit. United States v. Bustamante, 45 F.3d 933, 940 (5th Cir.1995)(*quid pro quo* not required to prove illegal gratuity).

---

5. In addition, bribery contracts violate public policy and are unenforceable. Providence Tool Co. v. Norris, 69 U.S. (2 Wall.) 45 (1864).

6. See also United States v. Anderson, 509 F.2d 312 (D.C.Cir.1974), in which a regis-tered lobbyist was convicted for bribing a Senator with campaign contributions in exchange for his taking a position on postal rate legislation.

Violations of these statutes are hard to prove and there are not many prosecutions. United States v. Head, 641 F.2d 174 (4th Cir.1981), held that an "appearance fee" paid to a Member of Congress to attend a meeting was not per se a bribe, even if all the Member did was attend. Such payments are made to get the candidate elected, to obtain general good will, or, at most, to gain access to the legislator, rather than to obtain an improper quid pro quo. In United States v. Biaggi, 909 F.2d 662 (2d Cir.1990), the court found that the promise of a future job to a retiring politician was an illegal bribe. However, the court acknowledged that public officials regularly leave public service to return to private employment and occasionally formalize these arrangements while in office, without the offer of a job constituting a bribe. And in McCormick, supra, the Court held (on the facts) that receipt of a campaign contribution was not extortion.

Validity of legislation. Is legislation passed with the help of a corrupted legislator invalid? In Fletcher v. Peck, 10 U.S. (6 Cranch) 87 (1810), the Court dealt with a statute which had granted land to some people who had bribed the legislators to pass the legislation. The Court held that the bribe was not grounds for invalidating the statute. The corrupt legislative process was not a sufficient basis for deciding that the law which passed was not a "law." However, the Fletcher decision actually protected a bona fide purchaser from someone who had originally obtained the land through bribery. The Court's specific holding was that the land grant was a contract which could not be impaired by the State as against the interests of a bona fide purchaser. Suppose the State tried to take back the land from the corrupt original acquirers?[7]

Payments to voters. Money or something else of value might also flow from the candidate to the voter, rather than to a candidate. Buying votes is obviously as illegal as bribing a legislator. However, some kinds of value promised by a candidate will not support a charge of "buying votes."

In Brown v. Hartlage, 456 U.S. 45 (1982), the State of Kentucky declared an election void because the victorious candidate had announced to the voters during his campaign that he would serve at a salary less than that "fixed by law." The State argued that reducing tax burdens by waiving part of the official salary was an attempt to buy votes or to bribe the voters. Candidate Brown argued that this interpretation violated the First Amendment free speech guarantee. The Supreme Court upheld the candidate's position, noting (1) that the money did not come from the candidate's personal wealth (it was just a voluntary reduction in government salary); (2) that it was not a payment for a particular vote but only benefited people if the majority elected the candidate; and (3) that the benefit accrued to all taxpayers, not just those who voted for the candidate.

---

7. At the state level, there are cases in which state courts overturn local government legislation if a legislator violates a state conflict of interest statute and casts the deciding vote. In Wilson v. Iowa City, 165 N.W.2d 813 (Iowa 1969), the court went further and voided a resolution passed by the city council even when the offending council member did not cast the deciding vote. Local city councilmen knew that property in which they had an interest was included in an urban renewal project on which they voted.

Suppose state voters have been asked to vote on the legality of gambling. Businesses which stand to gain from an affirmative vote promise every voter (based on public records) a percentage of the gambling revenue. The payment is not limited to those who voted *for* legalized gambling but is not provided to every state resident or taxpayer. Is this a distortion of the political process which might violate a state law against bribing voters? See USA TODAY, November 2, 1995, Thursday, Final Edition, p. 9A (initiative to allow slot machines for tribal casinos in Washington State required that voters get a 10% cut of machine gambling revenues; the initiative failed). How, if at all, does this differ from candidate Brown taking a salary reduction, if elected?

b) Outside Income

If you are worried about the impact of money on legislative politics but are concerned that bribery, etc. is hard to prove, you might adopt rules which limit or prohibit various forms of outside income and, also, require disclosure of such income to the public in the hope that publicity (picked up by the media) would have a chastening effect. These rules vary among jurisdictions and are often changed. The subsequent paragraphs provide a checklist of the important issues.[8]

(1) The following outside income must be considered:

Gifts, travel and entertainment (distinguishing between benefits related to official duties and those which are not so related);

Outside earnings (including honorariums and book royalties);

Post-legislative jobs (especially lobbying).

(2) The rules must be written with the legislator's relatives in mind.

(3) Effective sanctions must be adopted. Most of these rules are internal legislative rules, whose violation can subject the legislator to reprimand, censure, or expulsion from the legislature. Even if the rules appear in legislation, they are usually an exercise of the legislature's internal rulemaking power and can be superseded by the House or Senate acting alone to govern their own behavior.[9] Occasionally, the rules appear in statutes imposing civil or criminal sanctions as well.

(4) Income disclosure rules must provide information which allows enforcement of the substantive rules, but will often cover broader categories of income (such as investment income) which are not explicitly limited or prohibited.

---

8. For a survey of state rules, see The Council of Governments, COGEL Blue Book: Campaign Finance, Ethics & Lobby Law, pp. 144–45, tbl. 26 (Joyce Bullock ed., 8th ed. 1990).

9. See, e.g., Ethics Reform Act of 1989, Pub. L. 101–194, 103 Stat. 1716 (1989). The Act in some respects followed recommendations of the Report of the President's Commission on Federal Ethics Law Reform (1989).

Gifts, etc. The House and the Senate recently banned gifts (including travel and entertainment), except under certain circumstances, which vary slightly between the two chambers. Here are some excerpts from the House Rule, LII, adopted November 16, 1995. Nothing is simple.

SECTION 1. AMENDMENT TO HOUSE RULES.

Rule LII of the Rules of the House of Representatives is amended to read as follows:

1. (a) No Member, officer, or employee of the House of Representatives shall knowingly accept a gift except as provided in this rule.

(b)(1) For the purpose of this rule, the term "gift" means any gratuity, favor, discount, entertainment, hospitality, loan, forbearance, or other item having monetary value. The term includes gifts of services, training, transportation, lodging, and meals, whether provided in kind, by purchase of a ticket, payment in advance, or reimbursement after the expense has been incurred.

(2)(A) A gift to a family member of a Member, officer, or employee, or a gift to any other individual based on that individual's relationship with the Member, officer, or employee, shall be considered a gift to the Member, officer, or employee if it is given with the knowledge and acquiescence of the Member, officer, or employee and the Member, officer, or employee has reason to believe the gift was given because of the official position of the Member, officer, or employee.

(B) If food or refreshment is provided at the same time and place to both a Member, officer, or employee and the spouse or dependent thereof, only the food or refreshment provided to the Member, officer, or employee shall be treated as a gift for purposes of this rule.

(c) The restrictions in paragraph (a) shall not apply to the following:

(1) Anything for which the Member, officer, or employee pays the market value, or does not use and promptly returns to the donor.

(2) A [lawful campaign] contribution * * *.

(3) A gift from a relative * * *.

(4)(A) Anything provided by an individual on the basis of a personal friendship unless the Member, officer, or employee has reason to believe that, under the circumstances, the gift was provided because of the official position of the Member, officer, or employee and not because of the personal friendship.

(B) [describing considerations affirming or negating whether gift provided on the basis of personal friendship].

(5) Except as provided in clause 3(c) [dealing with payments by a registered lobbyist and by an agent of a foreign principal], a contribution or other payment to a legal expense fund established for the benefit of a Member, officer, or employee that is otherwise lawfully made in accordance with the restrictions and disclosure requirements of the Committee on Standards of Official Conduct.

(6) [omitted]

(7) Food, refreshments, lodging, transportation, and other benefits—

(A) resulting from the outside business or employment activities (or other outside activities that are not connected to the duties of the Member, officer, or employee as an officeholder) of the Member, officer, or employee, or the spouse of the Member, officer, or employee, if such benefits have not been offered or enhanced because of the official position of the Member, officer, or employee and are customarily provided to others in similar circumstances;

(B) customarily provided by a prospective employer in connection with bona fide employment discussions; or

(C) [omitted]

(8–16) [omitted]

(17) Free attendance at a widely attended event permitted pursuant to paragraph (d).

(18) Opportunities and benefits which are [generally available to the public on the basis of a list of categories not targeted on members of Congress].

(19) [omitted]

(20) Anything for which, in an unusual case, a waiver is granted by the Committee on Standards of Official Conduct.

(21) Food or refreshments of a nominal value offered other than as a part of a meal.

(d)(1) A Member, officer, or employee may accept an offer of free attendance at a widely attended convention, conference, symposium, forum, panel discussion, dinner, viewing, reception, or similar event, provided by the sponsor of the event, if—
(A) the Member, officer, or employee participates in the event as a speaker or a panel participant, by presenting information related to Congress or matters before Congress, or by performing a ceremonial function appropriate to the Member's, officer's, or employee's official position; or

(B) attendance at the event is appropriate to the performance of the official duties or representative function of the Member, officer, or employee.

(2) A Member, officer, or employee who attends an event described in subparagraph (1) may accept a sponsor's unsolicited offer of free attendance at the event for an accompanying individual.

(3) A Member, officer, or employee, or the spouse or dependent thereof, may accept a sponsor's unsolicited offer of free attendance at a charity event, except that reimbursement for transportation and lodging may not be accepted in connection with the event.

(4) For purposes of this paragraph, the term "free attendance" may include waiver of all or part of a conference or other fee, the provision of local transportation, or the provision of food, refreshments, entertainment, and instructional materials furnished to all attendees as an integral part of the event. The term does not include entertainment collateral to the event, nor does it include food or refreshments taken other than in a group setting with all or substantially all other attendees.

(e) No Member, officer, or employee may accept a gift the value of which exceeds $250 on the basis of the personal friendship exception in paragraph (c)(4) unless the Committee on Standards of Official Conduct issues a written determination that such exception applies. No determination under this paragraph is required for gifts given on the basis of the family relationship exception.

(f) [omitted]

2.   (a)(1) A reimbursement (including payment in kind) to a Member, officer, or employee from a private source other than a registered lobbyist or agent of a foreign principal for necessary transportation, lodging and related expenses for travel to a meeting, speaking engagement, factfinding trip or similar event in connection with the duties of the Member, officer, or employee as an officeholder shall be deemed to be a reimbursement to the House of Representatives and not a gift prohibited by this rule, if [various disclosure requirements are satisfied].

(d) For the purposes of this clause, the term "necessary transportation, lodging, and related expenses"—(1) includes reasonable expenses that are necessary for travel for a period not exceeding 4 days within the United States or 7 days exclusive of travel time outside of the United States unless approved in advance by the Committee on Standards of Official Conduct;

(2) is limited to reasonable expenditures for transportation, lodging, conference fees and materials, and food and refreshments, including reimbursement for necessary transportation, whether or not such transportation occurs within the periods described in subparagraph (1);

(3) does not include expenditures for recreational activities, nor does it include entertainment other than that provided to all attendees as an integral part of the event, except for activities or entertainment otherwise permissible under this rule; and

(4) may include travel expenses incurred on behalf of either the spouse or a child of the Member, officer, or employee.

(e) The Clerk of the House of Representatives shall make available to the public all [ ] disclosures of reimbursement filed pursuant to paragraph(a) as soon as possible after they are received.

Outside earnings. Outside earnings are also the subject of specific rules. House and Senate members are not allowed to receive honoraria, defined to include payments for an appearance, speech, or article. In lieu of an honorarium, up to $2,000 can be paid to a charitable organization, on condition that the organization does not benefit the member or his family. The ban on honoraria was originally imposed only on House members when their pay was raised above that of Senators. The Senate later voted salary raises to match the House and banned honoraria for Senators. 5 U.S.C. App. (Ethics in Government Act), §§ 501(b-c), 505(*l*).

The outside earned income of House and Senate members is capped at 15% of their salary (in 1995, 15% times $133,600 = $20,040). 5 U.S.C. App. (Ethics in Government Act), § 501(a). "Outside earned income" is expressly defined for House members to exclude copyright royalties *only if* they are paid by an established trade publisher in line with customary contract terms. House of Representatives Rule XLVII, § 3(e)(5). The idea is to subject to the 15% ceiling any sweetheart deals for book royalties not paid as part of normal publishing practice. This rule is intended to discourage a·practice which had been exploited by a former Speaker of the House.

House and Senate members are in general prohibited from receiving compensation for the following: practicing a profession which involves a fiduciary relationship; affiliating with a firm which practices such a profession; serving on the board of an entity for compensation; receiving compensation for teaching unless approved by the relevant Ethics Committee. House of Representatives Rule XLVII, § 2; Senate Rule XXXVII, §§ 5, 6.

Post-legislative work. Members are subject to civil and criminal penalties if they lobby Congress during the one year period after leaving office. 18 U.S.C. § 207(e).

Disclosure. In addition, there are requirements for annual reporting and for public disclosure of income and assets in various categories, including investment income, and subject to exceptions for de minimis amounts and for transactions with relatives. 5 U.S.C. App. (Ethics in Government Act), § 102(a). In addition, 5 U.S.C. App. (Ethics in Government Act), § 102(e), requires disclosure of certain income of spouses and dependent children, including—spousal earnings and honoraria; gifts and reimbursements to a spouse or dependent child, unless received totally independent of the relationship to the member of Congress; and the investment and business property of a spouse or dependent child, unless they are the sole responsibility of the spouse or dependent child, do not derive from the member's wealth or activities, and from which the member does not benefit. Blind trusts are exempted from these disclosure rules. 5 U.S.C. App. (Ethics in Government Act), § 102(f).

c) CONTRIBUTION AND EXPENDITURE LIMITS

A special source of concern about the impact of money on politics has been campaign contributions and independent political expenditures by supporters of candidates and by the candidates themselves. As noted earlier, these concerns extend beyond buying votes and include the following:

1. Appearance of corruption;

2. Special access to legislators;

3. Undue influence on the public through the media;

4. Fund raising takes too much time away from political work.

Which of these concerns explain the legislation discussed in the following cases and which of them are legitimate or compelling state interests, capable of overriding any free speech concerns protecting the use of money in politics?

Also consider whether these concerns about money in politics apply (a) to contributions; (b) to total political spending (whether from contributions, by independent supporters of a candidate, or out of a rich candidate's own funds); and/or (c) to referendums and initiatives dealing with issues rather than election of candidates?

You should also be alert to three additional questions:

1. Is money in politics sometimes good; would money combat the advantages of incumbency; would small contributions from many contributors be desirable?

2. Is the problem of money in politics so difficult to address, especially by self-interested legislators, that we might as well abandon attempts to impose limits?

3. Is public financing the only effective remedy and is it a good idea?

i) BUCKLEY v. VALEO

Buckley v. Valeo, 424 U.S. 1 (1976), dealt with a federal statute limiting contributions and expenditures in federal elections. In the following excerpt, the Court distinguished between contributions to election campaigns and independent political expenditures to achieve political goals. Do you find the distinction persuasive?

Per curiam. * * *

The Act's contribution and expenditure limitations operate in an area of the most fundamental First Amendment activities. Discussion of public issues and debate on the qualifications of candidates are integral to the operation of the system of government established by our Constitution. The First Amendment affords the broadest protection to such political expression in order "to assure [the] unfettered interchange of ideas for the bringing about of political and social changes desired by the people." * * * This is no more than reflects our "profound national commitment to the principle that debate on public issues should be uninhibited, robust, and wide-open." In a republic where the people are sovereign, the ability of the citizenry to make informed choices among candidates for office is essential, for the identities of those who are elected will inevitably shape the course that we follow as a nation. As the Court observed in Monitor Patriot Co. v. Roy, 401 U.S. 265, 272 (1971), "it can hardly be doubted that the constitutional guarantee has its fullest and most urgent application precisely to the conduct of campaigns for political office."

The First Amendment protects political association as well as political expression. The constitutional right of association explicated in NAACP v. Alabama, 357 U.S. 449, 460 (1958), stemmed from the Court's recognition that "[e]ffective advocacy of both public and private points of view, particularly controversial ones, is undeniably enhanced by group association." Subsequent decisions have made clear that the First and Fourteenth Amendments guarantee " 'freedom to associate with others for the common advancement of political beliefs and ideas,' " a freedom that encompasses " '[t]he right to associate with the political party of one's choice.' "

It is with these principles in mind that we consider the primary contentions of the parties with respect to the Act's limitations upon the giving and spending of money in political campaigns. * * *

A restriction on the amount of money a person or group can spend on political communication during a campaign necessarily reduces the quantity of expression by restricting the number of issues discussed, the depth of their exploration, and the size of the audience reached. This is because virtually every means of communicating ideas in today's mass society requires the expenditure of money. The distribution of the humblest handbill or leaflet entails printing, paper, and circulation costs. Speeches and rallies generally necessitate hiring a hall and publicizing the event. The electorate's increasing dependence on television, radio, and other mass media for news and information has made these expensive modes of communication indispensable instruments of effective political speech.

The expenditure limitations contained in the Act represent substantial rather than merely theoretical restraints on the quantity and diversity of political speech. The $1,000 ceiling on spending "relative to a clearly identified candidate," 18 U.S.C. § 608 (e)(1)(1970 ed., Supp. IV), would appear to exclude all citizens and groups except candidates, political parties, and the institutional press from any significant use of the most effective modes of communication. Although the Act's limitations on expenditures by campaign organizations and political parties provide substantially greater room for discussion and debate, they would have required restrictions in the scope of a number of past congressional and Presidential campaigns and would operate to constrain campaigning by candidates who raise sums in excess of the spending ceiling.

By contrast with a limitation upon expenditures for political expression, a limitation upon the amount that any one person or group may contribute to a candidate or political committee entails only a marginal restriction upon the contributor's ability to engage in free communication. A contribution serves as a general expression of support for the candidate and his views, but does not communicate the underlying basis for the support. The quantity of communication by the contributor does not increase perceptibly with the size of his contribution, since the expression rests solely on the undifferentiated, symbolic act of contributing. At most, the size of the contribution provides a very rough index of the intensity of the contributor's support for the candidate. A limitation on the amount of money a person may give to a candidate or campaign organization thus involves little direct restraint on his political communication, for it permits the symbolic expression of support evidenced by a contribution but does not in any way infringe the contributor's freedom to discuss candidates and issues. While contributions may result in political expression if spent by a candidate or an association to present views to the voters, the transformation of contribution into political debate involves speech by someone other than the contributor.

Given the important role of contributions in financing political campaigns, contribution restrictions could have a severe impact on political dialogue if the limitations prevented candidates and political committees from amassing the resources necessary for effective advocacy. There is no indication, however, that the contribution limitations imposed by the Act would have any dramatic adverse effect on the funding of campaigns and political associations. The overall effect of the Act's contribution ceilings is merely to require candidates and political committees to raise funds from a greater number of persons and to compel people who would otherwise contribute amounts greater than the statutory limits to expend such funds on direct political expression, rather than to reduce the total amount of money potentially available to promote political expression.

The Act's contribution and expenditure limitations also impinge on protected associational freedoms. Making a contribution, like joining a political party, serves to affiliate a person with a candidate. In addition, it enables like-minded persons to pool their resources in furtherance of common political goals. The Act's contribution ceilings thus limit one important means of associating with a candidate or committee, but leave the contributor free to become a member of any political association and to assist personally in the association's efforts on behalf of candidates. And the Act's contribution limitations permit associations and candidates to aggregate large sums of money to promote effective advocacy. By contrast, the Act's $1,000 limitation on independent expenditures "relative to a clearly identified candidate" precludes most associations from effectively amplifying the voice of their adherents, the original basis for the recognition of First Amendment protection of the freedom of association. See NAACP v. Alabama, 357 U.S., at 460. The Act's constraints on the ability of independent associations and candidate campaign organizations to expend resources on political expression "is simultaneously an interference with the freedom of [their] adherents," Sweezy v. New Hampshire, 354 U.S. 234, 250 (1957)(plurality opinion).

In sum, although the Act's contribution and expenditure limitations both implicate fundamental First Amendment interests, its expenditure ceilings impose significantly more severe restrictions on protected freedoms of political expression and association than do its limitations on financial contributions.

The Court went on to hold that (1) the dollar ceilings on contributions to particular candidates by all contributors (such as the $1,000 limit on individual contributions to candidates), and (2) an overall $25,000 dollar ceiling on contributions to all candidates by individuals, were constitutional because the prohibitions dealt with the "appearance and reality of corruption." The expenditure limits to support a candidate (in contrast to contributions to the candidate) were struck down. The Court did not deal directly with longstanding legislation prohibiting both contributions *and* expenditures by corporations and unions to influence federal elections. This issue comes up in later litigation discussed below.

———

Some states continue to be dissatisfied with the impact of both independent political expenditures and campaign contributions on elections and have tried some imaginative ways to overcome the decision in Buckley v. Valeo. Some states, like Minnesota, adopt a program of public subsidies to candidates in exchange for sticking to spending limits. This is similar to the federal scheme for Presidential elections and is not objectionable. Minnesota has gone further, however. The following case dealt with a state law, which tried to discourage independent political expenditures and to drastically lower certain campaign contribution limits. The court struck down both aspects of the state law.

Day v. Holahan

34 F.3d 1356 (8th Cir.1994).

■ Bowman, Circuit Judge. * * *

Among the 1993 changes and additions to the Minnesota campaign finance and ethics laws was this provision directed to independent expenditures:

> Independent expenditures; limits increased. (a) The expenditure limits [on what a candidate can spend] are increased by the sum of independent expenditures made in opposition to a candidate plus independent expenditures made on behalf of the candidate's major political party opponents, other than expenditures by an association targeted to inform solely its own dues-paying members of the association's position on a candidate.
> * * *
>
> (c) * * * [The Minnesota Ethical Practices Board] shall pay each candidate against whom the independent expenditures have been made, if the candidate is eligible to receive a public subsidy and has raised twice the minimum match required, an additional public subsidy equal to one-half the independent expenditures. The amount needed to pay the additional public subsidy under this subdivision is appropriated from the general fund to the board.
>
> * * *

[B]y advocating a candidate's defeat (or her opponent's victory) via an independent expenditure, the individual, committee, or fund working for the candidate's defeat instead has increased the maximum amount she may spend and given her the wherewithal to increase that spending—merely by exercising a First Amendment right to make expenditures opposing her or supporting her opponent. Thus the individual or group intending to contribute to her defeat becomes directly responsible for adding to her campaign coffers. To the extent that a candidate's campaign is enhanced by the operation of the statute, the political speech of the individual or group who made the independent expenditure "against" her (or in favor of her opponent) is impaired.

* * * It is [   ] clear that [this law] infringes on that protected speech because of the chilling effect the statute has on the political speech of the person or group making the independent expenditure. As the potential "independent expenders" allege in their briefs (and as at least one sponsor of the legislation intended), the mere enactment of [this law] has already prevented many if not most potential independent expenditures from ever being made. The knowledge that a candidate who one does not want to be elected will have her spending limits increased and will receive a public subsidy equal to half the amount of the independent expenditure, as a direct result of that independent expenditure, chills the free

exercise of that protected speech. This "self-censorship" that has occurred even before the state implements the statute's mandates is no less a burden on speech that is susceptible to constitutional challenge than is direct government censorship.

Our conclusion that the most fundamental of rights is infringed by [this law] does not end our inquiry, however. We now must decide whether the statute is content-neutral or content-based, "not always a simple task." [Editor—The court goes on to state that no governmental interest was sufficient to justify the dampening of political speech through independent expenditures, whether the state law was or was not content-neutral.]

* * * Under [another section] of the campaign reform law, a political committee or political fund cannot "accept aggregate contributions from an individual, political committee, or political fund in an amount more than $100 a year." We hold that the $100 limit is so low as to infringe upon the citizens' First Amendment right to political association and free political expression.

As emphasized by the Supreme Court's decision in Buckley v. Valeo, it is clear that state-enforced limits on campaign contributions and expenditures stifle First Amendment freedoms. Here, because the limit applies to contributions both by and to political committees and funds, the limit affects not only free political speech but also free association, the "tradition of volunteer committees for collective action. * * * By collective effort individuals can make their views known, when, individually, their voices would be faint or lost."

It also is well established that Minnesota's declared purpose in enacting its $100 limit—to avoid corruption or the appearance of corruption in the political process that could result from large amounts of special interest money circulating in the system—is a compelling state interest.

But the fighting issue here is whether a $100 limit on contributions to political committees or funds is narrowly tailored to serve the state's interest, given the burden it imposes on political speech. We hold that it is not. "Given the important role of contributions in financing political campaigns, contribution restrictions could have a severe impact on political dialogue if the limitations prevented candidates and political committees from amassing the resources necessary for effective advocacy." And the concern of a political quid pro quo for large contributions, which becomes a possibility when the contribution is to an individual candidate, is not present when the contribution is given to a political committee or fund that by itself does not have legislative power.

The Buckley Court, eighteen years ago, found that a $1000 limit—ten times the limit at issue here—was sufficiently high to pass constitutional muster as narrowly tailored to serve the state's concern for the integrity of the political system. We realize that the

Buckley limit was never declared to be a constitutional minimum, but it does provide us with some guidance and a frame of reference in evaluating the constitutionality of Minnesota's $100 limit.

Among the undisputed facts relied upon by the District Court is the fact that a $100 contribution in 1976 would have a value of $40.60 in 1994 dollars, or approximately four percent of the $1000 limit approved in Buckley. * * * Based on these facts, we agree with the District Court that a $100 limit on contributions to or by political committees and funds significantly impairs the ability of individuals and political committees and funds to exercise their First Amendment rights. An annual $100 limit on contributions to or by political funds and committees is too low to allow meaningful participation in protected political speech and association, and thus is not narrowly tailored to serve the state's legitimate interest in protecting the integrity of the political system. Accordingly, we hold that the $100 limit violates the protections afforded by the First Amendment for free political speech and free association.

ii) CURRENT LAW AND "REFORM" PROPOSALS

We will look more closely in the following pages at post-Buckley v. Valeo litigation about legislating limits on money in politics. As background, here is some information about current law (some of which has been the subject of litigation), and various law reform proposals.

(A) Current law

Under current federal law, the contribution ceilings for federal elections are different for individuals and for multicandidate political committees (primarily PACs, described below). A multicandidate committee is, in general, one which has registered with the Federal Election Commission and receives contributions from more than 50 persons, and has contributed to five or more candidates for federal election.

An individual can give up to $1,000 to a candidate or to the candidate's political committee per election (a primary election is separate from election for office), $20,000 to a national party committee, and $5,000 to other political committees (primarily PACs). Multicandidate political committees (primarily PACs) can give $5,000 to a candidate or to the candidate's political committee (more than the $1,000 applicable to individual donors), $15,000 to a national party committee, and $5,000 to other political committees. A national party committee includes a House and Senate campaign committee. In addition, there is an overall $25,000 cap on the total campaign contributions which *individuals* can make per year, but not on other donors. 2 U.S.C. § 441a(a)(1–4).

Political parties are also subject to separate caps on expenditures which would be considered independent expenditures, if they were made by individuals or PACs. 2 U.S.C. § 441a(d).

The higher ceiling for contributions to and by PACs rests on the theory that they raise money from many sources. PACs were originally set up to avoid the absolute prohibition on contributions and expenditures by unions and corporations "in connection with any [federal] election." 2 U.S.C. § 441b. These organizations then created PACs, which were ostensibly independent of the union or corporation, to receive contributions from stockholders, executives and union members, and then make political contributions of their own. Under current law, 2 U.S.C. § 441b(b)(2)(C) permits "the establishment, administration, and solicitation of contributions to a separate segregated fund to be utilized for political purposes by a corporation, labor organization, membership organization, cooperative, or corporation without capital stock." Contributions can, in general, only be solicited from corporate shareholders, union members, and their families. 2 U.S.C. § 441b(b)(4)(A).

Today, PACs have expanded far beyond these traditional categories. First, PACs support general economic interests, such as those favored by trade associations, and more ideological objectives, such as free enterprise and free choice for abortion. Second, some politicians, seeking greater national power, have formed PACs to funnel contributions to other candidates. These "member" or "leadership" PACs may help legislators maintain or achieve leadership positions in Congress. Powerful politicians have always helped others raise funds, but member PACs are a more direct way of controlling the flow of funds from one legislator to another. There is some evidence that these PACs may help challengers as well as incumbents.

The political impact of PACs is still evolving and the evidence about their effect still being debated. The power of PAC money is probably one reason for the decline of party control, because it gives candidates political clout outside of the party structure. This may interfere with the ability of parties to mediate compromise. Thus, while the Court defers to government policy discouraging third parties and independent candidates on the theory that the two-party system has advantages, the growth of PACs may work in the opposite direction.

There are five other possible impacts of PAC money. First, it may favor incumbents. Second, it may encourage a candidate to respond to interests funded from outside his constituency. One study of contributions to House elections showed that virtually all PAC contributions come from outside the House district and over 80% from outside the state.[10] The greatest impact of contributions from outside the electoral district may be on members of all-purpose committees, not linked to particular constituent interests, such as the tax and appropriations committees. PAC money seems to flow in larger amounts to members of those committees. Third, a PAC may reinforce the power of political interest groups which already have significant influence. Fourth, fundraising from PACs (and other contributors) may sour candidates on seeking public office. Fifth, PAC influence may further disillusion the public about politics, whatever their actual impact.

10. M. Fiorina, Congress: Keystone of the Washington Establishment 127 (1989).

It is important to note that these federal monetary limits on individuals and corporations do not apply to "soft money" contributions to a political party for certain activities, such as electing candidates for state office, or for voter registration and "get out the vote" drives.

(B) "Reforms"

The present system of financing elections continues to attract proposals for reform. As of 1996 some of the enthusiasm for change has died out at the federal level, but in April 1992 a House/Senate conference agreed on a campaign finance bill (S.3), which President Bush vetoed (20 Weekly Comp. Pres. Doc. 822 (1992))—referred to below as the "1992 bill."

Source of money. Some proposals are concerned with the source of money. For example, PAC contributions would be banned. A more refined target of some legislative proposals is "bundling" of individual contributions by a PAC to be transferred to a candidate, far in excess of the PAC contribution limit. With "bundling," the individuals are still the contributors, but the PAC gets a lot of the credit for arranging the contributions.

The 1992 bill would have prohibited leadership or member PACs. It also prohibited bundling of separate contributions by unions, corporations, trade associations, and PACs which associate with these entities, and by political party committees.

Those concerned with the source of contributions sometimes favor lower ceilings on contributions from outside the candidate's state. Should out-of-state money be a special concern? Doesn't it broaden the legislators perspective beyond the economic interests of constituents? Or does it just give an advantage to economic interests with national impact? Does it favor national ideological preferences, either from the political Left or Right?

A variation on the concern with funding sources focuses on the total amount received from certain sources, such as PACs. Thus, the law might provide that no more than $100,000 could be received from PACs, without changing the total contribution ceiling from each PAC. For example, the first 20 PACs could give $5,000 for a $100,000 total, and no more PAC money could be received for that campaign.

The 1992 bill provided caps on what a candidate could receive from PACs and individuals, which is increased if there is a close primary fight. (a) Total PAC contributions were capped at $200,000. Supporting data in the Committee Report note that 46% of the funds spent by successful candidates in 1990 came from PACs, up from 31% in 1980; and that 55% of the winners received more than ½ their money from PACs, up from 24% in 1980. (b) Total contributions from individuals of more than $250 each are capped at $200,000. Expenditures of the candidate's own funds count against the $200,000. (c) In addition, contributions from national, state, and local parties cannot total more than $5,000, to prevent their influencing close races.

Total spending; public financing. Another group of proposals deals with the total amount of money spent on political campaigns. They would cap campaign spending (varying by state) if the candidate accepted public financing. The public financing carrot is meant to avoid constitutional objections to expenditure limits created by Buckley v. Valeo. That case had held, in the context of Presidential campaign financing, that a candidate could be required to adhere to dollar expenditure ceilings and to refuse contributions (except to make up for public financing shortfalls) in exchange for public money.

In these days of budgetary constraints, however, public financing is neither politically palatable nor likely to be a generous enough alternative to private financing. Some recent proposals would therefore provide public support in the form of free broadcast time, media ads at bargain rates, and low-rate postal privileges. Expenditure ceilings and public financing can also be combined with rules dealing with the source of money. For example, a candidate might be allowed to supplement public financing up to a specified total from small contributions (e.g. $100,000 from $100 contributions for House elections).

The 1992 bill contained the following public financing provisions for House elections. To obtain public financing, spending by House candidates was limited to $600,000 during each election year period. No more than $500,000 could be spent in the general election. There was no separate ceiling on primary spending, and in the case of a close primary (a win by 10% or less), the candidate could spend an additional $150,000.

The House was sensitive to the argument that spending limits might hurt political competition because of the incumbent's advantage. The House Committee Report (H.R. No. 102–340(I), 102d Cong., 1st Sess. (1991)) stated that the

> $600,000 figure was * * * based largely on experiences from House elections in the last decade, i.e., five election cycles. According-ing to a Congressional Research Service study, in 1990, the median amount spent by House winners in the closest races (decided by 10% or less) was $544,000, while $556,000 or less was spent by fully 75% of all successful House candidates and $538,000 or less was spent by 75% of those challengers who defeated incumbents. Clearly, the $600,000 would provide that critical latitude needed in most races which engender the highest degree of competition.

To qualify for public financing, a candidate had to raise $60,000, counting only contributions of less than $250 and the first $250 of larger contributions. The candidate could not spend more than $50,000 of his or her own money.

The first $200 of each contribution would be matched with public funds up to $200,000. One piece of mail could be sent to each voting age resident at third-class mail rates.

Spending limits were increased, more public money was available, or both, if certain contingencies occurred—an opponent refused to follow the spending limits; independent expenditures against a candidate or for an opponent exceeded $10,000; or an opponent spent a lot of his or her own money.

The 1992 bill would also have prohibited independent expenditures to support a candidate by PACs associated with registered lobbyists.

Soft money. A major weakness in the rules controlling campaign spending is the failure to deal with so-called "soft money" spending by national political party organizations, and the contributions by individuals, corporations, and unions made to such organizations for "soft money" purposes. Soft money includes spending to support state candidates (when federal candidates are also running and their views and political fortunes are linked). It also includes spending on voter registration and get-out-the-vote campaigns, with impact on the election of a favored candidate.

The 1992 bill would have limited electioneering spending (to get-out-the-vote and register voters) by state and national party organizations after April 1 in Presidential election years and June 1 in other election years.

———————

Proposals for "reform," such as those discussed above, must be considered against a backdrop of constitutional concerns raised by Buckley v. Valeo, and by the cases described below. More specifically, as you read these cases, consider whether the following would be constitutional:

banning PAC contributions *to* candidates;

limits on independent expenditures *by* PACs to support a candidate;

limits on total contributions received *from* PACs.

Does your answer change if the PAC is an ideological PAC, rather than one associated with profit-making organizations (corporations) or other economic interests (labor unions)?

iii) PACS AS CONTRIBUTORS AND INDEPENDENT SPENDERS; PARTY SPENDING

California Medical Association v. Federal Election Commission, 453 U.S. 182 (1981) dealt with the $5,000 limit on individual contributions to PACs (not candidates). A plurality of the Court upheld the contribution limit. The contributors argued that their contributions were like independent expenditures, because the PAC was not controlled by a candidate. The plurality concluded that they were not the kind of independent expenditure that Buckley v. Valeo protected because they supported speech by someone other than the contributor. Moreover, the anti-corruption goals underlying the limits on candidate contributions by individuals supported the $5,000 limit on contributions to PACs, because unlimited contributions to PACs could circumvent the limit on individual contributions to candidates. A fifth justice concurred in the judgment because the PAC was formed to make contributions to candidates (although the candidate did not control the PAC), not to make independent expenditures.

In Federal Election Comm'n v. National Conservative Political Action Committee (NCPAC), 470 U.S. 480 (1985), the Court dealt with a provision (not mentioned above) limiting independent expenditures by independent political committees to further the election of Presidential candidates to $1,000, if the candidate's campaign received public financing. The Court described NCPAC as

> a nonprofit, nonmembership corporation * * * registered with the (Federal Election Commission) as a political committee. * * * It is governed by a three-member board of directors which is elected annually by the existing board. The board's chairman and the other two members make all decisions concerning which candidates to support or oppose, the strategy and methods to employ, and the amounts of money to spend. Its contributors have no role in these decisions.

This case returns to the question, left unresolved in California Medical Association, of how much government control is permitted when a group makes independent expenditures to support a candidate (neither controlled by a candidate, nor contributions to a candidate), but are speech by proxy in the sense that the contributors to the group are not themselves making direct political expenditures.

The Court held that the ceiling on independent expenditures by PACs was an unconstitutional infringement of First Amendment protections. Justice Rehnquist stated:

> The FEC [Federal Election Commission] urges that these contributions do not constitute individual speech, but merely "speech by proxy," see California Medical Assn. v. FEC, 453 U.S. 182, 196 (1981)(Marshall, J.) (plurality opinion), because the contributors do not control or decide upon the use of the funds by the PACs or the specific content of the PACs advertisements and other speech. The plurality emphasized in that case, however, that nothing in the statutory provision in question "limits the amount [an unincorporated association] or any of its members may independently expend in order to advocate political views," but only the amount it may contribute to a multicandidate political committee. Unlike California Medical Assn., the present cases involve limitations on expenditures by PACs, not on the contributions they receive; and in any event these contributions are predominantly small and thus do not raise the same concerns as the sizeable contributions involved in California Medical Assn.
>
> Another reason the "proxy speech" approach is not useful in this case is that the contributors obviously like the message they are hearing from these organizations and want to add their voices to that message; otherwise they would not part with their money. To

say that their collective action in pooling their resources to amplify their voices is not entitled to full First Amendment protection would subordinate the voices of those of modest means as opposed to those sufficiently wealthy to be able to buy expensive media ads with their own resources.

[Editor—Existing law prohibits independent expenditures by corporations and unions to support a candidate. The Court distinguished NCPAC this way. "[T]he groups and associations in question, designed expressly to participate in political debate, are quite different from the traditional corporations organized for economic gain." It referred to "the evil of potential corruption [which] had long been recognized" in the case of corporations and unions.]

The Court went on to discuss the government's interest in restricting the expenditures. It held that "preventing corruption or the appearance of corruption are the only legitimate and compelling government interests thus far identified for restricting campaign finances," and that the "hallmark of corruption is the financial *quid pro quo*." It emphasized that the amounts given to the PAC were small, and, by definition, uncoordinated with the candidate. The potential for corruption was therefore "slight." It refused to treat as dispositive the possibility that the candidate might take notice of and reward those responsible for PAC expenditures.

A dissent rejected the Buckley v. Valeo distinction between independent expenditures and contributions. The dissent commented on the "credulous acceptance of the formal distinction between coordinated and independent expenditures" in a "realm of tacit understandings;" and argued that, even if Buckley v. Valeo was still valid, limits on PAC expenditures were more like limits on contributions than on independent expenditures. The dissent emphasized that the contributors in this case were not using their own money to express their own views, but giving money to others in the expectation that they will use the money to express views with which they agree. This, in the dissent's view, took their activity out of the category of protected speech, just as it did in the California Medical Association v. FEC (upholding ceilings on gifts to PACs).

The freedom PACs have to make independent expenditures could be used to circumvent limits on contributions to candidates if the PACs were really under the control of candidates. Congress has responded to this problem by defining an "independent expenditure" as an expenditure made "without cooperation or consultation with any candidate, or any authorized committee or agent of the candidate, and which is not made in concert with, or at the request or suggestion of, any candidate, or any authorized committee or agent of the candidate." 2 U.S.C. § 431(17). Needless to say, it may be difficult to determine whether there is "cooperation or consultation," rather than simply parallel points of view.

In Colorado Republican Federal Campaign Committee v. Federal Election Commission, 116 S.Ct. 2309 (1996), the Court dealt with the federal dollar ceiling on expenditures by campaign committees of political parties to help a federal candidate get elected. The statutory dollar ceiling rested on the assumption that such expenditures were likely to be coordinated with the candidate (without actual proof of coordination) and therefore testable under the standards applicable to contributions, not independent expenditures. The lower court upheld the law (59 F.3d 1015 (10th Cir.1995)), but the Court reversed, revealing a continued inability to agree on how best to analyze political expenditures. Three Justices (Breyer, O'Connor, Souter), applied the bifurcated contribution-expenditure analysis of Buckley v. Valeo, and struck down the statutory limits on independent party expenditures. These three judges, however, refused to reach another question—whether expenditures by parties which *were* in fact coordinated with the candidate could be treated as contributions to the candidate and subject to the limits applicable to contributions. Four Justices reached this second question (Kennedy, Rehnquist, Scalia, and Thomas), holding that *coordinated* party-candidate spending could not constitutionally be limited; it was entitled to the same protections as independent expenditures. One of these four Justices—Thomas—would overrule Buckley v. Valeo's distinction between all contributions and independent expenditures and hold them both protected by the First Amendment (recall that some Justices had wanted to eliminate this distinction for the opposite reason—to permit limits on both types of spending). Finally, two Justices (Stevens and Ginsburg) would have upheld the statute placing a ceiling on independent party expenditures.

As you read excerpts from the opinions, consider these questions.

(1) Is empirical information about the reality of the political process relevant in deciding whether caps on party expenditures are constitutional?

(2) Do any of the judges adopt criteria for determining constitutionality that are different from those adopted in Buckley v. Valeo?

(3) If independent nonparty expenditures cannot be capped and PAC spending has proliferated, does it make any sense to limit party spending? Would you rather have PACs and independent nonparty spending or party spending as the major source of campaign financing?

Colorado Republican Federal Campaign Committee v. Federal Election Commission

116 S.Ct. 2309 (1996).

■ Justice Breyer announced the judgment of the Court and delivered an opinion, in which Justice O'Connor and Justice Souter join. * * *

* * * [F]or present purposes, the Act now prohibits individuals and political committees from making direct, or indirect, contributions that exceed the following limits:

(a) For any "person": $1,000 to a candidate "with respect to any election"; $5,000 to any political committee in any year; $20,000 to the national committees of a political party in any year; but all within an overall limit (for any individual in any year) of $25,000. 2 U.S.C. §§ 441a(a)(1), (3).

(b) For any "multicandidate political committee": $5,000 to a candidate "with respect to any election"; $5,000 to any political committee in any year; and $15,000 to the national committees of a political party in any year. § 441a(a)(2).

FECA [Federal Election Campaign Act] also has a special provision, directly at issue in this case, that governs contributions and expenditures by political parties. § 441a(d). This special provision creates, in part, an exception to the above contribution limits. That is, without special treatment, political parties ordinarily would be subject to the general limitation on contributions by a "multicandidate political committee" just described. See § 441a(a)(4). That provision, as we said in (b) above, limits annual contributions by a "multicandidate political committee" to no more than $5,000 to any candidate. [T]his contribution limit governs not only direct contributions but also indirect contributions that take the form of coordinated expenditures, defined as "expenditures made * * * in cooperation, consultation, or concert, with, or at the request or suggestion of, a candidate, his authorized political committees, or their agents." § 441a(a)(7)(B)(i). Thus, ordinarily, a party's coordinated expenditures would be subject to the $5,000 limitation.

However, FECA's special provision, which we shall call the "Party Expenditure Provision," creates a general exception from this contribution limitation, and from any other limitation on expenditures. It says:

"Notwithstanding any other provision of law with respect to limitations on expenditures or limitations on contributions, * * * political party [committees] * * * may make expenditures in connection with the general election campaign of candidates for Federal office * * *." § 441a(d)(1) (emphasis added).

After exempting political parties from the general contribution and expenditure limitations of the statute, the Party Expenditure Provision then imposes a substitute limitation upon party "expenditures" in a senatorial campaign equal to the greater of $20,000 or "2 cents multiplied by the voting age population of the State," § 441a(d)(3)(A)(i), adjusted for inflation since 1974, § 441a(c). The Provision permitted a political party in Colorado in 1986 to spend about $103,000 in connection with the general election campaign of a candidate for the United States Senate. * * *

In January 1986, Timothy Wirth, then a Democratic Congress-man, announced that he would run for an open Senate seat in November. In April, before either the Democratic primary or the Republican convention, the Colorado Republican Federal Campaign Committee (Colorado Party), the petitioner here, bought radio adver-tisements attacking Congressman Wirth [which exceeded the statu-tory dollar limits].

The summary judgment record indicates that the expenditure in question is what this Court in Buckley called an "independent" expenditure, not a "coordinated" expenditure that other provisions of FECA treat as a kind of campaign "contribution." [Editor—Discussion of summary judgment record omitted.] * * *

Given [   ] established principles [distinguishing between contri-butions and independent expenditures], we do not see how a provision that limits a political party's independent expenditures can escape their controlling effect. A political party's independent ex-pression not only reflects its members' views about the philosoph-ical and governmental matters that bind them together, it also seeks to convince others to join those members in a practical democratic task, the task of creating a government that voters can instruct and hold responsible for subsequent success or failure. The indepen-dent expression of a political party's views is "core" First Amend-ment activity no less than is the independent expression of individu-als, candidates, or other political committees.

We are not aware of any special dangers of corruption associat-ed with political parties that tip the constitutional balance in a different direction. When this Court considered, and held unconstitu-tional, limits that FECA had set on certain independent expenditures by political action committees, it reiterated Buckley's observation that "the absence of prearrangement and coordination" does not eliminate, but it does help to "alleviate," any "danger" that a candidate will understand the expenditure as an effort to obtain a "quid pro quo." The same is true of independent party expendi-tures.

We recognize that FECA permits individuals to contribute more money ($20,000) to a party than to a candidate ($1,000) or to other political committees ($5,000). We also recognize that FECA permits unregulated "soft money" contributions to a party for certain activi-ties, such as electing candidates for state office, see § 431(8)(A)(i), or for voter registration and "get out the vote" drives, see § 431(8)(B)(xii). But the opportunity for corruption posed by these greater opportunities for contributions is, at best, attenuated. Unreg-ulated "soft money" contributions may not be used to influence a federal campaign, except when used in the limited, party-building activities specifically designated in the statute. See § 431(8)(B). Any contribution to a party that is earmarked for a particular campaign, is considered a contribution to the candidate and is subject to the contribution limitations. § 441a(a)(8). A party may not simply chan-nel unlimited amounts of even undesignated contributions to a candidate, since such direct transfers are also considered contribu-tions and are subject to the contribution limits on a "multicandidate political committee." § 441a(a)(2). The greatest danger of corrup-tion, therefore, appears to be from the ability of donors to give sums up to $20,000 to a party which may be used for independent party expenditures for the benefit of a particular candidate. We could understand how Congress, were it to conclude that the potential for evasion of the individual contribution limits was a serious matter, might decide to change the statute's limitations on contributions to political parties. But we do not believe that the risk of corruption present here could justify the "markedly greater burden on basic freedoms caused by" the statute's limitations on expenditures. Contributors seeking to avoid the effect of the $1,000 contribution limit indirectly by donations to the national party could spend that same amount of money (or more) themselves more directly by making their own independent expenditures promoting the candi-date. If anything, an independent expenditure made possible by a $20,000 donation, but controlled and directed by a party rather than the donor, would seem less likely to corrupt than the same (or a much larger) independent expenditure made directly by that donor. In any case, the constitutionally significant fact, present equally in both instances, is the lack of coordination between the candidate and the source of the expenditure. This fact prevents us from assuming, absent convincing evidence to the contrary, that a limita-tion on political parties' independent expenditures is necessary to combat a substantial danger of corruption of the electoral system.

The Government does not point to record evidence or legisla-tive findings suggesting any special corruption problem in respect to independent party expenditures. To the contrary, this Court's opin-ions suggest that Congress wrote the Party Expenditure Provision not so much because of a special concern about the potentially "corrupting" effect of party expenditures, but rather for the constitu-tionally insufficient purpose of reducing what it saw as wasteful and excessive campaign spending. In fact, rather than indicating a special fear of the corruptive influence of political parties, the legislative history demonstrates Congress' general desire to en-hance what was seen as an important and legitimate role for political parties in American elections. S. Rep. No. 93–689, p. 7 (1974)("[A] vigorous party system is vital to American politics * * *. Pooling resources from many small contributors is a legitimate function and an integral part of party politics"); id., at 7–8, 15.

We therefore believe that this Court's prior case law controls the outcome here. We do not see how a Constitution that grants to individuals, candidates, and ordinary political committees the right to make unlimited independent expenditures could deny the same right to political parties. [Editor—Does the "equality" argument work in the other direction? Why not decide that it is absurd to deny political parties rights enjoyed by individuals, but hold that neither parties nor individuals can make independent expenditures?] * * *

[Editor—The Justices then address the claim that the party's expenditures should be presumed coordinated, based on administrative and congressional findings.]

The Government does not deny the force of the precedent we have discussed. Rather, it argued below, and the lower courts accepted, that the expenditure in this case should be treated under those precedents, not as an "independent expenditure," but rather as a "coordinated expenditure," which those cases have treated as "contributions," and which those cases have held Congress may constitutionally regulate. * * *

* * * [T]he Government points to a set of legal materials, based on FEC interpretations, that seem to say or imply that all party expenditures are "coordinated." * * *

The Government argues, on the basis of these materials, that the FEC has made an "empirical judgment that party officials will as a matter of course consult with the party's candidates before funding communications intended to influence the outcome of a federal election."

* * * The FEC materials, however, do not make this empirical judgment. For the most part those materials use the word "coordinated" as a description that does not necessarily deny the possibility that a party could also make independent expenditures. [They] appear[ ] without any internal or external evidence that the FEC means it to embody an empirical judgment (say, that parties, in fact, hardly ever spend money independently) or to represent the outcome of an empirical investigation. * * *

Finally, we recognize that the FEC may have characterized the expenditures as "coordinated" in light of this Court's constitutional decisions prohibiting regulation of most independent expenditures. But, if so, the characterization cannot help the Government prove its case. An agency's simply calling an independent expenditure a "coordinated expenditure" cannot (for constitutional purposes) make it one. * * *

Finally, the Government and supporting amici argue that the expenditure is "coordinated" because a party and its candidate are identical, i.e., the party, in a sense, "is" its candidates. We cannot assume, however, that this is so. See, e.g., W. Keefe, Parties, Politics, and Public Policy in America 59–74 (5th ed. 1988)(describing parties as "coalitions" of differing interests). Congress chose to treat candidates and their parties quite differently under the Act, for example, by regulating contributions from one to the other. See § 441a(a)(2)(B). And we are not certain whether a metaphysical identity would help the Government, for in that case one might argue that the absolute identity of views and interests eliminates any potential for corruption, as would seem to be the case in the relationship between candidates and their campaign committees.

[Editor—The Justices then explain why they do not reach the broader question of whether, "in the special case of political parties, the First Amendment forbids congressional efforts to limit coordinated expenditures as well as independent expenditures."]

For these reasons, the judgment of the Court of Appeals is vacated, and the case is remanded for further proceedings.

■ Justice Stevens, with whom Justice Ginsburg joins, dissenting.

In my opinion, all money spent by a political party to secure the election of its candidate for the office of United States Senator should be considered a "contribution" to his or her campaign. * * *

I am persuaded that three interests provide a constitutionally sufficient predicate for federal limits on spending by political parties. First, such limits serve the interest in avoiding both the appearance and the reality of a corrupt political process. [Editor—What does "corrupt" mean here? Is it what Buckley v. Valeo means when it speaks of avoiding the appearance of corruption?] A party shares a unique relationship with the candidate it sponsors because their political fates are inextricably linked. That interdependency creates a special danger that the party—or the persons who control the party—will abuse the influence it has over the candidate by virtue of its power to spend. The provisions at issue are appropriately aimed at reducing that threat. The fact that the party in this case had not yet chosen its nominee at the time it broadcast the challenged advertisements is immaterial to the analysis. Although the Democratic and Republican nominees for the 1996 Presidential race will not be selected until this summer, current advertising expenditures by the two national parties are no less contributions to the campaigns of the respective frontrunners than those that will be made in the fall.

Second, these restrictions supplement other spending limitations embodied in the Act, which are likewise designed to prevent corruption. Individuals and certain organizations are permitted to contribute up to $1,000 to a candidate. Since the same donors can give up to $5,000 to party committees, if there were no limits on party spending, their contributions could be spent to benefit the candidate and thereby circumvent the $1,000 cap. We have recognized the legitimate interest in blocking similar attempts to undermine the policies of the Act. See California Medical Assn. v. Federal Election Comm'n, 453 U.S. 182, 197–199 (1981)(plurality opinion)(approving ceiling on contributions to political action committees to prevent circumvention of limitations on individual contributions to candidates); id., at 203 (Blackmun, J., concurring in part and concurring in judgment).

Finally, I believe the Government has an important interest in leveling the electoral playing field by constraining the cost of federal campaigns. * * * It is quite wrong to assume that the net effect of limits on contributions and expenditures—which tend to protect equal access to the political arena, to free candidates and their staffs from the interminable burden of fund-raising, and to diminish the importance of repetitive 30–second commercials—will be adverse to the interest in informed debate protected by the First Amendment. [Editor—One commentator has suggested that the Court might uphold maximum spending limits on candidates on the ground that their purpose was to reduce the inordinate amount of time spent raising funds, which distracts representatives from their lawmaking activities. V. Blasi, Free Speech and the Widening Gyre of Fund–Raising: Why Spending Limits May Not Violate the First Amendment After All, 94 Colum. L. Rev. 1281 (1994). Although the Court did not directly address that argument, it may have implicitly rejected Justice Stevens' concern about the burdens of fund-raising.]

Congress surely has both wisdom and experience in these matters that is far superior to ours. I would therefore accord special deference to its judgment on questions related to the extent and nature of limits on campaign spending. * * *

Accordingly, I would affirm the judgment of the Court of Appeals.

■ Justice Kennedy, with whom the Chief Justice and Justice Scalia join, concurring in the judgment and dissenting in part. * * *

We had no occasion in Buckley to consider possible First Amendment objections to limitations on spending by parties. While our cases uphold contribution limitations on individuals and associations, political party spending "in cooperation, consultation, or concert with" a candidate does not fit within our description of "contributions" in Buckley. In my view, we should not transplant the reasoning of cases upholding ordinary contribution limitations to a case involving FECA's restrictions on political party spending.

The First Amendment embodies a "profound national commitment to the principle that debate on public issues should be uninhibited, robust, and wide-open." Political parties have a unique role in serving this principle; they exist to advance their members' shared political beliefs. A party performs this function, in part, by "identifying the people who constitute the association, and * * * limiting the association to those people only." Having identified its members, however, a party can give effect to their views only by selecting and supporting candidates. A political party has its own traditions and principles that transcend the interests of individual candidates and campaigns; but in the context of particular elections, candidates are necessary to make the party's message known and effective, and vice versa.

It makes no sense, therefore, to ask, as FECA does, whether a party's spending is made "in cooperation, consultation, or concert with" its candidate. The answer in most cases will be yes, but that provides more, not less, justification for holding unconstitutional the statute's attempt to control this type of party spending, which bears little resemblance to the contributions discussed in Buckley. Party spending "in cooperation, consultation, or concert with" its candidates of necessity "communicates the underlying basis for the support," i. e., the hope that he or she will be elected and will work to further the party's political agenda.

The problem is not just the absence of a basis in our First Amendment cases for treating the party's spending as contributions. The greater difficulty posed by the statute is its stifling effect on the ability of the party to do what it exists to do. It is fanciful to suppose that limiting party spending of the type at issue here "does not in any way infringe the contributor's freedom to discuss candidates and issues," since it would be impractical and imprudent, to say the least, for a party to support its own candidates without some form of "cooperation" or "consultation." The party's speech, legitimate on its own behalf, cannot be separated from speech on the candidate's behalf without constraining the party in advocating its most essential positions and pursuing its most basic goals. The party's form of organization and the fact that its fate in an election is inextricably intertwined with that of its candidates cannot provide a basis for the restrictions imposed here.

We have a constitutional tradition of political parties and their candidates engaging in joint First Amendment activity; we also have a practical identity of interests between the two entities during an election. Party spending "in cooperation, consultation, or concert with" a candidate therefore is indistinguishable in substance from expenditures by the candidate or his campaign committee. We held in Buckley that the First Amendment does not permit regulation of the latter, and it should not permit this regulation of the former.
* * *

I would resolve the Party's First Amendment claim in accord with these principles rather than remit the Party to further protracted proceedings. Because the plurality would do otherwise, I concur only in the judgment.

■ Justice Thomas, concurring in the judgment and dissenting in part * * *. [Editor—Justices Rehnquist and Scalia joined that part of Thomas' opinion which reached the same conclusion as Justice Kennedy—coordinated party-candidate expenditures are constitutionally protected in the same manner as independent expenditures. However, Justice Thomas wrote Part II of his opinion for himself alone—holding that the Buckley v. Valeo distinction between contributions and expenditures should be rejected in all situations. Portions of Part II are excerpted below.]

Critical to Justice Breyer's reasoning is the distinction between contributions and independent expenditures that we first drew in Buckley v. Valeo, 424 U.S. 1 (1976)(per curiam). Though we said in Buckley that controls on spending and giving "operate in an area of the most fundamental First Amendment activities," we invalidated the expenditure limits of FECA and upheld the Act's contribution limits. The justification we gave for the differing results was this: "The expenditure limitations * * * represent substantial rather than merely theoretical restraints on the quantity and diversity of political speech," whereas "limitations upon the amount that any one person or group may contribute to a candidate or political committee entail only a marginal restriction upon the contributor's ability to engage in free communication." This conclusion was supported mainly by two assertions about the nature of contributions: first, though contributions may result in speech, that speech is by the candidate and not by the contributor; and second, contributions express only general support for the candidate but do not communicate the reasons for that support. Since Buckley, our campaign finance jurisprudence has been based in large part on this distinction between contributions and expenditures.

In my view, the distinction lacks constitutional significance, and I would not adhere to it. As Chief Justice Burger put it: "Contributions and expenditures are two sides of the same First Amendment coin." Contributions and expenditures both involve core First Amendment expression because they further the "discussion of public issues and debate on the qualifications of candidates * * * integral to the operation of the system of government established by our Constitution." When an individual donates money to a candidate or to a partisan organization, he enhances the donee's ability to communicate a message and thereby adds to political debate, just as when that individual communicates the message himself. Indeed, the individual may add more to political discourse by giving rather than spending, if the donee is able to put the funds to more productive use than can the individual. The contribution of funds to a candidate or to a political group thus fosters the "free discussion of governmental affairs," just as an expenditure does. Giving and spending in the electoral process also involve basic associational rights under the First Amendment. As we acknowledged in Buckley, " 'effective advocacy of both public and private points of view, particularly controversial ones, is undeniably enhanced by group association.' " Political associations allow citizens to pool their resources and make their advocacy more effective, and such efforts are fully protected by the First Amendment. If an individual is limited in the amount of resources he can contribute to the pool, he is most certainly limited in his ability to associate for purposes of effective advocacy. And if an individual cannot be subject to such limits, neither can political associations be limited in their ability to give as a means of furthering their members' viewpoints. As we have said, "any interference with the freedom of a party is simultaneously an interference with the freedom of its adherents."

Turning from similarities to differences, I can discern only one potentially meaningful distinction between contributions and expenditures. In the former case, the funds pass through an intermediary—some individual or entity responsible for organizing and facilitating the dissemination of the message—whereas in the latter case they may not necessarily do so. But the practical judgment by a citizen that another person or an organization can more effectively deploy funds for the good of a common cause than he can ought not deprive that citizen of his First Amendment rights. Whether an individual donates money to a candidate or group who will use it to promote the candidate or whether the individual spends the money to promote the candidate himself, the individual seeks to engage in political expression and to associate with likeminded persons. A contribution is simply an indirect expenditure; though contributions and expenditures may thus differ in form, they do not differ in substance. As one commentator cautioned, "let us not lose sight of the speech."

Echoing the suggestion in Buckley that contributions have less First Amendment value than expenditures because they do not involve speech by the donor, the Court has sometimes rationalized limitations on contributions by referring to contributions as "speech by proxy." The "speech by proxy" label is, however, an ineffective tool for distinguishing contributions from expenditures. Even in the case of a direct expenditure, there is usually some go-between that facilitates the dissemination of the spender's message—for instance, an advertising agency or a television station. To call a contribution "speech by proxy" thus does little to differentiate it from an expenditure. The only possible difference is that contributions involve an extra step in the proxy chain. But again, that is a difference in form, not substance.

Moreover, we have recently recognized that where the "proxy" speech is endorsed by those who give, that speech is a fully-protected exercise of the donors' associational rights. In Federal Election Comm'n v. NCPAC, we explained that "the 'proxy speech' approach is not useful * * * [where] the contributors obviously like the message they are hearing from [the] organization and want to add their voices to that message; otherwise they would not part with their money. To say that their collective action in pooling their resources to amplify their voices is not entitled to full First Amendment protection would subordinate the voices of those of modest means as opposed to those sufficiently wealthy to be able to buy expensive media ads with their own resources."

The other justification in Buckley for the proposition that contribution caps only marginally restrict speech—that is, that a contribution signals only general support for the candidate but indicates nothing about the reasons for that support—is similarly unsatisfying. Assuming the assertion is descriptively accurate (which is certainly questionable), it still cannot mean that giving is less important than spending in terms of the First Amendment. A campaign poster that reads simply "We support candidate Smith" does not seem to me any less deserving of constitutional protection than one that reads "We support candidate Smith because we like his position on agriculture subsidies." Both express a political opinion. Even a pure message of support, unadorned with reasons, is valuable to the democratic process.

In sum, unlike the Buckley Court, I believe that contribution limits infringe as directly and as seriously upon freedom of political expression and association as do expenditure limits. The protections of the First Amendment do not depend upon so fine a line as that between spending money to support a candidate or group and giving money to the candidate or group to spend for the same purpose. In principle, people and groups give money to candidates and other groups for the same reason that they spend money in support of those candidates and groups: because they share social, economic, and political beliefs and seek to have those beliefs affect governmental policy. I think that the Buckley framework for analyzing the constitutionality of campaign finance laws is deeply flawed. * * *

Instead, I begin with the premise that there is no constitutionally significant difference between campaign contributions and expenditures: both forms of speech are central to the First Amendment. Curbs on protected speech, we have repeatedly said, must be strictly scrutinized. * * *

The formula for strict scrutiny is, of course, well-established. It requires both a compelling governmental interest and legislative means narrowly tailored to serve that interest. In the context of campaign finance reform, the only governmental interest that we have accepted as compelling is the prevention of corruption or the appearance of corruption, and we have narrowly defined "corruption" as a "financial quid pro quo: dollars for political favors." As for the means-ends fit under strict scrutiny, we have specified that "where at all possible, government must curtail speech only to the degree necessary to meet the particular problem at hand, and must avoid infringing on speech that does not pose the danger that has prompted regulation."

[Editor—Justice Thomas then explains why limiting contributions does not satisfy the "narrow tailoring" test—because bribery and disclosure laws are more precisely focused. One observation by Thomas on Stevens' opinion is especially interesting. Footnote 9 states:

Justice Stevens submits that we should "accord special deference to [Congress'] judgment on questions related to the extent and nature of limits on campaign spending," a stance that the Court of Appeals also adopted. This position poses great risk to the First Amendment, in that it amounts to letting the fox stand watch over the henhouse. There is good reason to think that campaign reform is an especially inappropriate area for judicial deference to legislative judgment. What the argument for deference fails to acknowledge is the potential for legislators to set the rules of the electoral game so as to keep themselves in power and to keep potential challengers out of it. Indeed, history demonstrates that the most significant effect of election reform has been not to purify public service, but to protect incumbents and increase the influence of special interest groups. When Congress seeks to ration political expression in the electoral process, we ought not simply acquiesce in its judgment.]

iv) CORPORATE POLITICAL EXPENDITURES

The Court has also considered the problem of independent expenditures in the context of corporate expenditures. In Federal Election Comm'n v. Massachusetts Citizens for Life, 479 U.S. 238 (1986), the Court dealt with a federal law prohibiting corporations from using their funds to make any expenditure "in connection with any election to public office." The appellee (MCFL) was a non-profit "right-to-life" corporation, which (among other things) published a newsletter supporting specific right-to-life candidates. It did not make contributions to the candidates. The law allowed the corporation to set up a separate segregated fund, composed of contributions earmarked by contributors for unlimited campaign spending. The appellee argued, however, that requiring it to set up a fund carried with it significant recordkeeping, disclosure, and formal organizational requirements that would not apply if it were not incorporated. The Court agreed that these requirements were unconstitutional burdens.

The Court (per Justice Brennan) made the following points, in distinguishing this corporation from the typical for-profit corporation.

Th[e] concern over the corrosive influence of concentrated corporate wealth reflects the conviction that it is important to protect the integrity of the marketplace of political ideas. * * *

Direct corporate spending on political activity raises the prospect that resources amassed in the economic marketplace may be used to provide an unfair advantage in the political marketplace. * * * The resources in the treasury of a business corporation * * * are not an indication of popular support for the corporation's political ideas. * * *

Regulation of corporate political activity thus has reflected concern not about the use of the corporate form *per se*, but about the potential for unfair deployment of wealth for political purposes. Groups such as MCFL, however, do not pose the danger of corruption. MCFL was formed to disseminate political ideas, not to amass capital. The resources it has available are not a function of its success in the economic marketplace, but its popularity in the political marketplace.

Finally, the Court concluded that one rationale against corporate political spending was inapplicable to MCFL. In the typical for-profit corporation, an individual shareholder's money might be used for purposes the individual does not support. Although the MCFL contributor may not be aware of the exact use to which a contribution will be put, the general purposes are known to those contributing to the non-profit corporation.

In Austin v. Michigan Chamber of Commerce, 494 U.S. 652 (1990), the Court dealt with a nonprofit corporation—the Michigan Chamber of Commerce—which was (in the Court's view) indistinguishable from a for-profit corporation. The Michigan State Chamber of Commerce comprises more than 8,000 members, three-quarters of whom are for-profit corporations. The Chamber's general treasury is funded through annual dues required of all members. State law prohibited independent expenditures by corporations in support of or opposition to candidates for election for state office, except through segregated funds of the type discussed in Massachusetts Citizens for Life (MCFL). The Chamber challenged the limitation on its use of general treasury funds to pay for a newspaper ad supporting a specific candidate. The Court (in an opinion by Justice Marshall) stated:

> The State contends that the unique legal and economic characteristics of corporations necessitate some regulation of their political expenditures to avoid corruption or the appearance of corruption. * * * State law grants corporations special advantages—such as limited liability, perpetual life, and favorable treatment of the accumulation and distribution of assets—that enhance their ability to attract capital and deploy their resources in ways that maximize the return on their shareholders' investments. These state-created advantages not only allow corporations to play a dominant role in the nation's economy, but also permit them to use "resources amassed in the economic marketplace" to obtain "an unfair advantage in the political marketplace." MCFL, 479 U.S., at 257. * * *
>
> * * * Regardless of whether th[e] danger of "financial *quid pro quo*" corruption may be sufficient to justify a restriction on independent expenditures, Michigan's regulation aims at a different type of corruption in the political arena: the corrosive and distorting effects of immense aggregations of wealth that are accumulated with the help of the corporate form and that have little or no correlation to the public's support for the corporation's political ideas. * * * We therefore hold that the State has articulated a sufficiently compelling rationale to support its restriction on independent expenditures by corporations.

The Court then concludes that the statute's coverage of corporations *without* great financial resources is not objectionable because of "the *potential* such corporations have for 'distorting the political process.' "

The Court also dealt with the Chamber's contention that the statute should not be applied to nonprofit ideological corporations like a chamber of commerce, which was like the Massachusetts Citizens for Life Corporation (MCFL). The Court distinguished MCFL on three grounds. First, the Chamber served many purposes which are not inherently political (e.g., compiling and disseminating information about social, civic, and economic conditions, training members, and promoting ethical business practices). Second, members (like shareholders) may be economically reluctant to withdraw as members even if they disagree with the Chamber's political expression. Third, the Chamber was not independent of influence by business corporations, and could therefore be a conduit for their expenditures.

Finally, the Court distinguished labor unions (not covered by the state law) from corporations on two grounds. Unions lack the legal advantages corporations have to amass wealth. And unions are constitutionally prohibited from compelling members to provide financial support for political activity of which they disapprove.

Recall the discussion in Chapter 4 about group formation. We noted that political groups were easier to form when people could derive other nonpolitical advantages from the group. Does the Austin case imply that some or all economic organizations have such a great advantage in forming groups that they should not be allowed to convert that advantage into political influence?

Justice Scalia dissented in Austin. He argued that Buckley v. Valeo settled the argument against the majority position when it held that independent expenditures do not raise a sufficient threat of corruption to justify prohibition. He characterizes the majority's view as adopting the "New Corruption"—specifically, that "expenditures must 'reflect actual public support for the political ideas espoused.' " He asks: "Why is it perfectly all right if advocacy by an individual billionaire is out of proportion with 'actual public support' for his positions?" Consider these answers: (1) the State helped the corporation amass wealth; does this argument apply equally to rich individuals; (2) a corporation is less entitled to free speech protection, which is grounded in part on providing personal fulfillment?

Finally, Justice Scalia dealt with the argument that the State could protect corporate shareholders (and, by inference, the Chamber's members) because shareholders can only avoid supporting the corporation's politics by selling their stock. He argues that shareholders must accept many politically unpalatable corporate actions as part of their profit-making activities. Their remedy is either garnering majority support to change corporate policy or exiting by sale.

Does the Michigan Chamber of Commerce case put to rest the question whether independent corporate and union expenditures for candidates can be prohibited? It uses the word "corruption" a lot. The Court also uses that word in cases dealing with contribution limits. Is the meaning the same in both contexts?

Suppose a state prohibits a for-profit corporation from making a contribution or expenditure regarding a referendum on an issue put to voters, not an election of a candidate, unless the issue materially affects the property, business or assets of the corporation. In First National Bank of Boston v. Bellotti, 435 U.S. 765 (1978), the Court struck down such a prohibition. The specific issue was a state constitutional amendment permitting a progressive state income tax on individuals. The Court distinguished issue elections from candidate elections, because there was no quid pro quo corruption potential. This is a more troublesome distinction than might at first be apparent.

(1) Why isn't there a danger of the "corrosive influence of concentrated corporate wealth?" If you say that issue elections do not corrupt candidates, you have abandoned the "New Corruption" approach—that aggregations of wealth distort political results.

(2) Perhaps the point is that shareholders are more likely to agree with the corporation's political objectives in issue elections, so the problem of spending shareholder money without their consent is reduced.

v) ISSUE ADVOCACY

Federal Election Commission v. MCFL, 479 U.S. 238 (1986), supra, which refused to treat a not-for-profit corporation like a for-profit corporation, also stands for an additional proposition that has recently become very important. In addition to holding that the particular non-profit corporation was exempt from limits on independent corporate political expenditures, it further held that only the "express advocacy" of a candidate's election could constitutionally be regulated by the government, whether the spender was a for-profit corporation or not. This meant that "issue advocacy," as contrasted with independent expenditures to support a candidate, could not be limited or regulated. The Court relied on a portion of Buckley v. Valeo, not previously quoted, which stated that "the term 'expenditure' encompassed 'only funds used for communications that expressly advocate the election or defeat of a clearly identified candidate.' 424 U.S., at 80." The MCFL Court went on to state that "an expenditure must constitute 'express advocacy' of a candidate in order to be subject to the prohibition [on corporate independent expenditures] of § 441b." This holding has important implications for for-profit corporations and unions, and anyone else whose political expenditures the government might want to regulate. It probably means that contributions to issue-advocacy PACs which do not contribute to candidates cannot constitutionally be limited. And it allows corporations and unions to spend unlimited funds for issue advocacy.

A lot therefore turns on what is meant by issue advocacy. MCFL involved "express advocacy" of a candidate through the use of "voter guides," because "[t]he publication not only urges voters to vote for 'pro-life' candidates, but also identifies and provides photographs of specific candidates fitting that description. The [guide] cannot be regarded as a mere discussion of public issues that by their nature raise the names of certain politicians. Rather, it provides in effect an explicit directive: vote for these (named) candidates. The fact that this message is marginally less direct than 'Vote for Smith' does not change its essential nature. * * * The disclaimer of endorsement cannot negate this fact." However, in the 1996 federal elections, expenditures which described the position (and gave the picture) of a candidate running for election—e.g., that he or she favored tax increases or right to life—without mentioning the fact that he or she was running for office, were thought by many to be "issue advocacy." The fact that enforcement of election spending rules will long post-date an election encourages people to push the law to its limits and worry about the consequences later.

The constitutional protection for "issue advocacy" is a major concern for those who believe that public financing should replace the current system and/or that expenditure limits on supporting candidates should be constitutional. Unlimited issue advocacy could undermine such reforms, unless a narrow definition of protected issue advocacy would be constitutional.

vi) LIMITS ON CANDIDATE PAC FUNDING

Suppose the law limits the total amount of contributions which can be *received* by a candidate from PACs. As of 1992, Wisconsin and five other jurisdictions (Hawaii, Montana, Arizona, Louisiana, and California) had such legislation. In Gard v. Wisconsin State Elections Board, 456 N.W.2d 809 (Wis.1990), the court dealt with the Wisconsin law, limiting total contributions which can be received from individual committees (that is, PACs) and party-related committees. A party-related committee is a political party committee (such as the Democratic or Republican State Party) or a legislative campaign committee (set up by the Democratic or Republican members of the State Assembly and Senate) to finance elections. The court upheld the limits, as follows:

> The Campaign Finance Law creates essentially two classes of committees. An individual committee other than a political party committee or legislative campaign committee is what is commonly referred to as a PAC or special interest group. Limits are set on the amounts an individual committee, other than a political party committee or legislative campaign committee, may contribute to each candidate, depending upon the political office sought. For example, in the 1987 Special Election, an individual PAC could contribute no more than $500 to an assembly candidate. The limits * * * apply only to PACs and not to political party committees and legislative campaign committees (party-related committees). Total contributions by each PAC to a party-related committee are also limited to $6,000 per year. In addition to the limits on individual PAC contributions to party-related committees, no party-related committee can receive over $150,000 from all PACs in a biennium. These limits on

committee contributions to other committees do not apply to transfers between party-related committees.

Section 11.26(9)(a), Stats., however, places a restriction on party-related committees by limiting the total amount of money a candidate may accept from all committees combined. The cap in sec. 11.26(9)(a), is set at 65 percent of the total disbursement level in sec. 11.31, Stats., which is the schedule of maximum disbursement levels for various political offices if public financing is accepted. Furthermore, sec. 11.26(9)(b), limits the total amount of money a candidate may accept from all PACs combined to 45 percent of the disbursement level. Thus, while a candidate may accept up to 65 percent of the fixed disbursement level in sec. 11.31, from all committees, a candidate may accept only 45 percent of that amount from PACs.

To illustrate, during the November, 1987 special election campaign, the total disbursement level for a candidate for representative to the assembly was $17,250. The limit on contributions that an assembly candidate could receive and accept from all committees combined was $11,213 or 65 percent of $17,250. Of that total, no more than $7,763 or 45 percent of the total disbursement level, could be received and accepted by an assembly candidate from all PACs. Furthermore, each PAC was limited in the amount it could contribute to an assembly candidate to $500. Thus, candidates have the discretion to accept funds from these different committees in any amounts they choose, so long as they abide by the 65 percent limit for all committees and the 45 percent limit on PACs. For example, an assembly candidate could have accepted all of the $11,213 from party-related committees or could have accepted $7,763 (45 percent) from PACs and the remaining $3,450 (20 percent) from party-related committees. In any event 20 percent of the candidate's disbursement level is reserved for party-related committees.

The court agreed to subject the law to strict scrutiny, requiring a compelling state interest to justify the statute. It then found a compelling state interest, relying in large part on the findings of Governor Lucey's Study Committee on Political Finance (the "Committee"), chaired by Professor Adamany, and on the following data.

* * * The Committee found that there was an enormous growth in the campaign financing role played by PACs and an increasing dependence by candidates upon such money.

The Committee is concerned with the impact of such an increase in reliance on these [PAC] funds on the campaign finance system. The ability of political committees having similar interests to join together and make large contributions tends to undermine the effectiveness and integrity of the present system of limits on contributions. It believes that the imposition of a ceiling on aggregate contributions from such committees would restore the integrity and effectiveness of the existing and constitutionally sound limits on contributions by any single such political committee, person or other individual to a candidate. * * *

A dramatic increase in PAC contributions and influence on individual candidates has also taken place at the state level. In Wisconsin, PAC contributions to state candidates rose by over 50 percent in just four years. More significant, however, is the potential impact of narrow interest PAC money, which is channeled through party-related committees, on an individual candidate.

To illustrate the potential impact of large PAC contributions on individual candidates and, therefore, the need for sec. 11.26(9)(a), Stats., in order to prevent domination of an individual candidate by narrow interest PAC money, we need only look at some statistics from the State Elections Board. Respondents point out that, despite the aggregate limits on the amount of money all PACs may contribute to a party-related committee ($150,000), these committees are primarily funded with PAC money. During the 1983–84 period, 77 percent of contributions to legislative campaign committees came from PACs. Shea, Legislative Campaign Committees: The Wisconsin Experience, p. 6 (a research report prepared for Common Cause in Wisconsin, available at the Legislative Reference Bureau). In 1987–88, 70 percent of contributions to legislative campaign committees came from PACs. As Petitioners point out, these contributions to legislative campaign committees are within the aggregate limits set forth in sec. 11.26(8)(a), which limit the total amount of money party-related committees may receive from all PACs to $150,000. While the $150,000 aggregate limit may have some significance in the context of a particular committee, that aggregate limit has little significance in the context of an individual candidate's campaign. That is, if a legislative campaign committee received a total of $150,000 in contributions from PACs, the corrupting influence of that money on any one candidate is diminished only if there is a limit set on the amount an individual candidate may receive from that committee. Without a limit (such as in sec. 11.26(9)(a)), any one of these PAC-dominated [legislative campaign] committees could contribute an unlimited amount of this money to any individual candidate, thereby resulting in a "special interest" candidate. Without sec. 11.26(9)(a), the restrictions on the amount an individual committee may contribute to a candidate become meaningless. Instead of being limited to contributing $500 to an assembly candidate, for example, a PAC could contribute $6,000 to a legislative campaign committee, which in turn could give that $6,000 to the assembly candidate. Without limits on the party-related committee, it could pass $6,000 from each PAC to an individual candidate, thereby rendering the $500 PAC-to-candidate limit meaningless. We note that sec. 11.26(9)(a), is in fact the only limitation on a party-related committee's contributions to an individual candidate. By placing restrictions on the party-related committee's ability to contribute, the corrupting influence of large contributions to that committee, is diffused.

Having described campaign financing in these terms, the court (not surprisingly) held that there was a compelling state interest in placing an aggregate limit on the contributions that an individual candidate may receive from all committees. It stated that the

purpose of sec. 11.26(9)(a), Stats., along with other restrictions on contributions to individual candidates, is to limit the impact of huge special interest contributions on a candidate and to encourage a broad and diverse base of support in order to prevent either actual corruption or the appearance of corruption. * * * All of the contribution limits set on PACs and party-related committees are necessary in order to prevent individual candidates from becoming unduly dependent upon large narrow interest contributions.

The court also concluded that existing rules to prevent contributors from earmarking gifts for particular candidates were not sufficiently effective to eliminate the need for dollar caps on committee contributions to candidates. Moreover, nothing prevented narrow issue PACs from proliferating into several committees to circumvent ceilings on contributions by each PAC to a candidate. Finally, the court considered the argument that the statute restricted a committee's ability to make a symbolic expression of support by banning contributions once the cap is reached. The court disagreed on several grounds. First, the ban is not absolute because the candidate can return contributions once the cap is reached so that others may contribute. Second, PACs (but not party-related committees) can still express themselves by making independent expenditures for a candidate. Third, party-related committees have other ways to express themselves besides independent expenditures. There are no dollar limits on their contributions, unlike the $6,000 limit on PACs, except for the contribution cap; 20% of the cap is reserved for party-related committees; party-related committees can make unlimited expenditures on generic party-building activities, such as "Vote Republican"; and party-related committees can act as a conduit for individual contributions by bunching them together, in which case the individual rather than the committee is the contributor.

Does the reasoning in Gard suggest that, with the proper factual base, a statutory limit on so-called "independent" PAC or party expenditures *for* candidates (not just contributions *to* them) could be justified? What factual showing would have to be made? Do the NCPAC and Colorado Republican Federal Campaign Committee cases, striking down dollar limits on independent expenditures, foreclose that possibility?

CHAPTER 17

THE LEGISLATURE

In this Chapter we move from the electoral to the legislative process. Chapter 17.01 looks at procedural requirements. We expect adjudication to follow well established procedures, some of which are constitutionally required. There are also constitutional requirements for the passage of legislation, but they are less familiar because they apply primarily to state legislation and are found in state constitutions. The adoption of federal statutes typically follows from traditionally accepted practices, such as committee deliberations, but these are not required by the U.S. Constitution.

Chapter 17.02 considers substantive limits on legislation based on procedural concerns. Once again, state constitutions are the primary source of law—e.g., (1) prohibiting statutes including more than one subject and (2) prohibiting special legislation.

Chapter 17.03 analyzes federal constitutional requirements of legislative rationality and the standards they impose on the legislative process.

It is no accident that state constitutions are the primary source of law in this area. While theorists speculate today about the role of private economic interests in legislatures, state legislatures in the 19th Century confronted some very raw examples of private feeding at the public trough. These were not examples of compromises between private interests about public interest legislation, such as the accommodation of worker and employee interests in Workers Compensation. They were balder attempts at gaining private benefits, such as obtaining public lands at low cost.

Chapter 16 considered what normative political theories might underlie constitutional law decisions about the electoral process. This Chapter also searches for normative theories—now focused on the legislative process. As you read the cases, consider what normative theory of legislation underlies the decisions. (1) Do they encourage an open deliberative legislative process? (2) Do they prevent one interest group from obtaining an unfair political advantage? (3) How effective are the decisions in achieving these goals?

17.01 PROCEDURAL REQUIREMENTS

State constitutions often require bills to follow certain procedures, designed to improve the deliberative process—slowing it down, making sure that people are aware of what they are voting on. These procedures include: prohibiting changes in a bill's purpose between introduction and passage;

requiring that the bill be read three times; insisting on a time period between introduction and voting. In addition, bills must usually begin with an enacting clause, to indicate to legislators that they are voting on something meant to have the force of law.

a) RESOLUTIONS, BILLS, AND ENACTING CLAUSES

A bill is the normal vehicle for enacting legislation. A bill contains an enacting clause which indicates that everything following that clause is to be enacted into law. At the federal level, a statute specifies that

> the enacting clause of all Acts of Congress shall be in the following form: Be it enacted by the Senate and House of Representatives of the United States of America in Congress assembled, * * *. 1 U.S.C. § 101.

Before the enacting clause, there is an identifying number. S.1, for example, would be the number of the first bill in the Senate during that Congress. H.R. 1 would be the first House of Representatives bill. A new Congress is constituted every two years, meeting in two annual sessions. If a bill becomes law, a Congress and Public Law number will replace the bill number. For example, Pub.L. 98–403, 98th Cong., 2d Sess., means that the statute is the 403rd public law passed by the 98th Congress and that it passed in the second of the two yearly sessions which make up one term of Congress.

A title which indicates the purpose of the legislation also precedes the enacting clause—for example:

> An Act to amend the Internal Revenue Code of 1954 to encourage economic growth through reduction of the tax rates for individual taxpayers, reduction of capital cost recovery of investment in plant, equipment, and real property, and incentives for savings, and for other purposes.

The title can be fairly long. Sometimes a preamble explaining the law's purpose will also appear before the enacting clause. Everything that precedes the enacting clause is not (technically) enacted into law but is sometimes referred to as an aid to interpretation.

After the enacting clause comes the main body of the legislation, adopting the operative language. A short title might precede the operative language. For example, the above Act amending the Internal Revenue Code stated that "This Act may be referred to as the 'Economic Recovery Tax Act of 1981.'" Another optional section after the short title is a statement of legislative findings and purposes, similar to a preamble, to explain why the statute is necessary and (sometimes) to indicate the constitutional authority under which it is adopted. Like a preamble, statements of findings and purposes might not receive close attention from legislators and they may contain rhetorical excesses written by strong advocates of the legislation. Finally, there is the language with direct legislative impact—for example, authorizing the expenditure of money, imposing a tax, creating enforcement mechanisms, defining statutory terms. An effective date usually appears at the end of the statute.

Preambles and purpose clauses are not always drafted to explain legislative objectives. They may instead have a more limited procedural goal. Passage of legislation often depends on which legislative committee considers a bill and that, in turn, may depend in part on what a preamble or purpose clause states. For example, a bill investigating Army intelligence activity languished in the Armed Services Committee but was later reintroduced with a title and accompanying statement focusing on enforcement of constitutional rights, which resulted in consideration by the more sympathetic Judiciary Committee.[1]

At the federal level, *joint* resolutions go through the same procedure as bills and are used to adopt public laws. They are approved by both Houses of Congress and the President, except that they are designated as Joint Resolutions; e.g., H.J. Res. or S.J. Res., rather than H.R.1 or S.1, depending on the originating body. A *concurrent* resolution at the federal level is adopted by both Houses of Congress but is not submitted to the President for his signature. Concurrent resolutions often correct errors in bills adopted by both Houses before the bill is sent to the President for approval, or express the sense of Congress without enacting law. A concurrent resolution is designated H. Con. Res. or S. Con. Res., as appropriate. At the state level the terms joint and concurrent resolution are sometimes used interchangeably.

The U.S. Constitution specifies that "Every Resolution * * * to which Concurrence of the Senate and House of Representatives may be necessary * * * shall be presented to the President of the United States; and before the Same shall take effect, shall be approved by him." U.S. Const., Art. I, sec. 7, cl. 3. This provision has never been interpreted literally to apply to concurrent resolutions, but only to joint resolutions, which are intended to be public laws. S.Rep.No. 1335, 54th Cong., 2d Sess. (1897).

A *simple* resolution at the federal level is passed by only one House (H. Res. or S. Res.) and affects only the business of that House. The procedural rules of each House are adopted by simple resolutions. All resolutions except simple resolutions are published in the Statutes at Large volumes. Simple resolutions appear in the Congressional Record.

––––––––––––

What happens if a legislature tries to legislate by concurrent resolution? In Moran v. LaGuardia, 1 N.E.2d 961 (N.Y.1936), the court refused to allow the legislature to repeal a prior law with a concurrent resolution, stating:

A concurrent resolution of the Legislature is not effective to modify or repeal a statutory enactment. To repeal or modify a

––––––––––––

1. Baskir, Reflections on the Senate In-   618, 649 (1974).
vestigation of Army Surveillance, 49 Ind. L.J.

statute requires a legislative act of equal dignity and import. Nothing less than another statute will suffice. A concurrent resolution of the two Houses is not a statute. A concurrent resolution, unlike a statute, is binding only on the members and offices of the legislative body. It resembles a statute neither in its mode of passage nor in its consequences. The form of a bill is lacking, and readings are not required. It does not have to lie on the desks of members of the Legislature for three legislative days. N.Y.Const. art 3, § 15. But more important, its adoption is complete without the concurrent action of the Governor, or, lacking this, passage by a two-thirds vote of each House of the Legislature over his veto.

In State v. Knapp, 171 P. 639 (Kan.1918), however, the court dealt with something called a concurrent resolution, which had followed all the procedures of a bill, including signature by the Governor. The text, however, began with the statement: "Be it *resolved* by the House of Representatives of the state of Kansas," instead of "Be it *enacted* by the Legislature of the state of Kansas." The state Constitution required that legislation begin with an "enacting" clause. The court upheld the law. The dissent objected on the ground that legislators used the enacting clause as a warning that what was coming was meant to be a law. Concurrent resolutions, by contrast, were used for such things as paying compliments and issuing denunciations. The Knapp decision was overruled in State v. Kearns, 623 P.2d 507 (Kan.1981).

b) ENROLLED BILL DOCTRINE

The "enrolled bill" rule is a doctrine by which courts abstain from questioning the legislature's violation of constitutional rules about how legislation should be made. In effect, some constitutional provisions lack a judicial remedy and are left to the legislature to enforce.

A bill is "enrolled" when it is prepared after passage by designated legislative officials for signature by the Chief Executive. The enrolled bill rule states that the law is the bill as enrolled, regardless of undisclosed defects.

The following case abandons the enrolled bill rule. Is there any reason why contemporary courts might be less likely to apply the enrolled bill rule? Are they less tolerant of procedural violations, or more willing to enforce constitutional norms? Or, to the contrary, is there any reason why contemporary courts should be *more* likely to apply the enrolled bill rule—that is, more lax in enforcing rules about legislative procedure?[2]

D. & W. Auto Supply v. Dept. of Revenue
602 S.W.2d 420 (Ky.1980).

■ Stephens, J. * * *

[Editor—This case involved an appropriations bill which passed by a 48–43 majority. Under the state constitution, appropriations

---

2. At least some courts refuse to abandon the enrolled bill rule. See Roehl v. Public Utility District No. 1 of Chelan County, 261 P.2d 92 (Wash.1953)(sticking to the enrolled bill rule because the legislature is a coordinate branch of government).

bills could become law only by an absolute majority of the 100 members of the legislature. Lafferty, referred to in the opinion, is an earlier case adopting the enrolled bill rule.]

Kentucky is not alone in adherence to the enrolled bill doctrine. At least 19 of our sister states follow the rule which conclusively presumes the validity of a bill passed by the legislature and signed by the legislative offices.

Nowhere has the rule been adopted without reason, or as the result of judicial whim. There are four historical bases for the doctrine. (1) An enrolled bill was a "record" and, as such, was not subject to attack at common law. (2) Since the legislature is one of the three branches of government, the courts, being coequal, must indulge in every presumption that legislative acts are valid. (3) When the rule was originally formulated, record-keeping of the legislatures was so inadequate that a balancing of equities required that the final act, the enrolled bill, be given efficacy. (4) There were theories of convenience as expressed by the Kentucky court in Lafferty.

The rule is not unanimous in the several states, however, and it has not been without its critics. From an examination of cases and treatises, we can summarize the criticism as follows: (1) Artificial presumptions, especially conclusive ones, are not favored. (2) Such a rule frequently (as in the present case) produces results which do not accord with facts or constitutional provisions. (3) The rule is conducive to fraud, forgery, corruption and other wrongdoings. (4) Modern automatic and electronic record-keeping devices now used by legislatures remove one of the original reasons for the rule. (5) The rule disregards the primary obligation of the courts to seek the truth and to provide a remedy for a wrong committed by any branch of government.

In light of these considerations, we are convinced that the time has come to re-examine the enrolled bill doctrine. * * *

It is clear to us that the major premise of the Lafferty decision, the poor record-keeping of the legislature, has disappeared. Modern equipment and technology are the rule in record-keeping by our General Assembly. Tape recorders, electric typewriters, duplicating machines, recording equipment, printing presses, computers, electronic voting machines, and the like remove all doubts and fears as to the ability of the General Assembly to keep accurate and readily accessible records.

It is also apparent that the "convenience" rule is not appropriate in today's modern and developing judicial philosophy. The fact that the number and complexity of lawsuits may increase is not persuasive if one is mindful that the overriding purpose of our judicial system is to discover the truth and see that justice is done.

The existence of difficulties and complexities should not deter this pursuit and we reject any doctrine or presumption that so provides.

Lastly, we address the premise that the equality of the various branches of government requires that we shut our eyes to constitutional failings and other errors of our coparceners in government. We simply do not agree. Section 26 of the Kentucky Constitution provides that any law contrary to the Constitution is "void." The proper exercise of judicial authority requires us to recognize any law which is unconstitutional and to declare it void. Without belaboring the point, we believe that under section 228 of the Kentucky Constitution it is our obligation to "support * * * the Constitution of this Commonwealth." We are sworn to see that violations of the constitution—by any person, corporation, state agency or branch of government—are brought to light and corrected. To countenance an artificial rule of law that silences our voices when confronted with violations of our constitution is not acceptable to this court.

We believe that a more reasonable rule is the * * * "extrinsic evidence" rule. Other jurisdictions have embraced this rule, which we hereby adopt as the law of this case and future cases. Under this approach there is a prima facie presumption that an enrolled bill is valid, but such presumption may be overcome by clear, satisfactory and convincing evidence establishing that constitutional requirements have not been met.

We therefore overrule Lafferty v. Huffman and all other cases following the so-called enrolled bill doctrine, to the extent that there is no longer a conclusive presumption that an enrolled bill is valid.

COMMENTS

1. *"Threatening the legislature."* Illinois flirted with abandoning the enrolled bill rule in Geja's Cafe v. Metropolitan Pier and Exposition Authority, 606 N.E.2d 1212 (Ill.1992)(failure to comply with three readings requirements), stating:

While plaintiffs make a persuasive argument, we decline their invitation [to abandon the enrolled bill rule]. We do so because, for today at least, we feel that the doctrine of separation of powers is more compelling. However, we defer to the legislature hesitantly, because we do not wish to understate the importance of complying with the Constitution when passing bills. If the General Assembly continues its poor record of policing itself, we reserve the right to revisit this issue on another day to decide the continued propriety of ignoring this constitutional violation.

In People v. Dunigan, 650 N.E.2d 1026 (Ill.1995), however, the Illinois Supreme Court later adhered to the enrolled bill rule.

2.   *Tolerance of legislative lapses.* Courts which do not follow the enrolled bill rule are not necessarily intolerant of legislative lapses. In McClellan v. Stein, 201 N.W. 209 (Mich.1924), the court was unsympathetic to the enrolled bill rule in a case involving the constitutional requirement that the bill should be read three times before passage.

> The object of these requirements of the Constitution is to guard against hasty and impulsive legislation, by giving each member opportunity and time to familiarize himself with and maturely consider the wisdom of a proposed law, and also to give the public time and opportunity to know what legislation is proposed and being enacted by their lawmaking body. The manifest important purpose of requiring the Legislature to keep a journal is that the people whom they represent may be able to learn whether a published law has in truth been constitutionally enacted, and to have a permanent and reliable primary record evidencing its validity. * * *

> The Constitution in no uncertain terms directs the Legislature to keep a record of its proceedings. If such record does not show that the constitutional requirements have been observed in enactment of the laws of the country, what was its purpose and why was it required to be kept? * * * We are therefore constrained to hold the law invalid, which leaves all preceding laws upon that subject in force.

Having said this, however, the court was willing to waive enforcement of the requirement of the first two readings, as long as the third reading occurred:

> [I]n view of the customary legislative rule and practice of supplying each member with a printed copy at least five days before passage of any bill, this court has declined to hold invalid laws so passed where the journal showed the third reading was in full. The question was disposed of in Hart v. McElroy, 72 Mich. 446, 40 N.W. 750, in part as follows:

>> The legislative practice of reading the same twice by title, and only once at length, has been maintained too long in this state to be now overthrown by the courts. * * * The Constitution, in terms, does not direct that the reading shall be at length, and, while such reading might be the better practice, we cannot hold that it is imperatively required that it should be so read more than once. This act, as it passed, was read once in each house at length, as appears from the journals.

What is the point of rejecting the enrolled bill rule but then being lax about enforcing constitutionally required procedures? Does that, in effect, make compliance discretionary with the courts? Are there clear judicial standards for determining whether compliance is adequate? If not, does the court have too much power to decide which laws to uphold?

3.   *Proving legislative lapse.* When a court does *not* follow the enrolled bill rule, it must decide where to find evidence that the legislature has violated procedural requirements. Some states permit *all evidence* of procedural violations to be considered. Some states follow the *journal entry* rule, which looks only at the legislative journal to see if procedural requirements have been followed. The *modified journal entry* rule allows courts to refer only to the journal and then only to determine whether a procedure which the constitution requires to be recorded in the journal has been so recorded.[3]

4. *Reference to journal to uphold law.* In Wilmington Savings Fund Society v. Green, 288 A.2d 273 (Del.1972), state law required a two-thirds majority to pass a law. The enacting clause of the statute did not specify that the required majority was received and the issue was whether the court could consider Senate and House journals to prove that a two-thirds vote was received. Although the court normally followed the enrolled bill doctrine, it refused to do so in this case, stating:

> The most recent case [Ingersoll] involving the application of the doctrine, however, clearly required a conclusive presumption [that an enrolled bill was valid] and discussed the policy underlying its decision. Citizen reliance on the correctness of an enrolled bill, thus avoiding the need for "title searches" through journals and other records to verify the bills' contents, was suggested as an important reasons underlying the theory which required a conclusive presumption of validity. * * *

> * * * We think the undue burden feared in Ingersoll does not arise where one is alerted to a possible irregularity in the legislative process by a defect apparent on the statute's face. Such an error arguably leads one to the legislative journals in search of an explanation for the flaw or omission—a procedure not logically resulting from a reading of a statute valid on its face. In short, in cases where a statute is defective on its face, we feel that the Enrolled Bill Doctrine does not apply fully. Furthermore, we believe the application of the conclusive presumption which here would require that we presume the statute invalid would not serve to fulfill either the policy reasons suggested in Ingersoll or traditionally urged for the rule's existence.

c) NOTE ON STATE VS. FEDERAL LEGISLATURES

Most of the procedural rules about legislation in state constitutions were adopted in the 19th Century. State legislatures traditionally consisted of poorly paid part time legislators who lacked resources of their own to research the issues and draft statutes. Private lobbying groups were (and are) frequently the source of both information and drafting assistance. Private economic interests often dominated state legislatures and obtained legislation for private gain.

---

3. See, e.g., Hoover v. Board of County Com'rs., 482 N.E.2d 575 (Ohio 1985)(a bill must be read three times); Independent Community Bankers Ass'n. v. State, 346 N.W.2d 737 (S.D.1984)(bill must be read two times).

The federal constitution does not contain many procedural rules designed to limit legislative power. In earlier times, such limits were probably not considered necessary because the Congress was delegated power to enact laws on only certain subjects. Today, limits on federal legislative power have all but evaporated as a result of an expansive interpretation of the Commerce Clause and the power to Tax and Spend for the General Welfare. However, the contemporary federal legislative process has none of the institutional weaknesses that led to severe limits on state legislatures in an earlier era. Legislators are not badly paid, they work full time, and they receive a lot of expert support. There is an Office of Legislative Counsel in both Houses of Congress to draft legislation. Staff personnel provide research and drafting services to both committee members and individual legislators. The Congressional Research Service, General Accounting Office, Congressional Budget Office, Joint Committee on Taxation, and Joint Economic Committee also provide legislators with technical support. Private lobbyists still feed congressmen with information and drafts of bills, but legislators in opposition to the lobbyist can get expert help of their own. If there is a problem at the federal level, it may be that there is too much information and too many staff personnel. There are complaints that the overload of information *creates* more work and interferes with the legislator's primary duty to debate and deliberate intelligently.

The following excerpt provides an updated look at state legislatures.[4] It comments on improvements in the state legislative process. Would you expect improvement in the state legislative process to lead to more or fewer states adopting the enrolled bill rule?

Rosenthal, The State of State Legislatures

11 Hofstra L. Rev. 1185 (1983).

Probably the greatest change to have taken place in state legislatures has been the enhancement of legislative capacity, consisting mainly of time, organization, assistance, and information. Legislatures have considerably more time to perform their legislative functions today than earlier, and they have started to make more effective use of it. There is, first of all, the tremendous increase in time spent in session. In 1960 the legislatures of only eighteen states met annually, while those in thirty-two states met every two years rather than every year. Today, by contrast, forty-three legislatures—by formal or informal arrangement—meet every year and only seven are still on biennial schedules. Moreover, there is the time spent in special sessions. In the 1981–82 biennium, for instance, thirty-four legislatures met in special session, primarily because of the need to adopt decennial reapportionment plans and to cut state budgets or raise state taxes. Constitutions in more than half the states limit the length of regular sessions to a specified

4. A somewhat less rosy picture of state legislatures is painted in Citizens Conference on State Legislatures, The Sometime Governments (1971).

number of calendar or legislative days. In the rest, however, there are no constitutional limits, and the number of days spent in session has increased steadily during recent years. * * *

Moreover, one of the most significant advances by legislatures has been in the use of the interim period—the period between one legislative session and the next. It is during this period that legislatures, through their regular standing committees or special committees, engage in intensive study of public policy and conduct oversight of department and agency activities. The scheduling of interim activity varies. In Florida, for example, when the legislature is not actively in session, members spend three or four days one week each month meeting with their standing committees and engaging in interim work. Some other states also have regular schedules, with committees meeting at specified times; but most permit their interim committees to meet at times specified by the chairman and the members—usually once or twice a month. * * *

Today, also, legislatures are organized more effectively than before. The most important aspect of a legislature's organization is the standing committee system. Twenty years ago, although standing committees could be found in every legislative chamber, with the exceptions of a few committees and a few chambers, they were paper committees only. Little time was spent screening or working over bills, and committees met only on occasion. * * * Committees were far from being the focal point of the legislative process that they are today.

Since the 1960's, committee systems virtually everywhere have been overhauled. In some places overhaul has been accompanied by a reduction in the number of committees. In some places it has meant a reduction in the number of assignments for legislators, so that in at least a few chambers individuals serve only one committee. Along with restructuring has been the staffing of committees by professionals, who sometimes are hired by the leadership and/or committee chairman but who normally are assigned to the committee from a bipartisan central staff agency. Currently, all standing committees are staffed by professionals in about thirty-five states. In the remainder only the major committees and/or the fiscal committees are staffed separately; the rest are served by a pool of professionals.

Regardless of number, respective member assignments, and staffing patterns, there can be little doubt that committees today are truly the "workhorses" of the legislature and that "[t]he quality and quantity of work done in committees is vital to the legislature in appropriating funds, enacting or changing laws, and overseeing state agencies. Standing committees provide a division of labor, opportunities for members, a degree of specialization, a more intensive scrutiny of substantive matters, and a broader distribution of influence within the legislature. * * *"

More than any other single factor, the expansion of professional staffing has contributed to the enhancement of state legislative capacity. Although the professional staffing of legislatures began half a century ago, with legislative reference bureaus and legislative councils, it was not until the 1970's that substantial growth occurred in most places. It is estimated that there are now more than 16,000 full-time, year-round staff members—professional, administrative, clerical—working for legislatures. As many as 25,000 are on the payroll during the course of legislative sessions. The large majority of legislatures currently have anywhere from 50 to 300 professional employees. * * *

Staff members are of differing types and perform different tasks, including bill drafting, policy research, fiscal analysis, post audit or program evaluation, and sometimes even research on science and technology. They serve a variety of clients, including legislative leaders, party caucuses, rank-and-file members, and, as previously mentioned, standing committees. Because of the assistance rendered by many and multi-talented professionals, the legislative process works better than before; greater attention is devoted to both major and minor issues. Greater continuity of concern is possible. All in all, with professional staff the legislature can tackle problems it could not otherwise address.

d) APPROPRIATIONS BILLS

Courts clearly exercise discretion in deciding whether to take account of legislative procedural lapses—either by deciding whether to adopt the enrolled bill rule or, more particularly, by deciding which lapses are fatal. This discretion also allows the court to make distinctions among different kinds of statutes, squinting harder at those which are more subject to abuse. Pennsylvania has taken this route with appropriations statutes. In the following case, the court is much less tolerant of violations of constitutionally-mandated procedures when they crop up in the passage of appropriations legislation.

The case refers not only to procedural requirements, but also to the one-subject rule. The one-subject rule is discussed in detail in Chapter 17.02. It requires a bill to cover only one subject which must be expressed in the bill's title. General appropriations laws are, however, usually exempt from this requirement (legislatures often appropriate money for multiple purposes in one bill). The case is especially interesting because it interprets the constitution to exact a "procedural" price in exchange for exempting general appropriations laws from the one subject requirement.

Common Cause of Pennsylvania v. Commonwealth

668 A.2d 190 (Pa.Cmwlth.1995).

■ Opinion by Judge Colins: * * *

I. BACKGROUND

On July 19, 1995, petitioner Common Cause of Pennsylvania (Common Cause) filed a petition * * *. Counts 1 through 3 of the petition for review allege constitutional defects in the procedure by which the [General Appropriation Act] GAA was enacted * * *.

II. ALLEGED PROCEDURAL CONSTITUTIONAL VIOLATIONS

A. CONSTITUTIONAL PROVISIONS

Common Cause asserts, in the procedural counts, that the manner of enactment of the GAA violated Article III, sections 1, 2, 3, 4, and 11 of the Pennsylvania Constitution. These sections provide as follows:

> Section 1. No law shall be passed except by bill, and no bill shall be so altered or amended, on its passage through either House, as to change its original purpose.

> Section 2. No bill shall be considered unless referred to a committee, printed for the use of the members and returned therefrom.

> Section 3. No bill shall be passed containing more than one subject, which shall be clearly expressed in the title, except a general appropriation bill or a bill codifying or compiling the law or a part thereof.

> Section 4. Every bill shall be considered on three different days in each House. * * *

> Section 11. The general appropriation bill shall embrace nothing but appropriations for the executive, legislative and judicial departments of the Commonwealth, for the public debt and for public schools. All other appropriations shall be made by separate bills, each embracing but one subject.

B. ENACTMENT OF THE 1995–96 GAA

The 1995–96 GAA was enacted as House Bill No. 1169 (HB 1169). As demonstrated by the stipulated facts, HB 1169, as originally introduced, was not a general appropriation bill, but rather was entitled "AN ACT Making appropriations from a restricted revenue account within the General Fund and from Federal augmentation funds to the Pennsylvania Public Utility Commission." With minor amendments, all germane to the Public Utility Commission (PUC) appropriation, HB 1169 was passed by the House of Representatives on March 21, 1995, after being considered on three different days.

HB 1169 then was referred to the Senate Appropriations Committee, which made further amendments, involving only the amount of money appropriated to the PUC. This version of HB 1169 was considered on three different days in the Senate and was passed on

April 24, 1995. Because the version passed by the Senate differed from the House version, HB 1169 was returned to the House, and was referred to the House Rules Committee. It is at this juncture that the alleged unconstitutional procedures began.

The House Rules Committee again amended HB 1169, and reported the bill with amendments on June 13, 1995. The amendments made by the House Rules Committee, however, encompassed considerably more than the appropriation to the PUC. Instead, the House Rules Committee converted HB 1169 into the GAA by inserting the entire state budget into the bill, while retaining the appropriation to the PUC. The bill in this form was passed by the House on June 14, 1995 by a vote of 126–77. Later that same day, the Senate also passed the amended bill by a vote of 30–20.

C. ARGUMENTS

Common Cause asserts that HB 1169, as originally introduced, was not a general appropriation bill, but rather was a specific appropriation bill that was unconstitutionally amended during its enactment to become a general appropriation bill in violation of Article III, sections 3 and 11. Common Cause argues that this procedure also violates Article III, section 1, in that HB 1169 was amended or altered during its passage so as to change its original purpose.

Because HB 1169, after its substantial amendment in the House Rules Committee, was not subsequently referred to committee in either chamber, Common Cause argues that Article III, section 2 has been violated. Furthermore, because HB 1169 was not again considered on three different days after its amendment by the House Rules Committee, Common Cause asserts a violation of Article III, section 4. * * *

D. JUSTICIABILITY

Initially, we agree that the GAA, as with all legislative enactments, is entitled to a strong presumption of constitutionality. The courts have abstained from consideration of many perceived procedural irregularities under the enrolled bill doctrine, which, as explained in Kilgore v. Magee, 85 Pa. 401, 412 (1877), states that:

> When a law has been passed and approved and certified in due form, it is no part of the duty of the judiciary to go behind the law as duly certified to inquire into the observance of form in its passage * * *. The presumption in favor of regularity is essential to the peace and order of the state.

While the enrolled bill doctrine operates as an appropriate exercise of judicial restraint to avoid intrusion by the judiciary into the prerogatives of a co-equal branch of government, the Treasurer recognizes that such abstention is dependent upon the situation presented. As our Supreme Court stated in Consumer Party v. Commonwealth, 510 Pa. 158, 178, 507 A.2d 323, 333 (1986):

> While it is appropriate to give due deference to a co-equal branch of government as long as it is functioning within constitutional constraints, it would be a serious dereliction on our part to deliberately ignore a clear constitutional violation.

The court went on to state that:

> We agree with the Attorney General that we must not inquire into every allegation of procedural impropriety in the passage of legislation. However, where the facts are agreed upon and the question presented is whether or not a violation of a mandatory constitutional provision has occurred, it is not only appropriate to provide judicial intervention, and if warranted a judicial remedy, we are mandated to do no less. In this case where the facts are stipulated we agree with appellants that judicial scrutiny is required.

Accordingly, we shall proceed to analyze the procedure employed by the Legislature in the passage of the GAA to determine whether it complies with the mandates of Article III.

E.   CHANGE OF PURPOSE, ARTICLE III, SECTION 1

We begin with Article III, sections 1 and 3. Article III, section 3, the "single-subject" requirement, provides that no bill shall contain more than one subject, which shall be clearly expressed in the title of the bill. Notably, however, Article III, section 3 further provides an express exception for a general appropriation bill. Article III, section 1 provides that no bill shall be so altered or amended as to change its original purpose. Our Supreme Court has determined that the requirements of Article III, section 1 are mandatory. Consumer Party, 510 Pa. at 179, 507 A.2d at 334.

The Treasurer cites numerous cases in which the single-subject mandate of Article III, section 3 as well as Article III, section 1's prohibition on changing the purpose of a bill have been broadly construed. For example, in Consumer Party, the challenged bill, as originally introduced, dealt with changes in laws relating to counties of the third through eighth class. Similar to the GAA now at issue, the bill was approved by the Senate and further approved by the House with amendments, still bearing the same title. A Committee on Conference, however, recommended substantial amendments to the bill, adding voluminous provisions relating to the salaries and compensation of certain public officials. Both the House and the Senate adopted the Conference Committee bill on the day of its submission.

Our Supreme Court affirmed the Commonwealth Court's determination that the change did not violate Article III, section 1. Chief

Justice Nix, writing for a unanimous Court spoke of the need for legislative discretion, stating that:

> The practice of sending legislation to a conference committee is by its nature designed to reach a consensus. It is therefore to be expected that the legislation that emerges from such a process may materially differ from the bills sent to the Committee for consideration. To unduly restrict this process would inhibit the democratic process in its traditional method of reaching accord and would unnecessarily encumber the heart of the legislative process, which is to obtain a consensus. Here there was no change in the bill's purpose after it left the Committee and that object was clearly stated in the new title. Indeed, the parties stipulate that the purpose did not change after the bill left the Committee and while it was presented for final passage before both houses.

As noted by the Commonwealth Court:

> The Consumer Party does not allege that any members were deceived as to the contents of the bill, making them unable to vote on it with circumspection. There is no submission by the Consumer Party that any part of the measure was secret.

> The expansive interpretation urged by appellants would suggest that any material change in a piece of legislation during its passage would cause it to be constitutionally suspect. Such an interpretation would be incompatible with the traditional legislative process. We have said that the purpose sought to be achieved by Article III, section 1 was to put the members of the General Assembly and others interested on notice so that they may act with circumspection. Here the bill in final form, with a title that clearly stated its contents was presented to each house for its consideration and adoption. Under these circumstances there is no basis for sustaining a challenge under Article III, section 1.

The Treasurer argues that the process challenged in Consumer Party is virtually on all fours with the procedure that took place in the enactment of the 1995–96 GAA. Common Cause, while agreeing that the procedures employed are nearly identical, contends that the fact that the amendment involved the GAA as opposed to substantive legislation is a critical distinction. Indeed, neither the cases cited by the parties nor our research has revealed a case involving an Article III, section 1 or 3 challenge to a general appropriation act.

Article III, section 11 provides that a "general appropriation act shall embrace nothing but appropriations for the executive, legislative and judicial departments of the Commonwealth, for the public debt and for public schools." Section 11 further provides that "all other appropriations shall be made by separate bills, each embracing but one subject." It is clear that Article III, section 11 restricts the legislature's discretion in enacting a general appropriation act. * * *

Therefore, unlike non-appropriation bills, we have held that Article III, section 11 imposes certain unique strictures on the legislature when enacting a general appropriation act. In fact, our Supreme Court has recognized that the "evils attendant" in excluding general appropriation bills from the single subject requirement of Article III, section 3 are minimized by the restrictions imposed by Article III, section 11 upon the content of such bills. * * *

It is apparent, then, that Article III section 11 was intended to restrict the power of the legislature as a trade-off for the provision in Article III, section 3 which excludes a general appropriation bill from the single subject requirement. Because a general appropriation bill of necessity contains multiple subjects, the Article III, section 3 exclusion was a practical necessity. However, the potential for legislative abuse was limited by requiring that such bills contain only appropriations in the five areas [listed] by Article III, section 11.

Under this interpretation, we must agree with Common Cause that the metamorphosis of a bill originally containing only an appropriation from a restricted account in the general fund to the PUC into the GAA violated Article III, section 1. * * *

Put another way, the judiciary is normally loathe to substitute its judgment for that of the legislative branch under the guise of determining whether the constitutional "purpose" of a bill has changed during the course of its passage through the legislative process. The "purpose" of a general appropriation act, however, is constitutionally defined by Article III, section 11, and the legislature is bound by that definition. When, as here, the constitutional bounds are exceeded, the judiciary must grant appropriate relief.

F. ARTICLE III, SECTIONS 2 and 4

Because we conclude that the enactment of the GAA violated Article III, section 1, we must also agree that the legislature violated Article III, sections 2 and 4. After the insertion of the GAA into HB 1169, it has been stipulated that the bill was neither referred to committee as required by Article III, section 2, nor was it considered in each house on three separate days, as mandated by Article III, section 4. In Parker v. Department of Labor and Industry, 115 Pa. Commw. 93, 540 A.2d 313, 328 (Pa.Cmwlth.1988), we adopted the rule followed by other jurisdictions in relation to whether or not an amended bill need be referred to committee and considered on three separate days. We concluded that it did not, if the amendments are germane to, and do not wholly change, the general subject of the bill. Since we have already determined that the legislature in fact did materially alter or amend the original bill by the insertion of the GAA in violation of Article III, section 1, we also conclude that such procedure also violated Article III, sections 2 and 4.

G.   SINGLE SUBJECT—ARTICLE III, SECTION 3

Finally, we also agree that the GAA, as enacted, violates Article III, section 3. The appropriation to the PUC, which constituted the original version of HB 1169, remained in the final GAA. * * * [T]he fact that the moneys are "earmarked" for a specific purpose and are to be appropriated solely for that purpose leads us to conclude that the PUC appropriation is not properly part of the GAA, but rather one of "all other appropriations" which shall be made by separate bills, each embracing but one subject pursuant to Article III, section 11. * * *

H.   REMEDY

In summary, we hold that the enactment of the GAA violated Article III, sections 1, 2, 3, 4 and 11 of the Pennsylvania Constitution * * *.

We are aware that our decision casts doubt upon the long-standing legislative practice of amending a GAA into an unrelated bill used as a "vehicle." We are further aware that requiring strict adherence to the specific procedural provisions contained in Article III will no doubt make the process of legislating more time consuming. In our view, however, the framers of our constitution did not envision that a complete and detailed budget could simply be agreed upon by legislative leaders behind closed doors and inserted as a fait accompli into any bill that happened to be so positioned in the legislative process so as to serve for a "vehicle" for the budget. Instead, we believe that the framers intended that a bill bearing the title of a GAA should be introduced, referred to committee and considered on three different days in each chamber, and in the process not amended to change its original purpose, thus ensuring both opportunity for public scrutiny as well as full legislative participation.

e) FEDERAL LEGISLATION

Field v. Clark
143 U.S. 649 (1892).

▪ Mr. Justice Harlan delivered the opinion of the Court. * * *

[Editor—The act in question repealed the previous tariff act and assessed new tariff rates. A section of the bill as passed by the House and Senate was not in the bill authenticated by the signatures of the presiding officers of the houses of Congress and approved by the President.]

The argument, in behalf of the appellants, is, that a bill, signed by the Speaker of the House of Representatives and by the President of the Senate, presented to and approved by the President of the United States, and delivered by the latter to the Secretary of State, as an act passed by Congress, does not become a law of the United States if it had not in fact been passed by Congress. In view of the express requirements of the Constitution, the correctness of this general principle cannot be doubted. There is no authority in the presiding officers of the House of Representatives and the Senate to attest by their signatures, nor in the President to approve, nor in the Secretary of State to receive and cause to be published, as a legislative act, any bill not passed by Congress.

But this concession of the correctness of the general principle for which the appellants contend does not determine the precise question before the court; for it remains to inquire as to the nature of the evidence upon which a court may act when the issue is made as to whether a bill, originating in the House of Representatives or the Senate, and asserted to have become a law, was or was not passed by Congress. This question is now presented for the first time in this court. It has received, as its importance required that it should receive, the most deliberate consideration. We recognize, on one hand, the duty of this court, from the performance of which it may not shrink, to give full effect to the provisions of the Constitution relating to the enactment of laws that are to operate wherever the authority and jurisdiction of the United States extend. On the other hand, we cannot be unmindful of the consequences that must result if this court should feel obliged, in fidelity to the Constitution, to declare that an enrolled bill, on which depend public and private interests of vast magnitude, and which has been authenticated by the signatures of the presiding officers of the two houses of Congress, and by the approval of the President, and been deposited in the public archives, as an act of Congress, was not in fact passed by the House of Representatives and the Senate, and therefore did not become a law.

The clause of the Constitution upon which the appellants rest their contention that the act in question was never passed by Congress is the one declaring that "each house shall keep a journal of its proceedings, and from time to time publish the same, except such parts as may in their judgment require secrecy; and the yeas and nays of the members of either house on any question shall, at the desire of one-fifth of those present, be entered on the journal." Art. 1, sec. 5. It was assumed in argument that the object of this clause was to make the journal the best, if not conclusive, evidence upon the issue as to whether a bill was, in fact, passed by the two houses of Congress. But the words used do not require such interpretation. * * *

* * * [T]he contention is, that [an enrolled act] cannot be regarded as a law of the United States if the journal of either house fails to show that it passed in the precise form in which it was signed by the presiding officers of the two houses, and approved by the President. It is said that, under any other view, it becomes possible for the Speaker of the House of Representatives and the President of the Senate to impose upon the people as a law a bill that was never passed by Congress. But this possibility is too remote to be seriously considered in the present inquiry. It suggests a deliberate conspiracy to which the presiding officers, the committees on enrolled bills and the clerks of the two houses must necessarily be parties, all acting with a common purpose to defeat an expression of the popular will in the mode prescribed by the Constitution. Judicial action based upon such a suggestion, is forbidden by the respect due to a co-ordinate branch of the government. The evils that may result from the recognition of the principle that an enrolled act, in the custody of the Secretary of State, attested by the signatures of the presiding officers of the two houses of Congress, and the approval of the President, is conclusive evidence that it was passed by Congress, according to the forms of the Constitution, would be far less than those that would certainly result from a rule making the validity of Congressional enactments depend upon the manner in which the journals of the respective houses are kept by the subordinate officers charged with the duty of keeping them. * * *

We are of opinion, for the reasons stated, that it is not competent for the appellants to show, from the journals of either house, from the reports of committees, or from other documents printed by authority of Congress, that the enrolled bill designated "H. R. 9416," as finally passed, contained a section that does not appear in the enrolled act in the custody of the State Department. * * *

QUESTIONS AND COMMENTS

1. *Unpassed law?* Suppose a bill had not yet been adopted by both Houses of Congress but was mistakenly enrolled and sent to the President, who signed it. Is it law? See State v. Savings Bank of New London, 64 A. 5 (Conn. S.Ct. of Errors 1906)(a bill, which was not passed but was mistakenly sent to Governor and signed, is not a law).

2. *What is the federal rule?* Field v. Clark is usually cited as establishing the enrolled bill rule for federal legislation,[5] but that may overstate the holding of the case.

---

5. The enrolled bill rule has also been applied to Amendments to the U.S. Constitution. See United States v. Thomas, 788 F.2d 1250 (7th Cir.1986) (16th Amendment certified as having passed despite the fact that the language approved by the majority of States

First, the Court will decide whether a statute violated the constitutional requirement that "all bills for raising revenue shall originate in the House of Representatives but the Senate may propose or concur with amendments as on other bills." U.S. Const., Art. I, sec. 7, cl. 1. It will be hard to find a violation, however. See United States v. Munoz–Flores, 495 U.S. 385 (1990)(the Constitution's reference to revenue "raising" refers only to general financing, not to legislation creating and financing a specific government program).[6] Justice Scalia argued that Field v. Clark should have applied in Munoz–Flores, because "uncertainty and instability [   ] would result if every person were 'required to hunt through the journals of a legislature to determine whether a statute, properly certified by the speaker of the house and the president of the senate, is a statute or not.'" He concluded that a statute with the designation "H.J.Res." should be conclusively presumed to originate in the House. The majority dismissed this argument on the ground that Field v. Clark did not apply to a constitutionally mandated procedure.

Second, in Missouri Pacific Ry. Co. v. Kansas, 248 U.S. 276 (1919), the Court held that the constitutional requirement of a two-thirds vote to overturn a Presidential veto referred to two-thirds of the quorum required to vote on legislation (which is a majority of the entire body), not two-thirds of the membership of the House and Senate. The Court assumed without deciding that inquiry into legislative compliance with this constitutional requirement was permitted, even though the statute had been certified as having passed over the President's veto.

Third, in United States v. Ballin, 144 U.S. 1 (1892), the Court assumed without deciding that it could examine the congressional journal to determine whether a quorum was present to pass a law. The Constitution defines a quorum as a majority of membership. The Constitution also states that, at the request of ⅕th of those present, the Yeas and Nays shall be entered on the journal. This mandates a recorded vote in the journal when properly requested, and implicitly requires the journal's record of the vote to reveal a quorum. So understood, the case implemented the modified journal entry rule, which allows courts to consider whether procedures constitutionally required to be recorded in the legislative journal are so recorded.

Would it make sense for the court to enforce the Origination Clause but not quorum requirements? Which violation is more serious? Which violation is less likely to be controlled by the political process itself?

was not that passed by Congress; court upheld the amendment); Leser v. Garnett, 258 U.S. 130 (1922)(Field v. Clark precluded Court from questioning validity of state ratification of 19th Amendment on the ground that state constitutional procedures were violated). See also Coleman v. Miller, 307 U.S. 433 (1939) (state ratification must be contemporaneous, but Congress, acting through control of the certification process, makes final decision). Congress took no chances with the recent 27th Amendment, which prohibited compensation changes for Members of Congress until after the next election for the House of Representatives. Ratification occurred over a two hundred year period and Congress explicitly accepted the Archivist's certification in H. Con. Res. 320, 138 Cong.Rec. D605 (May 20, 1992), and S. Con. Res. 120, 138 Cong. Rec. S6948 (May 20, 1992).

6. Challenges based on the Origination Clause typically involve House bills whose language is completely replaced by the Senate. See, e.g., Texas Ass'n of Concerned Taxpayers, Inc. v. United States, 772 F.2d 163 (5th Cir.1985).

f) Enforcing Procedural Rules Not Required by the Constitution

The situation we have been discussing so far must be sharply distinguished from one in which the rules Congress violates are found in earlier statutes or resolutions, not the Constitution.[7] There is no doubt that Congress can disregard its own procedural rules concerning how it adopts statutes, assuming they are not constitutionally required. This is true even if the rules are contained in a prior statute, rather than in a resolution adopting rules at the beginning of the legislative session.[8]

The judicial instinct to enforce rules is hard to suppress, however, especially if the rules seem to implement some worthy policy, such as a meaningful deliberative process. State court decisions which selectively enforce state constitutional procedures betray a similar discretionary approach. In federal cases, the opportunity to enforce legislative rules indirectly sometimes arises when a court interprets a statute.

For example, complete agreement between House and Senate on the text of the same bill is necessary for passage. It is not sufficient that an H.-numbered and an S.-numbered bill contain the same text. When there is disagreement, the bill can go back and forth between the Houses (a process known as "amendments between the Houses"), until there is agreement. This is the most common procedure, except for major legislation. For major legislation, a House/Senate conference is usually convened to reconcile differences. The rules of each house prohibit the conference from agreeing to exceed the "scope of the differences" or deal in a matter not in disagreement. Thus, if the House and Senate versions appropriate $10 and $20 billion respectively, the conference cannot agree on a $25 billion figure. Moreover, if both versions agree on a $10 billion figure, the appropriation could not be deleted. Nor could a conference agree on a new appropriation not contained in either the House or Senate version.

The court's opportunity to enforce these rules indirectly through statutory interpretation might arise in the following circumstance. Suppose that a conference committee deletes language appearing in both House and Senate versions of a bill. The deletion exceeds the authority of the conference committee, if it removes a provision with substantive effect, because that goes beyond resolving differences between the House and Senate. Deletion of a provision could be interpreted, however, to mean that the law, even without the deleted language, reached the same result as the deleted material. The deleted language was simply superfluous, accomplishing what the statute already provided. Because deletion of language with substantive effect violates internal legislative rules, a court might tilt towards interpreting the statute as though the deleted language was superfluous to avoid the conclu-

---

7.   Article I, § 3, cl. 2 of the U.S. Constitution allows each House of Congress to adopt its own rules.

8.   Metzenbaum v. Federal Energy Regulatory Comm'n, 675 F.2d 1282 (D.C.Cir.1982).

But cf. Mulroy v. Block, 569 F.Supp. 256 (D.N.Y.1983) (court suggests that the enrolled bill rule applies to procedural rules not required by the constitution), affirmed, 736 F.2d 56 (2d Cir.1984).

sion that Congress violated its own rules. See, e.g., Union Electric Co. v. E.P.A., 427 U.S. 246, 262 (1976).

The trouble with this approach is that the legislature often purposely violates the letter or spirit of its procedural rule about the scope of differences in a conference, without undermining the deliberative process. There are several ways the rule can be circumvented, which include the following. First, in the House, there are two procedures to avoid the rules limiting what a conference can do. "Special rules," which are issued by the House Rules Committee and adopted by the House, may govern debate on a bill and prevent a representative from raising a point of order. A House vote to suspend the rules has a similar effect.

Second, the Senate also has ways around limits on conferees. Unanimous consent by Senators can prevent raising points of order. Or the Senate as a body can overrule a Chair's ruling on a point of order. Such overruling is often based on political considerations concerning the bill's substance, not an effort to judge the correctness of the procedural decision. This politicizing of rules is an accepted part of Senate practice.

Third, the conferees can report a matter beyond the scope of differences in "technical partial disagreement," thereby avoiding limits on what the conference can do. In that case, the items in disagreement are voted on separately as part of the "amendments between the Houses" procedure.

In addition to these procedural opportunities to go outside the scope of differences, a bill might pass despite violating the "scope of differences" rule because a point of order is not raised. There can be many reasons for this, all of which are consistent with Congress purposely violating its own rules. These include a sense of collegiality, or political agreement with the conference result.

A court cannot therefore assume that a bill has complied with procedural rules about the scope of differences in a conference. It will also have trouble interpreting the implications of what Congress has done. It is hard to know whether the rules were purposely violated and whether violation undermines a desirable deliberative process. In sum, indirect enforcement of legislative procedures through statutory interpretation is very tricky business because it is often difficult to unravel the political significance of procedural maneuvering.

17.02 SUBSTANTIVE LIMITS BASED ON PROCEDURAL CONCERNS

In addition to state constitutional rules about legislative procedure, state constitutions also routinely provide substantive limits on state legislation. The rationale for both the substantive and procedural rules is similar—preventing private interest legislation and encouraging a deliberative legislative process. These substantive rules include the "one-subject" rule, the prohibition of substantive law in an appropriations bill, and the requirements that a statute have a public purpose and not be special legislation. In the following cases you will often encounter lax enforcement of these limitations, sometimes to the point of the rules being almost a dead letter (analogous to the enrolled bill rule for procedural requirements). Why don't courts apply the rules rigorously?

a) "No Law Shall Embrace More Than One Subject Which Shall Be Stated in its Title"

A typical state constitutional provision prohibits a law from having more than one subject and requires the subject to be stated in its title. There are usually exceptions for general appropriations laws and, sometimes, for "codes." For example, Pennsylvania Constitution, Article III, sections 3 and 11 provide as follows:

> Section 3. No bill shall be passed containing more than one subject, which shall be clearly expressed in the title, except a general appropriation bill or a bill codifying or compiling the law or part thereof.

> Section 11. The general appropriation bill shall embrace nothing but appropriations for the executive, legislative and judicial departments of the Commonwealth, for the public debt and for public schools. All other appropriations shall be made by separate bills, each embracing but one subject.

i) RUUD, NO LAW SHALL EMBRACE MORE THAN ONE SUBJECT, 42 Minn.L.Rev. 389 (1958)

> A one-subject rule for laws has found its way, in one form or another, into the constitutions of forty-one of our states. * * *

> The primary and universally recognized purpose of the one-subject rule is to prevent log-rolling in the enactment of laws—the practice of several minorities combining their several proposals as different provisions of a single bill and thus consolidating their votes so that a majority is obtained for the omnibus bill where perhaps no single proposal of each minority could have obtained majority approval separately.

> Another stated purpose for the provision is to prevent "riders" from being attached to bills that are popular and so certain of adoption that the rider will secure adoption not on its own merits, but on the merits of the measure to which it is attached. This stratagem seems to be but a variation of log-rolling.

> Another purpose served by the one-subject rule is to facilitate orderly legislative procedure. By limiting each bill to a single subject, the issues presented by each bill can be better grasped and more intelligently discussed. * * *

> [Editor—Another reason for the "one subject" rule is to protect the Governor's veto. Governors usually can veto specific items, not just the entire bill, in an appropriations bill (called a "line item" veto,

discussed in Chapter 18), but usually cannot veto specific items in other laws. The one subject rule makes it harder to lump together unrelated items, which cannot be individually vetoed.]

The constitutional provision embodying the one-subject rule also contains an independent requirement that each bill contain a title and that that title express the subject or object of the bill. However, these requirements have independent operation; independent historical bases; and separate purposes. The constitutional title requirement finds its American historical basis in the notorious Yazoo Act of the Georgia legislature of January 7, 1795. Because it was felt that the act, making substantial grants to private persons, was smuggled through the legislature under an innocent and deceptive title, public demand arose for a constitutional requirement that each bill contain a title which adequately expresses the subject matter of the bill. [Editor—The title referred to "An act * * * for the payment of late state troops" and "declaring the right of this state to the unappropriated territory [   ] for the protection and support of the frontiers of this state, and for other purposes." Mayor and Aldermen of Savannah v. State, 4 Ga. 26, 38 (1848).] At the instance of General James Jackson, a provision to this effect was inserted in the Georgia constitution of 1798. The primary purpose of the title requirement is to prevent surprise and fraud upon the people and the legislature. If a title fails to express adequately the subject matter of the act or is misleading in its expression of the subject of the act, then a portion or all of the act is held invalid. While it is the purpose of the title requirement to prevent legislation by stealth, the one-subject rule also aids in the eradication of this practice and complements its sister requirement. Judicial expressions of the purpose of constitutional provisions * * * generally combine in one statement the purposes of the two requirements of these provisions. Thus, the isolation of the separate purposes of the two requirements of the single constitutional provision is often difficult. * * *

[Editor—There is still life in the "title" rule. See Lewis v. Captain's Quarters, Inc., 655 S.W.2d 26 (Ky.App.1983)(bill titled as dealing with Alcohol Beverage Control; bill invalid insofar as it included minimum wages for employees in the alcohol business).]

* * * [T]he issue of violation of the one-subject rule is squarely presented only where the body of the act contains two or more subjects and the act's title adequately expresses these subjects. In these cases, the courts generally hold the entire act void. The courts usually declare that they cannot choose between subjects in order to hold one valid and the remainder invalid; as they cannot determine which subject the legislature wished to be law, the courts find themselves unable to use the doctrine of severability and must declare the entire act invalid. Several cases, however, have suggested that the court should determine whether one of the subjects is of greater dignity or is the dominant subject so that it can be conclud-

ed that the legislature wished that subject to be law over the others or that the other subjects furnished no special inducement for the passage of the act. The portion of the act dealing with the dominant subject would thus be found valid and the other portions invalid.

It is very doubtful that the doctrine of severability is applicable to an act containing two or more subjects adequately expressed by its title. Where a portion of an act is unconstitutional, the doctrine of severability saves the constitutional portions and gives them effect, where to do so will carry out the legislative purpose. Unconstitutionality generally flows from lack of legislative power. The one-subject rule is not concerned with substantive legislative power. It is aimed at log-rolling. It is assumed, without inquiring into the particular facts, that the unrelated subjects were combined in one bill in order to convert several minorities into a majority. The one-subject rule declares that this perversion of majority rule will not be tolerated. The entire act is suspect and so it must all fall. If this is the rationale for the constitutional rule—and it certainly is the principal one stated by the courts, then it is manifestly unsound to employ severability to save the provisions dealing with one of the subjects. The necessary assumption that this will carry out the legislative purpose, assented to by a majority of the legislators, cannot be made.

[Editor—When there are two subjects one of which is expressed in the title, courts sometimes invoke the "title" rule first to reduce the statute to the one subject expressed in the title, which is then constitutional. This may be required by the state Constitution. See, e.g., Article IV, section 20, of the Oregon Constitution, which provides:

> Every Act shall embrace but one subject, and matters properly connected therewith, which subject shall be expressed in the title. But if any subject shall be embraced in an Act which shall not be expressed in the title, such Act shall be void only as to so much thereof as shall not be expressed in the title.

But some courts reach this result without specific constitutional authorization. Does this pay enough attention to the anti-logrolling, as opposed to the notice, policies which underlie the one-subject/title rule?]

There is one circumstance, however, in which it may be proper to find that an act deals with more than one subject and invalidate the provisions dealing with all but one of the subjects. It is said that one of the purposes of the one-subject rule is to prevent riders from being attached to popular bills so as to secure adoption of the rider not on its own merits but upon those of the remainder of the bill. The general appropriation act has, historically, presented a special temptation for the attachment of these riders. Where it is clear that a provision dealing with an unrelated subject had this tactical relationship to the rest of the act, it seems to be consistent with the rationale of the one-subject rule to hold only the rider invalid. The troublesome question, though, would seem to be one of determining when this situation exists. * * *

When the one-subject rule is examined from the purely pragmatic point of view of the advocate, the rule appears as a weak and undependable arrow in his quiver. The most remarkable fact that emerges from this investigation is that, while the rule has been invoked in hundreds of cases, in only a handful of cases have the courts held an act to embrace more than one subject. This seems to justify courthouse lore to the effect that an argument based on the one subject rule is often the argument of a desperate advocate who lacks a sufficiently sound and persuasive one. To the extent that this argument is considered the hallmark of a weak case, the advocate may consider it wise to use it very sparingly. * * *

[Editor—The author then comments on the fact that the one-subject rule does not prohibit logrolling. Majorities can still be constructed to logroll by passing two or more statutes. Still, the use of more than one bill might discourage logrolling, because there is always a risk that one bill will not pass, which may discourage forming logrolling coalitions.]

Many states apply the one subject rule in a very relaxed fashion. For example, in Dague v. Piper Aircraft Corp., 418 N.E.2d 207 (Ind.1981), the court dealt with product liability rules contained in a statute which also provided rules concerning the operation and jurisdiction of various Indiana courts. The Product Liability Act under consideration was passed as section twenty-eight of Public Law 141 of the Acts of 1978. Public Law 141 consisted of twenty-eight sections, and was entitled: "An Act to Amend I.C. 33 concerning courts and court officers and product liability." The first twenty-seven sections concerned the operation and jurisdiction of the various courts of Indiana.

In defense of a very liberal interpretation of the one subject requirement, the court adopted a "reasonableness" standard, stating:

For purposes of legislation, "subjects" are not absolute existences to be discovered by some sort of *a priori* reasoning, but are the result of classification for convenience of treatment and for greater effectiveness in obtaining the general purpose of the particular legislative act. And if, from the standpoint of legislative treatment, there is any reasonable basis for the grouping together in one "act" of various matters, this court cannot say that such matters constitute more than one subject. * * *

It is clear in the case before us that the legislature was aware of the contents of Public Law 141 when the act was passed. There is no basis for finding that some trick was employed to attach the Product Liability Act to the other provisions of the act, so that the public would be deceived by its location. In fact, the title of the act specifically mentions the subject matter of section twenty-eight. Plaintiff does not claim that these evils are present in Public Law 141 or, more particularly, in section twenty-eight of the act. The broad subject in the act is the construction, operation and jurisdiction of Indiana courts. Thus, it would not be clearly unreasonable to conclude that the Product Liability Act should fall under that heading. In view of these factors and the broad constructions we have given in the application of this constitutional provision, we cannot say that the grouping together of the subjects in this act was so unreasonable as to be repugnant to the Indiana Constitution.

Wasn't the court confusing the purposes of the one subject requirement (prevent logrolling) with the purposes of a requirement that the subject of the bill should be stated in the title (adequate notice)? (In fact, the Indiana Constitution does not even have a "title" provision; it only prohibits legislation with more than one subject.)

***

Does the following decision also confuse the "title" and "one subject" requirements? A Michigan statute, 1992 PA 270, made it a crime to engage in certain acts to assist suicide. The statute's title stated:

AN ACT to create the Michigan commission on death and dying; to prescribe its membership, powers, and duties; to provide for the development of legislative recommendations concerning certain issues related to death and dying; to prohibit certain acts pertaining to the assistance of suicide; to prescribe penalties; and to repeal certain parts of this act on a specific date.

As first introduced, the sole purpose of the bill was to create a commission to study death and dying. The title of the initial bill contained no reference to prohibiting assistance of suicide. After Dr. Kevorkian provided assistance to another suicide, the original bill was amended to contain a criminal prohibition on such assistance and the title was amended to read as above.

The issue was whether the statute violated the state constitution stating: "No law shall embrace more than one object, which shall be expressed in its title." (Notice that the Michigan Constitution requires that a law have only one "object," rather than "subject." It is unlikely that this textual difference would make a difference, but a court might say that it did.)

A lower court held that the statute violated the constitution, as follows:

Hobbins v. Attorney General

518 N.W.2d 487 (Mich.App.1994).

■ Fitzgerald, J. * * *

The Attorney General posits [that] both objectives [creating a study commission and creating a crime] are within the act's primary purpose of regulating assisted suicide. However, neither the original title of HB 4501 nor the title of 1992 PA 270 as enacted declare such a purpose. A fair reading of 1992 PA 270 reveals that, although encompassing a single "subject," the legislation has not one, but rather two, primary objectives. These objectives were originally the subjects of two distinct bills. One bill (HB 4501) encompassed the study of issues related to voluntary self-termination of life, with or without assistance, and another (SB 32) only encompassed the crime of criminal assistance to suicide. The suggestion that the amendment of HB 4501 to include the substantive provisions of SB 32 resulted in one primary purpose of "regulating assisted suicide" is unpersuasive in the absence of a comprehensive declaration of such a purpose in the title of the act.

Had the Legislature intended to codify or regulate the general "subject" of assisted suicide, it could have notified the public of this intention by declaring a single broad purpose and by joining the object contained in HB 4501 with the object contained in SB 32 together in one bill. This the Legislature did not do. This failure resulted in the body of the act containing two distinct objects. The fact that the title was amended to reflect the addition of section 7 does not cure the constitutional infirmity. The one-object provision may not be circumvented by creating a title that includes different legislative objects. We find, therefore, that 1992 PA 270 as enacted has two distinct objects which, although encompassing the same "subject," are not germane to each other, are directed toward different purposes and, when grouped together in one act, offend the constitutional one-object provision. * * *

Does this result make sense? How can drafting the title more broadly change the fact that the statute contains more than one object (or subject)? And, in any event, why would a broader title be a good thing? Isn't lack of specificity in a statute's title a good way to conceal what the legislature is doing?

The Michigan Supreme Court agreed that the lower court improperly confused the one-subject and title rules. In State of Michigan v. Kevorkian, 527 N.W.2d 714 (Mich.1994), the court stated:

The Court of Appeals majority suggested that the Legislature could have included the provisions regarding the commission and the criminal penalties in the same bill if it had used a more general title * * *.

This emphasis on the title is misplaced. It cannot be said that a statute has two objects if its title specifically describes its content, but only one if the title is general. Insofar as one of the purposes of the Title–Object Clause is to provide notice of the content of a bill to the Legislature and the public, a more specific title better achieves that purpose, particularly regarding a fairly short bill like the one in this case.

The court also stated that "the terms 'subject' and 'object' are largely equivalent for the purpose of analyzing these issues, and are often used interchangeably by the courts."

The following opinion by the Oregon Supreme Court in McIntire v. Forbes, 909 P.2d 846 (Or.1996)(en banc), also suggests that a statute's generally worded title might overcome the court's doubt about whether there is more than one subject. The court adopts the following approach:

(1) Examine the body of the act to determine whether (without regard to an examination of the title) the court can identify a unifying principle logically connecting all provisions in the act, such that it can be said that the act "embrace[s] but one subject."

(2) If the court has not identified a unifying principle logically connecting all provisions in the act, examine the title of the act with reference to the body of the act. In a one-subject challenge to the body of an act, the purpose of that examination is to determine whether the legislature nonetheless has identified, and expressed in the title, such a unifying principle logically connecting all provisions in the act, thereby demonstrating that the act, in fact, "embrace[s] but one subject."

Perhaps the point is that the court is willing to be educated as to the unifying single subject by the legislature's characterization, even if it is not at first apparent.

QUESTIONS

Do the following statutes violate the one subject rule?

1. A statute started as a tax bill in the State House of Representatives. The Senate passed the tax bill almost in tact but added an "ethics" provision dealing with the behavior of county council members. Porten Sullivan Corp. v. State, 568 A.2d 1111 (Md.1990).

2. The Uniform Commercial Code, including Article 2 on Sales, Article 3 on negotiable instruments, and Article 9 on secured transactions. Assume that the state constitution does *not* exempt codes from the one subject rule.

3. Legislation designed "to regulate political activity" created a political ethics commission as an autonomous entity within the department of state and provided for its composition, powers and duties; provided requirements for the establishment of candidate committees and provided for the filing of statements of organization and reporting of contributions and expenditures; set maximum limits on campaign expenditures; established a state campaign fund with a diversion of certain taxpayer-designated portions of income tax revenues to the fund for distribution to qualifying gubernatorial candidates;

proscribed political conflicts of interest; required designated official to file financial disclosures for themselves and members of their immediate families; required the registration and reporting of lobbying activities. In re Advisory Opinion on Constitutionality of 1975 Pa. 227, 240 N.W.2d 193 (Mich.1976).

ii) SEVERABILITY

Seals v. Henry Ford Hospital

333 N.W.2d 272 (Mich.App.1983).

■ Bronson, Presiding Judge.

The issue common to these appeals is the trial judge's holding that the Elliott–Larsen Civil Rights Act, M.C.L. § 37.2101 et seq.; M.S.A. § 3.548(101) et seq., is unconstitutional.

In each case, the trial judge held that the act violated the single-object clause of Const. 1963, art. 4, § 24. The arrest record and polygraph provisions of the act were found to be nongermane to its object. In each case, the trial judge held that provisions of a statute found to violate the single-object clause are not severable.

None of these cases involves the arrest record or polygraph provisions of the act. All of the parties concede, therefore, that we must first address appellants' contention that these provisions are severable. In holding that they are not, the trial judge in each case relied exclusively on the majority opinion in Advisory Opinion on Constitutionality of 1975 PA 227, 396 Mich. 123, 130–132, 240 N.W.2d 193 (1976), in which the Court stated:

"Severability is not available in instances challenging constitutionality on this ground. A prohibition against the passage of an act relating to different objects expressed in the title makes the whole act void." * * *

We cannot agree with the holdings of the courts below that a violation of the single-object clause always requires the invalidation of the statute in which it appears. Although some of the language used by the Supreme Court above is absolute, the reasoning used by the Court in the entire passage undermines an absolute rule. It would be unwise to impose a per se rule against severability on the basis of dicta, when such a rule is not supported by the well-known and long-accepted purposes underlying the constitutional provision. * * *

We find that the application of a per se rule against severability will not promote the purpose of the single-object clause when applied to amendments. Defendants here have asked us to hold that the Legislature's (at worst) inadvertence has resulted in the invalidation of a major piece of legislation. This case at least should raise the specter that minor nongermane amendments might be used to achieve the implicit repeal of other major statutory schemes.

Such a perverse result could only be achieved with the help of a judiciary which ignores the presumptive validity of legislative enactments; we refuse to play this role here.

The Elliott–Larsen Civil Rights Act was adopted in 1976 (1976 P.A. 453). The polygraph provisions were added by separate amendments in 1978 (1978 P.A. 610) and 1979 (1979 P.A. 91). Nothing else was contained in either amendatory act. From an examination of the statute alone, without reference to any extrinsic aids, we can determine that the 1976 act was passed without consideration of the amendments to be made in the future. To do so, we need not engage in the "idle speculation" condemned by the Supreme Court in Advisory Opinion, supra. Even a cursory examination of the original act, its amendments and their dates of enactment, leaves absolutely no room to doubt the Legislature's intent. We conclude that the polygraph provisions of the act are severable; we need not address the issue of their constitutional validity.

Appellants argue that the arrest record provisions of the act are also severable. We disagree. These provisions were in the act, as passed, in 1976. The act was amended by 1977 P.A. 162 to refer to these provisions in its title. Plaintiffs argue that the adoption of this amendment on its own merits indicates that it would have been enacted independent of the rest of the act. This argument, if accepted, would sustain only the arrest record provisions. The rest of the act was never passed without containing the arrest record provisions. We should not presume that the act would have passed in 1976 without those provisions. Since it is the validity of the remainder of the act which appellants wish to sustain, the severance argument cannot help them.

We have no reservations, however, about holding that the arrest record provisions of the act are germane to its object. * * *

We believe that the Legislature was correct in its determination that its goal of promoting the civil rights of disadvantaged persons could be advanced by prohibiting a prospective employer from examining an applicant's record of arrests without convictions. The federal courts have repeatedly sustained claims that the use of arrest records by prospective employers has a disproportionate adverse impact on the employment opportunities of black men. * * *

We conclude that the trial judges erred by ruling that the Elliott–Larsen Civil Rights Act is constitutionally invalid.

QUESTION

Are you completely sure that the polygraph provisions adopted in 1978 and 1979 were unrelated to the survival of the 1976 Act after either 1978 or

1979? Can you think of a set of facts which would relate the 1976 Act and later amendments?

b) SPECIAL VS. GENERAL LEGISLATION—HELPING PERSONS

In this section we consider state constitutional provisions aimed primarily at preventing legislation which benefits a relatively narrow group of people. We discuss (1) the rule that statutes must have a public purpose, and (2) doctrines prohibiting (a) "special legislation," (b) nonuniform and local laws, and (c) statutes which make "gifts."

These state constitutional doctrines, like the rules discouraging multi-subject logrolling, are intended to prevent distortion of the legislative process for the benefit of private interests. They are, however, more self-consciously aimed at statutes benefiting a limited group of people and are used to prevent that result even when there is no logrolling. They may also be concerned with fairness in financing the benefits, either through taxes imposed on the general public, or by helping one business competitor at the expense of another.

These doctrines have also been given a broader reading to promote conceptions of the appropriate role of government, beyond concerns with narrow private interest legislation and methods of financing. The cases may be concerned, for example, (1) with whether the government is interfering too much with how the private sector allocates resources, (2) with government ownership of production, (3) with fiscal soundness, (4) with general equal treatment concerns (not just narrow private interest legislation), (5) with the size of the government sector, and (6) with income distribution. As you read the following material, see which conceptions of the proper role of government are enforced. Is it legitimate for a court to adapt a doctrine aimed at discouraging private interest legislation to serve other goals?

i) PUBLIC PURPOSE

State legislation must be for a public purpose. This requirement is usually inferred as a limitation on state taxing power. Less often, it is inferred as a limit on legislative power. Common Cause v. State, 455 A.2d 1 n. 17 (Me.1983). Sometimes it is so basic to government that no explicit constitutional provision is cited for the requirement. In re Opinion of Justices, 154 A. 217 (N.H.1931).

A public purpose is required whenever the government harms a narrow group of people—for example, when private property is taken. Not only must the property owner be compensated, but the taking must be for a public purpose. That branch of the "public purpose" doctrine does not concern us here. We are interested in cases where the government is benefiting a relatively narrow group of people and the charge is made that this does not constitute a public purpose, whether or not a few people bear the burden.

1. *Defunct federal doctrines.* Most of the litigation about the use of legislative power for a public purpose arises under state constitutions and

our primary focus is therefore on state law. This is not surprising. States legislatures were most vulnerable to political pressure brought by private interests. You should, however, be aware of two now-defunct federal constitutional doctrines. In the 19th century, the federal constitution was sometimes applied to prohibit state government expenditures to help private industry on the ground that it was not a public purpose. In Citizens' Savings and Loan Association v. Topeka, 87 U.S. (20 Wall.) 655 (1874), the Court stated that this exercise of governmental "power can as readily be employed against one class of individuals and in favor of another, so as to ruin the one class and give unlimited wealth and prosperity to the other," and that "to lay with one hand the power of the government on the property of the citizen, and with the other to bestow it upon favored individuals to aid private enterprise and build up private fortunes, is none the less robbery because it is done under the forms of law and is called taxation." The opinion cited no specific constitutional authority for this conclusion, only that it is inherent in the concept of limited government. In later cases, however, the Citizens' Savings and Loan Association case was understood to be a statement about Illinois (that is, state) law, not to be a statement about federal constitutional law.[9]

A similar development occurred with the "public trust" doctrine, adopted in Illinois Central R. Co. v. Illinois, 146 U.S. 387 (1892). The State of Illinois sued to determine who owned rights to land in front of the water line of the City of Chicago on Lake Michigan. The case held that a State was not competent to deprive itself of ownership of submerged lands in the Chicago harbor by transferring the lands to a railroad. The prior transfer violated the State's obligation to hold the property in "public trust." The legal origin of this doctrine was obscure and in 1926 the Court held that it was a state law doctrine with no federal constitutional overtones. Appleby v. City of New York, 271 U.S. 364 (1926).

2. *Interpreting "public purpose"*. The public purpose requirement in state constitutions is usually interpreted today to permit government spending to help private industry where there is a public benefit, such as economic development and pollution control. Common Cause v. State, 455 A.2d 1 (Me.1983) is typical. The case held that bonding authority to help private developers of port facilities in Portland, Maine served a public purpose. The project was unique in its potential for extensive, long-term economic impact, and the potential for creating jobs. The court conceded that older cases required a direct benefit to the public, such as slum clearance, or production to which the public had access, such as rail transportation. Nonetheless, the court applied an evolving concept of public purpose to include indirect benefits to the public through economic development, despite the acknowledged risk that this encouraged legislation dominated by private interests. The court also refused to limit the taxing power to the same public purpose

9. Madisonville Traction Co. v. St. Bernard Mining Co., 196 U.S. 239, 260 (1905)(Holmes, J., dissenting). But see Carmichael v. Southern Coal & Coke Co., 301 U.S. 495, 515 (1937)(only a "plain departure from every public purpose which could reasonably be conceived" would violate the Fourteenth Amendment).

standard that applied when the government took private property for a public purpose in exercise of the eminent domain power.

The following case applies the public purpose doctrine to strike down government aid to private industry in the form of Industrial Revenue Bonds. These are bonds for which the government is only the nominal debtor; the creditor cannot collect from government funds. The loan is used to finance private industry, which is responsible for all debt and interest payments. Revenue bonds have usually been upheld as having a public purpose.[10]

QUESTIONS

Consider the following questions as you read the case:

1. Should the fact that the government's credit does not stand behind revenue bonds reduce or even eliminate the public purpose requirement?

2. What is the objectionable feature of the state law:

that the subsidy aids private enterprise which can (or should) make the expenditure on its own;

that only the timber industry benefits from the subsidy;

that only one business in the timber industry benefits;

that competitors of the beneficiary do not benefit?

Stanley v. Dept. of Conservation & Development

199 S.E.2d 641 (N.C.1973).

■ Sharp, Justice. * * *

[Editor—The petitioner alleged that Industrial Revenue Bonds violated Article V, sec. 2(1) of the State Constitution, requiring that taxes be spent only for a public purpose. In this case, the statute authorized such bonds to finance economic development and pollution control. The focus of the court's attention was a bond issued to help Albermarle Paper Co. construct pollution control facilities.]

Patently the Act was designed to enable industrial polluters to finance at the lowest interest rate obtainable, the pollution abatement and control facilities which the law is belatedly requiring of

---

10. See Kennecott Copper Corp. v. Town of Hurley, 507 P.2d 1074 (N.M.1973)(upholding revenue bonds to construct pollution control facilities); Marshall Field Co. v. Village of S. Barrington, 415 N.E.2d 1277 (Ill.App.1981)(upholding revenue bonds to encourage a retail store to move to a community, and refusing to inquire whether the bonds were really a factor in inducing the store to move); Wilson v. Board of County Commissioners, 327 A.2d 488 (Md.1974)(revenue bonds must satisfy public purpose requirement even though the state is not obligated; pollution control is a public purpose); Turner v. Woodruff, 689 S.W.2d 527 (Ark.1985)(revenue bonds for student loans, including out-of-state students, serve a public purpose).

them. As noted earlier, if it be held that the Authorities cannot constitutionally issue tax-free revenue bonds for that purpose the Act fails, for it has no other objective. * * *

Because the concept of public purpose must expand to meet the necessities of changed times and conditions, this Court has not attempted to confine public purpose by judicial definition but has "left each case to be determined by its own peculiar circumstances as from time to time it arises." Keeter v. Lake Lure, 264 N.C. at 264, 141 S.E.2d at 643. Our reports contain extensive philosophizing and many decisions on the subject. * * *

An activity cannot be for a public purpose unless it is properly the "business of government," and it is not a function of government either to engage in private business itself or to aid particular business ventures. It is only when private enterprise has demonstrated its inability or unwillingness to meet a public necessity that government is permitted to invade the private sector. [Thus] revenue bonds issued by two public housing agencies for the purpose of providing housing for low-income tenants were held to be for a public purpose. Governmental activity in that field was not an intrusion upon private enterprise, which had eschewed the field. Further, the primary benefits passed directly from the public agency to the public and not to a private intermediary.

Aid to a private concern by the use of public money or by tax-exempt revenue-bond financing is not justified by the incidental advantage to the public which results from the promotion and prosperity of private enterprises. * * *

Does the State serve a public purpose when it assists a private industry in financing the abatement and control of the pollution the industry creates? Beyond any doubt air and water pollution have become two of modern society's most urgent problems, and noise pollution is likewise a major modern evil. Such pollution knows no boundaries, for it cannot be contained in the area where it occurs. 61 Am.Jur.2d, Pollution Control, §§ 19–30, 53–60, 100 (1972). Regardless of where it occurs, the abatement and control of environmental pollution are immediately necessary to the public health, safety, and general welfare; and, in the exercise of the State's police power, the legislature has plenary authority to abate and control pollution of all kinds. * * *

It is stipulated that Albermarle's air and water pollution emissions are and have been in violation of the laws and regulations of the State; that it is and has been operating under temporary, conditional permits; and that if Albermarle is to continue its operation it must reduce its air and water emission to the legal limits. There is no finding that Albermarle is unable to provide the required facilities at its own expense and without outside assistance. Indeed, upon the argument of these cases, defendants conceded that

Albermarle is able to correct the pollution it creates and that construction of the necessary facilities is in progress.

It is recognized that the net result of revenue bond financing such as the Act authorizes "is that the municipality lends its tax-free bond issuing power to the private corporation or organization so that the interest on what would otherwise be a private bond issue becomes free of income tax and a low interest rate on borrowed money is obtained." 64 Am.Jur.2d, Public Securities and Obligations 109 (1972). Thus the Act would permit the Authorities to do indirectly for Albermarle that which the constitution forbids Albermarle to do for itself, that is, to issue tax-free revenue bonds to finance construction of an integral part of its plant. The cost of such construction is just one of the many expenses which a manufacturing enterprise must take into account in fixing the price of its product.

The conclusion is inescapable that Albermarle is the only direct beneficiary of the tax-exempt revenue bonds which the Halifax and Northampton Authorities propose to issue and that the benefit to the public is only incidental or secondary. It cannot be said that a benefit results to the public when the State assists a private industry in financing facilities the law requires the industry to construct without such aid. This is especially true when, as here, the industry is able to do its own financing.

Were the State to aid Albermarle by tax-free revenue bond financing, to that extent it would subsidize a particular pulp and paper mill which is in competition with other and unsubsidized pulp and paper mills, a violation of N.C.Const. art. V, § 2(1). * * * [Editor—"The power of taxation shall be exercised * * * for public purposes only * * *."] * * * [O]nce any industrial polluter receives the subsidy provided by tax-free revenue bond financing, all others—chemical producers, iron and steel mills, petroleum refineries, smelters, energy producing utilities, et cetera—would be equally entitled to the same subsidy. Incidentally, it can reasonably be anticipated that, were all their demands to be met, industrial revenue bonds would flood the bond market to the detriment of old fashioned municipal bonds backed by the full faith and credit of the municipality seeking to finance schools, sewerage disposal systems, fire equipment and other public ventures.

Pollution control facilities are single-purpose facilities useful only to the industry for which they would be acquired and to which they would be leased. If that industry were to become insolvent or, for any reason, default in its rental payments and guarantee of the bonds which an authority had issued to finance the facilities, those bonds would soon be in default. A few such defaults would certainly adversely affect the revenue-bond market and, almost certainly, also the credit rating of the county whose governing body had created the defaulting authority. These economic dangers demonstrate the wisdom of N.C. Const. art. V, § 2(1). * * *

Since the State may not directly aid a private industry by the exemption of its bonds for plant construction from taxation, it may not indirectly accomplish the same purpose by authorizing the creation of an authority to issue its tax-exempt revenue bonds for that same purpose. We hold, therefore, that the creation of the Halifax, Northampton, and Jones County Authorities for the purpose of financing pollution abatement and control facilities or industrial facilities for private industry by the issuance of the tax-exempt revenue bonds is not for a public purpose and that the Act which purports to authorize such financing violates N.C.Const. art. V, § 2(1).

3. *Government ownership*. The Stanley case suggests that the government cannot engage in business unless private business demonstrates an unwillingness to do so. Does this statement rule out government ownership of production when private industry is willing to act (that is, does it put a limit on socialism), or does it only limit public subsidies for private industry? In Madison Cablevision, Inc. v. City of Morganton, 386 S.E.2d 200 (N.C.1989), the government owned a cable TV service, even though private industry was willing to provide the service. The court permitted government ownership, stating that public utilities, hospitals, and waste disposal facilities (among others) would otherwise be illegal if "private industry willingness" were sufficient to make government ownership illegal.

4. *Private competitors*. Is it relevant that private competitors of a public enterprise might be hurt? See Ferch v. Housing Authority, 59 N.W.2d 849 (N.D.1953)(the fact that public housing for low income tenants would hurt someone who owned and rented private housing was irrelevant). See also Tennessee Electric Power v. T.V.A., 306 U.S. 118 (1939)(no right to be free from competition from government production and sale of electric power).

5. *Lending state credit*. The public purpose doctrine has been closely connected with state constitutional prohibitions on lending state credit to private persons. Some states treat the doctrines as coextensive, holding that lending credit for a public purpose is constitutional. Most states hold that the prohibition on lending credit is an additional constraint, apart from public purpose. There are many ways to get around this constraint, however. Direct state borrowing is often exempt, even if the money is then loaned to a private person, on the theory that only state guarantees of private borrowing have the seductive lure that the prohibition on lending credit was intended to prevent. Moreover, Industrial Revenue Bonds do not violate the rule against lending state credit because the state is not liable. See Common Cause v. State, 455 A.2d 1 (Me.1983).

6. *Wealth redistribution*. The public purpose doctrine was typically used to prevent public financing of private enterprise, but it was sometimes applied to limit government redistribution of wealth to the needy. This is not so surprising. You will recall from the Chapter 2 discussion of 19th Century legal history that judicial hostility to statutes built on but was not limited to

suspicion of special interest laws. This viewpoint manifested itself in some judicial applications of the requirement that statutes have a public purpose.

For example, in State ex rel. Walton v. Edmondson, 106 N.E. 41 (Ohio 1914), the court struck down aid to the needy blind as not serving a public purpose because the needy person's children or friend might be able to support them. In Auditor of Lucas County v. State ex rel. Boyles, 78 N.E. 955 (Ohio 1906), aid to the needy blind was prohibited because there was no way to draw a line short of equal distribution of wealth.

The approach in these Ohio cases would have erected barriers to the development of modern welfare legislation and many other states did not follow suit.[11] There may, however, still be some limits on public expenditures for social welfare. Would either of the following cases be decided differently today? Ferrie v. Sweeney, 72 N.E.2d 128 (Ohio Ct. Common Pleas 1946)(government operation of a free child care facility available to the middle class did not have a public purpose); Opinion of the Justices, 154 A. 217 (N.H.1931)(aid to the aged without regard to need did not serve a public purpose). What contemporary conception of public purpose might support the state expenditures in these cases?

Does the following revenue bond serve a public purpose? The loans would be used to finance housing for low and moderate income tenants. However, as many as 49% of the tenants could have unlimited income. Murphy v. Epes, 678 S.W.2d 352 (Ark.1984).

ii) SPECIAL LEGISLATION

The text of State constitutional provisions prohibiting "special legislation" varies. Some constitutions set forth a specific list of subjects on which special legislation is prohibited. Some states prohibit special laws whenever a general law exists on the subject or whenever general law could be adopted. Some states combine the prohibitions. For example, the Pennsylvania Constitution prohibits special legislation when general laws do or could exist on a subject and, in any event, prohibit special laws on a variety of subjects, including remission of fines, exemption of property from tax, regulation of labor, and creation of corporations. Pa. Const., Art. 3, § 32. These prohibitions might appear in the state bill of rights but are usually found in the constitutional rules dealing with legislative power. There are some old cases striking down legislation on the ground that it is "manifestly contrary to the first principles of civil liberty and natural justice" to favor a narrow group, without regard to any specific constitutional text. See, e.g., Holden v. James, 11 Mass. 396 (1814).[12]

---

11. See Opinion of the Justices, 154 A. 217 (N.H.1931)(aged needy with no more than $2,000 property can be aided); Denver R.G.R. Co. v. Grand County, 170 P. 74 (Utah 1917)(aid to mother with needy children permitted); Ferch v. Housing Authority, 59 N.W.2d 849 (N.D.1953)(low income housing allowed); City of Phoenix v. Superior Court of Maricopa County, 175 P.2d 811 (Ariz.1946)(temporary housing for returning war veterans permitted).

12. This case, although appealing to a principle that prohibits government favoritism, actually dealt with a statute suspending a statute of limitations for a plaintiff who was

Prohibitions of special legislation, whatever their source, were a reaction to the widespread practice of passing laws favoring those with special access to political power. For example, in 1872, only 43 out of 1113 laws passed by the Pennsylvania legislature were general laws. B. Abernathy, Constitutional Limitations on the Legislature 47 (1959). As stated in Cities Service Co. v. Governor, 431 A.2d 663 (Md.1981):

> [T]he object of the constitutional prohibition "was to prevent or restrict the passage of special, or what are more commonly called *private* Acts, for the relief of particular named parties, or providing for individual cases. In former times, as is well known and as the statute books disclose, Acts were frequently passed for the relief of named individuals, such as sureties upon official bonds, sheriffs, clerks, registers, collectors and other public officers, releasing them sometimes absolutely, and sometimes conditionally from their debts and obligations to the State."

You should not conclude, however, that special legislation was solely a 19th Century phenomenon, giving rise to the prohibition. Special legislation, such as granting corporate charters to specific people, had been the dominant style of legislation for a long time. The rejection of special legislation represented a shift in the underlying conception of government which left matters to individual choice operating under broad governmental statements of policy. Thus, during the 19th Century, general incorporation laws replaced special legislation creating corporations. A similar pattern developed with divorces. Statutes granting specific divorces were replaced by general statutes specifying the grounds for divorce. State constitutional rules prohibiting special legislation were consistent with this change in attitude towards government.

The prohibition of special legislation, like the public purpose requirement, prevents special treatment for some people. The public purpose requirement, however, is usually applied only to expenditures, but the special legislation prohibition applies to other kinds of legislation as well. For example, in Cities Service Co. v. Governor, 431 A.2d 663 (Md.1981), the court struck down an exemption from a state statute which prohibited oil producers from engaging in retail gas sales. The exemption permitted a subsidiary of an oil producer who had been selling gas before a certain date to continue to do so, but the exemption applied only to Montgomery Ward, a subsidiary of Mobil Oil.

The equal treatment implications of the rule prohibiting special legislation are sometimes carried very far. In Grace v. Howlett, 283 N.E.2d 474 (Ill.1972), the Illinois court dealt with a no-fault insurance statute which protected people injured by privately owned vehicles, but not government

then able to sue an administrator of an estate. The statute therefore involved special legisla- tion helping "Peter" and hurting "Paul."

owned vehicles. This limit on benefits violated the prohibition of special laws. Justice Schaeffer specifically rejected the argument that government benefit programs are allowed to go one step at a time, as follows:

> Unless the court is to abdicate its constitutional responsibility to determine whether a general law can be made applicable, the available scope for legislative experimentation with special legislation is limited, and this court cannot rule that the legislature is free to enact special legislation simply because "reform may take one step at a time."

But see Anderson v. Wagner, 402 N.E.2d 560 (Ill.1979), upholding legislation which applied a shorter statute of limitations period in medical malpractice because the legislation was a response to a well documented crisis.

Uniformity. State Constitutions often require that tax law be "uniform." This requirement serves the same purpose as prohibitions on special legislation—preventing favoritism—and may also prevent competitive advantage for a tax-favored business. The rules are usually interpreted, however, to permit special treatment when justified by public policy. For example, in Williams v. Mayor, 289 U.S. 36 (1933), a state law exempted a specific insolvent railroad from property tax. The Court held that the state's uniformity requirement was not violated if there was a relation, fairly discernible, between the good of the individual and the good of the community. In this case, the railroad line carried millions of passengers, and supplied the only railroad service between the capital of the state and its most populous city. The court did not require that other insolvent businesses be similarly favored. The public policy that made it wise in the judgment of the legislature to help this particular railroad and keep its business going was not necessarily applicable to other railroads.

At the federal level, the United States Constitution requires that duties, imposts and excise taxes (Art. I, sec. 8, cl. 1) and Naturalization and Bankruptcy laws (Art I, sec. 8, cl. 3) be uniform throughout the country. This has been interpreted to require geographical uniformity, not equal treatment of individuals. Even when different geographical areas receive different treatment, however, the statute might not violate the uniformity requirement, if there are sound public policy reasons for the distinction. In United States v. Ptasynski, 462 U.S. 74 (1983), for example, the Court upheld an exception from a tax on oil for "exempt Alaskan oil" because it was a unique class of oil that merited favorable treatment. Congress had before it ample evidence of the disproportionate costs and difficulties—the fragile ecology, the harsh environment, and the remote location—associated with extracting oil from this region. These were neutral factors justifying separate treatment. Moreover, a lot of Alaskan oil was still taxed and some offshore oil beyond the boundaries of any state was exempt.

However, in Railway Labor Executives' Ass'n. v. Gibbons, 455 U.S. 457 (1982), the Court struck down a statute providing protection for employees of only one regional bankrupt railroad. There were other railroads in bankruptcy at the time. The Court emphasized that the statute was in the nature of a private bill, favoring one railroad. The concurring opinion stressed that it was regional bias, not just the fact that the statute was like a private bill, that was offensive. Would a private bill without regional bias still violate the U.S. Constitution's uniformity requirements?

Local laws. Another state constitutional rule similar to the prohibition on special legislation prohibits "local" laws. The target of this rule is legislation helping one part of the state. The rule can be easily avoided if the problems of one part of the state are genuinely different and require special treatment, such as a city with the largest population. Occasionally, however, legislation will run afoul of the prohibition. In Christen v. County of Winnebago, 218 N.E.2d 103 (Ill.1966), the state statute authorized county boards to issue general obligation bonds for the construction, reconstruction or remodeling of courthouses without a referendum, which was usually required, if the county had a population between 200,000 and 1,000,000. The court noted that legislative classification based upon population is valid, if there is a reasonable relationship between the objectives sought to be accomplished by the law and the population differences fixed by the statute. The state argued, in defense of the statute, that conditions existed which justified the removal of the requirement of a referendum in the specified counties, while retaining it in all others. Specifically, the statute was supported on the ground that a particular intermediate population range bore a special relationship to the rate of population increase which, in turn, affected the degree of potential courthouse use. It was claimed that there was an accelerated growth factor in the specified counties, but the data did not support the claim. Some excluded counties had an even greater growth factor. Moreover, some included counties had no plans to build a new courthouse. The statute therefore violated the prohibition on "local" laws.

iii) GOVERNMENT "GIFTS"

In Fairfield v. Huntington, 205 P. 814 (Ariz.1922), the statute provided that Huntington should be paid for injuries arising out of and in the course of state highway employment resulting in permanent total disability. The State Constitution stated that "neither the state, or any county, * * * shall ever * * * make any donation or grant, by subsidy or otherwise, to any individual, association or corporation." The court stated:

> It is true that if the act were passed solely in the exercise of gratitude and charity and did nothing more than make a gratuitous present of the public funds, the payments authorized by it would be merely donations; but, since it is clear that it was the purpose of the Legislature in passing it to recognize a moral obligation then resting upon the state and founded upon equity and justice, regardless of the fact that the state was not liable therefor as a matter of law, the question presents itself whether an appropriation made out of considerations of this kind comes within the constitutional provision prohibiting donations. As used in section 7, article 9, this word has the meaning usually attached to it, which appears in Webster's International Dictionary as a "gift" or "that which is given as a present or gratuitously." The idea it conveys is that of help voluntari-

ly extended in obedience to a desire to do a charitable act where no duty except to aid a worthy cause demands it, there being no thought or intention on the part of the donor of discharging thereby either a legal or moral obligation due from him to the donee. It prevents the state from becoming a subscriber to a charitable object, either alone or with others; that is, from appropriating its funds to an individual, association, or corporation for a cause having no claim upon the state other than its admitted worthiness, but it does not prevent the recognition of moral obligations founded on justice and equity, even though the state is not liable therefor as a matter of law. Its effect is merely to prohibit the state from assuming the attitude of the person who says: "The cause is a good one, I will contribute to it," but it does not interfere with its taking the position of one who says of a just, though unenforceable obligation: "I owe that, here is your money in payment of it." * * *

It is difficult to define, with absolute accuracy, just what is included in the term "moral or equitable obligation," but in all those cases in which the appropriation of the public funds of the state has been upheld upon this ground the state has received some benefit as a state, or the claimant has suffered some direct injury "under circumstances where in fairness the state might be asked to respond—where something more than a mere gratuity was involved." * * *

* * * [I]t would be difficult to imagine a case calling more strongly for the discharge of [a duty to compensate] than that of an employee of the state seriously injured or killed in its service without fault on his part, but for whose injury or death the state, by reason of its Legislature's omission to enact a law to that effect, cannot be compelled to make any recompense whatsoever. Under the same circumstances an individual or corporation would be legally liable. Why then should the discharge by the state of such an obligation be regarded as a donation or as anything other than the payment of an honest debt, a thing that the State, as well as every good citizen, should do? * * *

It follows, therefore, that the appropriation in payment of appellee's claim does not constitute a donation, and, since the power of the Legislature to render the state liable for injuries of the character of appellee's is unquestioned, that chapter 169 does not violate section 7, article 9, of the Constitution.

In Cox v. State, 279 N.W. 482 (Neb.1938), however, the court held that a law creating liability for the tort of a state's agent committed against someone traveling on the highway violated the prohibition against special laws. It stated that "to uphold this legislation would require individuals, similarly situated, to knock at the door of the legislature and ask that an exception be made in their particular cases, while others, less fortunate, may not be able to obtain the relief sought."

Why doesn't the Arizona statute in Huntington, which helps the state employee injured on the job, require the employee "to knock at the door of the legislature?" Doesn't special legislation of this kind reduce the incentive to pass more general legislation? Would it really be difficult to enact a general law discharging the state's moral obligation to its employees?

———————

Cox and Huntington concern liability for injuries. Are state welfare laws invalidated by constitutional rules prohibiting donations or similar government expenditures? In Commonwealth v. Liveright, 161 A. 697 (Pa.1932), the court dealt with Art. 3, § 18, of the state Constitution, which provided:

> No appropriations, except for pensions or gratuities for military services, shall be made for charitable, educational or benevolent purposes, to any person or community, nor to any denominational or sectarian institution, corporation or association.

The case involved a statute providing poor relief for the unemployed without means of support. In a prior case the court had struck down a 1923 statute providing $1 a day to those seventy years or older even though they had $365 income during the year or $3,000 of assets. By the poverty standards of earlier times, these people were not "poor,"—that is, without means of support. The act was unconstitutional "as an effort to give the state's bounty to a definite class of persons who had means of support." The court stated, however, that

> [t]here is no direct prohibition against the use of state money to pay for the care and maintenance of indigent, infirm, and mentally defective persons, without ability or means to sustain themselves, and other charges of alike nature. They become direct charges on the body politic for its own preservation and protection. As such, in the light of an expense, they stand exactly in the same position as the preservation of law and order. To provide institutions, or to compensate such institutions for the care and maintenance of this class of persons, has for a long time been recognized as a governmental duty, and * * * such appropriations may well be sustained on this theory.

On that reasoning, the court upheld the appropriation for relief of the poor who had been driven into that situation through enforced unemployment. It referred to a "governmental duty" and a "pressing, governmental function," despite the volume of unemployed. "It is no answer to say that the people generally should take care of the situation; whether they are or are not able to do so does not relieve the state of its duty." The court did, however, state that those who refused work without good reason could not receive poor relief "even if the families of such persons suffer because the one responsible for their maintenance refuses to work."

This kind of litigation prompted Pennsylvania to protect its welfare statutes by constitutional amendment permitting payments "for pensions or gratuities for military service and to blind persons twenty-one years of age and upwards and for assistance to mothers having dependent children and to aged persons without adequate means of support." Pa. Const., Art. 3, § 29.

c) FEDERAL PRIVATE LEGISLATION

Congress has enacted private laws to benefit one or a few individuals since the country's beginning. The U.S. Constitution does not prohibit special legislation. Although Congress has limited legislative powers, the Constitution probably authorizes private legislation by the following provisions: the authority to pay debts (U.S. Constitution, Art. I, sec. 8) includes moral as well as legal debts; and the First Amendment guarantees the right "to petition the Government for a redress of grievances." Specific grants of legislative power, such as authority to adopt naturalization laws (U.S. Constitution, Art. I, sec. 8), also justify private legislation.

Private laws are nonetheless troublesome. They appear to be the exercise of a judicial power to decide the merits of individual cases. In recognition of their special status, they receive a "Private Law" designation and are published separately from Public Laws in the Statutes at Large volumes. In addition, Congress adopts procedures for private legislation which are more "judicial" than in the case of public laws, as the following excerpt explains.

Morehead, Private Bills and Private Laws: A Guide to the Legislative Process
Vol. 9, No. 3, The Serials Librarian 115 (1985).

* * * Succinctly put, "Private bills are lawmakers' admission of fallibility, for private bills generally are used to address some particular problem which public laws either created or overlooked." The framers of our constitution adopted this machinery from the British Parliament, but the venerable practice dates at least from Roman times. Based on the principle of equity, the private bill is intended to exempt "specific individuals, groups, or localities from the application of a [public] law that was not intended to apply to them."

Renowned House parliamentarian Asher C. Hinds, in his Precedents of the House of Representatives (1907), proposed this definition: "A private bill is a bill for the relief of one or several specified persons, corporations, institutions, etc., and is distinguished from a public bill, which relates to public matters and deals with individuals only by classes." And he added this caveat from the House Manual: "The line of distinction between public and private bills is so difficult to be defined in many cases that it must rest on the opinion of the Speaker and the details of the bill." Despite this difficulty, when a private bill becomes a private law it is routinely taken out of its chronological order and grouped in a separate section of the Statutes at Large.

At one time Title 44 of the United States Code provided an official definition of a private bill: "The term 'private bill' shall be construed to mean all bills for the relief of private parties, bills granting pensions, bills removing political disabilities, and bills for the survey of rivers and harbors." However, when the sections were renumbered (PL 90–620; 82 Stat. 1238, October 22, 1968), the definition was expunged. Nevertheless, the House and Senate have developed ample criteria for distinguishing between public and private measures.

In sum, the introduction of private legislation "seems premised on the belief that general laws cannot cover all situations equitably. It is felt that some way of coping with extraordinary circumstances is needed and that Congress has * * * the responsibility for creating 'equitable law' to cover such circumstances." * * *

* * * Individuals or institutions initiate the process [by which a private bill becomes a private law] directly or through an intermediary, such as an attorney or a lobbyist, by contacting the Representative or Senator in the appropriate jurisdiction. In almost all instances, the introduced measure is referred to the House or Senate Judiciary Committee, which in turn sends the bill to the relevant subcommittee or individual member. If the bill is reported favorably out of committee, it is placed on the Private Calendar in the House or on the Senate's Calendar of Business, where floor action takes place on certain predetermined days of the month.

Both chambers use a group of "objectors" to screen private bills for possible disapproval. House objectors review bills reported by the Judiciary Committee "before the bills are called up on the Calendar. If one of them objects during floor consideration, the bill is passed over for later consideration. If two or more object, the bill is recommitted. Often, this kills the bill." In the Senate this function is handled by the "Democratic and Republican Policy Committees. They screen private bills reported by the Committee on the Judiciary to ensure that objection will be voiced to bills that conflict with policy objectives."

The system of objectors, which has no counterpart in the passage of public legislation, is designed in part to prevent political pressures from overruling the merits of the measure. But if a private bill has strong support in the House or Senate Judiciary Committees, passage is likely.

Another way to de-politicize private laws is to refer a claim "involving determination of facts" to the United States Court of Federal Claims (previously called the U.S. Claims Court, and before that, the U.S. Court of Claims) for guidance. Usually the court's report is included in the report of the House or Senate Judiciary Committee supporting the private law.

The following examples of private bills are given by Morehead: a $50,000 award to an individual in settlement of a claim against the United States for his idea and development of a paper blanket; $9,940.31 as a gratuity for sacrifices made by a woman imprisoned for over eight years in Poland on espionage charges while employed in the U.S. Embassy; $50 to a person for loss of a typewriter left with a government attendant in the Government Publication Reading Room; $625,000 in satisfaction of a claim arising from administration of LSD to the individual without his knowledge by Army personnel as part of an Army drug testing program.

Congress may also enact the equivalent of private legislation in a public law. A recent example is the adoption of exemptions from the burdens imposed by the Tax Reform Act of 1986 for selected individuals. Other similarly situated individuals challenged these provisions in the following case. Despite serious misgivings, the court upheld the law. Does the court simply accept as inevitable the reality of the public choice model of lawmaking as favoring private interests, or does the court instead rely on positive features of the legislative process from a deliberative perspective?

Apache Bend Apartments, Ltd. v. United States

964 F.2d 1556 (5th Cir.1992).

■ Goldberg, Circuit Judge:

In an effort to dampen the impact of the radical changes brought about by the Tax Reform Act of 1986, Congress provided certain taxpayers exemptions from the new tax laws. In many instances, Congress designed these exemptions, known as "transition rules," to favor only one or a very few taxpayers. The method by which Congress selected those taxpayers that would enjoy the benefit of the transition rules is the subject of this lawsuit.

Plaintiffs are taxpayers that were not granted any relief under the transition rules. Claiming that they are similarly situated to those taxpayers to whom the transition rules do apply, they brought this lawsuit to challenge the constitutionality of the transition rules under the * * * equal protection component of the Due Process Clause of the United States Constitution. They argued that Congress exhibited favoritism to those taxpayers with strong congressional lobbies, and thus discriminated against those taxpayers, like plaintiffs, that "were not fortunate to have an ear in Congress." Plaintiffs * * * request[ed] the court [to] enjoin the enforcement of the transition rules so that no taxpayer could benefit from them. * * *

* * * A transition rule of general application, as opposed to these "rifle shot" transition rules, would have been far more costly in terms of tax revenue, albeit eminently fairer.

This method of doling out tax breaks raised more than a few eyebrows in Congress. Several members of Congress expressed concern that similarly situated taxpayers were not being treated equally. Others conceded their use of raw political power to obtain transition rules for favored constituents. Even in this court, the government acknowledges that "political considerations definitely played a significant role in the selection process * * * [and] the focus of the debate was on subjective factors [as opposed to objective factors]."

Plaintiffs contend that no rational basis exists for Congress' classification as between those taxpayers afforded relief under the transition rules and those who were not. They maintain that but for the fact that they did not have "the right people speaking for [them]" in Congress, they are similarly situated to those taxpayers who presently enjoy tax breaks accorded by the transition rules. In plaintiffs' view, this classification—providing benefits only to those taxpayers with connections in Congress and the political savvy to exploit those relationships—amounts to a violation of equal protection. * * *

* * * [T]he legislature has a legitimate governmental purpose in making exceptions from the general application of the Tax Reform Act to protect "substantial reliance interests." * * *

But that does not end our inquiry, for we must evaluate not only the purpose of the legislation, but the purpose and legitimacy of the classifications as well. To do that, we must first identify the classification. Plaintiffs take the position that:

> [w]hile assisting all taxpayers with general transition relief would be a valid and appropriate governmental purpose, the objective of providing selective exemptions to only a few, biased upon their access to politicians, is an illegitimate and prohibited objective * * *. There can never be a legitimate public purpose served by the arbitrary selection of a favored few from the general applicability of a taxing statute.

Plaintiffs would have us define the "favored" class as those taxpayers with "access to influential members of Congress."

Their argument is not without some foundation. * * * For example, the Chairman of the Senate Finance Committee confessed that

> [i]t would be foolish of me to say that, on occasion, politics did not enter those judgments. If the Speaker of the House requested the chairman of the Ways and Means Committee a transition rule, my hunch is that [he] would give it reasonably high priority in his thinking.

> If Senator Dole requested one of me, I would give it reasonably high priority in my thinking. 132 Cong.Rec. S 13,786 (daily ed. Sept. 26, 1986) (statement of Sen. Packwood). [Editor—Dole was Senate Majority Leader and Packwood was Chair of the Senate Finance Committee.] * * *

Moreover, it is quite plain that absent "access to the conference committee which enabled them to obtain a so-called transition rule so their activity could continue to be taxed under the old law," 132 Cong. Rec. s 13,810 (daily ed. Sept. 26, 1986)(statement of Sen. Levin), there was little, if any, chance that a taxpayer would receive transitional relief. As one Senator asked: "[W]hat about those who could not come to Washington and make their case? What about those who could not hire the lobbyists to present their appeal? Where is the fairness to them?"

While we recognize that politics played a part in determining to whom the transition rules would apply, we nevertheless believe that, in view of the great deference accorded by the Supreme Court to tax legislation, the classifications contain no constitutional malady. Congress sought to give transitional relief to those taxpayers who petitioned for relief and demonstrated, most convincingly, that they relied substantially on the old tax laws in making major investment decisions. Not every application for transitional relief was granted, however, political clout notwithstanding. Congressional staff members examined more than one thousand requests for rifle shot transition relief before recommending the inclusion of several hundred. As the Senate Finance Committee Chairman explained: * * * [We said] to the staff, "Here are the rules by which transitions are to be selected. Try to avoid violating those rules." * * * Congress could not grant every request for transitional relief, for that would have threatened the success of the Act, which, by design of the President and Congress, was to be revenue neutral, neither raising nor lowering the aggregate level of federal revenue collections.

* * * [A]s far as we can tell from the legislative history, Congress made their decisions based on the merits of the applications for transitional relief made to the Finance Committee. We realize that those taxpayers with political connections had better access to the Committee than others. Nevertheless, nothing suggests that Congress aimed to exclude others or that Congress designed the classifications with such a purpose in mind: "If the adverse impact on the disfavored class is an apparent aim of the legislature, its impartiality would be suspect. If, however, the adverse impact may reasonably be viewed as an acceptable cost of 'achieving a larger goal, an impartial lawmaker could rationally decide that that cost should be incurred.' " U.S. Railroad Retirement Bd. v. Fritz, 449 U.S. 166, 181 (1980)(Stevens, J., concurring in judgment).

Moreover, it appears that Plaintiffs never sought transitional relief from the Tax Reform Act. That places them in an especially difficult position to challenge the rifle shot rules. They did not ask for, and therefore did not receive, the congressional manna: Congress cannot be expected to search out on its own those taxpayers whose peculiar circumstances give them strong equitable arguments for special relief from general tax provisions; rather, such taxpayers must come to Congress. * * *

We hold that the classifications made by Congress were not arbitrary. It accorded transitional relief to those deserving taxpayers who applied for such relief and established most convincingly that they relied substantially on the old tax laws in making major investment decisions.

The Fifth Circuit reviewed the issue in Apache Bend in an en banc opinion and held that the taxpayers lacked standing. To what extent does the decision turn on the fact that the taxpayers did not apply to Congress for a tax break? Here are some of the majority and dissenting opinions.

Apache Bend Apartments, Ltd. v. United States

987 F.2d 1174 (5th Cir.1993).

■ E.   Grady Jolly, Circuit Judge: * * *

The Supreme Court has noted that "[t]he term 'standing' subsumes a blend of constitutional requirements and prudential considerations." To satisfy the requirements of Article III, the plaintiffs must have suffered an "injury in fact," caused by the challenged government conduct, which is likely to be redressed by the relief they seek. In addition to the constitutional requirements, the Court also has applied certain prudential principles in determining whether litigants have standing. Plaintiffs " 'generally must assert [their] own legal rights and interests,' " and their complaint must "fall within 'the zone of interests to be protected or regulated by the statute or constitutional guarantee in question.'" The Court further has stated that it will not adjudicate " 'abstract questions of wide public significance' which amount to 'generalized grievances,' pervasively shared and most appropriately addressed in the representative branches."

The prudential principle barring adjudication of "generalized grievances" is closely related to the constitutional requirement of personal "injury in fact," and the policies underlying both are similar. * * * Prudential principles are judicial rules of self-restraint, founded upon the recognition that the political branches of government are generally better suited to resolving disputes involving matters of broad public significance. * * *

We find it unnecessary to decide whether the plaintiffs have alleged a redressable injury sufficient to satisfy the requirements of Article III of the Constitution, because even if we assume that they have, it is clear that the prudential principles apply with particular force here, and preclude our adjudication of the constitutional issues raised by the plaintiffs.

The transition rules apply only to a very, very few taxpayers who requested such relief from Congress. The plaintiffs, claiming to lack political access, did not request such relief. In this lawsuit, they do not seek transition relief for themselves, but ask only that transition relief be denied to the favored taxpayers. Accordingly, they concede that any palpable injury they may suffer as the result of their own unabated tax liability cannot be redressed by the relief they seek. Therefore, "unequal treatment" is the only injury upon which the plaintiffs rely in support of their claim to standing. They contend that a decision in their favor will redress that injury, and give them the satisfaction of knowing that all taxpayers are being treated equally in accordance with the Constitution. [Editor—In a footnote, the court notes that the plaintiffs allege no competitive injury.]

The following prudential concerns convince us that the plaintiffs have not alleged an injury that is appropriate for judicial resolution.

First, it is important to note that the plaintiffs are not seeking to litigate their own tax liability, but the tax liability of taxpayers granted transition relief. The favored taxpayers, who are the only persons whose tax liability would be affected by the relief that the plaintiffs seek, are not before our court, and are thus unable to express their views. * * *

The injury of unequal treatment alleged by the plaintiffs is shared in substantially equal measure by a "disfavored class" that includes all taxpayers who did not receive transition relief. Like myriad taxpayers who did not request transition relief, the plaintiffs have not suffered any direct injury in the sense that they personally asked for and were denied a benefit granted to others. * * * [T]he Supreme Court has made it clear that "when the asserted harm is a 'generalized grievance' shared in substantially equal measure by all or a large class of citizens, that harm alone normally does not warrant exercise of jurisdiction." * * *

When the excess verbiage of the dissent has been shorn so that the essence of this case may be plainly seen, the plaintiffs only assert a generalized right to even-handed administration of tax laws, a right that they share with all taxpayers. This claim is exactly the sort of generalized grievance that, in our view, we should refrain from addressing under prudential standing principles. * * *

Because all taxpayers have an interest in the fair administration of the tax laws, the plaintiffs' stake in the outcome of this dispute is no greater than any other taxpayer's. * * *

The injury of inequality alleged by the plaintiffs essentially is nothing more than a claim to "an asserted right to have the Government act in accordance with law." The Supreme Court has repeatedly rejected standing under such circumstances. * * *

* * * Were we to accept the plaintiffs' claim of standing alone in this case, there would be no principled basis upon which to deny standing to any taxpayer wishing to challenge any of the countless provisions of the federal tax laws which treat some taxpayers more favorably than others. Such a broad expansion of standing would

enable the courts "to assume a position of authority over the governmental acts of another and co-equal department," and to become "virtually continuing monitors of the wisdom and soundness of Executive action." * * *

The plaintiffs' allegations of inequality resulting from the transition rules present " 'abstract questions of wide public significance' which amount to 'generalized grievances,' pervasively shared and most appropriately addressed in the representative branches."

Goldberg, Circuit Judge, with whom Politz, Chief Judge, Wiener, and DeMoss, Circuit Judges, join, dissenting: * * *

Contrary to the majority's statement that "[w]ere we to accept the plaintiffs' claim of standing in this case, there would be no principled basis upon which to deny standing to any taxpayer wishing to challenge any of the countless provisions of the federal tax laws which treat some taxpayers more favorably than others," the class of aggrieved taxpayers is limited to those taxpayers who are similarly situated to the taxpayers who are treated more favorably. Different treatment of taxpayers who are not similarly situated does not offend equal protection.

The class of taxpayers who are similarly situated to those taxpayers who received transitional relief may seem ad hoc. Undoubtedly, most equal protection challenges are brought by persons belonging to a class or group of persons which exists independently of the challenged law, as most laws distinguish between persons on the basis of some identifiable and general characteristic. By contrast, the transition rules, a truly unique legislative concoction, do not define their beneficiaries by general characteristics. For example, one of the transition rules exempts from the revised alternative minimum tax provision "corporations incorporated in Delaware on May 31, [1912]," a description which fits exactly one company. Since the transition rules offer tax relief to corporations which do not share any common attributes, except being burdened by the changes in the tax code and receiving the transitional tax relief, the aggrieved class of similarly situated taxpayers is necessarily a class artificially created by the transition rules themselves: Rules which benefit an ad hoc class necessarily injure an ad hoc class. Crucial to the prudential analysis at hand is that despite the ad hoc nature of the class of persons similarly situated to the beneficiaries of the transition rules, the class does not include all taxpayers, or even most taxpayers, and hence does not raise the prudential concerns over generalized grievances.

The class of aggrieved persons to which the Apache Bend plaintiffs belong is incomparably less general than the aggrieved classes in the precedents cited by the majority. * * * [T]he Apache Bend plaintiffs do not allege a grievance that is shared by all citizens, or by all taxpayers. * * *

The prudential limitations on standing are ultimately grounded in a concern about the role of courts in a democratic society. I firmly believe that the health of our constitutional democracy depends on the right of citizens to explicate in open court the purported irrationality of laws which they allege treat them unequally. "The very essence of civil liberty certainly consists in the right of every individual to claim the protection of the laws whenever he receives an injury." It is crucial that courts have the opportunity to determine whether the date of birth of a corporation is a rational criterion by which to distribute tax benefits. The majority opinion, in the name of prudence, eviscerates the Constitution's promise of equal protection to all Americans and diminishes the historic role of federal courts as protectors of individual rights.

17.03 LEGISLATIVE RATIONALITY—THE DELIBERATIVE MODEL

a) THE CONCEPT OF LEGISLATIVE RATIONALITY

1. *Will vs. reason*. Alexander Hamilton drew a distinction between legislative will and judicial rationality (he called it "judgment") in Federalist, #78. The image of legislation that pervades the Federalist Papers is one of legislative willfulness, to be checked by such techniques as bicameralism, executive veto, and judicial review. Legislative will, as depicted in these accounts, is not the harmonizing of diverse interests into an expression of public values, but the result of aggregating and accommodating partial and partisan interests. As noted in Chapter 4, recent commentary suggests that the Founders might have expected or at least hoped that a more general public good would emerge from a deliberative rather than willful legislative process.[13] One bit of evidence in this direction is the rejection in the first Congress of a right in state legislatures to issue binding instructions to Members of Congress as part of the First amendment, because such instructions would violate norms of legislative deliberation.[14] Nonetheless, legislative willfulness was certainly anticipated if not embraced from the outset.

The electoral process is supposed to legitimate the product of legislative will emerging from the legislative process, but there are some federal constitutional limits, which impose a higher standard on the legislature. If certain substantive interests are implicated (sometimes referred to as "fundamental interests" or "suspect classifications"), the legislative goals have to satisfy a "compelling" public interest standard, and the means chosen have to be the "least restrictive" to achieve the legislative goal.

In addition, the court will demand a high level of legislative rationality before those interests can be impaired. Legislative rationality in this context

---

13. Sunstein, Interest Groups in American Public Law, 38 Stan. L. Rev. 29 (1985)

14. See the discussion in Levmore, Precommitment Politics, 82 Va.L.Rev. 567, 591 & n.51 (1996).

consists of a clear legislative understanding and articulation of statutory ends and attention to the close fit between the statutory means chosen and the ends sought. We refer to this conception of rationality as the deliberative model of the legislative process. We are interested in this section in the level of legislative rationality required even when no fundamental interests or suspect classifications are involved.

2. *Justice Stevens*. Justice Stevens, who is probably more concerned with this issue than any other Supreme Court Justice, appeals to the Due Process Clause to enforce the deliberative model. He invokes that Clause to condemn a statute for failure to meet deliberative standards in his dissent in Fullilove v. Klutznick, 448 U.S. 448 (1980). In this case, the Court dealt with a federal statutory requirement that at least 10% of federal funds granted for local public works projects must be used by the state or local grantee to make purchases from minority owned businesses. "Minority" was defined as citizens who are "Negroes, Spanish-speaking, Orientals, Indians, Eskimos, and Aleuts." Rather than strike down the statute because of the substantive consequences of a racial quota, he embraced a requirement of legislative deliberation, as follows:

> A judge's opinion that a statute reflects a profoundly unwise policy determination is an insufficient reason for concluding that it is unconstitutional. * * * But the exercise of [legislative] powers is subject to the constraints imposed by the Due Process Clause of the Fifth Amendment. That Clause has both substantive and procedural components; it performs the office of both the Due Process and Equal Protection Clauses of the Fourteenth Amendment in requiring that the federal sovereign act impartially.

> * * * I am not convinced that the Clause contains an absolute prohibition against any statutory classification based on race. I am nonetheless persuaded that it does impose a special obligation to scrutinize any governmental decisionmaking process that draws nationwide distinctions between citizens on the basis of their race and incidentally also discriminates against noncitizens in the preferred racial classes. For just as procedural safeguards are necessary to guarantee impartial decisionmaking in the judicial process, so can they play a vital part in preserving the impartial character of the legislative process.

> In both its substantive and procedural aspects this Act is markedly different from the normal product of the legislative decisionmaking process. The very fact that Congress for the first time in the Nation's history has created a broad legislative classification for entitlement to benefits based solely on racial characteristics identifies a dramatic difference between this Act and the thousands of statutes that preceded it. This dramatic point of departure is not even mentioned in the statement of purpose of the Act or in the Reports of either the House or the Senate Committee that processed the legislation, and was not the subject of any testimony or inquiry in any legislative hearing on the bill that was enacted. It is

true that there was a brief discussion on the floor of the House as well as in the Senate on two different days, but only a handful of legislators spoke and there was virtually no debate. * * *

Although it is traditional for judges to accord the same presumption of regularity to the legislative process no matter how obvious it may be that a busy Congress has acted precipitately, I see no reason why the character of their procedures may not be considered relevant to the decision whether the legislative product has caused a deprivation of liberty or property without due process of law. Whenever Congress creates a classification that would be subject to strict scrutiny under the Equal Protection Clause of the Fourteenth Amendment if it had been fashioned by a state legislature, it seems to me that judicial review should include a consideration of the procedural character of the decisionmaking process. * * *

[R]ather than take the substantive position [that racial classifications are unconstitutional], I would hold this statute unconstitutional on a narrower ground. It cannot fairly be characterized as a "narrowly tailored" racial classification because it simply raises too many serious questions that Congress failed to answer or even to address in a responsible way. The risk that habitual attitudes toward classes of persons, rather than analysis of the relevant characteristics of the class, will serve as a basis for a legislative classification is present when benefits are distributed as well as when burdens are imposed. In the past, traditional attitudes too often provided the only explanation for discrimination against women, aliens, illegitimates, and black citizens. Today there is a danger that awareness of past injustice will lead to automatic acceptance of new classifications that are not in fact justified by attributes characteristic of the class as a whole.

When Congress creates a special preference, or a special disability, for a class of persons, it should identify the characteristic that justifies the special treatment. When the classification is defined in racial terms, I believe that such particular identification is imperative. [Editor—Justice Stevens goes on to find that Congress failed to "demonstrate that its unique statutory preference [was] justified by a relevant characteristic shared by members of the preferred class."]

See also Delaware Tribal Business Comm. v. Weeks, 430 U.S. 73 (1977) (Stevens, J. dissenting)(federal statute violated the Due Process Clause of the 5th Amendment when an unintentional exclusion of Indians was a "malfunction of the legislative process rather than a deliberative choice by Congress," resulting from a "legislative accident, perhaps caused by nothing more than the unfortunate fact that Congress is too busy to do all of its work as carefully as it should.")

The customary view of constitutional law is that a high standard of legislative rationality is *not* required unless there is a special concern with how people are treated because the statute impinges on a "suspect classification" or "fundamental interest." Stevens' opinion in Fullilove is more or less in that tradition. Even though the statute benefited rather than hurt minorities, his concern with racial stereotyping was palpable. Similarly, his objection to a "legislative accident" in the Delaware Tribe case protected American Indians, to whom the government had a "unique obligation." This customary view of constitutional law needs reexamining, and a Legislation course, with its focus on legislative process, is a good place to do it. Rather than duplicating the analysis and material you encounter in a constitutional law course, we will look at hints that there might be a meaningful requirement of legislative rationality even when suspect classifications and fundamental interests are not involved. In other words, does the deliberative model of the legislative process have some independent claim to judicial enforcement, or is deliberation something to which the legislature must aspire without a nudge from the courts?

3. *Administrative law*. Anyone who has studied how courts review administrative agency decisions will recognize that the concern with deliberation and rational decisionmaking pervades administrative law. You may have observed a "common law" of agency process, imposing standards of rational decisionmaking beyond those required by the Constitution or governing statutes. Administrators, however, are less subject to electoral checks than legislators and, for that reason, are more subject to rationality requirements than legislators.

The difference between the level of rationality required at the legislative and administrative levels is noted in Bowen v. American Hospital Ass'n, 476 U.S. 610 (1986):

> It is an axiom of administrative law that an agency's explanation of the basis for its decision must include "a 'rational connection between the facts found and the choice made.'" Agency deference has not come so far that we will uphold regulations whenever it is possible to "conceive a basis" for administrative action. To the contrary, the "presumption of regularity afforded an agency in fulfilling its statutory mandate," is not equivalent to the "minimum rationality a statute must bear in order to withstand analysis under the Due Process Clause." Thus, the mere fact that there is "some rational basis within the knowledge and experience of the [regulators]," under which they "might have concluded" that the regulation was necessary to discharge their statutorily-authorized mission, will not suffice to validate agency decisionmaking. Our recognition of Congress' need to vest administrative agencies with ample power to assist in the difficult task of governing a vast and complex industrial Nation carries with it the correlative responsibility of the agency to explain the rationale and factual basis for its decision, even though we show respect for the agency's judgment in both.

4. "*Some kind of hearing*". Deliberative rationality is also encouraged in the adjudicative and administrative process by legal requirements for "some kind of hearing."[15] A hearing requirement makes good sense in the adjudicative

---

15. Friendly, "Some Kind of Hearing,"
123 U. Pa. L. Rev. 1267 (1975).

and administrative setting when the issue is applying a rule to an identifiable group of people. It is useful for educating decisionmakers about the ends they are pursuing and what enforcing those ends through particular means will entail, as well as giving people a sense that they have not been treated arbitrarily. There is, however, no constitutional or statutory requirement for public participation in the legislative process. See, e.g., Minnesota State Board for Community Colleges v. Knight, 465 U.S. 271 (1984)("The Constitution does not grant to members of the public generally a right to be heard by public bodies making decisions of policy.") We must trust the representative process to provide adequate public participation.

Does a legislative rationality requirement nonetheless give an indirect nudge in the direction of "some kind of legislative hearing"? In Fullilove, supra, for example, Justice Stevens referred not only to the legislature's failure to explain its quota decision in committee reports (an explanation would be one indicator of a deliberative process), but also to the absence of testimony or inquiry at legislative hearings and of floor debate about quotas (that is, the absence of evidence of some kind of hearing). Perhaps evidence that some kind of hearing occurred could compensate for failure to demonstrate a reasoned deliberative process.

b) Mindless Borrowing of Legislative Text

The Supreme Court case that comes closest to adopting a constitutional requirement of legislative rationality, outside of the "suspect classification" and "fundamental interest" framework, is Schweiker v. Wilson, 450 U.S. 221 (1981). As you will see in the following opinion, even the majority disputes the dissent's criticism that the legislative process was more or less mindless, implying that some standard of rational deliberation must be met. Why does the dissent think the statute lacks rationality and how might the legislature have overcome the dissent's objection? Does the majority respond adequately or does it miss the point? Notice also who was disadvantaged by the legislature in this case. Was something like a suspect class or fundamental interest involved?

Schweiker v. Wilson

450 U.S. 221 (1981).

■ Justice Blackmun delivered the opinion of the Court.

The issue in this case is whether Congress constitutionally may decline to grant Supplemental Security Income benefits to a class of otherwise eligible individuals who are excluded because they are aged 21 through 64 and are institutionalized in public mental institutions that do not receive Medicaid funds for their care. * * *

In October 1972, Congress amended the Social Security Act (Act) to create the federal Supplemental Security Income (SSI) program, effective January 1, 1974. 86 Stat. 1465, 42 U.S.C. § 1381 et seq. "This program was intended [t]o assist those who cannot work because of age, blindness, or disability," S. Rep. No. 92–1230, p. 4 (1972), by "set[ting] a Federal guaranteed minimum income level for aged, blind, and disabled persons," id., at 12.

The SSI program provides a subsistence allowance, under federal standards, to the Nation's needy aged, blind, and disabled. Included within the category of "disabled" under the program are all those "unable to engage in any substantial gainful activity by reason of any medically determinable physical or mental impairment which can be expected to result in death or which has lasted or can be expected to last for a continuous period of not less than twelve months." § 1614 (a)(3)(A) of the Act, 42 U.S.C. § 1382c(a)(3)(A).

Although the SSI program is broad in its reach, its coverage is not complete. From its very inception, the program has excluded from eligibility anyone who is an "inmate of a public institution." § 1611(e)(1)(A) of the Act, as amended, 42 U.S.C. § 1382(e)(1)(A). Also from the program's inception, Congress has made a partial exception to this exclusion by providing a small amount of money (not exceeding $300 per year) to any otherwise eligible person in "a hospital, extended care facility, nursing home, or intermediate care facility receiving payments (with respect to such individual or spouse) under a State plan approved under subchapter XIX [Medicaid] * * *." § 1611(e)(1)(B), as amended, 42 U.S.C. § 1382(e)(1)(B). Congress thus, while excluding generally any person residing in a public institution, explicitly has tied eligibility for a reduced amount of SSI benefits to residence in an institution receiving Medicaid benefits for the care of the eligible individual.

Appellees brought this suit to challenge this resulting detail of Congress' having conditioned the limited assistance grant on eligibility for Medicaid: a person between the ages of 21 through 64 who resides in a public mental institution is not eligible to receive this small stipend, even though that person meets the other eligibility requirements for SSI benefits, because treatment in a public mental institution for a person in this age bracket is not funded under Medicaid.

Appellees attack this statutory classification as violative of the equal protection component of the Fifth Amendment's Due Process Clause. Their challenge, successful in the District Court, is twofold. First they argue that the exclusion of their class of mentally ill (and therefore disabled) persons bears no rational relationship to any legitimate objective of the SSI program. They assert, in fact, that their class was excluded inadvertently because of its political powerlessness. Second, they insist that because the statute classifies on the basis of mental illness, a factor that greatly resembles other characteristics that this Court has found inherently "suspect" as a means of legislative classification, special justification should be required for the congressional decision to exclude appellees. * * *

[Editor—The Court noted that the exclusion of inmates of public institutions left out many claimants who were not mentally ill and that mentally ill individuals could be covered if they were not in public institutions. Therefore, the statute did not appear to be directly targeted against the mentally ill.]

To the extent that the statute has an indirect impact upon the mentally ill as a subset of publicly institutionalized persons, this record certainly presents no statistical support for a contention that the mentally ill as a class are burdened disproportionately to any other class affected by the classification. The exclusion draws a line only between groups composed (in part) of mentally ill individuals: those in public mental hospitals and those not in public mental hospitals. These groups are shifting in population, and members of one group can, and often do, pass to the other group.

We also note that appellees have failed to produce any evidence that the intent of Congress was to classify on the basis of mental health. Appellees admit that no such evidence exists; indeed, they rely on the absence of explicit intent as proof of Congress' "inattention" to their needs and, therefore, its prejudice against them. As in Jefferson v. Hackney, 406 U.S. 535 (1972), the indirect deprivation worked by this legislation upon appellees' class, whether or not the class is considered "suspect," does not without more move us to regard it with a heightened scrutiny.

Thus, the pertinent inquiry is whether the classification employed in § 1611(e)(1)(B) advances legitimate legislative goals in a rational fashion. * * *

* * * As long as the classificatory scheme chosen by Congress rationally advances a reasonable and identifiable governmental objective, we must disregard the existence of other methods of allocation that we, as individuals, perhaps would have preferred.

We believe that the decision to incorporate the Medicaid eligibility standards into the SSI scheme must be considered Congress' deliberate, considered choice. The legislative record, although sparse appears to be unequivocal. Both House and Senate Reports on the initial SSI bill noted the exclusion in no uncertain terms. The House Report stated:

"People who are residents of certain public institutions, or hospitals or nursing homes which are getting Medicaid funds, would get benefits of up to $25 a month (reduced by nonexcluded income). For these people most subsistence needs are met by the institution and full benefits are not needed. Some payment to these people, though, would be needed to enable them to purchase small comfort items not supplied by the institution. No assistance benefits will be paid to an individual in a penal institution." H. R. Rep. No. 92–231, p. 150 (1971). * * *

The limited nature of Medicaid eligibility did not pass unnoticed by the enacting Congress. In the same bill that established the SSI program, Congress considered, and passed, an amendment to Medicaid, providing coverage of inpatient services to a large number of the juvenile needy in public mental institutions. See 1905(h) of the Act, 42 U.S.C. § 1396d(h); S. Rep. No. 92–1230, at 280–281; H. R. Conf. Rep. No. 92–1605, p. 65 (1972). Also, a Senate proposal for demonstration projects on the feasibility of extending Medicaid to cover all inpatient services provided in public mental institutions was simultaneously defeated. See S. Rep. No. 92–1230, at 281; H. R. Conf. Rep. No. 92–1605, at 65. Congress was in the process of considering the wisdom of these limitations at the time it chose to incorporate them into the SSI provisions. The decision to do so did not escape controversy. The Committee hearings contained testimony advocating extension of both Medicaid and SSI benefits to all needy residents in public mental institutions. See Social Security Amendments of 1971, Hearings on H. R. 1 before the Senate Committee on Finance, 92d Cong., 1st and 2d Sess., 2180, 2408–2410, 2479–2485, 3257, 3319 (1972). This legislative history shows that Congress was aware, when it added § 1611(e) to the Act, of the limitations in the Medicaid program that would restrict eligibility for the reduced SSI benefits; we decline to regard such deliberate action as the result of inadvertence or ignorance. See Maine v. Thiboutot, 448 U.S. 1, 8 (1980).

Having found the adoption of the Medicaid standards intentional, we deem it logical to infer from Congress' deliberate action an intent to further the same subsidiary purpose that lies behind the Medicaid exclusion, which, as no party denies, was adopted because Congress believed the States to have a "traditional" responsibility to care for those institutionalized in public mental institutions. The Secretary, emphasizing the then-existing congressional desire to economize in the disbursement of federal funds, argues that the decision to limit distribution of the monthly stipend to inmates of public institutions who are receiving Medicaid funds "is rationally related to the legitimate legislative desire to avoid spending federal resources on behalf of individuals whose care and treatment are being fully provided for by state and local government units" and "may be said to implement a congressional policy choice to provide supplemental financial assistance for only those residents of public institutions who already receive significant federal support in the form of Medicaid coverage." We cannot say that the belief that the States should continue to have the primary responsibility for making this small "comfort money" allowance available to those residing in state-run institutions is an irrational basis for withholding from them federal general welfare funds. * * *

We conclude that Congress did not violate appellees rights to equal protection by denying them the supplementary benefit. The judgment of the District Court is reversed.

■ Justice Powell, with whom Justice Brennan, Justice Marshall, and Justice Stevens join, dissenting.

The Court holds that Congress rationally has denied a small monthly "comfort allowance" to otherwise eligible people solely because previously it rationally denied them Medicaid benefits. In my view, Congress thoughtlessly has applied a statutory classification developed to further legitimate goals of one welfare program to another welfare program serving entirely different needs. The result is an exclusion of wholly dependent people from minimal benefits, serving no Government interest. This irrational classification violates the equal protection component of the Due Process Clause of the Fifth Amendment. * * *

The refusal to pay for treatment in public mental institutions has a lengthy history in the development of the federal medical assistance programs. * * * The residual exclusion of large state institutions for the mentally ill from federal financial assistance rests on two related principles: States traditionally have assumed the burdens of administering this form of care, and the Federal Government has long distrusted the economic and therapeutic efficiency of large mental institutions. See S. Rep. No. 404, 89th Cong., 1st Sess., 20 (1965).

The legislative history of § 1611(e) sheds no light on why Congress made the exclusion from reduced SSI benefits coextensive with the exclusion from Medicaid payments. [Editor—The dissent notes that the "only indication of congressional intent states: 'No assistance benefits will be paid to an individual in a penal institution.' H. R. Rep. No. 92–231, p. 150 (1971)."] The Secretary argues that Congress might rationally have concluded that the States have the primary responsibility for making payments of comfort allowances to appellees, because they already bear the responsibility for paying for their treatment. In accepting this justification, the Court adds that whether the States do, ever have, or ever will provide this benefit to residents of large mental institutions is irrelevant to the rationality of Congress' supposed judgment. * * *

The deference to which legislative accommodation of conflicting interests is entitled rests in part upon the principle that the political process of our majoritarian democracy responds to the wishes of the people. Accordingly, an important touchstone for equal protection review of statutes is how readily a policy can be discerned which the legislature intended to serve. When a legitimate purpose for a statute appears in the legislative history or is implicit in the statutory scheme itself, a court has some assurance that the legislature has made a conscious policy choice. Our democratic system requires that legislation intended to serve a discernible purpose receive the most respectful deference. Yet, the question of whether a statutory classification discriminates arbitrarily cannot be divorced from whether it was enacted to serve an identifiable purpose. When a legislative purpose can be suggested only by the ingenuity of a government lawyer litigating the constitutionality of a statute, a reviewing court may be presented not so much with a legislative policy choice as its absence. [Editor—The dissent observes in a footnote: "Congress' failure to make policy judgments can distort our system of separation of powers by encouraging other branches to make essentially legislative decisions. See Cannon v. University of Chicago, 441 U.S. 677, 743 (1979)(Powell, J., dissenting.)"]

In my view, the Court should receive with some skepticism *post hoc* hypotheses about legislative purpose, unsupported by the legislative history. When no indication of legislative purpose appears other than the current position of the Secretary, the Court should require that the classification bear a "fair and substantial relation" to the asserted purpose. This marginally more demanding scrutiny indirectly would test the plausibility of the tendered purpose, and preserve equal protection review as something more than a "mere tautological recognition of the fact that Congress did what it intended to do." U.S. Railroad Retirement Bd. v. Fritz, 449 U.S. 166, 180 (1980)(Stevens, J., concurring in judgment).

Neither the structure of § 1611 nor its legislative history identifies or even suggests any policy plausibly intended to be served by denying appellees the small SSI allowance. As noted above, the only purpose identified in the House and Senate Reports is the irrelevant goal of depriving inmates of penal institutions of all benefits. The structure of the statute offers no guidance as to purpose because § 1611(e) is drawn in reference to the policies of Medicaid rather than to the policies of SSI. By mechanically applying the criteria developed for Medicaid, Congress appears to have avoided considering what criteria would be appropriate for deciding in which public institutions a person can reside and still be eligible for some SSI payment. The importation of eligibility criteria from one statute to another creates significant risks that irrational distinctions will be made between equally needy people.

The Secretary argues, and the Court agrees, that the exclusion "is rationally related to the legitimate legislative desire to avoid spending federal resources on behalf of individuals whose care and treatment are being fully provided for by the state and local government units." The Secretary does not argue that appellees are not in present need of the comfort allowance; indeed, he concedes that "the statutory classification does not exclude [appellees] because they were thought to be less needy." Nor does the Secretary suggest that because a State provides health care and the necessities of life to inmates of mental hospitals, the State also will provide the inmate with a comfort allowance. Indeed, the probability that a State will pay a patient a comfort allowance does not increase when the Federal Government refuses to relieve it of part of the cost of the patient's medical care. The Court apparently recognizes this, as it states that whether or not a State actually provides a comfort allowance is irrelevant. Appellees simply are denied a benefit provided to other institutionalized, disabled patients.

But, it is argued, Congress rationally could make the judgment that the States should bear the responsibility for any comfort allowance, because they already have the responsibility for providing treatment and minimal care. There is no logical link, however, between these two responsibilities. Residence in a public mental hospital is rationally related to whether the Congress should pay for the patient's treatment. The judgment whether the Federal Government should subsidize care for the mentally ill in large public institutions involves difficult questions of medical and economic policy. But residence in a *public mental* institution, as opposed to residence in a state *medical* hospital or a *private* mental hospital, bears no relation to any policy of the SSI program. The monthly $25 allowance pays for small personal expenses, beyond the minimal care and treatment provided by Medicaid or "other programs." H. R. Rep. No. 96–451, pt. 1, p. 153 (1979). If SSI pays a cash benefit relating to personal needs other than maintenance and medical care, it is irrelevant whether the State or the Federal Government is paying for the maintenance and medical care; the patient's need remains the same, the likelihood that the policies of SSI will be fulfilled remains the same.

I conclude that Congress had no rational reason for refusing to pay a comfort allowance to appellees, while paying it to numerous otherwise identically situated disabled indigents. This unexplained difference in treatment must have been a legislative oversight. I therefore dissent.

Compare Schweiker with United States Railroad Retirement Board v. Fritz, 449 U.S. 166 (1980). Congress was concerned about the solvency of the railroad retirement system. It planned to solve the problem by eliminating dual benefits under both the railroad retirement and social security systems, but nonetheless still grandfathered dual benefits for certain employees. Somewhat simplified, dual benefits were continued for railroad employees who had enough years of employment to qualify under both systems if, on December 31, 1974 (the "cut-off date"), they had completed 25 years of railroad service, or performed railroad service in 1974 or during some recent period prior to the cut-off date. This left out employees with long but not recent service. The dissent cited evidence that Congress had simply delegated the job of drafting this law to labor and industry and that labor had sold out to its current members, leaving out employees with long service who had left the railroad industry a few years before the cut-off date.

In dissent, Justice Brennan described the legislative process this way:

Congress conducted hearings to consider the Joint Committee's recommendations, but never directed its attention to their effect on persons in appellee class' situation. In fact, the Joint Committee negotiators and Railroad Retirement Board members who testified at congressional hearings perpetuated the inaccurate impression that all retirees with earned vested dual benefits under prior law would retain their benefits unchanged. * * *

Of course, a misstatement or several misstatements by witnesses before Congress would not ordinarily lead us to conclude that Congress misapprehended what it was doing. In this instance, however, where complex legislation was drafted by outside parties and Congress relied on them to explain it, where the misstatements are frequent and unrebutted, and where no Member of Congress can be found to have stated the effect of the classification correctly, we are entitled to suspect that Congress may have been misled. As the District Court found: "At no time during the hearings did Congress even give a hint that it understood that the bill by its language eliminated an earned benefit of plaintiff's class."

The majority upheld the law, applying only the laxest standard of rationality review, basing its analysis of the statute on "plausible" reasons for the statutory classification. As for Justice Brennan's concern about misleading Congress, the Court stated:

[W]e disagree with the District Court's conclusion that Congress was unaware of what it accomplished or that it was misled by the groups that appeared before it. If this test were applied literally to every member of any legislature that ever voted on a law, there would be very few laws which would survive it. The language of the statute is clear, and we have historically assumed that Congress intended what it enacted. To be sure, appellee lost a political battle in which he had a strong interest, but this is neither the first nor the last time that such a result will occur in the legislative forum.

Even Justice Stevens was willing to rely on either the legislature's actual purpose or "a legitimate purpose which we may reasonably presume to have motivated an impartial legislature." Stevens found an actual purpose to help current employees analogous to the typical retirement plan's favoritism for recent retirees. This grounded the statute in what he called "relevant precedent," and it was therefore reasonable.

QUESTIONS

How does Schweiker differ from Fritz?

1. Was Congress more aware of what it was doing in Fritz than in Schweiker? Someone, presumably the unions, knew what they were doing. Can that knowledge be imputed to Congress, or is

the delegation of lawmaking to private parties with interests to advance as bad as mindless legislation?

2. Who are the disadvantaged groups in Schweiker and Fritz? Are the omitted beneficiaries more or less likely to be able to organize effectively in one case rather than the other?

3. Is the difference in subject matter relevant? Is the issue more "social and economic" in Fritz than in Schweiker?

4. What would be the implications for judicial review if the classification in Fritz had been struck down?

The problem in Schweiker was the arguably mindless borrowing of a standard from one statute for another. In Rubin, Legislative Methodology: Some Lessons from the Truth-in-Lending Act, 80 Geo. L. J. 233, 294 (1991), the author refers to the "beneficial role of habit" in legislative drafting, *once* the legislature has achieved some refinement in its approach. The particular issue he discusses is adoption in the Truth-in-Savings Act of the same cause of action provisions that appear in other federal consumer statutes (minimum damage award plus attorney's fees; maximum awards to prevent defendant's catastrophic losses; excusing financial institution's bona fide errors). He speaks favorably of congressional habit in this context, "despite shifting political alignments that might favor more stringent or a more lenient provision in specific cases." Would the dissenters in Schweiker agree that shifting political alignments should go unheeded? Is deferring to "habit" more troublesome in Schweiker than in federal consumer legislation?

c) OBSOLETE STATUTES

In Chapter 9, dealing with change, we discussed Professor Calabresi's views on adapting legislation to change, focusing on obsolete statutes. Judge Calabresi has written a concurring opinion in Quill v. Vacco, 80 F.3d 716 (2d Cir.1996), cert. granted, 117 S.Ct. 36 (1996), suggesting that old statutes which threaten fundamental interests or suspect classifications should be declared unconstitutional, without prejudice to the court reconsidering its conclusion if a modern legislature revisits the issue and suggests why the law might be defensible in a contemporary setting. The driving force behind his view is that legislation should be a rational/deliberative process which self-consciously makes political choices, at least when important constitutional values are at stake. Here is some of what he said.

■ Calabresi, Circuit Judge, concurring in the result:

The Court today strikes down the New York statutes prohibiting assisted suicide insofar as they apply to "terminally ill, mentally competent patients, who would self-administer drugs." It does so because it finds these statutes to be in violation of the Equal Protection Clause of the Fourteenth Amendment since they are not "rationally related to a legitimate state interest." [Editor—The majority objected to the distinction between allowing doctors to terminate life support systems but not allowing prescription of life-terminating drugs at the request of a terminally ill competent patient.] At the same time, the Court declines to hold that these statutes violate the Due Process Clause of the Fourteenth Amendment, because "the right to assisted suicide finds no cognizable basis in the Constitution's language or design."

Recently the Ninth Circuit, sitting en banc, held that analogous laws violated the fundamental Due Process rights of terminally ill patients. Compassion in Dying v. Washington, 79 F.3d 790, (9th Cir.1996)(en banc). The Ninth Circuit recognized that Equal Protection arguments for invalidity were "not insubstantial," but did not discuss them in view of its Due Process holding.

I agree with the Court that these statutes cannot stand. But I do not believe that the history of the statutes, and of New York's approach toward assisted suicide, requires us to make a final judgment under either Due Process or Equal Protection as to the validity of statutes prohibiting assisted suicide. What is not ready for decision ought not to be decided. I would therefore leave open the question of whether, if the state of New York were to enact new laws prohibiting assisted suicide (laws that either are less absolute in their application or are identical to those before us), such laws would stand or fall. Accordingly, I join the Court's result, but write separately to explain my unwillingness to reach the ultimate Due Process and Equal Protection questions. * * *

I. A Bit of History * * *

The statutes at issue were born in another age. New York enacted its first prohibition of assisted suicide in 1828. The statute punished any individual who assisted another in committing "self-murder" for first-degree manslaughter. This prohibition was tied to the crime of suicide, described by one contemporary New York Court as a "criminal act of self-destruction."

English authorities had long declared suicide to be murder. And the leading American case echoed these English authorities. * * *

[In 1881], however, the New York Legislature revised the Penal Code. The new code provided that an intentional attempt to commit suicide was a felony with a maximum penalty of two years' imprisonment. * * * The 1881 statute, echoing the earlier 1828 provision, punished assisting a successful suicide as manslaughter in the first degree. The Code also punished assistance in attempted suicide as an unspecified felony. * * *

The 1881 scheme was altered in 1919 when the prohibition against attempted suicide [ ] was removed. The Legislature, nevertheless, left in place the declaration of suicide as a "grave public wrong." And the prohibition of assisting suicide also remained on the books. But we have found no case in which a physician aiding a person who wished to commit suicide was, in fact, penalized in New York after 1919.

In 1965, the Legislature took the next step and deleted the declaration that suicide was a "grave public wrong." It, however, left in place redrafted versions of [the Code] stating: "A person is guilty of manslaughter in the second degree when * * * he intentionally causes or aids another person to commit suicide," and "[a] person is guilty of promoting a suicide attempt when he intentionally causes or aids another person to attempt suicide * * *."

The years since 1965 have brought further erosion in the bases for prohibiting assisted suicide with respect to terminally ill persons. Thus, in 1981, the New York Court of Appeals declared that "a doctor cannot be held to have violated his legal or professional responsibilities when he honors the right of a competent adult patient to decline medical treatment." The court applied this principle both to the withdrawal of life-support and to the refusal of blood transfusions. Furthermore, in 1986, the court stated: "In our system of a free government, where notions of individual autonomy and free choice are cherished, it is the individual who must have the final say in respect to decisions regarding his medical treatment * * *."

The New York Legislature itself acted accordingly. In the 1987 Orders Not to Resuscitate Act, it provided that an "adult with capacity" may create an "order not to resuscitate" in the event the patient "suffers cardiac or respiratory arrest." In the 1990 Health Care Agents and Proxies Act, it went further and permitted a competent person to designate an agent who has "authority to make any and all health care decisions on the principal's behalf that the principal could make." The statute explicitly stated that choices regarding the withdrawal of artificial nutrition and hydration are within the purview of a health care agent when the wishes of the principal are reasonably known to the agent.

Later, in 1994, the New York Task Force on Life and the Law, a group organized in 1985 at the request of Governor Cuomo and composed of doctors, bioethicists, and religious leaders, among others, prepared a report on the question. The report, in effect, said leave things as they are: permit suicide and attempted suicide, recognize the right of competent terminally ill patients—either on their own or through agents—to order the ceasing of nutrition and hydration and the withdrawal of life support systems, but do not alter the law to permit what petitioners seek today. The Legislature received the report and, not surprisingly, took no action, then or since.

From this historical survey, I conclude that 1) what petitioners seek is nominally still forbidden by New York statutes; 2) the bases of these statutes have been deeply eroded over the last hundred and fifty years; and 3) few of their foundations remain in place today.

Specifically:

The original reason for the statutes—criminalizing conduct that aided or abetted other crimes—is long since gone.

The distinction that has evolved over the years between conduct currently permitted (suicide, and aiding someone who wishes to die to do so by removing hydration, feeding, and life support systems) and conduct still prohibited (giving a competent, terminally ill patient lethal drugs, which he or she can self-administer) is tenuous at best.

The Legislature—for many, many years—has not taken any recognizably affirmative step reaffirming the prohibition of what petitioners seek.

The enforcement of the laws themselves has fallen into virtual desuetude—not so much as to render the case before us nonjusticiable, but enough to cast doubt on whether, in a case like that which the petitioners present, a prosecutor would prosecute or a jury would convict. And this fact by itself inevitably raises doubts about the current support for these laws.

II.   Constitutional Doubts

In the case of ordinary legislation none of this would matter much. We regularly uphold laws whose original reason has vanished, whose fit with the rest of the legal system is dubious, whose enforcement is virtually nil, and whose continued presence on the books seems as much due to the strong inertial force that the framers of our constitutions gave to the status quo as to any current majoritarian support. In a different context, I have argued that courts have used subterfuges and aggressive interpretations to rid the system of such laws. See Guido Calabresi, A Common Law for the Age of Statutes 163–66, 172–77 (1982). But I have also criticized such judicial action, at least in the absence of express legislative sanction. See Taber v. Maine, 67 F.3d 1029, 1039 (2d Cir.1995).

When legislation comes close to violating fundamental substantive constitutional rights or to running counter to the requirements of Equal Protection, however, there is, as I hope to demonstrate, a long tradition of constitutional holdings that inertia will not do. In such instances, courts have asserted the right to strike down statutes and, before ruling on the ultimate validity of that legislation, to demand a present and positive acknowledgment of the values that the legislators wish to further through the legislation in issue. And so it is to an examination of the substantive constitutional dubiety of the laws before us that I now turn.

There can be no doubt that the statutes at issue come close—at the very least—to infringing fundamental Due Process rights and to doing so in ways that are also suspect under the antidiscrimination principles of the Equal Protection Clause. * * *

[Editor—Calabresi cites Cruzan v. Director, Missouri Department of Health, 497 U.S. 261 (1990), and Planned Parenthood v. Casey, 505 U.S. 833 (1992) as authority. He notes that, in Cruzan, "the Court examined whether guardians could order withdrawal of an incompetent patient's life support when, contrary to the requirements of the State of Missouri, there was not clear and convincing proof of the patient's wish to have life support withdrawn. In deciding that the guardians could not so order, the majority opinion noted that 'the principle that a competent person has a constitutionally protected liberty interest in refusing unwanted medical treatment may be inferred from our prior decisions.'" And, in Casey, the Court noted that "our law affords constitutional protection to personal decisions relating to marriage, procreation, contraception, family relationships, child rearing, and education" and that "the Constitution places limits on a State's right to interfere with a person's most basic decisions about * * * bodily integrity." Casey borrowed from Justice Harlan's formulation in Poe v. Ullman, 367 U.S. 497, 543 (1961)(Harlan, J., dissenting), and defined liberty interests to include choices at the core of human existence. Following Harlan, it stated: "These matters, involving the most intimate and personal choices a person may make in a lifetime, choices central to personal dignity and autonomy, are central to the liberty protected by the Fourteenth Amendment. At the heart of liberty is the right to define one's own concept of existence * * *. Beliefs about these matters could not define the attributes of personhood were they formed under compulsion of the State."]

III. The Constitutional Remand

I contend that when a law is neither plainly unconstitutional * * * nor plainly constitutional, the courts ought not to decide the ultimate validity of that law without current and clearly expressed statements, by the people or by their elected officials, of the state interests involved. It is my further contention, that, absent such statements, the courts have frequently struck down such laws, while leaving open the possibility of reconsideration if appropriate statements were subsequently made. * * *

* * * [R]ecent opinions have applied constitutional remands directly. In Califano v. Goldfarb, 430 U.S. 199 (1977), for example, Justice Stevens provided the swing vote in the Court's five-to-four decision that the Social Security Act's grant of special benefits to widows was in violation of Equal Protection. He found that the law discriminated "against a group of males [and] is merely the accidental byproduct of a traditional way of thinking about females."

Significantly, he went on to say that "perhaps an actual, considered legislative choice would be sufficient to allow this statute to be upheld, but that is a question I would reserve until such a choice has been made."

[Editor—Rostker v. Goldberg, 453 U.S. 57 (1981), may be an example of an "actual, considered legislative choice" which saves a statute. Without dissent from Justice Stevens, the Court upheld exclusion of women from draft registration, stating:

> Congress did not act "unthinkingly" * * *. The question of registering women for the draft not only received considerable national attention and was the subject of wide-ranging public debate, but also was extensively considered by Congress in hearings, floor debate, and in committee.]

The powerful, and telling, concurring opinion by Justice O'Connor in Thompson v. Oklahoma, 487 U.S. 815 (1988), which provided the fifth vote to strike down state death penalty laws applicable to minors less than sixteen years of age, did the same thing. The fact that such laws were on the books in many states did not suffice to meet the strictures of the Cruel and Unusual Punishment Clause. The laws may have been there inadvertently or as a result of inertia, and many state legislatures seemed not to have realized that children could be executed under their statutes. Such laws, moreover, were virtually never enforced against minors under sixteen. Hence, the Justice reasoned, they were invalid. But if states reenacted them, consciously and clearly, the Court would then have to consider whether the statutes could actually meet the Clause's requirements.

Perhaps the most dramatic instance of this constitutional remand, or second look, approach occurred in our own Circuit, in a case bearing many similarities to the one before us today. In Abele v. Markle, 342 F.Supp. 800 (D.Conn.1972)("Abele I"), a three-judge district court was asked to examine the constitutionality of a Connecticut statute that banned abortion. Circuit Judge J. Edward Lumbard found the statute to be unconstitutional for reasons later echoed by the Supreme Court in Roe v. Wade, 410 U.S. 113 (1973). District Judge T. Emmet Clarie found no violation of due process for reasons akin to those adverted to in today's majority opinion. The key vote was by then-District Judge Jon Newman.

In his landmark opinion, now-Chief Judge Newman found that the Connecticut statute had been passed in 1860 to protect the health of pregnant women, and that this aim was no longer applicable in 1972 because childbirth endangered a woman's life more than abortion did. Yet he recognized that other valid grounds for the statute might exist, including, perhaps, the protection of unborn life (Roe v. Wade had not yet been decided). Newman pointed out, however, that the statute was not passed to protect unborn life. "If the Connecticut legislature had made [such] a judgment," Newman mused, "the constitutionality of such laws would pose a legal question of extreme difficulty * * *." Because "that legislative determination has not been shown to have been made," Newman found it "inappropriate to decide the constitutional issue that would be posed" if the Legislature in fact passed a law designed to protect human life. And since the statute before him, whatever its basis, raised strong constitutional doubts, Newman nullified the law while explicitly leaving the Legislature free to reconsider the issue. * * *

Today, Timothy Quill takes the place of Janice Abele in challenging another statute of nineteenth-century origin. As with the Connecticut abortion law, the rationale for the New York assisted-suicide prohibition has eroded with the passage of time. In the nineteenth century, both suicide and attempted suicide were crimes and assisting in those crimes was, derivatively, a crime as well. But suicide and attempted suicide are no longer crimes. Nevertheless, the prohibitions on assisted suicide might serve other valid ends. It is possible, for example, to imagine a state in which such statutes were part of an overall approach to the preservation of life that was so all-encompassing that the laws' validity might be upheld despite their infringement of important libertarian individual rights. * * *

Various amici for the respondents argue that the New York assisted suicide laws consciously adopt their particular vision of what life and death should be. Amicus United States Catholic Conference, for example, insists that suicide is antithetical to freedom, that it is not voluntary and that it is linked to psychiatric illness. But there is no reason to believe that New York has accepted these arguments. If it had, one would expect that New York would prohibit attempted suicide and that it would, for example, aggressively discourage suicide by the terminally ill, through legislative declarations defining it to be a "grave public wrong" or through some other means.

Other amici contend that the difference between what they call "active" assisted suicide (making lethal drugs available to those terminally ill who would self-administer them) and what they call "passive" behavior (actively removing life supports or feeding tubes, on demand, so that the patient may die) is fundamental. Even if I were to accept the distinction * * * there is no reason to believe that New York has consciously made such a judgment. Certainly New York has never enacted a law based on a reasoned defense of the difference.

The Attorney General of New York contends that its Legislature has, in fact, made just such a distinction by its inaction, by its failure to remove the prohibitions before us today. It left these in place after the prohibition on what could be called "passive" assisted suicide had been abrogated. Leaving aside the difficulties involved in arguing that legislative inaction should be given the same weight as legislative action in supporting the view that medical action and medical inaction are fundamentally different, the argument will not do. As the majority points out, we have not been given any clear statements of possible interests that the state actually believes would be served by the distinction. In their absence, how can we say that the distinction, which is anything but obvious, and which results in severe harm to the ability of some, but not all, individuals to determine crucial life and death choices for themselves, is mandated by the state's fundamental needs? * * *

I take no position on what I would hold were such an affirmative statement forthcoming from the state of New York. * * * What I do say is that no court need or ought to make ultimate and immensely difficult constitutional decisions unless it knows that the state's elected representatives and executives—having been made to go, as it were, before the people—assert through their actions (not their inactions) that they really want and are prepared to defend laws that are constitutionally suspect.

It is different when the Constitution speaks clearly. When a law violates the plain mandates of the text, history, or structure of the Constitution, no second look is warranted or appropriate. That law must fall. Laws that violate the core of the First Amendment and the core of the Takings Clause are but two examples. When that is not the case, when the Constitution and its history do not clearly render a statute invalid, when its validity depends instead, in part, on the strength of the state interests at stake, then a second look is not only appropriate, it is, in my view, usually required.

Without a second look by the people, courts are liable to err in either direction. They may uphold and thereby validate (as they all too often have) the infringement of rights upon which the states did not truly wish to encroach. Conversely, they may, ultimately and definitively, strike down laws, believing that the state interests involved are minor, when in fact these interests turn out to be highly significant.

In the end, a constitutional remand does no more than this: It tells the legislatures and executives of the various states, and of the federal government as well, that if they wish to regulate conduct that, if not protected by our Constitution, is very close to being protected, they must do so clearly and openly. They must, in other words, face the consequences of their decision before the people. Unless they do this, they cannot expect courts to tell them whether what they may or may not actually wish to enact is constitutionally permitted.

IV. Conclusion

I would hold that, on the current legislative record, New York's prohibitions on assisted suicide violate both the Equal Protection and Due Process Clauses of the Fourteenth Amendment of the United States Constitution to the extent that these laws are interpreted to prohibit a physician from prescribing lethal drugs to be self-administered by a mentally competent, terminally ill person in the final stages of that terminal illness. I would, however, take no position on whether such prohibitions, or other more finely drawn ones, might be valid, under either or both clauses of the United States Constitution, were New York to reenact them while articulating the reasons for the distinctions it makes in the laws, and expressing the grounds for the prohibitions themselves. I therefore concur in the result reached by the Court.

d) DIRECT DEMOCRACY—REFERENDUMS AND INITIATIVES

Should the rules designed to improve the legislative process apply to direct democracy; and, if so, with greater or lesser force than they apply to laws adopted by legislatures? We first define direct democracy—initiatives and referendums—and then look at some cases which explicitly or implicitly answer these questions. You will recall from Chapter 3 that direct democracy is associated in this country with the Populist and Progressive movements at the end of the 19th and beginning of the 20th Centuries and that it enjoyed considerable success in the western states.

i) DEFINITION

Eule, Judicial Review of Direct Democracy

99 Yale L.J. 1503 (1990).

Direct democracy comes in a multitude of forms. * * * For purposes of this Article, I shall divide instances of direct democracy into two basic subgroups. The first I will call *substitute* direct democracy; the second, *complementary* direct democracy.

Substitute direct democracy is direct democracy in its purest current form. Here the voters can completely bypass the legislative and executive branches of government. * * * In order to exercise this option the voters neither need legislative permission nor legislative assistance. A measure may be placed on the ballot by securing a specified number of signatures—usually set at some percentage of the votes cast in the preceding general election—and the measure is enacted if a majority of the voters signify their approval.

Ordinarily, such a form of plebiscite is called an initiative. Initiatives, however, are often subclassified as direct or indirect. The process just described is generally referred to as a direct initiative. An indirect initiative, on the other hand, requires that the voters' petition be submitted to the legislature before the issue is placed on the ballot. The legislature has a specified period of time in which to enact the proposal. If the legislature fails to do so, the measure is sent to the voters. * * *

While substitutive direct democracy offers a stripped down version of lawmaking free from the constraints—and, as I shall argue, the safeguards—of the legislative framework, *complementary* direct democracy adds an additional tier. This form of direct democracy is commonly called a referendum because the legislation is referred to the electorate for ratification. Here the voters and the legislature must act in concert before a law may take effect. Legislative passage is prerequisite but inadequate: Without voter endorsement the legislative effort fails; without legislative passage the electorate has nothing to vote on.

Referenda come in three versions, differentiated by who or what prompts the referral. In the first, the so-called mandatory or compulsory referendum, the state constitution commands submission of certain legislative enactments to the electorate. This version is often used for debt authorization and is necessary in forty-nine states for legislatively initiated amendments to the state constitution. In the second version, often styled the voluntary referendum, the legislature is given the option to refer measures to the voters. In its final form, usually known as the popular referendum, citizens can petition to force a referral of a previously enacted—but not yet effective—legislative measure.

Direct democracy, the conventional history tells us, was a response of the Progressive Reform movement to the widely perceived corruption and control of legislatures by corporate wealth. The Progressives' remedy curbed legislators by placing corrective power in the citizenry. Substitutive plebiscites, by circumventing the legislative framework, rectify corruption that impedes legislation. In contrast, the Progressives directed complementary plebiscites against corruption that produces legislation. Toward this end, the reformers added a new layer to the lawmaking process. Thus, the two Progressive reforms simultaneously made it easier and more difficult to enact laws. One dismantled the system of checks and balances. The other augmented it. * * *

ii) REFERENDUMS

Eule critiques "negative" complementary plebiscites (referendums on proposed legislative action) in which the voters can disapprove of legislation already passed by the legislature, as follows:

[T]hese "negative" complementary plebiscites pose a distinctive threat of majority tyranny. Complementary plebiscites enable popular majorities to prevent legislation that minorities have managed to convince legislative majorities to enact. Sometimes legislative sensitivity to minority interests, as well as debts incurred by the process of logrolling and compromise, result in minorities' being able to assert their legislative power in a positive rather than negative manner. Where the minority's legislative victory takes the form of passing rather than preventing legislation, complementary plebiscites—which make lawmaking more difficult—may deserve enhanced judicial attention.

Why should a constitutional vision of checks and filters be offended by the operation of an additional check? The protection the Constitution offers minorities is chiefly one against legislative action, not inaction. * * *

The picture of complementary plebiscite as additional check [on legislation] is a superficially appealing one. Viewed this way it looks a lot like bicameralism or executive veto or judicial review. Of course the complementary plebiscite is a filter that the Federal Constitution did not install, but surely the states are not barred from making it more difficult for government to act. The problem with this portrayal is that it assumes a filtering system that applies equally to all lawmaking. But that is not the reality of complementary plebiscites, which instead provide selective augmentation of the ordinary legislative process.

Not all complementary plebiscites are suspect merely because of their selectivity. It is entirely legitimate for states to require complementary plebiscites for constitutional amendment. Preventing momentary majorities—whether legislative or electoral—from altering the state's constitutive document appropriately calls for a procedure incorporating extra checks. The difficulty arises when subjects that disproportionately affect unpopular minorities—like blacks, latinos, aliens, or the poor—are singled out for an augmented checking system.

I have argued in this Article that substitutive plebiscites demand additional judicial attention because they bypass the legislative filtering system designed to protect minority interests. Complementary plebiscites pose a danger of a different sort. We frequently hear the praises of allowing the electorate to pass on the action of their representatives in a more focused manner than that afforded by periodic retention elections. But when the road to legislation is lengthened only sporadically, we must be extremely wary about the process for picking those moments. For while nothing may be wrong with allowing the voters to reject their agents' decisions, the selective use of the voter veto is fraught with danger to unpopular minorities.

When a state constitution or a city charter mandates that specific categories of legislation receive the dual approval of legislators and voters, courts should scrutinize this requirement itself for impermissible anti-minority bias. Thus it will not be necessary for judges to pass on the individual exercise of the plebiscitary veto— and indeed it may not be possible. * * * The Court's attention [is] correctly directed not at a particular electoral veto but at the constitutionality of the structural provision requiring submission of the issue to the voters. [I earlier] advocated an enhanced *substantive* review of the individual product of substitutive plebiscites. When it comes to complementary plebiscites my claim is rather that courts must look harder at the fairness of the *selective use of the process*.

How does the following case deal with the problems Eule identifies with referendums in particular and direct democracy in general? What image of direct democracy does the Court adopt?

James v. Valtierra
402 U.S. 137 (1971).

■ Mr. Justice Black delivered the opinion of the Court.

These cases raise but a single issue. It grows out of the United States Housing Act of 1937, which established a federal housing agency authorized to make loans and grants to state agencies for slum clearance and low-rent housing projects. In response, the California Legislature created in each county and city a public housing authority to take advantage of the financing made available by the federal Housing Act. At the time the federal legislation was passed the California Constitution had for many years reserved to the State's people the power to initiate legislation and to reject or approve by referendum any Act passed by the state legislature. Cal.Const., Art. IV, s 1. The same section reserved to the electors of counties and cities the power of initiative and referendum over acts of local government bodies. In 1950, however, the State Supreme Court held that local authorities' decisions on seeking federal aid for public housing projects were "executive" and "administrative," not "legislative," and therefore the state constitution's referendum provisions did not apply to these actions. Within six months of that decision the California voters adopted Article XXXIV of the state constitution to bring public housing decisions under the State's referendum policy. The Article provided that no low-rent housing project should be developed, constructed, or acquired in any manner by a state public body until the project was approved by a majority of those voting at a community election.

The present suits were brought by citizens of San Jose, California, and San Mateo County, localities where housing authorities could not apply for federal funds because low-cost housing proposals had been defeated in referendums. The plaintiffs, who are eligible for low-cost public housing, sought a declaration that Article XXXIV was unconstitutional because its referendum requirement violated * * * the Equal Protection Clause. * * *

California's entire history demonstrates the repeated use of referendums to give citizens a voice on questions of public policy. A referendum provision was included in the first state constitution, Cal.Const. of 1849, Art. VIII, and referendums have been a commonplace occurrence in the State's active political life. Provisions for referendums demonstrate devotion to democracy, not to bias, discrimination, or prejudice. Nonetheless, appellees contend that Article XXXIV denies them equal protection because it demands a mandatory referendum while many other referendums only take place upon citizen initiative. They suggest that the mandatory nature of the Article XXXIV referendum constitutes unconstitutional discrimination because it hampers persons desiring public housing from achieving their objective when no such roadblock faces other groups seeking to influence other public decisions to their advantage. But of course a lawmaking procedure that "disadvantages" a particular group does not always deny equal protection. Under any such holding, presumably a State would not be able to require referendums on any subject unless referendums were required on all, because they would always disadvantage some group. And this Court would be required to analyze governmental structures to determine whether a gubernatorial veto provision or a filibuster rule is likely to "disadvantage" any of the diverse and shifting groups that make up the American people.

Furthermore, an examination of California law reveals that persons advocating low-income housing have not been singled out for mandatory referendums while no other group must face that obstacle. Mandatory referendums are required for approval of state constitutional amendments, for the issuance of general obligation long-term bonds by local governments, and for certain municipal territorial annexations. California statute books contain much legislation first enacted by voter initiative, and no such law can be repealed or amended except by referendum. * * *

The people of California have also decided by their own vote to require referendum approval of low-rent public housing projects. This procedure ensures that all the people of a community will have a voice in a decision which may lead to large expenditures of local governmental funds for increased public services and to lower tax revenues. It gives them a voice in decisions that will affect the future development of their own community. This procedure for democratic decisionmaking does not violate the constitutional command that no State shall deny to any person "the equal protection of the laws."

QUESTIONS AND COMMENTS

1. How would you decide the following case? A city charter provision requires proposed land use changes to be ratified in a referendum by 55% of the votes cast. A landowner purchased land zoned for light-industrial use but sought a variance for multi-family, high rise apartments. Both the Planning Commission and City Council approved the request but it failed to get the required 55% approval in a referendum. The Court rejected the argument that the referendum procedure was an unconstitutional delegation of legislative power to the voters because reliance on a *more* democratic procedure—reserving power to the people—could not delegate legislative authority. The dissent thought that the referendum requirement was a violation of due process ("The essence of fair procedure is that the interested parties be given a reasonable opportunity to have their dispute resolved on the merits by reference to articulable rules. * * * I have no doubt about the validity of the initiative or the referendum as an appropriate method of deciding questions of community policy. I think it is equally clear that the popular vote is not an acceptable method of adjudicating the rights of individual litigants."). See City of Eastlake v. Forest City Enterprises, Inc., 426 U.S. 668 (1976).

2. What does this discussion of direct democracy suggest about the Court's decision in First Nat. Bank of Boston v. Bellotti, 435 U.S. 765 (1978) (discussed in Chapter 16.04civ). That case struck down a Massachusetts statute forbidding use of corporate funds to influence referendum votes on issues having no direct connection with the corporation's business—amending the state constitution to allow enactment of a graduated income tax on individuals.

3. The view that "more" democracy is good was not shared by many of the critics of the direct democracy movement in the early decades of the 20th century. You can hear a critical echo in Hawke v. Smith, 253 U.S. 221, 227 (1920), where the Court refused to allow a state legislature to refer ratification of a U.S. Constitutional amendment to a popular referendum. The Court contrasted a referendum with the two constitutional "methods of ratification, by legislatures or conventions," both of which "call[ed] for action by *deliberative* assemblages representative of the people, which it was assumed would voice the will of the people (emphasis added)."

iii) INITIATIVES

Eule also critiques substitutive democracy (initiatives) from the perspective of pluralist (meaning "public choice") and deliberative models of legislation, as follows:

> Our worst tendencies toward prejudice, suggests Derrick Bell, are chastened in legislative debate. Knowledge and exposure are effective weapons against prejudice. Debate and deliberation inevitably lead to better informed judgment. Enlarging one's exposure to competing ideas and perspectives induces greater sensitivity and checks partiality. Legislative hearings and the testimony of various interest groups widen the legislator's horizon. But hearings are only a part of legislative education. Perhaps a more important factor in generating empathy is the diversity of the legislature's membership itself. Racism is not always conscious. More often than not it occurs because of ignorance, oversight, or insensitivity. When minorities are part of the legislative "we," subordination of the "other" becomes both more visible and less comfortable. Group representation ensures that diverse views are continually expressed, increasing

"the likelihood that political outcomes will incorporate some under-standing of the perspectives of all those affected."

The substitutive plebiscite, on the other hand, has little capacity for deliberation. Public debate is infrequent. Exposure to minority perspectives occurs accidentally if at all. Voters may be confused and overwhelmed by the issues placed before them. Any efforts at self-education are thwarted by manipulative campaigns designed to oversimplify the issues and appeal to the electorate's worst instincts. Most important, voters register their decisions in the privacy of the voting booth. They are unaccountable to others for their preferences and their biases. Their individual commitment to a consistent and fair course of conduct can be neither measured nor questioned.

If the deliberative version of the legislative process sounds a little too much pie-in-the-sky to the reader, I share the sentiments. Whatever its normative force, it falls considerably short as descrip-tion. The deviations from an ideal model of deliberation are particu-larly marked at the state and local level. And it is to combat this failing that many commentators have urged judicial emphasis on due process of lawmaking. But it seems inconceivable that on balance the legislature does not come a whole lot closer to the ideal than the substitutive plebiscite. A pluralistic snapshot of the legisla-tive process shows an ongoing system of compromise, negotiation, vote-trading and tactical deals. This arrangement forces legislators to reckon with minority groups. Legislative logrolling over a broad agenda brings minorities into the process and allows resulting compromises to accommodate their interests.

Substitutive plebiscites, on the other hand, are one-shot, win-ner-take-all. The coalition process does not work in the sporadic and unwieldy world of citizen lawmaking. As Frank Michelman notes, you can't dicker with an electorate for support now in exchange for your support on something else later. Majoritarian preferences cannot be softened or diluted by political compromise. * * *

* * * The absence of structured factfinding in the substitutive plebiscite and the dangers of classification inherent in a process of naked aggregation [of preferences] suggest that the substitutive plebiscite may be one of those situations that warrants heightened ends-means review.

Eule argues for review of the results of substitutive democracy which is sensitive to its shortcomings. He distinguishes between judicial suspicion of initiatives which impinge on individual rights and equal application of the law (for example, official English requirements), and tolerance of initiatives improving the legislative process, such as regulation of lobbyists and cam-paign finance reform. He identifies fiscal measures, such as tax and spending limits, as likely to burden the underrepresented poor and minorities and to favor the upper-middle class. On this theory, it should have made a difference in James v. Valtierra, supra, that the constitutional amendment requiring referendums resulted from an initiative by the voters placing the amendment on the ballot for popular approval.

Initiatives dealing with economic regulation pose the most difficult problem. Courts generally avoid rationality review of such laws, as in Fritz, supra, but Eule questions whether traditional judicial restraint is equally appropriate for plebiscites. He discusses a California Nader-backed initiative rolling back insurance rates by 20% in response to legislative inattention to the problem and insurance company secrecy. The voter's approval came in the face of well-financed insurance company opposition, so adoption of the initiative could not be blamed on inadequate attention to the loser's point of view. But the complexity of the initiative was daunting, filling forty-two pages of small print in pamphlets mailed to voters. Eule labels the vote "more visceral than considered," lacking any connection to findings about industry profits and the type of insurance policy.

How valid is the charge that plebiscites are more visceral than legislation? Doesn't the legislature sometimes vote viscerally on the general theme of a statute with little attention to detail—for example, whether it is civil rights or quota legislation; tax reform or rate reduction for the rich? Even if many legislators vote viscerally, do many of them still pay more attention to detail than the general public? For example, it is sometimes said that minimum wages are not really pro-worker provisions, despite the general impression. Is the argument that they raise the cost of labor and put people out of work more likely to be aired during the legislative or plebiscite process? By what method does the legislature pay attention to detail?

In the following case, the U.S. Supreme Court struck down an amendment to the Colorado state constitution adopted in a popular election as the result of a voter initiative on the ground that it did not satisfy a minimum rationality standard. The amendment stated as follows:

> No Protected Status Based on Homosexual, Lesbian, or Bisexual Orientation. Neither the State of Colorado, through any of its branches or departments, nor any of its agencies, political subdivisions, municipalities or school districts, shall enact, adopt or enforce any statute, regulation, ordinance or policy whereby homosexual, lesbian or bisexual orientation, conduct, practices or relationships shall constitute or otherwise be the basis of or entitle any person or class of persons to have or claim any minority status, quota preferences, protected status or claim of discrimination.

The case pays no *explicit* attention to the fact that the amendment was the result of direct democracy, but that may have been relevant. This possibility is suggested by the difficulty of reconciling the decision with earlier cases.

First, in a prior case, Bowers v. Hardwick, 478 U.S. 186 (1986), the Supreme Court refused to establish sexual preference (between same-sex partners) as a protected suspect classification or fundamental interest. Although Bowers in fact dealt with conduct (making it criminal to engage in sodomy), you may wonder why the state could not express its disapproval of same-sex preferences once the Court concluded that it could criminalize same-sex sexual practices, *unless* there was something wrong with the political process in adopting that rule. (Of course, it is possible that the Court is moving towards protecting sexual preference as a suspect classification or fundamental interest.)

Second, another possible ground for the decision was that the "amendment [   ] singles out one form of discrimination and removes its redress from consideration by the *normal* political processes (emphasis added)." Because access to normal political processes is a fundamental right, the amendment cannot stand unless it has a compelling state interest, which the State cannot demonstrate. This was the basis on which the Colorado Supreme Court decided the case. The problems with this analysis, including the Supreme Court's tolerance of supramajority requirements, were discussed in Chapter 16.03bi, supra.

As you read the case, take note of the following:

1. Cultural choices are not always forbidden by the United States Constitution. If they were, states could not outlaw polygamy.

2. One reason for requiring that legislatures act rationally (that is, pay attention to ends and the means-end fit) is to force animus out into the open, where (we hope) it will not be enacted into law. The statute in the Moreno case, cited in the following Supreme Court opinion, prohibited households from being eligible for food stamps if they consisted of unrelated individuals, but this category was overbroad and underbroad from the point of view of the alleged purpose for the law—preventing fraud in applying for Food Stamps. The irrationality of the law in relation to its alleged purpose masked the statute's animus against "hippies," who formed unrelated households. However, it may be hard to describe the adoption of the Colorado amendment as an example of hidden animus. The political choice was clearly in the open.

Or was it? If you read the amendment carefully, stripping out intervening language, you can expose the following rule:

[No political unit in Colorado] shall [   ] enforce any [   ] policy whereby [gay] orientation, conduct, practices or relationships shall constitute or otherwise be the basis of or entitle any person or class of persons to have or claim any [   ] claim of discrimination.

As suggested by one of the briefs filed in the case, that language is so broad that it might allow the police to refuse to respond to a 911 call from a gay person. 1995 WL 862021, fn. 4. Perhaps *no one* in society can be subjected to such discrimination, which in effect treated homosexuals as outlaws. At least, they should not be exposed to this possibility by a popular initiative which is presented in the public debate primarily as a way to prevent special legislative treatment for gays, rather than as a broad denial of protection from hostile government administration.

Romer v. Evans

116 S.Ct. 1620 (1996).

■ Justice Kennedy delivered the opinion of the Court.

One century ago, the first Justice Harlan admonished this Court that the Constitution "neither knows nor tolerates classes among citizens." Plessy v. Ferguson, 163 U.S. 537, 559 (1896)(dissenting opinion). Unheeded then, those words now are understood to state a commitment to the law's neutrality where the rights of persons are at stake. The Equal Protection Clause enforces this principle and today requires us to hold invalid a provision of Colorado's Constitution.

I

* * * The impetus for the amendment and the contentious campaign that preceded its adoption came in large part from ordinances that had been passed in various Colorado municipalities. For example, the cities of Aspen and Boulder and the City and County of Denver each had enacted ordinances which banned discrimination in many transactions and activities, including housing, employment, education, public accommodations, and health and welfare services. What gave rise to the statewide controversy was the protection the ordinances afforded to persons discriminated against by reason of their sexual orientation. See Boulder Rev. Code § 12–1–1 (defining "sexual orientation" as "the choice of sexual partners, i.e., bisexual, homosexual or heterosexual"); Denver Rev. Municipal Code, Art. IV § 28–92 (defining "sexual orientation" as "the status of an individual as to his or her heterosexuality, homosexuality or bisexuality"). Amendment 2 repeals these ordinances to the extent they prohibit discrimination on the basis of "homosexual, lesbian or bisexual orientation, conduct, practices or relationships." Colo. Const., Art. II, § 30b.

Yet Amendment 2, in explicit terms, does more than repeal or rescind these provisions. It prohibits all legislative, executive or judicial action at any level of state or local government designed to protect the named class, a class we shall refer to as homosexual persons or gays and lesbians. The amendment reads:

No Protected Status Based on Homosexual, Lesbian, or Bisexual Orientation. Neither the State of Colorado, through any of its branches or departments, nor any of its agencies, political subdivisions, municipalities or school districts, shall enact, adopt or enforce any statute, regulation, ordinance or policy whereby homosexual, lesbian or bisexual orientation, conduct, practices or relationships shall constitute or otherwise be the basis of or entitle any person or class of persons to have or claim any minority status, quota preferences, protected status or claim of discrimination. This Section of the Constitution shall be in all respects self-executing.

* * *

II

The State's principal argument in defense of Amendment 2 is that it puts gays and lesbians in the same position as all other persons. So, the State says, the measure does no more than deny homosexuals special rights. This reading of the amendment's language is implausible. * * *

Sweeping and comprehensive is the change in legal status effected by this law. So much is evident from the ordinances that the Colorado Supreme Court declared would be void by operation of Amendment 2. Homosexuals, by state decree, are put in a solitary class with respect to transactions and relations in both the private and governmental spheres. The amendment withdraws from homosexuals, but no others, specific legal protection from the injuries caused by discrimination, and it forbids reinstatement of these laws and policies. * * *

* * * [W]e cannot accept the view that Amendment 2's prohibition on specific legal protections does no more than deprive homosexuals of special rights. To the contrary, the amendment imposes a special disability upon those persons alone. Homosexuals are forbidden the safeguards that others enjoy or may seek without constraint. They can obtain specific protection against discrimination only by enlisting the citizenry of Colorado to amend the state constitution or perhaps, on the State's view, by trying to pass helpful laws of general applicability. This is so no matter how local or discrete the harm, no matter how public and widespread the injury. We find nothing special in the protections Amendment 2 withholds. These are protections taken for granted by most people either because they already have them or do not need them; these are protections against exclusion from an almost limitless number of transactions and endeavors that constitute ordinary civic life in a free society.

III

The Fourteenth Amendment's promise that no person shall be denied the equal protection of the laws must co-exist with the practical necessity that most legislation classifies for one purpose or another, with resulting disadvantage to various groups or persons. We have attempted to reconcile the principle with the reality by stating that, if a law neither burdens a fundamental right nor targets a suspect class, we will uphold the legislative classification so long as it bears a rational relation to some legitimate end.

Amendment 2 fails, indeed defies, even this conventional inquiry. First, the amendment has the peculiar property of imposing a broad and undifferentiated disability on a single named group, an exceptional and, as we shall explain, invalid form of legislation. Second, its sheer breadth is so discontinuous with the reasons offered for it that the amendment seems inexplicable by anything but animus toward the class that it affects; it lacks a rational relationship to legitimate state interests.

Taking the first point, even in the ordinary equal protection case calling for the most deferential of standards, we insist on knowing the relation between the classification adopted and the object to be attained. The search for the link between classification and objective gives substance to the Equal Protection Clause; it provides guidance and discipline for the legislature, which is entitled to know what sorts of laws it can pass; and it marks the limits of our own authority. In the ordinary case, a law will be sustained if it can be said to advance a legitimate government interest, even if the law seems unwise or works to the disadvantage of a particular group, or if the rationale for it seems tenuous. See New Orleans v. Dukes, 427 U.S. 297 (1976)(tourism benefits justified classification favoring pushcart vendors of certain longevity); Williamson v. Lee Optical of Okla., Inc., 348 U.S. 483 (1955)(assumed health concerns justified law favoring optometrists over opticians); Railway Express Agency, Inc. v. New York, 336 U.S. 106 (1949)(potential traffic hazards justified exemption of vehicles advertising the owner's products from general advertising ban). The laws challenged in the cases just cited were narrow enough in scope and grounded in a sufficient factual context for us to ascertain that there existed some relation between the classification and the purpose it served. By requiring that the classification bear a rational relationship to an independent and legitimate legislative end, we ensure that classifications are not drawn for the purpose of disadvantaging the group burdened by the law. See United States Railroad Retirement Bd. v. Fritz, 449 U.S. 166, 181 (1980) (Stevens, J., concurring)("If the adverse impact on the disfavored class is an apparent aim of the legislature, its impartiality would be suspect.").

Amendment 2 confounds this normal process of judicial review. It is at once too narrow and too broad. It identifies persons by a single trait and then denies them protection across the board. The resulting disqualification of a class of persons from the right to seek specific protection from the law is unprecedented in our jurisprudence. * * *

It is not within our constitutional tradition to enact laws of this sort. Central both to the idea of the rule of law and to our own Constitution's guarantee of equal protection is the principle that government and each of its parts remain open on impartial terms to all who seek its assistance. * * * Respect for this principle explains why laws singling out a certain class of citizens for disfavored legal status or general hardships are rare. A law declaring that in general it shall be more difficult for one group of citizens than for all others to seek aid from the government is itself a denial of equal protection of the laws in the most literal sense. * * *

A second and related point is that laws of the kind now before us raise the inevitable inference that the disadvantage imposed is born of animosity toward the class of persons affected. "If the constitutional conception of 'equal protection of the laws' means anything, it must at the very least mean that a bare * * * desire to harm a politically unpopular group cannot constitute legitimate governmental interest." Department of Agriculture v. Moreno, 413 U.S. 528, 534 (1973). Even laws enacted for broad and ambitious purposes often can be explained by reference to legitimate public policies which justify the incidental disadvantages they impose on certain persons. Amendment 2, however, in making a general announcement that gays and lesbians shall not have any particular protections from the law, inflicts on them immediate, continuing, and real injuries that outrun and belie any legitimate justifications that may be claimed for it. We conclude that, in addition to the far-reaching deficiencies of Amendment 2 that we have noted, the principles it offends, in another sense, are conventional and venerable; a law must bear a rational relationship to a legitimate governmental purpose, and Amendment 2 does not.

We must conclude that Amendment 2 classifies homosexuals not to further a proper legislative end but to make them unequal to everyone else. This Colorado cannot do. A State cannot so deem a class of persons a stranger to its laws. Amendment 2 violates the Equal Protection Clause, and the judgment of the Supreme Court of Colorado is affirmed.

■ Justice Scalia, with whom the Chief Justice and Justice Thomas join, dissenting.

The Court has mistaken a Kulturkampf for a fit of spite. The constitutional amendment before us here is not the manifestation of a " 'bare * * * desire to harm' " homosexuals, but is rather a modest attempt by seemingly tolerant Coloradans to preserve traditional sexual mores against the efforts of a politically powerful minority to revise those mores through use of the laws. That objective, and the means chosen to achieve it, are not only unimpeachable under any constitutional doctrine hitherto pronounced (hence the opinion's heavy reliance upon principles of righteousness rather than judicial holdings); they have been specifically approved by the Congress of the United States and by this Court.

In holding that homosexuality cannot be singled out for disfavorable treatment, the Court contradicts a decision, unchallenged here, pronounced only 10 years ago, see Bowers v. Hardwick, 478 U.S. 186 (1986), and places the prestige of this institution behind the proposition that opposition to homosexuality is as reprehensible as racial or religious bias. Whether it is or not is precisely the cultural debate that gave rise to the Colorado constitutional amendment (and to the preferential laws against which the amendment was directed). Since the Constitution of the United States says nothing about this subject, it is left to be resolved by normal democratic means, including the democratic adoption of provisions in state constitutions. This Court has no business imposing upon all Americans the resolution favored by the elite class from which the Members of this institution are selected, pronouncing that "animosity" toward homosexuality, is evil. I vigorously dissent.

I

The central thesis of the Court's reasoning is that any group is denied equal protection when, to obtain advantage (or, presumably, to avoid disadvantage), it must have recourse to a more general and hence more difficult level of political decisionmaking than others. The world has never heard of such a principle, which is why the Court's opinion is so long on emotive utterance and so short on relevant legal citation. And it seems to me most unlikely that any multilevel democracy can function under such a principle. For whenever a disadvantage is imposed, or conferral of a benefit is prohibited, at one of the higher levels of democratic decisionmaking (i.e., by the state legislature rather than local government, or by the people at large in the state constitution rather than the legislature), the affected group has (under this theory) been denied equal protection. To take the simplest of examples, consider a state law prohibiting the award of municipal contracts to relatives of mayors or city councilmen. Once such a law is passed, the group composed of such relatives must, in order to get the benefit of city contracts, persuade the state legislature—unlike all other citizens, who need only persuade the municipality. It is ridiculous to consider this a denial of equal protection, which is why the Court's theory is unheard-of.

The Court might reply that the example I have given is not a denial of equal protection only because the same "rational basis" (avoidance of corruption) which renders constitutional the substantive discrimination against relatives (i.e., the fact that they alone cannot obtain city contracts) also automatically suffices to sustain what might be called the electoral-procedural discrimination against them (i.e., the fact that they must go to the state level to get this changed). This is of course a perfectly reasonable response, and would explain why "electoral-procedural discrimination" has not hitherto been heard of: a law that is valid in its substance is automatically valid in its level of enactment. But the Court cannot afford to make this argument, for as I shall discuss next, there is no doubt of a rational basis for the substance of the prohibition at issue here. The Court's entire novel theory rests upon the proposition that there is something special—something that cannot be justified by normal "rational basis" analysis—in making a disadvantaged group (or a nonpreferred group) resort to a higher decisionmaking level. That proposition finds no support in law or logic.

II

I turn next to whether there was a legitimate rational basis for the substance of the constitutional amendment—for the prohibition of special protection for homosexuals. It is unsurprising that the Court avoids discussion of this question, since the answer is so obviously yes. The case most relevant to the issue before us today is not even mentioned in the Court's opinion: In Bowers v. Hardwick, 478 U.S. 186 (1986), we held that the Constitution does not prohibit what virtually all States had done from the founding of the Republic until very recent years—making homosexual conduct a crime. That holding is unassailable, except by those who think that the Constitution changes to suit current fashions. But in any event it is a given in the present case: Respondents' briefs did not urge overruling Bowers, and at oral argument respondents' counsel expressly disavowed any intent to seek such overruling. If it is constitutionally permissible for a State to make homosexual conduct criminal, surely it is constitutionally permissible for a State to enact other laws merely disfavoring homosexual conduct. * * *

[Editor—Scalia argues that Bowers establishes a rational basis for the Amendment even if it defines the affected group as those who have a tendency towards homosexual conduct, because a statutory category need not be precisely tailored—"[W]here criminal sanctions are not involved, homosexual 'orientation' is an acceptable stand-in for homosexual conduct. A State 'does not violate the Equal Protection Clause merely because the classifications made by its laws are imperfect.' "]

III

The foregoing suffices to establish what the Court's failure to cite any case remotely in point would lead one to suspect: No principle set forth in the Constitution, nor even any imagined by this Court in the past 200 years, prohibits what Colorado has done here. But the case for Colorado is much stronger than that. What it has done is not only unprohibited, but eminently reasonable, with close, congressionally approved precedent in earlier constitutional practice.

First, as to its eminent reasonableness. The Court's opinion contains grim, disapproving hints that Coloradans have been guilty of "animus" or "animosity" toward homosexuality, as though that has been established as Unamerican. Of course it is our moral heritage that one should not hate any human being or class of human beings. But I had thought that one could consider certain conduct reprehensible—murder, for example, or polygamy, or cruelty to animals—and could exhibit even "animus" toward such conduct. Surely that is the only sort of "animus" at issue here: moral disapproval of homosexual conduct, the same sort of moral disapproval that produced the centuries-old criminal laws that we held constitutional in Bowers. The Colorado amendment does not, to speak entirely precisely, prohibit giving favored status to people who are homosexuals; they can be favored for many reasons—for example, because they are senior citizens or members of racial minorities. But it prohibits giving them favored status because of their homosexual conduct—that is, it prohibits favored status for homosexuality.

But though Coloradans are, as I say, entitled to be hostile toward homosexual conduct, the fact is that the degree of hostility reflected by Amendment 2 is the smallest conceivable. The Court's portrayal of Coloradans as a society fallen victim to pointless, hate-filled "gay-bashing" is so false as to be comical. Colorado not only is one of the 25 States that have repealed their antisodomy laws, but was among the first to do so. But the society that eliminates criminal punishment for homosexual acts does not necessarily abandon the view that homosexuality is morally wrong and socially harmful; often, abolition simply reflects the view that enforcement of such criminal laws involves unseemly intrusion into the intimate lives of citizens.

There is a problem, however, which arises when criminal sanction of homosexuality is eliminated but moral and social disapprobation of homosexuality is meant to be retained. The Court cannot be unaware of that problem; it is evident in many cities of the country, and occasionally bubbles to the surface of the news, in heated political disputes over such matters as the introduction into local schools of books teaching that homosexuality is an optional and fully acceptable "alternate life style." The problem (a problem, that is, for those who wish to retain social disapprobation of homosexuality) is that, because those who engage in homosexual conduct tend to reside in disproportionate numbers in certain communities, and of course care about homosexual-rights issues much more ardently than the public at large, they possess political power much greater than their numbers, both locally and statewide. Quite understandably, they devote this political power to achieving not merely a grudging social toleration, but full social acceptance, of homosexuality. * * *

That is where Amendment 2 came in. It sought to counter both the geographic concentration and the disproportionate political power of homosexuals by (1) resolving the controversy at the statewide level, and (2) making the election a single-issue contest for both sides. It put directly, to all the citizens of the State, the question: Should homosexuality be given special protection? They answered no. The Court today asserts that this most democratic of procedures is unconstitutional. [Editor—Note the reference to "this most democratic of procedures" to defend the Colorado amendment.] * * *

As I have noted above, this is proved false every time a state law prohibiting or disfavoring certain conduct is passed, because such a law prevents the adversely affected group—whether drug addicts, or smokers, or gun owners, or motorcyclists—from changing the policy thus established in "each of [the] parts" of the State. * * *

But there is a much closer analogy, one that involves precisely the effort by the majority of citizens to preserve its view of sexual morality statewide, against the efforts of a geographically concentrated and politically powerful minority to undermine it. The constitutions of the States of Arizona, Idaho, New Mexico, Oklahoma, and Utah to this day contain provisions stating that polygamy is "forever prohibited." See Ariz. Const., Art. XX, par. 2; Idaho Const., Art. I, § 4; N.M. Const., Art. XXI, § 1; Okla. Const., Art. I, § 2; Utah Const., Art. III, § 1. Polygamists, and those who have a polygamous "orientation," have been "singled out" by these provisions for much more severe treatment than merely denial of favored status; and that treatment can only be changed by achieving amendment of the state constitutions. The Court's disposition today suggests that these provisions are unconstitutional, and that polygamy must be permitted in these States on a state-legislated, or perhaps even local-option, basis—unless, of course, polygamists for some reason have fewer constitutional rights than homosexuals.

* * *

IV

* * * The Court's stern disapproval of "animosity" towards homosexuality might be compared with what an earlier Court [ ] said in Murphy v. Ramsey, 114 U.S. 15 (1885), rejecting a constitutional challenge to a United States statute that denied the franchise in federal territories to those who engaged in polygamous cohabitation:

> Certainly no legislation can be supposed more wholesome and necessary in the founding of a free, self-governing commonwealth, fit to take rank as one of the co-ordinate States of the Union, than that which seeks to establish it on the basis of the idea of the family, as consisting in and springing from the union for life of one man and one woman in the holy estate of matrimony; the sure foundation of all that is stable and noble in our civilization; the best guaranty of that reverent morality which is the source of all beneficent progress in social and political improvement.

I would not myself indulge in such official praise for heterosexual monogamy, because I think it no business of the courts (as opposed to the political branches) to take sides in this culture war. But the Court today has done so, not only by inventing a novel and extravagant constitutional doctrine to take the victory away from traditional forces, but even by verbally disparaging as bigotry adherence to traditional attitudes. To suggest, for example, that this constitutional amendment springs from nothing more than " 'a bare * * * desire to harm a politically unpopular group,' " quoting Department of Agriculture v. Moreno, 413 U.S. 528, 534 (1973), is nothing short of insulting. (It is also nothing short of preposterous to call "politically unpopular" a group which enjoys enormous influence in American media and politics, and which, as the trial court here noted, though composing no more than 4% of the population had the support of 46% of the voters on Amendment 2.)

When the Court takes sides in the culture wars, it tends to be with the knights rather than the villeins—and more specifically with the Templars, reflecting the views and values of the lawyer class from which the Court's Members are drawn. How that class feels about homosexuality will be evident to anyone who wishes to interview job applicants at virtually any of the Nation's law schools. The interviewer may refuse to offer a job because the applicant is a Republican; because he is an adulterer; because he went to the wrong prep school or belongs to the wrong country club; because he eats snails; because he is a womanizer; because she wears real-animal fur; or even because he hates the Chicago Cubs. But if the interviewer should wish not to be an associate or partner of an applicant because he disapproves of the applicant's homosexuality, then he will have violated the pledge which the Association of American Law Schools requires all its member-schools to exact from job interviewers: "assurance of the employer's willingness" to hire homosexuals. Bylaws of the Association of American Law Schools, Inc. § 6–4(b); Executive Committee Regulations of the Association of American Law Schools § 6.19, in 1995 Handbook, Association of American Law Schools. This law-school view of what "prejudices" must be stamped out may be contrasted with the more plebeian attitudes that apparently still prevail in the United States Congress, which has been unresponsive to repeated attempts to extend to homosexuals the protections of federal civil rights laws, see, e.g., Employment Non–Discrimination Act of 1994, S. 2238, 103d Cong., 2d Sess. (1994); Civil Rights Amendments of 1975, H. R. 5452, 94th Cong., 1st Sess. (1975), and which took the pains to exclude them specifically from the Americans With Disabilities Act of 1990, see 42 U.S.C. § 12211(a) (1988 ed., Supp. V). * * *

Today's opinion has no foundation in American constitutional law, and barely pretends to. The people of Colorado have adopted an entirely reasonable provision which does not even disfavor homosexuals in any substantive sense, but merely denies them preferential treatment. Amendment 2 is designed to prevent piecemeal deterioration of the sexual morality favored by a majority of

Coloradans, and is not only an appropriate means to that legitimate end, but a means that Americans have employed before. Striking it down is an act, not of judicial judgment, but of political will. I dissent.

The conclusion of Scalia's opinion contains an allusion to Hamilton's dichotomy between legislative will and judicial judgment. On the one hand, he accuses the Court of being willful. On the other hand, he defends the legislature's right to act willfully—even with animus—as a legitimate foundation for lawmaking. These foundations can be found in our traditions, which include animus towards homosexual relationships, polygamy and murder? There is, he says, an element of such will at the core of many legislative judgments.

And he is surely right about this. Will and judgment are intertwined. But this observation raises two questions. First, the fact that will and judgment are intertwined does not tell us how they should interact in specific circumstances. The majority is, in effect, requiring the lawmaker to be something more than *merely* willful, to include some exercise of rational judgment, to pay closer attention to the fact that the Colorado amendment may deny citizens protection from outlaw status. Scalia completely dichotomizes will and judgment, deferring to the merely willful legislature.

Second, if judges make judgments and judgments contain elements of willfulness, how can judges judge? The majority's answer in this case might have been that there *is* an element of judicial willfulness in *judicial* judgment, but it is not *merely* willful. Like the animus against homosexuality, it also rests on a tradition—one that assures people equal protection of the law—and marginalizing a group by making them outlaws denies them equal protection in the most literal sense of the word. What is Scalia's answer to this argument?

iv) STATE LAW REQUIREMENTS

Do not overlook state constitutional law provisions in challenging initiatives and referendums.

1. Requirements that accompanying explanatory statement be clear

State constitutions or statutes usually require that the public be adequately informed about the issues on which there will be an initiative or referendum. One such provision requires that the language on which there will be a vote be accompanied by an explanatory statement.

In Kimmelman v. Burgio, 497 A.2d 890 (N.J.Super.1985), the legislature drafted an explanatory statement accompanying a proposal for a constitutional amendment to be voted on in a referendum, but the court thought it was misleading. Under state law, if the legislature did not provide an explanatory statement, the Attorney General had to provide one if the question put to the public was not clear. Here is the original explanatory statement by the legislature and the court's suggested revision. What was the court worried about and did it do a good job of rewriting the statement?

The specific issue concerned an amendment to the state constitution which gave the legislature a legislative veto over state agency rules. The original statement by the legislature was as follows:

> State executive agencies are authorized by law to issue rules and regulations which have the force and effect of law. The Legislature has the duty to review those rules and regulations to see if they carry out the intention of the Legislature as contained in law and if they are efficient and effective. This amendment provides a constitutional recognition of this oversight role by permitting the Legislature to prohibit proposed rules from taking effect and to invalidate existing rules.

The suggested revision by the court was as follows:

> State executive agencies are authorized to issue rules and regulations which have the force and effect of law. The Legislature may review those rules and regulations from time to time in order to determine whether they conform with the intent of the statutes. The Supreme Court of New Jersey has ruled that under the New Jersey Constitution in general the Legislature may not invalidate an executive rule or regulation except by adopting legislation subject to the Governor's veto. This amendment addresses that Supreme Court ruling by modifying the New Jersey Constitution to allow the Legislature to invalidate executive rules and regulations without enacting legislation and without presenting the issue to the Governor. Its enactment would constitute a fundamental change in the relationship between the co-equal branches of government.

Does the *federal* Due Process Clause protect state voters from unclear summaries drafted by the legislature about constitutional amendments on which the people will vote? In Burton v. State, 953 F.2d 1266 (11th Cir.1992), the summary stated that the issue was whether "the General Assembly may authorize lawsuits against the state," when in fact the amendment cut back on suits against the state permitted by recent state court decisions. The federal court held that there was no federal constitutional violation unless the ballot summary was so misleading that voters could not recognize the subject of the amendment. Should the federal standard be higher?

2. One-subject rule

In the following two excerpts, the opinions discuss the one-subject rule in the direct democracy context.

Oregon Education Ass'n v. Phillips

727 P.2d 602 (Or.1986).

■ Linde, Justice, concurring. * * *

Rules governing the germaneness of provisions combined in a single bill are appropriate constraints within the legislative process. They are likely to be routinely respected in daily practice, and objections can be and often are raised by points of order in the legislative body. When a majority overrides the objection, at least it acts with notice of the contents of the bill and upon majority support for combining its several parts. It is doubtful whether a court later should invalidate such an institutional decision of the legislature, and Oregon courts in fact have not done so.

The initiative process, however, is quite different from that in the Legislative Assembly, and it poses greater institutional risks both for the internal rationality of measures and for the comprehension of the citizens who must vote on them. First, once the sponsors have drafted and submitted the text of a measure, there is no further opportunity to correct, refine, or clarify that text, even to fit it into existing statutes, no matter what obscurity, errors, or unintended implications the sponsors themselves or anyone else may discover in it. Second, there is nothing comparable to the hearings of legislative committees to raise questions and allow the presentation of different viewpoints in order to eliminate unacceptable aspects of a proposal and to produce an improved or at least defensible compromise with the help of staff members and other knowledge-able persons. Third, efforts to secure or to defeat passage of an initiative measure by the voters are bound to rely on slogans and oversimplified appeals that can be broadcast to the public at large by advertising techniques rather than on the give and take of debate among legislators chosen to represent, and sensitive to, constituents with divergent interests.

These differences are so substantial that they raised doubt whether under some circumstances replacement of the legislative process by the initiative would be inconsistent with the "Republican Form of Government" required for every state by Article IV, section 4, of the United States Constitution. It is these differences, also, that recently led the Florida Supreme Court to hold an initiative proposal to a tighter "one subject" standard than a proposal that has gone through a normal deliberative process. Fine v. Firestone, 448 So.2d 984 (1984). Although Oregon takes pains to provide carefully written explanatory ballot titles and to include both explanatory and argumentative statements about each measure in the official Voters Pamphlet sent to registered voters, the risks of mistake, confusion, and emotional responses to a single, yes-or-no choice divorced from the context of other laws or alternative measures cannot wholly be avoided.

Washington Federation of State Employees v. Washington

901 P.2d 1028 (Wash.1995).

[Editor—The court affirmed a prior decision that the one-subject/title rule applied to initiatives and referendums. See Fritz v. Gorton, 517 P.2d 911 (Wash.1974)(Const. art. 2, § 19 applies to initiatives), *reversing*, Senior Citizens League v. Department of Social Sec., 228 P.2d 478 (Wash.1951). It noted that only one of the seven states which have considered this issue had held that the one-subject/title rule did not apply to initiatives. The court also held that the state constitutional requirement mandating notice to the public of an initiative's contents (through a pamphlet with explanatory statement) did not obviate the need for a one-subject/title rule, because not everyone read this material and, in any event, adequate notice did not prevent logrolling. A concurring opinion stated as follows.]

■ Talmadge, J. (concurring in part/dissenting in part) * * *

The majority is correct in determining that art. 2, § 19 of the Washington Constitution applies to initiatives and referenda for the reasons articulated in the majority opinion. * * *

As the majority correctly discerns, these purposes must be met both for enactments by the Legislature and enactments by the people. Enactments by the people may, as with legislative enactments, be the product of logrolling or contain provisions that are not revealed to the average reader from the title of the act or the ballot question for the measure. Initiatives and referenda are a valuable tool in direct democracy for the people of the State of Washington. The potential for abuse of initiatives and referenda is, in many respects, more significant than the possibility of abuse of the legislative process. There is no public hearing process for initiatives and referenda, as for bills in the Legislature. Once submitted to the voters, initiatives and referenda cannot be amended. Once adopted, initiatives and referenda may be amended only by a super-majority for two years after enactment. Art. 2, § 1(c). As Justice Rosellini forcefully noted in Fritz v. Gorton, 83 Wash.2d 275, 333, 517 P.2d 911 (1974):

> Logrolling is an even greater danger to the democratic exercise of power in the initiative process. What is to prevent an individual or a group from including mildly objectionable legislation—that is, legislation which might benefit a small group and is mildly disfavored by the electorate as a whole—in an initiative measure which includes other legislation which has great popular appeal? In the legislature the committee process assures that such a provision will be detected; the amendment process provides the remedy. The legislature can delete parts of a proposal it disfavors; the electorate is faced with a Hobson's

choice: reject what it likes or adopt what it dislikes. Only article 2, section 19, preserves the integrity of the initiative process.

In determining whether or not a rational unity exists between the various subdivisions of a general enactment, courts should consider a number of questions. First, was the process by which the law was enacted open to public involvement? Plainly, greater latitude must be given where a very open and public process was utilized for the enactment of the initiative measure than where an initiative was prepared secretly by various special interest groups. * * *

Second, was the public given adequate notice of the contents of the enactment? The evidence of the campaign process, including the voters pamphlet, with respect to initiatives or referenda, is important to an art. 2, § 19 analysis. If the public knows that certain issues are treated together by the Legislature or initiative proponents, this ensures that the decision-makers are not misled in the enactment of the legislation.

Third, have the issues been considered together historically? * * *

Fourth, what was the subject matter of the enactment? The Legislature must be given greater latitude under art. 2, § 19 when the legislation is a budget bill, for example, than a more narrow enactment. Similarly, if the legislation is an omnibus bill designed by the Legislature or the people to address a larger subject area, the wishes of the Legislature or the people in addressing an issue comprehensively in a single bill may be respected. See, e.g., State v. Jenkins, 68 Wash. App. 897, 847 P.2d 488 (1993)(Uniform Controlled Substances Act of 1989 upheld). * * *

Finally, does the title of the enactment indicate a common unifying theme to the enactment? If the title of the enactment is a "laundry list" of the contents of the legislation, this is suggestive of the possibility that the Legislature or the proponents of a popular enactment could not articulate a single unifying principle for the contents of the measure. Similarly, a law containing subdivisions that allegedly relate to a subject such as "fiscal affairs," "government," or "public welfare" could violate the single-subject provision because the subject matter was excessively general.

QUESTION

Based on these critiques of direct democracy, do you think the following decision is correct in concluding that there *is* one subject? In Legislature of State of California v. Eu, 816 P.2d 1309 (Cal.1991), the California Supreme Court dealt with an initiative (Proposition 140) imposing term limits, limiting amounts which could be spent for legislative operations, and capping legislative pensions. It upheld the law against a "single subject" challenge, as follows:

> Petitioners appear to be confusing germaneness with functional relationship. As we have previously held, the single-subject provision does not require that each of the provisions of a measure effectively interlock in a functional relationship. It is enough that the various provisions are reasonably related to a common theme or purpose.
>
> The framers of Proposition 140 evidently believed that "the powers of incumbency" could be reduced or checked by making an extended career in public office both less available and less attractive to incumbent legislators, through term and budgetary limitations as well as reduced pension benefits. Budgetary reductions may have been deemed necessary to reduce the advantages incumbents possess vis-a-vis other candidates * * *. As for limited pension benefits, the measure expressly states that the limitation was appropriate because service in the Legislature is no longer "intended as a career occupation." The framers presumably did not believe budgetary or pension limitations were needed with respect to the other constitutional officers subject to the term limitations of the measure.
>
> Whether or not these various provisions are wise or sensible, and will combine effectively to achieve their stated purpose, is not our concern in evaluating the present single-subject challenge. Sensible or not, the separate aspects of Proposition 140 relate to the furtherance of a common purpose.
>
> We conclude that the various provisions of Proposition 140 are reasonably germane to the single subject of incumbency reform.

3. Permitting constitutional amendment but not "revision" by direct democracy

California distinguishes between the power to amend the constitution, which can be accomplished by initiative, and "revision" of the constitution, which requires a constitutional convention called by the legislature. This reflects some mistrust of the initiative process for certain constitutional changes.

Which of the following rises to the level of a "revision"? Is there anything in the prior discussion of direct democracy that suggests how to draw a line between amending and revising? See Legislature of State of California v. Eu, 816 P.2d 1309 (Cal.1991).

1. A proposal that state courts cannot provide procedural rights under the state constitution beyond what the federal Supreme Court provides under the federal constitution.

2. A proposal to limit state Senators to two terms and Assembly members to three terms.

EXECUTIVE–LEGISLATIVE RELATIONS

This Chapter deals with the relationship between the executive and the legislature. We first look in Chapter 18.01 at how courts deal with discrepancies between the text of a bill passed by the legislature and that signed by the chief executive. Textual discrepancies appear to raise important issues of political power—does the chief executive have a significant lawmaking role. But such discrepancies turn out in practice to be insignificant when compared to the fundamental legislative-executive conflicts that arise regarding the executive control of spending (impoundment of appropriated funds and the line item veto), and the legislative veto of actions taken by executive branch officials and administrative agencies.

Executive control over spending is discussed in Chapter 18.02, with primary attention to the line item veto (allowing the chief executive to strike out specific parts of an appropriations bill, rather than the entire legislation). The concerns giving rise to the line item veto in the majority of *state* constitutions are historically related to those discussed in Chapter 17—to discourage logrolling and secretive legislation. It compensates for the fact that the one-subject rule is usually inapplicable to general appropriations bills. The President also has a line item veto power, granted by congressional legislation in 1996, not by the U.S. Constitution. The President's line item veto power has a different history and raises different problems from the item veto in state constitutions.

The legislative veto is discussed in Chapter 18.03. The legislative veto allows one or both houses of the legislature (or, in some versions, its committees) to veto action taken by executive branch officials and administrative agencies without going through the normal legislative process (including signature by the chief executive).

Determining the validity and interpreting the scope of the exercise of the executive line item veto and the legislative veto obviously depends on the court's view of the respective lawmaking competence of both the executive and legislative branches, as well as on the judge's own sense of lawmaking authority.

Chapter 18.04 concludes with a discussion of lawsuits in which members of Congress try to enforce institutional rules about how law is made. It finds a place in this Chapter, because most of the cases concern relationships between the executive and the legislature. It is also a good place to conclude the course because the judicial role in hearing complaints by Members of

Congress focuses attention on what courts should be doing in our constitutional system.

18.01   DISCREPANCY BETWEEN BILL PASSED BY LEGISLATURE AND BILL SIGNED BY EXECUTIVE

Sometimes there is a discrepancy between the bill passed by the legislature and the bill signed by the chief executive because of a clerical error. If the enrolled bill doctrine does *not* apply to validate the version signed by the executive, courts must decide whether there is a valid law despite the discrepancy and, if there *is* a valid law, whether the operative law is that passed by the legislature or signed by the executive.

How can the law be that passed by the legislature, if a different law is signed by the executive?   (1) Is it because the executive is a minor player in the legislative process?   (2) Does the legislative version prevail only if there is evidence of executive intent to adopt the law as passed by the legislature? (3) What if the public is likely to rely on the text signed by the Governor?

a)   TWO CASES

Rice v. Lonoke–Cabot Road Improvement Dist. No. 11

221 S.W. 179 (Ark.1920).

■ Humphreys, J. * * *

[Editor—A statute providing for road building was mistakenly altered after legislative passage and before enrollment to exclude 19 sections of land in "township 4 north, range 9 west." The Governor signed the "incorrect" version. The lawsuit was about whether there was a statute authorizing road building. The court upheld the statute as passed by the legislature.]

The chief insistence for reversal is that the bill approved by the Governor was a different bill from the bill passed by the Legislature. An enrolled bill, in Legislative parlance, is a reproduction or copy of the identical bill passed by both houses of the General Assembly. The enrolling clerk or committee has no power or authority to modify a bill passed by the General Assembly in any respect. It follows that the purpose and intention of the Governor in signing an enrolled bill, or in allowing an enrolled bill to become a law without his signature, is to approve the bill passed by both branches of the Legislature, or to acquiesce in such bill becoming a law. In approving an enrolled bill, therefore, it may aptly be said that the Governor intends to, and does, approve the original or identical bill passed by the General Assembly. For this reason additions, omissions, or misprisions of the enrolling clerk in copying the bill to be signed by the Speaker of the House and President of the Senate and to be presented to the Governor do not impair or invalidate the act. Otherwise legislation would depend entirely upon the accuracy of the enrolling clerk and care of the enrolling committee. * * *

It is apparent from the face of the enrolled bill that lands in township 4 north, range 9 west, are intended to be included, but were omitted in copying from the original bill. * * * By reference to the original bill published by the Legislature it is apparent that the enrolling clerk omitted to incorporate in the enrolled bill the paragraph in the original bill describing 19 sections of land traversed by [a] proposed road. The paragraph was in the original bill and rendered the district symmetrical in form. It is true the omission from the enrolled bill constituted a material discrepancy between the enrolled and the original bill, but nevertheless the omission was a clerical error, apparent from the face of the bill, and what should have been incorporated in the enrolled bill is ascertainable from an inspection of the original bill in the office of the secretary of state. * * *

One judge did not agree with this opinion. He refused to view the Governor as "a mere automaton." He asked rhetorically: "[Is] it to be assumed that, because he is willing to give assent to the bill becoming a law which is presented to him, he would also assent that any other bill dealing with the same subject, although materially different, should likewise become a law?" He concluded that a material difference between the law signed by the Governor and passed by the legislature voids the law.

––––––––

Harris v. Shanahan

387 P.2d 771 (Kan.1963).

■ Fatzer, Judge. * * *

[Editor—The statute in question described state senatorial districts. The Kansas courts do not follow the enrolled bill rule. In this case the court voids the statute because of the discrepancy between the bill passed by the legislature and signed by the Governor. Is there anything about the issue in this case that justifies voiding this statute, but not the road building statute in the prior Rice case? What are the practical consequences of voiding the statute in each case?]

* * * [T]he minds of the house and senate met in common agreement that senate bill 440, as amended by the house, be passed. At some later time, after passage of the bill by both houses, a variation appeared in the language establishing senatorial district No. 15, notwithstanding the senate committee's report that the bill was correctly engrossed and enrolled. Unfortunately, [ ] the language relating to the city of Leawood was omitted, and the remain-

ing language of the house amendment was such as to give no warning of the omission. The enrolled bill * * * was approved and signed by the governor on April 17, 1963. * * *

* * * The parties candidly concede there is no ambiguity in that part of the bill which established senatorial district 15. What they ask this court to do is not to construe the statute, but in effect, enlarge it so that what was omitted by inadvertence or error, may be included within its scope. To supply the omissions under these circumstances would transcend the judicial function. * * *

We assume that the intention of both houses of the legislature and of the governor was to enact a law which gave adequate senatorial representation to every citizen of Kansas, including the residents of the city of Leawood. No one questions that fact. But we are confronted with what was done, not what the legislature may have really intended to do. * * * The long and short of this case is that the bill passed by both houses of the legislature was not the bill approved and signed by the governor and this court has no authority to insert what was omitted. The requirements of [the Constitution] are mandatory that the governor sign the same bill which passed the legislature. It follows that the enrolled bill the governor signed (Laws 1963, Ch. 13) was not made into law in the form and manner prescribed, and is a void enactment.

Due to the nature of senate bill 440 and its importance to the people of the state, we have examined the question somewhat at length. It is to be deeply regretted that as important a law as this, covering a subject of great public interest, should, because of gross carelessness of someone, be wiped bodily from the statute book. But the court is not responsible for this; nor can it usurp the functions of the legislature or the governor, and, by shutting its eyes to the undisputed legislative record, declare a bill as passed by both houses of the legislature, which was never presented to the governor nor approved by him, to be a valid law. It is lamentable that error on the part of engrossing clerks and legislative committees should defeat the action of the legislature. But the strict rule calling for full compliance with constitutional requirements is, in the long run, a good one. In some cases it may work a hardship, but, by and large, it is beneficial to our republican form of government.

b) Executive Intent

In State v. Wright, 163 P.2d 190 (Wyo.1945), a bill had been passed providing for disbursement of 23% of certain revenues to counties and 2% to cities and towns. The enrolled bill, however, which was signed by the Governor, provided that 25% of the revenues would go to counties and 2% to cities and towns. The Governor was aware of the mistake and stated in a letter accompanying signature of the bill that he wanted the law to go into effect because the 2% was badly needed by cities and towns. The court held that the law was that which passed the legislature, providing 23% to counties and 2% to cities and towns.

In State v. Hanson, 342 P.2d 706 (Idaho 1959), the Governor signed a tax bill specifying that tax rates would be 3.5%. The bill that passed the state legislature specified a 3% rate. A letter from the Governor indicated that he intended to sign legislation specifying the 3% rate adopted by the legislature. Admitting that the discrepancy was material, the court held that the 3% rate was law. Would anyone rely to their detriment on the 3.5% rate in the bill as signed by the Governor?

If there had been no expression of executive intent to adopt the law passed by the legislature in these two cases, how should the court have dealt with the discrepancy between legislative-passed and executive-signed bills?

18.02 EXECUTIVE CONTROL OF SPENDING

a) BACKGROUND OF LINE ITEM VETO

The President and every state Governor (except in North Carolina) has the power to veto an *entire* bill, subject to legislative override. At the state level, there is considerable variation in the legislature's power to override a veto, reflecting in part an historical antipathy to executive power. States may require a simple majority of those voting, a simple majority of the entire membership, a two-thirds, or a three-quarters vote to override a Governor's veto.

A line item veto (sometimes referred to as an "item veto") is more focused than the regular executive veto. It permits the chief executive to veto only a portion of an *appropriations* bill, rather than the entire legislation.[1]

Historically, the executive's line item veto grew out of the same suspicion of legislatures which produced the one subject rule, discussed in Chapter 17. The Governor was considered less subject to the kind of private interest pressures that were rampant in many legislatures. The item veto is, however, different from the one subject rule in an important respect. The item veto lets the *Governor* remove something from a law, but the one subject rule lets the *court* decide whether the statute has more than one subject. Moreover, the item veto leaves the rest of the law in tact, but a violation of the one subject rule has an uncertain impact on the survival of the entire statute.

The first item veto appeared in the Confederate Constitution but then became very popular in State Constitutions throughout the country after the

---

1. See generally Briffault, The Item Veto: A Problem in State Separation of Powers, 2 Emerging Issues in State Constitutional Law 85 (1989) (dealing with definition of vetoable item and appropriations bill).

Civil War. The item veto tended to perpetuate itself, as provisions were copied by new states from older constitutions.

44 Governors have this power under state constitutions.[2] (Congress has also given the executive an item veto in United States possessions.) In 10 states, the Governor can reduce items of appropriations as well as veto them. Usually, the override rules for a regular veto also apply to an item veto. The President has recently been given the equivalent of a line item veto by 1996 legislation.

Some support for an item veto rests on broader ideological grounds than just a concern with logrolling. The Governor, it is hoped, will use the veto to balance the budget and cut back on the size of government. This rationale has a more modern ring to it and probably underlies support for a Presidential item veto. It would justify an item veto to reduce, not just wipe out, an appropriation. Conversely, contemporary chief executives may also be players in the logrolling game. The item veto power may simply be one more bargaining tool in the executive-legislative interaction.

We look first at state constitutional provisions for an item veto. We then look at the impoundment power, which would allow an executive to refuse to spend appropriated funds. If allowed, it could serve as a substitute for an item veto. Finally, we examine the federal legislation giving the President an item veto.

b) STATE CONSTITUTIONS

The constitutional language implementing the item veto varies from state to state—allowing the item veto of "items," "parts," or "items or portions" of "appropriations"—but the cases suggest that more basic questions about the Executive's legislative role influence how these terms are interpreted. As the court said in Fairfield v. Foster, 214 P. 319 (Ariz.1923):

> * * * Attempts are generally made to base the decision on the precise language of the particular Constitution construed, but a careful examination of the reasoning in each case will disclose that the conclusion is really based on the view the particular court takes as to the general nature of the veto power and the purpose to be accomplished by the special constitutional provision .

i) PURPOSES

What is the nature of the item veto power and its purposes?   The following excerpts are typical judicial answers to this question.

---

2. As of 1985, 43 Governors had the line item veto. The Book of the States, Tables 2.4 & 3.20, pp. 67 & 157 (1990–91 Edition). Maine amended its Constitution in 1995 to provide the Governor with an item veto, dis-cussed in Opinion of the Justices, 673 A.2d 1291 (Me.1996) (interpreting the state constitution to allow the Governor to veto the entire bill after the legislature overrides a line item veto).

Commonwealth v. Barnett

48 A. 976 (Pa.1901).

　　* * * As inherited from the colonies and adopted in the early constitutions, the veto power was confined to approval or disapproval of the entire bill as presented, and this, in experience, was found to be inadequate to the accomplishment of its full purpose. The legislature, in framing and passing a bill, had full control over every subject and every provision that it contained; and the governor, as a co-ordinate branch of the lawmaking power, was entitled to at least a negative of the same extent. But by joining a number of different subjects in one bill the governor was put under compulsion to accept some enactments that he could not approve, or to defeat the whole, including others that he thought desirable or even necessary. Such bills, popularly called "omnibus bills," became a crying evil, not only from the confusion and distraction of the legislative mind by the jumbling together of incongruous subjects, but still more by the facility they afforded to corrupt combinations of minorities with different interests to force the passage of bills with provisions which could never succeed if they stood on their separate merits. So common was this practice that it got a popular name, universally understood, as "logrolling." A still more objectionable practice grew up, of putting what is known as a "rider" (that is, a new and unrelated enactment or provision) on the appropriation bills, and thus coercing the executive to approve obnoxious legislation, or bring the wheels of the government to a stop for want of funds. These were some of the evils which the later changes in the constitution were intended to remedy. Omnibus bills were done away with by the amendment of 1864 that no bill shall contain more than one subject, which shall be clearly expressed in the title. But this amendment excepted appropriation bills, and as to them the evil still remained. The convenience, if not the necessity, of permitting a general appropriation bill containing items so diverse as to be fairly within the description of different subjects was patent. The present constitution meets this difficulty—First, by including all bills in the prohibition of containing more than one subject, except "general appropriation bills" (article 3, § 3); secondly, by the provision that "the general appropriation bill shall embrace nothing but appropriations for the ordinary expenses of the executive, legislative, and judicial departments of the commonwealth, interest on the public debt, and for public schools; all other appropriations shall be made by separate bills each embracing but one subject" (Id. § 15); and, thirdly, by the grant to the governor of "power to disapprove of any item or items of any bill making appropriations of money, embracing distinct items, and the part or parts of the bill approved shall be the law, and the item or items of appropriation disapproved shall be void, unless re-passed according to the rules and limitations prescribed for the passage of other bills over the executive veto" (article 4, § 16). * * *

State v. Kirkpatrick

524 P.2d 975 (N.M.1974).

* * * [The item veto power is t]he power to disapprove * * *. This is a negative power, or a power to delete or destroy a part or item, and is not a positive power, or a power to alter, enlarge or increase the effect of the remaining parts or items. It is not the power to enact or create new legislation by selective deletions. Thus, a partial veto must be so exercised that it eliminates or destroys the whole of an item or part and does not distort the legislative intent, and in effect create legislation inconsistent with that enacted by the Legislature, by the careful striking of words, phrases, clauses or sentences.

Brown v. Firestone

382 So.2d 654 (Fla.1980).

Whether seeking to define "line item" or "specific appropriation," the concept embodied in those terms is essentially the same. A specific appropriation is an identifiable, integrated fund which the legislature has allocated for a specified purpose. It is necessarily a fluid concept which to some extent will vary as the contours of a general appropriations bill change. Thus, if the legislature deems it expedient to allocate $50,000,000 to the Department of Corrections without breaking the allocation down to its components, then that lump sum would be a specific appropriation [which is subject to an item veto] under article III, section 8(a). Conversely, if the legislature allocated $1,000,000 of the $50,000,000 to maintenance of the corrections system, then that would be considered a specific appropriation. In each instance the legislature has designated an identifiable, integrated fund for a specified purpose. The fact that in one case the designation is broad and in the other specific is a matter of legislative judgement as to the requirements of each funding project.

In the context of a qualification or restriction, a specific appropriation is the smallest identifiable fund to which a qualification or restriction is or can be directly and logically related. In practical effect this means that in most cases where a qualification or restriction includes the setting apart of an identifiable sum of money, that fund will be considered a specific appropriation, since it will most likely be the smallest identifiable fund to which the qualification logically relates.

The implications are obvious. If the legislature deems it wise to appropriate a specific fund in a qualification or restriction, then the governor will be able to veto that qualification as a specific appropriation, just as he could have had the legislature listed the fund as a separate line item. The fund mentioned in the qualification or restriction will of course also be nullified. This construction elevates substance to its rightful place over form. On the other hand, a qualification or restriction containing no express identifiable fund, if it logically relates even to a substantial specific appropriation, cannot be vetoed without the governor also vetoing the appropriation to which it relates. This affords the legislature substantial leverage, yet there is an internal check working upon the legislature in this regard. The fashioning of a substantial lump sum appropriation in order to avoid an executive veto would in some instances ill-serve legislative objectives, for it would merely give the governor greater latitude in directing expenditure of the money appropriated.

ii) APPROACHES

It has been easier to state the purposes of an item veto than to implement the veto in specific cases. Of special concern is whether provisos and conditions attached to particular spending can be vetoed, leaving the dollar appropriations in tact. Before you read several opinions, consider the following approaches.

(1) *Cancel funds.* One approach is to permit an item veto only when it cancels an expenditure of money. The idea is that the Governor can reject the legislature's spending decision but not retain power to spend the money. For example, suppose a law states that $1 million should be spent for roads on condition that the road be built in County X. Arguably, the Governor should not be allowed to veto the condition, leaving the Governor free to spend the $1 million on the roads. Some courts have nonetheless had trouble with this issue. Karcher v. Kean, 479 A.2d 403, 411–13 (N.J.1984), reversing in part, 462 A.2d 1273, 1288–90 (N.J.Super.1983), involved a statute in which $12 million had been appropriated, with the proviso that some of the funds be available for a particular highway at an estimated cost of $3 million. The Governor vetoed the $3 million proviso. The New Jersey Supreme Court held that the $12 million fund did not have to be reduced after the veto.

(2) *How related is the vetoed provision?* A second approach is to focus on whether the vetoed provision belongs in an appropriations bill, not whether the item itself requires an expenditure of money. This approach might *justify* vetoing provisos and conditions which do not require expenditures of money and leaving the appropriations in tact, if they bore *no* relationship to the underlying appropriation of money—such as conditioning spending for roads on the Governor's abandoning enforcement of an existing environmental program unrelated to road building. Conversely, this approach might *prohibit* the veto of some appropriation items, even though they would cancel expenditures, if they were integrally related to the total program rather than some peripheral or logrolled item.

(3) *"Institutional competence" issues.* Perhaps the only way to decide how carefully courts should scrutinize the Governor's item veto is to decide whether you are more suspicious of (1) legislatures sneaking in improper legislation (less judicial scrutiny so Governor has free hand) or (2) Governors

distorting legislative intent by striking statutory language (more judicial scrutiny). In addition, if you think courts cannot be trusted to review what the Governor has done, "less judicial scrutiny" may be the best course, even if it permits Governors too much power.

iii) A NOTE ON PROHIBITING SUBSTANTIVE LAW IN APPROPRIATIONS BILLS

The item veto is not the only way to reduce the legislature's ability to load appropriations bills with inappropriate provisions. Most state constitutions also prohibit substantive legislation in appropriations bills. For example, Art. III, § 12 of the Florida Constitution states that "Laws making appropriations * * * shall contain provisions on no other subjects." We take note of the prohibition on substantive law in appropriations bills in this Chapter for two reasons. First, it serves a similar function as the item veto in discouraging misuse of appropriations bills. Second, some state courts allow the Governor to item veto provisions which are unconstitutional substantive legislation in an appropriations bill.

Courts generally interpret the prohibition in the manner indicated in Brown v. Firestone, 382 So.2d 654 (Fla.1980), as follows:

> * * * The enactment of laws providing for general appropriations involves different considerations and indeed different procedures than does the enactment of laws on other subjects. Our state constitution demands that each bill dealing with substantive matters be scrutinized separately through a comprehensive process which will ensure that all considerations prompting legislative action are fully aired. Provisions on substantive topics should not be ensconced in an appropriations bill in order to logroll or to circumvent the legislative process normally applicable to such action. Similarly, general appropriations bills should not be cluttered with extraneous matters which might cloud the legislative mind when it should be focused solely upon appropriations matters.

> * * * [A]n appropriations bill must not change or amend existing law on subjects other than appropriations. This is, of course, subject to our statement in In re Advisory Opinion to the Governor, 239 So.2d at 10, that a general appropriations bill may make "allocations of State funds for a previously authorized purpose in amounts different from those previously allocated or [substitute] adequate specific appropriations for prior continuing appropriations." Were we to sanction a rule permitting an appropriations bill to change existing law, the legislature would in many instances be able to logroll, and in every instance the integrity of the legislative process would be compromised. * * *

> [The state constitution] will countenance a qualification or restriction only if it directly and rationally relates to the purpose of an appropriation and, indeed, if the qualification or restriction is a major motivating factor behind enactment of the appropriation. That is to

say, has the legislature in the appropriations process determined that the appropriation is worthwhile or advisable only if contingent upon a certain event or fact, or is the qualification or restriction being used merely as a device to further a legislative objective unrelated to the fund appropriated?

QUESTIONS

Like all tests designed to permit legislation only if it is part of a related program, the prohibition of substantive legislation in appropriations bills is difficult to apply. What should the result be in the following situations, taken from the following cases: Brown v. Firestone, 382 So.2d 654 (Fla.1980); Department of Education v. Lewis, 416 So.2d 455 (Fla.1982); Henry v. Edwards, 346 So.2d 153 (La.1977).

1. A proviso in an appropriations bill for penal institutions required a reduction in inmate population at one penal institution.

2. A proviso in an appropriations bill stated that no monetary aid to postsecondary institutions could be used to assist any organization that recommends or advocates sexual relations between unmarried persons.

3. An appropriations bill dealing with medical education required expenditures for a new teaching hospital, but the spending had not previously been authorized by legislation.

iv) CASES

The following cases reveal how much trouble the courts have deciding what the Governor can item veto. Can you define a vetoable item on the basis of either of the two approaches discussed above (is it an item of expenditure; does it belong in an appropriations bill), using these cases as examples?

(1) In Commonwealth v. Dodson, 11 S.E.2d 120 (Va.1940), the Governor vetoed a part of a bill providing for a Legislative Director at a salary of $6,000. The bill also provided that it "shall be the duty of the Legislative Director to cooperate with the Executive Director of the Budget and the State Comptroller in the supervision of the expenditures out of all appropriations made by the General Assembly, and to assist in the preparation of the biennial budget." This was held not to be a vetoable item, as follows:

> The creation of a new office, its holder to serve at a stated salary, without more, would be an "item" which the Governor at his election might veto, but if it be tied up with other budget provisions, then under the terms of the Constitution it can not be eliminated. Here he is to co-operate with the Executive Director of the Budget and the State Comptroller in the supervision of expenditures out of all appropriation made by the General Assembly. It may be that the Executive Director of the Budget and the State Comptroller are amply able to protect the interests of the Commonwealth in the expenditure of its appropriations. It may be that this office and

officer were not needed, but the Legislature thought it well that in addition they should have the benefit of an additional safeguard—of a Legislative Director. It is these three officers, and not any two of them, who are charged with this supervision. It is a duty extraordinarily important. To secure its efficient, faithful and intelligent performance we are given three supervisors; at times a three-judge court has been thought wise. The supervision of expenditures provided for in the budget bill is a wise provision and must be, if the intention of the Legislature is observed, supervised by those named to supervise—that is to say, this Legislative Director is given a coordinate measure of control over an indefinite number of budget items. If one supervisor may be eliminated, another might be, and this "item" or his office is not one which does not affect other approved "item" or "items." This Legislative Director is in part responsible for the proper use of many items in the appropriation bill and serves as another check on arbitrary action. For these reasons, this veto can not be sustained under section 76 of the Constitution.

(2) Opinion of the Justices to House of Representatives, 428 N.E.2d 117 (Mass.1981):

Question 5 asks whether the Governor has authority * * * to disapprove certain words and phrases in item 1201–0100 without disapproving or reducing the entire item.

The item appropriates funds for the administration of the Department of Revenue. * * * The provisions vetoed by the Governor began with the following language: "and provided further that no monies shall be allotted to said department unless the following provisions were implemented in the following quarter * * *." Detailed provisions follow directing the Governor to file periodic revenue reports with the Legislature, and, if revenues are less than a designated amount, to request that the Legislature reduce expenditures or increase taxes to compensate for the difference. * * *

The purpose of the appropriation is for the administration of the Department of Revenue. The elimination of the provisions does not affect the purpose of providing funds for the operation of the department. The provisions do not specify the way the appropriation is to be spent. Nor do they direct a more detailed itemization of the appropriation.

The disapproved language does not impose a restriction or condition on the expenditure of the appropriation. Although the item relates to the administration of the Department of Revenue, the provisions are aimed solely at the Governor. We recognize that the introductory language, quoted above, is cast in conditional terms, but skillful drafting will not convert a separable piece of general legislation to a restriction or condition on the expenditure of an appropriation. Looking to the substance of the provisions, we find that they are not restrictions or conditions on the appropriation.

Accordingly, we answer question 5 in the affirmative.

(3) Rios v. Symington, 833 P.2d 20 (Ariz.1992)(en banc)

■ Moeller, Vice Chief Justice:

* * * In response to the Governor's call [for a special session], the Legislature enacted House Bill[   ] 2001 * * *. House Bill 2001 is primarily a "fund transfer" bill that directs the transfer of various sums of money from special funds to the state's general fund. * * *

Viewed in isolation, the fund transfers themselves are not clearly "items of appropriation," because the transfers themselves do not constitute a legislative grant of spending authority, much less state a specified sum of money to be devoted to a specified purpose. However, we do not believe that such a narrow view reflects the proper interplay between the legislative and executive branches. When the Legislature transfers monies from a previously-made appropriation, the obvious effect is to reduce the amount of the previous appropriation. The Constitution does not permit such reductions free of gubernatorial oversight. To hold otherwise would permit the Legislature to do indirectly that which it may not do directly, and would seriously limit the Executive's constitutional role in the appropriation process.

If we were to accept the argument that such transfers are not subject to the line item veto, a future Legislature could, for example, enact an appropriation bill and, knowing the Governor's views and priorities, appropriate a sufficient amount for a given purpose so as to gain the Governor's approval, rather than a veto. The Legislature could then later direct that some or all of that fund be transferred to another fund. By placing the transfer provision within a larger transfer bill, the Legislature could evade the Governor's line item veto power notwithstanding the fact that the later transfers completely alter the original appropriation. Such procedures, if authorized, would eviscerate the line item veto power which the Constitution intended the Governor to have. Although we are urged to construe the Governor's line item veto narrowly and strictly, we hold that it should be construed in such a way as to carry out the obvious constitutional intent.

In our view, if the Governor's constitutional power to line item veto an appropriation is to mean anything, the Governor must be constitutionally empowered to line item veto a subsequent reduction or elimination of that appropriation. Therefore, we hold that the Governor validly vetoed the five special fund transfers in House Bill 2001.

(4) Rush v. Ray, 362 N.W.2d 479, 480–83 (Iowa 1985):

In this appeal a legislator challenges the legality of the Governor's action exercising his item veto power. The basic issue is whether use of the governor's item veto power to eliminate a provision in an appropriation bill which prohibits the expenditure or

transfer of appropriated funds from one department of state government to another is proper. The trial court held that such a veto is
proper. We conclude such a provision is a qualification or limitation
on the appropriation, rather than an item, and reverse.

During the 68th session of the Iowa General Assembly, the
legislature enacted five appropriation bills for specific purposes.
* * * Each bill contains a provision that either provided "notwithstanding section eight point thirty-nine (8.39) of the Code, funds
appropriated by this Act shall not be subject to transfer or expenditure for any purpose other than the purposes specified" or recited a
phrase similar in language and content. * * *

Appellant asserts that the vetoed portions of these five acts are
provisos or limitations, not items; thus, they were not subject to the
governor's item veto power. On the other hand, the Governor
asserts that the language stricken from the five appropriation bills
constituted distinct, severable "items" within the meaning of article
III, section 16 of the Iowa Constitution, that could be removed from
the appropriation bills by the use of the item veto.

We have twice passed on the legality of the governor's exercise
of the item veto power. On each occasion, we discussed whether
the vetoed portion of the legislative bill was a condition or qualification of the appropriation, not subject to veto, or an item, properly
deleted. Welden v. Ray, 229 N.W.2d 706, 710 (Iowa 1975); State ex
rel. Turner v. Iowa State Highway Commission, 186 N.W.2d 141, 151
(Iowa 1971). * * *

The problem presented in Turner arose when the legislature
appropriated funds to the primary road fund, and the governor
vetoed a portion of the bill that additionally prohibited removing
certain established offices from their present location. 186 N.W.2d at
143. When this item veto was challenged, we upheld the veto. We
established certain principles to be used in interpreting the term
"item" and distinguished items, which are subject to veto, from
provisos or conditions inseparably connected to an appropriation,
which are not subject to veto. We approved another court's statement that an "item" is "something that may be taken out of a bill
without affecting its other purposes and provisions. It is something
that can be lifted bodily from it rather than cut out. No damage can
be done to the surrounding legislative tissue, nor should any scar
tissue result therefrom." Id. at 151 (quoting Commonwealth v.
Dodson, 11 S.E.2d 120, 124 (Va.1940)). * * *

When the governor's authority to exercise his item veto power
was challenged in Welden, we reached a different result than in
Turner, holding that the attempted vetoes by the governor were
beyond the scope of his constitutional power. 229 N.W.2d at 715
(two justices dissenting). The vetoed items in the appropriation bills
provided limitation on how the money appropriated for each department was to be spent. Specifically, these provisions included limita-

tions on the number of employees in a department, limitations on the percent of the appropriation that could be used for salaries, prohibition against construction of buildings, prohibition against spending beyond budget, and elimination of matching fund grants if the federal funds were discontinued—with the further provision that unused state matching funds would revert to the general fund. We held that these clauses were lawful qualifications upon the respective appropriations rather than separate, severable provisions. * * *

In the present case the trial court determined that the vetoed portion of each appropriation bill did not change the basic purpose of the legislation; thus, the provision is properly considered a severable item rather than a legislatively-imposed condition. We agree with appellant's contention that "the effect of this veto was to make money from the treasury available for purposes not authorized by the legislation as it was originally written, contrary to the clear intent of the legislature." The Governor has used the item veto power affirmatively to create funds not authorized by the legislature. The vetoed language created conditions, restricting use of the money to the stated purpose. It is not severable, because upon excision of this language, the rest of the legislation is affected. The appropriated money is no longer required to be used only for the stated purpose; it could be used for other purposes.   Thus, these are not items which are subject to veto.

This case is unlike Turner in which the deletion of directions concerning office changes had no effect on the appropriation of funds. We find it closer akin to Welden in which the governor had deleted provisions which dictated how and for what purposes the appropriated funds were to be expended. In the present case the legislature clearly limited the expenditure of the appropriated funds to specified purposes. The veto distorted the obvious legislative intent that the funds only be spent for the appropriated purposes and created additional ways the funds might be spent. This was use of the veto power to create rather than negate. We hold that the language vetoed constituted qualifications on the appropriations rather than separate items subject to veto. * * *

A dissenting opinion stated:

The majority holding is a rejection of the definition of "item" which we established in State ex rel. Turner v. Iowa State Highway Comm'n., 186 N.W.2d 141, 150–52 (Iowa 1971), and a far-flung expansion of our majority holding in Welden v. Ray, 229 N.W.2d 706 (Iowa 1975). The result at once deprives the executive branch of a proper item veto and the right to veto legislation that repeals the operation of an existing statute. I respectfully dissent. * * *

The experience in other states shows that, at best, there tends to be a blurred line between an "item" (which can be vetoed from an appropriation bill) and a proviso or condition on how the funds are to be spent (which cannot). It does however seem clear that the

line, no matter how blurred, is crossed when legislation (even if labeled a proviso or condition) is appended to an appropriation bill in violation of the single subject provisions of a state constitution.
* * *

The majority recites, and seems to acknowledge the validity of, the "scar-tissue test", but does not follow it. Under the test the provisions in question here were proper subjects of item vetoes. Each appropriation was earmarked to a department of government which could use the funds only for the purpose specified by the legislature. The vetoes here in no way modified the legislative plan of how the department could use the funds. The vetoed provisions related only to funds which might remain unused. The power of the governor to transfer unused funds under section 8.39, acting after notice to and "review and comment by" appropriate legislative chairpersons, has been statutorily provided for more than forty years. See Iowa Acts (49 G.A.) ch. 62, § 5 (1941). All branches of Iowa government have become quite used to it. It is, to put it in simple terms, the way our state government works.

If the legislature were to pass an act calling for the repeal or suspension of section 8.39 the act would be subject to an executive veto. Under the scar tissue rule the governor should not be robbed of this veto power by the simple process of attaching the repeal or suspension of this existing statute to an appropriation bill. This is a textbook example of why we and states elsewhere adopted the scar tissue rule. The trial court should be affirmed.

Vetoing unconstitutional provisions. The discussion in Rush v. Ray suggests another basis for an item veto—the unconstitutionality of substantive legislation in an appropriation bill. This would include not only (1) an unrelated proviso, but also (2) changes of prior law (see the dissent in Rush v. Ray) and (3) provisos which might impinge on free speech and other individual rights. Courts do not agree on whether an unconstitutional proviso can, on that account alone, be item-vetoed. See Benjamin v. Devon Bank, 368 N.E.2d 878 (Ill.1977)(a requirement that no funds be spent to establish an Unemployment Office within 500 feet of a school was invalid substantive legislation in an appropriation bill but could not be item vetoed because it was not an "item of appropriation"); Brown v. Firestone, 382 So.2d 654 (Fla.1980)(an unconstitutional proviso in a general funding law for jails, dealing with inmate population in one institution, cannot be item-vetoed). But see Henry v. Edwards, 346 So.2d 153 (La.1977)(item veto of an unconstitutional proviso, prohibiting salaried assistant district attorney from electioneering in a specific parish, is allowed).

Remember why it matters whether an unconstitutional provision is subject to an item veto. An item veto allows the Governor to get rid of the unconstitutional provision *before* it becomes law, subject to later judicial challenge. By contrast, an unvetoable but unconstitutional provision remains on the books until rejected by a court in a later lawsuit. Second, an item veto would allow the Governor to sever and strike out the unconstitutional portion, whereas a challenge to the unconstitutional provision might result in a decision that the unconstitutional portion cannot be severed from the rest of the bill and the entire bill might fall.

v) VETOING LETTERS, WORDS, AND NUMBERS

Whatever you think of the operation of the item veto so far, you cannot help but wonder at the Wisconsin approach. The State Constitution, Article V, section 10(1) states:

> (a) Every bill which shall have passed the legislature shall, before it becomes a law, be presented to the governor.

> (b) If the governor approves and signs the bill, the bill shall become law. Appropriation bills may be approved in whole or in part by the governor and the part approved shall become law.

In State v. Conta, 264 N.W.2d 539 (Wis.1978), a statute was passed as follows:

> "(1) Every individual filing an income tax statement may designate that their income tax liability be increased by $1 for deposit into the Wisconsin Election Campaign Fund for the use of eligible candidates under § 11.50."

Acting Governor Schreiber exercised his partial veto by lining out the words, "that their income tax liability be increased by," and the words, "deposit into." The section as changed by the partial veto read:

> "(1) Every individual filing an income tax statement may designate $1 for the Wisconsin Election Campaign Fund for the use of eligible candidates under § 11.50."

The bill as enrolled would have required taxpayers to "add on" to their tax liabilities the sum of $1 if they wished that sum to go to the campaign fund. As changed by the Governor's partial veto, a taxpayer instead could elect to designate that the sum of $1 be "checked off" or expended from the state general funds for the purposes of the Election Campaign Fund.

The court stated:

> [T]he power of the Governor to approve or disapprove a bill "in part" is a far broader power than that conferred upon Governors under the partial-veto provisions of most state constitutions. In most instances, the power of the Governor is confined to the excision of the appropriations or items in an appropriation bill. * * *

> [In Wisconsin] * * * the test of severability has clearly and repeatedly been stated by this court to be simply that what remains be a complete and workable law. The power of the Governor to disassemble the law is coextensive with the power of the Legislature to assemble its provisions initially. * * *

In the present case it is undisputed that what remained after the Governor's partial veto is a complete, entire, and workable law. As such, it is severable and reflects the proper exercise of the partial-veto power conferred on the Governor by the Constitution of the state. * * *

* * * Under the Wisconsin Constitution, the governor may exercise his partial-veto power by removing provisos and conditions to an appropriation so long as the net result of the partial veto is a complete, entire, and workable bill which the legislature itself could have passed in the first instance. * * *

The dissent noted:

In recent years, partial vetoes have not only increased greatly in number; they have been applied to ever smaller portions of bills. Several years ago, an attempt was made to exercise the power so as to strike the digit "2" from a $25 million bonding authorization. Even this may not mark the limits of the use of the power. Advisors to a recent governor were reported to have considered striking the letter "t" from the word "thereafter" in order to alter the effective date of a liquor tax increase. Only the limitations on one's imagination fix the outer limits of the exercise of the partial veto power by incision or deletion by a creative person. At some point this creative negative constitutes the enacting of legislation by one person, and at precisely that point the governor invades the exclusive power of the legislature to make laws.

* * * In the scheme of our constitution, the governor is to review the laws and not to write them. He is not, by careful and ingenious deletions, to effectively "write with his eraser" and to devise new bills which will become law unless disapproved by two-thirds of the legislators who are elected by the people of the state. * * *

The dissent's test for the item veto was as follows:

* * * The [item veto] * * * is not a power to reduce a bill to its single phrases, words, letters, digits and punctuation marks. Rather the partial veto power should be exercised only as to the individual components, capable of separate enactment, which have been joined together by the legislature in an appropriation bill. That is, the portions stricken must be able to stand as a complete and workable bill. * * *

The approach here set forth would effectively define the limits of the constitutional role of the governor. He would be able to veto independent elements of multi-subject appropriation bills, and would in most cases be unable to effectively add elements to the bills enacted by the legislature. His veto would be directed to portions of an appropriation bill which were grammatically and structurally distinct, and he would not be able to deal individually with numbers or words, or single digits or letters.

In State v. Thompson, 424 N.W.2d 385 (Wis.1988), the court affirmed the broad implications of Conta, that the Governor could veto letters and numbers. This included a power to reduce appropriations. The court explicitly rested the item veto power on the Governor's affirmative power to participate in legislation, not just the negative power to deter logrolling. The only limit it imposed was that the veto not create something "totally new, unrelated, or non-germane."

An amendment to the Wisconsin Constitution adopted by the legislature and ratified in 1990 took away a bit of the Governor's broad item veto power. It specifies:

> In approving an appropriation bill in part, the governor may not create a new word by rejecting individual letters in the words of the enrolled bill. Enrolled Jt. Res. 76, 1987–1988 Wis. Legis., 1987 Wis. Laws 2180; Wis. St. J., Apr. 4, 1990, at 3A, col. 1.

The Governor can still delete the word "not," or one digit of a number.

The following Wisconsin case considered whether the Governor could reduce appropriations.

Citizens Utility Board v. Klauser

534 N.W.2d 608 (1995).

■ Wilcox, J. * * *

In at least nine instances, Governor Thompson crossed out dollar figures written in Arabic numerals and wrote in different, smaller numbers. The legislature did not attempt to override these partial vetoes by the governor * * *

* * *

Petitioners argue that Art. V., sec. 10 of the Wisconsin Constitution, while allowing the governor to approve an appropriation bill in whole or in part, only authorizes action as to those numbers that are physically part of an appropriation. * * *

Respondents counter that striking numerals in an appropriation and writing in other numerals to create a smaller dollar figure is no different than striking out individual digits to create a smaller dollar figure.

We conclude that the governor, acting within the scope of his powers derived from Art. V., sec. 10 of the Wisconsin Constitution, may strike a numerical sum set forth in an appropriation and insert a different, smaller number as the appropriated sum. * * *

The more difficult consideration as to the appropriateness of the governor's partial veto is a determination as to whether $250,000 is "part" of $350,000 so as to fall within the purview of powers authorized by Art. V., sec. 10(1)(b). [T]his court has recognized that the word "part" as used in sec. 10(1)(b) should be given its ordinary and accepted meaning. * * * [I]t is readily apparent that $250,000 is "part" of $350,000, because $250,000 is "something less than" $350,000, and $250,000 goes "to make up, with others * * * a larger number," i.e., $350,000. This "common sense" reading of the word "part," in terms of appropriation amounts, is what we believe is intended in sec. 10(1)(b).

The Petitioners contend that "if numbers can be written in so can words. * * * The governor might veto the words, 'State of Wisconsin' and write in 'City of Milwaukee,' because Milwaukee is part of Wisconsin." This contention can be addressed on several levels. First, both sides recognize that the governor never has written in a word and does not claim the authority to do so. Second, this court has already implicitly limited the governor's power in this area [ ] to reductions of amounts of appropriations. * * * We now make explicit the fact that a governor may only reduce an appropriation by a number contained within the original appropriation allotment. Third, while our prior cases have consistently recognized that a component of the governor's power to partially veto includes the power to reduce the monetary amount of an appropriation, this court has never discussed the conceptual "reduction" of any other elements of an appropriation bill (i.e., dates, times, counties, cities, groups, etc.). This recognition points up the fact that an important rationale of the partial veto is clearly linked to expenditure reduction and fiscal balance.

c) PRESIDENTIAL CONTROL OF SPENDING

The item veto is historically related to prevention of private interest logrolling. In the modern context, Presidential control over the budget is more concerned with the executive's role in determining spending priorities and with fiscal matters more generally (deficits, inflation, interest rates, etc.). In this section we consider the legal issues surrounding Presidential impoundment of funds and the legislation giving the President a line item veto. Before we consider these issues, however, we review the history of the budget process at the federal level.

i) OVERVIEW OF THE FEDERAL BUDGET PROCESS[3]

The Constitution suggests that Congress has control of the budget process. Article I, § 9, cl. 7 states that "No Money shall be drawn from the

---

3. See generally, Stith, Rewriting the Fiscal Constitution: The Case of Gramm–Rudman–Hollings, 76 Calif. L. Rev. 593 (1988); Dauster, Budget Emergencies, 18 J. Leg. 249 (1992); Joyce & Reischauer, Deficit Budgeting: The Federal Budget Process and Budget Reform, 29 Harv. J. Leg. 429 (1992).

Treasury, but in Consequence of Appropriations Made by Law." The Executive Branch is not supposed to spend without congressional authority. In fact, Congress has not done a very good job of keeping control of its own budget process and the Executive Branch has taken every opportunity (often with legislative authority or acquiescence) to expand its budgetary power.

During the 19th Century, Congress paid very little attention to controlling or coordinating the budget process. Congress typically made line item appropriations, setting down the amount that could be spent on specific projects. Line item appropriations did not, however, control the Executive. The practice grew up of shifting money between accounts specified in line items, and of over-obligating money, forcing "coercive deficiencies" for which Congress had to appropriate money as a practical matter. In 1905, Congress attempted to regain some control by passing the Anti–Deficiency Act, prohibiting executive obligation of funds in excess of appropriations (31 U.S.C. § 1341). The phenomenon of the government closing down at the end of a fiscal year when appropriations for the next year have not been passed stems from this prohibition. Congress usually deals with these crises by passing a stop-gap "continuing resolution," to allow spending at the previous year's rate.

After World War I, political events forced a change in the budget process. The war created a large deficit and the recently enacted income tax expanded revenues. Greater coordination of budgeting was needed, but it was the President rather than Congress who acquired that power. The Budget and Accounting Act of 1921 gave the President a central role in preparing a budget, and created the Bureau of the Budget in the Treasury (since 1970, this has become the Office of Management and Budget in the White House). Congress could still decide whether to accept the President's budget but the initiative shifted away from the legislature. Within Congress, there was still no unified budget process. That would not come until the Congressional Budget and Impoundment Act of 1974.

The growth of the federal government, especially during the New Deal, also contributed to a shift in budgetary control to the executive. Line item detail was replaced by lump sum programmatic appropriations. This gave administrators greater flexibility to implement government programs by "reprogramming" funds within broad categories. In contemporary practice, Congress often attempts to exercise the equivalent of line item control through committee reports specifying in detail how funds should be spent and through more informal committee-agency contacts. (See, e.g., H.Rep. No. 98–866, 98th Cong., 2d Sess. (1984)(over ten pages specifying funds for specific projects)). These committee specifications differ from a legislative veto (discussed later in this Chapter), which would give a committee the right to veto agency action, because the legislative veto is meant to be legally binding. Committee specifications about spending are only a matter of political comity between branches. See International Union, U.A.W. v. Donovan, 746 F.2d 855 (D.C.Cir.1984); 55 Comp. Gen. 307 (1975).

By 1974, three features of the budget process were apparent to Congress: within the legislature, there was inadequate control of fiscal matters (spending decisions were not integrated and revenue and spending were not coordinated); the President had immense control over the "purse," which was supposed to be a legislative responsibility; and (much less importantly until the 1980s) there was concern with deficits. The response was the Congressional Budget and Impoundment Act of 1974. Before explaining that Act, however, we must understand the terminology used in budget matters and the various ways the government can spend.

Contemporary practice draws a distinction, reflected in the legislative committee structure, between substantive "authorization" of a program, and budgetary "appropriations" to finance them. The first step in legislation is usually consideration by a substantive committee (such as Foreign Relations) about whether the government should be doing something. If the substantive legislation passes, the appropriations committee (acting through specialized subcommittees), proposes how much money can be spent, up to the ceiling in the authorizing legislation. Its spending proposals are then implemented through a multi-subject appropriations bill. In practice, the division between substantive authorizations and budget appropriations is less sharp. There are ways for substantive authorizations to force spending, and, at the federal level, there are no constitutional barriers to appropriations for amounts not previously authorized. Indeed, the appropriations process has recently become the vehicle for a lot of substantive law, because divided government blocks passage of free-standing legislation.

The appropriations process itself is more complex than this description suggests. A distinction must be made between the authority to obligate funds and the actual outlay of funds. These are called "budget authority" and "outlays" respectively. (The "authority" to obligate, provided in an appropriations law, should not be confused with the "authority" to spend, created by substantive legislation.) Budget authority is often multi-year, allowing obligation of funds over more than one year. Some budget authority is permanent, good for as long as the purposes of the legislation require. Actual outlays in a given year can therefore arise from the following sources: (1) obligations made in the prior year and not yet paid off (that is, no outlay has yet been made); (2) obligations authorized to be made in a given year, arising from prior-year budget authority legislation; (3) and any new obligational authority granted by Congress for the particular year.

There are also various forms of "backdoor spending" outside of the periodic appropriations process. These include "contract authority" given to various agencies; the right to borrow and spend without further legislative approval; and credit guarantees of private loans. In addition, the tax law can put funds into the hands of people indirectly by lowering their taxes if they engage in certain behavior, such as providing child care services, investing in housing, or cleaning up the environment. These "tax expenditures" do not involve outlays, but are indirect ways of bypassing *both* the authorization and appropriations process. These various forms of backdoor spending are very important because attempts to control the appropriations process will fail if they do not take them into account.

Finally, substantive legislation may contains permanent appropriations, immune from periodic appropriations review, as with Social Security and, until recently, most welfare entitlement programs.

The Congressional Budget and Impoundment Act of 1974 attempted to bring the budget process under coordinated congressional control by several means. It created Senate and House Budget Committees, backed up by the Congressional Budget Office (CBO) with a large professional staff to give Congress the kind of help the Executive gets from the Office of Management and Budget. These Committees were responsible for adopting a concurrent budget resolution (after working out their differences), specifying congressional targets for overall budget authority, revenue, outlays, the deficit, and public debt. If spending and revenue targets were not met, a "reconciliation" procedure required cutting spending to bring the totals within the targets. This process introduced new players into budget-making. At least on paper, the substantive and appropriations committees had to explain their decisions regarding spending and entitlement to the Budget Committees and cooperate with them in shaping an overall budget.

Not surprisingly, the politics of the budget proved overpowering and the 1974 Act did not give Congress effective budget control. The entire process worked only through internal legislative procedures (which were not "law"). These procedures are usually enforceable only by points of order, which are often ineffective means of control.

In 1981, President Reagan adapted the 1974 Act to serve the President's political agenda of cutting back on spending. He persuaded Congress to attach provisions to the May 15 resolution reconciling spending with the budget targets and then embodied the resolution in the longest legislation hitherto adopted by Congress (the Omnibus Budget and Reconciliation Act of 1981). The 1981 Act was remarkable in applying to some previously "uncontrollable" backdoor spending and in reducing authorizations contained in substantive legislation (though not without objection from chairs of the authorization committees). After 1981, Presidential control of the congressional budget process weakened, but Congress had as much or more trouble obtaining control over its own process as before. Congress often ignored the law's procedures and deadlines and its reconciliation targets.

Still, a certain tone had been set. Failure by Congress to obtain control of its budget was now an obvious political failure. It could not be concealed with the same ease as before. Moreover, the problem of the deficit, not just the power struggle between Congress and the President, became a central legislative concern. Congress was especially bothered by the fact that it was blamed for deficits, even though Presidential goals of increased defense spending and tax cuts were major contributors. These concerns led to the adoption in 1985 of the Gramm–Rudman–Hollings Act (GRH).

One objective of GRH was to try to make the internal budget procedures of the 1974 Act work better. Prior experience indicated, however, that internal legislative rules about budget-making were hard to translate into results. Deadlines continued to be missed, and the usual ways around points of order were often exploited. The major contribution of GRH was therefore its second objective of backing up its internal budget process rules with a mandatory sequestration procedure, which was supposed to force down total spending to meet deficit targets. If the deficit targets specified in GRH were not met, spending would be sequestered more or less uniformly in accordance with a formula. The formula, in general, was the overall spending ceiling as a percentage of total projected spending. The general idea was to prevent sequestration from altering the previously specified legislative spending priorities. For example, if the spending target was 16 and projected spending was 20, budget authority would be reduced more or less across the board to reduce outlays to 80% of projections.

Before 1987, the Congressional Budget Office (CBO) played an equal role with OMB in determining the figures on which sequestration would be based. In addition, the Comptroller General (head of the General Accounting Office) had the final authority for enforcing the GRH deficit reduction. In Bowsher v. Synar, 478 U.S. 714 (1986), however, the Supreme Court held that the Comptroller General could not be given this authority, because it would vest executive authority in a legislative official. Many thought that this decision meant the end of sequestration, but in 1987 Congress made CBO's role advisory and took away the Comptroller General's enforcement authority. The final authority to determine the relevant budget figures was given to OMB, which is part of the President's Executive Office.

A slowing economy produced mounting deficits which in turn created political turmoil. This was aggravated by the exemption of many programs from sequestration, such as social security and welfare, leaving a small percentage of the domestic budget fully subject to sequestration. Political stalemate ensued, with Congress unable to agree on a budget by the end of the fiscal year. This finally produced the 1990 Budget Enforcement Act, Pub. L. No. 101–508, tit. XIII, 104 Stat. 1388 (1990), which adopted a different approach to sequestration.

The key concept of the 1990 Act was that spending guidelines rather than the deficit would determine sequestration. Spending under existing programs would be insulated from sequestration. It could even increase, if the reason was the worsening economy. Thus, spending under existing unemployment insurance programs could increase free of a sequester, but newly legislated benefits would be vulnerable to sequestration reduction. In addition, there was a special pay as you go rule for entitlement programs and taxes; no legislated increase in entitlement programs (e.g., Medicare or Food Stamps) was possible unless other entitlement programs were reduced or taxes were increased. The 1993 Budget further tightened the rules, by adopting a *hard freeze* on all non-defense discretionary spending. This extended the tax-entitlement trade-off rule to most discretionary domestic spending—e.g., an increase for farmers must be offset by a decrease in something else, such as airport subsidies.

The statute had several built-in escape hatches. First, some spending could be declared off-budget, as was the case with the savings and loan bailout. Second, spending targets could be suspended in case of war or economic slowdown. 2 U.S.C. § 907a. Third, the President and Congress could agree to declare "emergency spending," exempt from spending limits. 2 U.S.C. § 901(b)(2)(D)(i). This was used sparingly (for example—Desert Storm, aid to the Kurds and Bangladesh, and domestic disaster and crop damage).

As of this writing (Fall 1996), the political salience of budget deficit issues is unclear. It has gone from the front-burner in 1995 (with both parties negotiating over the terms of a seven-year balanced budget), to a political hot potato in the form of a proposed and narrowly defeated balanced budget amendment to the Constitution, and then to the back-burner, with tax reductions as the more politically potent issue; and, after the November, 1996 elections, renewed talk of a balanced budget amendment. If a balanced budget is ever enacted, it will undoubtedly result in revision of the sequestration, trade-off, and other rules which Congress sets for the appropriations process.

In the remainder of this section, we focus on one aspect of the budget problem—the President's role in limiting spending. We first look at an old controversy—Presidential impoundment. We then consider the desirability and legality of a Presidential item veto.

ii) PRESIDENTIAL IMPOUNDMENT

(A) Background

Many Presidents have claimed an impoundment power to limit spending appropriated by Congress. Traditionally, impoundment was usually used to limit waste when Congress overappropriated for a particular purpose, or to stretch out nonmilitary appropriations during wartime. These impoundments often fit a category called "programmatic" impoundments, because they furthered or were at least consistent with the purposes of the program adopted by the legislature. Other impoundments sought to control military spending, where the President could appeal to his constitutional status as Commander-in-Chief. There were occasional controversial impoundments of nonmilitary spending, which resembled an item veto, but the practice was not widespread prior to 1968.

In 1968 President Nixon began an unprecedented exercise of the impoundment power. He employed impoundment to defeat programs with which he disagreed politically and to reduce overall spending. These are often called "policy" impoundments, because they are based on the President's policy, not on improving the operation of the legislative program. The following case grew out of President Nixon's clash with Congress and is the only Supreme Court case dealing with impoundment.

(B) Litigation

Train v. City of New York
420 U.S. 35 (1975).

■ Mr. Justice White delivered the opinion of the Court.

This case poses certain questions concerning the proper construction of the Federal Water Pollution Control Act Amendments of 1972, which provide a comprehensive program for controlling and abating water pollution. Section 2 of the 1972 Act makes available federal financial assistance in the amount of 75% of the cost of municipal sewers and sewage treatment works. Under § 207, there is "authorized to be appropriated" for these purposes "not to exceed" $5 billion for fiscal year 1973, "not to exceed" $6 billion for fiscal year 1974, and "not to exceed" $7 billion for fiscal year 1975. Section 205(a) directs that "[s]ums authorized to be appropriated pursuant to [§ 207]" for fiscal year 1973 be allotted "not later than 30 days after October 18, 1972." The "[s]ums authorized" for the later fiscal years 1974 and 1975 "shall be allotted by the Administrator not later than the January 1st immediately preceding the beginning of the fiscal year for which authorized * * *." From these allotted sums, § 201 (g)(1) authorizes the Administrator "to make grants to any * * * municipality * * * for the construction of publicly owned treatment works * * *," pursuant to plans and specifications as required by § 203 and meeting the other requirements of the Act, including those of § 204. Section 203 (a) specifies that the Administrator's approval of plans for a project "shall be deemed a contractual obligation of the United States for the payment of its proportional contribution to such project."

[Editor—In a footnote, the Court noted the difference between the funding method in this Act and the more usual funding mechanisms:

> The act thus established a funding method differing in important respects from the normal system of program approval and authorization of appropriation followed by separate annual appropriation acts. Under that approach, it is not until the actual appropriation that the Government funds can be deemed firmly committed. Under the contract-authority scheme incorporated in the legislation before us now, there are authorizations for future appropriations but also initial and continuing authority in the Executive Branch contractually to commit funds of the United States up to the amount of the authorization. The expectation is that appropriations will be automatically forthcoming to meet these contractual commitments. This mechanism considerably reduces whatever discretion Congress might have exercised in the course of making annual appropriations. The issue in this case is the extent of the authority of the Executive to control expenditures for a program that Congress has funded in the manner and under the circumstances present here.]

The water pollution bill that became the 1972 Act was passed by Congress on October 4, 1972, but was vetoed by the President on October 17. Congress promptly overrode the veto. Thereupon the President, by letter dated November 22, 1972, directed the Administrator "not [to] allot among the States the maximum amounts provided by section 207" and, instead, to allot "[n]o more than $2 billion of the amount authorized for the fiscal year 1973, and no more than $3 billion of the amount authorized for the fiscal year 1974 * * *." On December 8, the Administrator announced by regulation that in accordance with the President's letter he was allotting for fiscal years 1973 and 1974 "sums not to exceed $2 billion and $3 billion, respectively." * * *

Section 205(a) provides that the "[s]ums authorized to be appropriated pursuant to [§ 207] * * * shall be allotted by the Administrator." Section 207 authorizes the appropriation of "not to exceed" specified amounts for each of three fiscal years. The dispute in this case turns principally on the meaning of the foregoing language from the indicated sections of the Act.

The Administrator contends that § 205(a) directs the allotment of only "sums"—not "all sums"—authorized by § 207 to be appropriated and that the sums that must be allotted are merely sums that do not exceed the amounts specified in § 207 for each of the three fiscal years. In other words, it is argued that there is a maximum, but no minimum, on the amounts that must be allotted under § 205(a). This is necessarily the case, he insists, because the legislation, after initially passing the House and Senate in somewhat different form, was amended in Conference and the changes, which were adopted by both Houses, were intended to provide wide discretion in the Executive to control the rate of spending under the Act.

The changes relied on by the Administrator, the so-called Harsha amendments, were two. First, § 205 of the House and Senate bills as they passed those Houses and went to Conference, directed that there be allotted "all sums" authorized to be appropriated by § 207. The word "all" was struck in Conference. Second, § 207 of the House bill authorized the appropriation of specific amounts for the three fiscal years. The Conference Committee inserted the qualifying words "not to exceed" before each of the sums so specified.

The Administrator's arguments based on the statutory language and its legislative history are unpersuasive. Section 207 authorized appropriation of "not to exceed" a specified sum for each of the three fiscal years. If the States failed to submit projects sufficient to require obligation, and hence the appropriation, of the entire amounts authorized, or if the Administrator, exercising whatever authority the Act might have given him to deny grants, refused to obligate these total amounts, § 207 would obviously permit appropriation of the lesser amounts. But if, for example, the full amount provided for 1973 was obligated by the Administrator in the course of approving plans and making grants for municipal contracts, § 207 plainly "authorized" the appropriation of the entire $5 billion.

If a sum of money is "authorized" to be appropriated in the future by § 207, then § 205(a) directs that an amount equal to that sum be allotted. Section 207 speaks of sums authorized to be appropriated, not of sums that are required to be appropriated; and as far as § 205(a)'s requirement to allot is concerned, we see no difference between the $2 billion the President directed to be allotted for fiscal year 1973 and the $3 billion he ordered withheld. The latter sum is as much authorized to be appropriated by § 207 as is the former. Both must be allotted.

It is insisted that this reading of the Act fails to give any effect to the Conference Committee's changes in the bill. But, as already indicated, the "not to exceed" qualifying language of § 207 has meaning of its own, quite apart from § 205(a), and reflects the realistic possibility that approved applications for grants from funds already allotted would not total the maximum amount authorized to be appropriated. Surely there is nothing inconsistent between authorizing "not to exceed" $5 billion for 1973 and requiring the full allotment of the $5 billion among the States. Indeed, if the entire amount authorized is *ever* to be appropriated, there must be approved municipal projects in that amount, and grants for those projects may *only* be made from allotted funds.

As for striking the word "all" from § 205, if Congress intended to confer any discretion on the Executive to withhold funds from this program at the allotment stage, it chose quite inadequate means to do so. It appears to us that the word "sums" has no different meaning and can be ascribed no different function in the context of § 205 than would the words "all sums." It is said that the changes were made to give the Executive the discretionary control over the outlay of funds for Title II programs at either stage of the process. But legislative intention, without more, is not legislation. Without something in addition to what is now before us, we cannot accept the addition of the few words to § 207 and the deletion of the one word from § 205(a) as altering the entire complexion and thrust of the Act. As conceived and passed in both Houses, the legislation was intended to provide a firm commitment of substantial sums within a relatively limited period of time in an effort to achieve an early solution of what was deemed an urgent problem. We cannot believe that Congress at the last minute scuttled the entire effort by providing the Executive with the seemingly limitless power to withhold funds from allotment and obligation. * * *

What does the Train case tell us about how to analyze the legality of impoundments? Are Presidential impoundments based on policy reasons *necessarily* illegal?

The impoundment in Train reflected the President's substantive dis-agreement with the legislation, as evidenced by his earlier veto of the statute. The impoundment in Commonwealth of Pennsylvania v. Lynn, 501 F.2d 848 (D.C.Cir.1974), was different. The Secretary of Housing and Urban Development temporarily suspended expenditure of funds pending a study of whether the expenditures on low income housing were achieving the purpose Congress intended. The court was impressed with the fact that the reason for the impoundment was program-related, not objection to the general level of government expenditures. The Secretary's action was upheld.

(C) The Impoundment Control Act (ICA) of 1974

At the same time that Congress tried to bring its own budget process under control, it also tried to contain the exercise of impoundment power by the President. The Impoundment Control Act of 1974, Pub. L. 93–244, 88 Stat. 332, set forth procedures for the President to follow before impounding funds, such as notifying Congress of the impoundment. A rescission, which canceled an expenditure, was ineffective unless approved by concurrent resolution within 45 days. Deferrals, which postponed expenditures, were valid unless vetoed by either House. In addition, the Comptroller General had to inform Congress whether the President impounded funds without telling Congress and whether any deferrals were rescissions in disguise.

The Comptroller General was also given the power to sue the President to spend money where the ICA procedures had not been followed. President Reagan argued, in a signing statement accompanying amendments to the ICA, that the power to sue was an unconstitutional vesting of executive power in a legislative officer. The Comptroller General's power is important because it is doubtful whether private parties have the authority to sue to force the President to follow ICA procedures. Rocky Ford Housing Authority v. United States Dep't of Agriculture, 427 F.Supp. 118 (D.D.C.1977)(no private standing to object to President's failure to report impoundment to Congress).

The legal framework for impoundment under the ICA was thrown into disarray when the legislative veto (discussed later in this Chapter) was ruled unconstitutional. Specifically, this had the effect of invalidating the power of Congress to uphold rescission through a concurrent resolution or prohibit deferral through disapproval by one house. Legislative policy could only be made by legislation.

In 1987, the Balanced Budget and Emergency Deficit Control Reaffirmation Act of 1987, Pub. L. 100–119, amended the Impoundment Control Act of 1974 to deal with the unconstitutionality of the legislative veto. Presidential rescission was ineffective unless approved by a law, not just a concurrent resolution. In effect, a rescission is now a proposal for legislation. The legislative veto of deferrals was eliminated.

The 1987 amendments also addressed the question of the President's underlying impoundment power. It described the deferral power in the same terms as the old Anti–Deficiency Act, which had been adopted in the early 1900s (31 U.S.C. § 1512), stating:

> "deferral shall be permissible only—(1) to provide for contingencies; (2) to achieve savings made possible by or through changes in requirements or greater efficiency of operation; or (3) as specifically provided for by law." 2 U.S.C. § 684.

This statute obviously does not affirmatively authorize deferral for *policy* reasons, unless it is (improbably) "provided for by law" (in paragraph (3) *supra*). But does ICA affirmatively create *programmatic* deferral authority (in paragraphs (1) and (2), *supra*), which (again, improbably) is not already allowed by the underlying law authorizing spending in the first place? In this connection, consider the following provision in the ICA:

> Nothing contained in this Act, or in any amendments to this Act, shall be construed as * * * superseding any provision of law which requires the obligation of budget authority or the making of outlays thereunder. 2 U.S.C. § 681 (1988).

This presumably means that ICA does not *technically* authorize programmatic deferrals if they are not allowed by the basic appropriations legislation. But does it mean that the ICA has *no* impact on whether statutes providing for spending will be interpreted to authorize programmatic impoundments?

The statute seems to say two things: first, it suggests that programmatic deferral is allowed if certain procedures, such as notifying Congress, are followed; and then it rejects construction of the ICA to supersede any law which obligates funds. In a close case involving interpretation of the basic appropriations law, would the ICA push the court towards finding that the impoundment was in fact allowed, at least if the President followed the ICA procedures?

If you are unsure how to answer these questions, recall the discussion of statutory patterns in Chapter 15. Frequently, the interaction of statutes passed at different times is not well thought out, and this appears to be another example of that problem.

(D) Governor impoundment?

Do Governors have an impoundment power? If the Governor has an item veto power, does that make it more or less likely (1) that the Governor will try to impound funds, or (2) that a court will uphold such power? In New York, where the Governor has an item veto (New York Constitution, Art. 4, § 7), the court denied the legality of an impoundment. County of Oneida v. Berle, 404 N.E.2d 133 (N.Y.1980). Under state law, the Governor had an obligation to *submit* a balanced budget, but not to assure that the budget remains balanced throughout the budget year. Consequently, impoundment could not be used to balance the budget. See also 1980 Op. Atty. Gen. 786 (Iowa)(no impoundment power; Governor has item veto—Iowa Const. Art III, § 16); Rios v. Symington, 833 P.2d 20 (Ariz.1992)(en banc)(item veto but no impoundment power).

Some state constitutions are explicit about an impoundment power. In State v. Ashcroft, 828 S.W.2d 372 (Mo.1992), the State Constitution gave the Governor both an item veto power and a power to reduce spending when actual revenues fall below the revenue estimates on the basis of which the appropriations were based.

iii) PRESIDENTIAL ITEM VETO

In 1996, Congress passed a statute giving the President a line item veto power. Presidents of all parties had asked for the item veto for much of the 20th Century but Congress had been as reluctant to give this power to the President as they had been to acquiesce in Presidential impoundment. The reversal in Congress' position was a product of concerns over budget deficits and federal spending and the desire to do *something* which would at least appear to address these concerns.

At first blush, a *legislative* grant of line item veto power may seem legally doubtful. The Constitution specifies what a President can veto and there is no provision for vetoing *part* of legislation. The legislative solution, as you will see when you read excerpts from the law *infra*, is for Congress to delegate authority to the President to reject spending items contained in a law, much as Congress delegates rulemaking authority to agencies.

A Presidential line item veto would reduce though not eliminate the need for an impoundment power. The existence of the item veto might even lead a court to interpret legislation to narrow the scope of impoundment authority, but is that a reasonable judicial approach? After all, the veto wipes out a law from the outset, but impoundment can react to events which occur *after* passage of the law.

The Presidential line item veto legislation raises at least three issues— first, does it make good policy sense; second, is it constitutional; third, does it pose practical interpretation problems?

Policy issues. Are there relevant differences between state and federal governments which argue against the desirability of a Presidential item veto? Consider the following:

(1) The President already has a lot of budget control.

(2) More generally, legislative power is already weakened and an item veto gives the President one more way to keep a recalcitrant legislator in line (by threatening to veto a pet project, for example).

(3) The President might become a logrolling player, threatening an item veto unless projects he favors are adopted.

(4) Congress is less vulnerable to private interest control than state legislatures and certainly less vulnerable than 19th century state legislatures.

(5) Congress will be more not less irresponsible if there is an item veto, because it will vote for spending in the expectation that the President might veto it (especially if the President can reduce the expenditure, without totally vetoing it).

(6) A relatively small percentage of the federal budget would probably be subject to a veto. Big ticket items like social security and interest on the national debt would be untouched. In this connection, consider a General Accounting Office Report (B–244571), Jan. 22, 1992, which studied the likely impact of a line item veto based on the assumption that the President would veto items listed in Statements of Administrative Policy (SAPs). SAPs contain objections sent to Congress on behalf of the President by the Office of Management and Budget while appropriations are under consideration. SAP data indicate that the line item veto would have reduced the deficit and borrowing by about 6.7%, or a total of about $70 billion, assuming no congressional override. These figures probably overstate the reduction because they are based on budget authority, not spending figures. In addition, the SAPs probably objected to more appropriations than would be item vetoed, as indicated by the lesser amounts contained in Presidential rescission proposals during the same time period. The Report estimates that 72% of the savings would come from five functional areas: (1) transportation; (2) commerce and housing credit; (3) education, training, employment, and social services; (4) income security; and (5) natural resources and environment. The transportation budget would have been cut by 11.7%. Seventy one programs would have been terminated, including AMTRAK and the Legal Services Corporation.

(7) Congress has too many other ways to spend money, such as tax breaks and loan guarantees. These types of spending are not easily scrutinized by the public and should not be encouraged by permitting an item veto, unless the item veto applied to them.

When you read excerpts from the 1996 Line Item Veto Act, *infra*, see whether any of the concerns raised by these comments has been addressed— especially, backdoor spending, and treatment of existing entitlement programs, such as Social Security.

Constitutionality? The line item veto legislation tries to overcome constitutional objections by treating the issue as one of delegation of authority to the executive. Delegation of rulemaking is normally allowed if there are sufficiently clear standards to guide the executive's discretion. This is a notoriously vague and underenforced requirement, although there are some signs that the Supreme Court may now take it more seriously than it has since the late 1930s. Is there anything in the item veto legislation (*infra*) which addresses concerns about standardless delegation? Will a court be more inclined to squint hard at delegation to the executive when it threatens to undermine a fundamental separation of powers concern—the legislature's control over spending?

Interpretation problems. Does the line item veto legislation try to avoid the interpretive problems encountered under state constitutions about whether a proviso or condition can be vetoed—e.g., are reductions allowed; can provisos be vetoed?

Here is an extended excerpt from the Line Item Veto Act. It helps you to decide how this legislation answers some of the concerns expressed above about giving the President a line item veto. It also helps you understand how hard it is to go from a general political idea to the details of legislation, only a small portion of which is presented below.

LINE ITEM VETO ACT
Public Law 104–130, 104th Cong., 2d sess. (1996).

An Act

To give the President line item veto authority with respect to appropriations, new direct spending, and limited tax benefits.

Be it enacted by the Senate and House of Representatives of the United States of America in Congress assembled,

SECTION 1. SHORT TITLE.

This Act may be cited as the "Line Item Veto Act".

SEC. 2. LINE ITEM VETO AUTHORITY.

(a) In General.—Title X of the Congressional Budget and Impoundment Control Act of 1974 (2 U.S.C. 681 et seq.) is amended by adding at the end the following new part:

Part C—Line Item Veto

Sec. 1021. (a) In General.—Notwithstanding the provisions of parts A and B, and subject to the provisions of this part, the President may, with respect to any bill or joint resolution that has been signed into law pursuant to Article I, section 7, of the Constitution of the United States, cancel in whole—(1) any dollar amount of discretionary budget authority;

(2) any item of new direct spending; or

(3) any limited tax benefit [Editor—This is a form of backdoor spending];

if the President—

(A) determines that such cancellation will—

(i) reduce the Federal budget deficit;

(ii) not impair any essential Government functions; and

(iii) not harm the national interest; and

(B) notifies the Congress of such cancellation by transmitting a special message, in accordance with section 1022, within five calendar days (excluding Sundays) after the enactment of the law providing the dollar amount of discretionary budget authority, item of new direct spending, or limited tax benefit that was canceled. * * *

[Editor—How severely do these criteria limit the President's delegated authority?]

Sec. 1022. (a) In General.—For each law from which a cancellation has been made under this part, the President shall transmit a single special message to the Congress.

(b) Contents.—

(1) The special message shall specify—

(A) the dollar amount of discretionary budget authority, item of new direct spending, or limited tax benefit which has been canceled, and provide a corresponding reference number for each cancellation;

(B) the determinations required under section 1021(a), together with any supporting material;

(C) the reasons for the cancellation;

(D) to the maximum extent practicable, the estimated fiscal, economic, and budgetary effect of the cancellation;

(E) all facts, circumstances and considerations relating to or bearing upon the cancellation, and to the maximum extent practicable, the estimated effect of the cancellation upon the objects, purposes and programs for which the canceled authority was provided * * *.

(2) In the case of a cancellation of any dollar amount of discretionary budget authority or item of new direct spending, the special message shall also include, if applicable—

(A) any account, department, or establishment of the Government for which such budget authority was to have been available for obligation and the specific project or governmental functions involved;

(B) the specific States and congressional districts, if any, affected by the cancellation; and

(C) the total number of cancellations imposed during the current session of Congress on States and congressional districts identified in subparagraph (B).

* * *

Definitions

Sec. 1026. As used in this part:

* * *

(5) Direct spending.—The term "direct spending" means—

(A) budget authority provided by law (other than an appropriation law);

(B) entitlement authority; and

(C) the food stamp program.

[Editor—"Budget authority provided by law (other than an appropriation law)" includes borrowing and contract authority; "entitlement authority" refers to authority to make payments not provided in advance by appropriations laws, where the obligation is to those who meet requirements established by law (e.g., Social Security). See U.S. General Accounting Office, Glossary of Terms Used in the Federal Budget Process.]

* * *

(7) Dollar amount of discretionary budget authority.—

(A) Except as provided in subparagraph (B), the term "dollar amount of discretionary budget authority" means the entire dollar amount of budget authority—

(i) specified in an appropriation law, * * *;

(ii) represented separately in any table, chart, or explanatory text included in the statement of managers or the governing committee report accompanying such law;

(iii) required to be allocated for a specific program, project, or activity in a law (other than an appropriation law) that mandates the expenditure of budget authority from accounts, programs, projects, or activities for which budget authority is provided in an appropriation law; * * *

(B) The term "dollar amount of discretionary budget authority" does not include—

(i) direct spending;

(ii) budget authority in an appropriation law which funds direct spending provided for in other law;

(iii) any existing budget authority rescinded or canceled in an appropriation law; or

(iv) any restriction, condition, or limitation in an appropriation law or the accompanying statement of managers or committee reports on the expenditure of budget authority for an account, program, project, or activity, or on activities involving such expenditures.

(8) Item of new direct spending.—The term "item of new direct spending" means any specific provision of law that is estimated to result in an increase in budget authority or outlays for direct spending relative to the most recent levels calculated pursuant to section 257 of the Balanced Budget and Emergency Deficit Control Act of 1985.

(9) Limited tax benefit.—

(A) The term "limited tax benefit" means—

(i) any revenue-losing provision which provides a Federal tax deduction, credit, exclusion, or preference to 100 or fewer beneficiaries under the Internal Revenue Code of 1986 in any fiscal year for which the provision is in effect; and

(ii) any Federal tax provision which provides temporary or permanent transitional relief for 10 or fewer beneficiaries in any fiscal year from a change to the Internal Revenue Code of 1986.

(B) A provision shall not be treated as described in subparagraph (A)(i) if the effect of that provision is that—

(i) all persons in the same industry or engaged in the same type of activity receive the same treatment;

(ii) all persons owning the same type of property, or issuing the same type of investment, receive the same treatment; or

(iii) any difference in the treatment of persons is based solely on—

(I)   in the case of businesses and associations, the size or form of the business or association involved;

(II) in the case of individuals, general demographic conditions, such as income, marital status, number of dependents, or tax return filing status;

(III) the amount involved; or

(IV) a generally-available election under the Internal Revenue Code of 1986.

(C) A provision shall not be treated as described in subparagraph (A)(ii) if—

(i) it provides for the retention of prior law with respect to all binding contracts or other legally enforceable obligations in existence on a date contemporaneous with congressional action specifying such date; or

(ii) it is a technical correction to previously enacted legislation that is estimated to have no revenue effect.

* * *

Sec. 1027. (a) Statement by Joint Tax Committee.—The Joint Committee on Taxation shall review any revenue or reconciliation bill or joint resolution which includes any amendment to the Internal Revenue Code of 1986 that is being prepared for filing by a committee of conference of the two Houses, and shall identify whether such bill or joint resolution contains any limited tax benefits. The Joint Committee on Taxation shall provide to the committee of conference a statement identifying any such limited tax benefits or declaring that the bill or joint resolution does not contain any limited tax benefits. Any such statement shall be made available to any Member of Congress by the Joint Committee on Taxation immediately upon request.

(b) Statement Included in Legislation.—[Editor—This subsection allows inclusion in the legislation of the Joint Committee's exclusive list of limited tax benefits. If so included, the President's item veto of limited tax benefits applies only to items on that list. Absent such a list, the President's item veto extends to whatever meets the statutory definition.] * * *

(d) Congressional Identifications of Limited Tax Benefits.— There shall be no judicial review of the congressional identification under subsections (a) and (b) of a limited tax benefit in a conference report.

SEC. 3. JUDICIAL REVIEW.

(a) Expedited Review.—

(1) Any Member of Congress or any individual adversely affected by part C of title X of the Congressional Budget and Impoundment Control Act of 1974 may bring an action, in the United States District Court for the District of Columbia, for declaratory judgment and injunctive relief on the ground that any provision of this part violates the Constitution.

* * *

The Act takes effect on January 1, 1997 (after election of a new President in fall 1996) and expires on January 1, 2005. Would you predict that the Act will be renewed or will the line item veto expire?

18.03 LEGISLATIVE VETO

a) DESCRIPTION AND CRITIQUE

Congressional concern about executive decisionmaking is not limited to budgetary matters. One method of keeping some control of the executive is the legislative veto, by which executive action is effective only if not rejected by Congress. Legislative rejection can come in many forms—one or both houses of Congress (that is, a simple or concurrent resolution), or a negative vote by a congressional committee in one or both houses.

The legislative veto began in 1932 when Congress gave the President the authority to reorganize executive departments subject to a one-house veto. The practice then began to grow, eventually reaching the point where the House almost voted to adopt a legislative veto for all agency rules and regulations. The veto was useful for three different kinds of problems. *First*, there are deep divisions between the President and Congress built into the constitutional structure. The War Power is an example. Congress therefore authorizes the President a free hand to take military action for a limited period of time subject to a two-house legislative veto thereafter. *Second*, Congress lacks time to address issues involving specific individuals traditionally dealt with by private legislation. Immigration and naturalization is an example. Congress therefore authorizes the Attorney General to make these decisions subject to a legislative veto. The Chadha case, discussed below, which struck down the legislative veto at the federal level, involved this issue. *Third*, the regulatory state grows but Congress is unable to provide detailed rules, either because of insufficient knowledge, changes over time, or political stalemate about specifics. It therefore delegates authority to an agency but wants a second look, which it retains through a legislative veto.

On the merits, the veto might be more or less desirable depending on the context. Professor Strauss argues that the veto is desirable when the Constitution assigns significant roles to both the President and Congress, as in the case of executive reorganization, War Powers, and Impoundment. In such cases, a realistic sharing of authority through use of a legislative veto preserves the appropriate balance of power. With economic regulation, however, the President does not usually have a significant role, because Congress does not delegate authority to the President. Admittedly, the Office of Management and Budget exercises some general supervision over administrative rulemaking for the President but this power varies widely, depending on the agency, and is often not very effective. A legislative veto might therefore give too much power to Congress.[4]

One objection to a legislative veto, especially in the area of economic regulation, is that it allows excessive influence by special interests, operating through the committees that review executive rules subject to veto. Iron triangles involving agencies, committees, and interest groups obtain too much power. Consider this response to that objection by A. Maass, Congress and the Common Good (1983). First, a legislative veto by the entire house rather than a committee reduces opportunities for excessive influence by special interests. Second, special interests work wherever authority lies. If Congress elects to review agency rules and regulations for certain major programs, the lobbyist will work in the agencies to get them to draft agreeable rules and then in Congress to get the rules approved or vetoed. If Congress elects not to review agency rules and regulations, then the lobbyists will simply increase their efforts in the agencies. The corridors of the departments are as crowded with lobbyists as are those of the Capitol.

Another objection to the legislative veto appeared in Consumer Energy Council of America v. Federal Energy Regulatory Commission, 673 F.2d 425 (D.C.Cir.1982), *affirmed*, 463 U.S. 1216 (1983).

> Fundamentally, the argument for the legislative veto as a means of oversight comes down to a belief that the existence of powerful and unaccountable rulemaking bodies demands that Congress have an efficient and effective means of control * * *. The empirical evidence suggests that legislative vetoes are not all that efficient in practice, however, and this case presents an example of extreme

4. Strauss, Was There a Baby in the Bathwater? A Comment on the Supreme Court's Legislative Veto Decision, 1983 Duke L.J. 789; Strauss, The Place of Agencies in Government: Separation of Powers and the Fourth Branch, 84 Colum. L. Rev. 573 (1984).

disruption of the normal administrative process. [The agency] claims that it did not exercise its policymaking discretion because it believed that Congress wanted only a proposal to evaluate. Yet Congress appears to have delegated [authority] precisely to make use of [the agency's] policy expertise. The result was the agency assuming the bizarre position that it failed to exercise reasoned decisionmaking when it issued the rule.

[Editor—In a footnote, the court added the following: When the agency has difficulty in determining its mandate, the value of the administrative process, with its guarantee of equal opportunity to participate by all interested parties, diminishes sharply. The agency may tend to ignore parties' submissions since it knows Congress ultimately will review the rule prior to its implementation. As a result, the attempt to enhance the political accountability of agency rulemakers may actually backfire as administrators view their roles as proposers of appropriate policy rather than final decisionmakers who must listen to and attempt to reconcile competing interests.]

The current political implications of the legislative veto can only be understood in light of our changing attitudes towards administrative agencies and the contemporary split in party control between Congress and Presidency. When the administrative state blossomed during the New Deal, agencies and Congress had more or less parallel agendas. Greater regulation served the interests of the new liberal majority. That has changed. We are now suspicious that agencies are influenced by interest groups which may not prevail in Congress. Moreover, the President (supported by his agency appointees) may not be sympathetic with congressional purposes. In this political environment, striking down the legislative veto increases the power of the Executive branch which is often at odds with Congress. Faced with this reality, Congress can try to override agency rules legislatively, but will likely encounter a Presidential veto.[5]

b) CONSTITUTIONALITY

Presidents have routinely objected to the legislative veto on constitutional grounds. Sometimes they vetoed legislation containing a legislative veto, but they often signed the bills because they contained other desirable provisions. If the bill became law, the President might act as though the legislative veto was inoperative (because it was unconstitutional), but would often conform to the legislative veto procedures in the interest of congressional/Presidential accommodation. The issue finally came to a head in the following case.

Immigration and Naturalization Service v. Chadha

462 U.S. 919 (1983).

■ Mr. Chief Justice Burger delivered the opinion of the Court.

* * *

---

5. See Eskridge & Ferejohn, The Article I, Section 7 Game, 80 Geo. L. J. 523 (1992).

[Editor—In this case, an alien's deportation order had been suspended by the Attorney General pursuant to a delegation of discretionary authority from Congress to deal with deportation matters. Under the statute, the Attorney General's action could be negated by a one-house veto. The House Judiciary Committee considered the Attorney General's action and recommended a veto of Mr. Chadha's deportation suspension.

Justice Powell thought that this action was adjudicatory in nature and therefore beyond the scope of legislative power.

The Court did not adopt such a narrow approach. It struck down the legislative veto, stressing both the importance of bicameralism, which requires that legislative action be taken by both Houses, and the Presentment Clause, which requires Presidential assent to legislation, subject to a two-thirds legislative override. The relevant Constitutional provisions are found in Art. I, sec. 1, sec. 7 (clauses 2 and 3), referred to throughout the opinion. The reference to sec. 244 in the opinion is to the Immigration and Naturalization Act. The following excerpt from Mr. Chief Justice Burger's majority opinion and Justice White's dissent indicate very different approaches to the problem. The majority is very legalistic in striking down the veto and the dissent emphasizes the practical advantages of a legislative veto.]

The Constitution sought to divide the delegated powers of the new federal government into three defined categories, legislative, executive and judicial, to assure, as nearly as possible, that each Branch of government would confine itself to its assigned responsibility. The hydraulic pressure inherent within each of the separate Branches to exceed the outer limits of its power, even to accomplish desirable objectives, must be resisted.

Although not "hermetically" sealed from one another, the powers delegated to the three Branches are functionally identifiable. When any Branch acts, it is presumptively exercising the power the Constitution has delegated to it. When the Executive acts, it presumptively acts in an executive or administrative capacity as defined in Art. II. And when, as here, one House of Congress purports to act, it is presumptively acting within its assigned sphere.

Beginning with this presumption, we must nevertheless establish that the challenged action under § 244(c)(2) is of the kind to which the procedural requirements of Art. I, § 7 apply. Not every action taken by either House is subject to the bicameralism and presentment requirements of Art. I. Whether actions taken by either House are, in law and fact, an exercise of legislative power depends not on their form but upon "whether they contain matter which is properly to be regarded as legislative in its character and effect." S. Rep. No. 1335, 54th Cong., 2d Sess., 8 (1897).

Examination of the action taken here by one House pursuant to § 244(c)(2) reveals that it was essentially legislative in purpose and effect. In purporting to exercise power defined in Art. I, § 8, cl. 4 to "establish an uniform Rule of Naturalization," the House took action that had the purpose and effect of altering the legal rights, duties and relations of persons, including the Attorney General, Executive Branch officials and Chadha, all outside the legislative branch. Section 244(c)(2) purports to authorize one House of Congress to require the Attorney General to deport an individual alien whose deportation otherwise would be canceled under § 244. The one-House veto operated in this case to overrule the Attorney General and mandate Chadha's deportation; absent the House action, Chadha would remain in the United States. Congress has acted and its action has altered Chadha's status.

The legislative character of the one-House veto in this case is confirmed by the character of the Congressional action it supplants. Neither the House of Representatives nor the Senate contends that, absent the veto provision in § 244(c)(2), either of them, or both of them acting together, could effectively require the Attorney General to deport an alien once the Attorney General, in the exercise of legislatively delegated authority, had determined the alien should remain in the United States. Without the challenged provision in § 244(c)(2), this could have been achieved, if at all, only by legislation requiring deportation. Similarly, a veto by one House of Congress under § 244(c)(2) cannot be justified as an attempt at amending the standards set out in § 244(a)(1), or as repeal of § 244 as applied to Chadha. Amendment and repeal of statutes, no less than enactment, must conform with Art. I.

The nature of the decision implemented by the one-House veto in this case further manifests its legislative character. After long experience with the clumsy, time consuming private bill procedure, Congress made a deliberate choice to delegate to the Executive Branch, and specifically to the Attorney General, the authority to allow deportable aliens to remain in this country in certain specified circumstances. It is not disputed that this choice to delegate authority is precisely the kind of decision that can be implemented only in accordance with the procedures set out in Art. I. Disagreement with the Attorney General's decision on Chadha's deportation—that is, Congress' decision to deport Chadha—no less than Congress' original choice to delegate to the Attorney General the authority to make that decision, involves determinations of policy that Congress can implement in only one way; bicameral passage followed by presentment to the President. Congress must abide by its delegation of authority until that delegation is legislatively altered or revoked. * * *

[Editor—Chief Justice Burger then lists four examples in which the Constitution explicitly authorizes either House of Congress to act alone: House initiation of impeachments; Senate trial following impeachment; Senate approval of presidential appointments; and Senate treaty ratification. In addition, presentment to the President is not required for proposed constitutional amendments which have passed both Houses, and for internal legislative rules adopted by simple resolution, which bind only the House that adopts them.]

Since it is clear that the action by the House under § 244(c)(2) was not within any of the express constitutional exceptions authorizing one House to act alone, and equally clear that it was an exercise of legislative power, that action was subject to the standards prescribed in Article I. The bicameral requirement, the Presentment Clauses, the President's veto, and Congress' power to override a veto were intended to erect enduring checks on each Branch and to protect the people from the improvident exercise of power by mandating certain prescribed steps. To preserve those checks, and maintain the separation of powers, the carefully defined limits on the power of each Branch must not be eroded. To accomplish what has been attempted by one House of Congress in this case requires action in conformity with the express procedures of the Constitution's prescription of both Houses and presentment to the President.

The veto authorized by § 244(c)(2) doubtless has been in many respects a convenient shortcut; the "sharing" with the Executive by Congress of its authority over aliens in this manner is, on its face, an appealing compromise. In purely practical terms, it is obviously easier for action to be taken by one House without submission to the President; but it is crystal clear from the records of the Convention, contemporaneous writings and debates, that the Framers ranked other values higher than efficiency. The records of the Convention and debates in the States preceding ratification underscore the common desire to define and limit the exercise of the newly created federal powers affecting the states and the people. There is unmistakable expression of a determination that legislation by the national Congress be a step-by-step, deliberate and deliberative process. * * *

■ Justice White, dissenting. * * *

The prominence of the legislative veto mechanism in our contemporary political system and its importance to Congress can hardly be overstated. It has become a central means by which Congress secures the accountability of executive and independent agencies. Without the legislative veto, Congress is faced with a Hobson's choice: either to refrain from delegating the necessary authority, leaving itself with a hopeless task of writing laws with the requisite specificity to cover endless special circumstances across the entire policy landscape, or in the alternative, to abdicate its lawmaking function to the executive branch and independent agencies. To choose the former leaves major national problems unresolved; to opt for the latter risks unaccountable policymaking by those not elected to fill that role. Accordingly, over the past five decades, the legislative veto has been placed in nearly 200 statutes. The device is known in every field of governmental concern: reorganization, budget, foreign affairs, war powers, and regulation of trade, safety, energy, the environment and the economy. * * * [Editor—Justice White then reviews the historical development of the legislative veto, from the Reorganization Acts to the War Powers and Impoundment statutes, to regulatory laws.]

Even this brief review suffices to demonstrate that the legislative veto is more than "efficient, convenient, and useful." It is an important if not indispensable political invention that allows the President and Congress to resolve major constitutional and policy differences, assures the accountability of independent regulatory agencies, and preserves Congress' control over lawmaking. Perhaps there are other means of accommodation and accountability, but the increasing reliance of Congress upon the legislative veto suggests that the alternatives to which Congress must now turn are not entirely satisfactory.

The history of the legislative veto also makes clear that it has not been a sword with which Congress has struck out to aggrandize itself at the expense of the other branches—the concerns of Madison and Hamilton. Rather, the veto has been a means of defense, a reservation of ultimate authority necessary if Congress is to fulfill its designated role under Article I as the nation's lawmaker. While the President has often objected to particular legislative vetoes, generally those left in the hands of congressional committees, the Executive has more often agreed to legislative review as the price for a broad delegation of authority. To be sure, the President may have preferred unrestricted power, but that could be precisely why Congress thought it essential to retain a check on the exercise of delegated authority.

For all these reasons, the apparent sweep of the Court's decision today is regrettable. The Court's Article I analysis appears to invalidate all legislative vetoes irrespective of form or subject. * * *

c) Scope and Effect of Chadha

Chadha appears to have few limits. The hint in Chadha that the veto must "alter[ ] the legal rights, duties and relations of persons" was dispelled in E.E.O.C. v. Allstate Ins. Co., 570 F.Supp. 1224 (D.Miss.1983) and E.E.O.C. v. Hernando Bank, Inc., 724 F.2d 1188 (5th Cir.1984). In these cases, a one-House veto in the Reorganization Act of 1977 was struck down. The reorganization plan shifted enforcement of the Equal Pay Act from the Labor Department to the Equal Employment Opportunity Commission and did not affect legal rights.

Legislative vetoes of agency regulatory action have also been struck down. Process Gas Consumers Group v. Consumer Energy Council of America, 463 U.S. 1216 (1983). In this case, the Court also refused to distinguish one house and two house vetoes. It summarily affirmed vetoes of agency rulemaking in several cases, one of which provided for a two house veto.

Occasionally, a court upholds the legislative veto when Congress is not acting pursuant to Article I, §§ 1, 7, dealing with the legislative power and presentment. (1) Some judges have upheld a legislative veto applicable to certain actions of the District of Columbia government (United States v. Langley, 112 Wash. D.L. Rptr. 801 (D.C. Super. 1984); United States v. McIntosh, 112 Wash. D.L.Rptr. 789 (D.C. Super. 1984)), because the congressional power to legislate for the District of Columbia is derived from Article I, sec. 8, clause 17 of the Constitution. Contra Gary v. United States, 499 A.2d 815 (D.C.App.1985). (2) In National Wildlife Federation v. Watt, 571 F.Supp. 1145 (D.D.C.1983), a legislative veto was upheld, limiting the Executive's power to sell leases on federal lands. The Court held that Congress was acting under its power to "dispose of and make all needful Rules and Regulations respecting the Territory or other Property belonging to the United States" in Article IV, sec. 3 of the Constitution, not under its Article I power.

Congress has had mixed reactions to the Chadha case. The House Rules Committee refused in many instances to permit bills with legislative vetoes to come to a House vote. Nonetheless, many post-Chadha statutes were passed with legislative vetoes. See, e.g., Pub.L. 99–591, sec. 302 (committee veto). In some situations, political realities require the President to comply with an unconstitutional veto provision, or else suffer the consequence of legislative reprisals. Congress has also legislated to eliminate some unconstitutional vetoes, but not all of them. See 44 Cong. Quart. Weekly Rev. 3028 (1986). Several veto provisions were changed to head off constitutional concerns. The veto of District of Columbia laws was replaced by a requirement of a joint resolution of disapproval (a congressional joint resolution must be signed by the President). Pub.L. 98–473, § 131(b), 98 Stat. 1974 (1984). A different approach was taken under the 1984 Reorganization Act, authorizing the President to reorganize the Executive. The President is now authorized only to make proposals to Congress, which Congress can approve by passing a law. Pub.L. 98–614, § 3(a), 98 Stat. 3192 (1984).

Nothing the Supreme Court said about legislative vetoes prevents states from using them. That is a question of state law.[6] Two New Jersey cases hint

---

6. See Comment, The Legislative Veto: A Survey, Constitutional Analysis, and Empiri- cal Study of Its Effect in Michigan, 29 Wayne St. L. Rev. 91 (1982).

that states may show more flexibility in deciding which vetoes to reject, based on the breadth of the veto's coverage and its impact on executive activity. In General Assembly of State of New Jersey v. Byrne, 448 A.2d 438 (N.J.1982), the court struck down a legislative veto by concurrent resolution which applied to every "rule hereafter proposed by a State agency," except rules required by the federal government and rules adopted in cases of emergency affecting public health, safety, or welfare. But in Enourato v. New Jersey Bldg. Authority, 448 A.2d 449 (N.J.1982), the court upheld a legislative veto by concurrent resolution of proposed building projects that, in any event, would have required continuing appropriations from the legislature. The narrow scope of the veto did not threaten to disrupt a "coherent regulatory scheme" or interfere with executive functions.

However, most state courts which have passed on the legislative veto seem inflexible. They have struck down legislative vetoes on broad separation of powers grounds, whether the veto is by concurrent resolution, one house, or a committee. See State v. Hechler, 462 S.E.2d 586 (W.Va.1995); Martinez v. Department of Industry, Labor and Human Relations, 466 N.W.2d 189 (Wis.App.1991); Opinion of the Justices to the Senate, 493 N.E.2d 859 (Mass.1986).

QUESTIONS

1. *Delegation to congressional agency?* Could Congress solve its problem of controlling administrative decisions by delegating executive authority to agencies controlled by Congress? No. The Constitution gives the executive power to the executive branch, not the legislature. Congressional control over those charged with administering the law therefore violates Separation of Powers principles. Bowsher v. Synar, 478 U.S. 714 (1986)(Comptroller General, removable for cause by Congress, cannot share in administration of Gramm–Rudman Act).

2. *Severability?* If a veto provision is invalid, is it separable from the grant of authority subject to the veto or does the grant of authority also fail? In City of New Haven v. United States, 809 F.2d 900 (D.C.Cir.1987), the court held that the link between the impoundment power and the legislative veto in the original version of the 1974 Impoundment Control Act was not separable. However, Alaska Airlines, Inc. v. Brock, 480 U.S. 678 (1987) is more typical. The Court there severed the legislative veto from the underlying grant of rulemaking authority to the Secretary of Labor. The distinction between an inseverable legislative veto in statutes directly implicating a clash of power between the Congress and the President (as in the case of impoundment), and a severable legislative veto in the more routine case of a statute granting rulemaking power to an agency suggests that Professor Strauss, *supra*, was correct—the courts are sympathetic with Congress protecting itself in direct conflicts with the President but not with keeping too much control over the administrative rulemaking process.

d) ALTERNATIVES

The initial reaction to Chadha was that it destroyed a lot of legislation and was a judicial assault on Congress. However, Congress appears to be adjusting, using alternative means to contain executive discretion. Undoubtedly, the utility of different alternatives will vary with the situation. Here is a summary of the alternatives and some of the legal problems they might raise.

Limit agency discretion. First, Congress can limit executive discretion. It can legislate more narrowly, if it can agree on statutory language. There is some evidence that regulatory statutes are becoming more detailed, but this might be a response to different parties controlling the Presidency and Congress, rather than a reaction to loss of the legislative veto.

One way Congress might be prodded into limiting executive discretion would be a revival of the nondelegation doctrine, which would force Congress to provide more precise rulemaking standards when it delegates authority to executive agencies. Over a Justice Scalia dissent, the Court has reaffirmed a very broad delegation authority. Mistretta v. United States, 488 U.S. 361 (1989)(statute authorizing Federal Sentencing Commission to issue sentencing guidelines meets "intelligible principle" test for congressional delegation; Congress cannot operate without delegating under "broad general directives").

Sunset laws. Second, Congress can pass laws with a "sunset" provision, if it is willing to hazard the disruption this causes in the agency's work. The statute granting authority would automatically expire. Congress would then get a chance to review the agency's prior action and decide whether agency authority should be renewed or modified. The *in terrorem* effect of the review also encourages agency compliance with informal congressional pressure.

There is a tendency, however, to automatically renew sunset laws when the expiration date arrives, unless there is strong political pressure for review. It is unclear whether the sunset provision creates any greater pressure to review the law than there would be without the sunset provision.

Report to Congress. Third, statutes can impose a requirement that the agency report rules to Congress, accompanied by a waiting period before agency rules are effective. This "report and wait" procedure is often used. Congress can then use informal pressure or pass legislation to alter regulations of which it disapproves. The Claims Court held that the "report and wait" procedure was an unconstitutional legislative veto because it was followed by informal legislative pressure on the agency to alter its rules, but the Federal Circuit Court reversed, City of Alexandria v. United States, 737 F.2d 1022 (Fed.Cir.1984), stating as follows:

> We take notice that since early in the 19th Century there have been marked differences between the United States Congress and other parliamentary bodies. One is the greater development of the committee system here, as the statute illustrates. Committee chair-

men and members naturally develop interest and expertise in the subjects entrusted to their continuing surveillance. Officials in the executive branch have to take these committees into account and keep them informed, respond to their inquiries, and it may be, flatter and please them when necessary. Committees do not need even the type of "report and wait" provision we have here to develop enormous influence over executive branch doings. There is nothing unconstitutional about this: indeed, our separation of powers makes such informal cooperation much more necessary than it would be in a pure system of parliamentary government. * * *

According to the facts believed by the Claims Court judge, the administrator communicated informally with a committee chairman and learned that there would be so much opposition it would be unwise to make a formal report. This is not at all the same thing as conferring an outright veto power on a committee, because the administrator may have thought it prudent to yield in this and other such cases because he perceived that opposition on the committee's part could make itself felt in action by the full Congress in a constitutional way. If he couldn't persuade the committee, chances of persuading the full Congress were too slim to be worth the pursuit.

The Claims Court judge writes "[w]hat is reserved is the power to disapprove or to withhold approval without passing legislation." This is true: the committees can disapprove. The right question is not asked: What is the legal effect of disapproval? That it has great moral effect cannot be doubted: does the committee demand more? Thus there is nothing to show that the "report and wait" provision of this statute is unconstitutional as applied.

Oversight. Fourth, as the Federal Circuit Court notes, even without sunset laws or agency reporting requirements, Congress engages in a variety of informal interactions with agencies enabling it to review regulations and let its objections be known. Agencies and legislative committees frequently have close working relationships, whereby committees engage in continuous oversight of agency action.

There has been a renewed emphasis on oversight. Subcommittees have been given special oversight authority. Congress also makes more use of the Congressional Budget Office, the General Accounting Office, and the Congressional Research Service to study issues which agencies would otherwise know more about. However, congressional oversight has shortcomings. It comes in third on most legislators' lists of concerns, after constituent service and legislation. As a matter of practice, oversight often lacks the kind of policy review that the legislative veto affords. Instead, it concentrates on corruption, intervention in administrative minutiae, and the development of committee alliances with the agency. A recent book suggests that there has been a dramatic increase in oversight activities since the 1970s, although its effectiveness for policy review remains a question.[7]

When Congress engages in oversight, Members of Congress often contact agency rulemakers in an attempt to influence adoption of rules. In the following case, the court comments on the problem of ex parte contacts with Members of Congress. It is concerned with whether such contacts should be permitted, and whether they are ever used so improperly that the agency's rule is invalid.

Sierra Club v. Costle

657 F.2d 298 (D.C.Cir.1981).

■ Wald, Circuit Judge: * * *

* * * Where agency action resembles judicial action, where it involves formal rulemaking, adjudication, or quasi-adjudication among "conflicting private claims to a valuable privilege," the insulation of the decisionmaker from ex parte contacts is justified by basic notions of due process to the parties involved. But where agency action involves informal rulemaking of a policymaking sort, the concept of ex parte contacts is of more questionable utility.

Under our system of government, the very legitimacy of general policymaking performed by unelected administrators depends in no small part upon the openness, accessibility, and amenability of these officials to the needs and ideas of the public from whom their ultimate authority derives, and upon whom their commands must fall. As judges we are insulated from these pressures because of the nature of the judicial process in which we participate; but we must refrain from the easy temptation to look askance at all face-to-face lobbying efforts, regardless of the forum in which they occur, merely because we see them as inappropriate in the judicial context. Furthermore, the importance to effective regulation of continuing contact with a regulated industry, other affected groups, and the public cannot be underestimated. Informal contacts may enable the agency to win needed support for its program, reduce future enforcement requirements by helping those regulated to anticipate and shape their plans for the future, and spur the provision of information which the agency needs. * * *

[The petitioner—EDF] challenges the rulemaking on the basis of alleged Congressional pressure, citing principally two meetings with Senator Byrd. EDF asserts that under the controlling case law the political interference demonstrated in this case represents a separate and independent ground for invalidating this rulemaking. But among the cases EDF cites in support of its position, only D. C. Federation of Civil Associations v. Volpe seems relevant to the facts here.

7. J. Aberbach, Keeping a Watchful Eye 198–201 (1990).

In D.C. Federation the Secretary of Transportation, pursuant to applicable federal statutes, made certain safety and environmental findings in designating a proposed bridge as part of the interstate highway system. Civic associations sought to have these determinations set aside for their failure to meet certain statutory standards, and because of possible tainting by reason of improper Congressional influence. Such influence chiefly included public statements by the Chairman of the House Subcommittee on the District of Columbia, Representative Natcher, indicating in no uncertain terms that money earmarked for the construction of the District of Columbia's subway system would be withheld unless the Secretary approved the bridge. While a majority of this court could not decide whether Representative Natcher's extraneous pressure had in fact influenced the Secretary's decision, a majority did agree on the controlling principle of law: "that the decision [of the Secretary] would be invalid if based in whole or in part on the pressures emanating from Representative Natcher." In remanding to the Secretary for new determinations concerning the bridge, however, the court went out of its way to "emphasize that we have not found nor, for that matter, have we sought any suggestion of impropriety or illegality in the actions of Representative Natcher and others who strongly advocate the bridge." The court remanded simply so that the Secretary could make this decision strictly and solely on the basis of considerations made relevant by Congress in the applicable statute.

D. C. Federation thus requires that two conditions be met before an administrative rulemaking may be overturned simply on the grounds of the Congressional pressure. First, the content of the pressure upon the Secretary is designed to force him to decide upon factors not made relevant by Congress in the applicable statute. Representative Natcher's threats were of precisely that character, since deciding to approve the bridge in order to free the "hostage" mass transit appropriation was not among the decision-making factors Congress had in mind when it enacted the highway approval provisions of Title 23 of the United States Code. Second, the Secretary's determination must be affected by those extraneous considerations.

In the case before us, there is no persuasive evidence that either criterion is satisfied. Senator Byrd requested a meeting in order to express "strongly" his already well-known views that the SO_2 standards' impact on coal reserves was a matter of concern to him. EPA initiated a second responsive meeting to report its reaction to the reserve data submitted by the [National Coal Association]. In neither meeting is there any allegation that EPA made any commitments to Senator Byrd. The meetings did underscore Senator Byrd's deep concerns for EPA, but there is no evidence he attempted actively to use "extraneous" pressures to further his position. Americans rightly expect their elected representatives to voice their grievances and preferences concerning the administration of our laws. We believe it entirely proper for Congressional representatives vigorously to represent the interests of their constituents before administrative agencies engaged in informal, general policy rulemaking, so long as individual Congressmen do not frustrate the intent of Congress as a whole as expressed in statute, nor undermine applicable rules of procedure. Where Congressmen keep their comments focused on the substance of the proposed rule[,] and we have no substantial evidence to cause us to believe Senator Byrd did not do so here[,] administrative agencies are expected to balance Congressional pressure with the pressure emanating from all other sources. To hold otherwise would deprive the agencies of legitimate sources of information and call into question the validity of nearly every controversial rulemaking.

Limitation riders. Fifth, Congress can always limit the appropriation of money to the agency. Attaching so-called limitation riders to appropriations bills is a favorite way of slapping an agency on the wrist. The rider states that the agency cannot spend money for a certain purpose. This is the sort of thing that a state legislature probably could not do because it might be considered an improper intrusion of substantive legislation into an appropriations bill. Such provisos are not unusual, however, at the federal level.[8] Ultimately, the congressional power of the purse may be the most powerful form of legislative control over agency discretion. Its usefulness is qualified, however, because appropriations are often caught up in the rush of last minute legislative business and because the limits must be renewed with every appropriations law.

Remember to distinguish between a statutory limitation on appropriations and an appropriation committee report specifying how lump sum funding should be spent by an agency. Such committee reports are often used as *nonstatutory* controls on agency discretion, because they inform the agency of committee expectations and carry a veiled threat of retaliation if the agency does not comply. They are not, however, legally binding on the agency. For example, when the Navy failed to follow a committee report in awarding a contract, a contractor asked the General Accounting Office (GAO) to void the contract. The GAO ruled that the Report did not impose legally binding restrictions on otherwise broad statutory spending authority in an appropriations statute. 55 Comp. Gen. 307, 319 (1975).

Fast track legislation approving agency rule. The statute authorizing agency rules can require agency proposals to be affirmatively legislated if they are to become law. This "affirmative law" approach can be made to approximate the veto procedure if legislative procedural rules put such laws on a fast track. For example, every rule for which Congress wants the right of

---

8. See Parnell, Congressional Interference in Agency Enforcement: The IRS Experience, 89 Yale L.J. 1360, 1374 (1980)(no fiscal year 1980 funds could be used by the IRS to formulate or implement any new guidelines causing loss in tax-exempt status of private religious schools or denying deductions for contributions to religious schools for educational purposes).

approval would automatically be introduced as a bill, which must be voted up or down within a certain period (e.g., 90 days) after introduction. Any legislator could object through a point of order if this procedure is not followed, which means that it takes only one legislator to force the up or down vote on the agency rule. Does this simulate a one or two house veto?

Recall the criticism of the reenactment and inaction doctrines in Chapters 12.03–.04, when used to ratify an intervening agency rule, on the ground that there was often inadequate legislative awareness and approval of what the agency did. Would passage of a bill approving the agency rule under a fast track procedure overcome these criticisms and preclude judicial review of the agency rule for failure to comply with the original statute delegating rulemaking authority to the agency? If judicial review is precluded by use of the fast track procedure, is that a good result?

18.04 JUDICIAL ARBITER OF DISPUTES BETWEEN AND WITHIN POLITICAL BRANCHES

In recent years courts have been asked by Members of Congress to rule on the legality of disputes between Congress and the President, such as (1) the President's military action in Southeast Asia, El Salvador, and Iraq, (2) the President's termination of the Taiwan treaty, and (3) the pocket veto. They have also been asked to rule on *intra*-legislative disputes concerning (1) the allocation of committee membership between the two major parties and (2) Senate initiation of a major tax bill by amending a minor House bill, in possible violation of the constitutional rule that tax bills must originate in the House. Courts have been reluctant but not entirely unwilling to become involved in these political disputes, but have had trouble finding the right analysis for exercising judicial restraint. They have discussed standing, political question, ripeness, and equitable discretion doctrine. In the following opinion, the District of Columbia Court of Appeals explains why it adheres to the equitable discretion rationale. The broader question raised by these cases, as explained in Judge Bork's dissent at the end of this section, is the extent to which courts should ever become involved in these political controversies.

a) RIEGLE V. FEDERAL OPEN MARKET COMMITTEE, 656 F.2D 873 (D.C.CIR.1981)

■ Robb, Circuit Judge * * *

[Editor—A Michigan Senator sued to enjoin voting by private members of the Federal Open Market Committee (FOMC). This committee played an important role in determining the nation's money supply. The private members were elected by private banks. The Senator claimed that it was unconstitutional for any members of this Committee to act unless they represented the public as a result of Presidential appointment and advice and consent by the Senate. The Senator claimed injury by being denied the right to advise and vote his consent under the Appointments Clause of the Constitution, Art. II, sec. 2, cl.2.]

Senator Riegle alleges that both the defendant individuals, "[b]y acting as officers of the United States when their nominations have never been submitted to the Senate," and the defendant executive agency, "[b]y permitting the defendant individuals to act as officers of the United States when their nominations have never been submitted to the Senate," deprive him of his constitutional right to vote in determining the advice and consent of the Senate to the appointment of the five Reserve Bank members of the FOMC. When ruling on a motion to dismiss for want of standing, "both the trial and reviewing courts must accept as true all material allegations of the complaint, and must construe the complaint in favor of the complaining party." Warth v. Seldin, 422 U.S. 490, 501 (1975). We assume, therefore, that the procedure for constituting the FOMC contained in 12 U.S.C. § 263(a) of the Act results in a deprivation of Senator Riegle's constitutional right to advise and consent regarding the appointment of the defendant officers of the executive branch.
* * *

Two contradictory principles pervade the opinions of this court concerning the standing of congressional plaintiffs. First, no distinctions are to be made between congressional and private plaintiffs in the standing analysis. * * * Second, this court will not confer standing on a congressional plaintiff unless he is suffering an injury that his colleagues cannot redress. * * * We believe that these two contradictory principles create unnecessary confusion when applied to suits brought by congressional plaintiffs. As the former chief Judge of this court recently observed,

> There can be no peaceful coexistence between, on the one hand, the notion that legislators are treated like any other plaintiff for standing purposes, and, on the other, the idea that courts should rigorously scrutinize whether the congressional plaintiff's true quarrel is with his colleagues, rather than the executive. There is no general requirement that a private litigant employ self-help before seeking judicial relief. Nor should there be, because an ordinary plaintiff, having suffered injury in fact within the contemplation of the law he invokes, is entitled to his day in court. If the plaintiff passes the standing test and presents a justiciable dispute, it is assumed that the political branches have decided to commit such disputes to the judiciary and, barring extraordinary circumstances, that is a judgement which courts are bound to respect.

Hon. Carl McGowan, "Congressmen in Court: The New Plaintiffs," 15 Ga.L.Rev. 241, 254–255 (1981). Accordingly we shall proceed by applying to this case the traditional standing tests for non-congressional plaintiffs gleaned from opinions of the Supreme Court. Thereafter, we shall examine what additional considerations, if any, must enter our analysis by virtue of the plaintiff's status as a Member of the United States Senate. * * *

[Editor—The court then holds that Senator Riegle met standing requirements. (1) He was injured in fact because he alleged "such a personal stake in the outcome of the controversy as to warrant his invocation of federal-court jurisdiction and to justify exercise of the court's remedial power on his behalf." Warth v. Seldin, 442 U.S., at 498–99. (2) The causation requirement for standing was satisfied because prospective judicial relief, enjoining the vote by private members of the government agency, would remove the harm. (3) The Senator's interest was within the zone of interests protected by the Appointments Clause of the Constitution.]

Appellant's status as a Member of the United States Senate, however, raises separation-of-powers concerns which are best addressed independently of the standing issue. As we observed *supra* the principle that a legislator must lack collegial or "in-house" remedies before this court will confer standing has been a theme of our congressional plaintiff opinions. This principle is a departure from traditional standing analysis because it violates the principle of equality between legislator and private plaintiffs; non-legislator plaintiffs are not routinely denied standing because of the presence of an alternative remedy. * * *

[Editor—The court then argues that political question and ripeness doctrines do not adequately deal with Separation of Powers concerns in congressional standing cases. Political question doctrine finds nonjusticiability when there is a textual commitment of an issue to a non-judicial branch. Ripeness doctrine prevents adjudication before illegal action is reasonably certain to occur. In this case the Appointments Clause does not commit resolution of the advice and consent issue to Congress and the dispute was ripe for review.]

The most satisfactory means of translating our separation-of-powers concerns into principled decisionmaking is through a doctrine of circumscribed equitable discretion. Where a congressional plaintiff could obtain substantial relief from his fellow legislators through the enactment, repeal, or amendment of a statute, this court should exercise its equitable discretion to dismiss the legislator's action. For the reasons set forth below, this test avoids the problems engendered by the doctrines of standing, political question, and ripeness. The standard would counsel the courts to refrain from hearing cases which represent the most obvious intrusion by the judiciary into the legislative arena: challenges concerning congressional action or inaction regarding legislation. Yet this standard would assure that non-frivolous claims of unconstitutional action which could only be brought by members of Congress will be reviewed on the merits.

The above standard would counsel dismissal of a congressional plaintiff's claim in cases concerning legislative action or inaction because it is in these cases that the plaintiff's dispute appears to be primarily with his fellow legislators. In these circumstances, separation-of-powers concerns are most acute. Judges are presented not with a chance to mediate between two political branches but rather with the possibility of thwarting Congress's will by allowing a plaintiff to circumvent the processes of democratic decisionmaking. * * * Thus, where a congressional plaintiff has standing to challenge the actions of those acting pursuant to a statute which could be repealed or amended by his colleagues, or where he alleges an injury which could be substantially cured by legislative action, our standard would counsel judicial restraint. In all such cases, it is unlikely that an unconstitutional action or statute would go unreviewed. While we discourage congressional plaintiffs in such circumstances, it is probable that a private plaintiff could acquire standing to raise the issue of unconstitutionality before a court. Because such a private plaintiff's suit would not raise separation-of-powers concerns, the court would be obliged to reach the merits of the claim. In this case, for example, although prudential considerations warrant the dismissal of Senator Riegle's claim, one can easily conceive of a private plaintiff who could acquire standing to bring a similar claim. A person with significant economic interests in the open securities markets and prime lending rates, e.g., a major corporation, pension fund, or other major investor, might qualify for standing to challenge the constitutionality of a procedure which allegedly permits improperly appointed officials to so substantially influence the monetary policy of the United States, open market trading, and prime rates. * * *

In this case there can be no doubt that Senator Riegle's congressional colleagues are capable of affording him substantial relief. Indeed, a bill which would accomplish Senator Riegle's objective was introduced in Congress as recently as 1980. The Senator remains free to attempt to persuade his fellow legislators of the wisdom of his views. His colleagues, if so persuaded, are empowered to redress the alleged inadequacies of 12 U.S.C. § 263(a) of the Act through amending legislation. Senator Riegle's attempt to prohibit voting by the five Reserve Bank members of the FOMC is yet another skirmish in the war over public versus private control of the Committee which has been waged in the legislative arena since 1933. It would be unwise to permit the federal courts to become a higher legislature where a congressman who has failed to persuade his colleagues can always renew the battle.

Assuming that the current procedure for constituting the FOMC may be unconstitutional, we must nevertheless weigh the danger of permitting such a statute to stand against two countervailing concerns: (1) the potential for misuse of the judicial system inherent in hearing a case brought by this particular plaintiff, who, because of his congressional status, has adequate collegial remedies; and (2) the unwarranted interference in the legislative process which judicial action would represent at this time. We conclude that rendering a decision on the merits in this case would pose a greater threat to the constitutional system than would the principled exercise of judicial restraint. * * *

We hold that Senator Riegle has standing to bring this action but exercise our equitable discretion to dismiss the case on the ground that judicial action would improperly interfere with the legislative process.

b) PROCESS?

A better idea of what concerns the D.C. Circuit appears in Moore v. U.S. House of Representatives, 733 F.2d 946 (D.C.Cir.1984). House members sued because a minor House tax bill had been gutted by the Senate and used as a vehicle for a major Senate tax bill. Under the Constitution, tax bills must originate in the House. The House had in fact voted to overrule objections that the Senate amendments violated the Constitution. Case law grants standing to private parties to raise the "House origination" issue in private litigation,[9] and the court upheld a Member of Congress' standing to sue. It had to distinguish the denial of congressional standing in other cases where the President had refused to enforce a statute or had taken action not authorized by law. It based its distinction on the ground that such claims were generalized claims of illegality which did not involve the special concerns of Members of Congress.

Nonetheless, the court withheld relief as a matter of equity, stating that this was "not a claim founded on injury to the legislator by distortion of the process by which a bill became law—a process in which a legislator has a right and a duty to participate." This last quote suggests that the court might overcome its qualms about exercising equitable discretion if a dispute involves the process for enacting a law.

Assuming that process is important, doesn't the court adopt too narrow a conception of enforceable process requirements. After all, the Origination Clause of the Constitution is a process rule designed to assure that revenue raising starts in the most democratic house of Congress. Is the court's conception of process too "judicial," neglecting what is important about the legislative process?

The following case is an easier one for upholding a congressman's right to enforce legislative process. In Powell v. McCormack, 395 U.S. 486 (1969),

9. See, e.g., Rainey v. United States, 232 U.S. 310 (1914); United States v. Munoz–   Flores, 495 U.S. 385 (1990).

the Supreme Court held unconstitutional the exclusion of an elected representative from the House of Representatives. The Constitution permits exclusion for failure to satisfy age, citizenship, and residence requirements by majority vote. By contrast, expulsion from the House is permitted by two-thirds vote. The Court found that the House was acting under its exclusion power and was therefore limited to applying the exclusion criteria, even though the actual vote to exclude carried by more than two-thirds (sufficient for expulsion). The Court would not speculate on what the vote would have been if the House had acted under its expulsion power. Because Powell satisfied the criteria for membership, the House's exclusion action was unconstitutional and the issue was reviewable by the Court.

The Powell case seems easier than other cases for two reasons. First, the petitioner had a personal claim to the office from which he had been excluded. And the courts have been quite willing to vindicate personal claims by a Member of Congress in other settings. For example, in Boehner v. Anderson, 30 F.3d 156 (D.C.Cir.1994), the issue was whether a congressional pay raise was legal. In 1992 the Archivist of the United States certified the 27th Amendment to the Constitution, which states that "[n]o law, varying the compensation for the services of the Senators and Representatives, shall take effect, until an election of Representatives shall have intervened." A 1989 statute (passed before certification of the 27th Amendment) provides for a cost of living increase for Members of Congress salaries in future years. In 1993, there was such an adjustment based on a cost of living increase. A Member of Congress objected to the pay raise on the ground that it violated the 27th Amendment because each cost of living adjustment was a new "law" varying his salary before an election for the House of Representatives had intervened. The court held that the Member's interest in his own pay—even though objecting to a *raise*—was a personal right that must be resolved by the court. It stated: "Mr. Boehner's claim that the Ethics Reform Act unconstitutionally interferes with the amount and timing of his pay is a straightforward challenge to the constitutionality of a public law that directly affects his private interest as a government employee. He raises no 'dispute properly within the domain of the legislative branch * * *.' " On the merits, the court held that the pay raise did not violate the 27th Amendment.[10]

Second, the petitioner in Powell made a claim which vindicated the rights of those voters who had elected him. As we saw earlier in Chapter 16, a voter's right to representation is considered a fundamental interest. A concern for voters was also apparent in Michel v. Anderson, 14 F.3d 623 (D.C.Cir.1994). Individual voters objected to a House of Representatives rule granting delegates from the territories and the District of Columbia the right to vote in the Committee of the Whole. Legislative bodies often resolve

---

10. There might also be doubt about whether the 27th Amendment is valid, because its ratification took more than 200 years. Although more or less contemporaneous ratification of constitutional amendments is required, case law leaves it to Congress to decide whether this standard has been met. Coleman v. Miller, 307 U.S. 433 (1939). The House and Senate affirmed ratification on May 20, 1992 in separate concurrent resolutions (H. Con. Res. 320, 138 Cong.Rec. D605 (May 20, 1992), and S. Con. Res. 120, 138 Cong.Rec. S6948 (May 20, 1992)).

themselves into something called a committee of the whole to avoid some of the more formal procedural constraints that otherwise apply. Tentative decisions can be made through a less formal process and they are not binding on the legislature when it later ceases to act as a committee of the whole and acts as a legislative body. The House rules dealing with territory and D.C. delegates specified that, if the votes of these delegates affected the result, the House would cease to act as a Committee of the Whole and the House itself would vote *without* the delegates. The individual voters who brought the lawsuit objected on the ground that this procedure diluted their interests as voters by diluting the impact of their representative's vote in Congress. The court reached the merits of the case and held that this arrangement was constitutional. Because the individual voters had standing, the court did not decide whether the concerns of voters would independently support the right of Members of Congress to sue in their behalf.

The procedure in Moore (the Origination Clause case) was required by the Constitution (as was the procedure in Powell). You might therefore conclude that only constitutionally-required procedures could ever be the subject of a lawsuit by a Member of Congress. Vander Jagt v. O'Neill, 699 F.2d 1166 (D.C.Cir.1982), suggests otherwise. The case involved a lawsuit against Speaker of the House O'Neill by Republican members of Congress who objected to committee membership less than their proportional representation in Congress. Although Republicans were 44.14% of the House, their committee representation on several important committees was 34.29%, 40% and 31.25%. The majority withheld judicial involvement in this dispute as a matter of equitable discretion, but refused to rule out completely ever becoming involved in committee membership disputes. The Court stated:

> * * * As long as it is conceivable that the committee system could be manipulated beyond reason, we should not abandon our constitutional obligation—our duty and not simply our province—"to say what the law is."

The court, in other words, will not give up an option to decide a future case involving committee assignments under its equitable discretion power, even though the dispute is intra-legislative and the procedure is not required by the Constitution.

c) EXECUTIVE–LEGISLATIVE CONFLICT

Judicial expressions of concern about the legislative process remain a tantalizing hint as to what might support the right of a Member of Congress to overcome standing and equitable discretion barriers to a lawsuit. Another factor—indeed, a more powerful factor—seems to be a conflict between the executive and legislative branches. Here are several cases where the court reached the merits of the case, all involving executive-legislative conflict.

(1) In Barnes v. Kline, 759 F.2d 21 (D.C.Cir.1984), vacated sub nom. Burke v. Barnes, 479 U.S. 361 (1987), the court exercised equitable discretion to decide whether the President had exercised a pocket veto. The pocket veto allows the President to veto a law by not returning it to Congress, if Congress is not in session on the tenth day after the bill has been presented to the President for approval, as follows: .

> Every bill which shall have passed the House of Representatives and the Senate, shall, before it become a Law, be presented to the President of the United States; If he approve he shall sign it, but if not he shall return it, with his Objections to that House in which it shall have originated, who shall enter the Objections at large on their Journal, and proceed to reconsider it. If after such Reconsideration two thirds of that House shall agree to pass the Bill, it shall be sent, together with the Objections, to the other House, by which it shall likewise be reconsidered, and if approved by two thirds of that House, it shall become a Law * * *. If any Bill shall not be returned by the President within ten Days (Sundays excepted) after it shall have been presented to him, the Same shall be a Law, in like Manner as if he had signed it, *unless the Congress by their Adjournment prevent its Return, in which Case it shall not be a Law* (emphasis added).

The issue was whether a bill became law when the President failed to return it or whether the bill was "pocket-vetoed" because congressional adjournment prevented its return. Congress had adjourned its first session (every Congress lasts two years and meets in two annual sessions), and the ten day period for the President to return the bill expired during the adjournment. The court held that appointment in the House and Senate of agents to receive veto messages prevented a pocket veto. The court examined the historical rationale for the pocket veto and found that its purpose was to prevent congressional adjournment from defeating the President's ability to return a bill to Congress with objections. The Framers wanted to give the President a veto but also wanted to protect the right of congressional override (hence the bill becomes law in ten days if it is not signed). But the Framers also wanted to protect the President's right to object (hence the pocket veto provision, if congressional adjournment prevents the President's return of the bill to Congress). The court decided that appointment of congressional agents during the inter-session recess protected the President's right to object.

The court also discussed another reason for the pocket veto, which was the delay in determining whether there was a law if congressional adjournment was lengthy. It discussed Wright v. United States, 302 U.S. 583 (1938), where the Court held that *intra*session adjournments were short enough to prevent a pocket veto when legislative agents were appointed to receive veto messages. Barnes v. Kline, however, involved an *inter*session adjournment, and the court had to deal with an old precedent upholding the *inter*session pocket vetoes. See The Pocket Veto Case, 279 U.S. 655 (1929). The Pocket Veto Case was distinguished by the Court of Appeals on the ground that

Congress no longer took the five or six month adjournments prevalent when that case was decided.

(2) Goldwater v. Carter, 617 F.2d 697 (D.C.Cir.1979), vacated, 444 U.S. 996 (1979), was decided before the D.C. Circuit developed its equitable discretion approach. The Court of Appeals decided that Members of Congress had standing to challenge President Carter's termination of the Mutual Defense Treaty with Taiwan. On the merits, President Carter acted legally. (In the Supreme Court, four Justices refused to decide the issue on the ground that it was a political question; one Justice held that the issue was not ripe for decision.)

QUESTION

Suppose the President fails to follow the procedures for deferral of funds under the Impoundment Control Act (ICA), such as notifying Congress (discussed in Chapter 18.02ciiC). Can and should a court hear a lawsuit by a Member of Congress challenging the deferral?

d) PRIVATE PARTY STANDING

A sub-theme in some of the cases exercising equitable discretion not to hear a case brought by a Member of Congress is that a private party has standing to raise the issue in court. For example, in Riegle, the court stated:

> [I]t is probable that a private plaintiff could acquire standing to raise the issue of unconstitutionality before a court. Because such a private plaintiff's suit would not raise separation-of-powers concerns, the court would be obliged to reach the merits of the claim. In this case, for example, although prudential considerations warrant the dismissal of Senator Riegle's claim, one can easily conceive of a private plaintiff who could acquire standing to bring a similar claim.
> * * *

However, the decision to reach the merits in Barnes v. Kline (the pocket veto case) is inconsistent with this point of view. The statute involved a program which would have funded medical assistance and prospective beneficiaries of the program could have sued to object to the pocket veto. See also Melcher v. Federal Open Market Committee, 836 F.2d 561 (D.C.Cir.1987)(court exercised equitable discretion not to decide a claim, but explicitly refused to base its decision on whether private plaintiffs had standing).

e) REMEDY AVAILABLE FROM LEGISLATURE

In Riegle (membership on Federal Open Market Committee), the court which invoked equitable discretion to deny reaching the merits of the case referred to the fact that legislation passed by colleagues was an alternative in-house remedy for the aggrieved legislator. See also Humphrey v. Baker, 848 F.2d 211 (D.C.Cir.1988) (Senators challenged the mechanism for setting legislators' salaries, on the ground that the legislation delegated too much power to the President; the court exercised equitable discretion not to decide the case, stating that there was an in-house remedy if Congress did not like the delegation law); Gregg v. Barrett, 771 F.2d 539 (D.C.Cir.1985)(Members of Congress object to the inaccuracy of the Congressional Record; court exercises equitable discretion not to reach the merits because a remedy was available within the legislature); Skaggs v. Carle, 898 F.Supp. 1 (D.D.C.1995)(1995 House Rules prohibit income tax rate increase except by not less than three-fifths of the Members voting; 15 Members of the House sued on the ground that the Rule violated an implicit Constitutional requirement that majority rules; "equitable" discretion requires court to refrain from intruding in the name of the Constitution upon the internal affairs of Congress at the behest of lawmakers who have failed to prevail in the political process.)[11]

How persuasive is the "alternative legislative remedy" criterion? (1) Couldn't the legislature in Barnes v. Kline repass the law which the President had allegedly pocket-vetoed improperly? (2) Is this argument more persuasive when the claim does not involve an executive-legislative conflict? (3) What kind of "right" is it, if the court refuses to protect it just because a majority can provide the petitioner with relief?

f) OTHER GATEKEEPING RULES

Courts often refuse to hear cases similar to those described above on other "gate-keeping" grounds, such as political question, ripeness, and standing. For example, the court refused to decide two cases involving claims by Members of Congress that the President's commitment of troops improperly usurped Congress' power to declare war. Both decisions were based, not on the equitable discretion doctrine, but on the conclusion that the issue raised a nonjusticiable political question.[12]

In yet another case, Dellums v. Bush, 752 F.Supp. 1141 (D.D.C.1990), the court considered a challenge by Members of Congress to President Bush's power to initiate an offensive attack against Iraq without first obtaining a congressional declaration of war or other explicit congressional authorization. The court held that political question, standing, and equitable discretion doctrine did not bar a judicial decision, but that the issue was not ripe. The issue was not ripe for two reasons. First, as of December 1991, the President had not yet shown a commitment to a definitive course of action. Second, Congress had not yet acted to establish an impasse with the President. The court said that the issue would have been ripe, however, if a *majority* of Congress had sued. (Equitable discretion would not be a bar because there was no effective way to obtain relief from fellow legislators. Is that true? Couldn't Congress refuse to appropriate money? Would that provide the relief the legislators sought?)

---

11. For a debate over whether the 60% supra-majority rule is constitutional, see Comment: An Open Letter to Congressman Gingrich, 104 Yale L.J. 1539 (1995).

12. Sanchez–Espinoza v. Reagan, 770 F.2d 202 (D.C.Cir.1985); Mitchell v. Laird, 488 F.2d 611 (D.C.Cir.1973).

In Harrington v. Schlesinger, 528 F.2d 455 (4th Cir.1975), a congressman challenged the President's expenditures in support of military operations in Southeast Asia. Congress had passed statutes limiting expenditure of funds for this purpose and the President agreed that he was governed by the statute. There was disagreement, however, about what the statute meant. The court noted that private parties would not have standing to sue, based on Flast v. Cohen, 392 U.S. 83 (1968)(standing to challenge unconstitutional government expenditures limited to violations of specific limits on taxing and spending power, such as the Establishment Clause). Nonetheless, the court held that Members of Congress lacked standing. Their claim that a lawsuit declaring the President's action illegal would help them vote on impeachment proceedings was too generalized a complaint. The court also noted that the dispute was really about what the statute meant, so congressional petitioners had a remedy by passing a more precise statute limiting executive spending.

g) Bork's Dissent

If and when the Supreme Court decides whether a Member of Congress can obtain a judicial remedy for any of the above complaints, it will have to consider Judge Bork's objections, based on the concept of standing.[13] In the Barnes v. Kline case, 759 F.2d 21 (D.C.Cir.1984), vacated sub nom. Burke v. Barnes, 479 U.S. 361 (1987), he wrote a long dissent explaining why giving Members of Congress standing violated basic principles of Separation of Powers. Here is some of what he had to say. Do you agree with his conclusion that the D.C. Circuit's approach is (1) unprincipled, (2) and that the court's approach is "aesthetic?" Does "aesthetic" mean the same thing as "unprincipled"?

"Standing" is one of the concepts courts have evolved to limit their jurisdiction and hence to preserve the separation of powers. A critical aspect of the idea of standing is the definition of the interests that courts are willing to protect through adjudication. A person may have an interest in receiving money supposedly due him under law. Courts routinely regard an injury to that interest as conferring upon that person standing to litigate. Another person may have an equally intensely felt interest in the proper constitutional performance of the United States government. Courts have routinely regarded injury to that interest as not conferring standing to litigate. The difference between the two situations is not the reality or intensity of the injuries felt but a perception that according standing in the latter case would so enhance the power of the courts as to make them the dominant branch of government. There would be no issue of

---

13. If a Member of Congress lacks standing, Congress cannot even *give* the Member a right to sue—for example, by the provision in the Line Item Veto Act of 1996, giving an "adversely affected" Member of Congress a right to "bring an action" on the ground that the new law violated the constitution. See Lujan v. Defenders of Wildlife, 504 U.S. 555 (1992)(Congress cannot grant standing to sue where the constitutional standards for standing are not met).

governance that could not at once be brought into the federal courts for conclusive disposition. Every time a court expands the definition of standing, the definition of the interests it is willing to protect through adjudication, the area of judicial dominance grows and the area of democratic rule contracts. That is what is happening in this case. My disagreement with the majority, therefore, is about first principles of constitutionalism. * * *

The concept of congressional standing, as the majority opinion makes clear, rests upon the idea that members or Houses of Congress must be able to sue to vindicate powers or rights lodged in them by the Constitution. Nothing else is required to confer standing under the doctrine as it has been enunciated by this court. It follows, according to the majority, that appellants have standing to maintain an action against an officer of the Executive Branch to establish that the President's exercise of his pocket veto power was not within the terms set by the Constitution. This may sound unexceptional; it is, in fact, a constitutional upheaval.

The first problem with this court's doctrine of congressional standing is that, on the terms of its own rationale, the concept is uncontrollable. Congress is not alone in having governmental powers created or contemplated by the Constitution. This means that the vindication-of-constitutional-powers rational must confer standing upon the President and the judiciary to sue other branches just as much as it does upon Congress. "Congressional standing" is merely a subset of "governmental standing." This rationale would also confer standing upon states or their legislators, executives, or judges to sue various branches of the federal government. Indeed, no reason appears why the power or duty being vindicated must derive from the Constitution. One would think a legal interest created by statute or regulation would suffice to confer standing upon an agency or official who thought that interest had been invaded.

These points become obvious upon examination of the court's doctrine. If this extrapolation of that doctrine at first seems far-fetched, that is only because it points to a new and wholly unfamiliar legal and constitutional world. * * *

We may begin with Congress. Members of Congress, dissatisfied with the President's performance, need no longer proceed, as historically they always have, by oversight hearings, budget restrictions, political struggle, appeals to the electorate, and the like, but may simply come to the district court down the hill from the Capitol and obtain a ruling from a federal judge. The Pocket Veto Case, 279 U.S. 655 (1929), for example, need not have awaited suit by persons who thought themselves unlawfully deprived of monies: had the congressmen and courts of that time understood what this court now understands, an abstract ruling on the principle of the thing could have been obtained immediately after the President failed to sign the bill. * * * Members could sue the President about his law enforcement policies and priorities, claiming that their power to make laws under Article I, section 8, and his duty, arising under article II, section 3 to "take Care that the Laws be faithfully executed," had both been infringed. Examples of this sort could be multiplied indefinitely. * * *

[Editor—Judge Bork can find no distinction between objections to an invalid pocket veto and to the President's improper execution of the law. Both impair the Member's right to participate and vote on legislation. Thus, Bork argues, "the obligation to 'take Care that the Laws be faithfully executed' [is moved] out of article II of the Constitution and divide[d] between articles I and III."

He also argues that, if Congress can sue the President, the President can sue Congress (to object to a legislative veto) and judges could sue Congress (to object to withdrawal of jurisdiction).]

Intra-branch disputes also must succumb to this court's plenary interpretation of its own powers. * * * Congress, in short, is subject to judicial oversight to whatever degree this court, exercising its newly-invented powers of equitable discretion, decides supervision is warranted, or, as one of our cases puts it, not "startlingly unattractive." Vander Jagt, 699 F.2d at 1176 (quoting Davids v. Akers, 549 F.2d 120, 123 (9th Cir.1977)). It appears that our constitutional jurisdiction now rests less upon law than upon aesthetic judgments. * * *

To make its standing doctrine more palatable this court has adopted a doctrine of remedial or equitable discretion. This doctrine permits the court to say that a congressional plaintiff has standing, and hence that the court has jurisdiction, and yet refuse to hear the case because the court is troubled by the separation-of-powers implications of deciding on the merits. * * * By claiming that discretion, the court has created for itself a kind of certiorari jurisdiction—which it took an act of Congress to create for the Supreme Court. * * *

* * * The doctrine of remedial discretion removes separation-of-powers considerations from the jurisdictional inquiry and converts them into mere interests to be balanced. Thus, the doctrine relegates separation of powers to second-class status and subordinates the structure of our constitutional system to the discretion of this court. It is impossible for me to view that prospect with equanimity.

It is plain on the face of these developments that what we are observing constitutes a major aggrandizement of judicial power. Any lingering doubts on this score are laid to rest by this court's stated presumption in favor of exercising discretion to decide a case when, if a decision on the merits were withheld, "non-frivolous claims of unconstitutional action would go unreviewed by a court." Riegle, 656 F.2d at 882. The function of the article III case-or-controversy limitations, including the standing requirement, is, however, precisely to ensure that claims of unconstitutional action will go unreviewed by a court when review would undermine our system of separated powers and undo the limits the Constitution places on the power of the federal courts. * * *

At bottom, equitable discretion is a lawless doctrine that is the antithesis of the "principled decisionmaking" that was invoked to justify its manufacture. A doctrine of remedial discretion more than "suggests the sort of rudderless adjudication that courts strive to avoid," Vander Jagt, 699 F.2d at 1175–it *is* rudderless adjudication. * * *

Ultimately, the doctrine of equitable discretion makes cases turn on nothing more than the sensitivity of a particular trio of judges. One cannot, unfortunately, have any solid grounds for supposing that these aesthetic judgments, though subjective and varying, will at least mark out an irreducible realm of "startling[ ] unattractive[ness]." Vander Jagt, 699 F.2d at 1176. As the spectacle of public officials suing other public officials over abstract constitutional questions becomes familiar, the taint will wear off, and what seemed unattractive will appear inevitable. Alexander Pope's dictum, though grown trite, is too apt to ignore: "Vice is a monster of so frightful mien/As to be hated needs but to be seen;/Yet seen too oft, familiar with her face,/We first endure, then pity, then embrace." An Essay on Man, Epistle II, 1. 217. The combination of congressional standing and equitable discretion will very probably prove to have been but a way-station to general, continual, and intrusive judicial superintendence of the other institutions in which the Framers chose to place the business of governing.

Judge Bork certainly lays down the gauntlet. Are there really no standards to limit the court's choices? Are we on the slippery slope Judge Bork describes?

INDEX

References are to pages

ADJUDICATION
See also Common Law
Administrative agencies, compared to, 2, 6–7
Legislation, compared to, 2, 7–8, 86, 94–98, 289–320
Prospectivity, 316–320

ADMINISTRATIVE AGENCIES
Adjudication, compared to, 2, 6–7
Deference by courts, 488–516
    Chevron, 494–516
    Institutional competence, 491–493
    Legislative intent, 489–490
    Super-deference, 493–516
    Text, relation to, 488–489, 501–507
Institutional competence, 491–493, 507–516
    Litigating position, 507–509
    Notice and comment, 509–514
Interpreting statutes, 488–516
Legislative history, compared, 515–516, 528
Legislative veto, 913–927
Rationality requirement, 491–492, 836–837
Reenactment of law,
    After agency rule, 529–531
    Agency change rule after, 538–540
Report & wait, 922–923
Retroactivity, 507–514
State law, 515

BACKGROUND CONSIDERATIONS
See Context, External

CANONS, LINGUISTIC
See also Canons, Substantive
Avoid surplusage, 204–205
Close proximity, 198–204
Consistent meaning, 205–207
Ejusdem generis, 204
Expressio unius, 208–210, 299–300, 519
Outlandish definition, 210

CANONS, SUBSTANTIVE
See also Canons, Linguistic
Absurdity, 31, 238, 275–277, 373
Ad hoc approach, compared, 275–277
Curative statutes, 293–294
Derogation of common law, 23, 67–70, 76–78, 90–91, 118–123, 372
Federalism, 257–258, 279–289, 588–589, 610
Golden Rule, 31–32
Liberal construction, 123–124, 278, 691–692

CANONS, SUBSTANTIVE—Cont'd
No implied statutory repeal, 652–671
    Appropriations laws, 659–671
    Substantive law, 652–659
Plain statement requirements, 257–258, 278–316
Protecting States, 257–258, 279–289, 588–589, 610
Retroactive statutes, 289–316, 517–519
Rule of lenity, 90–91, 110–117, 378–381
Statutes overriding, 123–124

CARROLL, L., 4

CHANGE
Common law, 360–362
Future audience, 193–198
Judicial role, 360–403
Legal landscape, 362–365, 375–376, 382–388, 547–548, 556–565, 680–681
Legislative inertia, 341–342, 365–367, 385, 540–541, 575
    Asymmetries of, 365–367
Obsolete statutes, 367–376, 690
    Unconstitutionality, 373–375, 845–853
Statutory evolution, 376–394
    Common law context, 376–381
    No common law context, 381–394
Textualism and, 393–403

COMMITTEES
See Legislative History; Legislative Process

COMMON LAW
See also Adjudication; Common Law Power
Admiralty, 556–562, 578–579
Change, 360–362
Context for statute, 376–381
Federal courts, 575–602
    Unique federal interest, 578–580
Legislation, compared to, 2, 7–8, 28, 86, 94–98, 187–188, 289–320, 360–361
Perfection of reason, 28, 72
Statutes, as part of, 361–376
Statutes freeze, 372
Statutes, in derogation of, 23, 67–70, 76–78, 90–91, 118–123, 372

COMMON LAW POWER
See also Common Law; Judicial Role

941

†

1–56662–519–X

9 781566 625197

90000